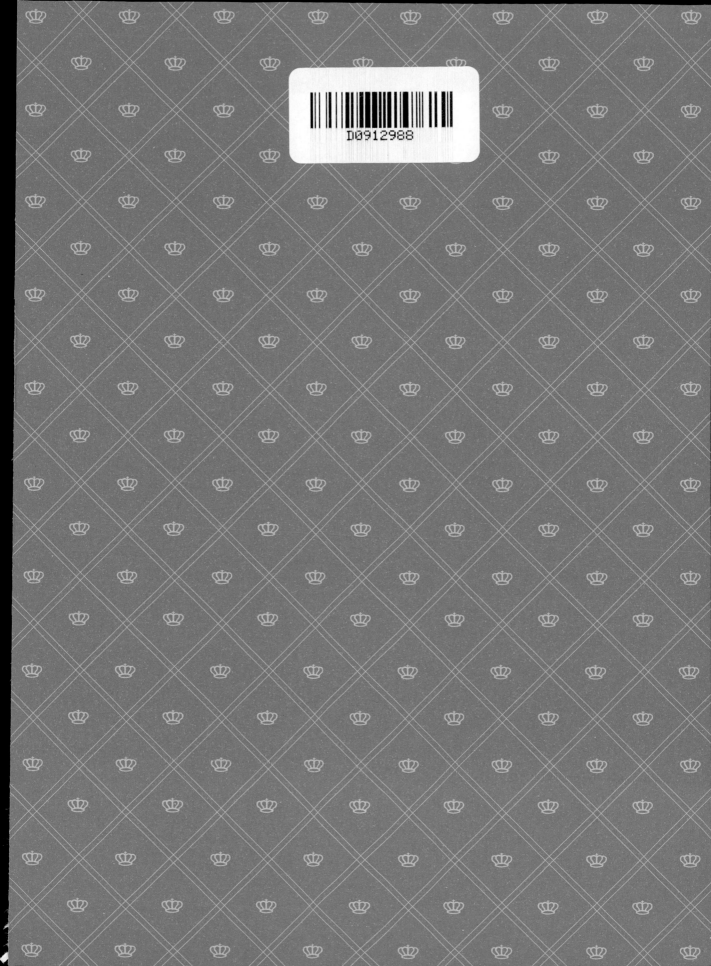

The

ESSENTIAL
COCKTAIL

The

ESSENTIAL
COCKTAIL

THE ART OF MIXING
PERFECT DRINKS

CLASSIC FAVORITES • NEW INGREDIENTS • MODERN TECHNIQUES

PHOTOGRAPHS BY DAVID KRESSLER

DALE DEGROFF

Clarkson Potter/Publishers
NEW YORK

Copyright © 2008 by Dale DeGroff
Photographs by David Kressler, copyright © 2008 by David Kressler

All rights reserved.
Published in the United States by Clarkson Potter/Publishers, an imprint of the Crown
Publishing Group, a division of Random House, Inc., New York.
www.crownpublishing.com
www.clarksonpotter.com

Clarkson N. Potter is a trademark and Potter and colophon are registered trademarks of
Random House, Inc.

Photographs on pages 88, 228, 255 (V-shaped), 256 (highball, chimney/Collins, and old-
fashioned), 257 (London docks and shot glass), and 258 (Irish coffee, flute, and hot toddy mug)
© by George Erml. Photograph on page 16 by James Ensing-Trussel; photographs on pages 32
(*The Modern Bartender's Guide*), 45, 49, 50, 182, 187, and 223 courtesy of the author. Rye on
page 49 and rums on page 182 from the collection of Stephen Remsberg.

Library of Congress Cataloging-in-Publication Data
DeGroff, Dale.
  The essential cocktail / by Dale DeGroff. — 1st ed.
    p. cm.
  Includes bibliographical references and index.
  1. Cocktails.   I. Title.
  TX951.D493   2008
  641.8'74—dc22   2007048044

ISBN 978-0-307-40573-9

Printed in China

Design by GOODESIGN

10 9 8 7 6 5 4

First Edition

*Dedicated to the
memory of my good friend*

GEORGE ERML

MANHATTAN, PAGE 32

PINK LADY, PAGE 96

CAIPIRINHA, PAGE 120

COSMOPOLITAN, PAGE 72

THE GIBSON, PAGE 107

NEGRONI, PAGE 94

GROG, PAGE 176

BLOOD & SAND, PAGE 68

MINT JULEP, PAGE 37

CONTENTS

Introduction   8

THE ESSENTIAL CLASSICS   10

THE ESSENTIAL MODERN CLASSICS   56

THE ESSENTIAL MARTINIS   102

THE ESSENTIAL SOURS   118

THE ESSENTIAL HIGHBALLS   142

THE ESSENTIAL TROPICALS   168

THE ESSENTIAL PUNCHES   192

THE ESSENTIAL SWEETS   210

THE ESSENTIAL INNOVATIONS   230

Appendix A: Basic Recipes   246

Appendix B: Garnishes   251

Appendix C: Glassware and Tools   255

Resources   264

Bibliography   266

Acknowledgments   267

Index   268

INTRODUCTION

In 1985 when I went to work for restaurateur Joseph Baum, first at Aurora Restaurant and later at the Rainbow Room in New York City, he was looking for a classic bar program featuring authentic recipes made with fresh, quality ingredients. The menu I developed at the Rainbow Room Promenade Bar included drinks that had not appeared on a menu since the 1930s, as well as a changing seasonal component. The menu caught the attention of the press and then the public, igniting a spark around the city and eventually around the country. We were on the way to the return of the essential cocktail with real ingredients and classic recipes, but this time there was a twist. Ingredients usually found only in the kitchen began to find their way into the cocktail. First a basil leaf and a strawberry, mashed together with a bit of lemon, honey, and gin. Then more exotic ingredients like hot chiles and yuzu-lemon juice, until at some restaurants it became hard to tell the garde manger station from the bar.

In those years, I used the lore and history of the cocktail to give young bartenders a sense that they were part of a real profession, a profession that had a history. The cocktail is one of the first truly American culinary arts and I wanted these guys to take pride in that heritage. The stories of classics, like the Manhattan and the Collins, the daiquiri and the Jack Rose, gave these guys a way to connect with their customers and infect them with their newfound enthusiasm for the great American cocktail. The stories also provided some small compensation for the rigorous preparation and attention to detail they had not been required to master as mere "beverage transporters," a term author Brian Rea once used to describe the post-Prohibition bartender.

The lore and history of the cocktail has been brought into sharp focus by the liquid archaeology of authors like David Wondrich and Eric Felton. Their meticulous research has revealed a culture of the barroom not unlike that of the bars in New York City where I spent years honing my craft—a culture that birthed and nurtured the cocktail into the strapping youth it is today. But as cocktails evolve, one essential element remains constant: they must taste good. A good bartender has to master the skill of crafting recipes that appeal to a wide audience while also understanding how to adapt each drink to the individual preference of the guest.

The Essential Cocktail is a cocktail handbook with recipes that work. Having said that, cocktail recipes are often just starting points. In the 1882 *Bartenders Guide*, Harry Johnson observed that "the greatest accomplishment of a bartender lies is his ability to exactly suit his customer." What makes the cocktail unique in the culinary landscape is its relationship with the customer. A cocktail is much more personal than the main course of a restaurant meal. Aside from a few classics chiseled in stone, people want to fiddle; they want to personalize their drink. In all my years working as a waiter (prior to being a bartender), I was never instructed by a customer on how the chef should prepare his hollandaise sauce, but, with very few exceptions, people have a lot to say about the preparation of their Bloody Mary, Manhattan, old-fashioned, and even the ultimate classic cocktail, a dry martini.

I have fine-tuned the recipes to find versions that will appeal to a wide swath of humanity—but not by dumbing them down. In fact a simple short list of ingredients can challenge the skills of the best bartenders even more than a complicated concoction. Simple does not mean easy. And I love that we have come full circle to a time when people can appreciate subtlety and excellence in their cocktails, a fact due in a large part to bartenders returning to the craft of the cocktail.

The Essential Cocktail has a simple mission: to enable every bartender, whether amateur or professional, to master the essentials—those hundred or so drinks that are the fundamental building blocks of the bar—along with another hundred important variations. The list embraces the original pre-Prohibition classics like the Bronx, the old-fashioned, and the mint julep; modern twentieth-century classics like the margarita and the Cosmopolitan; the martini in its various guises; sours like the Collins and the mojito; tropical classics like the mai tai; punches like sangria; after-dinner sweets like the Alexander; and, for good measure, the contemporary innovations that are an absolute must for forward-thinking bartenders, including those that take advantage of culinary ingredients, foams, and other approaches that were unheard-of a mere decade ago. Throughout the book I have included many of my original drinks and adaptations of classics, which are identified with asterisks.

These recipes are more than just a handful of ingredients poured into a glass. A bartender must learn to understand ingredients: what works and what doesn't work, and he or she must understand technique, garnish, and proper glassware. The sours entry, for example, supplies the reader with a formula that can be adapted to different flavor additions, kind of like a base sauce in cooking. There's also history and lore, anecdote and advice. After learning about each drink, the reader will be able to prepare it with confidence and maybe even tell a story or two. So this book does not offer recipes for 1,000 or 1,500 or even 2,500 drinks. Instead I present a master class on how to make the great cocktails, make them right, and most important, skillfully craft them to the individual's taste. A finely crafted cocktail is a marriage of creativity, history, and expression. So roll up your sleeves and immerse yourself in this simple, culinary pleasure.

The Essential
CLASSICS

ABSINTHE DRIP • ADONIS COCKTAIL • BLACK VELVET • BLUE BLAZER
BOBBY BURNS • BRONX COCKTAIL • CHAMPAGNE COCKTAIL
CHAMPAGNE PICK-ME-UP • CLOVER CLUB • EAST INDIA COCKTAIL • FLIP
JACK ROSE • MANHATTAN • MINT JULEP • OLD-FASHIONED
PIMM'S CUP • POUSSE CAFÉ • ROB ROY • SAZERAC
TODDY • WARD EIGHT

A lot of romance is associated with Prohibition—this was the Roaring Twenties of flappers in speakeasies, of Fitzgerald in New York and Hemingway in Paris, of bootleggers. People often think Prohibition was the classic era of cocktails, but nothing could be further from the truth. Although there was indeed a lot of drinking during the dry era, it was of bathtub gin and watered-down rum, mixed up in basements and served without ceremony.

The classic era of the cocktail was, in fact, the half-century that preceded Prohibition—from 1862, when Jerry Thomas published the first cocktail book, to 1912, by which point the Drys had made real inroads and Prohibition was already the law in two-thirds of the states. Punches, juleps, and slings had survived from the colonial era, and, with the addition of bitters, a new category was born, called *cocktails*. The industrial revolution also made the public bar possible with inexpensive ice made by machines, water saturated with gas, and beer pushed through lines and out of taps. Finally, the influx of European immigrants—particularly Irish and German—to the urban centers of the Northeast added an essential component: the longstanding tradition of communal drinking. And so the modern bar was born.

In these modern bars, the martini and the Manhattan were invented, as were the old-fashioned and the Rob Roy. As the number of bars grew and the culture of cocktails flourished, the invisible hand of market forces added its own fuel to the fire by turning homemade concoctions or unknown imports into widely available commercial products: fruit liqueurs and syrups, cordials and specialty spirits, American whiskey. As these ingredients spread across the land, bartenders got more creative in using them, and the profession flourished. This was the classic era, a time of invention and excitement, a time when the cocktail was king. ♛

ABSINTHE DRIP

INGREDIENTS

2 ounces absinthe or absinthe substitute
    (see Ingredient Note)
1 or 2 lumps of sugar, to taste

☞ Put the absinthe and 1 cube of ice in a good-sized tumbler. Place an absinthe spoon (a flat spoon with little holes in it) across the top of the glass and set 1 or 2 lumps of sugar on the spoon. Now pour water, drop by drop, on the sugar. The water melts the sugar, sweetens the drink, and lowers the alcohol level. Serve in a cloud of unfiltered cigarette smoke, preferably wearing a beret.

 After the first glass, you see things as you wish they were. After the second, you see things as they are not. Finally you see things as they really are, and that is the most horrible thing in the world. —OSCAR WILDE

There was a time in the nineteenth century when absinthe was one of the most popular alcoholic beverages in the world. Although it is still illegal in many countries, absinthe has experienced a rebirth as the European Union relaxed laws controlling its manufacture and sale. A large part of absinthe's appeal was its religiously observed ritual of consumption in the Drip. A small shot of the strongly flavored and incredibly potent (130- to 140-proof) liquor was placed in a glass. A special absinthe spoon—nearly flat, with very little concavity, perforated, and often ornately decorated—was set over the glass. A sugar cube was placed in the spoon. And then water was dripped onto the cube, melting the sugar into the drink, where the addition of these drops of water would turn the clear green absinthe into a cloudy yellow, sweetened and slightly diluted. With premium absinthes, though, sugar was often considered unnecessary, and the Absinthe Drip was then made using a special glass with a reservoir, replacing the spoon; cold water poured into this reservoir would slowly drip down into the absinthe.

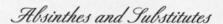

INGREDIENT NOTE

Absinthes and Substitutes

The ritual of the Absinthe Drip can still be undertaken today with one of the many absinthe substitutes. Pernod and Ricard, both from France, are the most popular and widely available. In the nineteenth century, the Pernod family bought the original absinthe recipe from its inventor, and today's Pernod tastes more like anise; Ricard, a popular Marseilles pastis, tastes more like licorice. Both of these are much sweeter than absinthe, and they are often served like premium absinthe with simply water, no sugar. Herbsaint, originally from New Orleans but now distilled in Kentucky, is our own perfectly fine American absinthe substitute. Absente, made in France using southwood, a variation of wormwood, is a high-quality 110-proof

liqueur that closely approximates the original; less sweet than Pernod and Ricard, it is one of the best substitutes for making the Absinthe Drip.

Interestingly, a New Orleans chemist named Ted Breaux recently bought two of the 1,100-liter stills, manufactured in 1901, that had been used to make the early-twentieth-century Pernod recipe for absinthe. Breaux has fired up these old stills, along with eight smaller ones, in Combier, France, and started making absinthe again. Breaux is using the same stills in the same town, using the same ingredients and often from the same sources as the original recipe did 150 years ago—he chemically analyzed a pre-ban bottle of Pernod Fils, which he

bought at auction. Ted's company, Jade Liqueurs, produces a few bottlings, all based on original formulas that he researched and chemically matched; these products are quite easy to find online. In 2007, Ted started distributing a bottling called Lucid Absinthe Supérieure, which is the first absinthe in nearly a century that's 100 percent legal in the United States—legal to sell, legal to buy, legal to drink, and more and more widely available at retail every day—because Ted figured out a way to provide the wormwood-oil flavor impact without any trace of the actual wormwood. (When Ted isn't making absinthe, he's an environmental microbiologist.)

ABSINTHE

In the few decades before it was internationally banned, absinthe was probably the most famous spirit in the world. It was thought of as an aphrodisiac and as medicine (it was prescribed by doctors to control fever), and was known as *la fée verte*—"the green fairy." Absinthe was strongly flavored with anise and had lighter notes from herbs including mint, coriander, chamomile, and something called wormwood, which, when taken in large quantities, was believed by some to attack the nervous system— sometimes fatally. (But wormwood too was originally thought of as medicine; the name, from the Middle Ages, refers to its use in drawing worms out of the digestive tract.) Absinthe was also thought to be the primary cause of the spread of alcoholism in France and a cause of epilepsy and suicide. It was rumored to be the fuel behind Vincent van Gogh's insane decision to lop off his own ear. And so it was banned—first in 1907 in Switzerland, where it was invented and manufactured, then in the United States in 1912, and finally in France, which gave up the green fairy in 1915.

As it turns out, contemporary chemists have proven that wormwood and absinthe could not have been guilty of the crimes with which they were charged; more likely, the drinking problems in France were caused by the utter lack of regulation in the industry—and hence the dangerous byproducts that could be found in many distilled spirits—combined with absinthe's very high proof.

ADONIS COCKTAIL

The Adonis was named for a long-running play that debuted on Broadway in 1884, about an Adonis statue that comes to life. The recipe below is my own variation, adapted from the classic to showcase Vya vermouth, which I think is the first American-made vermouth with character. Winemaker Andy Quady, of Madera, California, came up with the premium apéritif ten years ago, and it drives some spice into this twenty-first-century Adonis. I'd never serve Vya in a dry martini because it's not the traditional flavor and it would put off the traditional martini drinker. But on its own, or in a complex drink with other flavor notes, such as the Adonis, it's an intriguing, highly original apéritif. The sherry to use here is the dry style, called *fino*, as opposed to the fuller, usually sweeter *oloroso*.

INGREDIENTS

1 ounce Vya dry vermouth
½ ounce French dry vermouth
½ ounce fino sherry
1 ounce fresh-squeezed orange juice
2 dashes of Gary Regan's Orange
    Bitters No. 6
Flamed orange peel (page 249), for
    garnish
Nutmeg, for grating, optional

☞ Combine the Vya and dry vermouths, sherry, orange juice, and bitters in a mixing glass with ice and shake well. Strain into a chilled cocktail glass and garnish with the orange peel. Grate nutmeg over the top of the drink, if desired.

INGREDIENT NOTE

Bitters

This recipe calls for Gary Regan's Orange Bitters No. 6, which is definitely *not* Angostura bitters. Angostura and Peychaud's bitters, the two most widely known and available types, are bitters in the very real sense of having a flavor profile whose strongest note is the bitter herb gentian. Orange bitters are dominated by an orange flavor that's surrounded by sharp herbal notes. Bitters of any type impart strong flavor from little volume, and the different varieties are not at all interchangeable. So be forewarned that the word(s) in front of *bitters* are just as operative. For this recipe, Gary Regan's No. 6 is what I've been using, but you might also try Angostura's recently released, long-awaited orange bitters, which have received genuine rave reviews—not a surprise, given that their aromatic bitters have been unmatched in intensity, flavor, and favor for 180 years.

BLACK VELVET

In 1861, the death of Queen Victoria's husband, Prince Albert, set off a long period of deep mourning in the British Isles; they even draped their Champagne in black, hence the name Black Velvet. I have to admit the Black Velvet is not now and never has been a wildly popular drink in the United States, but it has always been drunk overseas, especially in the United Kingdom. The British have a long, strong tradition of mixing beers, ales, and stouts with one another and with other alcoholic beverages, such as in the Black and Tan (stout with ale). Stout is a rich, dark ale–style beer. To make stout, ale yeast is used, and the brew top-ferments at a higher temperature and quicker than beers made with lager yeasts. Ales can be light, like wheat beer, or very dark, like stout; the difference is the degree of barley roast. Stout is made from barley roasted until it's almost black, creating a very dark beer, perfect for shrouding your Champagne. And for most people the word *stout* means Guinness, the revered Irish brewery founded in 1759 by Arthur Guinness in Dublin. As unlikely as this combination of stout and Champagne sounds, David Embury explains in his 1949 book *The Fine Art of Mixing Drinks*, the result is "something like molasses and horse-radish. Actually, it is excellent. The champagne cuts the heavy, syrupy consistency of the stout, and the stout takes the sharp, tart edge off the champagne. Each is the perfect complement of the other. Be sure, however, that you use (a) a good bottling of the stout, (b) an extra-dry champagne—preferably a *brut* or *nature*."

INGREDIENTS

Guinness stout
Champagne

☞ In a pilsner beer glass—or a silver tankard, if you've got one lying around—slowly pour together equal parts stout and Champagne.

BLUE BLAZER

Okay, I have to be honest: You're not going to make this drink at home unless you're a professional who's practicing for a competition or a really insane amateur with a death wish. Why? First, it's made by pouring a stream of fire back and forth. Second, it's made by *pouring a stream of fire back and forth.* Otherwise, it's merely a variant of a toddy; the entire point of the Blue Blazer is the show of mixing it aflame. This show was first put on by Jerry Thomas, author of the first cocktail book and the godfather of my trade, who, according to legend, invented the Blue Blazer at the Occidental Hotel in San Francisco for a lucky prospector. This customer showed up at the bar carrying both a large ingot from the vein he'd hit and the bluster that comes from newfound fortune. He demanded, "Make me something special." Thomas went back to the kitchen, concocted the Blue Blazer, emerged to the bar, and served this dramatic show. The prospector drank it down hot, pronounced it a potent and spectacular success, and a legendary cocktail was born.

INGREDIENTS

1 teaspoon white sugar or less, to taste
1½ ounces boiling water
1½ ounces scotch, warmed
Lemon twist, for garnish

☞ Into a London dock glass—a stemmed glass meant to hold port or Sauternes but that works nicely for hot or warm mixed drinks—spoon the white sugar. Heat two silver-lined mugs using hot water. When they're nice and hot, pour the boiling water into one mug and the warmed scotch into the other. With a long-handled match (like a fireplace match or a nice-sized kitchen match), ignite the scotch; note that the scotch can also be lit with a flamed lemon peel, giving the opportunity for a bit more showmanship. Lower the lights. Pour the flaming scotch into the hot-water mug, then back into the now-empty other mug. Pour the flaming mixture back and forth a few times, partially to mix the drink but mostly for the pure drama of it. Each time the liquid is poured back and forth, carefully increase the distance between mugs— that is, if all precautions have been taken and you're feeling confident in your technique. Finally, pour the flaming mixture into the London dock glass, garnish with the lemon twist, and serve with a racing heart and immense pride.

Avoiding Immolation

THE TOOLS: Because you're igniting alcohol and handling it while it's on fire, you need the proper vessel, which is called, with uncanny appropriateness, a Blue Blazer mug. This is a mug that's lined on the inside with Sheffield silver, which has a high tolerance for heat, and has an insulated handle (the mug can't be *all* silver, or it'd immediately heat up too much to touch), a feathered rim (which allows you to pour cleanly without any dribbling), and a mouth wide enough to be a decently sized target. You probably won't find a bona fide Blue Blazer mug, but to avoid the emergency room, please do find a heat-resistant vessel with a feathered lip, like a Pyrex measuring cup. (I once tried this with a pair of silver creamers, and the flame flew up my hands.) Practice pouring water back and forth to make sure it doesn't dribble, and test for adequate insulation from boiling water.

THE INGREDIENTS: When Thomas invented the drink, 100 percent malt scotch was the only whiskey available from Scotland; blended scotch was still twenty years in the future. Scotch was expensive in the United States and thus not very popular, and the English really despised it, so it was a special ingredient at the time. Thomas specified Islay malt, the strongest, smokiest, peatiest of the malt scotches. Now, of course, scotch whiskey doesn't seem that remarkable, but the distinction is still important. When you're lighting your whiskey on fire and drinking it hot, you want it to be a good scotch and barrel-strength, which ignites more readily. And when using cask-strength scotch, pour the hot water and whiskey into the same mug; the overproof whiskey will ignite, even when not warmed in advance.

THE FLOOR: That's right—the floor. Of the room you're standing in to mix the Blue Blazer. That floor should be neither wood nor carpet; you want to be standing on a nice inflammable tile or some such.

THE FIRE EXTINGUISHER: Must be nearby.

THE LIGHTS: Okay, so now you're ready—you have the right vessels and ingredients, you've practiced, your friend has the fire extinguisher at the ready. Now turn the lights down so everyone can see this pyrotechnic feat; alcohol burns with a pale blue flame and is difficult to see in normal room light. When this pour is done properly in a dark room, it makes a wonderful show. With the lights on, though, it's wasted effort.

BOBBY BURNS

Before the Waldorf merged with the Astoria and moved uptown and over to Park Avenue, it stood on the Fifth Avenue site now occupied by the Empire State Building and was home to the cocktail palace and most famous pre-Prohibition bar in America, the Big Brass Rail, the watering hole for the robber barons and politicians and anyone else who ran New York City. It wasn't unusual to find Andrew Carnegie and John Jacob Astor sharing a drink at this bar, which had an oyster counter at one end and a cigar concession at the other. It was here that the Bobby Burns was invented—named for the Scottish poet and served on Robert Burns Day. Don't skip the shortbread cookie garnish. It's traditional, it's Scottish, and it's delicious.

INGREDIENTS

2 ounces Highland malt scotch
¾ ounce Italian sweet vermouth
½ ounce Benedictine
Shortbread cookie, for garnish

 Stir the scotch, vermouth, and Benedictine in a mixing glass with ice. Strain into a chilled cocktail glass and garnish with the cookie on the side.

*Let other poets raise a fracas
A'bout vines, an' wines, an'
drunken Bacchus
An' crabbit names an' stories
wrack us
   An' grate our lug,
I sing the juice Scotch bear can
mak' us,
   In glass or jug.*
—ROBERT BURNS,
 from "Scotch Drink"

KENTUCKY COLONEL

Until a few decades ago, it was not uncommon for high-end hotels to have their own bourbon, privately bottled and labeled. In the case of the Hotel Bel Air in Los Angeles, where I worked from 1979 to 1984, the private label was Jim Beam bourbon, which went into this variation of the Bobby Burns, which was one of our house cocktails.

INGREDIENTS

2 ounces bourbon
¾ ounce Benedictine liqueur
Dash of Angostura orange bitters

☛ Stir the bourbon, Benedictine, and bitters with ice. Strain into a chilled cocktail glass, with no garnish. Or serve in a rocks glass over ice, also with no garnish. *Note:* According to the regulars, the senior bartender at the hotel for thirty years prior to my arrival, Spence, dashed this drink with DeKuyper orange bitters, a tradition I continued until the day I emptied the last bottle and ordered another. The senior steward, exhibiting no tolerance for my obvious ignorance, gleefully announced that the stuff hadn't been made in years.

BENEDICTINE FOAM

The conservative makers of Scotch whiskey might balk at the idea of turning spirits to foam just to experience another texture. But then again, they also balk at drinking scotch with ice! Here, I pull the Benedictine flavor out of the cocktail (and of course omit it from the liquid part of the recipe) and reconstruct it as a foam ingredient on top of the drink. See page 250 for more information on making foam—you'll need some equipment.

Using the ½-liter cream canister will make enough foam for 15 to 20 drinks
2 gelatin sheets, each
    9 x 2¾ inches
¼ cup superfine bar sugar
6 ounces Benedictine
2 ounces emulsified egg whites

☛ Place the empty ½-liter canister with the top unscrewed in the refrigerator to chill; do not put it in the freezer. Fill a saucepan with 10 ounces water and place over low heat. Slowly stir in the 2 gelatin sheets, dissolving them completely. Turn off the heat, add the sugar, and continue to stir until dissolved. Let cool. Add the Benedictine and the egg whites, mix well, and fine-strain the mixture into a metal bowl; place the bowl in an ice bath, and stir occasionally until the mixture is cold.

Add 1 pint of the mixture to the canister. Screw the cap on very well, making sure it is completely tightened. Screw in the cream charger; you will hear a quick sound of gas escaping, which is normal. Turn the canister upside down and shake very well, and the foam is ready.

Store in the refrigerator between uses. Before each use, turn the canister upside down and shake well. Then hold the canister almost completely upside down and gently put pressure on the trigger mechanism, applying the foam slowly over the top of the drink, working from the inside rim of the glass in a circular fashion to the center. When the canister is empty, hold it over the sink and engage the trigger to be sure the gas is completely spent. Remove the top and clean according to the manufacturer's instructions.

BRONX COCKTAIL

INGREDIENTS

1½ ounces gin
½ ounce Italian sweet vermouth
½ ounce French dry vermouth
1 ounce fresh-squeezed orange juice
Dash of Angostura bitters, optional
Orange peel, for garnish

☞ Combine the gin, sweet and dry vermouths, orange juice, and bitters in a mixing glass with ice and shake well. Strain into a large cocktail glass and garnish with the orange peel.

 You're out of town. You're wearing your best suit, and your shoes are freshly shined. You haven't yet closed the deal, but you now know that tomorrow you will. So although it's premature to order the celebratory Champagne, it's exactly the right moment to order a traditional stiff drink at the five-star hotel's bar, taking your first deep, worry-free breath in what seems like forever. And so you shoot your cuffs, rest your wingtip on the brass foot rail, and order a Bronx, just like the fat cats did from Johnny Solon, who supposedly invented the Bronx at the Waldorf. Hold your chin high when you order your Bronx and imagine a long bar with no stools, a cigar counter at one end and an oyster counter at the other, and Wild Bill Hickok, in town for the Wild West Show, elbow to elbow with you at the Big Brass Rail.

ORANGE BITTERS FOAM

The Bronx has always presented a bit of a challenge for the bartender when it comes to figuring out how much juice to use in the drink. Early recipes indicate that juice was a very small part of the recipe, but at the Rainbow Room I quickly discovered the drink was popular only if I used at least 1 ounce orange juice. In a retooled twenty-first-century version I use the foam recipe below and reduce the amount of juice in the cocktail itself from 1 ounce to ½ ounce, providing the rest of the orange-spice flavors with the topping. For advice on making foam, including the equipment needed, see page 250.

Using the ½-liter cream canister will make enough foam for 15 to 20 drinks
2 navel oranges
2 gelatin sheets, each 9 x 2¾ inches
¼ cup superfine bar sugar

4 ounces fresh-squeezed orange juice, strained
2 ounces emulsified egg whites
3 ounces Grand Marnier
10 dashes of Angostura orange bitters

☞ Carefully cut away large sections of the orange peels with as little pith as possible. Set aside.

Place the empty ½-liter canister with the top unscrewed in the refrigerator to chill; do not put it in the freezer. Fill a saucepan with 8 ounces water and place over low heat. Slowly stir in the 2 gelatin sheets, dissolving them completely. Turn off the heat, add the sugar, and continue to stir until dissolved. Let cool. Add the orange juice, egg whites, Grand Marnier, and bitters, and mix well. Twist the reserved sections of orange peel over the mixture, expressing the oil into the mixture, and stir to combine. Strain the liquid through a fine strainer into

a metal bowl; place the bowl in an ice bath to chill.

Add 1 pint of the mixture to the canister. Screw the cap on very well, making sure it is completely tightened. Screw in the cream charger; you will hear a quick sound of gas escaping, which is normal. Turn the canister upside down and shake very well, and the foam is ready.

Store in the refrigerator between uses. Before each use, turn the canister upside down and shake well. Then hold the canister almost completely upside down and gently put pressure on the trigger mechanism, applying the foam slowly over the top of the drink, working from the inside rim of the glass in a circular fashion to the center. When the canister is empty, hold it over the sink and engage the trigger to be sure the gas is completely spent. Remove the top and clean according to the manufacturer's instructions.

VARIATION

SATAN'S WHISKERS

This variation of the Bronx, with the addition of Grand Marnier (why wouldn't you?), is adapted from the recipe of the Embassy Club in Hollywood, circa 1930.

INGREDIENTS

1 ounce gin
½ ounce Italian sweet vermouth
½ ounce French dry vermouth
½ ounce Grand Marnier
1 ounce fresh-squeezed orange juice
Dash of Angostura or orange bitters
Orange peel, for garnish

☛ Combine the gin, sweet and dry vermouths, Grand Marnier, orange juice, and bitters in a mixing glass with ice and shake well. Strain into a chilled cocktail glass and garnish with the orange peel.

 INGREDIENT NOTE

Grand Marnier

Grand Marnier is a younger cousin of the first orange liqueurs, curaçao and triple sec, but quickly surpassed them to become, as David Embury notes in his book *The Fine Art of Mixing Drinks*, "the absolute king of all liqueurs." Grand Marnier is found primarily in cocktails, but can also be sipped neat after dinner.

CHAMPAGNE COCKTAIL

INGREDIENTS

Sugar cube soaked in Angostura bitters
Champagne
Splash of cognac, optional
Lemon peel, for garnish, optional

 Place the Angostura-soaked sugar cube in the bottom of a Champagne glass and fill with Champagne. This drink is sometimes topped with a splash of cognac and garnished with a lemon peel, but the former is usually done in England, and the latter is never done in France.

TOASTING

Although the Greeks were the first to raise a glass as a welcome gesture (actually, it was to prove the wine wasn't poisoned), it was the Roman tradition of putting toasted bread in wineglasses—to make mediocre wine more palatable—that gave us the phrase.

 What a magically sophisticated pairing of words—just sàying "Champagne Cocktail" should make you feel civilized. This is one of the few original cocktails that appeared in the first (1862) edition of *How to Mix Drinks*, by Jerry Thomas, and the recipe has remained unchanged for nearly 150 years. The only difference is that in those days sugar cubes weren't available, so the recipe called for 1 teaspoon sugar. The cognac, which adds firepower, is a European addition, originated by the Café Royal in London; as a general rule, Americans don't use the cognac fortification. And the lemon twist, although traditional in America, is utter sacrilege in France and to Frenchmen no matter where they may be ordering their Champagne Cocktails. The French believe, with good reason, that the acid destroys the integrity of the fine wine. I include the peel only if the guest requests it.

The style bars of London employ a clever bit of business to make a show of the preparation by placing a small cocktail napkin over the mouth of the glass and setting the plain sugar cube on top of the napkin. The Angostura is carefully dashed over the cube, soaking it completely. Then the napkin is folded in half, creating a chute to drop the sugar cube into the glass.

INGREDIENT NOTE

It is called Champagne Cocktail, not Sparkling Wine Cocktail, so use the real stuff. Champagne is a region in the north of France, and this region's sparkling wine, produced since the end of the eighteenth century, is called *Champagne,* either blanc de blancs if made exclusively from chardonnay grapes or blanc de noirs if made from red wine grapes, usually pinot noir. Most Champagne is nonvintage, meaning the wines are a blend from different years. It is *brut* if dry, *demi-sec* if semisweet (literally "semi-dry"), and *doux* if sweet. Demi-sec used to be the most common type, but the drying out of Champagne, which began when Madame Clicquot (the widow, or *veuve*) made a concerted effort to appeal to the less-sweet-loving British palate, eventually surpassed the sweeter type. Sparkling wine is made elsewhere in the world—notably cava from Spain, prosecco and Asti in Italy, Sekt in Germany—and some of it is quite good, sometimes even great. But with the notable exception of the United States, which allows domestic sparkling wine to be mislabled "Champagne," the rest of the world reserves the capitalized word *Champagne* for the French wine that you should use for a proper Champagne Cocktail.

CHAMPAGNE PICK-ME-UP

INGREDIENTS

1 ounce VS cognac

1½ ounces fresh-squeezed orange juice

2 dashes of grenadine

3 ounces Champagne or other sparkling brut

Seasonal fresh fruit or berries, for garnish

☞ Combine the cognac, orange juice, and grenadine in a mixing glass with ice and shake well. Strain over ice into a white wine glass and top up with the Champagne. Garnish with whatever fruit is freshest.

 I prey thee let me and my fellow have
A haire of the dog that bit us last night.
—THOMAS HEYWOOD (1575–1641)

Champagne is one of those alcoholic beverages you can enjoy any time of day, even in the morning. It sounds foreign today, but in the eighteenth and nineteenth centuries it was utterly commonplace to drink alcohol throughout the day, because water was often undrinkable and other non-alcoholic beverages were often of questionable potability. So spirits were often consumed beginning at breakfast. The lighter, less alcoholic ones, like the Champagne Cocktail, were sensibly taken earlier in the day. The crowd-pleasing recipe here is from the Ritz Bar in Paris, circa 1936. Because the sparkling wine here is mixed with a few other assertive ingredients, it's permissible to use something less rarefied than genuine Champagne.

THE PICK-ME-UP

The hair-of-the-dog philosophy, though it sounds reasonable and certainly hints at a fun-loving life, is utter nonsense from a physiological point of view. The various degrees of hangover are all various degrees of alcohol poisoning. As David Embury pointed out in *The Fine Art of Mixing Drinks,* "You don't treat arsenic poisoning by taking more arsenic. . . . Why be so naïve as to imagine that you can cure alcohol poisoning by drinking more alcohol?" You can't, of course. The only way to cure a hangover is to get rid of the alcohol in your bloodstream, which more than anything is simply a function of resting and waiting.

While we're on the subject of overconsumption, allow me to speak to the responsibility a host has for his or her guests: It is the same concern a professional bartender must have by law, which is not to overserve customers. Alcohol begins to affect the human body only when it has left the stomach and entered the bloodstream. A host can do many things to slow that process. First, of course, is to reduce the speed with which the alcohol is consumed, and that a host or bartender can control, to a certain extent. Equally important is to fill the stomach with food and water to slow the progress of the alcohol to the bloodstream. I think a full glass of water should be served with each and every strong drink—a part of regular bar service that has been neglected in recent years. And making food and water available to your guests will make for a better evening all around.

RITZ COCKTAIL*

This is my tribute to the Ritz hotels of London, Paris, and Madrid, a cocktail designed as a sophisticated evening cocktail, not a pick-me-up. I substitute the great white cherry liqueur of the Adriatic and premium orange liqueur for the pick-me-up's grenadine, and add acid in the form of lemon. The Ritz Cocktail was the first drink that ever earned me national ink, in *Playboy* (1985). More than two decades later, I still think it's worth the ink.

INGREDIENTS

¾ ounce cognac
½ ounce Cointreau
½ ounce Luxardo Maraschino
   liqueur
½ ounce fresh-squeezed lemon juice
Champagne
Flamed orange peel (page 249), for
   garnish

☞ In a mixing glass, stir together the cognac, Cointreau, Maraschino liqueur, and lemon juice with ice. Strain into a large cocktail glass and fill with Champagne. Garnish with the flamed orange peel.

CLOVER CLUB

Yeats eyed the novel pink drink warily. At first, he was for waving it away. . . . Yeats tasted the cocktail, and smacked his lips. Another taste. His eye gleamed and his face lighted up. But, to the surprise of his hosts, he declined to gulp. This thing must be taken slowly. It was filled with a variety of flavors, and it must be tasted all the way down to the bottom of the glass. So he just sat and sipped that Clover Club Cocktail. When wine was brought and proffered him, he waved it away. —ALBERT STEVENS CROCKETT, *Old Waldorf Bar Days* (1931)

This pre-Prohibition cocktail was the invention of the Bellevue-Stratford Hotel in Philadelphia, which for a few early-twentieth-century decades was one of the premier hotels in the world. The Bellevue-Stratford hosted something of a Friar's Club called the Clover Club, from the late 1880s until at least the First World War, and this sour-style drink was named for that group. The recipe here is modified from one in *The Artistry of Mixing Drinks* by Frank Meier (published in 1936 by the Ritz Hotel, Paris). Harry MacElhone, who worked at the Plaza in the early teens, used lime juice instead of lemon. If you add a sprig of mint before shaking, you get a Clover Leaf. And if raspberries are in season and you're in the mood for something extra-fresh, omit the grenadine and instead muddle a half-dozen fresh raspberries in the shaker with the simple syrup; also, increase the syrup to 1 ounce. Then add the rest of the ingredients, shake, and double-strain (first with a Hawthorn strainer to pour the drink out of the shaker, then with a julep strainer set over the glass to catch any raspberry seeds) into a chilled cocktail glass. Another twist: Ted "Dr. Cocktail" Haigh revealed the secret sister of the Clover Club, the original Pink Lady (page 96), made by adding ½ ounce applejack to the recipe here. One final variant: With the same 1½ ounces London dry or Plymouth gin, add 2 teaspoons apiece of both Noilly Prat white and Martini & Rossi red vermouths. Note that the early-twentieth-century recipes used grenadine as the exclusive sweetener for the Clover Club and the Pink Lady. I added simple syrup because today we make larger drinks, and with the added sour ingredient it becomes necessary to help the grenadine and avoid a too-sour drink.

INGREDIENTS

1½ ounces gin
¾ ounce simple syrup (page 246)
¾ ounce fresh-squeezed lemon juice
½ teaspoon grenadine
White of 1 small egg (see Ingredient Note, page 30)

☛ In a shaker, combine the gin, syrup, lemon juice, and grenadine. In a small bowl, lightly whip the egg white. Add half of the whipped white to the shaker; save the other half for another cocktail. Shake vigorously—drinks with egg must be shaken harder and longer to emulsify the egg. Strain into a chilled cocktail glass.

EAST INDIA COCKTAIL

In its day (that day was back when East India was a place) this was a very popular cocktail, and its recipe appeared in every cocktail book. The first version appeared in O. H. Byron's 1884 classic *The Modern Bartender's Guide* and called for red curaçao, which is now extinct (the white version is also high on the endangered spirits list), as well as for "1 wineglass brandy," which is not a measure we continue to use. Here is my version of the Byron recipe adapted with updated measures and with orange in place of the red curaçao.

INGREDIENTS

2 ounces cognac
1 teaspoon raspberry syrup
1 teaspoon orange curaçao
2 or 3 dashes of Angostura bitters
2 or 3 dashes of Luxardo Maraschino
    liqueur
Lemon peel, for garnish

☞ In a mixing glass, combine the cognac, syrup, curaçao, bitters, and Maraschino liqueur with ice, and stir well. Strain into a cocktail glass, twist the lemon peel over the top, and serve.

PINEAPPLE-SPICE FOAM

In the 1980s, when I reconfigured the East India recipe at the Rainbow Room, I added some spice to the mixture. Two decades later, I reconfigured it again, delivering the same spice notes in a deconstructed version of a mid-nineteenth-century classic. When using this foam alternative, leave out the Angostura bitters, and of course you won't need to grate any nutmeg over the top. But you *will* need a foam canister. These are made by several manufacturers; I recommend Isi's Thermo Whip 0.5-liter canister. You'll also need two cream chargers. (See page 250 for more on making foam.)

Using the ½-liter cream canister will make enough foam for 15 to 20 drinks
4 nutmeg berries, each broken into pieces
2 gelatin sheets, each 9 x 2¾ inches
½ cup superfine bar sugar
8 ounces unsweetened pineapple juice
2 ounces emulsified egg whites
¾ ounce of Angostura bitters

☞ Place the empty ½-liter canister with the top unscrewed in the refrigerator to chill; do not put it in the freezer. Fill a saucepan with 12 ounces water and place over low heat. Add the nutmeg berries, and simmer for 15 minutes. Then slowly stir in the 2 gelatin sheets, dissolving them completely. Turn off the heat, add the sugar, and continue to stir until dissolved. Fine-strain the mixture to remove the solids. Let cool. Add the pineapple juice, egg whites, and the bitters, and stir well. Fine-strain the mixture into a metal bowl; place the bowl in an ice bath to speed up the chilling process.

Add 1 pint of the mixture to the canister. Screw the cap on very well, making sure it is completely tightened. Screw in the cream charger; you will hear a quick sound of gas escaping, which is normal. Turn the canister upside down and shake very well, and the foam is ready.

Store in the refrigerator between uses. Before each use, turn the canister upside down and shake well. Then hold the canister almost completely upside down and gently put pressure on the trigger mechanism, applying the foam slowly over the top of the drink, working from the inside rim of the glass in a circular fashion to the center. When the canister is empty, hold it over the sink and engage the trigger to be sure the gas is completely spent. Remove the top and clean according to the manufacturer's instructions.

TWENTIETH-CENTURY EAST INDIA COCKTAIL

This is from Harry Craddock's 1930 *Savoy Cocktail Book*, but I have taken the liberty of translating to ounces from Craddock's "parts," and I added the garnish.

INGREDIENTS

1½ ounces cognac
¼ ounce unsweetened pineapple juice
¼ ounce orange curaçao
Dash of Angostura bitters
Flamed orange peel (page 249), for garnish

☞ Combine the cognac, pineapple juice, curaçao, and bitters in a mixing glass with ice, and shake well. Strain into a cocktail glass and garnish with the orange peel.

MILLENNIUM COCKTAIL*

In 1999, more than one hundred years after Byron published his version of the East India Cocktail and fifty years after a guy named Bill Kelly published his in a book called *The Roving Bartender*, I decided to reinvent the East India. I called it the Millennium Cocktail in honor of the upcoming turn of the calendar and for the Millennium bottling by Courvoisier, which had hired me to create a drink for the special product. It was quite a bit juicier than the earlier versions, and had the additional garnishes of freshly grated nutmeg and a flamed orange peel. Soon after announcing my genius invention (pictured opposite), I learned of the prior versions, and I sheepishly acknowledged that I was not, after all, the inventor of this exceptional drink.

INGREDIENTS

1½ ounces Courvoisier Millennium cognac
1 ounce orange curaçao
1½ ounces unsweetened pineapple juice
Dash of Angostura bitters
Flamed orange peel (page 249), for garnish
Nutmeg, for grating

☞ Combine the cognac, curaçao, pineapple juice, and bitters with ice, and shake. Strain into a chilled cocktail glass and garnish by flaming the orange peel over the drink and dusting with freshly grated nutmeg.

FLIP

INGREDIENTS

2 ounces sherry

½ large egg, beaten (see Ingredient Note)

1 ounce simple syrup (page 246)

Nutmeg, for grating

☞ Combine the sherry, egg, and syrup in a mixing glass with ice and shake long and hard to emulsify the egg. Strain into a London dock glass and dust with freshly grated nutmeg.

Flips are a category of drinks dating from Shakespearean times, when it all started with a mixture of sherry, milk, and eggs called sherry sack posset. By the eighteenth century, Old World flips were pretty complex affairs. Both wine and beer were combined with eggs and all sorts of spices and milk. But when flips made the leap to New England, a strong spirit (usually rum) replaced the ale or wine. The drink was further simplified in the latter half of the nineteenth century to a combination of a spirit shaken with sugar and whole egg. All the spices were gone (save a dusting of nutmeg on top), as was the beer and the idea of shoving a scalding poker into the mix or cooking it over the hearth to create a hot drink. The modern American flip was cold. The most common versions were made with brandy, port, or sherry, though rum and whiskey were possibilities as well. No matter the liquor, this was a morning drink, an eye-opener, at a time when many drinks were thought of as appropriate for particular times of day—there was an egg in here, after all; it was practically breakfast on its own.

I can't say I've ever gotten a lot of orders for flips, but that doesn't mean I haven't served a lot of them. Back at the Rainbow Room, I used to suggest it with some frequency (especially if I had some spare egg lying around, left over from a fizz I'd just made). The flip is undoubtedly the forerunner of American eggnog, and, like eggnog, it's a perfect winter drink. I like to make it with sherry, but definitely not with the fino style, which is too dry and can't stand up to the egg and sugar. Instead, I use a rich oloroso or a nutty Amontillado. Dry sack (a misnomer if ever I've heard one, dry sack is not at all dry) or even a cream sherry like Bristol Cream would be good choices. And if you're going to make the flip with a strong spirit like cognac or whiskey, decrease the portion to 1½ ounces.

INGREDIENT NOTE

Eggs

The proper flip recipe calls for a small egg, but modern animal husbandry has made small eggs all but extinct in the United States. So find a medium egg and use three-quarters of it, or a large egg and use half. Either way, you're looking for about 1½ ounces beaten egg.

Now, about eggs in general. All drinks made with raw eggs must be shaken twice as hard and twice as long as other drinks to completely emulsify the egg. And, of course, you must observe the standard health cautions. But note that eggs used in cocktails don't constitute the same hazard as raw eggs used in, say, a béarnaise sauce, because the alcohol and acid in cocktails kill many of the dangerous bacteria.

JACK ROSE

Brett did not turn up, so about quarter to six I went down to the bar and had a Jack Rose with George the bar-man. Brett had not been in the bar either, and so I looked for her upstairs on my way out, and took a taxi to the Café Select. Crossing the Seine I saw a string of barges being towed empty down the current, riding high, the bargemen at the sweeps as they came toward the bridge. The river looked nice. It was always pleasant crossing bridges in Paris.
—ERNEST HEMINGWAY, *The Sun Also Rises* (1926)

Even if you're not Jake Barnes being stood up at the Crillon by the love of your life, the Jack Rose is a fantastic drink at quarter to six. And I love Hemingway's sentiment that Jake Barnes has a drink with George the bar-man, not a drink at the bar. The drink below is my adaptation for a modern palate, with the addition of simple syrup to turn it into more of a sour-style drink. The original recipe is too much about grenadine, especially now that 99 percent of the grenadine on the market is nothing more than artificially flavored and colored sugar water. Real grenadine—the original—is actually a pomegranate product and should *taste* like pomegranate (see Ingredient Note for homemade grenadine, page 96).

INGREDIENTS

1½ ounces applejack
¾ ounce simple syrup (page 246)
¾ ounce fresh-squeezed lemon juice
¼ ounce grenadine
Apple slice, for garnish
Maraschino cherry, for garnish

☛ Combine the applejack, syrup, lemon juice, and grenadine in a mixing glass with ice and shake well. Strain into a small cocktail glass and garnish with the apple slice and cherry.

INGREDIENT NOTE

Applejack

Applejack, also known as Jersey lightning (as in New Jersey), is a Calvados-like spirit that dates back to the colonial era. In fact, it may have been one of the earliest distilled spirits in the New World. In the eighteenth and nineteenth centuries, applejack was widely produced everywhere from New England down through New Jersey and into the Ohio River Valley—wherever there were apple orchards. One of the only brands left on the market is Laird and Company, which was established in 1780 (they claim to be America's first commercial distillery, with distillery license #1 issued) and is still owned by the same family. The regular Laird bottling of today is a blend of 35 percent apple whiskey with 65 percent neutral grain spirits, but they also produce a 100 percent apple whiskey called twelve-year-old Rare Apple Brandy.

In colonial times, homemade applejack was made without a still when the temperature dropped below freezing at night. You would take fresh-pressed apple cider and just leave it around to gather yeast and start fermenting. When you had naturally hardened cider, you put it in a shallow pan on your porch at night. In the early morning, there would be a thin layer of ice on top of the liquid. You skimmed off and discarded that ice, which is water, leaving behind the hardened cider; with each successive freeze-skim cycle, you removed more and more water, and stronger and stronger applejack was left behind.

MANHATTAN

INGREDIENTS

2 ounces blended whiskey
1 ounce Italian sweet vermouth
2 dashes of Angostura bitters
1 Maraschino cherry, for garnish (or your
special home-infused fresh cherry,
page 101)

☞ Stir the whiskey, vermouth, and bitters
in a mixing glass with ice. Strain into a
chilled cocktail glass and garnish with the
cherry.

Some things never go out of style, and the Manhattan is one of them. It is always in the top ten most-popular American cocktails. It is *the* rye cocktail (unless you happen to make it with brandy or bourbon) and was supposedly invented in 1874 by a bartender at the Manhattan Club, who created the drink when Jennie Churchill threw a party for Samuel James Tilden in honor of his election as governor of New York State. (However, according to the cocktail's historical oracle David Wondrich, a diligent researcher who's prone to ruining perfectly good stories with, um, facts, Jennie was in England having baby Winston on the date of the Tilden party.) In those days, curaçao was the preferred sweetener to take the edge off hard spirits. In *The Modern Bartender's Guide* by O. H. Byron (1884), two versions of the Manhattan (see page 34) arose in tandem with the inroads being made by both French and Italian vermouth into America and our cocktails.

GOLDEN AGE

THE FIRST MANHATTAN

The first Manhattan recipe appeared in the 1884 classic *The Modern Bartender's Guide: How to Mix Fancy Drinks* by O. H. Byron.

Whiskey for the Manhattan

Back in the nineteenth century, New York was a rye-drinking town, and it's safe to say that the early Manhattans were made with rye. But then Prohibition turned everything on its head, especially Americans' taste for whiskey, because none of it was produced in the United States for thirteen years. So the only good, aged, and relatively inexpensive whiskey was from Canada, and Crown Royal, a blend, had a lock on the North American premium-whiskey market. This is why the post-Prohibition generation drank blended if they drank whiskey, and that's how they took their Manhattans, right up through the 1950s. That's when bourbon, which is a bit spicier than Canadian blends, began a slow revival as America's brown spirit of choice.

We're now in the age of small-batch and single-barrel bourbons, and drinkers are moving in the direction of premium and super-premium spirits for everything, so those ingredients are now finding their way into Manhattans. Even rye, which has faced steadily diminishing sales since the 1960s, is starting to find a new audience—albeit a small one—via super-premium bottlings such as the thirteen-year-old from Pappy Van Winkle; Michter's ten-year-old; the 100-proof and twenty-one-year-old versions from Rittenhouse, in Kentucky; and the various bottlings of Old Portrero from Fritz Maytag, of Anchor Steam fame, especially his eleven-year-old Hotaling's Rye (see Ingredient Note, page 164).

THE ORIGINAL MANHATTANS

Below are the two Manhattan recipes that appeared in O. H. Byron's 1884 *Modern Bartender's Guide*. The first recipe doesn't include any instructions; the second, which is similar to the modern recipe, does. Following the second recipe was an entry for something called Martinez, with no recipe—just the line "Same as Manhattan, only you substitute gin for whiskey." This was the beginning of the saga of the martini. (For the measurements, note that a pony was equal to 1 ounce, and a wineglass was equal to 2 ounces.) It seems whiskey was a supporting actor and not the star in this early recipe. The first appearance of vermouth in a cocktail book was in 1869's stupendously long-titled *Haney's Steward & Barkeeper's Manual: A Complete and Practical Guide for preparing all kinds of Plain and Fancy Mixed Drinks and Popular Beverages, being the Most Approved Formulas Known in the Profession, designed for Hotels, Steamers, Club Houses, &c., &c., to which is appended recipes for Liqueurs, Cordials, Bitters, Syrups, etc., etc.* Remember that vermouth was still a cutting-edge ingredient in 1884.

MANHATTAN #1
- In a small wineglass
1 pony french vermouth
½ pony whiskey
3 or 4 dashes angostura
3 dashes of gum syrup

MANHATTAN COCKTAIL #2
2 dashes curaçao
2 dashes angostura bitters
½ wineglass whiskey
½ wineglass italian vermouth

 Fine ice; stir well. And strain into a cocktail glass.

VARIATION

BULL'S MANHATTAN*

Fortune magazine asked me to create cocktails to represent bulls and bears. Because Jack Daniel's is the best-selling American whiskey in the world, I thought it would be appropriate for the bull-market drink. Believe me, Old #7 is rarely seen in such fancy French company.

INGREDIENTS

2 ounces Jack Daniel's whiskey
¾ ounce French dry vermouth
¼ ounce Benedictine
Lemon peel, for garnish

☛ Stir the whiskey, vermouth, and Benedictine in a mixing glass with ice. Strain into a chilled cocktail glass and garnish with the lemon peel.

VARIATION

MANHATTAN EAST*

A Manhattan is a strong spirit combined with a wine product, and it's not that much of a stretch to replace the vermouth with sake, imparting an Eastern twist to the classic cocktail.

INGREDIENTS

2½ ounces bourbon
½ ounce Domaine de Canton
½ ounce dry sake
2 dashes of Gary Regan's Orange Bitters No. 6
Flamed orange peel (page 249), for garnish

☛ Stir the bourbon, ginger liqueur, sake, and bitters with ice. Strain into a chilled cocktail glass and garnish with the flamed orange peel.

MINT JULEP

Bracingly cold juleps were the first internationally known American cocktails, making their global debut in the late eighteenth century, when they were a mixture of cognac and peach brandy. (The name is derived from the Arabic *juleb*, which is a sweetened, herbal-infused water used as a health tonic.) But although the English took a small fancy to this cocktail—and since 1845 Oxford University has had a Mint Julep Day—it was the hot American summers that catapulted the drink to fame, for a julep is nothing if not icy cold and refreshing, filled with shaved ice inside the glass and a crust of it outside, chilling your whole body. When the julep was invented, there was rye whiskey in America but no such thing as bourbon—the corn whiskey idea didn't take root until the late eighteenth and early nineteenth centuries, with the settlers' movement west to areas of the continent where corn grew easily and rye was less prevalent. In the early nineteenth century the julep was strictly brandy and peach brandy, and, as late as 1869, in *Haney's Steward & Barkeeper's Manual*, the mint julep was a cognac-based drink with garnishes of orange and berries; there was also a whiskey variation that for some reason omitted the fancy fruit.

The mint julep made with bourbon achieved immense popularity in the American South and somehow became practically the signature cocktail of Kentucky. Every year since the late 1930s, America has had its own Mint Julep Day of sorts on the occasion of the Kentucky Derby at Churchill Downs in Louisville. In its heyday, the mint julep inspired the type of debate that today can be found swirling around the martini, as evidenced from this passage of Patrick Gavin Duffy's *Official Mixer's Manual*, first published in 1934: "There is no drink about which there is so much discussion as the Mint Julep. It is virtually impossible to find as many as two well-known bartenders who will agree as to the method of preparing it. We have given four of the better known Julep recipes, in the hope that one, at least, of them will be able to satisfy the most discriminating palate."

INGREDIENTS

2 sprigs of mint, preferably perky-looking spearmint
¾ ounce simple syrup (page 246)
2 ½ ounces bonded bourbon
Powdered sugar, for dusting, optional

☞ Gently bruise 1 of the mint sprigs in the bottom of a mixing glass with the syrup—use just enough pressure to release the mint's oils, but don't shred the leaves. Add the bourbon, but there's no need to mix here, because you're going to do a lot of it next. Strain into a highball glass or your favorite silver julep chalice filled with crushed ice (see page 38) and swirl the ice with a bar spoon until the outside of the glass frosts, which can take a few minutes for a thick glass or just a few seconds if you're using a proper silver julep cup (a 10-ounce sterling-silver chalice) or its approximation; if using glass, the thinner the better. Top off with a bit more crushed ice, as the level will have dropped with all that stirring, and stir briefly again. Garnish with the remaining mint sprig. If it's your preference, sprinkle the fine sugar over the top of the drink, which looks like yet more frosting of snow. Also, if it's your preference, insert two straws that are about 1 inch taller than the glass—ideally, these straws, as well as your cups, are sterling. Counsel your guests to hold the drink tightly, because all the frost makes it likely to slip through their grasp. One of the beauties of the proper julep cup is the reverse-tapered body, sometimes with a lip at the rim, allowing the imbiber every opportunity to rescue a slipping drink.

INGREDIENT NOTE

Bonded Bourbon

Bonded bourbon is certified by the United States government as straight whiskey from one distillery aged in oak for at least four years and bottled at 100 proof, allowing the bourbon to stand up to all that melting crushed ice. Old Forester is a good choice, or use one of the small-batch or single-barrel bourbons that are either cask strength or 90-plus proof: Look for Booker's, Blanton's, or even Maker's Mark. Stay away from 80-proof spirits; the higher proof is the best choice for crushed ice.

PROPER CRUSHED OR POWDERED ICE

Besides the generous serving of bonded Kentucky bourbon, the most pleasing aspect of the mint julep is the frostiness that builds up on the outside of the glass. This requires that you start with good ice. "Good ice?" you may ask. "Isn't all ice the same?" No. Ice can be extremely cold, dense, and dry when it's chipped off a block from an ice house, or it can be warm, thin, and wet when it's made from the ice machines that are ubiquitous in bars and the little alcoves off hotel corridors. Bad ice is made and maintained at the highest possible temperature—just at the freezing point—to produce copious amounts but at the expense of quality. Proper ice from an ice house (or from a good professional machine like Kold Draft or Scotsman) is colder and stays that way longer. What you want is to chip a fist-sized chunk off a nice cold block. Then you place your chunk in a canvas bag called a Lewis bag (that's right—there's a name for the bag you use to crush ice, made out of canvas to absorb any water created when you're crushing), fold over the bag, and place it on a secure cutting board away from small children or pets; however, if you have some larger children, this is a good job for them. (Also maybe if your pet is a really smart, obedient chimpanzee.) Then you grab a big square-headed wooden mallet—say, 5 to 8 pounds—and whale away until you've pulverized your block into a powder. This is proper powdered ice.

WHISKEY SMASH*

I created this drink because, frankly, I was a little bored by mint juleps, which have a tendency to be too sweet and too uncomplicated, with just whiskey and sugar water. So I mashed up some lemon with the mint and used curaçao instead of sugar, and I strained it into an old-fashioned glass, and . . . hey, it works so well you may win over a couple of vodka-drinking pals with this one. In summer, when peaches are sweet and inexpensive, I like to add a couple of peach slices to the mixing glass and muddle them along with the mint and lemon. I also add a slice of peach as a garnish along with the fresh sprig of mint. I fashioned the drink for bourbon or rye, but any American or Canadian whiskey will do, or even Irish. Steer clear of scotch for this drink, though, because its smoky profile would fight with the mint, and everyone would lose.

INGREDIENTS

4 mint leaves plus 1 sprig of mint
3 lemon quarters (Note: The sweet-sour balance of lemons can vary dramatically with seasonal changes, and the amount of curaçao will have to be adjusted up or down accordingly)
1 ounce orange curaçao
2 ounces bourbon or rye
Lemon slice, for garnish

☞ In the bottom of a bar glass, muddle the mint leaves, lemon quarters, and curaçao. Add the whiskey and ice; shake. Double-strain into an ice-filled rocks glass by using the Hawthorn strainer with the shaker while holding the julep strainer over the mouth of the serving glass to catch bits of mint or lemon. Garnish with the mint sprig and the lemon slice.

GRAPEFRUIT JULEP*

This original of mine takes serious liberty with the idea of a julep. I concocted it a few years ago after doing some work for both the grapefruit growers of Florida and for POM Wonderful pomegranate juice. Both grapefruit and pomegranate are pleasingly tart, like cranberry juice, and tart ingredients are excellent for mixing in cocktails. At the time I was exploring how to use sweeteners other than simple syrup and liqueurs. I was mixing different syrups together—honey with agave syrup, or honey, agave, and simple syrup all in the same cocktail. The unusual blends gave a warmly layered and complex sweetness that's impossible to achieve with plain simple syrup. The combination of all these elements yields a light, summery drink that's perfect by the batch for a picnic. (Or for the Academy Awards, at which it was served in 2005, under the name Pomegranate Martini.) A couple of years after I invented the Grapefruit Julep, Finlandia Grapefruit was released, and I think it may very well be the best of this ilk of flavored spirits, so that's what's used here.

INGREDIENTS

2 mint sprigs

½ ounce fresh-squeezed lime juice

½ ounce honey syrup (page 247)

½ ounce agave syrup (page 247)

1½ ounces vodka, preferably Finlandia Grapefruit

1½ ounces fresh-squeezed grapefruit juice

1 ounce POM Wonderful pomegranate juice

☛ In the bottom of a mixing glass, bruise 1 of the mint sprigs with the lime juice, honey syrup, and agave syrup. Add the vodka, grapefruit juice, pomegranate juice, and ice, and shake well. Strain it into a highball glass filled with crushed ice and stir to frost as you would a mint julep. Garnish with the remaining sprig of mint.

OLD-FASHIONED

INGREDIENTS

1 level teaspoon superfine bar sugar,
   or 1 to 2 sugar cubes, to taste
3 dashes of Angostura bitters
2 orange slices
2 Maraschino cherries
Splash of water or club soda
2 ounces bourbon

☞ In the bottom of an old-fashioned glass (what else?), carefully muddle the sugar, bitters, 1 of the orange slices, 1 of the cherries, and a splash of water or soda. Remove the fruit husks. Add the bourbon and ice, and stir. Garnish with the remaining orange slice and cherry.

For the Old-Fashioned, claimed by the Pendennis Club in Louisville, Kentucky, as their own, there are two philosophies: Muddle fruit, or don't muddle fruit. All other things being equal, I'm always partial to the flavor that's added from muddling—if you flip around in this book, you'll notice a lot of muddling—so I belong to the first school of thought, and here is the definitive muddled version. But the old-fashioned Old-Fashioned was simply a sugar cube, bitters, and water, muddled until dissolved, then chilled with ice and mixed with whiskey and garnished with a lemon peel—no fresh fruit. A very simple drink whose name refers to the almost identical presentation of the first cocktails in the first cocktail book, the 1862 edition of Jerry Thomas's *How to Mix Drinks*, which set the standard definition of the cocktail as a strong spirit of any kind, sugar, water, and bitters. The muddled fruit arrived in the twentieth century, which softened the Old-Fashioned into more of a punchy drink, and it has become a traditional Thanksgiving or Christmas pre-dinner cocktail in a lot of households.

ROYAL GINGERSNAP*

I was commissioned to create a cocktail for Crown Royal, and it turned out fine. I replaced the sugar with orange marmalade, making for a jolly holiday drink.

INGREDIENTS

Superfine sugar, for frosting the glass
Ground cinnamon, for frosting the glass
2 slices orange
1 Maraschino cherry
1 bar spoon (1 teaspoon) orange marmalade
¼ ounce Domaine de Canton
2 ounces Crown Royal
2 dashes of Angostura bitters
Flamed orange peel (page 249), for garnish

☞ Prepare a rocks glass: Combine equal measures superfine sugar and cinnamon in a plate, and frost the rim of the glass with this mixture and 1 of the orange slices according to the directions on page 137. In the bottom of a mixing glass, muddle the other orange slice and the cherry with the marmalade and ginger liqueur. Add the whiskey, bitters, and ice, and shake well. Strain into the prepared glass over ice, and garnish with the orange peel.

PIMM'S CUP

INGREDIENTS

1½ ounces Pimm's No. 1
7UP
Cucumber spear, for garnish
Green apple slice, for garnish

☞ Combine the Pimm's and 7UP in a highball glass over ice. Garnish with the cucumber spear and apple slice.

During my first week working at the Hotel Bel Air, in 1978, a guest ordered a margarita. I made it with the standard pre-mix and slid it across the bar. "I don't want that," the customer said. "I want a fresh margarita." I didn't know what the hell he was talking about, so I had to ask. The response was something along the lines of "With fresh juice, you idiot." It had never occurred to me that you could make a drink this way, and I immediately realized how ill-equipped I was to do—and keep—that job behind the famed bar at a hotel frequented by Armand Hammer and Laurence Olivier and the moguls and megastars who were too well established to bother with the starlets and riff-raff at the Beverly Hills Hotel. I'd never before been challenged behind the bar, and so I was ignorant—I didn't know what Sauternes was, didn't know how to mix a fresh drink, didn't know any drinks history.

So I had to do some quick footwork. I sought advice from senior bartenders who worked at other high-end joints around Hollywood and Beverly Hills. (They must have seen the seeds of a decent bartender buried beneath all the green.) Two veteran waiters in the lounge, Larry and Richard, started to fill me in on the regulars and what they drank. One of those drinks was a strange but popular concoction, an import from England, where it was served in a big pewter mug and garnished with the herb borage, or fresh mint sprigs when borage was unavailable, plus cucumber, apple, orange, lemon, lime, strawberries—or *all* of this fruit. I found out years later it was, and still is, the "mint julep" of the Wimbledon tennis championship. This cocktail, the Pimm's Cup, is made with the gin-based apéritif Pimm's No. 1, invented by James Pimm, who operated Pimm's Oyster Bar in the banking center of London in the mid-nineteenth century. James Pimm later sold his business and the rights to his name; his successors began to bottle the mixture for sale to other restaurants and bars, and it soon made its way abroad. This Pimm's was totally new to me—gin with a background hint of botanicals and quinine—and I loved it instantly. As I did the Pimm's Cup cocktail. I garnished it with a long spear of cucumber, dropping flavor into the drink along its entire face, and a slice of green apple, never red. I love a well-made Pimm's Cup, both for its flavor and for the journey on which it launched me.

INGREDIENT NOTE

Cynar

Cynar is another in the grand tradition of bitter European apéritifs, albeit with a surprising—you might even say astounding—flavor base: artichoke. Cynar, like Campari (which owns the brand), features a variety of herbal flavors. Also like Campari, Cynar is a tough sell to the American palate, especially as a primary ingredient; but as a minor note in a complex cocktail, it's an interesting addition, and in general it's a good alternative to Campari. Having said that, Cynar seems to have found a niche in the United States and shows up on back bars almost as regularly as Campari.

FRESH LEMONADE PIMM'S CUP*

When I became more comfortable using fresh juices, I began making the Pimm's Cup with fresh lemonade instead of what the English call lemonade, which is 7UP (or any lemon-lime soda). The version below mixes the both of them.

INGREDIENTS

1½ ounces Pimm's No. 1
¾ ounce fresh-squeezed lemon juice
1 ounce simple syrup (page 246)
Club soda
Splash of 7UP, optional, for a sweeter drink
Cucumber spear, for garnish
Green apple slice, for garnish

☛ In a cocktail shaker, combine the Pimm's, lemon juice, and syrup. Shake with ice. Strain over ice into a highball glass and top with the club soda and the 7UP, if using. Garnish with the cucumber spear and apple slice.

PIMM'S ITALIANO*

Here's an Italian-oriented riff on the English classic, created for the 2007 opening of Keith McNally's restaurant Morandi. Be sure to use bottled tonic, never the stuff from a gun.

INGREDIENTS

1 wheel of cucumber, cut crosswise, and 1 long slice of English cucumber, cut lengthwise
½ ounce Cynar (see Ingredient Note, opposite)
1½ ounces Pimm's No. 1
3 ounces tonic
Lemon slice, for garnish
Lime slice, for garnish

☛ Drop the wheel of cucumber and the Cynar into a tall serving glass. Smash the cucumber with a muddler. Add the Pimm's, tonic, and ice, and stir. Garnish with the long slice of cucumber and the slices of lemon and lime.

ROB ROY

Bill Grimes, in his fantastic book *Straight Up or On the Rocks*, found the origin of this drink in an 1890s Broadway show called (drumroll . . .) *Rob Roy*. It was created at the old Waldorf Hotel. Also called the Affinity, the Rob Roy is simply a Manhattan made with scotch instead of bourbon (this is how young bartenders remember the recipe). Back when Harry Craddock first wrote the *Savoy Cocktail Book*, in 1930, the standard recipe was equal parts scotch, sweet vermouth, and dry vermouth. That would be too sweet for today's palate, so the recipe here is in a drier style. It also includes bitters, which for a long time I didn't use because the cinnamon and allspice notes of Angostura weren't a good match with smoky scotch. But then I became more familiar with Peychaud's bitters, and its anise-cherry notes are actually a great match with scotch. So use Peychaud's if you have it, or no bitters. As for the scotch, blended is the traditional choice—usually a medium blend like Johnny Walker Red, or even a lighter style like J&B or Cutty Sark. But if you want to use single malt, steer clear of any tremendously smoky and peaty Islay malt or its kin and instead use a lighter style like Glenmorangie, which is really the first stop on the malt train after you've left the blended station—that is, the closest thing to a blend you'll find in single malt. That may not be what you want poured into a glass neat, but it *is* what you want mixed with sweet vermouth.

INGREDIENTS

2 ounces blended scotch
1 ounce Italian sweet vermouth
Peychaud's bitters to taste, optional
Lemon peel, for garnish

☛ Pour the scotch, vermouth, and bitters over ice in a mixing glass. Stir as you would a martini. Strain into a chilled cocktail glass and garnish with the lemon peel.

VARIATIONS

A PERFECT ROB ROY: 2 ounces scotch with equal parts dry and sweet vermouth, ½ ounce apiece, plus Peychaud's bitters.

A DRY ROB ROY, which in my years behind the bar I found was very popular, uses just ¾ ounce dry vermouth, no sweet, plus Peychaud's bitters.

SAZERAC

The Peychaud family were refugees from the 1790s slave uprising in Santo Domingo (which became Haiti), and Antoine Peychaud operated a pharmacy in New Orleans's Rue Royal. He was a Freemason, and his place often hosted lodge meetings. As refreshments, Peychaud would serve a drink based on cognac with his proprietary bitters. For many years, the colorful story of the birth of the word *cocktail* centered around the small two-sided egg cups in which Peychaud served his drink. The French called these cups *coquetries*, a word that Americans changed to *cocktay*, and then *cocktail*, in the early nineteenth century. Sadly, the Peychaud apothecary story is not the true derivation of the word: Cocktail was first defined in print in *Balance and Columbian Repository*, on May 13, 1806, when Peychaud was two years old. I hate it when a good story is ruined with the truth.

Although Peychaud's pharmacy wasn't the source of the word *cocktail*, it *was* the birthplace of the fantastic cocktail that became known as the Sazerac. In New Orleans at the time, the favorite cognac was made by Sazerac de Forge et Fils, in Limoges, France, and hence the name. This American classic is a sublime sipping drink, with all the spices and botanicals of the bitters and lemon oil mingling with the peppery rye and interacting with the bitter anise of absinthe. The Sazerac is made chilled but then served without ice, so the flavors open up immensely as it warms, delivering a new flavor burst with every sip.

The drink became legendary in New Orleans, where bars were named for it, like John Schiller's Sazerac Coffee House, which opened in 1859. (Locals were fond of referring to bars as *coffeehouses*, where women were always welcome to consume alcohol alongside their men, a custom that didn't take hold in the rest of the country until Prohibition, when speakeasies opened their doors to men and women alike . . . and why not? It was all illegal.) Note that the preparation of the Sazerac employs two rocks glasses, a tradition born of commonsense at a time when the bartender did not have an array of mixing tools and vessels.

INGREDIENTS

1 sugar cube, 2 for a sweeter drink

3 or 4 dashes of Peychaud's bitters

2 ounces rye whiskey

Splash of Lucid absinthe, Pernod, or another absinthe substitute (see Ingredient Note, page 12)

Lemon peel, for garnish

☛ Take two rocks glasses and fill one with ice to chill for serving while preparing the drink in the other. In the bottom of the prep glass, muddle the sugar cube and bitters until the sugar is dissolved; a splash of water can expedite the process. Add the rye and several ice cubes, and stir to chill. Take the serving glass, toss out its ice, and add the splash of absinthe or Pernod. Swirl it around to coat the inside of the glass, and then pour out any liquid that remains. Strain the chilled cocktail into this prepared glass. Garnish by twisting a lemon peel over the top and dropping it in the drink.

BLACK ROSE

This interesting take on the Sazerac is a bourbon variation—a long evolution from a cognac drink to a rye whiskey one to this Black Rose.

INGREDIENTS

2 ounces bourbon
1 dash of grenadine
2 dashes of Peychaud's bitters
Flamed lemon peel (page 249), for garnish

☛ Fill an old-fashioned glass three-quarters full with ice. Add the bourbon, grenadine, and bitters, and stir. Garnish with the lemon peel.

VARIATION

DALE'S SAZERAC*

As American tastes changed from cognac to whiskey over the years and centuries, the Sazerac cocktail came to be based on rye, instead of cognac. The recipe below, my own twist, incorporates the best of both worlds by using a mixture.

INGREDIENTS

1 ounce VS cognac
1 ounce rye whiskey
½ to ¾ ounce simple syrup (page 246), to taste
2 dashes of Peychaud's bitters
2 dashes of Angostura bitters
Splash of Lucid absinthe, Pernod, or another absinthe substitute (see Ingredient Note, page 12)
Lemon peel, for garnish

☛ Take two rocks glasses and fill one with ice to chill for serving while preparing the drink in the other. In the prep glass, combine the cognac, rye, syrup, and the two kinds of bitters. Add several ice cubes, and stir to chill. Take the serving glass, toss out its ice, and add the splash of absinthe. Swirl it around to coat the inside of the glass, and then pour out any liquid that remains. Strain the chilled cocktail into this prepared glass. Garnish by twisting the lemon peel over the top and dropping it in the drink.

ABSINTHE FOAM

I decided to have a little fun with the nineteenth-century Sazerac, giving it a twenty-first-century twist by removing the absinthe as a liquid ingredient and presenting its flavor in another form: as foam on top of the drink. When using the foam alternative, leave out the absinthe or absinthe substitute from the cocktail recipe. You'll need a foam canister; I recommend iSi's Thermo Whip 0.5-liter canister, along with two cream chargers. (See page 250 for more on making foam.)

Using the ½-liter cream canister will make enough foam for 15 to 20 drinks
2 gelatin sheets, each 9 x 2¾ inches
½ cup superfine bar sugar

4 ounces Lucid absinthe or absinthe substitute
2 ounces emulsified egg whites

☞ Place the empty ½-liter canister with the top unscrewed in the refrigerator to chill; do not put it in the freezer. Fill a saucepan with 10 ounces water and place over low heat. Slowly stir in the 2 gelatin sheets, dissolving them completely. Turn off the heat, add the sugar, and continue to stir until dissolved. Let cool. Add the absinthe and the egg whites, and stir well. Fine-strain the mixture into a metal bowl; place the bowl in an ice bath to chill.

Add 1 pint of the mixture to the canister. Screw the cap on very well, making sure it is completely tightened. Screw in the cream

charger; you will hear a quick sound of gas escaping, which is normal. Turn the canister upside down and shake very well, and the foam is ready.

Store in the refrigerator between uses. Before each use, turn the canister upside down and shake well. Then hold the canister almost completely upside down and gently put pressure on the trigger mechanism, applying the foam slowly over the top of the drink, working from the inside rim of the glass in a circular fashion to the center. When the canister is empty, hold it over the sink and engage the trigger to be sure the gas is completely spent. Remove the top and clean according to the manufacturer's instructions.

INGREDIENT NOTE

Rye Whiskey

From the colonial era up until the late twentieth century, rye whiskey was distilled in Pennsylvania in the Monongahela River Valley, the site of the 1794 Whiskey Rebellion; during the Revolutionary War, the distilleries of the Monongahela Valley supplied George Washington's army. But by 1990 the proud tradition of distilling came to an end in Pennsylvania, and since then rye whiskey has been primarily distilled in Kentucky. In 2006, distilling returned to Pennsylvania with Bluecoat Dry Gin, and potato vodka made from local potatoes may not be far behind.

TODDY

INGREDIENTS

½ ounce dark rum
½ ounce rye or bourbon whiskey
½ ounce fresh-squeezed lemon juice
1 ounce honey syrup (page 247)
3 to 4 ounces hot tea or hot water
Lemon peel, for garnish

☛ In a large goblet, mix together the rum, whiskey, lemon juice, and honey syrup. Add the hot liquid and stir a few times. Garnish with the lemon peel.

The toddy category—sugar, water, and a strong spirit of any kind—preceded the cocktail category (which is the same ingredients, plus bitters; slings had the same ingredients, but with the addition of a spice like nutmeg). The original toddies were served either hot or cold, more often the former, and that's the primary form in which they've endured. The name probably comes from something called a toddy stick, similar to a muddler, which was used in taverns and inns for smashing spices. In the colonial era, sugar usually came in loaves that had to be chipped. Then the chips were mashed into powder, and this may have been done with the toddy stick. (Legend has it that both the stick and the drink were named after Robert Toddy, the proprietor of a colonial tavern in New York called the Black Horse Tavern.) Anyway, the hot toddy that survives to this day isn't so much an exact recipe as it is a general idea, and I think of it mostly as a loose family recipe. It's hot tea or hot water or even hot apple cider; plus a sweetener that's usually honey but can also be maple syrup; plus lemon juice or lemon peel or both; and, finally, a spirit, most commonly rum but sometimes brandy up north and bourbon down south, and maybe applejack. The toddy is not a cocktail that many people order in bars, although it may appear on the menus of the more historically minded bartenders. But it is a cocktail you may want to find in your hand as you sit in front of a roaring fire, in a deep comfortable sofa, surrounded by friends and family in late December.

CHAI TODDY*

INGREDIENTS

1½ ounces spiced rum
1 dash of peppermint schnapps
1 teaspoon honey
4 ounces hot chai
Peppermint stick, for garnish

☞ In a mug or stem glass, combine the rum, schnapps, and honey. Add the hot chai and stir. Garnish with the peppermint stick.

Ten years ago, I'd never heard of chai, but then all of a sudden it was everywhere. The mixture of hot tea paired with peppermint is a natural, and it's not much of a leap to spike it with rum. Instead of the schnapps for the mint flavor, other premium European spirits like Goldschläger or Goldwasser would work well.

HOT BUTTERED RUM

INGREDIENTS

1 ounce dark rum or spiced rum
1 ounce light rum
¾ ounce simple syrup (page 246)
Hot water or hot cider
½ tablespoon Holiday Compound Butter (see opposite)
Cinnamon stick, for garnish

☞ In a goblet glass, combine the dark and light rums with the syrup. Add the hot water and stir to mix. Add the butter, stir a couple of times to start to melt it, and garnish with the cinnamon stick.

We may think of toddies as more medicinal than recreational (I remember getting toddies from my grandmother when I was sick—every grandma had her own version), but the hot buttered rum is definitely festive. If it's a few days before Christmas, you've just spent a long day skiing, and you return to the cabin cold and tired but happy and needing something to warm you up, this is absolutely the right drink. And now that rum has become a popular spirit again, the recipe could include spiced or heavy-bodied rum, and there's no reason you couldn't use brandy or cognac with the rum, and you could use dark-brown sugar syrup or even honey syrup instead of the simple syrup. Like the Bloody Mary, this drink is wide open for interpretation.

BLACK CURRANT TODDY*

When Hendrick's gin debuted, the company asked me to create some cocktails to promote the brand within the United Kingdom, where people are nuts about their jellies and jams. I wanted to use English ingredients in this promotion, so I played around with Earl Grey tea and the super-premium jellies and jams you find in abundance in London. These are fabulous ingredients for cocktails, almost like taking real fruit and mashing it with syrup, plus the bonus of having a little bit of the spice and citrus notes that preserves often include. Eventually I emerged from this testing ordeal with a wonderful toddy variation, a sweet-tart drink that I serve as a cold toddy, not a hot one.

INGREDIENTS

1½ ounces Hendrick's gin

¼ ounce John D. Taylor's Velvet Falernum

½ ounce honey syrup in a 2:1 ratio (page 247)

¾ ounce fresh-squeezed lemon juice

¾ ounce cold tea, such as Earl Grey or green tea, or water

1 level teaspoon high-quality black currant preserves or jelly

Flamed orange peel (page 249), for garnish

Spiral orange peel, for garnish

 Assemble the gin, Falernum, honey syrup, lemon juice, tea, and preserves in a mixing glass with ice. Shake well. Strain through a tea strainer into a chilled coupe glass. Garnish with the flamed orange peel dropped into the liquid and the spiral peel set on the rim of the glass.

HOLIDAY COMPOUND BUTTER

This will make a lot more than you'll need for any reasonable-sized party, but it's not any easier—in fact, it's harder—in smaller quantities, so just go with it. Soften 1 pound unsalted butter in a mixing bowl. Add 1 teaspoon ground cinnamon, 1 teaspoon freshly ground nutmeg, 1 teaspoon ground allspice, ½ teaspoon ground cloves, and ¼ cup dark brown sugar. Mix well to thoroughly combine. Using a sheet of wax paper, form the butter mixture into a log or a rectangle—your choice—and place in the refrigerator to set. When the butter is firm, you can slice it into individual-serving pats of about 1 teaspoon apiece, or just cut each piece as needed to serve. Either way, though, let the butter soften again and warm up before serving—you don't want to put cold butter directly from the fridge into a hot drink.

WARD EIGHT

Many drinks have unconfirmed stories of how they got invented by a certain bartender in a particular bar, tailored to a specific customer, for some reason or another, inspired by who knows what. Rarely are those stories both specific and verified, but the Ward Eight's is. It was created on Election Eve, 1898, by Tom Hussion of the Locke-Ober Café in Boston, to celebrate the impending victory of Democrat Martin Lomasney, a member of the Hendricks Club political machine, to the Massachusetts General Court. From the Eighth Ward, of course. (Eric Felton's diligent research for his book *How's Your Drink?* corrects the date of the election to 1896, not 1898, and casts doubt that the Ward Eight ever meant to celebrate Lomasney's election. Perhaps it did not. But if a drink was created and glasses were raised in honor of their benefactor in the Eighth Ward of Boston in 1898, it was surely in honor of Lomasney!) In the end, it was an ironic circumstance, because Lomasney turned out to be a staunch proponent of Prohibition, and yet the lasting impact of his political career was, basically, a whiskey sour with grenadine in it. Back in those days, bars were political action centers; congressmen and senators ran their campaigns from bars, not from rented storefronts. A bar was where you went—"to the local"—after the election to get your patronage job in the sanitation, police, or fire department. So you wanted to be true to your neighborhood bar, not just because the bartender remembered your favorite drink but also because cheating on your bar meant something bigger: It meant cheating on your candidate, your official, your party. It meant betrayal.

INGREDIENTS

2 ounces rye whiskey
1 ounce simple syrup (page 246)
¾ ounce fresh-squeezed lemon juice
¼ ounce grenadine
Maraschino cherry, for garnish

☛ Combine the whiskey, syrup, lemon juice, and grenadine in a mixing glass with ice and shake well. Strain into an old-fashioned glass or a special sour glass and garnish with the cherry.

The Essential

MODERN CLASSICS

AMERICAN BEAUTY COCKTAIL • BACARDI COCKTAIL • BEE'S KNEES • BELLINI
BIJOU • BLOOD AND SAND • COCTEL ALGERIA • COLONY COCKTAIL • COSMOPOLITAN
DUBONNET COCKTAIL • EL PRESIDENTE • GIMLET • IRISH COFFEE • KIR
LONG ISLAND ICED TEA • MARGARITA • MIMOSA • MONKEY GLAND • NEGRONI
PINK LADY • STORK CLUB COCKTAIL • WHITE LADY

I first used the phrase *modern classics* in relation to cocktails in the mid-1990s, when I was talking about the Cosmopolitan. Although the Cosmo is a contemporary recipe, it is clearly bigger than a fad—it is here to stay, taking on all the classic comers, and bound to become a permanent fixture in the standard bar repertoire. The Cosmopolitan is just the latest in a long tradition of post-Prohibition inventions that have stuck, and these can all be grouped into the category of modern classics. They're not the original classic cocktails, but they have endured the test of time.

A great many of these twentieth-century inventions are the result of a distinctly twentieth-century phenomenon: advertising. It wasn't until after Prohibition that beverage manufacturers discovered the power of inventing cocktails to promote brands. The Bloody Mary, the screwdriver, and the Moscow Mule (all in the *Highballs* chapter) were all born of Smirnoff's marketing campaign; Irish coffee brought Irish whiskey attention; the margarita practically introduced America to tequila; the Cape Codder was the brainchild of the cranberry collective; and the Dubonnet Cocktail, of course, was a showcase for Dubonnet. The Cosmopolitan itself was created as part of the test-marketing of a new product called Absolut Citron.

The compromises made by the advocates of Repeal—the compromises that enabled the end of Prohibition—gave state and local governments power over the consumption and sale of alcoholic beverages. The post-Prohibition era featured a byzantine maze of laws that stifled the rich cocktail culture of earlier years. Control states strictly directed the sale of alcohol and owned or controlled the retail stores. In this role, states purchased only those products that they perceived as bestsellers, leaving the bartender and the consumer wanting for a multitude of ingredients needed to make classic cocktails. In other states, whole counties remained completely dry. So a great many liquor manufacturers didn't even bother with anything other than the largest markets: New York, Illinois, and California. This made cocktail culture a lot less interesting than it had been before Prohibition. Not to mention that there was a pretty big Depression in full swing—followed quickly by a pretty big war.

So it wasn't until after World War II that the cocktail culture was finally revived. It was in these years that the country started to move away from whiskey and gin toward vodka, and a large proportion of the successful drinks invented in the ensuing half-century were vodka-based. But back in the 1950s, Manhattans and gin martinis were still enjoying their moment in the sun, along with bourbon Presbyterians and whiskey highballs, plus the house drinks of famed clubs like the Colony and the Stork. Then, in the 1960s, the whole cranberry thing really took off with lots of highballs, as well as the introduction of such exotic drinks as the margarita and the mimosa.

It all came to a screeching halt in the 1970s, when a whole generation of young people turned on and tuned out. Wine made giant inroads into the American market, and so recipes like the Kir enjoyed new popularity, and jug wine, which helped pot-smokers keep their mouths wet, took off. But all of a sudden the beverages of choice were chardonnay, Perrier, and Tab. There were barely any skilled bartenders anywhere. Soda guns had ruined highballs, powdered mixes had ruined sours, and Americans simply stopped ordering anything more complex than a highball.

This sorry state of affairs didn't end until the mid- to late 1980s, when the culinary revolution that was then in full swing—with fresh seasonal ingredients, fusion cuisine, big flavor, and unlimited dining options—started to affect cocktails. People began to say no to the culture of mediocrity that festered at the bar, rejecting the artificial mixes and shortcuts that had been created as a foil against unskilled labor. They demanded real, fresh, and seasonal ingredients in their drinks. Premium imported vodkas like Finlandia, Stolichnaya, and Absolut arrived; American whiskey-makers started producing single-batch bottlings with high price tags. The age of the luxury brand was ushered in.

When Joe Baum hired me to develop a beverage program for the fine dining restaurant Aurora, he said, "Dale, let's figure out a way to make great drinks so people will start drinking cocktails again." If people discovered they could get a properly made pisco sour using fresh lime juice and bitters on top, they would start drinking them again. This is what I worked on at Aurora. Then for the 1987 reopening of the Rainbow Room, I created a classic cocktail program, ushering in a new cocktail era. Journalists began writing about the high quality of the drinks, and of course there was the magic of the Rainbow Room itself—the stunning skyline views, revolving dance floor, live swing orchestra, classic service, classic dishes, and a return to romance complete with classic cocktails. Young bartenders all over started to rediscover the classic recipes—in New York, in San Francisco, and in little pockets in between. And the modern classic called the Cosmopolitan was born, rounding out a century of ups and downs—ending, thankfully, on the big up that continues today. ♛

AMERICAN BEAUTY COCKTAIL

The sweet ingredients in the splendid American Beauty are used in tiny amounts, as minor flavor notes; the dry vermouth, brandy, and orange juice keep the drink relatively dry; and the ruby port creates striations, which may very well have named the drink. It's a balanced, sophisticated drink, and with its pink color and striated texture, it's a beautiful thing to look at as well as to sip.

INGREDIENT NOTE

Vermouth

When vermouth is called for, I use French dry or Italian sweet. This is a personal preference but also an article of faith among many bartenders, especially those of my generation and older. Store vermouth, which is a wine product and not a hard spirit, in the refrigerator; if it darkens, you can still use it to deglaze your pan after sautéing a veal chop but not for making a cocktail. My advice is that unless you're running a commercial bar or enjoying a lot of martinis very wet, you should buy the small bottles so you don't end up wasting too much vermouth. Stick with French brands such as Noilly Prat for dry and the Italian Martini & Rossi for sweet. Vermouth—a manufactured wine product that's aged in barrels, flavored, filtered, cooked, and fortified with alcohol to preserve it—was invented in Italy in the eighteenth century, in Turin, probably by the Carpano family at their eponymous coffeehouse. Later, the first license for Turinese vermouth production was issued in 1840 to a firm that later became Martini & Rossi. For sweet vermouth, Italians did it first, and they still know how to do it best.

INGREDIENTS

¾ ounce brandy

¾ ounce French dry vermouth

¾ ounce fresh-squeezed orange juice

2 dashes of grenadine

2 dashes of simple syrup (page 246),
    optional

Dash of green crème de menthe,
    optional

½ ounce ruby port

1 rose petal, organically grown or well
    washed

☞ Combine the brandy, vermouth, orange juice, grenadine, and the optional syrup and green crème de menthe in a mixing glass with ice and shake well. Strain into a small cocktail glass, and float the port on top. Garnish with the rose petal.

BACARDI COCKTAIL

INGREDIENTS

1½ ounces Bacardi white rum
¾ ounce simple syrup (page 246)
¾ ounce fresh-squeezed lemon juice
1 teaspoon grenadine

☛ Combine the rum, syrup, lemon juice, and grenadine in a mixing glass with ice and shake well. Strain into a small cocktail glass.

The Bacardi cocktail has been the subject of a good deal of controversy over the years and was the subject of a ruling in the New York State Supreme Court on April 28, 1936, that required the drink to be made with Bacardi rum in order to be called a Bacardi cocktail. (Those were the days when the judicial branch recognized its priorities.) But no matter what it's called, and what brand of rum is in it, some people will assert that the Bacardi is nothing more than a daiquiri that uses grenadine instead of sugar. But those people have forgotten that the Bacardi cocktail was the Cosmopolitan of the post-Prohibition generation, a wildly popular drink that was the specialty of so many bars that the Bacardi company was prompted to file its almost-tongue-in-cheek but still successful lawsuit. That Depression-era drink was a little different than the version here; its only sweetener was pomegranate-based grenadine. I find that overly tart, and because real pomegranate grenadine is nearly impossible to find, I use the grenadine as a coloring, and sweeten the drink with simple syrup.

VARIATION

BACARDI COCKTAIL, RITZ VERSION

This is adapted from a recipe in *The Artistry of Mixing Drinks* by Frank Meier (published in 1936 by the Ritz Hotel, Paris), including an interesting touch that Meier added, probably to introduce a French product to the mix: vermouth.

 INGREDIENTS

1½ ounces white rum, preferably Bacardi
½ ounce French dry vermouth
½ ounce fresh-squeezed lemon juice
½ ounce simple syrup (page 246)
1 teaspoon grenadine

☛ Combine the rum, vermouth, lemon juice, syrup, and grenadine in a mixing glass with ice and shake well. Strain into a chilled cocktail glass.

INGREDIENT NOTE

Bacardi Rum

The Bacardi company was founded in 1862 in Santiago de Cuba, and it remained there, ever expanding as the most popular rum brand in the world, until the revolution of 1960. It is now based in New Providence, in the Bahamas, where for half a century it has continued its dominance, a remarkable feat of longevity. Founder Don Fecundo

Bacardi revolutionized the way rum was made by taking advantage of the then-new technology of the column still, which was able to produce a pure, neutral-style rum. This rum was barrel-aged for a year, then filtered to remove all color from the aging process, achieving a clean base for cocktails. But in today's age of big flavor, there's a move back toward more artisan-

style rums like rum agricole (made from sugarcane syrup rather than molasses), carving a market segment away from the neutral-style rums Bacardi practically invented. However, this style exemplar remains, 150 years after it was introduced, the best-selling rum in the world.

BEE'S KNEES

INGREDIENTS

2 ounces gin
¾ ounce honey syrup (page 247)
½ ounce fresh-squeezed lemon juice
Lemon peel, preferably flamed (page
    249), for garnish

☞ Combine the gin, honey syrup, and lemon juice in a mixing glass with ice and shake well. Strain into a chilled cocktail glass and garnish with the lemon peel.

Back in the gin-oriented 1930s, long before the ascendancy of vodka, the Bee's Knees was a sort of novelty cocktail, and it got bartenders thinking about using honey as a cocktail sweetener for the first time since the colonial era. Honey syrup imparts a warmth and flavor that sugar syrup simply can't provide, plus floral notes that do a great job of offsetting acid ingredients such as citrus and bitter ingredients such as aromatics and spirits. You wouldn't want to use honey as a sweetener for most clean, simple drinks with distinctive flavor profiles, like the daiquiri or the margarita, because its sweet floral notes would muck up the purity of the drinks. But the Bee's Knees is, in fact, based on honey, so it's not a mucking-up—it's defining the drink.

VARIATION

BEE'S KISS

This white rum version is made with cream and is a far richer cocktail.

INGREDIENTS

1½ ounces white rum agricole

1 ounce heavy cream

¾ ounce honey syrup (page 247)

 ☞ Combine the rum, cream, and syrup in a mixing glass with ice and shake well. Strain into a chilled cocktail glass.

INGREDIENT NOTE

Rum Agricole

For the rum in this drink, I recommend an artisan-style agricole, such as Niessan or La Favorite. Demerara rum from Guyana would also make a great Bee's Kiss, but ideally with simple syrup made from Demerara sugar (page 246) instead of honey syrup, which would make it into a drink that probably shouldn't be called a Bee's Kiss but could be called a tasty one.

BELLINI

INGREDIENTS

1½ ounces white peach purée, well
   chilled
4 ounces prosecco, preferably Mionetto
¼ ounce premium peach liqueur,
   preferably Marie Brizard, optional

 Put the chilled purée in the bottom of a bar glass—a bar glass only, never in the metal half of a Boston shaker, which would prevent the guest from enjoying the show. Hold a bar spoon in one hand and slowly pour the wine with the other hand down the inside of the glass to prevent the sparkling wine from foaming. Use the bar spoon to slowly pull the purée up the side of the glass, mixing ever so gently; don't stir briskly, or the prosecco will lose its effervescence. Strain into a flute, and float the optional peach liqueur on top.

It's tough to find people who don't want a Bellini—what's not to love?—so if you're making one, you might as well make a lot. Find a large glass pitcher— 46 ounces or so—that's wider at the top than at the bottom. Place 8 to 10 ounces peach purée in the bottom of the pitcher, and use the above pouring technique (and a very long bar spoon) to add an entire 750-milliliter bottle of sparkling wine, pouring the wine down the inside of the pitcher. Add the peach liqueur floats to individual servings, as desired.

In an out-of-the-way piazza off the Grand Canal in Venice, the Bellini was invented by Giuseppe Cipriani in 1945. That is to say, in 1945 the magical concoction was first mixed and served to customers. But it wasn't named until three years later, during an exhibition in Venice of the Renaissance artist Giovanni Bellini, that Cipriani named the drink for the painter. And it wasn't until another few decades that it appeared on seemingly every brunch menu in the world at last. This is a fantastic pre-noon pick-me-up. In fact, it's a great pre-anything drink.

INGREDIENT NOTES

Peach Purée and Prosecco

Originally, the Bellini was made only four months out of the year, when sweet white peaches were in season. But most recipes today use flash-frozen peach purée, the sort that chefs use to make sorbet, allowing for year-round Bellinis. These high-quality purées—from companies such as Perfect Purees of Napa, California, as well as Looza from Belgium and Funkin from the United Kingdom—are just beginning to emerge in the retail market, which will finally allow home mixologists and sorbet-makers to re-create the types of recipes that have long been the sole domain of professionals.

To make an authentic Italian Bellini, you'll need to use the Italian sparkler called prosecco, the grown-up version of Asti Spumante. Because of the widespread popularity of overly sweet Asti in the 1970s and 1980s, Americans got the idea that all Italian sparkling wine is treacly. But prosecco is much closer to Champagne, a dry wine with delicate floral notes that comes in a brut style, which is bubbly like Champagne, or *frizzante,* which is just lightly carbonated. I prefer the *frizzante* style for Bellinis because it doesn't foam (so you don't have to wait for the foam to subside when mixing and drinking); it imparts a pleasing sparkle on the tongue instead of creating lines of bubbles in the glass. A good *frizzante* may be difficult to find, so plan in advance and check with your favorite wine shop.

HARRY'S BAR

"Harry's Bar" sure doesn't sound like one of the most exclusive restaurants in Venice, let alone a traditional trattoria that was opened by Giuseppe Cipriani three-quarters of a century ago. But it's actually the namesake of an American named Harry Pickering, who, while spending the Venice leg of an escape-the-Depression grand tour getting plastered, became friends with Cipriani and eventually borrowed ten thousand lire from him. Then Harry disappeared. A year later, he showed up with the payback plus some, and a desire to own a bar, which opened for business in 1931; Harry put up the money, so the name was his. But Cipriani was the one who invented the restaurant and captained the nautically decorated room to immense success.

As is the case with some restaurants, it fell into favor with locals, then with rich locals, then with elite tourists, then with Ernest Hemingway, who set a good part of his bad novel *Across the River and into the Trees* there, and that led almost instantaneously to the type of international notoriety that attracts movie stars, kings and queens, and other world-famous jet-setters. At about the same time, Giuseppe had two brainstorms that earned Harry's a place in the firmament of twentieth-century restaurants. One was a dish of raw filet mignon pounded thin, invented to accommodate the diet of a regular customer; the other was a sparkling cocktail, invented to use up an excess supply of fresh peaches. Both were named for painters—the solid one for Vittore Carpaccio, the liquid one for Giovanni Bellini.

BIJOU

INGREDIENTS

1½ ounces Plymouth gin
½ ounce green Chartreuse
½ ounce Italian sweet vermouth
Dash of orange bitters
Maraschino cherry or cocktail olive,
   for garnish
Lemon peel, for garnish

☞ Combine the gin, Chartreuse, vermouth, and bitters in a mixing glass with ice and shake well. Strain into a chilled cocktail glass. Garnish with a cherry or an olive, squeeze a piece of lemon peel on top, and serve. (Note that these instructions, from Mr. Craddock, indicate to me that the lemon peel is discarded.)

The first drinks book ever published that included cocktail recipes was the 1862 edition of Jerry Thomas's *How to Mix Drinks*, which, despite its status as the progenitor of many volumes of cocktail books, is astoundingly stingy with its cocktail recipes; Thomas includes just ten in that first edition. One of them, the Fancy Gin Cocktail, with two important ingredient additions, is the Bijou ("Jewel"): One ingredient is vermouth, which gradually replaced curaçao as the accent sweetener of choice in many mid-nineteenth-century cocktails; the other was Chartreuse.

Vermouth reached our shores through the port of New Orleans as early as 1838, but it was not widely available for another thirty-five years—in fact, not a drop of it appears in Thomas's 1862 volume. When it became more widely available later in the nineteenth century, two of the iconic classics of the cocktail category were invented: the Manhattan and the martini. That's also when the Bijou was invented. The recipe here was adapted from *The Savoy Cocktail Book* by Harry Craddock, originally published in 1930, and borrowed by Craddock from a 1900 version that appeared in Harry Johnson's *Bartenders Manual*. I bumped up the gin and moderated the vermouth and Chartreuse (what the heck, I like it better my way). See the opposite page for Frank Meier's own idea for the Bijou. As Louis Armstrong said after a good improvisation on a theme, "I never met a melody that didn't need a little help."

 INGREDIENT NOTE

Chartreuse

One of the cordial immortals of all time. Like Benedictine and Certosa, Chartreuse is the product of monks—this time of the Carthusian Order, and formerly only at their establishment in the French Alps called Grande Chartreuse . . . Unfortunately this order was banished from France to Spain just after the turn of the century and, at Tarragona, they again set up with their secret formula compounded of elixirs from odd and rare herbs, water, sugar, and fine spirits . . . Naturally all of France sprouted imitations. Clever chemical folk pronounce it made up of the following essences: Sweet flag, orange peel, peppermint oil, dried tops of hyssop, balm, leaves of balm, angelica seeds and root, wormwood, tonka bean, cardamoms, as well as known spices such as mace, cloves and cinnamon. Nice, simple little formula, this!
—**CHARLES E. BAKER JR.,** *The Gentleman's Companion,* 1939

BIJOU, RITZ VERSION

This recipe is from Frank Meier's *The Artistry of Mixing Drinks* (1936); Meier reigned behind the bar of the Ritz Hotel in Paris. Note the absence of Chartreuse in the French version. For my money, these proportions make a fantastic drink. But there's a huge population in the drier camp these days who might prefer a Bijou made with 2½ ounces gin and only ½ ounce each curaçao and vermouth.

INGREDIENTS

1½ ounces gin
¾ ounce orange curaçao
¾ ounce French dry vermouth
Dash of orange bitters
Maraschino cherry, for garnish

☞ Combine the gin, curaçao, vermouth, and bitters in a mixing glass with ice and shake well. Strain into a chilled cocktail glass and garnish with the cherry.

DUBONNET COCKTAIL

INGREDIENTS

1 ounce Dubonnet Rouge
1 ounce London dry gin
Lemon peel, for garnish

☛ In an old-fashioned glass, combine the Dubonnet and gin over ice, and stir. Garnish with the lemon peel.

Dubonnet is one of those apéritifs that evolved from the nineteenth-century obsession with preventing malaria in French soldiers by spiking their wine with quinine. It was invented in 1846 by a chemist named Joseph Dubonnet, who named his concoction Dubonnet Quinquina, after the bitter quinine root that was the main ingredient. Dubonnet is sweetened more than most of the other bitter apéritifs like Campari, with major flavor notes from orange peel, coffee, cinnamon, manzanilla, and chamomile, which are added to wine that is then fortified with eau de vie and sweet grape juice and, finally, matured for three years. The result, in blanc and rouge versions, is an assertive, highly botanical apéritif that's usually served simply, mixed with lemon—juice or oil, in the form of peel—and on the rocks. There was one famous cocktail from the 1920s and 1930s called the ZaZa, but that's disappeared. What remains are the Dubonnet Cocktails; the Dubonnet Fizz, made with club soda and lemon juice, or the more ambitious version with Cherry Heering, orange juice, and lemon juice; and the Bentley, which is simply Dubonnet shaken with an equal part of applejack.

VARIATION

DUBONNET KISS*

In truth, the Dubonnet Kiss doesn't bear that much relation to the Dubonnet Cocktail—it's a very different drink, in fact. But there aren't many Dubonnet-based cocktails in the world, and I wanted to include this one, so here it is:

INGREDIENTS

1 ounce Dubonnet Rouge
½ ounce sour apple schnapps
1 ounce apple cider
¼ ounce fresh-sqeezed lemon juice
¼ ounce simple syrup (page 246)
1 thin slice Red Delicious apple, for garnish

☛ In a cocktail shaker with ice, combine the Dubonnet, schnapps, cider, lemon juice, and simple syrup, and shake well. Strain into a chilled cocktail glass and garnish with the apple slice.

EL PRESIDENTE

INGREDIENTS

1 slice orange

Splash of fresh-squeezed lemon or lime juice

1½ ounces white rum

¾ ounce orange curaçao

½ ounce French dry vermouth

Dash of grenadine

☞ In the bottom of a bar glass, muddle the orange slice with the lemon or lime juice. Add the rum, curaçao, vermouth, grenadine, and ice, and shake well. Strain into a small cocktail glass.

The daiquiri, the Cuba Libre, the mojito, El Presidente . . . Cuban rum-based drinks have certainly added a lot to the American cocktail repertoire. This one was created during Prohibition at the Vista Alegre in Havana and named for General Carmen Menocal, who was president of Cuba before Batista. American Prohibition led to a flourishing cocktail culture that was just a short jaunt from Miami, in Havana. For a long time Havana was home to one of the most prestigious bartending schools in the world at the Hotel Sevilla, turning out some of the best-trained, most technically astute, and most graceful bartenders ever to shake a cocktail. The original version of El Presidente was, in my opinion, a flawed drink, too sweet and with no acid. Here is my version, enhanced with muddled orange and fresh citrus juice.

VARIATION

PRESTIGE COCKTAIL*

I arrived at the Prestige by playing with the Presidente's ingredients until the progeny barely resembled the parent. This invention of mine won first place for Best Fancy Cocktail (the "best in show" award) at the Bacardi Martini Gran Prix in Spain, in 2002, where the year before I'd become the first American to win the decades-old international cocktail competition; in 2001, it had been for the Old Flame (page 95). The Prestige is my tribute to the great Cuban rum drinks of the Prohibition era.

INGREDIENTS

1 ounce Bacardi eight-year-old rum

¼ ounce Martini & Rossi dry vermouth

¾ ounce John D. Taylor's Velvet Falernum

1 ounce unsweetened pineapple juice

¼ ounce fresh-squeezed lime juice

Pineapple wedge, for garnish

Lime wheel, for garnish

☞ Combine the rum, vermouth, Velvet Falernum, pineapple juice, and lime juice in a mixing glass with ice and shake well. Strain into a large chilled cocktail glass. Decorate with the pineapple wedge and lime wheel.

GIMLET

INGREDIENTS

2 ounces gin or vodka
¾ ounce Rose's lime juice
Cucumber slice or lime wedge (or both),
   for garnish

 Combine the gin or vodka and lime juice in a mixing glass with ice and shake well. Strain into a small cocktail glass or serve over ice in an old-fashioned glass. Garnish with the cucumber slice or lime wedge.

INGREDIENT NOTE

Rose's Lime Juice

When the British navy finally realized the need for citrus of some kind to fend off scurvy on long voyages, the challenge became to preserve the citrus juice. The obvious answer was alcohol. British navy rum was then in plentiful supply, and one of the components of the blend was Demerara rum from Guyana, which served the purpose nicely of preserving lime juice. But the search still continued for a nonalcoholic solution to the problem; sailors falling out of the rigging were becoming a hazard for the officers on deck. Finally, in 1867, a Scottish merchant named Lauchlin Rose patented the process of preserving lime juice without using alcohol—and good timing, as that was the year the British government mandated by law that all British merchant ships have daily rations of lime juice for the crew to prevent scurvy. Rose's product was an instant success.

If you're committed to using the best fresh ingredients, the temptation with the gimlet is to substitute fresh lime juice for the preserved variety. But the veteran gimlet drinker would be disappointed. So this is one of the rare instances in which I counsel *not* to use fresh-squeezed juice except the lime squeeze garnish. The recipe is actually based on the flavor profile of preserved lime juice, which was invented hundreds of years ago to help prevent sailors from getting scurvy (vitamin C deficiency). The enlisted men drank their lime juice with rum (grog, which was two-thirds of the way to a modern daiquiri), while the officers cut theirs with gin.

CALIFORNIA GIMLET

If someone wants a gimlet, don't serve this fresh variety without discussing it first. The fresh lime juice here makes for a very different drink than the preserved lime juice that's been the gimlet standard for everyone's lifetime. A dash of the Rose's might be appropriate here to remind the drinker whence their potation came.

INGREDIENTS

2 ounces gin
3/4 ounce fresh-squeezed lime juice
Dash of Rose's lime juice, optional
1 ounce simple syrup (page 246)
Lime wheel, for garnish

☛ Combine the gin, lime juice(s), and syrup in a mixing glass with ice and shake well. Strain into a small cocktail glass or serve over ice in an old-fashioned glass, garnished with the lime wheel.

YUZU GIMLET*

When I was working in Hawaii at the Halekulani Hotel with Chef Daryl Fujita, I matched this gimlet spin-off with a Kona Kampachi Ceviche with Micro Greens and a Yuzu-Basil Emulsion. That's complicated-sounding food, and, admittedly, the drink itself isn't nearly as simple as the traditional gimlet, because it involves some sweeteners that probably aren't on your bar shelf—at least, not yet. Also, in this gimlet there are three sours—yuzu, fresh lime, and preserved lime—that I've balanced with three sweets. This is taking great liberty with a simple recipe, adding complexity of preparation and complexity of flavor but retaining the spirit of the original.

INGREDIENTS

1 1/2 ounces Plymouth gin
1/4 ounce Luxardo Maraschino liqueur
1/4 ounce yuzu extract or 1/2 ounce yuzu juice
1/4 ounce Rose's lime juice
1/2 ounce fresh-squeezed lime juice
1/2 ounce fresh-squeezed grapefruit juice
1 ounce triple syrup (page 248)
Lime wheel, thinly sliced, for garnish
Thin slice of seedless cucumber, for garnish

☛ In a cocktail shaker, assemble the gin, Maraschino liqueur, yuzu extract, Rose's and fresh-squeezed lime juices, grapefruit juice, and the triple syrup. Add ice and shake well. Strain into a chilled cocktail glass and garnish with the lime wheel and the cucumber slice.

IRISH COFFEE

INGREDIENTS

Unsweetened heavy cream
1½ ounces Irish whiskey
4 ounces fresh-brewed coffee
1 ounce brown-sugar or regular simple
   syrup (page 246)

☛ Whip the cream until bubbles no longer collect on the surface; it should be less than stiff and still pourable. In an Irish coffee glass or small white wine glass, combine the whiskey, coffee, and syrup, and stir to combine. Gently ladle 1 inch of cream on top of the coffee mixture, and serve immediately.

Irish coffee is one of the all-time great winter drinks, especially after dinner or for brunch. It is also one of the most abused drinks in the hands of careless purveyors. The size of the glass is critical. The classic Irish coffee glass is an 8-ounce stemmed glass in the shape of a tulip that makes it nearly impossible to ruin the drink. The glass forces you into the correct proportions, and that means not overpouring the coffee, which is a common mistake—you don't want the coffee-to-whiskey ratio to be any greater than 3:1, or the liquor will get drowned. It's tough to find a proper Irish coffee glass, so use a small white wine glass. Also, you should sweeten the coffee but never sweeten the cream, which you want to whip until it's faintly stiff but still pourable—much looser than the standard texture of whipped cream (and never, ever use an aerosol whipped cream); you should end up with a ¾- to 1-inch layer of cream that's cleanly floating on top of the coffee, creating a sharp demarcation between black and white. Finally, although some recipes call for the addition of green crème de menthe, don't give in to this vice.

VODKA ESPRESSO

This wonderful cocktail was created by Dick Bradsell at the ground-breaking Match Bar Group in London. It's important to make your espresso ahead of time and give it an opportunity to chill—hot espresso would melt too much ice, hence watering down the drink to an unpleasant degree. Use half Kahlúa with half Tia Maria to lighten the sweetness of the Kahlúa. When shaken very, very hard, it will get a *crema* on top (this is the foam on the top of a freshly made espresso) that lasts a long time, creating a beautiful drink that looks like a martini glass filled with espresso—in fact, so beautiful that it doesn't need a garnish. But I always love a good garnish, and so I often use ground cocoa nibs here, which are a little hard to find; if you can't find them or don't want to, by all means serve this gorgeous drink garnishless.

INGREDIENTS

Unsweetened ground cocoa nibs, for garnish, optional

Orange slice, for coating glass, optional

1 ounce vodka

1 ounce espresso, chilled

¾ ounce Kahlúa

¾ ounce Tia Maria

 If you're using the cocoa nibs, at least 15 minutes before serving, grind a couple of tablespoons to a powder with a mortar and pestle or an electric spice grinder. Use the orange slice and ground cocoa to dust the rim of a cocktail glass according to the directions on page 137. Place the glass in the freezer to chill and to allow the cocoa to dry and set on the rim of the glass.

When the glass is ready, shake the vodka, espresso, Kahlúa, and Tia Maria with ice. Strain into the prepared glass.

OTHER VARIATIONS

The basic idea of Irish coffee—mixing hot coffee with a spirit—is flexible, and here are some of the more popular international variations, all combined with a few ounces of hot coffee:

CALYPSO COFFEE: rum and Kahlúa

JAMAICAN COFFEE: rum and Tia Maria

MEXICAN COFFEE: tequila and Kahlúa

SPANISH COFFEE: Spanish brandy and Kahlúa

COFFEE ROYAL: cognac and sugar

KEOKE COFFEE: brandy and Kahlúa

PRESIDENT'S COFFEE: cherry brandy

KIR

INGREDIENTS

White wine, preferably a crisp Burgundy
½ ounce crème de cassis
Lemon peel, for garnish, optional

 Pour a glass of white wine, then slowly pour the cassis carefully down through the wine. The Kir is sometimes garnished with a lemon peel, but never for a Frenchman!

VARIATIONS

The KIR ROYALE is made with sparkling wine, usually Champagne.

The KIR IMPERIALE is a Kir Royale, made with Champagne but with the raspberry liqueur Framboise instead of the cassis.

 Despite Jake Barnes's preference for a pre-dinner Jack Rose at the Crillon (see page 31), if it's a quarter to six and you find yourself seated at a sidewalk café in Paris, and you order a drink, chances are it is—or it should be—a Kir. This white wine cocktail, with just a hint of a spirit in it, is named for Canon Felix Kir (1876–1968), who, when he was mayor of Dijon, served it to visiting dignitaries in order to boost a local product, crème de cassis. The drink was actually around long before Mayor Kir; it was then called a Blanc Cassis, after the black currant liqueur first commercially produced in the early nineteenth century in Dijon. But it was Mayor Kir who popularized the cocktail, so he deserves the name.

From left: Kir, Kir Royale, and Kir Imperiale.

LONG ISLAND ICED TEA

INGREDIENTS

½ ounce vodka
½ ounce gin
½ ounce rum
½ ounce tequila
½ ounce triple sec
¾ ounce simple syrup (page 246)
¾ ounce fresh-squeezed lemon juice
3 ounces Coca-Cola
Lemon wedge, for garnish

☞ In a mixing glass, combine the vodka, gin, rum, tequila, triple sec, syrup, and lemon juice with ice, and stir. Strain into a large iced tea glass with ice, top with the Coca-Cola, and stir. Garnish with the lemon wedge.

This crowd-pleasing drink—especially if the crowd is in the basement of a fraternity house—was supposedly invented by bartender Robert C. Butt, nicknamed Rosebud, of the infamous OBI (Oak Beach Inn) in Hampton Bays, which closed just a few years ago after a multi-decade run as one of the largest, most popular bars on all of Long Island. The OBI had a big pier with a bar on it, and customers would arrive by boat as well as by car, motorcycle, bicycle, and foot. It was a great happy-hour place, and the Long Island Iced Tea is a great happy-hour drink—if made properly. But despite the long-standing story about the OBI's invention, I was recently contacted by Craig Weisman, who from 1976 to 1979 tended bar at a catering facility called Leonard's in Great Neck, New York. Weisman claims that for big wedding receptions, the older bartenders at Leonard's would set out whiskey sours. But the younger bartenders—Weisman was eighteen at the time (the New York State legal drinking age was then eighteen)—recognized that the young bridal parties didn't want sours. So they prepared pitchers of what they called Leonard's Iced Tea, made with spirits from the premium well: Smirnoff, Bacardi, Beefeater, Cuervo Gold, and Cointreau. According to Weisman, the Leonard's bartenders taught this Iced Tea to the guys at the OBI. It wasn't until years later that Weisman realized the drink he and his pals had invented was now world famous as the Long Island Iced Tea—with an inaccurate invention claim.

Whichever story you believe, the key to making a pleasing Long Island Iced Tea is to use all the spirits in moderation, creating a fine-tasting, well-balanced drink with a total alcohol content of only 2½ ounces, the same as many other cocktails. On the other hand, the sure road to disaster—a bad drink and a badly drunk customer—is the common mistake made by young bartenders of putting a full ounce of each spirit in the glass with a little cola, creating a ghastly concoction with a full 5 ounces liquor in it. (Bartenders also sometimes use sour mix for this, which doesn't help either.) I taught myself how to make the Long Island Iced Tea properly at the Rainbow Room, because for some reason it was incredibly popular with the European tourists, especially Germans, who were a large part of our crowd. We also used premium spirits in our version, and the tourists ordered round after round, which we served in big iced tea glasses. I didn't want my customers "in the toilet." Neither do you.

FULL MONTE

The masterful Audrey Saunders created this spinoff with the sophisticated finish of Champagne instead of Coke.

INGREDIENTS

¼ ounce vodka
¼ ounce gin
¼ ounce rum
¼ ounce tequila
¼ ounce Luxardo Maraschino liqueur
½ ounce fresh-squeezed lemon juice
½ ounce simple syrup (page 246)
2 dashes of Angostura bitters
Champagne
Maraschino cherry, for garnish

☞ Combine the vodka, gin, rum, tequila, Maraschino liqueur, lemon juice, syrup, and bitters in a mixing glass with ice, and shake well. Strain into a flute, top with Champagne, and garnish with a stemless Maraschino cherry on a spear (with the tip of the spear not protruding into anyone's eyeball, please).

LONDON ICED TEA

This tea is actually a pared-down version, with only two strong spirits, plus the interesting addition of amaretto.

INGREDIENTS

¾ ounce gin
¾ ounce rum
½ ounce amaretto
¾ ounce fresh-squeezed lemon juice
½ ounce simple syrup (page 246)
Coca-Cola
Lemon wedge, for garnish

☞ Combine the gin, rum, amaretto, lemon juice, and syrup in a mixing glass with ice. Strain into a Collins glass over ice, top with Coca-Cola, stir, and garnish with the lemon wedge.

MARGARITA

INGREDIENTS

Kosher salt, for coating the rim of the
    glass
Lime slice, for coating the rim of the glass
1½ ounces pure agave tequila
1 ounce Cointreau
¾ ounce fresh-squeezed lime juice
¼ to ½ ounce agave syrup (page 247),
    optional (but possibly mandatory for
    those who grew up on the overly
    sweet frozen margaritas of the 1970s)

☞ Using the kosher salt and the lime
slice, prepare the salted glass (see
Technique Note, opposite) along half the
rim; chill the glass. Combine the tequila,
Cointreau, lime juice, and optional syrup
in a mixing glass with ice, and shake well.
Strain the drink into the prepared glass.
Note: Margaritas may be served over ice
in a rocks glass or without ice in a cocktail
or classic margarita glass (see glass chart
on page 255).

If you believe the Cuervo company, this incredibly popular drink was created by a Texas-based socialite named Margarita Sames at a 1948 Christmas party in her Acapulco villa, which was next to both the Flamingo Hotel and John Wayne's house. Whether this happened or not, many years later Ms. Sames did end up on the Cuervo payroll, claiming the story is true. And Hollywood did indeed end up embracing the margarita—especially Bing Crosby, who also had a home in Mexico and loved tequila so much that he imported the first popular brand, Herradura ("horseshoe"), to the United States.

But there are competing theories about the name. One compelling piece of information is that a drink called Tequila Daisy was served at Tijuana's Agua Caliente racetrack in the 1920s that was made with lemon juice, tequila, and a sweet ingredient—the makings of a margarita—and *daisy* translates to *margarita* in Spanish. But no matter who invented it, in sixty years the margarita has gone from an obscure secret of the Hollywood movie colony to one of the most popular cocktails in the United States; and although it's been in the

Salting a Glass

This is something that, when done without thought, is often done poorly. First off, you probably don't want to salt the entire rim of the glass, which requires that the drinker not only wants salt (some people don't) but also wants it with every single sip, which most people don't. You also don't want any salt on the inside of the glass, where it'll bleed down into the drink.

So here's what you do: First, pour a good amount of kosher salt—never iodized salt, which is too fine and too salty—into a shallow saucer or a small plate. Cut a slice of very juicy fresh lime to the exact thickness you would like your salt frosting to be—if you want ¼ inch salt, cut the slice ¼ inch thick. Now, hold your glass upside down so excess juice doesn't drip down it. Using the slice as a guide, wet the top portion of the outside rim of the glass along half the circumference of the glass. Dab the moistened half-circumference of the glass in the saucer of salt, pressing the glass into the salt for maximum adhesion, then tap the glass to remove any excess. Now you have a properly salted glass. It helps if you then put it in the freezer for a few minutes, not only for the obvious benefits of chilling the glass but also to help the salt-juice mixture crystallize and adhere to the rim.

United Kingdom for only thirty-five years and a well-kept secret until the last five, it's now a contender for the most popular cocktail in England. This parallels the rise in popularity of tequila, which, like Canadian whiskey and Caribbean rum, enjoyed a swell of popularity during Prohibition, when American distilleries were not operating. It was popular again during World War II, when American alcohol was repurposed from beverage to gunpowder ingredient. And then it saw another surge of interest from the late 1960s into the 1970s. But all of these periods of tequila popularity were almost entirely limited to the West; through the 1970s, it was difficult to find a bottle of tequila behind a New York bar.

And then the margarita caught on. It is a simple, three-ingredient drink that doesn't need any mucking up. Good tequila, the star of the show, is made from 100 percent blue agave, a green and peppery alcohol with mineral and vegetal notes. A good margarita doesn't require—or want—an aged tequila, because the oaky notes of the aging interfere with the pure flavors of the agave, lime, and orange. So use a *puro blanco*, aged under sixty days, if there's any aging at all; also use fresh lime juice—you can't make a good margarita with mixes; and use Cointreau, which is the cleanest-tasting and highest-proof of all the orange liqueurs (not that Grand Marnier is bad, but it has a lot of brandy and oak notes that don't belong in the margarita). All that said, there are some wonderful variations of the margarita, but nothing beats the original, simplest version.

PREMIUM MARGARITAS BY THE PITCHER

For the party animal, here's how to mix up a big batch:

1. First, add fresh-squeezed lime juice to fill about one-quarter of the pitcher.

2. Double the volume of liquid by adding Cointreau. Taste—it should still be a bit tart. You can add a little more Cointreau, but not much; you want to keep it on the tart side. The pitcher should now be half full.

3. Add the tequila of your choice to the three-quarter mark of the pitcher.

4. Adjust the sweetness with agave syrup (page 247) or simple syrup (page 246), but don't use more Cointreau (or its lesser cousin, triple sec), which would change the balance of citrus versus tequila.

5. Taste. The mixture should still be intense because the last ingredient hasn't yet been added.

6. Add ice to fill the pitcher. This will not only chill the pitcher but also mellow the drink and blunt the sharp alcohol attack. Stir vigorously and allow guests to help themselves. That is the easy way. My preference is to add the ice to a cocktail shaker (instead of the pitcher) and shake each drink individually for guests as they arrive. Whether shaken or from the pitcher, pour over new ice in a rocks glass or a stemmed margarita glass with a half-salted rim.

FROZEN MARGARITA

INGREDIENTS

1½ ounces pure agave tequila
¾ ounce Cointreau
1 ounce fresh-squeezed lime juice
1½ to 2 ounces simple syrup (page 246) or agave syrup (page 247)
Thin lime wheel, for garnish

☞ In a blender, combine the tequila, Cointreau, lime juice, and syrup with 1 cup cracked or crushed ice. Blend until thick and smooth. Pour into a traditional margarita or cocktail glass and garnish with the lime wheel.

♛ This wildly popular alternative requires a couple of ratio adjustments. Because you're adding so much more water by blending with ice, you need more of both the sweet and the tart to carry these flavors through the dilution, or your drink will end up tasting like slightly off tequila-water.

INGREDIENT NOTE

Tequila

For margaritas, I suggest using *puro* tequila, bottled exclusively in Mexico and made entirely from blue agave. Which is not as common as you might imagine. Over 90 percent of the tequila consumed worldwide is shipped out of Mexico in tankers and then bottled locally, sometimes after being unscrupulously diluted with neutral spirits and water. So always look for the words *Hecho en Mexico* ("Made in Mexico") as well as "100% blue agave." If you're serious about your margaritas, I suggest getting

a couple of bottlings to test the style you prefer, as you would with any spirit.

The best tequilas are generally from well-known distillers who own their own agave or purchase agave only from growers who adhere to their standards in managing the agave fields, as opposed to purchasing, packaging, and selling spirit made by another party. There are many notable tequila producers; a few of my favorites are Casa Cuervo's Tradicionale and Gran Centenario bottlings (in the case of the Gran Centenario, the

name Cuervo doesn't appear on the label), as well as any bottlings from the forward-thinking Herradura or those from El Tesoro and Don Julio, very old houses with traditional methods (which at El Tesoro include using an old stone wheel called a *tahona* to grind the agave, fermenting in wooden vats, and utilizing pot stills). Also, be sure to try the Partida family's tequila—they've been growing agave for generations and are now producing finished tequila as well.

VARIATION

RUBY PARTIDA*

Partida Tequila, created by entrepreneur Gary Shansby together with grower Enrique Partida, is an estate-grown premium tequila made from 100 percent blue agave that has been grown for generations by the Partida family in the heart of Mexico's historic Tequila Valley. Within the Tequila region, the Amatitán Valley has extraordinarily rich volcanic soil that results in superb agave, and the Partida family's land is in the heart of the production area. Their lowland-style tequilas are made in four distinct bottlings: Blanco; Reposado, which is aged for six months; Añejo, aged for eighteen months; and the superpremium Elegante, which had its first release in 2007. I designed the Ruby Partida as a showcase for their tequila. But the idea of this cocktail goes way back to the early tequila recipes of the 1920s: the sweet-tart berry flavor of cassis has always been a good match for the herbal, mineral, and vegetal notes of tequila. Finding things to combine with tequila isn't easy—this is one of the biggest challenges for the creative mixologist. As with grappa, anise-based spirits, and other spirits with bold idiosyncratic flavors, tequila tends to overpower almost anything it combines with. So cassis is something of a godsend.

INGREDIENTS

1½ ounces Partida Reposado tequila
½ ounce Cointreau
½ ounce fresh-squeezed ruby grapefruit juice
½ ounce fresh-squeezed lemon juice
½ ounce French crème de cassis, preferably Trenel Fils, Josoph Cartron, or Jules Theuriet

☛ In a cocktail shaker, combine the tequila, Cointreau, grapefruit juice, and lemon juice with ice. Shake well. Strain into a chilled cocktail glass, then dribble the cassis down through the drink. Serve with a stirrer on the side.

 OTHER VARIATIONS

A few other margarita variations are worth noting:

THE CADILLAC is the basic margarita recipe, but instead of using 1 ounce Cointreau, you use ½ ounce each Cointreau and Grand Marnier.

THF MILLIONAIRE is the Cadillac but using a super-premium tequila and the hundredth-anniversary bottling of Grand Marnier.

I like to make a STRAWBERRY MARGARITA (not the frozen one) with fresh strawberries. Begin the standard recipe by mashing a few fresh strawberries in the bottom of the shaker. Be sure to strain fully—preferably through a tea strainer—to avoid strawberry seeds in the cocktail. As is true whenever you're adding fresh fruit to a drink, additional sweetener may be necessary; try 1 teaspoon agave nectar here.

For a FROZEN STRAWBERRY MARGARITA, use the basic frozen margarita recipe previously described, throwing 3 or 4 fresh, hulled strawberries into the blender with the rest of the ingredients. Be sure to blend long and hard, until the strawberry flesh and seeds are totally pulverized.

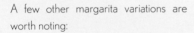

INGREDIENTS

2 ounces fresh-squeezed orange juice
4 ounces Champagne
½ ounce Cointreau float, optional
Orange zest, for garnish

☛ Pour the orange juice into a flute. Fill gently with Champagne, and the drink will mix itself; there's no need to stir, which would just wastefully dissipate the bubbles. Top with a ½-ounce float of Cointreau for an appealing little extra kick, and garnish with the orange zest.

I drink when I have occasion, and sometimes when I have no occasion.
—MIGUEL DE CERVANTES (1547–1616)

If you have no occasion to drink but are still doing it, chances are it's Champagne in your glass. Bubbly wine is appropriate (or at least not entirely inappropriate) any time of the day—quite possibly the perfect beverage. And the mimosa is certainly a testament to Champagne's pre-noon popularity—this is on pretty much every brunch menu ever written, along with the Bloody Mary. I think it's absolutely crucial to use fresh-squeezed orange juice, or the mimosa is just not the same. And if you're using fine French Champagne, does it make sense to mix it with carton juice? No, it doesn't.

MANGO MIMOSA*

Here's my tropical interpretation of the fizzy classic, combining both a fruit and an herb with alcohol, which is a type of combination that's intrigued me for a few years now.

INGREDIENTS

3 or 4 small pieces of mango
½ ounce mango-infused grappa
2 teaspoons Bevoir mango cordial
4 ounces prosecco
Orange peel, for garnish

☞ In the bottom of a Boston glass, combine the mango pieces, grappa, and mango cordial, and muddle well. Slowly pour the prosecco down the side of the glass while using a long-handled bar spoon to pull the flavors gently up from the bottom. Strain through a tea strainer into a flute, and garnish with the orange peel.

BUCK'S FIZZ

The progenitor of the mimosa was the Buck's Fizz, invented in the 1920s at the Buck's Club on Clifford Street in London. A bartender named McGarry at this gentleman's club came up with a sparkling wine combination with kicks of both gin and cherry brandy.

INGREDIENTS

2 ounces fresh-squeezed orange juice
Splash of gin
Splash of Peter Heering Cherry Heering
3 ounces Champagne
Spiral orange peel, for garnish

☞ In a mixing glass with ice, stir the orange juice with the gin and Cherry Heering to chill. Strain into a flute, and top with the Champagne. Garnish with the spiral peel.

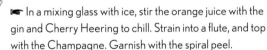

MONKEY GLAND

INGREDIENTS

Splash of absinthe or absinthe substitute
   (see Ingredient Note, page 12)
Orange slice, optional
1½ ounces gin
1 ounce fresh-squeezed orange juice
¼ ounce grenadine
Orange peel, for garnish

☞ Splash the absinthe into a mixing glass. Add the orange slice, gin, orange juice, grenadine, and ice, and shake. Strain into a small cocktail glass and garnish with the orange peel. Note that fresh juices are always preferred, but if using juice from the carton, toss in the slice of orange when shaking.

Strange name, isn't it? Instead, let's think of it as Victorian Viagra. In the early twentieth century, a Russian doctor named Serge Voronoff invented an odd surgical procedure that transplanted ape testicles into old men—human men, elderly *homo sapiens*—with the goal of renewing their sex drive. Questionable medicine, to be sure, but perhaps a stiff drink could also renew an older man's sex potency (though, sadly, the opposite is mostly the case), and hence the Monkey Gland. When this drink was invented by Harry MacElhone, owner of Harry's New York Bar in Paris and author of *ABC of Mixing Drinks*, it was made with absinthe, the anise-flavored concoction that has been illegal in the United States since 1912. The drink itself was a descendant of the nineteenth-century category of drinks called *daisies*, whose formulas were spirits with a juice and a sweetener, often grenadine. After it leaped across the pond, American bartenders began using Benedictine, a sweetened herbal liqueur, instead of the absinthe. So there are two utterly respectable versions of this odd-sounding drink: the American, with Benedictine; and Harry's, with anise or licorice flavoring. I'm partial to the original, so here is Harry's Monkey Gland.

VARIATION

ORANGE BLOSSOM

INGREDIENTS

1½ ounces dry gin
½ ounce Cointreau
1½ ounces fresh-squeezed orange juice
Orange peel, preferably spiral (page 154), for garnish

☞ Pour the gin, Cointreau, and orange juice into a mixing glass. Add ice and shake. Strain into a small, chilled cocktail glass. For a Prohibition-era presentation, serve in a stemmed goblet. Garnish with the orange peel.

The idea of mixing orange juice with spirits originated with the Bronx Cocktail (page 20) in the late nineteenth century. During Prohibition, when good liquor was, of course, difficult to procure, a well-made Bronx—with sweet and dry vermouths plus high-quality gin—became impossible to find. Hence the Orange Blossom was born. The goal was to mask the taste of bathtub gin with sweet orange juice and whatever liqueur was around. If you're feeling particularly Prohibition-y, put on a blindfold, choose a liqueur at random, toss in ½ ounce instead of the Cointreau, and have a taste of the unpredictable randomness of the Roaring Twenties.

NEGRONI

INGREDIENTS

1 ounce Campari
1 ounce Italian sweet vermouth
1 ounce gin
Orange peel, for garnish

☞ Combine the Campari, vermouth, and gin in an iced old-fashioned glass and stir. Garnish with the orange peel.

This famous drink was created in the bar of the Hotel Baglioni, on the Arno River in Florence, Italy, in 1925, when Count Camillo Negroni decided that the Americano (page 144) was too tame a drink. He asked the barman to spike his Americano with a splash of gin; the idea caught on and became popular as an Americano in the Count Negroni fashion, the name of which was eventually shortened to *Negroni*. The original recipe was equal proportions of gin and Campari served over ice, but lately the Negroni has evolved into a gin-heavy drink straight up in a cocktail glass, with the apéritifs receding to half-measures or just a splash. Sometimes vodka replaces the gin. I prefer the original 1:1:1 ratio, and I also prefer to serve it on the rocks. The effect of the melting ice cubes—big ones, please—is important in an all-spirits combination like this. Campari can be a challenge for those not familiar with the bitter apéritif, and I think it's easier consumed in this mixed fashion. Finally, some people use a lemon peel for the garnish, but I prefer orange for its pleasing match with Campari.

OLD FLAME*

This original of mine won the 2001 Bacardi Martini Gran Prix in Malaga, Spain. Which I considered immense good fortune, because it's a thoroughly accidental invention. I was in Dallas as part of a nationwide tour of cocktail dinners, matching cocktails to chef's food. I'd had Negronis made to go with the canapés and served a pair to a food journalist and her accompanying photographer, Nancy. They both took sips, and both rewarded me with the classic "ick" face, which is often the reaction Americans have to bitter-apéritif-oriented drinks, whose flavors differ so strongly from the sweet soda-pop flavors on which we're raised. So I took the Negronis back to the bartender and asked him to add fresh orange juice and Cointreau, reshake, and restrain. I presented the new glasses, and this time both women rewarded me with smiles. So I called it the Fancy Nancy, after the photographer, and soon after decided to enter it into the competition with a more universal handle, Old Flame, and lo and behold . . .

INGREDIENTS

1 ounce Bombay white-label gin
½ ounce Martini & Rossi sweet vermouth
½ ounce Cointreau
¼ ounce Campari
1½ ounces fresh-squeezed orange juice
Flamed orange peel (page 249), for garnish

☛ Combine the gin, vermouth, Cointreau, Campari, and orange juice in a mixing glass with ice and shake well. Strain into a chilled cocktail glass and garnish with the orange peel.

PINK LADY

In the far west of Greenwich Village, along Hudson River, there are now Richard Meier–designed buildings with residents including Martha Stewart and restaurants owned by Jean-Georges Vongerichten. But in the 1970s, when I was biking along the river with my wife and another couple, there was nothing but garages and warehouses and, along Christopher Street, a couple of bars. It was hot, we were thirsty, and there was nothing else around, so we went into a place called the Tool Box. Behind the bar was a guy wearing a motorcycle cap. "You sure you're in the right place?" he asked suspiciously. "We're just thirsty," I said. "We'll have a beer and go." So he gave us cans, which was how gay bars often operated back then, so they didn't have to worry about taps or kegs or other pricey, heavy equipment if they had to make a quick and permanent exit of the premises.

Halfway through our beers—and we were drinking pretty damn quickly—we heard a giant roar from outside, and fifteen or twenty bikes pulled up. A bunch of guys came in wearing full leather garb. The guy in front of the pack looked around the room and then at us, then back at his friends, and bellowed, "Pink Ladies all around." That was our cue to depart. And this was just a couple years after my arrival in New York, when, as it happened, I used to order this creamy after-dinner drink sometimes because I really didn't know what else to have—the Pink Lady was a part of pop culture, used in comic lines and plays, and I figured it had to be good. And the truth is, with the rose and cucumber notes from Hendrick's gin rather than the big juniper London dry style, it *is* a good drink. Not really a midday cycling-break-in-a-leather-gay-bar drink, but for, you know, less ridiculous circumstances.

INGREDIENTS

1½ ounces gin, preferably Hendrick's
¼ ounce grenadine
¾ ounce simple syrup (page 246)
1 ounce heavy cream
Maraschino cherry, for garnish

☛ Combine the gin, grenadine, syrup, and cream in a mixing glass with ice and shake well. Strain into a small cocktail glass and garnish with the cherry.

INGREDIENT NOTE

Homemade Grenadine

The bright red stuff you find on most grocery shelves—and in many cocktails—is nothing more than artificially flavored, sweetened, and colored water. Real grenadine is sweetened pomegranate juice, and here's how to make it: Put the seeds of three or four pomegranates into a sieve set over a bowl. With the back of a wooden spoon or a cocktail muddler, press gently on the seeds to break them open and release their juices. Don't press too hard, because you don't want to release any of the bitterness from the white center. You should end up with about 1 cup pomegranate juice. Combine this 1 cup juice with ½ cup rich simple syrup (page 246), strain, and there you have it: homemade grenadine.

VARIATION

THE ORIGINAL PINK LADY

Ted Haigh, a.k.a. Doctor Cocktail and author of *Vintage Spirits and Forgotten Cocktails*, has dedicated every minute that he's not performing his day job (as a graphic artist for Hollywood movies) to his real passion, cocktails. Doc has found what he says is the original Pink Lady recipe, which is a much drier cocktail than what the drink became in later years. To make this historical oddity a bit more palatable, I suggest using more than two good dashes of the grenadine, and maybe add a couple of dashes of simple syrup as well.

♛ INGREDIENTS

1½ ounces gin
½ ounce applejack
½ ounce fresh-squeezed lemon juice
White of 1 small egg (see Ingredient Note, page 30)
2 good dashes of grenadine

☛ Shake the gin, applejack, lemon juice, egg white, and grenadine very well with ice. Strain into a chilled cocktail glass.

APPLEJACK-POMEGRANATE FOAM

Behind Ted Haigh's passion for cocktails is a cool intellect. Doc analyzes all the data and comes up with exactitude in a subject that usually defies quantitative analysis, because even among the most intelligent observers, no one was sober enough to record anything! The addition of Jersey lightning, or applejack, to the Pink Lady is an example of Doc's determination to find the intended flavor in early cocktail recipes. The Pink Lady is also a perfect opportunity to display this flavor with a different textural impact: as a foam topping. If you're using this option, omit the apple brandy from the cocktail recipe. For full instructions on making foam, and information on the necessary equipment, see page 250.

Using the ½-liter cream canister will make enough foam for 15 to 20 drinks
2 gelatin sheets, each 9 x 2¾ inches
¾ cup superfine bar sugar
6 ounces pomegranate juice, preferably POM Wonderful
2 ounces emulsified egg whites
4 ounces Laird's Reserve apple brandy

☛ Place the empty ½-liter canister with the top unscrewed in the refrigerator to chill; do not put it in the freezer. Fill a saucepan with 6 ounces water and place over low heat. Slowly stir in the 2 gelatin sheets, dissolving them completely. Turn off the heat, add the sugar, and continue to stir until dissolved. Let cool. Add the pomegranate juice, egg whites, and apple brandy. Stir to combine, then fine-strain into a metal bowl; place the bowl in an ice bath, stirring occasionally until the mixture is well chilled.

Add 1 pint of the mixture to the canister. Screw in the cream charger; you will hear a quick sound of gas escaping, which is normal. Turn the canister upside down and shake very well, and the foam is ready.

Store in the refrigerator between uses. Before each use, turn the canister upside down and shake well. Then hold the canister almost completely upside down and gently put pressure on the trigger mechanism, applying the foam slowly over the top of the drink, working from the inside rim of the glass in a circular fashion to the center. When the canister is empty, hold it over the sink and engage the trigger to be sure the gas is completely spent. Remove the top and clean according to the manufacturer's instructions.

STORK CLUB COCKTAIL

INGREDIENTS

1½ ounces gin

¾ ounce Cointreau

1 ounce fresh-squeezed orange juice

½ ounce fresh-squeezed lime juice

Dash of Angostura bitters (the new Angostura orange bitters would make a fine substitute)

Flamed orange peel (page 249), for garnish

☞ Combine the gin, Cointreau, orange and lime juices, and bitters in a mixing glass with ice and shake well. Strain into a chilled cocktail glass and garnish with the orange peel.

When I was designing the first Rainbow Room menu in 1987, I looked through all the books about the grand old supper clubs of New York. We'd made it our stated mission to serve the house cocktails of the glorious clubs, restaurants, and hotels that had been in the shadow of the RCA Building in Rockefeller Center: the Colony, the Copacabana, the Knickerbocker, and the other celebrated nightspots of the 1950s where the stars and society hung out. Nowhere was a bigger hangout than the two-level, thousand-seat Stork Club, whose ultra-exclusive Cub Room—no one got in without a nod from the boss—was the progenitor of today's VIP rooms. This was the place, at 3 East Fifty-first Street, that world-famous Broadway columnist Walter Winchell called "the New Yorkiest place in New York."

The Stork Club Cocktail is a classic, if made properly—which means, above all, not substituting anything (such as triple sec or Grand Marnier) for the Cointreau, which is by far the most sophisticated, harmonious, and well balanced of the orange liqueurs. Cointreau is clean and bittersweet, without the brandy-driven wood notes of Grand Marnier; I love Grand Marnier, but not in most citrus cocktail applications. The downside, of course, is cost. As with so very many things.

VARIATION

VELVET FOG*

Flavored vodkas are here to stay (see Ingredient Note below), and I think the best way to use them is combined with fresh-fruit ingredients, as in this original recipe of mine, which uses orange vodka combined with fresh-squeezed citrus juices.

INGREDIENTS

1½ ounces Belvedere Pomarnacza vodka
½ ounce John D. Taylor's Velvet Falernum
1 ounce fresh-squeezed orange juice
½ ounce fresh-squeezed lime juice
2 dashes of Angostura bitters
Flamed orange peel (page 249), for garnish
Nutmeg, for garnish

☞ Combine the vodka, Velvet Falernum, orange and lime juices, and bitters in a mixing glass with ice and shake well. Strain into a chilled cocktail glass. Garnish with the orange peel and a dusting of freshly grated nutmeg.

INGREDIENT NOTE

Flavored Spirits

The snobbery camp of the cocktail world may turn up their well-trained noses at the increasing preponderance of flavored spirits. New brands and new variations are being released constantly, taking up an ever larger segment of the market. But the idea is actually a very, very old one, going back nearly five hundred years to the first vodkas, which were flavored with honey, herbs, and flower essences to mask the awful flavors of the pioneering distillates; and from the very beginning, rums were flavored and colored with spices and burnt sugar. If you want to get really technical about it, the Greeks flavored their wines two thousand years ago. So the idea isn't new; it's the *process* that's new. And it's true that modern flavorings are created in laboratories, not in kitchens (although you'll find many chefs today who question that distinction). If a manufacturer compounds sugar and artificial flavorings with a spirit, chances are the result will taste unnatural; but if he uses expensive essential oils and makes the effort to balance the flavors and maintain quality, the product can be good to excellent. Absolut Citron was the first of the contemporary crop to be made with care (and it was the test-marketing of this product that gave us the most popular modern cocktail, the Cosmopolitan). Recently, Finlandia introduced a grapefruit vodka I think is wonderful. Even the best of these flavored spirits—and certainly the worst of them—are used to most pleasant effect when combined with fresh flavors (for example, combining Absolut Citron with lime juice in the Cosmopolitan), which is what I recommend for all of these flavored spirits—not as a substitute for fresh flavors but as an augmentation of them.

WHITE LADY

INGREDIENTS

1½ ounces gin
1 ounce Cointreau
¾ ounce fresh-squeezed lemon juice

☞ Combine the gin, Cointreau, and lemon juice in a mixing glass with ice and shake well. Strain into a cocktail glass.

Harry Craddock was one of the great bartenders at the fine Hoffman House who was put out of a job—out of a profession—by Prohibition. Exiled by the law, he made his way to the Savoy Hotel in London, where he became head bartender of the American Bar, and where he wrote one of the all-time great bartending books, *The Savoy Cocktail Book,* first published in 1930. It was also where he invented the White Lady, named after a popular rose of the era, which in turn was named after White Lady Banks in 1807. Interestingly, Harry MacElhone, another famous bartender of the day who was exiled from his job (his was at the Plaza Hotel in New York City) by Prohibition, created a different drink called the White Lady at Harry's New York Bar in Paris, which he too published in another famous book, *ABC of Mixing Cocktails.* The two Harrys' White Ladies were in fact very unlike—MacElhone's was brandy, crème de menthe, and Cointreau, while Craddock's was gin, Cointreau, and lemon juice. It's the latter that survived as a popular cocktail.

Etymology aside, it's a good, simple three-ingredient drink, featuring orange liqueur married with lemon juice and all the botanicals in the gin to create a well-balanced yet complex cocktail with superb flavor. But speaking of well-balanced, here's an interesting note: Craddock's version called for equal parts of Cointreau and lemon juice. However, Craddock's drink was sure to be served in much smaller glasses than today's options, since all cocktails were smaller then. Glass sizes have increased to at least 5½ or 6 ounces, so it's important to reapportion some types of cocktails, especially ultrasimple ones where balance is everything—the sour ingredient tends to gain pronouncement as the drink grows in size. So in the modern version here, the sweet Cointreau is slightly larger than the sour lemon juice. That's progress for you.

AVIATION

The Aviation first appeared in print in *Recipes for Mixed Drinks*, published in 1916 by Hugo Ensslin, the head bartender at the Hotel Wallick in Times Square, New York. That original recipe included a shot of gin and ½ ounce lemon juice, plus 1 teaspoon each of two sweet liqueurs, Maraschino liqueur and crème de violette, the latter of which created a sky-blue drink—hence the name, from the earliest days of aviation. Alas, crème de violette is no longer available, and other palatable purple liqueurs haven't rushed in to fill the void, so an Aviation made today can't resemble the original blue drink. But the Internet-based cocktail geek squad has revived the Aviation, and you can now find it in the "Classics" section of a lot of forward-thinking (or, rather, retro-gazing) drinks menus. In fact, there's even a new gin, from Portland, Oregon, called Aviation, with its sights clearly set on being mixed up in this old favorite. There are rumblings from Ted Haigh, the guru of forgotten spirits, that our shores may again be graced by crème de violette or Parfait Amour by the time this book hits the shelves.

INGREDIENTS

2 ounces gin
¾ ounce Luxardo Maraschino liqueur
½ ounce fresh-squeezed lemon juice

☛ Combine the gin, Maraschino liqueur, and lemon juice in a mixing glass with ice and shake well. Strain into a chilled cocktail glass.

INGREDIENT NOTE

Maraschino Liqueur and Cherries

Maraschino liqueur is made from the marasca cherry, which grows around the Adriatic Sea; the liqueur was originally popularized in nineteenth-century Champagne punches. Like most liqueurs, the floral, sweet Maraschino has never been used as a cocktail base—always as an accent. Beginning in the 1880s, Maraschino cherries were available in the United States from the Luxardo com-pany, which bottled marasca cherries in actual Maraschino liqueur. But American companies began to replace the liqueur with a combination of almond oil, red food coloring, and sugar. By 1920, the American version had pretty much entirely replaced the Italian import. Luxardo is still the brand name of choice for Maraschino liqueur. But, sadly, real Maraschino cherries—marasca cherries bot-tled in Maraschino liqueur—are hard to come by. You can make your own by buying your favorite variety of fresh cherries, packing them in a jar with sugar for a day, and then pouring Luxardo's liqueur to fill the jar. Marinate for a week, then taste. The result should be Maraschino cherries, give or take another few days' marinating.

DRY MARTINI

INGREDIENTS

4 dashes of French dry vermouth
2½ ounces London dry gin or vodka
Pitted Spanish cocktail olive, no
    pimiento, chilled, for garnish
Lemon twist, for garnish

 Fill a mixing glass—and I mean a *glass*, because a martini should always be mixed in plain sight of the whole room— with ice. Add the dashes of vermouth first, then the gin or vodka. Stir 50 times if using large, dense, cold ice cubes, 30 times if using small, warmer cubes. (We want water in the drink from the melting ice; it is a critical ingredient that softens the alcohol jolt on the palate.) Strain into a chilled cocktail glass. Garnish traditionally with the pitted olive, and then twist a lemon peel over the top and drop it into the drink.

THE IMPORTANCE OF THE TWIST

Some people prefer a twist of lemon rather than an olive in their martini, about which David Embury, in his wonderful 1949 book *The Fine Art of Mixing Cocktails,* provides a perfect explanation: "When the bit of lemon peel is twisted over the glass, the surface of the cocktail should be sprayed as if by an atomizer with the oil of the lemon. This simple operation transforms a mediocre cocktail into a good one, and raises a good cocktail to the level of frankincense and myrrh!"

As a martini approaches the ideal of drier than dry, the choice of gin becomes more and more critical; the cocktail can become nothing more than cold gin. These days there's a pretty wide field of choice for gins, including the classic London Dry products such as Tanqueray and Beefeater, with their big Christmas-tree spices featuring juniper front and center. There's also the bright-tasting Tanqueray #10, with fresh botanicals like grapefruit, orange, and lemon peel in addition to the dried botanicals of juniper and coriander; and the revitalized Plymouth (which is in a category all its own, practically considered an AOC, distinct from London Dry), featuring coriander instead of juniper as the top note, which magnifies the impact of the citrus; and new bottlings like Miller's, which features herbal and anise notes, and Hendrick's from Scotland, which is heavy on cucumber and rose flavors. These latter gins won't produce a classic London dry martini, but they're worth trying, especially for neophytes who don't have a long sense-memory of the London dry style to set the standard for their brains via their palates.

Speaking of nonstandards: I sometimes like to replace the vermouth with up to ¼ ounce fino sherry, which works really well with either gin or vodka, and also substitute the lemon peel with orange peel, which is a wonderful natural partner for sherry; the sherry-orange combination helps soften the attack of the alcohol, and so it's much mellower and easier for someone who's not used to the tremendous kick of a martini. (If this drink is made with gin, it's called the Valencia, page 111: with vodka, it's a Flame of Love, page 110.) Remember that whether you're stocking the bar with dry vermouth or with fino sherry, these are wines, and they must be stored in the refrigerator.

Whichever version of the martini you're making, I think it's a good idea to mix the drink in front of your guests—the ceremony and the anticipation are a large part of the experience. Always chill your glasses in the freezer for at least a minute or two. (Or, to be the debonair, ever-prepared host, always leave a pair of glasses chilling in your freezer. Because you never know.) As for garnish, I think both lemon peel *and* an olive are perfectly acceptable in a classic martini—I like both in mine—but most people prefer one or the other, and they'll be sure to let you know; with martinis, people tend to let you know *exactly* what they think is right and what is wrong. The answer is that whatever the drinker wants is right, and whatever he or she doesn't want is wrong. But I suggest that if you're using olives, don't place more than three small ones in the glass itself, although you can serve extra olives on the side. Don't risk the type of scorn Frank Sinatra heaped upon the bartender at Manny Mateo's Saloon in Westwood, California, who made a martini and presented it to Frank, who commanded, "Throw a couple olives in there, kid." The eager-to-please young bartender then made the fatal mistake of asking, "Would you like a couple of onions, too, Mr. Sinatra?" To which Frank cracked, "Hey, kid, if I want a salad, I'll order it."

Here is my favorite dry martini.

EXTRA-DRY MARTINI

The dryness of a dry or extra-dry martini is a moving target. In Harry Johnson's 1888 *Bartender's Manual*, the recipe called for gum syrup, bitters, curaçao, Old Tom gin, and vermouth—that is, sweet vermouth, which was the type most readily available at the time. At the turn-of-the-century Knickerbocker Hotel in New York, it was Plymouth dry gin paired with Noilly Prat dry vermouth in equal measure, with a dash of orange bitters—a far, far cry from the late-twentieth-century dry martini. It wasn't until after Prohibition that the 3:1 martini came into vogue; forty years later, at the height of the Cold War, the true extra-dry martini arrived, in an 11:1 ratio (and that was followed quickly by the advent of the vodka martini, often dry or extra-dry). There's a movement back toward a wetter martini these days, but you'll still hear a lot of requests for extra-dry. Here's a good ratio:

 INGREDIENTS

2 dashes of French dry vermouth
2½ ounces gin or vodka
Cocktail olive, no pimiento, chilled, for garnish

☞ Stir the vermouth, the gin or vodka, and ice in a mixing glass 50 times if using large ice cubes, 30 times if using the small pellet-size cubes. If you're serving on the rocks, the cocktail should be mixed in the serving glass; if you're serving it up, strain it into a chilled cocktail glass. Either way, garnish with the cold olive.

INGREDIENT NOTE

Olives

The perfect martini olive is a little bigger than the manzanilla size, or the smallest of the queen sizes. You want your olive pitted, of course, but I think a pimiento or any other stuffing is generally a mistake. (Though I do think that blue cheese is a great partner for martinis—but as a nibble on the side, not stuffed into an olive and dropped in the liquor.) I also think nearly all olives could stand a little mellowing before they become a cocktail garnish, and here's how you do it: Remove from the brine the number of olives you need for the round of martinis; put them in a cup of mineral water for 90 seconds, no longer, to remove the acidic vinegar brine but to retain the olives' saltiness. By all means, keep your olives chilled, which is especially important for the larger varieties or if you're garnishing with a few of them. Using room-temperature olives is tantamount to putting a reverse ice cube into a nicely chilled drink. Not a good idea. Note that for some inexplicable reason, a few people insist on a standard canned black olive in their martini, and that variation is called Buckeye. If you choose a tasty Italian green olive with a pit, alert your guests ahead of time or they may bite down hard with an unhappy result.

THE GLASS

The classic V-shaped cocktail glass that became an icon of the cocktail age was part of an exhibit introduced in the famous 1925 Paris event called the Exposition Internationale des Arts Décoratifs et Industriels Modernes, a show that introduced the style we know today as Art Deco. The glass didn't catch on immediately—it wasn't until after World War II that it saw widespread use—but when it finally did take hold, it did so with a tenacity rarely seen, and it remains to this day an absolute must and the iconic vessel for any martini.

 VESPER

He looked carefully at the barman.

"A dry martini," he said. "One. In a deep champagne goblet."

"Oui, monsieur."

"Just a moment. Three measures of Gordon's, one of vodka, half a measure of Kina Lillet. Shake it very well until it's ice-cold, then add a large thin slice of lemon peel. Got it?"

"Certainly, monsieur." The barman seemed pleased with the idea.

—IAN FLEMING, *Casino Royale* (1953)

A few pages later, Bond was sharing a carafe of his unnamed cocktail, chilled in a bowl of ice, with a female agent. It turned out her name was Vesper.

"Can I borrow it?" He explained about the special martini he had invented and his search for a name for it. "The Vesper," he said. "It sounds perfect and it's very appropriate to the violet hour when my cocktail will now be drunk all over the world. Can I have it?"

And so a legend began when journalist Ian Fleming penned these words in 1952 while vacationing at his Jamaican estate, Goldeneye, not only inventing one of the most famous fictional characters of all time but also launching vodka onto a stratospheric path that within two decades would take it from obscurity to the most popular spirit in the United States. In real life, that original drink—a combination of vodka and gin with Lillet (which is not vermouth)—was invented by Gilberto Preti at the Duke's Hotel in London, which was Fleming's neighborhood bar. (Maybe that should read "In real-ish life," because this can't be considered real life for almost anyone in the world.) Fleming then went on to write another dozen Bond books, all of which were made into movies beginning with *Dr. No* in 1962. Most featured Agent 007 ordering a vodka martini. And so it was that John Martin, the genius behind the Smirnoff promotions that introduced vodka to the United States, contacted Albert Broccoli, the producer of the Bond flicks, with a product placement proposal. The instructions for the Bond martini were eventually shortened to "Vodka, shaken not stirred" in order to accommodate Smirnoff, which was paying a pretty penny to have their bottles sharing the screen with Sean Connery or Roger Moore. And this, oddly enough, is how the spirits world was transformed. In my first book, *The Craft of the Cocktail*, I made the mistake of pandering to vodka drinkers by switching the gin and vodka proportions to make the drink more appealing; now I have an opportunity to correct that error in judgment.

Here is Bond's original recipe, with my alteration of the garnish.

 INGREDIENTS

3 measures Gordon's gin
1 measure vodka
½ measure Lillet
Flamed orange peel (page 249),
   for garnish

☞ Combine the gin, vodka, and Lillet in a mixing glass with ice and shake well. Strain into a chilled cocktail glass and garnish with the orange peel.

INGREDIENT NOTE

Lillet

The Kina Lillet that Bond enjoyed—as did the Duchess of Windsor, who had a case sent ahead to wherever she was visiting—was more bitter and quinine-heavy than the Lillet of today. The apéritif, which had been invented in the nineteenth century, was reconfigured in 1985, and today's version is actually quite sweet (and has dropped the name *Kina* from the brand). Now it's just Lillet, blanc or rouge (the latter is pretty hard to find), made in Bordeaux and usually served over ice.

FLAME OF LOVE

INGREDIENTS

½ ounce fino sherry, preferably Tio Pepe or La Ina

3 orange peels, cut as for flaming (page 249)

2 ounces vodka

☞ Wash out a chilled cocktail glass with the sherry by swirling and then discarding the excess. Flame the oil from 2 of the orange peels into the empty glass, discarding the flamed peels after coating the glass with their oil. Chill the vodka in a mixing glass (although Pepe Ruiz preferred to shake) and strain it into the prepared glass. Flame the remaining peel over the surface of the drink, and drop it in.

Pepe Ruiz, a hometown hero in Los Angeles, was head bartender at the original Chasen's during its mid-twentieth-century heyday in Hollywood, when it was the clubroom to movie stars and moguls, the watering hole of the Rat Pack. One night, Dean Martin tells Pepe he's been coming to Chasen's for years—whenever they're not in Vegas, the whole Rat Pack is at Chasen's—and finally wants his own drink. So the next time Martin comes in, Pepe does this whole show of cutting four giant orange peels from one orange, igniting the peels to make a big light show, coating the whole inside of the glass with the flamed oil. Then Pepe seasons some ice with fino sherry—the driest of the sherry styles—which is a simpatico partner to orange. Finally, he mixes the drink, pours it into the prepared glass, and flames one final orange peel over the top. Martin absolutely loves the drink, gushing his thanks at Pepe. Later that night, he drags Frank Sinatra to the bar—not that Sinatra ever needed to be *dragged* to any bar—to try this magical cocktail. Sinatra too is blown away by it, so much so that he orders a cocktail for everyone in the restaurant—at least two hundred people—on him. Pepe calls the kitchen staff out to the bar to help, and they mix up the round, all two hundred drinks. Now that's what I call watering the infield.

VALENCIA

Also known as the Spanish martini, this drink was the preferred cocktail of the late Joe Drown, owner of the Hotel Bel Air in Los Angeles. The hotel grounds had been a stables and sales office for the visionary Alfonso E. Bell, who purchased the 600-acre Danziger Estate in 1922, eventually amassing 4,500 acres of the most beautiful canyons in the Santa Monica Mountains to create lush 1-acre properties that he named, collectively, Bel Air. The most beautiful of all those canyons was Stone Canyon, where the Bel Air Hotel was built by Joe in 1946 (the year after Bell died). I got to the Bel Air in 1978, when Joe was elderly and sick but still coming in for his nightly martini, prepared according to exact instructions since the 1940s: gin with fino sherry instead of vermouth, served in a 4-ounce carafe set into a little ramekin filled with crushed ice. Joe would pour a tiny bit into his glass at a time, maybe just a couple of sips, ensuring that every sip was ice cold. Here is that drink, except that Joe didn't take his with the flamed orange peel I use today.

INGREDIENTS

½ ounce fino sherry, preferably La Ina or Tio Pepe
2½ ounces gin or vodka
Flamed orange peel (page 249), for garnish

☞ Stir the sherry and the gin or vodka with ice in a mixing glass 50 times if using large ice cubes, 30 times if using the small pellet-shaped cubes. Strain into a chilled cocktail glass and garnish with the flamed orange peel.

THE FLAMED ORANGE PEEL

I first saw the flamed peel at Mama Leone's, the tourist trap in New York's Theater District, where waiters used to flame lemon peels into espressos, which were served in very close proximity to the presentation of the check. I was working on an advertising campaign, walking from table to table and doing something so silly that I claim I can't remember what it was—this was back in my aspiring-actor days, when I had a lot of odd jobs.

Fast-forward ten years, and I'm on Tom Snyder's television show along with Pepe Ruiz from Chasen's and Jim Hewes from the Willard Hotel in Washington, DC. Pepe had been at Chasen's for nearly four decades, was an old friend of Tom's, and was the elder statesman of this trio of bartenders. So even though I was getting some attention for flaming peels at the Rainbow Room—this was when the Cosmopolitan was really taking off and I was igniting peels like a mad arsonist for their garnishes—I decided not to flame anything during my part of the segment to avoid stepping on Pepe's toes. Jim does his Mint Julep and finally it's Pepe's turn, and Tom says, "I know what you're going to make," and we all do because it's Pepe's signature. Pepe steps out in front of the camera, and . . . freezes. Like a block of ice. He's petrified, shaking, can't get a word out. The segment turns into an utter disaster. When it's over and the camera is off, Tom asks Pepe how he's able to serve movie stars and kings and queens every single night—and during Reagan's presidency this was practically the Western White House—and yet freeze here. Pepe shrugs; It's the camera.

FRENCH MARTINI

INGREDIENTS

1 ounce premium vodka
1 ounce Chambord
2 ounces unsweetened pineapple juice

☞ Combine the vodka, Chambord, and pineapple juice in a mixing glass with ice and shake well. Strain into a chilled cocktail glass, with no garnish.

The French martini was imported from Europe, probably Paris, in the early 1990s. It first appeared on an American menu at Keith McNally's Pravda, when that vodka-themed lounge opened in 1996. This is the cocktail that kicked off the whole flavored "martini" craze that's redefining the American bar lexicon. But nomenclature aside, the French martini is a delicious cocktail, which, when shaken vigorously like the Flamingo (page 173), develops a great ½ inch of foam from the pineapple juice. (This foam, by the way, is not something you want to ruin with any garnish.) The French martini has never been as popular as its sister the Cosmopolitan, but it's a decently popular drink that I think deserves a wider audience.

INGREDIENT NOTE

Chambord

Chambord is a premium raspberry liqueur from France, but it was not developed by monks, nor is it an herbal or botanical liqueur like Benedictine or Chartreuse, nor is it made from a fermented mash of raspberries in the eau-de-vie family; it's a lower-proof, flavored, neutral grain spirit, and it fits more readily into the category of fruit liqueurs that includes curaçao, Grand Marnier, and cherry liqueur. Chambord became huge in the 1980s and 1990s because it was an ingredient in the disco drinks of that era, such as the Purple Hatter, the Lobotomy, and the Grape Crush, which all followed the elementary formula of a spirit plus a sweet. Chambord was the sweet, with the extra benefit of supplying some acid, which was useful in balancing the drinks. Chambord is packaged in a round glass bottle with a plastic gold belt around the middle and a crown on top. Nearly exactly the same package was used for a beloved pre-Prohibition spirit called Forbidden Fruit, which was based on shaddock fruit. It was the liqueur of the Bustanoby family of restaurateurs in New York City who lost everything after Prohibition; Forbidden Fruit was popular in many cocktails of the day.

PERFECT PASSION*

I created this drink for my friend Robin Massey, with whom I worked at the Rainbow Room. Robin was getting married in London; I was working and couldn't get there, but Robin asked me to design the cocktails for the event. I happily obliged with a list including this invention, named for her state of heart. My original idea was for a blanco tequila drink, but most of Robin's friends drank vodka, so we made the alteration; it also works well with gin. If you're going to make one of these at home, the recipe here works great; but if you're going to mix up a lot of them for a party (or if you're a professional), you can't be doing all this work for one drink at a time, so make a batch of the Strawberry-Lychee Marinade (below) and some Ginger Syrup (page 248) to replace the muddling stage; for each cocktail, use 1 ounce marinade and ¾ ounce ginger syrup along with the vodka and lemon juice. Note that despite my normally maniacal insistence on fresh ingredients, I'm not suggesting you use fresh lychees here: I think there's no noticeable difference between the fresh and the canned, and the fresh take a lot of effort that I don't think is worth it.

INGREDIENTS

1 nickel-sized piece of fresh ginger root

¼ ounce John D. Taylor's Velvet Falernum

3 fresh strawberries, 2 hulled for muddling, 1 for garnish

2 canned lychees

2 ounces vodka

1 ounce triple syrup (page 248)

½ ounce fresh-squeezed lemon juice

☛ In the bottom of a Boston shaker glass, mash the ginger with the Velvet Falernum. Add 2 of the strawberries and the lychees, and muddle well. Add the vodka, triple syrup, lemon juice, and ice, and shake well. Tea-strain into a chilled cocktail glass. Cut the remaining strawberry in half, make a slit in the bottom of one half, and set the rim of the glass into the slit, as garnish.

STRAWBERRY-LYCHEE MARINADE

This is essential for making Perfect Passions for a crowd; without it, you'll never cease muddling and mixing. Make it the night before.

6 pints fresh strawberries, washed and hulled

6 12-ounce cans lychees, plus syrup from 1 can

1 pint honey syrup (page 247)

1 liter simple syrup (page 246)

1 liter agave syrup (page 247)

Put the strawberries and lychees into a mixing bowl. With an immersion blender, roughly chop the fruit. Pour this mixture into a large container, and add the lychee syrup, honey syrup, simple syrup, and agave syrup, and stir.

Cover the pitcher tightly, and let marinate in the refrigerator for at least 3 hours but preferably overnight, stirring occasionally. Before using, strain through a china cap or fine-mesh sieve, and store, refrigerated, for up to 4 days.

LAZONE'S MARTINI*

INGREDIENTS

1½ ounces gin
1 ounce Southern Comfort
½ ounce fresh-squeezed lime juice
2 dashes of Peychaud's bitters
2 dashes of Herbsaint
Thin lime wheel, for garnish

☛ Combine the gin, Southern Comfort, lime juice, simple syrup, bitters, and Herbsaint in a mixing glass with ice and shake well. Strain into a chilled cocktail glass and garnish with the lime wheel. Note: Adjust sweetness with simple syrup.

The third anniversary of a wonderful New Orleans event called Tales of the Cocktail was 2005. For one of my presentations, I hosted a cocktail dinner at Brennan's. While in the Big Easy, I wanted to use classic New Orleans ingredients like Southern Comfort, Peychaud's bitters, and Herbsaint, and the result is this drink, which I named after the chef at Brennan's, Lazone Randolph.

GARNET*

INGREDIENTS

1½ ounces Tanqueray No. 10 gin
¾ ounce Cointreau
1 ounce pomegranate juice
1 ounce fresh-squeezed grapefruit
    juice
Flamed orange peel (page 249), for
    garnish

☛ Combine the gin, Cointreau, pomegranate juice, and grapefruit juice in a mixing glass with ice and shake well. Strain into a chilled cocktail glass and garnish with the orange peel.

This is one of my own contributions to the ever-broadening category of flavored martinis, this one a gin drink. The new-wave gin brands are taking aim at seducing the vodka drinker, with less emphasis on the Christmas-tree spices of the London dry style, and instead replacing the heavy juniper notes with more citrus as the top flavor. The Garnet is a fruity-style gin cocktail that takes advantage of this lighter taste profile.

STRAWBERRY NIRVANA*

This delicately fruity rum mixture is a luscious, aromatic, and well-balanced cocktail, like a flower in a glass. It's also a good amount of labor, with multiple syrups, fresh-squeezed juice, and some berry work. With berries, you want to use a fine-mesh or tea strainer on the finished mixtures because the tiny seeds can annoy the hell out of people—plus they float all over the place in the drink, a look I don't care for. Finally, for the garnish strawberry, you'll want to wash it, but don't hull it—a strawberry garnish is prettier with the greens still attached.

INGREDIENTS

3 medium strawberries, washed

¾ ounce fresh-squeezed lemon juice

1½ ounces Plymouth gin

¼ ounce Luxardo Maraschino liqueur

1 ounce triple syrup (page 248)

 Remove the hulls from 2 of the strawberries. In the bottom of a bar glass, muddle them with the lemon juice. Add the gin, Maraschino liqueur, triple syrup, and ice, and shake well. Tea-strain into a chilled cocktail glass. Cut the remaining strawberry in half, make a slit in the bottom of this one, and set the rim of the glass into the slit, as garnish.

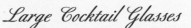

TECHNIQUE NOTE

Large Cocktail Glasses

I'm not a fan of large glasses for traditional cocktails, especially all-alcohol ones such as the martini and the Manhattan; for these drinks, big glasses result in either too much liquor or too much empty space, neither of which is good for the drinker. On the other hand, for juice-driven cocktails with a lot of volume, like the Garnet, an 8- or 10-ounce cocktail glass is appropriate. Most juice-driven cocktails are served over ice, often in highball glasses, so it's not often you find a drink of 6-plus ounces that's served up. But when you do, that's when you should reach for the jumbo V-shaped glass. Never, however, for the likes of a classic dry martini.

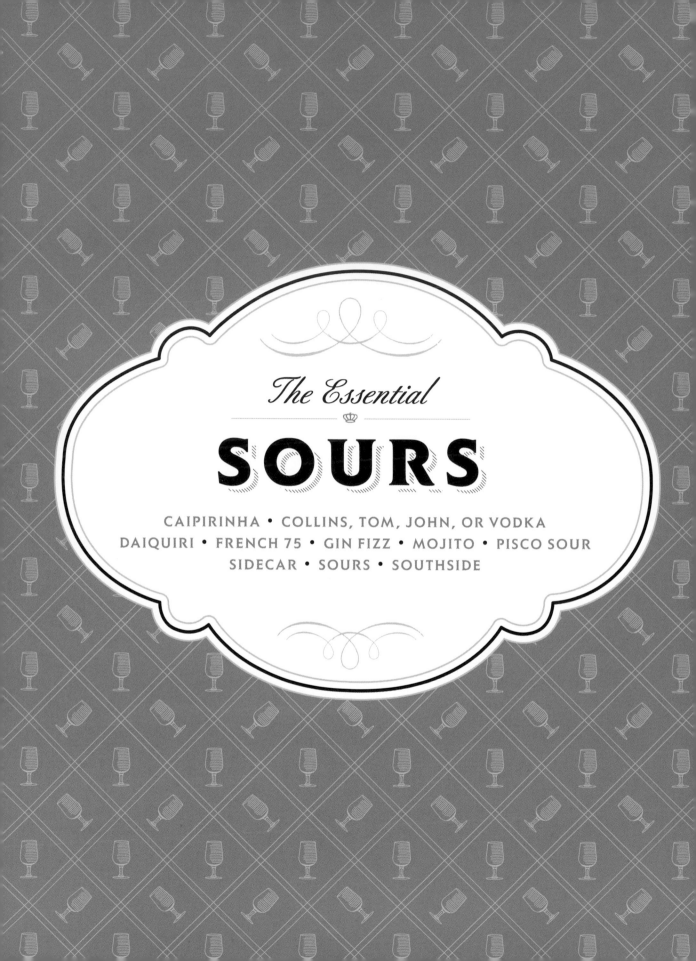

The Essential

SOURS

CAIPIRINHA • COLLINS, TOM, JOHN, OR VODKA
DAIQUIRI • FRENCH 75 • GIN FIZZ • MOJITO • PISCO SOUR
SIDECAR • SOURS • SOUTHSIDE

The sour formula looks simple: a combination of sweet, sour, and strong. But, oh, how looks can deceive! The sour is the sophisticated corner of the mixologist's art, putting the cocktail practitioner's skill on the line. When a chef tries his hand at classic, formal French cuisine, he opens up a whole world of challenges. Much the same can be said for a bartender—and for that matter a bar—serving real sours.

Why? Primarily, balance: It's simply hard to achieve a pleasing one, and there's little room for error because this type of balance is all about subtleties. Also, the sour is based on fresh fruit juices, which vary seasonally, require lots of handling, and can be expensive when mishandled; it's much easier and cheaper to buy the powdered mixes or shortcut bottles, which, as expected, are awful. The sour ingredient is almost always lemon or lime juice, but these days yuzu makes the occasional appearance, imparting an extra acid note. Bitters sometimes play a role, balancing the sweet with intense flavor. The sweet itself can be more than one ingredient—in fact, all three of the sweet, sour, and strong elements can include multiple ingredients, creating a richly layered, complex cocktail.

A properly made sour is a work of art, and sours have been many of the iconic drinks of the past century: the Sidecar in the 1930s, the Southside in the 1950s, and daiquiris across the decades. Today the sour of choice is the mojito, which is forcing bartenders to pay attention to the art of the sour for the first time in nearly forty years. It's still hard to get a drink made with fresh-squeezed lemon or lime juice in much of the country. But in the upper end of the business, you can get a real sour these days, and to me that's a crucial test of the health of the cocktail. If you can get a good sour, things are looking up. ♚

CAIPIRINHA

INGREDIENTS

½ lime, quartered

2½ teaspoons sugar or 1 ounce simple syrup (page 246)

2 ounces cachaça

¼ ounce John D. Taylor's Velvet Falernum, optional

☛ Fill a rocks glass with cracked ice. In the bottom of a mixing glass, place the lime quarters and the sugar or syrup. Muddle to extract the lime juice and the oil in the lime skin. Add the cachaça and the ice from the rocks glass, as well as the Falernum, if using, and shake well. Pour the entire contents of the mixing glass into the chilled rocks glass and serve. In the tradition of the Caipirinha, the muddled fruits—whether solely lime or with additional fruits—are used as the garnish.

I was introduced to the Caipirinha in 1989 by a pair of sophisticated, beautiful Brazilian women who used to come to the Rainbow Room to listen to their music teacher, who happened to be our guitar player. The first day they ordered Caipirinhas, I had to plead ignorance, and not just of the cocktail but of the spirit from which it is concocted. On the next visit, the women brought in a bottle of cachaça (pronounced "ka-sha-sa"), and one of them taught me how to make my first Caipirinha. Since then I've been a devotee of this farmer's drink that was born in the Brazilian countryside; the word *caipira* means "countryman," and the Caipirinha is a diminutive. Its base spirit is the wonderful sugarcane-based, rum-like cachaça, which for many years was dismissed as a peasant product by the higher classes in Brazil. But within the past decade a new generation of wealthy Brazilians has embraced cachaça as a heritage product and as the national spirit. There's now a law that requires the Caipirinha be made with cachaça Brasilerio (other cachaça-like products, with different names, are made elsewhere in South America). There are more than three thousand cachaça producers in Brazil, many of them small-scale family-run distilleries, and we get fewer than 1 percent of the brands here in the United States. I suggest using, if you can find it, an old-world artisanal-style cachaça such as Ypioca, Beleza Pura, Rochinha, or Velho Barreiro. The additional spice note from the Falernum is my own idea; it is not part of the traditional recipe.

VARIATION

GINGER-LYCHEE CAIPIROSKA*

A Caipirinha that's made with rum instead of cachaca is called a Caipirissima; made with vodka, which is how the Brazilian wealthy used to drink it before the surge of national pride in cachaca, it's called the Caipiroska. The variation here can be prepared with vodka, rum, or cachaca; all are equally delicious. Note that the tradition of the Caipirinha and its variations require that you retain the ice and the fruit you used to mix the drink. So rather than discarding the fruit, straining, and replacing with new ice, just shake the drink and then empty the entire contents into a serving glass as you would a regular Caipirinha.

♛ INGREDIENTS

1 small piece of fresh ginger root (about the size of your fingernail), or ³/4 ounce ginger syrup (page 248)

1 ounce simple syrup (page 246)

½ lime, quartered

2 canned lychees

2 dashes of John D. Taylor's Velvet Falernum

2 ounces vodka

☞ If using fresh ginger, muddle it in the bottom of a bar glass with the simple syrup; if using the ginger syrup, just place it in the bottom of the bar glass. Either way, muddle the resulting ginger-sugar mixture with the lime quarters, lychees, and Velvet Falernum. Add the vodka and cracked ice, shake well, and then pour the contents of the shaker—without straining—into a rocks glass.

DAIQUIRI

INGREDIENTS

1½ ounces white rum
1 ounce simple syrup (page 246)
¾ ounce fresh-squeezed lime juice
Thin slice lime, for garnish

☛ Combine the rum, syrup, and lime juice in a mixing glass with ice and shake well. Strain into a cocktail glass and serve up, with the lime slice as garnish. *Note:* To prepare frozen and frozen fruit–style daiquiris refer to the formula for a frozen margarita (page 88). The additional ice and fresh fruits mean you will need extra sweetener.

The daiquiri was invented in Cuba in 1898 by two men, Harry E. Stout and Jennings Cox, in a small village named Daiquiri near Santiago. (Even though, for all intents and purposes, grog [see page 176] is a daiquiri without ice. So the daiquiri invention can hardly be considered wheel-like.) Cox's original recipe called for the juice of 6 lemons, 6 teaspoons sugar, 6 cups Carta Blanca rum, 2 small cups mineral water, and crushed ice. This serves-a-crowd punch recipe soon evolved into a single-portion drink, and Admiral Lucius Johnson introduced it to Washington, D.C., at the Army-Navy Club. (Johnson also introduced it to the University Club in Baltimore, where the bartender insisted on adding bitters; to San Francisco, where it was not a hit; and to Honolulu, Guam, and Manila. He was quite the ambassador.) The daiquiri has long been one of America's favorite cocktails, especially in warmer weather, when the lime-rum combination is a great quencher. But note that unlike the mojito (page 131), the daiquiri isn't thinned with club soda or anything except the water in the syrup and lime juice, both of which do a remarkable job of hiding the alcohol content of the drink. Which is to say: Take it slow with daiquiris, because they can sneak up on you.

PAPA DOBLE

The great bartender Constantino Ribalaigua, of the Floridita Bar in Havana, must have been inspired by the cocktail muse when he added fresh grapefruit juice and Maraschino liqueur to the daiquiri, because the result is ambrosia. A. E. Hotchner, who was Ernest Hemingway's longtime friend, went down to Cuba to collect a story that was way overdue for *Life* magazine, and he ended up staying a year. In Hotchner's biography of his friend, *Papa Hemingway*, is a recipe for the Floridita's version, which omits sugar or syrup and includes only a small amount of Maraschino liqueur. I find Hotchner's version, called the Papa Doble, sour to the point of undrinkability, so I've sweetened it up.

For twenty years, Hemingway's primary residence was an estate called Finca Vigía, outside Havana; it was here that he wrote novels and stories and thousands upon thousands of letters and the short masterpiece *The Old Man and the Sea*, which earned him the Nobel Prize in 1954. After a hard day of writing and fishing and hunting, Hemingway would have a night of hard drinking, sometimes with the likes of Gary Cooper or Errol Flynn. As often as not, this drinking was done at the Floridita, whose version of the double daiquiri was Hemingway's usual choice, so they named it after him. Here is the Papa Doble as remembered by Hotchner, followed by my version for those who can't take the extra-sour original.

 INGREDIENTS

3 ounces white rum
Juice of 2 limes (1 to 1½ ounces)
½ ounce marsh grapefruit juice (see Ingredient Note)
6 drops of Luxardo Maraschino liqueur

 Blend the rum, lime juice, grapefruit juice, and Maraschino liqueur with ice. Pour into a coupé glass and serve without garnish.

INGREDIENT NOTE

Marsh Grapefruit

Marsh grapefruits, like all grapefruits, originated with the crossing of sweet oranges with shaddock (or forbidden fruit, as it is colloquially referred to). Marsh grapefruits are sought after because they are seedless and have sweet juice.

DALE'S HEMINGWAY DAIQUIRI*

INGREDIENTS

1½ ounces white rum
½ ounce Luxardo Maraschino liqueur
¾ ounce simple syrup (page 246)
½ ounce fresh-squeezed grapefruit juice
½ ounce fresh-squeezed lime juice

Combine the rum, Maraschino liqueur, syrup, and grapefruit and lime juices in a mixing glass with ice and shake well. Strain into a cocktail glass and serve up.

FRENCH 75

INGREDIENTS

1 ounce Plymouth gin or cognac
3/4 ounce simple syrup (page 246)
1/2 ounce fresh-squeezed lemon juice
3 ounces Champagne
Spiral lemon peel, for garnish

☛ Combine the gin or cognac with the syrup and lemon juice in a mixing glass with ice and shake well. Strain into a large goblet over ice. Top with the Champagne and garnish with the spiral lemon peel.

Hits with remarkable precision. —HARRY CRADDOCK, *The Savoy Cocktail Book* (1930)

The French 75 started as a gin drink in the Tom Collins style, with Champagne in place of club soda, but now is much more often made with brandy or cognac. Harry's New York Bar in Paris is often credited as the originator, but the backstory I prefer is a little more romantic: The doughboys of World War I, out in the French countryside, were longing for a Tom Collins or any other refreshing highball. They had gin and they had Champagne, and there was maybe a lemon tree nearby, but they didn't have access to much else, certainly not club soda. So they made a Tom Collins with the Champagne, *et voilà!* But whether it was a bow-tied barman at Harry's or an anonymous American soldier in the Somme, what we do know for certain is that the name comes from the 75-millimeter shell—a big one. The U.S. Army didn't have a good field piece, so the gunnery units used the new French-designed 75; Harry Truman, a young officer in World War I, commanded a unit that used the French 75. (And was heard to say, one busy afternoon, "I'd rather be here than be president of the United States.")

Anyway, the elusiveness of its origin is echoed in the elusiveness in the standard preparation. I've seen it prepared in a big fat goblet topped off with lots of fruit, in a slender flute with a little spiral of peel, and in a highball glass over ice with a cherry and an orange like a Tom Collins. And a great Nantucket restaurant called the Chanticleer specialized in a brandy-based French 75 that they served in a burgundy glass, over ice, and decorated with a cornucopia of fruit—strawberry and orange with mint—that was simply stunning; you couldn't watch one of these things go through the dining room without wanting to order one for yourself. This is how I sometimes serve it—as a fun, brunchy drink—although a purist would probably prefer to see it strained into a tall flute. But this is an ad lib drink, not something carefully invented by a mixologist using the best ingredients to create the ideal cocktail. It was improvised at its inception, and I think it's open season for you to improvise it today. I do.

GIN FIZZ

The Collins and the fizz are both spinoffs of the sour—they're really just sours with the addition of club soda—and the difference between them is nothing more than glass size and garnish. A Collins goes into a tall or Collins glass and is garnished with a cherry and an orange slice; a fizz is served in a short highball glass, once known as a Delmonico glass, without any garnish. In other words, a fizz is a Collins on the short plan. Both categories have embraced lots of drinks since aerated or charged water, now known as seltzer, became widely available in the nineteenth century. They are versatile, refreshing, flexible, and forgiving, lighter than martinis and other all-alcohol drinks, good for daytime or evening. Although the proportions are flexible and somewhat forgiving, you should never use more than 2 ounces soda, or the result will be too watery.

INGREDIENTS

1½ ounces gin
¾ ounce fresh-squeezed lemon juice
1 ounce simple syrup (page 246)
1 to 2 ounces club soda, to taste

☛ Combine the gin, lemon juice, and syrup in a mixing glass with ice and shake well. Strain into a highball glass with ice. Fill with club soda. Do not garnish.

VARIATION

SILVER FIZZ

This fizz is a slightly lighter, without the heavy cream, and slightly simpler, without the orange-flower water, variation on the Ramos (see page 129).

INGREDIENTS

1½ ounces gin
¾ ounce fresh-squeezed lemon juice
1 ounce simple syrup (page 246)
¾ ounce egg white
Club soda

☛ Combine the gin, lemon juice, syrup, and egg white in a mixing glass with ice and shake long and hard to completely emulsify the egg. Strain into a fizz or highball glass without ice, and top with soda but no garnish.

GOLDEN FIZZ

INGREDIENTS

1½ ounces gin

¾ ounce fresh-squeezed lemon juice

1 to 2 ounces simple syrup (page 246), to taste

Yolk of 1 small egg (see Ingredient Note on page 30)

Club soda

☛ Combine the gin, lemon juice, syrup, and egg in a mixing glass with ice; shake long and hard to completely emulsify the egg. Strain into a fizz or highball glass without ice, and top with soda.

To turn a Golden Fizz into a Royal Fizz, use the whole egg instead of just the yolk. These drinks must be shaken very, very hard and long to completely emulsify the egg.

THE RIGHT GLASS

When bars stocked the full complement of glassware, including specialty glasses designed for specific drinks, the bartender's job was easier, and the customer could have greater confidence that the drink would arrive in the proper proportions—in a lot of cases, the size of the glass would nudge the bartender into mixing a well-balanced drink. A Tom Collins was made in a tall, narrow Collins glass filled with ice cubes (the glass was only 1 cube wide), a shot of gin, and the other ingredients were simply what fit into the glass; same for the fizz, in its 8-ounce Delmonico glass. But you won't find an 8-ounce highball behind many bars today— nearly all highballs are 12 or 14 ounces. So if a bartender takes one of these glasses, pours in a shot of spirit, balances it with the right amount of lemon juice and syrup, and then fills the glass with soda . . . the customer gets an awfully watery mess of a drink. Which is too bad. Alas, there's no glass these days that'll prevent the inexperienced bartender from drowning the drink in soda.

RAMOS OR NEW ORLEANS FIZZ

Over the years, I've soothed thousands of hangovers with this famous eye-opener. The Ramos Fizz, also known as the New Orleans Fizz, was originated by Henry C. Ramos in 1888 when he opened his Imperial Cabinet Bar at the corner of Gravier and Carondelet streets in New Orleans. The drink caught on so tremendously that by the time he opened his soon-to-be-famous Stag Saloon in 1902, the Ramos Gin Fizz was one of the best-known drinks in the country and ordered by practically everyone who entered the Stag. But this presented a big logistical challenge, because a proper Ramos Fizz must be mixed and then shaken long and shaken hard, and the Stag had a lot of customers every night, seemingly all of whom wanted the same drink. So Ramos's ingenious solution was at once eminently practical and an awfully good show: He employed nearly three dozen "shaker boys"—this was back when it wasn't prohibitively expensive to have lots of employees (it wasn't unusual to have a half-dozen guys behind every bar, where today we usually have just one or two)—and at any given moment there were about twelve of the boys back behind the long bar. Every Ramos Fizz order would start at one end of the bar and be shaken by each guy in turn for a few seconds, the shaker going down the whole line, creating a spectacular show for the house specialty. I myself have never worked behind a bar with a dozen colleagues, but I have been known to pass the fizz shaker around the room to guests—it's great fun. (But first check that the shaker has a nice tight seal, or it'll be no fun at all.)

As long as you shake long and hard, use both lemon *and* lime juice, fresh-squeezed of course, and, most important, use orange-flower water and *not* orange juice, you will produce an ambrosial drink. Orange-flower water is an essence made by steeping orange-flower petals in alcohol. There is no substitute for this ingredient. If you can't find orange-flower water, put off making this fizz until you can; instead, make the Silver Fizz (page 127). The old Hotel Roosevelt in New Orleans, which bought the rights to the trade name Ramos Gin Fizz, is now called the Fairmont; don't leave New Orleans without a visit to its bar, where they carry on the tradition of the Ramos Fizz in grand style.

INGREDIENTS

1½ ounces gin
½ ounce fresh-squeezed lemon juice
½ fresh-squeezed lime juice
1½ to 2 ounces simple syrup (page 246), to taste
2 ounces heavy cream
¾ ounce egg white
2 drops of orange-flower water
Club soda

☛ Combine the gin, lemon and lime juices, syrup, cream, egg white, and orange-flower water in a mixing glass with ice and shake long and hard to completely emulsify the egg. Strain into a highball glass without ice. Top with soda but no garnish.

MOJITO

In Cuba, the mojito is a farmers' drink (as compared to the more sophisticated urban drinks, daiquiris and El Presidentes). Havana was once a primary source of U.S. slaves, and it is not a stretch to imagine plantation owners and slave traders enjoying a few juleps on the expansive porches of southern plantations; the mojito may have been inspired by the southern julep. Although ice wasn't available commercially in Cuba until the 1890s, a wealthy slaver had the ships and the means to maintain a private supply if required. In Cuba in the early twentieth century, when the artificial ice plants opened and charged water also became available, the mojito became a reality for the general population. But despite its immense popularity, I'm pretty sure the cocktail didn't appear on any American menu until the 1960s, when Joe Baum served it at his groundbreaking pan-Latin restaurant La Fonda del Sol. (But in 1936, a well-known barman named Eddie Woelke, who had worked in Paris and Havana before returning to New York after Prohibition, won the *Madison Avenue Week* cocktail competition with a drink called the Madison Avenue, which contained mint leaves, white rum, lime juice, bitters, and Cointreau. He had clearly paid attention while in Cuba, because this winning recipe looks a lot like a mojito.) On Joe's menu, it was called mojito Criollo (Creole), which is a product used for seasoning meat and fish. Now, you'll see it everywhere as simply *mojito*. And you'll also see it overproduced with mint that's shredded and shaken throughout the drink, which I think makes it overly herbal and often bitter. In Cuba, the mojito is not even shaken—the mint is simply bruised in the bottom of the glass to release some flavor—and the drink is kept simple and easy, an adult limeade. That's my preference.

INGREDIENTS

2 sprigs of tender, young mint
1 ounce simple syrup (page 246)
3/4 ounce fresh-squeezed lime juice
1 1/2 ounces white rum
2 dashes of Angostura bitters, optional
1 1/2 ounces club soda

☛ In the bottom of a highball glass, bruise the leaves from 1 of the mint sprigs with the simple syrup and the lime juice. Add the rum and bitters, if required; top with no more than 1 1/2 ounces of club soda; and stir. Garnish with the second sprig of mint.

INGREDIENT NOTE

Rum

Rums can be categorized as light, medium, or full-bodied, and then further depending on whether they're made in the French style from sugarcane syrup, usually called *agricole,* or in the Spanish style from molasses, which includes the rums from Cuba, Puerto Rico, and the other Spanish colonies. Although as a rule I prefer the agricole style of rum, the light Spanish style perfected by Bacardi is better for drinks such as the mojito, where you want to keep the flavors simple and straightforward to produce a clean, limy, minty cocktail.

PISCO SOUR

The pisco sour and the pisco punch (page 200) are totally different drinks that both feature the same unusual base spirit from South America. The sour, which is now probably the best-known pisco-based cocktail in the United States, is said to have been created in 1915 by Victor Morris, a native of Berkeley who owned the Morris Bar in Lima, Peru. The American version of the pisco sour has traditionally used lemon juice, as with all sours. But my Peruvian friend Diego Loret de Mola tells me that the citrus fruit used in Peru is green and more like a lime. The drink itself is quite good when prepared with lime juice, so the citrus choice is really yours.

INGREDIENTS

1½ ounces Bar Sol Pisco
1 ounce simple syrup (page 246)
¾ ounce fresh-squeezed lemon or lime
    juice
1 ounce egg white
Several drops of Angostura bitters

☞ Combine the pisco, syrup, lemon juice, and egg white in a mixing glass with ice and shake long and hard to completely emulsify the egg. Strain into a small cocktail glass. Garnish by dropping a sprinkling of bitters on top of the egg-white foam.

INGREDIENT NOTE

Pisco

It is perfectly colourless, quite fragrant, very seductive, terribly strong, and has a flavour somewhat resembling that of Scotch whiskey, but much more delicate, with a marked fruity taste. It comes in earthen jars, broad at the top and tapering down to a point, holding about five gallons each. We had some hot, with a bit of lemon and a dash of nutmeg in it. . . . The first glass satisfied me that San Francisco was, and is, a nice place to visit. . . . The second glass was sufficient, and I felt that I could face small-pox, all the fevers known to the faculty, and the Asiatic cholera, combined, if need be.

This is how pisco was described by an anonymous writer way back in 1872. Pisco comes in four styles: *pisco aromatico,* which is how Chileans usually make it; *pisco puro,* nonaromatic, which is the Peruvian's preferred style; *pisco acholado,* a blend of the aromatic and nonaromatic muscat grape clones; and *pisco mosto verde,* made from partially fermented grape juice. A number of brands are available in the United States, including Bar Sol, Alto del Carmen, Capel, Biondi, Don Cesar, La Diablada, Montesierpe, and Bauza. Bar Sol has several bottlings that illustrate three of the four styles of pisco. The easiest to find in the United States is Quebranta (which is also the grape name), the nonaromatic variety, a dry-style pisco that's a good choice for cocktailian pursuits; Acholado, also fairly easy to find, is made from a combination of Italia, a fragrant muscat variety, and Quebranta. Both of these are good choices for the pisco sour. Finally, Bar Sol also produces both Torontel and Italia, earthy and aromatic bottlings that are my choices for the pisco punch.

PISCO BELL-RINGER

This is a pisco sour with extra flavor via dashes of rum and bitters and a seasoned glass—an approach that could be extended to dozens of drinks, using different fruit and alcohol. The Bell-Ringer was adapted by Julie Reiner at the Flatiron Lounge in New York City from an original recipe that appeared in the *Esquire* drinks database created by David Wondrich, *Esquire* magazine's resident cocktail historian.

INGREDIENTS

1½ ounces Bar Sol Pisco Acholado
½ ounce Bacardi eight-year-old rum
½ ounce fresh-squeezed lemon juice
½ ounce simple syrup (page 246)
White of 1 egg (see Ingredient Note, page 30)
Dash of orange bitters
Dash of Angostura bitters
Dash of apricot liqueur, preferably Marie Brizard Apry
Lemon wheel, for garnish

☛ Combine the pisco, rum, lemon juice, syrup, egg white, and both bitters in a mixing glass with ice and shake well. Pour the apricot liqueur into a chilled cocktail glass, swirl it to coat, and then discard the liquid. Strain the pisco-rum mixture into the glass. Garnish with the lemon.

CUZCO

The Cuzco was invented by Julie Reiner of the Flatiron Lounge. In the words of pisco expert Diego Loret de Mola, both the Cuzco and the Bell-Ringer are "brilliantly crafted cocktails expressing the perfect combination of elements in a Pisco libation (whether served straight up or on the rocks): the right style of pisco, bitter modifiers, citrus elements, and a unique flavor touch." The Cuzco takes much of its unique character from Aperol, which is the darling ingredient of the bar-chef these days. It's kind of like Campari for beginners, with all the same notes but not as bitter, and so it is easier to mix and more friendly to the American palate.

INGREDIENTS

2 ounces Bar Sol Italia Pisco
¾ ounce Aperol
½ ounce fresh-squeezed lemon juice
½ ounce fresh-squeezed grapefruit juice
¾ ounce simple syrup (page 246)
Dash of kirschwasser
Grapefruit twist, for garnish

☛ Combine the pisco, Aperol, lemon and grapefruit juices, and syrup in a mixing glass with ice and shake well. Pour the kirschwasser into a highball glass, swirl it around to coat, and then discard the liquid. Strain the pisco mixture into the prepared highball over ice. Garnish with the grapefruit twist.

SIDECAR

INGREDIENTS

Sugar, for frosting the glass
Orange slice, for frosting the glass
1½ ounces cognac
¾ ounce Cointreau
¾ ounce fresh-squeezed lemon juice
Flamed orange peel (page 249), for
garnish

☛ Prepare a sugar-crusted rim on a cocktail glass using the sugar and orange slice, as explained in the Technique Note on page 137. Chill the glass. Now, make the drink. Combine the cognac, Cointreau, and lemon juice in a mixing glass with ice and shake well. Strain into the prepared glass, and garnish with the orange peel.

The Sidecar was invented at Harry's Bar in Paris, about 1930. But to say it was "invented" then is a bit misleading, because the Sidecar was nothing more than a modernized version of a very old drink—one of the original cocktails that appeared in the first edition of Jerry Thomas's *How to Mix Drinks*, seventy years earlier—called the Brandy Crusta, which was invented in New Orleans by a man named Santini, a Spanish caterer of some note. The word *crusta* referred to dipping the rim of the glass in sugar and letting it dry into a crust. That crusted rim is an ingredient and an essential part of the Sidecar's presentation. For the drink itself, I use equal parts Cointreau and lemon juice rather than my normal formula of slightly more sweet than sour, creating a drink that's on the tart side, because you'll be getting extra sweet from the sugared crust. Don't substitute triple sec for the Cointreau, as most brands are both too sweet and too low in alcohol for this sweet-and-tart drink (for, in fact, nearly any drink). And speaking of what you should and should not use: The Sidecar is a cognac drink, an elegant drink to be made with premium ingredients, which means not with regular brandy. Finally, the orange-peel garnish is my own addition—a lemon peel is more common—because it's a better match with the Cointreau and makes for a better drink all around.

And what about the name? You've probably heard that the drink was named for a regular customer at Harry's who arrived in a motorcycle that had a sidecar. But I don't believe it. The word *sidecar* means something totally different in the world of the cocktail: If the bartender misses his mark on ingredient quantities so when he strains the drink into the serving glass there's a bit left over in the shaker, he pours that little extra into a shot glass on the side—that little glass is called a *sidecar*. Every bartender should make sidecars, instead of pouring the extra down the drain, where it won't do anybody any good. And I think this may be where the cocktail got its name.

BETWEEN THE SHEETS

INGREDIENTS

1½ ounces cognac
½ ounce Benedictine
½ ounce Cointreau
¾ ounce fresh-squeezed lemon
   juice
Flamed orange peel (page 249), for
   garnish

☞ Combine the cognac, Benedictine, Cointreau, and lemon juice in a mixing glass with ice and shake well. Strain into a chilled cocktail glass and garnish with the flamed orange peel.

♔ The oft-found recipe for this wonderfully named spinoff of the Sidecar includes rum and brandy, in a 1:1 ratio, while the uncommon recipe in Ted Saucier's pulchritudinous *Bottoms Up* calls for just one base spirit, the brandy, with an accent of Benedictine; this is far superior. That said, if you have a particularly interesting rum with distinctive flavor notes, you can make that original version, 1:1 brandy-to-rum, with an additional 1 measure of the Cointreau and ¾ measure of lemon juice.

VARIATION

BULL'S BLOOD*

INGREDIENTS

¾ ounce rum
¾ ounce high-quality orange
   curaçao, such as Maria Brizard,
   Bols, or Hiram Walker
¾ ounce Spanish brandy, preferably
   Cardenal Mendoza
1½ ounces fresh-squeezed orange
   juice
Flamed orange peel (page 249), for
   garnish

☞ Combine the rum, curaçao, brandy, and orange juice in a mixing glass with ice and shake well. Strain into a cocktail glass and garnish with the flamed orange peel.

♔ The Between the Sheets inspired an original of my own where I do mix brandy and rum, as in the common recipe. But I think Spanish brandy is a friendlier companion to rum than French cognac, and I've replaced the Cointreau with a different orange flavor, curaçao. I've also replaced the lemon juice with orange juice because orange is a great flavor complement to Spanish brandy—in fact, it's that friendliness that drives this drink.

Frosting a Glass with Sugar

When you frost a glass with salt—for a margarita, for example—you do it at the moment you serve the drink, using a lemon or another tart citrus. But when you frost a glass with any kind of sugar—plain white, or brown, or flavored, or Demerara—it must be done way in advance, preferably several hours ahead of serving, to give the sugar time to crystallize, turning into nearly a lollipop consistency that stays on the rim during the course of consuming the drink. If you frost the glass right before serving, then you face multiple problems. First is that a good portion of the sugar comes off the glass with every sip, making the drink too sweet; second is that as the glass begins to sweat, the sugar migrates down the glass to the stem, turning it into a sticky mess.

Here's how to create the crust: Pour a good amount of sugar into a shallow saucer or small plate. Cut a slice of citrus—orange for the orange-accented Sidecar, but other fruits will do for cocktails with other flavors—to the exact thickness you want your crust to be (if you want ¼ inch of crust, cut the slice ¼ inch thick). Hold your glass upside down so excess juice doesn't drip down it. Using the slice as a guide, wet the top of the outside rim of the glass—never the inside—along its full circumference (when you're frosting with salt, I suggest using only half the circumference, but for sugar, go all the way around). Dab the moistened rim in the saucer of sugar, pressing the glass into it for maximum adhesion, and then gently tap the glass to shake off any excess. Now let the sugar crystallize at room temperature until totally hardened. When it is, transfer the glass to the freezer to chill.

SOURS

INGREDIENTS

1½ ounces base liquor
1 ounce simple syrup (page 246)
¾ ounce fresh-squeezed lemon juice
¼ ounce egg white, optional
Cherry, for garnish
Orange or lemon slice, for garnish

 Combine the base liquor with the syrup, lemon juice, and egg white, if using, in a mixing glass with ice and shake well. Strain into an old-fashioned glass and garnish with the cherry and the citrus slice—orange for the American version, lemon for the English.

How Sweet Is Too Sweet?

Back in the days when the standard cocktail was a mere 2 to 3 ounces, syrup was made in a stronger concentration of 2 parts sugar to 1 part water, packing a lot of sweetening punch into a small volume. But now that drinks have gotten so much larger, this concentration doesn't provide enough volume to stand up to the larger proportion of spirits in most drinks. Nowadays the syrup ratio you are looking for is 1:1.

If you ask me, it's the classic sour—whiskey, vodka, or rum—that separates the amateur bartender from the pro. This is an easy drink to screw up and a hard one to nail because the ratio of flavors is a precarious balance. The proper ratio is what's in this recipe, which is a variant on the classic punch formula (1 measure of sour, 2 of sweet, 3 of strong, 4 of weak, plus spice). I came up with these measures in 1985, when I had my first head-bartender job and was trying to figure out how to run a classic bar using only traditional recipes and fresh ingredients. This meant no modern conveniences, such as soda guns, and certainly no bottled sour mixes. In the end, 95 percent of drinkers are happy with the ratio here, which is applicable to all manner of sour-style drinks—not just the sour itself. If you err with this drink—and lots of people do—try to err on the side of sweet rather than sour because most guests will drink that. But if you err on the side of too sour, no one will, except the English, because their taste tends more to sour than their American cousins.

Finally, there's the question of base liquor. Whiskey was long the most popular for sours, which for a long time meant blended, either American or Canadian. But today bourbon has taken the lead, so that should be the default.

FITZGERALD*

We had a tradition at the Rainbow Room that if a customer asked for a drink to be designed for a specific taste, we'd do it, and we'd do it *à la minute*. A guy came in one crowded night and said he was bored with gin and tonic and wanted something else. I was getting slammed at the time but felt obliged to honor the tradition, and I came up with this gin-based sour. But before I served it, I realized the customer had probably had more than his fair share of gin sours as well, so I spiced it up with Angostura bitters. This was back in the cocktail dark ages of the early 1990s, when my friend Tony Abou Ganim used to quip, "What lasts longer, a bottle of Angostura bitters or your marriage?" So I was reasonably confident the customer hadn't had a bittered gin-based sour. I was right. The drink was a hit—even non–gin drinkers enjoy it—and I eventually put it on the Rainbow Room menu.

INGREDIENTS

1 1/2 ounces gin
1 ounce simple syrup (page 246)
3/4 ounce fresh-squeezed lemon
   juice
2 or 3 dashes of Angostura bitters
Lemon wedge, for garnish

☛ Combine the gin, syrup, lemon juice, and bitters in a mixing glass with ice and shake well. Strain into a rocks glass and garnish with the lemon wedge.

SOUTHSIDE

INGREDIENTS

2 sprigs of mint, preferably young
    spearmint tops
¾ ounce fresh-squeezed lemon juice
1½ ounces gin
1 ounce simple syrup (page 246)
1½ ounces club soda

☞ Prepare as you would a mojito: *Gently* muddle 1 of the mint sprigs with the lemon juice in the bottom of a mixing glass. Add the gin and syrup and shake well. Pour over crushed ice in a goblet and stir until the outside of the glass frosts. Top with a splash of soda—up to 1½ ounces, to taste—and garnish with the other sprig of mint.

This was the house drink of the famous 21 Club in New York City during its heyday, back when it was usually called Jack and Charlie's. Jack Kriendler and Charles E. Berns, cousins of Austrian descent, grew up in New York City. In the depths of Prohibition, they decided to go into the speakeasy business. In 1922 they opened their first speak in Greenwich Village, in the unseemly shadow and unpleasant roar of the Sixth Avenue elevated subway; in 1925 they moved across the street to a Spanish-themed speakeasy called Frontón. They were evicted that same year, when the city was condemning buildings to make way for a new underground subway to replace the el. So they moved uptown, to be among all the other fabulous nightspots, and opened their new space at 42 West Forty-ninth Street. It was there, finally, that Jack and Charlie's graduated to a more grown-up crowd, ushered in by Yale graduate Ben Quinn, who brought in other Yalies, including a good smattering of writers. Soon Jack and Charlie's was the favorite of Robert Benchley and Alexander Woollcott, of Dorothy Parker and Edna Ferber.

In 1929, Jack and Charlie were evicted once again, this time to make room for Rockefeller Center, and so they moved into a new space at 21 West Fifty-second Street, where Jimmie Coslove manned the peephole (he was called "Jimmy of the front door") and where they built an elaborate electrified system of secret doors and passageways to hide the liquor in case of a raid. After Repeal, the roving establishment that had been popularly known as Jack and Charlie's finally started using a permanent name. During the Great Experiment, they'd changed the name of the businesses regularly to help avoid successful prosecution (the changing names were evidence against a continuity of business). After a brief hiccup in the early 1930s, 21, as it was now known, flourished for decades, becoming one of the longest-running success stories in New York.

The Southside was 21's long-running house drink. A Southside is, for all intents and purposes, a mojito made with gin (a strong ingredient, a sour, a sweet, plus mint and soda). And it's up for grabs which came first, the mojito or the Southside, though it's fairly certain that both were preceded by the third in the triumvirate of minty drinks, the julep, which was being made as long ago as the eighteenth century. If you're a mojito lover, the Southside is a no-brainer of an alternative, and it's really far superior to the mundane gin-and-tonic as a summer quencher. For the gin itself, any variety will make a good Southside—Old Tom, London dry, Plymouth, or even Holland gins, those malty and grainy varieties that are now called *genever* (which are much more like white whiskeys than the other clean, vegetal gin styles). But for non–gin drinkers I'd suggest using one of the new-wave brands such as Tanqueray 10 or the more vegetal Hendrick's, which would shine in a recipe like this, or Citadel, with its citrusy and floral notes, or Aviation, with its lavender and cardamom hints. But whatever gin you use, avoid the hot-summer-day temptation to drown the drink with club soda, which won't make it more of a thirst-quencher but will just make it bad. I call for 1 ½ ounces, and you can stretch that to 2, but certainly no more. If what you're looking for is to drink club soda, then by all means drink club soda, and have the cocktail later.

The Essential

HIGHBALLS

AMERICANO • BLOODY MARY • CAPE CODDER
CUBA LIBRE • GIN RICKEY • HORSE'S NECK • MOSCOW MULE
PRESBYTERIAN • SCREWDRIVER • SLING • STONE WALL
TEQUILA SUNRISE

It is one of my fondest hopes that the highball will again take its place as the leading American drink. I admit to being prejudiced about this—it was I who first brought the highball to America, in 1895. —PATRICK GAVIN DUFFY, *The Official Mixer's Manual* (1934)

When I was a kid, I read Hemingway, where it seemed all the men sat around cafés drinking brandy and soda highballs while they read the newspaper. So when I was in college, I sat around cafés, drinking brandy and soda highballs while I read the newspaper, a practice that may have led to my premature departure from the University of Rhode Island. In the detective stories I read, the detective kept a bottle of whiskey in the drawer and a siphon of soda on the desk to mix up highballs. To me, the highball was a civilized twentieth-century staple, whether dry with soda or sweet with ginger ale. It was an icon of the country for a century. The gin and tonic was almost synonymous with the yacht club and summertime; after Labor Day, when you put away your white bucks and seersucker suit, you traded in the gin highball for a whiskey one.

What is this icon? The simple formula of a strong spirit, usually 1½ ounces, with 4 to 5 ounces mixer, usually club soda, tonic water, or ginger ale, served over ice in a 12- or 14-ounce glass. A twist of lemon can be the garnish, but many people prefer their highballs with no garnish. And all people prefer their highballs with only 1½ ounces spirit—no more. If they wanted a strong drink, they'd have a Manhattan or a martini. The reason they want a highball is to have a light drink, so don't overpour the liquor. (This goes double if you're a professional. Take note that bars make their money on highballs and their small dose of liquor, not on martinis and their glassfuls of expensive booze. So not only don't your guests want a strong drink, neither does your bottom line.) ♛

AMERICANO

INGREDIENTS

1½ ounces Italian sweet vermouth
1½ ounces Campari
2 to 3 ounces club soda, to taste
Orange slice, for garnish

☞ Pour the vermouth and Campari into an ice-filled highball. Top with club soda and garnish with the orange slice.

The Americano was invented as the Milano-Torino (the Campari was from Milano, the vermouth from Torino) in the 1860s at the Caffè Camparino in Milan, owned by Gaspare Campari, the inventor of the Campari apéritif. It wasn't renamed the Americano until Prohibition, when Americans flooded the Continent looking for a stiff drink. Many of them found their way to Campari's, where they ordered the drink en masse, and the Italians renamed the drink in honor of their new clientele. (Ironically, Campari itself wasn't illegal in the States during Prohibition because it was classified as a medicinal product, not an alcoholic beverage.) At one point, the Americano was so globally popular that the Martini & Rossi Company bottled and sold it around the world in a pre-mix that required the simple addition of club soda.

That's a lot of European history for a drink called the Americano. But history aside, I think the Americano is the premier summer cooler: It's light and refreshing, with just a touch of bittersweet. But be sure not to drown the drink in club soda—no more than 3 ounces. Once you get up to 4 or 5 ounces, you've drowned the spirits and the flavor, you've lost all the guts of the drink, and you've created off-tasting fizzy water, which is not really what anyone wants.

VARIATION

ARANCIO AMERICANO*

I designed this contemporary version of the Americano for Keith McNally's restaurant Morandi, which opened in New York City in early 2007. This variation replaces the club soda with sparkling Italian wine and includes a little orange juice for kicks of sweet and acid.

INGREDIENTS

¾ ounce Italian sweet vermouth, preferably Martini & Rossi
½ ounce Campari
1 ounce fresh-squeezed orange juice
2 ounces prosecco

☛ Build the vermouth, Campari, and orange juice over ice in an aperitivo glass. Fill with prosecco.

 INGREDIENT NOTE

Campari

Gaspare Campari was born in 1828. When he was fourteen, Campari left his home in the countryside to find his fortune in Turin, where he apprenticed at a liqueur producer. He eventually went out on his own and made his way to Milan, where he set up shop at Caffè Camparino as a *licoriste,* a category of artisan-shop-keeper-bartender (plus a small dash of pharmacist), whose origins dated to the fifteenth century. Licoristes were as much scientists as chefs, and were often favored members of the court; they were the guys who devised formulas for the cordials and *aperitivi* that were the proprietary drinks of caffès (some of these eventually became

commercially manufactured products, including more than a few vermouths from Turin and Milan), the forefathers of the nineteenth-century mixologists who pioneered the cocktail tradition. Campari's liqueur, first poured in 1862, was one of these proprietary house drinks. To this day it remains extraordinarily proprietary. Its formula is so closely guarded that the president of the company is the only person in the world who knows the full list of its eighty-six ingredients. Each week, the president, the technical director, and eight other employees—none of whom knows more than his particular piece of the puzzle—get together to produce the base

concentrate that's later mixed with alcohol to create the *aperitivo.* The only interesting thing that's widely known about the contents is that the red coloring agent is carminium, whose use is documented back to the Aztecs and Incas. Carminium is made from the dried bodies of a South American insect called the carmine cochineal. Campari is thus a bright red liqueur with a bittersweet taste. It is often served in Italy accompanied by nothing more than soda water on the side—and, in fact, the Campari-soda combination is also sold pre-mixed in single-serving bottles.

BLOODY BULL

INGREDIENTS

2 ounces vodka
2 ounces Campbell's beef broth
2 ounces Sacramento tomato juice
Dash of fresh-squeezed orange juice
4 dashes of Tabasco sauce
Dash of freshly ground black pepper
Orange peel, for garnish

☛ In a mixing glass, combine the vodka, broth, tomato juice, orange juice, Tabasco, and pepper. Add ice and shake. Strain into a goblet glass over ice, and garnish with the orange peel.

I did a version of the meaty Bloody Bull called a Foul Shot, made with pheasant consommé (the name is compliments of Milton Glaser, for whom I invented the drink). But the beef-broth version has always been the popular old-time steakhouse favorite. Although it sounds down-market and prefab, a can of Campbell's is the ideal ingredient for the Bloody Bull; it has the right balance of beefy and salty. If you insist on standing on gourmet ceremony and using homemade broth, you may want to add a dash of salt, but definitely don't use salt with canned broth. And unlike the Bloody Mary, you definitely want to shake the Bull—somehow, the beef broth prevents the mixture from getting unpleasantly foamy. Finally, garnish with a twist of orange peel, not the lemon wedge you use for other Bloody drinks. Why? At Aurora, we did a good business in Bloody Bulls, and Joe Baum liked the drink, but he was dissatisfied with the traditional lemon or lime wedge garnish, and thought it didn't make sense either visually or tastewise. But he couldn't tell me what he wanted instead, and this bothered me immensely. I won't claim I lost sleep over the Bloody Bull garnish, but it was definitely an issue. And then one day I sat down at a Chinese restaurant and for the first time noticed a menu item I'd never given much thought to. So I ordered it. And then before me was a dish of chunks of beef swimming amid orange peels. Wow. So back at Aurora, I mixed up a Bloody Bull with a couple of personal additions: a dash of orange juice and the oily twist from the orange-peel garnish. Apparently, beef likes the orange flavor much better than lemon or lime. And so did Joe.

VARIATION

BULL SHOT

This is a Bloody Bull without the tomato juice—a great lunchtime drink if you're dining in a joint with sawdust on the floor and aged beef on your plate.

INGREDIENTS

2 ounces vodka
4 ounces Campbell's beef broth
4 dashes of Tabasco sauce
2 dashes of fresh-squeezed orange juice
Dash of freshly ground black pepper
Orange peel, for garnish

 In a mixing glass, combine the vodka, broth, Tabasco, orange juice, and pepper. Add ice and shake. Strain into a goblet glass over ice, and garnish with the orange peel.

OTHER VARIATIONS

The Bloody Mary is fertile ground for improvisation and variation, and here are a few of the most noteworthy takeoffs:

The DANISH MARY replaces the vodka with aquavit, whose herbal flavors go well with the tomato juice. If aquavit were more available and known in this country, it'd probably quickly overtake vodka as the popular Bloody base.

The BLOODY MARIA substitutes tequila for the vodka.

The BLOODY CAESAR uses clam juice—actually, it uses Clamato, which was invented because of the Bloody Caesar. In 1969 Walter Chell, a bartender from Montenegro who relocated to Calgary, Canada, was working at the Calgary Inn. He was asked to create a drink for the opening of the hotel's new Italian restaurant, called Marco's.

Chell experimented for three months and came up with a combination that included hand-mashed clams and tomato juice as well as the other traditional Bloody Mary ingredients. This fantastic cocktail, the Bloody Caesar, inspired Duffy Mott, of the Mott's company, to develop and patent Clamato. After some dispute between Chell and Mott, the bartender became a spokesperson for Clamato, and the Bloody Caesar became Canada's national drink.

CUBA LIBRE

INGREDIENTS

1½ ounces Cuban-style rum, such as
    Matusalem or Brugal Silver
4 ounces Coca-Cola
Lime wedge

☞ Pour the rum over ice in a highball
glass, and then fill with Coca-Cola.
Squeeze in the lime wedge.

"Free Cuba!" was the battle cry of the Cuban revolutionaries and their allies from the United States, Teddy Roosevelt's Rough Riders, as they fought the Spanish at the end of the nineteenth century. But what does that have to do with this perennially favorite cocktail? Well, a century ago, the Coca-Cola Company made sure the boys had plenty to drink while on the job in Cuba. And the alcoholic fortification of choice in the local market was, of course, Cuban rum. Soldiers being soldiers, the heat being the heat, and necessity being the mother of invention, a beautiful drink was born. Note that the only difference between the Cuba Libre and the more pedestrian-sounding rum and Coke is that this drink has the juice of a lime wedge in it, as opposed to nothing (although the rum and Coke is often garnished with the wedge on the side—so you can turn it into a Cuba Libre with very, very little effort).

INGREDIENT NOTE

Coca-Cola

Coca-Cola—which has had a legal lock on the word *Coke* in the United States since 1920—is perhaps the most recognizable and popular consumer product in the world. It was invented by Dr. John Pemberton in Atlanta, Georgia, in 1886. Dr. Pemberton died a mere two years later, and the product was taken over by local drugstore owner Asa Chandler. The Coca-Cola Company was incorporated in 1892, and in the next decade it became a national brand. But it wasn't until World War II that Coke went truly international, proving, yet again, how it pays to have friends in government, especially during wartime. Sugar was rationed during the war, and so U.S. Coke consumption was down. But abroad was a different situation. So the company quickly opened sixty-four bottling plants overseas, ensuring that all the GIs got their Coke, while paving the road to many, many more customers around the globe.

GIN RICKEY

This drink took its name from "Colonel Joe" Rickey, a lobbyist in Washington in the late nineteenth century who regularly drank with members of Congress in Shoemaker's Bar. But Colonel Joe wasn't a colonel and didn't drink gin, and his Rickey was most certainly a whiskey one, though it's the gin version that became more popular. Colonel Joe later became the first major importer of limes to the United States, but it's unclear whether that had anything to do with this cocktail or not. The hundred-plus-year-old recipe is exactly the same as our modern version—it's really just a highball of gin and soda with lime. This recipe is pretty tart; feel free to add syrup or sugar. A Rickey can be made with a variety of bases, and the tartness of fresh lime juice works well with the sweetness of many liqueurs. The Rickey can even make a charming, tasty appearance in virgin form, made with grape juice (or any fruit juice), a little bit of sugar, fresh lime juice, and soda—variations on limeade. A more adult nonalcoholic version called the Lime Rickey is simply fresh lime juice with simple syrup, Angostura bitters, and club soda—the drinking man's nonalcoholic drink.

INGREDIENTS

1½ ounces London dry gin, such as Beefeater
¾ ounce fresh-squeezed lime juice
1¾ ounces club soda
Lime wedge, for garnish

☞ In a short highball glass or a rocks glass, stir together the gin, lime juice, and club soda with ice. Garnish with the lime wedge.

MOSCOW MULE

INGREDIENTS

1½ ounces vodka
4 ounces ginger beer
Lime piece, for garnish

☞ Combine the vodka and ginger beer in an iced glass. Garnish with the lime piece.

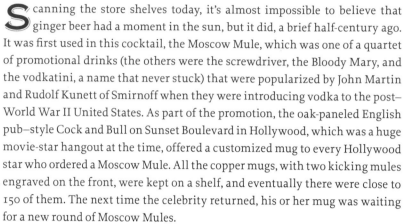

Scanning the store shelves today, it's almost impossible to believe that ginger beer had a moment in the sun, but it did, a brief half-century ago. It was first used in this cocktail, the Moscow Mule, which was one of a quartet of promotional drinks (the others were the screwdriver, the Bloody Mary, and the vodkatini, a name that never stuck) that were popularized by John Martin and Rudolf Kunett of Smirnoff when they were introducing vodka to the post–World War II United States. As part of the promotion, the oak-paneled English pub–style Cock and Bull on Sunset Boulevard in Hollywood, which was a huge movie-star hangout at the time, offered a customized mug to every Hollywood star who ordered a Moscow Mule. All the copper mugs, with two kicking mules engraved on the front, were kept on a shelf, and eventually there were close to 150 of them. The next time the celebrity returned, his or her mug was waiting for a new round of Moscow Mules.

At this time, Schweppes was probably the most popular ginger beer around, and the popularity of this interesting beverage lasted well into the 1960s. By 1970, although vodka had finally caught on, the Moscow Mule had all but disappeared; ginger beer was simply too spicy for the times, which favored bland and sweet over assertive and spicy. By the 1980s, even Schweppes ginger beer was gone. I was still serving the occasional ginger-beer drink during my time at the Hotel Bel Air in the 1970s and early 1980s (a period in which I also passed many a wonderful hour at the Cock and Bull, before it was, sadly, shuttered to make way for a car dealership). When I returned to New York in 1985, ginger beer was gone. But all things—or at least most things—are cyclical. So when big flavor returned in the 1990s with the popularity of spicy Latin and Asian cuisines, so did ginger beer, albeit no longer from Schweppes. Now the market is dominated by the spicy products from Jamaica, where ginger beer was invented, and they can be found in great variety in Texas, of all places, where you can sometimes choose among a dozen brands on a grocery shelf, ranging from the mild Barrett's to the ultra-spicy Old Tyme.

DARK AND STORMY

There's a lucky population of Americans and Europeans who while away their time sailing from Caribbean island to Caribbean island, rarely wearing socks or using a telephone. This is their drink, a sailor's drink. If we're to believe the Gosling family, makers of the eponymous dark rum, the Dark and Stormy hails from the Bahamas, as does their rum. But no matter on which island the drink or the rum is found, it must be bitter, dark rum, which is practically never taken alone but rather in cocktails or punches or strange-sounding concoctions like this one.

 INGREDIENTS

1½ ounces Gosling's or Myers's dark rum
4 ounces medium-spicy ginger beer, such as Reed's
Lime piece

☞ Pour the rum over ice in a highball glass. Fill with ginger beer and squeeze in the lime piece.

THE SMIRNOFF STORY

The Smirnov distillery in Moscow, opened in 1818 by Pyotr Arsenye-vitch Smirnov, grew into a behe-moth structure called the House of Smirnovka by the Iron Bridge that was producing 35 million cases per year by World War I. Then came the Russian Revolution, and the Smirnov family fled, taking their brand to Paris, where Vladimir Smirnov, the great-great-grandson of Pyotr, opened a new distillery and changed his name to Smirnoff. (Today the Smirnov descendants claim Vladimir never had the legal

rights to the name, and that might explain his name change in Paris.) This business was soon acquired by a Ukrainian named Rudolph Kunett, whose grandfather had been one of the major grain suppliers to Smirnov in Moscow. Kunett opened a plant in Connecticut right after Prohibi-tion, which was a bad move; on the heels of Repeal, Americans didn't want to explore unfamiliar spirits like vodka but just wanted their good old gin, whiskey, and rum back. In 1934, Kunett found a

buyer for his American operation, John G. Martin, the president of Heublein's of Hartford, Connecti-cut. Kunett remained after the sale as a consultant to assist in the marketing, and Martin took on Smirnoff as a pet project and a blank slate for his marketing genius. Under Martin's direction, and with the help of Kunett, Smirnoff led an unprecedented revolution in American spirits consumption over the next few decades.

SCREWDRIVER

INGREDIENTS

1½ ounces vodka

4 to 5 ounces fresh-squeezed orange juice, to taste

Orange slice, for garnish, optional

☞ Build the vodka and orange juice over ice in a highball glass. Garnish very optionally with the orange slice (traditionally, screwdrivers are not garnished).

When John Martin of Heublein made his big promotional push for Smirnoff in the years immediately following World War II, his main vehicles were four special cocktails: the Moscow Mule, with ginger beer; the vodkatini, with vermouth; the Bloody Mary, with tomato juice; and the screwdriver, with orange juice. The sun may have set on the Moscow Mule's popularity, but those other three cocktails slowly redefined the American bar over the subsequent half century, as vodka became increasingly popular every year. In 1967, vodka outpaced gin as the most popular white spirit in America; in 1976, vodka became the most popular spirit of any type in the United States. This was a span of about thirty years from the first promotions to ultimate success—an astoundingly short period if you're looking at it historically or an incredibly long-term testament to patience if you're looking at it from the perspective of a brand manager.

A number of stories are told about the origin of the screwdriver's name, but the one that seems to stick with the most adhesive is that when Martin introduced the vodka–orange juice combo in Texas, the wildcatters stirred it with the screwdrivers they all carried in their tool belts. Martin also once served the drink to all of Los Angeles by filling a tanker truck with vodka and orange juice and parking it on Hollywood Boulevard, handing out Smirnoff screwdrivers. That's how you build a brand the old-fashioned way.

Clockwise from left: Screwdriver, Harvey Wallbanger, Sicilian Root Beer, Italian Kiss

VODKA VERSUS GIN: A SNAPSHOT

One of the leading cocktail books of the post-Prohibition era was Patrick Gavin Duffy's *Official Mixer's Manual,* first published in 1934 and then in a new edition in 1940. Duffy organized his recipes by their base spirit, and he devoted 104 pages to 420 individual cocktails based on gin, 26 pages to those based on whiskey, 14 to rum, and 1 page to a mere 2 vodka-based cocktails (a long-forgotten concoction called the Barbara cocktail with cream and crème de cacao, which resurfaced years later as the White Russian, coffee liqueur replacing the cacao, and the Blue Monday Cocktail, with Cointreau and blue food coloring made from vegetable extract). Duffy also devoted 83 pages to drinks based on everything else, including, for example, 15 recipes for absinthe-based cocktails and 12 for those featuring applejack.

HARVEY WALLBANGER

Galliano's promotional group struck gold when they created a surfing character named Harvey, who would run into walls after drinking too many Wallbangers. The cocktail is nothing more than a screwdriver with a float of Galliano, using the now-traditional marketing approach of simply adding a product to an already hugely popular drink, the way people are shoving everything into Cosmopolitans these days. Note that this drink is really special with a cinnamon frosting on the rim of the glass; see page 137 for instructions, using a mixture of half sugar and half cinnamon. I created a takeoff on the Harvey Wallbanger that tastes like root beer, so I called it Sicilian Root Beer: 1 ounce each of vodka and Kahlúa, ½ ounce of Galliano, and Coca-Cola to fill a highball glass with ice, garnish with a lime wedge.

♛ INGREDIENTS

1½ ounces vodka
4 to 5 ounces fresh-squeezed
   orange juice, to taste
¾ ounce Galliano

☛ Pour the vodka into an ice-filled highball glass, then fill almost to the top with the orange juice. Float the Galliano on top and serve without garnish.

THE ITALIAN KISS*

Orange Julius was a big fad a quarter century ago, spawning shops to sell the stuff, which was fresh orange juice whipped up with some sort of dairy product. This cocktail is something of an adult Orange Julius: fresh orange juice, cream, and Galliano, spiked with Orangecello (a liqueur that's similar to the more popular Limoncello but based, of course, on oranges instead of lemons).

♛ INGREDIENTS

¾ ounce Galliano
¾ ounce vodka
1½ ounces fresh-squeezed orange
   juice
1 ounce heavy cream
½ ounce Orangecello
Ground cinnamon, for garnish

☛ Combine the Galliano, vodka, orange juice, cream, and Orange-cello in a mixing glass with ice, and shake. Strain into a chilled cocktail glass and dust with a bit of ground cinnamon.

INGREDIENTS

1½ ounces gin
½ ounce sweet vermouth
1 ounce fresh-squeezed lemon juice
¾ ounce simple syrup (page 246)
Dash of Angostura bitters
Club soda
Long spiral lemon peel (see Technique Note), for garnish

 Combine the gin, vermouth, lemon juice, syrup, and bitters in a mixing glass with ice and shake well. Strain over ice into a Collins glass, top with soda, and garnish with the spiral lemon peel.

The sling—defined as a strong spirit with water and a sweetener—is actually an older category than the cocktail; in fact, *cocktail* was defined as a bittered sling in a *Balance and Columbian Repository* article about the new category that dates back to the early nineteenth century. Over the years, a lot of license has been taken with slings, first in the nineteenth century, when there was a rage for hot slings based on whiskey, brandy, rum, or gin and topped with grated nutmeg. Then, in the early twentieth century, the sling took a sharp turn and got much more complicated. The sugar was replaced with liqueurs such as Cherry Heering, Benedictine, and Cointreau, and the nutmeg spice was expanded to the more complex flavoring of Angostura bitters. On the other hand, the choice of base liqueurs narrowed, and the sling became almost exclusively a gin drink instead of a whiskey, brandy, or rum drink. And then finally came the Singapore sling (opposite), which is a very different beast from the nineteenth-century drink. I think the original is overdue for a revival, so here's the gin version from the late nineteenth century that I tinkered with and put on my menu at the Rainbow Room.

TECHNIQUE NOTE

Spiral Lemon Peel

To make a long spiral peel, prepare the horse's neck garnish, which results in two long peels: the first cut, which is usually discarded, and the second cut, which is the horse's neck shape. The long spiral peel is the one that's usually discarded. See page 154 for instructions.

SINGAPORE SLING

Ted Haigh, curator of the Museum of the American Cocktail, believes the Singapore sling is the progeny of the drier Straits sling. The Singapore was invented in about 1915, at the Long Bar of the Raffles Hotel in, of course, Singapore; it was said that if you sat on the front porch of the Raffles long enough, eventually you'd meet everybody who was anybody. This is my favorite of the many Singapore sling recipes out there. It was faxed to me in 1989 by the head bartender of Raffles when I contacted him to verify that I was using the correct recipe. I was.

INGREDIENTS

1 ounce gin
½ ounce Peter Heering Cherry Heering
¼ ounce Cointreau
¼ ounce Benedictine
3 ounces unsweetened pineapple juice
½ ounce fresh-squeezed lime juice
Dash of Angostura bitters
Orange slice, for garnish
Cherry, for garnish

☛ Combine the gin, Cherry Heering, Cointreau, Benedictine, pineapple and lime juices, and bitters in a mixing glass with ice and shake well. Strain into a highball glass and garnish with the orange slice and the cherry.

STONE WALL

INGREDIENTS

Small piece of fresh ginger root, peeled
¼ ounce Demerara-sugar simple syrup
   (page 246)
1½ ounces fresh apple cider
1½ ounces strong rum
1½ ounces ginger beer
Lime wedge
Green apple slice, for garnish

☞ In the bottom of a mixing glass, muddle the ginger and the syrup. Add the cider, rum, and ice, and shake. Strain over ice into a rocks glass, and then top with the ginger beer. Squeeze in the lime wedge and garnish with the apple slice.

Apple juice and hard cider were used in two popular colonial-era drinks: the Stone Wall, with rum, and the Stone Fence (opposite), with rye whiskey. These may very well have been the first highballs, which were simple affairs: a shot of spirit topped up with cider. I re-created these two chestnuts with some enhancements. When I first updated the Stone Wall in a professional setting, the garnish was not a mere green apple slice; instead, I painted apple slices with cinnamon and sugar and dried them in a convection oven into crisp wafers that could sit on the rim of the glass. This may be a little much for home bartenders, so the simple slice will suffice. Whatever your garnish, the spice kick of ginger is a great match with apple, and this works wonderfully with either whiskey or rum. Both Stone highballs are great autumn drinks, which of course is when you can get apple cider; don't try them with regular apple juice.

INGREDIENT NOTE

Anchor Distillery's Hotalings Whiskey

One hundred years ago, earthquake, fire, and dynamite destroyed nearly 4.7 square miles of San Francisco, a swath of destruction that claimed 28,188 buildings and an incalculable number of lives. After the disaster, several clergymen asserted the catastrophe had been divine retribution, visited upon the city for its wicked ways. However, A.P. Hotaling & Co.'s Jackson Street whiskey warehouse survived. After the catastrophe, University of California at Berkeley professor Jerome Barker Landfield bumped into poet and wit Charles Kellogg Field. Field asked for a blank piece of paper on which to write. Landfield handed him a used envelope. On the back, Field penned these lines:

> If, as they say, God spanked the town
> For being over frisky,
> Why did He burn the churches down
> And save Hotaling's whiskey?

Fritz Maytag pays tribute to the San Francisco whiskey makers of the nineteenth century with a 100 percent malted rye whiskey. Its label reads simply "Hotalings Whiskey," without specifying *rye* whiskey, and that's because Fritz is ornery and decided to age in once-used charred-oak barrels, as the Scots do for the best malt whiskey in the world, instead of in new-charred American white oak wood barrels, which are required to call the resulting product *rye*.

STONE FENCE

It is said that good fences make good neighbors, which might lead you to believe that all the stone fences you see in New England were neighbor-improving devices. Not so. At the end of the Ice Age, receding glaciers left stones all over the place in the Northeast, including in the otherwise perfectly tillable fields. So people had to move all the stones out of the way, piling them up on the edge of their properties. And then, I like to imagine, they went to the porch and had a Stone Fence.

INGREDIENTS

Small piece of fresh ginger root, peeled
½ ounce Demerara-sugar simple syrup (page 246)
1½ ounces fresh apple cider
1½ ounces rye whiskey, preferably Old Potrero Hotaling's Whiskey
1½ ounces ginger beer
Lime wedge
Green apple slice, for garnish

☞ In the bottom of a mixing glass, muddle the ginger and the syrup. Add the cider, whiskey, and ice, and shake. Strain over ice into a rocks glass, and then top with the ginger beer. Squeeze in the lime wedge and garnish with the apple slice.

STONE POLE*

I invented this drink for the Silverleaf Tavern, the bar in the 70 Park Avenue boutique hotel. They wanted to give something of a colonial New York feel to the tavern, albeit with modern ingredients and recipes, so I devised a series of drinks based on the colonial favorite, the Stone Fence. This one uses the Polish vodka called Zubrowska (hence the name *Pole*), whose bison-grass inflection is a great pairing with apple.

INGREDIENTS

Small piece of fresh ginger root, peeled
¼ ounce Demerara-sugar simple syrup (page 246)
1½ ounces fresh apple cider
1½ ounces Zubrowka vodka
1½ ounces ginger beer
Green apple slice, for garnish

☞ In the bottom of a mixing glass, muddle the ginger and the syrup. Add the cider, vodka, and ice, and shake. Strain over ice into a rocks glass, and then top with the ginger beer. Squeeze in the lime wedge and garnish with the apple slice.

TEQUILA SUNRISE

INGREDIENTS

1½ ounces blanco tequila
4 ounces fresh-squeezed orange juice
¾ ounce grenadine

☛ Fill a highball glass with ice and build the tequila followed by the orange juice. Pour the grenadine slowly through to create the sunrise effect. Serve without garnish.

During Prohibition, the film colony spent a lot of time in Tijuana, where there was no law against almost any type of fun, including cocktails. A lot of the Hollywood elite also had houses farther down the coast, in Acapulco, where they could imbibe freely. One of the favorite Mexican hangouts was the Tijuana racetrack called Agua Caliente—literally, "hot water"—that featured not only a great restaurant but also a fabulous bar that made every effort to appeal to Americans with cocktails named Tequila Daisy and Tequila Sunrise. The track's Sunrise was a combination of tequila, lemonade, grenadine, cassis, and soda (recipe below). But when the recipe crossed the border into post-Prohibition America—with no experienced bartenders, a horrible distribution system for specialty spirits like French cassis, an unwillingness to make fresh lemonade when orange juice was so easily available, and a pretty rampant unfamiliarity with anything from Tijuana—the drink morphed into something quite different. Here's that modern American.

TEQUILA SUNRISE CIRCA 1920s

Here's the original Roaring Twenties recipe from the Agua Caliente racetrack in Tijuana, with a bit of my tinkering. An easy way to do this is to make a strong lemonade, very lemony and not so much water. First make a sugar syrup with a 1:1 sugar-to-water ratio, then mix this syrup in equal parts with fresh-squeezed lemon juice. Keep this mixture around to jump-start your Sunrise party.

INGREDIENTS

1½ ounces fresh-squeezed lemon juice
1 ounce simple syrup (page 246)
1½ ounces tequila
2 ounces club soda
½ ounce French cassis
¼ ounce grenadine

☛ In a mixing glass, stir together the lemon juice and syrup to make a tart lemonade. Fill a highball with ice and build the tequila, the lemonade, and the club soda. Slowly pour the cassis and grenadine down through the drink to create the sunrise effect. Serve without garnish.

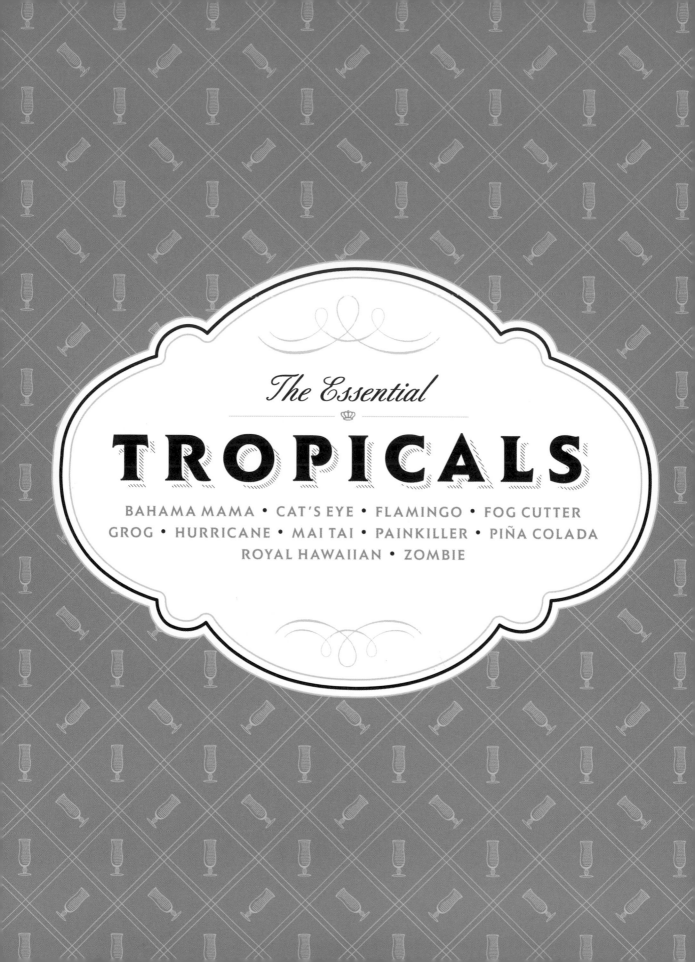

The Essential
TROPICALS

BAHAMA MAMA • CAT'S EYE • FLAMINGO • FOG CUTTER
GROG • HURRICANE • MAI TAI • PAINKILLER • PIÑA COLADA
ROYAL HAWAIIAN • ZOMBIE

What we think of as tropical drinks are, as Jeff "Beachbum" Berry pointed out, really faux tropical drinks; a true tropical drink would be made with an alcohol distilled from some obscure Asian root and mixed with the juice of a local fruit. But our tropical drinks are usually a mixture of two tropical traditions with an American filter in between: the rums, fruit juices, and spices of the tropical Caribbean, served with the set dressing of the tropical South Pacific and mixed according to the American approach to cocktails.

This is quite a cultural hodgepodge. But some of these drinks, using the best ingredients, are fantastic. While rum is the usual base spirit, other white spirits can be used in tropical drinks; seldom, though, will you find whiskey. Fruit cordials also play a large role, particularly curaçao. And spices are important—nutmeg and cinnamon are critical ingredients in a lot of these drinks.

The category evolved after Repeal, as a result of the American love affair that was kindled during Prohibition, when we often escaped to the Caribbean and Mexico to drink legally. And then a lot of Americans who spent quality time in the South Pacific during World War II brought back elements of the South Seas island culture, which lent the visual propping to the tropical drink movement. In short order, this movement morphed into an entire lifestyle complete with shirts and hats, thatched roofs and bars. At its worst, this became a parody of itself, and the drinks made with artificially flavored bottled mixes became overly sweet, syrupy, and silly.

But at its best? A well-made Mai Tai is a wonderful drink. And a tropical cocktail made in the actual tropics, with fresh-squeezed juices from exotic fruits that ripened in the fields, not in a warehouse, can be a sublime experience. Now that we live in an era in which it's possible to buy fresh guava and mango, take them home, and purée them with simple syrup, we can make the real stuff. ♛

BAHAMA MAMA

INGREDIENTS

³/₄ ounce white rum
³/₄ ounce añejo rum
³/₄ ounce Myers's dark rum
¹/₂ ounce coconut rum
3 ounces unsweetened pineapple juice
2 ounces fresh-squeezed orange juice
1 teaspoon grenadine
Dash of Angostura bitters
Maraschino cherry, for garnish
Orange slice, for garnish

☛ Combine the four rums, the pineapple and orange juices, the grenadine, and the bitters in a mixing glass with ice and shake well. Strain into a large goblet or a specialty drink glass such as a boca grande or hurricane, and garnish with the Maraschino cherry and orange slice.

The inventors of the modern rum cocktails—pioneers like Donn Beach and Victor Bergeron—realized something unique about this cane spirit: different rums, from different islands, made in different styles and strengths, like to be mixed with one another. This isn't true of any other spirit; you'd never mix, for example, two gins together, because their flavors would clash, and the sum would be a lot less pleasing than the individual parts. But something about the spice and sweet notes of rums makes them flexible partners. A combination of rum styles—light, dark, spiced, over-proof—in a mixed drink can create a much more complex, nuanced cocktail than the individual bottlings would produce. The Bahama Mama is a prime example, and it just wouldn't be the same drink without the combination of rum styles.

GOOMBAY SMASH

In the Bahamas, it seems as if tourists receive a packet of Bahama Mama vouchers at the airport—all the non-islanders order them at the bars. The locals, though, prefer this variation, made with the local Gosling's rum, which is widely available in the United States.

INGREDIENTS

1½ ounces Gosling's Black Seal dark rum
¾ ounce coconut rum
¾ ounce triple sec
3 ounces unsweetened pineapple juice
Pineapple slice, for garnish
Orange slice, for garnish

☛ Combine the dark rum, coconut rum, triple sec, and pineapple juice in a mixing glass with ice and shake well. Pour into a boca grande or hurricane glass over crushed ice, and garnish with the pineapple and orange slices.

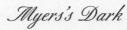

INGREDIENT NOTE

Myers's Dark

Myers's dark rum appears in many rum-punch recipes because it supplies a nicely bitter foundation. This distinctive style of rum is derived from Jamaica's manufacturing technique: They take spent mash from the fermentation vats and put it in the dunder pits to let bacteria grow; then they add some of the bacteria-laden spent mash, called *dunder*, to new mash. When you go anywhere near a distillery in Jamaica, you'll run into an awful aroma like a brick wall. This is the stench from the dunder pits, and it creates the distinctive deliciousness that's common to many Jamaican rums.

CAT'S EYE*

INGREDIENTS

1½ ounces Gran Centenario Plata
    tequila
1 ounce sweetened passion fruit purée
1 ounce fresh-squeezed orange juice
Flamed orange peel (page 249), for
    garnish

☛ Combine the tequila, passion fruit
purée, and orange juice in a mixing glass
with ice and shake vigorously. Strain into
a chilled cocktail glass and garnish with
the orange peel.

Here is an example of one of the holy grails of contemporary bartending—
a good tequila drink that's not a margarita. Passion fruit stands up nicely
to the strong flavors of tequila, and, in turn, because of its green and vegetal
notes, tequila is at home with the tropical flavors; just use a very good plata
tequila, with a lot of agave, green pepper, and mineral notes, which are a ter-
rific foil for the flavor and acidity of the passion fruit. I also add orange juice,
imparting a mellow, soft sweetness to round out the drink. Sometimes I'll also
put in just a tiny bit of a mixed berry juice such as Odwalla, to give it a little
color. If you have something like this lying around, it helps make a more
attractive drink and has a further mellowing effect on all the other acid. Without the berry juice, the drink has a yellow cat's-eye look to it, hence the name;
with the berry juice, and its addition of red, it looks like a demonic cat's eye.

FLAMINGO

B y the end of Prohibition, some of the best bartenders in the world were working in Havana—home to what was considered the best bartending school in the world—including a good smattering of exiled Americans, who imported their ideas of drinking establishments to Cuba. This is how it came to be that such unlikely names as Donovan's and Sloppy Joe's adorned the doors of bars in Old Havana. But one of the indigenous heroes was the legendary Constantino Ribalaigua of the Floridita, who invented the Flamingo in those days, when Douglas Fairbanks and Mary Pickford were regulars. Constante was the owner of the Floridita from the 1920s right up through the 1950s, and he's credited with some pretty famous drinks: not only the Flamingo but also the Hemingway daiquiri (also called the Papa Doble, page 125) and the Mary Pickford (a Flamingo plus orange curaçao). The unsung tropical Flamingo is fantastic and simple to make, even for a crowd. Mix up a pitcher, then shake with ice and pour as guests arrive. When shaken properly—vigorously, and for a while—the drink develops a wonderful, long-lasting layer of pink foam on top, the exact color of a pink flamingo.

INGREDIENTS

1½ ounces añejo rum
1 ounce unsweetened pineapple juice
½ ounce fresh-squeezed lime juice
2 dashes of grenadine
Dash of simple syrup (page 246), optional

☞ Combine the rum, the pineapple and lime juices, the grenadine, and, if using, the syrup in a mixing glass with ice. Shake very hard for a slow count of ten. Strain into a small cocktail glass. A beautiful layer of foam forms on top of the drink from shaking the pineapple juice very hard, and that foam is all the garnish you need.

THE REAL MCCOY

The Flamingo, like a lot of the great twentieth-century cocktails, was a rum-based drink invented overseas. William J. McCoy was one of the captains who snuck liquor to a stretch of the Atlantic coastline called Rum Row, ranging all the way from Boston down to Maryland, alongside the big cities. McCoy's fleet would stay beyond the three-mile limit in international waters, where they'd drop their liquor cases in nets attached to buoys, to be collected by speedboats adept at dodging the patrol boats. McCoy's was a top-flight operation, bootlegging scotch and gin through Canada and rum up from the Caribbean, supplying the gentleman's clubs and statehouses and the elite speakeasies. McCoy's top-notch product was known to be expensive but worth it—"the real McCoy."

FOG CUTTER

INGREDIENTS

2 ounces Brugal rum
1 ounce brandy
½ ounce gin
1 ounce fresh-squeezed lemon juice
1 ounce fresh-squeezed orange juice
½ ounce orgeat
½ ounce simple syrup (page 246),
    optional
Sherry, such as Bristol Cream or dry
    sack

☛ In a 14-ounce glass, build the rum, then brandy, then gin, lemon juice, orange juice, orgeat, and simple syrup, if using. Add cracked ice and shake. Pour into a tall glass with ice, and add the sherry float. Serve with straws. (These are Vic's instructions from his 1946 *Book of Food and Drink*. But he used 2 ounces lemon juice, and I don't believe anyone could drink a Fog Cutter with more than 1 ounce of the sour ingredient, so that's what I use.)

The Fog Cutter is one of those rare exceptions—along with Long Island Iced Tea and eggnog—to the general ban on mixing base spirits (except mixing types of rums, which is often done). But in this drink, which has an almond orgeat kick and is served in big goofy bowls with oversized garnishes, the mixture works. The key, as with Iced Tea, is to use the spirits in very small amounts. The Fog Cutter came out of the niche revolution in the post-Prohibition 1930s and 1940s, when Victor Bergeron in the Bay Area and Donn Beach in Los Angeles were responsible not only for practically singlehandedly (or doublehandedly, as it were) inventing the tropical style of drink but also introducing a new style of drinking in their exotic-themed destination bars, Trader Vic's and Don the Beachcomber. Here is Vic's original 1946 Fog Cutter recipe, to which I added simple syrup and specified sweet cream sherry, both to combat what's otherwise a very sour drink. But I kept Vic's specification of Brugal rum; in the post-Prohibition days when he started Trader Vic's, big flavor was the order of the day and Brugal, an assertive Dominican brand, was hugely popular. After World War II, American taste turned to bland, and spirits like Brugal fell from favor. Now Brugal is making a comeback, as are a lot of highly flavored or specialty spirits, with the streamlining of blue laws and the recently adventurous spirit of the American palate. And the cocktail world is once again alive with the possibilities that come from wide choice.

TRADER VIC AND DONN BEACH

Victor Bergeron's entrepreneurial streak began with a theme opposite from the one that made him a world-famous hospitality mogul: his restaurant Hinky Dink's, in Oakland, California, had a Northwestern theme complete with snowshoes, moose heads, and other outdoorsy décor. This was a good, profitable business. But then Victor heard about a hugely successful lounge-restaurant called Don the Beachcomber down in Los Angeles that was garnering lots of ink as a "sexy hideaway" and attracting a big-name, big-money clientele. So Victor paid a visit and met Donn Beach, who'd been around the world twice, collecting the tropical-themed clutter that defined his place. Victor loved everything about it and decided he wanted to open a similar business, and Donn was good enough to sell him some of his tiki stuff from the South Pacific. So Victor returned to Oakland, ripped down the moose heads, and opened Trader Vic's, which he soon moved to Emeryville, looking out at Treasure Island from the base of the Bay Bridge. This was when "ethnic" food in America meant Italian or Cantonese, and Trader Vic's totally phony blend of Americanized Polynesian and Chinese food discovered a previously undiscovered adventurous spot on the American palate; the cuisine wasn't genuine, but it sure was popular. As were the specialty drinks, many of them rum-based, for which Victor designed custom ceramic and glass serving vessels; every drink came in a different container.

Trader Vic's, like Don the Beachcomber, was a huge success, in no small part due to its focus on rum. Rum hadn't been all that popular in the United States since the colonial era, after which it was supplanted for a century and a half, first by gin and then by the long reign of whiskey. Prohibition not only devastated whiskey by shutting down American distilleries but also wrecked all but two of the Irish ones. This made for a difficult comeback after Repeal, because whiskey needs to age. So in 1933 you could get expensive Crown Royal from Canada or malts from Scotland, but you were still six years' worth of aging away from good, inexpensive American bourbon. Rum, on the other hand, was not only nearby and plentiful and already aged but also very, very cheap. Victor and Donn—both not only good bartenders but good businessmen and forward-thinking risk-takers—went to the Caribbean and bought whole production lots of aged rum, bottled it under their own names, and developed huge collections of house-brand and specialty rums. When World War II broke out, Donn's old friend Captain James Doolittle tapped his talents to travel to Europe and create R&R destinations for American pilots returning from harrowing bombing runs to Eastern Europe. When Donn returned from his officer's commission after the war, his business interests were owned and operated successfully by his former wife, Cora Irene Sund. Donn became a consultant at his former company,

and he practically opened Hawaii to tourism with his Hawaiian Village. But Cora had seen to it that Donn could use his name only outside the United States. He would never again see the success he had with the Beachcomber.

Victor's, on the other hand, was a rapidly growing empire. Soon after that first Trader Vic's, Bergeron opened a second, then a third, and quickly more and more, and today there are thirty Trader Vic's locations globally, including Abu Dhabi and Dubai. Bergeron created a second brand called Señor Picos, opening six around the world, although today only two are still open, one in Bangkok, the other in Oman. But by this time, with so many locations and such a huge business, Bergeron began to cut corners, including the fresh-ingredients aspect that's so vital to tropical drinks, and instead started creating mixes that were essentially sugar water with artificial flavoring. To be sure, the entire country—even the world—was undergoing the same transformation to shortcuts and artificial everything that swept the food and beverage business after World War II. Bergeron died in 1984, but today the company is being revitalized and attempting to move back to better-quality ingredients. Recently, they created a new expansion brand called the Mai Tai Bar, with two locations—Beverly Hills, California, and Estepona, Spain.

GROG

INGREDIENTS

1½ ounces rum, preferably Pusser's
　　Navy Rum
¾ ounce honey syrup (page 247)
½ ounce fresh-squeezed lime juice
1½ ounces water (hot or cold)

☞ Stir together the rum, syrup, lime
juice, and water. Serve over ice in a short-
stemmed footed goblet, or use boiling
water for a hot drink and serve in an
appropriate mug.

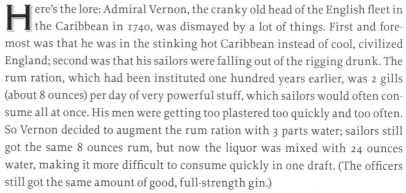

Here's the lore: Admiral Vernon, the cranky old head of the English fleet in the Caribbean in 1740, was dismayed by a lot of things. First and foremost was that he was in the stinking hot Caribbean instead of cool, civilized England; second was that his sailors were falling out of the rigging drunk. The rum ration, which had been instituted one hundred years earlier, was 2 gills (about 8 ounces) per day of very powerful stuff, which sailors would often consume all at once. His men were getting too plastered too quickly and too often. So Vernon decided to augment the rum ration with 3 parts water; sailors still got the same 8 ounces rum, but now the liquor was mixed with 24 ounces water, making it more difficult to consume quickly in one draft. (The officers still got the same amount of good, full-strength gin.)

Needless to say, this was an unpopular move, even though Vernon was beloved by his crews and considered the first admiral in the British navy to genuinely place the well-being of his sailors above all else (except, of course, victory). To forestall massive mutiny, Vernon begrudgingly sweetened the deal by mixing this watered-down rum with a little sugar and a little lime juice—in essence, serving the crew a rudimentary daiquiri. The sailors named this mixture after him—not after his name but rather the wool-silk blend of his coat, which was called *grogram*. Vernon was affectionately called Old Grogram, and the stuff he poured out to them was called *grog*.

But unsatisfyingly, conflicting lore bangs up against the popular Old Grogram story. Two decades before Vernon diluted the rum, an undefined drink called *grog* appeared in print; it's impossible to know whether this earlier grog was the same or a different drink. I doubt anyone thinks this mystery is worth Herculean excavations to unearth the truth, so in all likelihood we shall never know which came first, Grog or Old Grog. Perhaps the latter was named for the former, and not the other way around.

Finally, one odd little tidbit is that Admiral Edward Vernon was admired by George Washington's half brother, Lawrence, who served with Old Grog in Jamaica. Lawrence requested that his (and George's) father, Augustine Washington, rename their land overlooking the Potomac after his beloved admiral, and that was how this promontory came to be called Mount Vernon.

VARIATION

TRADER VIC'S NAVY GROG

When most people think of grog today, this is what they have in mind, from Trader Vic's.

INGREDIENTS

1 ounce Myer's dark rum

1 ounce Bacardi añejo rum

1 ounce Lemon Hart Demerara rum

½ ounce John D. Taylor's Velvet Falernum

½ ounce rock candy syrup

½ ounce Wray and Nephew Pimento Dram liqueur

½ ounce cinnamon syrup (page 249)

1½ ounces fresh grapefruit juice

¾ ounce lime juice

Sugarcane stick, for garnish

Spent half lime, for garnish

Mint sprig, for garnish

 Combine the three rums, Falernum, lime juice, syrup, Pimento Dram liqueur, cinnamon syrup, grapefruit juice, and lime juice in a mixing glass with ice and shake well. Strain into a Mai Tai glass over crushed ice and garnish with the sugarcane, lime, and mint.

INGREDIENT NOTE

Navy Rum

During the mid-seventeenth century, when a large contingent of the British fleet was battling the Spanish West Indian fleet for control of Jamaica, the tradition of rum rationing for British sailors began. Rum travels better than beer or wine because it's distilled and doesn't spoil, plus it's more concentrated and so it takes up less space. British navy rum was a blend of rums from the various West Indian islands, especially the British ones like Jamaica and Trinidad. The rums from each island, made as expressions of the local ingredients grown in the local climate and using always-differing techniques, had different styles; when they were blended, the complex mix was called *navy rum,* and it was always over 100 proof. Why? Because the shipboard rum was often stored next to the most important item on the ship, the gunpowder. If the rum leaked and mixed with the neighboring gunpowder, the gunpowder would be ruined—*unless* the rum was more than 50 percent alcohol, in which case the powder would still burn. So all the navy rum was over 100 proof—that is, "proved" for shipboard use. Lore has it that when Admiral Horatio Nelson, Britain's most beloved naval hero, was killed in the battle of Trafalgar in 1805, his body was preserved in a barrel of rum for the trip back to England. But upon arriving, when the cask was opened, it was discovered that the rum had been siphoned through a hole and consumed by the crew, hence the nickname Nelson's Blood.

HURRICANE

INGREDIENTS

1 ounce Myers's dark rum

1 ounce light rum

½ ounce Galliano

2 ounces fresh-squeezed orange juice

2 ounces unsweetened pineapple juice

1 ounce passion fruit nectar or, in a pinch, passion fruit syrup

¾ ounce fresh-squeezed lime juice

1 ounce simple syrup (page 246)

Dash of Angostura bitters

Fresh tropical fruit, such as pineapple and passion fruit, for garnish

☞ Combine the dark and light rums, Galliano, orange juice, pineapple juice, passion fruit nectar, lime juice, syrup, and bitters in a mixing glass with ice and shake well. Strain into an ice-filled hurricane glass and garnish with the fruit.

The first version of the Hurricane, made in the early twentieth century, contained cognac, absinthe, and Polish vodka (what a combo!); the contemporary rum-juice version was invented in the 1930s. There's one claim of invention from the descendants of a place called the Webb Lake Hotel, on Big Bear Lake in the north woods of Wisconsin, whose watering hole was called the Hurricane Bar. They claim that Pat O'Brien of New Orleans visited the hotel and then copied their drink at his own place, where he served it as an eye-opener for Carnival, dramatically presented in a 29-ounce hand-blown crested glass that resembled a hurricane lamp. No matter who invented the Hurricane—which itself is awfully derivative of Donn Beach's Zombie (page 190)—it was certainly O'Brien who popularized it, and, following in the steps of Victor Bergeron and other successful cocktail entrepreneurs, he ended up bottling a mix as well as a Hurricane powder mix. Yuck! As Americans have pursued convenience at all costs, the bottled mix has become the standard, and today the Hurricane is seldom made from scratch. Like all drinks that have met a similar fate, the pre-mixed version is a poor approximation of the original.

INGREDIENT NOTE

Galliano

Italians have always been the geniuses of cordials—they brought the idea of herbal-, fruit-, and nut-based liqueurs to France, then to the rest of the world. Relatively speaking, Galliano is one of the more recent additions; it dates from 1896 and has top flavor notes of lavender, anise, and vanilla. The brand was acquired with several other brands and brand groups by a new company, formed in 2006, Lucas Bols B.V., located in Amsterdam. The new company promises an aggressive return to the market for Galliano. Italians are also masters of product design, and the tall, lithe Galliano bottle is a great package—this is one bottle that is never thrown out when all the liquor is gone because all the women want to take it home. Galliano can be drunk unadulterated over finely crushed ice, but the liqueur found its audience mainly as an ingredient in the Harvey Wallbanger (page 161) and the Golden Cadillac (page 213).

MAI TAI

INGREDIENTS

1½ ounces añejo rum
½ ounce orange curaçao
½ ounce orgeat
½ ounce fresh-squeezed lime juice
Over-proof Lemon Hart rum, optional
Lime wedge, for garnish
Sugarcane stick, for garnish
Mint sprig, for garnish
Sonya orchid, for garnish, thoroughly
   optional but absolutely beautiful

☛ Combine the rum, curaçao, orgeat, and lime juice in a mixing glass with ice and shake well. Strain into a double (or triple, if you can find one) old-fashioned glass, and float the over-proof rum on the top, if using. Garnish with the lime wedge, sugarcane stick, mint sprig, and, if you're feeling exceedingly tropical, the orchid.

The Mai Tai was invented in 1944 by Victor Bergeron at his soon-to-be-famous Trader Vic's in Emeryville, California. Victor had just bought an entire distillery's worth of excellent sixteen-year-old Jamaican rum, which he designed a drink around and served to friends from Tahiti, who provided the name (from the superlative compliment *"Mai tai roa ae"*). But according to Donn Beach's last wife, Phoebe, she has evidence that it was Donn who invented the drink: a letter from syndicated newspaper columnist Jim Bishop describing a 1972 episode in San Francisco when Victor confessed that Donn really invented it. If this truly happened, I think Victor was just being nice to the pioneer who almost singlehandedly opened up Hawaii as a tourist destination. In any case, nobody makes Donn's version of the Mai Tai, published in Phoebe's book (cowritten with Arnold Bitner). I believe that recipe to be incomplete. It was taken from Beach's notes and, as published, it doesn't work. Victor's recipe is far simpler and superior, highlighting the great match of lime juice, orange curaçao, and rum, with the unexpected flavor accent from orgeat, the sweet, milky, almond syrup Italians traditionally use in baking. In Hawaii, where no one ever had access to Victor's special Jamaican rum, they used a rich, full-bodied rum as a base, then floated an over-proof rum, Lemon Hart, on top of the drink to give it the flavor dimension that was probably provided by the Jamaican specialty. That's the way I like to make the drink too, served in the specialty Mai Tai glass.

Like a lot of tropical drinks from the tiki culture, the Mai Tai suffers from abuse at the hands of well-meaning bartenders without the correct recipe or proper ingredients who, when called to task for their handiwork, all use the same phrase in their defense: "That's how we make them here!" If you can find a talented bartender, you will discover that the Mai Tai is a superb cocktail. (And a Mai Tai with the addition of orange juice is called, charmingly enough, a Suffering Bastard.)

DONN BEACH'S MAI TAI

While this frozen approach is not nearly as good as the Trader Vic's recipe, it's a contender of the original version, and it's worth remembering. Donn's wife, Phoebe, found the drink in his notes and published it in *Hawaiian Tropical Drinks and Cuisine*.

INGREDIENTS

1½ ounces Myers's Plantation Rum (Myers's dark)

1 ounce Matusalem añejo rum or other Cuban-style rum

½ ounce John D. Taylor's Velvet Falernum

¾ ounce Cointreau

1 ounce fresh-squeezed grapefruit juice

¾ ounce fresh-squeezed lime juice

2 dashes of Angostura bitters

Dash of Pernod

Shell of 1 squeezed lime

4 sprigs of mint, for garnish

1 spear of pineapple, for garnish

☛ Into a blender, place 1 cup crushed ice along with both rums, the Velvet Falernum, the Cointreau, the grapefruit and lime juices, the bitters, the Pernod, and the lime shell. Blend for 5 to 10 seconds on medium speed. (According to Beachbum Berry, this technique of quick-blending is vintage Donn Beach.) Pour into a double old-fashioned glass and garnish with the mint sprigs and pineapple spear. And, according to Donn, "Sip slowly through the mint sprigs until the desired effect results."

INGREDIENT NOTE

Matusalem Rum

Matusalem rum, originally made in Cuba, with three other pre-Castro Cuban rums; today Matusalem is produced in the Dominican Republic.

MANGO MAMA*

This is the surprisingly good vodka variation. You won't see too many Polynesian-type drinks whose base spirit is not rum, even though rum is the product of a completely different set of tropical islands on the other side of the world. But anyway, we all drink vodka these days, and this is a more interesting mixture for the most popular spirit in America than the usual juice with a dash of something.

INGREDIENTS

Ground cinnamon mixed with a small amount of sugar, for dusting the rim of the glass
Orange slice, for dusting the rim of the glass
4 pieces of mango, each about ¾ inch square
1 orange wedge
¾ ounce fresh-squeezed lime juice
½ ounce agave syrup (page 247)
½ ounce honey syrup (page 247)
¾ ounces Finlandia Mango vodka
¾ ounce vodka
2 teaspoons orgeat
Flamed orange peel (page 249), for garnish

☞ Using the cinnamon-sugar mixture and the orange slice, crust the rim of a cocktail glass according to the instructions on page 137. In the bottom of a mixing glass, muddle the mango and orange pieces with the lime juice, agave syrup, and honey syrup. Add the vodkas, orgeat, and ice, and shake well. Strain into the prepared cocktail glass and garnish with the flamed orange peel.

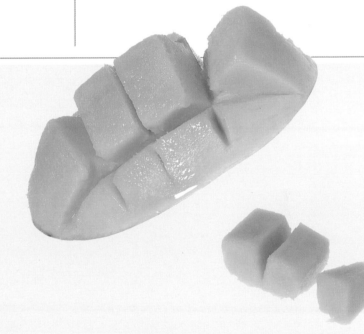

TECHNIQUE NOTE

Mango for Muddling

Stand the mango on end and cut two cheeks from either side of the pit Then slice as shown here.

PAINKILLER

INGREDIENTS

2 ounces Pusser's Navy Rum
1 ounce coconut cream such as Coco
    Lopez
2 ounces unsweetened pineapple juice
1 ounce fresh-squeezed orange juice
Fresh nutmeg, for garnish

☞ Combine the rum, coconut cream, pineapple juice, and orange juice in a mixing glass with ice and shake well. Strain over ice into a tall glass. Garnish by grating a light dusting of nutmeg over the top.

Drop anchor at White Bay, Jost Van Dyke, in the British Virgin Islands. Swim ashore to the Soggy Dollar Saloon, which is thus named because it's difficult to reach except by water, very often by swimming ashore from your boat. (And so the bar offers a clothesline on which to hang your soggy dollars up to dry.) Order this legendary drink of pineapple, orange, coconut cream, navy rum, and ground nutmeg, a boater's favorite that can be found in almost any Caribbean bar of note. The Soggy Dollar is mostly a beer and rum bar, but this is the famous cocktail of the place, which claims to use fresh coconut cream; the universally available Coco Lopez is pretty decent. (Or you could make it from scratch, sort of: Buy a can of unsweetened coconut cream and a can of coconut water, and mix together in equal measure, which is actually a very nice beverage on its own.) The original Painkiller was made to mind-numbing proportions of half rum, but a reasonable 2-ounce shot will do just fine.

Nutmeg

All spices are far superior when they're freshly ground or grated, but for none is that more true than nutmeg. Never use jarred, powdered nutmeg, especially considering that freshly grated nutmeg is easy. The nutmeg itself is actually the seed of an evergreen tree (mace is the seed's covering); it's not particularly expensive, it's widely available, and whole nutmegs will keep for years in a covered jar. Just finely grate a seed whenever you need some. Nutmeg is a spice of the Caribbean, and so it is at home in any number of punchy rum drinks, not just in the traditional egg-nog and cream drinks; I think it's vastly underused in cocktails. A couple of interesting notes: Nutmeg, when taken in sufficient quantities, is a hallucinogen; unfortunately, when taken in hallucinogenic quantities, it has some hugely unpleasant side effects.

LIME IN DE COCONUT*

I created this drink recently while conducting seminars in Puerto Rico and trying to use local products; I ended up serving it at a fund-raising dinner for the Museum of the American Cocktail. I think this is a good use of flavored vodkas—that is, paired with their flavorings' fresh fruits, juices, herbs, or spices. Here, it's Finlandia Lime combined with fresh lime juice. On their own, without the fresh form of the ingredients, I think these flavored vodkas are often too unnatural-tasting, especially when you think about how easy it is to infuse a bottle of vodka with fresh ingredients. But they *are* practical timesavers, taking the burden off the bartender to find a balanced mixture, so I have looked for good uses. The Lime in de Coconut is one of the better ones.

INGREDIENTS

1 ounce Finlandia Lime vodka

1 ounce unflavored vodka

1 ounce ginger syrup (page 248)

1 ounce fresh-squeezed lime juice

2 ounces coconut water

1 level tablespoon Coco Lopez coconut cream

1 lime slice, for garnish

1 long slice of English cucumber, cut lengthwise the full length of a highball glass, for garnish

1 mint sprig, for garnish

☛ In a cocktail shaker, assemble the vodkas, syrup, lime juice, coconut water, and coconut cream with ice. Shake well. Strain into a highball glass over ice, stir again, and add the garnishes of lime slice, cucumber slice, and mint sprig.

PIÑA COLADA

In Puerto Rico in the 1950s, Don Ramón Lopez-Irizarry invented a homogenized coconut cream that became Coco Lopez and later was generically known as *cream of coconut*, which become popular in tropical cooking, both sweet and savory. Then genius hit in 1957, when Ramon Marrero, a bartender at the Caribe Hilton in Puerto Rico, combined the coconut cream with rum, pineapple juice, and ice in a blender, and the piña colada was born. I like to spice it up by using two types of rum, light and Myers's or Gosling's dark, to add depth of flavor; I also like a bit of Angostura bitters, which very few people add to their piña coladas, because I think this drink deserves the extra jolt of spice. But it is usually made without the bitters, and just one rum instead of two; for that, I'd recommend Myers's light rum, which is a little more full-bodied than the Puerto Rican style of light that's the default base for this drink. And although the piña colada is much more famous as a frozen, blended drink, it can also be shaken and served straight up.

INGREDIENTS

1 ounce light rum
¾ ounce Myers's or Gosling's dark rum
1 ounce Coco Lopez cream of coconut
½ ounce heavy cream
2 ounces unsweetened pineapple juice
Dash of Angostura bitters
1 pineapple chunk, for the frozen version, plus 1 slice, for garnish
Orange slice, for garnish
Maraschino cherry, for garnish

☛ For a frozen drink: In a blender, combine the light and dark rums with the Coco Lopez, heavy cream, pineapple juice, bitters, and pineapple chunk. Add 1 cup crushed ice and blend until smooth. Pour into a goblet. For the shaken version: Combine the same ingredients, except the pineapple chunk, in a shaker with ice, then strain into a goblet with ice. Either way, garnish with the pineapple slice, orange slice, and cherry.

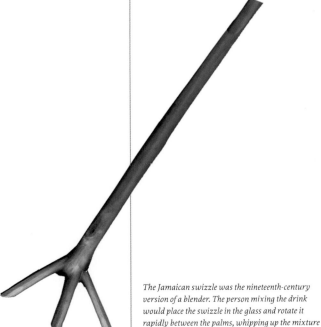

The Jamaican swizzle was the nineteenth-century version of a blender. The person mixing the drink would place the swizzle in the glass and rotate it rapidly between the palms, whipping up the mixture into a nice froth.

ROYAL HAWAIIAN

This drink was so popular at the Rainbow Room that we kept it on the Promenade Bar's menu for a full twelve years. Earlier, it had been the signature cocktail of the Royal Hawaiian Hotel, the granddaddy of the O'ahu resort hotels, which had been serving these types of fruity tropical drinks since the 1920s, especially a rum-based one called Kama'aina and a gin-based one called Princess Kaiulani; by the 1950s, the Princess Kaiulani had become known as the Royal Hawaiian. Although the hotel of that name still stands, its bar no longer serves the eponymous cocktail, which is similar to the famous Cuban-rum-based pineapple drink called the Mary Pickford, which itself was born during Prohibition, when Havana was the liquor-laden playground for East Coast drinkers. Hawaii was also a Prohibition hangout for the West Coast elite who could afford the luxury cruise to and from the islands, not to mention the expense of a resort like the Royal Hawaiian. And the Pacific islands did develop a tropical drink tradition all their own, involving a lot of extravagant garnishes. But not this one: The Royal Hawaiian is garnished with nothing more than the foam from the shaken pineapple juice, which, if you use your imagination and squint a bit, can look like the pounding Hawaiian surf.

INGREDIENTS

1½ ounces gin
1 ounce unsweetened pineapple juice
½ ounce fresh-squeezed lemon juice
¾ ounce orgeat

☛ Combine the gin, pineapple and lemon juices, and orgeat in a mixing glass with ice and shake well. Strain into a small cocktail glass and serve without garnish.

INGREDIENT NOTE

Orgeat

This milky-white almond-flavored syrup can be found in good Italian delis, bakeries, and grocery stores. When I was growing up, I spent some time in my mother's hometown of Westerly, Rhode Island, where the little grocery stores carried orgeat, which all the *nonnas* used for baking and to make soft drinks for kids by mixing it with water and juice; it was also a favorite with the men, who would put a dash in their espresso. The first time I bought a bottle was at Ferrara's, the famed pastry shop in New York's Little Italy, which is exactly the type of place you can still find it.

TROPICAL ITCH

The Hawaiian tropical drink culture was developed in large part by Harry Yee, the most famous of the O'ahu bartenders, who tended at the Hawaiian Village (later the Hilton Hawaiian Village) from the time it was built by Henry Kaiser in the late 1950s until Harry retired thirty-five years later. Yee was most famous for his Blue Hawaiian cocktail and for his use of unusual garnishes: He was the first to decorate a drink with a tiny parasol (the Tapa Punch, in 1959), and into this Tropical Itch he slipped a Chinese backscratcher that guests took away with them. Genius.

INGREDIENTS

½ ounce bourbon
½ ounce Lemon Hart 80-proof rum
¼ ounce orange curaçao
3 ounces sweetened passion fruit juice
Dash of Angostura bitters
151-proof Demerara rum

☞ Pour the bourbon, 80-proof rum, curaçao, passion fruit juice, and bitters into a shaker with ice. Strain into a large hurricane glass filled with crushed ice, float the over-proof rum on top, and garnish with a Chinese backscratcher.

VIRGIN ROYAL HAWAIIAN

This is one cocktail that can be very easily—and very successfully—refitted as a nonalcoholic specialty. I used to make this a lot at the Rainbow Room: 2½ ounces unsweetened pineapple juice, ¾ ounce fresh-squeezed lemon juice, and 1 ounce orgeat syrup. Shake with ice. Strain into a cocktail glass and serve up, as you would a fancy cocktail.

ZOMBIE

INGREDIENTS

1½ ounces medium-bodied Jamaican rum

½ ounce 151-proof Demerara rum

¼ ounce John D. Taylor's Velvet Falernum

½ ounce Donn's Mix #1 (page 249)

1½ ounces fresh-squeezed orange juice

¾ ounce fresh-squeezed lime juice

1 teaspoon grenadine

2 dashes of Angostura bitters

6 drops of absinthe or absinthe substitute (see Ingredient Note, page 12)

3 mint sprigs, for garnish

☛ In a blender with ¾ cup crushed ice, combine the two rums with the Falernum, Donn's Mix #1, orange juice, lime juice, grenadine, bitters, and absinthe. Blend for 5 seconds. Pour into a chimney glass, with more crushed ice if needed to fill the glass, and garnish generously with the mint sprigs.

Don the Beachcomber's wasn't just the first Tiki bar in America. Seventy years ago, it was also the most glamorous watering hole in Hollywood . . . You might be drinking with Charlie Chaplin, Orson Welles, Joan Crawford, or Buster Keaton. If Buster ordered a Martini it would be made in plain sight . . . But if he fancied a Zombie . . . the concoction would mysteriously appear from behind the back bar.
—JEFF BERRY, *Beachbum Berry's Sippin' Safari*, 2007

The quote above lays out the Zombie recipe problem precisely: Donn Beach was a really secretive guy—his recipes were his business plan, and he tried everything to protect them, including assembling a series of house mixes that were numbered, not labeled with any names that would make sense to anybody. So it's impossible to reconstruct with any degree of certainty which were the original recipes invented by Donn Beach, the man born Ernest Raymond Beaumont-Gantt in New Orleans, Louisiana.

Of all Donn Beach's inventions, perhaps none is more remembered than the Zombie. This terrifying-sounding cocktail immediately achieved notoriety because of the publicity-motivated rule that no customer was allowed to drink more than two on a given night. Putting aside the hype, a really well-made Zombie is a great drink. I won't tell you the preparation is easy—it's a multi-ingredient recipe, to say the least. And I can't tell you this is Donn's original recipe, because it's not. In fact, a totally different version was published posthumously by Donn's final wife, Phoebe, in 2001; she had cobbled together an assortment of Donn's notes, none of which indicated that any recipe was the definitive one. Donn was not only secretive but he also, like all bartenders who take the profession seriously, constantly messed about with his recipes, improving or sometimes simply changing them to accommodate new products or the loss of a key ingredient in an existing recipe. It turns out the "definitive" published version was flawed (for example, calling for a full 6 ounces of spirits with less than 2½ ounces of juice and other ingredients, which is a monstrously strong drink), so that can't really be the formula on which the empire was built.

Luckily, besides Donn's nondefinitive notes, other members of his staff—mostly Filipino waiters and bartenders—kept useful information in notebooks. With their private collection of recipes and other tips garnered from experience at the Beachcomber's, these guys could take the show on the road and open their own tiki bars anywhere; the only trick was that the recipes needed to be the real deal. One of the Beachcomber employees, a waiter named Dick Santiago, was willing to share his cherished little black book with writer Jeff Berry. In that notebook, Jeff found, in the 1937 notes, a Zombie recipe with the notation "old" next to it. That, with a couple of my changes—I'd call them improvements—is the recipe here.

The Essential

PUNCHES

BRANDY MILK PUNCH • CLARET LEMONADE
MATCH SPRING PUNCH • PISCO PUNCH • PLANTER'S PUNCH
PORT-WHISKEY PUNCH • SANGRIA
SCORPION PUNCH

Mozart, it was said, wouldn't perform unless he'd been served his bowl of punch.

This is where it all began, in seventeenth- and eighteenth-century London: the idea of mixed alcoholic beverages. Punches were the cocktails of their day, and punch bowls were the bars, where people gathered to imbibe. A young bachelor's standing was as much about his punch recipe as about his pocketbook or his looks. Although punches started out as five-ingredient drinks—sweet, sour, strong, weak, and spice—the formulas grew to twelve, even fifteen ingredients, getting more and more extravagant with fruit juices, multiple spices, wines, and different types of distilled spirits.

When punches crossed to the New World, Americans scaled down the recipes, resulting in the single-serving drinks that led to the cocktail. But punch's origin was in group drinking. The English even drank from the same cup, a tradition that appalled the French. (Much about the English appalled the French.)

In the middle of the nineteenth century, punches were still hugely popular—the first cocktail book published, by Jerry Thomas in 1862, featured *seven* times as many punch recipes as cocktail recipes. But then, from the late nineteenth into the twentieth century, the rise in popularity of bars and cocktails created an inverse decline in punch's popularity. Today you can find recipe books with a couple thousand cocktails but only three punches.

But what is a tropical drink except punch in a glass? Indeed, when I was at the Rainbow Room, I'd often take a nineteenth-century punch recipe and extrapolate backward to make a fun single-serving cocktail. And what about sours? They're directly descended from punches. We owe a lot to this category. As repayment of that debt, I think we should drink a punch every once in a while. Some of them are awfully good. And you don't necessarily need to make an entire bowl. ♛

BRANDY MILK PUNCH

INGREDIENTS

2 ounces cognac
4 ounces whole milk
1 ounce simple syrup (page 246)
Dash of pure vanilla extract, optional
Nutmeg, for garnish

☞ Combine the cognac, milk, syrup, and the optional vanilla in a mixing glass with ice and shake well. Strain into a large highball glass—14 ounces—and dust with the nutmeg.

This simple drink is a holiday favorite. It is an easier alternative to full-blown eggnog as well as the ideal choice if you don't want to serve or consume raw eggs. To simplify matters further, you can use sugar instead of the simple syrup called for here, but the syrup mixes better. Brandy milk punch was popular in New Orleans, where every bar had its own variation; many still do, and it's one of the preferred drinks as a morning-after stomach-coater. With the importance of the French influence in New Orleans, brandy in general, and especially cognac, was long the spirit of choice, through all of the eighteenth and most of the nineteenth centuries, until giving way to American whiskey. In the 1940 printing of Patrick Gavin Duffy's *Official Mixer's Manual*, the section entitled "Milk Punches" suggests the recipe can be made with applejack, Bacardi rum, bourbon, brandy, grenadine, Jamaica rum, rye, scotch, "and any other liquor with milk," all in the same fashion. Duffy's instructions also include, "Shake well with cracked ice for about three minutes"—a long shake indeed.

SIMPLIFIED EGGNOG

You can make simplified yet still delicious single-serving eggnog by dropping an egg into a brandy milk punch and shaking very, very hard. This is a great alternative to making a whole bowl of nog and is really the only option if just one person wants eggnog.

BOSOM CARESSER

I couldn't resist the title of this recipe from *Modern American Drinks,* published in 1900, because it begs somebody asking someone, someday, "How about a Bosom Caresser?"—a question that otherwise would probably be left unasked over the course of most lifetimes. Note that a touch of simple syrup might be necessary to find a wider audience for this novelty.

Fill a mixing-glass one-third full of fine ice; add a teaspoonful raspberry syrup, one fresh egg, one jigger brandy; fill with milk, shake well, and strain.

CLARET LEMONADE

INGREDIENTS

4 ounces red wine
1 ounce simple syrup (page 246)
½ ounce fresh-squeezed lemon juice
Lemon wheel, for garnish
Raspberries, for garnish, optional
Mint sprigs, for garnish, optional

☛ Combine the red wine, syrup, and lemon juice in the glass half of a Boston shaker. Pour back and forth between the two halves of the shaker to mix. Strain into a goblet over ice and garnish with the lemon wheel. In the nineteenth century, garnish was usually determined by seasonality. So if raspberries are in season, add a couple, along with a mint sprig.

👑 *To make a punch of any sort in perfection, the ambrosial essence of the lemon must be extracted....This, and making the mixture sweet and strong, using tea instead of water, and thoroughly amalgamating all the compounds so that the taste of neither the bitter, the sweet, the spirit, nor the element, shall be perceptible one over the other, is the grand secret, only to be acquired by practice.* —JERRY THOMAS, *How to Mix Drinks* (1862)

This eighteenth-century English summer cooler is basically lemonade made with red table wine instead of water. In New England in general and Boston in particular, the claret lemonade idea was eventually translated into the wine cooler—red wine mixed with 7UP—that was so wildly popular in the 1980s, and is still a working-class favorite in the Northeast. And this is not dissimilar to sangria (page 206)—but the *real* sangria, the way the Spanish make it, which is just lemon juice, sugar, club soda, and wine.

With very little fuss, claret lemonade can be imbued with delicate floral notes to become Claret and Lavender Lemonade, simply by replacing the simple syrup with lavender syrup: Combine 2 tablespoons dried lavender with 1 cup water; bring to a boil, then turn down the heat to a simmer; add 1 cup sugar and stir until dissolved, then simmer until the liquid is reduced by half; let cool. You can also try this syrup approach with other floral flavors, such as jasmine or chamomile.

VARIATION

HARRY JOHNSON'S CLARET LEMONADE

INGREDIENTS

Lemonade
Red wine

☛ Fill a tumbler with crushed ice, then three-quarters full with lemonade. Float the claret on top.

👑 Claret lemonade was the eighteenth-century English aristocracy's way to drink red wine in the summer, and their choice of wine was red French, which they called *claret*, and here's Harry Johnson's ultra-minimalist formula.

MATCH SPRING PUNCH

INGREDIENTS

1 ounce premium vodka, preferably
    Stolichnaya red
¾ ounce fresh-squeezed lemon juice
½ ounce Framboise
¼ ounce crème de cassis
¼ ounce raspberry syrup, preferably
    Monin
¼ ounce simple syrup (page 246)
Champagne
Lemon slice, for garnish
Raspberries, for garnish

☛ Combine the vodka, lemon juice, Framboise, cassis, and the raspberry and simple syrups in a mixing glass with ice and shake well. Strain into a tall glass over ice and top with Champagne. Garnish with the lemon slice and a few fresh raspberries.

London's cutting-edge style-bar scene is due, in large part, to the famous Dick Bradsell, whose Bramble cocktail appears on menus not just in the United Kingdom but around the United States as well. Dick created the equally superb Match Spring Punch for the Match Bars in London, and it quickly made its way to all the best cocktail menus in the West End and thence to the rest of the city—it became the Long Island Iced Tea of London—and then Australia and finally to the States. The style bars arose in London in the mid-1990s, first at the Atlantic Bar and Grill, as a serious culinary alternative to the dull place the cocktail had been stuck in for fifty years, a generic place of soda guns and artificial flavorings and processed everything. The style bar, on the other hand, introduced fresh and exotic fruits, herbs and other savory ingredients, and a whole new group of cocktails that are fun, flavorful, often food-friendly, and, above all, original. This is one of those drinks.

THE COMPASS CLUB

Here's another style-bar cocktail courtesy of Sam Jeveons, using raspberries that are shaken in the drink, as well as egg white, both hallmarks of the London scene. The Compass Club is based on the Asayla whiskey from Compass Box, a blend of grain and malt whiskeys that's very cocktail-friendly. Asayla is aged in first-fill American oak casks—that is, barrels that were used once in the United States for aging bourbon or rye, then shipped to the United Kingdom—which imparts a distinct flavor.

INGREDIENTS

2 ounces Asayla whiskey
¾ ounce fresh-squeezed lemon juice
1 ounce simple syrup (page 246)
5 whole raspberries
½ ounce emulsified egg white

☛ Combine the whiskey, lemon juice, syrup, 4 of the raspberries, the egg white, and ice in a cocktail shaker, and shake very hard. Fine-strain into a coupé glass, and garnish with the fifth raspberry.

PISCO PUNCH

INGREDIENTS

2 pineapple wedges without skin, plus
   1 pineapple wedge, skin on, for garnish
1 ounce unsweetened pineapple syrup
   (page 248)
2 ounces Bar Sol Pisco Acholado
¾ ounce fresh-squeezed lemon juice

☛ Mash the 2 skinless pineapple wedges with the pineapple syrup in the bottom of a mixing glass. Add the pisco, lemon juice, and ice, and shake well. Strain into a goblet, over ice, and garnish with the skin-on pineapple wedge.

The origin of pisco in the United States lies, as so many good commodity histories do, in nineteenth-century trade practices. But the story of the brandy called pisco is a much older one. The entire western coast of South America, from the tropical north in what's now Colombia down to the Antarctic tip in Tierra del Fuego, was once the vice-royalty of Peru, owned by the Spanish Crown. In the sixteenth century, Spanish settlers planted a lot of sweet grapes here—malvasia and muscat styles—that did extraordinarily well in the transversal valleys that sweep down from the mountains to the Pacific coast. The terroir was perfect, and from these grapes the colonists made good wine at excellent prices and shipped it back to Spain. The Spanish winemakers were unenthusiastic about the cheap imports, and they complained to the king, who appeased them by imposing a high tax on the colonial wine, making it unfeasible as an export product. The colonists responded by turning their wine into brandy, as early as the middle of the seventeenth century.

Fast-forward to the nineteenth century, just after gold was discovered in northern California and speculators were flocking to San Francisco by the only possible route at the time: around the horn of South America (this was before the Panama Canal). The port of Pisco was one of the few deepwater ports where ships could stop to take on provisions and water and where ships' captains could take on a side business: a cottage trade in brandy, buying it dirt cheap from the Peruvians and selling it in San Francisco, where spirits of any kind were expensive and hard to come by. One of the most famous San Francisco bars of the day was the Bank Exchange, on Montgomery Street, a truly magnificent saloon paved with marble floors and hung with oil paintings on the walls. And behind the Bank Exchange's bar was Duncan Nichol, who invented the Pisco Punch. (Nichol's recipe was buried with him; the recipe here is a best guess, employing some of the ingredients we know were in the original.) By the 1870s, Pisco Punch was far and away the most popular drink in San Francisco, particularly beloved by Jack London. And it was while sipping a Pisco Punch at the Bank Exchange that Mark Twain sat next to the fireman who was the inspiration for Tom Sawyer.

PISCO PUNCH ROYALE*

I prepared this recipe for the Match Bar Group in London, where it appeared on the Player Club menu. It's the sparkle from Champagne that makes it a royale variation.

INGREDIENTS

1 ounce Bar Sol Pisco Italia

¾ ounce pineapple syrup (page 248)

½ ounce fresh-squeezed lemon juice

¼ ounce John D. Taylor's Velvet Falernum

Champagne or other sparkling wine

Orange slice, for garnish

Pineapple slice, for garnish

☛ Combine the pisco, pineapple syrup, lemon juice, and Falernum in a mixing glass with ice and shake well. Strain into a medium white-wine goblet filled with ice. Top with about 3 ounces Champagne, and garnish with the orange and pineapple slices.

FALERNUM-SPICE FOAM

Jack London enjoyed Pisco Punch so much that he had it shipped in bulk to his home outside San Francisco, but he would never have imagined a version with a thick layer of spicy foam floating on top. (The equipment for making it hadn't been invented yet; you'll need a foam canister and two cream chargers. See page 250 for more on making foam.) As with other similar applications, the use of a flavor in the foam makes it superfluous as a liquid ingredient in the cocktail, so omit the Falernum from the Pisco Punch recipe.

Using the ½-liter cream canister will make enough foam for 15 to 20 drinks

6 whole cloves

½ cup superfine bar sugar

2 gelatin sheets, each 9 x 2¾ inches

4 ounces unsweetened pineapple juice

2 ounces emulsified egg whites

4 ounces Velvet Falernum

Place the empty ½-liter canister with the top unscrewed in the refrigerator to chill; do not put in the freezer. Fill a saucepan with 12 ounces water and the 6 cloves, and place over low heat. Simmer until reduced by half, but do not let the liquid come to a boil. Turn off the heat, add the sugar, and stir to dissolve. Add the 2 gelatin sheets, dissolving them completely. Let cool. Add the pineapple juice, egg whites, and Velvet Falernum, and whisk to combine. Fine-strain into a metal bowl; place the bowl in an ice bath and stir occasionally until well chilled.

Add 1 pint of the mixture to the canister. Screw the cap on very well, making sure it is completely tightened. Screw in the cream charger; you will hear a quick sound of gas escaping, which is normal. Turn the canister upside down and shake very well, and the foam is ready.

Store in the refrigerator between uses. Before each use, turn the canister upside down and shake well. Then hold the canister almost completely upside down and gently put pressure on the trigger mechanism, applying the foam slowly over the top of the drink, working from the inside rim of the glass in a circular fashion to the center. When the canister is empty, hold it over the sink and engage the trigger to be sure the gas is completely spent. Remove the top and clean according to the manufacturer's instructions.

PLANTER'S PUNCH

INGREDIENTS

¾ ounce Myers's dark rum

¾ ounce light rum

¾ ounce orange curaçao

½ ounce John D. Taylor's Velvet
    Falernum

1 ounce simple syrup (page 246)

¾ ounce fresh-squeezed orange juice

¾ ounce unsweetened pineapple juice

½ ounce fresh-squeezed lime juice

Dash of grenadine

Dash of Angostura bitters

Orange slice, for garnish

Maraschino cherry, for garnish

Pineapple wedge, for garnish

☛ Combine the dark and light rums, curaçao, Velvet Falernum, syrup, orange and pineapple and lime juices, grenadine, and bitters in a mixing glass with ice and shake well. Strain into a large glass filled with ice. Garnish with the orange slice, cherry, and pineapple wedge.

Planter's Punch was, literally, the punch of the plantation in the eighteenth and nineteenth centuries on the large sugar plantations of the Caribbean. The punch was usually a simple mixture of the local rum, often made from the residue of the plantation's sugar production, with citrus juice and cane syrup, which was also produced on the plantation. (Sometimes this cane syrup was spiced, which is the origin of the wonderful Velvet Falernum.) When I was at the Rainbow Room, I took this daiquiri-like simple drink and expanded it into something that's more like a Zombie (see page 190) than the Planter's Punch recipes that appear in many cocktail books; those versions were often called *ti* punch in the French islands, which was short for *petite*, or "small," a fitting name for a small recipe. Mine is a little larger—some might say extravagant—and here it is, circa 1989.

RAINBOW PUNCH*

The Rainbow Room had no small percentage of guests who were under-age—often way underage; this was a popular and family-friendly tourist destination. So I concocted something special for the younger set. Note that you want at least a little sparkle from a splash of club soda, but the drink can certainly take more than a splash. In fact, with nearly any punch, the soda quantity is totally flexible and can be adjusted based on taste or, for the professional, to make sure the glass is presented to the customer 100 percent full, with extra club soda taking up any empty space.

INGREDIENTS

3 ounces fresh-squeezed orange juice

3 ounces unsweetened pineapple juice

½ ounce fresh-squeezed lime juice

½ ounce simple syrup (page 246)

¼ ounce grenadine

2 dashes of Angostura bitters

Splash of club soda

Cherry, for garnish

Orange slice, for garnish

☞ Combine the orange, pineapple, and lime juices with the syrup, grenadine, bitters, and ice. Shake well. Strain into an iced tea glass, top with about a splash of soda, and garnish with the cherry and orange slice.

PORT-WHISKEY PUNCH*

INGREDIENTS

1½ ounces bourbon whiskey

1½ ounces fresh-squeezed orange juice

¾ ounce fresh-squeezed lemon juice

1 ounce simple syrup (page 246)

1 ounce ruby port

Orange slice, for garnish

Lemon twist, for garnish

☞ Combine the whiskey with the orange and lemon juices as well as the syrup in a mixing glass and shake well. Strain into a highball glass filled with ice, top with the port, and garnish with the orange slice and lemon twist.

I was inspired by the nineteenth-century practice of floating port or sherry on top of a cocktail; the floating looks pretty, and then the float will fall slowly into the rest of the cocktail, self-mixing. So I created what's basically a whiskey sour with a port float, which makes a delicious drink that tastes kind of punchy.

Velvet Falernum

When we opened the Rainbow Room, I bought a case of a spicy sugar syrup called Falernum because I'd seen it in old recipes for exotic classics such as Donn Beach's original Zombie recipe. I opened a bottle and tasted the stuff—*ghastly*. I used it to mix a couple of drinks—ruined. So I put the bottles aside, permanently. Then, at a party one evening, I was relating this experience to the president of United Distillers Glenmore (which no longer exists), who told me I must have the wrong product—Falernum is wonderful, he claimed. So he had a case sent to me of

John D. Taylor's Velvet Falernum from Barbados, and it was wonderful, tasting of almond, lime skin, and clove flavorings, with fortification from cane alcohol. The inclusion of the alcohol was probably originally intended to preserve the contents of the bottle, but it also had the benefit of allowing the mixture to be moved from grocery store shelves to liquor store shelves in states like New York, where the two are separated. Unfortunately, this movement to a more advantageous retail location was only an abstract possibility, because the reality was that Velvet Faler-

num wasn't available in this country at the time. But I was a big proponent, and so I went to an importer friend, Kay Olsen of Spirit of Hartford, and promised that if she'd bring it into the States, I'd do everything I could to promote the stuff. She agreed, and now it's around, albeit not in every corner liquor store in the land. If you have difficulty finding the Taylor brand, Joe Fee of Fee Brothers in Rochester, New York, a bitters and cocktail condiment supplier, also has a bottling of Falernum.

VARIATION

TAYLOR MADE*

It doesn't take a careful reading to notice I am a fan of John D. Taylor's wonderful Velvet Falernum (see Ingredient Note), and I was looking for a new way to use this unique syrup from Barbados, preferably with something other than the local favorite, rum—I was looking for something original. As I was scouring old menus, I came across a couple of recipes that featured bourbon with honey and citrus, so one thing led to another, and I came up with this punchy old-fashioned spinoff.

INGREDIENTS

1½ ounces bourbon

1 ounce fresh-squeezed grapefruit juice

1 ounce cranberry juice

½ ounce honey syrup (page 247)

¼ ounce John D. Taylor's Velvet Falernum

Grapefruit slice, for garnish

☞ Combine the bourbon, grapefruit and cranberry juices, honey syrup, and Velvet Falernum in a mixing glass with ice and shake well. Strain into a cocktail glass and garnish with the grapefruit slice.

SANGRIA

INGREDIENTS

6 pineapple wedges, each 1 inch thick

2 lemons, 1 cut into 8 wedges for muddling, 1 cut into thin slices for garnish

2 seedless oranges, 1 cut into 4 wedges for muddling, 1 cut into thin slices for garnish

4 ounces triple sec

2 ounces Spanish brandy

2 ounces simple syrup (page 246)

1 bottle Spanish red wine, such as Marquis de Riscal, or Australian shiraz

3 ounces fresh-squeezed orange juice

½ English cucumber, cut into thin wheels

Club soda

☞ Place the pineapple wedges, lemon wedges, and orange wedges in the bottom of a sangria pitcher. Add the triple sec, brandy, and syrup and muddle. Add the wine and orange juice and stir. To serve, fill a goblet with ice (or serve at room temperature) and 1 slice each of lemon, orange, and cucumber. Pour 2 ounces club soda into the glass, then strain the wine mixture on top of the soda to fill the glass. Stir again and serve.

Serves 4 to 6

*S*panish sangria was invented with the same inspiration as Italian vermouth: You have a middling, undistinguished table wine; it's a hot climate, and thus you might want your mediocre wine chilled; so you add some fortification with brandy (or vodka, though that's not common) to give it a little punch, plus fruit to give it extra flavor, sweeten it slightly, and there! You have something much more than palatable instead of something borderline. In fact, you have a great summer refresher, perfect for a picnic. The traditional sangria is made with red wine, but I've had great success with white, sparkling, port, and even Sauternes versions, so there are a few variations here. (After all, what are mulled wine and glögg except winter versions of sangria, with dried fruits and spices instead of fresh, served hot instead of cold?) In general, I wouldn't spend more than $15 per bottle for sangria wine, because you're going to obliterate any subtleties or finesse in it—that's the entire point of sangria. Some people like their sangrias to sit overnight, but as I muddle my fruit (as opposed to just dumping it in the pitcher), the fruits' flavor gets into the wine quickly, and this way the drink can be mixed and served *à la minute.*

WHITE OR ROSÉ SANGRIA

Although the red wine version is the classic, and appropriate for any season, I think a white or rosé version is more summery and picnic-y. You'll want your white or rosé to have no oak character, with forward fruit and rich color, such as Rosenblum Cellars Redwood Valley Grenache Rosé at about ten bucks.

INGREDIENTS

2 lemons, 1 cut into 8 wedges for muddling, 1 cut into thin slices for garnish

2 seedless oranges, 1 cut into 4 wedges for muddling, 1 cut into thin slices for garnish

1 ripe summer peach, cut into 4 wedges, for muddling

3 ounces Luxardo Maraschino liqueur

1 ounce Spanish brandy

2 ounces simple syrup (page 246)

1 bottle light white or rosé wine

6 frozen seedless grapes

½ English cucumber, cut into thin wheels

Club soda

☞ Place the lemon wedges, orange wedges, and peach wedges in the bottom of a sangria pitcher. Add the Maraschino liqueur, brandy, and syrup and muddle. Add the wine and stir. To serve, put 1 frozen grape and 1 slice each of lemon, orange, and cucumber in a goblet. Pour 2 ounces club soda into the glass, then strain the wine mixture on top of the soda to fill the glass. Stir again and serve.

Serves 4 to 6

SPARKLING SANGRIA

This is a more festive version, perfect for a holiday cocktail party.

INGREDIENTS

6 pineapple wedges, each 1 inch thick

2 lemons, 1 cut into 8 wedges for muddling, 1 cut into thin slices for garnish

2 seedless oranges, 1 cut into 4 wedges for muddling, 1 cut into thin slices for garnish

6 strawberries, 4 left whole for muddling, 2 cut into slices for garnish

3 ounces Luxardo Maraschino liqueur

2 ounces Spanish brandy

2 ounces simple syrup (page 246)

1 bottle sparkling wine

½ English cucumber, cut into thin wheels

Club soda

☞ Place the pineapple wedges, lemon wedges, orange wedges, and whole strawberries in the bottom of a sangria pitcher. Add the Maraschino liqueur, brandy, and syrup and muddle. Add the wine and stir gently. To serve, fill a goblet with ice cubes and 1 slice each of lemon, orange, strawberry, and cucumber. Pour 2 ounces club soda into the glass, then strain the wine mixture on top of the soda to fill the glass. Stir again and serve.

Serves 4 to 6

SCORPION PUNCH

INGREDIENTS

1½ bottles Brugal rum

2 ounces brandy

2 ounces gin

½ bottle white wine

1 cup (8 ounces) fresh-squeezed lemon juice

1 cup (8 ounces) fresh-squeezed orange juice

8 ounces orgeat

4 ounces Demerara-sugar syrup (page 246), plus more to taste

Gardenia blossom, pesticide-free and well washed, for garnish, thoroughly optional

Orange slice, for garnish, optional

Lemon slice, for garnish, optional

Mint sprig, for garnish, optional

☛ Pour the rum, brandy, gin, wine, lemon and orange juices, orgeat, and sugar syrup in a punch bowl with ice. Let stand for 1 hour. Adjust the sweetness to your taste with sugar syrup. Add more ice as needed to keep chilled, and serve individual portions garnished with a gardenia blossom, or with a slice each of orange and lemon and a mint sprig.

Makes 20 drinks

This punch is a mixture of rum and brandy—which are pretty common companions, as in eggnog and Between the Sheets, but here with the gin wild card tossed in. It also includes the interesting ingredient orgeat, an almond syrup whose use in cocktails, although uncommon, is a tradition that goes all the way back to the original 1862 edition of Jerry Thomas's *How to Mix Drinks*, which included something called the Japanese Cocktail (brandy, bitters, and orgeat). But by the 1869 edition of Thomas's book, the orgeat had been switched out for curaçao, and orgeat began a long life of use mostly in tropical drinks, as here in the Scorpion. Trader Vic made this punch famous, but when he first enjoyed the traditional Hawaiian concoction, at a luau in Manoa Valley, it was made with the local moonshine called *okolehao*, distilled from ti root. (That product is now available from Sandwich Island Distilling.) When the drink made the jump to the mainland, the local spirit was replaced by rum. And when Trader Vic's recipe made the jump into this book, I slightly adapted it. Although Vic didn't specify which type of wine to use, I suggest a fruity, not-too-dry white, possibly a California viognier; on the other hand, he did specify garnishing with a gardenia, but I suggest that any edible flower would be fine, or even just humble slices of orange and lemon and a mint sprig.

The Essential

SWEETS

ALEXANDER • BLACK RUSSIAN • COFFEE COCKTAIL • EGGNOG
GRASSHOPPER • SGROPPINO AL LIMONE • STINGER

You've eaten your last bit of dry-aged steak, swallowed your last sip of claret. You push your chair back a few inches, cross your legs, and think about what you want for dessert. You're definitely too full for the chocolate torte, but you still feel like you need something sweet. Maybe a little nip to drink, but you're not in the mood for a lethal eau-de-vie or a frozen Pear William, and you've had your fair share of ports and sherries. No, you want something else. You want a sweet cocktail.

Although a certain contingent will order a White Russian at any time of day, I think that sweet and creamy drinks are best as after-dinner delights and best enjoyed in limited quantities; the right number of sweet cocktails to consume in a given evening is almost always one. And they should never be consumed before or after other cocktails that feature heavy doses of citrus, because the combination could be a real stomach-churner.

But enough of what you *shouldn't* do. What you *should* do is find the best ingredients, especially when shopping for cream liqueurs and cordials, whose quality ranges vastly from the horrific to the sublime, but also for the base spirits—usually gin or brandy, but occasionally vodka or even tequila. Purchase the best brands you can afford. Although, to be historically accurate, you could also use bathtub gin; the reality was that many of these sweet and creamy drinks were invented during Prohibition to hide the bite of moonshine. A few of these confections preceded Prohibition—most notably Sgroppinos, the Italian *sorbetti*-based treats—but it was during the Great Experiment that the category was perfected. So although you may no longer need to spike your brandy with crème de menthe to make it palatable, the resulting liquid petit four called the Stinger is a fantastic digestif. ♛

ALEXANDER

INGREDIENTS

1 ounce high-quality brandy, preferably VS cognac, or gin
1 ounce dark crème de cacao
2 ounces heavy cream
Nutmeg, for grating

☞ Combine the brandy or gin with the crème de cacao and cream in a mixing glass with ice and shake well. Strain into a small cocktail glass and garnish with a pinch of freshly grated nutmeg.

INGREDIENT NOTE

Anisette

Marie Brizard was the first commercial brand of the anise-flavored liqueur called *anisette*—Madame Brizard started production in 1755—and it is still the best on the market. Luckily, the best in this case is also widely available, and you shouldn't have any trouble finding it.

The Alexander was born of Prohibition. As we all know, the thirteen-year illegality of alcohol didn't prevent it from being consumed, or being sold, or being made; it just made the former more exciting, the middle more lucrative, and the latter more, well, creative. Or haphazard. Or amateurish. However you want to characterize the production of bathtub gin, it was universally agreed that its flavor left something to be desired, and it was as smooth as a dirt road after a rainstorm. To take the bite off bathtub gin, it was mixed with fat and sweet—cream and sugar—in sufficient quantities to make it palatable; hence the Alexander became wildly popular, especially with women, as an after-dinner drink. (But it's not the best idea to start off a meal. As David Embury pointed out in his 1949 book *The Fine Art of Mixing Drinks*, the Alexander can be "a nice midafternoon snack in place of a half pound of bonbons, but deadly as a pre-prandial drink.") As the American palate abandoned gin as the white spirit of choice, the Alexander evolved into a brandy drink, so much so that the gin version is seldom seen; if you order an Alexander today, it's assumed to be a cognac or brandy cocktail, although the gin is equally pleasing. Oddly, although the drink was allegedly created by Harry MacElhone while he was working at Ciro's Club in London, around 1922, he doesn't give himself credit for this cocktail in his own book, *ABC of Mixing Cocktails*. If MacElhone really created the Alexander but didn't boast of it, he'd hold a unique place in the annals of mixology.

ALEXANDER FRAPPÉ

The Alexander can be enhanced, made richer and more decadent, by substituting a small scoop of vanilla ice cream for the heavy cream, then blending the drink to a frappé consistency and serving it in a large cocktail or even a standard Champagne coupé glass.

ALEXANDRA SPECIAL

This is modified from a recipe in *The Artistry of Mixing Drinks* by Frank Meier (published in 1936 by the Ritz Hotel, Paris), who was Hemingway's bartender; after Papa "liberated" the bar of the Ritz, it was renamed the Hemingway Bar. Meier was there both before and after the war—he was an exile of Prohibition from the famous Hoffman House bar in New York City. It was in Meier's book that brandy may have become the spirit of choice for this drink; it's the first printed recipe I've found for the brandy version.

INGREDIENTS

1½ ounces brandy
¾ ounce Marie Brizard anisette
1 ounce heavy cream

☛ Combine the brandy, anisette, and cream in a mixing glass with ice and shake well. Strain into a chilled cocktail glass.

GOLDEN CADILLAC

The Golden Cadillac was created at Poor Red's Saloon in El Dorado, California, near Sutter's Mill, two and a half hours east of San Francisco, which was Gold Rush territory, hence the name. This is not officially an Alexander spinoff, but it does fit into the same category of sweet, creamy, dessert-y drinks that are made from a spirit, a liqueur, and cream. The Golden Cadillac is a fine, upstanding member of this after-dinner cabal.

INGREDIENTS

1 ounce Galliano
1 ounce white crème de cacao
2 ounces heavy cream
Ground cinnamon, for garnish

☛ Combine the Galliano, crème de cacao, and cream in a mixing glass with ice and shake well. Strain into a chilled cocktail glass and garnish with a light dusting of cinnamon.

BLACK RUSSIAN

INGREDIENTS

1 ounce Kahlúa
1 ounce vodka

☞ In an old-fashioned glass, build the Kahlúa and vodka over ice. Garnish with nothing more than a slice of Cold War paranoia.

The Berlin Wall fell nearly two decades ago, and memories of the Cold War are beginning to fade even as the breeze begins to stiffen again from the east. But remember the 1950s and early 1960s? Sputnik and Khrushchev and *Dr. No*? Those were the days when the Black Russian was reputedly invented by Gustave Tops at the Hotel Metropole in Brussels, Belgium—a set of places and names that just drips with Cold War intrigue. The Black Russian came into its own as a popular drink in the late 1960s and 1970s, the ebb tide of cocktails, when it was almost impossible to find fresh ingredients and well-made drinks. These were the days of the one-glass bar—when such little care was taken with cocktails that in many places, every single drink was served in the same exact goblet glass. It was in these Dark Ages of mixology that vodka made its ascendance to the spirit of choice in America, and Kahlúa was the recipient of a heavy promotional budget that was wildly successful (Kahlúa was originally solely a Mexican product, but it is now so popular that most of it is made elsewhere in the world). And so back at this moment, the extraordinarily simple Black Russian—a sweet drink that's not cloying, and could be taken before dinner as well as after—enjoyed its moment in the spotlight. Today, in a more sophisticated era, Kahlúa has introduced a new bottling called Especial, at 70-proof with a bit more horsepower.

VARIATION

WHITE RUSSIAN

INGREDIENTS

1 ounce Kahlúa
1 ounce vodka
2 ounces heavy cream

☞ Shake the Kahlúa, vodka, and cream in a mixing glass with ice. Strain over ice in a rocks glass.

This crowd-pleaser is an absolute no-no pre-dinner, despite the devotees who swear by it any time of day, but it's an appropriately big hit for dessert. While the Black Russian achieved its peak of popularity in the 1960s and early 1970s, the White Russian shone in the late 1970s disco days, when a lot of people were awake late at night with a craving for something sweet. I seem to remember a lot of cravings in the late 1970s, late at night. The flappers had their Alexanders with crème de cacao, gin, and cream during Prohibition, and the disco babies had their White Russians.

ITALIAN EGG CREAM

INGREDIENTS

¾ ounce Amaretto di Saronno
¾ ounce white crème de cacao,
    preferably Marie Brizard
1 ounce whole milk
3 ounces prosecco brut

☛ In a white wine glass, build the Amaretto, crème de cacao, and milk over ice. Slowly pour in the prosecco while stirring gently with a spoon to create some foam atop the drink, but not so vigorously that you dissipate all the carbonation before the first sip is taken. Be sure to serve immediately, while there are still bubbles.

♛ Back in the Brooklyn soda-shop days, if you had money you ordered an ice cream soda, made with syrup and big scoops of vanilla ice cream, topped with soda, and finished off with a cherry. But if you had no money, you ordered an egg cream: a couple tablespoons milk, 1 tablespoon U-bets' chocolate syrup, and a few ice cubes, topped off with seltzer and stirred, with no cherry on top. This was the poor man's ice cream soda. Despite the total absence of egg or cream, it looked a bit like a whipped egg or a meringue, because of the foam on top, hence the name *egg cream*. The key to creating the foam is to stir constantly and vigorously while adding the soda, and it's the same technique that creates the foam in the drink here, which is not a poor man's anything.

SMITH AND CURRAN

INGREDIENTS

2 ounces dark crème de cacao
3 ounces whole milk or half-and-half
1½ ounces club soda

☛ Build the crème de cacao and milk in an iced highball glass. Top with soda while stirring as you would an egg cream—that is, constantly, pouring the fizzy water in slowly.

♛ After years—thirty of them—of making something with Kahlúa that I called the Smith and Kearns, my friend Eric Felton of the *Wall Street Journal* set me straight: two North Dakota oilmen concocted this unlikely but surprisingly tasty drink in 1952, but it turns out that their names were Smith and Curran, not Kearns; and their cocktail was made with crème de cacao, not Kahlúa. In 1982, when Jimmy Curran was informed that his drink was being made with Kahlúa, he retorted, "You tell them to cut that out." Sorry, Jimmy.

The Smith and Curran is reminiscent of an egg cream, made in exactly the same way, and it's actually a delicious drink. If you substitute cola for the club soda, this becomes a Colorado Bulldog, which tastes like coffee-and-alcohol-spiked Coke, which is a pretty interesting promise, isn't it?

MUDSLIDE

The 1980s spawned the Mudslide, with the addition of Baileys Irish Cream to the Black Russian recipe. Or sometimes Baileys instead of Kahlúa. Or sometimes just Baileys with, I guess, ice—the Mudslide was flexible. It was also Rod Stewart's favorite drink during my days at the Rainbow Room, when Mr. Stewart and his friends used to commandeer our not-open-to-the-general-public rooftop lounge (the then-defunct observation deck from the old RCA days at 30 Rockefeller Center). On a busy Saturday night, we'd mix up Mudslides by the pitcher and send them up into the sky above the bar. They'd have a blast up there on the roof, while down at the Promenade we could maintain our dress code of jackets for gentlemen without embarrassing anyone. To make a frozen version, replace the ice with a scoop of vanilla ice cream; whip in a blender until smooth.

INGREDIENTS

1 ounce Kahlúa
1 ounce vodka
1 ounce Baileys Irish Cream liqueur
1 ounce heavy cream

☛ Combine the Kahlúa, vodka, Baileys, and cream in a mixing glass with ice and shake well. Strain into an old-fashioned glass. Or replace the cream with a large scoop of vanilla ice cream and freeze in a blender for frozen mudslides. Either way, no garnish.

WILLIAM "THE ONLY WILLIAM" SCHMIDT

This oddly self-named character was the godfather of the Mudslide and a great many other sweet drinks. The recipes in his 1892 book, *The Flowing Bowl,* are swimming in milk, eggs, and sugar in guises including crème de roses liqueur and chocolate. He also anticipated the molecular gastronomy movement that was still a century in the future with his Bunch of Violets cocktail; beginning in his usual fashion with an egg in a mixing glass, he then added Benedictine, Maraschino liqueur, anisette, vino vermouth (red, possibly?), crème de vanilla, Chartreuse, and a whopping two ponies of cream. And, finally, the twenty-first-century touch, as written in the nineteenth: Fill the glass with ice, then "freeze into a jelly and strain into long glasses and serve." And here is his recipe for Chocolate Punch:

A Glass with an egg in the bottom
A teaspoonful of sugar
⅔ of brandy
⅓ of port
1 dash crème de cacao
1 pony (1 ounce) of cream

Fill your glass with ice, shake well, strain and serve.

COFFEE COCKTAIL

INGREDIENTS

1 egg, as small as you can find

1 ounce cognac

1 ounce ruby port or, for a drier cocktail, a ten-year tawny port

1 teaspoon sugar

Nutmeg, for grating

☛ If you can find a small egg, use the whole thing; if not, use three-quarters of a medium egg or half of a large egg. Beat the egg to emulsify the white and yolk. Combine the beaten egg, cognac, port, and sugar in a mixing glass with ice. Shake well—be sure to shake vigorously to emulsify the egg. Strain into a port glass and dust with nutmeg.

This specialty drink is from Jerry Thomas's 1887 *Bartender's Guide–How to Mix All Kinds of Plain and Fancy Drinks*. I was introduced to the Coffee Cocktail—which, oddly enough, contains no coffee, but does look like coffee with cream—by my boss at the Rainbow Room, Alan Lewis. The Coffee Cocktail preceded the turn-of-the-century Stinger as the gentleman's preferred nightcap, a dessert-y finale to a big evening. I once made this drink totally against my will in about 1994. The wine and spirits writer Alex Bespalof, who was writing a spirits column for *Penthouse*, called ahead to ask me to make a port cocktail for his drinking companion, who happened to own the port house Taylor Flagate. Boy, did I *not* want to serve a port-mixed drink to the owner of a venerable port house—this would be like making sangria out of first-growth Bordeaux and serving it to a Rothschild. But I obeyed my orders, prepared this drink, delivered it to the table, shook hands with both men, and returned to the bar. Ten minutes later, the guy was standing in front of me at the bar. "First of all," he said, "write it down for me." Then he explained, "My grandfather used to make a cocktail with our port, a recipe that went back a generation before *him*, but we lost the recipe. This is the drink. The house of Flagate finally has our recipe back." I was flattered. But as I continued my reading in old drinks books, I realized that the Port Flip could very well have filled the bill as the Flagate House cocktail. I'm sure the Port Flip—simply port, sugar, and egg, shaken together—was the drink from which the Coffee Cocktail sprang.

VARIATION

GOLDEN GIRL*

This invention of mine fits into a category that used to be tremendously popular: cocktails made with port (typically tawny, which tends to be less sweet and less viscous than ruby) and other wines, fortified or not. While working at the restaurant Blackbird and exploring the cognac-port-egg combination of the Coffee Cocktail, I hit on this assortment of ingredients. And I guess they worked, because this recipe went on to win the 2001 Bacardi Martini Grand Prix for fancy cocktail of the year.

INGREDIENTS

1 ounce Bacardi añejo rum
¾ ounce tawny port, preferably
    five- or ten-year
1 ounce unsweetened pineapple juice
½ ounce simple syrup (page 246)
½ small egg (or ¼ medium egg,
    or ⅛ large egg)
Orange zest, for garnish

☛ Shake the rum, port, pineapple juice, syrup, and egg in a mixing glass with ice—shake long and hard. Strain into a 5- or 6-ounce cocktail glass and grate a little orange zest over the top as garnish.

EGGNOG

INGREDIENTS

6 eggs, separated
1 cup sugar
1 quart whole milk
1 pint heavy cream
4 ounces bourbon
4 ounces Jamaican dark rum
Nutmeg, for grating

☛ In a punch bowl, beat the yolks until they turn almost white, adding ½ cup of the sugar as you beat. Stir in the milk, cream, bourbon, and rum, and grate in half of the nutmeg berry. Just before serving, beat the whites in a large mixing bowl with the remaining ½ cup sugar until peaks form. Fold the whipped whites into the liquor mixture. Nestle the punch bowl into a larger bowl filled with crushed ice to keep cold. To serve, grate a light dusting of fresh nutmeg over each cup.

Serves 6

INGREDIENT NOTE

Raw Eggs

Raw eggs are safe for alcoholic beverage use if they are handled properly, especially when mixed with 80-proof spirits or with acid from citrus fruit, as is the case in most beverages, because both the alcohol and the acid will kill nearly all harmful bacteria. Just follow commonsense rules: Buy the freshest eggs you can find; if you handle eggshells, wash your hands before touching other ingredients; and refrigerate eggs at all times.

In England, where they were invented, nogs and their cousins, flips and possets, were the exclusive options of the wealthy because eggs, dairy, and spices were all expensive. But when the tradition traveled to America, where these ingredients were not luxuries—we had plenty of empty land to devote to dairy and chicken farms—the eggnog became a much more proletarian drink. Ironically, it also lost the eponymous ingredient: *Nog* is a strong ale, but what Americans used was invariably the cheaper, much more widely available rum of the New World. In the 1862 edition of Jerry Thomas's *How to Mix Drinks*, his recipe calls for Jamaican rum, but he suggests brandy as an option for the more well-to-do. (Thomas also observes, "Every well stocked bar has a tin egg nogg [*sic*] shaker, which is of great aid in mixing this beverage.") And a further change from the homeland was that in America, eggnog was a cold concoction, made with cold ingredients and served in iced punch bowls, which was not how it was done in England, where eggnogs, flips, and possets were normally consumed at least warm, sometimes hot.

Anyway, to more modern history: The recipe here is from my Uncle Angelo, who left Calabria in 1915, when he was twelve, and made his way to Westerly, Rhode Island, where his family had already established itself. When I was growing up, Christmas Day always brought with it the taste of Uncle Angelo's famous eggnog (without the spirits, for us kids), which went on to win a contest sponsored by Four Roses whiskey and for a time appeared on that brand's Christmas packaging. Uncle Angelo's recipe was based on the popular Baltimore Eggnog—which was actually consumed year-round, not just in the winter—but differed in one key respect: Angelo used a mixture of heavy cream and milk, and the Baltimore variation used only the heavy cream.

FRIAR BRIAR'S SACK POSSET

This was the winning entry created by Kevin Armstrong from the English team of the 2006 International 42 Below (a New Zealand vodka) drinks contest.

INGREDIENTS

3 ounces 42 Below Manuka Honey Vodka
3 ounces Speights Old Dark Ale
1 ounce Tahiti Dark Rum
¼ ounce Benedictine
3 ounces cream
2 eggs
1 heaping teaspoon honey
Dash of Angostura bitters

☞ In a saucepan, combine the vodka, ale, rum, Benedictine, cream, eggs, honey, and bitters. Whisk all the ingredients over low heat, then char with a red-hot poker. Serve in a teacup.

ROYAL POSSET

We shall have a posset at the end of a sea-coal fire. —WILLIAM SHAKESPEARE (1564–1616)

This recipe is adapted from *Practical Housewife*, published in 1860 by Houlston & Wright, London.

INGREDIENTS

4 egg yolks
1 pint cream
2 tablespoons sugar
¼ nutmeg berry, grated
2 egg whites
½ pint ale

☞ In a large bowl, whip the egg yolks with the cream, sugar, and nutmeg. In a separate bowl, whip the egg whites. Add the ale and whipped egg whites to the yolk mixture, stirring well to blend. Place over a low fire and stir until thick, but do not boil. Remove from the fire and serve piping hot.

GENERAL HARRISON'S EGG NOGG

This personal favorite of mine, adapted from the original 1862 edition of Jerry Thomas's *How to Mix Drinks*, is a totally different take on the idea of eggnog. It's also made by the single-serving drink, not as a whole bowlful of punch, so it's a lot more convenient. Still, it includes a raw egg, so you have to shake the hell out of it. The bourbon is my addition; the original Thomas recipe was nonalcoholic.

INGREDIENTS

1½ ounces bourbon

4 ounces fresh apple cider

1 egg

1½ teaspoons sugar

Pinch of ground cinnamon, for garnish

☛ Assemble the bourbon, cider, egg, and sugar in a cocktail shaker with ice. Shake very well to completely emulsify the egg. Strain over ice into a large goblet and top with the pinch of ground cinnamon.

GOLDEN AGE

The first edition, from 1862, of Jerry Thomas's *How to Mix Drinks, or The Bon Vivant's Companion.*

GRASSHOPPER

INGREDIENTS

1 ounce green crème de menthe
1 ounce white crème de cacao
2 ounces heavy cream
Nutmeg, for garnish, optional

☞ Pour the crème de menthe, crème de cacao, and heavy cream into a shaker, and add ice. Shake vigorously for as long and as hard as you can muster the patience; with rich, sweet ingredients like these, you want a good amount of ice to melt, watering down the concoction so it isn't overly cloying. (And by the way: Although you or your guests might imagine that half-and-half or whole milk might be preferable to the cream, don't do it; what's enjoyable about this drink is its silken, ropy texture, which you can get only from the cream.) Strain into a chilled cocktail glass. Grate a light dusting from the whole nutmeg (do not use store-bought powdered nutmeg) directly over the center of the drink.

A grasshopper is a combination of green crème de menthe, crème de cacao, and crème de cow (heavy cream). That's a lot of crème, which makes the Grasshopper far more appropriate after dinner than before—it's something of a liquid liquored dessert. The two liqueurs actually don't include any cream whatsoever; all crème liqueurs, whether they're flavored with fruit and berries (most popularly banana and cassis, which is black currant), flowers or herbs (mint), or nuts (cacao), get their name from their heaviness on the palate, which is similar to cream's mouthfeel. But there's no dairy product in the bottle, so don't worry that these liqueurs must be refrigerated.

Liqueurs, which use plant essences to flavor alcohol, are not a recent invention, despite all the infused vodkas that seem like a new-fangled innovation these days. Alcohol infusions were pioneered in the thirteenth century by a Catalan chemist named Arnáu de Vilanova and perfected by monks throughout the Middle Ages (think of Benedictine and Chartreuse). The Grasshopper is a wonderful showcase for the sweet, rich flavors of the two classic crème liqueurs. As with other such heavy drinks, though, don't make it the theme of your party. The Grasshopper, to paraphrase the old Schaefer beer commercials, may be the one to have when you're having only one.

VARIATION

BANSHEE

The Grasshopper has been reinvented in several ways: A Coffee Grass-hopper replaces the crème de cacao with a coffee-flavored liqueur, such as Kahlúa; both the Vodka Grasshopper and the Flying Grasshopper use vodka, and no cream, with the ingredients in different proportions. But one variation stands on its own as a truly different drink: the Banshee. While the Grasshopper tastes something like a chocolate-mint-chip milkshake, the Banshee is a grown-up banana split. The name comes from Irish mythology; the banshee is a fairy from the Otherworld whose horrible wails are an omen for imminent death. (If you hear the wails, you're okay; it's the person who doesn't hear them who's done for.) But I have no idea how that relates to a banana-chocolate-flavored cocktail.

 INGREDIENTS

1 ounce crème de banane
1 ounce white crème de cacao
2 ounces heavy cream

☛ Shake the crème de banane, crème de cacao, and heavy cream in a mixing glass with ice in the same manner as for the Grasshopper. Strain into a chilled cocktail glass.

 INGREDIENT NOTE

Crème Liqueur

Don't economize on crème liqueurs. With all spirits, there's a noticeable difference between economy brands and the premium labels, but in no category is this difference more pronounced than liqueurs. I recommend you use Hiram Walker, from Canada (makers also of Canadian Club); Marie Brizard, from Bordeaux; or Bols, which, dating back to 1575 in what's now Rotterdam, may very well be the oldest commercial distiller in the world. And I hope that one day we will have the French Cartron brand of high-proof, high-quality cordials and crèmes available in the United States.

 TECHNIQUE NOTE

A Chocolate Rim

Both the Grasshopper and the Banshee can be dressed up for a special occasion with chocolate around the rim of the glass. For a chocolate rim, the easiest route is to buy any good brand of unsweetened powdered cocoa; the more ambitious (and somewhat more fun) technique is to buy unsweetened cocoa nibs, then grind them in a mortar and pestle to the consistency of sprinkles. Moisten the rim of the glass with an orange segment or simple syrup (page 246), and roll the rim in the cocoa powder. Be sure your chocolate is unsweetened; these drinks are sweet enough, and they don't need any sugar around the rim of the glass.

STINGER

1 ounce VS cognac (or better)
1 ounce white crème de menthe

☞ Combine the cognac and crème de menthe in a mixing glass with ice and shake very, very hard. Strain into an old-fashioned glass filled with crushed ice, and stir until the glass frosts.

This great nightcap—an adult after-dinner mint—dates to the 1890s, when it was the final drink of the evening for many high rollers. The only cocktail that can follow a Stinger is another Stinger, but you can't sit around knocking back these things, because they're all liquor—very, very strong—so one is pretty much the limit. But one properly made Stinger is a wonderful thing. Start with VS or better cognac—don't use house brandy here. Shake the Stinger very, very hard with ice; despite my general proscription against shaking all-alcohol drinks, the Stinger's combination of strong and sweet alcohol would produce something too cloying if stirred and served up, which might not dilute it sufficiently. Finally, strain into a rocks glass over crushed ice, and stir until the outside of the glass frosts nicely. Serve a Stinger after a heavy, sauce-driven meal—its strength and refreshing mintiness will cut right through all the butter.

The Stinger fell out of favor at the same time heavy, sauce-driven meals—that is, fancy French food—lost ground as the preferred meal of choice for the American upper classes in the late 1970s. But I'm on a mission to resurrect the after-dinner tradition of strong drinks such as the Stinger or even just a cordial glass of ice-cold high-proof eau-de-vie. I remember after a dinner at the Four Seasons, when I was about nineteen years old, the rolling trolley came out with frozen Poire William and other cordial bottles, all frosty on the outside, accompanied by an army of little glasses. I took a glass. Because of the name, I thought it would be some type of sweet, weak pear liqueur. So I knocked it back—and felt like my nostrils had been ignited with a blowtorch. Lesson learned. The next time I had such an after-dinner glass, I sipped it properly and loved the way the dry, fruit-driven alcohol cut right through the fat of the meal, leaving me feeling refreshed and satisfied at the same time. This is the same purpose a good Stinger can serve.

Although the recipe looks like it'll be terribly sweet—it's a 1:1 ratio of strong to sweet—it actually mixes up perfectly when done properly. If you think you can't tolerate all this sweetness, you can change the proportion to as much as 2:1 strong to sweet, but that's going to be a very strong cocktail. So have some type of fire extinguisher nearby.

WHITE SPIDER

Back in the late 1960s and early 1970s, when Americans started substituting vodka for all the other spirits in nearly any cocktail recipe, this Stinger spinoff became very popular. It's made exactly the same way as the original.

INGREDIENTS

1 ounce vodka
1 ounce white crème de menthe

☛ Combine the vodka and crème de menthe in a mixing glass with ice and shake very hard. Strain into an old-fashioned glass filled with crushed ice, and stir until the glass frosts.

INTERNATIONAL STINGER*

This is a similar variation made with the idiosyncratic Greek brandy called Metaxa, which is distinctively flavored with vegetal notes uncommon in other brandies that pair nicely with the botanical, herbal notes of Galliano.

INGREDIENTS

1 ounce Metaxa
1 ounce Galliano

☛ Combine the Metaxa and Galliano in a mixing glass with ice and shake very hard. Strain into an old-fashioned glass filled with crushed ice, and stir until the glass frosts.

SCORPION STINGER*

This shot is an altogether different species of scorpion, and I call it a Stinger because it's a strong spirit shaken with a liqueur and served very cold. It is a great showcase for mezcal and an interesting way to make that tough-to-take spirit palatable to a wider array of palates. Like grappa, mezcal is something of a rough customer—idiosyncratic, agave-heavy, with strong flavor and high alcohol.

INGREDIENTS

Unsweetened cocoa powder, for coating the rim of the glass
Dried ancho chile powder, for coating the rim of the glass
Granulated sugar, for coating the rim of the glass
Orange slice, for coating the rim of the glass
¾ ounce Scorpion Silver Mezcal
¾ ounce Kahlúa Especial (70-proof version)

☛ In a shallow plate, combine equal measures of the cocoa, chile powder, and sugar. Coat the rims of two shot glasses in this mixture with the orange slice according to the directions on page 137. In a cocktail shaker, combine the mezcal and Kahlúa with ice, and shake well. Strain into the prepared shot glasses. (You can also prepare this as a sipping cocktail instead of a shooter; just shake it up per the Scorpion directions.)

Makes 2 shooters or 1 cocktail

The Essential

INNOVATIONS

BIG SPENDER • CHAMPAGNE COBBLER • CHIARO DI LUNA
COPA VERDE • GREEN DREAM • LEGENDS COCKTAIL
MILLIONAIRE'S MANHATTAN • SEVILLA
STRAWBERRY JIVE

Mixologists have been inventing new cocktails since the invention of the mixed drink, adding a dash of this, a splash of that, substituting and finessing. There have been periods of great creativity and periods of stultifying stasis. When I started in the 1970s, we were at a low ebb. But I'm thrilled to say that today we are at an apex. Bartenders all over the world are embracing the use of fresh fruits and juices, high-quality ingredients, careful technique, and proper presentation.

We are also in a period of remarkable innovation. Beginning in the 1990s, the culinary world began to embrace the no-holds-barred advances of molecular gastronomy. And a young generation of forward-thinking London bartenders invented a new type of lounge that came to be known as a *style bar,* serving a new type of cocktail. A large part of this shift has been about melding the worlds of food and drink, with bartenders poking their noses into kitchens and vice versa. We are now using savory ingredients in mixed drinks—herbs like rosemary and sage, spices like black pepper and nutmeg, chiles, and fruits and vegetables. We are creating ethereal foams and viscous purées. We are playing with texture and temperature.

This is an exciting moment, at the cusp of an evolutionary mutation of the cocktail. A lot of the traditionalists may abhor these changes. But I find it exciting to enjoy a hint of rosemary in a cocktail, or the smooth texture of avocado with tequila. The cocktails in this chapter feature some of my innovations in this category, employing the types of ingredients and techniques I hope will one day be commonplace in sophisticated bars. But that doesn't mean I'm going to stop drinking a good old-fashioned gin martini when I'm in the mood. ♛

BIG SPENDER*

The margarita is such a perfect cocktail that it defies newcomers, so it's an immense challenge for bartenders to find new tequila drinks. But we keep trying. Here's one I created for the 2005 revival of *Sweet Charity* on Broadway while I was working for Gran Centenario Tequila. The cocktail was actually written into the script, held on the stage, and even sold in the theater. One of the important ingredients is blood orange juice, which used to be available only from Sicily during its season in late summer and early fall but is now also available from California from Christmas through summer, making for pretty wide availability; it's also produced by a lot of the big purée houses, such as Perfect Purée of Napa, and this form is perfectly acceptable for the Big Spender. The Liqueur Créole is rum-based, with orange notes, and is also called Créole Shrub, made by the rum producer Clément, out of Martinique. I first came across it when I was working at the Bel Air Hotel in the 1970s; it went off the market in the 1980s, but now it's available again, albeit spottily. Finally, for the wine here, you don't need to use Cristal—although, hey, it *is* the Big Spender—but it should be some type of sparkling rosé, such as Billecart Salmon Brut Rosé.

INGREDIENTS

1 ounce Gran Centenario Añejo tequila
1 ounce Liqueur Créole
1 ounce blood orange juice
Cristal Rosé Champagne
Flamed orange peel (page 249), for garnish
Spiral orange peel, for garnish

☞ Assemble the tequila, Liqueur Créole, and blood orange juice in a bar glass with ice, and stir to chill. Strain into a chilled flute and top with the sparkling wine. Flame the zest over the top of the drink and discard, and then garnish with the spiral orange peel.

CHAMPAGNE COBBLER*

INGREDIENTS

2 orange wedges
2 chunks fresh pineapple, each about
    3/4-inch square
2 lemon wedges
3/4 ounce Luxardo Maraschino liqueur
4 ounces Champagne
 Long spiral orange peel, for garnish

☛ In the bottom of a bar glass, muddle the orange wedges, pineapple chunks, and lemon wedges with the Maraschino liqueur. Add ice and the Champagne, and stir very gently. Strain into a Champagne flute and garnish with the orange peel.

 A lot of people think the cobbler was the very first shaken drink, a theory that's certainly supported by the name *cobbler shaker*, the standard three-piece shaker you find in most home bars. The cobbler shaker began as a small glass placed inside a larger glass (as opposed to the Boston shaker, which is a metal cup that fits into a larger glass). References to the cobbler predate the first cocktail recipe book ever published, Jerry Thomas's *How to Mix Drinks*, in 1862. Cobblers were a real nineteenth-century favorite; at that time, Harry Johnson claimed the cobbler was "without doubt the most popular beverage in this country, with ladies as well as with gentlemen. It is a very refreshing drink for old and young" (according to David Embury in *The Fine Art of Mixing Drinks*, 1949). Cobblers never really emerged from Prohibition as a popular category, but the idea of shaking fruit with spirits opens all sorts of possibilities. So I started playing around with this grandfatherly category, using Champagne, port, sherry, and other wines and spirits with fruits like orange, pineapple, and lemon. The fruit is mashed, the drink is shaken (unless it's made with sparkling wine, in which case you don't shake it, unless you want an explosion), and a liqueur sweetener is used, never a sugar syrup. The summery Champagne Cobbler here is my own invention, a twenty-first-century update to a nineteenth-century classic.

VARIATION

PORT COBBLER*

This is another contemporary cobbler of my own invention, a bit heavier than the Champagne Cobbler—maybe for a cool summer evening on the dock.

INGREDIENTS

1/2 orange, quartered, plus 1 orange slice, for garnish
2 wedges of fresh pineapple, one with skin and one without
1/2 lemon, quartered, plus 1 wedge, for garnish
3/4 ounce orange curaçao
1 ounce distilled water
4 ounces ruby port

☛ In the bottom of a bar glass, muddle the orange quarters, the skinless pineapple wedge, and the lemon quarters with the curaçao and distilled water. Add the port and ice, and shake. Strain into a double old-fashioned glass filled with crushed ice. Garnish with the orange slice, the skin-on pineapple wedge, and the lemon wedge.

CHIARO DI LUNA*

INGREDIENTS

Three 1-inch pineapple wedges
1 sprig of rosemary, halved
1 tablespoon orgeat
4 ounces prosecco brut

☛ In a bar glass, muddle 2 of the pineapple chunks and half the rosemary sprig with the orgeat. Add ice. Hold a bar spoon in one hand and use the other hand to slowly pour in the prosecco, using the spoon to gently pull the other ingredients up from the bottom of the glass. Strain into a chilled flute. Garnish with the remaining pineapple wedge and the other half of the rosemary sprig on the rim of the glass.

This drink—"Moonlight," in English—is a great example of cocktail evolution, taking a few cues from the Bellini: a botanical herb; a different fruit base, with the pineapple juice; and a third flavor element, the almond from the orgeat, creating a trio (almond, pineapple, and rosemary) that has been used to pleasant effect since the time of the Ancient Greeks.

PERO FRIZZANTE*

This is a drink I created for the Italian restaurant Morandi, whose chef, Jody Williams, insisted on a hard-spirit ban for their prosecco cocktail menu to avoid overpowering the delicate flavors of the food. At first I was doubtful of this approach, but it turns out a lot of great cocktails fit this food-friendly bill if we just open ourselves up to using culinary elements in mixed drinks.

INGREDIENTS

1 anjou pear, washed
Lemon wedge
3 fresh sage leaves
1 dried pitted purple plum (also known as a prune)
1 teaspoon honey syrup (page 247)
4 ounces *frizzante* prosecco, chilled

☛ First, prepare some pear-shaped pear slices: Stand the pear on end, with the stem up. Cut long ½-inch-thick slices from the top through the poles of the pear. Remove any seeds. Squeeze the lemon wedge over the pear to prevent the fruit from turning brown.

Now, make the drink: In the bottom glass of a Boston shaker, gently muddle 1 of the pear slices with 2 of the sage leaves, the plum, and the honey syrup. Hold a bar spoon in one hand and use the other hand to slowly pour in the prosecco, using the spoon to gently pull the other ingredients up from the bottom of the glass. Strain through a tea strainer into a chilled flute.

Finally, garnish the thing: Choose a pear slice based on the size of your glass. The fruit should look like it belongs. If you're serving in a little glass, for example, use the smallest pear slice. Cut a slit in an appropriate-sized slice, and tuck the remaining sage leaf in there, using this slit to hang the pear slice on the glass. Be sure to let the fruit hang into the glass, where it's doing some good in flavoring the drink, instead of on the outside of the glass, where it's doing nothing much except waiting to fall onto someone's dress. Note: If the pears are cut in advance, keep them in a mixture of lemon juice and water to avoid browning.

COPA VERDE *

INGREDIENTS

Chili powder, for frosting the rim of the glass, optional

Kosher salt, for frosting the rim of the glass, optional

Lime slice, for frosting the rim of the glass, optional

4 ounces Gran Centenario Plata tequila

½ avocado, ripe but not mushy, peeled and coarsely chopped

3 ounces agave syrup (page 247)

2 ounces fresh-squeezed lemon or lime juice

3 ounces bottled or filtered water

☞ If you want to frost the glasses with the chili-salt combination (or just salt, for the fainthearted), use the technique explained on page 87, using the lime slice to moisten 10 shot glasses. In a blender, combine the tequila, avocado, agave syrup, citrus juice, and water. Blend until completely smooth *without ice*. When thoroughly puréed, pour the mixture into a pitcher and refrigerate until ready to use. When ready to serve, transfer the mixture to a cocktail shaker with ice and shake very well. Strain into the prepared shot glasses and serve immediately.

Makes 10 shots, about 1½ ounces each

For many of us restaurant-goers, our first experience of having a cocktail with dinner was in a Mexican restaurant; none of the European cultures has the tradition of distilled spirits with food. But in Mexican joints, tequila-based cocktails often flowed throughout the meal, and that's what inspired this bizarre spinoff of the margarita. These shooters are a great accompaniment to Spanish or Mexican *tapas*, with the avocado completely liquefied to create the "green glass." But as delicious as this concoction is—really an amuse-bouche unto itself as well as a great pairing—don't try to serve it as a full-quantity cocktail, which is just too much. This recipe is perfect for a crowd.

GREEN DREAM

I was introduced to a mojito offshoot called the Strepe Chepe by the inimitable Colin Cowie, who knows how to throw a party like few others do. I added ginger, sake, honey, and agave, but retained the same base of vodka, lemon, and mint. What's more, I kept the idea of serving this as a blended, chilled, relatively-low-alcohol shot that's cool and refreshing, either as an intermezzo (a palate-cleanser between courses) or as a dancing drink, where guests can consume this one shot at a time without needing to keep track of their drinks while on the dance floor. Colin calls drinks like this Rocket Fuel, for their effect on the crowd. (A pretty good name for a great idea, when you think about it.) There's an Eastern flair to this drink with the sake and, if you want, with the flavoring of Hanger One Buddha's Hand Vodka, which is an excellent choice here. (The Buddha's Hand can be hard to find, so substitute plain vodka, not a citrus-flavored one.) And be sure to blend this mixture a good long time, until completely liquefied, especially the mint leaves.

INGREDIENTS

6 ounces vodka

1 handful of mint leaves

4 ounces agave syrup (page 247), cut
   with 4 ounces water

2 ounces triple syrup (page 248)

2 ounces ginger sryup (page 248)

2 ounces sake

2 ounces fresh-squeezed lemon juice

2 ounces fresh-squeezed lime juice

☛ In a blender, combine the vodka, mint, agave syrup, triple syrup, ginger syrup, sake, and lemon and lime juices. Add ³⁄₄ cup ice and blend on high speed until *completely* liquefied and no mint particles are floating around in there. Divide the mixture among 18 shot glasses and pass them around to dancers so they don't have to miss a beat.

Makes 6 drinks or 18 shooters

LEGENDS COCKTAIL*

INGREDIENTS

Sugar, for dusting the glass
Ground ginger, for dusting the glass
Orange slice, for dusting the glass
1 small piece of fresh ginger root
½ ounce Cointreau
½ ounce St. Germain elderflower
    liqueur
1½ ounces vodka
½ ounce white cranberry juice
¾ ounce fresh-squeezed lime juice
Lemon peel, preferably spiral (page 162),
    for garnish

☞ Frost the rim of a cocktail glass using a mixture of 4 parts sugar to 1 part ground ginger, as well as the orange slice, according to the instructions on page 137. Place the piece of ginger, Cointreau, and elderflower liqueur in the bottom of a bar glass, and muddle. Add the vodka, cranberry and lime juices, and ice, and shake well. Strain into the prepared glass and garnish with the lemon peel.

Over the long weekend of May 13 to 15, 2005, Oprah Winfrey hosted an extraordinary event called Legends, paying tribute to some of the legendary black women of the past half century. I designed and supervised the cocktail program for these two days in Santa Barbara, which included this signature cocktail, flavored with the delicate notes of elderflower in the St. Germain. I was pretty confident the guests wouldn't have had elderflower liqueur before unless they were part of the style-bar scene in London, which was the only place I'd really seen it, and hence the elderflower would be an original flavor for everyone, and of course originality was the point of creating a drink here. St. Germain comes in a beautiful bottle—one of the most striking product designs in the spirit world—and it's well worth giving this interesting cordial a try. (*Cordial* is an old-fashioned way of saying *liqueur* and often sounds better when beside a word like *elderflower.*) Cordials like Benedictine and Chartreuse, made by Italian monasteries half a millennium ago at the dawn of the Enlightenment, were among the first distilled spirits. They were probably invented for medicinal use, and the recipes traveled with the monks throughout Europe, including to Poland and Russia in the thirteenth century (when a delegation of monks taught the tsar to make vodka) and to Catherine de Médicis, who in turn brought liqueurs—and, some say, civilization—to the French.

Cointreau

In the nineteenth century, curaçao, a liqueur first made by the Bols company in Holland, was the sweetener of choice for American cocktails. Over the years it was available in red, green, and white in addition to the orange and blue we still have today; orange was always one of the preferred varieties. As William Schmidt noted in his 1891 book *The Flowing Bowl:*

This famous liquor is manufactured best in Amsterdam by infusing curaçao peel in very good brandy that has been sweetened with sugar syrup. The curaçao fruit is a species of the bitter orange, that grows mainly in Curaçao, one of the Lesser Antilles, north of Vene- zuela, and the greatest Dutch colony in the West Indies.

In the mid-nineteenth century, the Cointreau brothers took the idea of curaçao and cleaned it up to create a clear, high-proof, bright orange liqueur with a touch of bitterness along with the sweet. They called their product triple sec, or triple dry, referring to its distinction from the sweeter curaçao. Many manufacturers, trying to duplicate the Cointreaus' success, produced poor approximations that they also labeled triple sec. So Cointreau, to distinguish itself from the imitators they'd spawned, eventually removed triple sec from its label and relegated that phrase to the numerous products that remain, to this day, lesser versions. I see no reason why American companies can't manufacture liqueurs in the super-premium category that are as good as the French companies Marie Brizard and Cartron (of whose numerous excellent products we can get only two in the United States). But despite the ubiquity of top-quality base spirits—with super-premium luxury brands of vodka, gin, tequila, and rum available virtually everywhere—we continue to mix these high-quality spirits with the inexpensive, artificially flavored sugar waters called triple sec that sit on every bar in this country. Ugh.

MILLIONAIRE'S MANHATTAN

INGREDIENTS

Orange slice, for frosting the rim of the glass

Edible gold flakes, for frosting the rim of the glass

1½ ounces Woodford Reserve bourbon

½ ounce Grand Marnier Centenaire

1 ounce unsweetened pineapple juice

¼ ounce orgeat

☞ Frost the rim of the glass using the orange slice and the gold leaf, according to the instructions on page 137, and set in the freezer to chill. Shake the bourbon, Grand Marnier, pineapple juice, and orgeat in a mixing glass with ice. Strain into the prepared glass with no garnish other than the extravagantly decorated rim.

I freely admit I'm stretching the bounds of reasonable nomenclature to call this drink a Manhattan, but I have to cop to the fact that I simply like the alliteration. In truth, this is a fancy whiskey cocktail, so traditionalists and purists might be peeved at my liberal use of *Manhattan*, but I'll have to live with that. Also, traditionalists and purists, unless they happen to be cake-bakers who specialize in ornate items for big-ticket weddings, probably don't have edible gold leaf lying around, which is what I use to decorate the rim of the glass. This is, of course, optional. But it's a beautiful touch, and the gold leaf isn't as difficult to find nor as expensive as you might imagine. (But it is *gold*, so don't expect it to be cheap.)

SEVILLA *

Orange and Spanish sherry are *muy simpatico*, and I use these two elements together whenever I have the chance. This flavor combination is also used to great effect in the Flame of Love (page 110) and its cousin the Valencia (page 111). But here I've moved beyond the traditional cocktail realm to include ingredients more frequently found in the kitchen than behind the bar. First is cinnamon, for frosting the glass; the combination of orange and cinnamon is a classic pairing in North African cuisine, which had a huge influence on the Iberian peninsula, where sherry is made, and so all these flavors tie together in the regional tradition. The second and even more unusual ingredient is pepper jelly, to add heat to the affair. There are many types of pepper jelly—some hotter, some sweeter—and the only way for you to find one you like is to try a few. For the Sevilla, the jelly should provide not only spice but also sweetness, because the only other sweet ingredient, orange juice, isn't all *that* sweet. If you're going to omit the jelly, you'll probably want to add a bit of sugar syrup to compensate. But please do try it with the jelly, which imparts an unmistakable zingy sweetness that brings a lot to the drink.

INGREDIENTS

Orange slice, for frosting the rim of the glass
Ground cinnamon, unsweetened, for frosting the rim of the glass
1 ounce Appleton white rum
½ ounce Tio Pepe fino sherry
¾ ounce fresh-squeezed orange juice
¼ ounce fresh-squeezed lime juice
1 teaspoon pepper jelly
Flamed orange peel (page 249), for garnish

☛ Prepare an old-fashioned glass by frosting the rim with the orange slice and the unsweetened ground cinnamon (see page 137 for directions). Assemble the rum, sherry, orange juice, lime juice, and jelly in a mixing glass with ice, and shake well. Pass through a fine strainer into the prepared glass over ice, and garnish with the flamed orange peel.

STRAWBERRY JIVE*

INGREDIENTS

2 strawberries
4 mint leaves and 1 mint sprig
2 basil leaves
¾ ounce triple syrup (page 248)
1½ ounces Hendrick's gin
1 ounce fresh-squeezed orange juice
2 dashes of fresh-squeezed lemon juice

 In the bottom of a mixing glass, muddle the strawberries, 4 mint leaves, and basil with the syrup. Add the gin, orange and lemon juices, and ice, and shake well. Strain into an ice-filled rocks glass and garnish with the mint sprig.

INGREDIENT NOTE

Hendrick's Gin

This unique Scottish product, with hints of rose and cucumber, has developed quite a following since its debut just a few years ago. Hendrick's is one of the new-wave gins, meaning it doesn't follow the traditional formulas of London dry (juniper as the top, primary flavor note) or Holland (malty, something like corn wine). Hendrick's does share some of the same botanicals, like coriander, but they're arranged in a different formula. It's small-batch distilled, which is unusual for gin, and it doesn't adhere to some of the other production conventions so specifically mandated for gin in England. And, unlike the traditional England gins, I wouldn't use Hendrick's in a martini. But for the burgeoning culinary side of the cocktail world, it's a natural.

Italians have been combining strawberries and basil—a flavor match made in heaven—for decades in their kitchens, but it's not a combination that's been extensively utilized in cocktails. At least not until the style bartenders of London's West End, who have pioneered a variety of surprising matches for their culinary cocktail meanderings. This fruit-herb combination and the rose and cucumber notes of the new-wave Hendrick's gin—a lot of elements of the garden—create a layered, complex drink. Don't make the Strawberry Jive with the London dry or Holland styles of gin, because it's the unique flavor profile of Hendrick's that really creates the right balance with the strawberry and mint.

The biographer James Boswell noted that
"Drinking is an occupation that a good many people
employ a considerable portion of time, and to
conduct it in the most rational and agreeable manner is one
of the great arts of living."

A gentleman named Kurt A. Boesch wrote me a letter to tell
me how much he had enjoyed reading my first book,
The Craft of the Cocktail, and he described how the cocktail was
a thing of history, beauty, and expression, and what an interesting journey it was for him to collect the ingredients, tools,
supplies, fruits, glassware, etc., for his little home bar. He wrote:
"I create a marvelous thing, and I say a little prayer of thanks for a
simple, astounding pleasure."

Cheers,
AND TURN OFF THE LIGHTS WHEN YOU LEAVE.

BASIC RECIPES

SIMPLE SYRUP • HONEY SYRUP • AGAVE SYRUP • TRIPLE SYRUP • LEMONADE • GINGER SYRUP • PINEAPPLE SYRUP • DONN'S MIX #1 • CINNAMON SYRUP • FLAMED ORANGE PEEL • FOAM

SIMPLE SYRUP

As you would guess from the name, this isn't rocket science. But just because it's easy doesn't mean it's not important: It's actually impossible to make consistent, smooth, well-balanced cocktails without simple syrup. This is more and more true as we return to cocktails made with fresh-squeezed lemon and lime juices. Unfortunately, sugar doesn't dissolve well into strong spirits, and one of the all-time awful sensations is sipping something and finding your tongue coated with granules. So the sugar first must be combined with water. This can be done simply by stirring sugar into water, or by shaking the two in a closed container, which may take a minute or two. The colder the water and the coarser the sugar and the larger the quantity, the longer the process will take, but it's not a noticeable ordeal for a quart or two, especially if you're using superfine sugar, also known in my circles as bar sugar, which is widely available in grocery stores. Or you can heat the mixture on the stovetop, which is what I'd do for any larger quantity. Either way, after mixing, be sure to refrigerate the syrup if you don't plan to use it in the near future. If you don't keep it chilled, it will do what anything with sugar in it does: ferment. I don't recommend making more syrup than you'll use in a week—it's too easy and inexpensive to be worth batching up, and it'll pick up off-flavors after a week in the fridge. If

A NOTE ON WATER

The recipes below are the building blocks of many cocktails. In turn, one of their main building blocks is water. Unless you're unusually confident in the purity and neutral taste of your tap water, use filtered or bottled. You don't want a drink's flavor to come from the water—especially chlorine and other chemicals—and you certainly don't want to ruin a party because you couldn't be bothered to buy a few bottles of water.

you insist on making a lot, it's not a bad idea to throw in an ounce of vodka for every quart of sugar water to help kill any microbes.

Now, despite the syrup's simplicity, there's still something crucial to pay attention to: the ratio of sugar to water (which, by the way, should be portioned using a measuring cup). The ratio I use today, and what all the recipes in this book are built around, is 1:1. This is a lot less concentrated than the old-time simple syrups, which were usually more like 2:1 of sugar to water. That's because drinks used to be much smaller, with a standard spirit shot measuring 1 ounce; a cocktail usually fit in a 3-ounce glass. So you needed to pack more sweet into less volume. For decades now, the trend has been for larger drinks, with a shot of 2 ounces and a total cocktail of at least 3½ ounces, sometimes much more. Glassware has grown commensurately, with cocktail glasses measuring 8, 10, or even 12 ounces. You want to fill up these glasses, or you'll look like a stingy host; but you don't want to fill them with liquor, or you'll be an irresponsible host. The solution (if you'll pardon the

pun) is a more diluted simple syrup. If, however, you're following recipes from an old book, or you want to serve smaller drinks, you can make the more concentrated syrup we will call rich simple syrup, in a 2:1 sugar-to-water mixture; do this on the stovetop.

Finally, there's the question of sugar. As mentioned above, you can use superfine bar sugar for quick mixing, or regular refined white sugar of the sort now sitting in your pantry. But other sugars are out there—various textures of white and various hues of brown, as well as turbinado, light and dark muscovado, and (one of my favorites for syrup) Demerara sugar (see Ingredient Note), especially when working with rum. Sometimes I'll also make a brown-sugar syrup for Irish coffee or heavy rum-punch drinks, but not for regular cocktails, because its high molasses content overpowers most other ingredients. Syrup is not meant to be the leading man but rather the fantastic character actor who makes everyone else look better.

INGREDIENTS
1 part bottled or filtered water
1 part sugar

☞ For a small quantity of 2 quarts or less, it's probably easiest to mix directly in the container in which you'll store the syrup. Combine the water and syrup in the container, and stir until the sugar dissolves completely. If your container has a sealed cover, by all means shake the mixture, and the sugar will dissolve more quickly.

For larger quantities, use the stovetop method. Bring the water just to a boil, turn off the flame, add the sugar, and stir constantly until it dissolves, which should be a matter of seconds. (Besides quantity, the choice of sugar should also dictate the method. It's fine to stir or shake superfine sugar. For the larger crystals of Demerara or raw sugar, it's best to use heat. For the in-between texture of refined sugar, either method will do.) Let the syrup cool completely before transferring it to a covered container for storage. It'll keep in the refrigerator—preferably sealed—for a couple of days.

HONEY SYRUP

Honey is a great flavor for some cocktails—I think it pairs particularly well with whiskey and makes for a great whiskey sour. But honey itself is too thick to use, so you need to thin it to a syrup. I usually use honey syrup with another sweetener to avoid an overwhelmingly honey-flavored drink, unless the cocktail is very grapefruit-oriented or otherwise extra-tart. For cocktail use, I suggest sticking with good old clover honey and staying away from strong flavors. Exceptions are wildflower honey, which can be truly lovely in a botanical-oriented cocktail, and a local honey paired with other local ingredients, which will not only create a local-flavored drink but also may help combat allergies.

INGREDIENTS
1 part bottled or filtered water
1 part honey

☞ In a saucepan, warm the water. Turn off the flame. Add the honey and stir until completely combined. You can store this in the refrigerator, covered, for up to 1 week. Or you can leave it on the kitchen counter, and it'll ferment into mead, which is something different entirely.

AGAVE SYRUP

Agave nectar, or *miel de maguey*, comes from the heart of the *pina*, the agave plant. This *agua miele* ("honey water") is a rich, warm, slightly vegetal sweetener that's a wonderful addition to drinks that already include the agave flavor (that is, tequila), especially margaritas, for a real sweet-and-sour effect. But agave syrup is not a great idea for drinks with a very clean profile, like daiquiris, because the vegetal taste would fight with the citrus and overwhelm the rum. The agave product you'll find in the store (organic food shops, health food stores, gourmet stores, online, in whatever section includes the honey) is usually called *nectar*. To make the syrup for cocktails, dilute it with an equal amount of water.

INGREDIENTS
1 part bottled or filtered water, at room temperature
1 part agave nectar

☞ Combine the water and nectar and stir constantly until completely combined. This syrup can be stored refrigerated for 1 week.

INGREDIENT NOTE

Demerara Sugar

Demerara sugar, made primarily in Guyana, is less processed than white sugar. Sugar production is accomplished by boiling the cane to remove crystals; when the sugarcane is boiled until all the brown is gone, the result is a white sugar, with a dark brown molasses as a leftover product. But if you do less boiling and leave in more crystals, you get a darker sugar with a larger grain; this is known as *raw* or *Demerara sugar*, and it's a lot more flavorful, with notes of butterscotch and vanilla as well as the expected molasses. It's these spicy notes that separate Demerara from regular brown sugar, which is all about molasses and not nearly the same flavor experience. There's also a Demerara rum, which I love to use combined with a syrup made from the same sugar. (To make this syrup, be sure to use the stovetop heat method, which you'll need to dissolve the large crystals.) I also like to use Demerara syrup in cocktails with intense fruits like pineapple and mango because the strong flavor of the sugar can stand up to the strong fruits. It also makes for a good pairing with rum punches, hot toddies, and rum drinks in general, as well as the occasional whiskey drink. But I counsel against using Demerara syrup for vodka or gin cocktails, where you don't want to lose the delicate botanicals under an avalanche of strong sugar flavors.

FOAM

Following the lead of kitchen wizards like Ferran Adrià of El Bulli Restaurant in Spain, bartenders have adapted some cutting-edge culinary techniques for the bar. The most widely used of Adrià's innovations is flavored foam—*espuma*—to enhance or heighten a flavor note in a dish. Foam also happened to be the most ridiculed of the Spanish master's innovations, dismissed as all style and not much substance (literally, of course, that is true). On the satisfaction scale when dining, foam is right up there with painted plates from the days of nouvelle cuisine. But in a beverage, it can be an effective flavor enhancer; after all, there is no expectation of something solid to follow, as there is on the food side. This is simply flavored foam atop flavored liquid, a match already enjoyed in cocktails such as Irish coffee as well as in the broad category of foamy sours and fruit drinks.

To make foam, you'll need a proper canister, and for this I recommend the iSi Thermo Whip, ½-liter (or pint) size. You also need 1 cream charger (not a CO_2 charger), which you should be able to find wherever you buy your canister, and gelatin sheets, which you'll find at a baking-supply shop. Finally, you'll need a good recipe for the ingredient combination, which, here in this book, you can find with a half dozen of the individual cocktail recipes (the Bobby Burns, Bronx, East India, Pink Lady, Pisco Punch, and Sazerac). When making foam, be sure to (1) fill the canister with no more than 1 pint of liquid; (2) be sure the gelatin is entirely dissolved before loading the charger; (3) fine-strain the mixture before loading the canister; (4) chill the liquid as well as the canister before loading; (5) make all seals tight; and (6) shake well before each use.

GARNISHES

Garnish is an important part of a well-made, properly presented cocktail. But garnish doesn't mean dumping any old piece of citrus into a drink. First of all, your garnish *must* be fresh—if it's not, you're defeating the entire point of both the flavors and the visuals. A mangy piece of hardened lemon peel, brown at the edges, is what I'd call shooting yourself in the garnish foot, providing no flavor and a negative appearance. And it should be generous, or you're likewise defeating the point of the gesture. It should be clean and attractive—wash and dry your fruit, remove any stickers, and scrape away any stamps with a knife; *all* garnish that touches a drink must be thoroughly washed. The garnish should also be cold. If not, what you're accomplishing is adding a reverse ice cube. Think about the effect of assaulting an ice-cold martini with three large room-temperature olives or filling a Manhattan's glass with warm cherries. The garnish should also be in the proper scale—a humongous slice of orange on a tiny glass is preposterous, as is a single tiny picholine olive in a gigantic dirty martini.

Finally, the garnish should be appropriate to the ingredients of the drink. A garnish that's completely unrelated to the cocktail is a bad show, except in the rare case of certain flowers (for example, the Sonya orchid for a Mai Tai or other tropical or tea-based drinks). On the other hand, a garnish that picks up the cocktail's ingredients can bring beauty, flavor, and often both to the glass. Sometimes multiple garnishes are fun and appropriate, especially with the Pimm's Cup (page 42), where seemingly an entire vegetable patch is used in the glass. The most common multiple-garnish situation is the classic flag—a slice of orange (or lemon, if that's the citrus in the drink) with a Maraschino cherry, whose contrasting colors resemble a flag. In international bartending competitions and the occasional overzealous bar, you'll sometimes find unusual garnishes cut into the shapes of birds, or flowers, or other origami-type projects. I myself happen to think this is both silly and misses the point, which is to make the drink experience an optimal one, not to show off the knife skills of the bartender. So my advice is to stick to the basics and to garnishes that highlight an ingredient in the drink, and to do them well. Here they are.

TWISTS

The most common garnishes are citrus twists or peels, which provide color to the presentation and, more important, flavor from their oils. So a peel should be cut in a way that emphasizes the oil cells in the rind and minimizes the white pith, which is bitter. I like to cut the peel very, very thin, and I like to do it as shortly as possible before using, so the oil is fresh and flavorful. If you have to cut peels in advance, be sure to cover them with plastic wrap. And when serving, never just dump the peel into the drink or balance it on the rim of the glass, or you're getting only the visual benefit. In order to get the flavor benefit as well, you need to release the oils somehow—by twisting, snapping, or igniting it (see Flamed Orange Peel, page 249) over the drink, so the oil gets into the cocktail. Note that lime peels are not particularly useful because their skins aren't thick enough to release much oil. To get extra lime oil into a drink, it's a better idea to grate the peel—the green part only, not the white—over the cocktail.

If you have good knife skills, here's how to cut a proper twist, using a

JUICE VERSUS GARNISH

Not all fruit is created equal, but all ripe, fresh fruits have equally important uses: juice and garnish. For example, the Meyer lemon is a beautiful piece of fruit with a thick, lustrous peel that contains lots of oil. But the Meyer is incredibly stingy with its juice. So if what you're looking for is a great twist, the Meyer is your lemon. But if you're looking for juice, or for a wedge to muddle, then skip the pretty, expensive Meyer and find yourself a cheaper, thin-skinned, ugly-duckling lemon that'll provide much more juice (but that you'd never hang from the edge of a glass). When juicing, be sure your fruit is at room temperature; if you're taking it out of the refrigerator, soak the fruit in hot water for 10 to 15 minutes before squeezing to loosen it up. And it's not a bad idea to roll it across the countertop a few times, applying pressure with your palm, to break the membranes and release the juice.

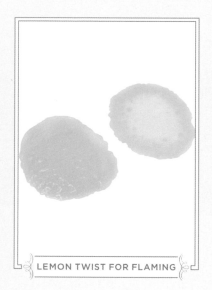

paring knife: Grasp the fruit firmly on the lower half, leaving the top clear for cutting. Beginning at the very top of the citrus, draw the knife carefully toward you, cutting as thin a peel as possible away from the fruit, about 1½ inches long, in the shape of an oval; the center of the oval might have a bit of white pith showing underneath, but the rest of the underside should just be the pithless peel. As your knife works its way around and down the peel, rotate the fruit toward you, always cutting from the top. When you get to the bottom of the fruit, you should have cut 10 to 12 twists that that will be perfect for releasing oil.

If you're not confident with a knife, here's a safer method. Cut ½ inch away from each pole, creating a level surface so you can set the fruit on its end. With the fruit on end, use your paring knife to slice downward, cutting away an oval with each slice, being careful to keep your fingers out of the guillotining blade.

LONG TWIST

This long twist is used in flutes or for Champagne drinks in any glass (though if you're doing it right, that should *always* be a flute). It is normally done with lemon.

SHORT, FAT TWIST

This rectangular shape is perfect for flaming.

HORSE'S NECK AND LONG SPIRAL PEEL

Cut this as you would peel an apple. See the instructions on pages 154 and 162.

WEDGES

Citrus wedges should look like the fruit they're cut from, a nice generous wedge that's recognizable as a portion of citrus. Don't butcher the fruit so much you can't discern the shape, but rather just remove about ⅛ inch from the poles (which get filled with dirt), then slice through the poles to halve the fruit. Lay each half on the cutting board, and divide each evenly into three or four wedges. Scrape away any seeds with the tip of a knife, then cover with plastic wrap until ready to use. Lemon wedges are fairly hardy and will last as long as a couple of days, but lime wedges oxidize quickly into something unattractive, so don't cut these until the last possible moment, and don't cut more fruit than you will use in a day. To make pineapple wedges for garnish, you want a slightly underripe pineapple. Leave the skin on, but cut off the ends. Cut the pineapple into round slices, about 1 inch thick. Then divide each disk into eight wedges.

PIECES FOR MUDDLING

I've done a lot of playing around with muddling—muddled fresh fruits are my signature, bordering on an obsession—and I've learned a few things. Fruit for muddling must be ripe and sweet, fresh and juicy. These are ingredients in your drinks, and, as part of the recipe, they must deliver their expected character, whether that's a sour note, a sweet ambrosial flavor, or the zinger aroma that makes the drink. Lemons and limes for muddling should be cut into eighths: one slice through the equator, then four slices to each half, creating a lot of surface area to the flesh. Oranges should be cut simply into slices. Pineapples should be skinned and cored, cut into thick slices, then those slices cut into eighths.

HORSE'S NECK GARNISH

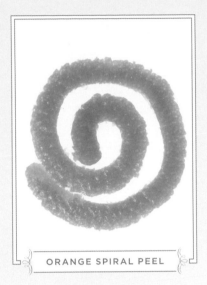

ORANGE SPIRAL PEEL

LEMON WEDGE

LIME WEDGE

PINEAPPLE WEDGE

LEMON FOR MUDDLING

LIME FOR MUDDLING

PINEAPPLE FOR MUDDLING

MANGO FOR MUDDLING

MINT GARNISH

MARASCHINO CHERRIES

SPRIGS

Herb sprigs, most notably mint, make their way into the occasional drink. For garnish, you want to choose a sprig from the very top of the plant, and the leaves from the very top of the sprig, which has the smallest leaves; the top 2 inches are what you should count on protruding from the drink, and the top of a good, healthy sprig should have 2 inches of pretty little leaves. If you have a choice, spearmint is the better variety for adorning a drink. For muddling after the topmost sprig is removed for garnish, simply strip the remaining leaves from the stalk and store them, refrigerated, until needed. I keep my herb garnish in water while using, but for storage I dry them off and place them in plastic bags in the fridge.

MARASCHINO CHERRIES

Today's Maraschino cherry is a poor relative of what was once a specialty food item—a Marasca cherry cured in a liqueur based on itself—that never really made it into the twentieth century, as post–industrial revolution American companies figured out a way to mimic the almond flavor of the original using artificial ingredients. But we have to use what we can find, and in the modern era that means looking for both the liqueur and the cherries made by Luxardo, or settling for the bright-red variety from the supermarket. For more on the Maraschino cherry, see page 101.

OLIVES

Olives are important to the martini drinker, so you should always provide them generously. And it's not a bad idea to match your olive size to the glass size. The classic martini olive has long been the pitted Spanish variety called *manzanilla*, with no pimiento. But with today's deplorable fad for giant martini glasses, the little manzanilla can look ridiculous. So if you or your guests insist on monstrous glasses, find some medium queen olives to put in them. Whichever size you use, remember: Keep your olives cold, or you'll ruin the martini. See the resource section (page 264) for good olive companies.

COCKTAIL ONIONS

Pearl onions, like perfect little moons packed in brine, are the key to the ultimate martini for select aficionados. For them, whether the spirit is gin or vodka, without the onion it is just another drink. If you count these devotees of the Gibson as friends, you can expect them to drop by on a regular basis if you keep a jar of Crosse and Blackwell cocktail onions in the fridge. Follow the same rules as with the olive: no more than three in a glass at a time, and the rest if desired on a small garnish plate; and chilled, please.

GLASSWARE AND TOOLS

GLASSWARE

Glassware evolved dramatically over the course of the past hundred years. At the beginning of the twentieth century, drinks were served in small glasses made of glass. Then the middle of the century saw an explosion in nonglass vessels, a trend pioneered by Victor Bergeron and Donn Beach, who served drinks in coconuts and bamboo, miniature rum kegs and old-fashioned sugar pots, metal and ceramic, anything. In the contemporary era, these gimmicky containers have mostly gone the way of curiosities and collectibles, and we're back to the realm of the all-glass bar. But many of these glasses have grown immensely, and the classic V-shaped cocktail glass—also known as a martini glass—that once held about 3 ounces is now produced in sizes up to 14 ounces. In *The Fine Art of Mixing Drinks* by David Embury, published in 1949, he says about cocktail glasses, "You will find them in sizes ranging from 2 to 3½ ounces. Get the large ones—not less than 3 ounces." If you came across a 3-ounce cocktail glass in a bar today, "large" would definitely not be the description to come to mind.

Whatever the glass, it must be cleaned. When it comes out of the cabinet, it needs dusting or polishing, at the very least; although modern dishwashers can turn out sparkling glassware, a streak or cloud can go a long way toward ruining a drinking experience. So polish with a lint-free cloth, or, in a pinch, use a paper towel.

You'll want to chill the glass for most drinks served in cocktail glasses, especially if the glasses are on the large side; a drink is never served in a cocktail glass with ice. So a chilled glass is your only way to keep the drink cold once it's in the drinker's hands. If your freezer can't accommodate all the glasses you want to chill, you can get it done on the counter. Fill the glasses with ice cubes and water, and they'll chill up nicely in a few minutes, albeit without the type of full-body frost that comes from the freezer's blast of enveloping cold.

Finally, it's crucial that the glass be appropriate to the cocktail, and the most important aspect of its appropriateness is size (although shape or material may also be crucial for the proper mixing of some drinks, such as the Pousse Café and mint julep). And size really does matter, but not in the bigger-is-better sense; I happen to think that today's giant glasses are not only an abomination, they're downright dangerous. A martini is not meant to be an 8-ounce drink—that's simply too much strong spirit. Most drinks are meant to be 3 ounces, maybe 4—that is, 12 to 15 good cold sips. But if you put this quantity into a 10-ounce glass, you look stingy. And if you fill a 10-ounce glass with something like a martini, you quickly have someone inebriated. The solution to the conundrum of the 10-ounce glass is simple: Don't use a 10-ounce glass.

COCKTAIL GLASSES

There are three shapes traditionally called *cocktail glasses*, and they are somewhat interchangeable. People sometimes call these things *martini glasses*, just as they call nearly anything served in a V-shaped glass a

V-SHAPED

NICK AND NORA

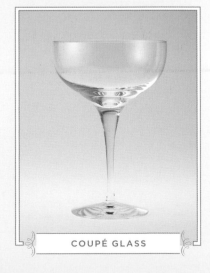

COUPÉ GLASS

martini; as the drink morphs from something specific into a generic idea, the name takes on different meanings. But I still refer to cocktails as cocktails, and cocktail glasses as cocktail glasses, and here they are:

V-SHAPED COCKTAIL GLASS

This is the iconic shape for martinis and Manhattans. The V-shaped glass made its debut in the 1925 Paris exhibition called the Exposition Internationale des Arts Décoratifs et Industriels Modernes, which eventually became known as the Art Deco show. But it wasn't until after World War II that this style of glass became truly popular, and it was in the 1950s and 1960s that the neon shape became the universal symbol for cocktail. Although these glasses are now available up to 12 ounces, I think it's a mistake to use anything larger than 5½ ounces.

NICK AND NORA COCKTAIL GLASS

If I'm serving a retro-oriented cocktail like the Bronx, I like to use this glass as a nod to history (and the history, in case you need it, is that Nick and Nora are the Charles couple in the *Thin Man* movie series, starring William Powell and Myrna Loy as socialite-detectives who were rarely cocktail-less); this was the standard cocktail glass in the early part of the twentieth century. The business portion of the glass is in the shape of a bowl, not a V.

COUPÉ

The coupé is a great shape for a straight-up daiquiri, El Presidente, margarita, and the nontraditional cocktail. (My martinis will always find a home in the V-shaped cocktail glass.) The coupé was originally called the Marie Antoinette glass because the shape of the bowl was supposedly designed to hold her breast—if not the actual flesh, then the idea of it. Like the V-shaped glass, it should be no larger than 6 ounces (Marie was not a Hooters waitress).

HIGHBALL

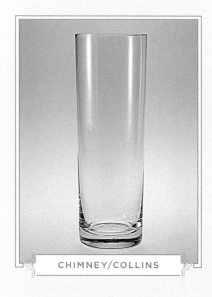

CHIMNEY/COLLINS

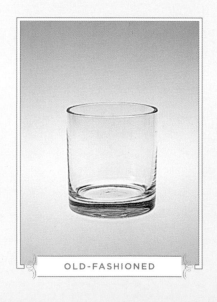

OLD-FASHIONED

HIGHBALLS

These tall, straight sided glasses should be 10 to 12 ounces.

HIGHBALL

The standard highball glass should be 10 to 12 ounces, suitable for nearly any highball cocktail with soda, and also for beer.

CHIMNEY OR COLLINS

These tall, skinny highballs are somewhat hard to find today, but they're elegant and cut a beautiful line for summer drinks like a Tom Collins or a sour, especially when accented with a really thin straw and delicately garnished. A chimney glass can be between 10 and 14 ounces; it is designed to be one ice cube wide, so the cubes stack one upon another to fill the glass.

DELMONICO OR FIZZ GLASS

Also somewhat hard to find, but easier if you look for it under the name juice glass. These 8- to 10-ounce glasses are appropriate for fizzes like the Ramos or the Golden, which are shaken with ice and then served without it.

ICED TEA GLASS

These big glasses are 14 to 16 ounces and are inappropriate for nearly every cocktail other than the Zombie (page 190) and the Long Island Iced Tea (page 84), but even those are nicely served in a Collins or chimney. I think the best use for an iced tea glass is for good old iced tea.

ROCKS OR OLD-FASHIONED GLASSES

For people who enjoy any spirit over ice, like a scotch, a rocks glass is essential. The key is a thick bottom, to give the glass heft, because there won't be much liquid in the glass to do the job—you never fill these more than one-quarter or, at most, one-third full. I happen to love the look and feel of an oversized rocks glass—8 to 12 ounces, instead of a mere 6 to 8—breaking my normal rule of preferring more modest-sized vessels. But with very little liquid in it, and even with no ice, the nice big glass has a feeling of generosity to it. There are a few variations:

OLD-FASHIONED

This is the standard short glass, 6 to 8 ounces.

DOUBLE OLD-FASHIONED, MAI TAI

This 10- to 12-ounce glass—really a huge container—is sometimes known as a bucket glass, but that version usually flares, having a thinner bottom and a wider top. It's appropriate for Mai Tais and larger drinks on the rocks.

CORDIAL AND OTHER SMALL GLASSES

UP-SOUR

For whiskey sours, pisco sours, and other similar drinks served up. You don't see the small old-fashioned glasses, so these cocktails now often go in V-shaped glasses, which I think is totally inappropriate. Instead, use a London docks or port glass.

LONDON DOCKS

This little glass with a short stem—sort of a dwarf wineglass—is the perfect size for a snort of fortified wine such as port or sweet wine such as Sauternes. It's also appropriate for straight liqueurs, cordials, even straight hard spirits that are served neat, without ice, as well as the occasional straight-up sour-style cocktail like the pisco sour. And many people prefer their cognac or brandy in a glass like this, as the French do, instead of a snifter; this shape allows the alcohol vapors to escape while retaining most of the aromas. England has long been the main market for port, Madeira, sherry, brandy—all the sweetened, fortified wine products, most of which were made by companies owned by the English. So a lot of this wine would end up, in barrels, on the London docks. To inspect the deliveries, an owner or his agent would pop the bung, put a little liq-

MAI TAI

LONDON DOCKS

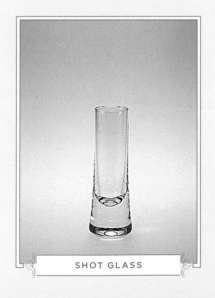

SHOT GLASS

uid into a glass he carried around, and taste to make sure he was getting what he was paying for.

PONY AND COPITA

Both of these miniature versions of the London docks or port glass are perfect for sherry; the pony is 1 ounce, while the copita is 1½ or 2 ounces. And I happen to think that fino sherry is nearly a perfect beverage, wonderful with food, especially any kind of cream soup. Both of these glasses are a great shape for toasting and a great size for sharing just a little something.

SHOT GLASS

A shot is actually a measure, not just a glass style; it's 1½ ounces. But these smaller glasses, grouped together under the name *shot glasses,* should be tailored to the specific drink. If you're using it for straight-spirit shooters, I think it should be ¾ ounce or at most 1 ounce, because the idea of the shooter is a little extra something—a side dish, not the entrée—and so you don't want a full 1½ ounces for that, which is too much alcohol. If you're mixing a regular cocktail and dividing it into shots, with a total of maybe ¼ to ½ ounce actual hard liquor in a given serving, then a full-sized shot glass might work perfectly. But for those incorrigible types who already have a drink in front of them and say, "Oh, man, let's do shots," what are you going to do? A nice, thick-bottomed ¾-ounce shot glass, that's what.

WINE AND BEER GLASSES

ALL PURPOSE WINEGLASS

This is the wineglass style that's neither explicitly for red (which can be a squat, bulbous balloon glass or a tall burgundy) nor explicitly for white (with straighter sides than the red glasses) but appropriate for either as well as for spritzers, wine coolers, and sangria.

PILSNER

If you're a big beer drinker, this glass—a very slight V that's slightly wider at the top, with a round disk on the bottom to keep it balanced—is the perfect vehicle for lager.

FLUTE

A lot of great cocktails are made with Champagne, including the most basic Champagne cocktail as well as a Pick-Me-Up and my own delicious version of a Champagne Cobbler. In the modern era, when we want to conserve our bubbles, they should be served in the tall flute with the reverse taper at the very top.

SPECIALTY GLASSES

HURRICANE

This flared glass is so named because it's shaped like a hurricane lamp, not because the drinks that come in it can wreak hurricane-like havoc.

BOCA GRANDE

Similar to a hurricane, but with more flare to the top and bottom.

IRISH COFFEE GLASS

Irish coffee is one of those cocktails that rely on the right glass to guide the bartender into the proper proportions, holding only 7 or 8 ounces; after a shot of liquor and the sugar are poured in, there's room for only the right amount of coffee, which prevents the bartender from overpouring and drowning the spirit. If you don't have an Irish coffee glass, use the smaller 8-ounce mug or a small white wineglass.

TEARDROP CHAMPAGNE

IRISH COFFEE

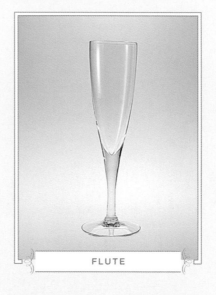

FLUTE

HOT TODDY MUG

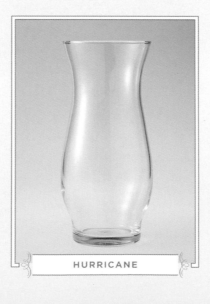

HURRICANE

POUSSE CAFÉ

CLASSIC PUNCH

HOT TODDY MUG

With a wide base that tapers to a thinner top, this mug retains the aromas and the heat while featuring a handle that prevents you from burning your hand.

WHISKEY TASTER

If you love whiskey, get a set of these glasses in the range of 3 ounces. They gather the aromas without trapping the heavy alcohol fumes.

POUSSE CAFÉ

A variant of the pony and copita, the Pousse glass is a little taller, with straighter sides. But the most important distinction is that it flares out at the top, instead of in, which allows you to get your spoon into the glass to construct the layered cocktail.

PUNCH BOWL AND GLASSES

I'm a big fan of punches, and I like them served in a proper bowl, ringed with 6-ounce cups. But this is a big investment—and takes up a lot of space. If you're not going to use it, I wouldn't put this item at the top of any shopping list.

BRANDY SNIFTERS

You probably need to a have a few of these around to have a truly well-appointed glassware repertoire; the snifter is a fine way to serve cognac or cognac-based cordials. Certain after-dinner drinks, like the White Russian, are sometimes requested in oversized snifters.

ABSINTHE GLASS

The nineteenth-century favorite was a squat, V-shaped glass with virtually no stem, usually decorated with faceted sides. These aren't easy to find, because neither is absinthe.

MARGARITA GLASS

This is the traditional glass for the Margarita straight-up or frozen, and is really the standard in Mexican restaurants. The shape says Margarita, and you shouldn't find any other drink in this glass.

MANHATTAN GLASS

In many bars today, Manhattans are served in the V-shaped cocktail glass. But in the 1950s the Manhattan always had its own glass, which is still available in classic cocktail lounges all around the country.

BRANDY SNIFTER

ABSINTHE TWO-PART

MARGARITA

MANHATTAN

COCKTAIL SHAKERS AND STRAINERS

The retail market is rich with choices for cocktail shakers, but nearly all the differences are about ornamentation and aesthetics, not function. There have ever been, and still are, only two categories of shakers: The Boston shaker is a two-piece model (a glass and a metal cup), and the Cobbler shaker is a three-piece affair (a large cup, a top, and a twist-off cap, all usually made of metal). The Cobbler shaker is the one with the more complex and highly stylized designs—if you can imagine a shape, someone has probably created a Cobbler shaker in it. But the Boston shaker is more versatile, easier to use, and the choice of most professionals. The glass is usually 16 ounces, fitting snugly into the larger metal cup of 26 or more ounces; you use a separate strainer to decant the liquid into the serving glass. Both the Boston and the Cobbler have the same downside: It's difficult to separate the pieces because pressure builds up and a seal is created while you shake the cold liquids. But the Boston seal is usually easier to break. With the glass on top and holding both parts firmly, use the heel of your hand to sharply hit the rim of the metal part. And the Boston has the important advantage of serving two purposes—shaking and stirring—while the Cobbler is really only good for shaking, because you don't want to stir in a metal container, ever. Stirring is a ceremony and a show, and people should be able to see the action—the ice spinning around and around as a pack, led by a glass rod or a bar spoon, hearing the quiet clink against the glass through the thirty hypnotic revolutions, anticipation building as the drink chills, dilutes, gets ready for the mouth. It would be a crime to hide this in a metal cup. So by all means use a Cobbler for shaking—shake hard, holding with both hands, creating a sound reminiscent of a machine gun. But you should still have a Boston shaker around for stirring.

With your Boston shaker, you'll need a strainer, of which there are also two basic types: the Hawthorn strainer (the one you'll find behind most professional bars) has a spring around the perimeter, and the julep strainer, which looks like a short-handled version of a cooking skimmer or strainer. Both are fine—the Hawthorn is the better choice for the metal part, while the julep is preferable for the glass (with the bowl-shaped side forming a small bucket to hold the ice and other solids). It's best to strain by pouring down the side of the glass, to avoid spilling, and it's a good show to pour in a circle and then to pull the shaker away from the glass for a final flourish. If you're straining a drink that has bits of muddled fruit and herbs in it, strain from the metal portion of the Boston shaker, then double-strain through the julep strainer held over the top of the serving glass. Indeed, sometimes a third strainer is needed, because with today's culinary style of cocktail recipes, all kinds of berries and spices are ending up in the shaker. For these fine bits, strain through a tea strainer held over the glass; the V-shaped tea strainers are preferred for this operation, since they direct the flow of liquid directly into the glass.

JIGGERS AND BAR SPOONS

Jiggers are the little measuring devices, with two different-sized cups on either side, which are essential for getting the proper proportions. If you have two jiggers—one of ¾ ounce over 1½ ounce, the other ½ ounce over 1—you're covered on 90 percent of the measurements you'll need to make to mix cocktails. And bar spoons should take care of the other 10 percent of the measures: When you fill the common twisted-handle spoon twice, you have ¼ ounce (see page 263 for common conversion factors for the bar).

SHAKEN VERSUS STIRRED

When do you shake, and when do you stir? The answer is that you shake when the finished cocktail would benefit from the resulting effervescence. This is most true for sour or fruity drinks, where you want to tone down the sweetness by filling your mouth with millions of little air bubbles to go along with the sugar. On the other hand, you want to stir those cocktails that are pure spirit, with no juice, such as the martini and the Manhattan. The texture and the weight of the liquid are paramount—you want it to be cold, heavy, and silky, which is what you get from stirring, not frothy, light, and effervescent, which is what shaking will get you. When you hold up a martini, you want to see straight through it; when you take a sip of a margarita or a daiquiri, you want it to feel light and bubbly. That's the difference between stirred and shaken.

And there's also in-between: For a Bloody Mary, stirring wouldn't suffice, but shaking would break down the integrity of the tomato juice, creating a foamy liquid with no weight, a very unsatisfying drink. So here you want to employ what's probably the oldest drink-mixing technique, rolling: You pour the ingredients back and forth from one container to another until well mixed.

BOSTON SHAKER SET

MODERN HAWTHORN STRAINER

VINTAGE HAWTHORN STRAINER

JULEP STRAINER

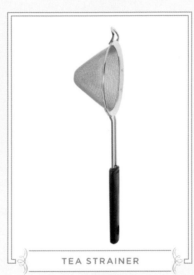

TEA STRAINER

JIGGERS

COCKTAIL SPOONS

SANTOKU & PARING KNIFE

CHANNEL KNIFE

ALL-PURPOSE GRATER

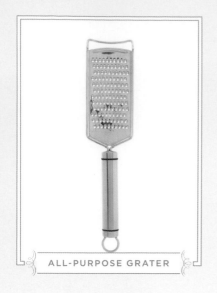

PEELER

NUTMEG GRATER

PUG & TAG BAR MUDDLERS

HAND JUICER

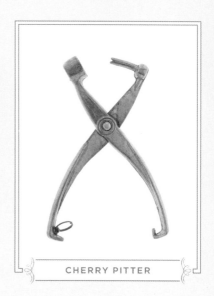

CHERRY PITTER

TONGS

KITCHEN SHEARS

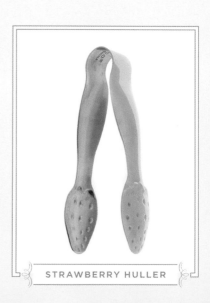

STRAWBERRY HULLER

KNIVES AND OTHER SHARP THINGS

You'll need an 8- or 10-inch chef's knife for cutting pineapple and other larger fruits, but otherwise a 4-inch paring knife should serve nearly all of your garnishing needs. The exception is for cutting the horse's neck garnish (page 154), for which you should really have a zester (also called a *channel knife*); this will also make quick work of cutting citrus peels. I have a small wood-handled channel knife that I purchased from barproducts.com whose blade cuts a bit deeper than the average channel knife, creating a spiral peel with more substance that holds together well. You can also use a vegetable peeler for extracting a wide but thin citrus peel without any pith (I have an OXO model that does a good job of this) as well as for plain old peeling. If you're doing a lot of slicing and peeling but don't have a lot of confidence in your knife skills, cut-resistant gloves might be a good idea. And I often use a grater for grating the peel of citrus (particularly limes) and spices as a dusting over the top of a drink: A flat grater with a little handle is good for citrus and even horseradish, and a tiny little rasp is perfect for nutmeg, and it is meant to live in the jar with the whole nutmegs.

MUDDLERS

Muddlers are a crucial tool for the contemporary bar, to release the flavors of fresh fruit and herbs; I like the Mister Mojito brand or the Pug Muddlers from Chris Gallagher (see Resources, page 264). The muddler should be made of hardwood and should not be varnished in any fashion (the varnish eventually comes off—into your drinks). In a pinch you can use a wooden cooking spoon, preferably a very thick one, or a pestle can also suffice. I think you should have two or three muddlers on hand because more and more cocktail parties are hands-on affairs rather than the passive chitchat sessions they used to be.

JUICERS

A lot of electric options are available for jucing and they certainly have their uses, especially if you're going to get involved with fresh vegetable juices or tropical fruit juices (papaya and mango, for example). But for run-of-the-mill citrus in reasonable quantities, hand juicers do the trick just fine, and they won't cost a fortune or dominate your counter space.

OTHER HANDY TOOLS

I have several tools I use only seasonally or occasionally when a recipe requires. They are not critical for everyday preparations, but I am glad to have them when the occasion arises. When summer rolls around, I give my cherry pitter a workout for Cherry Caipiroskas and other muddled drinks with cherry flavors. Tongs are a welcome tool when adding ice cubes or olives to a cocktail. And when I clean up a pineapple for display on my tiki bar setup, a pair of kitchen shears is indispensable; shears also come in handy when cutting lemon and orange peels to size and shape for fancy twists. A small funnel for filling decorative bottles with homemade syrups is much better than trying to hit a 1/2-inch-wide hole at the top of a bottle with a 1/2-inch stream of liquid. And, finally, I use a strawberry huller to avoid cutting away the whole top of the strawberry when I remove the green tops.

NOTE

Measures for the Bar

1 dash = 6 drops

1 teaspoon = 1 bar spoon = 12 dashes = 1/8 ounce

1 splash = 1/2 ounce

2 teaspoons = 2 bar spoons = 1/4 ounce

3 teaspoons – 3 bar spoons = 1/2 ounce = 1 tablespoon

2 tablespoons = 1 ounce = 1/8 cup = 1 pony = 3 centiliters

1 shot = 1 1/2 ounces

2 ounces = 1/4 cup

1 cup = 8 ounces = 1/2 pint = 1/4 quart

1 pint = 2 cups = 16 ounces = 1 mixing glass

1 quart = 2 pints = 4 cups = 32 ounces

1 wine bottle = 750 milliliters = 25.4 ounces = a fifth (which means 1/5 gallon)

1/2 bottle = 375 milliliters = 12.7 ounces

1 split = 187 milliliters = 6.4 ounces

RESOURCES

INDUSTRY NEWS, INFORMATIONAL WEBSITES, AND INSTRUCTIONS

WWW.ALCOHOLREVIEWS.COM
Online monthly beer, wine, spirits, and cocktails magazine.

WWW.ARDENTSPIRITS.COM
Gary Regan's e-mail newsletter, entertaining and informative, reaches more than 7,000 consumers, bartenders, and industry professionals worldwide. Gary also offers a Bartender Database that puts liquor companies and restaurants in touch with professional bartenders all over the globe. To subscribe contact: gary@ardentspirits.com.

WWW.BEVERAGEALCOHOL
RESOURCE.COM
A series of comprehensive spirits and mixology training programs designed to provide a complete education in spirits and mixology. Contact: kingcocktail@aol.com.

BURTON AND REA (BAR)
John Burton and Brian Rea's bimonthly newsletter featuring marketing trends, recipes, liquor laws, product review, bar management, and the history of the beverage business. To subscribe contact: johncburton@msn.com or barguru@aol.com.

WWW.CANTILEVERBARS.COM
This amazing cantilevered sink handles waste of all kind and never clogs or overflows.

WWW.COCKTAIL.COM
Martin Doudoroff and Ted Haigh's cocktail database is a great source for recipes and spirits information.

WWW.DRINKBOY.COM
Robert Hess's mixology-dedicated chat room was the first of its kind and remains the most popular mixologist website for exchanging information and ideas. Hess also offers a product guide, classic cocktail recipes, tools, and articles.

WWW.EXTREMEBARTENDING.COM
For videos, information, and competitions in flair bartending.

WWW.KINGCOCKTAIL.COM
Dale DeGroff presents award-winning cocktail recipes, information on bar training courses and events, and a mixology instructional DVD: *Making Great Cocktails*.

WWW.MISSCHARMING.COM
Extensive bartending information and bar novelty items.

WWW.THEMODERNMIXOLOGIST.COM
Tony Abou-Ganim's bartending website. *Modern Mixology: Making Great Cocktails at Home with Tony Abou-Ganim,* an instructional video, is available from various sources.

WWW.SMALLSCREENNETWORK.COM
"The Cocktail Spirit with Robert Hess" podcast. Cocktail videos with technique and recipe information.

WWW.SPIRITJOURNAL.COM
Paul Pacult's quarterly newsletter rating spirits, wine, and beer.

MUSEUMS

MUSEUM OF THE AMERICAN COCKTAIL (WWW.MUSEUMOFTHE AMERICANCOCKTAIL.ORG)
A nonprofit organization founded by a group of renowned mixologists, spirits experts, and food and drink writers for the purpose of advocating education in mixology and preserving the rich history of the cocktail. Its unique exhibit, designed by Ted Haigh and located at the Riverwalk Mall in New Orleans, celebrates two hundred years of the cocktail and includes Prohibition-era literature and music; vintage cocktail shakers, glassware, tools, and gadgets; memorabilia; and photographs from the collections of the founders.

VIRTUAL ABSINTHE MUSEUM (WWW.OXYGENEE.COM)
The premier absinthe resource on the Net, with history, art and antiques, distillation, drinking ritual, comprehensive absinthe FAQ, and absinthe collectors' forum.

SOUTHERN FOOD AND BEVERAGE MUSEUM (WWW.SOUTHERNFOOD.ORG)
A nonprofit organization based in New Orleans, dedicated to the discovery, understanding, and celebration of the culture of food and drink in the South. Located at the Riverwalk Mall in New Orleans.

SOUTHERN FOODWAYS ALLIANCE
An institute headquartered at the University of Mississippi in Oxford, Mississippi, that documents and celebrates the diverse food cultures of the American South.

PROFESSIONAL ASSOCIATIONS

BEVERAGE ALCOHOL RESOURCE (WWW.BEVERAGEALCOHOL RESOURCE.COM)
A series of comprehensive spirits and mixology training programs designed to provide a complete education in spirts and mixology.

U.S. BARTENDERS GUILD
(WWW.USBG.ORG)
The USBG works to enhance the prestige and status of the professional bartender, and to improve the image of the beverage industry.

GENERAL BAR SUPPLIES, GLASSWARE, AND BAR DESIGNS

WWW.BARPRODUCTS.COM
Wonderful resource for all bar tools at great prices.

WWW.BARWORKS.COM
Bartending products and supplies for bar owners and flair bartenders.

WWW.CANTILEVERBARS.COM
Calabrese sinks are available as a stand-alone unit, or as part of Cantilever bars. Contact: kingcocktail@aol.com

WWW.CORRECTPRODUCTS.COM
Full line of bar tools and other cocktail essentials for wholesale purchases.

WWW.ISINORTHAMERICA.COM
iSi products, Thermo cream canisters, and soda siphons for foam (espuma) preparations. Call 800-447-2426 for iSi North America Inc.

WWW.KOLD-DRAFT.COM
Manufacturer of ice machines that produce cold dense ice cubes in three sizes. Call 800-840-9577.

WWW.MINNERSDESIGNS.COM
Kevin McGrinder's Manhattan showroom for all types of bar glassware.

WWW.ULTIMATEBARCHEF.COM
Top-quality products including premium spirits, mixers, garnishes, bar tools, glassware, and services.

NOVELTY AND HARD-TO-FIND ITEMS

Corkscrews and wine accessories: www.FinelyCorked.com.

Lewis Ice Bag: www.beverage factory.com.

Mini martini glasses: www.4yourparty.com or 877-228-3701.

Moscow Mule copper mugs: Bridge Kitchenware (212-688-4220 or www.bridgekitchenware.com).

Muddlers: Excellent quality muddlers can be purchased online from www.themodernmixologist.com or JCGallagher08@hotmail.com or www.mistermojito.com.

Silver and gold edible flecks: www.easyleafproducts.com or lynnneuberg@nnigroup.com or 800-569-5323.

Speed pourers: The type you'll find in most bars are 285-50; the one with the wider cork is a 285-60. Both available at www.evo-lution.org.

Tiki bar, palapa kit, and palm thatch: Bikini Tiki Bar Factory; cigar gifts and accessories: www.MensGifts4Less.com.

FOODS

Frozen fruit purées: Perfect Purée of Napa Valley (www.perfectpuree.com) offers a line of all-natural frozen fruit purées through their website to consumers in the United States, Canada, and Mexico.

Fruit and spice syrups: Sonoma Syrups Co. (www.sonomasyrup.com or karincampion@sbcglobal.net) for fruit and spice syrups and extracts for food and cocktail preparation.

Demerara sugar: The Gilway Company Ltd. (17 Arcadian Avenue, Paramus, NJ 07652, mail@thegilway company.com).

Depaz cane syrup: Imported from Martinique, this nonalcoholic, pure Depaz cane syrup contains only two ingredients: cane sugar and filtered water. Available from dozens of online sources.

Cocktail cherries: Luxardo cherries are distributed by Preiss Imports, available through their website www.preissimports.com.

Premium cocktail olives: Dacosta (contact Valerie Oldham at 856-854-6060, or Voldham@ ChaseSalesCo.com).

Pickled vegetables: Metzger Specialty Brands (212-957-0055) for Tillen Farms' exceptional range of perfectly pickled vegetables grown in Washington State.

Ginger beer: www.ajstephans.com.

Peychaud's Bitters and Gary Regan's Orange Bitters #6: www.BuffaloTrace.com.

Fee Brothers Bitters: An extensive line of bitters and other cocktail condiments is available at www.FeeBrothers.com.

Stirrings cocktail ingredients: Made from all fresh and natural ingredients; available at www.stirrings.com.

BIBLIOGRAPHY

BAKER, CHARLES H., JR. *The Gentleman's Companion: Being an Exotic Drinking Book or, Around the World with a Jigger, Beaker and Flask.* New York: Derrydale Press, 1939.

BEACH, PHOEBE, AND ARNOLD BITNER. *Hawaii Tropical Rum Drinks and Cuisine by Don the Beachcomber.* Honolulu, HI: Mutual Publishing, 2001.

BERGERON, VICTOR. *Trader Vic's Book of Food and Drink.* Garden City, NY: Doubleday, 1946.

———. *Trader Vic's Rum Cookery and Drinkery.* Garden City, NY: Doubleday, 1974.

BERRY, JEFF, *Beachbum Berry's Sippin' Safari.* San Jose, CA: SLG Publishing, 2007.

———. *Beachbum Berry's Taboo Table.* San Jose, CA: SLG Publishing, 2005.

———. *Beachbum Berry's Intoxica!* San Jose, CA: SLG Publishing, 2002.

BYRON, O. H. *The Modern Bartender's Guide.* New York: Excelsior, 1884.

CONSIDINE, BOB. *Toots.* New York: Meredith, 1969.

CRADDOCK, HARRY. *The Savoy Cocktail Book.* London: Constable, 1930.

CROCKETT, ALBERT STEVENS. *Old Waldorf Bar Days.* New York: Aventine, 1931.

DOXAT, JOHN. *The World of Drinks and Drinking.* London: Ward Lock, 1971.

DUFFY, PATRICK GAVIN. *Official Mixer's Manual.* Alta, 1934.

EMBURY, DAVID. *The Fine Art of Mixing Cocktails.* Garden City, NY: Doubleday, 1949.

FELTON, ERIC. *How's Your Drink?* Chicago, IL: Surrey Books, 2007.

HAIGH, TED. *Vintage Spirits and Forgotten Cocktails.* Beverly, MA: Quarry, 2004.

HANEY, JESSE. *Haney's Steward & Barkeeper's Manual: A Complete and Practical Guide for preparing all kinds of Plain and Fancy Mixed Drinks and Popular Beverages, being the Most Approved Formulas Known in the Profession, designed for Hotels, Steamers, Club Houses, &c., &c., to which is appended recipes for Liqueurs, Cordials, Bitters, Syrups, etc., etc.* New York: Jesse Haney, 1869.

KAPPELER, GEORGE J. *Modern American Drinks: How to Mix and Serve All Kinds of Cups and Drinks.* Akron, OH: Saalfield, 1900.

MACELHONE, HARRY. *ABC of Mixing Cocktails.* London: Dean & Sons, 1919.

MACCIONI, SIRIO, WITH PETER ELLIOT. *Sirio: The Story of My Life and Le Cirque.* Hoboken, NJ: Wiley, 2004.

SCHMIDT, WILLIAM. *The Flowing Bowl: When and What to Drink.* New York: Charles L. Webster, 1892.

WONDRICH, DAVID. *Imbibe! From Absinthe Cocktail to Whiskey Smash.* New York: Perigee, 2007.

Acknowledgments

Thank you to Chris Pavone for taking my bartender's ramblings and turning them into a lively book.

Thank you to extraordinary photographer David Kressler, "Mr. Digital," and to my sons Leo and Blake for making our days in the studio a creative journey that ended with beautiful photography.

Thanks to my agent, Susan Ginsburg, for her continued support and for her good advice and commonsense approach to solving problems.

Special thanks to Brian Rea for access to his extraordinary library of vintage cocktail books.

Thank you to Rica Allannic, my editor at Clarkson Potter, for her keen eye and intelligent editing. She nudged and poked at the manuscript, ferreting out the ambiguities and inconsistencies.

Thank you to everyone at Clarkson Potter for making it possible to share my cocktail adventures with readers everywhere.

Thank you to Will Shine and Aisha Sharpe of Contemporary Cocktails for their help in the "laboratory."

Thank you to Minner's Designs for the loan of their vintage and classic glassware.

Finally, thank you to Jill, my wife, for her love and support in all my projects, but mostly for her extraordinary talent and creativity in our business and in her art.

INDEX

absinthe and substitutes, 12, 13; foam, 49
Absinthe Drip, 12
Adonis Cocktail, 14
agave syrup, 247
ale: in Friar Briar's Sack Posset, 221; in Royal Posset, 221
Alexander, 212–13
Alexander Frappé, 213
Alexandra Special, 213
amaretto, in London Iced Tea, 85
Amaretto di Saronno, in Italian egg cream, 216
American Beauty Cocktail, 59
Americano, 94
Americano Highball, 144–45
Anchor Distillery's Hotaling's Whiskey, 164
añejo rum: in Bahama Mama, 170; in Donn Beach's Mai Tai, 182; in Flamingo, 173; in Golden Girl, 219; in Mai Tai, 180; in Trader Vic's Navy Grog, 177
Angostura bitters, 14
anisette, 212
Aperol, in Cuzco, 133
applejack, 31; in Jack Rose, 31; in the original Pink Lady, 97; -pomegranate foam, 97
apple schnapps, in Dubonnet Kiss, 74
Appleton white rum, in Sevilla, 243
apricot liqueur, 69; in Coctel Algeria, 69
aquavit, in Danish Mary, 149
Arancio Americano, 145
Armstrong, Kevin, 221
Asayla whiskey, in The Compass Club, 198
Aviation, 101

B-52, 45
Bacardi rum, 61, 131; cocktail, 60–61; in Golden Girl, 219; in Pisco Bell-Ringer, 133; in Prestige Cocktail, 76; in Trader Vic's Navy Grog, 177
Bahama Mama, 170–71
Baileys Irish Cream: in B-52, 45; in Mudslide, 217

Banshee, 225
Bar Sol Pisco: in Bell-Ringer, 133; in Coctel Algeria, 69; in Cuzco, 133; in Pisco Punch, 200; in Pisco Sour, 132; in Punch Royale, 201
Baum, Joseph, 8, 58, 69, 70, 131, 148
Bay Breeze, 150, 151
Beach, Donn, 68, 170, 174, 175, 178, 190
Beach, Phoebe, 180, 182, 190
Bee's Kiss, 63
Bee's Knees, 62
Bellini, 64
Benedictine, 18, 112, 240; in Between the Sheets, 136; in Bobby Burns, 18; in Bull's Manhattan, 35; foam, 19; in Friar Briar's Sack Posset, 221; in Golden Age Pousse Cafés, 45; in Kentucky Colonel, 19; in Singapore sling, 163
Bergeron, Victor (Trader Vic), 170, 174, 175, 178, 180, 208
Berns, Charles E., 140
Between the Sheets, 136
Big Spender, 233
Bijou, 66–67
bitters, 14
Black and Tan, 15
Black Currant Toddy, 53
Black Rose, 48
Black Russian, 214–17
Black Velvet, 15
Blanc Cassis, 82
Blood and Sand, 68
Bloody Bull, 148
Bloody Caesar, 149
Bloody Maria, 149
Bloody Mary, 57, 146–49, 160
Blue Blazer, 16–17
Bobby Burns, 18–19
Bosom Caresser, 195
bourbon, 34, 175; in Black Rose, 48; bonded, 37; bonded, in Mint Julep, 37; in Collins, 122; in eggnog, 220; in General Harrison's Egg Nogg, 223; in Horse's Neck, 154; in Kentucky Colonel, 19; in Manhattan East, 35; in Millionaire's

Manhattan, 242; in Old-Fashioned, 40; -port punch, 204–5; in Presbyterian, 159; in sours, 138; in Taylor Made, 205; in Toddy, 50; in Tropical Itch, 189; in Whiskey Smash, 38
Bradsell, Dick, 198
brandy: in Alexander, 212; in Alexandra Special, 213; in American Beauty Cocktail, 59; in Bosom Caresser, 195; in Chocolate Punch, 217; in Fog Cutter, 174; in Golden Age Pousse Cafés, 45; in Keoke coffee, 81; in Pousse Café, 44; in Scorpion Punch, 208; see also cherry brandy; Spanish brandy
Brandy Milk Punch, 194–95
Bronx Cocktail, 20–21
Brugal rum: in Fog Cutter, 174; in Scorpion Punch, 208
Buck's Fizz, 91
Buhen, Ray, 68
Bull's Blood, 136
Bull Shot, 149
Bull's Manhattan, 35
Butt, Robert C. (Rosebud), 84
Byron, O. H., 28, 29, 32, 34, 106, 123

cachaça, in Caipirinha, 120
The Cadillac, 89
Caipirinha, 120
Caipiroska, Ginger-Lychee, 121
California gimlet, 79
Calypso coffee, 81
Campari, 42, 145; in Americano Highball, 144; in Arancio Americano, 145; in Negroni, 94; in Old Flame, 95
Campari, Gaspare, 144, 145
Cape Codder, 57, 150–51
Cat's Eye, 172
Chai Toddy, 52
Chambord, 112; in French martini, 112
Champagne, 22, 64; in Big Spender, 233; in Black Velvet, 15; in Buck's Fizz, 91; Cobbler, 234; Cocktail, 22; in French 75, 126; in Full Monte,

85; in Kir Imperiale, 82; in Kir Royale, 82; in Match Spring Punch, 198; in mimosa, 90; Pick-Me-Up, 24–25; in Pisco Punch Royale, 201

Chartreuse, 66, 112, 240; in Bijou, 66; in Golden Age Pousse Café, 45

Chell, Walter, 149

cherry brandy, in President's coffee, 81

cherry liqueur, *see* Luxardo Maraschino liqueur; Peter Heering Cherry Heering

Chiaro di Luna, 236–37

Chocolate Punch, 217

chocolate rim, 225

cinnamon syrup, 249

Cipriani, Giuseppe, 64, 65

Claret and Lavender Lemonade, 196

claret lemonade, 196–97

Clicquot, Madame, 22

Clover Club, 27

Clover Leaf, 27

Coca-Cola, 152

coconut rum: in Bahama Mama, 170; in Goombay Smash, 171

Coctel Algeria, 69

Coffee Cocktail, 218–19

coffee cocktails, 80–81

Coffee Royal, 81

cognac: in Between the Sheets, 136; in Brandy Milk Punch, 194; in Champagne Cocktail, 22; in Coffee Cocktail, 218; in Coffee Royal, 81; in East India Cocktail, 28; in French 75, 126; in Millennium Cocktail, 29; in Ritz Cocktail, 25; in Sidecar, 134; in Twentieth-Century East India Cocktail, 29; *see also* VS cognac

Cointreau, 241; in Between the Sheets, 136; in The Cadillac, 89; in Coctel Algeria, 69; in Cosmopolitan, 72; in Donn Beach's Mai Tai, 182; in Garnet, 116; in Legends Cocktail, 240; in margaritas, 86–89; in mimosa, 90; in Old Flame, 95; in Orange Blossom, 92; in Ritz Cocktail, 25; in Sidecar, 134; in Singapore sling, 163; in Stork Club Cocktail, 98; in White Lady, 100

Collins, 122–23, 127, 128

Collins, John, 122

Colony Cocktail, 70–71

The Compass Club, 198

Cook, Cheryl, 72

Copa Verde, 238

Cosmopolitan, 57, 58, 72, 111, 112

Craddock, Harry, 29, 46, 66, 100, 126

crème de banane, in Banshee, 225

crème de cacao: in Banshee, 225; in Chocolate Punch, 217; in Golden Cadillac, 213; in Grasshopper, 224; in Italian egg cream, 216; in Pousse Café, 44; in Smith and Curran, 216

crème de cassis: in Kir, 82; in Match Spring Punch, 198; in Ruby Partida, 89

crème de menthe: in American Beauty Cocktail, 59; in Grasshopper, 224; in Pousse Café, 44; in Stinger, 228; in White Spider, 229

crème liqueur, 225

Crown Royal, in Royal Gingersnap, 40

Cuba Libre, 152

curaçao, 112, 241; in Golden Age Pousse Café, 45; in Pousse Café, 44; *see also* orange curaçao

Cuzco, 133

Cynar, 42; in Pimm's Italiano, 43

daiquiri, 124–25

Dale's Hemingway daiquiri, 125

Dale's Sazerac, 48

Danish Mary, 149

Dark and Stormy, 157

Demerara rum, 78; in Trader Vic's Navy Grog, 177; in Zombie, 190

Demerara sugar, 247

dirty martini, 106

Domaine de Canton: in Ginger-Lemonade Highball, 123; in Manhattan East, 35; in Royal Gingersnap, 40

Donn Beach's Mai Tai, 182

Donn's Mix #1, 249

Don the Beachcomber, 68, 174, 175, 190

Dry Rob Roy, 46

Dubonnet Cocktail, 57, 74

Dubonnet Kiss, 74

Duffy, Patrick Gavin, 37, 143, 194

East India Cocktail, 28–29

eggnog, 220–23; simplified, 195

eggs, 30, 220

El Presidente, 76

Embury, David, 15, 21, 24, 104, 146, 212, 234

Ensslin, Hugo, 101

Falernum-spice foam, 201

Fancy Gin Cocktail, 106

Finca Vigía, 125

fino sherry, 104; in Adonis, 14; in Flame of Love, 110; in Sevilla, 243

Fitzgerald, 139

Flame of Love, 104, 110–11, 243

Flamingo, 112, 173

Flip, 30

foam, 250; absinthe, 49; applejack-pomegranate, 97; Falernum-spice, 201; pineapple-spice, 28

Fog Cutter, 174

Framboise: in Kir Imperiale, 82; in Match Spring Punch, 198

French 75, 126

French dry vermouth, 59; in Adonis, 14; in American Beauty Cocktail, 59; in Bacardi cocktail, Ritz version, 61; in Bijou, Ritz version, 67; in Bronx Cocktail, 20; in Bull's Manhattan, 35; in El Presidente, 76; in martinis, 104, 105, 106; in Satan's Whiskers, 21

French martini, 112–17

Friar Briar's Sack Posset, 221

Full Monte, 85

Galliano, 178; in Golden Cadillac, 213; in Harvey Wallbanger, 161; in Hurricane, 178; in International Stinger, 229; in The Italian Kiss, 161

Garnet, 116, 117

garnishes, 251–54

General Harrison's Egg Nogg, 223

Gibson, 107

gimlet, 78–79

gin, 58, 107, 175; in Alexander, 212; in Aviation, 101; in Bee's Knees, 62; in Bijou, Ritz version, 67; in Bronx Cocktail, 20; in Buck's Fizz, 91; in Clover Club, 27; in Fitzgerald, 139; in Fog Cutter, 174; in French 75, 126; in Full Monte, 85; in Garnet, 116; in gimlet, 78–79; in London Iced Tea, 85; in Long Island Iced Tea, 84; in Martinez, 106; in martinis, 105, 106, 116; in Monkey Gland, 92; in Negroni, 94; in Old Flame, 95; in Orange Blossom, 92;

gin *(continued)*
    in Pimm's Cup, 42; in Pink Lady, 96–97; in Royal Hawaiian, 188; in Satan's Whiskers, 21; in Scorpion Punch, 208; in sling, 162–63; in Stork Club Cocktail, 98; in Vesper, 109; vodka vs., 160; in White Lady, 100; *see also* Hendrick's gin; London dry gin; Plymouth gin
Gin Fizz, 127–29
ginger ale, 154
Ginger-Lemonade Highball, 123
Ginger-Lychee Caipiroska, 121
ginger syrup, 248
Gin Rickey, 153
glasses, 105, 117, 255–59; chocolate rim for, 225; frosted with sugar, 137; salting of, 87; for sours, 127, 128
Golden Cadillac, 178, 213
Golden Fizz, 128
Golden Girl, 219
Goombay Smash, 171
Gosling's dark rum: in Dark and Stormy, 157; in Goombay Smash, 171; in Piña Colada, 187
Gran Centenario tequila, 88; in Big Spender, 233; in Cat's Eye, 172; in Copa Verde, 238
Grand Marnier, 21, 87, 98, 112; in B-52, 45; in The Cadillac, 89; in The Millionaire, 89; in Millionaire's Manhattan, 242; in Satan's Whiskers, 21
grapefruit, marsh, 125
Grapefruit Julep, 39
grappa, in mango mimosa, 91
Grasshopper, 224–25
Green Dream, 239
grenadine, 96
Greyhound, 150, 151
grog, 176–77
Guinness stout, in Black Velvet, 15

Haigh, Ted (Dr. Cocktail), 27, 97, 101, 163
Harry Johnson's Claret Lemonade, 196
Harvey Wallbanger, 161, 178
Hendrick's gin, 104, 140, 244; in Black Currant Toddy, 53; in Pink Lady, 96; in Strawberry Jive, 244
Herbsaint: as absinthe substitute, 12; in Lazone's martini, 116
Hewes, Jim, 111

Hewett, Mike, 72
Holiday Compound Butter, 53
honey syrup, 247
Horse's Neck, 154
horse's neck lemon peel, 154
Hot Buttered Rum, 52
Hurricane, 178
Hussion, Tom, 55

ice, proper crushed or powdered, 38
International Stinger, 229
Irish coffee, 57, 80–81
Italian egg cream, 216
Italian sweet vermouth, 59; in Americano Highball, 144; in Arancio Americano, 145; in Bijou, 66; in Bobby Burns, 18; in Bronx Cocktail, 20; in Manhattan, 32; in Martinez, 106; in Negroni, 94; in Rob Roy, 46; in Satan's Whiskers, 21

Jack Daniel's, in Bull's Manhattan, 35
Jack Rose, 31
Jamaican coffee, 81
Jeveons, Sam, 198
jiggers and bar spoons, 260, 261
John Collins, 122
John D. Taylor's Velvet Falernum: in Black Currant Toddy, 53; in Donn Beach's Mai Tai, 182; in Perfect Passion, 115; in Pisco Punch Royale, 201; in Planter's Punch, 202; in Prestige Cocktail, 76; in Taylor Made, 205; in Trader Vic's Navy Grog, 177; in Velvet Fog, 99; in Zombie, 190
Johnson, Harry, 9, 66, 105, 106, 196, 234
juicers, 262, 263
juice vs. garnish, 251

Kahlúa: in B-52, 45; in Black Russian, 214; in coffee cocktails, 81; in Mudslide, 217; in Scorpion Stinger, 229; in White Russian, 214
Kentucky Colonel, 19
Keoke coffee, 81
Kir, 58, 82
knives, 261, 262, 263
Kriendler, Jack, 140

Lazone's martini, 116
Legends Cocktail, 240
lemonade: claret, 196–97; fresh,

Pimm's Cup, 43; recipe for, 248
Lemonade-Ginger Highball, 123
Lemon Hart 80-proof rum, in Tropical Itch, 189
Leonard's Iced Tea, 84
Lewis, Alan, 218
Lillet, 109; in Vesper, 109
Lime in De Coconut, 185
Liqueur Créole, in Big Spender, 233
London dry gin: in Collins, 122; in dry martini, 104; in Dubonnet Cocktail, 74; in Rickey, 153
London Iced Tea, 85
Long Island Iced Tea, 84–85, 174
Loret de Mola, Diego, 132, 133
Luxardo Maraschino liqueur: in Aviation, 101; in Champagne Cobbler, 234; in Dale's Hemingway daiquiri, 123; in Full Monte, 85; in Pousse Café, 44; in Ritz Cocktail, 25; in sangria, 207; in Strawberry Nirvana, 117; in yuzu gimlet, 79
Lychee-Ginger Caipiroska, 121
Lychee-Strawberry Marinade, 115

MacElhone, Harry, 27, 100, 146, 212
McGarry (bartender), 91
Madison Avenue, 131
Madras, 151
Mai Tai, 180–83
mango for muddling, 183
Mango Mama, 183
mango mimosa, 91
Manhattan, 32–35, 117
Manhattan Club, 32
Manhattan East, 35
maraschino liqueur and cherries, 101, 254; *see also* Luxardo Maraschino liqueur
margarita, 57, 58, 86–89, 233; frozen, 88, 89; other variations for, 89
Marie Brizard anisette, 212; in Alexandra Special, 213
Marrero, Ramon, 187
Martin, John, 109, 156, 157, 160
Martinez, 106
Martini & Rossi, 59; in Arancio Americano, 145; in Old Flame, 95; in Prestige Cocktail, 76
martinis, 102–17; dry, 104–7; French, 112–17
Match Spring Punch, 198
Matusalem rum, 182; añejo, in Donn Beach's Mai Tai, 182

measures for the bar, 263
Meier, Frank, 27, 61, 67, 213
Metaxa, in International Stinger, 229
Metropolitan, 72
Mexican coffee, 81
mezcal, in Scorpion Stinger, 229
Millennium Cocktail, 29
The Millionaire, 89
Millionaire's Manhattan, 242
mimosa, 58, 90–91
mint julep, 37–39
mojito, 69, 131, 140
Monkey Gland, 92
Moris, Victor, 132
Morning Glory Fizz, 123
Moscow Mule, 57, 156–57, 160
muddlers, muddling, 262, 263; pieces for, 252, 253
Mudslide, 217
Myer's dark rum, 171; in Bahama Mama, 170; in Dark and Stormy, 157; in Donn Beach's Mai Tai, 182; in Hurricane, 178; in Piña Colada, 187; in Planter's Punch, 202; in Trader Vic's Navy Grog, 177

Negroni, 94–95
New Orleans or Ramos Fizz, 129
Nichol, Duncan, 200
nutmeg, 185

O'Brien, Pat, 178
Old-Fashioned, 40
Old Flame, 76, 95
Old Potrero Hotaling's Whiskey, in Stone Fence, 165
olives, 105, 254
onions, cocktail, 107, 254
orange bitters, 14; foam, 20
Orange Blossom, 92
orange curaçao: in Bijou, Ritz version, 67; in Bull's Blood, 136; in El Presidente, 76; in Mai Tai, 180; in Millennium Cocktail, 29; in Planter's Punch, 202; Port Cobbler, 234; in Tropical Itch, 189; in Twentieth-Century East India Cocktail, 29; in Whiskey Smash, 38
orange peel, flamed, 111, 249
orgeat, 188

Painkiller, 184–85
Papa Doble, 125

peach liqueur, in Bellini, 64
peach purée, 64
Perfect Passion, 115
Perfect Rob Roy, 46
Pero Frizzante, 237
Peter Heering Cherry Heering, 68; in Blood and Sand, 68; in Singapore sling, 163
Petiot, M. Fernand (Pete), 146
Peychaud's bitters, 14
Pimm, James, 42
Pimm's Cup, 42; fresh lemonade, 43
Pimm's Italiano, 43
Piña Colada, 187
pineapple-spice foam, 28
pineapple syrup, 248
Pink Lady, 27, 96–97
pisco, 132; see also Bar Sol Pisco
Pisco Bell-Ringer, 133
pisco punch, 132, 200–201
Pisco Punch Royale, 201
Pisco Sour, 69, 132–33
Planter's Punch, 202–3
Plymouth gin, 104, 105; in Bijou, 66; in Strawberry Nirvana, 117; in yuzu gimlet, 79
pomegranate-applejack foam, 97
port: in Chocolate Punch, 217; see also ruby port; tawny port
Pousse Café, 44–45
Presbyterian, 159
President's coffee, 81
Prestige Cocktail, 76
Preti, Gilberto, 109
prosecco, 64; in Arancio Americano, 145; in Bellini, 64; in Chiaro di Luna, 236; in Italian egg cream, 216; in mango mimosa, 91; in Pero Frizzante, 237; in Sgroppino al Limone, 226
Pusser's Navy Rum: in grog, 176; in Painkiller, 184

Rainbow Punch, 203
Ramos, Henry C., 129
Ramos or New Orleans Fizz, 129
raspberry liqueur, see Chambord; Framboise
Reiner, Julie, 133
Ribalaigua, Constantino, 125, 173
Ritz Cocktail, 25
Rob Roy, 46
rolling, 146
rosé sangria, 207

Rose's lime juice, 78
Royal Gingersnap, 40
Royal Hawaiian, 188–89
Royal Posset, 221
Ruby Partida, 89
ruby port: in American Beauty Cocktail, 59; Cobbler, 234; in Coffee Cocktail, 218; -whiskey punch, 204–5
Ruiz, Pepe, 110, 111
rum, 131, 175, 177; in Bull's Blood, 136; in Calypso coffee, 81; in Cuba Libre, 152; in Full Monte, 85; in Jamaican coffee, 81; in London Iced Tea, 85; in Long Island Iced Tea, 84; in Shore Breeze, 151; in Stone Wall, 164; see also añejo rum; Brugal rum; coconut rum; Demerara rum; Pusser's Navy Rum
rum, dark: in Dark and Stormy, 157; in eggnog, 220; in Friar Briar's Sack Posset, 221; in Hot Buttered Rum, 52; in Toddy, 50; see also Gosling's dark rum; Myer's dark rum
rum, light or white: in Bahama Mama, 170; in daiquiri, 124; in Dale's Hemingway daiquiri, 123; in El Presidente, 76; in Hot Buttered Rum, 52; in Hurricane, 178; in mojito, 131; in Papa Doble, 125; in Piña Colada, 187; in Planter's Punch, 202; see also Appleton white rum; Bacardi rum
rum, spiced: in Chai Toddy, 52; in Hot Buttered Rum, 52
rum agricole, 61, 63, 131; in Bee's Kiss, 63
rye whiskey, 34, 49; in Dale's Sazerac, 48; in Sazerac, 47; in Stone Fence, 165; in Toddy, 50; in Ward Eight, 55; in Whiskey Smash, 38

sake: in Green Dream, 239; in Manhattan East, 35
Salty Dog, 150, 151
sangria, 69, 206–7
Santiago, Dick, 190
Satan's Whiskers, 21
Saunders, Audrey, 85
Sazerac, 47–49
Schmidt, William, 45, 217, 241
Scorpion Punch, 208
Scorpion Stinger, 229

scotch: in Blood and Sand, 68; in Blue Blazer, 16–17; in Bobby Burns, 18; in Morning Glory Fizz, 123; in Perfect Rob Roy, 46; in Rob Roy, 46

screwdriver, 57, 160–61

Sea Breeze, 150, 151

Sevilla, 243

Sgroppino al Limone, 226

shaken vs. stirred, 260

shakers and strainers, cocktail, 260, 261

sherry: in Flip, 30; *see also* fino sherry

Shore Breeze, 151

Sidecar, 119, 134–37

Silver Fizz, 127

simple syrup, 246–47

Singapore sling, 163

sling, 162–63

Smirnoff, story of, 157

Smith and Curran, 216

Solon, Johnny, 20

sours, 138–39

Southern Comfort: in Colony Cocktail, 70–71; in Lazone's martini, 116

Southside, 119, 140

Spanish brandy: in Bull's Blood, 136; in sangria, 206–7; in Spanish coffee, 81

Spanish coffee, 81

sparkling wine, 22; in Kir Royale, 82; in Pisco Punch Royale, 201; sangria, 207; *see also* prosecco

Spence (Hotel Bel Air senior bartender), 19

spirits, flavored, 99

sprigs, 254

Stinger, 228–29

Stone Fence, 165

Stone Pole, 165

Stone Wall, 164–65

Stork Club Cocktail, 98–99

Strawberry Jive, 244

Strawberry-Lychee Marinade, 115

strawberry margarita, 89; frozen, 89

Strawberry Nirvana, 117

sweetness, 138

tawny port, in Golden Girl, 219

Taylor Made, 205

tequila, 57, 88; in Bloody Maria, 149; in Full Monte, 85; in Long Island Iced Tea, 84; in margaritas, 86–89; in Mexican coffee, 81; in The Millionaire, 89; *see also* Gran Centenario tequila

Tequila Sunrise, 166

Thomas, Jerry, 11, 16, 17, 22, 40, 44, 66, 106, 122, 193, 196, 208, 218, 220, 223, 234

Tia Maria, in coffee cocktails, 81

toasting, 22

toddy, 50–53

Tom Collins, 122, 126, 128

tools, 260–63

Trader Vic's, 174, 175, 180, 208; Navy Grog, 177

triple sec, 98; in Goombay Smash, 171; in Long Island Iced Tea, 84; in Pousse Café, 44; in sangria, 206

triple syrup, 248

Tropical Itch, 189

Twentieth-Century East India Cocktail, 29

twists, 104, 251–52

Valencia, 104, 111, 243

Velvet Falernum, 205; -spice foam, 201; *see also* John D. Taylor's Velvet Falernum

Velvet Fog, 99

vermouth, 59; in Adonis, 14; in Dry Robb Roy, 46; in original Manhattans, 34; in Perfect Rob Roy, 46; in sling, 162; *see also* French dry vermouth; Italian sweet vermouth; Martini & Rossi

Vernon, Edward (Old Grogram), 176

Vesper, 109

Virgin Royal Hawaiian, 189

vodka, 58, 69, 107; in Bay Breeze, 151; in Black Russian, 214; in Bloody Bull, 148; in Bloody Mary, 146; in Bull Shot, 149; in Cape Codder, 150; in Collins, 122; in Colony Cocktail, 70–71; in Cosmopolitan, 72; Espresso, 81; in Flame of Love, 110; in Friar Briar's Sack Posset, 221; in Full Monte, 85; in gimlet, 78; in Ginger-Lemonade Highball, 123; in

Ginger-Lychee Caipiroska, 121; gin vs., 160; in Grapefruit Julep, 39; in Green Dream, 239; in Greyhound, 151; in Harvey Wallbanger, 161; in The Italian Kiss, 161; in Legends Cocktail, 240; in Lime in De Coconut, 185; in Long Island Iced Tea, 84; in Madras, 151; in Mango Mama, 183; in martinis, 104, 105, 106, 112; in Match Spring Punch, 198; in Metropolitan, 72; in Moscow Mule, 156; in Mudslide, 217; in Perfect Passion, 115; in Salty Dog, 151; in screwdriver, 160; in Sea Breeze, 151; in Sgroppino al Limone, 226; in Stone Pole, 165; in Velvet Fog, 99; in Vesper, 109; in White Russian, 214; in White Spider, 229

VS cognac: in Alexander, 212; in Champagne Pick-Me-Up, 24; in Dale's Sazerac, 48; in Stinger, 228

Ward Eight, 55

water, 246

wedges, 252, 253

Weisman, Craig, 84

whiskey, 34, 58, 175; in Irish Coffee, 57, 80; in Manhattan, 32; in original Manhattans, 34; in Presbyterian, 159; in sours, 138; *see also* bourbon; Jack Daniel's; rye whiskey; scotch

Whiskey Smash, 38

White Lady, 100–101

White Russian, 214

White Spider, 229

wine, 58; *see also* Champagne; port; prosecco; rosé sangria; sparkling wine; vermouth

wine, red: in claret lemonade, 196; in Harry Johnson's Claret Lemonade, 196; Spanish, in sangria, 206

wine, white, in Kir, 82; sangria, 207; in Scorpion Punch, 208

Woelke, Eddie, 131

Wondrich, David, 133

yuzu gimlet, 79

Zombie, 178, 190

Introduction to Law and Legal Systems

LAW AND THE REAL ESTATE BUSINESS

Many aspects of the real estate business are closely associated with law. In fact, only the world of finance may be more closely controlled by law. Almost any professional activity of a broker, salesperson, appraiser or investor involves certain legal restrictions. Thus, people with these positions or many others in real estate have a genuine need to know about the law and legal systems; the more extensive their knowledge, the more effective their job performance will be.

Real estate professionals deal not only with lawyers but also with recording clerks, building inspectors, tax officials, planning board employees and personnel from state and federal housing agencies. All of these people have specialized functions in the legal system. Understanding what they do and some of the responsibilities of their jobs increases the real estate professional's ability to work effectively with them. Many private sector individuals with whom salespeople and brokers come in contact also have specialized knowledge of the law; loan officers and appraisers are examples. Real estate professionals who have similar knowledge will be able to work more effectively with other specialists and improve their professional image at the same time.

Legal knowledge is especially important to people who sell real estate. They are involved in the real estate transaction at a critical point as far as legal input is concerned. Clients and customers will often question them about legal matters or the advisability of consulting an attorney. Although sales personnel should never give legal advice, a knowledge of law will help them develop an awareness of situations in which a lawyer should be consulted. Because legal knowledge is considered so important, some states require salespeople and brokers engaged in selling real estate to complete a formal course in real estate law.

Although this book is devoted to a study of real estate law, to some extent that designation is misleading. Real estate law cannot really be separated from other types of law. A famous jurist once said, "Law is a seamless web"; nevertheless, because of the complexity of law, people who want to understand it often consider it in small segments. The boundaries of these segments are never exact, nor is there general agreement on what each segment includes. So the reader must realize that although much of what is said about real estate law applies to law in general, some strands of the "seamless web" are more important to the real estate business than others. This book deals primarily with these strands.

Most of this book discusses specific rules important to real estate people. In this first chapter, however, the book takes a broader look at law and the legal system. This chapter attempts to clarify the law by looking at where law is found and the structure in which it operates.

SOURCES OF LAW

The answer to many legal questions comes from life's experiences. As a person learns in school, on the job or through daily living, laws important to that person become part of his or her knowledge of the manner in which things operate. Sometimes legal questions arise that are not answerable from experience. How does one find the answers to these questions? To what source does the student, the real estate professional, the lawyer or the judge turn to find out what the law is?

One of the prevailing myths about law is that all laws are found in nicely indexed, officially published volumes of statutes enacted by a legislative body. According to this belief, all a person has to do to answer a legal question is to locate the correct page in the right book, and the law will be there in clear black letters. Unfortunately, few legal questions are answered this simply.

Thousands of cases, statutes and administrative regulations are published each year. As a result, determining what the law is has become increasingly difficult. Computers have, during the past 25 years, provided a tool that enhances the potential for legal professionals and the general public to access the sources of law more effectively. The speed and manipulative power of the computer allow increased control over the burgeoning quantities of legal information.

To answer a legal question involving real estate, a person might have to examine one source or a number of different sources. Sometimes an answer will be found in a state constitution or the federal Constitution. Most often, however, people find the answer to real estate law questions in court opinions, often referred to as *precedents,* in statutes and in the regulations of administrative agencies. The different sources of law are discussed in the paragraphs that follow.

CONSTITUTIONS

A basic source of law, constitutions provide the framework within which the federal and state governments must operate. Ordinarily one does not associate real estate law with constitutional problems, but at least two functions of constitutions are important to the real estate business. First, the U.S. Constitution allocates power between the states and the federal government. Because the states generally have retained power over local matters, most real estate law is state law. However, as the states have given the federal government power to regulate businesses affecting interstate commerce, numerous federal statutes apply to the real estate business. At present, many people in the field are concerned about how federal statutes relating to anti-trust concerns, such as the Sherman Act and the Clayton Act, are affecting real estate. Bankruptcy statutes and consumer protection laws such as Truth-in-Lending, the Real Estate Settlement Procedures Act and environmental protection legislation are other examples of federal law that apply to real estate.

A second function of constitutions—both state and federal—is the protection of individual rights, including private property. Constitutional provisions require that the law be applied equally to all; in addition, they prohibit government from depriving a person of life, liberty or property without due process. This means that an individual's property can be taken by government only under limited circumstances. But the protection accorded the individual is far from absolute. Both the power of eminent domain and the police power allow government to restrict private property.

PRECEDENT

◆ **A published opinion of an appellate court that serves as authority for determining a legal question in a later case with similar facts.**

A distinctive feature of the law of English-speaking countries is its reliance on cases decided by appellate courts as a source of law. Reports of these cases are published as opinions, which provide the answers to many legal questions.

CASE EXAMPLE

Clayborne and his adult daughter lived in a house that Clayborne owned. At the request of the daughter, Dexter painted the house. Clayborne did not authorize the work, but he knew that it was being done and raised no objection. Clayborne refused to pay Dexter, arguing that he had not contracted to have the house painted.

Dexter asked his attorney if Clayborne was legally liable to pay him. The attorney told Dexter that in their state several published appellate court decisions had established that, when a homeowner allows work to be done on his home by a person who would ordinarily expect to be paid, a duty to pay exists. The attorney stated that, based on these precedents, it was advisable for Dexter to bring a suit to collect the reasonable value of the work that he had done.

In the legal system of countries that followed the English system, judges are obligated to follow principles established by prior cases (precedents). This obligation, also referred to as *stare decisis,* is ingrained in our system. The extent to which a court is governed by precedent is difficult to assess. Although the practice of following precedent is not a legal duty, it is definitely more than a tradition. A judge who failed to follow precedent would not be convicted of a crime, but he or she ordinarily would be reversed and in extreme cases censured or possibly impeached. People trained in our system generally consider reliance on precedent an effective and fair way to reach a decision, and the concept is fundamental to U.S. law.

The obligation to follow precedent is limited by a number of factors. A court need not follow precedent established in another state, although in reaching decisions courts sometimes consider case decisions from other states when their own state has no case law on the subject. Lower courts are bound to follow decisions rendered by higher courts of their state. Again, failure to do so may result merely in the lower court's decision being reversed. The highest appellate court in a state can overrule its own precedent. Although this occurs on occasion, most state appellate courts overrule reluctantly because they believe that certainty is a desirable characteristic of law. The reluctance to overrule is often seen in private areas such as real estate law, for certainty is deemed very important where property rights are involved. A court will overrule a prior decision when the rule of law was applied incorrectly in the first place or when the rule is not considered applicable because of a change in circumstances. In addition, only that part of a court's opinion that is *necessary* to resolve the dispute between the parties, called the *holding,* creates a precedent for future cases. Any discussion not necessary to settle the legal issue in question is *dicta,* and need not be followed in subsequent decisions.

Courts and attorneys frequently avoid the effect of a previous case by distinguishing it from the case under consideration. A case is distinguished when a significant factual difference can be pointed out between the two situations. For example, assume that, in defending Clayborne in a suit brought by Dexter, Clayborne's attorney asks the court to dismiss the case because she has found the published decision of a case with like facts where the appellate court held that the homeowner was not required to pay. Dexter's attorney argues that in that case the homeowner was on vacation and did not know the work was being done. As Clayborne knew that his house was being painted, the two cases are different and can be distinguished. If the court agrees the two cases are significantly different, that is, can be distinguished, it will decide that the earlier decision is not precedent and therefore not controlling in deciding the case before the court.

Law that evolves from published opinions of appellate courts, or precedent, is often called *judge-made law* or *decisional law.* In England, reliance on previous decisions or cases and on custom and tradition created a law that was common to the entire country. Therefore, the law based on prior opinions is often referred to as *common law.* Sometimes people have difficulty accepting the idea that in these opinions statutes are not involved in any manner. In fact, often no statute exists that can be used to settle the dispute. The United States adopted the English common law approach. Most of the non-English speaking nations have *civil law* systems relying exclusively on statutory or code law.

A modern example of judge-made law is found in those appellate decisions that impose responsibility on builders of defective homes. Before World War II, the builder of a defective home had little legal responsibility for injury or property damage once the home was sold. The buyer was required to make his or her own inspection of the premises. On the basis of this inspection, the buyer accepted responsibility for all defects, relieving the builder of responsibility for any defective construction. The courts were applying the ancient doctrine of *caveat emptor*—let the buyer beware.

During the 1950s and the 1960s, courts began to recognize the unfairness of this rule. They began to allow buyers of new homes to recover for personal injury and property damage resulting from defective construction. In numerous states, this modification of the law from *caveat emptor* to *caveat venditor* (let the seller beware) was accomplished without legislation. As one state court commented:

> If at one time . . . the rule of caveat emptor had application to the sale of a new house by a vendor-builder, that time is now past. The decisions and legal writings herein referred to afford numerous examples and situations illustrating the harshness and injustice of the rule when applied to the sale of a new house by a builder-vendor. . . . Obviously, the ordinary purchaser is not in a position to ascertain when there is a defect in a chimney flue, or vent of a heating apparatus, or whether the plumbing work covered by a concrete slab foundation is faulty.
>
> The caveat emptor rule as applied to new houses is an anachronism patently out of harmony with modern home buying practices. It does a disservice not only to the ordinary prudent purchaser but to the industry itself by lending encouragement to the unscrupulous, fly-by-night operator and purveyor of shoddy work. *Humber v. Morton, 426 S.W.2d 554 (Tex. 1968).*

STATUTORY LAW
◆ **Law enacted by local and state legislative bodies and by Congress.**

The Role of Statutes. Although for many years the opinions of courts were the chief source of real estate law in English-speaking countries and for the legal system generally, during the past 100 years statutes have gradually assumed this role. Among the many reasons for this trend are that statutes are more comprehensive, statutes can modify the law more rapidly, statutes can treat an entire problem rather than just a part and statutes are usually more understandable than cases.

During the past 75 years, statutes have been used to bring greater uniformity to state law. Economic expansion after the Civil War has been characterized by the growth of regional and national markets. States, however, have often adopted different laws to solve common problems occurring in these markets. This practice has increased the cost of doing business and caused confusion and uncertainty.

In 1890, the National Conference of Commissioners on Uniform State Law was established to alleviate this problem. The commission is charged with determining what uniform laws are necessary, drafting a uniform statute and trying to get states to adopt it. More than 100 uniform laws have been recommended, although few have been adopted by all or even a majority of the states.

The commission has proposed a number of laws that deal with real estate. These include a uniform condominium act, a uniform residential landlord-tenant act, a uniform simplification of land transfers act and a uniform eminent domain code. However, the impact of these uniform laws on real estate has been minimal to date.

Court Interpretation of Statutes. Despite the growing importance of statutes as a source of law, court opinions continue to play a significant role in shaping the law. Many statutes are broadly written. Often their meaning is not clear until they have been interpreted by a court. It is probably safe to say that, in a majority of instances, a lawyer looking for the answer to a legal question will first check for an appropriate statute and then review relevant court opinions interpreting that statute.

Codification of Appellate Judge-Made Law. Another reason that court opinions continue to be important is that statutes often are merely a codification of the cases dealing with a particular legal problem. When a legislative body codifies the law, it adopts a statute that reflects the decisional law. For example, when the courts in some states decided that the act of selling real property implied a warranty of fitness for habitation, the state legislature passed statutes mirroring the court's decisions.

ADMINISTRATIVE RULES AND REGULATIONS

In our dynamic, complex society, much of the work of government is done by administrative agencies. Both Congress and state legislatures create administrative agencies as part of legislation that aims to cure some social ill. The agency is empowered to enforce and implement the goals of the legislation. A substantial number of administrative agencies significantly influence the real estate business. Among such federal agencies are the Department of Housing and Urban Development, the Environmental Protection Agency and the Federal Home Loan Bank Board. State administrative agencies also have a far-reaching influence on the real estate business. They are the source of rules pertaining to such matters as licensing and disciplining real estate sales personnel, zoning, safeguarding the environment, and landlord and tenant rights.

Administrative agencies perform several functions. They are authorized to settle disputes and, in doing so, act like courts; this is called *administrative adjudication.* The procedures used in administrative adjudication are generally much less formal than those used by the courts, making reaching a settlement less time-consuming and costly. Another benefit of administrative adjudication is that the agency personnel resolving the dispute are experts in the subject area of the dispute and can therefore resolve the case more effectively than is sometimes possible in a court.

Many agencies also have the power to make rules and regulations that have the force of law. In this respect they act like legislatures. An agency's authority to make rules and regulations is granted in the legislation that created the agency. If the rule or regulation issued by the agency is constitutional, proper procedures have been followed and the agency has not exceeded the power and authority granted to it by the legislature, the rule or regulation is immune from modification or invalidation by the courts.

COURT STRUCTURE

People in the real estate business sometimes become involved in litigation, so it is helpful for them to know something about the structure of the system that applies the law.

TRIAL AND APPELLATE COURTS

Two types of courts are fundamental to the operation of the legal system: trial and appellate courts.

Trial Courts. The function of a trial court is to determine the facts and to apply the relevant law to these facts. A jury usually makes the factual determination, but in some cases the parties are not entitled to a jury, or they waive this right. Disputed facts are then decided by the judge. Whether a judge or jury makes the factual determination, findings are based on evidence. In most instances evidence is the oral testimony of witnesses who are questioned by attorneys for the parties.

The testimony of most witnesses is valuable because the witness has personal knowledge of the facts. One important type of witness often does not have personal knowledge of the situation, but does have expertise related to a disputed fact. This person is the expert witness. The testimony of the expert witness is not permitted until the trial court judge is convinced that the witness is qualified. When qualified, the expert witness may answer a hypothetical question that covers technical aspects of a disputed fact. Real estate brokers and appraisers often testify as expert witnesses in cases involving disputed land values.

Appellate Courts. If either party thinks that a legal error has been made by the trial court judge, the party may ask a higher court to review the case. This procedure is called an *appeal,* and the court hearing the case is an appellate court. The function of the appellate court is quite different from that of the trial court. This court is not concerned with deciding disputed facts; rather, it corrects legal mistakes. For this reason, there is no jury in an appellate court; there is a panel of judges. Instead of hearing the testimony of witnesses, the judges read briefs in which the parties explain what they believe the law to be. The attorneys may also present oral arguments. After the judges decide which party is correct, one of the judges will write an opinion presenting the views of the majority. If the court finds that an error has been made, the court may, in its opinion, order the lower court to correct its mistake. These opinions constitute the judge-made law explained earlier.

STATE AND FEDERAL COURTS

A first step in understanding the American legal structure is to recognize that the federal government and each of the states have their own system of trial and appellate courts. Each of the systems—state and federal—in most instances is the final authority within its own jurisdiction. One exception to this principle is that federal courts do have authority over state courts in questions involving the federal law.

Jurisdiction of State Courts. The authority of state courts is extensive. It includes cases involving violations of the state's criminal statutes as well as statutes that involve matters as diverse as divorce, education, public health and social welfare. Most contract cases and those involving personal injuries are also heard in state courts. In fact, state courts have jurisdiction over all matters except those the Constitution or Congress has given exclusively to the federal courts or has denied to the states.

Jurisdiction of Federal Courts. The jurisdiction of federal courts is limited to that given to them by the Constitution and the federal statutes that create them. As a result, federal courts hear only cases that involve the Constitution, treaties between the U.S. and a foreign nation, federal statutes, and citizens of different states. In the following case, the jurisdiction of the federal courts to decide a case brought against New Orleans real estate brokers is questioned.

McLAIN v. REAL ESTATE BOARD OF NEW ORLEANS, INC.

U.S. Supreme Court
444 U.S.232 (1980)

BACKGROUND. McLain and others (petitioners) brought a class action on behalf of real estate purchasers and sellers. The action was against real estate trade associations, firms and brokers (respondents). The complaint stated that the respondents had engaged in a price-fixing conspiracy in violation of the Sherman Act, a federal statute.

The petitioners' complaint alleged the following: (1) that respondents' activities were "within the flow of interstate commerce and have an effect upon that commerce"; (2) that respondents assist their clients in securing financing and insurance involved with the purchase of real estate and that much of this financing and insurance comes from outside the state. The purpose of these allegations is to show the interstate connection of the respondents' activity, thereby raising a federal Sherman Act issue.

The U.S. District Court dismissed the complaint, finding that respondents' activities involving real estate were purely local in nature and did not substantially affect interstate commerce. The U.S. Court of Appeals affirmed, and the petitioner appealed.

DECISION. The U.S. Supreme Court remanded the case for trial.

MR. CHIEF JUSTICE BURGER. The question in this case is whether the Sherman Act extends to an agreement among real estate brokers in a market area to conform to a fixed rate of brokerage commissions on sales of residential property.

• • •

The broad authority of Congress under the Commerce Clause has, of course, long been interpreted to extend beyond activities actually *in* interstate commerce to reach other activities that, while wholly local in nature, nevertheless substantially *affect* interstate commerce. During the near century of Sherman Act experiences, forms and modes of business and commerce have changed along with changes in communication and travel, and innovations in methods of conducting particular businesses have altered relationships in commerce. Application of the Act reflects an adaptation to these changing circumstances.

The conceptual distinction between activities "in" interstate commerce and those which "affect" interstate commerce has been preserved in the cases, for Congress has seen fit to preserve that distinction in the antitrust and related laws by limiting the applicability of certain provisions to activities demonstrably "in commerce." It can no longer be doubted, however, that the jurisdictional requirement of the Sherman Act may be satisfied under either the "in commerce" or the "effect on commerce" theory.

Although the cases demonstrate the breadth of Sherman Act prohibitions, jurisdiction may not be invoked under that statute unless the relevant aspect of interstate commerce is identified; it is not sufficient merely to rely on identification of a relevant local activity and to presume an interrelationship with some unspecified aspect of interstate commerce. To establish jurisdiction, a plaintiff must allege the critical relationship in the pleadings and, if these allegations are controverted, must proceed to demonstrate by submission of evidence beyond the pleadings either that the defendants' activity is itself in interstate commerce or, if it is local in nature, that it has an effect on some other appreciable activity demonstrably in interstate commerce.

To establish the jurisdictional element of a Sherman Act violation, it would be sufficient for petitioners to demonstrate a substantial effect on interstate commerce generated by respondents' brokerage activity. Under the Sherman Act, liability may be established by proof of *either* an unlawful purpose or an anticompetitive effect.

...

On the record thus far made, it cannot be said that there is an insufficient basis for petitioners to proceed at trial to establish Sherman Act jurisdiction. It is clear that an appreciable amount of commerce is involved in the financing of residential property in the Greater New Orleans area and in the insuring of titles to such property. The presidents of two of the many lending institutions in the area stated in their deposition testimony that those institutions committed hundreds of millions of dollars to residential financing during the period covered by the complaint. The testimony further demonstrates that this appreciable commercial activity has occurred in interstate commerce. Funds were raised from out-of-state investors and from interbank loans obtained from interstate financial institutions. Multistate lending institutions took mortgages insured under federal programs which entailed interstate transfers of premiums and settlements. Mortgage obligations physically and constructively were traded as financial instruments in the interstate secondary mortgage market. Before making a mortgage loan in the Greater New Orleans area, lending institutions usually, if not always, required title insurance, which was furnished by interstate corporations. Reading the pleadings most favorably to petitioners, for present purposes we take these facts as established.

At trial, respondents will have the opportunity, if they so choose, to make their own case contradicting this factual showing. On the other hand, it may be possible for petitioners to establish that, apart from the commerce in title insurance and real estate financing, an appreciable amount of interstate commerce is involved with the local residential real estate market arising out of the interstate movement of people, or otherwise.

To establish federal jurisdiction in this case, there remains only the requirement that respondents' activities which allegedly have been infected by a price-fixing conspiracy be shown "as a matter of practical economics" to have a not insubstantial effect on the interstate commerce involved. It is clear, as the record shows, that the function of respondent real estate brokers is to bring the buyer and seller together on agreeable terms. For this service the broker charges a fee generally calculated as a percentage of the sale price. Brokerage activities necessarily affect both the frequency and the terms of residential sales transactions.

Ultimately, whatever stimulates or retards the volume of residential sales, or has an impact on the purchase price, affects the demand for financing and title insurance, those two commercial activities that on this record are shown to have occurred in interstate commerce.

We therefore conclude that it was error to dismiss the complaint at this stage of the proceedings. The judgment of the Court of Appeals is vacated, and the case is remanded for further proceedings consistent with this opinion.

VACATED AND REMANDED.

The power of federal courts to hear cases that arise under the Constitution, treaties and federal statutes is called *federal question* jurisdiction. Most federal question matters involve the application or interpretation of one of the many federal statutes, such as the Clean Water Act, the Civil Rights Act or the Internal Revenue Code.

The power of federal courts to hear cases involving citizens of different states is called *diversity jurisdiction.* Diversity jurisdiction exists because, at the time the Constitution was adopted, many people believed that a citizen of one state would not get a fair trial if sued in another state. Consequently, those who drafted the Constitution included in it a provision extending federal judicial power to disputes between citizens of different states. Because diversity jurisdiction places a substantial burden on the federal courts as they are often applying state law, Congress has limited the diversity jurisdiction of these courts to cases in which the dispute involves more than $75,000.

CASE EXAMPLE

Able was a resident of New Hampshire and Baker a resident of New York. The two entered into a contract in which Baker agreed to purchase a large resort hotel in New Hampshire from Able. Baker breached the contract, and Able sued her in the New Hampshire courts for $850,000 in damages. Baker may transfer the case to the federal district court since the parties are residents of different states and the amount in controversy exceeds $75,000.

Most real estate litigation is brought in state courts because the dispute does not involve a federal statute or U.S. Constitutional question, and the parties are usually residents of the same state. In addition, most real estate legal disputes concern land located within the state, and there is no basis here for federal court jurisdiction. An exception would be land disputes involving Indian tribal rights, which are brought in federal court.

STATE COURT SYSTEM

As there are 51 independent court systems operating within the United States, understanding the structure of American courts might seem an impossible task. The task is, however, simplified by the existence of a pattern common to both the federal and the 50 state systems. This structure can be visualized as a pyramid with two or sometimes three levels.

State Trial Courts. Trial courts are at the base of the structural pyramid. Trial courts can be classified into three broad groups. This classification is based on the court's power to hear a case, which is termed its *jurisdiction.*

Courts of general jurisdiction. Each state usually has a trial court of general jurisdiction. In some states these are called *superior courts.* Other states call them *county courts, district courts, circuit courts* or *courts of common pleas.* These courts have the power to hear a wide variety of civil and criminal cases. Ordinarily, there are no limits on the court's monetary jurisdiction, and the court has the power to grant extraordinary remedies, such as the injunction and specific performance. An injunction is an order forbidding a person to do a particular act. Conversely, an order for specific performance commands that a particular act be performed.

In a number of states these courts hear appeals from administrative agencies and courts of limited jurisdiction (see Figure 1.1). Trial by jury is available for most cases. The court generally has statewide jurisdiction but is organized on a district or county basis. These courts are generally considered the cornerstones of judicial administration.

Courts of limited jurisdiction. Many of the more populous states have created trial courts that are limited to hearing cases in which the damages are less than a certain amount, fixed by statute. Depending on the state, this amount ranges from a few hundred to thousands of dollars. These courts also generally have criminal jurisdiction over cases involving petty crimes and misdemeanors. *Municipal courts* is a common name for these courts. Other states call them *justice courts, magistrates courts* or *district courts.*

Generalizations about courts of limited jurisdiction are difficult to make. Their authority differs widely from state to state. In metropolitan areas their monetary jurisdiction is sometimes extensive, and the courts are manned by full-time judges with large staffs. In some rural areas these courts hear only the most trivial cases and may be presided over by part-time judges with no legal training. Courts of limited jurisdiction are important to the legal system because they take some of the pressures off the courts of general jurisdiction.

Courts of special jurisdiction. Either because of tradition or because of the peculiar needs of judicial administration, many states have established special courts to resolve a wide variety of disputes. Traffic offenses are one type of case often tried in a court of special jurisdiction. Traffic cases are generally tried in a special court or a special division of a trial court as so many traffic offenses are processed that they would clog the regular judicial machinery.

FIGURE 1.1 *A Typical State Judicial System*

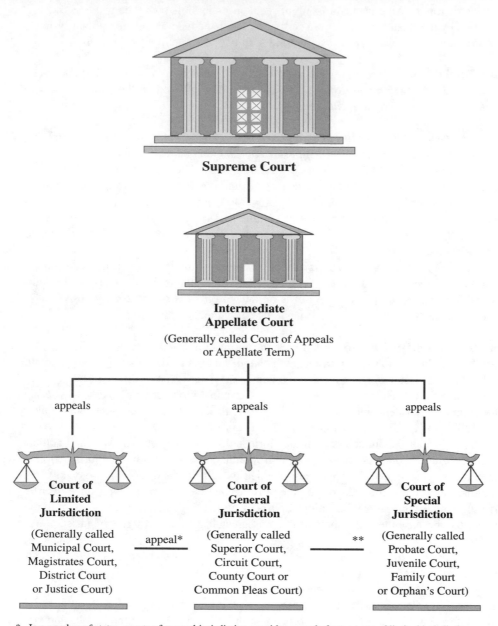

Supreme Court

**Intermediate
Appellate Court**

(Generally called Court of Appeals
or Appellate Term)

appeals   appeals   appeals

**Court of
Limited
Jurisdiction**

(Generally called
Municipal Court,
Magistrates Court,
District Court
or Justice Court)

appeal*

**Court of
General
Jurisdiction**

(Generally called
Superior Court,
Circuit Court,
County Court or
Common Pleas Court)

**

**Court of
Special
Jurisdiction**

(Generally called
Probate Court,
Juvenile Court,
Family Court
or Orphan's Court)

*   In a number of states, courts of general jurisdiction consider appeals from courts of limited jurisdiction.

** In many states these courts are part of the court of general jurisdiction.

Juvenile and domestic relations cases are also heard by a special court. These courts provide privacy and informal procedures that are effective in dealing with juvenile and family matters.

Numerous states also have separate probate courts that exercise jurisdiction over the administration of decedents' estates. When a real estate broker or sales associate is involved in a transaction that has to do with a decedent's real property, the broker or sales associate often has to deal with a probate court. In some states, probate courts have jurisdiction in guardianship, adoption, and competency proceedings.

State Intermediate Appellate Courts. About half the states have, by constitution or statute, established an intermediate level of appellate courts. The purpose of these courts is to lighten the burden of the state's supreme court. Some intermediate appellate courts have limited powers to act as trial courts. Usually this involves the power to issue extraordinary writs. However, the primary function of these courts is to provide appellate review. Although the extent of appellate jurisdiction is generally broad, some states place limits on the appeals that can be heard, possibly on the type of case or the maximum monetary amount. An intermediate appellate court might be permitted to hear civil appeals or civil appeals only in cases wherein the amount in controversy is under $30,000.

State Supreme Courts. At the apex of a state's judicial system is the state supreme court, which in most states hears appeals in all civil and criminal matters. This jurisdiction is often concurrent with that of the intermediate appellate court. Because of the extensiveness of the review process and the large number of appeals, most states allow their court of last resort to accept for review only cases that the justices or judges consider important. Appeals as a matter of right may, however, often be taken in important cases, such as those that involve constitutionality of a state or federal statute or the death penalty.

FEDERAL COURT SYSTEM

U.S. District Courts. The *U.S. District Courts* are the trial courts of the federal system. The United States is divided into 94 districts, each with a single district court. Almost all federal cases are initiated in these courts as they have the power to hear all types of federal cases except those assigned by Congress to special courts such as the tax court.

U.S. Courts of Appeal. The federal intermediate appellate courts are called *U.S. Courts of Appeal.* In 1985 the United States was divided into 12 geographic areas called *circuits,* with a court of appeals for each. These courts hear appeals from the federal district courts that are included in their circuit. They also hear appeals from administrative agencies. In addition, there is a Court of Appeals for the Federal Circuit which hears special appeals, for example, those from the Court of International Trade.

U.S. Supreme Court. The United States Supreme Court is the final appellate court in the federal system. Most of the cases the Supreme Court reviews come from the U.S. Courts of

Appeal and from the state supreme courts. The Supreme Court may review state supreme court decisions involving the federal Constitution or a federal statute.

In certain cases the Supreme Court must hear an appeal. One example is a case in which a U.S. Court of Appeals has held a state statute unconstitutional. Another is when a lower federal court has held a federal statute unconstitutional and the United States is a party. In most cases the party seeking review must first ask the Supreme Court to hear the case by petitioning for a writ of certiorari. This is a writ in which a superior court orders a lower court to supply a record of a particular case. The Supreme Court denies most petitions for certiorari as it does not consider the case important enough to hear.

ALTERNATE DISPUTE RESOLUTION (ADR)

◆ **A means of settling legal disputes without using the courts.**

Alternative dispute resolution (ADR) can take many forms. For instance, it can take the form of mediation when a neutral third party listens to both sides and tries to facilitate a compromise. The mediator cannot force the parties to reach a compromise. Many people argue that ADR is faster, cheaper, and less emotionally draining than traditional litigation.

Arbitration is another form of ADR. It may involve the formal submission of the dispute to a nonjudicial third person. The expertise of the arbitrator may be as a business professional. The expertise of the judge in litigation is the law. A person may get into arbitration by way of a contractual agreement, by statute, or by court order. Usually the arbitrator's decision is binding on the parties. A contractual agreement to arbitrate a dispute is the most common situation today.

Frequently, arbitration clauses are included in contracts dealing with development and sale of real estate, especially in construction contracts. The following case illustrates the use of a mediation/arbitration clause in a real estate sales contract.

LEE V. HEFTEL
Supreme Court of Hawaii
911 P.2d 721 (1996)

BACKGROUND. In May 1990, the Lees purchased a home from Cecil and Joyce Heftel for the purchase price of $3,100,000.

On May 23, 1990, the parties executed a Deposit Receipt, Offer and Acceptance (DROA) contract, for the sale of the aforementioned residential property. Paragraph 5.3 of the DROA's Addendum No. 1 provides:

Mediation and Arbitration. If any dispute or claim in law or equity arises out of this DROA, Buyer and Seller agree in good faith to attempt to settle such dispute or claim by mediation under the Commercial Mediation rules of the American Arbitration Association. If such mediation is not successful in resolving such dispute or claim, then such dispute or claim shall be decided by neutral binding arbitration before a single arbitrator in accordance with the Commercial Arbitration rules of the American Arbitration Association. Judgment upon the award rendered by the arbitrator may be entered in any court having jurisdiction thereof.

On July 7, 1992, the Lees filed a complaint in circuit court alleging intentional or negligent misrepresentation, fraudulent concealment, breach of warranty, dual agency, and malicious and wanton conduct. On September 1, 1992, the Heftels filed their motion to stay and contended that the DROA expressly provided that "any dispute or claim in law or equity must first be submitted to mediation and then, if necessary, binding arbitration under the rules of the American Arbitration Association." The Lees opposed said motion and argued that "when a [p]laintiff seeks 'revocation' of a contract, Hawaii [S]tatutes expressly provide that an arbitration clause will not be enforced."

On January 6, 1993, the circuit court filed its order granting the Heftels' motion to stay.

"[W]hen presented with a motion to compel arbitration, the court is limited to answering two questions: (1) whether an arbitration agreement exists between the parties; and (2) if so, whether the subject matter of the dispute is arbitrable under such agreement."

DECISION. The Hawaii Supreme Court affirmed the lower court granting the Heftels' motion to stay the proceedings pending arbitration.

JUSTICE NAKAYAMA. In this case, there is no dispute between the parties as to the existence of the arbitration clause provided in Addendum No. 1, paragraph 5.3 of the DROA. Rather, the controversy exists as to the determination of the second prong of the two-part test. The Lees argue that, because they were fraudu-

lently induced into purchasing the transferred property, mere allegations of such fraud revoke the contract, including the arbitration clause.

Because the pertinent language of HRS s 658-3 is virtually identical to the language of the federal arbitration statute, and due to the absence of [Hawaii] law regarding the scope of the trial court's role when faced with a motion to compel arbitration, we look to federal authority for guidance. In *Prima Paint Corp. v. Flood & Conklin Manufacturing Co.,* (1967), the United States Supreme Court heard a case involving circumstances analogous to those in the present case. The contract in *Prima Paint,* as in the present case, contained an arbitration clause, providing that "[a]ny controversy or claim arising out of or relating to this Agreement, or the breach thereof, shall be settled by arbitration." One party in that case alleged that the other had committed fraud in the inducement of the contract, although not of the arbitration clause in particular, and sought to have the claim of fraud adjudicated in court. The Supreme Court held that, notwithstanding a contrary state rule, consideration of a claim of fraud in the inducement of a contract "is for the arbitrators and not the courts." Accordingly, if the claim is fraud in the inducement of the arbitration clause itself—an issue which goes to the "making" of the agreement to arbitrate—the federal court may proceed to adjudicate it. But, the statutory language does not permit the federal court to consider claims of fraud in the inducement of the contract generally . . . . We hold, therefore, that in passing upon a[n] application for a stay while the parties arbitrate, a federal court may consider only issues relating to the making and performance of the agreement to arbitrate.

Thus, absent a state law to the contrary, arbitration clauses are separable from the contracts in which they are embedded, and where no claim was made that fraud was directed to the arbitration clause itself, a broad arbitration clause will be held to encompass arbitration of the claim that the contract itself was induced by fraud.

Like *Prima Paint,* no claim has been advanced by the Lees that the Heftels fraudulently induced them to enter into the agreement to arbitrate any controversy or claim arising out of or relating to this agreement, or the breach thereof. Additionally, there is no Hawaii statute contrary to the holding in *Prima Paint.* Thus, because the Lees' general allegations were based on fraud in the inducement of the contract as a whole, rather than fraud in the

inducement of the arbitration clause, we hold that the claim should be decided first by mediation, and then, if necessary, by arbitration, in accordance with the terms of the DROA contract.

In reaching this conclusion, we emphasize the importance of utilizing alternative methods of dispute resolution in an effort to reduce the growing number of cases that crowd our courts each year. This court has long recognized the strong public policy supporting Hawaii's arbitration statutes.

AFFIRMED.

REVIEW AND DISCUSSION QUESTIONS

1. Name the courts in your state having (a) general jurisdiction, (b) limited jurisdiction and (c) final jurisdiction.

2. (a) Define the doctrine of precedent. (b) Indicate limitations on the use of precedent.

3. During the past 50 years, statutory law has gradually replaced judge-made or decisional law. Explain the reasons for this.

4. Do you think that the courts' recognition of binding arbitration clauses in contracts will undermine the "right to a day in court?" Explain.

CASE PROBLEMS

1. Sorensen, a licensed real estate broker, entered into a listing agreement with Schomas. Sorensen located a buyer who submitted a purchase offer. Schomas refused to accept the offer or to pay Sorensen the commission that was clearly owed. Enraged, Sorensen threatened to "take the case to the United States Supreme Court, if necessary." Explain why Sorensen probably would be unable to do this.

2. Taylor was involved in litigation involving a real estate problem. Taylor's friend Bennett testified in Taylor's behalf at the trial. Bennett's testimony was critical to the outcome of the case. Taylor lost the case and decided to appeal. When Taylor informed Bennett of his intention to appeal, Bennett told him that he could not testify a second time as the experience had drained him emotionally. Taylor told Bennett that it would not be necessary for him to testify again. Explain why.

3. Stanley Beck purchased a remote farm to which he moved with his family. After living there for a time, Beck became disturbed because his children had a long walk to the school bus. The walk was especially dangerous during the winter because there were no sidewalks and the road was often icy. Beck asked an attorney whether the purchase could be rescinded on the grounds of fraud. Beck contended that the seller, knowing Beck had school-age children, should have informed him that the walk to the bus stop could be dangerous in winter.

The attorney told Beck that, in their state, silence could not be the basis for fraud unless the seller, knowing of a hidden defect in the property that could cause injury, failed to disclose it. The attorney stated that there was no precedent for the proposition that a long walk on an icy road to a school bus is a hidden defect that a seller is bound to reveal. Explain what the attorney meant by *precedent* and why the fact that no precedent existed was significant.

land also had important political connotations in both England and the United States. For many years in England and in most of the United States, only landowners were permitted to vote.

One result of the historic importance of land is a distinction in the law of English-speaking countries between it and other forms of wealth. Because of land's economic significance, the early common law provided extensive protection to landowners. A landowner ousted from possession could immediately bring an action to recover the land (called an *action in ejectment*). In contrast, the right of an owner of personal property against one who wrongfully took that property was limited to a lawsuit for money (called *damages*). Legal actions like ejectment that protect the rights of owners in their land were known as *real actions,* and that is the reason land is called *real property* or *real estate.* The lawsuit for money of a person who lost control of something of economic value other than land, usually a movable item, was known as a *personal action* because the items involved were personal property. In modern law, as will be discussed later, the distinction between real and personal property continues to be recognized in many areas.

Personal property generally is characterized as being movable. Historically, the items of personal property of importance were tangible things such as cattle, farm equipment and the tools of a person's trade. Today, many intangible forms of wealth exist. An example would be a franchise. These intangible rights are also personal property. Over the centuries these forms of personal property have expanded, and personal property has become more equivalent to real property as wealth. One result has been a narrowing of the legal distinctions between the two, but differences continue to exist and to influence American law.

REAL AND PERSONAL PROPERTY: LEGAL PROBLEMS

The fact that real and personal property continue to be treated differently in the law of English-speaking countries causes many problems. For example, a deed, the written document transferring ownership of real estate, conveys only real property, separate from personal property. This sometimes results in confusion when a home or business is sold. The potential buyer of a home, an apartment for investment, a factory or a farm examines the premises from a functional, not a legal, viewpoint. If the real estate is a residence, the buyer is thinking about a place to live, not about the distinction between real and personal property. Items such as the stove, refrigerator, storm windows and perhaps a bar are functionally related to the reason for the purchase. The buyer understandably considers these items integral parts of the building. At the same time the seller, perhaps having purchased the items separately, often thinks of them as independent of the structure. If the law considers these articles part of the real estate, they pass to the buyer by deed unless specifically excluded by agreement. If the items are deemed personalty and hence not part of the real estate, they are not covered by the deed, and the buyer does not get them.

> ## CASE EXAMPLE
>
> David, by deed, conveyed land to Bessie. A hay barn containing equipment for unloading hay was located on the land. The equipment consisted of a track, hangers to support the track, a carrier, a hay harpoon, two pulleys and rope. The hangers were bolted to the rafters, and the track was attached to the hangers. David removed the equipment. Bessie demanded that he return it, claiming that it was real estate, as it was a part of the barn. Although a court would find for Bessie if David refused to return the equipment, the problem could have been avoided if David and Bessie had agreed in the contract how the equipment was to be treated.

The distinction between real and personal property is also significant in real estate financing. A debt secured by a mortgage is secured only by the real estate. Personal property is not part of the security. For example, if a bank takes back a mortgage on a motel as security for a debt, the furniture that is integral to successful operation of the business is not covered. Of course, the furniture could also be used as security if designated as such by a separate security agreement.

> ## CASE EXAMPLE
>
> National Bank lent funds to a small manufacturing company and took back a mortgage on realty owned by the company. On the premises was a 2,000-gallon tank set on concrete blocks. The tank was used to store gas and was connected to a garage by lines that ran above ground. The bank was forced to foreclose because the debt was not paid. Both the bank and the company claimed the tank. If the court held the tank to be part of the real estate, the tank could be sold at the foreclosure sale.

Whether an item is real or personal property also raises important insurance, tax and inheritance questions. Sometimes state statutes help provide answers to these questions, but most continue to be settled by case law. Contracts and mortgages should make clear what property the parties intend to be personal property and what they intend to be real property. Sometimes, as in the case that follows, the parties do not have an opportunity to reach an agreement regarding the status of the property.

HASLEM V. LOCKWOOD
Supreme Court of Connecticut
37 Conn. 500 (1871)

BACKGROUND. On the evening of April 6, 1869, Haslem employed two men to gather into heaps manure that lay scattered on and along the side of a public road. The men piled the manure into 18 heaps between 6 P.M. and 8 P.M., and then left without removing them.

The manure was made chiefly by horses hitched to posts on the street along side a Borough of Stamford park. Lockwood discovered the heaps the next morning, and after unsuccessfully trying to find out who made them, removed the heaps around noon. Neither party requested permission from the Borough, from whose land it was scraped, to take the manure. No sign was left on the heaps by Haslem's men. The value of the manure was estimated to be $6. Haslem sued Lockwood for the value of the manure. The trial court ruled for Lockwood.

DECISION. The Connecticut Supreme Court reversed the judgment of the trial court and ordered that the plaintiff be given a new trial.

JUDGE PARK. The plaintiff claimed that the manure was personal property which had been abandoned by its owners and became by such abandonment the property of the first person who should take possession of the same, which the plaintiff had done by gathering it into heaps, and that it was not and never had been a part of the real estate of the borough. He further claimed that if it was a part of the real estate, it was taken without committing a trespass, and with the tacit consent of the owners of such real estate, and that thereby it became his personal property.

The defendant claimed that the manure being dropped upon and spread out over the surface of the earth was a part of the real estate, and belonged to the owner of the fee, subject to the public easement; and that, unless the heaps became personal property, the plaintiff could not maintain his action. The defendant further claimed that if the manure was always personal estate, or became personal estate after being scraped up into heaps, the plaintiff, by leaving it from eight o'clock in the evening until noon the next day, abandoned all right of possession which he might have had, and could not, therefore, maintain his action.

We think the manure scattered upon the ground, under the circumstances of this case, was personal property. The cases referred to by the defendant to show that it was real estate are not in point. The principle of those cases is, that manure made in the usual course of husbandry upon a farm is so attached to and connected with the realty that, in the absence of any express stipulation to the contrary, it becomes appurtenant to it. The principle was established for the benefit of agriculture. It found its origin in the fact that it is essential to the successful cultivation of a farm that the manure, produced from the droppings of cattle and swine fed upon the products of the farm, and composted with earth and vegetable matter taken from the land, should be used to supply the drain made upon the soil in the production of crops, which otherwise would become impoverished and barren; and in the fact that manure so produced is generally regarded by farmers in this country as a part of the realty and has been so treated by landlords and tenants from time immemorial.

But this principle does not apply to the droppings of animals driven by travelers upon the highway. The highway is not used, and cannot be used, for the purpose of agriculture. The manure is of no benefit whatsoever to it, but on the contrary is a detriment; and in cities and large villages it becomes a nuisance.

The manure originally belonged to the travelers whose animals dropped it, but it being worthless to them was immediately abandoned; and whether it then became the property of the Borough of Stamford which owned the land on which the manure lay, it is unnecessary to determine; for, if it did, the case finds that the removal of the filth would be an improvement to the borough, and no objection was made by any one to the use that the plaintiff attempted to make of it. At all events, we think the facts of the case show a sufficient right in the plaintiff to the immediate possession of the property as against a mere wrong doer.

The defendant appears before the court in no enviable light. He does not pretend that he had a right to the manure, even when scattered upon the highway, superior to that of the plaintiff; but after the plaintiff had changed its original condition and greatly enhanced its value by his labor, he seized and appropriated to his own use the fruits of the plaintiff's outlay, and now seeks immunity from responsibility on the ground that the plaintiff was a wrong doer as well as himself.

It is further claimed that if the plaintiff had a right to the property by virtue of occupancy, he lost the right when he ceased to retain the actual possession of the manure after scraping it into heaps.

We do not question the general doctrine, that where the right by occupancy exists, it exists no longer than the party retains the actual possession of the property, or till he appropriates it to his own use by removing it to some other place. If he leaves the property at the place where it was discovered, and does nothing whatsoever to enhance its value or change its nature, his right by occupancy is unquestionably gone. But the question is, if a party finds property comparatively worthless, as the plaintiff found the property in question, owing to its scattered condition upon the highway, and greatly increases its value by his labor and expense, does he lose his right if he leaves it a reasonable time to procure the means to take it away, when such means are necessary for its removal?

A reasonable time for the removal of this manure had not elapsed when the defendant seized and converted it to his own use. The statute regulating the rights of parties in the gathering of seaweed, gives the party who heaps it upon a public beach twenty-four hours in which to remove it, and that length of time for the removal of the property we think would not be unreasonable in most cases like the present one.

JUDGMENT IS REVERSED, AND A NEW TRIAL GRANTED.

FIXTURES

◆ **Separately identifiable items that were once personal property but that have become real property generally through annexation to land or buildings.**

Chandeliers, carpeting, electric hot water heaters and shrubbery are common examples of fixtures associated with residential real estate. All these items are personal property while part of the seller's inventory, but when annexed to land or buildings they are generally considered part of the real estate. On a farm, items such as cattle stanchions, water pumps and fencing would ordinarily be fixtures. Many items associated with industrial or commercial real estate are also classified as fixtures. How would you classify the mirror behind the bar in your favorite restaurant or the overhead track for moving heavy material in a factory? Both could be readily detached without harm to the building, and they appear movable as is personal property, but they, too, are probably fixtures.

The chief test in determining whether an item is a fixture is the intention of the party who attached it to the real estate. Intention will, however, be determined by the manner in which the one who affixed the item acted, not by his or her secret intention. In the case that follows, intention is clearly established by the evidence.

FEDERAL LAND BANK OF OMAHA V. SWANSON
Supreme Court of Nebraska
231 Neb. 868 (1989)

BACKGROUND. On April 8, 1983, Jerald E. and Pamela A. Swanson (codefendants) gave a note and mortgage on their farm to the Federal Land Bank of Omaha (plaintiff—appellant). In September 1983, the Swansons borrowed money from Arlington State Bank (defendant—appellee) to purchase two grain bins. The loan was evidenced by a properly executed promissory note and secured by a security agreement on the grain bins. A financing statement was thereafter filed. In 1986, the Swansons defaulted on their mortgage loan and voluntarily surrendered the real estate to the Federal Land Bank.

The Arlington State Bank initiated a procedure to obtain possession of the grain bins, so they could sell them at an auction. On November 5, 1986, the Federal Land Bank obtained a temporary restraining order prohibiting the sale. On July 27, 1987, the district court dissolved the temporary restraining order and awarded possession of the grain bins to the Arlington State Bank on grounds that the bins were the personal property of the Swansons. The Federal Land Bank appealed.

DECISION. The Nebraska Supreme Court affirmed the judgment of the lower court.

JUSTICE WHITE. The appellant's claim to the grain bins and accessories necessarily arises from its interest in the Swansons' real estate pursuant to the April 1983 mortgage. The appellee bank contends the grain bins and accessories are personalty in which it has a valid security interest because of the promissory note and financing and security agreement. Hence the threshold question is whether the grain bins are, as the district court found, personalty.

In *Metropolitan Life Ins. Co. v. Reeves,* this court said:

> Three main factors determine whether an article, or combination of articles, is a fixture. They are (1) whether the article or articles are actually annexed to the realty, or something appurtenant thereto; (2) whether the article or articles have been appropriated to the use or purpose of that part of the realty with which it is or they are connected; and (3) whether the party making the annexation intended to make the article or articles a permanent accession to the freehold. . . .
>
> . . . [T]he third factor, the intention of the annexing party to make the article or articles a permanent accession to the realty, is the factor which is typically given the most weight.

With respect to the first factor, the evidence shows that the disputed bins are utilized for drying and storing grain. One bin is a

30-foot-diameter eight-ring bin with a 14,000-bushel capacity, and the other is a 24-foot-diameter seven-ring bin with a 6,000-bushel capacity. The bins are provided with several accessories for drying and moving the grain, such as drying fans, heaters, and augers. Each bin sits on a concrete slab. On the bottom ring of each bin is an angle ring which lies flush on top of the concrete slab. Clips, which are not part of the bin structure, are placed over the lip of the angle ring and are attached to bolts protruding from the concrete slab around the outside of the bin. The clips are adjustable and can easily be slid off the lip of the angle ring, allowing removal of the bin. The contractor, Isadore Stoetzel, whose company erected the bins, testified that the bins were designed to sit on top of the concrete and that the purpose of the clip anchoring system was to prevent the bin from blowing away in the wind. Though Stoetzel has never moved this particular type of grain bin before, he has moved several bins similar to the ones in dispute. Stoetzel stated that on one occasion it took him only 4 hours to move two larger, 36-foot-diameter bins. On cross examination, the following testimony occurred:

Q. Did you ever discuss with [Jerald Swanson] whether [the bins] were ever going to be moved or not?
A. He asked me if they could be moved prior to signing the contract.
Q. And you told him—
A. I told him basically what I am telling you, that they can be moved.

The evidence also demonstrates that the accessories are items which are either attached to the grain bins or are readily movable. Accordingly, we find that the grain bins and accessories are not annexed to the real estate, and for the remainder of this opinion we treat the accessories as part of the grain bins.

The evidence going to the second factor, whether the grain bins have been appropriated to the use or purpose of that part of the realty with which they are connected, showed that Jerald Swanson used the bins to store crops raised on the surrounding land. However, on one occasion he did store some of his neighbor's grain for a short period of time.

Though finding that the evidence satisfied the second factor, as stated above, the third factor, regarding the intent of the annexing party, is given the most weight. We note that the evidence shows that Jerald Swanson purchased the grain bins in August 1983, approximately 5 months after the mortgage was executed. The loan from the appellee bank was used exclusively for the purchase and erection of the two bins. During a deposition, Jerald Swanson testified as follows:

Q. ... [W]ere you giving something to the [appellee] bank when you signed [the financing statement and security agreement]?
A. Well, you were giving an agreement that you were going to pay them back, I guess, for the property that they had. I guess they had the right to it until you paid it off.
Q. And the property that you are referring to then would be what?
A. My personal property, which you know.
Q. Would that include the grain bins?
A. Right, yes . . . .
Q. So if you did not pay off the loan, it was your intention that the bank would be entitled to the grain bins?
A. Yes.

In addition, every year appellee bank required a property statement from Jerald Swanson. On the 1984 statement, Jerald Swanson listed the grain bins as farm equipment and noted that appellee bank held a lien on the bins. Based on the foregoing, it is clear that Jerald Swanson's intention was that the bins were his personal property subject to a lien held by the appellee bank. He never intended the grain bins to be fixtures. Thus, we find that the evidence clearly establishes that the grain bins were personal property and not fixtures. The appellant failed to establish by a preponderance of the evidence each factor to support its claim to relief.

Because of our finding, it is not necessary to address appellant's other assignments of error except to note, with regard to its third assignment of error, that appellant cannot claim a superior interest in the grain bins on the alleged weakness of appellee bank's failure to perfect its security interest.

Accordingly, the judgment of the district court for Cheyenne County is affirmed.

AFFIRMED.

Many problems arise in identifying fixtures because infinite variations in facts complicate legal analysis. For parties involved in a real estate transaction, the most effective way to prevent these problems is for them to agree in writing as to whether particular items are to be treated as personalty or real property (fixtures).

TRADE FIXTURES

◆ **Items annexed to land or buildings by a tenant to be used in the tenant's trade or business.**

We have seen that items of personal property, annexed to realty with the intention that the item become part of the realty, are fixtures. *Fixtures are real estate* and usually may not be removed or treated separately unless the parties agree. It is clear, however, that a business firm leasing real estate would be seriously hampered if this rule applied to items needed to operate a plant or shop effectively. Therefore, the legal system differentiates between fixtures and trade fixtures, the latter being personalty attached to real estate in order to carry on a trade or business. A tenant may generally remove trade fixtures. Agricultural fixtures have been treated in a similar manner. In order to remove a trade or agricultural fixture, the tenant must restore the premises to their original condition and remove the trade fixture before the lease terminates.

Allowing tenants to remove trade fixtures has social benefits. It encourages both the use of land and efficiency in business. Tenants are more likely to invest in new and improved equipment if they can remove these items after they have been attached to the realty. Statutes in a number of states establish tenants' rights to remove trade fixtures.

Although the law allows tenants to remove trade fixtures at the end of a lease even if the lease does not mention this point, parties to a commercial lease should include provisions that express their agreement as to how trade fixtures will be treated when the lease ends. They might agree that the tenant shall not remove items that ordinarily would be trade fixtures. On the other hand, a lease provision stating the tenant's right to remove those items added to carry out the business or trade shows the intention of the parties and lessens possibilities for disagreement and litigation as to whether or not the items may be removed.

GROWING CROPS

Traditionally, courts classified growing crops in two categories. An annual crop that was the product of human effort was referred to as *fructus industriales*. This classification included crops such as wheat, corn, oats, cotton and rice. Crops that were produced on perennial roots such as trees, bushes and vines were categorized as *fructus naturales*. Fructus naturales were crops such as citrus fruits, apples, berries and grapes. As a general rule, fructus industriales were considered personal property and fructus naturales real property.

Today, in most states, for most purposes the classification of fructus industriales has been broadened considerably. In general, it includes any crop that owes its value to human care and labor. Thus, fruit and berry crops as well as crops like hay are classified as fructus industriales. In a limited number of states the courts consider the produce of perennial roots fructus industriales, although the trees, vines and bushes that produce the crop are fructus naturales.

Although these classifications continue to be of importance when a dispute arises involving growing crops, modern courts consider a number of other factors when determining whether a crop is realty or personalty.

One significant factor in some states is the maturity of the crop. The more mature the crop, the more likely courts are to consider it personal property. In addition to maturity, courts often consider factors such as the relationship of the parties, their intentions and the type of transaction. Many present-day legal problems involving growing crops are solved by statutes, which individual states have adopted because of the uncertainty of the case law.

One of the most significant of these statutes is the Uniform Commercial Code (UCC), which has been adopted by all states. Article 2 of the UCC deals with the sale of goods. "Goods" under the UCC are always personal property. Furthermore, the UCC defines growing crops as goods whether they are grown on annual or perennial roots. This definition eliminates the traditional legal distinction between fructus industriales and fructus naturales, at least for UCC purposes. The UCC also states that growing crops become goods if they can be removed without harm at the time buyer and seller contract for their sale even if they are part of the real estate at the time. Thus, Christmas trees and sod grown on the land become personal property before severance if they are identified as the subject of a contract.

Although statutes such as the UCC bring some certainty to the law, the real estate practitioner should realize that the most effective method of preventing controversy is to have the parties agree how the crops are to be treated. This agreement should then be included in the lease, deed, purchase offer or other written documentation that covers the transaction.

SECURED TRANSACTIONS

◆ **A transaction in which the parties agree that personal property or fixtures will secure a loan or the purchase of an item on credit.**

Lenders use various types of personal property to secure repayment of loans. Sellers, too, often retain an interest in goods being sold on credit to ensure payment of the purchase price. Secured transactions of this nature are very important to the economy of the United States. They range from relatively minor purchases of appliances and television sets by consumers

4. Thatcher was interested in buying a business. She finally located a gift shop and agreed to buy it. The business was located in a building that Thatcher leased for three years. In order to increase the shop's business, she purchased several new display cases. These were attached to the floor. The business was successful; however, the landlord notified Thatcher that the lease would not be renewed. Does Thatcher have the right to remove the display cases? Support your answer.

3

Land, Water and Air Rights

LAND

◆ **The solid surface of the earth and the natural elements (water and minerals) associated with it.**

It is the land, air and water in combination that make planet Earth different from other planets, and a place where humans can live. Until recently, the idea that people could exist for any length of time apart from land was inconceivable. Even today, when the idea of human beings living out their lives on islands in space is a possibility, human destiny remains linked with land. Since time immemorial, humans have taken their living directly or indirectly from the land. Because land and people have always been inseparable, the ways in which land has been viewed are as diverse as the world's communities.

Much of the conflict between the American Indians and Europeans who settled this hemisphere resulted from attitudes toward land. Land, to the Indians, was a resource possessed by the tribe. It was not subject to individual ownership. Some native groups in Africa, Australia and South America hold similar views today. In western Europe during the late Middle Ages, the idea of community ownership in some lands existed, but by the time major colonization occurred in North America, the concept of individual property rights prevailed. Most settlers who came to this country after 1700 wanted to own their own land. Although themes other than individual ownership can be discerned in the way Americans regard land, a majority, especially those living in the United States, continue to consider it a commodity to be owned individually.

Probably the most important factor in viewing land as a commodity is rooted in our economic philosophy. Our pioneer ancestors were individualistic in economic matters. The men and women who wrested arable land from the great forests of the East and from the prairies of the West were acquiring wealth for themselves and their families. They saw land, like any commodity, as something that could be bought and sold or passed on to their children. These people also believed in personal freedom. They regarded private ownership of land as a bulwark against both the intrusion of the state and the inquisitiveness of their neighbors. Finally, traditional economic theory in the Western world includes land as an important factor of production. Land is an important good that, with labor and capital, can be put to work to provide profit for the owner.

REAL ESTATE
◆ **Land and its improvements; mines, minerals and quarries under the land; air and water rights associated with land; and other rights and privileges related to land.**

Although it is a commonly used term, the meaning of *real estate* varies from place to place and from situation to situation. For example, in a number of states, leases are not considered real estate. In some states, the duration of the lease determines whether the tenant's interest is real estate; in other states it does not. In addition, *real estate* sometimes has more than one statutory definition within a single state, some definitions being broader than others. It is difficult to give real estate one definition because the sense in which it is used in everyday speech does not always correspond to its specific legal meaning.

In some contexts the terms *real estate* and *land* are used interchangeably; however, the meaning of *real estate* is generally broader than the meaning of *land.* Real estate includes not only land but also improvements on the land, such as a house, a barn and other structures. Many rights and privileges associated with land are considered to be real estate as well. For example, if one has a right-of-way from his or her own land across the land of a neighbor to reach a road, that right-of-way is real estate and can be sold or transferred as such in many instances. Water rights, mines, minerals and quarries are also considered real estate for most purposes.

Real property is a term lawyers and judges often use as a synonym for real estate. This chapter discusses real estate, or real property, principles in greater detail.

LAND AS A NATURAL RESOURCE
Although the view of land as a commodity has been dominant in the United States, this is but one view of land. A contrasting view of land as a social resource that must be preserved for future generations has gained increasing acceptance in recent years. As a result of this trend, vast areas of our nation have been set aside as a public domain, and governments at all levels have adopted legislation to control land use for the benefit of society. Some commentators are urging that the nature of land as essential for human survival necessitates that we cultivate a duty of stewardship toward the land, along with our emphasis on private property rights. Land has become the subject of a large body of law as our nation tries to cope with the problems involved with its use and disposition.

As traditionally defined by courts and commentators, land encompasses the surface of the earth, everything above that surface and all that is below. Land has been described as an inverted pyramid extending upward indefinitely into space (air rights) and downward to the center of the earth. Many items such as water, minerals, oil and gas can be separated from the land. Because these things are both scarce and desirable, they are often severed and treated as independent commodities. The result has been that detailed laws regulating their use have developed throughout the United States. These laws differ from place to place and from time to time as they reflect the needs of people in a particular area during a particular era. Consider how life today would have been affected had the opposite result been reached in the *Thrasher* case.

THRASHER V. CITY OF ATLANTA

Supreme Court of Georgia
173 S.E. 817 (1934)

BACKGROUND. Thrasher lived adjacent to the municipal airport. Though it was the advent of the age of the airplane, the flights across Thrasher's land were low and becoming more frequent. The plaintiff sued the City of Atlanta as the owner of the airport from which the flights originated. The plaintiff contended that the flights constituted an illegal trespass, violated his constitutional rights to private property, and perpetuated a nuisance on him and his family. The portion of the case reproduced here focuses on the issue of the trespass only. The trial court found for the defendant.

DECISION. The appellate court affirmed the decision for the defendant.

JUSTICE BELL. The Civil Code (1910), sec. 3617, declares that "the right of an owner of lands extends downward and upward indefinitely." In section 4477 it is stated that "the owner of realty having title downwards and upwards indefinitely, an unlawful interference with his rights, below and above the surface, alike gives him a right of action." These statements as to ownership above the surface are based upon the common-law maxim *cujus est solum ejus est usque ad coelum*—who owns the soil owns also to the sky. These provisions of the code should therefore be construed in the

light of the authoritative content of the maxim itself. As a matter of fact, the language of the code that the title to land extends upwards indefinitely would seem to be a limitation upon the ad coelum doctrine, indicating by implication that the title will include only such portions of the upper space as may be seized and appropriated by the owner of the soil. Such a construction of the code provisions would materially minimize the difficulties in the present case; but even if the code was intended to express the ad coelum theory in its entirety, and this we assume in the present case, it remains true that the maxim can have only such legal signification as it brings from the common law.

What is the sky? Who can tell where it begins or define its meaning in terms of the law? When can it be said that a plane is above the sky or below it? How can there be an unqualified tangible right in a thing so indeterminate and elusive? What and where is the res (thing) of which a court may assume jurisdiction in a case involving a private claim of title? Possession is the basis of all ownership and that which man can never possess would seem to be incapable of being owned. In order to recover for a trespass it is necessary to show title or actual possession. The space in the far distance above the earth is in the actual possession of no one, and, being incapable of such possession, title to the land beneath does not necessarily include title to such space. The legal title can hardly extend above an altitude representing the reasonable possibility of man's occupation and dominion, although as respects the realm beyond this the owner of the land may complain of any use tending to diminish the free enjoyment of the soil beneath. The maxim to which reference has been made is a generalization from old cases involving the title to space within the range of actual occupation, and any statement as to title beyond was manifestly a mere dictum. For instance, a court in dealing with the title to space at a given distance above the earth could make no authoritative decision as to the title at higher altitudes, the latter question not being involved. The common-law cases from which the ad coelum doctrine emanated were limited to facts and conditions close to earth and did not require an adjudication on the title to the mansions in the sky. Accordingly, the maxim imported from the ancient past consists in large measure of dicta, and to that extent cannot be taken as an authentic statement of any law. It follows that the literal terms of the code sections referred to must be discounted or qualified in like measure.

But the space is up there, and the owner of the land has the first claim upon it. If another should capture and possess it, as by erecting a high building with a fixed overhanging structure, this alone will show that the space affected is capable of being possessed, and consequently the owner of the soil beneath the overhanging structure may be entitled to ejectment or to an action for trespass. However, the pilot of an airplane does not seize and hold the space or stratum of air through which he navigates, and cannot do so. He is merely a transient, and the use to which he applies the ethereal realm does not partake of the nature of occupation in the sense of dominion and ownership. So long as the space through which he moves is beyond the reasonable possibility of possession by the occupant below, he is in free territory—not as every or any man's land, but rather as a sort of "no man's land." As stated above, however, the occupant of the soil is entitled to be free from danger or annoyance by any use of the super-incumbent space, and for any infringement of this right he may apply to the law for appropriate redress or relief.

Affirmed.

WATER

Water is an element essential to human survival. Without water, land is of little value. Consequently, lands adjacent to water or having water readily available are usually more valuable than other lands. Because of water's importance, disputes sometimes develop between property owners attempting to take advantage of this valuable resource. Efforts to solve these disputes have led to an extensive law of water rights.

Whatever the legal system, several factors appear to have a major influence on water rights law. The most significant is water's scarcity or abundance. The influence of this condition is clearly evident in U.S. law. Another important factor is the type of economy prevailing in the area. Climate and technology are also significant in determining rights of individuals to water. Historically, water rights law in the United States has been concerned mainly with problems of surface water. In more recent times, however, legal questions have also arisen concerning water that flows underground and water that percolates into the subsurface from rain and snow melt.

SURFACE WATER
◆ **Water upon the surface of the earth in flowing streams and lakes.**

Lakes and streams that are the subject of water rights can be navigable or nonnavigable. A navigable body of water is one that has the capacity to be useful for commerce or travel. The U.S. Constitution allocates power to Congress to regulate navigable waters, but until Congress acts, the states also may regulate. Although Congress frequently has taken actions that involve navigable waters, it has not, except in limited instances, such as the Clean Water Act, restricted the rights of owners of land along these waterways. As Congress has not asserted all its powers over navigable waters, the power of the state over waters within its jurisdiction is paramount, just as it is for nonnavigable waters.

Riparian Land. Riparian lands are those that border on a stream or watercourse. Riparian lands extend away from the stream, including the stream's drainage area or watershed, although all of the drainage area is not necessarily riparian land. The riparian area of the watershed is only that portion under ownership of a person whose property fronts on the waterway. A landowner's property might be in the watershed of a stream, but the landowner is not a riparian owner unless his or her property fronts on the stream.

Littoral Land. Littoral lands are those that border on an ocean, a sea, or a lake. In some states *littoral* applies only to lands that border on a tidal body such as an ocean or a sea. Other states use the term to describe lands that border on lakes as well. In many states the term is not used at all: *riparian* is used to designate lands bordering on lakes, oceans and seas as well as those bordering on flowing streams.

In general, the rights of owners of littoral lands are the same as those of the owners of riparian lands. These rights are discussed in the paragraphs that follow. However, at least one difference exists between riparian owners and littoral owners. Littoral owners do not own the land to the water. They own only to the line to which the high tide rises. This is called the *high-water mark*. From the high-water mark to the water (the *low-water mark*), the property is owned by the state. Therefore, the states have the power to control and regulate from the high-water mark to the low-water mark.

OWNERSHIP OF OIL AND GAS

U.S. courts have not been consistent in their treatment of the nature of the landowner's interest in oil and gas under the surface. Some courts have attempted to solve legal disputes involving oil and gas ownership by applying principles developed in cases involving ownership and mining of solid minerals. The theory that evolved is known as the *ownership theory*. Other courts recognized that oil and gas migrate under the ground from high-pressure to low-pressure areas. These courts applied rules similar to those applied to questions involving the ownership of wild animals and migratory birds. This theory is called the *non-ownership theory*. A discussion of the two theories follows.

OWNERSHIP THEORY

◆ **The theory under which oil and gas are minerals and are therefore as subject to absolute ownership as coal or any other solid mineral.**

"Absolute" is the key to this theory. In fact, the term *absolute* is often used in place of *ownership*. The ownership theory is not applicable logically to gas and oil because they are migratory within the earth. However, many states apparently have adopted this theory. In addition to Texas (see the following Case Example), states following this principle include Arkansas, Colorado, Kansas, Pennsylvania, Tennessee and West Virginia.

CASE EXAMPLE

S. R. Hill executed a lease of oil and gas rights to Mid-Kansas Oil and Gas Co. The county assessed a tax against the company based on the lease. At the time, no oil or gas had been taken from the ground. The company argued that it could not be taxed because oil and gas in place cannot be owned. This argument was based on the premise that, until oil or gas is brought to the surface, owners of adjacent land may lawfully appropriate the oil or gas.

The question of tax liability was decided in favor of the county. The court stated: "[G]as and oil in place are minerals and realty, subject to ownership, severance, and sale while embedded in the sands or rocks beneath the earth's surface, in like manner and to the same extent as coal or any other mineral." *Stephens County vs. Mid-Kansas Oil and Gas Co., 113 Tex. 160, 254 S.W. 290(1923).*

Under the ownership theory, the landowner may sever oil and gas by deed just as he or she would sever solid minerals or a portion of the surface itself. The person who acquires the oil or gas gets the same property rights that are acquired when buying a lot on the surface.

NONOWNERSHIP THEORY

◆ **The theory that oil and gas are not the subject of ownership because of their migratory nature.**

Under this theory, the landowner has no ownership of oil and gas in place. Each landowner has an exclusive right to drill on the land and becomes the owner when the oil is brought to the surface. The right can be transferred by sale or otherwise. Although the right to search for oil and gas is an interest in land, it is not real property. Some states by statute attribute to this interest many rules applying to real property. Ohio, Louisiana, New York, Alabama, Indiana and Kentucky are among the states in which courts generally adhere to the nonownership theory.

Although the nature of oil and gas ownership differs under these two theories, many significant aspects of oil and gas law are the same under both. For example, although drilling near the boundary line of one's land in most states is not an illegal interference with the rights of owners of adjoining land, a slanted well that goes under the surface of another's land is a trespass. Under both theories, government has the power to regulate operating and production practices, waste is not permitted and no driller may unreasonably injure the reservoir. Additionally, the important *rule of capture* is recognized under both.

RULE OF CAPTURE

◆ **The rule that states that the owner of the surface has the right to appropriate all oil and gas from wells on his or her land, including oil and gas that have migrated from the land of another.**

Whether a jurisdiction recognizes the ownership or the nonownership theory, as oil and gas migrate under the ground, the person whose wells produce the oil and gas owns it. This principle is applied in jurisdictions accepting the ownership doctrine even though oil brought to the surface does not always originate beneath the land of the driller. Similarly, ownership of oil and gas that migrate away from the surface owner's lands is lost. The rule of capture is a logical approach to ownership of oil and gas. It is impossible to distinguish oil that has seeped from under the land of another from that originally under the surface on which the well is located.

CASE EXAMPLE

Hastings owned 165 acres of land in northern Ohio. The Ohio Oil Co. owned oil and gas rights in several large parcels of land partially surrounding Hastings's acreage. Although the company had ample space to locate wells elsewhere, it drilled several wells at 400-foot intervals 25 feet from the Hastings property line. Hastings sought an injunction prohibiting the company from operating oil wells at any point within 200 feet of Hastings's farm. He argued that much of the oil produced from the company's wells percolated from under his land. Ohio courts refused to grant the injunction, thus recognizing the rule of capture. *Kelley v. The Ohio Oil Co., 57 Ohio St. 317 (1897).*

The rule of capture allows each landowner to appropriate oil and gas produced by all wells on his or her property. Early cases even permitted the wasteful disposal of whatever these wells produced. In some states an operator may increase flow from wells by pumping, although this practice draws oil from adjoining land. The only protection available to a neighbor is to drill and pump on his or her own land.

STATE STATUTES

During the past 25 years, court opinions and statutes in a number of states have extended the rights of all landowners to share in a common source of oil and gas. Waste is prohibited, and each landowner is permitted a reasonable opportunity to obtain a just and equitable share of the oil or gas in the pool. This is known as the doctrine of *correlative rights*. The gas under the ground may go wherever it will, but an operator may not draw off gas from a neighbor's land in a manner that will unnecessarily deplete a common pool.

A few states have adopted legislation defining the amount of land that must surround a well or requiring a specific distance between wells. These are known as *spacing statutes*. Their purpose is to prevent waste and to give each surface owner an opportunity to take from the common pool.

Other states attempt to control production so that each owner has a reasonable opportunity to recover a fair share of the oil and gas under his or her tract by pooling or prorating the allowable production of oil. Extensive regulation by the state is a fact of life where oil is involved.

AIR RIGHTS

Until recently, the traditional theory that whoever owns the soil owns to the heavens was sufficient to solve most disputes involving invasion of airspace. Airspace problems, which usually concerned overhanging branches, bushes or eaves, were important to the parties but of little significance to society. With the advent of the airplane as a major means of transportation, courts and legislative bodies had to reconsider the old concept of absolute control of airspace. The early English rule that airspace was an appurtenance to land, giving absolute and exclusive right to the owner "to the highest heavens," was repudiated. In general, the courts recognize that the public interest in efficient transportation outweighs any theoretical trespass in airspace. As long as air flight does not interfere with the owner's right to the effective use of the space above his land, airplanes passing through this space are not trespassing. In brief, a landowner's exclusive domain extends at least to a height that makes it possible for the land to be used in a reasonable manner. To this extent the owner of the surface has absolute ownership of the space above his or her land.

Recently some important developments in real estate have been possible because the ownership of airspace may be separated from ownership of the surface. As population has expanded, investors have turned to space above land to satisfy both commercial and residential needs. When an individual purchases a high-rise condominium, that person is acquiring title to airspace. In metropolitan areas such as New York City and Chicago, railroads owning downtown property have separately conveyed airspace above the tracks to be used for commercial buildings. The purchaser acquires air rights above the area needed by the railroad for its trains and a surface easement sufficient to support construction and facilities. As interest has grown in recent years in alternative, renewable sources of energy, questions arose regarding air rights to sunlight and to wind. The following case illustrates the point.

PRAH V. MARETTI
Supreme Court of Wisconsin
321 N.W.2d 182 (Wis. 1982)

BACKGROUND. Glenn Prah constructed a house in a subdivision, installing a solar system, including roof collectors, to supply energy to heat his house and water. Later, Richard Maretti purchased an adjoining lot for the purpose of building a house and acquired all the requisite government approvals to commence construction. Prah requested that Maretti move his proposed house further south on the lot than he planned so that it would not shade Prah's solar panels. Maretti refused the request and commenced construction.

Prah sued Maretti claiming that he was entitled to unrestricted access to the sun for solar power under the doctrine of private nuisance and sought to enjoin construction. Maretti moved for summary judgment for failure to state a cause of action. The trial court granted the motion for summary judgment.

DECISION. The Wisconsin Supreme Court reversed the trial court holding that Prah had stated a valid claim for relief and should be granted a trial to prove the claim.

JUSTICE ABRAHAMSON. This state has long recognized that an owner of land does not have an absolute or unlimited right to use the land in a way which injures the rights of others. The rights of neighboring landowners are rela-

tive; the uses by one must not unreasonably impair the uses or enjoyment of the other. When one landowner's use of his or her property unreasonably interferes with another's enjoyment of his or her property, that use is said to be a private nuisance.

The private nuisance doctrine has traditionally been employed in this state to balance the conflicting rights of landowners and this court has recently adopted the analysis of private nuisance set forth in the Restatement (Second) of Torts. The Restatement defines private nuisance as "a nontrespassory invasion of another's interest in the private use and enjoyment of land." The phrase "interest in the private use and enjoyment of land" is broadly defined to include any disturbance of the enjoyment of property.

Although the defendant's obstruction of the plaintiff's access to sunlight appears to fall within the Restatement's broad concept of a private nuisance as a nontrespassory invasion of another's interest in the private use and enjoyment of land, the defendant asserts that he has a right to develop his property in compliance with the statutes, ordinances and private covenants without regard to the effect of such development upon the plaintiff's access to sunlight. In essence, the defendant is asking this court to hold that the private nuisance doctrine is not applicable in the instant case and that his right to develop his land is a right which is per se superior to his neighbor's interest in access to sunlight. This position is expressed in the maxim, "cujus est solum, ejus est usque ad coelum et ad infernos," that is, the owner of land owns up to the sky and down to the center of the earth. The rights of the surface owner are, however, not unlimited.

The defendant is not completely correct in asserting that the common law did not protect a landowner's access to sunlight across adjoining property. At English common law a landowner could acquire a right to receive sunlight across adjoining land by both express agreement and under the judge-made doctrine of "ancient lights." Under the doctrine of ancient lights if the landowner had received sunlight across adjoining property for a specified period of time the landowner was entitled to continue to receive unobstructed access to sunlight across the adjoining property. Under the doctrine the landowner . . . could prevent the adjoining landowner from obstructing access to light.

Although American courts have not been as receptive to protecting a landowner's access to sunlight as the English courts, American courts have afforded some protection to a landowner's interest in access to sunlight. American courts honor express easements to sunlight. American courts initially enforced the English common law doctrine of ancient lights, but later every state which considered the doctrine repudiated it as inconsistent with the needs of a developing country. Indeed, for just that reason this court concluded that an easement to light and air over adjacent property could not be created or acquired and has been unwilling to recognize such an easement.

This court's reluctance in the nineteenth and early part of the twentieth century to provide broader protection for a landowner's access to sunlight was premised on three policy considerations. First, the right of landowners to use their property as they wished, as long as they did not cause physical damage to a neighbor, was jealously guarded.

Second, sunlight was valued only for aesthetic enjoyment or as illumination. Since artificial light could be used for illumination, loss of sunlight was at most a personal annoyance which was given little, if any, weight by society.

Third, society had a significant interest in not restricting or impeding land development. This court repeatedly emphasized that in the growth period of the nineteenth and early twentieth centuries change is to be expected and is essential to property and that recognition of a right to sunlight would hinder property development.

Considering these three policies, this court concluded that in the absence of an express agreement granting access to sunlight, a landowner's obstruction of another's access to sunlight was not actionable. These three policies are no longer fully accepted or applicable. They reflect factual circumstances and social priorities that are now obsolete.

First, society has increasingly regulated the use of land by the landowner for the general welfare.

Second, access to sunlight has taken on a new significance in recent years. In this case, the plaintiff seeks to protect access to sunlight, not for aesthetic reasons or as a source of illumination but as a source of energy. Access to sunlight as an energy source is of significance both to the landowner who invests in solar collectors and to a society which has an interest in developing alternative sources of energy.

Third, the policy of favoring unhindered private development in an expanding economy is no longer in harmony with the realities of our society. The need for easy and rapid development is not as great today as it once was, while our perception of the value of sunlight as a source of energy has increased significantly.

Courts should not implement obsolete policies that have lost their vigor over the course of the years. The law of private nuisance is better suited to resolve landowners' disputes about property development in the 1980s than is a rigid rule which does not recognize a landowner's interest in access to sunlight. "What is regarded in law as constituting a nuisance in modern times would no doubt have been tolerated without question in former times."

Yet the defendant would have us ignore the flexible private nuisance law as a means of resolving the dispute between the landowners in this case and would have us adopt an approach favoring the unrestricted development of land and of applying a rigid and inflexible rule protecting his right to build on his land and disregarding any interest of the plaintiff in the use and enjoyment of his land. This we refuse to do.

Private nuisance law, the law traditionally used to adjudicate conflicts between private landowners, has the flexibility to protect both a landowner's right of access to sunlight and other landowner's right to develop land. Private nuisance law is better suited to regulate access to sunlight in modern society and is more in harmony with legislative policy and the prior decisions of this court than is an inflexible doctrine of non-recognition of any interest in access to sunlight across adjoining land.

We therefore hold that private nuisance law, that is, the reasonable use doctrine as set forth in the restatement, is applicable to the instant case. Recognition of a nuisance claim for unreasonable obstruction of access to sunlight will not prevent land development or unduly hinder the use of adjoining land. It will promote the reasonable use and enjoyment of land in a manner suitable to the 1980s. That obstruction of access to light might be found to constitute a nuisance in certain circumstances does not mean that it will be or must be found to constitute a nuisance under all circumstances. The result in each case depends on whether the conduct complained of is unreasonable.

We do not determine whether the plaintiff in this case is entitled to relief. In order to be entitled to relief the plaintiff must prove the elements required to establish actionable nuisance, and the conduct of the defendant herein must be judged by the reasonable use doctrine.

REVERSED.

COMMON LAW LIMITATIONS

There are limitations created by the common law on the rights of owners to unrestrictively use their land. Such common law limitations are imposed by the law for the benefit of surrounding landholders.

NUISANCE
◆ **An unreasonable interference by one party with another's use or enjoyment of his or her land.**

The notion of nuisance is an ancient creation to protect landowners from unfettered and wrongful use of land by a neighbor. It does not require a physical invasion of the complainant's land, as does trespass. Such things as noise, dust, vibration and odors may constitute a nuisance. A party who is victimized by a nuisance will be able to get compensatory damages and may be able to enjoin the nuisance. Most states, however, will grant an injunction only after balancing the equities between the parties and determining that the benefit of the injunction will outweigh the ensuing detriment to the perpetrator of the nuisance. As a result of this balancing process, injunctions are not readily available to small landowners complaining about a nuisance created by a large industrial or commercial facility. For instance, in a case entitled *Boomer v. Atlantic Cement Co., 26 N.Y.2d 219, 257 N.E.2d 870 (1970)*, New York's highest court was unwilling to enjoin the operation of the $45 million plant, though admitting that there was a substantial nuisance to several nearby landowners. Prior to this case, New York had been more liberal than most states in granting injunctions in nuisance cases.

TRESPASS

◆ **A wrongful, physical invasion of the property of another.**

This common law remedy may be available to the landowner to put a stop to physical encroachments, whether they occur on the land's surface, in the air above or on the ground beneath.

JOHNSON V. MARCEL

Supreme Court of Virginia
465 S.E.2d 815 (1996)

BACKGROUND. Debra Johnson and Karlista Brennan by separate agreement became cotenants of a townhouse owned by Grace Marcel. Subsequently, when Johnson rebuffed Marcel's efforts to develop a business venture with her, Marcel demanded that Johnson vacate the premises prior to the lease's expiration. Johnson had prepaid her rent and refused to vacate. When Brennan refused to help Marcel evict Johnson, she ordered Brennan to vacate the premises within 24 hours. Brennan refused. Marcel proceeded to make harassing calls to the tenants at work and at home, she changed the locks on their garage, and she entered the townhouse without permission when the tenants were at work. On November 16, 1993, the tenants obtained a court order restraining Marcel from harassing and attempting to evict the tenants. On November 18, 1993, about midnight, Marcel pulled the tenants' downstairs phone from the socket, blocked their driveway, and began screaming, banging on doors and threatening them. The tenants vacated the premises in fear, despite the prepaid rent, lost their security deposit, and incurred the expense of temporary housing.

Johnson and Brennan sued Marcel alleging a common law trespass and seeking to recover for their financial losses described above, and for their emotional distress. The trial court dismissed their complaint for failure to state a cause of action.

DECISION. The Virginia Supreme Court reversed the trial court and remanded the case for a trial.

JUSTICE STEPHENSON. Although Marcel owned the premises, the plaintiffs, as tenants, had the right of possession. Therefore, under the circumstances of the present case, Marcel had no right to enter the premises without the plaintiffs' consent. According to the allegations in the amended motion for judgment, however, Marcel entered the premises without the

plaintiffs' consent. Despite the injunction, she also changed the locks on the plaintiffs' garage, ripped the downstairs telephone out of the wall socket, blocked the plaintiffs' driveway, and continually threatened, abused, intimidated, and harassed the plaintiffs. We think these allegations state a claim of common law trespass. We also think the plaintiffs may claim damages for emotional distress. Where, as here, the alleged trespass is deliberate and accompanied by aggravating circumstances, damages for emotional distress may be recoverable in the absence of physical injury.

We hold, therefore, that the amended motion for judgment states a cause of action for deliberate trespass and that the trial court erred.

REVERSED AND REMANDED.

Actual damages need not be shown in order to recover for a trespass to land, but as a practical matter the landowner is likely to get only nominal damages where he or she does not actually show loss.

REVIEW AND DISCUSSION QUESTIONS

1. Outline those arguments supporting individual ownership of land. Evaluate these arguments.

2. Compare the riparian doctrines of reasonable use and natural flow. What limitations exist upon reasonable use? From a public policy viewpoint, which doctrine is most valuable? Why?

3. (a) List the four methods of acquiring mineral rights. (b) What are the major legal differences among them?

TENURE

In the tenurial system, the king owned the land and parceled it out. Land was not owned in the sense that we think of ownership today. There were a number of legal restrictions which made it more like a tenancy. Under certain situations the land would revert to the king or lord.

As a tenant, the occupant owed certain services to his immediate overlord that arose because he had possession; for example, he was required to provide "rents" and military service. In turn the overlord protected the landholder. Under feudalism the land was to always have an occupant; otherwise, it would not serve the purpose of producing services. Lords who were seised of large tracts of land would transfer smaller tracts by the ceremony of *livery (delivery) of seisin* to sublords. The ceremony involved the transfer of a clod of earth or twig from the lord to the sublord. All the witnesses at the ceremony would remember the transfer in the event they were called on to testify as to ownership. This ceremony was later replaced by transfer of the deed.

TENURE IN THE UNITED STATES

In the eastern part of the United States, some of the early colonial grants were based on tenure. The proprietor held his land directly from the king. The small monetary payment required as a token of this relationship was called a *quitrent.* When the proprietor of a colony granted smaller tracts to individual settlers, each owed a quitrent by an extension of the feudal theory. These quitrents were very often ignored because of the ready availability of land on the frontier. In Massachusetts, Rhode Island and Connecticut, the tenurial system never existed; land there was held privately. After the Revolution, quitrents were abolished, and the notion prevailed that a person who owned land had an absolute title limited only by the state.

Vestiges of feudalism and tenure are retained in U.S. real property law. One example is the law of *escheat,* in which the state is paramount, with land reverting to it if a person dies without heirs. Probably more important is the English concept of estates in land, for our legal system continues to recognize the idea that separate divisible interests can exist simultaneously in the same piece of land.

ESTATES

◆ **The extent and character of a person's possessory rights and interests in land.**

The feudal notion of tenure is the foundation of the doctrine of estates in land. This doctrine has substantially influenced the rights that individuals may have in real property. The term *estate,* as used in this context, has a restrictive and technical meaning. Estate is derived from the word *status,* connoting the status that the king conferred upon a favored subject of the realm. It should not be confused with more common usage—that is, as a synonym for all of a person's assets.

In the system of tenure as it developed in England, land was separated from interests that might exist in it. Because land was one thing and interests in it another, several people could possess interests or estates in the same piece of land. This idea continues to be a feature of the law of English-speaking countries. Although a complete estate in land may exist at the present moment, it can be divided into various slices in such a way that each slice is regarded as existing now.

CASE EXAMPLE

Lansing Thomas owns a large farm. He directs by will that, upon his death, the property pass to Beverly Lane, his only daughter, for life and then to her oldest son. When Lansing dies, two estates exist in the land simultaneously.

Lansing's daughter Beverly has a *life estate*. This is a possessory estate because she is entitled to the rents and profits from the farm for her life. Beverly's oldest son has a *future estate*. Upon his mother's death he is entitled to the farm, but he can claim nothing in possession until she dies.

Although the nature, quality and extent of their interests often differ, each holder of an estate invariably has a present or future right of possession. Sometimes this right may be deferred until a future time, or it might even be conditional. During his mother's life, the son in the preceding example does not have a right to occupy the land or profit from it. He does, however, possess an interest or estate that would be recognized in American courts as it was in medieval England. Further, he has rights to prevent *waste* of the property by the life tenant.

As there are many possible interests in land, estates have numerous dimensions. Several classifications of estates have developed reflecting these differences. This chapter distinguishes between two types of estates characterized by the duration of the owner's right to possession: freehold and nonfreehold estates. Nonfreehold estates are discussed in full in Chapter 7. Freehold estates, including future estates are discussed in this chapter. Chapter 5 treats multiple ownership estates.

FREEHOLD ESTATE

◆ **An estate of uncertain duration.**

Numerous freehold interests exist in land. Although they all have in common uncertainty as to their termination, other rights of the owners differ. The holders of most freehold estates may pass their interests along to their heirs. These are generally called *freehold estates of inheritance*. The most usual is the *fee simple* or *fee simple absolute*. Life estates are also freehold estates since their duration is uncertain. Life estates, however, are not estates of inheritance because they terminate upon the owner's death.

Some estates are created for a fixed period of time. The principal estates of this nature are the estate, or tenancy, for years and the tenancy from period to period. At common law, these nonfreehold estates were distinguished from freehold estates. For many purposes, they were treated as personal, not real, property. The holder of a nonfreehold estate did not have the same status or legal rights as the holder of a freehold estate. Tenancies at will and tenancies at sufferance are other estates less than a freehold, all discussed in Chapter 7.

FEE SIMPLE OR FEE SIMPLE ABSOLUTE

◆ **The most extensive interest in land that a holder might possess; one that is potentially indefinite in duration.**

Most land in the United States is held in fee simple. A *fee simple* is a freehold and the most extensive estate known to the law. The holder of a fee simple title possesses all rights commonly associated with property or ownership. Possession is one of these rights. Subject to limitations by the state, the owner may sell the estate or give it away during his or her lifetime; the owner may direct the disposition of the estate by will; if the owner dies without a will, the fee simple will be disposed of according to the laws of the jurisdiction in which the fee simple is located. Creditors may levy against the estate, or the owner may use it as security. The holder of a fee simple may voluntarily limit uses to which it may be put or carve out lesser estates from it. Use limitations will be recognized by the courts if they do not violate public policy. Although the term has its roots in feudal times, in most respects the holder today of a fee simple has the rights of private ownership.

Except in cases of conveyances to institutions such as corporations or government, the common law required the grantor to use specific words to create a fee simple. The words *"and his heirs"* continue in common use today, although in most states any words that indicate an intention to create a fee simple are sufficient. Thus, the granting clause in a deed will generally state "to [grantee] and his heirs." In some parts of the country, this estate is referred to simply as a *fee*.

DEFEASIBLE FEE

◆ **A fee simple that terminates upon the happening of some future stated event.**

The holder of a fee simple or lesser estate has the right to create other estates in the land, which may be limited in several ways. Although this factor has complicated property law of English-speaking countries, it has also provided variety in the uses to which real property may be put. A grantor, by using the defeasible fee, is often able to benefit society and, at the same time, protect interests he or she considers important. The two types of defeasible fees next discussed have been used for self-serving, narrow-minded purposes, but they also have been used in a manner benefiting the entire community. In this context, it is important to remember that, until a defeasible fee terminates because the stated condition has occurred, the interests of the owner are the same as those possessed by the owner of a fee simple absolute.

> ## C A S E   E X A M P L E
> Mrs. Zahn, who is an environmentalist, owns a large tract of land in Wisconsin on which she desires to establish a wildlife sanctuary. She proposes to do this by giving the land to the National Wildlife Society. Although the directors of the society have agreed to administer and maintain the sanctuary, Mrs. Zahn fears that, as time passes and the land becomes more valuable, her original intent might be forgotten.

The law provides a number of methods for Mrs. Zahn to accomplish her objective and ensure that her intentions are honored. One of these would be to limit the future use of the land by imposing conditions in the deed. This task can be accomplished by creating either a fee simple determinable or a fee simple subject to condition subsequent.

Fee Simple Determinable. The *fee simple determinable,* sometimes called a *fee simple with a special limitation,* is a fee simple that automatically terminates when a stated condition is fulfilled. If the granting clause in the deed to the wildlife society states, "to the National Wildlife Society and its successors and assigns so long as the property is used as a wildlife preserve," a fee simple determinable would be created. The fee is indefinite in duration because it is a fee simple, but the grantee's interest terminates automatically and reverts back to the grantor upon the occurrence of the event, in this case when the property ceases to be used as a wildlife preserve. The language creating such a fee will ordinarily include words of limitation such as "so long as," "as long as," or "until."

Fee Simple Subject to Condition Subsequent. This is a fee simple that may be terminated by the grantor or the grantor's successor when a stated condition is fulfilled. This estate is very similar to a determinable fee. The major difference is that termination is not automatic. The estate continues when the stated condition is fulfilled unless the grantor or the grantor's successors take steps to terminate it. The grantor or successor is said to have a *power of termination.* The environmentalist might create an estate of this nature by stating in the deed: "to the National Wildlife Society and its successors and assigns forever on condition that the land is used as a wildlife preserve, but if the land is used for any other purposes, Mrs. Zahn and her heirs shall have a right of entry and repossession." The language creating such a fee will ordinarily include words of limitation such as "subject to the following," "subject to the conditions and restrictions," or "but if."

FUTURE ESTATE
◆ **An interest in an estate that may become possessory in the future.**

The common law accepted the idea that several estates of different duration could exist in land at the same time. Our legal system continues to recognize this concept. Only one of these interests is possessory, but because of the estate concept, the party in possession does not necessarily have all interests associated with ownership. If *A*, the holder of a fee simple, grants a life estate to *B*, *B*'s interest terminates with death and something obviously is left over. As *A* has a fee simple, *A*'s estate, from which the grant to *B* was carved, is infinite in duration. If *A*'s grant to *B* said nothing about what was left after *B*'s death, *A* and his heirs have a future interest. This is an interest that entitles them to possession at that time in the future when *B* dies. This particular type of future interest is called a *reversion,* as the residue reverts back to *A* or his heirs.

Suppose, however, that *A*'s deed is worded "to *B* for life, remainder to *C* and her heirs"; then *C* has a future interest. Although *C* has no present right to possession, her future interest is probably more valuable than *B*'s life estate, for upon the death of *B, C* or her heirs acquire a fee simple absolute. *C*'s interest is called a *remainder.* As *C*'s interest is not subject to any contingency except *B*'s death, the remainder is said to be *vested.*

In addition to the reversion and the remainder, other future interests also exist. An example is the previously mentioned fee simple determinable. In creating this estate, the holder does not make an absolute grant of his or her entire interest. When the condition limiting the grant is fulfilled, the interest of the party in possession automatically terminates. The grantor and his or her heirs thus have a possibility of regaining possession at some time in the future. This future interest is called a *possibility of reverter.*

The creation of a fee simple subject to a condition subsequent also creates a future interest. This future interest is referred to as a *right of reentry* or a *power of termination.* When the possessory estate terminates because the condition is fulfilled, the holder of the right of reentry may get the land by filing suit.

Current Status of the Future Interest. The acceptance of the concept of possessory estates in land followed by a future interest lends flexibility to the disposition of real property; in many instances, however, future interests exist because a grantor wishes to limit the free transferability of land. Often the creator of the estate wishes to control the use of the land not only during his or her lifetime but after death as well. Conditional and defeasible fees have been used in the past for this purpose and continue to be so used today.

The right of reentry and the possibility of reverter cause especially serious problems. The fees that give rise to these interests are created to last forever and often do last for many years. As a result, the right of reentry and the possibility of reverter are merely expectant interests with almost no present economic value. Often the current possessors of these interests are remote descendants of the original creator. Frequently they are unaware that another interest exists. When a title search reveals the existence of these interests, a person attempting to clear the title is presented with a difficult, if not insoluble, problem arising from the fact that often it is impossible to contact many of the parties who might retain an interest in the land because of the future interest.

A small but growing number of states have attempted to solve this problem through legislation. This legislation often places limitations on the time a future interest can last. Another type of legislation places limitations on the time during which a future interest can be enforced. Other states have adopted legislation that ensures that a person who has an unbroken chain of title extending over a given number of years has a fee simple free of future interests.

The next case involves the interpretation of the intention of the grantor as determined by an examination of the language in the deed.

MITCHELL v. JERROLDS

Tennessee Court of Appeals
1991 TENN. APP. LEXIS 201

BACKGROUND. The Jerrolds conveyed developed real estate to the Turkey Baptist Church, as a gift. The deed stated: "LIMITATIONS. This land is given by us to the Church for the purpose for the home for the Missionary Baptist Pastor and no Pastor shall occupy said place as a home unless he preaches that you are saved by Grace through Faith in Jesus Christ and not by works. And in the event he refuses to preach such doctrine he will not be permitted to reside in said pastorium." The church sought permission from the court to sell the property in order to purchase new property and construct a new pastorium. Heirs of the co-grantor contended that the property under the language of the deed must revert to them. The trial court held in favor of the church and the heirs of the co-grantor appealed.

DECISION. The Tennessee Court of Appeals affirmed the trial court decision.

JUDGE WILLIAMS. It is the insistence of the defendants that because the subject language begins with the word "limitations," such fully describes the intent of the grantors to create a determinable fee. . . .

Under the now well-accepted rule in construing a deed, we determine the estate conveyed in the deed by trying to determine the intentions of the parties. . . .

In [*Bailey v. Eagle Mountain Telephone, Inc.*], the Tennessee Supreme Court spelled out the long and well-established principles of law and rules of construction to be employed by the courts in determining whether the language in a deed established a determinable fee . . . or merely a statement of purpose for the grant

and not sufficient to create a determinable fee. The question presented in *Bailey* was whether the following language created a determinable fee with a possibility of reverter to the heirs of the grantor, "In consideration of love and interest we have in Education, we this day deed, transfer and convey a certain lot or parcel of land . . . To have and to hold for school purposes . . . so long as the aforesaid lot of land is used for the aforesaid purposes."

In holding that the language did, indeed, create a fee simple determinable subject to a possibility of reverter, the Supreme Court proceeded to contrast examples of when a determinable fee was created and when not.

Old examples of determinable fees are limitations to one and his heirs "as long as the Church of St. Paul shall stand" or "until the grantee go to Rome"; the most appropriate words to create a determinable fee being, during, so long as, till, until, whilst, etc., such words fitly prefacing a limitation.

A determinable fee may either arise from and be dependent upon a condition, or arise from a limitation, the essential difference being that in a case of a condition the estate is not terminated [automatically] by the happening of the event upon which it may be defeated, while in the case of a limitation it passes at once by way of reverter to the grantor. . . . It results from this distinction that the usual technical words by which a limitation is expressed relate to time, differing from those expressing a condition. . . .

It is plain that the subject language for construction in the Jerrolds' deed does not contain any apt word expressing a limitation in relation to time. Compare the words in the *Bailey* case

◆ *Dower.* **Life estate of a widow in one-third of any real property to which her spouse had legal title during marriage.**

For many generations, dower was an important right that a widow acquired in her husband's real property upon his death. This right minimally entitled her to a one-third interest in his lands for life. The widow was entitled to dower as well as any gifts made in the husband's will, unless the will clearly stated that the gifts were in lieu of dower. If it was clear that the bequests were in lieu of dower, the widow had to elect one or the other.

While the husband was alive, the wife's right, which did not materialize unless the husband died before she did, was protected against both the husband's acts and claims of his creditors arising after the marriage. The wife's interest, which was called *inchoate dower,* was a potential estate. She acquired a legal estate only if she survived her husband.

> ### CASE EXAMPLE
> Mary and Ed were secretly married in 1974. At that time, Ed owned a large office building. In order to modernize the building, Ed borrowed a substantial amount of money in 1976 and gave a mortgage to secure the loan. As a result of depressed economic conditions, Ed could not meet payments on the loan, and the mortgage was foreclosed. Any purchaser at the foreclosure sale would be subject to Mary's inchoate right of dower.

In order for dower to be allowed, the parties must have been legally married at the time of the husband's death. Consequently, in most states the right to dower is terminated by divorce. A wife can ordinarily release her inchoate right of dower by joining in any conveyance of the husband's real property. In the event a husband mortgages his property, the wife will release her inchoate right of dower if she signs the mortgage, but dower is restored upon payment of the debt. Today, states that recognize dower extend it to protect the husband as well as the wife.

HOMESTEAD EXEMPTION LAWS
◆ **Laws that (1) exempt the family from a forced sale of its home by certain classes of creditors; (2) may prevent an owner from selling or mortgaging the home without consent of the spouse; and (3) allow the designated family homestead to be used for the family's benefit after the head of the family dies.**

Homestead laws, which have been adopted in most states, provide heads of families with some exemptions from creditors' claims. A family is defined in various ways, but most courts take a very liberal approach. They consider that a family exists when two or more persons reside together with one having a legal or moral obligation to support the others. A common and certainly more restrictive definition used in some states limits the family to a currently married husband and wife or a widow or widower still living in the homestead. Some states have extended the exemption to single, unmarried persons.

Homestead exemptions are intended to protect the household. The exemption rests upon an expression of public policy. A legislature adopting a homestead exemption statute indicates it believes that a person's obligation to support dependents is at least as important as payment of debts. The expressed objective of homestead statutes in most states is to secure a family home beyond the reach of financial misfortune.

In addition to requiring that the owner have a family, most state homestead laws require that the exempt real estate be the permanent residence of the family. Several states also require the owner to formally declare a particular piece of real estate as a homestead. In the case that follows, the court discusses the policy underlying its state's homestead statute.

IN RE GRINDAL
United States Bankruptcy Court
30 B.R. 651 (1983)

BACKGROUND. Grindal and his wife owned a home and operated a business in Charleston, Maine. As the business was doing poorly, Mr. Grindal secured employment in East Millinocket, Maine. In order to avoid commuting expenses and because they believed that they were going to lose their home through foreclosure, the Grindals moved to East Millinocket on November 20, 1982. On November 30, they filed a bankruptcy petition, claiming an exemption in the Charleston house under Maine's homestead statute. The trustee in bankruptcy asked the court to disallow the exemption.

DECISION. The bankruptcy court held that the Grindals did not qualify for the exemption.

BANKRUPTCY JUDGE JAMES A. GOODMAN. The debtors claim their exemption under [Maine's state statute], which provides an exemption in real or personal property that the debtor (or his dependent) uses as a "residence." The critical time for determining the debtors' entitlement to the exemption is the date the bankruptcy petition is filed (here, ten days after the debtors moved to East Milli-

nocket). Thus, the issue to be decided is whether the Charleston property was the debtors' residence on November 30, 1982.

The concept of "residence" is a flexible one, and must be construed in light of the policies underlying the exemption statute. ("The words 'permanent residence' may have a variety of meanings depending upon the context in which the term is used.") In general, the purpose of exemption statutes is to secure for the debtor the means to support himself and his family. In particular, homestead statutes promote the stability and welfare of the state by encouraging property ownership, and they secure to the householder a home for himself and his family. While the homestead exemption should be liberally construed in order to afford all the relief the legislature intended, it must not be so broadly construed as to ignore the Maine legislature's clearly expressed intention to favor homeowners over non-homeowners. The legislature chose to "opt out" of the federal exemption scheme, which provided non-homeowners an exemption in other property equal in amount to the homestead exemption, and in its place granted non-homeowners a limited exemption. Thus, it appears that the

Maine homestead exemption is intended to help homeowners to maintain that status; but not to provide the debtor funds for other purposes. (The homestead exemption is "for the benefit of the family as a place of actual residence not as a refuge from the law's exactions. . . .")

Given the purposes of the homestead exemption, a finding that the debtors actually occupied the homestead on the filing date is neither necessary nor sufficient to qualify for the exemption. Occupancy may be constructive as well as actual. The primary factor is the debtor's intention on the filing date. A debtor who does not actually occupy the homestead on the filing date, but who intends to return when circumstances permit, may qualify for the exemption.[1] Conversely, a debtor who actually occupies the homestead on the filing date, but who intends to sell it and not purchase another home, may not qualify for the exemption.

In the case before the court, the debtors were not, on the filing date, actually occupying the Charleston property, having moved to East Millinocket ten days before. The facts show clearly that the debtors' move was meant to be permanent—they moved to be closer to Mr. Grindal's new place of employment while believing that the loss of the Charleston property was a certainty. Nothing before the court indicates that the debtors either intended to return to Charleston or that they have any intention of purchasing another home in East Millinocket. On the evidence before it, the court is compelled to conclude that on the date of filing the debtors had abandoned their Charleston property, and that they do not qualify for the homestead exemption. . . .

[1] Similarly, it has been held in some jurisdictions that the homestead exemption extends to proceeds from the sale of the home when the debtor intends to use the proceeds within a reasonable time to purchase another home. See *Field v. Goat,* 70 Okl. 113, 173 P. 364 (1918); *Annot.,* 1 A.L.R. 483 (1919), supp. 46 A.L.R. 814 (1927). Such an interpretation would seem to be consistent with a liberal construction of the homestead exemption, as it would further the purpose of aiding homeowners in maintaining their *status* as homeowners. Debtors often must sell their homes, perhaps to purchase less expensive homes, perhaps to pursue distant employment opportunities. It seems unlikely that the Maine legislature intended to aid only those homeowners who never move, for such an interpretation would often deny the exemption to those who most need it in order to maintain their homeowner status.

Exempt property usually includes a lot and improvements up to a stated dollar or acreage amount. Some states use a combination of acreage and dollars. The dollar amounts vary widely. They range from a few thousand dollars to the full value of the homestead. California and Florida are the more generous states granting homestead protection.

In rural areas, exempt acreage is frequently 160 acres; urban area exemptions are one-third to one-half acre. As a general rule, if the value or extent of the homestead exceeds the exemptions, creditors may force a sale of part of the property. The debtor retains the amount of the exemption.

> **CASE EXAMPLE**
>
> Richard Rainey owned and occupied a 250-acre farm. He incurred a number of debts that he was unable to pay. When his creditors obtained judgments against him and attempted to sell the farm, Rainey claimed his homestead exemption. State law limited the exemption to 160 acres, and the court ordered 90 acres sold and the proceeds applied to pay Rainey's debts. As was customary, the unsold portion included the residence.

Although the homestead exemption provides some protection to a debtor and his or her family, the exemption does not protect the debtor against all claims. The following claims are often given priority by state law:

■ An existing mortgage or deed of trust

■ A mortgage or deed of trust given to secure purchase of a residence

■ Real property taxes and assessments

■ Mechanics' liens

■ Debts incurred before the homestead was acquired

The homestead exemption is probably an anachronism in today's economy. Most exemption statutes were enacted at a time when the American economy was primarily agricultural. The statutes protected the farmer and his family and helped to ensure that food would be available to the nation. Today, many families live in apartments or rented homes. Homestead exemptions provide them with limited protection. Although the amount of the exemption has been increased recently in some states, many of the homestead exemptions are set at such low levels that the debtor's equity often exceeds them. The result is a forced sale and loss of the home. The owner does get the amount of the exemption in cash, but usually this amount is small and not sufficient to purchase a new home.

Homestead Property Tax Exemption. A number of states also use the term *homestead exemption* for statutes that afford property tax relief to older people of limited income and to people with limited income who are permanently and totally disabled. These statutes provide for a reduction of the taxable value of a person's residence if the person has reached a certain age—usually 65—or if a person is totally disabled. In both instances, to qualify for benefits, that person's income must not exceed an amount, usually quite low, specified by statute.

REVIEW AND DISCUSSION QUESTIONS

1. (a) What is the chief characteristic of an *estate?* (b) Explain how the concept of estates has influenced the development of real estate law.
2. Distinguish between a freehold estate and a nonfreehold estate. Give an example of each.

JOINT TENANCY

◆ **A form of co-ownership significant in that the entire estate passes to the survivor upon the death of the other joint tenant or tenants.**

The principal feature of the joint tenancy is the *right of survivorship*. Upon the death of one of the co-owners, that person's interest passes automatically to surviving joint owners.

CASE EXAMPLE

Tom Casicollo conveys Blackacre in fee simple to his wife Helen and son Tony "as joint tenants." Helen dies. Tony becomes the sole owner of the fee. As this is a joint tenancy, upon Helen's death her interest in Blackacre does not become part of her inheritance estate, but automatically becomes Tony's property.

Joint tenancy with the right of survivorship is an additional example of the manner in which law tends to reflect existing economic and social conditions. During the feudal period, when English property law was developing, ownership of an estate by a single individual facilitated the lord's collection of the dues and services to which he was entitled. As a result, when a deed or will created rights in co-owners, the common law courts presumed that a joint tenancy was intended unless some other form of co-ownership was clearly indicated. In those days, even if Tom had not stated that Helen and Tony were to hold as joint tenants, the law would have presumed that they did. The survivor possessed the entire fee. The estate was in the possession of one owner, and the overlord had only to deal with a single individual.

Additional forms of co-ownership developed during the feudal period, and after feudalism ended, the joint tenancy with its right of survivorship continued to meet the needs of English society. Throughout the 17th and 18th centuries, the wealth and power of the English aristocracy was based on large landholdings. Land was a principal source of political power, the chief source of wealth and the basis of social status. If the landholding had become fragmented because of too much division of property among multiple owners or through inheritance, the power of the English upper class would have been diluted. Because joint tenancy helped to prevent this dilution of power, it continued to be the dominant form of co-ownership and the form assumed by the courts to have been selected when the grantor's intention was not clear.

Although joint tenancy played a role in colonial American real property law, it was never as important in this country as it was in England. The reason for this was the marked difference in social and economic conditions between the two countries.

As forms of wealth other than land have become important, joint tenancy gradually has been replaced by other types of co-ownership. Most of these developed because they were more readily adapted to modern society's need for the free transferability of property.

RIGHTS OF JOINT TENANTS

Each co-owner who holds as a joint tenant has an equal right to possession of the entire property. This is referred to as an *undivided interest.* Although a joint tenant may not exclude other joint tenants from possession, strangely enough the law considers occupancy by one as occupancy by all. In the above example, if Tony Casicollo occupied Blackacre as a residence without his mother's objection, he would not be responsible to her for a proportionate share of the rent; neither would he be required to share income with her if Blackacre were a farm or commercial real estate. Helen Casicollo, however, has the same rights; hence, if each tenant is to benefit, all must agree to share the proceeds of the property. Where agreement cannot be reached, the tenancy must be terminated.

SEVERANCE OF JOINT TENANCY

A number of different methods exist to sever or terminate a joint tenancy. Traditionally, for a joint tenancy to be created or to continue, four "unities" are required. First, the *unity of possession* requires that each have an undivided right to possession. Second, the *unity of interest* requires that each receive a similar estate. For example, one joint tenant cannot hold as a life tenant while the other holds in fee simple. Finally, they have to take effect at the same time (*unity of time*) and from the same instrument (*unity of title*). If any of these unities terminates, the joint tenancy also ends. The new form of ownership is tenancy in common, a form in which the right of survivorship does not exist.

TENANCY IN COMMON

◆ **A form of concurrent ownership in which each owner possesses an undivided right to the entire parcel of land, with each owner's rights similar to those possessed by a sole owner.**

In the United States today, the tenancy in common is probably the most frequently occurring form of concurrent ownership. Although tenancy in common developed contemporaneously at common law with joint tenancy, the joint tenancy was for centuries the favored form of multiple ownership. This is no longer true. Many states have abolished the joint tenancy. In those that have retained it, a tenancy in common is implied unless a joint tenancy is clearly indicated by the instrument creating the concurrent estate. Hence, the tenancy in common is now the "default drive."

CASE EXAMPLE

By a provision in his will, Patrick Cross gave all his property to his sons, Thomas and William, "share and share alike, or to the survivor of them." William died before Thomas, and Thomas's heirs claimed the property, arguing that their father was a joint tenant with the right of survivorship. The court held that William and Thomas were tenants in common, not joint tenants; as a result, the share of each, upon death, became part of his separate estate. *Cross v. Cross, 324 Mass. 186, 85 N.E.2d 325 (1949).*

Rights of Tenants in Common

Like joint tenants, each tenant in common has an undivided right to possession of the entire parcel. Normally, a tenant in common will not be responsible to the co-owners for any benefits obtained through exclusive occupancy unless he or she excludes the others from participating. At the same time, no tenant in common is entitled to the exclusive use of any part of the land. The result is that problems arise when one cotenant wrongfully excludes the others, or when it is practical for the property to be occupied by only a single tenant. Under the circumstances, in a number of states, the cotenants not in occupancy will be entitled to a fair compensation for the use of the property. Similar problems arise where a cotenant not in possession receives benefits from the property exceeding those of his or her co-owners. These types of problems may best be solved by agreement among the parties, as can problems involving liability of cotenants for upkeep and improvements. When agreement cannot be reached, partition of property may be the only solution.

Partition

◆ **An action by which a co-owner obtains a division of property terminating any interest of other co-owners in the divided portion.**

Partition is the historic method by which unwilling concurrent owners of real property may terminate the interests of fellow co-owners. Although courts traditionally ordered partition even when no statute authorized them to do so, today partition exists in some form by statute in every state. Many states make the remedy available to some holders of future interests.

Partition may be voluntary or compulsory. Voluntary partitions are the result of agreement among the co-owners to end the relationship. They are usually carried out by deeds in which each co-owner is allocated a described portion of the realty by all the other part owners. It is also possible for all the co-owners to convey to a third party, the third party in turn conveying to each former co-owner his or her agreed-upon parcel. Although a few states recognize oral voluntary partitions, a written instrument is usually required, primarily to permit recording in the public records. Voluntary partition requires not only the consent of all the parties to the act, but also agreement as to the division of the estate. Compulsory partition by judicial action is necessary when one or more of the multiple owners desire to terminate the relationship and agreement cannot be reached for dividing the property.

The right to partition appears to be absolute unless the parties themselves have agreed they will not use the remedy. A co-owner may demand partition without regard to the size of his or her share. The fact that the interest of a co-owner is subject to a mortgage or other lien, though it is a complicating factor, will not defeat the right. So extensive is the right to partition that state condominium statutes must specifically prohibit the right of condominium owners to seek partition of the condominium elements that are owned in common.

Partition is accomplished in one of three ways. The preferred method is by a physical division of the property. The court orders the property divided, allocating to each co-owner a share that is equivalent to his or her interest. Often, however, physical division is not practicable or desirable, and in these cases the property will be sold and the proceeds divided among the co-owners in relation to their interests. The third method effectively results in one or more of the co-owners purchasing the interests of the other co-owners.

TENANCY BY THE ENTIRETY

◆ **Co-ownership of property by husband and wife, that is nonseverable without the consent of both; upon the death of either, the survivor remains as sole owner.**

Nearly half the states recognize tenancy by the entirety, a type of co-ownership existing only between husband and wife. This type of co-ownership is based on an ancient legal fiction by which the common law regarded husband and wife as a single legal person. One result was that, if the two acquired equal interests in real estate by the same instrument, the property was considered owned as an indivisible legal unit. Upon the death of either, the survivor remained as the parcel's sole owner. This result has long been accepted by modern law. Today, a right of survivorship similar to that existing for the joint tenancy exists for the tenancy by entirety. In a small estate, this right benefits the surviving spouse as it avoids the necessity and cost of probate proceedings.

CASE EXAMPLE

Jim Seaver and his wife, Helen, purchased an apartment building and took title in both their names. Jim died without making a will, and children by a former marriage claimed that a part interest in the property vested in them. They argued that Jim and Helen were tenants in common. The court held that Helen was the absolute owner because, when a husband and wife take title in both their names, a tenancy by the entirety is created unless otherwise indicated.

The result would not be the same in all states that recognize a tenancy by the entirety. Some of the states that accept this type of tenancy do so only if it is expressly stated in the granting instrument.

TERMINATION OF THE TENANCY BY THE ENTIRETY

A tenancy by the entirety is a more stable type of co-ownership than joint tenancy. Because the marital partners are considered a single unit, neither husband nor wife can sever the tenancy without the other's consent. Unlike joint tenancy, a sale by either the husband or the wife does not terminate the tenancy or end the right of survivorship.

In many jurisdictions, a tenancy by the entirety cannot be terminated by the forced sale of the husband's or wife's interest. This means that if either spouse individually incurs debts and then refuses to pay them, the creditor cannot *execute upon,* that is, judicially seize, the property. This rule has been criticized because it permits the debtor to escape responsibility while owning an interest in a valuable asset. For this reason a number of states in the last decade have abolished the tenancy by the entirety. Some states permit the separate creditors of either spouse to levy upon and sell the share of the debtor, whether husband or wife. If the non-debtor spouse survives, the creditor is deprived of his or her interest. If the creditor holds a joint judgment against both spouses, resulting from an obligation both incurred, the creditor can attach the estate held by the entirety.

Tenancies by the entireties are terminated by divorce because the marital relationship is essential to this form of co-ownership. Upon divorce the parties become tenants in common.

The common law allowed the husband almost complete control of all of his wife's property. This included her individual share in a tenancy by the entirety. The husband, thus, was entitled to all the income from the estate, and he had sole discretion as to occupancy and use. In fact, the husband could even sell the real estate, although sale was subject to the wife's right of survivorship.

A husband's absolute power over his wife's property was terminated by the passage of a number of married women's acts during the past century. These statutes entitle the wife to control and benefit from her property. Today, in most states that recognize tenancy by the entireties, the wife has the same rights in the property as her husband.

ESTATE TAX PROBLEMS OF JOINT INTERESTS

Co-ownership often is the source of complicated problems involving both estate and gift taxes. Most of these are beyond the scope of this book, but one common misconception needs clarification at this point. As we know, in both the joint tenancy and the tenancy by the entirety, the share of a deceased co-owner automatically passes to the survivor or survivors. Because of this, people sometimes wrongly assume that the estate of a deceased co-owner is not subject to state or federal estate tax on the jointly owned property.

It is true that for the tenancy by the entirety probate is unnecessary. Estate taxes on the decedent's estate may be avoided on the interest of the first spouse to die.

TENANCY IN PARTNERSHIP

◆ **A form of co-ownership in which each partner owns partnership property together with the other partners; each partner's share is treated as personal property; partnership property of a deceased partner passes to the surviving partners.**

The common law did not recognize the partnership as a legal entity. As a result, property could not be held in the partnership name. This not only caused confusion but also frequently led to complex legal problems when a partner died or experienced financial difficulty. Creditors of an individual partner could then attach specific partnership assets; upon the death of a partner, his or her share in specific partnership property passed to that person's estate, and an individual partner could terminate the relationship by selling his or her interest in a particular property.

> ### CASE EXAMPLE
> Kane and Waldron entered into a partnership agreement to operate a creamery. Partnership funds were used to purchase real estate to operate the business. Title was taken in both Kane's and Waldron's names. A short time later, Kane died. At common law, his interest in the real estate would pass to his heirs, not to the surviving partner.

Most states have now adopted the Uniform Partnership Act, which creates the tenancy in partnership. Specifically, the Uniform Partnership Act permits the firm to buy, hold and sell real estate in the partnership name. Individual partners share ownership in particular property only as members of the firm. Spouses, heirs and creditors of individual partners have no rights in partnership property.

Individual partners may not assign partnership property unless the assignment involves the rights of all partners. Although an individual partner can transfer partnership real property, any such transfer is made only as an agent for other partners of the firm.

Upon the death of any partner, his or her share passes to the surviving partners. In the previous example, Waldron, as the surviving partner, acquires Kane's share. Waldron, however, possesses this property only for the purpose of liquidation inasmuch as Kane's death terminates the partnership. During liquidation, Waldron can operate the business without interference from Kane's legal representatives.

Kane and his heirs—in fact any partner—all have a valuable interest in the partnership. The interest stems from the individual's right to share in the profits and surplus of the firm. The interest is not in specific firm property. Under the Uniform Partnership Act, this interest is regarded as personalty, not real property. The partner's interest is unlike the interest of a joint tenant or a tenant in common. If the partner's interest is sold separately, the partnership is destroyed and the interest is not subject to partition.

COMMUNITY PROPERTY
◆ **A form of co-ownership between husband and wife in which each has a one-half interest in property acquired through the labor of either during the marriage.**

Several jurisdictions in the United States apply the doctrine of community property to real estate owned by a husband or wife. Generally, the community property states are those located in the Southwest; the law of these states was influenced by the laws of France and Spain, countries that have traditionally used the concept of community property in determining property rights of married persons. The states in which community property is an integral part of the legal system are Arizona, California, Idaho, Louisiana, Nevada, New Mexico, Texas and Washington. Other states have from time to time adopted some of the community property ideas. Since community property ownership is statutory, each state varies the characteristics of the system to fit its own needs. It is therefore difficult to generalize about a community property doctrine. When decisions are to be made, legal advice should be obtained in the particular state involved.

Community property is based on the marital relationship. In community property jurisdictions, the husband and wife are regarded as partners. Each spouse becomes a co-owner with the other in all property acquired through the labor or skill of either or both while the two are married. This fact applies even if title to the property is held individually by the husband or wife.

CASE EXAMPLE

Tanya and Bob Blunt, residents of California, were married in 1949. Tanya, following the traditional role of homemaker, managed the domestic establishment and cared for the family. Bob successfully practiced his profession as a doctor. From 1959 until 1977, Bob's practice prospered, and he earned a great deal of money. Some of this was invested in real estate, which was held in Bob's name. When Bob died in 1977, one-half of this real estate, which was community property, belonged to his wife; the other half would be in Bob's estate.

Community property is at odds with the law in other states, which recognize that property held in the name of one of the spouses is solely the property of that person, although the other spouse usually has some rights in relation to the property upon the death of the owner and in some instances upon the termination of the marriage by divorce.

SEPARATE PROPERTY

◆ **Property owned by the husband or wife prior to marriage and property acquired during marriage by gift, inheritance or will.**

Not all property owned by husband and wife in the community property states is community property. The parties retain separate title to property they owned separately before marriage and to property each acquired by gift or inheritance during marriage.

CASE EXAMPLE

The will of John Earles, who died in 1933, gave a one-third interest in a 1,600-acre ranch to his son, Jesse. The remaining two-thirds was given to Helen Earles, John's wife. Jesse was married in 1940. In 1948 Helen Earles, retaining a life interest in her two-thirds share, transferred title to her portion of the ranch to Jesse. Upon Jesse's death the ranch would pass as a part of his separate estate, not as community property.

Real property purchased with the separate property of one spouse who takes title in his or her name remains separate property. In the example involving Tanya and Bob Blunt, if Bob had inherited money from his mother and invested it in real estate, the real property acquired would be separate property. In some community property states, rents and profits from separate property are considered separate property. In others, rents and profits from separate property become community property. Nonetheless, the property may lose its separateness if its character changes, as the next case illustrates.

IN RE WALRATH

Court of Appeals of California
51 Cal. App. 4th 1504 (1997)

BACKGROUND. Gilbert and Gladys Walrath were married in 1992 and separated three years later. The parties filed for a dissolution of the marriage. Before the marriage, the husband deeded the property (known as the Lucerne property) to himself and his wife. At that time the property had a value of $228,000, an $82,000 mortgage and equity in the amount of $146,000. The wife later paid $20,000 out of her separate marital property to reduce the mortgage further.

At the time of the separation, the Lucerne property was valued at $240,000. The couple refinanced the home, borrowing $180,000. They used $60,000 of the loan proceeds to pay off a portion of the first mortgage, another $62,000 to pay off the mortgage on another piece of property in Nevada, and another $40,500 to acquire and improve an investment property in Utah. They placed another $16,000 in a joint savings account.

The husband sought reimbursement for the amount he contributed to the Nevada and Utah properties and the amount placed in the joint savings account, arguing that this was part of his separate property. The trial court disagreed, ruling that the husband had no claim to reimbursement from the assets acquired with the loan proceeds. The case was appealed to the California Court of Appeals.

DECISION. The Court of Appeals affirmed the decision.

JUDGE CORRIGAN. [U]nder the Family Code, spouses who make separate property contributions to a community asset are entitled to reimbursement upon dissolution of the mar-

riage. Here we encounter an issue of first impression. When the original community asset is leveraged and loan proceeds are used to acquire new community properties, may a spouse seeking reimbursement for his original separate property contributions look to these new community properties acquired with loan proceeds?

Here, it is undisputed that the Lucerne property was transmuted to community property, and thus acquired by the community, when [the] Husband converted title to joint tenancy. Thereafter, the proceeds of the refinanced loan secured by the Lucerne property were community property. If, instead of refinancing, the parties had divorced, each would have been entitled to reimbursement for their separate property contributions to the Lucerne property. The parties did not divorce. Instead they made a joint decision to borrow against their community asset, thus reducing its value. They took the money gained and acquired new community assets. The community would profit or suffer loss as those new assets rose or fell in value. Each party retained the right to reimbursement from "the property" to which they had made their separate property contributions. That property was the Lucerne home, the value of which the parties had consciously diminished.

Section 2640, subdivision (h) provides that the contributing spouse shall be reimbursed for contributions to the acquisition of the property "to the extent the party traces the contributions to a separate property source." Husband contends he is entitled to reimbursement from the new community assets because he can trace the moneys used to acquire those

> **CASE EXAMPLE**
>
> Anna, Ben and Carla Lane formed a limited partnership to invest in real estate. Anna, the general partner, invested $10,000 and agreed to manage the property. Ben and Carla, as limited partners, contributed $25,000 each. The project failed after accumulating debts of $65,000. Individual assets of Anna could be reached to cover any claims of creditors not satisfied on liquidation. Ben's and Carla's individual assets could not be reached by the syndicate's creditors beyond the amounts of their initial investment.

If limited partners participate in the "control of the business," they lose their defense against liability to creditors. However, the ULPA does not define what constitutes "taking part in control." This has been left to the courts. Generally they have interpreted "taking part in control" in a manner that significantly restricts the limited partner's ability to participate without forfeiting limited liability. In addition, under the ULPA, if the limited partner's name appears in the partnership name, the limited partner becomes liable as a general partner. This is intended to protect creditors who extend credit to the business on the basis of the financial resources of a person who is actually only a limited partner.

The RULPA specifically allows a limited partner to act in a number of situations for the business without forfeiting limited liability. For example, the revised act permits a limited partner to be a contractor for or an agent or employee of the limited partnership. A limited partner can also consult with and advise a general partner, act as a surety for the partnership and approve or disapprove an amendment to the partnership agreement. In addition, the act permits a limited partner to vote on the:

▋ dissolution and winding up of the business;

▋ sale, exchange, lease, mortgage, pledge or other transfer of all or substantially all of the assets of the limited partnership;

▋ incurrence of indebtedness by the limited partnership other than in the ordinary course of business;

▋ change in the nature of the business;

▋ admission or removal of a general partner.

More important, under the RULPA, a limited partner is liable only to persons who transact business with the partnership with actual knowledge of the limited partner's participation in control. Additionally, to recover, a plaintiff must be misled into reasonably believing the limited partner is a general partner. If, however, the limited partner's participation is substantially the same as that of a general partner, the limited partner will be liable to any person who transacts business with the partnership.

◆ **Joint Venture. A business entity in which two or more persons have agreed to carry out a single undertaking for a profit.**

A joint venture is a form of business organization very similar to the partnership. Most of the law that applies to partnerships also applies to the joint venture. Like a partnership, the joint venture is based on agreement, and the members have a fiduciary relationship to each other. They share profits and losses; each enjoys the right to manage and direct the venture; and the venture is treated as a partnership for federal tax purposes.

The major difference between the partnership and the joint venture is that the latter is usually created to carry out a single transaction. Although some limited partnerships are created for a single purpose, most partnership operations are more extensive, carrying out a general business for a period of years. Other differences also exist between a partnership and a joint venture. In a joint venture, each participant has limited power to bind the others. However, the participants can agree that each will have this power. Finally, death of a joint venturer does not automatically dissolve the joint venture.

◆ **Real Estate Investment Trust (REIT). An organization in which trustees own real estate or loans secured by real estate that they manage for beneficiaries who hold transferable shares representing their respective interests.**

During the late 19th century, the American economy was expanding rapidly. Large sums of money were needed for investment in many segments of the economy. Real estate was no exception. Unfortunately, the corporate form of business organization that was used to attract capital into most business activity could not be used in real estate because most of the states prohibited ownership of real property by corporations. The business trust, or Massachusetts trust, evolved to circumvent this prohibition. The trust had many advantages of the corporation, such as limited liability, ready transferability of shares and continuous existence. Because the trust was not a corporation, it was a permissible form of enterprise for real estate investment.

With the passage of time, state prohibitions against corporate ownership of property were abolished, but the business trust continued to be important. It provided investors with a major tax advantage over the corporation. For tax purposes the trust was treated as a conduit through which income passed. Income it earned was not taxable to it as long as the income was distributed to the trust beneficiaries. Corporate income is not treated in this favorable manner but is taxable to the corporation and also to the shareholder when distributed. The tax advantage enjoyed by the business trust was eliminated in 1935 by a number of court decisions that emphasized the corporate characteristics of the trust and held these sufficient to classify the trust as an association taxable as a corporation.

These rulings had little immediate impact because of the depressed economic conditions of the 1930s and, later, the influence of World War II. The need for capital in the real estate market was limited. Conditions changed late in the 1940s as the postwar U.S. economic boom created a need for large sums of money to be invested in real estate. About this time, an effort was made to restore to the business trust the pre-1935 tax advantage that it had enjoyed. This effort was finally successful in 1960 when Congress approved legislation that allowed business trusts and investment trusts dealing in real estate to once again serve, under certain prescribed conditions, as a conduit through which income passes without being taxed twice. REITs are discussed in more detail in Chapter 6.

Government Regulation of Syndicates. Many real estate syndicates are financed by the public sale of participation certificates, which are securities. The public sale of securities is regulated extensively by both state and federal law.

The term *security* is defined broadly by federal and state statute. An investment in which a person is induced to participate with another person or entity expecting to profit substantially through the efforts of that person or entity is usually subject to regulation as a security. Many real estate syndications fit this description. In addition to real estate syndication, statutes regulating the sale of securities have been applied to transactions as diverse as the sale of lots in undeveloped land and the sale of resort condominiums that are to be rented, with profits to be divided among condominium owners. During the past decade, enforcement of federal and state statutes regulating the marketing of investments to the public has intensified. People in the real estate industry should expect this trend to continue.

State "blue-sky" laws generally require those who sell securities to be registered in the state. Practically all states also require that the security sold be registered. Usually these state laws include standards against which the quality of the security can be measured. This permits state officials to refuse to register securities that do not qualify or are fraudulent.

Two important federal statutes also regulate the sale of most securities. They are the Securities Act of 1933 and the Securities Exchange Act of 1934. Both statutes are discussed in more detail in Chapter 6.

REVIEW AND DISCUSSION QUESTIONS

1. Compare and contrast a *joint tenancy,* a *tenancy by the entirety* and a *tenancy in common.*

2. Under what circumstances will a court order the property owned by tenants in common to be partitioned?

3. During the past 15 years, the S corporation and the limited partnership have been used extensively in real estate syndication. What factors account for this?

4. Outline some of the problems that real estate sales personnel face as a result of co-ownership of real property.

CASE PROBLEMS

1. Lars Olsen is a general partner and Swen Nielson a limited partner in Olsen and Sons, a limited partnership engaged in the construction and sale of bowling alleys. Nielson had been in the construction business for many years but had retired because of ill health. Olsen has been in the construction business for a short time but had served as Nielson's accountant for a number of years. Although Olsen makes all business decisions, he frequently phones Nielson for advice. When asked for advice, Nielson usually replies, "Lars, I'm not telling you how to do it, but if I were doing it, I would do it this way." Olsen generally follows Nielson's advice. (a) If the venture fails, could Nielson be held liable as a general partner? Discuss. (b) Would the result be different if the business had been run by Nielson prior to his retirement? Explain.

2. Matilda Schomas owned a small apple orchard, which was operated by her son. Matilda did not wish to write a will, but she wanted her son to succeed to the property upon her death. Without the aid of counsel, she decided that she and her son should hold the orchard as joint tenants. Matilda then conveyed the orchard to herself and her son "as joint tenants, not as tenants in common." When she died, the son claimed the orchard by right of survivorship. Was a joint tenancy created? Explain why or why not.

3. Marie Rodesney and Fred Rowlett owned property as tenants in common. They had acquired the property for speculative purposes, each agreeing to use his or her best efforts to sell it at a profit. While they owned the property, Rowlett rented it to a Mr. Wood for a used car lot. Rentals under the agreement amounted to $5,230. Rowlett disbursed $3,511.52 for taxes and improvements, leaving a net balance of $1,718.48; however, the reasonable rental value of the property while it was owned by Rodesney and Rowlett was $15,900. Upon sale of the property, Rodesney contended that in addition to her share of the proceeds she was entitled to one-half of the reasonable rental value. Is her contention correct? Discuss. *Rodesney v. Hall, 307 P.2d 130 (Okla. 1957).*

4. James Huff and Carol Burns owned a condominium as tenants in common. From February 1978 until September 1985, they lived in the condominium as a family with Burns's minor child. During this period, Huff paid the maintenance expenses on the condominium. In 1985, the two quarreled and Burns changed the locks to the condominium, excluding Huff. Huff petitioned to partition the condominium and the property was sold. In addition to his half share from the sale, Huff argued that he was entitled to half of the maintenance expenses and half of the rental value during the period that he was excluded from the property until the judicial sale. Is Huff correct? Discuss treating each claim separately.

5. Ellen and Jack Slaney lived in a community property state. Jack was employed as an accountant. Ellen managed the home. When Ellen became pregnant, they decided to build a home and purchased land upon which to do so. After the baby was born, Jack changed his mind, as he preferred apartment living. Several years later, Ellen inherited money from an uncle. She used the inheritance for the construction of a home on the land. Is the land community property? What about the home? Support your answers.

6

Condominiums, Cooperatives, Time-Shares, and Real Estate Investments

The condominium and the cooperative afford techniques for obtaining an ownership interest in a dwelling or office. They are in many ways similar, but they also have marked differences. This chapter will focus initially on the condominium and will then describe and contrast the cooperative.

The chapter also discusses various types of time-share agreements and real estate syndications.

CONDOMINIUM

◆ The fee simple ownership of one unit in a multiple-unit structure, combined with an ownership of an undivided interest in the land and all other parts of the structure, held in common with the owners of the other individual units in the structure.

The concept of condominium ownership has blossomed in the United States since the mid-1960s. The notion of fee ownership, coupled with a release from the repair and maintenance chores of home ownership, made condominiums attractive to many people, especially to the elderly and to single-person households.

Condominiums did not present any fundamental legal problem. The common law had long recognized separate ownership of individual rooms or floors in a structure, which in essence is the nature of a condominium. Common or joint ownership of land and building was equally well established. Condominium ownership as a specific form, however, not only was new but also was a complex form of residential ownership. Describing the co-ownership, joint management, cross-easements and enforcement of individual responsibilities was part of the complexity. To provide some clarity and uniformity for this new area, states quickly began to adopt permissive condominium legislation. By 1968 all the states had adopted some form of condominium law. Although the terminology differs, there is a great deal of similarity in the statutes adopted by the various states.

This chapter discusses condominium ownership as it applies to residential units. The condominium form is also being used in commercial and some industrial property. The legal principles are the same, regardless of the use to which the condominium unit is put.

FORMATION OF A CONDOMINIUM

The developer may purchase an existing multiple-family apartment building for conversion into a condominium. Alternatively, he or she may purchase land and obtain a construction mortgage for erecting the condominium structure. The completed condominium units are then sold to individuals. The individual purchasing the condominium unit attains a fee simple interest in the apartment unit. In addition, the individual becomes a tenant in common with the other unit owners of the land and all structures outside the walls of the individual apartments. These are known as the *common elements.*

The condominium owner, if necessary, obtains a mortgage on his or her individual unit. Payment at the time of purchase is made to the condominium developer, who in turn pays off the construction mortgage as it pertains to that individual unit and its appropriate share of the common elements and has them released from the lien of the construction mortgage.

CASE EXAMPLE

Greg and Helene Burnside purchase a condominium unit from Condo Developers Inc. for $128,000. They obtain a mortgage on the unit for $110,000 from Security Bank, provide $18,000 of their own cash and deliver a check for $128,000 to Condo in exchange for a deed to the unit. Condo pays its mortgagee an amount sufficient to obtain a release for the Burnsides' unit and for 1 percent of the common elements. (There are 100 units of equal value in the development.)

DECLARATION

◆ **A document required by state law, which must accompany and be recorded with the master deed for the condominium development.**

The declaration, one of three documents commonly mandated by state law, contains a description of the property, restrictions on use and the detailed legal requirements that attach to ownership of a condominium unit. The other two documents are the bylaws and the deed to each individual unit.

The declaration is required for both new construction and for conversion of an existing building. It is filed in the county where the property is located, and it is maintained by the county clerk in the condominium records for the county. The declaration must contain a legal description of the property; a general description of each unit, including square footage and identification by floor and unit number; a description of any area that is subject to limited control, such as carports and garages; a description of the common areas and each apartment's fractional interest in the entire condominium regime. Any changes or alterations to these declarations must be filed with the county clerk.

Since the association is generally mandated by state law, it is quasigovernmental in nature. Its actions may be treated as "state action" and thus subject to the proscriptions in the constitution. For instance, when a unit owner is subjected to sanctions provided in the declaration for nonpayment of an assessment, the unit owner is entitled to due process (notice and hearing). Similarly, the right of first refusal cannot be utilized by the association to exclude prospective purchasers on the basis of race, religion, color, sex, national origin, familial status, or handicap. Although the boundaries of constitutional responsibility of associations are unclear, it appears certain that some restrictions such as those mentioned above will be imposed.

ASSESSMENTS

◆ **The regular monthly payments for upkeep of the common elements, as well as payments required for special expenses or improvements to those common elements.**

State legislation generally provides that the bylaws establish the rules for regular and special assessments. The association's board of directors, or a project manager appointed by the board, normally collects the assessments and uses them in maintaining the condominium property. The original setting of the amount of the regular assessment, the changing of that amount and the imposition of a special assessment are determined by the terms of the bylaws. The bylaws are likely to place responsibility for establishing these assessments with the association or its board of directors.

CASE EXAMPLE

The newly elected board of directors of a high-rise condominium discovered that the building had serious structural defects and that the association was in debt. The board of the Tower West Condominium discussed the woes at length and then levied a $100,000 special assessment to be paid proportionately by the unit owners. Papalexion and several other unit owners refused to pay the assessment contending that according to the bylaws a vote of the full association was necessary unless there was "an extreme emergency." They argued that this was not such an emergency.

The court held that the unit owners had to pay the assessment. Based on the structural problem and the poor financial condition of the condominium association, the board acted reasonably in concluding that this was an extreme emergency as intended under the bylaws. *Papalexion v. Tower West Condominium, 167 N.J. Super. 516, 401 A.2d 280 (1979).*

When a unit owner refuses or is unable to pay an assessment, he or she is subject to enforcement procedures that are usually stated in the bylaws. In at least two states, the statute permits the association to cut off utilities ten days after notice of delinquency is given. The normal route, however, makes any unpaid assessment a lien on the property with priority over all other liens except those designated in the statute. Generally, the liens designated in the statute are the most common forms: tax liens, prior mortgages, mechanics' liens and the like.

The procedure for foreclosing on this lien is the same as that followed under the state's mortgage foreclosure law, unless otherwise stated. At the foreclosure sale, the association is permitted to purchase the delinquent unit unless the practice is proscribed by the declaration. The main disadvantage of the foreclosure procedure is that the other unit owners must bear the expense of the delinquency during what may be a protracted foreclosure action.

The association also has the option of bringing an action for money damages, and this action does not preclude the subsequent lien foreclosure action described above. If delinquency is caused by a unit owner's shortage of funds, generally an action for money damages is not advisable.

In states that have homestead laws, seizure of the place of residence may be prohibited. Often the residential condominium qualifies as the homestead. A second lien method that circumvents these laws is the trust and lien upon sale technique. This technique permits recovery of the delinquent amount from the proceeds at the time the delinquent unit is sold. Because the proceeds are considered to be in trust, the assessment lien must be satisfied prior to any distribution to the seller of the condominium unit. The legal implications for the buyer are unclear. A cause of action may lie against the buyer who receives the proceeds prior to a satisfaction of the assessment lien.

Again, this technique may force the other unit owners to bear the burden of the delinquency for an extended period of time. However, it should circumvent the difficulty under the homestead laws existing for the previously described lien technique.

The *Beachwood Villas* case which follows provides a good insight into the roles that the state condominium statute, the declaration, and the board of directors play in regulating condominium use.

BEACHWOOD VILLAS CONDOMINIUM V. POOR

District Court of Appeal of Florida
448 So.2d 1143 (1984)

BACKGROUND. The board of directors of Beachwood Villas Condominium adopted two rules regulating unit rentals and the occupancy of units by guests during the owner's absence. Earl and Iris Poor, owners of a condominium unit, were unhappy with the rules and sued to have them declared invalid because they exceeded the scope of the board's authority. The trial court agreed with the Poors, deciding that the board exceeded its authority.

DECISION. The District Court of Appeals reversed the judgment of the trial court.

JUDGE HURLEY. Rule 31, the rental rule, requires that: (1) the minimum rental period be not less than one month, (2) the number of rentals not exceed a specified number which is calculated to the size of the unit, (3) tenants not have pets without the approval of the board, and (4) a processing fee of $25.00 be paid.

Rule 33, the guest rule, requires: (1) board approval for the "transfer" of a unit to guests when the guests are to occupy the unit during the owner's absence, (2) the number of transfers (either by rental or guest occupancy) not exceed six per year, and (3) that the occupancy rate not exceed a specified number which is calculated to the size of the unit.

Hidden Harbour Estates, Inc. v. Basso, (1981), suggested that condominium rules falling under the generic heading of use restrictions emanate from one of two sources: the declaration of condominium or the board of directors. Those contained in the declaration "are clothed with a very strong presumption of validity . . . ," because the law requires their full disclosure prior to the time of purchase and, thus, the purchaser has adequate notice. Board rules, on the other hand, are treated differently. When a court is called upon to assess the validity of a rule enacted by a board of directors, it first determines whether the board acted within its scope of authority and, second, whether the rule reflects reasoned or arbitrary and capricious decision making.

The reasonableness of rules 31 and 33 was not questioned below and, therefore, we are concerned only with the scope of the board's authority. Inquiries into this area begin with a review of the applicable statutes and the condominium's legal documents, i.e., the declaration and by-laws.

By express terms in the statute and in the declaration, the association has been granted broad authority to regulate the use of both the common element and limited common element property.

In general, that power may be exercised as long as the exercise is reasonable, is not violative of any constitutional restrictions, and does not exceed any specific limitations set out in the statutes or condominium documents.

Since there has not been any suggestion that either rule violates the Condominium Act, Section 718, Florida Statutes (1983), we begin by viewing the Beachwood Villas declaration of condominium. Article X provides that "[t]he operation of the condominium property shall be governed by the By-Laws of the Association which are . . . made a part hereof." In turn, Article IV of the by-laws states that "[a]ll of the powers and duties of the Association shall be exercised by the board of directors. . . ." More specific is Article VII, Section 2, which states that "[t]he Board of Directors may, from time to time, adopt or amend previously adopted rules and regulations governing and restricting the use and maintenance of the condominium units. . . . "

It is obvious from the foregoing that the board of directors is empowered to pass rules and regulations for the governance of the condominium. The question remains, however, whether the topics encompassed in rules 31 and 33 are legitimate subjects for board rulemaking. Put another way, must regulations governing rental of units and occupancy of units by guests during an owner's absence be included in the declaration of condominium? A declaration of condominium is "the condominium's constitution." Often, it contains broad statements of general policy with due notice that the board of directors is empowered to implement these policies and address day-to-day problems in the condominium's operation through the rulemaking process. It would be impossible to list all restrictive uses in a declaration of condominium. Parking regulations, limitations on the use of the swimming pool, tennis court and card room—the list is endless and subject to constant modification. Therefore, we have formulated the appropriate test in this fashion: provided that a board-enacted rule does not contravene either an express provision of the declaration or a right reasonably inferable therefrom, it will be found valid, within the scope of the board's authority. This test, in our view, is fair and functional; it safeguards the rights of unit owners and preserves unfettered the concept of delegated board management.

Inasmuch as rules 31 and 33 do not contravene either an express provision of the declaration or any right reasonably inferable therefrom, we hold that the board's enactments are valid and plainly within the scope of its authority. Accordingly, we reverse the order on appeal and remand the cause for further proceedings consistent with this opinion.

REVERSED AND REMANDED.

COOPERATIVE

◆ **A form of ownership in which the land and buildings are (usually) owned by a corporation; individual unit residents own stock in the corporation and have a proprietary lease in a specific unit or apartment.**

Unlike the condominium unit owner, the cooperative owner or tenant does not have a fee simple interest in the apartment. Instead, the owner has shares of stock in the corporation that owns the land and building, along with a long-term *proprietary lease*. Occasionally, the cooperative ownership is in a trust or partnership form rather than a corporate form.

The notion of a proprietary lease connotes that, unlike typical tenants, the cooperative tenants participate in the running of the cooperative through their stock interest in the corporation. The participation may be direct, when an individual is elected as a member of the board of directors, or indirect, when voting for directors or giving opinions to the elected directors. Despite the proprietary nature of the lease, however, it continues to be a lease and is governed by landlord-tenant law. One must be cautious, however, because the state may choose to treat cooperatives differently than a traditional lease.

CASE EXAMPLE

Drew Associates, a cooperative developer, challenged the New Jersey Cooperative Recording Act as unconstitutional. One of Drew's grounds was that the statute created an illegal restraint on the alienation of land by requiring that all transfer documents be recorded, and that it contain the consent of the board of managers of the cooperative. These conditions are not placed on other leases or even condominium transfers.

The Court upheld the statute stating that cooperative ownership is a "hybrid" form of property and does not fall within traditional notions of either realty or personalty. It is reasonable, therefore, for the state to impose conditions on cooperative transfers not imposed on other forms of transfer. *Drew Associates of N.J. v. Travisano, 122 N.J. 249, 584 A.2d 807 (1991).*

FINANCING A COOPERATIVE

In a typical situation, an investor purchases a multiple-unit dwelling to convert it into a cooperative. To finance the conversion, the investor takes out a mortgage with a bank for 80 percent of the dwelling's value. The remaining 20 percent is paid initially by the investor but is recouped through the issuance of stock in the cooperative corporation to the future tenants. Future tenants pay their share of the 20 percent by purchasing stock when they enter the cooperative. In addition, each makes monthly payments that cover his or her share of the mortgage payment as well as operating expenses.

In addition to the mortgage share, each tenant as part of the monthly rent will pay a share of any other debt, taxes and operating expenses. As in a condominium, the share of these expenses may be on a per-unit basis or may vary with the relative value of the apartment. The amount of the annual or monthly assessment is determined by the board of directors of the corporation.

DIFFERENCES BETWEEN CONDOMINIUMS AND COOPERATIVES

One difference between a cooperative and a condominium is the type of mortgage obtained. In the condominium each unit owner arranges for his or her own mortgage; in the cooperative there is a *blanket mortgage* for the entire building. The blanket mortgage may be more difficult to obtain.

In the cooperative there are restrictions on the ability of the tenants to sell their interest. Generally, the tenant needs the approval of the board of directors for the proposed new tenant. This procedure is a little more stringent than the right of first refusal used in the condominium area. These restrictions on the cooperative go beyond the outright sale and may prevent a tenant from assigning or subletting his or her share of the premises. The purpose behind these restrictions is to ensure that a compatible group of tenants is assembled in the cooperative.

The cooperative form of ownership has advantages for the tenant compared with the usual landlord-tenant situation. The tenant is not subjected to annual rent increases and does not risk having the lease terminated arbitrarily. The cooperative tenant has a long-term lease and participates in any decision to raise the rent.

Like the condominium owner, the cooperative owner or tenant is subject to an extensive set of rules and regulations governing the cooperative. Failure to comply with the terms of the regulations may permit the board of directors to cancel the tenant's lease or to take some other action provided in the rules for redressing the violation.

Upon the death of the tenant, any successor—an heir under the tenant's will or by law—must clear the screening of the board of directors. There is no automatic right on the part of successors to be able to continue the cooperative lease. This differs from a condominium, where the unit is owned in fee and can freely be passed on to successors.

There are some distinct advantages to fee simple ownership, of which the condominium owner is the beneficiary. The notion of fee ownership itself carries a certain feeling of security and psychological confidence that is not matched by the lease of the cooperative arrangement. Many of these advantages are tangible and specific.

The condominium owner is responsible for his or her own mortgage and is not as vulnerable to default as the cooperative owner, who shares a blanket mortgage with everyone else in the cooperative. If the unit is rented, the condominium owner can directly take advantage of certain tax benefits, such as property tax deduction, interest deductions, casualty loss deductions and depreciation allowance. Although residential cooperatives may be able to take advantage of some federal tax benefits, such as property tax and interest deductions, these benefits are not available individually to the cooperative owners. Under Section 528 of the Internal Revenue Code, however, a condominium owner is permitted to make a tax-free contribution to the association for capital expenses, maintenance and operating expenses provided the association meets the requirements of Section 528. Thus, a condominium owner can make a tax-free payment to the association for a new roof or for the pool lifeguard. A payment for similar expenses to a cooperative would not qualify.

On the sale of a condominium unit, the owner can sell at market value and pay the reduced capital gains rate on the gain, subject to postponement and rollover provisions. The cooperative owner generally must sell the stock back to the cooperative at a stipulated price. Often the stipulated price is the original price.

Cooperatives can be troublesome during difficult economic times. Initially, it may be more difficult to get a blanket mortgage loan than to get a mortgage loan on an individual condominium unit. Given the nature of the interdependence created by the blanket mortgage, the default of one or several cooperative owners can cause a default on the mortgage. On default, all cooperative owners stand to lose their investments, even those who can afford to keep up their share of expenses. In a condominium, on the other hand, the default on an individual mortgage does not affect the other condominium owners. Nevertheless, the financial straits that caused the mortgage default are likely to prevent payment of condominium assessments; in this respect, delinquencies can place a financial strain on the other condominium owners.

One advantage the cooperative has over the condominium is that it is relatively easy to get rid of an incompatible tenant. A tenant who refuses to comply with the rules of the cooperative can be evicted in summary proceedings in most instances. Although a condominium owner who is in default on assessments can be ousted through a lien foreclosure, the procedure is likely to be more prolonged and expensive.

LEVANDUSKY V. ONE FIFTH AVENUE APARTMENT CORP.

Court of Appeals of New York
553 N.E.2d 1317 (1990)

BACKGROUND. Ronald Levandusky lived in an incorporated residential cooperative. Seeking to increase the kitchen area of his apartment, he had renovation plans prepared and presented to the cooperative's board of directors. The board approved the plans, and executed with Levandusky an "Alteration Agreement" which incorporated "Renovation Guidelines." The guidelines provided that special written approval was required for any alteration to the building's heating system, and none was indicated in the initial plan. It later came to the board's attention that Levandusky intended to move the steam pipes. At a later meeting the board reaffirmed its existing policy against relocating vertical steam pipes, and modified Levandusky's plan approval to reflect that limitation. Levandusky hired a contractor and proceeded with the work. The board issued a stop order pursuant to its "Renovation Guidelines." Levandusky sued to have the stop order set aside.

The trial count dismissed Levandusky's petition and ordered him to restore the steam pipes. The intermediate appellate court affirmed in a split decision (3-2). One of the major issues discussed by each of the courts was the role courts should play in reviewing disputes between boards of directors and unit owners/tenants in condominiums and cooperatives.

DECISION. The Court of Appeals affirmed the decision of the lower courts.

JUDGE KAYE. As cooperative and condominium home ownership has grown increasingly popular, courts confronting disputes between tenant-owners and governing boards have fashioned a variety of rules for adjudicating such claims. In the process, several salient characteristics of the governing board/homeowner relationship have been identified as relevant to the judicial inquiry. The cooperative or condominium association is a quasi-government—"a little democratic sub-society of necessity." The proprietary lessees or condominium owners consent to be governed, in certain respects, by the decisions of a board. Like a municipal government, such governing boards are responsible for running the day-to-day affairs of the cooperative and to that end, often have broad powers in areas that range from financial decisionmaking to promulgating regulations regarding pets and parking spaces. Authority to approve or disapprove structural alterations, as in this case, is commonly given to the governing board.

Through the exercise of this authority, to which would-be apartment owners must generally acquiesce, a governing board may significantly restrict the bundle of rights a property owner normally enjoys. Moreover, as with any authority to govern, the broad powers of a cooperative board hold potential for abuse through arbitrary and malicious decisionmaking, favoritism, discrimination and the like.

On the other hand, agreement to submit to the decisionmaking authority of a cooperative board is voluntary in a sense that submission to government authority is not; there is always the freedom not to purchase the apartment. The stability offered by community control, through a board, has its own economic and social benefits, and the purchase of a cooperative apartment represents a voluntary choice to cede certain of the privileges of single ownership to a governing body, often made up of fellow tenants who volunteer their time, without compensation. The board, in return, takes on the burden of managing the property for the benefit of the proprietary lessees. It is apparent, then, that a standard for judicial review of the actions of a cooperative or condominium governing board must be sensitive to a variety of concerns—sometimes competing concerns. Even when the governing board acts within the scope of its authority, some check on its potential powers to regulate residents' conduct, lifestyle and property rights is necessary to protect individual residents from abusive exercise, notwithstanding that the residents have, to an extent, consented to be regulated and even selected their representatives. At the same time, the chosen standard of review should not undermine the purposes for which the residential community and its governing structure were formed: protection of the interest of the entire community of residents in an environment managed by the board for the common benefit.

We conclude that these goals are best served by a standard of review that is analogous to the business judgment rule applied by courts to determine challenges to decisions made by corporate directors. A number of courts in this and other states have applied such a standard in reviewing the decisions of cooperative and condominium boards. We agree with those courts that such a test best balances the individual and collective interests at stake.

Developed in the context of commercial enterprises, the business judgment rule prohibits judicial inquiry into actions of corporate directors "taken in good faith and in the exercise of honest judgment in the lawful and legitimate furtherance of corporate purposes." So long as the corporation's directors have not breached their fiduciary obligation to the corporation, "the exercise of [their powers] for the common and general interests of the corporation may not be questioned, although the results show that what they did was unwise or inexpedient."

We emphasize that reference to the business judgment rule is for the purpose of analogy only. Clearly, in light of the doctrine's origins in the quite different world of commerce, the fiduciary principles identified in the existing case law—primarily emphasizing avoidance of self-dealing and financial self-aggrandizement—will of necessity be adapted over time in order to apply to directors of not-for-profit homeowners' cooperative corporations. So long as the board acts for the purposes of the cooperative, within the scope of its authority and in good faith, courts will not substitute their judgment for the board's. Stated somewhat differently, unless a resident challenging the board's action is able to demonstrate a breach of this duty, judicial review is not available.

As this case exemplifies, board decisions concerning what residents may or may not do with their living space may be highly charged and emotional. A cooperative or condominium is by nature a myriad of often competing views regarding personal living space, and decisions taken to benefit the collective interest may be unpalatable to one resident or another, creating the prospect that board decisions will be subjected to undue court involvement and judicial second-guessing. Allowing an owner who is simply dissatisfied with particular board action a second opportunity to reopen the matter completely before a court, which—generally without knowing the property—may or may not agree with the reasonableness of the board's determination, threatens the stability of the common living arrangement.

Levandusky's argument that having once granted its approval, the board was powerless to rescind its decision after he had spent considerable sums on the renovations is without merit. There is no dispute that Levandusky failed to comply with the provisions of the "Alteration Agreement" or "Renovation Guidelines" designed to give the board explicit written notice before it approved a change in the building's heating system. Once made aware of Levandusky's intent, the board promptly consulted its engineer, and notified Levandusky that it would not depart from a policy of refusing to permit the movement of pipes. That he then went ahead and moved the pipe hardly allows him to claim reliance on the board's initial approval of his plans. Indeed, recognition of such an argument would frustrate any systematic effort to enforce uniform policies.

AFFIRMED.

TIME-SHARES

Time-sharing has become a popular marketing device for resort developments in the United States. Time-sharing includes several very different types of ownership. Some of these forms include ownership of an interest in the real property, and other forms are mere rights of use with no interest in the property itself.

Time-sharing arrangements can be built on several different legal principles. In some instances the arrangement is a variation of the tenancy in common. In others it is a variation of a cooperative. It could also be a lease. When it is built on one of these types of legal ownership of property, it always includes a limitation as to the time of use. For example, a tenancy in common is an estate that includes more than one owner, with each co-owner owning an undivided interest. A time-sharing arrangement based on the legal principles of the tenancy in common would introduce the characteristic of time with respect to possession of the property. An ordinary tenant in common has an equal right to possession with the other cotenants. The time-share agreement limits the right to possession to a specific time period each year.

The time-sharing arrangement can also include principles of contract, partnership, license or corporate law. For example, a time-sharing arrangement based in contract would include the right to use a specific piece of property at a definite time each year for a certain number of years. At the expiration of that period, the property would be owned by the developer, not the owner of the time-share.

Much of the criticism of time-sharing arrangements is a result of misleading marketing practices. The legal rights associated with time-sharing arrangements can vary significantly from development to development. The variety of legal rights that are being marketed as time-shares coupled with deceptive and misleading information by salespersons has prompted some states to enact legislation dealing specifically with time-shares.

REAL ESTATE SECURITIES

◆ **Any syndication whereby a person invests money in a common enterprise involving real estate with the expectation of attaining profits from the efforts of a promoter or some other third party.**

A normal transaction for the sale or lease of real property is not a security within the context of federal and state security laws. When a person or promoter offers an interest in the arrangement to the public, however, it may become a security. On other occasions, a person will sell a business, and the assets include real property. In many states, real estate securities and business opportunity sales have separate and distinct control schemes from the usual real estate transactions.

If the transaction constitutes the issuance of a security, unless exempted, the promoter must comply with federal and (probably) state regulations.

CASE EXAMPLE

Fafner offers a group of his friends and neighbors an opportunity to be investors with him in a piece of mountaintop property he is about to acquire. The property has multiple-unit housing on it, and the investors will share in the profits. This purchase is a real estate security and must be registered as described later in this section.

One of the chief federal regulations in the area of securities is the 1933 Securities Act. The language of Section 2 of the act covers any investment contract or profit-sharing arrangement and is therefore broad enough to encompass almost any real estate syndication. The key factors are that transactions be a common enterprise and that there be management of the investment by a third party for the benefit of a passive investor. When an agency or court makes the decision as to whether or not a transaction involves a security, the emphasis is on the substance and economic reality rather than on the form the transaction takes. In defining what is a security, or any other regulation hereinafter discussed, the investor must take care to research the provisions of the state "blue-sky" laws, which regulate security transactions as well.

CONDOMINIUMS AS SECURITIES

The offering of a condominium unit is not normally treated as a security, but as a sale of real estate. Thus, the sale is not subject to the regulation of the Securities and Exchange Commission (SEC) or to similar state laws.

CASE EXAMPLE

Joyce entered a purchase agreement for a condominium unit, which he planned to use for his personal residence. Joyce sued the condominium project owner, contending that his contract was an "investment contract" and subject to federal securities laws. The security had not been registered, nor had Joyce received a prospectus as required by federal securities law.

The federal district court held that a condominium purchase does not fall within the definition of an investment contract. An investment contract presumes that the investor hopes to realize a profit from the investment due to the activity of a third party. This is not the case where a typical condominium is purchased as a personal residence. *Joyce v. Ritchie Tower Properties, 417 F. Supp. 53 (D. Ill. 1976).*

Nevertheless, several states have extensive regulations of condominiums as securities. It is clear, however, that in any state if condominium advertisements or other documents make any reference to providing rental services for the buyer for the period the buyer is not using the condominium, the purchase will be treated as an investment contract and the above-mentioned security regulations will apply. For more detail, SEC Release No. 33-5347 (January 4, 1973) provides guidelines for determining when condominium offerings are securities.

HOCKING v. DUBOIS

United States Court of Appeals, Ninth Circuit
885 F.2d 1449 (1989)

BACKGROUND. After visiting Hawaii, Gerald Hocking, a resident of Nevada, contacted a Hawaii real estate agent, Marylee Dubois. Hocking asked Dubois to search for a condominium for him to invest in. He indicated that he wanted to buy directly from the developer, to be "a first person buyer." Dubois brought a condominium to Hocking's attention in a resort complex being built by Aetna Life Insurance Co. The particular condominium unit Dubois referred to was owned by the Libermans, but Dubois apparently assured Hocking that he was buying from the developer. She told Hocking that a rental pool arrangement (RPA) would be available if he chose to buy the unit; that

units in the complex were renting for an average of $100 a day, or about $2,000 to $3,000 per month. Hocking intended to use the income to make his monthly payments on the unit.

Hocking purchased the condominium unit and joined the RPA, thereby contracting with Hotel Corporation of the Pacific (HCP) to manage his rentals. The contract could be terminated by Hocking on 30 days' written notice, and by HCP if the participation of the number of units in this complex fell below 40 percent. He handled all these matters through Dubois.

Hocking purchased the unit for $115,000, with a $24,000 down payment and installments due thereafter until final payment in June 1982.

Subsequently, Hocking "cancelled" his investment and refused to make payments because the rental income did not live up to Dubois's predictions. He alleged that his investment was entirely passive, that he relied on Dubois to select, manage, and protect his investment, and that he relinquished all control over the unit except for two weeks each year. Hocking sued Dubois, contending that she violated the antifraud provisions of the Securities and Exchange Commission Act of 1934. The trial judge ruled for Dubois, granting a summary judgment.

DECISION. The U.S. Court of Appeals reversed the trial court's decision and remanded the case for a trial on the issues.

CHIEF JUDGE GOODWIN. The term "investment contract" has been interpreted to reach "[n]ovel, uncommon, or irregular devices, whatever they appear to be . . . " "It embodies a flexible rather than a static principle, one that is capable of adaptation to meet the countless and variable schemes devised by those who seek the use of the money of others on the promise of profits." In *Howey* (1946), the Supreme Court found that the combined sale of land and a land service contract, under which the purchaser relinquished all control over the land for a 10-year period, was an investment contract. The Court there put forward the classic definition of an investment contract: [A]n investment contract for purposes of the Securities Act means a contract, transaction or scheme whereby a person invests his money in a common enterprise and is led to expect profits solely from the efforts of the promoter or a third party, it being immaterial whether the shares in the enterprise are evidenced by formal certificates or by nominal interests in the physical assets employed in the enterprise. *Howey* rejected the suggestion "that an invest-ment contract is necessarily missing . . . where the tangible interest which is sold has intrinsic value independent of the success of the enterprise as a whole."

Subsequent cases have merely refined the three prongs of the *Howey* test. While the first prong, an investment of money, has proved relatively simple, the other two have evolved with time. As discussed below, the second prong's requirement of a "common enterprise" has been construed by this Circuit as demanding either an enterprise common to the investor and the seller, promoter or some third party (vertical commonality) or an enterprise common to a group of investors (horizontal commonality).

While *Howey*'s third prong demanded an expectation of profits "solely from the efforts of the promoter or a third party," we have dropped the term "solely" and instead require that "the efforts made by those other than the investor are the undeniably significant ones, those essential managerial efforts which affect the failure or success of the enterprise.

We must therefore determine whether Hocking's purchase of a condominium and rental pool was (1) an investment of money, (2) in a common enterprise, (3) with an expectation of profits produced by the efforts of others.

In *Howey,* as here, the investors purchased real estate and at the same time relinquished much of the right to use or enter the property. In *Howey,* as here, the investors were not obligated to purchase the service contracts, and in fact some decided to purchase the land without a service contract. In *Howey,* as here, the investors were generally nonresidents who lacked the skill, knowledge and equipment necessary to manage the investment.

Hocking, however, did not purchase the condominium in the initial offering from the developer. He purchased in the secondary market from the Libermans. Further, Hocking entered into the rental pool agreement with HCP, and has, defendants argue, failed to demonstrate any link between HCP and the developer. Finally, unlike the investors in *Howey*, Hocking could legally terminate the RPA according to its terms and regain control over the condominium. We must determine therefore whether these differences from *Howey* make Hocking's alleged transaction into an ordinary real estate purchase or whether it nevertheless could prove to be the purchase of a security.

In 1973 the SEC issued a release in order to "alert persons engaged in the business of building and selling condominiums . . . to their responsibilities under the Securities Act and to provide guidelines for a determination of when an offering of condominiums or other units may be viewed as an offering of securities."

The SEC points out that Release 5347 applies to "persons engaged in the business of building and selling condominiums . . . ," and not to brokers in the secondary market.

Given the SEC's position, we do not rely on Release 5347 in determining whether Hocking was offered a security. We instead examine the alleged transaction entirely in terms of the *Howey* test.

The *Howey* Test

A. INVESTMENT OF MONEY. Defendants attempt to pull apart the package into two separate transactions. They argue that even if Hocking did invest money in the condominium, he did not invest money in the RPA, and it is the RPA that provides the elements necessary to satisfy the *Howey* test's other requirements. Therefore, they claim, Hocking did not satisfy this first requirement. Admittedly, there would be an argument as to whether the "investment of money" requirement had been met if someone who already owned a condominium de-

cided to place the condominium into a rental arrangement, independent of the decision to purchase the condominium. If, however, the condominium and rental agreements were offered as a package, there can be no serious argument that Hocking did not invest money in the package. Since Hocking has created an issue of fact over whether the condominium and RPA were sold as a package, he has met this first requirement of *Howey* for purposes of summary judgment.

B. COMMON ENTERPRISE. The simple purchase of real estate lacks any horizontal commonality, as no pooling of interests or profits is involved. The purchase of real estate combined with an RPA, however, does evidence horizontal commonality. The participants pool their assets; they give up any claim to profits or losses attributable to their particular investments in return for a pro rata share of the profits of the enterprise; and they make their collective fortunes dependent on the success of a single common enterprise. Because in this case Hocking has raised facts supporting horizontal commonality, we need not consider vertical commonality.

Of course, whether Hocking can prove horizontal commonality at trial will depend on whether he can show that Dubois offered a package which included the RPA. As discussed above, Hocking has raised a genuine issue of fact as to that question.

C. EXPECTATION OF PROFITS PRODUCED BY THE EFFORTS OF OTHERS. This third prong of *Howey* forms the greatest hurdle for Hocking, assuming he can prove at trial that the condominium and rental agreements were part of one package. He must show an expectation of profits produced by the efforts of others, that the efforts of others are "those essential managerial efforts which affect the failure or success of the enterprise."

The crux of defendants' argument on this point is that the rental agreements allowed Hocking to maintain a high degree of control over his condominium, thus making any managerial efforts of Dubois or HCP nonessential to the success of Hocking's investment.

Hocking was not required to enter into any of the rental agreements as a prerequisite of purchasing the condominium. He elected to delegate control of the condominium to HCP. Further, the rental agreements gave Hocking various termination rights described above, allowing him to regain control over the use and management of his investment.

The record presents a material question of fact: was Hocking dependent on Dubois or HCP, and unable to exercise control over his investment? Hocking claims to be an unsophisticated, inexperienced investor, lacking any special training or education. He resides thousands of miles away from the location of the investment. He is not in the business of managing condominiums or other real estate. He has raised a genuine issue of fact whether he requested and received an offer of management services.

Further, Hocking observed that the condominium complex was "operated like a hotel from the lobby," and that HCP distributed brochures and advertisements on the mainland. Numerous other condominium owners participated in the RPA, and HCP reserved the right to terminate the RPA if the number of participating units fell below 40 percent of the units in the complex.

Hocking's affidavit and deposition raise a genuine issue of fact whether he intended his investment to be entirely passive, and whether, as alleged, he "relied solely on Dubois to select, manage, and protect" his investment.

In the context of isolated resales, each case requires an analysis of how the condominium was promoted to the investor, including any representations made to the investor, and the nature of the investment and the collateral agreements. The investor's intentions and expectations as communicated to the broker would be relevant in determining what investment package was actually offered.

If the *Howey* analysis is undertaken, the securities laws are found to apply, and the application of the securities laws places undue burdens on developers, real estate brokers, or condominium owners, changes in the law should be sought from Congress or the Securities and Exchange Commission. *Howey*, on this record, requires this case to proceed beyond summary judgment.

REVERSED AND REMANDED.

If the security regulations apply, registration of the entire offering must be made with the SEC. About half the states follow the disclosure rule: the prospect must be fully informed so that an intelligent decision can be made. In the other states, full disclosure as well as minimum standards of "fairness" apply to the condominium offering when treated as an investment contract.

EXEMPTIONS

◆ **Transactions that would otherwise meet the definition of a security but that have been statutorily excused from the law's restrictions.**

Exemptions from registration are made in the case of two types of transactions: intrastate sales and private offerings.

Intrastate Offerings. This exemption is provided in Section 3(a)(11) of the statute and applies to offerings that are made *solely* to residents of the state where the offerer or issuer is a resident and doing business. A key word in this exemption is *solely*. If one sale is made to a single nonresident of the relevant state, or if the issue is not wholly owned by residents up to nine months after the distribution of the issue is complete, the exemption will not apply.

> **CASE EXAMPLE**
>
> Referring back to the earlier example, Fafner, using the intrastate offering exemption, sells a share in his mountaintop venture to Thorsen. It takes six months to sell the full interest in the investment. If Thorsen, prior to completion of the sale, sells her share to her brother-in-law who lives out of state, Fafner's offering would no longer qualify under the intrastate offering exemption.

To use this exemption, therefore, the promoter must have assurances that the purchasers do not intend to resell. The burden of proving this exemption is on the promoter. For a sizable issuance, it is very risky to rely on this exemption in light of its restrictive character. Note that, despite its exemption under the federal statute, the issue may have to comply with the state law regarding securities. An array of remedies is available against an issuer who has relied on the intrastate exemption but who has failed to meet all the requirements of the exemption. Recovery of damages for the price paid for the security, plus interest, is among those remedies. For further clarification of the meaning of this exemption, see SEC Rule 147.

Private Offering. This exemption applies to offerings that are made to knowledgeable investors who have adequate information to evaluate fully the risks entailed in the transaction. It is the intent of this exemption that the offering be made to investors who are adequately informed so that they do not need the protective umbrella of the SEC disclosure rules. The purpose behind the exemption is to exclude such issues from expensive and time-consuming regulations.

> **CASE EXAMPLE**
>
> When the SEC challenged an offering made to employees under the private offering exemption by Ralston Purina Company, the Supreme Court adopted a several-fold test in determining the availability of the exemption.
>
> The court stated that these questions should be asked: Were the offerees the type of persons who could fend for themselves? Did the offerees have access to the same type of information that would appear in a registration statement? Were the securities purchased for the investor's own account? *Securities and Exchange Commission v. Ralston Purina Co., 346 U.S. 119 (1953).*

The determination of whether or not an offering is private is based on numerous factors, including the number of offerees, the sophistication of the offerees, the number of units in the issue and their denomination and the manner of the offering, that is, personal contact or public advertising. There are no hard and fast rules, but the SEC will weigh the above factors in deciding whether or not the issue is a private one.

The SEC has adopted Regulation D, SEC Release No. 6389 (1982) as a "safe harbor" for those seeking to take advantage of the private offering exemption. If Regulation D is adhered to, the issue is exempt from registration requirements but not the antifraud, civil liability or other provisions of the SEC Act. The exemption applies only to the original issuer of the security. The requirements of Regulation D are complex and detailed and are not amenable to a brief summary here. The regulation should be followed closely to ensure compliance and the protection of the "safe harbor."

REGISTRATION OF SECURITIES

◆ **The listing of an issuance that meets the definition of a security—and is not otherwise exempted—with the SEC and (perhaps) with state officials.**

Prior to making any offering of a nonexempt security, the promoter must register the issuance with the SEC. No sales can take place before the SEC declares the *registration statement* to be effective. During the period between the filing with the SEC and its approval, the promoter can make oral offers or even written offers by way of a preliminary prospectus, but no investor can be bound and no sale concluded until the registration is declared effective by the SEC.

> **CASE EXAMPLE**
> MacLeish has filed a prospectus and supporting documents with the SEC. While waiting approval, he begins to contact potential investors, providing them with a copy of the preliminary prospectus explaining the benefits of the investment. MacLeish asks for no commitments from these prospects. There would be nothing illegal about MacLeish's conduct.

If the promoter makes any sale prior to SEC approval, all investors have the right to rescind the transaction and get their money back, plus interest.

PROSPECTUS

◆ **A written document containing all the information necessary for an investor to make an independent and intelligent decision regarding a securities offering.**

The prospectus must be filed with the SEC registration and must be provided to prospective investors. The registration also will include the financial statements for the promoter's operation and the operating statements for the property (for example, statements indicating the income received from the property for the past five years). Any publicity regarding the offering should be avoided prior to filing with the SEC.

The SEC, in examining the proposed registration, compares the annual earnings history with the yearly cash distributions proposed by the issuer. The SEC attempts to see that the information alleged in the prospectus is complete and accurate; it does not pass on the merits of the issue.

For example, the SEC examiner explores the registration documents to determine whether the 6 percent annual return in investment asserted in the prospectus is realistic in light of past performance. The examiner does not comment on the fact that a 6 percent return, given existing market conditions, might be a poor investment.

Under federal law, the offeror is required to give full and fair disclosure and is not permitted to give advice on the wisdom of the investment opportunity. In some states, the state regulatory agency evaluates the merits of the offering as well as determining that the prospectus is accurate.

FORMS OF OWNERSHIP

The modes of ownership or ways of setting up a real estate syndication are varied. A simple vehicle such as concurrent ownership (tenancy in common), discussed in Chapter 5, can be used. Traditional forms of doing business—partnerships, limited partnerships and corporations—are utilized. Less common techniques such as trusts, particularly the real estate investment trust (REIT), have gained popularity.

Each method of ownership has its intrinsic advantages and disadvantages. Tenants in common retain direct individual control over their investment fates, but the death of a tenant can suddenly propel an heir into the ownership picture as an unwanted tenant. Partners can retain control over decision making, but, as with tenants in common, operational rules must be clearly provided or chaos may ensue. Partners avoid the dual taxation that exists in a corporate form but do not enjoy the limited liability of corporate shareholders. Limited partners enjoy some of the best of both the partnership world and the corporate world since they generally avoid dual taxation and have limited liability. Nevertheless, tax risks exist in the limited partnership technique in the form of income tax recapture penalties that may be imposed on the investor above the loss of the initial investment capital. Because of the additional risks, the limited partnership form has been confined largely to sophisticated investors by choice of both the promoters and the investors.

Each of these techniques is used broadly within and outside the real estate investment area. A complete explanation of them would require an entire textbook; they are usually covered in a separate course of study. It may be useful, however, to discuss in more detail the trust device and the real estate investment trust in particular. It might be helpful to review the general discussion of trusts in Chapter 5 prior to reading about the specialized real estate investment trust.

REAL ESTATE INVESTMENT TRUST (REIT)

◆ **A tax shelter that exempts certain qualified real estate investment syndications from corporate taxes where 95 percent or more of the ordinary income is distributed annually to the beneficiaries or investors.**

The Real Estate Investment Trust Act was passed by Congress in 1960. The rules governing these statutory trusts are very complex and must be strictly adhered to by those attempting to take advantage of the form. The real estate investment trust can exist only where it is permissible under state law.

The REIT is a conduit for getting income to certificate holders while avoiding the taxation of the trust as a corporation that would normally occur. For example, a group of friends invest some funds by purchasing certificates in a REIT. The trustee of the REIT, an independent manager, uses their money to purchase an apartment complex for the purpose of attaining a return on that investment through rental income from the units. The net profits from the rentals are distributed to the group of friends (and any fellow investor in the REIT). These profits are taxed as ordinary income to all the investors, but the trust does not pay tax on the distributed portion of the profits.

The major conditions for creating a REIT are as follows:

∎ There must be 100 or more certificate holders.

∎ A minimum of 95 percent of the gross income of the REIT must be derived from passive investments, such as rents, dividends and interest.

∎ At least 75 percent of the gross income of the REIT must be derived from transactions connected to real estate, such as rents from real estate, mortgage interest, gains on the sale of real property and the like.

∎ The trustees must have centralized authority over the trust.

∎ At least 95 percent of the earned income from the trust business must be distributed to the certificate holders.

∎ There are additional restrictions on income produced by assets held for less than six months.

There are some distinct advantages to using the REIT form, in addition to the avoidance of dual corporate taxation. Other factors include centralized management, limited liability to the investors and the availability of real estate experts to do the investing. Nevertheless, the investments are limited to passive ones, and these may not provide the highest return on the investment dollar. Because of the size of trust distribution (100 or more certificate holders), the trust must generally register with the SEC, which is an expensive procedure.

Due to the complexity of the REIT qualifications, this simplified description of the procedure should not be relied on by anyone interested in forming this type of trust. State laws may provide further restrictions on REITs.

REVIEW AND DISCUSSION QUESTIONS

1. Match the following terms with their correct definitions:

   a. declaration
   b. bylaws
   c. individual unit deed

   (1) Document prepared for each individual condominium unit in the development
   (2) Document, required by state law, that must accompany and be recorded with the master deed for condominium development
   (3) Document outlining the rules governing the internal operation of a condominium development

2. What are the common elements in a condominium arrangement? Distinguish between general common elements and limited common elements.

3. A condominium unit owner surrenders in writing her right to use the swimming pool, one of the common elements. Does that action relieve her of the responsibility of sharing the cost of maintaining the pool?

4. Compare and contrast condominiums with cooperatives.

5. Roberta Geist is undertaking to promote a shopping center construction project. To obtain the necessary capital, Geist is considering offering shares in the venture to 20 business associates and friends.

   (a) Geist and all the offerees live in Nebraska. Discuss with Geist the pros and cons of not registering with the SEC and utilizing the intrastate offerings exemption.
   (b) All of Geist's proposed offerees are experienced businesspersons. Would you advise her to take advantage of the private offerings exemption? Why?

6. What advantages accrue to investors entering a joint real estate venture who use the real estate investment trust form?

CASE PROBLEMS

1. Lynne Voyant inherited $50,000 upon the death of her rich uncle. Voyant is exploring investment possibilities and is considering investing in a real estate venture promoted by a friend, Percy Shifter. Shifter has assured Voyant that the investment is an excellent opportunity to make her money grow since the offering is registered with the SEC. Voyant has a premonition that there is more to consider than this. Clarify the situation for her.

2. Enterprise, Inc., purchased an existing shopping center and converted the commercial rentals into commercial condominium units. Jack Jackson, owner and operator of Jackson's Drug Store, tenant in the shopping center, sued to enjoin the conversion, contending that (1) condominium formulation is illegal for commercial units; (2) the conversion requires the issuance of a prospectus; and (3) it is illegal to deny him a vote since the day-to-day operation of the common elements will be done by the board of directors and not all the members of the condominium association. Was Jackson correct? Why?

3. The original officers and directors of Avila S. Condominium Association contracted with Kappa Corp. to provide the association with recreational facilities. These officers and directors were also officers and directors of Kappa Corp. Other members of the condominium association sued the original officers and directors, contending that they were unjustly enriched as a result of their involvement with the Kappa Corp. Discuss. *Avila S. Condominium Ass'n. v. Kappa Corp., 347 So.2d 599 (Fla. 1977).*

4. Kellogg owned an individual unit within a condominium. He decided that he wanted to put an additional story onto his unit and to expand the width of the existing story. He got the approval of the town zoning officials but did not get the consent of the other condominium owners. The bylaws of the condominium indicate that unanimous consent of the owners is necessary for a unit owner to make a private use of the common elements. Kellogg claims that he is not using the common elements, but only unused air space. What do you think of Kellogg's argument as to (a) the horizontal expansion? (b) the vertical expansion? *Grey v. Coastal States Holding Co., 22 Conn. App. 497, 578 A.2d 1080 (1990).*

7

The Leasehold

LEASEHOLD ESTATE

◆ **An estate created when the owner of property, known as the lessor or landlord, conveys a possessory interest in the real property to another, known as the lessee or tenant, for a specific period of time in exchange for the tenant's payment of rent.**

An unusual aspect of a lease is that it is rooted firmly in two distinct areas of law: contract law and real property law. As a contract, the lease must contain the essential elements of any contract—offer, acceptance and consideration—in order to be enforceable. Because it relates to real property, the lease involves a conveyance of an estate in land, or a leasehold estate. The landlord surrenders his or her possessory rights to the premises for the duration of the lease. The tenant must pay for that possession during the term of the lease. Because the tenant is getting an estate in land, he or she is required by law to pay the rent even if there is no specific agreement regarding rent. Possession is exchanged for rent.

The granting of a leasehold estate gives to a tenant the *exclusive possession* of the premises for an agreed-upon term with a reversion at the end of the term to possession by the landlord. This exclusive right of possession deprives the owner of the premises during the lease. Even where tenants fail to comply with the leasehold bargain, landlords can remove them from the premises only by bringing formal eviction proceedings.

Four different kinds of leasehold estates can be created. They are term tenancy, periodic tenancy, tenancy at will and tenancy at sufferance.

TERM TENANCY

◆ **An estate for a specified period of time that has a specific beginning date and a specific ending date. When the ending date arrives, the estate is terminated without notice by either party.**

This tenancy, also known as an *estate for years,* terminates without any action by either party upon expiration of the term stated in the agreement. It should be noted that if the parties' lease stipulates notice or other conditions for termination of the tenancy, as written leases often do, then these conditions must be met. In the absence of a statute or an agreement to the contrary, the term tenancy is considered personal property and will pass as such to those entitled to take personal property from the estate of the deceased tenant.

If the parties fail to stipulate the amount of rent due, a reasonable rent is required. A reasonable rent is based on prevailing rental rates in the vicinity. Under the common law, however, the rent is not due until the end of the tenancy. By way of contrast, most modern leases require the rent to be prepaid since landlords are understandably unwilling to wait until the end of the term to receive payment of rent.

PERIODIC TENANCY

◆ **An estate from period to period, continuing from period to period until terminated by proper notice from one of the parties.**

The periodic tenancy is normally from year to year or month to month but can be for any period up to a year. It can be created in several different ways. One way is by express agreement. If *A* leases her property to *B* "from month to month beginning April 1, 1990," a periodic tenancy is created.

This type of estate can also evolve from a term tenancy when the tenant remains, or "holds over," after the expiration of the term tenancy. The holdover tenancy will be discussed in more detail later in this section.

The periodic tenancy can be terminated by either party upon giving adequate notice. The parties may contractually agree on what will constitute adequate notice. Absent such an agreement, adequate notice will be one period's notice up to six months.

CASE EXAMPLE

Karen Kaiser leases Greenacre to Franks "from year to year beginning April 1, 1996." She leases Brownacre to Martin "from month to month beginning April 1, 1996." To terminate the lease to Greenacre, either Kaiser or Franks would have to give six months' notice unless they had an agreement to the contrary. The Brownacre lease could be ended by either party with one month's notice of termination, absent a contrary agreement.

These common law notice periods have been altered by statutes in many states. For example, the Uniform Residential Landlord and Tenant Act has been adopted in part in several states. This act provides that a week-to-week tenancy requires a written notice of ten days. A month-to-month tenancy requires a notice of at least 60 days. Year-to-year tenancies are not mentioned in the act because they almost inevitably apply only to agricultural lands and not to residential premises.

Notice given by the terminating party must reach the other party a full period early. The general rule is that the notice must be given one calendar period in advance, although some cases have held to the contrary.

Where there is uncertainty as to the period of the tenancy, a good indicator is the rent payments. If the rent is paid yearly or monthly, it is a good indication that the parties have a year-to-year or month-to-month periodic tenancy. An exception occurs when the yearly rent is stated in the lease but the payment is due monthly. This would be treated as a year-to-year period.

CASE EXAMPLE

The Smits, experienced dairy farmers, entered an oral agreement with the Prescotts to rent their farm. The parties agreed to a lease beginning May 1, for a period of three years, with an annual rental of $14,400 payable in equal monthly installments. The Smits moved onto the land and began paying rent before the written lease was prepared. By the time the written lease was ready, the Smits were having problems with some cows dying and others becoming sick. The problem was apparently a contaminated water supply. The Smits refused to sign the lease, and after several months stopped paying rent and abandoned the farm. The Prescotts sued for nonpayment of rent.

Among other things, the court held that the lease was a term tenancy and that the term was year to year. The court reasoned that it was a year-to-year term because the rent, though payable monthly, was stated in annual terms in their oral agreement. The conclusion was reinforced by the fact that it was a farm lease, and such leases are traditionally entered on a yearly basis. *Prescott v. Smits, 505 A.2d 1211 (1985).*

TENANCY AT WILL

◆ **A tenancy that exists until either party chooses to terminate it.**

This type of estate may arise by express agreement. For example, a lease may state "to Franks at the will of Kaiser." This wording creates a tenancy at will. Despite this restrictive language, tenancies at will can be terminated by either party.

A tenancy at will is more likely to arise by implication.

CASE EXAMPLE

In the Prescott case discussed above, the court had to decide whether the oral lease was an at-will tenancy or a periodic tenancy. In the parties' state, an oral lease for a period longer than one year is unenforceable. Since the three-year term agreed to by the parties

(Continued)

was not legally enforceable, the court had to decide what type of tenancy had been created.

As stated above, the court found that the lease was a year-to-year tenancy. If the situation had been altered so that the Smits had not yet moved onto the land, or the amount of the rent was left uncertain, the court probably would have found that a tenancy at will arose by implication.

Under the common law, no notice was required to end a tenancy at will. Many states now have statutes that require a minimum notice period, thereby softening the harshness of the common law rule. Although the estate exists wholly by permission, all the rights and duties of the landlord-tenant relationship exist. Unlike the previously mentioned leasehold estates, however, a tenancy at will is terminated by the death of either party or by the sale of the property to a third party.

TENANCY AT SUFFERANCE

◆ **Created when a person is wrongfully in possession of another's land without a valid lease.**

The tenant at sufferance is similar to a trespasser. The major difference is that the tenant at sufferance entered the property legally. Usually he or she is the holdover tenant from a term tenancy. The landlord owes this tenant no duties, and the tenant can be evicted at any time. The classification of a person as a tenant at sufferance, not as a trespasser, actually works to the tenant's disadvantage. The tenant is unable to possess the property adversely against the landlord and eventually gain an ownership interest, although a trespasser could.

HOLDOVER TENANT

◆ **One who failed to vacate or surrender possession of the premises on the ending date of a term tenancy.**

The term *holdover tenant* is sometimes used in relation to a periodic tenancy, where the tenant stays on despite the landlord's adequate notice to vacate. Under these circumstances, a landlord who permits the tenant to remain has technically waived the notice and allowed the continuation of the periodic tenancy.

The term tenant who holds over after the expiration date of a lease temporarily becomes a tenant at sufferance. All options shift into the landlord's hands when the tenant holds over. The landlord has the option of evicting the tenant or of holding him or her for another term.

CASE EXAMPLE

Anton leases a house and lot to Glenn and Sarah Williams. The terms of the agreement stipulate that the lease commences on July 1, 1995, and terminates on June 30, 1996. On July 1, 1996, the couple is still living in the house. Anton has the option of beginning eviction proceedings against the Williamses, who are now tenants at sufferance, or of unilaterally extending their lease until June 30, 1997.

Once the landlord exercises the option to hold the tenant for an additional period, the estate becomes a periodic tenancy. The maximum length of the period will be one year, or more accurately year to year, even where the term tenancy was for a longer period. If the original term tenancy was for less than one year, the holdover tenant will be held to a periodic tenancy for that particular period, such as week to week or month to month.

The terms of the holdover tenant's new lease will be the same as those of the original lease except as to length of time, as noted above. One exception arises when the landlord notifies the tenant before the expiration of the lease that he or she is changing the terms (for example, raising the rent). The tenant is usually held to the altered terms.

If the holdover is involuntary and for a short period of time, courts will not hold the tenant for an additional term. For instance, if the holdover is caused by a tornado, a snowstorm, a death in the family or a one-day delay of the moving van, the court is not likely to hold the tenant for an additional period. The following case involves a less dramatic reason for holding over.

J.M. BEALS ENTERPRISES, INC. V. INDUSTRIAL HARD CHROME, LTD.

Appellate Court of Illinois
648 N.E.2d (1995)

BACKGROUND. Charles Therkildsen, doing business as Industrial Hard Chrome Ltd. (IHC), leased real property from Beals Enterprises (Beals) commencing in 1985 and expiring December 31, 1992. In July 1992, a dispute arose between the parties over what equipment and materials were part of a 1985 sale of IHC by Beals to Therkildsen. The dispute was settled by agreement on December 10, 1992, and IHC was to perform considerable work on the premises prior to vacating on December 31.

IHC was unable to complete the work by the date the lease expired, and was refused an extension by Beals. IHC remained on the premises through January 18, 1993, solely for the purpose of completing the work under the December 10th agreement. Beals filed suit under the state holdover tenant statute that would entitle it to double rent and other fees and costs. After oral argument the trial judge granted a summary judgment to Beals.

DECISION. The Illinois Appellate Court reversed the trial court's decision and remanded the case for trial.

JUSTICE EGAN. The Holdover Statute, the interpretation of which is the heart of this case, provides as follows:

"If any tenant willfully holds over any lands after the expiration of his or her term or terms, and after demand made in writing, for the possession thereof, by his or her landlord the person so holding over, shall, for the time the landlord or rightful owner is so kept out of possession, pay to the person so kept out of possession, at the rate of double the yearly value of the land."

The issues as raised by IHC are two-fold: Does the record disclose, as a matter of law, that IHC withheld possession from Beals; and, if so, does the record disclose, as a matter of law, that IHC's holding over was willful within the meaning of the Holdover Statute? One general principle recognized everywhere is that whether a tenant is a holdover and whether the holding-over was willful are questions of fact.

IHC argues that it was not a holdover tenant at all because it did not deprive Beals of possession. We have no doubt that whether IHC was a holdover is, at least, a question of fact, The statute does not define the term "willful", but one of the earliest cases decided under the statute, Stuart v. Hamilton (1872) gives us some guidance:

"The courts have held that when the lease had expired according to its terms, the holding over, although intentional, is not within the statute, unless it was knowingly and willfully wrongful; that where the tenant continued to hold under a reasonable belief that he was doing so rightfully, he does not incur the penalty, and yet the language [of the statute] would embrace such a case as reasonably as if the term had been ended by the landlord by enforcing a forfeiture of the lease."

Although most of the cases which refuse to enforce the double rent statute involved bona fide disputes over the right to possession, we refuse to make such a narrow pronouncement that only a bona fide dispute over the right to possession will excuse a tenant under the statute. We believe the better rule is that where a tenant remains in possession for colorably justifiable reasons, he should not be charged under the statute. In other words, the tenant, to be liable under the statute, must know that his retention of possession is "wrongful." With that understanding we turn to the agreement.

Under the agreement, IHC agreed to leave certain equipment on the premises "in operating condition"; and to remove certain equipment, including a boiler and cooling tower connections and piping, dust collectors and a tank ventilator system, including air duct piping, electrical wiring connections and all other personal property. IHC was also required to "remove or cut off flush with [the] surface, all fasteners, brackets, bolts and attachments in floors, walls and ceilings used to secure or serve equipment removed; [to remove] all depressed concrete pits; [to repair] all roof and/or wall openings resulting from removal performed by IHC pursuant to the agreement." The agreement further provided that on or before March 1, 1993, IHC was to inspect the premises to determine "compliance" with the agreement; that Beals would provide IHC notice of any claims of Beals "regarding any defaults" by IHC of the settlement terms. IHC would have 30 days after receipt of Beals' default claims to "cure each of the" claims. It is obvious that the parties recognized the possibility that IHC would not complete the removal of equipment by December 31. The agreement also recognized the possibility that IHC would be required to return to the premises after March 1, 1993, to complete work required by Beals.

A reasonable inference may be drawn that IHC was confronted with a formidable task in completing what was required in 21 days. IHC had a Hobson's choice in walking away from the premises on December 31 in compliance with Beals' demand for possession or staying on the premises in an attempt to comply with the agreement. Whether IHC's actions were knowingly wrongful raise at least a question of fact.

REVERSED AND REMANDED.

LEASE

◆ **A contract, either written or oral, that transfers the right of possession of the premises to the lessee or tenant.**

The relationship of lessor and lessee usually arises from an express contract on the part of the parties called a *lease*. As previously stated, the lease is firmly rooted in the law of contracts. The lease or contract, sometimes referred to as a rental agreement, normally includes terms giving the lessee the right to possession and entitling the lessor to a certain amount of rent. To this extent these contractual components overlap the possession-rent aspects that arise inherently from the real property notion of a conveyance of an estate in land. The lease-contract is likely to specify the terms of the possession and the amount of the rent, as well as many other factors that together compose the essence of the lessor and lessee's agreement.

ESSENTIAL ELEMENTS OF THE LEASE

The purpose of the lease is to detail the rights and duties of each of the parties in the contract. It is incumbent upon the parties to take great care in drafting the lease, especially if the terms of the agreement are complex or the duration of the lease is long. To do otherwise is to invite a lawsuit.

A Valid Contract. Since a lease is a contract, it must contain the essential elements of a contract. There must be a mutual consent to enter the agreement, and the agreement must be supported by consideration (rent in exchange for possession). The lease agreement will not require the use of any particular prescribed words. Essentially, it must be shown that it was mutually intended for the tenant to have possession and that the landlord retained a *reversionary* interest in the land (that is, the right to have the property back when the lease expired).

The consideration that supports the lease contract is usually the rent. Nevertheless, the periodic payment of rent is not necessary to have a valid contract. The requirement is merely that consideration, or something of value, be given at some time to the landlord.

The other elements of a valid contract, such as the capacity of the parties (both must be sane and of legal age) and legality of purpose, must be met as well.

Statute of Frauds. Prior to 1677, under the common law originally operating in England, leases did not have to be in writing. With the adoption of the Statute of Frauds, however, leases for a term in excess of three years had to be in writing to be enforceable beyond those three years. A few states have adopted the English version of the Statute of Frauds and require writings for leases in excess of three years. In most states, however, the Statute of Frauds provision necessitates a writing if the lease exceeds one year.

The intent of this requirement is to reduce fraud in the area of leases. It should be made clear that the statutory minimum, usually one year, does not indicate that leases for one year or less should not be in writing. The careful landlord and tenant will benefit if all terms of their agreement are reduced to writing in order to minimize the opportunity for misunderstanding or outright fraud.

It should be emphasized that an oral lease within the maximum term of the Statute of Frauds is every bit as valid as a written lease. If a dispute arises over an oral lease, however, the proof may be more difficult to derive. If a dispute arises over a lease that has gone beyond the allowable period under the Statute of Frauds, the estate is treated as a tenancy at will.

Parties. The lease must identify the parties as lessor and lessee, and both parties should sign the document. The signature of the lessor, the owner of the property, is normally mandatory. Under the Statute of Frauds, the signature of the party against whom the lease will be enforced is required.

The spouse of the lessor should sign the lease as well, if he or she has an outstanding interest or potential interest in the property. For example, if a married couple owns the premises jointly, both parties must sign the lease since the spouse is a concurrent owner. The wife should also sign the lease where the state recognizes a dower interest, inasmuch as her potential interest may come into effect during the term of the lease.

Under some contracts, a lessee may have the power to sublease or to assign the property to a third party, in which case the person signing as "lessor" of the property may not be the actual owner of the premises. For this reason, a lessee should make certain that the non-owner lessor has the authority to sublet and convey all or part of the interest to another. Subleasing will be discussed in more detail in the following chapter.

If the lessor is an individual, he or she must have the *capacity* to contract—that is, be mentally competent and of legal age. If the lessor is a fiduciary, entering the lease for another as guardian, executor or trustee, for example, the lessee must be assured that the authority to lease is within the fiduciary's powers. Similarly, if the lessor is a corporation that is not in the business of leasing real estate, the lessee must verify the authorization of the corporation's board of directors to be assured that it is entitled to lease the premises.

Description of the Premises. In order to avoid a future dispute, the premises should be described clearly. If the landlord's entire conveyed premises are being leased, then the description as contained in the deed or deeds is satisfactory. A lot number or block number used for assessment purposes may be used if it is complete and accurate. A street number may not be adequate in itself because it relates only to the building and not to the land that is probably part of the leasehold as well.

When the lessor is leasing something less than all that he or she has, the lease should state clearly and exactly what is to be leased. In the absence of an agreement to the contrary, the lease of a building will be construed to include the use of everything reasonably necessary for the enjoyment of the land. It is up to the lessor expressly to exclude a use, or exclusive possession may pass to the lessee.

C A S E   E X A M P L E

Arthur leases one-half of an apartment house to Melanie, who has three small children. Unless the lease specifically excludes use of the fenced-in backyard, Melanie can use it for ingress and egress and as a play area for the children.

It is also to the lessee's benefit to have the precise nature of his or her use or possession spelled out in the lease, rather than to rely on the uncertain notion that he or she is entitled to certain unstated uses.

Statement of a Lease Term. The term of the lease should be stipulated clearly. Stating the beginning and ending dates as well as the length of the term will reduce doubt as to date of entry and the like. The lease should state, for example, "for one year beginning January 1, 1996, and terminating December 31, 1996." Where the beginning date is not spelled out, some doubt may exist as to whether the tenant began the term on the date the lease was signed, the first of the following month or some other date. If the beginning date is not stated, the commencement of the lease should be related to some event or ascertainable time so that the beginning of the lease is clear.

C A S E   E X A M P L E

Sanchez leased to Williams for one year beginning upon the surrender of possession by the present tenant or April 1, 1996, whichever comes first.

The courts do not favor leases of unlimited duration. If the time of termination is not fixed, the courts may interpret the agreement to be a tenancy at will, which is probably not what the parties intended. In a periodic tenancy, of course, the time of termination is fixed, although the tenancy is subject to automatic renewal upon the existence of certain conditions, such as failure to give notice of termination.

Some courts have been inclined to hold that leases that are too long—for instance, 100 years or more—are barred by statute. The theory behind the term limitation is that when the lease gets to be too long it defies the temporary aspect, or right of reversion, inherent in a leasehold estate. The result of these statutes and judicial rulings has been to popularize the 99-year lease. Similarly, in a few states, there is a restriction on the length of leases for agricultural lands.

There is a correlation between the length of the lease and the care with which the lease must be drawn. If the lease is as long as 75 years, the likelihood increases that the structures will need to be replaced. Some agreement should be reached to cover contingencies of this sort that will occur during the long period of the lease.

◆ **Rent.** **The compensation paid by the lessee for the possession of the leased property.**

Normally, rent takes the form of a money payment. It could, however, take the form of a percentage of the crops harvested from the land or of relief for the lessor of an obligation owed to the lessee. A statement of the amount of rent is one of the essential terms of a lease; nevertheless, where it has been omitted, courts have declared that the landlord is entitled to a "reasonable rent," based on the area's prevailing rental rates.

In the usual practice is to state in the lease that the rent will be paid in advance. If such a statement is lacking, the rent is due at the end of the period. The rationale behind this rule is that the lessee is paying for the possession that he or she has enjoyed, and nothing is due until he or she has had the enjoyment.

In addition to how much and when, the lease should indicate where the rent is to be paid. Absent such an indication, it is payable at the leasehold premises.

Unless stipulated to the contrary, the total rent is due on the date set for payment. The usual practice is to require in the lease monthly, quarterly or annual payments.

> ## CASE EXAMPLE
> Karen leases Greenacre to Frank for a rent of $2,400 annually, payable in advance and on the first of each month in installments of "$200, and presented at the residence of the lessor."
> This wording covers each of the above considerations.

For short-term residential leases, it is most common to have a straight rental fee, such as $200 per month. In commercial leases, however, a variety of methods are used for determining the rent. The net lease, percentage lease and ground lease will be discussed later. Another technique is to assess rent on a *graduated* basis. A lease might stipulate a rent of $2,400 the first year, $3,600 per year for the following two years and $4,800 per year for the last two years. If the lessee is operating a new business, under the graduated rental the amount of rent is smallest in the start-up period and increases as the business (theoretically) grows.

Other techniques include basing the rent on the consumer price index or on some other criterion that is particularly relevant to the parties, to the business or to the lease itself. In short, the days of the straight or flat rental fee as the sole method for calculating rent, especially in business leases, have long since passed.

LEGAL USE OF THE PREMISES

If the lease gives no indication as to the uses that can be made of the premises, the general rule is that the lessee can make any legal use of the land he or she wants. Some courts, however, would limit the lessee to "reasonable uses" where the agreement is silent on the matter.

The question of reasonable use is a factual question that the court will examine in light of the type of premises involved and the prior uses of the property. If the building was constructed and has been used as a residence from its inception, for example, it would be unreasonable to use it now as a cheese factory.

Although it is appropriate for the lessor to limit the lessee's use by the agreement, careful drafting is warranted. If the lessor limits the use to a clearly designated purpose, courts will uphold that limitation. If the lessor indicates a *specific* purpose to which the premises can be put—for example, ". . . can be used for a beauty shop"—and nothing more, however, this wording will not prohibit the lessee from making use of the land other than as a beauty shop. The rationale behind these rules is that the law favors unrestricted use of the land conveyed. In short, ambiguities will be construed against the lessor and toward maximizing the lessee's use. If the lessor's limitations on permitted uses are not designated clearly, the lease will be construed to favor the lessee. If the lessor, by permitting use as a beauty shop, has not clearly shown an intent to limit use to that purpose alone, the lessee will be able to make any other use as well. The careful drafter would have stated, ". . . for use as a beauty shop only."

CASE EXAMPLE

Ewing leased five acres of land to Adams for a five-year term. The lease contained a clause stating that the land was to be used for a drive-in movie theater. Adams used the land as an outdoor theater for a period of time but then attempted to discontinue that use and to use it for other commercial purposes. Ewing objected, contending that Adams was confined to the use stipulated in the lease.

The court found for the lessee, Adams. It stated that absent clear and specific words of limitation, the lease is strictly construed against the lessor. The clause confining use to a drive-in movie theater was merely descriptive and not intended to restrict the use of the premises to that sole purpose. *Ewing v. Adams, 573 So. 1364 (1990).*

Where the lessee's use of the property has been made illegal by a change in the law, the lease is not usually invalidated. If the lease permits other legal uses, the lessee can change the type of use. If, however, the lease limits the lessee to the now illegal use, the change in the law will invalidate the lease. The fact that the lessee's business has become unprofitable or that the property no longer suits him or her for a residence will not excuse performance under the lease contract.

A tenant who leases only part of a building for commercial purposes should be careful to reach some agreement with the lessor regarding the leasing of other parts of the building to competitors and use by the lessor as a competitor with the lessee. Without such an agreement, the lessor is free to put the remainder of the property to a competitive use.

Besides the terms of the lease, the tenant should also be careful to check the public regulation restrictions on his or her use. The zoning code may well prohibit uses that the lessor has not prohibited.

RIGHT OF POSSESSION

◆ **In all jurisdictions the right of possession implicitly resides in the tenant; that is, no one will have possessory rights inconsistent with those granted to the tenant.**

In a majority of jurisdictions, the landlord covenants to give the right of possession and nothing more. If there is a wrongdoer in possession at the time the tenant's lease commences, the landlord has not violated his or her implied promise of giving the *right to possession.* The fact that the tenant may have to bring a lawsuit to obtain possession is an excellent reason why the tenant should be careful to see to it that the lease contains a provision ensuring that the landlord will give *possession* of the premises, not merely the right to possession. The possibility of the landlord's being unable to deliver actual possession is not terribly remote. Holding over by former tenants is not a rare incident.

In some jurisdictions the landlord implicitly covenants to deliver the possession of the premises. The onus then falls on the landlord to take necessary action (for example, eviction proceedings) to recover possession for the tenant.

It should be remembered that normally the tenant's possession is exclusive. Even the landlord, who may be the owner of the premises in fee simple, is not permitted to invade that exclusive possession without authorization. The landlord would be a trespasser, and the tenant could bring the appropriate legal action against him or her.

RECORDING THE LEASE

The practice of recording leases is permitted in most states since a lease is a conveyance of an interest in land. It is uncommon to record residential and other short-term leases, however, because actual possession by the tenant is notice to everyone of the tenant's interest in the land. Upon finding a tenant in possession, a potential taker of an interest in the land would have actual notice of the possession and would have the duty to inquire as to the possessor's right to be there. Failing to inspect the premises, he or she would still have constructive notice of the possession.

There is, however, more of an inclination to record leases that are for a longer period (three years or more). In about one-third of the states, the rule holding that possession is constructive notice has been abolished where the lease exceeds a given period of time (usually either one year or three years). In these states it is very important that the tenant record the lease for his or her own protection.

TYPES OF LEASES

It was indicated earlier that several types of leases exist. Four of these will be discussed in more detail here. Most are used primarily in commercial applications.

◆ **Gross Lease. A lease in which a flat or fixed amount of rent is paid by the tenant.**

Generally, under a gross lease the tenant pays the rent and the landlord is responsible for expenses incurred in operating the premises. The landlord pays the taxes, insurance, special assessments and the like. Responsibility for ordinary repairs may be bargained for separately. In residential leases the gross rental fee may or may not include heat and other utilities. It would seem to be to the benefit of both parties, and society as a whole, to exclude heat and utilities from the fixed rent in order to encourage the tenant to minimize the costs by reducing the consumption of energy and water.

Where long-term leases are desired, gross leases have gradually fallen from favor because of inflation and the fluctuation in the value of the dollar. Unless there is some provision in the lease to compensate the lessor for the gradually diminishing value of the periodic rent check, rental property becomes a questionable investment.

◆ **Net Lease. As contrasted with the gross lease, a type of lease in which the tenant agrees to pay the taxes, insurance, repairs and other operating expenses of the premises.**

This type of lease assures the lessor of a steady income from the property and relieves him or her of the responsibility of overseeing the operations on the property. In short, the lessor has a real estate investment without most of the problems that usually accompany this type of investment.

Like the gross lease, the net lease does not necessarily take into account the loss of purchasing power due to inflation. Net leases can be drawn up that tie the amount of periodic rent that is payable to some recognized indicator, such as the consumer price index. In this way the lessor will have the same purchasing power at the end of a long-term lease that existed at the beginning.

◆ **Ground Lease. A specialized type of net lease in which the lessor leases a piece of vacant land to the lessee, usually with the stipulation that the lessee at his or her own expense will construct a building thereon.**

The ground lease is a type of net lease in that the lessee agrees to assume the operating expense of the property. Once the building is constructed, it becomes part of the realty and title passes to the lessor. Therefore, several elements are common to the lease agreements in ground lease situations. The term of the lease is either for the life expectancy of the building or, at least, for a long period. When the term of the lease is not tied to the building's life expectancy, provisions must be made for the building at the expiration of the lease. The parties may agree that the lessor will have to pay the lessee the appraised value of the building at the time the lease expires. Of course the parties can write any agreement that suits them on this matter.

The rent agreement can be for a fixed rate but is often tied to the appraised value of the land. In this way the lessor retains the benefit of the land's appreciating value.

In most such leases the lessee needs financing to construct the building. If this is the case, provisions must be made to accommodate the mortgagee as well as the parties to the lease. The lessor will have to agree to permit the building to be mortgaged while excluding himself or herself from liability on that mortgage. Likewise, the mortgagee will insist upon the untrammeled right to sell the property in the case of a foreclosure. In addition, the mortgagee will usually insist that the term of the ground lease extend significantly beyond the duration of the mortgage so that the tenant does not lose the incentive to make mortgage payments during the latter years of the obligation.

◆ **Percentage Lease.** **A lease whose rental is based in part on the gross sales made by the tenant on the premises.**

The lessee in such a lease is required to pay a fixed periodic rental, the amount of the rent to be less than the property's full rental value. In addition, the lessor is entitled to a percentage of the gross sales made by the lessee.

A common practice is to charge a flat minimum rent (perhaps $200 per month) plus a percentage of the gross sales over a stipulated figure (for example, $200 per month plus 2 percent of the gross sales over $30,000). If the lease has a long term, the percentage lease provides some hedge against inflation. As inflation grows, theoretically so do gross sales; once sales exceed $30,000, the rent increases proportionately. Since the flat minimum rent is usually lower than the maximum amount the landlord would expect, the percentage lease is a hedge for the commercial lessee against bad times.

Percentage leases have become very popular in the leasing of commercial property. The percentage may be very low (1 or 2 percent) in the case of a supermarket or very high (70 to 80 percent) where a parking lot is involved. Regardless of the type of business or the percentage agreed upon, it is critical that the parties carefully draft their agreement. The lease should make clear exactly what is encompassed within the term *gross sales* and should establish the right of the lessor to examine records of the business. From the lessor's perspective, in addition to the protection of a carefully drafted lease, the lessee should be selected carefully to ensure a sound credit rating and good business history.

The Papa Gino's case deals with a percentage lease and shows a court struggling with the meaning of the term *gross sales* used in the lease. The case speaks loudly for the premise that parties to a lease should be as precise as possible in drafting its terms.

**PAPA GINO'S OF AMERICA, INC. V.
BROADMANOR ASSOCIATES, LTD.**
Appellate Court of Connecticut
500 A.2d 1341 (1985)

BACKGROUND. In 1978, Papa Gino's entered into a written lease for the rental of commercial premises at the Manchester Shopping Parkade with Broadmanor Associates' predecessor in title. The lease was for a 10-year term with options to renew. The lease provided a fixed, monthly, minimum rental payment and additional rent equal to 5 percent of Papa Gino's "annual gross sales in excess of $285,000." Papa Gino's had a practice of providing meals free of charge or at a discount to employees and making discount coupons available to the public. When a discount coupon was presented by a purchaser, the face value of each coupon was deducted from the price of the food.

Broadmanor Associates purchased the Parkade in 1981 and in 1982 notified Papa Gino's that it was deficient in its rental payments because under the percentage of gross sales provision, it had not included the value of the free and discounted meals to employees or the face value of the discount coupons. Papa Gino's paid the amount demanded under protest and sued Broadmanor Associates, seeking a declaration by the court that it was not deficient in the payment of its rent. The trial court held that the term *gross sales* in the lease included the face value of the discount coupons, but not the contested meals to employees. Papa Gino's appealed the ruling on the discount coupons.

DECISION. The Appellate Court of Connecticut reversed the ruling of the trial court on the issue of the discount coupons.

JUDGE DALY. The plaintiff has raised the following issues on appeal: (1) whether the trial court erred in failing to declare that the term "gross sales" in the lease does not include the face value of the discount coupons made available to the public, because the plaintiff receives no monetary compensation for the amount discounted in sales to coupon holders; and (2) whether the trial court erred in denying the return of the escrow fund to the plaintiff. We find that the trial court was in error on both points.

A lease is a contract. In its construction, three elementary principles must be kept constantly in mind: (1) the intention of the parties is controlling and must be gathered from the language of the lease in the light of the circumstances surrounding the parties at the execution of the instrument; (2) the language must be given its ordinary meaning unless a techni-

cal or special meaning is clearly intended; and (3) the lease must be construed as a whole and in such a manner as to give effect to every provision, if reasonably possible.

A lease which provides for a percentage rent added to a fixed rent is a common arrangement for the rental of commercial premises. The percentage lease gears the landlord's return to the productivity of his location, such productivity being measured by the tenant's gross dollar volume in sales. In addition to a percentage lease arrangement, the lease in question defined "gross sales" to mean "the entire gross income from the use or occupancy of the leased premises (including advertising and demonstrations) and of all business threat. These terms shall also include the full price of all sales made and services rendered at the lease premises. ... There shall also be deducted, to the extent to which they shall be included in the sales price, the amount of sales or other taxes which may be imposed by law on the purchaser."

The definition of the term "gross sales" has no definitive judicial meaning, is imprecise, and depends principally upon the wording established by the parties in particular contract. The term "sale," as ordinarily defined and popularly understood, means the transfer of property for money *paid* or to be paid; this is the usage of the term in the lease with which we are here concerned. The term "receipts" indicates money received from a sale. Further, under the Connecticut sales tax laws, cash discounts are not included as taxable income and not considered as "gross receipts." In the hotel business, total gross revenues from room rentals do not include credit card discounts. It would appear, then, that "gross sales" and "receipts" indicate money or cash that is actually received, and therefore would not apply to the discount coupons.

"The courts do not favor constructions in derogation of the course of conduct of the parties." The purpose of the coupons, presumably, is to lure customers into the plaintiff's restaurant with the expectation that they will purchase other items as well. By this method, the landlord receives a benefit from the gross sales. To give the landlord that value of the inducement as well (the coupon) would be to construe the lease as allowing the landlord an additional, uncontemplated kind of "double recovery." We conclude that this is unwarranted under the circumstances and, therefore, that the trial court incorrectly included the face value of the discount coupons offered to the restaurant patrons in the calculation of gross sales generated by the plaintiff's business.

The judgment is set aside and the case in remanded with direction to render judgment that the term "gross sales" shall not include the value of the subject discount coupons, and the amounts held in escrow shall be awarded to the plaintiff.

REVERSED.

Other Types of Leases. Leases are as variable as the parties are creative. Some types of leases, such as the variety that relates rent to the consumer price index or some other index, may come into vogue temporarily as a reaction to unstable economic conditions. Others, such as the graduated lease, are tailored to meet the needs of a new business. Here the rent rises over time as the anticipated growth of the business takes place. Still others, such as the sale and leaseback arrangement, are attractive for large firms, which sell their real estate and lease it back from the new owner in order to release investment capital for future expansion. Partners under this type of lease are investors who have capital to invest in order to ensure an agreeable rate of return from the rents on the leased-back property. These examples represent only a few types of leases that have been adapted to the special needs of the parties.

LEASE RENEWAL

Depending on the type of leasehold estate that was conveyed by the landlord or on the terms of the parties' agreement, the lease will terminate on its own or on appropriate notice by either party. It is not unusual, however, to include in the lease a term that provides for the renewal of the lease. The renewal provision may be one that requires the tenant to give notice of renewal by a specified period of time prior to the termination of the lease. Alternatively, the renewal may be automatic, absent notice of nonrenewal by either party.

A renewal is a new lease. Unless otherwise stated, the renewal is under the same terms and conditions as the original lease. The parties may agree that the rent will be altered to reflect the present value of the land. For instance, each renewal may require a reappraisal of the land and a rent adjustment to reflect a specified percentage of the appraised value. Except where the agreement is for an automatic renewal of the lease, the parties should indicate whether the renewal clause will be operative in the second lease and in succeeding renewed leases.

Another method of renewal is by holding over. The legal implications for the holdover tenant were discussed in a preceding section.

REVIEW AND DISCUSSION QUESTIONS

1. Match the following:
   - a. Tenancy at sufferance
   - b. Term tenancy
   - c. Tenancy at will
   - d. Periodic tenancy

   (1) Has a specific beginning and ending date.
   (2) Exists as long as neither party chooses to terminate it.
   (3) Continues from period to period until terminated by one of the parties giving proper notice.
   (4) Exists when a person is wrongfully in possession of another's land without a valid lease.

2. Name two ways in which a periodic tenancy can be created.

3. Define the term *holdover tenant.*

4. List and briefly describe four terms that should be specified in a lease contract.

5. What risks are involved in entering an oral lease?

6. Distinguish between "the landlord gives possession of the premises" and "the landlord gives the right of possession of the premises."

7. Match the following:
   - a. Net lease
   - b. Gross lease
   - c. Percentage lease
   - d. Ground lease

   (1) The rent is based in part on the gross sales made by the lessee.
   (2) The lessor leases a piece of vacant land to the lessee, usually with the stipulation that the lessee at his or her own expense wil construct a building.
   (3) The tenant agrees to pay taxes, insurance, repairs and other operating expenses of the premises.
   (4) The rent is a fixed or flat amount.

8. Describe and discuss those rules of landlord-tenant law that no longer seem appropriate given present-day expectations of lay parties.

CASE PROBLEMS

1. China Doll Restaurant, Inc., leased premises from Schweiger. China Doll agreed to pay a base rent of $600 per month and an amount equal to 5 percent of the restaurant's first $288,000 of gross sales. The owners of China Doll had considerable experience in operating a Chinese restaurant.

   The lease also contained a provision in which lessee agreed to use the premises "for conducting and operating a restaurant business." Before the expiration of the lease, China Doll moved to new and larger premises. At this time they stated that they intended to open a Mexican restaurant at the former China Doll location. Little was done to accomplish this, but they continued to pay the base rental of $600 per month. During this period the premises were unoccupied. Has China Doll violated the terms of the lease? *China Doll Restaurant, Inc. v. Schweiger, 19 Ariz. 315, 580 P.2d 776 (1978).*

2. Chapman rented farmland to Walker on a year-to-year basis beginning each year on January 1. Chapman sold the property to Gregory with a stipulation that Gregory was to have possession as of January 1, 1963. On July 1, 1962, Chapman gave Walker notice to vacate at the end of the year. Is this notice sufficient in a state following the traditional common law rule? *Gregory v. Walker, 239 Ark. 415, 389 S.W.2d 892 (1965).*

3. Regency Inn leased a rental office in the lobby of its hotel to Americar, a car rental agency. Wagner rented a car from Americar, and while walking through the hotel parking lot to reach her rental car, she was robbed and raped. Wagner sued Regency Inn for damages alleging that they maintained a public nuisance. A clause in the lease held that Americar was responsible to indemnify Regency Inn for any damages suffered due to the operation of the car rental agency. At the time of assault on Wagner, Americar was a holdover tenant. Can Regency Inn claim indemnification under these conditions? *Wagner v. Regency Inn Corp., 463 N.W.2d 450 (1990).*

4. Doyle owed Byrne $5,000 for services performed in rewiring Doyle's house. After six months, Doyle had paid nothing on the $5,000 bill and, upon being confronted by Byrne, admitted that it was unlikely that he could pay the bill in the near future. Byrne suggested that he would take a lease for a year on Doyle's camp on the lake. Doyle said "fine," and the conversation ended. In the spring, Byrne moved into Doyle's camp and occupied it without incident until mid-July. At that time, Doyle arrived at the camp and ordered Byrne to evacuate. Byrne refused, claiming that he had a one-year lease. Doyle retorted that there was nothing in writing, that no rent was stipulated and that the services for electrical work could not be used in lieu of cash payments for rent. Discuss the validity of Doyle's arguments.

8

The Landlord-Tenant Relationship

The signing of a lease creates obligations on the part of both the lessor and the lessee. Failure by either party to comply with obligations imposed either by contract or by law gives rise to the availability of certain legal remedies. The remedies available depend on the nature of the obligation breached and on the present circumstances of the parties. For example, did the lessee remain in possession, or were the premises abandoned? Some problems result from actions taken by one of the parties to the transaction—the lessee may have sublet the premises, for example—or from actions involving not the parties but other persons, as when a visitor falls down the stairs of the leased premises. These occurrences lead to legal responsibilities on the part of the parties to the lease. Obligations imposed by the lease contract, by the relationship itself and by the law are the topics of this chapter.

LESSOR'S SECURITY

Several forms of protection have evolved over time to protect landlords from tenants who mistreat the leased premises.

RENT PAID IN ADVANCE

◆ **A normal requirement for modern leases is that rent payments are due prior to the beginning of the lease period.**

Under common law, where it is not otherwise specified, rent is due at the end of the rental period. The modern practice of requiring advance payment of the rent in the lease gives the landlord some additional assurance of stability. Where the rent is not forthcoming from the tenant by the first day of the rental period, the landlord is given some lead time in pursuing remedies for nonpayment. If the rent were not due until the end of the rental period, the landlord would lose additional time pursuing the remedies.

SECURITY DEPOSIT

◆ **Money deposited by the tenant for the security of the landlord, usually at the inception of the lease, over and above the advance payment of rent.**

The security deposit is usually equivalent to one month's rent or more. Its purpose is to secure the landlord against damage done to the premises by the tenant or to clean or repair the premises, over and above normal wear and tear, when the tenant vacates. It may also provide a wider margin of security against a tenant who wrongfully abandons the premises. It has the practical effect of inducing the tenant who wants the security deposit returned to maintain the premises carefully during occupancy and to clean the premises thoroughly upon leaving. In some states, there is a limit on the amount the landlord can demand as a security deposit.

The security deposit is held by the landlord in trust for the tenant. The parties may agree that interest will be paid on this money. In some states, it is mandatory that the landlord of multiple-unit housing pay interest on any security deposit.

Because the security deposit is not a form of liquidated damages, the landlord can retain only as much as is necessary to pay for the damage done by the tenant. If the payment is a security deposit and not an advance rental, the tenant cannot use it in lieu of payment of rent for the last month. Whichever it is should be stipulated clearly by the parties.

Some states have adopted parts of the Uniform Residential Landlord and Tenant Act, which is geared toward promoting uniformity in landlord-tenant law. The act provides strict regulation of the security deposit. It would limit the amount deposited to one month's rent, require a written explanation of the purpose for and handling of the funds as well as an indication of the reasons for retaining any of the deposit and provide for the return of any unneeded funds to the tenant within 14 days after the termination of the lease. It also provides for penalties in case the landlord mishandles any of the security deposit funds. Most of the states have tailored these provisions to fit their needs.

THIRD-PERSON GUARANTY OF RENT

◆ **The landlord who has doubts about the capacity or reliability of the tenant in meeting the conditions of the lease may require a third person to guarantee performance.**

In a commercial or industrial lease where the tenant is thinly capitalized, a personal guaranty by the individuals actually running the business under the corporate veil may be required. Also, where the tenant has a poor credit rating, the landlord may insist on the assurance of a more reliable third person. The guaranty would have to be in writing and signed by the guarantor. The guaranty agreement may be a part of the lease or a separate agreement usually appended to the lease.

COGNOVIT

◆ **A confession of judgment that permits the landlord, upon default by the tenant, to obtain a judgment against the tenant without the need for formal legal proceedings.**

When this clause is present, the tenant has agreed in the lease that in case of his or her default, the landlord can obtain a confession of judgment without the necessity of going to court to obtain the decree. Usually, the cognovit is executed by the landlord's attorney, who files an affidavit stating that the default occurred. Such a judgment, like any other, constitutes a lien on any real property in the jurisdiction of the leased premises.

The effect of a cognovit is to expedite the landlord's collection process after a default. It creates a situation ripe for abuse by the landlord, and in some states it is illegal for a tenant to execute such an agreement until after the default has taken place.

LESSOR'S OBLIGATIONS

The landlord is bound by any promises made to the tenant in the lease. In addition, certain obligations have been imposed on the landlord by the law over and above the contractual understanding. The following covenants and warrants are the major ones with which the parties must be concerned.

COVENANT OF QUIET ENJOYMENT
◆ **A warrant by the landlord that the tenant will have the premises free from interference by the landlord or anyone claiming better right to the premises than the landlord.**

There is no general guarantee by the landlord against wrongful intrusion by third persons. Should such an intrusion take place, the tenant will have satisfactory legal avenues through which to redress the interference. For centuries, however, the general common law rule has been that the tenant is protected from a wrongful intrusion by the landlord or someone claiming better rights than the landlord or tenant.

The covenant of quiet enjoyment is breached only upon eviction by the landlord or by a third person, either actual or constructive. Actual eviction consists of a physical removal of the tenant from the premises. Constructive eviction could occur when there is a substantial interference with the tenant's enjoyment of the premises.

CASE EXAMPLE

HTM leased commercial property from Goldman, Sachs and Company. Goldman failed to pay the mortgage, resulting in the mortgagee foreclosing on the property and ousting HTM from its lease. HTM sued for breach of implied covenant of quiet enjoyment.

The court noted that in every lease of land there is, absent an agreement to the contrary, an implied covenant of quiet, peaceful enjoyment of the premises. Unfortunately for HTM, a clause in their lease stated that they accepted the premises subject to all mortgages. The mortgage preceded the HTM lease so that HTM had waived their implied convenant of quiet enjoyment by "agreeing to the contrary." *HTM Restaurants, Inc. v. Goldman, Sachs and Company, 797 S.W.2d 326 (Texas, 1990).*

Generally, in the case of either an actual or a constructive eviction the tenant must have vacated the premises before asserting a breach of the covenant of quiet enjoyment.

COVENANT TO DELIVER POSSESSION

◆ **The landlord promises to deliver the right of possession to the tenant at the time the lease is scheduled to start.**

This covenant is quite limited. It does not warrant against a wrongdoer being in possession of the premises at the time the lease commences, but only that the tenant will have the *right to possession.*

CASE EXAMPLE

Reichman leased premises from Emery for a term of five years. The lease was to commence on July 1. At the time the lease was executed, the property was occupied by Drake, whose term expired on June 9. Drake, however, refused to vacate, and Reichman commenced an action to evict her. Several months later this suit was successful. After Drake was evicted, Reichman commenced a damage action against her as he had been unable to occupy the premises during the eviction proceeding. Drake argued that she had no liability to Reichman as she had no *contractual* relationship with him. An appellate court concluded that Drake's action violated Reichman's *property* rights and awarded damages. *Reichman v. Drake, 89 Ohio App. 222, 100 N.E.2d 533 (1951).*

Should a wrongdoer be in possession, the tenant has the obligation to evict him or her. A few jurisdictions have adopted the so-called English Rule, which requires the landlord to deliver *possession,* not merely the *right* to it. This interpretation is consistent with the usual expectancy of the parties upon entering the contract.

One aspect of this covenant that is sometimes misunderstood by residential landlords is that the tenant's right to possession is exclusive. This excludes the landlord as well as others.

COVENANT OF FITNESS OF THE PREMISES

◆ **An assurance that the premises are fit for habitation.**

The common law rule is that the landlord does not implicitly warrant that the premises are fit for habitation. Some jurisdictions still follow the dictate of this rule, but even in these a few exceptions have been created. Where the lease is for a furnished apartment or is intended for a short duration (a few days, weeks or months), there is an implied warranty that the premises are habitable upon entry. Similarly, when the landlord knew of latent

In a significant number of states, statutes have been passed imposing a duty on the land-lord to perform repairs. The parties should be careful, given the variability of the rules regarding repairs, to make the terms of their agreement clear. When the landlord has the duty to repair and fails to do so, the tenant may sue the landlord for damages or make the needed repairs and deduct the cost from the rent.

If the landlord agrees in the lease to perform repairs, there is a split of authority over the responsibility for rebuilding a structure destroyed by a fire or other catastrophe. Some courts hold that the obligation to repair includes rebuilding; others claim that "repairing" is narrower than "rebuilding." Under the latter rule, once the building is substantially destroyed, it would not be encompassed within the obligation to repair.

If the landlord has agreed to rebuild, whether expressly or by implication in consenting to repair, the failure to rebuild would terminate the tenant's obligation to pay rent, at least where the building is the major concern of the lease.

DUTY TO PAY TAXES

◆ **Absent a contrary agreement, the landlord has the duty to pay the property taxes.**

As the owner of the fee interest in the premises, the landlord is responsible for paying the taxes. If the property is sold at a tax sale for nonpayment, the sale is subject to the existing lease. Where the tenant makes improvements to the property that cause the taxes to rise, the tenant will probably be liable to pay for the increase.

BUILDING CODE COMPLIANCE

◆ **Most cities have adopted building codes for the purpose of protecting the public health, safety and welfare by regulating building and construction standards.**

Through the requirement of obtaining a building permit or a certificate of occupancy for new construction or substantial alteration of an existing structure, city officials inspect structures for violations of the building code. The code is usually divided into special areas, such as plumbing code, electrical code and fire code. As a result of the division, there may be several inspectors and a multitude of permits. Failure to comply with the building code may result in the landlord's being fined.

The codes are applicable to existing buildings as well, and the code process usually comes into play when there is a tenant complaint about a violation. Often the result of these complaints is that the tenant receives a notice to vacate the premises at the earliest legal opportunity. Naturally, this discourages tenant complaints. Due to this landlord reaction, some jurisdictions have created the affirmative defense of retaliatory eviction. Under this defense a tenant cannot be evicted for complaining, at least until a legislated period (some-times 90 days) has lapsed after the complaint has been remedied. This provides only tem-porary protection to the tenant, and the landlord is free to terminate the tenancy after the time stated in the statute.

LESSOR'S REMEDIES

If one of the parties does not comply with the lease agreement, the other party will have an array of potential remedies. The chief remedies of the landlord will be discussed here.

EVICTION BY THE LANDLORD

◆ **The term usually associated with the legal procedure by which a landlord has the tenant removed from the premises because the tenant has breached the lease agreement.**

Under the common law, the covenants of a lease were mutually exclusive, and therefore the breach of a covenant by the tenant would not entitle the landlord to dispossess the tenant. The landlord would have a cause of action for damages resulting from the breach.

In the modern landlord-tenant situation, generally there is a provision in the lease, or the right may be provided by state statute, that the landlord can sue to regain possession of the premises in case of the tenant's failure to comply with the covenants in the lease. Though the agreement or the statute may not provide for dispossession in the case of *any* breach of a covenant, it normally applies to the failure to pay rent, the violation of the use provisions of the lease, the unlawful use of the premises or the violation of state and local health codes.

The eviction process will be used to dispossess a tenant who has received legal notice to vacate the premises and has failed to do so. Where the basis for the eviction is nonpayment of rent, the landlord will be required to notify the tenant of the possibility of eviction and make a demand for the rent prior to beginning the eviction proceedings.

The eviction of the tenant terminates the obligation to pay future rents. However, many business leases contain "survival clauses" under which the obligation to pay rent continues despite the eviction of the wrongdoing tenant. When it is a long-term lease, however, the right to sue accrues only at the termination of the lease, unless a clause in the lease indicates otherwise. It may be impractical to delay the suit for ten or more years until the lease period ends.

The term *eviction* is used to describe the wrongful dispossession of the tenant by the landlord as well as the legal action of the landlord described above. Wrongful eviction will be discussed under the lessee's remedies below.

WRONGFUL ABANDONMENT

◆ **The tenant's vacating of the premises without justification and with the intention of no longer performing under the terms of the lease.**

When the tenant wrongfully abandons the premises, the landlord has two options: either to do nothing until the lease period ends and then to bring an action for nonpayment of rent or to reenter the premises and reassert possessory rights.

The common law rule is that the landlord is free to do nothing and recover the full amount of unpaid rent at the termination of the lease. In some states, however, a duty arises to mitigate damages, thereby compelling the landlord to reenter and attempt to relet the

---

CASE EXAMPLE

Lubin leases commercial shop space to Murphy. In order to sell her cards and gifts, Murphy installs shelves that are attached to brackets and the brackets are affixed to the wall. Prior to the end of the lease Murphy can remove the shelves and brackets as long as the removal does not significantly or materially injure the shop.

The exception to the general rule is based on the idea that it was the presumed intent of the parties to permit removal, and public policy supports rules that will encourage trade through flexibility.

Several things should be noted about trade fixtures. First, the question of whether an item is a trade fixture may be treated as one of fact and left up to the trier of fact (the jury). More certainty can be obtained by stipulating in the lease how these fixtures will be handled. Second, removal can be executed only where serious injury will not result to the premises. Finally, removal is not permitted after the termination of the lease. Upon termination of the lease, trade fixtures become the permanent property of the landlord.

LESSEE'S REMEDIES

The lessee has several remedies available when the lessor violates the conditions of the lease.

WRONGFUL EVICTION

◆ **An act that occurs when the landlord without justification deprives the tenant of possession of the premises.**

A tenant who has been wrongfully evicted (also referred to as an *actual eviction*) can sue for recovery of possession of the premises or for damages caused by the breach of covenant of quiet enjoyment. In a somewhat punitive aspect of this area of law, if the landlord wrongfully evicts the tenant from only part of the premises, the tenant may retain the remainder of the property but will have no obligation to pay any rent until the partial wrongful eviction ceases.

A wrongful eviction and breach of the covenant of quiet enjoyment will exist also where the tenant is ousted because a third person has proved rights superior to those of the landlord. In such a case the tenant will have an action for money damages.

CONSTRUCTIVE EVICTION

◆ **An occurrence that results when the actions of the landlord so materially interfere with the tenant's enjoyment as to make the premises untenable.**

Theoretically at least, the right to assert a constructive eviction occurs when the tenant is forced by the condition of the premises to vacate. The tenant must notify the landlord of the conditions, where appropriate, and give the landlord a reasonable time to remedy the situation. Finally, the tenant must actually vacate the premises to be able to allege constructive eviction.

The concept of constructive eviction is a judicial construction. It is used to offset the fact that the landlord normally inserts in the lease a provision permitting the eviction of the tenant for failure to comply with the terms of the lease. Leases do not normally provide for comparable rights for the tenant. The Blackett case discusses the defense of constructive eviction.

BLACKETT V. OLANOFF
Supreme Judicial Court of Massachusetts
358 N.E.2d 817 (1977)

BACKGROUND. Jerrold Olanoff leased residential premises to Arthur Blackett. Olanoff leased other residential premises in the vicinity and also leased commercial premises to another for use as a bar and cocktail lounge. The noise emanating from the lounge in the late evening and early morning hours was substantial. Blackett complained about the noise to his landlord, who attempted unsuccessfully to control the noise from the lounge. After a reasonable time, Blackett vacated the premises contending that the noise made the premises untenable, thereby breaching his implied warranty of quiet enjoyment.

Olanoff brought this action against Blackett to recover unpaid rent. Blackett offered the defense of constructive eviction. Olanoff contended that he was not responsible for the noise created by the proprietors, employees and patrons of the lounge. Olanoff did not contend that the noise was not loud enough to cause a constructive eviction. The trial judge concluded that Blackett was constructively evicted.

DECISION. The Supreme Judicial Court of Massachusetts affirmed the trial court's decision.

JUSTICE WILKINS. Our opinions concerning a constructive eviction by an alleged breach of an implied covenant of quiet enjoyment sometimes have stated that the landlord must perform some act with the intent of depriving the tenant of the enjoyment and occupation of the whole or part of the leased premises. There are occasions, however, where a landlord has not intended to violate a tenant's rights, but there was nevertheless a breach of the landlord's covenant of quiet enjoyment which flowed as the natural and probable consequence of what the landlord did, what he failed to do, or what he permitted to be done. Although some of our opinions have spoken of particular action or inaction by a landlord as showing a presumed intention to evict, the landlord's conduct, and not his intentions, is controlling.

The judge was warranted in ruling that the landlords had it within their control to correct the condition which caused the tenants to vacate their apartments. The landlords introduced a commercial activity where they leased premises for residential purpose. The lease for the lounge expressly provided that entertainment in the lounge had to be conducted so that it could not be heard outside the building and would not disturb the residents of the leased apartments. The potential threat to the occupants of the nearby apartments was apparent in the circumstances. The landlords complained to the tenants of the lounge after receiving numerous objections from residential tenants. From time to time, the pervading noise would abate in response to the landlord's complaints. We conclude that, as matter of law, the landlords had a right to control the objectionable noise coming from the lounge and that the judge was warranted in finding as a fact that the landlords could control the objectionable conditions.

This situation is different from the usual annoyance of one residential tenant by another, where traditionally the landlord has not been chargeable with the annoyance. Here, although the clash of tenants' interests was only a known potentiality initially, experience demonstrated that a decibel level for the entertainment at the lounge, acoustically acceptable to its patrons and hence commercially desirable to its proprietors, was intolerable for the residential tenants.

Because the disturbing condition was the natural and probable consequence of the landlords' permitting the lounge to operate where it did and because the landlords could control the actions at the lounge, they should not be entitled to collect rent for residential premises which were not reasonably habitable. Tenants such as these should not be left only with a claim against the proprietors of the noisome lounge. To the extent that our opinions suggest a distinction between nonfeasance by the landlord, which has been said to create no liability, and malfeasance by the landlord, we decline to perpetuate that distinction where the landlord creates a situation and has the right to control the objectionable conditions.

JUDGMENTS AFFIRMED.

DAMAGES, REFORMATION AND RESCISSION

◆ **Actions a tenant may bring where an implied warranty of habitability exists and the landlord has failed to maintain the premises in a tenable condition.**

The remedies made available to the tenant when the implied warranty of habitability is breached are of a complementary nature. That is, the tenant is afforded relief short of vacating the premises or withholding rent, both of which may be risky remedies.

The tenant may sue for damages measured by expenses incurred as a result of the landlord's refusal to perform the covenants in the lease. The tenant may seek reformation of the contract due to the conduct of the landlord in refusing to perform repairs. The reformation could take the form of reducing the amount of rent due in order to conform to the lessened value of the unrepaired premises. If the breach of covenant has reduced the value of the lease to the tenant significantly, prior to the tenant's entry he or she may seek to have a court rescind or negate the entire agreement.

> ## CASE EXAMPLE
> Laferty, the landlord, has agreed to provide repairs in his lease with Manne. The roof leaks into a small bedroom. Despite requests by Manne to Laferty to repair the roof prior to Manne's moving in, the roof remains unrepaired. Manne *needs* the bedroom for a child and seeks rescission of the lease. The tenant's attorney chooses this as a safer, albeit more time-consuming, remedy for the tenant than vacating after entry and contending constructive eviction. Under constructive eviction Manne would run the risk of the court's disagreeing with his contention that the premises are "untenable" and charge him for unpaid rent.

RENT WITHHOLDING

◆ **The practice, allowed in some states under limited circumstances, in which the tenant withholds rent as an inducement to force the landlord to perform repairs.**

It should be remembered that at common law the obligation to pay rent arises from the possession of the land and from the covenant to pay in the lease. Each covenant in the lease is independent. Therefore, the tenant normally has the duty to pay the rent despite the landlord's failure to perform some aspect of his or her obligation.

In some states, including New York, Illinois, Connecticut, Vermont and Michigan, tenants are legislatively authorized to withhold rent in cases where the landlord has failed to obtain a certificate of occupancy as required by the municipal housing code. Similarly, welfare agencies are authorized to withhold rent payments that they normally make directly to the landlord for the welfare tenant. A statute establishes the conditions for rent withholding and the procedures for utilizing the right. It affords protection to the tenant from being evicted.

It should be noted that rent withholding is not a broadly applicable remedy, and local and state law will have to be checked carefully to determine whether the right exists and to what extent.

THIRD-PARTY-RELATED TRANSACTIONS

On occasion a person other than the landlord or tenant becomes involved with the leasehold agreement. Because of a job change, for example, a tenant may seek a substitute to complete the tenancy. Or a person visiting the tenant may fall down the hall stairway in the apartment due to poor lighting or a faulty railing. These and other third-party incidents affecting the lease are discussed next.

SUBLEASE

◆ **A transfer of part of the leasehold interest of the tenant, with the tenant retaining a reversionary interest.**

ers have advanced the theory that a more modern and just viewpoint should be applied in situations such as the present; that the rule applicable in ordinary breach of contract cases, requiring efforts to mitigate damages after breach, should be applied to leases; and in furtherance of this view that a lessor should be obligated to accept a suitable subtenant offered by the lessee.

We feel that we must adhere to the majority rule. In reaching this conclusion we are motivated by the fact that the language of the assignment provision is clear and unambiguous and that many leases now in effect covering a substantial amount of real property and creating valuable property rights were carefully prepared by competent counsel in reliance upon the majority viewpoint. It would seem clear from the language adopted in all such cases that the lessors therein are entitled to place full reliance upon the responsibility of their respective lessees for the rentals they have contracted to pay. Should a lessee desire the right to assign or sublet to a suitable tenant, a clause might readily be inserted in the lease similar to those now included in many leases to the effect that the lessor's written consent to the assignment or subletting of the leased premises should not be unreasonably withheld. There being no clause in the present lease to such effect, we are compelled to give its terms their full force and effect as have the courts of a majority of other jurisdictions.

AFFIRMED.

Impact of an Assignment. At the beginning of the preceding chapter, some care was taken to describe a lease as a conveyance of an estate in land as well as a contractual obligation. In the area of assignment, the dichotomy is important. Upon taking a transfer by lease, the tenant enters into a dual relationship. Under the estate-in-land aspect of the agreement, the landlord and the tenant are said to have *privity of estate.* Under the contractual side of the agreement, the parties have created *privity of contract.* As explained earlier, privity connotes the mutuality that binds parties to their agreement.

A tenant who assigns the lease to a third person surrenders possession and transfers the *privity of estate* to the assignee. The assignee literally stands in the legal shoes of the tenant, since he or she received all that the tenant has, and privity of estate now exists between the landlord and the assignee. The assignee's right to possession makes him or her liable directly to the landlord for payment of rent. Possession automatically gives rise to the obligation to pay rent.

By way of contrast, there is no *privity of contract* between the landlord and the assignee. There is no contract, or mutual agreement to be bound, created by the assignment. An outgrowth of this is that the tenant/assignor continues to be bound by the terms of the lease-contract to the landlord.

As the result of privity of estate existing between the landlord and the assignee, the landlord can sue the assignee for nonpayment of rent. If, when the assignment takes place, the assignee agrees to assume the obligations of the lease and to be bound to the lessor for rent, he or she will have privity of contract with the lessor as well as the privity of estate previously discussed.

SALE OF THE LEASED PREMISES

The landlord is free to convey the leased premises at any time. The buyer takes subject to the leasehold interest of the tenant. The buyer has the right to collect all subsequent rents once the tenant has been notified of the sale.

The buyer is the successor in title to the lessor's land; the tenant has an obligation, arising out of the notion of a conveyance of real property, to pay the rent to the new owner. It would not, therefore, be necessary to have an assignment of the lease, or the lessor's contract rights to the buyer, in order to collect the rent. However, unless the lease or contract provides otherwise, the lessor would continue to be liable for covenants he or she made to the lessee in the lease.

PARTIES' TORT LIABILITY

◆ **In general, the person who has possession and control of the premises owes a civil duty to third parties to maintain the premises in a reasonably safe condition.**

The leased premises are normally in the possession and under the control of the tenant, and the tenant must use reasonable care in maintaining those premises in a safe condition. Failure to do so is a civil wrong, or tort. As a consequence of this rule, and the rule that does not require the landlord to repair or make the property habitable, generally the landlord owes no duty to the tenant or to third parties when they are injured as the result of a defective condition of the premises. However, the general rule is under siege where jurisdictions have adopted a warranty of habitability. It should be kept in mind, however, that technically warranty is a contract theory, and the extent of damages recoverable in case of a breach may be limited to contract damages (the cost of repair, not personal injury).

Even without the modern trend applying a warranty of habitability, there are exceptions to the rule holding that the landlord owes no duty in tort. When the landlord retains control over portions of the premises, such as stairways and halls, he or she will owe a duty to use reasonable care to maintain safe conditions. This is consistent with the general rule because the landlord retains control of these areas.

In addition, where the landlord is aware of latent defects on the premises and fails to notify the unknowing tenant, he or she will owe a duty to the tenant and other third parties. Also, where the lease is for a furnished apartment and the tenant has no opportunity to inspect, the landlord will be liable in tort. Likewise, the landlord will be liable where he or she carelessly performs repairs.

YOUNG V. GARWACKI
Supreme Judicial Court of Massachusetts
402 N.E.2d 1045 (1980)

BACKGROUND. Garwacki and Mastello leased a second-story apartment from LaFreniere as tenants at will. In 1977, Mastello invited a friend, Young, to dinner. Young was helping in the meal preparation. When Mastello left the apartment to pick up another dinner guest, Young went onto the second story porch to yell down to him to bring back certain groceries. As she leaned on the porch railing with her hands, it gave way and she fell to the ground below. Young was injured.

The landlord was aware that the railing was dangerous. He had informed the tenants in 1976 that the railing was faulty, and he had purchased materials to fix it but had not performed the repairs. Young sued the landlord and tenants to recover damages for her personal injuries suffered in the fall. She argued that the railing was negligently maintained. At the trial court, a judgment was entered against the tenants, but not the landlord. Young appealed the decision as to the landlord.

DECISION. The Supreme Judicial Court of Massachusetts reversed the lower court finding for the plaintiff against the landlord.

JUSTICE LIACOS. In the absence of the landlord's express agreement to keep the rented premises in repair, is he liable to his tenant's guest for injuries resulting from his negligent failure to maintain the safety of the premises? Common law rules defining a landowner's liability in negligence to people coming onto the land reflected the needs of an agrarian society. The landowner was a petty

sovereign within his boundaries. The character of his duty to an injured party varied with the party's relationship with the sovereign. Thus, the common law distinguished several classes of tort plaintiffs; among them, trespassers, licensees, invitees, and tenants.

The traditional approach to tenants turned on the concept of a lease as a conveyance of property. The tenant "bought" the leasehold at his peril, so he could not expect the landlord to have repaired preexisting defects, and at the time of the letting, the landlord ceded to the tenant his dominion over the rented premises. Under this ancient view, the axiom was "there is no law against letting a tumbledown house." The landlord might have been liable for negligent maintenance of common areas, but was not generally liable for the negligent maintenance of the premises themselves.

The landlord "was under a separate and limited duty toward each tenant and that tenant's visitors to exercise reasonable care to maintain the common areas in a condition not less safe than they were, or appeared to be in, at the time of the letting to the particular tenant." As to the demised premises, *caveat emptor* reigned. The tenant took the premises as he found them. "The general rule is that the landlord is not liable to the tenant for defects in the premises existing at the time of the letting unless they are hidden defects of which he is aware and does not warn the tenant."

The ordinary agreement for consideration by which a landlord is to make repairs is construed as an agreement to repair on notice. Failure to repair under such an agreement gives rise only to a contract action for the cost of the repair. Tort liability will exist, however, for negligently made repairs. In the absence of such a specific agreement to repair, no agreement will be implied from the mere letting of the premises, and any repairs made will be treated as gratuitous.

After seven years of reconsideration and reform, little remains of this obsolete machinery of the common law. "Recent decisions of this court clearly reflect . . . a shift in philosophy with regard to status distinctions in tort standards of care. We did away with the legal significance in tort of categories of licensee and invitee and held that a landowner owes a duty of reasonable care to all lawful visitors. We said: "The problem of allocating the costs and risks of human injury is far too complex to be decided solely by the status of the entrant, especially where the status question often prevents the jury from ever determining the fundamental question whether the defendant has acted reasonably in light of all the circumstances in the particular case."

In the landlord-tenant field, we have held that a landlord is liable to a tenant's guest for failing to exercise due care in maintaining common passageways under the landlord's control without regard to their condition at the time of the letting. We extended the landlord's general and continuing duty to exercise reasonable care as to the safety of common passageways to include tenants as well as their visitors.

We have also attacked the theory on which the tenant's status classification depends. In the line of cases creating and applying the implied warranty of habitability, we have overthrown the doctrine of caveat emptor and the notion that a lease is a conveyance of property. Moreover, we have invoked the doctrine of warranty to afford a tenant compensation not only for economic loss, but for personal injury.

Thus, at least to the extent required by the relevant housing and building codes, a landlord may be liable to his tenant for failing to maintain areas not under the landlord's control.

Today, we do away with the ancient law that bars a tenant's guest from recovering compensation from a landlord for injuries caused by negligent maintenance of areas rented to the tenant. Like the other rules based on status, this rule has prevented a whole class of people from raising the overriding issue: whether the landlord acted reasonably under the circumstances. The practical result of this archaic rule has been to discourage repairs of rented premises. In cases like the one before us, a landlord with knowledge of a defect has less incentive to repair it. And the tenant, who often has a short-term lease, limited funds, and limited experience dealing with such defects, will not be inclined to pay for expensive work on a place he will soon be leaving. Thus, the defect may go unrepaired until an unsuspecting plaintiff finds herself with a lawsuit that care could have prevented.

Henceforth, landlords as other persons must exercise reasonable care not to subject others to an unreasonable risk of harm. A landlord must act as a reasonable person under all of the circumstances including the likelihood of injury to others, the probable seriousness of such injuries, and the burden of reducing or avoiding the risk. We think this basic principle of responsibility for landlords as for others "best expresses the principles of justice and reasonableness upon which our law of torts is founded."

The former rule was not without its reasons. When a landlord rents an apartment to a tenant, he gives up his right to enter. Matters of control, like matters of status, can be components of familiar negligence analysis; they can affect such questions as reasonableness and

3. Lubin owns an apartment in a college town. Many units in the building are rented to college students. Lubin retains keys to these apartments. From time to time she visits the tenants. Although she always phones first, if the tenants are not available she will use her duplicate key to enter. The main purpose of Lubin's visit is to ensure that the utilities, appliances and plumbing are functioning properly. If she does not interfere with the tenants' occupancy, is Lubin's conduct legally proper? Discuss.

4. Addison leased a unit in an apartment building from Seikely. He tripped over a loose board on an exterior stairway and was injured. He sued Seikely, claiming negligent maintenance of the common stairway. Seikely offers as a defense that a clause in the lease excuses him from liability for any injury incurred on the premises. Discuss the validity of Seikely's defense.

5. Gokey rented a mobile home (part of the realty) to the Bessettes at a monthly rent of $400. During the tenancy, the Bessettes complained of numerous problems, including a leak in the roof, a broken furnace and a break in the sewer line. The Bessettes complained to code enforcement officials about the sewer line because noxious liquids lay under the trailer for up to four months, causing foul odors to fill their home. Should the Bessettes move out? Should they stop paying rent? Explain. *Gokey v. Bessette, 580 A.2d 488 (1990).*

9

Easements and Other Nonpossessory Rights

EASEMENT

◆ **A nonpossessory interest in real property; the right to use another's real estate for a limited purpose.**

Most of the ownership interests considered in prior chapters provide the holder with a current or future right of possession. In these forms of ownership, the owner enjoys or will enjoy in the future the right to proceeds from the property and the right to occupy it to the exclusion of all others.

Some people have interests in real estate that are limited to use, not possession. These are referred to as *nonpossessory rights.* One important nonpossessory right is the easement. Easements are used extensively in real estate. For example, they are essential to the operation of utilities. They also provide a legal basis for condominium ownership, scenic and open-space protection and preservation of historic buildings. Indeed, few land developments would be successful without the extensive use of easements. Although easements are interests in real estate, the person who has an easement is never entitled to possession of the land itself—only use.

The holder of an easement has a right to use another's land or buildings for a specified purpose. That purpose might be as simple as crossing the land to reach a beach or as complicated as using a portion of a neighbor's building to support one's own.

The person who owns an easement has neither title nor estate in the land burdened by it. The easement holder's limited interest is, however, protected against interference by third parties, and the easement cannot be terminated at the will of the owner of the land that it burdens.

Frequently, easements authorize a person to perform a particular act. An example would be a right to use a neighbor's driveway to reach the back portion of a lot. These authorizing easements are called *affirmative easements.* Others, called *negative easements,* prohibit the owner of the land from doing something that ordinarily an owner would be entitled the death of its holder. For this reason, if the parties wish to have the easement continue or to have any value, they must to tie it to a dominant estate. If this is done, it would be appurtenant and would run with the land.

Traditionally, the courts have treated easements in gross granted for commercial uses differently. Because of their importance to the public, they are considered freely transferable. For example, a utility easement can be sold or assigned by one utility company to another. Although transferable, an easement given for a specific purpose, such as a sewer, cannot be used for another purpose, such as an electric line. However, an easement in cable used for telephone transmission may ordinarily be assigned to a cable company for use in television transmission. Here, the character of the easement has not substantially changed.

Inasmuch as the easement in gross is not intended to benefit a parcel of land, it is considered a personal right in another's property.

PROFIT À PRENDRE

◆ **A nonpossessory interest in real property that permits the holder to remove part of the soil or produce of the land.**

Most authorities consider the profit, correctly known as the *profit à prendre,* a type of easement. Others distinguish the profit from the easement, as the profit allows the holder to take specified resources from the land, such as soil, produce, wild animals, coal and timber. A person who has an easement does not have this right. Suppose, for example, that Stump grants the Cazenovia Lumber Company the right to take "any and all standing timber" from his property at Lake Feather. Although the lumber company does not have title to the timber, it has a right to remove it from the land. This is a profit.

Few differences exist between easements and profits. Like other types of easements, a profit is an interest in land, but it is nonpossessory and limited to a particular purpose. The holder of the profit has a right of reasonable ingress and egress in order to use the right advantageously. In most states, unless specifically limited by the agreement, the owner of land does not lose the right to use the resource that is the subject of the profit. Like easements, profits may be appurtenant or in gross. The usual profit is in gross. This makes it a personal right not related to a dominant estate. Unlike the noncommercial easement in gross, however, the profit à prendre is freely transferable.

CREATION OF EASEMENTS

An easement is generally created in one of three ways: by deed, by implication or by prescription.

CREATION OF AN EASEMENT BY DEED

The most common method of creating an easement is by deed. Among other things, a deed describes the land and, in the case of an easement, describes the location of the easement.

Deeds are discussed in Chapter 17. Most courts are reluctant to accept the idea that an easement may be created orally. The reason is that an easement is an interest in real estate, and statutes in all states require that an interest in real estate—such as an easement—be created only by a written instrument.

> ### CASE EXAMPLE
> Paul Brangs owned a lot at Lake Feather next to his home. Paul wished to sell the lot but was having difficulty because it was narrow. Paul's driveway bordered the lot. To induce Nan Crampton, a prospective purchaser, to buy, Paul agreed to grant her an easement over his driveway to reach the back portion of the property. At the closing, Paul delivered a deed passing title to the lot and a separate deed conveying an easement over his driveway to Crampton.

The granting of an easement may be an independent transaction. Utility companies often seek easements when they need to run their lines over another's property. In many states the law gives these companies the right of eminent domain if the landowner refuses to grant the requested easement. Gas pipelines, sewers and roads are based on easements from property owners.

Deeds creating easement may do so by express grant or express reservation.

◆ **Express Grant.** **An easement created by an owner expressly granting in a deed or other instrument a specific right to another to use the property.**

> ### CASE EXAMPLE
> Morgan owns two adjoining lets at Lake Feather. She sells one to Betterman. Morgan's lot includes a private alley, and Morgan's deed to Betterman *expressly grants* by deed to Betterman the use of this alley.

An easement may also be created by a *contract* between the parties. This is not a preferred method, but if the courts will enforce by specific performance or injunction an agreement in which one party promises to allow another to use land for a limited purpose, an easement has been created. A few courts have even enforced oral contracts that create a limited interest in land. Usually, these involve something like a common driveway or access road.

◆ **Express Reservation.** **An easement created when an owner of property conveys title to another by deed while specifically reserving an easement in his or her favor.**

> ### CASE EXAMPLE
> Morgan sells Betterman the lot with the alley and keeps the other for herself. Morgan's deed includes a clause that *expressly reserves* her right to use the alley.

Provisions expressly reserving an easement are usually found in a deed; some easements are created by will, but easements may also be included in a mortgage or lease.

CREATION OF AN EASEMENT BY IMPLICATION

Courts sometimes presume that the parties intend to create an easement because certain facts exist when real estate is conveyed. The easement supposedly reflects the intention of the parties and is called an *easement by implication*. Courts have traditionally assumed easements by implication in two situations. In both, the easement results only if one or more parcels are severed from a larger tract under common ownership.

In the first situation, the effective use of one parcel (the dominant estate) depends on continuation of a use already being made of the other (the servient parcel). As a result, the easement is sometimes referred to as an *easement implied from prior use*. The other situation occurs if the severed portion is landlocked and cannot be used without passage across the other. This type is generally referred to as an *easement by necessity*. This second example is much less common than the first. Support for the creation of easements by implication is found in the idea that a sale of real estate includes that which is necessary to use the property beneficially.

Easement Implied from Prior Use. If a property owner visibly and continuously has used one part of land for the benefit of another, and this use is reasonably necessary for the fair enjoyment of the other, an easement is actually created when either part is sold separately. This is true even when neither party expressly makes any commitment creating the easement. The case that follows involves creation of an easement implied from prior use.

CASH V. CRAVER
Court of Appeals of North Carolina
302 S.E.2d 819 (1983)

BACKGROUND. Ted Cash (plaintiff) and Mary Craver (defendant) own adjoining tracts of land. Both tracts had been part of a larger tract of land owned by W.J. Roberts. In 1917, the 170-acre Craver tract was severed from the whole by deed. The 70-acre Cash tract was severed from the whole by deed in 1942. Roberts School Road ran across the Cash and Craver tracts before the severance. The road had always been used by the plaintiff, the defendant and others as a schoolway and farm-to-market road, as well as a general means of ingress and egress to interior lands for farming and transfer to major highways abutting the tracts.

In 1981, Cash sued for a permanent injunction barring Mary Craver and others from using the portion of Roberts School Road that crosses Cash's property. The trial court refused to grant this injunction, ruling that the defendants owned an easement by implication. Cash appealed.

DECISION. The appellate court affirmed.

JUDGE HILL. We hold, in affirming its order, that the trial court properly denied plaintiff's motion for a permanent injunction and found an easement by implication in favor of defendants....

It is apparent from [the judge's] order that he found an easement implied from prior use. The elements of proof for easements implied from prior use are: (1) separation of title; (2) prior use "so long continued and so obvious or manifest as to show that it was meant to be permanent," and (3) that the claimed easement was "necessary to the beneficial enjoyment of the land."

The plaintiff, who apparently concedes the existence of severance and prior use, contends ... that necessity has not been shown. While we need not discuss the sufficiency of the evidence in order to reach our conclusion, we briefly consider the question to dispel any confusion regarding the degree of necessity required for an easement implied from prior use.

A showing of strict necessity is not required for an easement arising from prior use. It is sufficient to show such physical conditions and such use as would reasonably lead one to believe that [the] grantor intended [the] grantee should have the right to continue to use the road in the same manner and to the same extent which his grantor had used it,

because such use was reasonably necessary to the "fair" ... "full" ... "convenient and comfortable"... enjoyment of his property.

The party must establish ... that the easement is reasonably necessary to the beneficial enjoyment of the land. The presence of a second or alternate way onto the property is not conclusive proof that an implied easement arising from prior use is unnecessary. Indeed, perhaps of greater significance is evidence that supports the inference that the parties intended the use to continue after severance.

In the present case, the road had been used regularly for farm and travel purposes before severance. That the road has been regularly and similarly used by defendants, their predecessors in title, lessees and neighbors is certainly probative of their right to use the road. While there was evidence of another road on the Craver property by which access to a major abutting highway could be gained, there was also evidence that (1) the road would require major repairs to be passable; and (2) use of the road might necessitate defendants' crossing land belonging to others over which they have no enforceable right-of-way. In any event, the prior, regular and continuous nature of the use and the difficulties inherent in exploiting an alternate way, if one does exist, amply support the [trial court's] findings.

AFFIRMED.

◆ **Easement Implied from Necessity.** An easement permitting the owner of a landlocked parcel to cross a portion of land of which the easement formerly was a part.

Most courts consider the easement by necessity a form of implied easement. They reason that the parties intended that the grantee of a landlocked parcel have a means of access to his or her land. Without a right to cross the lands of the grantor, the grantee would derive no benefit from the conveyed property. A few courts have taken the position that presumed intent is not necessary. These courts feel that sound public policy dictates that no land should be inaccessible. Whatever theory prevails, two factors must be established for an easement to be created by necessity:

TERMINATION OF EASEMENTS

Although an easement is actually a nonpossessory interest, in many respects it resembles a possessory interest. Like an estate, an easement may be created for a specific period, for life or for a designated purpose. Stump, who you recall granted an easement across his property to reach Lake Feather, might have limited the easement to a designated number of years or until a road was constructed to the lake. When an easement is created for a period of time or a designated purpose, it terminates when either the time expires or the purpose is accomplished. Easements for life terminate when the measuring life ends. An easement created by necessity does not last once the necessity disappears. Most easements, however, do not expire automatically. Like the fee simple, they have the potential to last forever.

A number of methods exist for terminating easements that do not expire automatically, including release, merger, estoppel, abandonment, prescription, conveyance and eminent domain. Each of these methods is discussed below.

RELEASE

The holder of an easement appurtenant or in gross may extinguish it by means of a written agreement to give up the right. This document is referred to as a *release*. An oral release alone is ineffective. Except for automatic termination of easements, extinguishing by release is probably the most common method.

MERGER

An easement terminates by merger when the holder of either the dominant or servient estate acquires the other. An easement establishes a right to use land owned by someone else. As a result, a person cannot have an easement in his or her own land. The principle applies whether the easement is in gross or appurtenant. Either expires if ownership changes in this way.

ESTOPPEL

◆ **A doctrine by which a person is not permitted to deny the consequences of facts that are inconsistent with his or her previous actions or statements.**

Two factors must unite before the doctrine of estoppel is applied. First, a person must act in a manner that causes another to believe something. Second, the other person must rely on the belief and stand to suffer some loss if reliance on such belief should be barred or penalized.

An easement is extinguished by estoppel if the holder causes the servient estate owner to believe the easement will no longer be used and the servient owner relies on this belief and suffers some damage as a result. The belief might be the result of a statement made by the easement holder or might be inferred from the person's conduct.

> **CASE EXAMPLE**
> Stump asked Bach to use another path across Stump's property to reach Lake Feather. Bach orally agreed to do so. Stump then built a tennis court that was partially on the original right-of-way. Bach found the new path inconvenient and demanded to be allowed to use the old recorded right-of-way. Bach's easement had been terminated by estoppel.

Nonuse of an easement for a substantial period of time is generally not a sufficient basis on which to terminate an easement by estoppel.

ABANDONMENT

Although nonuse alone does not extinguish an easement, it may indicate an intention to abandon it. For an easement to terminate by abandonment, the holder's intention to give it up must be clearly established. This can be done if the holder discontinues use, states his or her intention to do so or acts in a manner consistent with discontinued use.

> **CASE EXAMPLE**
> Suppose Bach purchases additional land giving him frontage on Lake Feather. He builds a fence along his line abutting on Stump's land and clears a path across the newly acquired tract to Lake Feather. Bach has probably abandoned his easement across Stump's property.

PRESCRIPTION

An easement may be extinguished after the owner of the servient estate acts in a manner adverse to the easement for the prescriptive period. This use must be open, notorious and uninterrupted. That is, the servient owner must act in a manner similar to that which occurs when an easement is created by prescription.

> **CASE EXAMPLE**
> Stump builds a garage on his property, blocking Levit's right-of-way to Lake Feather. Levit does nothing about the garage because he has no interest in reaching Lake Feather. The prescriptive period in the state is seven years. Levit's easement will terminate by prescription unless he asserts his right before the end of the period.

CONVEYANCE

An easement is sometimes terminated when the servient estate is sold to a person who has no knowledge of the easement's existence. When a written easement is not recorded, or when the easement is not visible from indications on the property, the servient estate may become free of the easement. Easements created by necessity and by prescription, however, are not subject to this doctrine.

EMINENT DOMAIN

The right of the state to take private property for public use applies to easements. If the state takes the servient estate for a purpose that is not consistent with the continued use of the easement, the dominant tenant loses his or her right to continue this use. This is true even if the dominant estate itself is not taken. The owner of the dominant estate is entitled to compensation for the loss in value of his or her easement right. Similarly, condemnation of the dominant estate may terminate the easement. This occurs if the condemnation and the new use destroy the usefulness of the easement.

LICENSE

◆ A personal privilege to enter another's property for a specific purpose.

> ### CASE EXAMPLE
> Able and Baker are neighbors. Baker is having work done on his driveway, and Able gives him permission to park in Able's driveway for two weeks. Baker has a license.

Purchasing tickets to attend the theater or a sporting event and obtaining a camping permit at a state park are other examples of licenses. Although both easements and licenses are intangible, an easement is an interest in land; a license is not. It is a right that is personal to the licensee, the party to whom it was given. Without a license, if Baker had parked in Able's driveway, Baker would be a trespasser.

Licenses may be created orally or may be in writing. Because a license is personal, the licensor may revoke it at any time. If the license was created by a contract, the revocation is a breach of the contract. Nevertheless, although the licensee may collect damages, he or she cannot require the licensor to honor the agreement by specific performance because the licensee has no interest in the realty. If Baker had paid for permission to park in Able's driveway, Able could revoke the license. Although Able would be responsible for money damages because of the revocation, Baker could not get a court order requiring Able to make space available.

Because licenses are personal, they are usually invalidated by the licensee's death and may not be transferred. An exception exists when the individual's license is coupled with an interest in the real estate. Under these circumstances the license is irrevocable. Instead of merely giving Baker permission to park in the driveway, Able sells Baker timber on Able's property. Because of his interest in the timber, Baker has, in addition, an irrevocable privilege to enter and remove it. Baker's license to enter the land is irrevocable because of the interest in the timber. The license is said to be *coupled with an interest*.

CASE EXAMPLE

Durell had an oil and gas lease and was operating wells on property owned by Freese. A former owner had orally given Durell permission to place equipment on the land to aid in pumping oil. Freese removed this equipment on the grounds that all Durell had was a license that could be revoked at any time. Durell could get an injunction prohibiting Freese from removing the equipment because the license was irrevocable, as it was coupled with the oil and gas lease. *Durell v. Freese, 151 Okla. 150, 3 P.2d 175 (1931).*

REVIEW AND DISCUSSION QUESTIONS

1. Compare and contrast an *easement appurtenant* and an *easement in gross.*
2. Explain the factors that must exist for an easement to be created by prescription.
3. What is a license? How does it differ from an easement?
4. What is a profit? How does it differ from an easement? In what ways is it similar?
5. Is an easement an estate? Support your answer.
6. Is an easement property? Support your answer.
7. Name seven ways an easement may terminate and give an example of each.

CASE PROBLEMS

1. Hamilton and Tucker owned adjoining farms. For more than 40 years, Mrs. Tucker, her predecessors in title, her agents and her employees had reached her farm by a roadway across the Hamilton farm.

   At one time, the two farms had been a single unit, but it had been divided in 1884 by Mrs. Tucker's grandfather. He had given approximately 200 acres to each of his two sons. The Hamiltons had purchased their farm in 1972 from the widow of one of the sons.

   Upon purchasing the farm, the Hamiltons blocked the roadway to the Tucker place. Mrs. Tucker seeks an injunction to restrain this action. Will she succeed? Discuss. *McIlroy v. Hamilton, 539 S.W.2d 669 (Mo. Ct. App. 1976).*

2. Anderson owned and operated a small motel in a resort area. One of the area's principal attractions was a well-known golf course. Although it was difficult to reach the clubhouse by automobile from the motel, the clubhouse was within easy walking distance.

   In order to provide easy access to the clubhouse for his guests, Anderson acquired an easement over a neighbor's land "for use as a connecting walk by guests of the Anderson Motel." Three years later Anderson sold the motel to a national franchise, which doubled the room capacity. The neighbor attempted to stop motel guests from crossing the land, and the new owner sought an injunction prohibiting interference. Would the new owner be successful? Present arguments for both the neighbor and the new owner.

3. Soergel owned lot A. He granted Smith, who owned lot B directly to the west of lot A, a ten-foot-wide easement for installation of a sewer line. Smith sold lot B to Preston, who owned lot C directly to the west of lot B. Preston began to install a sewer line from his house on lot C across lots B and A. Soergel sought an injunction prohibiting Preston from constructing the sewer line. Was Soergel successful? Support your answer. *Soergel v. Preston, 367 N.W.2d 366 (Mich. Ct. App. 1985).*

4. Devlin leased a restaurant in a shopping center. The owner of the shopping center did not object when Devlin erected a sign in the parking lot advertising the restaurant. When the shopping center was sold, the new owner demanded that the sign be removed. (a) If Devlin refused to remove it, could the new owner do so legally? (b) Would the result be the same if Devlin had permission from the former owner to erect the sign? Discuss. *Devlin v. The Phoenix, Inc., 471 So.2d 93 (Fla. Dist. Ct. App. 1985).*

5. Todd operated a business that provided laundry machines for use in apartments. In 1979, Todd entered into an agreement with Lake Feather Realty giving him the exclusive right to install and maintain laundry equipment in an apartment building owned by Lake Feather Realty. The contract was for a ten-year period and purported to be binding "on the heirs, successors and assigns" of the parties.

    When the apartment building was sold in 1981, the new owner demanded that Todd remove the machines. Todd sought a permanent injunction to prevent the removal of the machines, arguing that the contract gave him an easement to maintain them. What do you think was the result? Why?

6. Elaine Owens owned property in Lake Feather Village. For 25 to 30 years, during the summer, people had used the property as a shortcut to reach the beach. In the spring and fall, the property was used by children as a baseball diamond or a football field.

    When Owens built a fence around the property, Fink, an abutting owner, sued to prevent the area from being blocked. Would Fink be successful? Support your answer.

Basic Contract Law

CONTRACT

◆ **A promise or an agreement between two or more parties that the courts will enforce.**

Citizens are obliged to obey laws the government imposes on them. No one likes to pay taxes, but failure to do so results in penalties. The obligation to pay taxes arises from a legislative act. Obligations may also arise by individual agreement. Two or more persons may come together in agreement to be bound by their own "private legislation." The law will enforce that agreement through the courts if certain ingredients are present. Such an agreement is called a *contract*.

Contracts are the essential fabric of commercial transactions. Most people enter into contracts on a daily basis, by asking for fuel at a gas station, ordering a sandwich to carry out or purchasing a paper from a newsstand. Real estate listing and purchase agreements, leasehold agreements, options to buy and mortgages are more complex forms of contracts. Each of these agreements is governed by contract law. Every state has its own body of contract law, derived from the common law and from statutes. The general body of contract law applies to all commercial agreements, including real estate agreements.

Not every agreement entered into between parties is enforceable. The law enforces agreements arising in a commercial context, assuming that certain other ingredients discussed in this chapter are present. The law will not, however, enforce a purely social arrangement.

An offeror has the power to control the terms of a contract. The offeror may make a reasonable offer or an unreasonable offer. If it is to ripen into a contract, the offeree must accept the terms of the offer.

If unaccepted, an offer may terminate in several ways, including revocation, rejection, lapse of a reasonable time, destruction of the subject matter, death of the offeror, insanity of the offeror or illegality of the subject matter of the offer.

Revocation. Generally, an offeror may withdraw an offer any time before the offeree's acceptance. The revocation becomes effective upon actual communication to the offeree. If the offeree receives a revocation prior to acceptance, the offer is terminated. Any purported acceptance after receipt of a revocation merely operates as a new offer (counteroffer), which the original offeror may accept or reject. The revocation need not in every instance be communicated by the offeror to the offeree in order to be effective. A communication to the offeree's agent is normally effective.

C A S E   E X A M P L E

Behee made a written offer to the Smiths to purchase their real estate for $42,500 plus $250 for a dinner bell and flower pots. The offer was mailed on March 3. The Smiths signed the proposed agreement. Before Behee was notified of the acceptance, he withdrew the offer by notifying the Smiths' real estate agent.

The Missouri Court of Appeals held that the withdrawal was an effective revocation of his offer, because "an offeror may withdraw his offer at any time before acceptance and communication of that fact to him. . . . Notice to the agent, within the scope of the agent's authority, is notice to the principal. . . ." *Hendricks v. Behee, 786 S.W.2d 610 (Mo. Ct. App. 1990).*

Sometimes a revocation is implied. An implied revocation occurs when the offeree learns from a reliable source that the offeror has acted in a manner incompatible with the outstanding offer.

C A S E   E X A M P L E

Frank makes a valid offer in writing to Dale to sell his residence to Dale. Before Dale accepts, Dale learns from Jackie, Frank's agent, that Perry purchased Frank's property. The communication of such information to Dale results in an implied revocation of Frank's offer. See *Dickinson v. Dodds, 2 Ch. D. 463 (1876).*

Rejection. An offeree may simply reject an offer by communicating to the offeror a refusal to accept the offer. If the offeree makes a counteroffer, an implied rejection of the offer results. An offeree who communicates a rejection of an offer and then decides to accept the offer has actually rejected the offer. The purported acceptance merely results in a counteroffer, which the original offeror is free to accept or reject.

> ### CASE EXAMPLE
>
> Mr. and Mrs. Leavey owned the Hereford Ranch in Wyoming. They desired to sell the ranch. Edward Murray, a real estate broker, learned the ranch was for sale and actively looked for buyers. Verne Woods and A. Trautwein were interested in purchasing the property for $2,300,000. After negotiations, the Leaveys made an offer that was communicated by Murray to Woods and Trautwein. Woods and Trautwein signed the agreement but attached three material amendments to the instrument. The Leaveys refused to accept the agreement with the amendments because "they changed the whole deal." After learning of the Leaveys' refusal to accept the amendments, Trautwein advised Mr. Leavey that the amendments were removed and the original offer acceptable. The Leaveys refused to sell the property to Woods and Trautwein, who sued for breach of contract. The court held that the Woods-Trautwein amendments constituted a rejection of the Leaveys' offer, which terminated the offer. Consequently, the subsequent assent to remove the amendments did not result in a contract. *Trautwein v. Leavey, 472 P.2d 776 (Wyo. 1970).*

Lapse of Reasonable Time. An offeror may specify an expiration date for an offer. A purported acceptance after the specified date is ineffective. If no date is specified, then the offer lapses after a reasonable period of time. What is considered reasonable varies from case to case, depending on the circumstances. In general, however, an offer to purchase realty will not expire as rapidly as, for example, an offer to purchase shares of stock because the price of stock normally fluctuates more rapidly than that of realty.

Destruction of the Subject Matter. Destruction of the subject matter of the offer before acceptance results in a termination of the offer. If a seller offers to sell land and the house on it to a prospective purchaser, the offer will automatically terminate, before acceptance, upon the destruction of the house. This would be true even if the prospective purchaser was unaware of the destruction. (Nevertheless, a *contract,* as distinguished from an *offer,* does not necessarily terminate because of the destruction of the subject matter.) Obviously, one who willfully destroys the subject matter of the contract will not be excused from performance but will be liable for damages. Normally, the contract specifies who bears the loss in the event the property is destroyed by accident.

Death of the Offeror. Death of the offeror results in a termination of the offer whether the offeree knows of the death or not. If the offeree accepts the offer and then the offeror dies, a contract exists. Death will normally not excuse performance of one's contractual obligation unless the performance involves personal services. If a seller who was bound under a purchase contract to sell realty dies, the seller's representative, pursuant to probate law, is required to execute a good deed conveying the property to the buyer. If the buyer dies, the purchase price will be paid out of the proceeds of his or her estate, and the seller will convey the deed directly to the buyer's estate, heirs or next of kin, as the law provides.

Insanity of the Offeror. An offer terminates before acceptance in the event the offeror becomes insane. Otherwise, the offeror would be at a disadvantage because an insane person (like a deceased person) does not possess the faculties necessary to decide to revoke an offer. A contract for the sale of realty, however, is not affected should a party become insane after entering the contract; the guardian or other representative of the insane person is required to perform.

Illegality of the Subject Matter. A change in the law may cause an offer that was legal when made to become illegal. Such a change causes an offer to terminate. Assume, for example, that a corporation offers to spray fruit groves. Thereafter, a law is passed that prohibits the particular "spray" that is required under the contract. The offer would automatically terminate due to illegality. Similarly, a valid contract that later becomes illegal due to a change in law is generally unenforceable.

ACCEPTANCE

◆ **Assent to the terms of an offer.**

Acceptance is the second component of the agreement. The offeree has the power to create a contract merely by communicating an acceptance. The offeree does not have the authority to modify the terms of a proposal. As mentioned earlier, should the offeree change the terms of the offer, the variation creates a *counteroffer,* which actually constitutes a rejection of the original offer. The original offeror may then reject or accept the counteroffer.

At times an offeree appears to add terms to an offer when in fact the new terms were implied within the original offer. In such a case the purported terms will not defeat the acceptance.

CASE EXAMPLE

Allen offers to sell Solid Rock to Baldoro for $70,000. Baldoro responds by saying, "I accept, provided the title is good." Since the law implies in Allen's offer that Allen will tender good title, Baldoro has added no new terms and the acceptance is valid.

The offer and the acceptance constitute the agreement. It may not always be feasible or possible to determine which party made the offer and which party accepted. In many instances, after final negotiations, the entire agreement is reduced to writing. Both parties then sign the agreement. It is only academic in such a case to break the agreement down to the offer and acceptance components. However, the party who signed first could be considered the offeror and the second signer the offeree. In reality this is not always true, since a contract may have resulted prior to the signing of the agreement. In such a case the signing is merely the evidence of the oral agreement.

Manifest Intent. Courts often articulate that no agreement exists without a "meeting of the minds." This subjective test requires an examination of the inner psyche of each of the parties, which is, of course, impractical and usually impossible. The more acceptable approach is the *objective test,* one that is designed to determine whether the parties manifested an *intent* to be bound. Regardless of the mind of the offeror, if a reasonable offeree believes an offer to have been communicated seriously, then an acceptance of the offer ripens into a contract. This is true even when the offer was made in excitement, or jest, as contended in the following case.

LUCY V. ZEHMER
Supreme Court of Virginia
196 Va. 493, 84 S.E. 2d 516 (1954)

BACKGROUND. Mr. Lucy sought to purchase the Ferguson Farm from its owners, the Zehmers. He made contact with them at a restaurant Mr. Zehmer operated. Lucy said, "I bet you wouldn't take $50,000 for [the farm]." Zehmer replied, "Yes, I would too; you wouldn't give fifty." Lucy asked Zehmer to write up the agreement. On the back of a restaurant check Zehmer wrote, "We do hereby agree to sell to W.O. Lucy the Ferguson Farm for $50,000 complete." It was signed by Mr. and Mrs. Zehmer. Both Lucy and Zehmer had been drinking.

The Zehmers attempted to back out of the transaction contending that the agreement was signed in jest. W. O. Lucy and J. C. Lucy, husband and wife, sued A. H. Zehmer and Ida S. Zehmer for specific performance of the contract. The trial court found in favor of the defendants, the Zehmers.

DECISION. Supreme Court of Virginia reversed and remanded the case to the trial court, ordering specific performance of the contract in favor of the plaintiffs, the Lucys.

JUSTICE BUCHANAN. In his testimony Zehmer claimed that he "was high as a Georgia pine," and that the transaction "was just a bunch of two doggoned drunks bluffing to see who could talk the biggest and say the most." ... [This] is contradicted by other evidence as to

the condition of both parties, and rendered of no weight by the testimony of his wife that when Lucy left the restaurant she suggested that Zehmer drive him home. The record is convincing that Zehmer was not intoxicated to the extent of being unable to comprehend the nature and consequences of the instrument he executed, and hence that instrument is not to be invalidated on that ground. . . .

The appearance of the contract, the fact that it was under discussion for forty minutes or more before it was signed; Lucy's objection to the first draft because it was written in the singular, and he wanted Mrs. Zehmer to sign it also; the rewriting to meet that objection and the signing by Mrs. Zehmer; the discussion of what was to be included in the sale; the provision for the examination of the title; the completeness of the instrument that was executed; the taking possession of it by Lucy with no request or suggestion by either of the defendants that he give it back, are facts which furnish persuasive evidence that the execution of the contract was a serious business transaction rather than a casual, jesting matter as defendants now contend.

If it be assumed, contrary to what we think the evidence shows, that Zehmer was jesting about selling his farm to Lucy and that the transaction was intended by him to be a joke, nevertheless the evidence shows that Lucy did

> **CASE EXAMPLE**
>
> Burnside promises to pay Yerkes $25,000 for Needleacre, and Yerkes promises to sell Needleacre to Burnside for $25,000. All the material details of the contract are reduced to writing. Since there is a promise for a promise, a bilateral contract exists. Each promise is supported by consideration supplied by the other's promise.

An *act* may constitute good consideration for a promise. If the promisor is bargaining for the act, the performance of the act usually constitutes a legal benefit to the promisor as well as a legal detriment to the promisee. Such a contract is termed *unilateral* because there is only one promise.

> **CASE EXAMPLE**
>
> Burnside promises to convey Needleacre to Johannes if Johannes cares for Burnside's mother for her life. Johannes cares for Burnside's mother for her life. Since there is a promise for an act, the contract is unilateral. The act is sufficient consideration to support Burnside's promise since it was bargained for and results in a detriment to Johannes.

Consideration also may take the form of a *forbearance*. Such a contract is also unilateral, since there is only one promise.

> **CASE EXAMPLE**
>
> Burnside promises to convey Needleacre to Lasser if Lasser refrains from smoking for ten years. Lasser refrains. Since there is a promise for a forbearance, the contract is unilateral. The forbearance is sufficient consideration to support the promise since it was bargained for and results in a detriment to Lasser. See *Hamer v. Sidway, 124 N.Y. 538, 27 N.E. 256 (1891).*

In a unilateral contract, the act or forbearance constitutes both the consideration and the acceptance. If the promisor is looking for a promise and receives an act, the act does not constitute sufficient consideration because it was not "bargained for and given in exchange." Similarly, in the event the promisor is looking for an act, a return promise is insufficient consideration.

Promissory Estoppel. *Promissory estoppel* is a doctrine that prevents a party from denying that a promise is supported by consideration. The doctrine of promissory estoppel is applicable when no consideration exists, but it is necessary to enforce a promise in order to prevent an injustice. The following elements must also be present: (1) a promise calculated to induce reliance, (2) actual justified reliance by the promisee and (3) injury.

> ### CASE EXAMPLE
>
> Montrasor is in arrears on her mortgage payments and requests additional time from the mortgagee to permit her to pay the arrearage. The mortgagee extends the time by 90 days. There is no consideration to support the promise to extend. Thirty days thereafter Montrasor makes substantial improvements to the property in reliance on the mortgagee's promise. The mortgagee files an action in foreclosure prior to the expiration of the 90 days. Since the ingredients of promissory estoppel are present, the mortgagee's promise not to foreclose for 90 days is enforceable.

LAWFUL PURPOSE

A contract must have a legal purpose. For example, a landlord-tenant lease that states that the purpose is for gambling would be unlawful. Any contract that runs afoul of a statute or public policy is illegal and hence void.

A party to an illegal bargain will not normally be assisted by the courts. Simply, the courts will leave the parties in the same position as they are found. There are, however, some exceptions to this rule.

Sometimes the parties to the contract are not deemed to be *in pari delicto*—that is, not at equal fault. A landlord who lets property to a tenant who uses the property to traffic drugs may be innocent of the illegal purpose for which the property was intended. In that instance, the courts aid the innocent party in the collection of the rents. An elderly man who is tricked out of his real estate or other property will be protected in many jurisdictions regardless of the fact that he was a willing participant in an unscrupulous scheme.

When a contract involves an illegal provision, the courts may excise that portion and enforce the remainder of the contract. However, if the illegal provision is so interconnected with the whole as to render it nonseverable, the entire contract will be rendered void.

A number of states have passed civil forfeiture statutes that authorize the government to confiscate property that has facilitated the commission of a crime. The following case decided by the United States Supreme Court considers the constitutionality of such statutes.

AUSTIN V. UNITED STATES

Supreme Court of the United States
509 U.S. 602 (1993)

BACKGROUND. After a state court sentenced Austin on his guilty plea to one count of possessing cocaine with intent to distribute in violation of South Dakota law, the United States filed an action in Federal District Court against his mobile home and auto body shop under a statute that provides for the forfeiture of real property used, or intended to be used, to

> **C A S E   E X A M P L E**
>
> Walter and Thelma Terry entered into a contract to sell real property to William and Shirley Born, husband and wife. The Borns agreed to pay the purchase price in monthly installments over a specified period of years. A provision within the contract stated that the contract was "not assignable nor [could] the buyer convey the property without the seller's written consent." The Borns subsequently contracted to assign the contract to Rollins without the Terrys' consent. The Terrys commenced an action against the Borns seeking forfeiture of the contract. The appellate court held that the provisions prohibiting assignment were unreasonable restraints on trade unless necessary to protect the sellers' security. The case was returned to the trial court to determine whether the Terrys' security would be impaired by the Borns' conveyance to Rollins. *Terry v. Born, 24 Wash. App. 652, 604 P.2d 504 (1979).*

An assignee is bound to perform the obligations the assignor promised the seller, including payment of the purchase price. Failure to perform on the part of the assignee constitutes a breach of the agreement and results in liability for damages. An assignment does not relieve the assignor from obligations under the contract. In the event that the assignee does not perform, the seller may hold the original purchaser (assignor) responsible to perform in accordance with the agreement.

The seller, as a party to an executory contract, has an equitable interest in the purchase price; the seller has a right to receive the purchase price in accordance with the terms of the contract. The seller may assign the right to receive this purchase price. The same rules that apply to the assignment of a purchaser's rights apply to the assignment of a seller's rights.

BREACH OF CONTRACT

◆ **The unexcused failure to perform an obligation under a contract.**

The failure of a purchaser to tender the purchase price for the property at the appointed time is one example of a breach of contract. Another example is the seller's failure to tender title to the purchaser at the appointed time. Any nonperformance of a term within the contract may give rise to a breach of that contract. The law provides remedies in the event of breach. This serves as an incentive to both parties to live up to the terms of the agreement.

ANTICIPATORY BREACH

◆ **A breach of contract that occurs as a result of repudiating a contract before the due date for performance.**

It is not always necessary to await the day designated for performance to determine that a party is in breach. Sometimes an anticipatory breach occurs. In order to constitute an anticipatory breach, the nonperforming party must clearly communicate to the other party an intention not to perform. Or, an intention not to perform may be clearly determined from a party's behavior.

> **CASE EXAMPLE**
>
> R. Brower, a contractor, agreed to paint John Dooley's home for $2,500. Pursuant to the contract, the work was to begin August 1. Thereafter Brower informed Dooley that he was going out of business and asked him to find someone else to do the work. On July 15, Dooley learned from a reliable source that Brower went out of business, sold all of his equipment and had dishonored all of his existing contracts. Under such a circumstance, Dooley may treat Brower as in anticipatory breach of contract and immediately sue for damages.

SUBSTANTIAL PERFORMANCE

◆ **The amount of compliance under the terms of a contract that discharges a party from further obligation where a party has failed to perform totally under the contract.**

The law recognizes that humans, frail as they are, cannot always perform certain contracts according to the exact specifications. Consequently, if the closing date is set for April 5 and the purchaser desires it to be moved to April 7, the two-day delay does not amount to a material breach, barring a provision in the contract to the contrary or exceptional circumstances. In the area of building contracts, a contractor who builds a home and incurs minor deviations from the specifications may nonetheless have substantially complied with the contractual provisions. In such a case, the contractor will be entitled to the contract price less the cost to remedy the deviations to the property. If, for example, a contractor complies with all the specifications under a $60,000 building contract but fails to paint 3 out of 14 window panels, the contractor is entitled to $60,000 less the cost of having the window panels painted.

> **CASE EXAMPLE**
>
> Thomas Haverty Company entered into a contract with Jones whereby Haverty agreed to build and install plumbing, heating and ventilation equipment in Jones's building for $27,332. The total cost of the building was $186,000. After completion Jones refused to pay a balance of $10,123 to Haverty Company. Jones maintained that Haverty's performance was defective. The company sued Jones for the balance. The trial court held that Haverty's performance deviated from the contract specifications in 12 respects, that 9 could be resolved at a cost of $99, that the remaining 3 defects could not be remedied without a greater expenditure than was justified and that the damage to the building as a result of the three deviations amounted to $2,180. The court found that the deviations were made as a result of mistakes and misinterpretations. Finding that the contract had been substantially performed, the court awarded $7,844 ($10,123 minus $99 and $2,180) to Haverty Company. The appellate court affirmed the decision. *Thomas Haverty Co. v. Jones, 185 Cal. 285, 197 P. 105 (1921).*

There is no substantial performance if the utility of the property or its purpose is significantly affected by the contractor's deviation. If the specifications in the contract called for gas heating and the contractor installed oil heating instead, the deviation would amount to a breach, and the contractor would not be entitled to any compensation. Some courts do, however, permit the contractor to recover the reasonable value of the services rendered and goods supplied where a substantial deviation is not willful.

REMEDIES FOR BREACH OF CONTRACT

Before a party is entitled to a remedy, he or she must show a readiness, willingness and ability to perform the obligations under the contract. A seller must tender (offer) the deed, and a buyer must tender the purchase price, unless it is clear from the circumstances that the tender would be fruitless. The common remedies enjoyed by each party in the event the other breaches the contract are specific performance, rescission, damages and foreclosure.

◆ **Specific Performance.** **A court decree mandating a party to perform according to the contract.**

Specific performance is ordinarily applicable to contracts involving a unique subject matter. Every parcel of real estate is considered unique and irreplaceable. Therefore, should the seller refuse performance, a court may award specific performance requiring the seller to execute a deed in favor of the buyer. Refusal by the seller to comply with the decree may result in contempt of court and punishment. The court may also execute a deed in the buyer's favor, or, in the event of the seller's refusal to perform in accordance with the decree, the very court decree may be deemed to pass title to the buyer. In many jurisdictions specific performance is also available to a seller against a defaulting buyer. A decree of specific performance in such a case compels the purchaser to pay the purchase price and accept title to the property.

A court will grant specific performance only if the party seeking it has "clean hands." If one of the parties has taken advantage of the other's unsound condition, for example, or has been guilty of fraud, the court will deny this equitable relief.

◆ **Rescission.** **Cancellation of a contract that results in the parties being restored to the position they were in before the contract was made.**

A buyer, upon a seller's default, may elect to *rescind* the contract. Under such a remedy, the seller must return to the buyer all payments received. The remedy is especially desirable for the buyer when the real estate has depreciated in value below the contract price. In the event the buyer is in breach of the contract, the seller may elect the remedy of rescission, thus restoring the parties to their original position.

Either party may seek rescission on grounds of fraud, innocent misrepresentation, mistake, duress or undue influence. In addition, a contract may be rescinded by mutual consent of the parties.

◆ **Damages. Money recoverable by one suffering a loss or injury due to breach of the contract.**

A buyer may, for example, incur actual damages when the seller breaches the obligation to tender the deed. The damages may be in the nature of the loss of the bargain. Translated into monetary terms, loss of the bargain is the difference between the market value of the property at the date set for closing and the contract price. That difference represents the value of damages to which the purchaser is entitled, assuming that the market value of the property at the time of breach is greater than the contract price. In addition, damages may include the deposit made by the purchaser and actual costs incurred incidental to the contract. Incidental expenses include attorney fees for handling the purchase transaction as well as the expense related to a title search.

CASE EXAMPLE

Joe Deal, seller, refused to tender his deed to John Tiehl, purchaser, on March 13, the date set for closing. Tiehl had previously paid Deal $5,000 to be applied to the purchase price of $85,000. Tiehl additionally expended $500 for a title search of the property. The market value of the property was $90,000 on March 13. In an action by Tiehl against Deal for damages, Tiehl will be entitled to $5,500, computed as follows: $90,000 (market value) − $85,000 (contract price) = $5,000 + $500 (title search). Tiehl will also be entitled to a return of the $5,000 deposit.

When the buyer breaches the contract, the seller is entitled to retain any deposit the buyer made and to keep the real property. In the event the market value of the property falls in an amount greater than the deposit forfeited, the seller may also sue for damages. Damages in such a case are computed by deducting the market price from the purchase price minus any earnest money payment forfeited to the seller.

A court judgment for damages becomes a general lien on all real property a party owns until the judgment is satisfied. (This is discussed in greater detail in Chapter 16.) As a judgment creditor, a party may foreclose on the real property to satisfy the judgment. Other means of satisfying a judgment can include the attachment and sale of the debtor's personal property and garnishment of his or her wages.

◆ **Liquidated Damages. An amount of money stipulated in a contract that will be awarded in the case of a breach, which amounts are reasonably calculated to approximate the actual damages.**

Some real estate purchase contracts contain a liquidated damage clause that will state, for example, the per diem dollar award in the event of breach. The amount must be reasonably calculated to approximate the actual damages in the event of breach. It may not be a penalty. For example, a buyer may be planning on moving out of an apartment on the day of the closing of a purchased house. In the event that the house does not close due to the breach by the

However, if the contract involves personal services, the rule is different. Assume, for example, that a carpenter agrees to build a tree house. Death of the carpenter will result in a discharge of obligations under the contract because of the personal nature of carpentry services. The same rule holds regarding insanity of a party. A party to a contract who is unable to complete a personal service contract due to insanity is excused from performance.

When a contract that was legal when entered into becomes illegal, the parties are discharged from performance. Suppose, for example, that a contractor enters into a contract with a shipper to transport specified building materials from a foreign country. Should the U.S. government issue an embargo forbidding the transport of goods from that foreign country, the parties will be discharged from their contractual obligations.

Finally, the law has evolved to recognize that certain contracts cannot be performed because it is commercially impracticable to do so. Some courts have discharged parties from their obligations in these types of cases. The impetus for this rule emanates from Section 2-615 of the Uniform Commercial Code, which reads in part:

> Delay in delivery or non-delivery in whole or in part by a seller . . . is not a breach of his duty under a contract for sale if performance as agreed has been made impracticable by the occurrence of a contingency the non-occurrence of which was a basic assumption on which the contract was made. . . .

Courts have not limited this doctrine to the traditional sale of goods cases but have extended it to other cases as well.

CASE EXAMPLE

Northern Corporation entered into a contract with Chugach Electric Association. Under the contract, Northern was to install protective riprap on a dam located on Cooper Lake, Alaska, owned by Chugach. The work required Northern to transport rock and install it on the face of the dam.

The contract was silent as to the method for transporting the rock to the dam site. Apparently the parties contemplated that it would be transported across the frozen lake during the coming winter.

Attempts to haul the rock across the ice were frustrated by the unsafe condition of the ice. On one occasion two trucks broke through the ice, resulting in the drivers' deaths.

Northern ceased performance and sought a ruling discharging it from any further obligations under the contract. Chugach countersued, seeking damages for breach of contract. In upholding the trial court's ruling in favor of Northern, the Supreme Court of Alaska said:

(Continued)

> Under [the doctrine of commercial impracticality], a party is discharged from his contractual obligations, even if it is technically possible to perform them, if the cost of performance would be so disproportionate to that reasonably contemplated by the parties as to make the contract totally impractical in a commercial sense. . . .
>
> [The concept of commercial impracticality]—which finds expression both in case law and in other authorities—is predicated upon the assumption that in legal contemplation something is impractical when it can only be done at an excessive and unreasonable cost. . . .
>
> There is ample evidence to support [the findings that] "the ice haul method of transporting riprap was within the contemplation of the parties and was part of the basis of the agreement which ultimately resulted in the contract amendment," and that that method was not commercially feasible within the financial parameters of the contract. . . .
>
> *Northern Corporation v. Chugach Electric Association, 518 P.2d 76 (Alaska 1974).*

REVIEW AND DISCUSSION QUESTIONS

1. (a) Which agreements will a court enforce? (b) Which agreements will a court not enforce? (c) Why?

2. Name five elements of a contract and define each.

3. Explain the rationale behind the objective test of contract formation.

4. Give an example of when the doctrine of promissory estoppel will be applied.

5. When does a breach of contract occur? What is the consequence of a breach of contract?

6. (a) Explain the remedies available to a buyer when the seller breaches the contract for the sale of real property. (b) Explain the remedies available to the seller in the event of the buyer's breach.

7. Name ways in which parties to a contract may be discharged from their obligation to perform by operation of law.

CASE PROBLEMS

1. Burns and Pugmire entered into a contract for the sale and purchase of real estate. The contract stated that the purchase price was $79,500, to be paid in installments of $675 per month, including taxes and insurance for the contract "period remaining, or until buyer elects to refinance." The contract was silent as to the closing date, which party was to pay closing costs and when transfer of title and delivery of a deed would take place. Is this agreement sufficiently definite and certain? Explain. *Burns v. Pugmire, 194 Ga. App. 898, 392 S.E.2d 62 (1990).*

2. The Bakers made a written offer to purchase Nelson's home. Nelson was unhappy with the down payment provision and formulated an addendum which was added to the Bakers' original offer and returned to them. The Bakers signed it. Nelson then purported to accept

11

Real Estate Purchase Contract

The earlier chapter on basic contract law (Chapter 10) provided the background necessary for a specific look at real estate purchase contracts. The purchase contract is the instrument that legally obligates the buyer and seller to perform. Normally, the total understanding of the parties is contained within that agreement. Consequently, the conduct of the parties will be largely dictated by its terms. For that reason, careful attention to the form and substance of the real estate contract is important. This chapter details the prerequisites for a valid real estate purchase contract and the provisions customarily contained in that contract.

REAL ESTATE PURCHASE CONTRACT

◆ **An agreement whereby a seller promises to sell an interest in realty by conveying a deed to the designated estate for which a buyer promises to pay a specified purchase price.**

Generally, contracts need not be in writing to be enforceable. Real estate purchase contracts, however, fall within a unique class of contracts that necessitate a writing. They are governed by the Statute of Frauds.

STATUTE OF FRAUDS

◆ **A statute that necessitates that certain contracts, in order to be enforceable, must be supported by a written memorandum and signed by the party against whom enforcement is sought.**

The British Parliament enacted the Statute of Frauds in 1677. This statute modified the common law that enforced oral contracts for the sale of real estate. The Statute of Frauds was intended to protect against fraud and perjury. Prior to the Statute of Frauds, it was not uncommon for a person to pay witnesses to fabricate testimony to support a nonexistent oral contract for the sale of realty. Section 4 of the statute required a contract for the sale of an interest in land to be in writing, or supported by a written memorandum, and signed by the party to be charged. Nearly every state has modeled its version of a statute of frauds after the English statute. The Ohio statute, for example, reads in part:

> No lease, estate, or interest, either of freehold or term of years, in lands . . . shall be assigned or granted except by deed, or note in writing, signed by the party assigning or granting it, or his agent thereto lawfully authorized. . . .

CASE EXAMPLE

Wayne Gibbens and Mark Hardin entered into a joint effort to purchase three parcels of real estate. A purchase offer of $2.4 million for the property was accepted. Gibbens claimed that there was an oral agreement that required Hardin to make a 3.075 acre boundary adjustment to the property in favor of Gibbens. Gibbens would receive the two houses located on Parcel #3 and an easement of access to one of the houses. Hardin denied this. The Supreme Court of Virginia found "[t]he alleged oral boundary agreement . . . unenforceable because it fails to comply with Virginia's statute of frauds." *Gibbens v. Hardin, 389 S.E.2d 478 (Va. 1990).*

◆ **Memorandum.** **A writing that contains essential terms in satisfaction of the Statute of Frauds.**

Normally, the entire agreement of the parties—the real estate purchase contract—is reduced to writing. This writing will, of course, satisfy the memorandum requirement of the Statute of Frauds. The entire agreement of the parties need not be in writing, however, to satisfy the Statute of Frauds. The statute only requires a written memorandum, which may be the skeleton of the contract. A memorandum must ordinarily contain:

▮ the names of the parties to the contract,

▮ a description of the property,

▮ the purchase price,

▮ other essential terms and conditions of the sale, and

▮ the signature of the party against whom enforcement is sought (a few states also require the signature of the party seeking to enforce the transaction).

The memorandum may be prepared anytime before suit on the contract is commenced. Loss or destruction of the memorandum does not render the contract unenforceable. In such a case, the existence of the memorandum may be proved by witnesses or other documents. In most jurisdictions the Statute of Frauds is deemed waived unless it is pleaded as a defense in court. The memorandum need not be contained within one instrument. It may be gleaned from a series of related writings, such as letters or faxes. Or, as in the next case, an ordinary check may satisfy the statute.

CLARENCE V. LARKIN

Supreme Court of Kansas
172 Kan. 284, 239 P.2d 970 (Kansas 1952)

BACKGROUND. Plaintiffs, Clark and Musser, are residents of Hutchinson and Kansas City, Missouri, respectively. Defendant is a resident of Wichita. For some time prior to March 31, 1950, plaintiffs were the owners of and were in possession of six lots, known as 405 East A, in the city of Hutchinson. The property was a well-improved tract on a corner of the intersection of Avenue A and Elm Street. Prior to that date, plaintiffs had advertised the property for sale and had placed it in the hands of Scott Clark, husband of one of the plaintiffs, with oral authority to sell. On March 31, 1950, defendant came to Hutchinson for the express purpose of purchasing a residence property, and, through a mutual acquaintance, contacted Scott Clark. Clark and defendant then went to the property, at which time defendant made a careful inspection, including the improvements. They agreed on a purchase price of $17,000—$1,000 to be paid down, $7,000 to be paid on approval of abstract of title, and the balance of $9,000 to be paid in 5 years with interest at the rate of 5 percent per annum. At the suggestion of defendant, he and Clark then went to the latter's office for the purpose of consummating the agreement of purchase and sale. Defendant produced his checkbook on The Security Bank of Blackwell, Oklahoma, and requested Clark to make out a check for the downpayment. Clark did as requested, and defendant signed the check and delivered it to Clark. This check, including notations on it, a copy of which was attached to the amended petition as an exhibit, is as follows:

"No, 45

Blackwell, Oklahoma, Mar. 31, 1950

Pay to the Order of Opal F. Clark $1,000
One Thousand & no/100 DOLLARS

To apply on 405 East 'A' at $ 17,000.00 . . . $ 7,000.00 to be paid on approval of abstract & $9,000.00 to be paid in 5 years at 5 %.

Jon. P. Larkin

To The Security Bank

Blackwell, Oklahoma."

Plaintiffs, in due course of business, deposited the check, properly endorsed, with a bank in Hutchinson. In the meantime defendant caused payment of the check by the Blackwell bank to be stopped. Upon inquiry as to the reason therefor he advised plaintiffs that due to his wife's request and insistence he was refusing to go through with the deal.

Plaintiff sued, and the trial court denied defendant's motion to dismiss.

DECISION. The Kansas Supreme Court affirmed.

JUDGE PRICE. In this court defendant contends, as he did in the court below, that the memorandum (check) is too indefinite and uncertain to take the alleged oral agreement for the sale of the property out of the statute of frauds the pertinent portions of which read as follows:

> "No action shall be brought whereby to charge a party upon . . . any contract for the sale of lands, tenements, or hereditaments, or any interest in or concerning them; . . . unless the agreement upon which such action shall be

brought, or some memorandum or note thereof, shall be in writing and signed by the party to be charged therewith, ... "

The general rule as to the sufficiency of a written memorandum to meet the requirement of the statute is as follows:

"Generally speaking, a memorandum in writing meets the requirements of the statute of frauds that certain contracts shall be evidenced by writing if it contains the names of the parties, the terms and conditions of the contract, and a description of the property sufficient to render it capable of identification."

On the question whether a check may constitute a sufficient memorandum under the statute ... a check, given in connection with the sale of lands, bearing notations or references to papers or matters which, by the rules of contract and evidence, may properly be deemed a part thereof, and which contains the essential terms of the contract of sale, is sufficient.

In the nature of things and in the light of common, everyday business dealings, the check and notations upon it clearly indicate that defendant, as maker, was purchasing from payee, as owner, certain real estate described as "405 East 'A'," for the sum of $17,000; that the amount of the check ($1,000) was a down payment; that the sum of $7,000 was to be paid upon approval of the abstract of title; and that the balance of $9,000 was to be paid in five years with interest on such latter sum at the rate of 5 percent. The names of the parties, as payee and maker of the check, are thus designated as seller and purchaser, respectively, with no uncertainty. There is nothing left to conjecture or speculation with respect to the purchase price, the amount being paid down, or as to when the balance of $16,000 was to be paid. To place any other construction on the instrument would do violence to the plain and ordinary meaning of the very language used.

Defendant strenuously argues that the location and identity of the property are not given with reasonable certainty, and that on account of the check being given on a Blackwell, Oklahoma, bank it is logical to assume the property is located in that city. It is true that nowhere on the check and its notation is the location of the property, as to city, county or state, listed.

On the other hand, it is to be remembered that by the allegations of the amended petition the property is specifically described as being located on a corner of the intersection of Avenue A and Elm Street in the city of Hutchinson, known as 405 East A. It is further alleged that it was the only real estate owned by plaintiffs known and described as 405 East A; that it was the only tract with that description placed for sale with Scott Clark, and that defendant personally inspected the same.

We think that under the above rules there can be no question but that the description of the property as "405 East A" is sufficient to satisfy the statute. It cannot be said defendant is being in any way misled by the use of that description. He knew exactly the property for which he was bargaining, and that it was the property described by its street address on the check. The statute of frauds was enacted to prevent fraud and injustice, not to foster or encourage it, and courts will, so far as possible, refuse to allow it to be used as a shield to protect fraud and as a means to enable one to take advantage of his own wrong.

Holding as we do, that the memorandum in question is a sufficient compliance with the statute of frauds, the court did not err in [failing to dismiss the plaintiff's Complaint] and its ruling is therefore ...

AFFIRMED.

Party Against Whom Enforcement Is Sought. In many jurisdictions a contract for the sale of real estate may be enforced only against the party who signed the memorandum. Consequently, it is very possible that a purchaser of a parcel of real estate may not be legally able to enforce the contract against the seller, while the seller may be legally able to enforce the contract against the purchaser. The reverse is also true.

CASE EXAMPLE

Bill Barley, seller, contracts with John Harley, buyer, for the sale of Lodgeacre, with complete details of the sale contained in a writing. Barley signs the writing, but Harley neglects to sign. The contract is enforceable against Barley but not against Harley, because Harley failed to sign the writing.

The best way to ensure compliance with the Statute of Frauds is to require that all parties sign the real estate purchase contract. Although the entire agreement of the parties need not be reduced to writing, as a practical matter it is best to do so. This prevents uncertainty and provides a controlling document to resolve disputes.

Part Performance. There are certain exceptions to compliance with the Statute of Frauds. The most notable exception is the doctrine of *part performance*. There are various views as to what constitutes an act of part performance sufficient to remove a contract from the Statute of Frauds so that a writing will not be required. Some courts take the position that part performance is satisfied if a purchaser takes possession pursuant to an oral contract. Other courts require both possession and payment of the purchase price to prevent the seller from raising the defense of the statute. Still others require that possession be accompanied by a substantial improvement to the property. Finally, other jurisdictions limit the scope of the doctrine of part performance by requiring payment of the purchase price, the purchaser's possession and a change of position in reliance on the contract that would result in irreparable harm unless the contract were enforced.

CASE EXAMPLE

Brown entered into an oral contract to purchase a farm from Burnside. Brown took possession of the farm, made several improvements, tore down an old farmhouse, paid taxes and made payments on the purchase price. Burnside thereafter refused to deed the farm to Brown. Brown sought specific performance of the contract. The court held for Brown on the theory that the Statute of Frauds does not apply when there has been partial or complete performance, as under these circumstances. *Brown v. Burnside, 94 Idaho 363, 487 P.2d 957 (1972).*

PAROL EVIDENCE
◆ **Oral or other evidence extraneous to the written instrument.**

Parol evidence is not admissible for the purpose of varying or contradicting the terms of a contract. Parol evidence is permissible if:

■ it is consistent with the writings of the parties.

■ its purpose is to clarify ambiguous terms in the contract or prove that the writing was induced by fraud, illegality, duress, undue influence or mistake.

■ it is a subsequent agreement that alters the previous writings.

CASE EXAMPLE

Jim Hutchins and Jerry Bolen enter into a real estate contract for the sale of Hutchins's property. Afterward they enter into a contract canceling the prior real estate contract. The introduction into evidence of the new contract containing the cancellation does not violate the parol evidence rule, since it was entered into after the purchase contract.

BROKERS' AUTHORITY

Many localities use preprinted purchase contract forms that have been approved by the local attorney bar association and the association of real estate brokers. The provisions within these form contracts are designed to reflect the practices within the locality. Normally, the broker assists the parties in filling in the blanks in such a contract, including the names of the parties, a description of the property, the price and such,. A standard real estate purchase contract is shown in Figure 11.1. Sometimes it is necessary to delete certain inapplicable provisions from the form. Often lengthy additions are necessitated by the particular nature of the transaction. To what extent a broker may prepare a purchase contract without engaging in the offense of unauthorized practice of law differs from state to state. Some states prevent a broker from drafting a purchase contract because that act constitutes the practice of law. Other states permit such brokerage activity on the theory that it is normally incident to the practice of a broker's profession. Although most states permit brokers to fill in the blanks, there is often a thin line between filling in the blanks and drafting.

CULTUM v. HERITAGE HOUSE REALTORS, INC.
Supreme Court of Washington
694 P.2d 630 (Wash. 1985)

BACKGROUND. Yvonne Ramey, a real estate agent for Heritage House Realtors, Inc. (Heritage), prepared a real estate purchase contract (earnest money agreement), setting forth Cultum's offer to purchase Smith's home. The agreement was prepared on standard forms drafted by attorneys. Ramey filled in the blanks and also prepared an addendum which stated:

"This offer is contingent on a Satisfactory Structural Inspection, to be completed by Aug. 20...." The Smiths accepted the offer. Based upon the inspection report Cultum found the condition of the house unsatisfactory. He demanded return of a $3,000 deposit. Heritage refunded the money and Cultum sued Heritage for loss of use of the money during the period Heritage held it, and sought a permanent injunction restraining Heritage from engaging in the practice of law.

DECISION. The trial court found in favor of Cultum, holding that Heritage engaged in the unauthorized practice of law and it granted damages and permanently enjoined Heritage from "completing, filling in the blanks, or otherwise preparing any clause with respect to any real estate purchase or sale agreement...." The Supreme Court of Washington affirmed the damage award but found that Heritage was not engaged in unauthorized practice of law.

JUSTICE PEARSON. At issue in this appeal is whether the completion by a real estate salesperson of a form earnest money agreement containing a contingency clause constitutes the unauthorized practice of law....

...

[A]lthough the completion of form earnest money agreements might be commonly understood as the practice of law, we believe it is in the public interest to permit licensed real estate brokers and salespersons to complete such lawyer prepared standard form agreements; provided, that in doing so they comply with the standard of care demanded of an attorney.

For a long time suppression of the practice of law by nonlawyers has been proclaimed to be in the public interest, a necessary protection against incompetence, divided loyalties, and other evils. It is now clear, however, as several other courts have concluded, that there are other important interests involved. These interests include:

(1) The ready availability of legal services.

(2) Using the full range of services that other professions and businesses can provide.

(3) Limiting costs.

(4) Public convenience.

(5) Allowing licensed brokers and salespersons to participate in an activity in which they have special training and expertise.

(6) The interest of brokers and salespersons in drafting form earnest money agreements which are incidental and necessary to the main business of brokers and salespersons.

We no longer believe that the supposed benefit to the public from the lawyers' monopoly on performing legal services justifies limiting the public's freedom of choice. The public has the right to use the full range of services that brokers and salespersons can provide. The fact that brokers will complete these forms at no extra charge, whereas attorneys would charge an additional fee, weighs heavily toward allowing this choice.

Another important consideration is the fact that the drafting of form earnest money agreements is incidental to the main business of real estate brokers and salespersons. These individuals are specially trained to provide buyers and sellers with competent and efficient assistance in purchasing or selling a home. Because the selection and filling in of standard simple forms by brokers and salespersons is an incidental service, it normally must be rendered before such individuals can receive their commissions. Clearly the advantages, if any, to be derived by enjoining brokers and salespersons from completing earnest money agreements are outweighed by the fact that such conveyances are part of the everyday business of the realtor and necessary to the effective completion of such business.

The interest of protecting the public must also be balanced against the inconveniences caused by enjoining licensed brokers and salespersons from completing form earnest money agreements. Although lawyers are also competent to handle these transactions, lawyers may not always be available at the odd hours that these transactions tend to take place. . . .

In a few instances earnest money agreements may be complicated and one or both parties may realize the need for a lawyer to prepare the contract rather than use a standardized form. In fact, if a broker or salesperson believes there may be complicated legal issues involved, he or she should persuade the parties to seek legal advice. More often, however, these transactions are simple enough so that standardized forms will suffice and the parties will wish to avoid further delay or expense by using them.

It should be emphasized that the holding in this case is limited in scope. Our decision provides that a real estate broker or salesperson is permitted to complete simple printed standardized real estate forms . . . approved by a lawyer. . . . These forms shall not be used for other than simple real estate transactions actually handled by such broker . . . or salesperson and then without charge for the simple service of completing the forms.

The trial court awarded Cultum damages . . . representing the interest lost during the time that Heritage retained her earnest money. If a real estate broker fails to exercise reasonable care and skill, the real estate broker is liable to the client for damages resulting from such failure. Based on this rule and our conclusion that Ramey failed to exercise the reasonable care and skill of a practicing attorney, we affirm the trial court's award of damages. . . .

AFFIRMED IN PART AND REVERSED IN PART.

A broker should exercise caution when rendering advice to a party or giving detailed explanation of the terms of the contract; these activities may be deemed the unauthorized practice of law.

PROVISIONS OF THE REAL ESTATE PURCHASE CONTRACT

It is important to note that, in addition to the essential elements of a basic contract—offer, acceptance, consideration, capacity, lawful purpose—there are major provisions peculiar to a real estate purchase contract. Some of these provisions included within the real estate purchase agreement are there to satisfy the Statute of Frauds. Others are present to clarify the details of the agreement. Common real estate contract provisions include the date, the names of parties and other elements presented on the following pages.

FIGURE 11.1 *Real Estate Purchase Contract*

Real Estate Purchase Contract
Adopted by The Columbus Board of Realtors
and by The Columbus Bar Association

REALTOR®

It is recommended that all parties
be represented by legal counsel

_____, 19____

The undersigned Buyer agrees to buy and the undersigned Seller agrees to sell, through you as Broker, upon the terms hereinafter set forth, the following real estate

located in the State of Ohio, County of _____

1. On the following terms:

2. Possession:

3. Evidence of Title: Seller shall furnish and pay for an owner's title insurance commitment and policy [ALTA Form B (1970 REV. 10-17-70 & REV. 10-17-84)] in the amount of the purchase price, with copy of subdivision or condominium plat. The title evidence shall be certified to within 30 days prior to closing with endorsement as of 8:00 A.M. on the business day prior to the date of closing, all in accordance with the standards of the Columbus Bar Association, and shall show in Seller marketable title in fee simple free and clear of all liens and encumbrances except: (a) those created by or assumed by Buyer; (b) those specifically set forth in this contract; (c) zoning ordinances; (d) legal highways; and (e) covenants, restrictions, conditions and easements of record which do not unreasonably interfere with present lawful use. Buyer shall pay any additional costs incurred in connection with mortgage insurance issued for the protection of Buyer's lender. If Buyer desires a survey, Buyer shall pay the cost thereof.
If title to all or part of the real estate is unmarketable, as determined by Ohio law with reference to the Ohio State Bar Association's Standards of Title Examination, or is subject to liens, encumbrances, easements, conditions, restrictions or encroachments other than those excepted in this contract, Seller shall within thirty (30) days after written notice thereof, remedy or remove any such defect, lien, encumbrance, easement, condition, restriction or encroachment or obtain title insurance without exception therefor. At closing Seller shall sign an affidavit with respect to off-record title matters in accordance with the community custom.

4. Deed: Seller shall convey to Buyer marketable title in fee simple by transferable and recordable general warranty deed, with release of dower, if any, or fiduciary deed, as appropriate, free and clear of all liens and encumbrances not excepted by this contract, and excepting the following:

5. Taxes and Assessments: At closing, Seller shall pay or credit on purchase price all delinquent taxes, including penalty and interest, all assessments which are a lien on the date of contract and all agricultural use tax recoupments for years prior to the year of closing. At closing, Seller shall also pay or credit on the purchase price all other unpaid real estate taxes which are a lien for years prior to closing and a portion of such taxes and agricultural use tax recoupments for year of closing prorated through date of closing and based on 365 day year and, if undetermined, on most recent available tax rate and valuation, giving effect to applicable exemptions, recently voted millage, change in valuation, etc., whether or not certified.
Seller warrants that no improvements or services (site or area) have been installed or furnished, or notification received from public authority or owners' association of future improvements of which any part of the costs may be assessed against the real estate, except the following:

_____ (None, if nothing inserted.)

6. Rentals, Interest, Condominium Charges, Insurance, Utilities and Security Deposits: Adjustments shall be made through date of closing for: (a) rentals; (b) interest on any mortgage assumed by Buyer; (c) condominium or other association periodic charges; and (d) transferable insurance policies, if Buyer so elects. Seller shall pay, through date of possession, all accrued utility charges and any other charges that are or may become a lien. Security deposits shall be transferred to Buyer.

7. Damage or Destruction of Property: Risk of loss to the real estate and appurtenances shall be borne by Seller until closing provided that if any property covered by this contract shall be substantially damaged or destroyed before this transaction is closed, Buyer may (a) proceed with the transaction and be entitled to all insurance money, if any, payable to Seller under all policies covering the property, or (b) rescind the contract, and thereby release all parties from liability hereunder, by giving written notice to Seller and Broker within ten (10) days after Buyer has written notice of such damage or destruction. Failure by Buyer to so notify Seller and Broker shall constitute an election to proceed with the transaction.

FIGURE 11.1 *Real Estate Purchase Contract (Continued)*

8. **Fixtures and Equipment:** The consideration shall include any fixtures, including but not limited to: built-in appliances; heating; central air conditioning; and humidifying equipment and their control apparatus; stationary tubs; pumps; water softening equipment (unless leased); roof antennae; attached wall-to-wall carpeting and attached floor coverings; curtain rods and window coverings excluding draperies and curtains; attached mirrors; light, bathroom and lavatory fixtures; storm and screen doors and windows, awnings, blinds, and window air conditioners, whether now in or on the premises or in storage; garage door openers and controls; attached fireplace equipment; security systems and controls (unless leased), smoke alarms; satellite TV reception system and components; all exterior plants and trees; and the following:

The following shall be excluded:

9. **Inspections:** Before closing, Seller shall furnish and pay for: (a) a report on FHA/VA approved form, by an Ohio Certified Pest (Termite) Control Applicator stating whether based upon an inspection of the areas visible or accessible, the inspector discovered any evidence of infestation or damage by termites. Infestation and resulting damage by termites or other wood destroying insects shall be treated and repaired at Seller's expense, provided that if the cost of repair exceeds 1% of the purchase price, Seller may terminate this contract unless Buyer agrees to pay the cost of such repair in excess of 1% of the purchase price; (b) a written guaranty from a gas line repair company or a licensed plumber, guaranteeing the non-existence of gas leaks at the time of transfer of gas service to Buyer, including all repairs and alterations to gas lines, valves, meters not owned by the local natural gas distribution company, vents, connected gas appliances sold with the premises, and restoration of premises (excluding grass, shrubs & trees,) necessary to accomplish the transfer; and (c) a written health department report showing in essence that the water from the primary water supply, other than that provided by a municipality or water supply utility or company, is bacterially safe and that any individual sewage disposal system is in operating condition. Seller warrants that at time of closing, water is available in sufficient quantities for ordinary household purposes.

10. **Property Inspection:** (Not applicable if number of days not inserted.) Buyer, at Buyer's expense, shall have _____ days after the acceptance hereof to have the property and all improvements, fixtures and equipment inspected. Seller shall cooperate in making the property reasonably available for such inspection(s). If Buyer is not, in good faith, satisfied with the condition of the property as disclosed by such inspection(s), Buyer may terminate this contract by delivering written notice of such termination to Seller, along with a written copy of such inspection report(s), within the time period specified above, which notice and report(s) shall specify the unsatisfactory conditions. Failure of Buyer to so deliver written notice and copy of the inspection report(s) within such time period shall constitute a waiver of Buyer's right to terminate pursuant to this provision.

11. **Home Maintenance Plan:** Seller, at Seller's expense, shall provide _____ (Not applicable if plan name not inserted.)

12. **Deposit:** Buyer has deposited with Broker the sum receipted for below, which shall be returned to Buyer, upon Buyer's request, if no contract shall have been entered into. Upon acceptance of this contract by both parties, Broker shall deposit such amount in its trust account to be disbursed, subject to collection by Broker's depository, as follows: (a) if Seller fails or refuses to perform, or any contingency is not satisfied or waived, the deposit shall be returned; (b) deposit shall be applied on purchase price or returned to Buyer when transaction is closed; (c) if Buyer fails or refuses to perform, this deposit shall be paid to Seller, which payment, or the acceptance thereof, shall not in any way prejudice the rights of Seller or Broker(s) in any action for damages or specific performance.

In the event of a dispute over the disposition of the deposit, Broker shall retain the deposit until (i) Buyer and Seller have settled the dispute; (ii) disposition has been ordered by a final court order; or (iii) Broker deposits said amount with a court pursuant to applicable court procedures.

13. **Miscellaneous:** Buyer has examined all property involved and, in making this offer, is relying solely upon such examination with reference to the condition, character and size of land and improvements and fixtures, if any. This contract constitutes the entire agreement and there are no representations, oral or written, which have not been incorporated herein. Time is of the essence of all provisions of this contract. All provisions of this contract shall survive the closing. In compliance with fair housing laws, no party shall in any manner discriminate against any purchaser or purchasers because of race, creed, sex or national origin.

14. **Duration of Offer and Closing:** This offer shall be open for acceptance to midnight _____, 19_____, days after acceptance hereof, unless the parties agree in writing to an extension. This contract shall be performed and this transaction closed within _____

The undersigned agrees to and accepts the foregoing offer.

Buyer acknowledges receipt of a copy of this contract.

Seller shall pay a brokerage fee of _____ of the purchase price in connection with this transaction.

Seller acknowledges receipt of a copy of this contract.

_____ Phone _____
(Buyer)

_____
(Seller)

Address _____

Address _____ Phone _____

Deed to _____

Signed this _____ day of _____ 19_____

Name of Buyer's Attorney _____

Name of Seller's Attorney _____

©CBR and CBA 1989

Broker acknowledges receipt of the sum of $_____ by cash/check which shall be held, deposited and disbursed pursuant to paragraph 12, above.

By _____

DATE

A contract comes into being when the purchase offer is accepted. The contract should be dated. The date may appear at the beginning or the end of the contract or in both places. Failure to include the date does not render the contract unenforceable. However, the question of the date of the signing may arise in several situations. The contract may contain provisions that require the happening of events by reference to the date the contract came into existence. For example, a clause within a contract might read, "Buyer shall obtain financing within 45 days of the signing of this contract." In some instances the statute of limitations may begin to run on the date the contract was signed. The statute of limitations is the time period within which one must sue or be barred from recovery. Some states require that a suit for breach of a written contract be commenced within six years of the signing of the contract, while other states permit a longer period of time. Also, certain legal ramifications attach on the date the contract comes into being. For example, the buyer becomes the equitable owner of the property. As equitable owner, the buyer may enforce the contract by specific performance in the event the seller fails to perform.

PARTIES

In order to satisfy the Statute of Frauds, the names of the parties must be included within the writing. Care should be taken to ensure that the names of the buyer and seller are accurate. An attorney who later draws up the deed may derive the names to insert in the deed from the contract. Accurate spelling prevents problems at a later date when a title search may otherwise uncover discrepancies.

The marital status of the seller should be included; if the seller is married, then the spouse should be named as well. A seller's spouse possesses certain legal rights that must be relinquished by signature in order for the buyer to be assured of a good title. For this reason, the spouse should sign the contract.

There may be more than one seller or buyer. All parties should be named. If there are multiple buyers, it is essential to include a statement of the type and fraction of ownership interest each will receive.

Sometimes a party to the sale (seller or buyer) designates an agent to negotiate and/or sign the contract. This practice should be reserved for extreme cases where it is not feasible for the actual party to act. When a party designates an agent, such appointment should be evidenced by a written power of attorney. A copy of the power of attorney should be attached to the contract and, in some states, recorded. Even here problems may occur because no one can be absolutely sure that the power of attorney has not been revoked by subsequent act or event.

CASE EXAMPLE

Howard Moore, owner of a tract of land that is for sale, is planning a visit to Australia. To prevent his absence from the country from impeding the sale, he executes a power of attorney, giving his real estate broker power to negotiate, contract and sign the deed of conveyance. Hugh Fine, a farmer, enters into a contract for the sale of Moore's land. The broker appears at the closing and executes a deed in behalf of Moore. Fine takes possession and learns later that before the date of closing Moore was killed in Australia in a hunting accident. Since death revokes a power of attorney, Fine's title is seriously impaired.

PROPERTY DESCRIPTION

Property descriptions contained in the contract must sufficiently identify the property. Courts are rather liberal in upholding descriptions of real property contained within the contract. Consequently, a contract for the purchase of "all my lands" has been held sufficient to identify the subject of the sale and to comply with the Statute of Frauds. Even where the quantity of the lands to be sold is not accurate, it is enough if the terms within the description are sufficient to identify the subject property accurately.

CASE EXAMPLE

Vander Graff contracted to sell "all my lands lying on the Miami River, in the State of Ohio, 1,533⅓ acres . . . in my name." Should the actual quantity be greater than the acreage mentioned, the sale would include the excess of the quantity stated in the contract.

Parol evidence is admissible to clarify specific lands. However, parol evidence will not be admitted to reform a description to include lands not specifically referred to by the description.

CASE EXAMPLE

"December 13, 1950, received of P. H. Pilgreen ten dollars ($10) as binder on 20 acres of land and timber; price to be $200 for land and timber. Deed to be made later." Parol evidence will not be admitted in this particular case because the description as written does not allude to a definite parcel of property.

It is best to include in the real estate purchase contract a complete and accurate legal description of the property so that there is no room for any alternative interpretations. In many jurisdictions, however, it is customary to include only the street address for sales of residential property.

PRICE

To satisfy the Statute of Frauds, the amount of the purchase price must be clearly ascertainable. Consider this example:

> The total purchase price shall be $60,000 payable as follows:
>
> ■ $500 upon the signing of the contract,
>
> ■ $5,500 in cash or the equivalent to be paid at closing upon delivery of the deed, and
>
> ■   the balance to be paid by assuming the existing mortgage on said property in the amount of $54,000 held by Citizens Saving & Loan Company.

In the event the purchase price is not specified, it must be subject to ascertainment by computation. For example:

> The acreage of the property is to be determined by survey, and the price is to be computed by multiplying the number of acres and any fraction thereof by $5,000.

The usual and safest form of payment is cashier's or certified check or the equivalent. These forms of payment prevent the buyer from stopping payment after tender, which could occur if a personal check were issued.

CONTINGENCY CLAUSE

◆ A provision within a contract that makes performance under the contract conditional upon the occurrence of a stated event.

A contingency clause may be inserted within a contract to benefit a purchaser or a seller. A common contingency within a purchase contract conditions performance on the buyer's obtaining financing. The details of the acceptable financing are normally specified, for example, "The within obligations of the buyer are conditional upon buyer obtaining a 25-year loan from a financial institution in the amount of 80 percent of the purchase price at 10 percent interest; otherwise this contract to become null and void." This contingency is for the benefit of the purchaser. In the event that the purchaser cannot obtain terms as favorable, he or she could elect to waive the contingency and proceed with the purchase. Other contingencies that benefit a buyer may be contained within a purchase contract, for example, making the contract conditional upon the sale of buyer's house or upon the change of a zoning regulation.

Contingencies may also be included within a contract for the seller's benefit. The seller may desire to make performance under the contract conditional upon confirmation of a job transfer by a present employer. Or perhaps other circumstances make it desirable for the seller to include other contingencies within the contract.

CASE EXAMPLE

Pete Perry owns a home in Tulsa, Oklahoma, and he is interested in selling that home and moving to Seattle, Washington. Perry enters into a valid purchase contract with Sam Sells whereby Perry is to buy Sells's residence for a stated sum. After signing the contract, Perry is not able to sell his residence in Tulsa and consequently is unable to accumulate the funds necessary to close on the Seattle property. Nonetheless, Perry is obligated to perform. A contingency clause as follows would have adequately protected Perry against such a misfortune: "The purchase of Sells's residence is contingent upon Perry selling his residence in Tulsa at market price within at least 30 days prior to the date set for closing."

Contingency clauses are often cunningly drafted in an attempt to permit a party to be relieved of obligations at the party's whim. Courts will often construe such clauses in such a way as to require good faith and honesty on the part of the party the contingency benefits.

CASE EXAMPLE

Brenda Rodgers enters into a purchase contract to buy Hedgeacre. A contingency clause within the contract reads, "Said contract contingent upon buyer obtaining a 10 percent loan for 80 percent of the sales price." Brenda had a change of mind about Hedgeacre and refused to attempt to obtain financing. Brenda's refusal would be considered a lack of good faith and would constitute a breach of contract.

POSSESSION

The date the seller is required to surrender possession to the buyer is usually negotiable. In many contracts, the date the purchaser is entitled to possession coincides with the closing. Ordinarily, in absence of a possession provision, the buyer is entitled to possession upon payment in full. This usually occurs at the closing. The parties can always agree to a different date of possession. It is not uncommon for the parties to agree for the buyer to take possession upon the signing of the contract, especially when the property is vacant. Sometimes a purchaser is impliedly entitled to immediate possession; for example, when the contract requires the purchaser to maintain the premises from the date the contract is signed.

There are dangers to the seller associated with the purchaser's possession before payment. The purchaser in possession may commit waste to the property and then fail to make payment to the seller pursuant to the contract. Or the purchaser might remain on the property and refuse to close the transaction. If this occurs, the seller may have to engage in a lengthy suit before possession is legally returned to the seller or some other favorable remedy is achieved. From the seller's viewpoint, it would be much better for the buyer who takes possession before payment of the purchase price to be characterized as a tenant until payment. In this event the seller would be in a position to evict the purchaser/tenant, an action that would normally result in a quick return of possession to the seller.

Sometimes in residential sales the contract allows the seller to maintain possession rent free for a period of time after closing, such as 30 or 60 days. In such a case, a danger exists that the seller will holdover or commit waste to the premises. For protection against this possibility, the purchaser may require a security deposit, returnable to the seller if the premises are vacated in the condition they were in at the time of contract, reasonable wear and tear excepted.

EVIDENCE OF TITLE

◆ **A document such as an abstract or title insurance verifying ownership of property.**

The seller is not under any affirmative obligation to prove that title to the realty is *marketable*—that is, free of liens or other encumbrances. If a general warranty deed is used, the seller personally warrants that the property is free and clear of encumbrances other than those specifically excluded and that the seller will warrant and defend the title against the lawful claims and demands of all persons. A purchaser may maintain an action for damages against the seller under the general warranty in the event of a breach of the warranty against encumbrances. However, the warranty is only as good as the seller's net worth. When making an investment in realty, the purchaser should take extreme precaution. Toward that end, the purchaser may hire an attorney to effect a title search and render an opinion as to the marketability of the title. Or the purchaser may purchase title insurance from a reputable company. (Title search and title insurance are discussed in Chapter 20.) Still better, the purchaser may insist on a clause in the contract that the seller provide evidence of title in the form of an abstract of title or an owner's title insurance policy. The prevailing custom within the real estate industry in many localities is for the seller to provide such proof of title. The standardized real estate purchase contract within the locality normally reflects the common and approved practice within the area.

FORM OF DEED

The type of deed to be conveyed by the seller may be controlled by the terms of the contract. It is most desirable for the contract to specify the type of deed, whether it be a general warranty deed, bargain and sale deed, quitclaim deed or some other type. In the absence of agreement, the law within the jurisdiction governs the type of deed the seller is required to convey. Under this circumstance some jurisdictions obligate the seller to convey a general warranty deed, whereas other jurisdictions require only a quitclaim deed.

PRORATION

Certain expenses or income associated with the realty at the time of closing may be due but unpaid. Other expenses or income may have been prepaid. Because these expenses and income are related to the use of the premises, in part by the seller and in part by the buyer, apportionment is necessary. A clause within the contract may read:

Taxes, insurance, utilities, assessments, and rental income shall be apportioned pro rata as the interests of the parties may appear at closing.

Taxes on real property, for example, may be payable annually, semiannually or otherwise. The fiscal year may not correspond to the calendar year; the tax assessment period may be, for example, July 1 to June 30. To complicate matters, some local jurisdictions run six months to a year behind in their billing so that the owner is always paying taxes due in the past. Fairness demands that an adjustment be made so that the seller is charged with accrued but unpaid taxes.

CASE EXAMPLE

Olivieri pays $260 a year for real estate property taxes on her home. The fiscal period for tax purposes is July 1 to June 30. Olivieri is billed $130 twice a year, in December and June. Each installment of $130 covers the previous six months. On March 31, 1998, Olivieri appears at a closing on her house. The contract provides for apportionment of taxes as of the date of closing. Olivieri is current in her payments of taxes and presents a paid receipt for the December installment. Olivieri will owe $65 for accrued and unpaid taxes for the period January 1 to March 31, which amount will be credited to the buyer against the selling price.

Hazard insurance policies may be transferred from the seller to the buyer. However, the transfer may necessitate an apportionment. Insurance is often payable in advance, and the unaccrued portion that was paid by the seller for a period during which the purchaser has the use of the premises must be reflected in the apportionment.

Sometimes it is possible to notify the insurance carrier to refund the unaccrued portion to the seller and bill the purchaser for the applicable amount. Another method is for the seller to cancel the insurance policy and receive a rebate for the unused premium and for the buyer to purchase another policy.

Other expenses, such as fuel, electricity, water and other assessments, are often prorated. Usage of these utilities is not always the subject of exact computation. The parties can notify the respective companies to read the utility meters as of the date of closing and divide the bill accordingly.

Income from rentals is often apportioned as of the date of closing. Normally, rentals are paid in advance. If the closing occurs in the midst of a rental payment period, an adjustment is required because the seller in such an event receives from the tenant a rental payment covering a portion of the time after ownership has passed to the buyer.

CASE EXAMPLE

Jerry Rogers, seller, and Ronald Dodge, buyer, are to close July 15 on commercial property owned by Rogers. A tenant is under a leasehold agreement for such property and pays $350 per month on the first of each month. A clause within the real estate purchase contract requires apportionment of rentals as of the date of closing. On July 15 the buyer would be entitled to $175, which represents the unused portion of the rental.

Prorations are also covered in Chapter 14.

PROPERTY INSPECTION

The condition of the property may be the subject of dispute at closing or thereafter. To reduce the possibility of such a dispute, the contract may contain an inspection clause. Inspection clauses may permit the buyer to have the premises inspected or may require the seller to produce certificates evidencing the results of an inspection. Types of inspection include termite, gas line, electrical, structural and plumbing.

In the event that the inspection shows a defect, the contract governs as to the responsibilities of the parties. The following is an example of a contractual provision:

> Seller shall make all repairs to the property not to exceed 5 percent of the purchase price. In the event Seller fails to make said repairs Buyer may make the repairs and deduct the amount from the purchase price at closing. In the event the cost of repairs exceeds 5 percent of the purchase price and Seller agrees to make the repairs, the Buyer may (1) close the sale with the completed repairs or (2) terminate the contract.

Under such a provision, assume that the purchase price of a home is $200,000. A termite inspection reveals termite infestation and structural damage. The cost of repair is $8,000. The seller must make the necessary repairs. If, however, the cost of repairs is over $10,000 (over 5 percent), the seller does not have to make the repairs. In such a case the contract is rescinded. In the event that the seller agrees to make the repairs, the buyer may accept the repairs or refuse the repairs and terminate the contract.

HOME WARRANTY PLAN

Many contracts contain protection for the buyer through home warranty plans. Various private companies, for a fee, will contract to repair major systems and appliances for a period of time, normally one year. The cost may range from $250 to $500, depending on the location and terms of the plan. In the event that a home maintenance provision is not included within the purchase contract, the option is usually open for the buyer to pay for and obtain coverage.

EARNEST MONEY

A real estate purchase contract normally calls for the purchaser to deposit earnest money. Contrary to popular belief, this deposit is not necessary to validate the contract. Sufficient consideration exists in the form of mutual promises contained within the agreement.

Earnest money may be a nominal sum, such as $100, or it may be as substantial as 10 percent of the purchase price or more. Normally, the real estate broker holds the deposit in an escrow account pending closing. At closing the earnest money may be returned to the purchaser or credited against the amount due to the seller.

SIGNING

A contract for the sale of real estate should be signed (executed) by both parties. A writing not executed by all parties is arguably not the agreement of any party who has failed to sign.

An agent acting in behalf of a party to the contract may bind a principal by signing the contract. Authority of the agent in some states may be oral; nevertheless, even in those states written authority is preferable. If an agent lacks proper authority, then only the agent is bound. An unauthorized act of an agent may be subsequently ratified (approved) by a principal.

Only a few states require that a contract for the sale of realty also contain a *seal*. A vestigial remnant of the seal can be seen in some form contracts that have a mark, *L.S.* (for *locus sigilli*), the Latin initials meaning "place of the seal."

ATTESTATION AND ACKNOWLEDGMENT

In most jurisdictions a contract for the sale of realty need not be witnessed (attested). The parties who sign the writing need not acknowledge their signatures as genuine before a notary public. However, some jurisdictions do not permit recording of a contract that is not witnessed and so acknowledged. A contract, however, does not have to be recorded in order to be considered binding between the parties. (Some jurisdictions require that the land installment contract, discussed in Chapter 22, be recorded.) Recording a contract would provide protection for the buyer; anyone considering purchasing the property under contract would have notice of the buyer's ownership interest in that property. The seller may, however, for good reason, object to recording because of potential problems it may cause. In the event the buyer defaults on the contract, it may be costly and burdensome to remove the encumbrance that the recorded contract presents.

CLOSING

The contract normally states the date and place of closing. The closing is discussed in detail in Chapter 14. At closing the buyer makes payment to the seller and the seller passes title by signing and conveying the deed in accordance with the terms of the contract. In the event that the time and place of closing are not specified within the contract, the law presumes that the parties intended that the closing take place within a reasonable time at a reasonable location.

Normally, time is not of the essence in real estate closings. Hence, even if a date is specified, failure to close on that date is not considered critical as long as the noncomplying party has acted in good faith and is able to close within a reasonable time thereafter. The parties, of course, may agree within the contract that time is of the essence, and under such a clause, even a day's delay on the part of a party would be deemed a breach of contract.

Under certain circumstances, time is of the essence even in absence of express language in the contract to that effect. Time is of the essence when parties are dealing in highly speculative land transactions that are subject to rapid fluctuations in value. In addition, when one party is made aware of particular circumstances that make the timing of the closing date critical (such as the necessity for the buyer to vacate an apartment the day of closing), time is deemed as an essential element to the contract.

A buyer who appears at the closing unattended by the seller must be ready, willing and able to perform. The buyer must tender the purchase price by depositing it in escrow or through a show of the money to witnesses in attendance. Conversely, a seller makes tender by showing a readiness, a willingness and an ability to deliver marketable title to the buyer.

UNCONSCIONABLE CONTRACT

The Uniform Commercial Code (UCC), which has been enacted into law at least in part by all states, applies to the sale of goods but not to the sale of real property. Nevertheless, trends in the law of real property may be derived from an examination of certain provisions within the UCC. Courts often reason by analogy from this code in reaching results in non-code-governed cases. Section 2-302(1) of the UCC recognizes that some contracts, or provisions within contracts may be unconscionable.

If the court as a matter of law finds the contract or any clause of the contract to have been unconscionable at the time it was made, the court may refuse to enforce the contract, or it may enforce the remainder of the contract without the unconscionable clause, or it may so limit the application of any unconscionable clause as to avoid any unconscionable result.

In a seller's market, the seller can dictate provisions on a take-it-or-leave-it basis. A buyer may be compelled to sign a contract including the provision "Buyer represents that he has examined the entirety of the property and asserts that he has not relied upon any representation made by the seller." The effect of such a clause may be to prevent the buyer from raising the defense of fraud or misrepresentation should their existence be revealed later. Some courts may relieve a buyer of this helpless position by striking the clause as unconscionable, thus treating it in a way similar to the way the UCC does when dealing with transactions involving the sale of goods.

REVIEW AND DISCUSSION QUESTIONS

1. What are the elements necessary to satisfy the Statute of Frauds?
2. (a) Why does the Statute of Frauds apply to sales of interests in real estate? (b) Give an example of a case involving a real estate transfer that is excepted from the Statute of Frauds.
3. What is the purpose of the parol evidence rule?
4. What limitation may a broker confront when preparing real estate purchase contracts?
5. Describe five major provisions contained within the real estate purchase contract.
6. (a) What is a contingency clause? (b) What purpose does it serve? (c) Whom does it benefit?
7. When does the closing occur? Explain.
8. Explain how the Uniform Commercial Code influences real estate transactions.

CASE PROBLEMS

1. A trustee of real property held a public auction to sell the property. Charles McCabe was the highest bidder. There was no written contract or memorandum of sale. The next day, when the trustee of the property submitted a deed for delivery, McCabe refused to pay the price. The trustee sued for specific performance. Who wins and why? *Watson v. McCabe, 527 F.2d 286 (6th Cir. 1975).*

2. The Roths entered into a contract to purchase real property from Loye Ashton and his co-owners. There was no writing evidencing the sale. The Roths paid most of the purchase price for the property and constructed a building on the property in which they were operating a business. Is it possible for Ashton to rescind the agreement? Explain. See *Williston Co-op Credit Union v. Fossum, 459 N.W.2d 548 (N.D. 1990).*

3. The Whites entered into an agreement with the Rehns to purchase "all land west of road running south to the Rehn farmstead containing 960 acres." Nothing within the description pinpointed exactly which 960 acres was to be transferred. Immediately before the purchase agreement was to be signed, the extent of the specific parcel was explained orally to Mr. White. (a) Should the Rehns desire to back out of the sale, what argument could they make? (b) How should the Whites respond? *White v. Rehn, 103 Idaho 1, 644 P.2d 323 (1982).*

4. River Birch Associates, a developer, entered into a plan to develop a 144-unit town home project on 19.6 acres. River Birch agreed to convey fee simple title to the "common area" to the Homeowner's Association of the project. The specific identity of the common area was not designated in the contract. Can the Homeowner's Association resort to extrinsic evidence to clarify the quantity and the specific identity of the common areas? Explain. What extrinsic evidence may be helpful? *River Birch Associates v. City of Raleigh, 326 N.C. 100, 388 S.E.2d 538 (1990).*

5. A contract of sale required the Laddons, the buyers, to pay, as part of the purchase price, a $1,000 deposit to be held by Rhett Realty, the broker, "in escrow on behalf of seller until settlement." The contract further provided that the deposit would be forfeited to the sellers in the event the Laddons breached the contract. In such a case, under the terms of the contract, Rhett Realty would be entitled to 50 percent of the amount forfeited. The contract was contingent upon the buyers obtaining financing, which they were unable to do. Who is entitled to the earnest money? Explain. *Laddon v. Rhett Realty, Inc., 63 Md. App. 562, 493 A.2d 379 (1985).*

6. 805 Third Avenue Co. (Third Avenue) and M.W. Realty Associates entered into a contract whereby Third Avenue was to purchase M.W. Realty's air rights. Third Avenue needed the air rights to construct an office building. Third Avenue obtained a city permit authorizing it to commence construction, and it began to excavate and enter into contracts for the erection of the structure. M.W. Realty refused to complete its obligations under the purchase contract, insisting on a modification of the contract on terms less favorable to Third Avenue. Knowing that any delay would result in serious injury, Third Avenue agreed to the unfavorable terms. (a) What remedy is now available to Third Avenue? (b) What is the legal justification for the remedy? *805 Third Avenue Co. v. M.W. Realty Assoc., 58 N.Y.2d 447, 461 N.Y.S.2d 778 (1983).*

12

Agency and Brokerage

AGENCY

◆ **A legal relationship in which one party, called the principal, authorizes another, called the agent, to act in the principal's behalf in dealing with third parties.**

Agency is a useful legal relationship in business and personal transactions. A substantial amount of business in the United States is done through agents, both by corporations and partnerships that are unable to act for themselves and by individuals, who find acting through agents convenient and efficient in their business and private affairs.

AGENCY AND REAL ESTATE TRANSACTIONS

The agency relationship is used extensively in many phases of the real estate business. It is especially prevalent in selling and leasing residential and commercial property. Owners of these types of properties often retain agents to help them find buyers or tenants, as agents usually have extensive knowledge of the market as well as contacts with potential occupants.

Agencies created to bring about the sale or lease of real estate differ in two significant ways from agencies in many other businesses. One difference is that in all states an agent appointed to sell or buy real estate must be licensed. License requirements for real estate agents will be discussed later in the chapter.

A second difference between the real estate agent and other agents is the extent to which the real estate agent has the power to contract on behalf of the principal. In many, if not most, business agencies, the agent has this power. For example, if the president of a corporation that is developing land for a shopping mall signs a contract to have the land cleared, the contract is binding on the corporation. However, in most transactions that involve the sale or lease of real estate, the agent does not have the power to contract for the principal. If the owner wishes the agent to have this authority, the owner must execute a written document called a power of attorney. The power of attorney grants the agent, usually referred to as an attorney-in-fact, the authority to contract for the owner.

Creation of Agency

The usual method of creating an agency is by agreement. The principal authorizes the agent to act in the principal's behalf, and the agent agrees to do so. As a general rule, no particular formality is required to create an agency; the agreement may be oral or in writing. This rule ordinarily does not apply to transactions involving the sale or lease of real estate. To be valid, a power of attorney must be in writing. In addition, almost half the states by statute require that the appointment of an agent to procure a buyer or tenant for real estate be in writing.

Broker

◆ **An agent who for a commission or fee brings parties together to negotiate or conducts negotiations to complete a transaction, usually involving the sale or exchange of property or the acquisition of contract rights.**

A broker is an intermediary or go-between whose primary function is to facilitate a transaction. In many fields, brokers play important roles in bringing business dealings to fruition. Although stockbrokers and real estate brokers are common examples, the long list of brokers includes those who arrange the sale of yachts, produce, hides and furs and, in some societies, even marriage. What brokers do and the authority they enjoy differ from one business to another, but brokers almost always represent buyers or sellers in some capacity.

Most states have statutory provisions that define real estate brokers and sales personnel for the purpose of licensing and regulation. These statutes frequently designate brokers in terms of activities relative to real estate transactions. When people engage in these activities for others and for a commission or fee, they are brokers or salespersons for regulatory purposes and must be licensed.

The statutes contain words such as *auctions, sells, offers for sale, buys, solicits prospective sellers or buyers, negotiates the sale* and *exchanges.* Similar broad terminology is used to describe activities relative to rental of real property. In some statutes, activities such as finding borrowers or lenders, negotiating or collecting loans and arranging investments secured by real estate also are included in the statutory definition of broker.

A corporation or a partnership may be a real estate broker. In most states, members of the firm who actively engage in the brokerage business must be licensed. A few states require that anyone actively engaged in management be licensed as well. In some states one member of the firm may be designated on the license as a broker and others as associate brokers or sales personnel. License requirements will be discussed more fully later in this chapter.

INDEPENDENT CONTRACTOR

◆ **A person who is retained to do a job and uses his or her own judgment as to how the work will be done.**

The broker is in a technical sense retained by the seller as an agent. Nevertheless, the agency agreement establishes only the broker's authority to act, not the manner in which the broker is to accomplish the result. The broker controls the hours, methods and details of the job. As the broker's actions are not controlled by the seller, the seller is not liable for negligent harm caused by the broker unless the act causing harm was authorized or within the broker's inherent powers. In addition, as the broker is not an employee but an independent contractor, the seller does not have to withhold federal or state income taxes or make contributions to the Social Security or unemployment compensation funds on the broker's behalf.

LISTING

◆ **A contract between a seller of real estate and a broker authorizing the broker to secure a buyer for the property upon specified terms in return for a fee if the broker is successful.**

The listing creates the agency relationship between the seller and the broker. A number of states require by statute that a listing be in writing. In these states, if there is no written listing, the broker is not entitled to a fee. In the absence of a statute requiring a writing, an oral listing is enforceable. This question should not come up, however, since both the prudent seller and the broker would insist on a written contract clearly spelling out the rights and obligations of the parties. An appreciable portion of the litigation that centers around suits for brokers' commissions could be prevented by carefully drawn brokerage agreements. This problem as well as some others that can be alleviated by a writing will be discussed later.

In those states that recognize the oral listing, a broker may establish employment by implications arising from a property owner's actions.

CASE EXAMPLE

Frewert owned a home that he had been trying to sell. Carlson, a real estate salesperson, obtained permission to show the home to the Coopers. Carlson obtained an offer, which she presented to Frewert. In discussing the transaction, she told Frewert that she was representing him. Frewert then quoted a minimum net price that he wanted for the property and discussed possession with her. Carlson obtained a second offer from the Coopers that was slightly less than Frewert's minimum net price. Frewert rejected this offer. Two days later, he signed a contract directly with the Coopers and refused to pay a commission.

In a successful suit against Frewert for a commission, the court stated, "[W]hile a contract of employment is necessary to create an agency relationship . . . no particular form is required. Ordinarily, all that is necessary is that the broker act with consent of his principal either by written instrument, orally, or by implication from the conduct of the parties." *Dickerson Realtors, Inc. v. Frewert, 16 Ill. App. 2d 1060, 307 N.E.2d 445 (1974).*

The listing agreement should contain all the important elements of any contract: the amount of compensation, duration of the listing, point at which the commission is earned and the like. The contract should also outline defects and encumbrances to which the title is subject, terms upon which the owner will sell and details as to possession. The listing should also indicate whether it is a nonexclusive, or open, listing or an exclusive one.

◆ **Exclusive Agency. A listing in which the seller gives one broker authority to procure a buyer for property but retains the right to procure a buyer for the property himself or herself.**

The exclusive agency is one of the two types of exclusive listings common in the United States. In this type of exclusive listing, if the seller procures the buyer the broker is not entitled to a commission.

◆ **Exclusive Right To Sell. A listing in which the seller gives one broker authority to procure a buyer for property. The broker is entitled to a commission even if the buyer is procured by the seller.**

The *exclusive right to sell* differs from the *exclusive agency* in that the exclusive right to sell entitles the broker to a commission even if the seller procures the buyer without the broker's assistance. Courts in most states require unequivocal language in a listing before accepting it as an exclusive right to sell. These courts reason that the ordinary seller should be clearly informed that even if he or she makes the sale alone, the commission must be paid.

Both types of exclusive listings protect the broker against appointment by the seller of any other broker. Brokers prefer these types of listings because they provide added assurance that time and money spent procuring a buyer will be rewarded. The broker does not have to fear loss of a commission if another broker arranges a prior sale of the property.

Most exclusive listings are given for a specified period of time. They terminate automatically at the end of that period unless renewed. For a broker to take an exclusive listing for an indefinite period is generally considered poor practice. In many states an indefinite exclusive listing is illegal. This protects sellers who, unaware that the exclusive listing is still in effect, list with another broker and thus find themselves liable for two commissions. If an exclusive listing is open-ended, it is subject to cancellation upon notice. A few states allow the broker a reasonable period of time to arrange the desired transaction. In any case, most courts agree that a seller may not terminate a listing where the only objective is to bypass the broker and sell to a buyer with whom the broker has been negotiating.

◆ **Open Listing. A listing that entitles the broker to compensation only if his or her activities bring about the desired result.**

The open or nonexclusive listing is common in some states. Unless the agreement clearly indicates otherwise, courts presume that a listing is open. A seller who enters into an open listing agreement may list the property with any number of brokers. The broker who brings about the sale is entitled to the commission. Authority of all of the brokers is automatically revoked without notice if and when the seller enters into a contract to sell the property.

In an open listing, the seller retains the right to negotiate a sale on his or her own. If the sale is effected by the seller without the aid of a broker, no commissions are due and all listings are automatically terminated. Ordinarily, an open seller listing has no time limit and the seller can withdraw at any time. The seller has no commitment until the broker has procured a buyer ready, willing and able to buy. In order to escape paying a commission, a dishonest seller, suspecting that a broker is about to submit an offer, might revoke the broker's authority and attempt to deal directly with the potential buyer. A seller who revokes in bad faith under these circumstances is subject to liability if the property is sold to a buyer located by the broker. Some open listings contain provisions entitling the broker to a commission after the expiration of the listing if the property is purchased by one to whom it has been shown by the broker.

◆ **Multiple-Listing Service. An organization in which brokers have contracted with each other to share their exclusive listing contracts.**

Multiple listing is a marketing strategy that brokers have developed among themselves to increase their effectiveness in brokering real estate. Brokers participating in the service have agreed to pool their exclusive listings and to divide the commission received for negotiating a sale. Multiple-listing services are common in most areas of the United States.

In a transaction involving broker members of a multiple-listing service, the selling broker was traditionally considered to be a subagent of the listing broker. The subagent relationship is no longer required in many jurisdictions. A selling broker may choose to represent the buyer in the transaction rather than be a subagent of the seller. Each of the brokers involved receives a percentage of the commission that had been negotiated by the listing broker with the seller. The split of that percentage that each broker receives is determined by them. Some multiple-listing services allow their members to withhold certain real estate from multiple listing; others require that all listings be submitted. Multiple-listing services also generally allow the listing broker a period of time to attempt to sell the property before registering it with the organization. Since brokers have limited rights to delegate their authority, the members of a multiple-listing service should be sure that their contracts with the owners permit them to submit property to multiple listing.

AUTHORITY
◆ **Term used in the law of agency denoting the agent's power to perform acts authorized by the principal.**

The broker is a special agent with limited authority, usually restricted to a single transaction. In addition, although many people in real estate—and often the courts—refer to a broker's authority to sell, most listings merely authorize the broker to find a buyer, not to enter into a contract on behalf of the principal.

CASE EXAMPLE

Vance entered into an exclusive-listing agreement for three months with Management Clearing, Inc. His wife did not sign the listing, although community property was involved. Management Clearing, Inc., obtained an offer on terms identical to the listing, but Vance rejected it. Management Clearing, Inc., sued for its commission.

Vance defended on grounds that in a community property state, a husband alone cannot authorize the sale of community real estate. The court refused to accept this defense. The court stated, "[A] brokerage contract places only the duty on the broker of finding a buyer. . . . It does not authorize the broker to sell the property." *Management Clearing, Inc., v. Vance, 11 Ariz. App. 386, 464 P.2d 977 (1970).*

The broker does not bargain as to terms but assists the parties in arranging terms upon which agreement can be reached. Although the seller may give the broker authority to execute a contract of sale, this authority must be clearly spelled out in the listing. Because brokers usually do not have the power to contract for a seller, a buyer should demand evidence of the broker's authority to do so if the broker signs on the seller's behalf. Brokers who are employed as property managers or rental agents often have the authority to contract for their principal.

◆ **Express Authority. Authority a principal confers upon an agent explicitly and distinctly; may be conferred orally or in writing.**

An agency authorization in the listing contract between the broker/agent and the owner/principal is the foundation upon which the broker's authority rests. Such authorization establishes certain tasks the broker is given the power to accomplish.

IMPLIED AUTHORITY

◆ **An agent's authority to do those things necessary and proper to accomplish the express terms of the agency.**

Implied authority includes activities such as advertising, showing the property and transmitting from buyer and seller proposals relating to the sale. The broker has the implied authority to do these things as they are necessary to achieve the result sought by his or her express authority, that is, to find a ready, willing and able buyer.

The broker also has the implied authority to make certain representations about the property. A real estate broker, however, is a special agent. This means that the broker's implied authority is confined strictly to the terms of the agency, and the broker is bound by his or her obligation as an agent to obey the directions of the principal.

CASE EXAMPLE

Mustafa Ali owned a profitable bakery that he desired to sell. He listed the business and property with Dave Gould Realty, Inc., for $150,000.

Gould obtained an offer for the property, which Ali accepted; a $1,500 deposit to be held by Gould accompanied the offer. The contract provided that the deposit on the purchase price would be paid to the seller if the buyer defaulted. The buyer refused to close the sale because of alleged defects in the title. Without contacting Ali, Gould returned the $1,500. Because the contract did not close as scheduled, Ali sold the property to another. If Gould sued for a commission, the court would rule against him because he had no implied authority to modify the contract by returning the deposit to the buyer.

The extent of the broker's authority is a critical issue in determining the seller's responsibility for representations made by the broker about the property. In a majority of jurisdictions, these statements are binding upon the seller. If the statement is material and untrue, the buyer may rescind the contract and in some cases collect damages. These results follow even if the broker thought the statement was true or if the seller was unaware that the statement was being made. As a general rule, courts consider statements made by a broker within the scope of the broker's implied authority. Any loss occasioned by these statements should be borne by the seller, who selected the broker, and not by the buyer, who was misled by the false statement.

Brokers generally are chosen for their knowledge, skill and judgment. The relationship between the broker, or the brokerage firm, and the seller is personal, and generally the broker has no authority to delegate to another the tasks that he or she has been hired to perform. This rule applies, however, only to broker's actions that are discretionary, such as determining the terms of the sale.

A broker may delegate to another the authority to perform acts that are ministerial or mechanical in nature. Thus the broker may assign to a salesperson the task of showing the property or finding a buyer, inasmuch as these acts do not involve the broker's discretion. When a ministerial task is accomplished by a broker through a subagent, the broker is entitled to collect a commission even if the subagent's relationship to the broker was unknown to the seller.

CASE EXAMPLE

Dave Gould Realty, Inc., was authorized to sell property that belonged to Edna Philbrick. Gould mentioned this to Arthur Clairmont, a fellow broker. Several days later, Clairmont obtained Gould's permission to show the property to one of Clairmont's customers. Clairmont described the property and terms to this buyer. The buyer on his own examined the property and entered into an agreement with Philbrick, who refused to pay Gould a promised commission. Philbrick argued that she had not authorized Clairmont to procure a buyer.

Courts would ordinarily find for Gould in this situation, as Clairmont's verbal description and transmittal of terms represented a mechanical act.

BROKER'S DUTIES TO SELLER

A real estate broker owes his or her principal, the seller, essentially the same duties that any agent owes to a principal. Like other agents, the broker is a fiduciary. A fiduciary is a person who acts primarily for the benefit of another in a relationship founded on trust and confidence. In selecting the broker as agent, the seller has relied on the broker's integrity, fidelity and ability. This relationship of confidence and trust requires high standards of conduct, and the broker must exercise good faith and loyalty in all matters relating to the agency.

Good Faith and Loyalty. Good faith and loyalty require the broker to advance the principal's interest even at the expense of his or her own. A broker may not purchase the seller's property unless the seller has complete knowledge of all the facts and freely consents to the sale. This prohibition applies even if the broker can show that the transaction was beneficial to the seller and the seller was not injured in any way.

The duty of good faith and loyalty controls situations in which the broker can represent both parties. If a broker has the authority *to enter into a contract for either buyer or seller,* the broker violates the fiduciary duty if he or she accepts compensation from both. Courts reason that it is impossible for a broker under these circumstances to satisfy the diametrically opposed interest of both parties.

In the common brokerage agreement, however, the broker is employed merely to bring the parties together. In this situation the broker may act as a dual agent and receive a commission from each as long as this dual capacity has been fully disclosed and is agreed to in writing by both buyer and seller. In the effort to bring the parties together, the broker who is to receive compensation from buyer and seller must be certain to act impartially.

Abstract terms such as trust, good faith and loyalty indicate the general scope of the broker's responsibility to his or her principal. In reality a broker must take at least three positive actions to meet these general requirements:

1. The broker must fully disclose to the principal all matters relating to the agency.
2. The broker must obey the principal's lawful instructions.
3. The broker must account to the principal for any proceeds of the agency coming in to his or her hands.

Full disclosure requires that the principal be informed of all offers, the identity of purchasers, commission-splitting arrangements with other brokers, relationships between buyer and broker, financial limitations of the purchaser and the selling price of comparable property.

CASE EXAMPLE

Neibert listed property with Alfred C. Moore, a broker. One of Moore's salespeople obtained a purchase offer for the property. The offer acknowledged receipt of $3,000 from the buyer and provided that the deposit should be "forfeited as liquidated damages" if buyer failed to close.

(Continued)

Unknown to Moore, the deposit was in the form of a promissory note, not cash. Moore discovered this later but failed to inform Neibert, since the buyer assured Moore that the note would be honored. When the sale did not close, Neibert demanded the deposit to cover losses incurred. The buyer refused to pay the note.

In an action affirming the real estate commission's 60-day suspension of Moore's license, the court recognized that the temptation to withhold information is "especially strong when it is only a matter of disclosing bad news which may improve." The court added that "it is an agent's duty to give his principal timely notice of every fact or circumstance which may make it necessary for him to take measures for his security." *Moore v. State Real Estate Commission, Pa. Commw. Ct. 506, 309 A.2d 77 (1973).*

Skill and Care. In addition to meeting the high standards of conduct of a fiduciary, the broker must not be negligent in carrying out the duties of the agency. A broker is negligent if he or she acts in an unreasonable or careless manner and this action is the proximate cause of loss to the principal.

CASE EXAMPLE

Ponia Towski, who could neither read nor write English, owned a house in Camden, New Jersey. There was a vacant lot on each side of the house. Between the lot on the east and the house was an alley. Towski's house was on the boundary of the west lot. Because of this, Towski wished to purchase that lot and erect a dwelling, using his west wall as a party wall.

All of this was explained to Joshua Griffiths, a real estate broker. Through Griffiths, Towski purchased what he thought was the lot on the west and built an adjoining structure with a party wall. Unfortunately, Griffiths had negotiated a sale with the owner of the eastern lot. Because Towski did not own the property on which the adjoining building was located, his tenants were forced to vacate the premises. Towski then brought a successful damage action against Griffiths. *Towski v. Griffiths, 91 N.J.L. 663, 103 A. 192 (1918).*

Although the facts of this case are unusual, in finding for Ponia Towski the court applied a test that is relatively common. It held the defendant liable because he had not used the degree of care and skill ordinarily employed by people engaged in the brokerage business.

Liability for negligence depends on factors that vary from one case to another. As a result, it is impossible to say that a broker is negligent because of acting in a particular manner. A slight variation in the circumstances might cause a court or jury to consider a particular act careless in one instance and not in another. There are, however, a number of relatively common situations in which principals have brought successful negligence actions against their brokers or have used the broker's conduct as a defense in an action brought for commissions. Cases exist in which brokers have been found negligent because they did not use ordinary care and skill in securing an adequate purchase price, investigating encumbrances, preparing papers relative to the sale, collecting payments due the principal and filing discharges for mortgages and liens.

It has been held that a broker who fails to make a determined effort to sell, especially a broker with an exclusive agency, is liable to the principal. Other cases have held that a broker charged with renting property is liable for failure to properly investigate prospective tenants who later damage the property.

Numerous remedies are available to the principal when the broker violates these duties. The principal may:

- sue for breach of contract;
- bring a tort action for negligence;
- withhold the commission requiring the broker to bring a suit against the principal;
- discharge the broker without compensation;
- force the broker to account; or
- recover for loss and misuse of the principal's property.

BROKER'S DUTY TO BUYER

Business relationships between buyers and brokers arise in one of two ways. In the typical real estate sale, the seller lists his or her property with the broker. The listing authorizes the broker to act as the seller's agent in procuring a buyer for the property. The buyer is a third party. In negotiations with third parties (buyers), the broker is acting in the seller's behalf and, like the seller, deals at arm's length with the buyer. In an arm's-length transaction each party acts in his or her own interest. In the past, courts have applied the principle of caveat emptor, that is, let the buyer beware, to the relationship between the seller's broker and the buyer.

Seller's brokers are liable to buyers in some situations. Traditionally, to recover against a broker representing the seller, the buyer needed to rely on some tort theory, not on any duty the broker owed to the buyer arising out of the relationship between them. Sellers' brokers are liable to buyers for misrepresentation of material facts about the property or for actively concealing any defects. If the misrepresentation is intentional, the broker is liable for fraud; if the misrepresentation is made innocently, the broker is liable, but the buyer's remedies may be limited. Fraud and misrepresentation are discussed in Chapter 13.

The liability of the seller's broker to the buyer for fraud or misrepresentation has been expanded in a number of states during the last 20 years. Many courts have held sellers' brokers liable to buyers for failing to disclose material facts about the property. For example, buyers have recovered against sellers' brokers who have not disclosed a termite problem, a defective sewer, a leaky basement or personal interest in the property. Currently being litigated are cases involving "stigmatized property," where houses are reputedly haunted, or the site of a murder, or are in a neighborhood where a child sex offender lives. At this juncture it is difficult to predict the outcome of these cases.

Courts holding that sellers' brokers have a duty to disclose material facts to buyers justify this stance in several ways. Some have applied a theory of negligence or negligent misrepresentation. To establish a claim of negligence, the buyer must show that the broker owed the buyer a duty to conform to a certain standard. In a number of cases, to establish this standard, courts have referred to standards in ethical codes promulgated by state real estate commissions and/or the Code of Ethics of the NATIONAL ASSOCIATION OF REALTORS®. These codes impose upon the broker a duty to treat all parties fairly. In other cases, courts have held sellers' brokers to a high standard of care in relations with buyers on grounds that state legislation licensing real estate brokers must be interpreted in the light of its obvious purpose of protecting the public. A broker does not stand in the same shoes as a seller. Brokers owe the buyer the same duties of integrity owed the public at large. They must be answerable at law for breaches of statutory duty to the public. In addition, courts have stated that the broker's license is a privilege conferred by the state in return for which the broker must act in the public interest.

HOFFMAN v. CONNALL
Supreme Court of Washington
736 P. 2d 242 (1987)

BACKGROUND. In January 1983, Bryan and Connie Connall signed a listing agreement with Cardinal Realty, Inc., to sell five acres of land. Shortly thereafter a Cardinal broker went to the site with one of the sellers. The seller pointed to a stake that marked the southeast corner, and the broker noted that the stake lined up with a fence line to form the west boundary. The seller had built a corral and horse barn six inches inside the fence line, and assured the broker that the fence and other improvements were inside the property line. The seller pointed out that the southwest corner stake lined up with a row of poplar trees to form the west boundary. The seller located also the approximate location of the northwest corner.

James and Verna Hoffman saw an advertisement for the property and contacted the broker who took them to the site. The broker pointed out the corner stakes and other locational information given him by the seller. The Hoffmans owned a horse so the fence, corral, and horse barn were important to them. The Hoffmans bought the property in February, and in May were notified by a neighbor that according to his recent survey the fence and part of the corral and horse barn encroached on his property by 18 to 21 feet. The buyers determined that the cost of moving the improvements was about $6,000. The buyers sued the sellers and the broker for misrepresenting the true property line. The trial court held that the broker did not breach the duty of acting like a reasonably prudent real estate broker. The Court of Appeals reversed holding that a broker is liable for innocent misrepresentations to the buyer.

DECISION. The Washington Supreme Court reversed the Court of Appeals affirming the trial court's decision in favor of the broker.

JUSTICE ANDERSEN. A real estate broker is held to a standard of reasonable care and is liable for making "negligent," though not "innocent," misrepresentations concerning boundaries to a buyer. The Restatement (Second) of Torts defines the tort of innocent misrepresentation as follows:

> One who, in a sale, rental, or exchange transaction with another, makes a misrepresentation of a material fact for the purpose of inducing the other to act or to refrain from acting in reliance upon it, is subject to liability to the other for pecuniary loss caused to him by his justifiable reliance upon the misrepresentation, even though it is not made fraudulently or negligently. The Restatement, however, leaves open the question of whether such a cause of action lies against real estate brokers.

We recognize that some other jurisdictions have agreed with the viewpoint of the Court of Appeals in this case and have held real estate brokers liable for making innocent misrepresentations on which buyers justifiably rely. Courts that so hold do so because of their belief that the innocent buyer's reliance tips the balance of equity in favor of the buyer's protection. The courts justify placing the loss on the innocent broker on the basis that the broker is in a better position to determine the truth of his or her representations.

This approach has been criticized for imposing a standard of strict liability for all misrepresentations that a broker might make or communicate, however innocent, in a real estate transaction. Another commentator observes the obvious—that there is a problem with subjecting brokers to liability for innocent misrepresentations without imposing a corresponding duty of inspection for defects, and that without such a duty, a broker may be tempted to provide less information to a buyer, fearing that his or her chances of exposure to liability for innocent misrepresentations will multiply with the quantity of information provided.

At the other end of the spectrum from liability for innocent misrepresentation is the view that a real estate broker is an agent of the seller, not of the buyer, and is protected from liability under agency law. Thus, an agent would be permitted to repeat misinformation from his principal without fear of liability unless the agent knows or has reason to know of its falsity. This principle has been upheld by approximately half the jurisdictions that have addressed the issue of broker liability for innocent misrepresentations. The Supreme Court of Vermont recently reaffirmed this rule, holding that "[r]eal estate brokers and agents are marketing agents, not structural engineers or contractors. They have no duty to verify independently representations made by a seller unless they are aware of facts that tend to indicate that such representation[s are] false."

A recent decision of our Court of Appeals declared a middle ground that we find persuasive. At issue in *Tennant v. Lawton,* was a broker's liability for misrepresenting that a parcel of land could support a sewage system and thus was "buildable." The *Tennant* court echoed the Vermont court in holding that a broker is negligent if he or she repeats material representations made by the seller and knows, or reasonably should know, of their falsity. The court went on, however, to hold that a broker has a limited duty toward a purchaser of real property.

The underlying rationale of [a broker's] duty to a buyer who is not his client is that he is a professional who is in a unique position to verify critical information given him by the seller. His duty is to take reasonable steps to avoid disseminating to the buyer false information. The broker is required to employ a reasonable degree of effort and professional expertise to confirm or refute information from the seller which he knows, or should know, is pivotal to the transaction from the buyer's perspective.

We perceive no persuasive reason to hold real estate brokers to a higher standard of care than other professionals must satisfy. We have held that lawyers must demonstrate "that degree of care, skill, diligence and knowledge commonly possessed and exercised by a reasonable, careful and prudent lawyer in the practice of law in this jurisdiction.

Of relevance in this connection is RCW 18.85.230(5), which provides that a real estate license may be suspended or revoked if the holder is found guilty of [k]nowingly committing, or being a party to, any material fraud, misrepresentation, concealment, conspiracy, collusion, trick, scheme or device whereby any other person lawfully relies upon the word, representation or conduct of the licensee.... Under this statute, a broker is only guilty of knowingly committing a misrepresentation.

Absent a legislative directive to the contrary, we do not consider it appropriate to impose liability on a real estate broker without a similar requirement of knowledge. Knowledge, or any reasonable notice, that the boundaries pointed out by the seller were incorrect is absent in this case, as the trial court found in its findings of fact.

There was no evidence on the property which suggested to [the broker] he should investigate the boundary lines further. There was nothing in the surrounding circumstances that would have put [the broker] . . . on notice that there may have been something wrong with the property lines.

In short, a real estate broker must act as a professional, and will be held to a standard of reasonable care. If a broker willfully or negligently conveys false information about real estate to a buyer, the broker is liable therefor. We decline, however, to turn this professional into a guarantor. Real estate agents and brokers are not liable for innocently and nonnegligently conveying a seller's misrepresentations to a buyer.

The broker did not breach the standard of care of a reasonable prudent broker.

The improvements on the property were important to the buyers because they wanted to raise and ride horses. The broker saw markers for some of the boundaries when he walked the property with the seller, but could not locate all of the boundaries with certainty. Trees and other physical features on the land supported the seller's representations regarding the boundaries, however, and the broker testified that the seller assured him that the improvements were inside the property line.

The trial court is sustainable in its view that the broker in this case had no notice that anything was wrong with the boundaries as represented by the sellers. While hindsight suggests that the broker would have done well to check on the alleged survey, there was no testimony that such a check was the prevailing practice in the real estate business. Moreover, natural and man-made boundaries reinforced the seller's representations concerning the legal boundaries. Accordingly, the trial court did not err in finding and concluding that the broker in this case was not negligent.

REVERSED.

In most states that recognize a duty on the part of the seller's broker to disclose all material facts to the buyer, the duty is limited to facts the broker actually knew or should have known. In addition, most of these states hold the broker liable only if the buyer has no reasonable opportunity to discover the information himself or herself. One intermediate appellate court in California, in *Easton v. Strassburger* (1984), however, has held in a case involving residential property that the broker has not only a duty to disclose material facts but also an affirmative duty to conduct a reasonable inspection to discover all facts materially affecting the value or desirability of the property.

Though no other state court has gone as far as the *Easton* court, the decision triggered a flurry of new legislation. Apparently promoted by the National Association of REALTORS® and beginning in California, a significant number of state legislatures have enacted disclosure laws. Though there are wide variations among the new laws, generally they require that a buyer be provided with a disclosure form completed by the seller containing specified information about the property to the extent known by the seller. Some statutes prescribe use of a specific form, others are quite vague on the disclosure requirement. It should be recognized that the early submission of the disclosure forms to the buyer is very important. A few state statutes use the disclosure forms in lieu of the buyer's common law agency protections discussed in this chapter. Despite the disclosure form, the buyer must undertake an inspection of the premises as a protection against overpayment and to establish reasonable reliance for a possible fraud claim.

◆ **Buyer's Broker.** A broker who has contracted to locate real estate for a buyer.

In most real estate transactions, the seller hires a broker to procure a buyer for the property. However, in some transactions the agency relationship is created by a buyer who authorizes a broker to negotiate for the purchase of real estate suitable for the buyer's needs. In these transactions, the broker's fiduciary duties are owed to the buyer.

SALAHUTDIN V. VALLEY OF CALIFORNIA, INC.

California Court of Appeal
29 Cal. Rptr.2d 463 (1994)

BACKGROUND. Shaucat Salahutdin and his wife, Jeannie, immigrants from Korea, engaged David Seigal, a Coldwell Banker broker, to find property that they could purchase in Hillsborough. They informed him that it was essential that the property could be subdivided so that they could leave one-half to their daughter. Seigal informed the Salahutdins that a parcel had to be larger than one acre in Hillsborough for them to be able to subdivide. The Salahutdins agreed to wait as long as necessary to find a parcel large enough to subdivide. Later, Seigal found a parcel listed by another Coldwell Banker broker (the name under which Valley of California, Inc., did business) called the Black Mountain property that was shown as larger

◆ Dual Agency.   A transaction in which an agent represents both principals.

In a real estate transaction, a dual agency would exist if a broker were to represent both buyer and seller or owner and tenant. Undisclosed dual agency is generally considered to be illegal. Courts reason that an agent cannot adequately fulfill his or her fiduciary duty of loyalty to both principals. If representing the seller, the broker is obligated to obtain the best price for the seller's property. If representing the buyer, the broker's obligation is to obtain the property for the lowest possible price.

There are conditions, however, under which dual agency is permissible. The key seems to be for the broker to obtain the consent of both parties. The two principals must clearly understand that the agent is representing both of them and the broker must obtain their consent in writing. In a dual agency situation, the broker cannot disclose to either party confidential information the broker possesses. The broker should confine disclosures to matters concerning the property itself. In some states it is illegal for the broker to collect a fee from both principals even though both have agreed.

CASHION v. AHMADI ET AL.

Supreme Court of Alabama
345 So.2d 268 (1977)

BACKGROUND. Phillip and Donna Cashion (plaintiffs, appellants) purchased a home from Timothy and Nettie Ahmadi (defendants, appellees) through the realty firms of Pope and Quint (defendants, appellees) and Vergos Realty Company (defendant, appellee). After the purchase, the Cashions discovered a serious water seepage problem in the basement. They tried, unsuccessfully, to have this stopped, and then moved out. The Cashions then sued the former owners and the realty companies. The defendants moved for summary judgment. The trial court dismissed the case and plaintiffs appealed. Additional facts are in the opinion.

DECISION. The appellate court affirmed in part; reversed in part; and remanded.

JUSTICE ALMON. Marge Mills, realtor for Pope and Quint, was initially contacted by Mrs. Cashion because of a newspaper advertisement either about the house in question or another house. The house in question had been previously listed by Pope and Quint, but at the time Marge showed it to Mrs. Cashion, it was listed under an exclusive contract with Vergos Realty and Bauer Realty (not a party to this suit). At no time did the Cashions converse directly with Gus Vergos or the Ahmadis.

The Cashions sued the appellees alleging a confidential relationship existed between themselves and the Ahmadis, Pope and Quint, and/or Vergos Realty, and because of the confidential relationship, any one or all of the appellees had a duty to disclose that the house had a water problem which the appellees knew about. The trial judge dismissed the counts based on confidential relationship, apparently on the basis that the facts alleged did not show such a relationship.

By amendment, the Cashions alleged further (1) that they employed Pope and Quint to find them a residence to purchase, that they reposed trust and confidence in Pope and Quint, that Pope and Quint knew about the water problem, and that Pope and Quint breached their obligation arising out of their confidential relationship in failing to inform the Cashions about it, and (2) that Vergos Realty, as agent for the Ahmadis, negligently failed to disclose the water problem.

The Cashions contend they should have been allowed to prove that Pope and Quint was their agent, or, alternatively, that a confidential relationship existed because of the "particular circumstances" associated with this case.

A real estate broker may be hired to find a buyer or to find a seller. In either case the broker owes a duty of faithfulness to his principal.

> A broker is a fiduciary and holds a position of trust and confidence. He is required to exercise fidelity and good faith toward his principal in all matters within the scope of his employment, and to account for all funds or property rightfully belonging to his principal. He cannot put himself in a position antagonistic to his principal's interest, by fraudulent conduct, acting adversely to his client's interests, or by failing to communicate information he may possess or acquire which is or may be material to his employer's advantage, or otherwise.

The more common situation appears to be where the broker is hired by the seller to find a buyer for a percentage of the sale price, to be paid by the seller. From there, the house may be placed on a multiple listing, whereupon any number of realty firms may partake in the commission by finding a buyer.

In the instant case the house was listed under an exclusive contract with Vergos and Bauer Realties. However, Pope and Quint was allowed 50 percent of the commission for finding a buyer. In essence, the sale was treated as if it were a multiple listing.

The question raised by the Cashions is where did Pope and Quint's duty of faithfulness lie in this sale, with the sellers, the Ahmadis, or the buyers, the Cashions? Interestingly, Marge Mills, Frank Hicks (ex-broker for Pope and Quint), and Gus Vergos all acknowledged that if they were aware of a material defect in a residence they were selling, they should and would inform the buyer of the defect.

The Cashions contend that Pope and Quint was their agent and that it violated its duty of faithfulness to them in not disclosing the water problem. A broker, as well as any agent, may be an agent for both parties in a sale transaction; however, he opens himself to possible liability when he does so without full disclosure to both parties. Any broker, though especially a broker working with a multiple listing in which he has to work through another broker who deals directly with the seller, often finds himself in the precarious situation of seeking the trust and confidence of the prospective buyer while still claiming faithfulness to the seller. He cannot have it both ways.

Whether one is an agent of another is normally a question of fact to be determined by a jury. We believe that whether the total circumstances of this case require the conclusion that Pope and Quint, via their agent, Marge Mills, was an agent of Cashions, regardless of whether it may have been also an agent of the sellers, the Ahmadis, is a question for the jury under our scintilla evidence rule.

As to the question of whether Pope and Quint knew about the water problem, we note that while Marge Mills, Frank Hicks (ex-real estate agent for Pope and Quint) and Arthur

Pope deny such knowledge, Dr. Ahmadi was sure that he had informed Hicks about the problem, though what seepage problem existed while he owned the house had been remedied several years prior to the sale to the Cashions. Dr. Ahmadi also stated that dampness in the basement was the reason the price of the house was reduced, though such is denied by the realtors.

The judgment in this cause is affirmed as to the Ahmadis and Vergos Realty Company and reversed as to Pope and Quint, Inc.

AFFIRMED IN PART; REVERSED IN PART; AND REMANDED.

During the 1980s the unintentional dual agency problem was of major concern to the real estate industry. Many consumer protection groups and regulatory agencies sought a solution to it that would protect both buyers and the reputation of the real estate industry. As a result, a number of state legislatures and administrative agencies charged with regulating real estate sales personnel mandated that the agency relationship be disclosed in every transaction in which a broker is involved.

The rules and regulations that evolved require the broker to disclose to the parties the party he or she represents. The disclosure must be in writing, usually on a standard form that has been prescribed by the state's real estate regulatory body. (See Figure 12.1.) Additionally, disclosure must occur before the submission of an offer to purchase. Dual agency is not prohibited as long as the parties agree and proper disclosure is made.

Transaction Brokers. With some recent success, brokers have been lobbying for independent contractor status. Under this approach, brokers act as finders, putting sellers and buyers in contact with one another, thereby facilitating the progress of the deal. The broker's only responsibility, in order to be paid, is to conclude the deal. The broker is not within the control of either party. The good news for the seller and buyer is that neither would be liable for the illegal acts of the transaction broker. The bad news is that many of the remedies provided by agency law to the seller and buyer may be eliminated. Most state statutes that permit the transaction broker, or independent contractor, status do require that the broker act reasonably and in good faith.

One of the fears concerning the transaction broker is that it will only add to the existing confusion over the primary loyalties of the broker. Sellers and buyers who pay brokers' commissions expect loyalty from that broker. Whatever the outcome, the existence of transaction brokers is increasing.

FIGURE 12.1 *Notice to Prospective Real Estate Purchasers/Tenants*

In Ohio, real estate licensees are required to disclose which party they represent in a real estate transaction. Under Ohio law, a real estate licensee is considered to be an agent of the owner of real estate unless there is an agreement to the contrary and that agreement is disclosed to all parties.

Some duties of the licensee, as the agent of the owner, are to:

■ treat all parties to a transaction honestly;

■ offer the property without regard to race, color, religion, sex, ancestry, national origin, familial status, or handicap;

■ promote the best interest of the owner;

■ obtain the best price for the owner;

■ fully disclose to the owner all facts which might affect or influence a decision; and

■ present all offers to the owner.

As a buyer, if you choose to have a real estate broker represent you as your agent, you should enter into a written contract that clearly establishes the obligations of both you and your agent and specifies how your agent will be compensated.

Under Ohio law, the disclosure statement below must be submitted to the prospective purchaser/tenant in each transaction. This form has been approved by the Ohio Real Estate Commission for use by Ohio real estate licensees. Please sign below.

AGENCY DISCLOSURE STATEMENT

The listing broker and all agents associated with the listing broker represent the owner. The _____ (Selling Broker) and _____ (Selling Agent) represent (please check one): the purchaser/tenant _____ ; the owner _____ .

If a broker/agent is representing both the purchaser/tenant and the owner as a dual agent, he/she must attach a copy of the agreement signed by the purchaser/tenant and owner acknowledging their agreement to this arrangement.

By signing below, the parties confirm that they have received, read and understood the information in this Agency Disclosure Form and that this form was provided to them before signing a contract to purchase/lease real estate.

_____   _____
Purchaser/Tenant   *Date*   *Owner*   *Date*

_____   _____
Purchaser/Tenant   *Date*   *Owner*   *Date*

Any questions regarding the role or responsibilities of real estate brokers or agents in Ohio can be directed to an attorney or to:

State of Ohio
Department of Commerce
Division of Real Estate
Telephone: In Ohio 1-800-344-4100 or in Columbus 614/466-4100

◆ **Ready, Willing and Able.** **Capable of present performance.**

To be entitled to a commission, the broker must procure a buyer "ready, willing and able" to complete the transaction. The test of whether the buyer is ready and willing is his or her intention at the time the contract is made. Intent at the time the contract is to be consummated (closed) is not material. Most courts infer readiness and willingness if the buyer submits an offer on terms stipulated by the owner.

A buyer is said to be able if he or she has the financial ability to complete the transaction.

CASE EXAMPLE

Chester Winkelman, a real estate broker, brought suit against J. R. Allen to recover a commission. The basis of Winkelman's action was that he had procured a ready, willing and able buyer. The evidence indicated that Allen had listed his ranch with Winkelman at $350,000. The listing was open. Winkelman showed the ranch to Russell Bird and his father, Randall. Randall Bird was a prosperous rancher. Russell, age 22, had appreciable ranching experience but little capital.

The Birds and Allen discussed the sale on several occasions. On one of these, Allen was informed that only Russell, the son, was to sign the contract. After apparent agreement was reached on terms satisfactory to Allen, a written offer signed by Russell and a $1,000 deposit were submitted. Allen held the offer for several days and then sold the property to another.

After a lower court found in Winkelman's favor, an appellate court reversed and ordered judgment for Allen. The court stated, "[W]here the only available source from which the money is to come is . . . admittedly in the possession of a third person . . . who is in no way bound . . . such a purchaser cannot be considered able to buy. . . ." *Winkelman v. Allen, 214 Kan. 22, 519 P.2d 1377 (1974).*

In the *Winkelman* case the broker did not produce a ready, willing and able buyer. No commission was due. A buyer is considered financially ready and able to buy under any of three conditions:

1. The buyer has cash on hand to complete the sale.
2. The buyer has sufficient personal assets and a strong credit rating that ensures with reasonable certainty that he or she can complete the sale.
3. The buyer has a binding commitment for a loan with which to finance the sale.

When Commission Is Earned. In most states, the broker has procured a buyer when the broker submits a binding, enforceable offer from a buyer on the seller's terms. The result is that, as long as the buyer is financially able, the broker has earned the commission at that time. The broker and seller may, and frequently do, agree that the commission will be earned on conditions other than submission of a binding offer. Their contract may state that the commission is due on closing of title or out of the proceeds of the sale. If this is the case, the broker's commission has not been earned until that condition is met. As a general rule, if the broker procures a counteroffer that deviates in price or otherwise from the specified terms, the seller may accept or decline. If the seller accepts, the commission is due the broker for services rendered.

Recent case law in some states modifies the traditional general rule as to when the commission is earned. Courts in these states hold that the broker is not entitled to a commission if the buyer defaults on the contract. As a result, the broker does not earn the commission until the transaction closes.

Several reasons exist for this change. For one, most sellers listing property with a broker anticipate paying the broker's commission out of the proceeds of the sale. If the sale fails to close through no fault of theirs, sellers feel that they should not be responsible for a commission. A second reason is that the rule obligating the seller to pay a commission upon contracting places upon seller the burden of determining the buyer's financial ability. But the seller is the wrong person to make this decision. Determining the prospect's financial status and willingness should rest with the broker, for ordinarily that person has had closer contacts with the buyer and is better able to measure financial capacity and willingness. From the point of view of paying a commission, the time when financial ability and willingness are important is not when the agreement is signed, but at the time of closing. If the buyer refuses or is unable financially to perform at that time, the broker has not really done the job. If, however, failure to complete the transaction results from the seller's wrongful act or refusal, the broker has a valid claim for the commission.

Traditionally, the broker's compensation has been based on a percentage of the selling price. Most brokers in the same market customarily charge a similar commission, although even informal agreement among brokers to do so is illegal. In the late 1970s and early 1980s, as competition in the real estate industry increased, some brokers adopted alternative methods for determining fees. An obvious competitive strategy was to reduce the percentage charged to below that being charged by other brokers in the market. Another approach was to charge a flat fee instead of a percentage of the selling price. A third approach was to separate or "unbundle" the services provided a client and charge for each on an individual basis. For example, a broker might determine a separate fee for appraising the property and suggesting a selling price, advertising and showing the home, conducting negotiations or assisting at the closing. Clients could select the services desired and be billed only for these. Although discounting, flat fees and unbundling have been resisted in the industry, they probably will be used more frequently as real estate brokerage becomes more competitive.

TERMINATION OF AGENCY

The agency relationship may be terminated in numerous ways. Probably most agencies terminate upon accomplishment of the purpose for which the agency was created or on expiration of the time agreed upon for performance. The latter is important in real estate as many exclusive listings contain a date on which the listing will end. In fact, regulations in many states require that a listing include a specific termination date. Of course, the agency will continue if the parties renew the agency at that time.

By Acts of the Parties. As agency is a consensual relationship, either party has the power to end it at any time. However, the fact that one has the power to terminate the agency does not necessarily mean that he or she has the right to do so. For example, if a seller gives a broker an exclusive-right-to-sell listing for 90 days, the seller has the power to revoke the broker's authority before 90 days have passed, but if the seller revokes without justification, the broker can sue for damages.

CASE EXAMPLE

Hague owned 240 acres of farmland. He listed 80 acres with Hilgendorf, a licensed broker. Before the listing expired, Hague terminated it as he had encountered financial problems and decided to sell the entire farm. The farm was not listed with Hilgendorf.

Hilgendorf found a ready, willing and able buyer for the 80 acres. When Hague refused to accept the buyer's offer, Hilgendorf sued for his commission. Hague argued that Hilgendorf's duty of loyalty required him to give up the listing. Both the trial and appellate courts rejected this argument. The appellate court stated that "[i]n performing agency functions an agent does indeed occupy a fiduciary position, and his duty requires him to place the principal's interests first. But in the contract of agency . . . neither of the parties is acting for the other; each is acting for himself."

On this basis the appellate court rejected Hague's argument and awarded damages to Hilgendorf. The court stated that, although the principal has the power to terminate an unexpired agency, the principal subjects himself to damages for doing so. *Hilgendorf v. Hague, 293 N.W.2d 272 (Iowa 1980).*

By Operation of Law. In addition to termination by the acts of the parties, the agency relationship terminates automatically by operation of law if any of the following events occur:

- Death, incompetency or bankruptcy of principal or agent
- Destruction of the subject matter
- Change in law making the agent's duties illegal
- Loss of license required by either principal or agent
- Conflict of interest

Although termination for any of the above reasons is easy to understand, a difficult termination problem arises when an unusual change in conditions related to the agency takes place. For example, if a broker is authorized to sell land at a specified price and the value of the land suddenly increases substantially, has the original authority terminated? Most courts would say so.

◆ Agency Coupled with an Interest. An agency that cannot be revoked by the principal.

Although ordinarily an agency can be terminated at the will of either party, an agency coupled with an interest is irrevocable. In this type of agency, the principal has given the agent certain powers and coupled these with a financial or security interest in the subject matter of the agency. As a result, the principal does not have the right to revoke the agent's power. In addition, when an agent has authority coupled with an interest, the death, incompetency or bankruptcy of the principal does not terminate the agency.

One common example of the agency coupled with an interest is a mortgage in which the borrower gives the lender the power to have the security sold if the mortgage debt is in default (see Chapter 21 and discussion of power of sale foreclosure). A less common example would be a business arrangement in which a broker advances funds to a contractor to complete a home on speculation. In addition to agreeing to repay the loan, the contractor gives the broker an exclusive right to sell the property when the home is completed.

REAL ESTATE SALES ASSOCIATE

◆ **A person employed by a real estate broker who, under the broker's direction, lists and sells real estate.**

In many real estate transactions, much of the work is done by sales personnel who are not licensed brokers. Although many state licensing statutes use the designation *salesman* for both male and female sales personnel, the term *associate* is becoming more common. That word will be used in this chapter.

All states require real estate sales associates to be licensed. The procedures that are followed to license sales associates are similar to those for licensing brokers; however, the requirements for obtaining a sales associate's license are less demanding. For example, to obtain a broker's license a person is usually required to have experience in selling real estate, but experience is not necessary to obtain a sales associate's license. If a competency examination is required to obtain a sales associate's license, it is almost always less comprehensive than the licensing examination for brokers.

In large firms, sales associates do much of the legwork for the business. A sales associate prospects for buyers and sellers, assists the seller in determining price and completes listings and sales contracts. Sometimes the sales associate helps to arrange financing and may provide assistance to lenders and attorneys with regard to title evidence and documents necessary to complete the sale of real property.

A sales associate is required by law to be associated with a broker. The broker holds the sales associate's license and directs and supervises his or her work. Commissions on each sale are collected by the broker. The sales associate receives as compensation a previously agreed-upon percentage of the commission. There is some judicial disagreement as to the relationship between broker and sales associate. A majority of courts conclude that the sales associate is an independent contractor, not an employee. Under this view, the broker is not responsible for workers' compensation, unemployment insurance premiums or withholding taxes. Some recent cases, however, tend to view the relationship between broker and sales associate as that of employer-employee. Where this view is taken, the broker has the same legal responsibility to the sales associate that all employers have to their employees. Actually, whether an employer-employee or independent contractor relationship exists depends on the facts of the particular relationship.

> ## CASE EXAMPLE
>
> Several purchasers bought condominium units constructed by Salishan Properties, Inc., in a resort area in Oregon. Due to erosion from the ocean, their lots were severely damaged. The owners sued the developer/builder, contending that it had held itself out as an expert in resort-type construction and was, therefore, negligent in selecting an appropriate site for construction of its condominium units. Salishan countered that it had no liability since it was powerless to control the erosion problem.
>
> The court held that the developer could not be held liable for latent defects. It could, however, be held liable for negligence in site selection. Since the developer held itself out as an expert in resort construction, it was required to take reasonable precautions to assure that the lots were suitable for residential construction. *Beri, Inc. v. Salishan Properties, Inc., 282 Or. 259, 580 P.2d 173 (1978).*

Once the land is acquired, the developer undertakes to install the infrastructure for the development. The roads, sewer and water lines, power and telephone wires, gutters and sidewalks, and site grading must be completed. Most of these items are installed to specifications established by federal, state, county or municipal governments.

When the infrastructure is in place, the developer, when not also the builder, undertakes to market the lots to one or more homebuilders. The lot or lots may be sold outright to the builder. When a poor market exists for housing, the developer may agree to postpone full payment for the improved lot until the house is sold by the builder.

The Developer and Government Agencies. It is the developer's responsibility to obtain governmental approval for the site and for the individual installations. The land must be zoned properly for the type of housing that will be constructed. If it is zoned inappropriately, the developer seeks to have the zone changed to dovetail with the planned development.

Once the zoning is correct, the developer must obtain subdivision approval from the municipal planning board. The board will check to see whether the developer's plans comply with its regulations. For instance, the roads must be adequate in width and depth of roadbed, sewer lines must be adequate for anticipated flow and drainage layout must prevent flooding or ponding problems.

The most extensive cost in many subdivisions is that of installing utilities (using that term to encompass the full range of items that go into site preparation). These costs may be handled in a variety of ways. Some municipalities will bond (borrow) for the full cost of the utilities, recouping their money for bond retirement from the increased taxes obtained from the new homeowners in the subdivision. In other cases, the locality will bond for only a fixed amount for utilities, generally on a per-lot basis. If costs exceed that amount, the developer bears the financial obligation to pay the difference between the cost and the municipal bonding limit. In still other municipalities, the developer must pay the full cost of utilities without the assistance of public bonding. In the case of power and telephone lines the utilities themselves may bear the cost of installation up to a fixed maximum.

The developer is legally responsible for the construction to specification of any utility installed by it. Many times the municipality will demand that the developer provide a performance bond to guarantee that the utilities will be properly installed. The bond will be released in stages as portions of the utility installation are constructed and found to conform to public regulations.

The legal relationship lies between the municipality and the developer. The actual builder contracts for the purchase of lots with the developer, but the developer remains primarily responsible for compliance with local laws. One area where this lack of legal connection between the municipality and the builder causes trouble is final site grading. The developer grades the site pursuant to municipal specifications. Final grading on each lot, however, is usually the responsibility of the builder upon completion of construction of the house. It is the builder's contractual obligation with the developer to grade the site properly, but it is the developer that will be held accountable by the municipality.

There are various other approvals that the developer must obtain, depending on local laws. Sewer installations may need state or county health department approval. An environmental impact statement or other environmental permits may be mandated. In all of these, generally the developer has primary responsibility for compliance.

ARCHITECT
◆ **A professional person hired to prepare the plans and specifications for the construction of a house.**

The subdivider or contractor uses the architect to design the model home plans that he or she will sell to buyers. Also, the architect may lay out the design or configuration of the subdivision, locating the roads, the home lots and the drainage flow. The architect may, in addition, be employed to oversee construction. For an individual home, supervision may be confined to spot-checking materials that come onto the site and labor that is being performed. In larger projects, the architect may be hired to be on the site continuously to oversee the quality of work.

In any event, the architect who is hired by the buyer, owner or subdivider in one or more of these capacities has certain authority to act and certain rights and duties that arise from that authority.

The Authority of the Architect. The architect and buyer enter a personal service contract. Selection is based on the architect's skill as well as his or her reputation for honesty and fairness in business dealings. Although the basis of the authority granted is spelled out specifically in that contract, some generalizations can be made.

When the architect is hired to design a subdivision or an individual residential unit, an employer-employee relationship arises between the hiring party (the buyer) and the architect. This relationship requires the architect to follow the general instructions of the buyer in drafting the design. No architect is required to comply with instructions that would make the structure unsafe or would violate the regulatory ordinances of the community.

Since the architect is hired because of particular skills and characteristics, the contract is not assignable to another architect without the hirer's consent. If a firm of architects is hired, then any architect within that firm can do the design work unless otherwise stipulated in the contract.

When the architect is hired to supervise the construction, a principal-agent relationship arises between the architect and the buyer.

CASE EXAMPLE

Forty-O-Four Grand Corp. hired the architectural firm of Roland A. Wilson and Associates to supervise construction of a luxury apartment building in Des Moines. A dispute arose over the performance of the architect, and the owner withheld the architect's fee.

In an action by the architect for the remainder of his fee, the court described the parties' legal relationship. When one employs an architect to supervise construction, the architect is the agent of the one who employs him or her. The architect is bound to use reasonable care to see that the work is done properly with the proper materials. *Roland A. Wilson & Assoc. v. Forty-O-Four Grand Corp., 246 N.W.2d 922 (Iowa 1976).*

The architect has no general authority to bind the buyer but has the authority to do what is reasonably necessary to complete the job according to the plans and specifications provided.

Although the extent of the architect/agent's authority is specified in the contract, certain implied authority exists unless prohibited. The architect is implicitly authorized to make minor changes in the plans needed to correct errors made but does not have the authority to alter the plan materially without the buyer's approval. In addition, the architect has the implied authority to inspect materials that come onto the site to assure that they are of the requisite quality.

The architect has a third type of authority that does not neatly fall into a traditional legal category. When supervising construction, the architect has the implied authority, if not otherwise expressed, to settle disputes that arise between the buyer and the contractor. Though hired by the buyer and primarily responsible to that buyer, the architect is under a duty to resolve these disputes impartially. The architect must apply notions of equity to the dispute resolution and lay aside any duties owed to the buyer, which may put the architect in an uncomfortable position at times.

The Architect's Rights and Duties.   The architect who designs a subdivision or residential unit has a duty to perform in a workmanlike manner. Design work must be completed on time, or within a reasonable time if a date is not stipulated in the contract. An architect who fails to perform in a timely fashion will be liable in damages for that tardiness.

When the architect is the construction supervisor and therefore an agent, the fiduciary relationship demands the duty to act in good faith and with loyalty. The architect is prohibited from having a financial interest in the contract or in any way benefiting personally from the contract unless there is full disclosure and consent by the buyer.

The architect does not warrant a perfect job but does assure that the contract will be supervised with reasonable care. Failure to use reasonable care or to be loyal will make the architect susceptible to a suit for money damages by the buyer and to the withholding of the fee for failure to perform adequately. In the case cited above, the court stated that "this obligation does not make the architect a guarantor of the contractor's work. Instead, it requires the architect to exercise reasonable care in supervision and inspection of the work to protect the owner against payment of money to the contractor for work not performed or materials not delivered."

If the buyer fails to pay the architect for services performed, the architect has a mechanic's lien on the property. The architect can compel judicial sale of the structure if the lien is not satisfied. Lien rights are discussed in more detail in Chapter 16.

CONTRACTOR (BUILDER)
◆ **The person or firm that undertakes to construct a house at a given price.**

The term *contractor* or *builder* can mean several different things, depending on the building arrangement that is made by the buyer. Generally, the buyer hires a general contractor to construct the building to certain plans and specifications. The general contractor is obligated to provide the materials and labor necessary to construct the planned house. Much of the work is performed by subcontractors, whom the general contractor will hire and be solely responsible for. The general contractor is neither an employer nor an agent of the buyer, like the architect, but is classified legally as an independent contractor. The independent contractor agrees to provide a house to specifications, but the buyer has no direct control while the contractor is performing the services contracted for.

The general contractor may be constructing homes in a subdivision in compliance with the model home selected by the buyer or may be hired to construct an individually designed house on a lot owned by the buyer. Also, the general contractor may be building homes on speculation, hoping to sell them during or after construction. Although these are the most common arrangements, others exist as well. The buyer may choose to act as his or her own general contractor, hiring and coordinating the subcontractors or unit contractors.

The contractor may be selected personally by the buyer or may be obtained through a bidding process. If a bidding process is used, the potential contractors will be requested to bid on plans and specifications for a specific house. The bid entered by the contractor is an offer, and the buyer is free to select from among the various offers unless he or she has previously agreed to accept the lowest bid without reservation. There is no contract until the bid is accepted by the buyer. Any attempt to alter the bid materially by the buyer will be treated as a rejection of that bid.

The contract to build entered into by the contractor and the buyer will be governed by the usual rules of contract discussed in Chapter 10. The contractor's authority is simply to provide a final product, a house that complies with the plans and specifications provided by the buyer or the architect.

The chapter on contracts provides a thorough discussion of the various legal problems surrounding contracts. Satisfactory performance, delays in performance, mutual or unilateral mistake, modification of the contract and various actions for damages are discussed there. These general contract principles apply as well to the contracts entered into by the parties discussed in this chapter and will not be covered here.

The requirement of a building permit from a municipal official prior to beginning construction of a house is nearly universal. Failure to obtain a building permit allows the municipality to halt construction at any time and order compliance. Prior to issuing a building permit, the municipal official examines the plans for the house to ensure that no municipal code violations will occur.

If the building permit is issued and the contractor carelessly or willfully violates the municipal code, the contractor will be required to allow a reduction of the contract price equal to the cost of remedying the defects. If payment has already been made, a suit for money damages by the buyer is the appropriate remedy.

Rights and Duties of the Contractor. One of the chief responsibilities of the contractor is to coordinate the work of the subcontractors. If the general contractor fails to coordinate the work reasonably and that failure causes injury to the buyer or to a subcontractor, the general contractor will be liable in a suit for damages.

The contractor has the duty to inspect the materials brought onto the construction site. If such materials have defects that are reasonably discoverable upon an inspection and the contractor fails to inspect them or inspects but does not reject the defective materials, the contractor will be liable for injury caused by those materials. Injury includes the final product being a less valuable house, and the contractor will be liable for money damages for the difference between the value of the house contracted for and the one actually built.

The contractor, and any commercial home seller, implicitly warrants that the house he or she constructed is habitable. If the house proves not to be habitable or otherwise does not conform to any express warranty given by the contractor, the contractor will be liable in damages for the injury caused the owner.

C A S E   E X A M P L E

David and Patricia Elmore purchased a new home from a builder, Robert Blume. The Elmores told Blume that they planned on carpeting and making a recreation room in the basement. Blume assured them that the basement, which contained standing water upon inspection, would be dry when the gutters and windows were in place. After the Elmores took possession of the home, it continued to have a wet basement, and they sued for the cost of drain tiles.

The court stated that the contractor/vendor gives an implied warranty of habitability to the vendee in the contract for the sale of a house. Water damage caused by faulty construction would breach that warranty. *Elmore v. Blume, 31 Ill. App. 2d 643, 334 N.E.2d 431 (1975).*

If the house is destroyed by fire, flood or other natural disaster during the period of construction and the contract does not address this contingency, the contractor continues to be liable to provide a house completed to specifications. Once the building is finished, the contractor's responsibility to replace the house in case of destruction not due to the contractor's negligence terminates. If the buyer tells the contractor what lot to build on and supplies the builder with plans, the contractor is not legally responsible for soil characteristics that make the area unsuitable for construction nor for structural weaknesses in the house.

In general, the contractor agrees to perform in a workmanlike manner commensurate with accepted community norms. In exchange, the buyer agrees to make payments without unreasonable delay as they come due. If there is unreasonable delay in payment, the contractor may be justified in abandoning the job.

REVIEW AND DISCUSSION QUESTIONS

1. What are the two types of exclusive listings? Explain how they differ.

2. Compare and contrast express authority and implied authority. Provide some examples of implied authority.

3. Although appreciable differences exist in the United States as to what constitutes unauthorized practice of law, two principles are commonly accepted. State these principles.

4. Explain how the authority of an architect supervising construction differs from the authority agents generally enjoy.

CASE PROBLEMS

1. Ed Kelly gave Dave Gould Realty an exclusive listing on property owned by Kelly. Gould showed the property to Nadine McNicols, a real estate developer. McNicols had numerous questions relating to zoning, and Gould referred her to Kelly's attorney, who answered her questions and supplied her with additional information.

   When McNicols learned that Gould was showing the property to other prospective buyers, she made an offer directly to Kelly. Kelly accepted the offer but refused to pay Gould a commission. (a) What argument could be made for Kelly? (b) For Gould? (c) Who would win if Gould sued? Why?

2. Sam Guidi, a real estate broker, learned from a friend that Arro, Inc., was interested in buying vacant land for a warehouse. Knowing that Byron Lane owned land that he was trying to sell, Guidi phoned Lane, who quoted him a price of $35,000 for the parcel. Lane knew that Guidi was a broker, but no commission or other arrangements were discussed. Guidi obtained an offer of $28,000 from Arro, which Lane rejected. Shortly thereafter Lane contacted Arro directly and entered into a contract at $33,000. In a suit by Guidi against Lane for a commission, what resulted? Why?

3. Caldwell listed property with Burnette, a broker, at $3,000 per acre. The listing was open. Burnette showed the property to Donaldson, who stated that the price was too high. He requested Burnette to persuade Caldwell to reduce it. Burnette submitted an offer of $2,750 to Caldwell, but Caldwell would not accept the lower price.

   Several months later, Caldwell listed the property with Crutchfield at $2,500. Crutchfield showed the property to several prospective purchasers, including Donaldson. Donaldson offered $2,750 and the property was sold to him at that price. When Burnette heard of this, he demanded a commission. When Caldwell refused, Burnette sued. Would Burnette be successful? Support your answer. *Leon Realty, Inc. v. Hough, 310 So.2d 767 (Fla. Dist. Ct. 1973).*

4. Lewis, a licensed real estate sales associate, listed residential property owned by Flavin. Flavin informed Lewis that the property was in the South West School District. Actually the property was in the Columbus School District. Flavin, however, did not know this because he had no children and had frequently received mailings from the South West schools. In addition, children who lived next door attended schools in the South West District.

Katz and her husband were looking for a home, but they did not want to buy property in the Columbus district because children were bused substantial distances to achieve racial balance. The Katz family was interested in Flavin's home and agreed to buy it after Lewis assured them that it was in the South West District. Would the erroneous statement made by Lewis be a basis for Katz to recover damages? Discuss.

Fraud and Deceit

FRAUD

◆ **A deceptive act or statement deliberately made by one person in an attempt to gain an unfair advantage over another.**

No evidence exists that misrepresentation and fraud are more prevalent in real estate than they are in other sectors of the economy. However, deceptive acts that occur in real estate transactions probably have a greater impact than they do in other areas for several reasons. First, most real estate transactions involve large sums of money; as a result, people who feel deceived are more apt to complain or take legal action to assert their rights. A second reason is that licensing laws in every state have placed substantial supervisory responsibility on brokers for the conduct of sales associates, as was seen in Chapter 12. Unauthorized and even unintentional deception by the sales associate can subject the broker to liability, including the fraud of license. Finally, in many transactions little direct contact takes place between buyer and seller. Inasmuch as information is often transmitted through a third party, misunderstanding and error can result in the buyer, seller or both feeling that they have been deceived.

Many definitions exist for fraud; however, fraud can be classified into two major categories, based on the intent of the one who practices it. *Actual fraud,* or misrepresentation, is based on intentional deception and is usually accomplished by misstating or concealing a material fact. Actual fraud is often called *deceit,* and the two terms are used synonymously in this chapter. *Constructive fraud,* on the other hand, is not based on *intentional* deception. Constructive fraud often consists of a breach of duty arising out of the fiduciary relationship discussed in previous chapters.

Liability for constructive fraud may be based on a negligent or even an innocent misrepresentation. The law reads fraud into the actor's conduct because of its tendency to deceive another or to injure the public interest.

Those who enter into an agreement because they have been deceived by a misrepresentation are entitled to some form of remedy for any injury suffered as a result. The remedy available often depends on the extent to which the person making the misrepresentation intended to deceive. Remedies will be discussed more fully later in the chapter.

ACTUAL FRAUD

Almost any of the parties involved in a real estate transaction is potentially liable for fraud or deceit: buyer, seller, broker or sales associate. A defendant is liable for fraud if plaintiff can establish that defendant *intentionally misstated* a *material fact* on which plaintiff *justifiably relied.* Additionally, the plaintiff must be able to prove damages. Although it is relatively simple to list these elements, their application in practice is much more difficult.

Intentional. An intentional, conscious misrepresentation is an essential element of actionable frauds. Courts usually refer to this as an *intention to deceive.* The technical term *scienter* is also used. *Scienter* exists if a person knowingly makes a false statement or asserts that something is true or false without actual knowledge of whether or not this is the case. An evil intention is not necessary, nor is it required that the speaker intend to injure the other party.

Early cases found the requisite intent only in those situations in which the speaker had actual knowledge of the falsity of the representation; the courts equated intent to deceive with knowledge of falsity. This restrictive interpretation did not long survive. Today all American jurisdictions find *scienter* not only when the speaker knew the representation to be false but also when the representation was made either without belief in the statement's truth or with reckless disregard of its truth or falsity. Included are statements made by a person who realizes that he or she does not have sufficient basis or information to justify them.

CASE EXAMPLE

Gertrude Hall contracted to exchange her home for one being built by Haskins. The agreement was conditioned upon rezoning her property from residential to commercial use. After the property was rezoned, Haskins asked her to sign a blank deed. Mrs. Hall questioned this and inquired of Wright, her attorney, about the title to the Haskin property. Although Wright had never examined the title, he told her to sign the deed and that he would see that she got an abstract showing clear title.

Hall moved into the Haskins property. Some time later, Wright discovered that it was heavily mortgaged. Hall refused to make the mortgage payments, and she was ousted from possession. She then sued Wright for fraud. Wright defended on the grounds that he had not intended to deceive her. This defense was unacceptable to the court on the grounds that Wright spoke without knowledge. *Hall v. Wright, 261 Iowa 758, 156 N.W.2d 661 (1968).*

A majority of courts in the United States will not award damages for fraud if the speaker honestly believes, upon the basis of creditable evidence, that the representation is true. A substantial and growing minority do not accept this limitation when the innocent misrepresentation is made in a transaction involving the sale, rental or exchange of real estate. In these transactions the courts allow damages but limit them to the difference in value between what the listener has parted with and the value of what has been received and retained.

CASE EXAMPLE

Glenn, a father of two preschool children, leased a house from Takio on a five-year term. The rental was $600 per month. Takio had innocently represented to Glenn that a new school was to be built in the neighborhood. Takio did not know that plans had been canceled. When Glenn discovered the cancellation, he sued Takio for damages, claiming deceit. Glenn was able to prove that the rental value of the property without the new school was $450. The court awarded damages to compensate him for the reduced value of the property.

In all jurisdictions, even an honest misrepresentation of fact supplies the plaintiff with grounds to *rescind* the agreement. *Rescission* is the disaffirmation or cancellation of a transaction.

Misstatement of a Past or Present Material Fact. An important premise of American contract law is that adults are competent and have the ability to make rational decisions. As a result, courts do not aid those who rely on statements not worthy of belief. Judges reason that the rational person discounts statements that are not factual.

CASE EXAMPLE

Elfrieda A. Scantlin contracted to purchase a house being constructed by Superior Homes (Superior). In the course of the negotiations leading to the sale, an agent for Manning Real Estate, the builder's broker, stated that Superior was "a good builder and constructed excellent homes." After Scantlin took title, she found several things wrong with the building. When Superior did not repair these defects satisfactorily, she sued both Superior and Manning Real Estate. Scantlin claimed that the statement made by the agent was fraudulent. Scantlin's case against Manning was dismissed as the court held the agent's statement was merely his opinion. *Scantlin v. Superior Homes, 627 P.2d 825 (Kan. Ct. App. 1981).*

Although the rule that only factual statements that are misrepresented can be the basis for fraud is clear, often it is difficult to determine what statements are factual. A fact is something that is knowable, a physical object that actually exists or existed or an event that is under way or has taken place. Understanding what the law means by a statement of fact is often clarified by examining statements that courts generally consider as not factual. These include opinions and estimates (as illustrated by the previous case), predictions, guesses and promises.

Promises require a special word of caution. As discussed in Chapter 10, one who breaks a promise may be liable for breach of contract. Fraud is not the basis for the injured party's action. This makes a difference in the damages that the injured party can recover. For example, in a contract action, the successful plaintiff is entitled to compensatory damages only. If successful in a suit based on fraud, however, the plaintiff can collect punitive damages as well.

Puffing. Sellers have a natural tendency to commend the item they are selling. Such expressions as "I built it with the best," "It's the best building in town" and "You have nothing to worry about; it's a good well" are examples. Statements of opinion like this, made by a seller to induce the purchaser to buy, are often referred to as *puffing* or *dealer's talk*. Such statements are not actionable as fraud, even when false, since courts treat them as expressions of opinion. A leading American jurist, Judge Learned Hand, explained why in the following language.

> There are some kinds of talk which no sensible man takes seriously, and if he does he suffers from his credulity. If we were all scrupulously honest, it would not be so; but as it is, neither party usually believes what the seller says about his opinions, and each knows it. Such statements, like the claims of campaign managers before election, are rather designed to allay the suspicion which would attend their absence than to be understood as having any relation to objective truth. *Vulcan Metals Co. v. Simmons Mfg. Co., 248 F. 853 (2nd Cir. 1918).*

Although generally the law does not protect the credulous buyer who relies on the seller's opinion, a number of situations exist in which courts allow recovery for fraud based on nonfactual statements. Opinions expressed by (1) a person who enjoys a relationship of trust and confidence or has superior knowledge, (2) an expert hired to give advice or (3) a person who actually does not have this opinion are all actionable.

In the following examples, assertions that ordinarily would have been treated as opinion became the basis for fraud. In each case the court determined that the other party had a right to rely on the representation. Courts often rule this way when a pattern of deceptive conduct exists, or when the speaker has concealed something that fairness dictated should be revealed.

C A S E   E X A M P L E

Mel Erickson, a licensed real estate broker, specialized in investment properties. Tillitz, a wealthy rancher, wished to invest in a multifamily dwelling. Erickson showed Tillitz several properties. After inspecting one large unit, Erickson stated, "That's a fine building, and the return on your investment would be substantial." At the time, Erickson had never inspected the records and was unaware of some major problems with the heating units.

Tillitz purchased the building, lost money and sued Erickson for fraud. Because of Erickson's superior knowledge, many courts would consider the statement as the basis for fraud.

In the case that follows, a statement is clearly opinion, but the speaker is asserting an opinion that she doesn't actually have.

CASE EXAMPLE

Grover and his wife owned a house on a bluff overlooking Lake Michigan. For a number of years, the Grovers and their neighbors had been concerned with erosion along the shore and the safety of their homes. In fact, a group of people from the area, including the Grovers, had met with the Army Corps of Engineers to work out a solution to the erosion problem.

A prospective buyer of the Grover property expressed concern as to the safety of the house. Mrs. Grover responded, "The house is perfectly safe. We are living here, aren't we?" In an action to rescind the contract of sale, the Grovers defended upon the grounds that the statement was merely an expression of her opinion. This defense would not be successful, inasmuch as the Grovers did not actually have this opinion. See *Groening v. Opsota, 67 Mich. 244, 34 N.W.2d 560 (1948)*.

During the past 50 or 60 years, the trend has been to expand the type of statement that can serve as the basis for fraud. Courts look beyond the form of the statement and consider the circumstances in which it was made when attempting to determine whether there was deceit. One example is the manner in which most state courts treat statements of law made by a layperson. Courts traditionally considered these statements of opinion. They arbitrarily reasoned that all laypeople had comparable knowledge of the law; as a result, the person to whom that statement was made had no right to rely on it. Today, the law in most states differs. Courts generally examine the context in which such statements are made. In many instances, they conclude that the circumstances are such that a reasonable person has the right to rely on what the layperson says the law is.

Both buyers and sellers of real estate have been successful in actions for fraud, even when specific words concerning particular facts were never spoken. Most actions for fraud are based on oral or written statements, but numerous other methods are used to deceive. Actions, failure to act, concealment and silence can all be employed to mislead another.

CASE EXAMPLE

Lawson purchased land in a development called Vanderbilt Hills. He had a house constructed on this property. After a few months, the house began to sink. Upon investigation, Lawson discovered that the developer had filled a large gully with logs, stumps and other types of debris and covered this with clay. The land apparently was level, and enough clay had been dumped into the gully so that excavation for the foundation did not disclose the fill. Lawson was successful in a suit against the developer for fraud, inasmuch as the court held that the seller had a duty to disclose what he had done because the purchaser could not discover this through a reasonable inspection. *Lawson v. Citizens So. Nat'l Bank of South Carolina, 259 S.C. 477, 193 S.E.2d 124 (1972)*.

---

258 REAL ESTATE LAW

In the following situations, courts in most states have ruled with consistency that a person must speak out about relevant circumstances and facts known to him or her:

■ A hidden defect exists that is likely to result in personal harm to persons using the property.

■ A hidden defect exists that is likely to limit a use the seller knows the buyer intends to make of the property.

■ The seller enjoys a confidential relationship with the buyer.

■ The buyer has asked a question that the seller has answered truthfully, but the situation changes and the answer is now false.

Another troublesome problem exists where the seller has made an oral or written representation that is only partially true. Like silence and concealment, the "half-truth" is a misrepresentation actionable as fraud. In many cases, a half-truth is more misleading than a statement that is completely false. The half-truth can more easily lull the listener into accepting other representations that are made.

CASE EXAMPLE

Franks owned property on the outskirts of town. Although sewer lines had been constructed to the area, Franks's property was not yet connected. A prospective buyer asked Franks if the property was connected to a sewer. Franks replied, "The sewer line is across the street." Later, the buyer discovered that sewage from the house was being piped to the back end of the property. She sued Franks for the cost of having the property hooked to the sewer. Franks argued that his statement was true, but the court awarded damages to the buyer. *McWilliams v. Barnes, 172 Kan. 701, 242 P.2d 1063 (1952)*.

Reliance. To be successful in an action for fraud, the injured party must prove that (1) he or she acted in reliance on the false information, and (2) the reliance was justified. A person cannot have relied on false information if the information was acquired after the person acted, nor may a person rely on statements that investigation indicates are false.

CASE EXAMPLE

Grace Kiner was interested in purchasing a music store from Helen Little. Kiner's marketing strategy required a large volume of potential customers. Little informed Kiner that on the average 250 people came in daily. Little knew that this was false.

Upon several occasions, Kiner visited the store, remaining for appreciable periods of time. After Kiner purchased the store, it became apparent that Little's statement was false. As a result, Kiner sued to rescind. Rescission would be denied if the jury determined that Kiner had relied on her own inspection, not Little's statement.

In spite of the previous example, the fact that a purchaser makes an independent investigation does not in itself show reliance only on his or her own judgment. In these situations the courts must weigh the circumstances of the particular case to determine whether continued reliance on the misrepresentation after investigation is justifiable. Critical factors are such elements as the (1) background of the person investigating, (2) amount of time available to investigate, (3) sources of information available and (4) techniques needed to secure correct information.

Courts use different criteria to determine whether reliance is justifiable. Some states measure the plaintiff's conduct against that of a reasonably prudent person. If a jury decides that a reasonably prudent person, one who uses ordinary care under the circumstances, would not have relied on the statement, the plaintiff's reliance was not justified. Most states have rejected this standard. The test that is applied is tailored to the particular individual to whom the misrepresentation has been made. Courts in these states take the position that the law should not protect positive, intentional fraud practiced on the simpleminded or unwary. At the same time, a person who has special knowledge and competence is not justified in relying on statements that the ordinary person might believe. Similarly, a person whose background and information are those that a normal person might have is not barred from recovery because he or she carelessly accepts a misrepresentation; but if the alleged fact is preposterous, reliance is not justified, and recovery for fraud will be denied.

Material. Not only must the misrepresentation be relied upon; it must also be material. A person is not justified in acting on a false statement that is trivial in relation to the entire transaction. Inconsequential information of this nature is not material and thus not grounds for suit. On the other hand, some false statements that in themselves seem to be of no significance are important in particular situations. Consider the following examples, in both of which the representations are false.

CASE EXAMPLE

Rex Todor is purchasing a house in Memphis, Tennessee. The sales associate states, "Elvis Presley's uncle once lived here."

CASE EXAMPLE

Rex Todor is purchasing an inn in Memphis, Tennessee. The sales associate states, "Elvis Presley often stayed here."

In the first example, the misrepresentation would not be material. A reasonable person would not consider this a significant factor. If, however, the speaker knew that this was important to the buyer, the result would be different. Courts ordinarily will not allow a person knowingly to practice a deception, even though the supposed fact might be unimportant to most people. In the second example, the misrepresentation is material. The fact that Elvis Presley had often stayed at a particular inn would increase the property's value as an attraction for tourists.

Materiality also has a second dimension, which causes some legal problems. Frequently, a false statement is only one of several reasons that cause the person to act. A difficult factual question exists when the plaintiff has numerous bits of valid information upon

260 REAL ESTATE LAW

which a decision could logically be reached but, in addition, has been given some information that is false. Most courts hold that for the false information to be material, it must have contributed substantially to the plaintiff's decision to act. If without this information the injured party would not have contracted, the false information may be the basis of an action for deceit. Whether the information is material is a question for the jury. As noted in Chapter 1, the parties may waive a jury trial. If they do so, the judge is the trier of the facts.

Remedies Available to the Injured Party. A majority of courts in the United States have taken the position that a party deceived by an innocent misrepresentation is entitled to rescind the contract but not to collect damages. A few courts have held that even an innocent misrepresentation may justify an award of both rescission and damages.

If the misrepresentation is intentional, the injured party may proceed in a number of ways. He or she may:

- refuse to perform, using the deceit as a defense if sued for breach of contract;
- affirm the contract and sue for damages; or
- ask a court for a decree rescinding the contract.

In a number of states, courts will not allow the party who rescinds to collect damages except for the return of any consideration that has been given up. Courts in these states reason that rescission is based on a theory that no contract ever existed. Thus rescission is inconsistent with an award of damages for breach of contract. The trend in most states is to allow the deceived party who rescinds to collect damages notwithstanding the rescission.

CASE EXAMPLE

Mrs. Slade sold her house to Garrity. At the time that Garrity inspected the property, Slade informed him that the heating unit was new. Actually, the unit had been installed several years earlier.

In a suit for fraud based on the deceit, Garrity would be entitled to damages. These would be related to the cost of installing a new unit. He could also, if he desired, rescind the contract and recover the expenses involved in replacing the old unit.

Although U.S. courts generally have been solicitous of people injured by deceit, they recognize the potential harm to the defendant who is charged unjustly. Allowing recovery against a person for fraud or deceit can affect many aspects of that individual's life. His or her ability to earn a livelihood and to purchase a home or other items on credit are sorely jeopardized. As a result, the law has been reluctant to find against a defendant in a fraud action unless the plaintiff's case is sound and evidence clearly establishes all the necessary elements.

Damages. In an action for fraud and deceit, a plaintiff is not entitled to recover damages unless actual monetary loss can be proved. Ordinarily, this requirement is met easily because usually the relationship between the misrepresentation and monetary injury is clear. Few people would sue for misrepresentation unless they believed the deception caused them to lose money. The costs and trauma of litigation make it an expensive way to prove a person a liar if the plaintiff lost nothing.

Generally, the more acute legal problem involves the amount of the damages, not their existence. The following case, *Kramer v. Chabot,* discusses different theories of damages in cases involving fraud and negligent misrepresentation.

KRAMER V. CHABOT
Supreme Court of Vermont
564 A.2d 292 (1989)

BACKGROUND. Marilyn Kramer (plaintiff, appellant) sued Lee Chabot (defendant, appellee) for breach of professional duty and misrepresentation in his inspection of a house on her behalf. The trial court awarded her $50 in damages. Plaintiff appealed from the determination of damages. Additional facts are included in the opinion.

DECISION. The appellate court vacated and remanded for further proceedings.

JUSTICE GIBSON. In June of 1979, plaintiff decided to buy a house in Manchester, Vermont, for $42,500. Prior to the purchase, she signed an agreement with the seller stating, inter alia, that the purchase was contingent upon plaintiff's obtaining a favorable inspection report on the property. Plaintiff hired defendant, a builder, to carry out this inspection.

Defendant gave plaintiff a one-page report which stated that the house (including the foundation, structural timbers, plumbing, electrical wiring, and roof) was in good condition. Plaintiff, relying on the report, then completed the purchase.

Despite the representations made in defendant's inspection report, plaintiff discovered, after the sale, numerous defects in the house which required substantial repairs. In the course of the next few years, she spent over $25,000 to put the house into shape, and then sued the defendant to recover the sums she had expended, alleging that he had a duty to perform the inspection in a professional manner, and that his breach of that duty was the proximate cause of damage to plaintiff. In addition, plaintiff claimed that defendant either negligently or intentionally misrepresented certain facts about the property, and that she relied on his representations in deciding to purchase it.

Defendant did not appear personally for trial, although his attorney was present, and the trial court entered a default judgment against him on the issue of liability. The court then proceeded to take evidence on the issues of damages. Plaintiff claimed damages totaling $25,214.10, the amount she had spent on repairs after buying the house.

Acknowledging that the "sole question" before it was the amount of damages to be awarded, the court concluded that compensating plaintiff for all her reasonable expenses in bringing the house into line with the inspection report would produce "an eminently unfair result," since evidence showed that the value of the property at the time of trial, some seven and one-half years after the purchase, was in

NEGLIGENT MISREPRESENTATION

The rules of negligence apply to a false representation made carelessly in a business transaction. The person supplying false information who fails to exercise reasonable care in obtaining or communicating it is responsible for actual loss suffered by the listener. Because there was no intent to deceive, the speaker's liability is more limited than in a case of intentional misrepresentation. In addition, the defendant may assert defenses, such as plaintiff's contributory negligence, that are not available in an action for deceit.

WAIVER

◆ **Intentional surrender of a known right or privilege.**

Under certain circumstances, one who has been induced to enter a contract because of fraud or deceit waives the available remedies. Generally, waiver occurs when a person discovers the fraud and then does nothing about it. American courts generally hold that a person learning of deceit must take some action, or the contract based upon the deception will be confirmed.

In a majority of U.S. jurisdictions, if the contract is wholly *executory*—that is, neither party has performed—the defrauded party upon discovery of the fraud must rescind. Often courts in these jurisdictions do not allow the injured party to recover damages when an executory contract is rescinded. This rule is open to criticism because it denies the injured party the benefit of any bargain that has been made.

If a contract has been substantially performed, the injured party may elect to rescind or affirm the contract and sue for damages. Some action, however, must be taken, and the position of the person defrauded must be made clear to the perpetrator of the fraud. Waiver occurs if, after discovery of the fraud, the injured party merely continues to perform. This is not to say that the injured party need proceed with the contract. Completion of the contract and a subsequent suit for damages is an available option, but the injured party's position must be established, and within a reasonable period of time.

Real estate contracts sometimes contain provisions stating that the purchaser has not relied on any representations made by the owner or broker. A modification of this is a statement that the purchaser has personally examined the property and enters the contract relying solely on his own inspection. A typical example is a clause such as "buyers agree that they have entered into this contract relying upon their own knowledge and not upon any representations made by the seller or any other person." Clauses of this type do not waive the injured party's rights to sue for fraudulent representations made by an owner or a broker. The courts reason that to accept such clauses as defenses would provide the seller and the seller's agent with a license to commit fraud. Most buyers would neither recognize the significance of the language nor consider that it applied to outright deception. To allow its enforcement would violate the clear public policy of protecting people who act on the basis of deceptive statements.

REVIEW AND DISCUSSION QUESTIONS

1. Explain the difference between actual and constructive fraud.

2. What is the meaning of *scienter?*

3. A limited number of situations exist in which silence can be the basis for a successful action based on fraud. Discuss these situations.

4. (a) How does the benefit-of-the-bargain rule for measuring damages differ from the out-of-pocket rule? (b) Which is more beneficial to the injured party?

5. Under what circumstances might a court award punitive damages in a case involving fraud?

6. Many courts refuse to award damages for fraud if a contract is wholly executory. Critically evaluate this rule.

CASE PROBLEMS

1. Able hired a contractor to repair several cracks in the walls of his home. The cracks were the result of settling, but the contractor never mentioned this fact to Able. Somehow Able got the impression that the cracks were caused by green lumber. When Able later tells Baker, a prospective purchaser, about the cracks, he explains the cause as green lumber. Baker purchases the property. When additional cracks appear and Baker discovers their true cause, he sues Able for fraud. Is Able liable? Discuss.

2. J. B. Williams was an experienced businessman. In 1977, he entered into a written contract to buy realty from Threlkeld and Murray for $1 million. During the negotiations, Van Hersh, who represented the sellers, stated that New York Life had made a commitment to loan $6 million to develop the property. The terms of this loan were never discussed, nor did the parties ever talk about interest rates or any possible conditions. Williams did not check with New York Life.

    When Williams discovered that the life insurance company had not made a commitment, he attempted to rescind the contract on the grounds of fraud. Would he be successful? Discuss. *Williams v. Van Hersh, 578 S.W.2d 373 (Tenn. 1978).*

3. Kaye was interested in buying a large piece of land from Katzenberry, who lived nearby. Katzenberry did not want to sell the land to a buyer who would use it for commercial purposes; he asked Kaye what he planned to do with the property. Kaye told Katzenberry that he was going to build a house on part of it and probably would use the rest for a garden. This was true, but before the closing Kaye changed his mind and made plans to build a hamburger stand next to his house. Katzenberry learned of this and refused to convey the property. Kaye sued for breach of contract; the defense claimed fraud. Would Kaye be successful? Discuss.

4. Hayes owned a valley home that he wanted to sell. He listed the property with Watkins, a local broker. Hayes knew that the basement of the house was subject to extensive flooding, especially during the spring. He did not inform Watkins of this. Watkins did know that rains and melting snow in the spring often caused a flooding problem for valley property.

    During the fall, Hayes showed the house to Morris, who was from out of state. While the two were examining the basement, Morris expressed concern about obvious water damage. Watkins, who stood nearby, said nothing. Later, while talking to Hayes, Morris asked about basement flooding. Hayes stated that in the spring, water sometimes seeped into the basement. Watkins, who listened to the conversation, again said nothing.

Morris purchased the property. The following spring the basement was damaged by severe flooding. Morris sued both Hayes and Watkins for fraud. What defenses, if any, are available to Hayes and Watkins? Will Morris be successful? Support your answer.

5. Hattie Griffin agreed to give a lot to Charles Spence, a self-educated itinerant preacher, and his wife. Mrs. Griffin had befriended the Spences and they had provided her with spiritual comfort upon the death of her son. The transfer was conditioned upon the Spences building a church on the lot and allowing Mrs. Griffin the right to use the church parking facilities as a parking lot for her restaurant on an adjoining lot. The parties had also agreed that the lot was to revert to Mrs. Griffin if it wasn't used for a church.

At the closing, which was hastily arranged, Mrs. Griffin read the deed, but not carefully. Both Spence and his attorney assured her that it was "drawn up like you asked." However, the deed did not contain wording that restored the property to Mrs. Griffin if it was not used for a church. At the trial the attorney testified that he had tried to explain the contents of the deed to Mrs. Griffin, but he felt she didn't understand it.

When problems arose concerning the use of the parking facilities by Mrs. Griffin's customers and financing a building on the lot, Mrs. Griffin sued for rescission on grounds of fraud. Would she be successful? Discuss.

6. Reilley owned a small ranch that he planned to sell. The ranch was in a rural area, and the exact boundaries were not clear. Although a survey of the ranch existed, Reilley felt that it was incorrect. As a result he hired Gavin, a licensed surveyor, to resurvey the ranch. Reilley placed stakes in the ground at what he believed to be one of the corners, and Gavin surveyed with that as the starting point.

When Reilley placed the property on the market, he used Gavin's survey as the basis for the description of the property. Herman contracted to purchase the ranch on the basis of the Gavin survey. During the negotiations, Herman and Reilley walked what Reilley informed Herman were the boundaries. Reilley did not inform Herman of the questionable boundaries or the existence of the first survey.

After Herman took the title, he discovered that boundaries were questionable and that another survey existed. This survey indicated that the ranch was smaller than the Gavin survey indicated. Herman sued to rescind, arguing fraud in that Reilley had not informed him of the questionable boundaries and the discrepancy between the two surveys. Would Herman be successful? Support your answer.

14

Closing the Real Estate Transaction

CLOSING OR SETTLEMENT

◆ The final stage of the real estate purchase transaction during which the deed and the purchase money are exchanged.

After the buyer and the seller sign a real estate purchase contract, they need time to prepare for the closing. The buyer ordinarily must search for financing, while the seller needs time to prepare evidence of title. Other documents need preparation as directed by the purchase contract, laws and local customs. There is a deed to be drawn, inspection certificates to be obtained, expenses and income to be apportioned, and other preparatory matters to be completed. The interval between the signing and the closing date is intended to provide the necessary time to accomplish these matters.

The date of closing is normally specified in the contract. The date may be as early as two weeks from the date of the contract or as long as two months and occasionally even longer. One difficulty with a long interval is that lending institutions normally do not extend a loan commitment for more than 30–60 days without some additional cost to the borrower.

A postponement of the closing date does not result in a breach of the purchase contract as long as the adjournment is reasonable. On the other hand, if the contract specifies that "time is of the essence," even a one-day postponement could be considered a breach for which the law would afford a remedy to the innocent party.

When the contract does not provide for a closing date, a reasonable time is implied. Since the purpose of the interval is to provide the necessary time to accomplish certain tasks, a reasonable time would be a period within which these tasks could reasonably be accomplished.

The rights and obligations of the parties are defined by the contract. To a large extent, the contract governs the closing format. Local custom, to the extent that it does not contradict contractual provisions, also shapes the closing. Some localities, for example, customarily use the *escrow closing,* wherein the deed and purchase price are delivered to a third party, who is directed to close the transaction outside the presence of the parties. The escrow closing is the subject of the next chapter. In other jurisdictions the parties meet each other face to face at the closing. This conference type of closing is the subject of this chapter.

The object of the closing is to complete the transaction so that the purchaser is vested with title to the realty and the seller receives the purchase price. Various persons who may be responsible for the closing proceedings (other than the buyer and seller) include the real estate broker, attorney and settlement clerk.

BROKER

The broker has an economic interest in the closing; at this stage the real estate commission is paid by the broker's principal, who is normally the seller. For that reason the broker usually participates in the closing preparation and is present at the closing.

State law varies concerning the broker's permissible role in the closing. Some states permit the broker actually to draw up legal documents, whereas other states relegate the broker to a more passive role. Often the broker facilitates the closing by communicating with the lending institution, the purchaser, seller and/or their representatives on last-minute details. The broker may hand-deliver closing documents to the parties or their legal representatives to minimize the risk of a breakdown in the critical last hours before closing. The broker may be responsible for reminding the parties what documents they need to bring to the closing. To the extent permitted by local law, the broker may even assist in the computation of prorations and the preparation of closing statements. In absence of an attorney representing the seller, the broker will explain to the seller the closing process as it unravels, thus reducing anxiety and confusion at the closing.

ATTORNEY

The attorney's role at the closing varies, depending on state law, the type of closing and local custom. Although not every real estate closing involves attorney representation, when it does occur, purchasers are more apt to be represented than sellers. Perhaps this is because it is legally more difficult to ascertain whether a purchaser has received good marketable title to the real estate than whether the seller has received the full purchase price prescribed by the contract. In other words, the lay seller is in a better position to ensure receipt of the full purchase price than the lay buyer is to ensure receipt of marketable title to the real estate.

At the ordinary closing, the attorney's role is routine, being confined to explaining the various documents to the client. Most of the attorney's preparation for the closing—examination of documents such as the deed, abstract or title insurance policy, mortgage, mortgage note and closing statements—occurs in advance. If the attorney has properly prepared in advance, the routine closing is normally smooth and may seem anticlimactic. An attorney has a more important role, however, in the rare closing where a difficult legal problem arises. Since no one can determine beforehand whether the closing will present an extraordinary problem, it is best for all parties to be represented by counsel. When parties are represented by attorneys, closings are likely to be smoother and less confusing because each party generally has confidence in his or her legal representative.

The seller is responsible for delivering a deed in conformity with the contract. For this reason the seller must hire an attorney for the preparation of the deed or permit the lending institution's attorney to prepare it, in which event the fee will be charged to the seller. The purchaser's attorney will examine the deed to ensure that the description of the property is accurate and that compliance with the necessary formalities for execution of the deed has occurred. The seller may be responsible, pursuant to the terms of the contract, for producing an abstract showing the history of the transactions that relate to the title of the property. An abstract may be prepared by the seller's attorney; in some jurisdictions professional abstractors who are not attorneys may perform this service. Based on the abstract, the buyer's attorney may be called upon to provide a certificate or letter of opinion regarding the marketability of the title. An attorney who negligently renders a wrong opinion to the buyer will be liable for damages.

SETTLEMENT CLERK

◆ **The person who is designated to coordinate the execution of documents at the closing.**

The settlement clerk is responsible for ensuring that all documents are properly signed and delivered to the appropriate party. The settlement clerk may be an attorney, real estate broker, employee of the lending institution or title insurance company or any other designated person. A few states require the settlement clerk to be licensed. The deed and other documents may require acknowledgment before a notary. Hence, it is advisable that the settlement clerk be a notary public. Otherwise, a notary public should be present.

At the closing, a lot of paper changes hands. The closing is routine for the settlement clerk, who has undoubtedly performed numerous closings; for the buyers and sellers, however, it may be bewildering. Unless the settlement clerk is sensitive to that fact, the closing may be less than successful. Each document and transaction should be briefly explained to the parties, either by the clerk or by the attorney representing the client. Most problems that emerge at the closing can be remedied by thoughtfulness and a calm spirit.

PREPARATION FOR CLOSING

Preparation is the key to a successful real estate closing. Both the buyer and the seller need to take care of certain items preliminary to the closing. Failure to do so may result in a breakdown at the closing. The laws and customs that govern the buyer's and seller's conduct in preparation for closing do not vary greatly from state to state.

BUYER'S PREPARATION

The buyer's preparation involves obtaining financing, examining the title, securing hazard insurance, calculating the amount needed at closing, and inspecting the premises.

Obtaining Financing. The buyer ordinarily lacks the available cash to pay for the property and must therefore search for a loan. The prudent purchaser selects a lending institution on the basis of the best buy available, comparing interest rates and other charges. A difference of one half of one percent in the interest rate may be very substantial over the life of the loan. A lending institution requires an application, a credit check and an appraisal before it will approve a loan. Various federal laws related to the loan, discussed later in this chapter, place certain obligations upon the lender.

The real estate contract is usually contingent upon the buyer obtaining a loan. If, after exercising good faith, the buyer is unable to obtain the necessary financing, the parties are discharged from any further obligations under the contract. However, as the next case illustrates, the failure to obtain the loan must occur in spite of the exercise of good-faith efforts to obtain the loan.

DUNCAN V. ROSSUCK

Supreme Court of Alabama
621 So.2d 1313 (Ala. Sup. Ct. 1993)

BACKGROUND. The Duncans signed a contract to purchase a house from the Rossucks for $148,000. The contract stated in part: "This contract is subject to purchaser being able to obtain a suitable loan in the approximate amount of $118,400. The purchaser agrees to exert all reasonable effort and diligence to obtain such loan and to make application for such loan within 10 days." The Duncans sought financing at seven banking institutions, although they only applied in writing to one. Because they were experiencing difficulty in obtaining a loan, the Rossucks extended the closing date for 10 days. They also arranged for the Duncans to assume an existing mortgage on the property for about $79,000. A bank agreed to lend the Duncans the remaining amount on condition that they pledge additional property as security for the loan. The Duncans refused. The Rossucks then agreed to lend the Duncans the remaining amount upon the same or more favorable terms as the bank. The Duncans would not agree. The Rossucks

sued. The trial court found in favor of the Rossucks.

DECISION. The Supreme Court of Alabama affirmed the trial court decision.

JUDGE STEAGALL. When the parties signed the contract, the Rossucks advised the Duncans that the term "suitable financing" meant that they must do their best to obtain the financing to purchase the real estate. The closing date was set for August 15, 1990.

In its order the trial court did not find any ambiguity in the term "suitable financing." The record shows that when the Duncans sought financing from the Bank . . . they specified their own terms in the written application and thus tailored their application to reflect what they considered to be a "suitable" loan. . . . The evidence contained in the record supports the trial court's conclusion that the term "suitable financing" was not ambiguous.

The Duncans next argue that, because the "suitable financing" provision was a contingency that did not come to fruition, their duty to perform under the contract never arose. This Court has previously held that a contract provision making the contract subject to the procurement of a loan to finance the purchase price is a valid condition precedent to performance; however, the purchasers have the implied duty to attempt to obtain financing through a reasonable good faith effort. In this case, this duty was an express part of the contract.

In its order, the trial court specifically found that the suitable financing provision was a valid condition precedent to performance under the contract; however, the court found that the Rossucks offered such financing to the Duncans, and that the Duncans refused the financing solely because they wished to be relieved from performing under a contract that they had become disenchanted with. The Duncans' own testimony contained in the record fully supports the trial court's findings; thus, we find no merit in the buyer's argument on this point.

AFFIRMED.

The lending institution that loans money to the buyer will require the buyer to sign a note promising repayment, plus a mortgage of the property, which secures repayment by giving the lender an interest in the property. At the closing, the lending institution will make sure that these instruments are signed by the buyer before disbursing the proceeds from the loan.

Examining Title. The contract may call for the seller to provide evidence of title in the form of an abstract, certificate of title or title insurance. The buyer should insist on the evidence of title prior to closing so that an attorney can scrutinize the documents to ensure their reliability. An abstract should be up to date and contain no gaps in the chain of title. A certificate of title should be signed by an attorney. Title insurance policies should be checked to ascertain what encumbrances, if any, are excluded from protection. These exclusions may draw attention to title problems.

The purchaser is entitled to a marketable title in absence of a provision in the contract to the contrary. Marketable title is one for which a reasonable, prudent purchaser would be willing to accept and pay fair value. A marketable title is free from objections or encumbrances that would significantly interrupt the owner's peaceful enjoyment and control of the land or impair its economic value. In order to be marketable, it is not necessary that the title be free from every possible encumbrance or suspicion of encumbrance. It need only be free of a reasonable possibility of contentious litigation. Nobody wants to purchase a lawsuit, and, indeed, the law will not require a person to do so.

the gas lines are free from leakage. Heating, plumbing, electrical, sewerage or any other system may be the subject of required certificates showing the systems to be in good working order and free from defects. The seller should be prepared to produce the appropriate certificates at closing.

ACTION AT THE CLOSING

The place of the closing is controlled by local custom. Commonly the closing is conducted at the office of the lending institution where the purchaser has obtained financing to purchase the property. Other possible places of closing include an attorney's office or the office of the real estate broker, title insurance company or seller's mortgagee.

Both seller and buyer have responsibilities at the closing. Each is discussed below.

SELLER'S ACTIONS

At the closing the seller tenders the deed, provides evidence of title, if required, and delivers any necessary assignment of leases.

Tendering the Deed. The seller is obligated to tender the deed to the buyer or to the settlement clerk for delivery to the buyer. The buyer should carefully check the deed to make sure its specifications are in accord with the contract. The deed should be of the type the grantor agreed to give. Any encumbrances that are excepted in the deed should be compared to the contract to ascertain whether they are found there. The description should be double checked against the description contained in the prior deed of conveyance or another reliable source. The names of the grantor(s) and grantee(s) should be checked for accuracy. Even a minor misspelling of a name may cause future problems that will take time and money to remedy. Particular attention should be directed to the form of the execution to ensure conformity with state law. If, for example, the state law requires that the grantor subscribe the deed by signing an alphabetical signature, then a mark of the grantor should not be accepted. If the state law requires that two witnesses sign in the presence of each other, a deed otherwise witnessed is unacceptable. If the state law requires acknowledgment before a notary, the notary seal and notary commission expiration date should be examined for authenticity.

Evidencing Title. The seller may be required to provide evidence of title in the form of an abstract or attorney's opinion, sometimes called a *certificate of title*. Judgments or other encumbrances can intervene between the date of the abstract or attorney's opinion and the date of closing. For that reason, it is most advisable for the purchaser to make a final search of the title down to the moment of closing. Such a search, however, is not always practical. One way to protect the buyer who is unable to make a final search is to close in escrow, which is the subject of the next chapter. Under this closing procedure, the settlement clerk or other escrow agent holds the executed deed and the purchase price pending a final check of the title. Upon notification by the buyer or buyer's attorney that the title is in order, the deed is transferred to the buyer and the purchase price to the seller. Sometimes the seller will be required to give the buyer an affidavit of title (as shown in Figure 14.1), which covers objections that might not appear in the title search.

Assigning Leases. In the event the property is sold subject to a lease, the seller should deliver a proper assignment of the lease to the buyer. In addition, the seller should deliver to the buyer any security deposited by the tenants along with letters to tenants notifying them of the sale and advising them to pay future rentals to the purchaser.

PURCHASER'S ACTIONS

The buyer's responsibilities at the closing include tendering the purchase price and closing the loan extended by the lender.

Tendering Purchase Price. The purchaser is obligated to tender the purchase price to the seller. Normally, in absence of an excuse by the seller, the purchase price must be produced and offered to the seller. It is normally not a sufficient tender for the purchaser to appear at the closing and maintain that he or she has access to the purchase money elsewhere. The purchaser must actually make a show of the money with the intent to deliver it to the seller. Of course, this is not necessary if the tender would be futile, for example, should the seller not appear at the closing.

Payment is usually made by some form of check, usually a cashier's or certified check. However, whatever medium the contract calls for must be honored.

> ### CASE EXAMPLE
> Benjamin Chertok entered into a contract to purchase realty from Aroosiag Kassabian. Chertok made a deposit and agreed to pay the remainder in cash at the closing. At closing Chertok tendered a third person's certified check to Kassabian. Kassabian requested that he cash the check, and Chertok refused. After Kassabian refused to tender the deed, Chertok sought a return of his deposit. The court held that Chertok's tender was not the equivalent of payment in cash, and consequently he was in breach and not entitled to a return of his deposit. *Chertok v. Kassabian, 255 Mass. 265, 151 N.E. 108 (1926).*

Mortgaging the Property. Lending institutions charge closing costs, normally computed as a percentage of the amount borrowed. Closing costs are charged by the lending institution to cover the cost of services performed in connection with the loan and for servicing the loan. Closing costs vary among lending institutions.

If the buyer is financing the purchase through a new loan, the lender supplies a mortgage and a note for the borrower to sign at closing. Any existing mortgage on the property will be satisfied out of the purchase price, and a satisfaction of mortgage signed by the seller's lender will be given to the settlement clerk for recording.

In reality, most closings involve two distinct but related transactions. First, the sale of the property is closed between the seller and the buyer, with the seller receiving the purchase price and the buyer the deed. Second, the loan extended by the lending institution is closed

FIGURE 14.1 *Affidavit of Title*

State of Ohio
County of Hamilton

Rod Ross, being first duly sworn, on May 1, 1998, deposes and says that:

1. He resides at 6415 Stover Avenue, in the City of Cincinnati, County of Hamilton, State of Ohio, and has resided at such place for approximately 10 years; he is a citizen of the United States, over the age of 18 years; he is the seller named in the contract of sale dated March 10, 1998, with Bert Haas as purchaser, and is the owner of the real property therein described.

2. He has been such owner since on or about July 1988, having acquired the same from Harry Blythe by deed; ever since his acquisition affiant has been in peaceful and undisturbed possession of such real property and neither his possession nor his title thereto has been disputed or denied by anyone.

3. Affiant's predecessor in interest was in peaceful and undisturbed ownership and possession of the same real property for approximately eight years prior to conveyance to affiant.

4. No use, tenancy exchange or occupancy of such real property or any part thereof has been such as to give rise to any claim of title or interest by adverse possession.

5. All taxes and assessments levied against the property have been paid when due, and such property is free and clear of any tax lien except for current taxes not yet due or delinquent.

6. The real property is free of any encumbrance by mortgage, deed of trust, or otherwise except restrictive covenants specified in the deed.

7. Plaintiff has not suffered any judgment or decree in any court and no judgment lien has ever attached against such property during affiant's ownership thereof, or during the ownership of affiant's predecessor in interest, to the best of affiant's knowledge and belief.

8. No lien for unpaid income taxes has been filed or is outstanding against the property.

9. No laborer has worked on the premises, nor has anyone supplied materials used on the premises who remains unpaid.

10. Affiant is not married.

11. In acquiring title to the real property described in the contract of sale, and in all subsequent transactions relating to the property, affiant has been designated and described only by the name subscribed hereto.

12. The reason for making this affidavit is to induce the purchaser named in the contract of sale to accept title to the real property therein described and pay the agreed purchase price therefor; the affidavit is made with the intent and understanding that each statement contained herein shall be relied upon.

_____   _____
Witness   Rod Ross, Seller

_____
Witness
                    Affirmed to before me this 1st day of May, 1998

_____
Notary Public

FIGURE 14.2 *Transactions Involved in a Real Estate Closing*

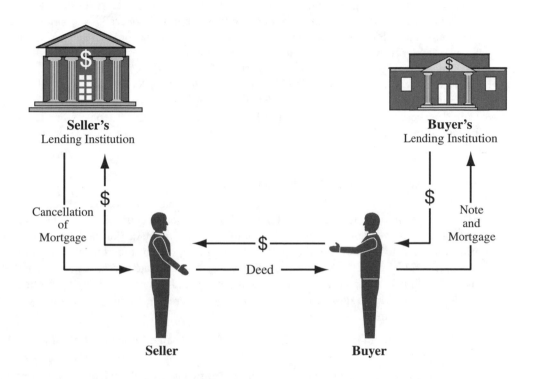

between the lender and the borrower (buyer), with the borrower receiving the proceeds of the loan (which are used to pay the seller) and the lender receiving a note and mortgage from the borrower securing repayment of the loan. After the closing, the seller pays off the old mortgage and the seller's lending institution cancels the old mortgage. These transactions are illustrated in Figure 14.2.

REAL ESTATE SETTLEMENT PROCEDURES ACT (RESPA)

◆ A federal law that requires lending institutions to disclose certain information to purchasers of residential real estate and prohibits those institutions from engaging in specified activities.

A borrower who seeks a mortgage loan needs full information from lending institutions in order to select a lender prudently. RESPA requires the lending institution to make certain disclosures designed to help the borrower make informed judgments. Generally, RESPA is applicable to first mortgage loans made for the purchase of residential real estate. Residential real estate includes one-family to four-family properties. Cooperatives, condominiums and mobile home lots can qualify as residential real estate. The act applies only to purchases where a lender (other than the seller) takes a purchase-money mortgage to secure the loan. A purchase-money mortgage in which the seller takes a mortgage back to secure the unpaid purchase price is not covered by RESPA. The requirements of RESPA are applicable only to lenders involved in a "federally related mortgage loan." The definition of *federally related* is very broad and includes any lending institution whose deposits are federally insured or regulated.

SETTLEMENT COSTS BOOKLET

RESPA is administered by the Department of Housing and Urban Development (HUD). HUD has prepared a settlement costs booklet. Every lender is required to provide an applicant for a mortgage loan with the contents of this booklet on the day of the loan application or, failing that, to deposit it in the mail to the applicant within three business days of the application. The booklet contains information about the real estate purchase process, including negotiating a sales contract and home loan financing. Under the heading "Selecting the Lender," the booklet suggests certain inquiries a borrower should make in order to compare lenders. For example:

▪ Am I required to carry life or disability insurance? Must I obtain it from a particular company?

▪ Is there a late payment charge? How much? How late may the payment be before the charge is imposed?

▪ If I wish to pay off the loan in advance of maturity, must I pay a prepayment penalty? How much? If so, for how long a period will it apply?

▪ Will the lender release me from personal liability if my loan is assumed by someone else when I sell my house?

▪ If I sell the house and the buyer assumes the loan, will the lender have the right to charge an assumption fee, raise the rate of interest or require payment in full of the mortgage?

▪ Will I be required to pay monies into a special reserve account to cover taxes or insurance? If so, how large a deposit will be required at the closing of the sale?

In addition, the booklet contains information regarding home buyers' rights and obligations, settlement services and escrow accounts, as well as a sample work sheet to calculate the settlement costs.

GOOD-FAITH ESTIMATE

Another RESPA requirement is that the lender must provide the borrower with a good-faith estimate of settlement charges at the time of the application. These charges may be expressed as a range. A lender who fails to provide the required information on the date must deposit the information in the mail within three business days of the application. The good-faith estimates include the breakdown of the costs of settlement charges rendered by the mortgagee, for example, loan origination fee, credit report fee, appraiser's fees, title search charges, attorney fees, surveys and document preparation. The complete schedule of all settlement charges is contained in Section L of the Uniform Settlement Statement (see Figure 14.3). The good-faith estimate does not have to include prepaid hazard insurance premiums or reserves deposited with the lender such as escrow for taxes and insurance since this information is not usually available to lenders at the application stage. Although the estimates must be made in good faith, they are subject to change as the market alters the costs of the various settlement charges.

INSPECTION OF UNIFORM SETTLEMENT STATEMENT

A closing or settlement statement is normally prepared by the settlement clerk handling the closing. The settlement statement (see Figure 14.3) consists of a summary of the buyer's (borrower's) and the seller's transactions, broken down into various categories. For some items it may be necessary to apportion income and expenses between the parties. For example, assume that the seller has paid the real estate taxes for six months in advance. Credit should be given to the seller for the portion paid that covers any period after closing. Apportionment of the taxes ensures that each person bears the expense only for the months that person had use of the premises. Other expenses often apportioned include water and sewer assessments, fuel and insurance. Rental income may also be adjusted for unearned rentals received by the seller in advance.

RESPA requires that a lender permit the borrower a right to inspect the Uniform Settlement Statement (USS) one day before closing. The USS is a form settlement statement that contains a summary of the borrower's and seller's transactions and an itemization of the settlement charges as allocated to the borrower and seller. In the event that this information is unavailable the day before closing, the lender is relieved of the responsibility. In this case, the completed statement must be given to the buyer no later than the closing. This requirement may be waived by the buyer, but in the event of such waiver the USS must be mailed at the earliest practical date. Where there is a closing without an appearance of the buyer or the buyer's agent, the lender need only mail the statement to the buyer as soon as practical after the closing. The lender need not provide a USS to the buyer when there are no settlement charges to the buyer or when the settlement charges are a fixed amount communicated to the borrower at the time of the loan application. However, here the lender must provide the borrower with an itemized list of services provided within three days after closing.

In all transactions covered by RESPA, the USS must be used. Otherwise, a statement resembling that form is normally used.

FIGURE 14.3 *HUD Settlement Statement (Continued)*

L. Settlement Charges

				Paid From Borrowers Funds at Settlement	Paid From Seller's Funds at Settlement
700.	**Total Sales/Broker's Commission based on price $**	@	% =		
	Division of Commission (line 700) as follows:				
701.	$	to			
702.	$	to			
703.	Commission paid at Settlement				
704.					
800.	**Items Payable In Connection With Loan**				
801.	Loan Origination Fee	%			
802.	Loan Discount	%			
803.	Appraisal Fee	to			
804.	Credit Report	to			
805.	Lender's Inspection Fee				
806.	Mortgage Insurance Application Fee to				
807.	Assumption Fee				
808.					
809.					
810.					
811.					
900.	**Items Required By Lender To Be Paid In Advance**				
901.	Interest from to @$	/day			
902.	Mortgage Insurance Premium for	months to			
903.	Hazard Insurance Premium for	years to			
904.		years to			
905.					
1000.	**Reserves Deposited With Lender**				
1001.	Hazard insurance	months@$	per month		
1002.	Mortgage insurance	months@$	per month		
1003.	City property taxes	months@$	per month		
1004.	County property taxes	months@$	per month		
1005.	Annual assessments	months@$	per month		

FIGURE 14.3 *HUD Settlement Statement (Continued)*

1006.			months @ $	per month	
1007.			months @ $	per month	
1008.			months @ $	per month	
1100. Title Charges					
1101. Settlement or closing fee			to		
1102. Abstract or title search			to		
1103. Title examination			to		
1104. Title insurance binder			to		
1105. Document preparation			to		
1106. Notary fees			to		
1107. Attorney's fees			to		
(includes above items numbers:					)
1108. Title insurance			to		
(includes above items numbers:					)
1109. Lender's coverage	$				
1110. Owner's coverage	$				
1111.					
1112.					
1113.					
1200. Government Recording and Transfer Charges					
1201. Recording fees: Deed $	; Mortgage $	; Releases $			
1202. City/county tax/stamps: Deed $	; Mortgage $				
1203. State tax/stamps: Deed $	; Mortgage $				
1204.					
1205.					
1300. Additional Settlement Charges					
1301. Survey to					
1302. Pest inspection to					
1303.					
1304.					
1305.					
1400. Total Settlement Charges (enter on lines 103, Section J and 502, Section K)					

ABUSIVE PRACTICES

One reason Congress passed RESPA was because certain abusive practices inflated closing costs. "Kickbacks" are one such practice expressly prohibited by RESPA. Kickbacks occur, for example, when a person or an entity gives a fee to another for business referrals.

> ### CASE EXAMPLE
> ABC Savings and Loan has an agreement with Alfred Hillman, attorney, whereby for every person ABC refers to Hillman for legal services in connection with real estate transactions, Hillman pays ABC 10 percent of the fees generated. This is an illegal kickback under RESPA. In addition, Hillman would be violating the attorney's code of ethics and would be subject to disciplinary measures.

There are similar prohibitions against the payment of a "phantom" charge, a fee that is given where no service has been performed. Both kickbacks and phantom fees may result in a violation for which criminal penalties may attach. Also, an aggrieved party may sue to recover three times the amount of the kickback or the phantom fee. As the next case illustrates, not every service in connection with a real estate transaction is covered by the "anti-kickback-phantom fee" provisions of RESPA.

EISENBERG V. COMFED MORTGAGE CO., INC.
U.S. District Court
629 F. Supp. 1157 (D. Mass. 1986)

BACKGROUND. The Eisenbergs sought a $164,000 loan from Comfed in order to finance the purchase of a home being built for them. The loan was to be secured by a mortgage on the new home, and then it was to be assigned to Comfed's parent, the Bank. One provision required the Eisenbergs to pay two and one-half percent of the face value of the loan as a "mortgage origination fee." One-half percent of that amount was to be paid to Comfed as a commission and the remainder to the Comfed branch manager and to Comfed's overhead.

The Eisenbergs sued Comfed and its parent, the Bank, contending that the provisions allocating percentages were in violation of the anti-kickback provision of the Real Estate Settlement Procedures Act.

DECISION. The Federal District Court dismissed plaintiff's suit and found in favor of the defendants on the basis that the allocation of the percentages was not an illegal kickback for services rendered, in violation of RESPA.

JUDGE YOUNG. The Eisenbergs contend that one point of their two and one-half point mortgage origination fee constituted the "payment of a thing of value" bearing no reasonable relationship to the value of services received by them from Comfed. The percentage fee charged by Comfed was, they argued, "received for the rendering of a real estate settlement service in connection with a transaction involving a federally related mortgage" and bore no relation to "services actually performed."

The Eisenbergs support this contention by pointing to the fact that Comfed has admitted that the one point commission and overhead fee was arrived at, if not arbitrarily, at least with considerations in mind other than the actual cost of processing the Eisenberg loan. They further point out that, "although the same routine, mechanical services are provided for each borrower and in each loan transaction, the dollar amount equivalent to the points paid, determined solely on a percentage basis, varies dramatically from mortgage to mortgage." Thus the Eisenbergs paid much more for their comparatively large loan than would a mortgagor with a smaller loan, even though Comfed provided for each substantially the same services.

Even accepting . . . the Eisenbergs' description of Comfed's point system of calculating mortgage origination fees, this Court refuses to stretch the words of the Act to cover that system. First, there has not been any "referral" shown. Comfed did not receive a fee in return for a referral of business to its owner, the Bank. It received a commission for the origination of the loan, and fully assigned its rights in the mortgage to the Bank; it was not a referral of business but a transfer of . . . interests.

More important, however, this Court rules that the making of a mortgage loan is not a "settlement service" within the meaning of the Act. [The Act] defines the term "settlement services" as follows:

The term "settlement services" includes any service provided in connection with a real estate settlement including, but not limited to, the following: title searches, title examinations, the provision of title certificates, title insurance, services rendered by an attorney, the preparation of documents, property surveys, the rendering of credit reports or appraisals, pest and fungus inspections, services rendered by a real estate agent or broker, and the handling of the processing, and closing or settlement. . . .

Clearly, the making of mortgage loans is not included in the list. Moreover, although the list is not meant to be complete, the Sixth Circuit in *United States v. Graham Mortgage Corp.* concluded that each of the "settlement services" in the illustrative list was "an ancillary or peripheral service that, unlike the making of a mortgage loan, is not directly related to the closing of a real estate sale" covered by the Act. . . . The *Graham* court concluded that "Congress's failure to specify the making of a mortgage loan in listing settlement services seems inexplicable unless the omission was intended."

This Court finds logic of the *Graham* decision compelling. The system of charging mortgage origination fees based on percentages of loan amounts is industry-wide. In the absence of a more unambiguous statement of Congressional intent, this Court refuses to disturb that practice by construing the words of the Act to cover a type of transaction not specifically mentioned in it.

. . .

DISMISSED.

addition to the purchase price of the house, Darrow has arranged to purchase the curtains for $300. County taxes on the property are $1,200 per year, payable semiannually. The county is six months behind on billing and collecting taxes; Liz's last payment was made January 15, 1998. The seller prepaid $200 on January 1 for hazard insurance, which covers the calendar year. The house is heated by oil; 50 gallons of home heating oil costing $1.50 per gallon remain in the tank on the day of closing. Seller's tenant has paid $600 advance rent for the month of May.

Darrow is paying $20,000 as a down payment, which will be paid at the closing. The payoff by the seller of the first mortgage on the home, as of the date of closing, is $37,120.

Water and sewer assessments are payable quarterly at an even billing of $45 per quarter at the end of March, June, September and December. Nodler made the March 31 payment. Every six months a reading is taken to determine the actual usage for the six-month period, and adjustments are made at the end of the year. Average adjustments for the last five years have resulted in an additional assessment of $40 at the end of the year.

A listing agreement with Decade Today Realtors requires the seller to pay a 6% commission. The loan origination fee was 2 percent. Seller, pursuant to the terms of the contract, was to pay two mortgage discount points (2 percent). The appraisal fee of $120 and $35 for a credit report was paid by Darrow at the time of the loan application. The survey fee of $175 to Survey Plat, Inc., is payable by the buyer at closing.

Assume that simple interest based on a 360-day calendar year is to be paid at closing for the 17-day period encompassing May 15 to May 31. Darrow will be required to deposit two months' taxes escrow at closing into. Attorney fees for preparation of the deed to be borne by the seller are $35. The buyer's attorney fees for services connected with the closing are $350, payable to Lincoln, Todd and Harrison Law firm at closing. The seller obtained a joint title insurance policy, as required per contract, to fully cover the lender and the owner. The cost to the seller, to be disbursed at closing to ABC Title, Inc., is $650. The buyer's charge for recording fees for the deed and the mortgage amounts to $5 for each document. The seller must pay the recording fee for the release of the existing mortgage.

Additionally, a .01 percent county transfer conveyance fee is assessed against the seller. Seller, pursuant to the contract, agreed to pay for termite and gas line inspection costs. She employed Exterm Pest Control to do the termite inspection; the charge was $50 for the inspection and $240 for repair work. The seller employed the city to do the gas line inspection at a cost of $75. Using the HUD forms on pages 282 through 285, prepare the closing statement.

Escrow Closing

REAL ESTATE ESCROW

◆ A deed delivered by a grantor to an escrow agent, who is directed to deliver the deed to a grantee when specified conditions are met.

In the previous chapter, we examined a conventional closing, where buyer and seller come face to face to exchange the deed for the purchase price. The real estate escrow closing is a modification of this procedure that is practiced in some localities. Instead of the buyer and seller coming face to face, a third party acts as an intermediary. The third party, commonly called an *escrow agent*, is charged with certain responsibilities designed ultimately to invest the seller with the full purchase price and the buyer with good title to the property.

The subject of the escrow transaction is a written instrument. The written instrument in the normal real estate escrow transaction involves a deed. Technically, the term *escrow* characterizes the instrument—the deed itself—while it is held by the third party. This strict terminology has been relaxed, however, and it is common to refer to "depositing a deed into escrow." In this regard the escrow is the "receptacle" of the instrument rather than the instrument itself. Courts refer to escrows in both senses, and either reference is acceptable.

ESCROW CLOSING DISTINGUISHED

The escrow closing should not be confused with the escrow account. Many mortgages include a clause requiring the mortgagee to set up an escrow account to be used to disburse payments for real estate taxes and/or hazard insurance. The particulars of this escrow account vary from jurisdiction to jurisdiction. Generally, the mortgagor pays into the escrow account monthly an amount equal to one-twelfth of the amount of the yearly property tax and hazard insurance. This constitutes an additional amount above the normal mortgage payment. The mortgagee then makes payments directly from the escrow account to pay taxes and insurance when they become due. This type of escrow procedure is required for

FHA-insured loans and for most conventional loans; it is suggested for VA-guaranteed loans.

These escrowed funds are normally placed in non-interest-bearing accounts; depositors are not paid for the use of the funds. There is, however, a trend in recent years for buyers, particularly in commercial transactions, to require the escrowed money to be deposited in an interest-bearing account in favor of the buyer.

THE ESCROW TRANSACTION

In the most elementary real estate escrow transaction, a seller and a buyer enter into a contract for the purchase of specified real property. They agree to close the transaction in escrow, and they appoint a bank or other escrow agent to be responsible for handling the closing. As part of the agreement between the parties, the seller then deposits a fully executed deed with the escrow agent. The escrow agent is instructed to deliver the deed to the purchaser after receipt of the purchase price. When the purchase price is deposited by the purchaser, the escrow agent delivers the deed to the purchaser and the purchase price to the seller. At this point the escrow closing is complete (see Figure 15.1).

Another typical example of the real estate escrow transaction involves conditions relating to title. In this arrangement the seller deposits the deed, and the purchaser deposits the purchase price with the escrow agent. When the purchaser's attorney approves the title to the property, the escrow agent is bound by the purchase contract or other agreement to deliver the deed to the purchaser and money to the seller. The escrow agent may be instructed to record the deed in favor of the purchaser as soon as the purchaser deposits the money, even before the title to the property is approved. Then, in the event the title cannot be approved, the purchaser is entitled to a return of the purchase money upon reconveying the deed to the seller. A variation of this procedure requires the purchaser to execute a quit-claim deed in favor of the seller and deposit it with the escrow agent at the time the purchase money is deposited and the deed is recorded in favor of the purchaser. In the event that title cannot be approved, the escrow agent is required to record the quitclaim deed and return the purchase money to the purchaser, thus returning the parties to their previous position.

The real estate escrow device is not confined to money transactions but may also be used when the seller and purchaser are merely interested in exchanging deeds to real estate.

CASE EXAMPLE

Rocky Hayes owns a five-acre tract of land in Florida and is interested in selling his land and moving to Colorado. Johnny Ruskin owns a five-acre tract of land in Colorado and is interested in moving to Florida. A real estate broker brings the two together, and an even exchange of property is agreed upon. Hayes deposits his deed to the Florida property with Jerry Bloom, a third party, on condition that the Florida deed be delivered to Ruskin upon receipt of the deed to the Colorado property. When Ruskin deposits the deed to the Colorado property, Bloom will deliver it to Hayes and deliver the deed to the Florida property to Ruskin, thus completing the escrow transaction. See *Morris v. Davis, 334 Mo. 411, 66 S.W.2d 883 (1933).*

FIGURE 15.1 *Escrow Transaction*

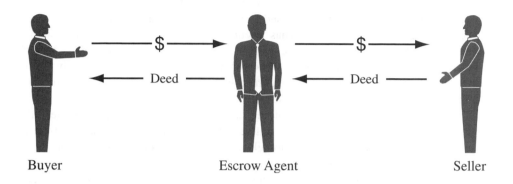

ADVANTAGES OF ESCROW

The objective of the escrow transaction is to ensure that the buyer is invested with clear title to the property and the seller receives the purchase price. The use of the escrow device in closing sales of real estate enjoys the advantages of convenience and protection against a party's change of mind.

CONVENIENCE

Sometimes it is simply inconvenient for parties to be present at a closing. The escrow method of closing enjoys the advantage of facilitating interstate transactions or other closings where it is not feasible for the parties to appear at the closing.

> **CASE EXAMPLE**
> Junior Wells, a resident of California, owns farmland in Kentucky that he desires to sell. Senior Johnson, a resident of Kentucky, desires to buy the farmland. The cost of Junior Wells's appearance at a closing in Kentucky is prohibitive. The parties enter into a purchase contract for the sale of the farmland and agree to close in escrow. Wells mails a fully executed deed for his Kentucky farm to Kentucky Loan & Trust Co., which is instructed to deliver the deed to Johnson upon receipt of the purchase price. When Johnson delivers the purchase price, Kentucky Loan & Trust, as previously instructed, delivers the deed to Johnson.

ASHER V. HERMAN
Supreme Court of New York
49 Misc. 2d 475, 267 N.Y.S.2d 932
(Sup. Ct. App. Div. 1966)

BACKGROUND. Pursuant to the terms of a real estate purchase contract, the purchaser left a deposit with Irvin Dickman, the escrow agent and the seller's attorney. Dickman embezzled the funds. The buyer sought the deposit from the sellers.

DECISION. The Appellate Division of the Supreme Court of New York entered judgment in favor of the defendants.

JUSTICE SHAPIRO. The question posed for decision in this case is who, as between the plaintiffs (vendees) and the defendants (vendors) must suffer the loss of moneys deposited by the vendees under real estate contract with an escrowee who has converted the funds to his own use.

. . .

The contract of purchase sale provided that "The seller shall give and the purchaser shall accept a title such as the Security Title and Guaranty Company will approve and insure."

It is undisputed that at the time of the closing the vendors were unable to deliver to the plaintiffs a good and marketable title by reason of the fact that a New York Estate Tax against a party in the chain of title had not been fixed and paid nor had an order of exemption been obtained.

The Security Title and Guaranty Company refused to approve and insure title to the premises by reason of the outstanding estate tax except that it would insure against collection out of the premises up to a sum not exceeding $797. This was unacceptable to the vendees. An offer by the vendors to deposit a specific sum of money as security for the payment of the estate tax was likewise rejected by the vendees. In refusing to accept such an arrangement, the vendees were within their rights, since no one could foretell whether the deposit would be ample. In any event, the vendors could not deliver a title which the Security Title and Guaranty Company would "approve and insure," and since no request was made by the vendors for an adjustment to perfect their title, the plaintiffs were entitled to receive back the moneys deposited by them under the contract.

The vendees contend that since the escrowee was the attorney for the vendors it is they, the vendors, who must suffer the loss....

Where, in light of the general principles above set forth, should the result of the escrowee's dereliction fall? . . .

. . .

The rule . . . seems to be well settled and generally applied that if property is embezzled or lost by an escrow holder, the loss, as between seller and buyer, falls on the one who owned the property at that time. In this case the vendors were never entitled to receive the moneys deposited in escrow because they never had a title which the plaintiffs were obligated to accept. Under the circumstances, the escrow moneys at all times remained the property of the plaintiffs-vendees. When they were embezzled, it was the property of the plaintiffs that was embezzled and they are the ones that must suffer the loss.

. . .

The plaintiffs . . . contend that the clause in the contract which provides that,

In the event that the seller is unable to convey title in accordance with the terms of this contract, the sole liability of the seller will be to refund to the purchaser the amount paid on account of the purchase price and to pay the net cost of examining the title, which cost is not to exceed the charges fixed by the Security Title and Guaranty Company, and upon such refund and payment being made, this contract shall be considered canceled.

specifically imposes upon the defendants "the liability to refund the down payment to the plaintiffs" and that by agreeing to this clause, the defendants became a guarantor of the escrow agent, who was also their attorney.

The clause in question is the stock clause found in a contract for the sale of real estate. It is applicable where the vendor receives the down payment under the contract and is, therefore, obligated upon his default "to refund" it. Such a clause cannot be deemed applicable to a situation where the vendor has nothing "to refund to the purchaser" because he has obtained nothing from the purchaser. It is also obvious that the escrow clause was intended to be solely applicable to the fact situation at bar.

• • •

Judgment is, therefore, directed for the defendants-vendors, dismissing the plaintiffs' complaint on the merits. . . .

Of course an escrow agent who embezzles or otherwise misappropriates funds is liable to the person upon whom the loss falls. As a practical matter, however, it is very difficult to collect against an absconding or incarcerated escrow agent.

Escrow Agreement

◆ **An agreement that directs the escrow agent regarding terms and conditions under which the deed or other instruments are to be delivered to the parties and the disposition of the deed or other instruments on default.**

The escrow agreement need not be reduced to writing. Even so, in retrospect many buyers and sellers regret their failure to do so. Some lawyers who draft escrow agreements include the terms of the escrow agreement in the purchase contract; others include them in an entirely separate instrument. The escrow agreement should be sufficiently detailed in writing to express the intent of the parties and to cover various contingencies. Some of the terms commonly included within an escrow agreement are:

▌ names and addresses of seller, buyer and escrow agent;

▌ description of the property that is the subject of the escrow;

▌ obligations of buyer and seller regarding the deposit of instruments and money into escrow;

▌ directions to escrow agent regarding the recording of the deed and disbursement of the purchase money;

▮ the specific condition upon which title is to pass;

▮ directions to the escrow agent regarding procedure in the event the condition is not met;

▮ payment of escrow brokerage and attorney fees, recording charges and other costs; and

▮ signatures of the seller, buyer and escrow agent.

The escrow agent is bound by the terms of the escrow agreement and may not deviate from it in any respect, unless of course, it is contrary to law. Where a conflict exists between the terms of the purchase contract and the escrow agreement, the agent is bound to follow the instructions contained in the escrow agreement. The escrow agent may not follow oral instructions that contradict the terms of the written agreement. A typical escrow agreement is shown in Figure 15.2.

When the condition upon which title is to pass occurs, the escrow agent must deliver the deed to the grantee. If the condition does not occur, under the terms of the agreement the escrow agent is normally charged with returning the purchase money to the purchaser and redelivering the deed to the grantor.

An escrow agreement is a contract; it is not revocable by any party without the consent of all the parties to the agreement. In the event that one of the parties attempts to revoke and demands the return of the deposit, the escrow agent must ignore the demand. When conflict or doubt as to interpretation of the agreement arises, a judicial declaration should be sought.

Under the Federal Rules of Civil Procedure as well as many state laws whose civil rules are patterned after the federal rules, an escrow agent who is faced with conflicting claims of liability or ownership may secure a judicial declaration by *interpleading* the claimants. The practical result of this procedure is to force the parties to litigate their rival claims in one court action. The escrow agent becomes a stakeholder who holds the contested property pending the outcome of the lawsuit. The interpleader device is not available to an escrow agent who is guilty of misconduct in the escrow transaction.

CONDITION

Before an instrument can be considered an escrow, its deposit with the escrow agent must be coupled with the depositor's intention that it not take effect until the happening of a specified condition. This condition is essential in order to suspend passage of the instrument to the buyer. If there is no specified condition, then delivery of a fully executed deed to the escrow agent immediately vests title in the purchaser.

The escrow may be used to require any number of conditions to attach before the deed and purchase money pass to the respective parties. Buyers' conditions may include, for example, conditioning the passage of title on the buyer's obtaining financing, making payment of the purchase price, selling a house or securing a zoning change. Sellers' conditions may include providing evidence of title, proof that the property is free from wood-destroying insect infestation or proof that the electrical system in the house is free from defects. Before the grantee is entitled to delivery of the deed, the specified condition must occur. Until such occurrence, the legal title to the deed remains with the seller. In the event the depositary delivers the deed over to a grantee prior to the happening of the condition, no title actually passes since the delivery is unauthorized.

FIGURE 15.2 *Escrow Agreement*

This agreement is entered into between Rocky Sylvester [hereafter referred to as Seller] and Andora Klimer [hereafter referred to as Buyer]. Whereas the Seller and Buyer have entered into a contract dated May 20, 1998, of which a true copy is attached, for the sale of premises described in Plat Book No. 13, page 33, Parcel 17 of Wilona Township.

Now, therefore, it is mutually agreed:

That Henry Earnest is hereby appointed escrow agent and empowered to carry said contract and this agreement into effect;

That the Seller will deposit with said escrow agent a fully executed deed to said premises to the Buyer with general warranty that the title is good and unencumbered except use restrictions and easements of record, if any, and taxes and assessments for the year 1998 and thereafter;

That the buyer will deposit with said escrow agent the sum of $125,000, being the balance of the purchase price of $137,500;

That said escrow agent is directed to file said deed for record and make disbursements when the terms of said contract can be complied with, and provided he can furnish to the Buyer a certificate of title showing record title to said premises to be good and unencumbered;

That the escrow agent shall return any deposit if all deposits and requirements necessary to closing are not made within 45 days from this date;

That Seller shall pay for the preparation of deed, the cost of obtaining a certificate of title, and one-half of the costs of the escrow charges;

That Buyer will pay the fees for filing the deed and one-half of the cost of the escrow charges;

That taxes and assessments, prepaid insurance premiums and rents will be prorated as of the date of closing, and no adjustments are to be made by the escrow agent for water or other utilities.

Dated this 20th day of May, 1998.

_____   _____
Seller   Buyer

_____
Escrow Agent

TITLE PASSAGE

In a completed escrow transaction, there are two deliveries. The first delivery is accomplished when the grantor surrenders control over the deed and delivers it to the escrow agent. The second delivery occurs when the escrow agent surrenders the deed to the purchaser after the occurrence of the condition. As soon as the condition occurs upon which the escrow is predicated, the grantee is entitled to delivery of the escrow. The trend in authority is that title actually passes to the grantee when, pursuant to the escrow agreement, the grantee is entitled to the delivery.

RELATION BACK

◆ **A legal doctrine whereby the title acquired by a deed relates back to the moment of the first delivery to an escrow agent.**

In some instances the *second delivery* of the deed is accounted as taking effect as of the time of the first delivery to the agent. This doctrine of relation back is applied when an event that would otherwise thwart the intent of the parties or cause a manifest injustice intervenes between the first and second deliveries.

Death and Disability. The doctrine of relation back avoids complications that might normally arise where death or insanity of the grantor intervenes between the first and second deliveries. The death of the grantor whose deed is held in escrow does not invalidate the escrow. Upon the happening of the escrow condition, the grantee is entitled to delivery. The delivery relates back in time to the original moment of transfer to the escrow agent. Under this doctrine of relation back, title passage is deemed to have occurred while the grantor was living. Similarly, if after the delivery of a deed in escrow the grantee dies, the grantee's representative will be entitled to delivery upon the happening of the condition. Under the doctrine of relation back, the passage of title is deemed to have occurred at the time of the first delivery, during the life of the grantee.

> ### CASE EXAMPLE
> Birdie H. Fuqua executed a contract for the sale of a 50-acre tract of property to Selected Lands Corporation (SLC). Shortly thereafter she signed a deed and placed it in escrow. Under the terms of the agreement, the escrow agent was to deliver the deed to SLC when SLC's attorney approved the closing papers. Before the approval, Birdie died. Thereafter the attorney approved the papers. The court held that the death of the grantor did not invalidate the instrument and that upon the occurrence of the condition, the grantee was entitled to the deed. Under the doctrine of relation back, title would be deemed to pass as of the date of the first delivery. *Fuqua v. Fuqua, 528 S.W.2d 896 (Tex. Civ. App. 1975).*

The doctrine of relation back is similarly applicable to a case where the grantor becomes insane or otherwise incompetent to effect a transfer after delivering the deed to the escrow agent but before delivery to the purchaser. Under the doctrine, upon the happening of the condition, the grantee is entitled to passage of title, which is deemed to have occurred on the date of the first delivery, thus avoiding frustration of the intent of the parties.

Dower. The doctrine of relation back may protect the purchaser from dower claims by the seller's wife where the wife of a deceased seller had no dower expectancy at the time the deed was deposited into escrow. This may occur as a result of a marriage by the seller after delivery of the deed into escrow but before the second delivery to the purchaser. In such a case, upon the happening of the condition, the title passage relates back to the date of the first delivery; consequently, the seller's wife has no dower interest.

CASE EXAMPLE

Seth Nathan, unmarried, executes a deed and deposits it in escrow. The escrow agent is directed to deliver the deed to the buyer when the buyer secures financing and deposits the purchase price. Before the deposit of the purchase price, Seth marries; thereafter, the buyer deposits the purchase price. Seth's wife refuses to release dower interests in the property. Regardless, the escrow agent is charged with conveying the deed to the grantee, who takes possession free of spousal interests pursuant to the doctrine of relation back.

Intervening Liens. Application of the doctrine of relation back may avoid problems caused by liens, encumbrances and judgments that attach between the time of the first and second deliveries. When a seller conveys title by deed to a third party who has knowledge that the deed is the subject of an escrow, the doctrine of relation back normally protects the original purchaser. Under this doctrine the purchaser is deemed to have taken title at the first delivery; consequently, the seller was without power to convey good title to the third party. If the third party is a bona fide purchaser for value without notice that the instrument is the subject of an escrow, however, the courts are less likely to apply the doctrine to defeat the third party's title. The same rules apply where the grantor creates an encumbrance on the property during escrow. If the lienholder is without knowledge of the escrow, the lienholder has priority. Otherwise the doctrine of relation back will protect the grantee since the grantor's title is deemed cut off at the time of the first delivery.

Follow the reasoning in the next case involving the application of the doctrine of relation back.

HARTMAN V. WOOD
Supreme Court of South Dakota
436 N.W.2d 854 (1989)

BACKGROUND. The Woods entered into a contract for the sale of a parcel of real property to Garrett Ranch, Inc. (Garrett). The contract required the Woods to deliver fee title to the property when Garrett completed all of the payments called for in the contract for deed. Delivery of the fee title was to be accomplished through an escrow. The Woods executed a warranty deed to the property, naming Garrett as grantee, and deposited the deed with an escrow agent (escrowee). The escrow was to deliver the deed to Garrett when Garrett made all the payments for the property. Prior to the condition being met, Garrett transferred the contract for deed to a related partnership, which interests were then assigned to Connecticut Mutual Life Insurance Company as security on a mortgage. Connecticut Mutual foreclosed its mortgage and purchased the contract for deed at a sheriff's sale. Connecticut Mutual assigned its interest in the property to First National Bank of Minneapolis, who assigned its interest to Hartman. Hartman completed all of the payments required under the contract for deed and the Woods accepted the payments. Hartman asked Woods to convey a new warranty deed to the property, in effect bypassing the original deed that was placed in escrow. The Woods authorized release of the original deed in escrow to Hartman but refused to give a new deed.

Hartman brought an action for specific performance to execute a new deed. The trial court granted summary judgment in favor of the Woods.

DECISION. The Supreme Court of South Dakota affirmed.

JUSTICE MILLER. The question is whether an assignee of a purchaser under a contract for deed is entitled to a warranty deed from the vendor when the vendor has previously deposited a warranty deed with an escrow for delivery to the purchaser on payment of the purchase price.

Generally, title to property under a deed deposited into escrow transfers when the [escrowee] delivers the deed or when conditions placed upon its delivery have been met. There is an exception to this rule holding that transfer of title by deed will be treated as relating back to the deed's original deposit into escrow where resort to this fiction is necessary to give the deed effect. Thus:

Where the grantee in an escrow deed, after the deposit of the instrument in escrow but before the performance of the condition upon which it was to be delivered, makes a conveyance of the land to a third person, the escrow deed relates back to the original deposit, upon the performance of the condition, so as to validate the conveyance made by the grantee.

This is precisely the situation confronted in this case. Prior to performance of the conditions for delivery of the escrow deed, Garrett assigned its interest in the property to another party. Successive assignments were made to additional parties until Hartman performed the conditions for delivery of the escrow deed. Applying the above rule, the escrow deed should be treated as having vested title to the property in Garrett at the time the deed was placed in escrow. This would have the effect of validating the "subsequent" conveyances of the property by Garrett and its successors in interest (e.g., the sheriff's deed and the . . . warranty deed to Hartman).

Based upon the foregoing discussion, Hartman's action for specific performance against Woods was not an appropriate means of removing some cloud that he may have perceived on his title. Hartman had a deed to the property validated by the escrow deed's vesting of title to the property in Garrett prior to Garrett's conveyance of the property. . . .

We additionally observe that Woods performed all of their obligations under the contract for deed when they deposited the warranty deed into escrow. Specific performance against Woods was, therefore, unavailable because there was nothing left for Woods to specifically perform.

AFFIRMED.

OTHER USES OF ESCROW

Two other uses of escrow are notable. They are the long-term escrow and the mortgage escrow.

LONG-TERM ESCROW

The long-term escrow is a tool for financing a real estate transaction. A long-term escrow may range in duration from 1 year to 30 or more years. It is actually a combination of the land installment contract and the escrow.

A buyer may not be in a position to borrow funds. Nonetheless, a seller may desire to sell the land to such a purchaser by requiring installment payments. To secure the payment of the purchase price, the seller may withhold the deed from the buyer until the final installment is paid. Under such an arrangement, the seller delivers into escrow a fully executed deed with instructions to the escrow agent to deliver the deed to the buyer upon full payment of the purchase price.

CASE EXAMPLE

Jake Rubin owns 50 acres of farmland that has been on the market for two years, listed at $100,000. Lance Lane desires to buy the land but is unable to obtain financing from a lending institution. Rubin and Lane enter into a land installment contract whereby Lane pays $10,000 down and agrees to pay the remaining $90,000 over nine years at 9 percent interest. Rubin executes the deed in favor of Lane and deposits it with Fidelity Trust Co., an escrow agent that is directed by the terms of the escrow agreement to deliver the deed to Lane upon receiving receipts evidencing that the purchase price has been paid in full. Rubin does not have control over the deed as long as Lane does not default on the terms of the installment contract. After nine years of timely payments, Lane is entitled to the deed. See *Been Corp. v. Shader, 198 Neb. 677, 255 N.W.2d 247 (1977).*

If a purchaser fails to make the timely payments, the escrow agent is normally charged with returning the deed to the seller pursuant to the escrow agreement.

One major disadvantage of the long-term escrow is risk; the buyer takes a chance that the seller will convey the property by deed to another or mortgage the land in an amount that would interfere with the buyer's equity in the property. Since the seller remains the titleholder of record, a bona fide purchaser for value without notice of the contract may take from the seller and defeat the buyer's interest. However, if the installment buyer is in possession, then the purchaser has constructive notice of the buyer's interest and would not take good title. The installment buyer may also be protected by recording the land installment contract. This would be sufficient to give notice to subsequent grantees or mortgagees and thus protect the contract buyer. In fact, many states require a land installment contract to be recorded.

REAL ESTATE LAW

MORTGAGE ESCROW

A mortgagee may desire to set up an escrow in order to be protected. In this event, the money to be lent to the mortgagor is deposited in escrow, awaiting proof that there are no outstanding liens on the property. Upon such assurance, the mortgage can be recorded and the funds released to the mortgagor as directed; the mortgagee is secure as a first lienor. The surrender of the money into escrow is deemed to be the creation of a debt, which is necessary for a mortgage to be a valid lien on property.

REVIEW AND DISCUSSION QUESTIONS

1. Name the parties to an escrow transaction and describe the flow of documents.
2. What are the advantages of an escrow transaction?
3. Name the six requirements of an escrow and briefly describe each.
4. What are the responsibilities of an escrow agent?
5. Name some conditions upon which an escrow may be predicated.
6. When does the loss due to embezzlement of funds held by an escrow agent fall upon the seller?
7. Describe the doctrine of relation back and give some examples as to how it affects the buyer.
8. What is a long-term escrow and when is it used?

CASE PROBLEMS

1. Tillie Ganser entered into a contract with her four children whereby Tillie agreed to convey a specified tract of land to each child upon the payment by each child of a specified sum. It was agreed that an escrow would be used to handle the transaction. Tillie deposited four valid deeds with the escrow agent, but before any of the children paid the agent the amount due under the contract, Tillie died. Tillie's executor seeks to set aside the land sales as mere offers revoked by Tillie's death. (a) Will the executor be able to set aside the contracts for the sale of the land? Explain. *See Ganser v. Zimmerman, 80 N.W.2d 828 (N.D. 1956).*
(b) Would the following fact pattern present a different result? Tillie deposited four valid deeds, executed in the names of each of her four children, with her attorney, accompanied by instructions to convey the deeds to her children when all contracts for the sale of the property were negotiated. Before any contracts could be negotiated, Tillie died. *See Merry v. County Bd. of Educ., 264 Ala. 411, 87 So.2d 821 (1956).*

2. Ellen Love deposits a fully executed deed in escrow. Pursuant to a purchase contract and escrow instructions, the deed is to be delivered to Sarah Gibson when the zoning of the property is changed from residential to commercial. After the zoning change occurs, but before the escrow agent delivers the deed to Gibson, a judgment creditor of Gibson seeks to levy on the property. Will the judgment creditor be successful? Explain. *See Sturgill v. Industrial Painting Corp., 82 Nev. 61, 410 P.2d 759 (1966).*

3. Robert O'Neal agreed to sell to Thomas Ryan a parcel of land. The parties agreed to handle the transfer through an escrow agent. According to the escrow agreement, O'Neal was to deposit a valid deed executed in Ryan's name with the escrow agent. The agent was to deliver the deed to Ryan when Ryan deposited $12,000 with the escrow agent. Before Ryan or O'Neal performed their obligations under the agreement, O'Neal informed the escrow agent that the property was worth much more than $12,000 and that O'Neal would not deliver the deed unless Ryan paid $13,000. (a) Since neither party has performed his contractual duties, can O'Neal alter the terms of the escrow agreement? Why or why not? (b) What if Ryan agrees to the additional amount? Does that change the result? *See Gelber v. Cappeller, 161 Cal. App. 2d. 113, 326 P.2d 521 (1958).*

4. The Caulfields entered into a contract to purchase property owned by the Freddie Thomas Foundation, Inc., with a condition that the contract was subject to "the necessary Supreme Court approval authorizing this conveyance." The deed and closing papers were held in escrow, pending the Court's approval. The Caulfields took possession of the property on October 1. On October 4, the premises were partially destroyed by fire. Court authorization for the sale was obtained on October 29. Under the purchase agreement the risk of loss was to remain with the seller until the "closing." Whose insurer (the buyer's or the seller's) is responsible for the loss? Explain. *Caulfield v. Improved Risk Mutuals, Inc. 486 N.Y.S.2d 531 (Sup. Ct. App. Div. 1985).*

5. Maxum and Nelson reached a tentative agreement for the exchange of a parcel of land owned by Nelson for a parcel owned by Maxum. Maxum had not seen the Nelson property, located in a distant state, and so planned to visit the site before consummating the deal. Before leaving, Maxum deposited a valid deed to his property with Wallace. Maxum instructed Wallace that if he found the property suitable he would write to Wallace and direct him to deliver the deed to Nelson. The delivery of Maxum's deed was contingent on Nelson delivering the deed to his land to Wallace. Nelson delivered his deed to Wallace. Maxum, after examining the property, found it unsatisfactory and promptly wrote to Wallace, instructing him not to deliver the deed to Nelson. Nelson objected to Maxum's action. Nelson claims that a valid escrow agreement was formed and, upon the tender of his deed to Wallace, Wallace was bound to deliver the Maxum deed to Nelson. Is Nelson correct? Discuss. *See Nelson v. Davis, 102 Wash. 313, 172 P. 1178 (1918).*

6. Mr. Konopka and Mr. Zaremba negotiated a contract for the sale of Konopka's residence to Zaremba. The parties agreed to establish an escrow account with Ms. Wourms, Konopka's real estate agent. The escrow agreement required that Zaremba immediately deposit a down payment of $2,500 with Wourms, which he did. The ultimate sale of the residence was contingent on Zaremba's obtaining a mortgage loan of $20,500. Zaremba obtained the loan, at which time Konopka requested delivery of the down payment from Wourms. Wourms admitted that she was unable to deliver the money because she had used the money to pay her business creditors. Konopka refused to close the deal until Zaremba paid the contract price to him. Zaremba contended that he owed the contract price less the $2,500 he had already paid to Wourms. (a) Who was right? Upon whom did the loss of the money fall? Why? (b) Was it relevant that Wourms was employed by Konopka to act as his real estate agent? Explain. *See Zaremba v. Konopka, 91 N.J. Super. 300, 228 A.2d 91 (1967).*

16

Liens Against Title

LIEN

◆ **A claim against another's property securing either payment of a debt or fulfillment of some other monetary charge or obligation.**

Liens are important in all spheres of commercial law. They take many forms and are subject to extensive variations from state to state. Despite these differences, the underlying concept of all liens is much the same. The purpose is to provide security for a debt obligation or duty. A lien cannot exist in the absence of a financial claim against another person.

CASE EXAMPLE

Revisi, a contractor, obtained a long-term lease on land outside of Utica, New York, for construction of a small warehouse. Wilson Building Supply furnished all materials for the project. When Revisi did not pay his bills, amounting to $275,000, Wilson obtained a material supplier's lien (mechanic's lien) on the building.

Shortly thereafter, the state acquired Wilson's lumberyard as part of a slum clearance project. This left the company without facilities, and it demanded possession of Revisi's building on the basis of the lien.

Although courts sometimes refer to liens as property, a lien is not a property right in the thing itself. The lienholder has neither title nor the rights of a titleholder. His or her only right is to have a monetary obligation satisfied out of proceeds from the sale of the property. A lien thus differs from an estate, which is the right to possess realty, or an easement, which is the right to use realty. No court would award Wilson Building Supply possession of Revisi's warehouse on the basis of the material supplier's lien, even if the lien exceeded the value of the property. A lien simply does not give the holder of the lien title or the right to possession or use.

Because the fundamental nature of a lien is security, interests in real estate are frequently the subject of liens. Land and buildings provide excellent security. They are valuable, their value is relatively stable and they are difficult, if not impossible, to move or conceal. Further, in the United States, land is subject to a system of recording that gives constructive notice to the world of the existence of any liens against a parcel of land. For example, Wilson Building Supply, in obtaining its lien, had to follow a procedure designed to notify other creditors of Revisi of its claim against the property.

TYPES OF LIENS

Liens are either voluntary or involuntary. Voluntary liens are those the owner places against his or her land, usually to secure repayment of long-term debt. Funds are advanced to the property owner, who agrees to repay the debt and provide a lien on the property as security for repayment. In many states a real estate mortgage is regarded as a lien. Real estate mortgages are discussed extensively in Chapter 21.

A number of involuntary liens are also important to real estate practitioners. Involuntary liens, discussed in this chapter, are created by law to protect interests of persons who have valid monetary claims against the owner of real property. The claim might arise out of a judgment, sale or furnishing of a service of some kind. Involuntary liens also aid government in the collection of taxes and special assessments.

Liens may also be classified as *general* or *specific*. Specific liens apply to a specific parcel of realty only. The mechanic's lien, treated in this chapter, is an example. Other specific liens considered in the chapter are the vendor's lien and the property tax lien. A general lien is a lien against all the realty of a person in a given jurisdiction. Thus, a judgment against Jones in a lawsuit in Washington County imposes a lien against *all* of his realty in that county, not just against one or more specific parcels owned by him in Washington County. This type of general lien is known as a *judgment lien.* The federal tax lien, also discussed in this chapter, is a general lien.

MECHANIC'S LIEN

◆ **The right of one who renders services or supplies materials in connection with the improvement of real property to seek a judicial sale of the realty to satisfy unpaid claims.**

By statute in most states, contractors and suppliers who work on real estate or furnish material for such work are entitled to a lien if they are not paid. The lien provides them with a means of compelling payment because it allows the property to be sold to satisfy the claims. Generally, the lien attaches to both buildings and the land, and the work must have been done at the owner's request. The mechanic's lien, also known as a *material supplier's lien* or *contractor's lien,* is not the only action an unpaid supplier or contractor may take. By filing the lien, the supplier or contractor does not lose the right to recover on the contract.

> **CASE EXAMPLE**
>
> Eldon Horn and his wife purchased a lot. Shortly thereafter they contracted with Jamco Builders for the construction of a home on the lot. Jamco subcontracted some of the work to Mid-American Homes. Mid-American, as required by law, notified the Horns of its right to place a lien against the real estate. Jamco did not pay for the subcontracted work, and Mid-American filed a mechanic's lien against the property. This established its right to petition a court to have the property sold and the proceeds applied against the debt.

Valid reasons exist for granting contractors and suppliers a special lien against real property. In collecting for services and materials, they are at a disadvantage when compared with sellers of personal property on credit. When not paid, the seller of personal property, who has a valid security agreement, can usually repossess the item. This remedy does not exist for suppliers whose materials have been incorporated into a structure. Similarly, a contractor or laborer cannot get back time and effort expended on the job. Except for the mechanic's lien, such claimants are limited to suing for the contract price. Litigation such as this is time-consuming and expensive, and the winning plaintiff may have difficulty collecting the judgment. There is also the question of priority of distribution in the event there are a number of general judgment creditors. A mechanic's lienor will secure a higher priority than the general judgment lienor.

The lien also has nuisance value in that, until the debt is paid, a purchaser takes title subject to the lien. The mechanic's lien laws thus aid many small entrepreneurs who might be reluctant or financially unable to take judicial action to collect an unpaid claim.

Mechanic's lien laws did not exist at common law. They are the result of 19th-century state legislation that was necessary to protect the contractors, laborers and suppliers who were crucial to the building of American cities.

Every state in the United States now has some type of mechanic's lien legislation. Since this legislation is often merely the ad hoc response to problems of a particular area and time, it is extremely varied and often complicated. In those jurisdictions that have a basic mechanic's lien statute, political pressures may lead to substantial amendments, which increase variability and add further complications. Any person in real estate working with transactions involving mechanic's lien laws must be particularly concerned with local statutes on the subject. These statutes are usually quite technical, and their requirements must be followed strictly for the lien to be valid.

Claimants. Mechanic's lien statutes generally include several categories of potential claimants. A typical statute might name mechanics, material suppliers, contractors, subcontractors, lessors of equipment, architects, engineers, and surveyors. In addition, a statute usually includes a catchall provision that allows anyone to claim a mechanic's lien who has performed labor upon, or supplied materials to improve, property. Courts, too, have interpreted such statutes in a manner that extends the classes of persons who may claim mechanic's liens for making improvements to realty.

> **CASE EXAMPLE**
>
> Reet Development was constructing a large office building. It hired Francis Trucking Company to deliver materials to the site and Payne to serve as watchman. When Francis and Payne were not paid, they filed mechanics' liens. Reet argued that they were not entitled to liens, as their labor did not improve the premises. Although courts in numerous states would disagree, it is reasonable to hold that the services improved the premises, as they were necessary for ultimate completion of the job. These services could thus be the basis for a mechanic's lien.

Ownership Interest. Mechanic's lien laws apply to various ownership interests in real property. Absolute ownership is not required, but the lien ordinarily attaches only to the interest of the party ordering the work. Usually when the term *owner* is used in a statute, that term has been defined broadly. In addition to persons having fee simple title, other owners include those who have life estates, persons with remainder interests, and tenants under lease. As the following case example illustrates, in some situations an owner's interest may be subject to a mechanic's lien even though the owner did not contract for the improvements.

> **CASE EXAMPLE**
>
> Balbo purchased property from Sanchez on a land installment contract. The contract was recorded. Balbo commenced to build on the property, serving as his own contractor. Balbo contracted with American Wallboard to put in the walls. American purchased the necessary wallboard from Tri-City Building. Although Balbo paid American, American did not pay Tri-City. When the wallboard was delivered, Tri-City notified Sanchez of delivery, although Sanchez had not ordered the material. Most courts would hold that this notice was sufficient to establish mechanic's lien rights against Sanchez inasmuch as Sanchez had ownership rights.

In a land installment contract (see Chapter 22), the buyer pays the purchase price on an installment basis. The owner/seller—Sanchez in the example above—retains title until the purchase price is paid.

In most states, statutes allow a noncontracting owner to block a lien against his or her interest by posting a *notice of nonresponsibility*. In general, these statutes require the owner to post a written notice indicating that he or she will not be responsible for the improvements. The notice must be in some conspicuous place on the land and be posted within a short time after the owner finds out about the work being done. Depending on the state, the time ranges from three to ten days.

Type of Work. The statutes that establish mechanics' liens use various general terms to describe the type of work for which a lien may be obtained. Frequently, the terms are defined in the statutes themselves. When they are not defined by statute, the courts as a rule have tended to interpret these general terms broadly.

A number of statutes use the term *improvement(s)*. This term has been defined to include demolition, erection, alterations or repairs. Some courts have refused to allow mechanics' liens for tearing down a building unless the term *demolition* is included in the statutory definition or is necessary for improvement. Terms such as *building, structure* and *appurtenance* usually have also been defined broadly when included in mechanic's lien laws. Mechanic's lien laws in a number of states use *improvements* as a synonym for *building* or *structure,* not to indicate the type of work for which a lien may be granted.

Consent. In order for property to be subject to a mechanic's lien, most states require that improvements be made with the consent and knowledge or at the request of the owner. A contract is the basis for a mechanic's lien in most states, but a contract between an owner and a person seeking a lien is not required. As a result, numerous circumstances exist in which a lien may attach even when the owner has not personally entered into a contract with the lienor.

Consent of the owner may be express or implied. One example of implied consent is when a lease provision requires a tenant to make alterations or specific improvements. If a lease contains this type of provision, the lessor's interest is subject to a lien in most jurisdictions even if the modifications are made at the tenant's expense. On the other hand, a lease that contains the usual covenant that the tenant maintain or repair the premises and nothing more does not establish implied consent. In addition, except in states that have implied consent based on knowledge, mere knowledge by a lessor that improvements are being made is not sufficient to establish a lien against the lessor's interest.

The owner may give consent through an agent. Some states have, by legislation, established classes of persons as statutory agents for the owner. These people have the implied authority to consent in the owner's behalf. The statutory agents are contractors, subcontractors, architects, builders and any others who are in charge of work. An artisan or material supplier dealing with one of these persons is ordinarily entitled to a lien.

Permanency. The concept that work or materials to be lienable must result in a *permanent benefit* underlies most mechanic's lien laws. *Permanent* refers to material and labor that become part of the premises. Permanent labor and materials are distinguished from those that are part of the contractor's plant or equipment in the project, which are not lienable.

CASE EXAMPLE

ABC Plumbing had a contract to furnish plumbing fixtures to a developer. The contract required delivery of fixtures to the individual units. In order to protect its delivery truck and to store fixtures, the company built a small storage shed at the site. When the company was not paid, it filed a notice of lien that included $1,500, the cost of the structure. A court would probably hold that this amount was not included in the lien against the premises since the benefit was not permanent.

Permanent is construed broadly to last as long as the item remains part of the premises. As a result, many improvements of short duration as well as items detached from the structure may be the basis for a mechanic's lien. This includes work done to protect a permanent installation or even a structure not intended to be permanent but designed to be removed at a future time. Electrical signs, telephones and telephone equipment have been the basis for mechanics' liens. Items such as tables and benches have been considered permanent when necessary to the normal use of a structure and furnished for this use. Services such as mowing, trimming and spraying plants as well as weeding and raking lawns are not permanent improvements.

◆ **Perfection of Lien. The performance of those steps required by statute to sell real property under mechanic's lien laws.**

The time periods and procedures involved in and required for perfecting a mechanic's lien vary appreciably from state to state. They also frequently vary within the same state for different categories of claimants as well as for different types of benefits conferred. For example, in a number of states the steps that a subcontractor must take to perfect a lien differ from those the prime contractor must follow. Material suppliers usually have to follow procedures different from those required of the artisan supplying labor. Despite these and other differences, two almost universal requirements for perfecting a mechanic's lien are notice to the owner and the filing of a mechanic's lien claim in the county or city land records.

Notice. Statutes generally require a lien claimant to notify the owner before filing a lien. In most states, a defective notice or failure to provide the owner with notice invalidates a lien. The purpose of this requirement is to warn the owner not to pay a contractor against whom outstanding claims exist in favor of laborers, subcontractors or material suppliers. Knowing of the existence of these claims, the owner may protect himself or herself against paying twice by retaining funds due to the contractor until the lien claimant is paid, or obtaining a lien waiver signed by the claimant.

Notice to the owner ordinarily includes the following information: the name and address of the lienor, the name of the person with whom the lienor contracted if not the owner, the labor performed or material furnished, dates when the work was started and completed, the balance due and a description of the property and the owner's interest. Most states require the notice to be in writing; some require an affidavit as to the amounts due. Usually the statute gives the potential lienor a limited time period of 20, 30 or sometimes 60 days after the work is completed to notify the owner of the claim.

Some categories of claimants are excused by statute from giving a preliminary notice, for example, laborers working for a daily wage. The reason for this exception is to protect these people from losing the lien right because of a technicality of which they might not be aware. In a number of states, preliminary notice is necessary only if the lien claimant did not deal directly with the owner. In jurisdictions following this rule, a prime contractor would not be required to give notice, but a subcontractor would. A few states permit notice to the owner after the lien has been filed.

Filing. A second critical point in perfecting a lien is filing for record. Doing the work or furnishing the materials merely gives the claimant a right to acquire a lien. In some states this right is referred to as an *inchoate lien.* Usually the statute requires that the claimant file meaning of services or materials as contemplated in the mechanic's lien law statutes. Accordingly, Daniels' notice to hold and claim a lien, for the profits allegedly owing to him is invalid. Therefore, the summary judgment in favor of Deseret is affirmed.

Some states attempt to solve the problem of determining when completion has occurred by allowing the owner to file a notice of completion. This notice is the equivalent of completion and begins the time period within which the lien claim must be filed.

When a premature notice of completion is filed, the time period for filing commences from the date of actual completion. If the par-

ties disagree as to whether there was actually "substantial completion" when the notice of completion was filed, litigation similar to that in the previous case is the only means of settling the dispute.

Although proper filing of a lien is necessary for its validity, the lien is often effective from an earlier date. In many states the properly filed lien reverts back to the time construction began. In these states the lienholder's claim thus acquires priority over claims against the premises recorded or filed before the lien claim was filed but after the work was begun.

AFFIRMED.

C A S E   E X A M P L E

Scarlet and Grey Construction Company contracted to build a stable for Perry. Work began on November 10. On December 5, before the job was completed, Perry executed a mortgage on the property in favor of Betz. The stable was finished on December 12, but a portion of the contract price was not paid. Scarlet and Grey filed a lien against the property on January 3. In many states this lien would have priority over Betz's mortgage because the lien reverts back to November 10, the day work began.

In a few states, the lien attaches as of the time the original contract was made. In others, the lien attaches from the date materials were first furnished at the site.

Termination. Mechanics' liens may be extinguished in numerous ways. Probably the most common is by payment of the obligation upon which the lien is based. Other procedures are also widely used.

Ordinarily, discharging a debt terminates existing liens securing the debt and precludes a future lien based on the same debt. In some jurisdictions, however, mechanic's lien rights of subcontractors and suppliers survive payment to a principal contractor. In these states, the subcontractors may obtain liens for the full value of their respective claims *even if the principal contractor has been paid*. This practice is known as the *Pennsylvania Rule*. In states following this rule, the subcontractor's lien is considered direct, not a right that derives from the general contractor. These jurisdictions consider the contractor the owner's agent; thus, through an agent, the subcontractor is deemed to have contracted directly with the owner. When a state has a mechanic's lien statute of this type, the owner may be required to pay twice.

CASE EXAMPLE

Randolph Estates contracted with the ABC Pool Company for construction of a $28,000 pool. The pool was to serve residents of an apartment complex being constructed by Randolph Estates. ABC subcontracted excavation and grading to Montefresco Company for $1,500. Upon completion of the pool, Randolph paid ABC as per the contract. When ABC went bankrupt, Montefresco filed a mechanic's lien against the premises. In states following the Pennsylvania Rule, Randolph would have to pay the $1,500 again, this time to Montefresco, in order to extinguish the lien.

Probably the majority of states follow what is called the *New York Rule*. In these jurisdictions, a subcontractor's lien is limited to the amount still owed the general contractor at the time the lien is filed. The owner is not compelled to pay more than the contract price, inasmuch as any subcontractor's lien derives from the principal contractor. The result is that the owner may pay the principal contractor as work progresses without fear of a subcontractor's lien for the same work.

Many jurisdictions permit the owner to release an existing lien not only by paying the claim it represents but by giving a bond or paying cash into court to cover potential claims by contractors and/or subcontractors and artisans. If the claim is disputed, this process protects both the owner and the claimant. The owner is protected because the funds are controlled by the court; the claimant is protected because monies are available to pay any valid claim. This procedure is also valuable to the owner since the property is not tied up during litigation by being subject to a filed mechanic's lien.

Liens may also terminate by *waiver*. The waiver may be made before the improvement as part of the contract, as a *no-lien* provision. This provision must be clear and unambiguous. Any doubts will be resolved against the waiver. Some state courts have held that a waiver by a principal contractor is also applicable to subcontractors claiming through him or her. In other states, a subcontractor is bound by this type of provision only if he or she had actual knowledge of or expressly consented to the contractor's waiver.

Mechanics' liens are also extinguished by the lienor's *failure to foreclose* within a reasonable time. This period is often short. Six months and a year are common, although in some states a two-year limitation is applicable. A number of jurisdictions shorten the time further by permitting the owner to demand that the lienholder commence an action to foreclose the lien. Failure of the lienor to begin foreclosure proceedings within the allowed time results in forfeiture of the lien. The purpose of these statutory provisions is to eliminate the cloud on the title resulting from a properly filed mechanic's lien claim.

JUDGMENT LIEN

◆ **A lien that automatically attaches to real property of a defendant when a plaintiff wins a judgment in the jurisdiction in which the property is located.**

> ### C A S E   E X A M P L E
>
> Justin Lane purchased a lot for $10,000. Lane was the defendant in a tort case, and a judgment was entered against him for $8,500. Lane refused to pay the judgment as he believed it to be unfair. When Lane attempted to sell the lot, the purchaser's attorney refused to certify that the title was marketable because of a judgment lien resulting from the tort case.

Collecting a money judgment in a civil case is often almost as difficult as winning it. In most instances, the losing defendant does not rush up to the winning plaintiff with check in hand, but is very reluctant to pay. If the judicial process by which the money judgments are awarded is to be respected, the law must assist plaintiffs in collecting their judgments.

The ultimate method is the forced sale of enough of the defendant's property, real and personal, to cover the judgment. Although some property may be exempt by statute, the nonexempt property of a defendant may be seized and sold to satisfy the judgment. This is known as an *execution* or a *levy of execution.* It is accomplished by a writ from the court. The writ authorizes a court officer, usually the sheriff, to sell the property.

A judgment lien is an involuntary lien attaching to real property when a judgment is obtained against the owner. The lien establishes the claim of the *judgment creditor* against the defendant's real estate in the jurisdiction of the court that awarded the judgment and helps to ensure that the plaintiff will eventually collect the judgment. While the lien exists, a sale or mortgage of the property is subject to the judgment creditor's interest. As a result, the defendant often pays the judgment to free the property from the judgment creditor's lien. If the judgment is not paid, the real estate can be levied against and sold. Some states use a process similar to that used to foreclose a mortgage.

A judgment creditor can also obtain a lien against a defendant's personal property. Personal property, unlike real estate, must be levied against by a court order before being subject to a lien. This type of lien is generally referred to as an *execution lien.* In most states the execution lien and judgment lien are treated in a similar manner. Ordinarily, the personal property must be used to satisfy the judgment before the real property becomes available for that purpose.

Judgment liens did not exist at common law. They are created by statute, and their existence and operation depend on the statutory provisions establishing them. Not all states have provided the judgment creditor with this method of enforcing a judgment. If no judgment lien statute exists in a state, a lien against real property, like one against personal property, arises only when proper execution and levy have occurred.

A judgment lien is a general lien. It applies to all real estate owned by the defendant in the county where the judgment was rendered. The lien may be made specific by levy of execution. Most states have a simple procedure for extending the lien to other real estate owned by the defendant within the state. This is done by filing a transcript of the judgment in other counties in which the judgment debtor has real property. Federal statutes provide that a judgment of a United States district court sitting in a state having a judgment lien statute is a lien to the same extent as the judgments of a state court of general jurisdiction.

Requirements. The time at which a judgment lien attaches depends on state statute. This time is important because it determines the conflicting claims of creditors. In a few states the lien commences when the judgment is rendered; however, most state statutes require that the judgment be made part of the public record in some manner before the lien is created. This is a reasonable requirement. Official records should be available to third parties dealing with a judgment debtor so that they have a source whereby they can determine potential problems. A common requirement for establishing general notice of the judgment is that it must be filed, docketed (officially listed) and indexed before a lien based on it is effective. Some states require only that the judgment be filed and docketed.

In a few states, legislation provides that when a judgment is indexed the lien reverts to some earlier date. Sometimes this is the first day of the court term during which the judgment was rendered; more often it is the day the judgment was rendered. The *doctrine of relation back* means that the judgment lien might be superior to interests created before the lien became part of the public record.

Not all judgments rendered create liens. Of course, it is critical that the judgment be rendered validly by a court having jurisdiction. Another basic requirement is that the judgment be final. An interlocutory judgment or one that settles some intermediate plea or motion is not final and cannot give rise to a judgment lien. In addition, the judgment must be for a specific sum of money. In most states, liens are based on the judgments of any court of record. Frequently, however, state statutes require judgments of inferior courts to be filed with the statewide court of original jurisdiction before becoming a lien.

Legal Effect. As a general rule, liens and other interests in realty rank in the order in which they are created. This is the principle of "first in time, first in right." As a result of this principle, judgment liens have important consequences for two classes of people: buyers from a judgment debtor and other creditors of the judgment debtor.

If a judgment lien has been perfected before the signing date of a contract for the sale of realty, the buyer takes the real property subject to the lien. Because the real property is subject to a judgment lien, the real property may be sold by the sheriff to satisfy the judgment debt. As the lien existed at the time the buyer obtained his or her interest, the buyer will lose the real property unless the debt is paid off.

Creditors of a judgment debtor are also affected by a judgment lien. A valid judgment lien has priority over the claims of creditors who have not established a security interest in the debtor's real property prior to the judgment. The reason is that the judgment lien was created first. Prospective creditors also consider real property less valuable as security to the extent of judgment liens against it. If a loan is made and the debtor defaults, when the property is sold any judgment is satisfied out of the proceeds before the secured creditor's claim is paid.

Termination. In most instances, statutes creating the judgment lien also establish the lien's duration. Usually the period is short. Periods of three to five years are common. In only a few states are judgment liens enforceable for more than ten years from their commencement. A few states extend the life of a judgment lien if the plaintiff obtains a levy of execution based on the lien.

The circumstances under which a plaintiff is entitled to attach defendant's property are regulated in detail by the various state statutes. Requirements for obtaining an attachment order usually are strict. In general, the statutes allow attachment only if the plaintiff is seeking money damages. In a number of states, the monetary amount of the plaintiff's claim must be fixed or undisputed and only its validity contested.

A minority of states have unlimited attachment statutes. In these states the plaintiff is permitted to attach defendant's property in actions for money damages without showing special circumstances. Most states, however, require the plaintiff to show that some special reason exists to attach defendant's property. Permissible reasons are indicated by the state statute establishing the attachment remedy.

Typical state statutes allow attachment of the property of nonresident defendants. They also allow attachment of property that might easily be concealed or where facts indicate that the defendant might leave the jurisdiction. Ordinary business or pleasure trips outside of the state, openly made, are not within the contemplation of the statute as grounds for attachment. In many jurisdictions the fact that a defendant cannot be found is sufficient for the issuance of a writ of attachment. In almost all cases, a defendant may obtain the release of attached property by posting sufficient bond.

VENDOR'S LIEN
◆ **In some states, a right of a seller to a lien against land conveyed for any unpaid or unsecured portion of the purchase price.**

CASE EXAMPLE

Dwayne and Beulah Blankenship contracted to exchange their ranch in Bonner's Ferry, Idaho, for one owned by Roy C. Myers and his son Ron. In addition, Roy Myers agreed to pay them $105,000 in contracts and cash.

Myers delivered the contracts and cash to his agent, Patrick, who converted $50,000 of these assets to his own use. A short time later Myers conveyed his entire interest in the Bonner's Ferry ranch to his son. Both the senior Myers and Patrick became insolvent, and the Blankenships asserted a vendor's lien against the Bonner's Ferry property.

Although a lower court refused the lien on grounds that the Blankenships were not unpaid, the Idaho appellate court reversed. The appellate court stated, "if through no fault of the seller the seller never receives such consideration or collateral from the buyer, then the seller is unpaid and unsecured and has a vendor's lien." *Blankenship v. Myers, 97 Idaho 356, 544 P.2d 314 (1975).*

The term *vendor's lien* is used in several ways. In some situations, if the buyer does not pay the full purchase price, the seller reserves a lien in the deed. This is frequently referred to as an *express vendor's lien*. A lien of this type is very similar to a mortgage. It provides security for the unpaid seller just as a mortgage would. Like the mortgage, the express vendor's lien is the result of agreement between the parties. Although most of the states allow express vendor's liens, they are not in common use in this country. The probable reason is that a mortgage to the unpaid seller provides greater protection because the buyer also signs a note for the debt. In a few states, however, the vendor's lien is an important element in real estate sales when the seller is not fully paid at the closing.

In a number of states, a vendor's lien arises by implication if the buyer does not pay the full price and the seller takes no other security. This is the type of lien involved in the Bonner's Ferry case. The implied vendor's lien exists without express agreement. It is based on the principle that a person who has acquired another's property should not be allowed to keep it without paying for it. An unpaid seller should be allowed to satisfy the debt from the proceeds of a foreclosure sale of the property. Courts in some states also justify the vendor's lien on the theory of implied trust. These courts consider the buyer a trustee for the seller, holding legal title for the seller's benefit until the price is paid.

Courts and legislative bodies have often been critical of the implied vendor's lien. They consider the lien unfair because it is secret. They contend that third parties dealing with the buyer have no way of knowing of the lien's existence. Public records show that the buyer has legal title and no security interests exist against the property. As a result, a third party might be induced to buy the property or grant credit with the property as security. Although the public record is clear, a seller might have a lien that could be a cloud on the title or take priority over a mortgage. To eliminate this injustice, many states, by statute or judicial opinion, hold the vendor's lien unenforceable against encumbrances or purchasers in good faith who do not know of the lien's existence. For example, if Ron Myers had sold the Bonner's Ferry ranch to a bona fide purchaser prior to the Blankenships' efforts to assert a vendor's lien, the property would no longer be subject to the lien. Even so, a vendor's lien is not without value; it may be asserted against the seller, the seller's heirs or those who take from the seller knowing of the lien's existence.

Requirements. In those states in which it is recognized, the vendor's lien is created the moment the seller transfers legal title to the buyer. In order for the lien to exist, however, the seller must not have accepted some other type of security for the unpaid portion of the purchase price. For instance, if the seller takes back a mortgage, the lien is waived. Taking other land or personal property as security also waives the lien. In a number of states, a seller who agrees to pass a title free of encumbrances is not entitled to a vendor's lien unless one has been expressly reserved in the deed. Retention of possession by the vendor after passing title also generally negates a vendor's lien. The vendor, however, does not waive the lien by instituting an action to recover the unpaid purchase money.

Priority. As has been noted, in many states the vendor's lien has no priority against the interest of a bona fide purchaser from the vendee or security rights in the property given to a creditor without notice. In most states the vendor's lien is also subject to a mechanic's lien for home construction, even if construction takes place after sale. The vendor's lien does have priority over the claims of unsecured creditors. These priority rules do not apply if an express vendor's lien is reserved in the deed and the deed is recorded. Under these conditions, third parties have a means of knowing that the lien exists.

In some sections of the United States, the interest of a person who sells real estate under a land contract is considered a vendor's lien. The vendor holds the legal title as security. If the vendee defaults, the vendor may foreclose the vendee's interest and apply the proceeds of the sale to the purchase price.

TAX LIEN

◆ **A lien imposed against real property for payment of taxes.**

The power of government to levy taxes is commonly coupled with the right to place liens on real and personal property to facilitate tax collection. Liens are encountered as part of the tax structure at all levels of government. In addition to federal and state governments, counties, cities, towns and villages as well as nonpolitical units such as school and irrigation districts are authorized to use liens as security when taxes are unpaid.

Many types of taxes when unpaid create liens on property. These include both real and personal property taxes, income taxes and estate taxes, as well as local assessments for sidewalks, sewers, water distribution systems and so on. Less frequently, liens may be used to collect contributions to unemployment funds, wages that have been withheld and unpaid Social Security contributions.

Although tax liens may be placed against both real and personal property, liens on real property are generally more effective than those on personal property for several reasons. Personal property is easier to conceal than real property. Personal property can be moved from the taxing district or disguised with little difficulty. Real property's value is relatively stable, whereas many types of personal property deteriorate when used. As a result, personal property is often not of sufficient value to cover the defaulted tax.

Tax liens are not restricted to the property subject to taxation. In some jurisdictions, taxes assessed on personal property may be the basis for a lien on real property. A state may also collect taxes assessed against one parcel of real estate within its jurisdiction by proceeding against other parcels owned by the same person. A lien on property other than that against which the tax was assessed is limited to property owned when the taxes became collectible. Inasmuch as tax liens are statutory creations, the legislature has the authority to exempt certain types of property. Property exempt from tax liens varies considerably from state to state. Usually the statutory provision establishing lien exemption parallels statutes exempting property from taxation in general.

Priority. People who are unable to pay a particular tax generally have other financial problems. Often, many claims exist against their property. These claims may have been the basis for liens for other taxes, judgments or mortgages. The result is that litigation involving tax liens often concerns priority problems.

Legislative bodies have usually made tax liens superior to all other liens against the property, even those liens in existence before the tax lien. The rule of "first in time, first in right" does not ordinarily apply to tax liens.

> ## CASE EXAMPLE
> Graceland Savings and Loan held a mortgage on property owned by Ron Blue. The mortgage was recorded properly. Blue failed to pay his general property tax, and a lien was assessed against the property. The tax lien had priority over Graceland's mortgage.

State statutes ordinarily set forth any priorities existing between liens for different types of taxes. In the absence of a specific statute, the lien for general taxes is coequal with liens of other taxing units. Tax liens for general taxes are usually superior to liens for special assessments even if the special assessment lien was prior in time. The reason is that the claim for the necessary support of government is a higher obligation than the demand for the costs of a local improvement. Maintenance of civil government is the first and paramount necessity for social order, personal liberty and private property, and government cannot exist without revenue. Only upon specific legislative direction will the priority of the sovereign claims of the state be denied.

Foreclosure of Tax Liens. Sale of tax liens on real property is one method commonly used in the United States to collect delinquent taxes. When taxes that are a lien against real property are in default, tax collectors in most states are authorized to sell the lien. These sales are usually by public auction. The successful bidder acquires the right to receive the overdue taxes and interest as these are paid. If there are no bidders, the taxing unit acquires the tax lien.

A successful bidder at a tax sale of the lien does not get title to the property but a lien against it. This lien is evidenced by a tax certificate. If the delinquent taxes are not paid after a period of time, the holder of the tax certificate can foreclose against the property. Usually this period of time is two or three years. During this time the property owner may redeem the property by paying the delinquent taxes, interest and any penalties.

The purchaser at the foreclosure sale obtains title to the property. In most jurisdictions the foreclosure procedure is very similar to that for a mortgage. A few jurisdictions continue to allow certain taxing units to conduct an absolute sale of real property at public auction if taxes are delinquent. The highest bidder acquires immediate title to the property on payment of the bid and delivery of the deed.

Federal Tax Lien. The federal taxing authority uses liens against real property to aid in the collection of federal income, estate and gift taxes. Federal tax liens for income taxes are not valid against a mortgagee, pledgee, mechanic's lienor, purchaser or judgment creditor until a notice of lien is filed. Liens for federal estate taxes do not require recording or filing. They come into existence against all of a decedent's taxable assets automatically upon that person's death. Relatively simple procedures have been developed to release a decedent's real property from the tax lien. These are designed to facilitate sale of the property. They ordinarily require a bond by the estate or partial payment of the tax. Federal gift taxes also attach automatically upon all gifts made. If the tax is not paid, the donee can be personally liable up to the value of the gift.

REVIEW AND DISCUSSION QUESTIONS

1. When a contractor improves real property, the work is done on the basis of a contract with the owner. A contractor who is not paid can sue for breach of that agreement. Explain why a contractor should also be entitled to file a mechanic's lien against the property.

2. Mechanic's lien law differs appreciably from state to state. (a) Indicate at least five of these differences. (b) What public policy concerns might explain some of these variations?

3. Judgment lien law differs appreciably from state to state. (a) Indicate at least five of these differences. (b) What public policy concerns might explain some of these variations?

4. What is the chief criticism of the vendor's lien? Is this criticism justified?

5. For what reason does the tax lien enjoy a superior status? Do you agree? Explain.

CASE PROBLEMS

1. Kile borrowed $15,000 from Chatfield, giving her a promissory note to cover the debt. The note was unsecured, but Chatfield knew that Kile owned substantial unmortgaged real property. A short time later, Hude won a judgment against Kile for $150,000. When Kile filed as a bankrupt, both Chatfield and Hude claimed priority in the real estate. Which of the two has the superior claim? Explain.

2. Wood owned several hundred acres of land in Texas. In 1952 he decided to explore for oil on the land and leased an oil-drilling rig from Cabot. Under the terms of the lease, Cabot was responsible for moving the rig to the Wood property. Cabot then hired White Heavy Haulers to transport the equipment. White Heavy Haulers was not paid and filed a mechanic's lien against Wood's property. (a) Is the lien valid? Discuss. (b) Would your answer differ if under the lease the expense of moving the rig was to be borne by Wood? Explain.

3. Ransonne won a judgment against Sneed for $120,000. A certified copy of the judgment was filed in the office of the county recorder of Mesa County, a county in which Sneed owned real property with a market value of about $80,000. A short time later, Sneed contracted to sell this property for $82,000. Ransonne immediately sued to enjoin the sale on the basis of her judgment lien. She contended that the property would appreciate in value over the next few years and could then be sold to satisfy the judgment. Discuss the validity of her contention.

4. Jethro Construction Co., Inc., (Jethro) was the general contractor on two separate construction projects. Lasater Electric Co. (Lasater) was the electrical subcontractor on both projects. Lasater purchased its materials for their projects as well as others from Mac's Electrical Supply (Mac's). Lasater maintained an open account with Mac's. Over several projects, payments by Lasater to Mac's had been increasingly slow, and Mac's was worried about Lasater's ability to pay. What steps should Mac's take to ensure mechanics' liens against the projects if Lasater fails to pay?

5. A state statute created a mechanic's lien in favor of all persons "bestowing skill or other necessary service on . . . the construction . . . either in whole or in part, of any building, structure, or other work of improvement . . . " In the course of supplying general engineering services to subdivide land into residential lots, Nolte located boundaries and set monuments in the ground to mark them. When Nolte was not paid, he filed a mechanic's lien. The owner argued that Nolte's lien was invalid because it was not related to any "building, structure, or other work of improvement," as the mechanic's lien statute required. Is the lien valid? Support your answer. *Nolte v. Smith, 189 Cal. App.2d 140, 11 Cal. Rptr. 261 (1961)*

6. Tabet Lumber Company supplied materials for a house being constructed for Richard and Jan Baughman. The Baughmans paid the contractor in full and moved into the house on October 25, 1985. On January 15, 1986, the contractor hung two mirrors in the bathrooms, installed handrails on the stairs and weather-stripped two basement doors. These items were included in the original agreement. The contractor did not pay for all of the materials, and on April 15, 1986, Tabet filed a lien claim for the unpaid portion. The Baughmans asked the court to dismiss, contending that this filing was invalid as the state's mechanic's lien statute required filing within 90 days of completion. Their view was that substantial completion was sufficient and the 90-day period started running in October. Should the case be dismissed? Support your answer.

7. Ohio requires that a subcontractor file a notice of furnishings in order to perfect a mechanic's lien. The notice provides a public record that the subcontractor is furnishing work and/or materials. The statute requires that it be filed within 21 days from the time that the subcontractor receives notice that work has commenced.

   Masonry, Inc., contracted with General Contractors, Inc., to do masonry work for The Southside Church. Masonry, Inc., did not file the notice of furnishings until the 30th day. General Contractors went bankrupt, and Masonry, Inc., was not paid. Masonry, Inc., looked to the Church, who maintained that it paid General Contractors. The Church insisted that Masonry, Inc., remove its filing. Masonry, Inc., refused to do so until the Church paid it. What should Masonry, Inc., do and why?

17

Deeds

DEED

♦ **A legal instrument conveying title to real property.**

The deed is the primary method of transferring title to real estate. Title is the totality of rights and obligations possessed by an owner. The term is also used in the sense of evidence of ownership. Therefore, the deed is one of the critical documents in the real estate transaction. Although problems involving deeds are ordinarily the concern of the attorney, the real estate professional needs to be familiar with the various types of deeds, the elements of a deed and the method for executing a deed.

The deed is a two-party instrument. One party, called the *grantor,* conveys real estate to the second party, the *grantee.* A deed does not have to follow any particular form to be valid. Any written document containing the essential elements will be effective. Most states, however, have adopted statutory forms for the different types of deeds. The statutory forms are almost always short, often a single page, and all the essentials are included. Although the statutory form is acceptable for all transactions, lawyers sometimes prepare a longer, more formal document.

The use of statutory forms cuts the costs of recording and reduces the space necessary to preserve records and deeds. In some areas of the United States, especially heavily populated areas, space has become so acute a problem that many recording offices have turned to microfilm or microfiche storage or computerized systems to preserve the public records.

Several types of deeds are common in the United States. Ordinarily, in a real estate transaction, the type of deed that the seller uses is agreed upon in the contract of sale. This is one of several reasons why each party should consult an attorney before signing the agreement. A seller is bound to furnish the type of deed stipulated by the real estate sales contract, and this is what the buyer must accept, even though another type of deed might provide the buyer more protection. The most common types of deeds are the warranty deed, bargain and sale deed, quitclaim deed and fiduciary deed.

WARRANTY DEED

◆ **A deed that conveys title and warrants that the title is good and free of liens and encumbrances.**

Custom often influences what type of deed will be agreed upon in the contract. Real estate attorneys like to use the instrument in general use in a particular locality. In some areas, one type of deed is standard for residential sales, whereas a different type of deed is used to convey commercial property. Parties should remember, however, that the type of deed is subject to negotiation at the time of contracting.

CASE EXAMPLE

Olvic's contract with Ziebarth called for a general warranty deed. At the closing, Olvic offered another type of deed customarily used in the area. Nonetheless, Ziebarth was entitled to a general warranty deed.

There are two types of warranty deeds—the general or full warranty deed and the special or limited warranty deed.

General Warranty Deed. The *general* or *full warranty deed* is more commonly used. A general warranty deed conveys the seller's title and contains covenants of title respecting the title. These covenants provide the buyer with some protection against claims that might interfere with ownership.

The covenants in a general warranty deed vary from one locality to another, but five covenants are customary: covenant of seisin, covenant against encumbrances, covenant of quiet enjoyment, covenant of warranty and covenant of further assurances (see Figure 17.1). In some states, such as Illinois, the general warranty covenants are implied by statute by simply "warranting" the title. By use of a grant deed, California accomplishes the same result. The warranties are implied. Other states require express reference to the warranties.

By *covenant of seisin* the seller guarantees his or her ownership of the property and existence of a right to convey. The covenant has also been construed to mean that the seller has an estate of the quantity and quality purportedly conveyed. This covenant is sometimes referred to as the *covenant of right to convey.*

The *covenant against encumbrances* is the seller's assurance that, at the time of conveyance, the property is free of *encumbrances.* Typical encumbrances are leases, easements, liens, and mortgages, discussed more fully in Chapters 7, 8, 9, 16 and 21. The covenant does not apply to those encumbrances specifically excepted in the deed because the buyer has agreed to accept them. In many states, encumbrances that are open and visible and that benefit the land are also excluded from the covenant against encumbrances.

FIGURE 17.1 *General Warranty Deed*

General Warranty Deed

This general warranty deed is made the seventeenth day of May, 1998, between Honus Grantor and Elsie Grantee.

Witness that Grantor, in consideration of $1.00 and other good and valuable consideration, paid by Grantee, does hereby grant and release to Grantee and assigns forever, the following described real estate, together with the appurtenances and all the estate and rights of Grantor in and to said premises:

[Insert description here]

And Grantor covenants as follows:

1. That Grantor is seised of said premises in fee simple, and has good right to convey the same.

2. That Grantee shall quietly enjoy the said premises.

3. That the said premises are free from encumbrances.

4. That the Grantor will execute or procure any further necessary assurance of the title to said premises.

5. That Grantor will forever warrant the title to said premises.

In witness hereof, Grantor has hereunto set his hand on the above date.

_____   _____
Witness   Grantor

_____
Witness

Acknowledged before me this 17th day of May, 1998.

_____
Notary Public

CASE EXAMPLE

Al Wilson purchased a lot from Bonnie McConnell. The lot and several others in the area were subject to certain building restrictions. At the time Wilson contracted he knew of these restrictions, but they were not mentioned in the contract. Wilson refused to accept a deed from McConnell on grounds that the restrictions violated the covenant against encumbrances. Because Wilson knew of the restrictions and they benefited the land, however, this argument would be unsuccessful.

The *covenant of quiet enjoyment* and the *covenant of warranty* are very much alike. The covenant of quiet enjoyment warrants that the buyer will not be evicted by someone with a superior title. This covenant is not breached unless the buyer is actually evicted by a third party who has a superior title. The covenant of warranty warrants that the warrantor will defend title on behalf of the purchaser against all lawful claimants.

In some states the general warranty deed also contains a *covenant of further assurances*. This covenant obligates the grantor to perform all acts necessary to confirm the grantee's title, including the execution of any additional conveyances to accomplish the assurance.

The covenant of quiet enjoyment, the covenant of warranty and the covenant of further assurances protect future purchasers as well as the immediate purchaser. They are regarded as future covenants and are said to *run with the land.* As a result, their breach may be the basis for suit by a remote buyer against a previous seller who has given a warranty deed. This suit may occur many years after the particular defendant sold the property. The phrase *run with the land,* discussed more fully in Chapter 9, is used because these covenants attach to the land and pass from one person to another as title is transferred.

CASE EXAMPLE

Several years after buying the property from Olvic, Ziebarth sold it to Lance Murphy. Ziebarth did not convey by a general warranty deed. Murphy's title was contested, and he was evicted from the property. Unable to sue Ziebarth, Murphy commenced an action against Olvic. Olvic defended on the grounds that he had not sold the property to Murphy. In this litigation, a court would find for Murphy on the grounds that the covenants of quiet enjoyment and warranty run with the land and extend to future owners.

Covenants in a warranty deed do not assure the buyer that the seller has title or guarantee any rights to the buyer. All they do is give the buyer a right to sue if a covenant is broken. Although they provide the buyer with some protection, that protection is limited by many factors. The seller who has given the covenants might become insolvent or leave the jurisdiction. In that case, any judgment against the seller would be difficult to obtain or of little value. Many states limit the seller's liability to the original purchase price. In these states, improvements or appreciation in value is not included as part of the buyer's losses. Not covered by the traditional covenants are invalid claims and threats of litigation. Because of the limited nature of the protection offered, a buyer should never rely only upon a warranty deed. Additional assurances such as title insurance, discussed in Chapter 20, should be obtained.

Special Warranty Deed. A *special* or *limited warranty* deed restricts the extent of the seller's warranties. In this type of instrument, the seller guarantees only against acts that he or she has done that might affect title. Of course, the deed conveys the seller's title to the property.

> ### CASE EXAMPLE
>
> Ziebarth's conveyance to Lance Murphy was by a limited warranty deed. When Murphy discovered that Ziebarth's title was defective because of an undischarged mortgage given by Olvic in 1977, Murphy brought suit against Ziebarth. Because the defect arose before Ziebarth had acquired title, the limited warranty had not been breached. Murphy did, however, have a good cause of action against Olvic, who had conveyed by general warranty deed.

BARGAIN AND SALE DEED
◆ **A deed that conveys title with no warranties.**

The bargain and sale deed conveys title but contains no warranties. Sometimes the bargain and sale deed contains covenants against the seller's acts. When this is the case, the bargain and sale deed has the same effect as the limited or special warranty deed.

The bargain and sale deed may be used when, for example, there are some known encumbrances that the buyer will assume and that will be adjusted in the purchase price.

◆ **Fiduciary Deed. A deed that conveys title and contains no warranties except that the grantor has the authority to transfer title.**

An important variation of the bargain and sale deed is the fiduciary deed. A *fiduciary* is a person who has been placed by law in a position of trust regarding property that is not his or her own, for example, the administrator or executor of a decedent's estate. The fiduciary might need to convey title to the decedent's real property but would not want to make guarantees or warranties concerning the title. In that case a special form of deed, similar to the bargain and sale deed, may be used. In it the fiduciary guarantees only that he or she has been properly appointed and authorized to sell and convey. The deed does not make any other warranties.

In many states it is customary to use a sheriff's deed to convey foreclosed property to the purchaser at public auction. This is a type of fiduciary deed.

QUITCLAIM DEED
◆ **An instrument that conveys the grantor's interest only.**

Unlike the warranty deed and the bargain and sale deed, the quitclaim deed does not purport to convey title; it merely releases whatever interest the grantor possesses. If the grantor has title, the quitclaim deed conveys that title as effectively as a warranty or bargain and sale deed. A grantee who takes title by a quitclaim deed does not acquire any of the covenants that are given to a grantee accepting a warranty deed. If the contract does not mention the type of deed to be used, many states permit the seller to give a quitclaim deed.

One of the most common applications of the quitclaim deed is to transfer a spouse's interest in the marital residence to the other spouse as part of a divorce property settlement. The quitclaim deed is also commonly used to clear a *defective* title by having a third person who has a possible claim against the realty convey whatever rights he or she has back to the owner. The defect could be an outstanding lien, an easement or a potential dower right.

CASE EXAMPLE

Martin Russo contracted to sell property to Elmer Hunter. At the time, Russo was single, but he married before he signed and delivered the deed. Only Russo signed the deed. In their state, Russo's wife has a right of dower. Upon discovering the marriage, the attorneys for both parties asked Mrs. Russo to execute a quitclaim deed releasing her right to Elmer Hunter. In executing and delivering this instrument, Mrs. Russo would surrender any interest she might have in the property.

ESSENTIAL ELEMENTS OF A DEED

A deed is a serious instrument that should be drafted by an attorney. A properly drafted and executed deed is critical to any real estate sale. Errors in a deed may cause problems not only for the current owner but also for future generations of owners. Sale of the property, financing and even occupancy can be affected by errors that seem inconsequential. In order to help prevent these errors, the real estate salesperson needs some knowledge of the basic requirements of a valid deed. Since the deed should be drafted by an attorney, the salesperson's knowledge need not be extensive, but it should be sufficient to "flag" potential problems. With this background, the salesperson should be able to alert the drafter to issues that might lead to errors in the deed.

In order to be valid, a deed must include words of conveyance, a competent grantor, an identifiable grantee, and an adequate legal description. The instrument must be signed by the grantor, witnessed, and notarized, and a valid delivery and acceptance must occur. State statutes may require other terms, for example, the name and address where the tax bill should be sent.

WORDS OF CONVEYANCE

The heart of a deed is the granting clause. A deed must contain words of conveyance sufficient to transfer an estate from one party to another. No particular words are necessary, provided that those used express an intention to convey title. Words customarily used are *grant, convey* and *bargain.* A typical granting clause might read as follows: "Grantors . . . do by these presents grant, bargain, sell, and convey unto the said grantees forever. . . . " The words *quitclaim* or *release* are words of conveyance commonly found in quitclaim deeds.

A deed without words of conveyance does not transfer title; the courts have, however, been indulgent in interpreting words in order to a give a deed effect, when it was clearly the intent of the grantor to convey the property.

CASE EXAMPLE

Mary A. Searle conveyed land to her four children as tenants in common. Approximately seven years later, the four joined in the execution of an inartfully drawn instrument, which purported to change their rights as cotenants and to convey to others their interests.

The granting clause of this document stated, "Said premises are to be held so that as each of said parties shall die, the property shall vest in the survivors or survivor for their respective lives. . . . " Remainders were created using as granting words "to go," "to be his," and "shall go." In an action to establish who had title, plaintiffs argued that the operative words of grant "are to be held" and the phrases used to grant the remainder interests were insufficient and that the instrument was not a valid deed.

The court did not agree, stating, "To be effective to transfer an interest in realty, a deed necessarily must contain words of present grant. . . . But no particular verbal formula is required under our rule of construction as previously given. The quoted words express an intention to create among the original cotenants new incidents of survivorship and power of sale, and to grant remainder interests to other persons subject to defeasance upon the exercise of the power of sale. The instrument was not ineffective as a deed for lack of a sufficient granting clause." *Dennen v. Searle, 149 Conn. 126, 176 A.2d 561 (1961).*

COMPETENT GRANTOR

To be valid, a deed must have a competent grantor. Any natural person except a minor or a person who lacks mental capacity may convey real estate by deed. Corporations also have the capacity to convey real property.

Minors. Deeds made by minors are not void, but they are *voidable,* which means that the minor acquires the option of either ratifying or disaffirming the transfer.

The minor wishing to disaffirm a transfer by *deed* cannot ordinarily do so until reaching the age of majority, but a minor can avoid a *contract* to buy land at any time during minority and for a reasonable time after reaching majority. Today, in most states the age of majority is 18. Once having reached majority, the minor must institute proceedings to disaffirm within a reasonable time. If this is not done, the right is lost.

CASE EXAMPLE

John Spencer and his sister inherited land from their father. At the time, John was a minor. He attained majority five months later. John's sister was of full age at her father's death. Before John attained his majority, he and his sister sold the property to Alpheas MacLoon. Shortly thereafter, MacLoon conveyed part of the property to the Lyman Falls Power Company and the residue to William Hutchins. Three years later the power company commenced substantial improvements on the land. John Spencer attempted to disaffirm. The company's attorney pleaded that Spencer had a right to disaffirm when he reached majority, but the right had been lost because he failed to assert it within a reasonable time. This argument was adopted by the court called upon to rule on the issue.

MENTAL CAPACITY

To cancel a deed for lack of mental capacity, evidence of a grantor's incompetency must be clear and convincing. The test of mental capacity to make a deed is the grantor's ability to understand the nature and effect of the act at the time the deed is signed.

CASE EXAMPLE

Florence Woodward owned a 120-acre farm near Verna, Oklahoma. When she was nearly 80, she became ill and moved to a nursing home. While a resident at the home, she conveyed the farm to a nephew. After Woodward's death, a niece contested the validity of the deed on grounds that the grantor was incompetent.

Conflicting testimony was given at the trial concerning Florence Woodward's competency. Witnesses testified that prior to her hospitalization she was often confused and vague. Her concentration was described as poor. There was testimony that her home was untidy, and she often took care of her cattle at odd hours, such as midnight. A nurse from the nursing home testified that in her opinion Woodward would not have understood the effect of signing a deed, but she always recognized her nephews and would talk about her property. Other witnesses testified that Woodward was generally alert, competent and normal.

The court held the deed valid, stating that fragmentary evidence of isolated instances of failing memory or confusion is insufficient to overcome evidence that the grantor was competent. *Matter of Woodward, 549 P.2d 1207 (Okla. 1976).*

Corporate grantor. A number of special rules apply to transfers of real property by corporations. The corporate officer who executes a deed must be authorized to do so. This authorization is obtained from the board of directors, which adopts a written resolution permitting the officer to act. In most states, if the corporation sells real estate that is a substantial portion of the corporation's assets, statutes require the sale to be approved by a designated portion of the shareholders, usually two-thirds or more. Nonprofit corporations are often required by statute to obtain approval of a majority of members before selling real estate.

A partnership is not a legal entity for certain purposes—taxation, for example. However, all states have adopted the Uniform Partnership Act or a similar statute. These acts make it clear that a partnership is an entity for purposes of transferring title to real estate and holding title in its own name. Holding title in the name of the partnership avoids any problems associated with an interest in dower, since no dower attaches to a partnership interest.

IDENTIFIABLE GRANTEE

A deed does not convey title unless it names an existing identifiable grantee. Of course, few transactions exist in which the grantee does not legally exist. One example might be a deed that designated an unincorporated association as the grantee. A deed naming this group would be invalid. It would need to name the legal trustees of the association. However, as the next case example illustrates, courts permit extrinsic evidence to determine the identity of the grantee.

CASE EXAMPLE

I. A. Garraway and Mrs. I. A. Garraway signed a general warranty deed conveying to "The Trustees of Oak Grove Consolidated High School and Their Successors" a parcel of land. The deed was delivered and recorded. The trustees built a public school on the property and operated it for 28 years until the school was closed. The Perry County Board of Education succeeded to all rights of the former trustees of the high school. The Garraways' heirs sought to have the warranty deed declared null and void on the legal theory that no legal person was named as trustee in the deed. The trial court rejected the theory and the Supreme Court of Mississippi affirmed the trial court. The court stated:

> In the first place, the Trustees of the Oak Grove Consolidated High School were indeed a corporate body politic. . . . In any event, the conveyance is effective because all our law requires is that the grantee be described in such terms that by reference to objective evidence otherwise available, his identity may be ascertained with reasonable certainty. . . . There are minutes before the court reflecting that . . . the Trustees of the Oak Grove Consolidated High School were W. A. Hegwood, Forrest Cochran, Arthur Breland, H. I. Breland and Charlie Herring.

Garraway v. Yonce, 549 So.2d 1341 (Miss. 1989).

Ordinarily, the determination of the proper designation of the grantee is a responsibility of the attorney or other person who drafts the deed. The real estate professional can aid the drafter by informing him or her of unusual circumstances regarding the name or marital status of the grantee. For example, during negotiations the real estate salesperson may learn of the grantee's use of another name or a variation in spelling.

ADEQUATE LEGAL DESCRIPTION

Problems involving descriptions in deeds are, like those involving designation of the grantee, not primarily the concern of real estate personnel but of legal personnel. Sales personnel, however, are apt to be aware of boundary controversies, which may result from, or indicate, description problems. Legal description and controversies involving boundaries are discussed in Chapter 18.

The salesperson who is aware of a boundary or description issue should urge the seller to obtain a solution before placing property on the market. This will save time and embarrassment as well as prevent hard feelings that arise when these issues come up after agreement is reached.

It is not difficult to inadvertently transpose words or omit portions of a description when copying it from one deed to another. Descriptions probably cause more litigation than any of the other formal requirements of the deed. Property to be conveyed must be described well enough in the deed to identify it with reasonable certainty. An imperfect description does not necessarily render a deed invalid, but the description must accurately depict the land in question. Presumably the grantor intended to convey *something;* the deed will usually be upheld unless the description is so vague or contradictory that the particular land cannot be identified.

Most courts interpret words of description liberally in order to uphold a conveyance. The basic rule in construction of deeds is to ascertain and carry out the real intention of the parties. To accomplish this, courts first look to the document itself, but they will accept extrinsic evidence if the description furnished a guide to identifying the property conveyed.

CASE EXAMPLE

Plaintiff and defendant owned adjoining land. A former owner of plaintiff's property had conveyed a ten-foot strip of ground to the township to be used as a drainage ditch. The ditch drained defendant's land as well as that of other landowners. The description in the deed to the township indicated a point of beginning and described the ditch as "running due south for 2,200 feet." For several years defendant had maintained the ditch, which was at the time of suit six feet wide.

Plaintiff commenced a trespass action against defendant, asking for an injunction prohibiting defendant from maintaining and using the ditch. Plaintiff argued that the deed to the township was ineffective because the description contained no boundaries. The court rejected this argument on the grounds that logically the line described was intended as the center of the ditch. The description thus furnished the means by which the property could be identified. *Franz v. Nelson, 183 Neb. 122, 158 N.W.2d 606 (1968).*

PROPER EXECUTION

To be valid, a deed must be signed by the grantor; however, the grantee's signature is unnecessary. A few states require that a deed be signed at the end of the instrument. Otherwise the signature does not have to be in any particular place, but the signature must clearly apply to the entire instrument. Customarily, even when not required, a deed is signed at the end.

FIGURE 17.2 *Special Power of Attorney*

POWER OF ATTORNEY

I, Eberly Furston, do hereby invest my attorney-in-fact, Leroy Stutz, with full power and authority to sign a deed in my name in my stead and on my behalf and to execute all other documents necessary to transfer title to my real estate located at 1100 Wilder Ave. N., Decatur, Illinois, to Francine Harbaugh for the purchase price of $125,000.

_____   _____
Witness   Eberly Furston

_____ Date: 11-8-98
Witness

Eberly Furston, known to me, did execute this Power of Attorney on November 8, 1998.

_____
Notary Public

My commission expires on April 1, 1999.

Signature may be by the grantor's mark or by any writing the grantor intends as a signature. If a grantor signs by a mark, the name should appear near the mark, and the act should be witnessed.

Attestation is the act of witnessing the execution of an instrument and subscribing as a witness. In general, the law does not require witnesses to a grantor's signature to establish a deed as valid. Witnessing and attestation, however, are almost universal prerequisites to recording. The attesting witness subscribes the document for the purpose of verifying and identifying it. Usually two witnesses are required.

Acknowledgment is the act by which a grantor declares, before a duly authorized official, that a deed is genuine and executed voluntarily. Acknowledgment, like attestation, is in most states a prerequisite to recording rather than an essential requirement of a valid deed. The purpose of acknowledgment is to prevent forgery and fraud. The official witnessing the grantor's signature is charged with determining the grantor's identity. Each state by statute prescribes the officials before whom an acknowledgment must be made and the general form the acknowledgment must follow. Attestation and acknowledgment are discussed more fully in Chapter 20, which deals with recording.

Power of attorney. A power of attorney is a written instrument authorizing a person, the attorney-in-fact, to act as agent on behalf of another to the extent indicated in the instrument (see Figure 17.2).

A deed executed by an agent for the grantor, in the grantor's absence, is invalid unless the agent has a power of attorney. In a real estate transaction, the parties should use a special power of attorney instead of the all-inclusive general power of attorney. Courts strictly construe the power of attorney, and thus the power must specifically authorize the attorney-in-fact to convey the real estate. A general power to sell does not grant the power to convey. In some states, the *equal dignities* rule requires that a power of attorney in a real estate conveyance be executed with the same formalities that are required to execute the deed properly. In some states, a deed executed by a person with a power of attorney cannot be recorded unless the power of attorney is also recorded.

Normally, a power of attorney may be revoked at any time. In most cases the death of either the principal or the attorney-in-fact also revokes the power of attorney. Therefore, the purchaser taking a deed signed by an attorney-in-fact should be extremely cautious. The power of attorney should not be old, and the purchaser should require evidence that the principal is living. The purchaser should also insist that the power of attorney be recorded. This provides some protection because an unrecorded revocation is ineffective against a recorded power of attorney. Regardless, the seller's power of attorney may not be acceptable to parties involved in the transaction, for example, the mortgagee and the purchaser.

Delivery and Acceptance

A deed does not transfer title until delivered by the grantor and accepted by the grantee. Although manual transfer of the instrument is the common method of delivering a deed, manual transfer alone is insufficient to pass title. The grantor must *intend to pass title* and *surrender control of the instrument*. Unless these two components exist, the fact that the grantor has given up physical possession of the deed is of no consequence.

> ### Case Example
> Beatrice Curtiss executed a quitclaim deed to herself and to her granddaughter, Marilyn Feriss, as joint tenants. Although the deed was recorded, Mrs. Curtiss continued to occupy the property and paid all maintenance and insurance expenses. Both Mrs. Curtiss and other members of the family stated and acted as if Mrs. Curtiss were the sole owner. Mrs. Feriss was regarded and spoken of as "the inheritor." Mrs. Feriss never occupied the property or stayed there longer than a single night.
>
> In litigation involving the Feriss title, the appellate court stated that "the deed in question did not operate to pass an interest in the property . . . to Marilyn Feriss as the grantor did not intend for it to do so." *Curtiss v. Feriss, 168 Colo. 480, 452 P.2d 38 (1969).*

Conversely, even though physical transfer is the generally accepted procedure, delivery can be effective without it. Constructive or implied delivery, which is delivery without change of possession, is valid, although rare. As with actual delivery, the essence of constructive delivery is the intention of the parties, not the manual act of transfer. If the grantor, by words or acts, manifests an intention to be divested of title and for it to vest in another, the law determines that delivery is sufficient, even if the instrument itself (but not control) remains in the hands of the grantor.

C A S E E X A M P L E

On August 10, 1940, Frank and Elizabeth Agrelius, husband and wife, executed two warranty deeds, one deed conveying 80 acres of land to Clair T. Agrelius, the other deed conveying a nearby 80 acres to Paul Kenneth Agrelius. Neither deed was recorded during the lifetime of either grantor.

   On July 27, 1944, a safety deposit box was leased . . . in the names of Mr. and Mrs. Agrelius, who signed the lease at that time. Clair was also named as lessee, although he did not sign the lease contract until 1962. The deeds were placed in the safety deposit box. At some later time in 1944 . . . Mr. Agrelius told Clair of the two deeds executed in 1940. . . . At this time Mr. Agrelius handed Clair a key to the safety deposit box and said this would constitute delivery of the deed to him. After the death of Mrs. Agrelius in 1967, Clair removed the two deeds from the box and had them recorded.

   The trial court held that ". . . when Frank and Elizabeth Agrelius told Clair they had executed a deed conveying one 80-acre tract to him and another deed to the other 80-acre tract to Kenneth and placed the deeds in their lock box and then handed the key to the box to Clair, such actions constituted an effective constructive delivery of the deeds, and all the circumstances showed a purpose on the part of the grantors that there should be an immediate vesting of title in Clair and Kenneth, enjoyment only being postponed until the death of the grantors." *Agrelius v. Mohesky, 280 Kan. 790, 494 P.2d 1095 (1972).*

Delivery is ineffective unless the grantor parts with legal control of the instrument during his or her lifetime. The grantor may not retain the power to recall the deed from either the grantee or a third party. Once a valid delivery has occurred, the deed may, however, remain in the grantor's custody or be returned to the grantor for safekeeping.

A deed may be effective even if it contains a provision that it is not to become operative until the grantor's death. Delivery must take place during the grantor's lifetime. Delivery can be made directly to the grantee, who holds the deed until the grantor's death. Whatever the situation, the grantor must be effectively divested of control of the deed. This does not occur if the grantor places the deed with private papers or merely leaves the instrument in a mutually accessible trunk, as the next case illustrates.

JONES V. JONES

Supreme Court of Alabama
470 So. 2d 1207 (Ala. 1985)

BACKGROUND. Sanford and Daisy Lee Jones had two children, Alfred and Arthur. On December 7, 1981, Sanford and Daisy executed a deed to certain lands to Alfred Jones and his wife Luverne. Daisy died on March 3, 1983, and Sanford Jones died on June 13, 1983. The deed from Sanford and Daisy to Alfred and Luverne was not recorded until July 29, 1983.

Arthur Jones filed suit questioning the validity of the deed, and the trial court judge held that the deed was void due to lack of a valid delivery. Alfred and Luverne appealed.

DECISION. The Supreme Court of Alabama agreed with the trial court judge that the deed was void for lack of delivery.

JUSTICE ADAMS. The single issue for our review is whether the trial court's judgment that the deed was void for lack of a valid delivery was supported by the evidence.

• • •

Alfred Jones testified at trial that he received two earlier deeds—one dated January 8, 1980, and the other dated May 7, 1980. He testified that he recorded the January 8 deed the following day, and the May 7 deed the same day it was executed and delivered to him. In fact, one of the two deeds executed on December 7, 1981, was recorded by Alfred Jones on December 8, 1981; yet the deed in question, executed on the same day, was not recorded until July 29, 1983, approximately six weeks after the death of Sanford Jones.

There was also testimony adduced at trial that on August 16, 1982, Alfred told Arthur that he had found the deed in their father's trunk.

The trunk was located in the bedroom of their father's house, and was used by their father to store his valuable papers.

Alfred testified that Sanford Jones never divested himself of control over the title to the property and could have sold it at any time. Sanford Jones also retained all the incidents of ownership of the property, as he was the one who paid taxes, collected the rent, and paid for repairs to the property from December 7, 1981, until his death one and one-half years later.

Finally, Alfred testified that he went to an attorney's office on December 7, 1981, and left with one deed, which he read to his family and placed in a drawer with some other deeds. Later, he testified that he had two deeds, but only recorded one of them. He stated that the reason he did not record the deed in question was that his father was still collecting rent on the property.

The trial court had the chance to view the witnesses and observe their demeanor, and after considering all the relevant factors before it, found that there was no valid delivery of the deed. We simply cannot say that the court's finding is clearly erroneous or against the great weight of the evidence in this case. Therefore, the judgment of the trial court is affirmed.

AFFIRMED.

A grantor may deposit a deed with a third party to satisfy the legal requirement of delivery. This is an effective delivery if the grantor has surrendered all control over the instrument and is powerless to recall it. A deed delivered to a third party is effective from that time even if the grantor dies or becomes insane before the grantee obtains possession of the instrument.

The estate created by the deed may be conditioned upon the performance of some act or occurrence of some event. Until the condition is fulfilled, the grantee's estate does not come into existence.

> ### CASE EXAMPLE
>
> M. A. Hinkson, while suffering from a paralytic stroke, called Hazen, an attorney, to his bedside. Acting upon Hazen's advice, Hinkson signed and acknowledged a deed naming his two daughters, Mrs. Young and Mrs. Bury, as grantees. This deed was given to Hazen with instructions not to record it but to deliver it to the grantees upon Hinkson's death. Hinkson recovered and attempted to secure possession of the deed from Hazen. Hazen refused to return it.
>
> Later, Hinkson made a will leaving all his real property to Young. Upon Hinkson's death, Hazen turned the deed over to Bury. In litigation involving Young and Bury, the court held that the deed effectively conveyed title to the two daughters when delivered to Hazen. *Bury v. Young, 98 Cal. 446, 33 P. 338 (1893).*

Escrow. A means by which delivery may take place, escrow is a process by which money and/or documents are held by a third party until the terms and conditions of an escrow agreement are satisfied. Escrow is discussed in detail in Chapter 15. In a number of localities, real estate transactions customarily close through a third party called an *escrow agent* or *holder*. This system is prevalent in some of the western states, including California. The escrow holder may be an attorney, a bank, a title insurance company or an independent escrow agent.

Buyer and seller in an escrow closing agree to submit the necessary documents and funds to the escrow holder (agent). The escrow holder is responsible for seeing that the transaction closes upon the conditions agreed to by the parties. As stakeholder, the escrow holder retains the funds and mortgage documents submitted by the buyer. When the seller has delivered to the escrow holder a properly executed deed to the property, and the holder is assured the seller is passing good title, the funds and mortgage documents are turned over to the seller. Completion of an escrow transaction may depend upon other conditions. The escrow holder is responsible for seeing that these conditions are fulfilled before delivering the deed or disbursing the funds.

Consideration. A deed does not have to state a consideration to be valid. The owner of land has the right to convey it as a gift as well as to sell it. The primary function of a deed is to convey title.

Deeds generally do state a consideration. A transfer without consideration is vulnerable against the grantor's creditors. If a deed states a consideration, and there is consideration equal to the market value of the property, it is more difficult for the grantor's creditors to assert claims against the property. If creditors can prove that the grantee gave no consideration, they may successfully levy against the property even though ownership has been transferred. Under the recording acts in all but a few states, the grantee must have given value in order to be protected. As will be seen in Chapter 20, most recording statutes provide protection only for bona fide purchasers for value.

Customarily, deeds will recite a nominal consideration such as "one dollar ($1.00) and other good and valuable consideration." This is done because buyers are often reluctant to have the actual purchase price shown, although the actual price paid is usually available through the auditor's office or some other public record. A recital of a nominal consideration is effective, for if the question of actual consideration arises, the courts allow the parties to prove by extrinsic evidence the actual purchase price.

DEED RESTRICTIONS

In addition to passing title, a deed may be used to regulate land use. This is accomplished through a condition in the instrument or a covenant. Conditions must be included in the deed; covenants usually are, but a valid covenant may be created by an ancillary document.

Chapter 4 discussed the use of conditions to limit the use of an estate. That chapter indicated that, when a condition in a deed is fulfilled, the owner's estate is subject to termination. In some instances, depending on the wording of the condition, termination is automatic; in others, termination depends on some action being taken by the person holding the reversionary or remainder interest.

Sometimes a purchaser of land will agree that it not be used in a particular manner. This type of commitment is called a *covenant*. Although both a covenant and a condition limit land use, the legal effects of the two differ. When a condition is fulfilled, the owner's interest terminates or is subject to termination. When a covenant is broken, the owner may be sued for damages or enjoined from breaking the contract, but the owner does not lose title to the property.

RESTRICTIVE COVENANT

◆ **A provision in a deed limiting uses that may be made of the property.**

Restrictive covenants are an important tool used by developers to ensure consistency in land use. Persons selling a portion of their land use them also to prevent undesirable uses of the property by the buyer. Restrictive covenants are in effect a private type of zoning regulation. By accepting delivery, the grantee is bound by restrictions in the deed.

Typical restrictive covenants limit property to residential use, provide minimum setback and acreage requirements, prohibit certain types of buildings, limit the number of structures or set a minimum cost for housing to be constructed. Because restrictive covenants limit land use, courts do not always favor them. Today, however, most restrictive covenants will be enforced if they do not violate public policy. An example of a covenant violating public policy would be one restricting ownership of the land to members of a particular racial or religious group.

AFFIRMATIVE COVENANT

Affirmative covenants are recognized in most states. Typical affirmative covenants involve agreements to build fences, maintain party walls, provide railroad crossings and join and pay dues or an annual assessment to a homeowners' association for maintenance of roads, parks or similar facilities. In a few states, affirmative covenants are not recognized as valid because courts feel that they are too difficult to enforce.

TERMINATION

Although many covenants are part of a planned pattern of land use, they also constitute a burden on the land. Frequently, buyers and sellers wish to terminate covenants because they interfere with more profitable uses of the property. A few states have passed legislation that provides for the elimination of stale restrictions after a fixed period of time or when the limitation no longer substantially benefits those for whom it was created. Most states, however, do not have legislation of this nature. In these states, deed covenants often interfere with real estate development unless they can be eliminated.

Although several methods exist for eliminating covenants, each is either costly to accomplish or legally impractical. Covenants may be terminated by a release, by waiver or by abandonment, but these methods are usually impracticable since several people often have the right to enforce a single covenant. Other methods are by acquisition of the property subject to the covenant by the owner of the property benefiting or by litigation showing that conditions in the neighborhood have so changed as to nullify the benefits of the covenant. In the following case a medical doctor sought to show just that.

HEWGLEY V. JOSE VIVO
Court of Appeals of Tennessee
1997 Tenn. App. Lexis 153

BACKGROUND. Jose Vivo, a physician, converted one of his homes in a subdivision into a medical clinic. The subject property was in a subdivision containing 37 lots on the outskirts of Tullahoma. The deed to each lot contained a restrictive covenant limiting the use of the lots to residential purposes and authorized any of the subdivision's property owners to bring suit to enforce the covenants.

The subdivision has remained residential despite the development of the surrounding area. The golf course originally located to the west of the subdivision has been replaced by a high school. North Jackson Street has been expanded from two to five lanes. A hospital has been built in the area, and numerous commercial and retail establishments, including a shopping mall, have been constructed along North Jackson Street across from the subdivision.

Dr. Vivo was aware of the restrictive covenant in his deed when he purchased the lot. He believed that the noise, pollution and traffic in the area rendered the location unsuitable for residential purposes. Consequently, he had the property rezoned and began making alterations, including paving the front yard for a parking lot, building an additional room on the back of the house, and erecting an illuminated sign near North Jackson Street.

Neighbors filed suit seeking to enforce the restrictive covenant. The trial court upheld the validity of the covenant, and enjoined Dr. Vivo from using the property for commercial purposes. Dr. Vivo appealed.

DECISION. The appellate court affirmed the ruling of the trial court.

JUDGE KOCH, JR. [Dr. Vivo argues] that the restrictive covenant no longer benefits the property because of the substantial changes in the character of the surrounding property. While extensive commercial development has occurred in the area surrounding the subdivision, we concur with the trial court's conclusion that enforcing the restrictive covenant will benefit the subdivision as a whole.

Persons who develop property may place restrictions on its future use for their own benefit and for the benefit of the other property owners in the development. These restrictions are commonly known as restrictive covenants. They need not have specific time limits, and are binding on remote grantees when they appear in the chain of title or when the grantee actually knew about the restrictive covenant when it acquired title.

Like other contracts restrictive covenants are enforceable according to the clearly expressed intent of the parties. Grantees under a common development plan may enforce their rights under a restrictive covenant against other grantees.

In most circumstances, restrictive covenants cannot be released without the consent of the purchasers and grantees for whose benefit they were imposed. Restrictive covenants can, however, lose their force when they fail to serve a useful purpose. Thus, they may be rendered unenforceable if radical changes in the character of the entire neighborhood completely defeat the purpose of the covenant.

When determining whether a restrictive covenant continues to derive any useful purpose, the courts must be concerned primarily with the continuing value of the restrictive covenant to the entire neighborhood, not the hardship to the parties attempting to avoid the restrictive covenant. While rezoning of property covered by a restrictive covenant is some evidence of a change in the character of the use of the property, rezoning alone does not require the courts to conclude that the restrictive covenant no longer serves a useful purpose.

During the past forty years, the City of Tullahoma has sprawled toward and past the subdivision involved in this case. Extensive commercial development has unquestionably taken place along North Jackson Street, and this development has affected the residential desirability of the houses facing North Jackson Street. But notwithstanding the development of the surrounding area, most of the property in the subdivision has retained its residential character.

The value of the protection afforded to residential property by restrictive covenants is reflected in the price of the property. Purchasers of residential property will pay a premium for the protections that restrictive covenants provide. While the value of the front-tier lots in a subdivision may decline because of the development of the surrounding property, this decline in value does not render the restrictive covenants unenforceable as to the front-tier lots if the surrounding development has not altered the residential character of the subdivision as a whole.

[Dr Vivo's] arguments . . . have two significant shortcomings. First, the commercial development along North Jackson Street has not altered the essential character of the entire subdivision. Second, the commercial development had already occurred by the time the [doctor] purchased the property. [He is] not entitled to

...relief when [he] knew or should have known that the existing conditions would affect the residential use of [his] property and when [he has] already benefitted from the effects of the surrounding development by paying a lower price for the property.

AFFIRMED.

REVIEW AND DISCUSSION QUESTIONS

1. Explain the assurances provided a grantee by (a) covenant of seisin, (b) covenant of quiet enjoyment and (c) covenant of warranty.

2. Explain the difference between (a) *general warranty deed* and a special or *limited warranty deed* and (b) *bargain and sale deed* and a *quitclaim deed.*

3. What is the effect of a purchaser's failure to record a deed on (a) the purchaser's title and (b) a subsequent purchaser who relies upon the seller's recorded title?

4. Why is it important for a purchaser to acquire additional assurances, such as title insurance, when acquiring title by warranty deed?

5. Name the essential elements of a deed and give an example of each.

6. List the difference between a covenant and a condition within the deed and the benefits of each.

CASE PROBLEMS

1. Dunlap owned a large farm, which he worked for many years with his son, Sam. Dunlap had a daughter, Celeste, who lived in the city. Dunlap had often told Sam, Celeste and various relatives that Sam was to inherit the farm; nevertheless, nothing was ever done to ensure that it would happen. As Dunlap aged, he became senile and difficult to live with, but in lucid moments he talked about Sam's inheriting the farm. Because Sam knew that his father had no will, Sam had a deed prepared conveying the property to himself. Dunlap signed the deed. The execution of the instrument was done properly, according to state law. Two years later Dunlap died and Sam had the deed recorded. Celeste has sued to have the deed declared invalid. What arguments should she make? What counterarguments should Sam make?

2. Everett Wine conveyed his property by deed to his son, Benjamin. He failed to read the deed before signing it. He was very old and suffered from lung disease, cirrhosis and chronic brain syndrome. Concerning his mental capacity, his doctor wrote: "Mr. Wine's mental state fluctuated from psychotic to perfectly appropriate. There were times when Mr. Wine understood fairly well what he was doing, and there were times he was out of touch with reality." What additional evidence would you like to pursue in order to determine whether Mr. Wine possessed the legal competency to sign a deed? See *Harper v. Rogers, 387 S.E. 2d547 (W. Va. 1989).*

3. Cossette Furr deeded land to Peidmont and Western Investment Corporation. At the time of the conveyance, Peidmont and Western Investment Corporation's charter had been dissolved by the Secretary of State for failure to file any report or return or to pay taxes or fees. Thereafter, the corporation was reinstated. Did the deed operate to convey title to the property? Explain. *Peidmont and Western Investment Corp. v. Carnes-Miller Gear Co., Inc., 384 S.E.2d 687 (N.C. Ct. App. 1989).*

4. Clarence and Helen Haines deeded property to Ray and Barbara Mensen described as follows:

> Part of the Northeast Quarter of the Northeast Quarter of Section 9 Township 16 North Range 13 East all in Douglas County Nebraska.

> Comment on the adequacy of the description of the property. See *Haines v. Mensen, 446 N.W. 2d716 (Neb. 1989).*

5. Stephen Takacs and his son, John, purchased property as tenants in common. After sharing the costs of building a house, father, son and the son's wife lived together on the premises for two years. During this period Stephen paid $40 per month for his room and board.

   While the parties were living together in the home, the three went to the office of an attorney. The attorney, at Stephen's insistence, prepared a quitclaim deed conveying Stephen's interest to John Takacs and Mabel R. Takacs, John's wife.

   At the time there was an understanding that the deed would become effective on Stephen's death and would not be recorded during his lifetime. The deed, however, was delivered to John. It was never in Stephen's possession, nor did Stephen reserve the right to recall it. Shortly thereafter, John died. Mabel Takacs recorded the conveyance and attempted to sell the property.

   Stephen sued to set aside the deed. Will he be successful? Discuss. *Takacs v. Takacs, 26 N.W.2d 712 (Mich. 1947).*

6. Chris Stevens, a farmer, owned 40 acres of land that he did not use. He leased the land for three years to Orlando Baron. The lease was for farming purposes. Before the lease expired, Stevens conveyed the property by general warranty deed to Morgan Kettlewell. Kettlewell planned to subdivide the property. He had no knowledge of the lease and believed the crops on the land were Stevens's. What right, if any, does Kettlewell have against Stevens? How could Stevens have protected himself?

18

Land Descriptions

LEGAL DESCRIPTION

◆ **A description of a parcel of land that will be accepted by courts because it is complete enough to locate and identify the premises.**

This chapter deals primarily with descriptions found in real estate instruments. Boundary disputes are also discussed, as an intricate relationship exists between descriptions and boundaries. A description in a real estate instrument sets forth the physical dimensions of what is being conveyed. Boundaries are based on this description. They establish the property on the earth's surface. Often they are imaginary lines, but sometimes they are marked by an object.

With only a few exceptions, U.S. law requires a written instrument to transfer an interest in real estate. To be enforceable in a court of law, the written instrument must contain a valid description of the property involved. The courts will not enforce the written instrument if the description is incorrect or ambiguous. A seller or lessor who has agreed to transfer an interest in real estate is in breach of contract if the instrument executed does not properly describe the property. Even if the physical boundaries of a property are clear, no interest will pass if the property is not described properly.

The chief purpose of the description is to furnish a means for identifying a particular parcel of land. In addition, the description must describe an area that is bounded completely. In other words, the boundaries indicated by the description must close the parcel.

For a deed or other conveyance to be enforceable in a court of law, the description must make possible positive identification of the land. Courts consider this accomplished if a surveyor or other person familiar with the area can locate the property and determine its boundaries using the description in the conveyance. Although a description by street and number is not advisable, it passes title if the property is located in a municipality that has established a standard system of numbering, and the property is identified to the exclusion of all others.

A technically accurate description that provides all the information necessary to locating land is preferable to one that needs clarification by other evidence. Courts, however, are exceedingly liberal in allowing outside evidence to clarify an ambiguous description. Testimony of the circumstances surrounding the transaction, the interpretation placed on the description by the parties, statements of surveyors, neighbors and public officials as well as the physical elements of the area may be introduced. What the courts are searching for is the intent of the parties.

CASE EXAMPLE

The Rogers owned a large piece of land. The land included a lake in which there were several islands. Seventy acres of land jutted into the lake, forming a peninsula. When the tides were high and the wind right, this peninsula was separated from the mainland by a watercourse. Boats could traverse the watercourse at these times. At other times, only an inch or two of water was in the watercourse.

The Rogers deeded all their mainland holdings to Inches and the islands to Burgess. A dispute arose between Burgess and Inches over ownership of the 70 acres. Burgess contended that the jutting piece of land was an island and belonged to him. Inches argued that it was part of the mainland and he was the owner. A court eventually resolved this dispute in favor of Inches. In doing so, it considered the testimony of fishermen who sometimes traversed the watercourse, aerial photographs, the original government survey (which didn't show the watercourse), a motion picture of a boat navigating the watercourse and the testimony of surveyors. *Burgess v. Pine Island Corp., 215 So.2d 755 (Fla. 1968).*

The description in the deed in this transaction was general, not specific. Almost all courts will try to sustain a deed even though it contains a general description. They are reluctant to declare the instrument void. Judges reason that the parties must have intended to do something or they would not have been involved in the transaction.

BUTKOVICH v. SUMMIT COUNTY

Supreme Court of Utah
556 P.2d 503 (1976)

BACKGROUND. Summit County took title to the parcel in question as the result of a tax sale due to tax delinquency of a former owner. Subsequently, in July 1964 the Butkovichs purchased the land from the county, receiving a quitclaim deed. A year later the county issued a deed to correct the original quitclaim deed containing the following description: "All unplatted land in this Block (29 P.C.) and all land West of this Blk. and Pt. lot 1: Pt. lot A." Since that time the Butkovichs have held title and paid taxes on the property. Summit County argues that its quitclaim deed is invalid because it lacks an adequate description of the property. The trial court decided for the Butkovichs.

DECISION. The Supreme Court of Utah affirmed the trial court's decision.

JUSTICE CROCKETT. It is not to be questioned that in order to be valid, a deed must contain a sufficiently definite description to identify the property it conveys. But the rules which are generally applicable to controversies over the meaning of documents are also applicable to deeds. The problem lies in ascertaining the intent with which it was executed. It should be resolved, if possible, by looking to the terms of the instrument itself and any reasonable inferences to be drawn therefrom; and if there then remains any uncertainty or ambiguity it can be aided by extrinsic evidence. If from that process the property can be identified with reasonable certainty, the deed is not invalid for uncertainty.

The county's argument that the description in the deed is insufficient is based upon the use of certain abbreviations therein as shown in the first two lines thereof: All unplatted land in this Block (29 P.C.) and all land West of this Blk. and Pt. lot 1: Pt. lot A.

No serious question is raised as to the commonly used abbreviations of Blk for "block," or Pt. for "part," of the named lots. The principal defect complained of is the use of the initials "P.C." which must be read as "Park City" to give the deed meaning and effect. Even if it be assumed that those initials might leave some doubt as to the designation of one of the main towns in the county, when it is aided by the later statement in the same deed referring to "the Park City Townsite," and is considered in the light of the rules herein above stated concerning the interpretation of deeds, it is our opinion that there is a sound basis for the trial court's conclusion that the description in the deed was sufficiently definite to convey the property in question to the defendants Butkovich.

AFFIRMED.

One type of general description that courts have consistently upheld conveys all the grantor's land in a particular area. This is sometimes referred to as a "Mother Hubbard" description. Similarly, if a deed describes a particular plot in fairly general terms but provides a clue to the land's location in a specific city, county or state, the description is effective if evidence indicates the grantor owned no other land in the designated area.

Although courts are liberal in accepting outside evidence, a deed conveying land will be invalid if the description does not identify the specific parcel or at least provide a key to identifying property to the exclusion of all other sites.

CASE EXAMPLE

The City of Atlanta owned land at the foot of Climax Place. Berchenko owned all the land on the north of Climax Place, a frontage of 1,035 feet. Berchenko also owned a tract on the south, which had a frontage of 195 feet. Climax Place was only 22 feet wide, and the city wished to widen it to 50 feet.

(Continued)

In order to accomplish this, the city obtained from Berchenko a deed to "a 28-foot strip along Climax Place." The city then demanded that Berchenko remove a building that encroached on the north of Climax Place. Berchenko refused, claiming the deed invalid because the description was uncertain and insufficient. Both the lower court and the appellate court agreed. The appellate court stated, "no surveyor, however expert, could take the description contained in the instrument just mentioned, and by the aid of any extrinsic evidence, locate the precise body of land." See *City of Atlanta v. Atlanta Trailer City Trailer Park, 213 Ga. 825, 102 S.E.2d 23 (1958).*

REFERENCE TO OTHER DOCUMENTS

As illustrated by the *Burgess v. Pine Island Corp.* case, different kinds of outside evidence may be used to clarify a description. Included in this type of outside evidence are testimony, photographs, and original surveys. The most effective clarification is provided by a deed's reference to a survey, map, plat or some similar document that correctly describes the land. The details of this extrinsic document become part of the description and can be used to resolve ambiguities or to locate the parcel. In fact, many deeds describe a parcel of land by reference to a master survey, plat or map. This is a common practice that saves time and provides clarity.

Because of the complicated nature of boundaries and the economic importance of real property, the art of surveying has been in use since antiquity to establish and verify boundaries. The Babylonians, Assyrians, Egyptians, Hebrews, Greeks and Romans perfected the art. In the Americas, the Indian peoples such as the Incas and Mayans were remarkable surveyors.

In the sophisticated technological world of today, surveys by trained professionals are an integral part of the real estate business. Although the basis of a real estate conveyance is what the parties agree to as the boundaries, agreement is seldom reached without the help of a survey. An agreed-upon boundary cannot be changed by a survey, but a survey is generally used to establish new boundaries. Only in rare instances would a tract be subdivided without a survey or would unplatted land be sold without being mapped. In these situations, the surveyor's work is the basis for any description in a deed or other real estate instrument. Where title to land has been established either through an informal survey by the parties or by a prior professional survey, the surveyor's sole function is to help determine the boundaries of the grant. In litigation involving this type of boundary problem, the surveyor often testifies as an expert witness, giving an expert's opinion as to what the grantor's intention was. The surveyor's work is a critical factor in each of the three types of descriptions discussed in this chapter and commonly used in the United States: metes and bounds, the rectangular survey, and plats and maps.

METES AND BOUNDS

◆ **A method of describing land by specifying the exterior boundaries of the property using compass directions, monuments or landmarks where directions change and linear measurement of distances between these points.**

As the eastern United States was settled and developed, probably the most common method of describing land was to name the parcel. For example, the property would be described as the Jacktown plantation or the Ebenezer Smith farm. Usually boundaries were indicated by naming the owners of adjoining property or by natural landmarks called *monuments*. An early 19th-century deed in a trespass case described the property as follows:

A certain tract or parcel of land, including the mill-seat and mill known as the "Jethro R. Franklin Mill," the said tract situated in the county of Gates, embracing as far as the highwater mark, and bounded as follows: on the north by the lands of Richard E. Parker, Reddick Brinkley, and others, on the east by the lands of Harrison Brinkley and others, south by the desert road, west by the lands of Josiah H. Reddick and others.

A description based primarily on *adjoiners* (names of owners of contiguous property, a road or something similar) and monuments is still used if the costs of a survey are out of proportion to the amount of money involved. Descriptions of this nature may cause problems if some impermanent monuments are selected.

Metes-and-bounds descriptions provide a more sophisticated method of describing real property. A metes-and-bounds description is based upon a survey that commences at a beginning point on the boundary of the tract and follows compass directions, called *courses,* and distances around the area to the point of beginning. Monuments are placed at the corners or at points where directions change. Monuments are visible objects, sometimes natural but often artificial. They can be posts, iron pipes, piles of stone, trees, streams or similar objects. By following the courses and distances, a person should be able to walk the boundaries of the property.

A typical metes-and-bounds description follows:

Beginning at an iron pipe marked A and thence running South 8 degrees 15 minutes East 75 feet to a pipe marked B thence North 78 degrees 27 minutes East 34-$\frac{3}{10}$ feet to a pipe marked C thence North 11 degrees 28 minutes West 74-$\frac{9}{10}$ feet to a pipe marked D thence South 78 degrees 27 minutes West 30-$\frac{2}{10}$ feet to the place of beginning containing 2410.7 square feet, more or less.

In reading a metes-and-bounds description, one always says "north" or "south" first and then announces the number of degrees east or west of that north or south line. The number of degrees east or west of the north or south line cannot exceed 90. Thus, to say "North 95 degrees East" as a designation for Line A in Figure 18.1 is incorrect. The correct reading is "South 85 degrees East."

Metes-and-bounds descriptions based on a survey provide a very accurate method of designating the physical dimensions of a particular tract of land. When the land itself is supplied with permanent markers at each corner or angle, the parcel can be readily located for

FIGURE 18.1 *Metes and Bounds*

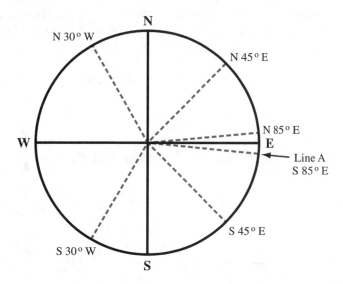

a long period of time. This method of describing land continues to be used extensively in the eastern United States. Metes-and-bounds descriptions are also used extensively in other areas of the country in conjunction with the rectangular survey to designate small parcels.

◆ **Call.** **A term used to refer to the different monuments, courses and distances that make up a metes-and-bounds description.**

Metes-and-bounds descriptions are not always based on a survey. Sometimes natural monuments used as calls are destroyed; in other instances, conflicting calls are the result of human error. To solve problems resulting from conflicting calls, courts have established a general order of preference to be given to calls when the intention of the parties is not clear. Natural monuments are preferred because they are considered more reliable than courses and distances. The general order of preference is:

1. natural monuments,
2. artificial monuments,
3. courses,
4. distances, and
5. quantity of acreage.

Adjoining landowners (adjoiners) are also important elements in some descriptions and receive a high degree of priority. Unless the adjoiner is clearly a mistake, it ranks with monuments, prevailing over courses, distances and quantity of acreage.

CASE EXAMPLE

Jones and Morrison purchased contiguous parcels from a common grantor. The deed to Jones described the east line of his property as being from the center of Edison Street south to a bois d'arc tree, a distance of 79 feet. Morrison's deed described his property's east line as being from the center of College Street north to a bois d'arc tree, a distance of 210 feet. Actually, the distance from the center of Edison Street to the tree was 86 feet; from the center of College Street the distance was 207 feet, as shown on the map.

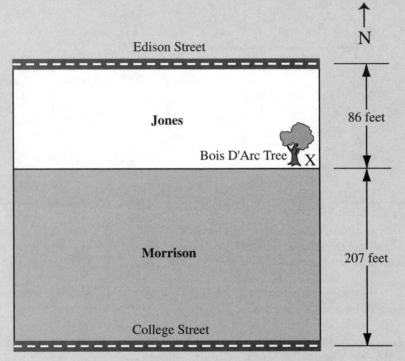

Morrison constructed a building on the property that encroached upon what Jones believed was his land. Jones sued to require the removal of the encroaching portion of the building. In finding for Jones, the court stated, "[t]his makes the case a classic example . . . for application of the rule that courses and distances must yield to natural monuments . . ." *Morrison v. Jones, 58 Tenn. App. 333, 430 S.W.2d 668 (1968).*

RECTANGULAR SURVEY SYSTEM

◆ **System of land description that applies to most of the land in the United States.**

After the Revolutionary War, the United States acquired a vast area of land west of Pennsylvania and north of the Ohio River. This area, known as the Northwest Territory, was acquired when states ceded their claims to the United States as a means of paying their war

FIGURE 18.2 *Starting Point for a Survey*

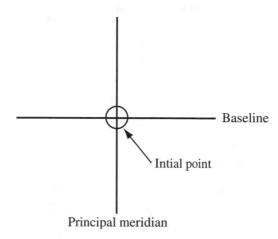

debts. Faced with pressures from land speculators and settlers as well as the need for revenue, Congress in 1785 passed legislation to prepare these lands for disposal.

An important element of this legislation was the establishment of a *rectangular survey system*, also known as the U.S. Government survey system. Although the government survey was criticized and attacked by the private land companies, it eventually became the foundation on which vast areas of the West were surveyed and sold.

With the exception of Texas, land descriptions in all states west of the Mississippi, the five states formed from the Northwest Territory and most of Alabama, Florida and Mississippi are based on this massive survey. Eventually, the survey covered more than two million square miles in the continental United States. It has been extended to Alaska, where hundreds of thousands of square miles remain unsurveyed. Although modified by legislation from time to time over the 200 years that the system has been used, the fundamentals of the rectangular survey have remained fairly consistent.

Initially, a large area is selected for survey and a starting point is chosen (see Figure 18.2). This initial point is chosen by astronomical observation. A line called a *baseline* is run east and west through this point. A perpendicular line also runs north and south through the initial point. This is called the *principal meridian*. The survey for the entire district is based on these two lines. Over the long history of the government survey, 32 baselines and 35 principal meridians have been established.

Principal meridians and baselines are designated in various ways. At first they were numbered, but later they were given names. The first principal meridian is the western boundary of Ohio. The 41st parallel is its accompanying baseline. All land descriptions in a particular area surveyed with reference to a principal meridian will refer to it. The basic unit of the survey is the *township*.

FIGURE 18.3 *U.S. Public Land—Rectangular System of Subdividing*

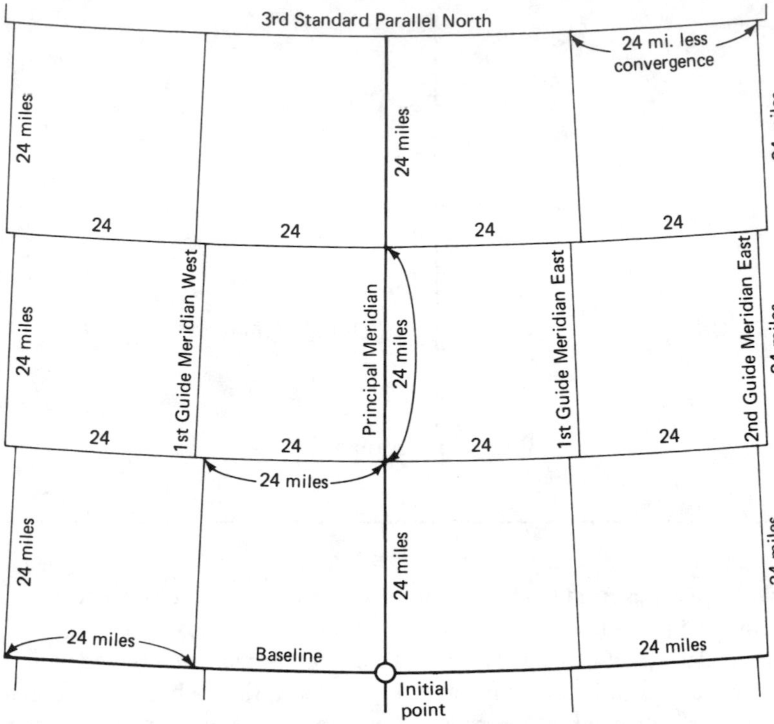

3rd Standard Parallel North

24 mi. less convergence

24 miles / 24 / 24 / 24 / 24

1st Guide Meridian West

Principal Meridian

1st Guide Meridian East

2nd Guide Meridian East

24 miles / 24 / 24 / 24 / 24

24 miles

24 miles

Baseline

Initial point

Division of Land into Tracts 24 miles square.

◆ **Township** **An area of land approximately six miles square, containing as nearly as possible 23,040 acres and divided into 36 sections, each one mile square.**

Legislation guiding the surveyors required a township to be a square, as nearly as possible six miles on a side. Because the lines that run parallel to the principal meridian converge toward the north, townships in the north would be smaller than the required 36 square miles. To remedy this, correction lines are run parallel to a baseline at 24-mile intervals north and south. These lines are called *standard parallels* or *correction lines*. Lines called *guide meridians* are then surveyed east and west at 24-mile intervals with a standard parallel as a base. Although the townships in the north are slightly smaller than those in the south, the constant correction kept the difference at a minimum. Some early surveys established correction lines at intervals much greater than 24 miles, leading to substantial discrepancy in township size. Continuous establishment of guide meridians and standard parallels reduced the compounding effect of surveying errors.

Each guide meridian and standard parallel, as shown in Figure 18.3, is designated by numerical order and compass direction from the appropriate principal meridian and

FIGURE 18.4 *Township Designations*

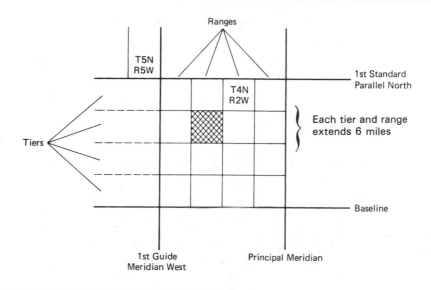

baseline. The intersections of guide meridians and standard parallels create square blocks or tracts 24 miles on each side. Townships are created by dividing these 24-mile tracts at 6-mile intervals. The result is 16 township units approximately six miles square in each tract.

Although these 24-mile-square blocks are not a factor in describing real estate, townships are an integral part of a land description. Over an entire area surveyed, tiers of townships are numbered north and south from the baseline. They are also numbered consecutively east and west from the principal meridian. The east-west tiers are called *ranges.* Each township as a result has two numbers and two directions. These numbers and directions thus provide a specific designation for each. Since all townships and ranges are numbered in reference to a particular principal meridian and baseline, no two have the same designation.

The shaded unit in Figure 18.4 is tier 3 north, range 3 west of a principal meridian. This would be indicated as T3N, R3W. Townships are not only important elements in many land descriptions, they also are often important political subdivisions.

◆ **Section.** An area of land approximately one mile square, containing as nearly as possible 640 acres.

Each township of approximately six miles square is further divided into sections. A township thus contains 36 sections. The sections in a township are numbered consecutively, beginning in the northeast corner with the number 1. Six sections are numbered westerly along the far north of the township. Section 7, just south of section 6, commences a row

FIGURE 18.5 *U.S. Public Land Survey—Typical Method of Numbering Sections*

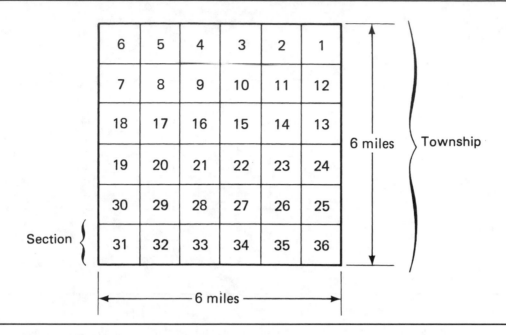

numbered in an easterly direction (see Figure 18.5). This pattern of alternating west-east numbering is followed, with section 36 being the southeast unit in the township.

Although a different numbering system was used in some of the early surveys, most of the land surveyed has sections designated in this manner. As a result, the number of the section is also a key element in describing a particular parcel of land.

Commercial realities of land disposal often resulted in a need to divide each section further. Half sections, quarter sections, and even smaller units were needed. This division is readily accomplished by surveying and designating smaller units by their geographic location within the section.

A half section may be described as the north one-half of section 15 and a quarter section as the northwest one-quarter of section 15. As each section consisted of 640 acres, the number of acres in each of these smaller units is easy to determine. A half section is 320 acres; a quarter section is 160. Figure 18.6 indicates additional divisions of a section that are commonly used. As each township has a numerical designation in relation to a particular baseline and each section a number, any of these smaller plots is precisely located within the square mile of which it is a part.

The section designation of a description using the rectangular survey system might read as "the east ½ of the SW¼." This would be the shaded portion of Figure 18.6. If the tract conveyed were in two quarters, the quarter section designations would be joined by "and." For example, the description might be worded as "the east ½ of the northwest ¼ and the east ½ of the southwest ¼."

FIGURE 18.6 *Divisions of a Section*

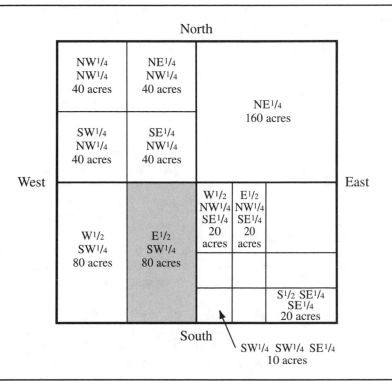

Governmental surveys were not made under ideal conditions. Errors often resulted because of weather, harsh terrain, hostile Indians, primitive equipment and plain ineptitude. The prevailing legal rule, however, has consistently been that, once land has been conveyed on the basis of a government survey, the conveyance will not be disturbed even if error is found in the survey. This is indicated in the case that follows.

BISHOP V. JOHNSON

District Court of Appeals of Florida
100 So. 2d 817 (1958)

BACKGROUND. Ralph and Francis Johnson (plaintiff, appellees) obtained title to a peninsula extending into Water Pen Lake. Their title was based on an official government survey and plat made in 1894. In 1949, a private survey of the lake showed a second peninsula just south of the first. This peninsula and adjacent land were conveyed to Wilbur Bishop (defendant, appellant).

Later it became clear that the official survey was erroneous. There was no peninsula as indicated on the official plat. The only peninsula was that indicated by the private survey. Both Bishop and the Johnsons claimed the peninsula and the Johnsons brought a suit to quiet title to the area. Their title was affirmed by the trial court and Bishop appealed.

DECISION. The decree quieting title in the Johnsons was affirmed.

JUDGE WIGGINTON. Suit was brought by plaintiffs, the appellees here, to quiet title to portions of a certain peninsula of land which extends westerly from the eastern shore of and into the navigable waters of Water Pen Lake, commonly known as Cow Pen Lake, in Putnam County.

A copy of the map showing the contended location of the disputed lands is here inserted for convenience and clarity of explanation.

During the last quarter of the year 1849 an official federal government survey was made of lands now constituting Sections 20, 21, 22, 27, 28 and 29 of Township 10S, Range 23 East. From this survey, and the field notes compiled as an incident thereto, an official township plat was constructed, approved and recorded.

This peninsula as it is identified by the government survey plat is depicted . . . by the letter "P", and consists of Lot 9 of Section 21, containing 12.10 acres, and Lot 3 of Section 22 containing 40.13 acres.

By patent dated November 18, 1903, the United States conveyed Lot 9 of Section 21 and Lot 3 of Section 22, both lying in Township 10 S, Range 12 E, to the State of Florida. Thereafter, on September 16, 1927, the Trustees of the Internal Improvement Fund conveyed both

lots to one Phillip Bersch, who, on August 8, 1953, conveyed them to the appellees. It is under title thus dereigned that appellees based their claim.

Late in 1949 a private survey was conducted from which it was concluded that the peninsula, designated as Lots 9 and 3, was actually situated south and west of the point shown on the official plat. According to this private survey, the peninsula is appended to the mainland at the Northwest corner of Lot 1, in Section 27, as shown by the letter "E" on the . . . map. In reliance upon this private survey, and under the mistaken belief that there existed a second peninsula, the Trustees of the Internal Improvement Fund issued to appellants as grantees a deed which purported to convey, by metes and bounds, the peninsula described in the aforementioned private survey. Some time after July 6, 1950, the date of the last mentioned deed, appellants acquired title to the northern portion of Lot 1, Section 27. Appellants rely upon the deed of July 6, 1950, and the subsequent deed to Lot 1 in asserting their title to the disputed peninsula.

It is admitted by the parties hereto that there is, in fact only one peninsula extending westwardly from the east shore of the lake and into the waters thereof.

It is to be noted at the outset that the government survey of 1849 did not merely ascertain or identify the disputed lands, but created Lots 9 and 3, in Sections 21 and 22 respectively, being that peninsula lying in Township 10 S, Range 23 East. The mere fact that a subsequent private survey shows an error by the United States Deputy Surveyor in locating the peninsula on the official plat is immaterial, since the latter survey is not admissible in evidence to affect or change the lines or location of land sold in accordance with an official government survey and plat.

It is well settled that the description of land and plats from field notes of an original survey filed in the General Land Office are conclusive, and section lines and corners as laid down therein are binding upon the General Government and all parties concerned. When lands described in a deed are by reference to or in accordance with a plat or survey, the courses, distances and other particulars appearing on the plat are to be as much regarded as if expressly set forth in the deed itself. The plaintiff and his predecessors in title acquired the land in question with reference to the official government plat which showed the property purchased to be a peninsula of land designated as lying in Sections 21 and 22, and extending from the eastern shoreline westward into the lake. The defendants are charged with knowledge, either actual or constructive, that the peninsula in question had been surveyed, platted and conveyed by the sovereign with reference to and in accordance with the official plat and that title thereto had become vested in the plaintiffs long before the defendants sought to acquire the lands by reference to a private resurvey. A resurvey that purports to change lines or distances or to otherwise correct inaccuracies and mistakes in an old plat is not competent evidence of the true line fixed by the original plat. Accordingly, it must be concluded that, as between the parties hereto, the government survey is paramount.

Accordingly, the decree appealed from must be and is hereby affirmed.

AFFIRMED.

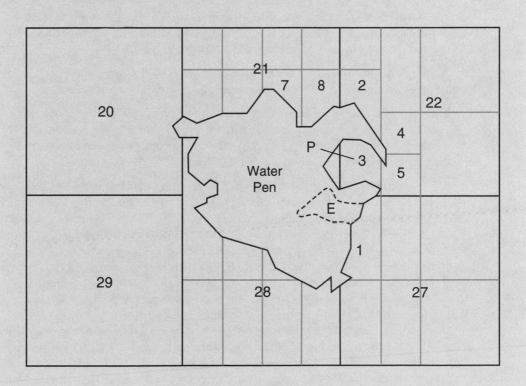

In most cases a survey does not create boundaries. Boundaries are created by the agreement of parties. The official government survey of the public land does, however, create boundaries. An original government survey, whether correct or erroneous, controls the boundaries of a section and parcels of land surveyed and platted from it. Courts feel that the parties who purchase property based on a plat from an official survey have a right to rely on it. If the survey is confirmed by the proper officials of the Department of the Interior, attack in the courts is no longer permitted when the property is sold.

PLAT

◆ **A map showing items such as natural and artificial monuments, lots, blocks and streets in a town or subdivision; generally drawn from a survey.**

A third method of describing land is by reference to a recorded plat or map. This method is used frequently in metropolitan areas. Usually it is used in conjunction with the rectangular survey or a metes-and-bounds description of a larger tract that is being divided. The property to be divided is surveyed and laid out in lots that are numbered in sequence. These lots are platted and when sold are described by their designated numbers. A description of this kind might read as follows:

> All of lot 8 in block 41 in Taylors Astoria, an addition within the corporate limits of the City of Astoria, Clatsop County, State of Oregon, as said addition was laid out and recorded by the Peninsular Land & Trust Company.

Although the deed does not contain the description of the entire survey, the United States Supreme Court in an early case supported this system. The court stated:

> . . . when lands are granted according to an official plat of the survey . . . the plat itself along with all its notes, lines, descriptions, and landmarks becomes as much a part of the grant or deed . . . as if such descriptive features were written out upon the face of the deed . . . *Cragin v. Powell, 128 U.S. 696 (1888).*

The use of maps and plats of surveys has become an important means of describing land in the United States. Plats are readily available because almost all states and many localities require a developer, when subdividing property, to have the property surveyed and a plat of it made by a competent surveyor. A typical plat is shown in Figure 18.7.

Although requirements vary, the plat generally shows the proposed streets, blocks and lots of the subdivision. The plat will also show such items as easements, rights-of-way and topographical details, such as elevations, as well as other physical features. School sites and recreational areas are indicated on plats for larger developments. Blocks and lots are designated in some manner, usually by number but sometimes by letter.

In most areas subdivision plats must be approved by some governmental body before land is sold. Usually this is a local planning board or a designated official such as the county engineer. The approved plat is then recorded in a *plat book* as part of the public land records. The property in the subdivision is thus accurately described by reference to this record. In

FIGURE 18.7 *Plat Adapted from Davis v. DeVore, 16 Ill. App. 334, 306 N.E.2d 72 (1974)*

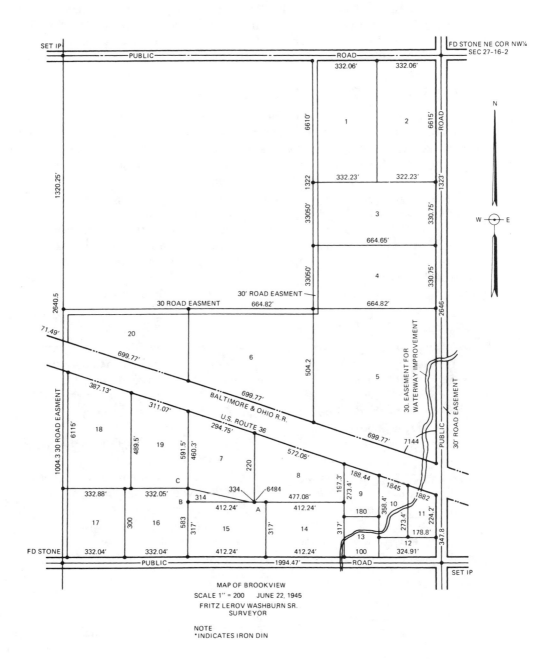

MAP OF BROOKVIEW
SCALE 1″ = 200   JUNE 22, 1945
FRITZ LEROV WASHBURN SR.
SURVEYOR

NOTE
*INDICATES IRON DIN

addition, recording of the plat serves to dedicate to public use land indicated on the plat as streets, parks and school and church sites.

In preparing land for a subdivision, the surveyor must carefully mark with permanent monuments physical boundaries of the parcels involved. The survey actually fixes the boundaries of the property, and these are reflected in the plat. If the plat and the boundaries fixed by the survey differ, the boundary as established by the physical monuments prevails.

BOUNDARY DISPUTES

Courts have adopted several rules in efforts to solve boundary disputes equitably. A fundamental principle is that the intention of the parties establishing a boundary should prevail. Although the plain meaning of the words used in a description is the best indication of intention, conflicting and ambiguous designations of boundaries must often be resolved by other rules. An example is the doctrine of "agreed boundaries."

For the doctrine of agreed boundaries to apply, the owners of adjoining property must be uncertain as to the true boundary. They must then agree as to what the true boundary is. This agreement does not have to be in writing. A minority of states require that there be some visible evidence of the boundary to be established. In any case, the boundary agreed on must be definite and certain. In a few states, the parties must continue to agree for a period equal to that required in cases of adverse possession. In most states, acquiescence for a shorter period is sufficient; however, the period varies greatly from state to state.

CASE EXAMPLE

Rouse owned a quarter section of land. In 1932 he sold the west portion to Cooper. In 1944 Rouse sold the east portion to Huggans. At the time of the sale to Cooper, the parties did not determine the exact boundary between the two properties but described the property using an old fence as one line. When Rouse conveyed the east parcel to Huggans in 1944, the description in the deed referred to the west boundary of the Huggans tract as the Cooper fence.

Huggans used the land up to the fence from 1944 until 1978. In 1978 the Cooper property was acquired by Weer. A survey at that time established the true property line 60 feet east of the fence. Upon acquiring the information, Weer attempted to remove the Cooper fence and Huggans petitioned the court for a temporary restraining order.

Huggans claimed that he had title to the 60-foot strip up to the fence, based upon adverse possession and the doctrine of agreed boundaries. This claim was rejected by the court because he had not met statutory requirements for adverse possession and proof of an agreed boundary was not clear and convincing. *Huggans v. Weer, 615 P.2d 922 (Mont. 1980).*

Intention in many situations is determined by what courts presume or infer the parties probably desire to occur. An example is found in the common solution to the substantial litigation involving title to a public thoroughfare. When land abutting on a public road or street is conveyed, the grantee takes title to the centerline unless the description specifically excludes this area. This rule applies even if the description designates the tract as "bounded by" or "bordering on" the particular public way. The reason is that courts consider it unlikely that a grantor conveying land on a public way had any intention of retaining title to the area dedicated to public use. Since the grantor has conveyed the abutting property, the small strip of land is of little value to him or her. It is, however, important to the grantee, who now owns the adjacent land. On the other hand, if the conveyance specifically reserves the narrow strip for the grantor, the intention of the parties will be honored, as this intention is the most significant factor.

SALES PERSONNEL AND PROPERTY DESCRIPTION

Property description is an important element of almost every real estate transaction. Although it is ordinarily the concern of the real estate lawyer, all real estate sales personnel should be aware of its important legal aspects. If problems involving descriptions are discovered early in the proceedings, before the deed or other document involving the property is prepared, time can be saved and trouble averted.

Sometimes real estate personnel obtain information about boundary problems when listing property or drawing up a contract. These should be carefully noted and an effort made to have the owner resolve the problems before entering serious negotiations with prospective buyers. Because boundary disputes may indicate description problems, a sales associate who becomes aware of a boundary controversy when negotiating a sale of real estate should alert the seller's attorney so that the description can be verified.

REVIEW AND DISCUSSION QUESTIONS

1. Sketch an imaginary principal meridian and baseline and indicate the location of (a) Township 3 North, Range 3 East and (b) Township 1 South, Range 3 West.

2. Define the following terms and indicate their relationship to the rectangular survey system: (a) principal meridian, (b) baseline, (c) township and (d) section.

3. The sketch below represents a section. Indicate the correct rectangular survey designation for the shaded portions labeled A and B.

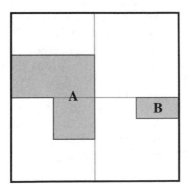

4. Locate the following tracts of land in a section and indicate the acreage of each.
    (a) E½ of the SE¼
    (b) NW¼ of the NW¼ of the NW¼

CASE PROBLEMS

1. A contract for sale of real estate described the property as follows:

    > Property of Greene D. Spillman located at Spillman, La., in Sections 48 and
    > 49, T1S, R2W, West Feliciana Parish, La., and improvements. Bounded on
    > the North by lands of Merrick, on the South by lands of Thoms and heirs of
    > C. H. Bickham, on the East by Hwy. 967 and on the West by Mills Creek. The
    > grounds measuring about 275 acres as per title for the sum of Sixty Thousand,
    > Five Hundred Dollars.

    Engquist signed a contract to purchase this property. A survey indicated that the farm
    contained only 223.64 acres. When Engquist refused to perform, the owner sued for breach
    of contract. (a) Would the owner be successful? Support your answer. (b) What is the mean-
    ing of the terms T1S, R2W? *Adams v. Spillman, 290 So.2d 726 (La. 1974).*

2. Sketch the following parcel.

    > Beginning at a point 447.18 feet East of the N.W. corner of SE¼ SE¼, said
    > Sec. 21; thence North 88 degrees 57'30" East 402.00 feet; thence South
    > 987.68 feet; thence North 89 degrees 56' West 401.93 feet; thence North
    > 979.48 feet to the point of beginning. *LeBaron v. Crimson, 412 P.2d 705
    > (Ariz. 1966).*

3. Brasker, a real estate broker, claimed an interest in one and one-half acres in Lot 4 on the
    north end of Sapelo Island. Brasker supported his claim with a deed that included the
    following description: "All of that certain lot, tract or parcel of land situate, lying and being
    in the 1312 District, G.M., McIntosh County Georgia, at Raccoon Bluff on Sapelo Island,
    containing Twenty-One (21) acres, more or less and being Lot Four (4) of the Raccoon
    Bluff Subdivision of William Hillary. Said property being bounded Northerly by Lot 3;
    Easterly by Blackbeard Island River; Southerly by Lot 5; and Westerly by the lot line of
    Raccoon Bluff Tract. This being that same property conveyed to Ben Brown by deed and
    plat from William Hillary dated July, 1882 and recorded in Deed Book 'U' at Page 298 and
    299, to which said deed and plat reference is hereby made for all intents and purposes."

    A plat showed one-acre and four-acre tracts out of Lot 4 established by a surveyor in
    1882. The defendant argued that the deed was ineffective. Who is correct? Support your
    answer. [Adapted from *Brasker v. Tanner, 356 S.E.2d 478 (Ga. 1987).*]

4. Brasker also claimed an interest in a three-acre tract on Sapelo Island. The three acres were
    conveyed from a larger lot in a 1907 deed to Jack Handy. The defendants argued that the
    deed was ineffective because the tract's boundaries were not clear. The legal description
    from the warranty deed from Jack Handy's heirs was as follows: "that certain tract of land
    in McIntosh County on Sapelo Island, three (3) acres, more or less, and being in the 1312
    District, and bounded on the North by Toni Handy and brothers, on the East by public Road,
    South by John Bailey and West by Sam Roberts."

    Is the description adequate? What is the key factor in determining the description's
    adequacy?

19

Involuntary Transfers

The conveyance of real property by deed, sometimes called *voluntary alienation*, was discussed in Chapter 17. A conveyance by deed is generally the result of a mutual agreement set forth in a real estate sales contract. There are, however, several circumstances under which title to real property is transferred involuntarily.

INVOLUNTARY ALIENATION

◆ **The transfer of title to land without the owner's consent.**

Involuntary alienation includes forced sales resulting from liens and foreclosures, discussed in Chapter 21. This chapter treats other forms of involuntary transfers: adverse possession, transfer by natural forces and transfers upon death.

ADVERSE POSSESSION

◆ **Acquisition of title to real property by means of wrongful occupancy for a period of time established by statute.**

Adverse possession is based on the statute of limitations. As a general rule, a person in possession of realty has good title against everyone but the true owner. The true owner has a right to bring legal action to gain possession if the occupant wrongfully withholds it. The statute of limitations requires that this cause of action be brought within a certain time. The time varies from state to state but is commonly 12, 15, 20 or 21 years. If the owner does not sue within the statutory term, the adverse possessor, upon meeting certain conditions, acquires title to the land.

Although the adverse possessor actually acquires title to the property, litigation is usually necessary to establish clear title before it can be sold. The reason is that the public records of land ownership show someone other than the adverse possessor as the owner.

The Elements of Adverse Possession.   A number of conditions must be met for a person to acquire title to land by adverse possession. Both case law and statutes establish requirements, although they differ from state to state and even from case to case. Some common qualifications are that such possession must be open, hostile, continuous and exclusive. Other adjectives sometimes used are *adverse, notorious, under claim of title* and *under color of title.* These requirements express a judicial and legislative intention that possession must be sufficiently evident to give the owner notice of what is happening.

C A S E   E X A M P L E

Marengo Cave Company owned land upon which the only entrance to a large cave was located. The cave was occupied exclusively by the company for the statutory term and was used as a tourist attraction. When Ross, an adjoining landowner, discovered through a survey that a portion of the cave extended under his land, he brought a quiet title suit. The court found that, even though the company's possession was widely publicized in connection with the tourist business, it was still not "open and notorious" because an ordinary observer on the land could not have readily seen that the owner's rights were being invaded. Hence, Marengo Cave Company did not gain title by adverse possession. *Marengo Cave Co. v. Ross, 212 Ind. 624, 10 N.E.2d 917 (1937).*

The courts also require that possession be *exclusive and continuous* for the entire statutory period. This means that, if the land is abandoned or the true owner reenters either in the absence of the adverse possessor or simultaneously, the statutory term is interrupted and must start over again. A brief absence, such as a vacation, by the adverse possessor is probably not enough to defeat this requirement, however.

A related issue arises when there is a succession of adverse possessors. Most jurisdictions allow the "tacking" of one possessor's term to that of another if one acquired directly from the other, as with a sale or conveyance by will.

C A S E   E X A M P L E

Martin was the owner of a lot, but Boyer was in possession for five years from 1940 to 1945. Then Boyer purported to sell the lot to Lucas, who possessed it for eight years and devised it to Tenton in 1953. Tenton, however, did not enter the land. When Tenton died in 1956, his heirs took possession. They sued to quiet title in 1969.

The heirs would lose this suit in a jurisdiction with a 20-year statute because even tacking Boyer's term to Lucas's would bring the total to only 13 years. During the three years the lot was empty (1953 to 1956), possession reverted to Martin, the true owner. Adverse possession was not exclusive and continuous for the requisite 20 years. The heirs would win in a state with a 12-year statute, however, since their own entry and possession in 1956 would start the running of the statutory term.

When Adverse Possession Does Not Apply. In addition to these elements of adverse possession, statutes and case law also often provide that in some situations statutes of limitations are prolonged or do not run at all. For example, adverse possession cannot be applied against the state or against one whose interest is not yet a possessory right, such as a holder of a future interest. It cannot be applied against those who have certain disabilities, such as infants, the mentally incompetent and the insane. For a disability to prevent the running of the statute, however, it must exist at the time a right to sue accrues, usually when the adverse possessor enters the land. An intervening disability does not bar the running of the statute. In addition, the disability is personal to the owner and cannot pass to his or her successors.

The Purpose of Adverse Possession. To many, adverse possession seems like a legal way of acquiring land without compensating the owner, and some question whether, with modern legislation like model title acts, recording acts and the like, society needs this ancient doctrine. Nevertheless, public policy has historically supported the doctrine. Those who defend adverse possession argue that the state has certain duties to citizens:

▪ It should eliminate stale claims since evidence and witnesses may be unavailable.

▪ It should discourage *laches*—that is, delayed enforcement of one's rights.

▪ It should encourage full and efficient use of land.

▪ It should facilitate land transfer by providing a means to remove old title problems and thus quiet titles.

It seems likely that adverse possession will continue to be an aspect of property law for the foreseeable future. The prudent owner of vacant land held for development or investment will make periodic inspections of the property to check for adverse possessors. The mere posting of "no trespassing" signs is probably not sufficient to protect the owner's interest.

EMINENT DOMAIN

◆ **The power of government to take private property for public use with just compensation afforded to the property owner.**

The power of eminent domain is one of the major attributes of sovereignty. In the United States, both federal and state governments are sovereign and may exercise this power. No specific constitutional grant is necessary for government to have the right to take private property for public use, although several state constitutions do contain provisions allocating the power of eminent domain to the state.

Eminent domain is a power that government may delegate. The result is that eminent domain is often exercised by villages, cities and counties as well as public bodies such as school boards and sanitation districts. The power can also be delegated to private corporations such as railroads, power companies and other public utilities. Upon a proper delegation, eminent domain may be exercised by individuals and partnerships. For a delegation to be proper, the property must be devoted to a public use.

◆ **Public Use.** **A use that benefits the community.**

The Fifth Amendment to the U.S. Constitution and the constitutions of the individual states require that property acquired through eminent domain be used to benefit the public and that just compensation be paid to the owners. Historically, in the United States, eminent domain has been used mostly to acquire land for public transportation systems and to satisfy government's need for space to conduct its business. As government has become increasingly involved in many aspects of life, the use of eminent domain has likewise increased. Today, government may use the power to acquire interest in land for diverse purposes such as parking lots to relieve congestion and traffic hazards, scenic beauty along highways and public recreation.

CASE EXAMPLE

Before 1967 most of the land in Hawaii that was not owned by the state or federal government was owned in fee simple by 72 private landowners. These landowners, who had acquired their titles through the descendants of Polynesian chiefs, refused to sell land. They would only lease it on long-term leases. At the termination of a lease that was not renewed, the land and improvements reverted to the landowners.

In 1967 the Hawaiian legislature, using its power of eminent domain, enacted a Land Reform Act designed to extend the fee simple ownership of Hawaiian land. The act created a mechanism for condemning residential tracts and transferring ownership to existing lessees, while affording the landowners just compensation.

The owners of the fee simple estates challenged the constitutionality of the legislative action. They argued that their property was not taken for a public use or purpose because the government itself never possessed or used the land but transferred it to individuals. The United States Supreme Court determined that the statute was constitutional. The court stated that correcting inequities in the housing market satisfied the constitutional requirement that land be taken for a public use or purpose. *Hawaii Housing Authority v. Midkeff, 467 U.S. 229 (1984).*

Although land taken by eminent domain must be used for a public purpose, different interpretations exist as to what this means. A number of jurisdictions require that the property actually be used by the public. Even in these jurisdictions, the facility does not have to be open to the public, as long as some arm of government actually supervises the operation. Thus, public use is satisfied if a utility acquires property by eminent domain even though the general public cannot use the facility. A public utility commission supervises the overall business of the company and ensures that the property is used in the public interest.

In most jurisdictions, the public use requirement is met if some benefit to the public results from the acquisition of the property. The benefit does not have to be direct, nor does all of the public have to receive some advantage. Courts have allowed the state to transfer lands acquired by condemnation to a private firm to build a plant that would increase employment in the area and to a developer to eliminate a slum. And, as the next case indicates, a physical invasion of the land is not necessary in order for eminent domain to occur.

UNITED STATES V. CAUSBY

Supreme Court of the United States
328 U.S. 256 (1946)

BACKGROUND. Appellant, the United States, repeatedly operated aircraft passing 83 feet over the respondents' (the Causbys) farm property. The aircraft passed 63 feet above their barn and 18 feet above the highest tree. Respondents claimed this amounted to a taking of their property and that they were entitled to just compensation. They sued and the U.S. Court of Claims agreed, awarding them $2,000. The government appealed to the United States Supreme Court.

DECISION. The United States Supreme Court agreed with the Court of Claims that a taking occurred, but remanded the case to that court to determine precisely what property was taken and its value.

MR. JUSTICE DOUGLAS. This is a case of first impression. The problem presented is whether respondents' property was taken, within the meaning of the Fifth Amendment, by frequent and regular flights of army and navy aircraft over respondents' land at low altitudes.

Respondents own 2.8 acres near an airport outside of Greensboro, North Carolina. It has on it a dwelling house, and also various outbuildings which were mainly used for raising chickens. The end of the airport's northwest-southeast runway is 2,220 feet from respondents' barn and 2,275 feet from their house. The path of glide to this runway passes directly over the property—which is 100 feet wide and 1,200 feet long. Since the United States began operations in May 1942, its four-motored heavy bombers, other planes of the heavier type, and its fighter planes have frequently passed over respondents' land and buildings in considerable numbers and rather close together. They come close enough at times to appear barely to miss the tops of the trees and at times so close to the tops of the trees as to blow the old leaves off. The noise is startling. And at night the glare from the planes brightly lights up the place. As a result of the noise, respondents had to give up their chicken business. As many as six to ten of their chickens were killed in one day by flying into the walls from fright. The total chickens lost in that manner was about 150. Production also fell off. The result was the destruction of the use of the property as a commercial chicken farm. Respondents are frequently deprived of their sleep and the family has become nervous and frightened. . . . The air is a public highway, as Congress has declared. Were that not true, every transcontinental flight would subject the operator to countless trespass suits. Common sense revolts at the idea. To recognize such private claims to the airspace would clog these highways, seriously interfere with their control and development in the public interest, and transfer into private ownership that to which only the public has a just claim.

But that general principle does not control the present case. For the United States conceded on oral argument that if the flights over respondents' property rendered it uninhabitable, there would be a taking compensable under the Fifth Amendment. . . . If, by reason of the frequency and altitude of the flights, respondents could not use their land for any purpose, their loss would be complete. It would be complete as if the United States had entered upon the surface of the land and taken exclusive possession of it.

...

There is no material difference between the supposed case and the present one, except that here enjoyment and use of the land are not completely destroyed. But that does not seem to us to be controlling. The path of glide for airplanes might reduce a valuable factory site to grazing land, an orchard to a vegetable patch, a residential section to a wheat field. Some value would remain. But the use of the airspace immediately above the land would limit the utility of the land and cause a diminution in its value.

...

As we have said, the flight of airplanes, which skim the surface but do not touch it, is as much an appropriation of the use of the land as a more conventional entry upon it.... While the owner does not in any physical manner occupy that stratum of airspace or make use of it in the conventional sense, he does use it in somewhat the same sense that space left between buildings for the purpose of light and air is used. The superadjacent airspace at this low altitude is so close to the land that continuous invasions of it affect the use of the surface of the land itself. We think that the landowner, as an incident to his ownership, has a claim to it and that invasions of it are in the same category as invasions of the surface.

The airplane is part of the modern environment of life, and inconveniences which it causes are normally not compensable under the Fifth Amendment. The airspace, apart from the immediate reaches above the land, is part of the public domain. We need not determine at this time what those precise limits are. Flights over private land are not a taking, unless they are so low and so frequent as to be a direct and immediate interference with the enjoyment and use of the land. We need not speculate on that phase of the present case. For the findings of the Court of Claims plainly establish that there was a diminution in value of the property and that the frequent, low-level flights were the direct and immediate cause. We agree with the Court of Claims that a servitude has been imposed upon the land.

...

Since on this record it is not clear whether the easement taken is a permanent or a temporary one, it would be premature for us to consider whether the amount of the award made by the Court of Claims was proper.

The judgment is reversed and the cause is remanded to the Court of Claims so that it may make the necessary findings in conformity with this opinion.

REVERSED AND REMANDED.

◆ **Just Compensation.** **The award the owner is entitled to, when property is taken by the government under its power of eminent domain, measured by the property's fair market value.**

The government and the landowner often dispute what constitutes proper compensation to the owner for taking his or her land. State constitutions and the U.S. Constitution require that such compensation be "just" or "reasonable." In each case, just or reasonable compensation must be determined by balancing the interests of the taxpaying public against those of the property owner to arrive at a result fair to both parties.

Compensation should not be more extensive than the owner's loss. The principal measure of the owner's loss is the fair market value of the property at the time. The U.S. Supreme Court has held that market value and just compensation are synonymous. Market value is normally determined by what a willing buyer would pay in cash to a willing seller in an arm's-length transaction. The seller is entitled to have the property valued at its highest and most profitable use, even if the property is not currently being used in that manner.

CASE EXAMPLE

The state of Maryland condemned Kamin's property for a highway improvement project. The property was zoned as Rural-Agricultural (R-A). Based on the present use and zoning of the property, experts appraised the Kamins' property at about $136,000. Kamins produced evidence at the condemnation hearing that if the condemnation did not take place, the property could be rezoned to EIA, an Employment and Institutional use Area. A planning supervisor for the Maryland Planning Commission testified that had an application for a zoning upgrade to EIA been made, it would have been granted. Because the court concluded that there was a reasonable probability of rezoning of the property to EIA within a reasonable period of time, it assigned a value commensurate with that higher use, $500,000. *State Roads v. Kamins, 572 A.2d 1132 (Md. App. 1990).*

The most common method of determining value is to compare the property being taken with similar land recently sold. This information is generally presented to the courts through the testimony of expert witnesses. Real estate sales personnel are often expert witnesses in condemnation cases because they are familiar with the selling price of land. A good expert witness must be very familiar with the parcel of land involved as well as the selling price of comparable property.

◆ **Condemnation.** Legal proceeding by which the government exercises the right of eminent domain, acquiring private land for a public use.

The Fourteenth Amendment to the U.S. Constitution prohibits state government from taking private property without due process of law and the Fifth Amendment imposes like restraints on the federal government. As a result, some type of notice and some type of legal proceeding are required when a landowner is unwilling to convey to a condemning authority for the price offered. Due process does not ensure any particular manner of proceeding, and federal and state law vary extensively as to the method and procedures that will be used. For example, many states use juries extensively in condemnation cases. However, as long as the state legislature has provided a fair method of evaluation of eminent domain "takings," by providing the parties ample opportunity to be heard and to present evidence, due process is satisfied.

Even within a state, condemnation procedures may vary. A number of states have established a general procedure by statute, but this procedure may be ignored or modified by the legislature for particular situations. Constitutional protections are not violated so long as the special procedure affords the property owner reasonable notice of the proceeding and a reasonable opportunity to establish just compensation.

Several states require the condemning authority to attempt to negotiate a voluntary settlement before commencing a condemnation action. Even when not a statutory requirement, this practice is followed in almost all cases. If the condemnor's offer is rejected, the most common procedure is to condemn by judicial proceeding. This action requires filing a petition in court, giving notice to the owners and others having an interest in the land. Ordinarily, the condemning authority has the burden of establishing the right to acquire the property. Once this right is established, the owner must prove the value of the property taken and any additional damages to which he or she is entitled. Upon the court's making the condemnation award, the interest necessary for the condemnor's purpose passes to the governmental authority involved. This interest may be an estate for years, an easement, or a fee simple absolute, but it may not exceed what is necessary to accomplish the public purpose for which the property was taken.

ACCESSION
◆ **The bundle of rights and principles the law uses to deal with changes in the size and shape of land due to natural causes, usually the actions of bodies of water.**

Accretion refers specifically to a gradual increase in riparian or littoral property as a result of deposits of sediment made by a body of water so as to create dry land where there once was only water. *Alluvion* is the term used for the land so created. *Reliction* is the word applied when water recedes and creates dry land without depositing more material. *Erosion* is simply the decrease in size of a piece of property as the result of water washing away material from the shore. Finally, *avulsion* is an abrupt and perceptible change in the size and shape of a tract as a result of unexpected events, such as a change in the course of a stream.

The general rule is that when accretion or reliction occurs, the riparian or littoral landowner's boundary line and land area are extended to take in the alluvion; but when avulsion occurs, it effects no change in boundary or title. One reason often given for the doctrine of accretion is that the landowner, who is subject to a diminution in the size of his or her tract through erosion, should have the corresponding benefit when the land is enlarged by natural processes. Another rationale for the rule is that the riparian or littoral owner is usually the only one in a position to use the land efficiently. A third explanation is the desirability of preserving the riparian owner's access to the water. The exclusion of avulsion from the general title-by-accretion rule is intended to mitigate the hardship that would result to abutting landowners when a river or stream abruptly changes course.

C A S E   E X A M P L E

Cummings owned shoreline property on the Arkansas River. Surveys from the late 1800s showed the existence of Beaver Dam Island near his property. Cummings contends that Beaver Dam Island was completely washed away in the flood of 1927, that subsequently a sandbar gradually built out into the river from his property and that by slow accretion, the land now constituting Beaver Dam Island resulted. The court held against Cummings, saying: "When the formation begins with a bar or an island detached and away from the shore and by gradual filling in by deposit or by gradual recession of the water, the space between bar or island and mainland is joined together, it is not an accretion to the mainland in a legal sense and does not thereby become property of the owner of the mainland." *Cummings v. Boyles, 242 Ark. 38, 411 S.W.2d 665 (1967).*

Because of these underlying policies, one necessary element of accretion, reliction or erosion is that it be a gradual and imperceptible change. Another frequently stated requirement is that of *contiguity;* that is, that there be no separation between the riparian owner's original tract and the alluvion. It is not generally required that the alluvion be the result of natural causes alone. For example, if an upstream owner builds a breakwater that affects water flow so as to increase accretion, the downstream riparian owner can still acquire title. An owner, however, cannot use the doctrine to enlarge property boundaries through his or her own acts.

Much of the case law in this area has to do with how to draw the boundaries once accretion, reliction or erosion has altered the shape of the land. Arising most often in suits for damages, declaratory judgment actions, quiet title cases or actions for ejectment, this issue is usually resolved by reliance on two general principles: (1) that the share of each party should be proportionate in size and quality to the prior holding and (2) that each party should have a fair share of the access to the water. The actual method of line drawing necessarily varies greatly depending on the topography in each case. The courts will strive for an equitable solution and favor compromise settlements by the parties. The law varies somewhat from state to state, and the applicable rule is that of the jurisdiction in which the accretion occurred.

TRANSFER OF PROPERTY UPON DEATH

When a person dies, title to that person's property can be transferred in one of two ways. If the decedent has made a valid "last will and testament," title to the decedent's property is transferred to the beneficiaries named in the will, subject to limitations imposed by the state. The person who has made a valid will is called a *testator* and is said to have died *testate.* A person who dies without making a valid will is said to have died *intestate.* State statutes direct to whom an intestate's property is transferred.

INTESTATE SUCCESSION

◆ **Distribution of property of a person who dies without leaving a will or whose will is invalid.**

The general philosophy underlying the laws of intestate succession is that property should descend to those persons the intestate individual probably would want to own it. If the decedent expressed no preference by executing a will, society assumes that he or she would want the property to go to those closely related by blood or marriage. Society also benefits from this assumption because it keeps property within the family and tends to strengthen that important institution.

Laws of intestate succession are statutory. No one has a constitutional or natural right to a decedent's property. People inherit because the legislature says that they can. The law might direct that all property of an intestate decedent revert to the state, as it did in England immediately following the Norman Conquest. This system was opposed by powerful tenants of the king, however, and the English rulers were soon forced to recognize the principle of inheritance by members of the tenant's family.

In modern U.S. real estate law, the concept of inheritance by family members is integral to the succession to property upon death. The idea that the state should acquire the property of an intestate is offensive to the sense of justice of almost all Americans. The state acquires title to the property only when the decedent has no relatives. Later in this section we will discuss this alternative (escheat) in greater detail.

Historical Background. The origin of state statutes of intestate succession is found in English law. Primarily because of the importance of land to the political and social structure of England, English law treated the transfer of real property upon the owner's death very differently than the transfer of personal property.

Until 1926 in England, when an owner died intestate, title to that person's real property passed directly to the heirs according to statutes of descent. Title to personal property went initially to an administrator. After the administrator had paid the claims against the estate, the personal property passed according to the Statute of Distribution.

Currently, in England and a majority of jurisdictions in the United States, the laws of intestate succession no longer distinguish between real and personal property. Statutes, commonly referred to as *statutes of descent and distribution,* treat the two types of property in the same manner.

◆ **Statutes of Descent and Distribution.** **Statutes that provide for the distribution of the property of a person who dies without a valid will.**

Today in the United States, the distribution of the estate of an intestate is modeled, in a general way, on the English Statute of Distribution. Both current American and English statutes provide for distribution of the entire estate, not just personal property. American law also focuses primarily on provision for the surviving spouse and children.

A surviving husband or wife ordinarily is entitled to a half or a third share of the decedent's property. Many states increase this portion if the couple had no children. Some states give the surviving spouse a specific dollar amount and a fraction of the net estate exceeding that amount. Community property states normally differentiate between intestate distribution of separate property and that of community property.

In every state, a surviving spouse and children share all of the intestate's estate. The children take whatever remains after the spouse's share. If there is no surviving spouse, the entire estate passes to the children, who divide the assets equally.

◆ **Per stirpes distribution.** Distribution of intestate property to persons who take the share allocated to a deceased ancestor.

A difficult question of fundamental fairness arises when a child who has children dies before a parent. When the grandparent dies, should the surviving grandchildren share equally with their aunts and uncles, or are they entitled only to the share of the deceased parent?

> ### CASE EXAMPLE
> Trent Hightower died intestate. His wife had predeceased him by many years. They had three children: Stephanie, Joseph and Douglas. Stephanie and Joseph survived their father, but Douglas died before him. Douglas, however, left three children of his own: Trent, Jr., Eliza and Anne. Trent Hightower's estate was divided into thirds, with one-third going to Stephanie, one-third to Joseph, and one-third to the children of Douglas. This allocation is *per stirpes* distribution.

In some states, when the only distributees are grandchildren, distribution is by modified per stirpes. In these states each grandchild takes in his or her own right as in *per capita* distribution. The decedent's estate is divided by the *number* of grandchildren.

◆ **Per capita distribution.** Distribution of intestate property to persons who take equal shares as members of a class, not as representatives of an ancestor.

> ### CASE EXAMPLE
> Jennie E. Martin died intestate, leaving as distributees three grandchildren: Alice E. Martin, Bourke Martin and Ned Martin. Alice E. was the daughter of Earl Martin; Bourke and Ned were the sons of Charles Martin. Both Earl and Charles had died before their mother died. The court divided Jennie Martin's estate into three parts, giving one to each grandchild. Alice E. Martin argued that the distribution should have been per stirpes and that she should have received one-half.
>   The appellate court affirmed the lower court's action. The court stated, "those who take as a class take equally. . . . We hold that it was the intention of the legislature that grandchildren, who alone survive the ancestor, should take equally. . . ." In other words, they should take as heirs, not by representation. *In re Martin's Estate, 96 Vt. 455, 120 A. 862 (1923).*

Order of distribution. In the absence of children, American distribution statutes generally distribute the intestate's property to parents, subject to the share of a surviving spouse. In a few states, brothers and sisters share with parents. Issue of deceased brothers and sisters take their parents' share. In a number of states, the amount of the estate determines the relative shares of parents, brothers and sisters.

Statutes provide for the property to go to the "next of kin" if no specific relatives survive and in some states, if there are no relatives or next of kin, to stepchildren. Most states by statute provide a method for determining next of kin. Usually the method is based upon that used in England to determine kinship under the Statute of Distribution. Other than the surviving spouse, relatives by marriage ordinarily are not entitled to the intestate's property (see Figure 19.1).

◆ **Escheat.** **Reversion of property to the state when a person dies intestate with no heirs or when property is abandoned.**

> **CASE EXAMPLE**
>
> Gene DiMond, who inherited property in St. Augustine from his only brother Henri, had no immediate surviving relatives. His parents were dead, and Gene had never married. Although he had one aunt, she had died many years before, leaving no children. Upon Gene's death, the state claimed the St. Augustine property because Gene had died without leaving a will and without heirs.

As we have seen, statutes in each of the states indicate the categories of relationship of those who are a decedent's heirs. Generally, these statutes are narrowly drawn, restricting the term *heirs* to the spouse and those closely related to the decedent by blood. If the decedent dies intestate without heirs, decedent's property escheats to the state. Because most decedents have heirs or make a will, escheat is not a common method by which a state acquires title.

Escheat is an incident of state sovereignty. Because the people possess the ultimate property in land, land should revert to the state for the people's benefit when no heirs exist. State constitutions in some instances contain provisions for escheat. Ordinarily, rules governing the details of escheat are statutory.

Some type of judicial proceeding is necessary to establish the state's right to the property. In a number of jurisdictions, title vests immediately in the state when a landowner dies intestate without ascertainable heirs. In these states, the judicial proceeding will be in the probate court and similar to proceedings to establish heirship. Other states require a more extensive action; in these states, title to escheated property does not vest in the state until a court so orders, after a hearing or trial. Escheat statutes are not favored by the courts and, as a result, are strictly construed.

TESTATE SUCCESSION

◆ **Transfer of property when a person dies leaving a will.**

The right of an owner of property to direct to whom it should go upon death has always been subject to significant limitations. Initially, the right to will one's property applied only to personal property. This right evolved in England shortly after the Norman Conquest in 1066.

FIGURE 19.1 *A Statute of Intestate Succession*

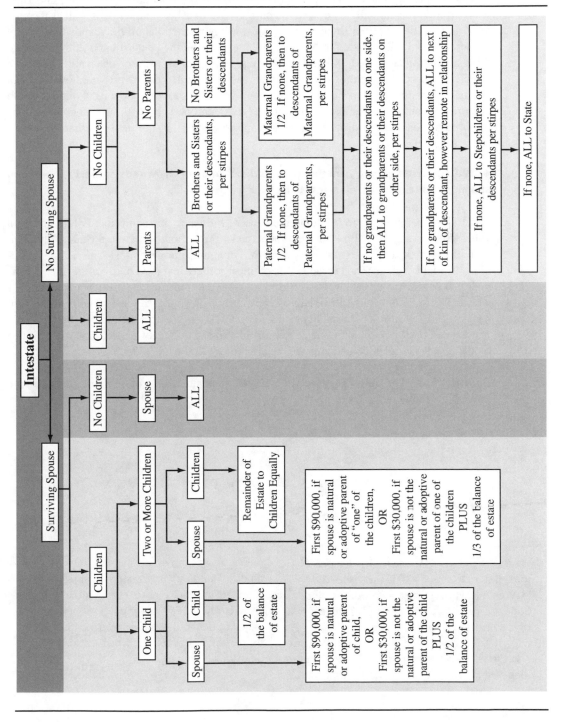

Historical Background. It was not until the enactment of the Statute of Wills in 1540 that English law granted real property owners a limited right to transfer it by will. This right was curtailed substantially by dower and curtesy, discussed in Chapter 4, as well as the customs and traditions of the English aristocracy. Many restrictions on the disposition of real property by will also existed in the United States. During the late 19th and 20th centuries, these restrictions lessened. As land became less important as a source of wealth in relation to personal property, statutes in both England and the United States provided owners with comparable rights to dispose of both real and personal property by will. Today, in both countries, a person can dispose freely of both types of property by will, subject to limitations imposed by the state to protect the family and to ensure that the debts of the decedent's estate are paid.

◆ **Will.** **A written instrument that permits distribution of an owner's property after death and must contain certain elements to be legally enforceable.**

Our English legal heritage has had an extensive influence on requirements for making a valid will. As a result, similar requirements exist throughout the United States, although individual states deviate significantly from the common pattern. In most American jurisdictions, formality is a general characteristic of the procedure involved in executing a will. Formality is predicated upon a legislative desire to prevent fraud, undue influence, coercion or a testator's impetuousness. Legislatures apparently believe that ceremony helps to prevent rash actions. In addition, formality helps to memorialize the transaction. To be legal and valid, a will must be signed by one of sound mind, free of undue influence, in writing, signed by the testator, witnessed and attested (see Figure 19.2 on page 382).

Sound Mind. The following case illustrates the requisites for a sound mind, free of undue influence, for the purposes of making a will.

HENDERSON V. ESTATE OF HENDERSON

Court of Appeals of Arkansas
1997 Ark. App. Lexis 324

BACKGROUND. Lindsey Henderson committed suicide at age 43. He had executed a will leaving all his property to Ms. Allison and Ms. Edge, no relations. He left out his closest relative, a brother, Larry Henderson.

The decedent lived with his mother until shortly before his death. He had a sketchy work record and some type of intellectual impairment. He had relied on his brother for assistance in handling his personal business.

Lindsey could read on a second grade level. He had been diagnosed as being mentally retarded and suffering from an inadequate personality, anxiety neurosis, and perhaps delusional thinking.

The decedent met one of the beneficiaries, Ms. Edge, at a night club. They became friendly and she referred him to an attorney when he said he desired to make a will. She accompanied the decedent to the attorney's office but waited in another room while he talked to the attorney. The attorney noticed that the decedent was a "little strange," such that he asked him to return with a medical note stating that he was competent to make a will. This the decedent did not do. Nonetheless he returned the next day with two witnesses and the will was executed.

The decedent met the other beneficiary, Ms. Allison, at a club where she tended bar. They had a sexual relationship. The decedent's brother filed a will contest maintaining that his brother was under undue influence when he executed the will and that he lacked the mental capacity to execute a will.

The Probate Court judge entered a decision denying the contest of the will.

DECISION. The Court of Appeals affirmed the decision of the Probate Court Judge.

JUDGE JOHN PITTMAN. The questions of undue influence and mental capacity are so closely interwoven that they should be considered together. When the mind of the testator is strong and alert, the facts constituting undue influence must be far stronger in their tendency to unduly influence the testator than when the mind of the testator is impaired. Undue influence sufficient to void a will must not spring from natural affection but must result from fear and coercion so as to deprive a testator of his free will and direct the benefits of the will to particular parties. Influence by a person over the maker of a will becomes undue so as to invalidate the will only when it is extended to such a degree as to override the discretion and destroy free agency of the testator.

Our generally expressed rule for testamentary capacity is that the testator must be able to know the natural objects of his bounty and the extent of his property; to understand to whom the property is being given; and to realize those who are being excluded from the will. In fact, it has been stated that it requires less mental capacity to make a will than it does to make a contract. Our probate law does not require that a testator mete out exact justice in the division of his property; so long as he has the capacity to make a will, he may be unfair, eccentric, injudicious, or capricious in making distribution. He may also be acting out of frivolity or revenge, and may take into account his estrangement from relatives.

From our review of the record, we are convinced that the findings of the probate judge are not clearly erroneous. The evidence shows that Lindsey had a real affection for Ms. Edge and Ms. Allison and clearly intended to omit [his brother] from his will. Although Ms. Edge introduced Lindsey to Mr. Leslie, she left the room while the will was being discussed, and neither she nor Ms. Allison was present when the will was actually signed. Further, the preparation of the will was Lindsey's idea, and it was he who drove, with his witnesses, to Mr. Leslie's office. Mr. Leslie was satisfied that Lindsey was capable of making a will and that he was not operating under undue influence. Although Lindsey clearly suffered from some intellectual impairment, the evidence adequately supports the probate judge's finding that he possessed the requisite mental capacity to make a will. We therefore cannot say that the probate judge erred in her evaluation of the evidence or that her findings are clearly erroneous.

AFFIRMED.

FIGURE 19.2 *Last Will and Testament*

Last Will and Testament
of
Will B. Done
1775 College Road
Columbus, Ohio 43210

I, Will B. Done, over the age of twenty-one years, a legal resident of the county of Franklin, State of Ohio, and being of sound mind and memory and not acting under menace, duress, fraud or undue influence, do make, publish and declare this to be my Last Will and Testament, hereby revoking all other Wills and testamentary writings heretofore made by me.

Item I. I direct my executor to pay out of my estate all of my just debts and funeral expenses as soon as reasonably practical after death.

Item II. I hereby devise and bequeath all property of whatsoever kind, real and personal, wheresoever situate, to my wife, Ima, if she shall survive me.

Item III. In the event that my wife, Ima, does not survive me, I give, devise, and bequeath all the residue and remainder of my estate, real and personal, of whatsoever kind and wheresoever situate, absolutely and in fee simple to the children of our marriage, share and share alike, or to the survivor, per stirpes.

Item IV. In the event my wife, Ima, does not survive me then I appoint Harold Greene and Sally Greene or the survivor as guardians over the person and property of said children under the age of twenty-one (21). Said guardians shall hold the money in trust for each minor until said child attains the age of twenty-one (21) and use such money until then for the support and education of the minor child. When each child attains the age of twenty-one (21), the guardians shall transfer the remaining funds held in trust for that child to said child and the guardianship of that child shall terminate.

Item V. I hereby appoint my wife, Ima, as executor of my Last Will and Testament if she survives me and is otherwise qualified; otherwise I nominate, constitute and appoint Rhesa Andrews, Columbus, Ohio. I hereby authorize and grant my executor full power without order of the Court to settle claims in favor of or against my estate, to sell at public or private sale for cash or credit, to mortgage, lease or convey all or any part of my estate, real or personal, of whatsoever kind wheresoever situate, without application to or confirmation by any court or government agency.

Item VI. In the event that my wife and children do not survive me, then I give, devise and bequeath all the residue and remainder of my estate, real and personal, of whatsoever kind, wheresoever situate, absolutely and in fee simple to my brother, Lance, my sister, Elgin, and my brother-in-law, Peter, share and share alike. I have intentionally not included my brother Conley because I know that adequate provision has already been made for him through other sources.

In testimony whereof, I have hereunto set my hand at Columbus, Ohio this 15th day of August 1999.

Will B. Done

Signed and witnessed in the presence of the testator and in the presence of each other.

Witness   Witness

Written. All states require a will to be in writing, but a limited number of states do permit oral wills of personal property under limited circumstances. Generally, oral wills are valid if made by military personnel in actual service or under certain conditions by a person suffering a terminal illness. A will written entirely in the testator's own hand, known as a *holographic* will, is considered valid in a number of states, even though it was not witnessed.

Signed. American courts are liberal in their interpretation of what constitutes a signature. A mark or an initial is sufficient if intended as a signature. Usually, the testator must sign personally, but someone else may if directed to do so by the testator. Usually, this must be done in the testator's presence. Generally, a signature any place on the document is sufficient if the intention is to validate the will. Some states require the signature to be at the end of the instrument. In those states, the entire document is invalid if the signature is in some other place.

Witnessed. Most state laws require only two witnesses for a will to be valid. Any competent adult may ordinarily act as a witness. In some states, a beneficiary under a will should not be a witness; that person's testimony is sufficient to sustain the will in court, but he or she is not entitled to take under the will.

The common practice is for the testator to sign first in the presence of the witnesses. In many states the actual signing does not have to be viewed by the witness if the testator later acknowledges the signature.

Attested. Attestation is a requirement in all jurisdictions for most wills. Attestation means that the person must intend to act as a witness and must sign for the purpose of validating the will. In a very few states, the witness need not sign the instrument, but attestation is necessary even in those states. In order to validate the will, witnesses must be able to testify at a later date that the testator signed or acknowledged the signature in their presence.

In the vast majority of cases, a will includes an attestation clause. This clause appears at the end of the will following the testator's signature. Each witness signs the attestation clause, which recites the witness's observation of the formalities necessary for the proper execution of the will.

Rights of the Family. Prevailing public policy in the United States is to encourage provisions for spouse and children out of a decedent's estate. As noted earlier, if a person dies intestate, inheritance statutes in all states provide first for the decedent's immediate family. State laws also furnish some protection for the spouse and, to a lesser degree, the children of a person who fails to provide for them by will. Historically, many of these laws applied specifically to real estate. Dower, curtesy and homestead rights discussed in Chapter 4 are examples. Today, protection for a decedent's spouse in most states is accomplished by giving the spouse a right to elect a share against the will. The right of election is charged against the entire estate, both real and personal.

◆ **Elective Share.** A share of a deceased spouse's estate that a surviving spouse may claim if the decedent spouse's will did not provide at least this amount.

Dower and curtesy have been replaced in many states by the right of a surviving spouse to elect a share against the decedent's will. The right of election is based on statute, and the share varies from state to state. Inasmuch as the right of election is a relatively recent trend in the law, state legislation usually reflects modern developments for this purpose, such as the elimination of distinctions between real and personal property, and similar treatment of husband and wife.

The right of election is also influenced by past laws and customs. Many state legislatures regard it as a substitute for dower. Thus, the survivor's elective share is often set at a fractional amount, such as one-third of the decedent's estate. In a number of states, the share is less if the couple has children. However, children may be disinherited by their parents, and no state has a law that provides children an elective share.

C A S E   E X A M P L E

Royce and Helen Hurley were married for many years. Early in their marriage Royce made a will leaving Helen $100,000. At the time, this was the bulk of Royce's estate. Over the years, Royce prospered but did not change his will. When Royce died in 1975, his net estate was more than $500,000. State statute gave Helen a right to take under the will or to elect to take a one-half share against the will. She elected to take one-half share ($250,000) instead of the $100,000 legacy.

One of the objections to dower was that in small estates the surviving spouse was provided for inadequately if reliance upon dower was necessary. Although a right of election ordinarily provides more for a surviving spouse because it includes personal property, the fractional share in some estates is insufficient to adequately support the survivor. In most cases this problem never arises because the decedent provides adequately for the surviving spouse in the first place.

ADMINISTRATION OF ESTATES

◆ **A general term used to describe the management and settlement of a decedent's estate by a person appointed by the courts.**

Many of the procedures for settling the estate of a decedent are similar for both testate and intestate decedents. A very important initial step is the appointment of a personal representative to act for the estate. The person charged with administration of the estate of an intestate decedent is called an *administrator;* the person who is appointed to administer the estate of a decedent who dies testate is an *executor.* Sometimes the person nominated in a will as an executor is unable or unwilling to serve. Under these conditions, the court appoints an *administrator with the will annexed.*

The administration of a decedent's estate is ordinarily supervised by a special court, frequently referred to as a *probate* or *surrogate's court.* The appointment of a personal representative is an important element in administering a decedent's estate. In the will, the testator almost always nominates a personal representative. The personal representative may be either a person or an institution such as a trust company. The decedent's nominee is usually appointed by the court, unless that person is not qualified or refuses to serve.

◆ **Probate. Proof that an instrument is genuine and the last will and testament of the maker.**

In the vast majority of cases, probate is a straightforward procedure. Ordinarily, the person nominated in the will as personal representative files a written application or petition for probate. In many jurisdictions, the probate court supplies the proper forms for this procedure. The petition alleges the testator's death and domicile at the time of death. The will is usually attached to the petition unless it has been filed previously with the court. Usually the names, relationships and residences of the heirs at law, as well as those receiving gifts under the will, must be included because they will be notified of the proceeding. Some states permit probate without notice to interested parties. Although the practice is legal, it can adversely affect land titles in case someone with a claim presents it later.

If a petition is unopposed, the court may order probate on the documents filed. Usually, a limited hearing is conducted in which the court takes testimony on the validity of the will. A number of states have developed less formal probate procedures for small estates, especially when no real property is involved.

Probate establishes that the will is valid and genuine. After the petition for probate is granted, the will can no longer be attacked on the ground of forgery, improper execution or revocation except in a proceeding to set aside probate. Probate does not establish the validity or meaning of particular provisions of the will. If the court is satisfied that the nominated personal representative is qualified to serve, this person will be furnished with *letters testamentary* as evidence of authority to settle the estate.

State statutes prescribe the persons eligible for appointment as administrator and the order in which they must be considered. The order, based on relationship to the decedent, parallels the order of intestate inheritance in most states. Preference is given to the surviving husband or wife. If there is no husband or wife, the relative next entitled to distribution is selected as administrator. The court selects, from among those who stand in equal right, the person best qualified to manage the estate. Usually, preference is given to residents of the jurisdiction. The court grants *letters of administration* to the person appointed to administer the intestate's estate.

The personal representative, whether an executor or administrator, is authorized by the court to settle the decedent's estate. He or she is responsible for ensuring that assets are distributed in an orderly manner to those who are entitled to them. Although the personal representative has a wide variety of miscellaneous chores, four basic steps are integral to the settlement of the estate:

1. Collection of estate assets
2. Processing and payment of claims against the estate
3. Management of estate assets
4. Accounting and distribution of estate assets

Proof of Death. It is axiomatic that neither a will nor an inheritance statute is operative until a property owner dies. Ordinarily, the occurrence and time of death are easy to determine, but problems arise in at least two instances. One instance is a disaster in which several closely related people die at approximately the same time; another is a situation in which a property owner has been missing for an extensive period.

Many wills solve the problem of determining who has died first in a common disaster by including a provision in the instrument.

CASE EXAMPLE

Lance Beck and his wife, Hilda, were killed in a common disaster. Because of the nature of the accident, determining which one had died first was impossible. Lance's will left all his property to his wife if she survived him. If she did not, his estate was to go to his parents and to charity.

Lance's will contained the following provision: "In the event my wife and I shall die under such circumstances that there is insufficient evidence to determine the survivor, it shall be conclusively presumed that I survived her." As a result of this provision, the estate went to Lance's parents and the charities that he had named, not into his wife's estate.

Most states by statute make special provisions for applying distribution rules when close relatives are killed under circumstances that make it impossible to determine the survivor. Almost all states have adopted the Uniform Simultaneous Death Act. In general, this act provides that in a common disaster each decedent's property shall be disposed of as if that decedent had survived.

States also solve by statute the problem caused by a missing owner. Generally, these statutes provide that a person whose absence is unexplained for seven years is presumed dead. The presumption, however, may be rebutted, if, for example,there is convincing evidence to believe that the person is alive.

REVIEW AND DISCUSSION QUESTIONS

1. What are the major arguments for allowing a person to acquire title by adverse possession?
2. Do you agree with the general rules surrounding the law of accession? Explain?
3. Explain the difference between per stirpes and per capita distribution.
4. Briefly indicate some of the limitations that exist upon the transfer of real property by will.
5. Discuss the major duties of a person appointed to settle a decedent's estate.

CASE PROBLEMS

1. Kittrell owned four house trailers that were parked on the edge of his property. Unknown to Kittrell, the trailers extended a few feet onto his neighbor's property. This condition was discovered by a survey after the trailers had been there several years. At the time, Kittrell

offered to buy the strip of land upon which the trailers encroached. The owner refused to sell, but, because permanent plumbing had been installed, did not order the trailers to be moved. Several years later the property was sold and the new owner demanded that Kittrell remove the trailers. Kittrell claimed ownership of the strip by adverse possession because the trailers had encroached on the land for more than ten years, the statutory period in the state. Discuss the validity of Kittrell's claim. *Kittrell v. Scarborough, 287 Ala. 177, 249 So.2d 814 (1971)*.

2. The Nollans purchased a beachfront lot in Ventura County, California. The lot contained a small bungalow, which was in disrepair. They desired to demolish the bungalow and replace it. They sought a permit to do so from the California Coastal Commission. The Commission granted the permit subject to the condition that the Nollans allow the public an easement to pass across a portion of their property to make it easier to get to a nearby county park. The Commission reasoned that the new bungalow would increase blockage of the view of the ocean and thus would prevent the public "psychologically" from realizing the benefit of a stretch of coastline. Is the condition constitutional? Explain. *Nollan v. California Coastal Comm'n, 483 U.S. 825 (1987)*.

3. Berman owned a department store on property in a District of Columbia slum. The property was well maintained, and no building violations existed. Using the power of eminent domain, the District of Columbia Redevelopment Agency acquired Berman's property, along with that of others in the area. The purpose of the acquisition was for "the development of blighted territory." Berman argued that the taking was unconstitutional as his property was not substandard and, after redevelopment, was to be managed privately. Discuss the validity of Berman's contention. *Berman v. Parker, 348 U.S. 26 (1954)*.

4. The statute of descent and distribution of the State of Y is as follows:

   If a person dies intestate, his or her real and personal property, if any, shall pass:

   (a) If there is no surviving spouse, to the children of the intestate or their lineal descendants, per stirpes.
   (b) If there is a spouse and one or more children or their lineal descendants surviving, the first $60,000 to the spouse, plus one-half of the remainder to the spouse and the balance to the children equally or to their lineal descendants, per stirpes.
   (c) If there are no children or their lineal descendants, the whole to the surviving spouse.
   (d) If there is no spouse and no children or their lineal descendants surviving, to the parents of the intestate equally or to the surviving parent.
   (e) If there is no spouse, no children or their lineal descendants and no parent surviving, to the brothers and sisters equally or their lineal descendants, per stirpes.
   (f) If there is no spouse, no children or their lineal descendants, no parents and no siblings surviving, to the next of kin.
   (g) If there is no next of kin, escheat to the state.

   Answer the following hypothetical questions based on this statute.

   a. Graham dies, leaving a valid will that bequeaths his entire estate to his sister-in-law, Ruth. He is survived by Ruth and by his mother, his grandson and his brother. What is the result under the statute?

    b.   Willis died intestate and is survived by his wealthy wife, Angela; his poverty-stricken mother, Rose; and his deserving second cousin, Ned. How will the estate be distributed?

    c.   Susan died intestate, survived by her son, Jack, and by three grandsons, Dennis, Randy and Rob. Dennis and Randy are the sons of Susan's deceased oldest son, David, and Rob is the only child of Susan's deceased daughter, Cheryl. How will the estate be divided?

    d.   Rebecca died intestate, survived by her husband, Gus; her father, Bruce; her daughter, Nancy; and her grandchildren, Chuck and Jill, the children of her deceased son, Rick. The net probate estate is $50,000. How will it be divided?

5. Martha had two children, Peter and Mary. Upon Martha's death, neither Peter nor Mary were living. Mary left three children and Peter left two children. Assuming all of Martha's property was left to Peter and Mary, how much will each grandchild get if the property devolved per stirpes? How much if it devolved per capita?

6. John and Larue Morgan were married in 1960. In 1965 Larue disappeared. Although extensive efforts were made to locate her, she was never found. In 1973 John brought a legal action to have Larue declared dead. At the hearing, Larue's brother attempted to introduce as evidence a Christmas card that he had received from her in 1967. The judge refused to accept this evidence and declared Larue dead because she had been missing for more than seven years. Was the judge correct? Discuss.

Recording and Assurance of Title

RECORDING STATUTES

◆ **Laws that require the entry into books of public record the written instruments affecting the title to real property.**

Under common law, deeds and other instruments affecting the title to real property were not *recorded*—officially entered into the public records. Problems arose for the owners when they lost or misplaced these deeds and other documents. Even more important, third parties had no way of knowing that a prior transaction had taken place. The person making a conveyance to an innocent third party may have previously conveyed to another and therefore had nothing to give to this subsequent party. These difficulties gave rise to the need for recording statutes. *The primary intent of these statutes is to protect third persons by giving them notice that a prior transaction has occurred.*

The recording statutes that have been adopted by all states provide a means for notifying third parties as to the ownership or other interests existing in a given parcel of land. The recording takes place when a deed, mortgage, easement or other legal instrument affecting the title to land is copied into the public record so that interested persons can discover the status of the title to the land. All entries regarding that title constitute the title history, also known as the *chain of title*.

Many centuries ago, land could be transferred by a symbolic gesture such as the giving of a handful of soil or a wild rose branch. Since England enacted the Statute of Frauds in 1677, however, a transfer of an interest in land must be in writing to attain legal recognition. The written document serves as proof of the transfer between the parties to the transaction—the buyer and the seller—and to anyone else who is aware of the writing. However, a prospective buyer unfamiliar with any prior transactions would have only the word of the seller as assurance as to what previously occurred. The buyer or the buyer's attorney can gain certainty about any prior transfer of an interest in the real estate by referring to the public records to find the recording of the transaction. If the transaction is duly recorded, one can rely on it with relative safety. (Limitations on reliance upon the recording will be discussed later.) If the public records do not reveal that the seller owned the parcel, the prospective buyer would normally choose not to buy it. The risk is that the seller is not telling the truth or that some other interest is outstanding in the land. To take a conveyance under these circumstances is to invite a lawsuit; under normal conditions it is too great a risk to the buyer. Thus the purpose of the recording act is to give to the prospective buyer and to the public *legal notice* of the status of a particular property.

LEGAL NOTICE

◆ **A knowledge of another's interest in real property sufficient to make the adverse interest legally binding to the prospective purchaser or any other party acquiring interest in the property.**

The public recording gives legal notice to third persons as to the existence of a transaction. Under the principle of *caveat emptor,* a prospective buyer or lender is charged with the responsibility of determining whether or not the seller holds title to the property and whether or not there are any encumbrances that would adversely affect the title. If an individual has legal notice of a defect or an encumbrance before acquiring an interest, he or she takes *title subject to those prior rights.* Legal notice may take the form of actual notice, implied notice or constructive notice.

◆ **Actual Notice. Title information that is acquired personally by the interest holder.**

A prospective purchaser may gain information from the seller or from other parties and from firsthand observation of the property.

CASE EXAMPLE

McCredy is negotiating an agreement to purchase Nagy's summer home. When McCredy inspects the premises, he finds several neighbors have been using a well on the property. If the neighbors have acquired and recorded an easement, that fact will appear on the record. If no easement is on the record, the users may have a prescriptive easement; that is, one imposed by law based on the extended use by the neighbors. If so, McCredy has actual notice of their easement.

An agreement between two parties gives *actual notice* to these two parties even if it is not recorded. However, unless a third party has actual notice of the parties' interests, an unrecorded deed gives no legal notice to the third party. Likewise, when a prospective purchaser is shown a house that is being occupied by someone other than the seller, the purchaser is put on notice that the occupant may have some kind of interest. The purchaser is thus obligated, under the theory of actual notice, to ascertain the status of this third party.

◆ **Implied Notice. Legal notice that is imposed by the law when conditions exist that would lead a reasonable person to inquire further into the condition of the title.**

If a prospective interest holder has implied notice of a possible claim, he or she is said to have legal notice of any interest that would be discovered during the course of a reasonable inquiry into the condition of the title. Failure to pursue such an investigation does not exempt the interest holder from notice.

Implied notice occurs in some states when the conveyance of property by quitclaim deed is a release of rights rather than a conveyance. In such states, use of a quitclaim deed is considered to give the purchaser implied notice that there may be defects in the title. In states where a quitclaim deed is considered a conveyance, no legal notice of adverse claims is implied merely by the existence of that type of deed.

◆ **Constructive Notice. The knowledge of certain facts that might be discovered through a careful inspection of public records, provided that such information is within the history of title, or discovered through an inspection of the premises.**

Under the concept of constructive notice, a prospective interest holder is considered to have legal notice of any information recorded within the history or chain of title, whether or not that individual has actual notice of the existence of the document.

Constructive notice also charges the prospective interest holder with any information contained within recorded documents. In addition, a person has constructive notice of all facts that would be revealed by an inspection of the property. For instance, constructive notice of an easement exists for a plainly visible drainage ditch that crosses the property. Notice occurs even if the person never visits the property or examines the public records, which may or may not reveal the existence of the easement.

CASE EXAMPLE

Sebastian leased land to Conley, who recorded the lease. The lease was for oil and gas exploration. Although the description in the lease was inaccurate, it did designate the land. Later Sebastian leased what he thought was adjoining land to Loeb. Part of the land leased to Loeb was the Conley parcel. Claiming that the record provided constructive notice of his interest, Conley sued to prevent Loeb from using the land. Both the lower court and an appellate court agreed that Loeb had constructive notice of Conley's interest and ordered Loeb to allow Conley access to the tract.

The appellate court stated as follows:

The constructive notice furnished by a recorded instrument, insofar as the boundary of the land and every other material fact recited therein is concerned, is equally as conclusive as would be actual notice acquired by a personal examination of the recorded instrument, or actual notice acquired by or through other means. Every person must take notice of its contents to the same extent as if he had personal knowledge of every fact that it recites. This is the very purpose of our recording law. *Loeb v. Conley, 160 Ky. 91, 169 S.W. 575 (1912).*

In addition to notice of all items contained in the public records, prospective interest holders are also considered to have constructive notice of all taxes that attach to the property.

TYPES OF RECORDING STATUTES

Although all have a similar purpose, the recording statutes vary markedly from state to state. They are designed to give notice to parties who are considering acquiring an interest in land. Reliance upon a warranty given in the deed is inadequate. The warranty gives the buyer the right to a lawsuit for damages but not to the land in which he or she is primarily interested. The two general types of recording statutes are race-notice and notice.

◆ **Race-Notice Statutes. Statutes that provide that a subsequent buyer will prevail only if he or she has no notice of the prior transaction at the time of conveyance and he or she records first.**

Under these statutes the subsequent taker must get to the recorder's office before the predecessor does.

> **CASE EXAMPLE**
> Nagy conveys Laneacre to McCredy. Later, to acquire funds for his permanent relocation to South America, Nagy offers Laneacre to Brennan. Brennan does not know of the prior conveyance to McCredy, and the public record does not show that McCredy recorded his deed. Brennan decides to take the proffered conveyance and beats McCredy to the recorder's office.

Brennan would prevail if he recorded before McCredy *and* since he had no knowledge that Nagy had previously conveyed Laneacre to McCredy.

◆ **Notice Statutes. Statutes that provide that the subsequent buyer prevails over all interested parties who have not recorded their interest at the time the buyer accepts the conveyance and pays consideration for the land without notice of the preexisting conveyance.**

There is no *race* under these statutes. So long as the subsequent buyer takes without notice of the previous conveyance, he or she prevails over the previous conveyance. It is irrelevant that the first deed holder records thereafter or the subsequent buyer never records.

CASE EXAMPLE

On May 9, 1860, Dignowitz executed a deed to McMillan for land in San Antonio. The deed was signed by Dignowitz's wife, who testified that she did not know whether it was delivered to McMillan, but she assumed that it was. This deed was not recorded until 1889.

In 1875, several years after the death of her husband, Mrs. Dignowitz conveyed the land to the City of San Antonio. Shortly thereafter the city conveyed the parcel to the United States, to be a part of a military reservation. At the time, the mayor of San Antonio orally mentioned a possible outstanding claim; but after an exhaustive search of the record, the attorney for the United States approved the title.

In a claim against the United States for trespass brought in 1889, the U.S. Supreme Court stated, "The inevitable conclusion as a matter of law is that the United States acquired a good and valid title, as innocent purchasers for valuable consideration, and without notice of a previous conveyance to McMillan." The Supreme Court did not consider the oral mention by the mayor of an outstanding claim as actual notice of the pre-existing conveyance. *Stanley v. Schwalby, 162 U.S. 255 (1896).*

It may seem unfair for the law to permit Dignowitz to make multiple conveyances of the same property. Theoretically, she no longer owns the property after the initial conveyance to McMillan and should be powerless to convey anything to San Antonio. This would be the case under the common law. Nevertheless, the impact of the recording statutes is to pry that title loose from McMillan and other nonrecording takers and to vest it in subsequent takers like the City of San Antonio.

The recording statutes are chiefly geared to protect good-faith purchasers for value. Consequently, these statutes do not afford protection to persons who acquire the land through gift or inheritance. To attain the protection of the statutes, the purchaser must give consideration, that is, a value of some sort. The value need not be equal to the fair market value of the premises, but neither can it be nominal or merely recited in the deed without actual payment. It must be a real value.

THE RECORDING PROCESS

Although the name of the specific office and official will differ, deeds are recorded at a county office created for that purpose. The recorder will be authorized under state law to record deeds, mortgages, easements, contracts for sale and, in some states, leases and any other transactions affecting the title to land. In addition, the recorder or some other county official will record notices of judgments, secured transactions, pending litigation, inheritance taxes and other dealings that may also encumber the free transfer of land. Each document either conveys a part of the owner's property rights or creates an encumbrance or lien on the parcel.

> ## CASE EXAMPLE
>
> George sells the western half of Laneacre to Herman. In the deed of conveyance, George grants an easement to Herman to use George's driveway to get to and from the garage. To purchase the land, Herman borrows money from the bank and executes a mortgage for the western half of Laneacre to the bank in order to secure the loan. The deed conveys title to half of Laneacre and conveys an easement to Herman to use a part of the other half, and the mortgage to the bank is a lien on Herman's portion of Laneacre. Each of these documents is recorded to secure the rights of the party receiving an interest thereunder.

The early recordings under the recording statutes were handwritten, verbatim accounts of the deed or other instrument. Later these recordings were typed, and today they are in large measure photocopies of the original documents. The document presented for recording must be the original.

The recording process begins with the presentation of the instrument to the recorder, usually by the party seeking protection (for example, the buyer in a sales transaction). On payment of a recording fee, the recorder stamps the instrument, showing the precise time it was filed with that office. The instrument is later photocopied and entered into the deed books. These numbered books contain exact copies of all deeds ever filed in that county. Simultaneously, the names of the grantor and grantee are indexed in separate grantor and grantee index books, with a reference to the deed book number and page where a copy of the deed can be found. A similar procedure would be followed if the instrument were a mortgage, easement or other document transferring an interest in the land.

Approximately ten states use a tract index that simplifies the title searching process. In addition to the grantor and grantee indexes, the tract index lists in a single place all the transactions that have occurred affecting the parcel concerning the searcher. Once the correct page is located, all deeds, mortgages and other transactions are listed for the searcher's convenience. The title searcher can rely on this page (or pages) as containing all the relevant transactions affecting the concerned piece of property.

The act of recording in no way legitimizes an instrument. If a deed is forged or was never delivered, recording will not remove this impediment to its validity.

CHAIN OF TITLE
◆ **The recorded history of events that affect the title to a specific parcel of land, usually beginning with the original patent or grant.**

Documents filed at the recorder's office are within the chain of title if they concern the parcel and are recorded during the period in which each grantee has title to the parcel of land. If the title searcher were to begin the search anew today, the chain of title would begin with the present owner's deed (who is also the last grantee of record). That deed would contain a recital stating from whom the present grantee's seller got the parcel. Continuing the example above, the last recorded deed would have as grantor, Herman, to grantee, Isaac, and something like the following: "being all of the same premises conveyed on June 16, 1968, by George to Herman and being contained in Deed Book 202 at page 1121." Normally each deed in the chain of title contains a recital of this nature so that the searcher can trace the title back to the original patent or grant.

The attorney or other agent doing an original title search examines the grantor index from the day the present grantee got the parcel until the day the search is being done, in order to ascertain whether or not the present grantee conveyed any interest in the land to another. He or she follows the same procedure for each preceding grantee, for the period of that grantee's ownership as recited. Any conveyance in the grantor index during this time period must be checked to see whether it affects the concerned parcel. Similarly, the mortgagor index is examined to ensure that no mortgage is outstanding against the parcel. The county records must also be examined to determine whether there are any unsatisfied judgments, pending litigation, mechanics' liens or secured transactions against the grantee. Each of these is an encumbrance on the land and normally must be satisfied prior to a buyer's acceptance of the deed.

If every transfer of property involved a title search going back to the original deed, title searches would be cumbersome and expensive. In many states the title is merely reviewed for transactions that have taken place since the last conveyance, inasmuch as the seller will supply his or her search for the previous title history.

Any transaction that is found within the chain of title is deemed to be constructively known by the buyer. Constructive notice is as valid a notice of the status of the parcel as that of which the buyer has personal knowledge. If a recorded transaction does not appear within the chain of title, however, the buyer is not charged with constructive notice of the facts contained therein.

> ## CASE EXAMPLE
>
> In 1984 George conveys to Herman, who does not record the deed. In 1985 George conveys the same parcel to Isaac, who records the deed. In 1986 Herman finally records his deed. Later that year, Isaac enters an agreement to sell the parcel to Jeremy. When Jeremy has a title search done, the deed from George to Herman is not in the chain of title. The title searcher does not examine the records for possible conveyances by George after 1985, when Isaac became the new owner. Since Jeremy is not charged with constructive notice of the deed to Herman, he takes the parcel free and clear of the prior deed to Herman. Herman has the right to sue George for damages but not for title to the land.

Some encumbrances on real estate do not appear in the chain of title, yet the buyer is charged with knowledge of them. These encumbrances include zoning laws, building restrictions, property taxes for the year of sale and subsequent years, and special assessments or taxes.

If the reconstruction of the chain of title reveals a gap or a flaw in the title, then the buyer is excused from the purchase agreement because the seller cannot deliver *marketable* or *unencumbered title* for which the purchaser contracted. A *gap* occurs when the recorded documents do not indicate who owned the parcel during a given period. An example of a *flaw* in the title occurs when the buyer, in the purchase agreement, has been promised an unencumbered fee simple interest and a life estate is found outstanding in the title to the parcel. In either of these situations, it is said that there is a *cloud on the title*. A cloud on the title is created whenever doubt is created as to the validity of the grantor's title. The property is unmarketable so long as a cloud on the title exists. If the seller is willing, a *quiet title action* may be brought in order to get a judicial (court) ruling that the title is marketable. The seller joins as defendants all those parties who have a potential interest in the land. The plaintiff-seller requests that the court declare his or her title valid, thereby "quieting title" to the land. The buyer can then rely on the judicial assurances of good title and consummate the deal.

ACKNOWLEDGMENT

◆ **A formal declaration by the person who executes an instrument that he or she is freely signing it; this signing is attested to by a public official, usually a notary public.**

The recorder does not pass judgment on the legitimacy of the instrument upon recording it, nor does the fact of recording add any degree of validity to a document that is otherwise defective or void. Most states have, however, established some prerequisites that must be satisfied before a document is acceptable for recording. The chief requirement is that the deed or other instrument be *acknowledged*.

For instance, when preparing the deed, the seller of land may sign the deed and a separate acknowledgment before a notary public. The notary public then indicates in the acknowledgment that he or she has witnessed the seller's affirmation or signature. The witnessing of the signature by a disinterested public official gives reasonable assurance that the signature on the deed is that of the seller and not an impostor. Under the statutes, the deed is then acceptable for recording.

It should be noted that in most states the failure to have the deed acknowledged or to meet any other prerequisite for recording prevents the deed from serving as constructive notice to anyone. The rule seems to be overly technical and may be unfair since the subsequent purchaser doing a title search has notice of the conveyance and yet because of the mistake in the acknowledgment, can ignore it. As a result, some states have passed statutes to the effect that an unacknowledged or mistakenly acknowledged instrument will be notice to subsequent purchasers and to creditors.

The chief importance of the acknowledgment lies in recording, not in conveyancing itself. A deed need not be acknowledged to effectuate a conveyance because title will pass to the grantee upon delivery and acceptance of the deed, whether it is acknowledged or not.

MISTAKES IN RECORDING

◆ **Errors made by the recorder.**

The rule in most states is that a person who has properly presented an instrument for recording has satisfied his or her duty; the instrument will be constructive notice to a subsequent taker. The result is that a mistake made by the recorder initially falls upon the future taker, even though that taker could not have discovered the instrument because of the mistake.

> **CASE EXAMPLE**
>
> Brownstein purchased a parcel of land from Peterson in 1951. In 1962 Brownstein conveyed a 20-foot drainage easement to the city. The city official presented the written easement for recording, but the recorder failed to enter Brownstein's name in the grantor index. In 1996 Brownstein conveyed the parcel to Jackson. Brownstein's conveyance to the city does not appear in the chain of title for the parcel. Jackson has no legal recourse against Brownstein or the city but would be able to recover against the recorder on that official's security bond.

A mistake by the recorder is a difficult dilemma for courts to resolve because neither the party presenting the instrument for recording nor the subsequent taker is at fault. A minority of courts, recognizing that the primary concern of the recording statutes is with good-faith purchasers for value, hold that the subsequent taker does have recourse against the grantor.

> **CASE EXAMPLE**
>
> Brownstein purchased a parcel of land from Peterson and presented the deed for recording. The recorder misplaced the deed and it was never recorded. Brownstein later enters a purchase agreement with Jackson in which he agrees to convey "good and marketable title" to him. When doing the title search, Jackson discovers that the deed by which Brownstein took title is missing. In some states Jackson would have a legal claim against Brownstein for breach of contract.

Regardless of which rule is adopted, the injured party has recourse against the recorder on his or her security bond.

MISTAKES IN THE INSTRUMENT
◆ **Errors made in the preparation of the instrument to be recorded.**

A mistake in the instrument recorded may affect the validity of the notice given. If the mistake is minor, it will not deter the instrument from being legal notice. For example, the grantor's name listed as Franc*is* Brown rather than Franc*es* Brown in a deed would be adequate notice to a third party. However, if the nature of the mistake is such that the instrument would no longer put the third party searcher on notice to inquire further, the instrument will not be constructive notice. Thus, if the grantor's name is George Thomas but is typed in the deed Thomas George, it will be listed in the grantor index under *G* for George and not *T* for Thomas. This deed will not be notice to a subsequent purchaser.

The following case illustrates a situation in which a failure of the grantees to record their deed did not cause them, or their successors in title, to lose their property interest. Why not? The case raises the issue of notice discussed earlier in the chapter.

GRAHAM V. LYONS

Superior Court of Pennsylvania
546 A.2d 1129 (1988)

BACKGROUND. In 1952, Paul and Helen Lyons delivered a deed conveying a parcel of land to Mr. and Mrs. Mitchell in exchange for $100. The deed was lost by the Mitchells and never recorded. In 1971, the Mitchells sold the land to Thomas and Laura Graham, who promptly recorded their deed. In 1968, before the Mitchells' conveyance to Grahams, the Lyons reconveyed the same parcel to their four sons. Many years later, the Grahams entered an agreement to sell the parcel, but during the course of the title search, the unrecorded deed was discovered. The Grahams sued the Lyons and their sons in a quiet title action to obtain a declaration from the court that their title was valid so that they could consummate the sale. The trial court decided in favor of the Grahams, and the Lyons appealed.

DECISION. The Pennsylvania Superior Court affirmed the trial court judgment.

JUDGE DEL SOLE. Appellants (Lyons) who claim to be the rightful owners of the property in question, contend that the trial court erred when it failed to take into account the fact that Mr. and Mrs. Lyons had conveyed the subject property to William H. Lyons, Paul G. Lyons II, Lynn C. Lyons, and Samuel H. Lyons on October 28, 1968, the deed to which was recorded the next day. Appellants maintain that the Pennsyl-

vania Recording Act protects their title since the conveyance was set down in writing and was recorded prior to the transfer of the property to appellees. (Grahams)

The argument advanced by Lyons must be dismissed since it is based on the faulty premise that the subject property was transferred in the 1968 conveyance. The deed conveying property from Mr. and Mrs. Lyons to their sons contains the following reservation:

> Also, Excepting and Reserving five (5) campsites sold by Paul C. Lyons and Helen M. Lyons, his wife, to third parties totalling approximately eight (8) acres, more or less.

A title abstractor who testified at trial performed a title search and indicated that during his examination he discovered four recorded deeds transferring four different campsites. None of the four deeds consisted of a transferred campsite from Mr. and Mrs. Lyons to Mr. and Mrs. Mitchell. The trial court concluded that the unrecorded "lost" deed executed in 1952 to Mr. and Mrs. Mitchell was the fifth campsite which was "excepted and reserved" in the conveyance from Mr. and Mrs Lyons to their sons. Although this conveyance was not recorded, the recording of a deed is not essential to its validity or to the transaction of title. The title to real estate may be passed by delivery of a deed without undertaking a recording since the recording is essential only to protect by constructive notice any subsequent purchasers, mortgagees and new judgment creditors. The question of whether Appellants had constructive notice that the property at issue was conveyed to the Mitchells is not at issue since Appellants' deed contains an exception which excludes this property from the description of the land transferred by the Lyons to their sons.

Since the property in question passed by means of a valid conveyance to Mr. and Mrs. Mitchell, who in turn transferred the property to Appellees (Grahams), and since the deed executed in 1968 from the Lyons to their sons excludes from its description the property at issue, the trial court properly ruled in favor of Appellees in this quiet title action.

ORDER AFFIRMED.

ASSURANCE OF TITLE

The average real estate buyer is not competent to determine on his or her own the status of the title to the parcel in question. Depending on the state, or often the local or county practice, the attorney hired by the buyer will have to provide evidence of the marketability of the title. This evidence of title may be provided by the lawyer's own research relating to the title. It is more often the case, however, that attorneys retain a title search firm or title insurance company to provide the necessary information. Specifically, evidence of title will be provided by abstract, by title insurance or by certificate.

ABSTRACT OF TITLE

◆ **A summary of all the recorded transactions, including deeds, mortgages, judgments and the like, that affect the title to a specific parcel of land.**

The title searcher or abstractor will examine the chain of title, making a descriptive notation of all recorded transactions affecting the concerned parcel. Depending on local practice, the abstractor may be required to examine the title back to the original grant or only back to the preceding conveyance. The abstractor prepares for the party employing him or her a document—an *abstract*—that contains a description of the concerned parcel and a brief description in chronological order of all the instruments affecting the land that fall within the chain of title.

CASE EXAMPLE

The abstractor will examine the grantor index for the name George Lang for conveyances between the years 1975 and 1985, the period during which Lang was the record owner of Laneacre. Having noted the deed book pages of all such conveyances, the abstractor will look at the deeds to see whether they affect Laneacre in any way.

---

arising prior to the registration of the Torrens certificate will be precluded from attacking the present owner's or any subsequent owner's title unless his or her interest was recorded on the original certificate. To ensure that the Torrens certificate is always up to date, any conveyance, mortgage, lien or other encumbrance upon the parcel will not be valid until it is entered on the original certificate. Further, title does not pass until the registration takes place. If there is a defect of title, suit is usually against the state for the loss. A limited state fund is provided for such lawsuits.

As with the normal recording system, under the Torrens system it is usually necessary to go beyond the recorder's office (or the certificate) to determine whether there are unpaid taxes or special assessments, zoning and building restrictions or federal court judgments that may affect the parcel.

For reasons not completely clear, the Torrens system has not been widely used. Perhaps the title searching apparatus already in place has successfully resisted the abolition of the title search. There is also the initial expense of having the title registered and the fact that the system is voluntary, both of which militate against its wide adoption. The Torrens system has been adopted to some degree by 15 states, but it does not seem to be spreading rapidly and is not likely to replace the present recording system in the foreseeable future.

PETITION OF ALCHEMEDES/BROOKWOOD
Minnesota Court of Appeals
546 N.W.2d 41 (1996)

BACKGROUND. Beatrice Bell and Walter and Stella Kaluznick originally owned their apartments as condominiums. In 1985, the condominiums were converted to apartments. Bell and the Kaluznicks received leases with lifetime renewal options from the new owner, Brookwood Estates. The lease agreements were kept secret and not recorded in the certificate of title. The apartment complex is registered Torrens property.

In 1985, Brookwood granted a mortgage to Midwest Federal Savings & Loan Association (Midwest or Midwest Federal). The mortgage was registered on the Torrens title certificate, and applied to the whole apartment complex. The mortgage stated that "the premises are free from all encumbrances except as set forth on Exhibit B." One of the exceptions listed in Exhibit B was unrecorded leases, without further identification. Midwest went into receivership and the Resolution Trust Corporation (RTC) obtained the mortgage. Alchemedes purchased the mortgage from RTC. Later, Brookwood defaulted on the mortgage, and Alchemedes foreclosed. Subsequently, Alchemedes petitioned to have a new Torrens title certificate issued in its name. Bell and the Kaluznicks sought to have their leases memorialized in the new title certificate. The district court found that Midwest had actual and constructive notice of the leases, and that they should be recorded with priority over the foreclosed mortgage.

DECISION. The Minnesota Court of Appeals reversed the District Court decision.

JUDGE DAVIES. Under the Torrens system, a party holding a certificate of title for property generally holds title free of all encumbrances except those memorialized on the certificate. This is to ensure that a person dealing with registered property "need look no further than the certificate of title for any transactions that might affect the land." The Minnesota Supreme Court has recognized one exception to the Torrens principle, that the Torrens Act does not do away with the effect of actual notice. Both parties agree that in determining whether there was actual notice, we examine the knowledge of Midwest Federal rather than that of Alchemedes. This case involves an apartment complex. Midwest Federal, therefore, knew that the property was subject to many leases. Midwest Federal undoubtedly made sure of that reality and even calculated the resulting cash flow. But, contrary to the district court ruling, that information did not provide notice of any long-term leases because leases of registered property for three years or more must be noted on the certificate. Thus, the district court erred in its conclusion that Midwest Federal's notice of "[u]nrecorded leases" constituted actual notice of the tenants' long-term leases. Midwest Federal could reasonably conclude that the leases of which it had actual notice and the leases referenced in Exhibit B were short-term leases. In addition, the Torrens law provides:

> Neither the reference in a registered instrument to an unregistered instrument or interest nor the joinder in a registered instrument by a party or parties with no registered interest shall consti-

tute notice, either actual or constructive, of an unregistered interest. This provision prevents the mortgage's reference to "unrecorded leases" from providing Midwest Federal with actual notice of any lease longer than three years. Midwest Federal's in-house counsel testified that at the time of the mortgage transaction, "no one knew about leases in excess of three years for this property." He also testified that if he had known of the leases, he "would not have allowed the loan to be closed...." The record contains no contradictory evidence suggesting that Midwest Federal had actual knowledge of these specific leases.

Alchemedes argues that the district court erred in its determination that Midwest Federal had constructive notice of the unrecorded leases because the doctrine of constructive notice does not apply to Torrens property. In *Juran* (case), the court stated that the Torrens Act "abrogates the doctrine of constructive notice except as to matters noted on the certificate of title." Because the leases were not recorded on the certificate, the principle of constructive notice does not apply.

Alchemedes did not have actual notice that any lease was for a period beyond three years, neither from the reference to unrecorded leases in the mortgage nor on any other basis. The doctrine of constructive notice does not apply. The leases should not be memorialized on the new certificate.

REVERSED.

REVIEW AND DISCUSSION QUESTIONS

1. (a) Explain the purpose of recording statutes. (b) What must a plaintiff establish to be protected by this type of legislation?

2. Define *constructive notice* and explain how it might affect a person who purchases real estate.

3. What is the difference between a race-notice and a notice recording statute?

4. What is a tract index? How does it facilitate the title searching process?

5. Describe the title searching process.

6. What are the prerequisites that must be met for an instrument to be recorded?

7. Explain why title insurance is often advisable even when the grantee receives a warranty deed.

8. What are the limitations in relying on title insurance for protection?

CASE PROBLEMS

1. Russell Ulrich claimed ownership of 38 acres of land through a chain of title dating back to a conveyance from the Loefler family to Ulrich's family in 1888. The Loeflers' claim to the land dates to an unrecorded deed prior to 1888. The Pennsylvania Game Commission (Commission) claims ownership to the same parcel through a conveyance from Handwerk. The origin of the problem is due apparently to a change in how land surveyors do surveys. The Commission argues that because the basis of Ulrich's claim is an unrecorded deed, his title is invalid. Does the Commission have a legitimate defense? *Commonwealth v. Ulrich, 565 A.2d 858 (1989).*

2. In an agreement dated March 9, 1964, Jaynes granted Lawing an option to purchase real property. The option was open for two calendar years. Before the option expired, Lawing took it up, but Jaynes refused to transfer the property. In April 1966, Lawing sued. Lawing's action was awaiting trial in March 1971 when Jaynes conveyed the property to McLean. When Lawing instituted his litigation in 1966, he filed a notice of his claim in the county registrar's office. The notice had been indexed improperly. In a suit by Lawing to have the deed from Jaynes to McLean declared void, what must McLean establish for a successful defense? *Lawing v. Jaynes, 206 S.E.2d 162 (N.C. 1974).*

3. Dowse sold land to Pender by warranty deed dated April 1, 1994. The deed was recorded on June 3, 1994. On May 29, 1994, Dowse fraudulently sold the same land to Petez. Petez recorded his deed on June 4, 1994. Petez had no actual knowledge of the deed to Pender. Between Pender and Petez, who has the superior claim in (a) race-notice jurisdiction? (b) notice jurisdiction? Explain.

4. Gagner purchased a parcel of land in 1969 after his attorney provided him with a certificate of title stating that the land was marketable and unencumbered by easements. In fact, a water district had previously been deeded a water pipe easement across the land, but the easement was not recorded until 1973. Although the easement was not in Gagner's chain of title, there were references in the chain indicating that the water district had certain rights in a larger parcel that included Gagner's land. The attorney relied on oral assurances from the seller, Crena, that these references did not affect the Gagner parcel. (a) Is the easement valid as to Gagner? (b) If it is valid, does Gagner have a remedy against the attorney? *See Gagner v. Kittery Water District, 385 A.2d 206 (Me. 1978).*

5. McDaniel discovered the existence of a utility easement along the eastern edge of his property that was not mentioned in his deed or noted in his title insurance policy. Since the title insurance policy purported to guarantee McDaniel fee simple ownership, he sued the title insurance company for the reduction in the fair market value of his land caused by the easement. The utility easement is recorded. Will McDaniel succeed? *McDaniel v. Lawyer's Title Guaranty Fund, 328 So.2d 852 (Fla. 1976).*

21

Mortgages

MORTGAGE

◆ **A written instrument that uses real property to secure payment of a debt.**

A mortgage is used in a loan transaction in which real estate is the security. The purpose of the mortgage is to provide security for repayment of the debt. Without the existence of a debt, a mortgage has no effect.

CASE EXAMPLE

Anders Plumbing Company, Inc., owned a valuable building. The company needed money and sold stock to Lance and Jean Billingham. In order to induce the Billinghams to purchase the stock, they were given a mortgage on the property.

Lee Sickles, a contractor, made improvements on the property. When he was not paid, Sickles attempted to enforce a mechanic's lien. The Billinghams argued that their mortgage had priority over the lien. In a suit by Sickles, the court would hold the mortgage invalid because it was not given as security for a debt.

SECURED DEBTS

From the purchase of a family's modest first home to the million-dollar commercial sale, financing is the key to almost every successful real estate transaction. People and institutions lend money because lending is profitable; much of the profitability stems from the risk entailed. A lender's risk is reduced when its loan is secured by property—an automobile, real estate, a firm's inventory or some other kind of valuable asset. When a loan is secured, the lender has a right to sell the security and apply the proceeds against the debt if the borrower fails to pay or violates some other term of the loan agreement.

In a mortgage relationship, the debtor is termed the *mortgagor*. The lender who takes the mortgage to secure repayment of the loan is referred to as the *mortgagee*.

The true nature of a mortgage, no matter what its form, is to establish a security right against a debtor's interest in real property. Most often the debtor's interest will be fee simple ownership, but legally mortgages may cover almost any interest in real estate that may be sold or assigned. Mortgages may be applied to rental income, life estates, estates for years, remainders and reversions, as well as other valuable property rights.

Mortgages are also used sometimes to secure obligations that are quite unrelated to the property mortgaged.

CASE EXAMPLE

Ray Adams wished to go into business for himself as a plumbing and heating contractor. He planned to hire one or two employees and open up a small showroom from which to sell plumbing fixtures. Although Ray had saved enough money to get started, he was advised by some of the manufacturers whose lines he wished to carry that he should have a line of credit with a local bank. Ray's bank was willing to give him a $45,000 line of credit; as security the bank asked for a mortgage against rental property that he owned.

NOTE

◆ **A written instrument signed by a borrower containing the provisions of a loan and a promise to repay according to the terms of the agreement between borrower and lender.**

In addition to security aspects, mortgage transactions often involve the borrower's personal liability to pay the debt. Usually the borrower makes the commitment by signing a note promising to pay the debt. In some states, the borrower signs a bond. The note or bond serves as evidence of the debt for which the mortgage is the security. The typical note contains the amount of the loan, the interest rate and the time and method of repayment, as well as the borrower's obligation to pay. This instrument is sometimes referred to as a *promissory note* or *mortgage note*.

The existence of the note and mortgage provide the lenders with two remedies if the debt is not paid: (1) to sue on the note and to obtain a personal judgment against the debtor or (2) to have the real estate sold and the proceeds applied against the debt. If the lender wins a personal judgment on the note, the judgment may be collected by attaching other property of the debtor or by garnishing the debtor's wages. In addition, if when sold the security does not bring enough to pay the debt, a personal action can be brought on the note. A few states require the lender to choose one of the two methods, either to sell the collateral to pay the debt or to sue on the note.

TITLE AND LIEN THEORY

The historical theory that the mortgage conveys title to the mortgagee continues to be used in some states, referred to as *title theory* states. Even in these states, however, although the mortgagee acquires title, the mortgagee does not acquire the right of possession unless the mortgagor defaults.

Most states recognize that in reality a mortgage is a lien. It is a device used by debtors and creditors to secure a debt. The mortgagee is interested primarily in having the security sold and the proceeds applied to the debt if the mortgagor fails to pay or violates some other mortgage provision. States taking this position are called *lien theory* states.

In some states that consider the mortgage a lien, the mortgagee of real property has more rights than most other lienholders. Sometimes these rights are very similar to those a title holder would have. For example, in several states, by statute the mortgagee is entitled to oust a defaulting mortgagor from possession. Most other types of liens permit the holder only to have the security sold and proceeds applied to the debt. Since vestiges of title theory appear in the law of lien theory states and lien theory remains in some title theory jurisdictions, few states can be classified rigidly.

FORMS AND CONTENT OF MORTGAGE

Currently, the mortgage most commonly used in the United States is a two-party instrument. By its terms, one of the parties, the mortgagor, creates a security interest in property for the other, the mortgagee. Because historically the mortgage was a conveyance, the mortgage often has many provisions similar to those of a deed. In some states, it is called a *mortgage deed.* Legislative bodies in a few states have adopted statutory mortgage forms. Although they contain all elements essential to a valid mortgage, use of the statutory form is not required.

In general, for an instrument to be effective as a mortgage, it should include at least the following information:

- Names of the parties
- Legal description of the premises
- Language indicating that the instrument is given as security for a debt
- Statement of the debt secured
- Terms for repaying the debt

Additionally, the mortgage must be signed by the mortgagor and executed according to the laws of the state in which the property is located.

Most mortgages contain substantially more information than minimal requirements. Because the parties insert many provisions designed to protect their rights, mortgage instruments tend to be lengthy. The recording process is expensive and requires a great amount of storage space. A number of states have adopted statutes that allow mortgagees to record a *master mortgage* containing the desired covenants and clauses. This practice permits execution and recording of a mortgage that incorporates by reference the provisions of the master mortgage. Stated are the recording date, file number, volume and page of the master mortgage.

Deed of Trust

◆ **A written instrument that transfers title to real property to a trustee as security for a debt owed by the borrower to the lender, who is the beneficiary of the trust.**

In an increasing number of states, the typical real estate security instrument involves three parties and is based on the law of trusts. Instead of executing a mortgage in favor of a lender, the borrower transfers title to a trustee through a deed of trust. The important difference between the mortgage and the deed of trust is that in a deed of trust, legal title passes to the trustee. The trustee holds this title for the benefit of both the borrower and the lender. When the debt secured by the deed of trust is repaid, the trustee must reconvey title to the borrower. In the mortgage, title remains in the borrower.

The law of trusts, which has developed over hundreds of years, requires trustees to act in utmost good faith and fairness. Like the real estate broker, the trustee is a fiduciary. In addition to this fiduciary duty, the trustee has specific obligations and powers stated in the deed of trust. A trustee who fails to meet these obligations is personally accountable.

Importantly, the trustee has the power to sell the property if the borrower fails to maintain payments on the debt or breaches some other condition of the loan agreement by failing to keep the buildings insured, by selling the property or by committing waste. The power-of-sale provision makes judicial foreclosure procedure unnecessary, although the trustee usually can elect such procedure. Because judicial foreclosure can be avoided, collection from the security is more rapid and economical than through the court procedure. Additionally, the lender may remain anonymous in a deed of trust.

Compared with the mortgage, a distinct disadvantage of the deed of trust lies in discharging the instrument. In most states a mortgage is discharged when the mortgagee executes a simple document called a *satisfaction of mortgage* or a *release of mortgage*. The deed of trust requires a reconveyance by the trustee. The trustee will refuse to reconvey the property without assurance that the underlying obligation has been paid. Otherwise, the trustee would be personally liable to the lender for any amount still due. If the trustee is an individual, the problem of reconveyance can become especially acute because the person might be difficult to locate. For this reason, the preferred practice is to name a corporate trustee.

Loan Application and Commitment

Today, most mortgage loans start with an application made on a printed form supplied by the lender. The information needed to complete the application is ordinarily given to a loan officer, and the form is signed by the party requesting the loan.

The application serves two purposes: it supplies the lender with information necessary to decide whether the loan should be granted and it serves as the borrower's *offer* to enter into a contract. If the lender approves the loan, it notifies the borrower and furnishes a formal commitment, often called a *loan approval.* The commitment, if it does not modify the terms in the application, is an acceptance of the offer. The parties have entered into a contract to make a loan with real property as security. Ordinarily, the commitment contains a clause terminating the contract if the borrower does not take advantage of the loan within a specified time.

If the lender refuses to honor the contract, the borrower's damages are relatively easy to calculate. They are the increased cost of obtaining the loan from some other source. If the borrower does not use the funds, damages to the lender are very difficult to measure. In a number of cases, the courts have held that the lender is entitled only to nominal damages. Because of problems associated with measuring the damages, many commitments for major loans contain provisions for a nonrefundable commitment fee paid by the borrower.

In the following case, the lender changed the terms of the commitment at closing.

LEBEN v. NASSAU SAVINGS & LOAN ASSOCIATION

Supreme Court, Appellate Division
40 A.D.2d 830 (N.Y. 1972)

BACKGROUND. The Lebens contracted with Smithtown Park, Inc., for a lot and a dwelling to be constructed by the seller. The contract provided that they were to apply for a mortgage loan from lending institutions designated by Smithtown. The mortgage was to be for $22,400, to run for 30 years and to bear interest at the rate of 6% per annum. A different provision of the contract provided that in the event the maximum allowable rate should change, the Lebens "will accept the . . . mortgage at the maximum rate which is in effect at the date of the closing of the permanent mortgage loan."

The Lebens applied to Nassau Savings for a mortgage loan. On December 6, 1967, Nassau Savings advised them by letter of its approval of the loan. The letter stated "Terms of this mortgage will be at the interest rate of 6%, in accordance with the terms of your contract, for a period of 30 years."

On October 4, 1968, the Lebens appeared at Nassau Savings for the closing of title. They were informed for the first time that the loan would bear interest at the rate of 7¼%. The Lebens had already moved into their new house and had cancelled the lease on their apartment. They were told there would be no closing unless they acceded to the higher interest rate. In order to protect themselves, but over their objection, they signed an assumption, release and modification providing for the increased interest rate and title was closed.

Shortly thereafter they sued for a declaration that the mortgage agreement dated December 6, 1967, is a legal, binding commitment obliging Nassau Savings to make the loan at 6% for 30 years. Additionally, they asked that the closing documents be reformed to comply with the December 6th letter of approval. The trial court dismissed their complaint and the Lebens appealed.

DECISION. The appellate court reversed the trial court and ordered the documents reformed to comply with the terms of the letter of approval.

PRESIDING JUDGE HOPKINS. In our opinion, the mortgage commitment agreement between plaintiffs and defendant clearly obligated defendant to make a mortgage loan at an interest rate of 6%. The addition of the phrase "in accordance with the terms of your contract" at best created an ambiguity and should be construed most strongly against defendant, the party who prepared it. Defendant is not named in the contract between the plaintiffs and Smithtown; nor does it appear that the provision with reference to the maximum allowable rate was made for its benefit.

In our opinion plaintiffs signed the assumption, release and modification agreement as the result of economic duress. The terms of that agreement . . . must be reformed to reflect the agreed upon rate of 6%.

REVERSED.

RIGHTS AND OBLIGATIONS OF PARTIES

A substantial amount of mortgage litigation involves disputes concerning the rights and obligations of the mortgagor and mortgagee. The well-drafted mortgage will reduce the possibilities of litigation by incorporating provisions that clearly indicate each party's rights and obligations.

Often a mortgage instrument that does not cover a problem arising between the parties will be used. When this is the case, public policy—reflected in legislation or case law—directs the parties. Inasmuch as questions involving possession, disposition of rents and profits and protection of the security are common, numerous rules exist to solve these problems.

POSSESSION
◆ **The right to occupy and control real estate to the exclusion of all others.**

The right to possession of mortgaged premises depends on the theory of mortgages followed in a particular state. In title theory states, the common provision allows the mortgagor to remain in possession and enjoy the benefits of ownership until default. Several title theory states have statutes prohibiting the mortgagee from taking possession until default.

In lien theory states, the mortgagee has no right to possession. This principle, however, is frequently modified by a provision in the mortgage allowing the mortgagee to take possession on default. A number of lien theory states have reached a similar result by statute.

As a general practice, either by statute or by mortgage terms, most mortgagors have the right to remain in possession of mortgaged premises until default. In a few states with statutory right-of-redemption laws, the mortgagor is allowed to remain in possession even after a foreclosure sale. This right to possession exists until the redemption period terminates unless limited by a provision in the mortgage.

The status of a mortgagor in possession differs from that of a mortgagee. Generally, the mortgagor in possession is entitled to all of the rights of ownership as long as the value of the security remains unimpaired. A mortgagee who takes possession has special, but limited, rights that revolve around protecting the security and applying proceeds to pay the debt.

RENTS AND PROFITS

Possession is an important factor in determining who has a right to rents and profits from the property. The well-established general rule is that a mortgagor who remains in possession is entitled to these earnings.

> ### CASE EXAMPLE
> Teal executed several mortgages to Walker on farmland and property in Portland, Oregon. The mortgages contained provisions allowing Teal to retain possession of the land but permitting Walker to take possession upon default. When Teal defaulted, Walker demanded possession of the properties. Teal refused to yield possession, collecting earnings from the property until ousted from possession by a foreclosure sale. As the proceeds of the sale fell far short of paying the debt, Walker sued for the rents collected after Teal's refusal to surrender possession. The United States Supreme Court . . . determined that the mortgagee was entitled to rents and profits only if actually in possession. *Teal v. Walker, 111 U.S. 242 (1884).*

A mortgagee who takes possession has a right to earnings from the property, but they must be applied to extinguish the debt. Amounts collected that exceed expenses are first applied to interest and then to principal.

Most mortgages that cover commercial property contain provisions in which the parties allocate rents, profits and earnings. One approach is for the mortgagor to assign the rents and profits as additional security from the date of the mortgage. A more common provision allows the mortgagee to collect the rents upon default. Until that time, rents go to the mortgagor. In both lien and title theory states, the mortgagee has a right to appoint a receiver to collect the rents and manage the property when there is a default. This right is based on either statute or the right to protect the value of the security.

PROTECTING THE SECURITY

A mortgagee has a right to protect the value of the security. Actions that have been held to impair the value of the security include cutting, removing and selling timber; removing machinery; removing a dwelling; failing to pay liens, and failing to keep the property repaired. The mortgagee's right to protect the value of the security may be asserted against third parties as well as against the mortgagor.

Insurance. Although the right to maintain the value of the security is important to the mortgagee, insurance is the best protection against many risks. The law is clear that both mortgagor and mortgagee have an insurable interest in the property. With a few exceptions, the law is equally clear that neither is required to insure for the other's benefit in the absence of an agreement to do so. Commonly, in the United States, a mortgagor agrees to insure for the benefit of the mortgagee. The typical proviso not only commits the mortgagor to insure but also authorizes the mortgagee to obtain insurance if the mortgagor fails to procure it and add the premium to the debt.

In addition to allocating responsibility for obtaining insurance, a well-drafted mortgage should contain a provision covering the application of insurance proceeds. A standard approach is a requirement that the mortgagor obtain a policy, making loss payable to himself or herself and the mortgagee "as interest may appear."

TAXES AND ASSESSMENTS

Taxes and assessments are the responsibility of the mortgagor. Mortgages frequently authorize the mortgagee to pay taxes if the mortgagor does not. The mortgagee can then add these payments to the debt. Even without this provision, the mortgagee probably has the right to pay the taxes and add them to the debt. The reason is that the mortgagee has a right to protect the value of the security. A tax lien takes precedence over a mortgage. In the event of foreclosure, the mortgagee recovers only after taxes have been paid.

In the housing boom that followed World War II, numerous financial institutions adopted the practice of requiring mortgagors to pay a portion of taxes and insurance premiums each month, usually $\frac{1}{12}$ of the estimated yearly total. These funds are held in escrow by the mortgagee, usually without interest.

PRIORITIES

Mortgage priority problems generally occur when a debt is in default or probability of a default exists. Under these circumstances, each secured creditor attempts to ensure that its lien has first claim to the proceeds if the security must be sold. Sometimes the rank of a creditor will be determined by a provision in the security document. At other times the creditor's position is established by case law or, more often, by some statute such as the recording acts.

The fundamental principle determining priority is "first in time, first in right," but modifications of this rule affect the mortgagee's position. As a result of the recording statutes treated in Chapter 20, the first in time priority generally belongs to the first party to deliver the security instrument for recording. In a majority of states, this priority is not accorded if the person recording has actual knowledge of a prior unrecorded claim. Some states do have "race to the record" statutory provisions that apply to mortgages, as described in Chapter 20. Under these statutes, the first mortgage on the record has a superior right even if the mortgagee knows of a prior unrecorded mortgage.

MORTGAGES AND LEASES

In general, the "first in time" rule applies to the priority relationship between mortgages and leases. If a lease is executed before a mortgage, the lease has priority. In a foreclosure sale, the purchaser would take subject to the lease. A lease entered into after a mortgage is subordinate to the mortgage if the mortgage has been recorded. In the event of a foreclosure sale, the purchaser of the property would take it free of the lease.

In practice, most mortgages on commercial property contain agreements by the mortgagee authorizing the mortgagor to lease the premises. Under these circumstances, a lease made by the mortgagor is not subject to the mortgage lien. Unless a lease contains unfavorable terms, a mortgagee entitled to possession will often recognize a lease made after the mortgage. Although the mortgagee has a right to eject the tenant, the mortgagee will be more interested in continued rental income, which can be applied against the debt.

MECHANICS' LIENS AND MORTGAGES

Litigation as to priority between mechanics' lienholders and mortgagees is widespread. Its outcome varies appreciably from state to state, even when the facts are similar. Although all state courts apply the fundamental rule of "first in time," state law differs as to when the mechanic's lien attaches, and it is time of attachment that establishes the first position. At least three different approaches are taken in the United States as to when the mechanic's lien becomes effective against other claims:

1. The lien, when properly filed, reverts back to commencement of construction, no matter when the work was done or materials furnished.

2. The lien, when properly filed, reverts back to the time the claimant began work or furnished materials.

3. The lien attaches when the claimant files his or her claim.

Mechanics' liens were discussed in Chapter 16.

DEFAULT

◆ **Nonperformance of a duty or obligation accepted by either party as part of the mortgage transaction.**

The mortgagee cannot institute a foreclosure action until the mortgagor defaults. The most commonly recognized default is the failure to pay the interest or principal. Obligations other than the payment of principal and interest found in most mortgages include payment of taxes, assessments and insurance. Often these commitments are worded in such a manner that failure to carry them out constitutes a default. Some mortgage instruments merely give the mortgagee the right to make the payment if the mortgagor fails to do so. The mortgagee can then add the amount to the mortgage debt, but in such cases, the mortgagee cannot foreclose since there has not been a default.

Many mortgages are worded so that the mortgagor's failure to comply with statutes, ordinances and governmental requirements affecting the premises constitutes default. Other relatively common provisions that can result in default are related to bankruptcy or the mortgagor's failure to keep the property repaired. Some mortgages provide that a mortgagor who files a voluntary petition in bankruptcy or makes an assignment for the benefit of creditors is in default. Permitting waste or allowing anything to be done on the premises that weakens the security of the mortgage are additional prohibitions often included in mortgages. If the covenant not to permit waste is breached, the mortgagor is in default.

A critical legal question when default has occurred is the mortgagee's right to collect the entire debt. This problem arises when the mortgagor breaches a covenant that is not related to payment or when the debt is to be repaid periodically and a payment is missed. What can the mortgagee do under these circumstances to protect his investment? The solution to this problem is a clause making the entire debt payable in the event of default. This is called an *acceleration clause.*

CASE EXAMPLE

Frederick defaulted on an installment of his $80,000 mortgage loan. The mortgagee, Northwest Bank, brought a foreclosure action and notified Frederick of its option to accelerate the entire debt. The notice stated that if Frederick paid the amount past due plus interest, he could cure the default. Frederick made no payment within the 30-day period. However, during the trial he proffered payment of the delinquent installments plus interest. Northwest refused to accept the amount, and Frederick moved to dismiss. The court refused to do so, holding that the notification of acceleration matured the entire debt, which was no longer payable in installments. *Northwest Bank v. Frederick, 452 N.W.2d 316 (N.D. 1990).*

EQUITY OF REDEMPTION

◆ **The right of the mortgagor or another person with an interest in the property to reclaim it after default but before foreclosure.**

In both title and lien theory states, the mortgagor has a right to redeem the property after default. Redemption can be accomplished by paying the full amount of the debt, interest and costs. To be effective, the right of redemption must be asserted prior to foreclosure. The purpose of foreclosure is to terminate the equitable right of redemption. Once the foreclosure sale has been confirmed, the mortgagor can no longer redeem the property, except in several states in which statutes provide an additional period. This statutory right of redemption is discussed later in the chapter.

In addition to the mortgagor, other parties having an interest in the property may redeem. Junior mortgagees, tenants under a lease, judgment creditors and grantees who have acquired through the mortgagor have this right. The junior mortgagee who redeems acquires the rights of the senior mortgagee, not title to the premises. A mortgagor redeeming has a superior right. Since the debt has been paid, he or she acquires the unencumbered fee.

sions granting a mortgagee or third party the power to sell the real estate at a public sale if the mortgagor defaults. Generally, the sale is authorized without court intervention, but a few states require judicial confirmation, and many have statutes that prescribe procedures that must be followed.

Some states by specific legislation require foreclosure by judicial action. Statutes of this type effectively prohibit the use of a power of sale. Most states, however, do allow the power-of-sale foreclosure, and it is the prevailing practice in several states.

At one time, the power-of-sale foreclosure was touted as the solution to many of the problems of judicial foreclosure, but this expectation was not fulfilled. Lawyers representing potential purchasers are wary of the process because the title acquired is not based on a judicial proceeding that establishes regularity. In addition, the purchaser's title is subject to attack because the sale does not have the official sanction of a court order. This attack can be made not only by the mortgagor but also by others who have an interest in the property.

Statutes in many states and case law in others provide some protection for the mortgagor whose real property is subject to a power of sale. These statutes generally require notice, usually by advertisement, and a sale that is conducted fairly in order to produce a good price. A sale will not be valid if factors exist that tend to stifle competition among the bidders. In conducting the sale, the mortgagee is representing the mortgagor's interest as well as its own.

CASE EXAMPLE

Union Market National Bank held a $9,800 mortgage on property owned by Missak Derderian. The mortgage was in default, and the bank advertised a sale under a power included in the mortgage. The advertisement stated, in addition to a $500 cash down payment at the time of sale, "other terms to be announced at the sale."

At the sale, the auctioneer announced that a $500 deposit would be required of anyone prior to that person's bid being accepted. This was a very unusual condition, and Derderian's brother, who was planning to bid, refused to comply. The auctioneer as a result refused to accept his high bid of more than $10,000 and sold the property to the mortgagee for $8,500. All parties at the sale knew that Derderian's brother was financially responsible.

When Derderian challenged the sale as improperly conducted, an appellate court agreed with him. The court stated that "[a] mortgagee with the power to select the methods of sale must act as a reasonably prudent man would to obtain a fair price. . . . If the conditions announced at the sale . . . operate to prevent free bidding, it is the mortgagee's duty to change them." *Union National Bank v. Derderian, 318 Mass. 578, 62 N.E.2d 661 (1945).*

STRICT FORECLOSURE

◆ **A judicial procedure that, by terminating the mortgagor's equity of redemption, gives the mortgagee absolute title to mortgaged real estate without a sale of the property.**

Judicial foreclosure and power-of-sale foreclosure are identified with the lien theory of mortgages. These procedures establish a mortgagee's right to have the property sold following default. The proceeds of the sale are used to pay the debt and expenses of the sale. If a balance remains, it is turned over to the mortgagor.

At common law, the mortgagee had a more extensive right. The mortgage gave the mortgagee a conditional or defeasible title. If the debt was not paid when due, the mortgagee's title became absolute. If the debt was paid when due, the mortgagor reacquired title.

Strict foreclosure is no longer common in the United States except in two or three states. Some states expressly prohibit strict foreclosure by statute; others accomplish the prohibition by requiring that the property be sold to compensate the creditor. The principal reason for the decline is that often strict foreclosure severely penalizes the mortgagor. At the same time the mortgagee has the potential for a windfall profit.

◆ **Deed in Lieu of Foreclosure. A procedure in which the mortgagor conveys the mortgaged real estate to the mortgagee, who promises in return not to foreclose or sue on the underlying debt.**

> ### CASE EXAMPLE
> As security for a $50,000 loan, Naomi Tilson executed a mortgage to the Pike County National Bank. After making two payments on the loan, she defaulted. At the time of her default, the market value of the property was slightly in excess of $50,000. Because Naomi and her family were valued customers, the bank offered to accept a deed to the property instead of foreclosing. After discussing the consequences of this action with her attorney, Naomi agreed to convey the property to the bank.

The use of a deed in lieu of foreclosure is a common practice in the United States. In conveying to the mortgagee, the mortgagor surrenders any rights to a foreclosure sale and to redeem the property. In return, the mortgagee cancels the underlying debt and becomes the owner of the real estate.

Potentially, the transaction can benefit the mortgagor in a number of ways. For example, Naomi Tilson's credit rating would be protected. The conveyance would be carried out in the same manner as any sale, and adverse publicity that might accompany foreclosure would not exist. Economically, she could anticipate three important benefits. First, any obligation for taxes and assessments would terminate. Foreclosure costs would also be saved. Probably most important of all, she would not be responsible for any deficiency.

The deed in lieu of foreclosure is also advantageous to the mortgagee. Long delays usually associated with foreclosure by judicial sale are avoided. In addition, the mortgagee escapes the poor public relations that are often the result of resorting to a judicial sale. On the other hand, the mortgagee faces the problem of disposing of the security. Until the property is sold, the mortgagee has to maintain it, and expenses of the sale must be borne by the mortgagee because it now owns the real estate.

An important legal consideration involves junior liens on the property. The purchaser at a foreclosure sale takes title free of such liens, but a mortgagee who acquires title to real estate by deed in lieu of foreclosure is subject to these interests. If Naomi Tilson had not paid for improvements on the property and a mechanic's lien existed, the Pike County National Bank's deed would be subject to that lien. A deed in lieu of foreclosure is also subject to attack under the Bankruptcy Act. Were Naomi to file for bankruptcy within a period of, say, 90 days after delivery of the deed to the bank, the bank could be treated as a preferred creditor. The deed would be set aside as a preferential transfer.

TYPES OF MORTGAGES

Many different types of mortgages exist. The principal reason for this is that mortgage lenders, in order to be competitive, in fact often to survive, have to adapt the mortgage loan to reflect prevailing economic conditions and needs.

The evolution of the flexible-rate mortgage during the 1970s is an example of adjustments made between governmental regulations and economic pressure. During the late 1960s and the early 1970s, financial institutions, especially savings and loans, which traditionally carried between 35 and 40 percent of residential mortgage debt, experienced major problems because of interest rate increases. The result was that thrift institutions frequently found themselves caught in a credit squeeze. They had extended credit for long terms at fixed rates, depending on additional deposits to meet reserve requirements and new commitments. When they experienced difficulty in attracting and retaining deposits because competing investments offered higher interest yields, they were often forced to liquidate existing mortgages at a loss to maintain reserves and meet new commitments. Mortgage funds thus dried up, and as new home purchases and construction slowed, the entire economy felt the pinch. The flexible-rate mortgage was an attempt to lessen the strain of "interest rate risk" on lending institutions.

The first mortgages with flexible rates appeared in the late '70s. They were known as variable rate mortgages (VRMs). In 1979, the Federal Home Loan Bank Board (FHLBB) authorized federally chartered savings and loans to make this type of loan. State and federal action authorizing lenders to make VRMs contained provisions to protect borrowers. Regulations limited the amount that interest could be increased over the life of the loan or at any single period, as well as the dollar amount that a periodic payment could increase. These limits are referred to as *caps*. In 1982, the FHLBB authorized lenders to make adjustable-rate mortgages.

ADJUSTABLE-RATE MORTGAGE (ARM)
◆ **A mortgage that contains a provision permitting the mortgagee to adjust the interest rate based on an index contained in the mortgage.**

ARMs tie the interest rate to an index that reflects short-term money market conditions. The index should be outside the control of the lending institution, and it should be readily verifiable by the owner. Indexes that have been used include the Federal Reserve rediscount rate, the Treasury bill rate and national mortgage loan rates compiled by the FHLBB or the Federal Housing Administration. Although one difference between the ARM and the VRM is that the ARM can be written with or without caps, most ARMs are written with caps. Some ARMs limit the amount that the interest rate can be adjusted at any one payment period and the amount the periodic payment can increase.

PURCHASE-MONEY MORTGAGE

◆ **A written instrument given by a buyer to secure part of the purchase price and delivered contemporaneously with the transfer of title to the buyer.**

> ### CASE EXAMPLE
> Martin Sankovich purchased a small dairy farm from his uncle for $250,000. He paid $40,000 down and assumed an existing mortgage of $110,000. His uncle agreed to take back a purchase-money second mortgage for $100,000. At the closing, Martin executed a mortgage and note in favor of his uncle, who in turn conveyed title to him.

The purchase-money mortgage provides some protection for a seller who takes back a mortgage for part of the purchase price. The principal benefit to the mortgagee is that the purchase-money mortgage takes priority, or preference, over liens against the buyer that might immediately attach to the property. Suppose, for example, that Martin at the time of closing had an outstanding judgment against him for $8,000. A judgment lien would usually attach immediately to his interest in the dairy and would be superior to his uncle's mortgage. However, the law assumes that the delivery of the deed and the purchase-money loan are one transaction. The result is that there is no time for an intervening lien to attach. The judgment, though prior in time, is inferior in right to the seller's mortgage. In states that recognize dower and homestead rights, the purchase-money mortgage takes priority over them. If the dairy were in a state that recognized dower, Martin's wife would have an immediate inchoate right of dower when Martin acquired title to the property. Even if she did not sign the mortgage, her right would be inferior to that of the purchase money lender.

In a few states, only a seller who takes back a mortgage is afforded the limited benefits of a purchase-money mortgagee. Most jurisdictions, however, have extended purchase-money safeguards to any lender who advances funds that are applied to the purchase price. If Martin had borrowed $210,000 from a bank to purchase the dairy, the bank would have purchase-money status if the funds were advanced simultaneously with the transfer of title to Martin.

The important protection provided by a purchase-money mortgage is illustrated by the following case.

GARRETT TIRE CENTER, INC.
v. HERBAUGH
Supreme Court of Arkansas
740 S.W. 2d 612 (1987)

BACKGROUND. On April 26, 1984, Garrett Tire Center obtained a judgment against Robert Herbaugh. Garrett Tire was unable to collect on the judgment as no assets could be found. In 1984, Farmers and Merchants Bank made a purchase-money mortgage loan to Herbaugh. A purchase-money mortgage was filed on January 30, 1985, five minutes after the deed to Robert Herbaugh was filed.

In October 1986, Farmers and Merchants Bank filed for foreclosure on its purchase-money mortgage. Garrett Tire intervened claiming that its judgment lien was superior to the bank's mortgage. The bank moved for summary judgment and the trial court rendered judgment in its favor. Garrett Tire appealed.

DECISION. The appellate court affirmed the summary judgment in favor of the bank.

JUSTICE PURTLE. The chancellor granted summary judgment in favor of a purchase money mortgagee over a prior judgment lien holder. The appellant argues that his judgment lien was superior because it attached before the appellee's mortgage lien. We hold that the appellee's purchase money mortgage had priority.

When a deed and a purchase money mortgage are a part of one continuous transaction, they are treated as being executed simultaneously. A prior judgment lien cannot attach because the purchaser never obtains title to the land, but acquires only an equity interest subject to the payment of the purchase money.

It is a general rule, to which there is little dissent, that a mortgage on land executed by the purchaser of the land contemporaneously with the acquirement of the legal title thereto, or afterwards, but as a part of the same transaction, is a purchase money mortgage, and entitled to preference as such over all other claims of liens arising through the mortgagor, though they are prior in point of time; and this is true without reference to whether the mortgage was executed to the vendor or to a third person.

The appellant argues that under [the Arkansas statute in question] a mortgage, including a purchase money mortgage, is not valid against a third party until recorded. Therefore appellant's judgment lien attached during the five minute space of time after the deed was filed and before the purchase money mortgage was recorded. Appellant relies on *Western Tie & Timber Co. v. Campbell*, where the state obtained a statutory lien on a defendant's real property for the criminal fines and costs adjudged against the defendant. Subsequently, the defendant simultaneously purchased land and executed a purchase money mortgage on it. The purchase money mortgage was recorded eight months later. The priority between the state's lien and purchase money mortgage became the issue on appeal.

The *Western Tie* court correctly stated the law as follows:

It is quite well settled by the authorities that a mortgage, given at the time of the purchase of real estate to secure the payment of purchase money, whether given to the vendor or to a third person, who, as part of the same transaction, advances the purchase money, has preference over all judgments and other liens against the mortgagor.

Nonetheless the court held that the legislature intended to give the state a lien against an unrecorded mortgage; so, under the circumstances the prior state lien was superior to the purchase money mortgage.

Despite the result in *Western Tie,* there is no dispute that a purchase money mortgage, executed as a deed as part of one continuous transaction, and recorded within a reasonable time to prevent detrimental reliance by a third party, is superior to any other lien. In the present case appellee Farmers and Merchants Bank obtained a promissory note secured by a purchase money mortgage as part of one transaction and recorded its lien within a reasonable time. The appellant did not in any way rely on the deed before the purchase money mortgage was recorded. The fact that the purchase money mortgage was filed five minutes after the deed was recorded did not affect the validity of the mortgage. We hold that the deed was encumbered by the purchase money mortgage at the time it was filed.

AFFIRMED.

CONSTRUCTION MORTGAGE

◆ **A mortgage given to secure funds advanced to construct or improve a building.**

Construction loan is a term frequently used in the real estate industry. Like many common terms, it has a variety of meanings. Sometimes people use it in a general sense when discussing sources of funds to remodel or make relatively minor improvements. More specifically, the term refers to a number of industry practices that provide substantial funding for construction or renovation. A common characteristic of these practices is that the lender agrees to advance a total sum but supplies the funds over a period of time as work progresses. The loan is secured by a construction mortgage.

For some lenders, the construction mortgage does not differ materially from a regular mortgage except that funds are advanced periodically, not in a lump sum. On completion of the work, the lender carries the mortgage as a permanent investment or assigns it to another lender. Some financial institutions will not make short-term construction loans, either based on internal decisions or because they are prohibited from making these loans by law. If financing through one of these institutions, the property owner first must obtain a short-term loan from an interim lender. When construction is completed, permanent financing is arranged. Usually this is based on a prior agreement made by the permanent mortgagee to provide long-term financing.

Both the construction mortgage and the mechanic's lien look to the property as security. The periodic advances made by the lender are secured by the increased value of the property stemming from the completed work. At the same time, if those working on the structure are not paid, they have a right to a lien against the real estate. The time when the mechanic's lien attaches is critical to the rights of the parties. For example, in a number of states, a mechanic's lien dates back to the start of construction. If a construction mortgage is not recorded until work commences, the mechanic's lien is superior even if perfected later. A number of states separate buildings from the land when attempting to adjust the interest of the construction mortgagee and the mechanic's lienholder. In these states the mechanic's lien has superior rights in the building even if a construction mortgage has been recorded against the property. Other states have different rules relating to time of attachment.

In order to establish the priority right of the construction mortgagee and to ensure that workers will be paid, state statutes provide the lender with a preferred position in the security if provisions for disbursing funds are followed. The construction mortgagee must be certain to follow these provisions exactly. Usually they involve two steps: obtaining detailed statements from contractors and subcontractors of the work that has been done and, when funds are disbursed, obtaining proper waivers from the parties to whom payments have been made. Not all states have statutes regulating construction loans. In those that do not, the construction mortgagee must develop procedures to ensure that the mortgage rights will be superior to the mechanics' liens.

OPEN-END MORTGAGE
◆ **A mortgage that permits the mortgagor to borrow additional funds, usually up to the original amount of the debt.**

Traditionally, in most American jurisdictions, a mortgage to secure future advances provides the lender with priority over liens intervening between the recording of the mortgage and the future advance. This principle is especially well established when the future advance is obligatory.

CASE EXAMPLE

Midge and Tony McLaughlin, a young married couple, executed a $25,000 mortgage to United National Bank for funds advanced to purchase a small house. Midge and Tony planned to have a family and knew that additions would have to be made to the house. When they explained this to the loan officer, he suggested an open-end mortgage. A provision was included in the mortgage requiring the bank to lend them additional funds up to the original amount of the loan.

Several years later, Midge and Tony requested those additional funds. During the intervening years, a judgment had been entered against Midge as a result of an automobile accident. Despite this judgment, United National advanced the money; the original mortgage provided security for the additional funds.

In most open-end mortgages, the mortgagee is not required to advance the additional funds. If the mortgagee has this option, the priority of the lien over an intervening encumbrance in most states depends on notice of the intervening claim. If the mortgagee has actual notice of an intervening lien and elects to advance the funds, any lien that results is inferior to that of the intervening claimant. In the previous example, if the mortgage was nonobligatory and United National had knowledge of the judgment against Midge, a lien resulting from any later advance would be inferior to the judgment lien.

Although the law generally agrees that actual notice of the intervening claim limits the priority of the open-end mortgage, the states are divided as to whether a recorded lien provides notice. A majority hold that the mortgagee does not have notice merely because a subsequent lien is recorded. In other states, the mortgagee is charged with notice of any subsequently recorded interest. In these states the mortgagee whose instrument is nonobligatory must reexamine the record before advancing additional funds.

PACKAGE MORTGAGE
◆ **A mortgage secured by both personal and real property.**

Package mortgages are used today primarily in financing residential real estate, although they can also be used to finance commercial and industrial ventures. The mortgage covers not only the real property but also personal property essential to the operation of a home or business. In residential financing, a package mortgage lien attaches to real estate and to equipment needed to make the home livable. This might include a stove, refrigerator, dishwasher or freezer. In a commercial transaction, the package mortgage would include items necessary to operate the business. In a mortgage covering a motel, for example, most lenders would require a lien on the furniture and other items necessary to operate the business. In the event of a foreclosure, the security would be much more valuable if it included equipment necessary for operation. Unless these items were included in the mortgage, the purchaser would have to buy them separately because the owner would have a right to remove them.

Benefits. For several reasons, the package mortgage might be beneficial to the buyer/mortgagor. First, the mortgagor is able to finance appliances at the same low rate of interest provided in the real estate mortgage. This rate is considerably lower than the rate for consumer loans. Second, the purchase price of these appliances can be spread over the entire term of the mortgage, thereby reducing monthly payments. Finally, some lenders contend that a package mortgage reduces the potential for default, especially for families buying their first home. Usually these people have to purchase all their appliances in addition to the realty. With a package mortgage, they are not saddled with additional payments for appliances simultaneously with initial payments on real estate debt. The cost of all items is included in the mortgage payment. The chief argument against the package mortgage is that the buyer, in paying for the appliances over the term of the real estate mortgage, is paying for them long after their useful life has expired.

ROLLOVER MORTGAGE
◆ **A mortgage that must be refinanced every few years in order to adjust the interest rate up or down in response to prevailing money market conditions.**

Rising interest rates create a substantial problem for financial institutions that make long-term loans. In recent years this problem has been especially acute for savings and loan institutions, which, in order to compete for funds, have to pay savers short-term rates. As interest rates increase, the return on mortgage money, invested at fixed rates often up to 30 years, lags well behind rapidly increasing short-term rates. The variable-rate mortgage (VRM) was one effort to solve this problem. The rollover, or renegotiated-rate, mortgage is another.

A rollover mortgage is written for a short term, generally three, four or five years. At the end of that period, the loan is renegotiated to reflect prevailing interest rates. To protect borrowers, a maximum increase is sometimes established, for example, two percentage points per year and five percentage points over the life of the mortgage. Other protections for the mortgagor include a requirement that the lender renew, formal foreclosure if the lender wants to terminate the loan and the right to pay off the loan in full with no penalty after 90 days. Many mortgagors object to rollover mortgages because they could lead to substantially higher costs if interest rates climb. On the other hand, if interest rates drop, the mortgagor will benefit when the loan has to be renegotiated.

REVERSE MORTGAGE
◆ **A mortgage loan in which the mortgagee advances funds to a homeowner based on the homeowner's equity in the real estate.**

The reverse mortgage appeals to people who have a substantial equity in their home but have reduced income because of retirement or death of the primary breadwinner. Instead of being forced to sell to take advantage of the equity, the homeowner is able to remain in the home. Payments from the mortgagee supplement income and can be used in any manner the homeowner desires.

A number of different types of reverse mortgages exist. The simplest type is one in which the mortgagee makes monthly payments to the owner-mortgagor. In some instances, instead of monthly payments, a line of credit is established. On the death of the mortgagor or at some future time fixed by the parties, the property is sold to pay off the mortgage debt. The danger of this approach is that the mortgagor surviving beyond the fixed date might be forced to vacate the real estate.

A more sophisticated approach is the reverse annuity mortgage. In this type of reverse mortgage, the mortgagor purchases an annuity with a lump sum payment provided by the mortgagee. A portion of the annuity is used to pay the interest on the mortgage debt. The balance of the income is paid to the mortgagor, who remains in the property for life.

MORTGAGE INSURANCE

◆ **Insurance provided by certain government agencies or private corporations protecting mortgage lenders against loss caused by a borrower's default.**

Authorities estimate that more than 25 percent of real estate mortgage loans are covered by some type of mortgage insurance. This type of insurance has numerous social benefits. Probably the most important is *liquidity*—the ease with which an asset can be converted to cash. Insured mortgage loans are much more liquid than those that are not insured. Liquidity is greater because firms initiating insured loans must follow established standards and procedures. These procedures include an approved appraisal of the structure as well as approval of the creditworthiness of the borrower. When a loan is insured, not only the lender but also the insurer must be convinced that the property value covers the loan and the borrower has the ability to repay.

Another benefit of mortgage insurance is a reduction in the number of foreclosures. When an insured loan is in default, the insurer pays the debt and takes over the property. The insurer then attempts to sell the property to cover its losses. Today, two federal agencies and several private firms share the mortgage insurance business.

FHA INSURANCE

◆ **Insurance provided lenders under Title II of the National Housing Act of 1934.**

The National Housing Act is administered by the Department of Housing and Urban Development (HUD); the Federal Housing Administration (FHA) is an organizational unit of HUD. The FHA administers several programs providing insurance to lenders financing real estate transactions. Loans can be insured for the purchase, construction, repair and improvement of housing. Rental housing, cooperatives, condominiums, low-cost and moderate-income housing, housing for the elderly and nursing homes are among the many types of dwellings covered by FHA programs. Mortgages insured by the FHA are known as *FHA mortgages.*

The mortgage loan insurance program that resulted from Section 203 of the National Housing Act is the most important to have arisen over the years. This section authorizes insurance for loans to finance the purchase of one- to four-unit dwellings. Four common provisions of FHA insured mortgage loans are:

1. long term for repayment,
2. full amortization over the term,
3. low down payment, and
4. interest rates generally below market.

Applications for mortgage insurance on one- to four-family dwellings have two requirements: approval of the property based upon an appraisal and approval of the purchaser's credit. Borrowers pay a one-time premium, which is a percent of the amount borrowed. From these premiums and fees, the FHA accumulates reserves to cover expenses and losses on properties acquired because of borrower default. All FHA loans tack on a ½ percent per year charge for insurance.

DEPARTMENT OF VETERANS AFFAIRS LOAN GUARANTEES

◆ **Guarantees provided by the Department of Veterans Affairs to lenders that finance housing construction and purchases by eligible veterans.**

The loan guarantee program of the Department of Veterans Affairs provides protection to private lenders financing homes for veterans. As a result of the guarantee, veterans have been able to buy or build homes on long-term loans with no down payment. Loans may be guaranteed on one- to four-unit structures; the veteran must occupy one of the units. Most DVA-guaranteed loans are for the purchase of single-family homes, mobile homes and units in condominium projects.

Although the loan may be for any amount, the guarantee covers only 60 percent of the loan or a maximum of $50,750, whichever is less. The amount of the loan that the DVA guarantees is called an *entitlement*. As in the FHA insurance program, the DVA guarantees a loan only upon an approved appraisal of the property. In addition, before the loan is guaranteed, the Department of Veterans Affairs must be convinced that the veteran is a satisfactory credit risk.

DVA-guaranteed loans have several advantages for the veteran. No down payment is required, and the loan may be paid in part or in full at any time with no penalty. If the veteran has financial problems, the DVA will arrange for a modification of terms. The loan may be assumed by any buyer, veteran or nonveteran, who is an acceptable credit risk. In addition, the veteran has the benefit of DVA appraisal, construction supervision and oversight of the lender's activities.

REGULATIONS AFFECTING MORTGAGE LOANS

Both state and federal regulations influence mortgage lending. Usually these regulations favor borrowers as legislators recognize that the borrower's bargaining position is weaker than the lender's. Usury statutes, the Truth-in-Lending Act and the Equal Credit Opportunity Act are examples of regulations with which lenders must contend.

USURY

◆ **The practice of charging interest on a loan in excess of a rate allowed by law.**

Religious disapproval of interest resulting in usury laws has influenced relationships between borrowers and lenders for centuries. The importance of usury laws depends to a large extent on economic conditions. When money is scarce, lenders are able to charge higher rates for loans, and usury becomes a factor that they must consider. Almost every state has laws prohibiting lenders from charging excessive interest. These statutes vary appreciably from state to state. Not only do the permissible rates differ, but major differences exist in the transactions that are covered and the penalties levied against the usurious lender.

In 1980, to provide additional stimulus to residential sales, Congress adopted legislation limiting state usury laws in some situations. The federal legislation called the Depository Institution Deregulation and Monetary Control Act (DIDMC) eliminated state interest ceilings on first mortgage loans made by financial institutions and secured by residential real estate. Individuals financing the sale of their own homes were also exempted. The DIDMC permitted states to override the federal law if they did so prior to April 1, 1983. Fourteen states elected to do so. In these states, usury statutes continue to apply to residential mortgage loans as they have traditionally.

TRUTH-IN-LENDING
◆ **The popular name given to part of the Consumer Credit Protection Act of 1968, the federal statute that requires lenders to disclose the cost of consumer credit so that users can better compare terms available from different sources.**

The purpose of the Truth-in-Lending Act is to foster the informed use of consumer credit, that is, credit extended to an individual to be used primarily for personal, family or household purposes. This legislation in no way fixes maximum or minimum charges for credit.

Real estate credit is only one of many types of credit covered by the act. To come within the scope of the act, real estate credit must be extended to a natural person and be granted to finance acquisition or initial construction of the borrower's principal dwelling. Thus, mortgage loans to corporations and to individuals for business purposes are excluded. Credit extended to the owner of a dwelling containing more than four units is also exempt.

The key to understanding Truth-in-Lending is *meaningful disclosure*. Provisions of both this act and of Regulation Z, the Federal Reserve Board's interpretations of the act, require that borrowers be furnished with the facts they need to make intelligent decisions on the use of credit. To accomplish this, information must be presented using terminology specified in the act and Regulation Z. This information must be clear, conspicuous and in writing. Generally, the information must cover all costs of credit, including in most cases the finance charge and the annual percentage rate.

◆ **Finance Charge.** **Dollars-and-cents total of all charges a borrower must pay, directly or indirectly, for obtaining credit.**

Prior to Truth-in-Lending, some lenders presented credit to borrowers in a manner that concealed or even misrepresented costs. Although institutions furnishing real estate credit were not generally as flagrant in this practice as other suppliers of consumer credit, some confusing practices did exist in the mortgage lending market. A relatively common practice was to charge a borrower for extras, loan fees, service charges or points that were not quoted with the interest rate. The 1968 act requires lenders to disclose the dollar total of *all costs* of credit. Extra charges cannot be tallied separately if they are a cost of credit but must be included in the finance charge.

Costs that a buyer would pay regardless of whether or not credit is extended need not be included in the finance charge. Items such as title examination fees, title insurance premiums, survey costs and legal fees fit into this category. These costs must be itemized and disclosed to the borrower separately if included in the total financed. One exception is a first purchase-money mortgage on residential property, for which the mortgagee is not required to state the total dollar finance charge.

◆ **Annual Percentage Rate. The relationship between the total finance charge and the amount to be financed in annual percentage terms.**

Disclosure of the annual percentage rate (APR) allows consumers to compare finance charges on a comparable basis, making the cost of credit more understandable. Based on a time period of a year, the APR is similar to simple annual interest, a concept with which many consumers are expected to be familiar.

Credit Advertising. Regulation Z defines *credit advertising* broadly. The definition covers commercial messages that either directly or indirectly promote a credit transaction. Thus, developers or real estate brokers are subject to the act if their advertisement includes terms to be granted by a creditor. Although the definition of *advertising* includes oral as well as written communication, it does not encompass a broker or developer responding to a buyer's questions about available credit.

Equal Credit Opportunity Act

◆ **Federal statute making it unlawful for any creditor to discriminate against an applicant regarding any aspect of a credit transaction on the basis of race, color, religion, national origin, sex, marital status, age or receipt of public assistance.**

The Equal Credit Opportunity Act (ECOA) prohibits a lender from refusing credit to an individual on the basis of sex, marital status or other classification protected by the act. The act also limits the type of information that can be asked for on credit applications and requires the creditor to notify the applicant within 30 days of action that has been taken. If credit is refused, the creditor must furnish the reason if requested to do so by the applicant.

The purpose of ECOA is to ensure that a person who applies for credit will be considered on the basis of ability to pay. Although the act applies primarily to consumer credit, business credit, when not excluded by action of the Federal Reserve Board, is also covered.

Under ECOA, creditors may ask questions about a person's spouse, marital status or age, but use of this information is permitted only for the purpose of determining creditworthiness. For example, a borrower applying for a joint account might be asked about his or her marital status if the spouse is to be permitted to use the account or the borrower is relying upon alimony, child support or separate maintenance payments to repay the credit. Information about age may be used to evaluate a borrower's length of employment or length of residence.

Creditors may not ask questions about a person's sex, race, color, religion or national origin, except in the case of a home mortgage; creditors are allowed to collect this information to show that they are complying with the law. The borrower does not have to supply answers, and failure to do so will not affect the credit application. Although a borrower can be asked to select a title such as *Ms., Miss, Mr.,* or *Mrs.,* the application must first indicate that this is optional.

An individual who is denied credit and can establish that the creditor has violated the Equal Credit Opportunity Act may recover his or her actual damages plus punitive damages up to $10,000. The plaintiff who brings a successful action under ECOA is also entitled to reimbursement for court costs and reasonable attorney fees.

FINANCIAL INSTITUTIONS REFORM, RECOVERY AND ENFORCEMENT ACT

The Financial Institutions Reform, Recovery and Enforcement Act (FIRREA) affects several aspects of residential mortgage financing. FIRREA strengthened the Home Mortgage Disclosure Act of 1975 (HMDA) and the Community Reinvestment Act of 1977. Both of these acts emphasized the economic responsibility of lending institutions to their communities. This responsibility exists as lending institutions are granted franchises to accept deposits from the community.

The HMDA requires lending institutions to disclose the geographic pattern of its lending practices. Disclosure is accomplished by requiring the lender to publicly report by census tract the locality of its residential mortgage loans. Any institutional redlining practices will be apparent from this disclosure. As a result, federal and state officials should be able to more effectively enforce equal credit opportunity statutes. Additionally, public pressure can be brought against institutions where reported data indicate redlining.

FIRREA expanded the types of institutions subject to the HMDA. Prior to FIRREA, HMDA applied only to depository institutions. Now nondepository institutions such as mortgage banks must report as well. Additionally, as a result of FIRREA, institutions required to report must report on all loan applications, not just those that closed.

FIRREA also strengthened the Community Reinvestment Act (CRA). When evaluating applications for mergers or new deposit facilities, CRA requires federal agencies to consider a lender's record in meeting the credit needs of the community. As a result of FIRREA, these evaluations must be made public. This public disclosure increases the effectiveness of community pressure designed to induce lender compliance with CRA's objectives.

SALE OF MORTGAGED REAL ESTATE

CASE EXAMPLE

Hal Zenick owned a home encumbered with an $85,000 mortgage at 9 percent interest. The mortgage was held by the Harper Hill Savings and Loan Association (Harper Hill). Hal, who had purchased the property for $98,000, had lived there for about a year when he was transferred and forced to sell. During the year, interest rates had risen considerably in Hal's area, and the broker with whom he listed the property suggested that Hal might sell his home more quickly and for a better price if the mortgage were retained. The buyer would not have to finance at the higher interest rates and might save in other ways.

Whether Hal lives in a title or a lien theory state, he has an interest in the property that he can sell. He cannot, however, escape personal liability for the mortgage debt unless Harper Hill, the mortgagee, releases him. In addition, the property remains subject to Harper Hill's lien. Nothing that Hal can do short of paying the underlying debt can eliminate the lien so long as the mortgage is recorded properly. Hal's right to sell his interest without discharging the mortgage may be restricted by a clause in the mortgage instrument, referred to as a *due-on-sale clause.*

DUE-ON-SALE CLAUSE

◆ **A provision found in some mortgages requiring the mortgagor to pay off the mortgage debt if the property is sold.**

A due-on-sale clause limits the mortgagor's right to convey the real property without discharging the mortgage. The clause treats the sale of mortgaged premises as a default; since almost all mortgages also contain a clause making the entire debt due upon default, the mortgagee may call the loan when the mortgagor sells the property. Of course a mortgagee such as Harper Hill can negotiate a modification of the debt with the mortgagor and the grantee and not call the mortgage. In Hal's case, Harper Hill might do this if the grantee were willing to pay interest at a rate that was closer to that the association was obtaining on new loans.

If Hal's mortgage does not contain a due-on-sale clause, two major approaches exist to the manner in which he may sell the property without discharging the mortgage. The property may be sold with the grantee agreeing to "assume and pay" the mortgage, or the property may be sold "subject to" the mortgage.

ASSUMPTION

◆ **A contract between a grantor-mortgagor and a grantee in which the grantee agrees to assume responsibility for the mortgage debt.**

Assume that Hal's broker found a buyer who was willing to pay $100,000 for Hal's residence. The buyer had $15,000 in cash and was anxious to assume the mortgage. The purchase offer that the buyer submitted to Hal contained the following provision: "Buyer assumes and agrees to pay the obligation secured by mortgage to Harper Hill Savings and Loan Association recorded in ____ according to the terms of the mortgage and the note accompanying it." When Hal accepted this purchase offer, a contract was created, one provision of which was the buyer's promise to pay the mortgage debt. This is a typical assumption agreement. Ordinarily, agreements of this nature originate in the contract of sale, but they may be made in a separate instrument.

In some states, an oral assumption, if provable, is binding, although certainly oral assumptions are not a preferred practice, and several states by specific statute require assumption to be in writing. In many cases the deed also contains an assumption clause. This binds the grantee upon acceptance of the deed even when only the grantor signs the instrument.

The assumption agreement does not relieve the mortgagor/grantor of personal liability for the debt. Hal continues to be responsible to Harper Hill, but he has acquired the right to sue the buyer if the debt is not paid. This right is based on the contract between them in which the buyer has assumed the debt. As the buyer is assuming to pay the mortgage loan, if the buyer and Harper Hill Savings modify the terms of the loan, Hal is released from liability for the debt.

Implicit in the assumption agreement is the buyer's commitment that the seller may look to the land for reimbursement if forced to pay the debt. For Hal, additional monetary responsibility exists only if the land becomes less valuable than the debt.

The land, however, remains subject to the mortgage, and if the debt is not paid, the mortgagee may foreclose. In addition, the mortgagee without foreclosing may sue the buyer on the assumption. The mortgagee's right exists in spite of the fact that it was not a party to the assumption agreement.

NOVATION

◆ **A mutual agreement in which a creditor agrees to discharge an existing debt and to substitute a new obligation and a new debtor in its place.**

A novation differs from an assumption to which the mortgagee has consented (see page 434). In the assumption, the original mortgagor has a secondary liability even after the property is sold. In a novation, the original mortgagor is discharged and the old debt is extinguished. Few mortgagees will consent to a novation during periods of increasing interest rates unless the new debtor agrees to pay interest at the prevailing rate.

"SUBJECT TO"

◆ **Refers to a sale in which buyer agrees to purchase property subject to the lien of the mortgage.**

Assumption

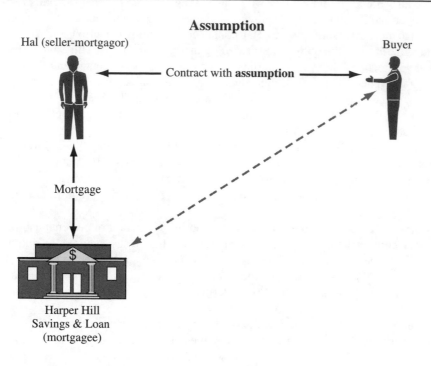

Novation

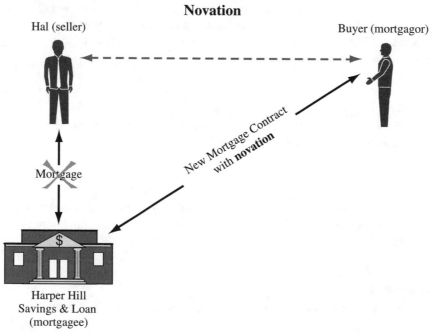

Perhaps the buyer found by Hal's broker would not be willing to assume the mortgage debt. Under these circumstances, the buyer would pay Hal for his equity in the property. Any interest acquired by the buyer is subject to the lien of the mortgage. If there is a default, the property will be foreclosed, but the buyer has not agreed to become personally liable.

As noted, if a buyer takes property subject to the mortgage, he or she has no personal obligation. Both the mortgagee and the seller/mortgagor must look to the land to collect the debt in the event of default. If proceeds from a foreclosure are not sufficient, the deficiency is the seller/mortgagor's responsibility. A number of states have, however, extended the buyer's responsibility with the doctrine of implied assumption. In these states, the buyer is personally liable even when no promise to assume exists, when the amount of an existing mortgage is deducted from the purchase price and the buyer pays the difference.

CASE EXAMPLE

Metcalf contracted to sell property to Lay for $29,000. The property was encumbered with a $20,000 mortgage. The contract did not mention the existing mortgage because Lay anticipated financing without it. This financing did not materialize, and the salesperson for the seller suggested that Lay merely purchase the equity. Lay agreed. Lay never talked with the seller, and no express assumption was discussed. At the closing, the price of the property was clearly shown as $29,000 with a $20,000 credit for the mortgage. The deed to Lay excepted the existing mortgage. When the debt was not paid, the mortgagee foreclosed. Not realizing enough from the sale to pay the debt, the mortgagee sued Metcalf, who in turn sued Lay. Lay would be held personally responsible although he had not assumed the mortgage if the court applied the doctrine of *implied assumption*.

ASSIGNMENT

◆ **The present transfer of a property right from one person (the assignor) to another (the assignee).**

One of the chief incidents of ownership is the right to assign, or to transfer to another, that which is owned. This principle applies to intangible as well as tangible property.

CASE EXAMPLE

South Central Savings financed the purchase of a residence for Marlene Jefferson. As a part of the transaction, Jefferson executed the customary note and mortgage in favor of South Central. South Central wished to obtain additional funds for lending and assigned the mortgage and note as part of a package to the Britan Insurance Company. The company discounted the notes and paid funds to South Central. Jefferson would be obligated to pay the insurance company because it now owned her obligation to South Central Savings.

The example illustrates a common situation in which mortgages and notes are assigned. South Central is the *assignor,* and Britan Insurance Company is the *assignee.* The mortgagor, Marlene Jefferson, is referred to as the *obligor.*

Understanding the mechanics of mortgage assignment is complicated by the dual nature of the mortgage transaction. Remember that a mortgage loan includes both a note, which is the borrower's personal promise to pay, and the mortgage, which is security for the debt. An assignment that is properly drafted transfers ownership of both the note and the mortgage. The assignee becomes the owner of both the obligation and the security.

DISCHARGE

◆ **A statement releasing property from the lien of the mortgage.**

Mortgages are commonly discharged by one of four methods: merger, release, running of the statute of limitations or payment of the mortgage debt.

Merger is a combination of the interest of the mortgagor and the mortgagee in the same person. It ordinarily occurs when for some reason or other the mortgagor conveys title to the mortgaged land to the mortgagee. Although a mortgage usually formally releases the land when the debt is paid, a mortgage may be released either in whole or in part under other circumstances.

A blanket mortgage often contains a partial *release* provision. A provision of this nature is necessary when a mortgage covers a large tract of land that is to be divided and developed. In order to obtain financing to build or sell residences on the smaller tracts, the developer must be able to release them from the lien of the blanket mortgage.

Statutes of limitations that apply to enforcement of mortgage liens vary widely from state to state. The application of the statute of limitations to bar foreclosure actions is further complicated by the dual nature of the mortgage transaction. In general, states have adopted shorter limitation periods for debts evidenced by a note than they have for enforcement of a mortgage. This creates a problem when collection of the note is barred by a statute of limitations but the statutory period for a foreclosure action has not yet expired.

CASE EXAMPLE

On July 29, 1959, Carl Lundberg executed a promissory note payable on demand to M. E. Tegels. The note, which was secured by a second mortgage, was for $9,100, with interest at 6 percent. Lundberg never paid any amount on the principal or the interest. No action was taken on the note, and by the time of Tegels's death payment was barred by the statute of limitations.

In 1971, Northwestern National Bank, trustees under Tegels's will, attempted to foreclose on the property. At this time Lundberg contended that the running of the statute of limitations on the note was a bar to the foreclosure action. Both the lower court and the Supreme Court of Minnesota disagreed. *Lundberg v. Northwestern National Bank, 299 Minn. 46, 216 N.W.2d 121 (1974).*

Courts in a number of states have ruled that, if collection of a debt is barred by the statute of limitations, the mortgage can no longer be foreclosed.

The period established by statutes of limitations is effectively extended by various actions taken by the mortgagor or mortgagee. A mortgagor's part payment of the debt or new promise to pay starts the statute anew. His or her absence from the jurisdiction discontinues or, in legal terms, *tolls* the statute for the duration of the absence. The mortgagee may also toll the statute through a promise to extend the time for payment. As a result, the fact that a mortgage is old is not a reliable guide to its enforceability. Because of this, several states have adopted statutes that void a mortgage a specified period of time after maturity, usually 20 years. In addition, marketable title acts discussed earlier provide for the elimination of stale mortgages unless some notice of claim is filed.

Payment of the mortgage debt is the usual method of discharging a mortgage. Payment of the debt, however, does not clear the public record; this must be done by entering in the record an instrument releasing the mortgage. Various names are given to this instrument. In some places it is known as a *satisfaction*. In other areas it is called a *discharge* or a *release*. At one time, it was a common practice merely to endorse on the margin of the recorded mortgage that it had been satisfied. A number of jurisdictions continue to follow this practice. Most states have statutes that provide for a monetary penalty if a mortgagee refuses to execute a release.

In those jurisdictions where the deed of trust is the popular form of financing instrument, the trustee who holds legal title will execute a release deed or deed of reconveyance when presented with the canceled notes indicating that the debt has been paid. Obtaining a deed of reconveyance or a satisfaction is important to the debtor. Unless these actions are taken, questions as to marketability of title may be raised.

REVIEW AND DISCUSSION QUESTIONS

1. Explain how the legal rights given to a mortgagee by a mortgage differ from the legal rights given by a note.

2. Discuss the difference between the lien and title theories of mortgages.

3. Explain the differences between a mortgage and a deed of trust.

4. Explain the rights and privileges of a mortgagee who takes possession of mortgage premises upon the mortgagor's default.

5. (a) List the three different approaches taken in the United States as to when a mechanic's lien becomes effective. (b) In your opinion which of these is the most equitable? Why?

6. What is a foreclosure by power-of-sale? How does it differ from judicial foreclosure?

7. Define the following as each is related to adjustable-rate mortgages: (a) caps (b) negative amortization.

8. The terms *finance charge* and *annual percentage rate (APR)* are important in Truth-in-Lending legislation. Explain what each means.

9. What is the basic premise underlining the Home Mortgage Disclosure Act and the Community Reinvestment Act?

10. What is a due-on-sale clause? Explain why this clause has become increasingly important in recent years.

11. Compare and contrast the rights and obligations of the grantor/mortgagor with those of a grantee assuming responsibility for the mortgage debt.

CASE PROBLEMS

1. Tom Hildebrant purchased a four-unit rental property for $175,000. River National Bank lent him $155,000 to complete the purchase. The loan was secured by a mortgage on the property. Because of a severe recession in the area caused by closing of several steel mills, Hildebrant was unable to consistently rent all of the units, and he defaulted on the debt. As a result the bank foreclosed. At the foreclosure sale, the property sold for $145,000. Does Tom have any liability on the unpaid portion of the debt? Discuss.

2. McCorriston purchased rental real estate in a lien theory state. The purchase was secured by a mortgage loan from the First Bank of Crooksville. When McCorriston defaulted, the bank attempted to collect the rents from the property to be applied against the loan. The mortgage did not contain a provision allowing it to do so. However, the bank argued that as McCorriston had defaulted, it was entitled to the rents. Was the bank correct? Support your answer.

3. Able, Baker and Charlie purchased a farm for investment. They took title as tenants in common. Part of the purchase price was secured by a purchase-money mortgage on the property. The mortgage and note were signed by Able and Baker but not Charlie. When the parties defaulted, the seller joined the three in a foreclosure action. Charlie defended on grounds that she has not signed the mortgage and note. Would she be successful? Support your answer.

4. Oellerich and his wife sold real estate that they owned. The purchasers assumed the mortgage. The assumption agreement provided that the Oellerichs were not released from liability on the original debt if the purchasers defaulted on the note. Shortly thereafter the lender and purchasers executed a modification agreement that increased the interest on the note. The Oellerichs were not parties to this agreement. Did the modification agreement affect the rights of the parties? Explain how and why. *Oellerich v. First Fed. Sav. & Loan Assn., 552 F.2d 1109 (5th Cir. 1977).*

5. Albert owns real property worth $35,000. He borrows $28,000 from Martin and executes a mortgage on the property in Martin's favor. The term of the mortgage is 15 years. Seven years later, Albert sells the property to Bobb for a cash amount with the mortgage remaining on the property. What difference, if any, will it make to Bobb if the deed from Albert states "subject to a mortgage indebtedness of _____" or "subject to a mortgage indebtedness of _____, which said indebtedness the grantee assumes and agrees to pay"?

6. Larson owned a commercial building that he had inherited from his mother. The original mortgage on the building had been satisfied. In January 1974, Larson leased a portion of the building to Hutchins for a five-year term. The lease was immediately recorded. In March 1975, Larson borrowed $75,000 from the Belville Bank, giving it a mortgage on the property. The mortgage was for a term of ten years. It was recorded on April 11, 1975. The $75,000 was used to renovate the property. In 1977, because the debt was not paid, the bank foreclosed.

(a) Kane, the purchaser at the foreclosure sale, wished to use the entire building and brought an action to eject Hutchins. Would Kane be successful? Discuss.

(b) Assume that, on March 27, Anderson began electrical work that was part of the renovation. The work was not completed until June. When Anderson was not paid, he filed a mechanic's lien. What are Anderson's rights vis-à-vis the Belville Bank? Discuss.

7. Smith agreed to purchase property from Layton. As part of the contract, Smith assumed and agreed to pay the existing mortgage. Smith immediately contracted to sell the property to Young. Layton agreed to convey directly to Young, who assumed the mortgage in the deed to him. Smith never had title to the property. The mortgage was not paid, and the foreclosure took place. There was a deficiency, and the mortgagee sued Smith. Would the mortgagee be successful? Discuss.

8. Lon Gabele is the president of Gabele Builders as well as its chief salesperson. Fredericktown Savings agrees to finance homes built by Gabele at a rate of 10½ percent if the buyer makes a $2,500 down payment. Gabele places an advertisement in the local paper indicating that homes can be purchased at $2,500 down. The only other information in the advertisement is the offering price, Gabele's name and the location of the development.

Prior to the advertisement's appearance, a number of buyers had visited the homes that Gabele had for sale. When asked about financing, Gabele informs them that it is available at 10½ percent. He provides no additional information but refers them to Fredericktown Savings. Has Gabele violated the credit advertising provisions of the Truth-in-Lending Act? Support your answer.

22

Land Installment Contracts

LAND INSTALLMENT CONTRACT

◆ **A legally enforceable agreement between buyer and seller whereby the buyer promises to make periodic installment payments to the seller toward the purchase price of real property and the seller promises to convey title to the property upon receipt of the last installment.**

Chapter 11 considered the real estate purchase agreement, the ordinary contract for the sale of real estate. This agreement defines the rights and duties of the seller and buyer in preparation for the closing of the transaction, which is discussed fully in Chapter 14. Between the signing of the purchase contract and the closing, there is a short interval ranging from about one to three months. During this interval the seller is expected to prepare an abstract or secure other evidence of title and the buyer attempts to obtain financing, typically through a lending institution.

Sometimes the buyer is unable to obtain financing from a lending institution. Lacking the necessary cash, the buyer may be forced to defer purchase until his or her financial situation improves. Several alternatives are open, however, that may enable the buyer to purchase the property. If the seller is willing to extend financing to the buyer for the purchase price, one alternative is the purchase-money mortgage, which is discussed in Chapter 21. Under that method, the seller transfers the deed to the property to the buyer and the buyer signs a mortgage in the seller's favor. The mortgage secures the remaining unpaid purchase price owed to the seller. The land installment contract, also known as a *land contract* or *contract for deed,* is another method of seller financing.

For the buyer, the land installment contract is a method of financing a real estate transaction through the seller; for the seller, it secures the payment of a debt. The rules that attach to ordinary contracts also apply to land installment contracts. The agreement must be supported by consideration and entered into by parties who possess the requisite capacity. Nevertheless, some obvious distinctions separate the land installment contract from the ordinary real estate purchase contract. In an ordinary real estate purchase contract, the buyer's right to possession is deferred until closing or thereafter. Under a land installment contract, possession is normally immediate and does not await final payment. In addition, the relationship between the parties to a real estate purchase agreement is of rather short duration, usually ceasing at the closing, when title is conveyed. The legal relationship of the parties to a land contract lasts longer. Such a contract may endure for as long as the seller is willing to extend the financing, perhaps 20 years or more, although shorter periods are more common. Often the seller extends a payment schedule based upon a 20- to 30-year payback period but requires the entire balance to be paid in full after a shorter period, for example, three to five years. The final payment is known as a *balloon payment* and normally requires the buyer to find outside financing to meet the payment. Before final payment, the seller holds legal title, whereas the purchaser is normally in possession of the property and enjoys *equitable title.*

TITLE PROBLEMS

Upon completion of all terms of the contract, including payment of the last installment, legal title passes to the buyer, and the deed can be recorded in the buyer's name. Until the last installment is paid, the property remains in the seller's name. During this interval, the seller may encumber the property with mortgages or other liens. Unless the buyer is protected, he or she may pay the entire purchase price and find the property totally encumbered. By recording the land installment contract, however, the buyer can secure protection against most future encumbrances. Recording places all prospective mortgagees and lienors on notice of the buyer's interest in the property, and title problems are less likely to arise.

If the contract is unrecorded and the seller encumbers or sells the property, the installment contract buyer may be without remedy. A claim against the seller for damages will not necessarily help the buyer should the seller be insolvent. Sellers often discourage or impede the recording, since it is easier to resell the property upon the buyer's default if the contract is not recorded. However, some states by statute require a land installment contract to be recorded.

Liens that attach before the creation of the installment contract may go unnoticed if the buyer fails to investigate the title beforehand. Title insurance protects the buyer's interest in the property. Normally this form of assurance is required when a third-party lender is involved. In land installment contracts, however, there is no third-party stimulus because the seller finances the transaction. The uneducated buyer may fail to have the title examined. The prudent buyer should require proof of title in the seller as a condition of entering into the contract, should be sure the contract is immediately recorded, and should require a clause within the contract clarifying that the seller agrees to tender a deed to the property free of all liens and other encumbrances.

AFTER ACQUIRED TITLE

In some cases, the seller does not have title at the time of entering into the contract but subsequently acquires it. In this event, the buyer is entitled to "after acquired title" when the time comes for the deed to be transferred to the buyer.

> **CASE EXAMPLE**
>
> Jim Ferguson, seller, enters into a land installment contract with Bill Hodd, buyer, whereby Ferguson is to tender a free and unencumbered deed to 20 acres of farmland designated as the Hill property, upon Hodd's completion of 60 monthly payments of $300 each. At the time the contract was entered into, Ferguson possessed only a leasehold interest. Thereafter, however, he acquired the property in fee simple absolute from the lessor. Upon completing the last installment payment, Hodd is entitled to the fee under the doctrine of after acquired title. *See Bull v. Goldman, 30 Md. App. 665, 353 A.2d 661 (1976).*

Should the buyer learn, after signing the contract, that the seller does not possess marketable title, in some jurisdictions the buyer may rescind the contract and seek return of the installment payments previously paid.

CONTRACT TERMS

Basic rules of real estate purchase contracts treated in Chapter 10 also govern land installment contracts. Since a land contract involves an interest in land, it must comply with the Statute of Frauds, which requires that the contract be supported by a written memorandum. Normally, the land installment contract must be properly executed before it can be recorded. State statutes vary and should be consulted to ascertain the particular requirements for proper execution. Ordinarily, it must be signed and witnessed and notarized.

The parties are free to agree on the terms of the land contract, and the courts will enforce those terms to the extent that they do not offend public policy. Over the years, certain typical terms have emerged. Generally, the specifics of the terms reflect the relative bargaining strength of the buyer and seller. It appears that the seller has traditionally possessed the upper hand. Nonetheless, the courts will give effect to the intent of the parties. The following case well illustrates the necessity of making that intent clear within the writing.

McKONE v. GUERTZGEN

Supreme Court of Wyoming
811 P.2d 728 (Wyo. 1991)

BACKGROUND. McKone sold his land to the Guertzgens under an installment contract. The contract provided that the Guertzgens would have possession of the property, but that the deed would not pass until all payments had been made under the contract.

The Guertzgens converted the property from a service station into a liquor store/lounge. The Chief of the town's fire department ordered the removal of the underground fuel tanks because they violated the fire code. Each party argued that it was the responsibility of the other to undertake the expense of removal.

The purchaser brought an action against McKone, the vendor, seeking to hold him liable for the removal. The trial court judge found the vendor responsible. The vendor appealed.

DECISION. The trial court decision is affirmed.

JUSTICE CARDINE. . . . [W]e acknowledged that the purchaser under a contract for deed has an "equitable interest" in the property. Thus, we agree that the Guertzgens fit the Code's definition of owner because their equitable interest in the property is also a contingent interest, which the Code includes under the definition of owner. The parties' agreement provides that the warranty deed remains in escrow until the Guertzgens have made all the payments under the agreement and the warranty deed is conveyed to them.

Professor Rudolph has summarized the legal principles of the contract for deed:

> The contract [for deed] typically provides for the payment of the purchase price in installments over a period of years and

for retention of title in the seller until the purchase price is fully paid, but gives the buyer a right to possession from the execution of the contract.

. . . Until there has been a conveyance of the warranty deed, McKone continues to hold legal title and remains the legal owner of the property.

. . . [W]e hold that McKone is the party responsible for the removal of the tanks because he was the owner of the property when they were abandoned.

AFFIRMED.

CHIEF JUSTICE URBIGKIT DISSENTING. When . . . McKone entered into a transaction with . . . [the Guertzgens] to sell a business lot . . . none of them expected that abandoned underground petroleum tanks would come back to haunt both the seller and buyers. Events change rapidly in this society in which we live and society came back to them to look with disdain, suspicion and active antagonism upon the abandoned underground petroleum product storage tanks.

The buyers bought the property "as is, where is." Unfortunately, in acceptance of an invalid legend of the advantages of the escrow deed arrangement for installment contract for sale . . . the parties were faced with events occurring since sale which have severely impacted the property's value—abandoned underground petroleum product storage tanks.

The buyers paid promptly and properly on the installment contract for about eight years until notice by the fire marshal of current law changes and regulations regarding abandoned underground petroleum product storage tanks....

We are now faced ... with society's imposition of an expensive cost upon the landowner and are asked who is to pay—the seller or the buyers? I would really like to believe that some part of the responsibility should be placed upon whoever advised these parties to use the installment sale technique ... instead of a note and mortgage, but those other parties are not here before us. We have a seller, buyers and an imposed cost by the government.

For this case I would hold that the buyers, by their agreement, bought problems of future governmental action with land purchased in specific accord with the "as is, where is," provisions of the written agreement. I would reverse the district court's judgment.... Further, I would determine that the unknown and unforeseen go with the risk of purchase and do not remain with the equity of retained sale price obligation. The owner of the premises should be the possessor with rights to the property, not the holder of a security device for purchase payment.

JUSTICE GOLDEN DISSENTING. I respectfully dissent. When resolving this sort of dispute this court looks first to the parties' agreement. If the writing was unambiguous it expresses and controls the parties' assignment of rights and obligations. I believe we need go no farther than the language of the written agreement to decide this case.

The majority applies this principle, but finds the provisions asserted by McKone do not address this particular contingency, and looks beyond the agreement language to determine liability for the cost of removing the abandoned tanks. In his dissent Chief Justice Urbigkit also looks to the agreement and resolves the issue to his satisfaction by applying "as is, where is" provisions of the written agreement.

I agree with the majority that the provisions McKone relies on do not allocate the burden of removal costs, but do note they evidence the intent of the parties that the Guertzgens would shoulder all responsibilities connected with the property when they assumed possession. I cannot identify an "as is, where is," provision, but I find that another agreement term does assign responsibility for removing the tanks in a manner consistent with the delegations in the provisions offered by McKone....

We are not concerned here so much with allocation of risk of loss as we are with determination of which party is responsible for compliance with laws. The agreement assigns this responsibility to the Guertzgens where it states that buyer agrees to purchase and take property

SUBJECT TO easements, reservations and restrictions of record and to Zoning *and other laws.*

Price. Normally the buyer pays a modest down payment and periodic installments. The installment payments include principal and interest. The installments may be payable monthly, quarterly, annually or at any other agreed-upon interval. Unless otherwise stated, taxes and insurance are the seller's responsibility because the seller is the legal owner of the property until the entire purchase price is paid. Neither statute nor custom prevents an allocation of taxes and insurance to the parties on the basis of their respective interests in the property. In most cases, however, the bargaining position of the seller is strong enough to require the buyer to assume the whole burden of these charges. This is not an unreasonable burden, considering that the buyer receives the present beneficial use of the property and expects full ownership in the future.

Waste, Removal and Inspection. The buyer is normally in possession of the premises in an installment contract. Consequently, the installment buyer is in the best position to maintain the premises and keep it in good repair. Customarily, the parties include a clause in the contract that makes the buyer responsible for the maintenance. Similarly, the installment contract may include a clause prohibiting waste or removal of fixtures or improvements without the consent of the seller. Failure of a buyer to comply with these clauses is a breach of the contract that gives rise to various remedies discussed later in this chapter.

The seller needs the right to inspect the premises in order to police these provisions. For that reason a clause similar to the following is often included: "Seller shall have the right to enter on and inspect the property and the buildings and improvements thereon after giving reasonable notice to do so."

◆ **Indemnification.** **The act of compensating another in the event of loss.**

In the event that the buyer fails to keep the property in repair or causes waste, damages may result from either loss of property value or consequent injury to occupiers of the property. Mechanics' liens (discussed in Chapter 16) may also encumber the property if the purchaser fails to pay the workers or suppliers for renovations, repairs, improvements or other authorized work. An indemnification clause such as the following may be included for the seller's protection:

> Buyer shall hold seller free and harmless from any and all demands, loss, or liability resulting from the injury to, or death of, any person because of the negligence of the buyer or the condition of the property at any time after the date possession is delivered to the buyer. Buyer shall further indemnify seller for the amount of any and all mechanics' liens or other expenses or damages resulting from any renovations, alterations, building repairs, or other work ordered by the buyer.

Should the buyer fail to pay the tax assessments or insurance as agreed upon, the seller's security is jeopardized. The government, deprived of its taxes or assessments, may place a tax lien on the property and even foreclose for failure to pay. The seller's security would also be jeopardized should the property be destroyed by fire unless hazard insurance is maintained. If there is a mortgage on the property, the mortgagee may foreclose in the event taxes, assessments and/or insurance payments are in arrears. To protect the seller against these risks, a clause such as the following may be included within the installment contract:

> Should buyer fail to pay any amount pursuant to this contract for taxes, assessments, or insurance within ten (10) days before that amount becomes delinquent, the seller may pay the amount and buyer agrees to repay to seller the amount paid by the seller together with interest at the rate of ten (10) percent per annum.

Assignment. In the absence of a provision in the contract prohibiting assignment, the buyer is free to transfer his or her interest in the land contract. Assignment does not, however, relieve the installment buyer of the obligation to continue making installment payments to the seller. The seller may desire to limit the buyer's right of assignment, being concerned that the assignee (one to whom the property is transferred) may be more likely to jeopardize the seller's interest in the property than the installment buyer. For this reason, the installment contract normally includes a provision prohibiting assignment without the seller's written consent. In absence of such a clause, the buyer may assign the contract, and the seller must respect that assignment.

CASE EXAMPLE

Wayne and Lucille Hickox entered into a written agreement for the sale and purchase of 864 acres of real estate with Barbara and Billy Bell. The purchase price was $700,000, payable $50,000 as a down payment and the remainder in installments, with the first five years' interest payments only. Under the contract, the purchasers had the option, as payments were made, to have the sellers sign a warranty deed in favor of buyers to such land as paid for based on $815 per acre. The Bells faithfully made payments the first four years and then assigned the contract to the Hesses, who made payments thereafter. The Bells requested that the Hickoxes execute a warranty deed conveying 83.67 acres based on the amount of principal paid to date. The Hickoxes refused to credit any amount of the payments made by the Hesses because it was not paid by the Bells.

Finding in favor of the Bells, the Illinois Appellate court said:

> [W]hen a valid assignment is executed, the assignee (1) acquires all of the interest of the assignor in the property that is transferred and (2) stands in the shoes of the assignor. . . . [We] find that the money paid by the Hesses under the contract is to be credited to the Bells as payment under the contract.

See *Hickox v. Bell*, 195 Ill. App. 3d 976, 55 2 N.E. 2d 1133 (1990).

At any time before title passes, the seller is free to transfer the property to someone other than the installment buyer. Installment payments are then directed to the new owner. The sale is subject to the rights of the installment buyer, who still remains entitled to the property upon fulfillment of the terms of the installment contract. The seller's power to assign may be limited by agreement, but normally is not because of the purchaser's weaker bargaining position.

Mortgage. Mortgages are discussed in detail in Chapter 21. A typical clause regarding the seller's right to mortgage the property, pending the full payment of the purchase price, is often included within the land contract. A clause similar to the following is not uncommon: "The seller may mortgage the property, but in no event may such mortgage exceed the amount of the balance due on the contract."

> **CASE EXAMPLE**
>
> Norma Livingston sells real property to Howard Kessler on a land installment contract for $120,000, payable $20,000 down and $5,000 annually thereafter at 10 percent interest for 20 years. After five years, Livingston desires to borrow money and gives a mortgage in the property to the Second National Bank as security for the loan. Livingston may mortgage the property up to $75,000, the balance due on the installment contract.

In addition, the buyer may be contractually safeguarded against the consequences of a seller defaulting on a mortgage by inclusion of a clause similar to the following:

The seller shall keep any mortgage on the property in good standing, and if the seller defaults on any mortgage, seller agrees that the buyer may pay the delinquency and receive credit toward payment due under the terms of the contract.

An installment buyer who desires to borrow money from a bank or other lending institution may use as collateral the realty that is the subject of the land contract. Unless the contract expressly states otherwise, the buyer is entitled to mortgage the property to the extent that its value exceeds the amount owed on the land installment contract. A provision in the contract prohibiting assignment does not prevent the installment buyer from mortgaging his or her interest.

> **CASE EXAMPLE**
>
> Jaurel and Edna Fincher entered into a land contract whereby Lester Stacey and his wife agreed to purchase a one-half acre tract of land from the Finchers. The purchase price was $1,200, payable $200 down with the remainder payable in installments of $47.50 per month. Paragraph seven of the contract provided that the "Buyers may not assign their rights hereunder in whole or in part." Later the Staceys entered into an agreement with Miles Homes to purchase a precut home for erection on the tract for $6,378. The Staceys made a down payment and signed a promissory note for the balance due. The note was secured by a mortgage on the tract of land purchased. Miles Homes delivered the materials to the site in accord with the contract. The Staceys made payments to the Finchers but defaulted after the death of Mrs. Stacey. Similarly, the Staceys defaulted on their obligation to pay Miles Homes. The Finchers canceled the contract (with the consent of Mr. Stacey), reacquired possession of the land and sought a judicial order determining that the Miles Homes' lien was invalid. The court concluded that the prohibition against assignment did not prohibit the Staceys from entering into a valid mortgage and that the Finchers owned the property subject to the Miles Homes' lien. *Fincher v. Miles Homes, 549 S.W.2d 848 (Mo. 1977).*

If the buyer mortgages the property and then defaults on obligations under the land installment contract, a serious question arises concerning the mortgagee's rights. The seller must notify the mortgagee of the default before taking any action regarding the property. In some jurisdictions, the mortgagee is entitled to acquire title to the property by paying the seller the amount due under the installment contract. In this circumstance, the mortgagee may receive more value than the balance due on the mortgage loan. Other jurisdictions limit the mortgagee's recovery to the amount of the mortgagor's indebtedness due by requiring the mortgagee to invoke foreclosure, as discussed in Chapter 21. Under such an action the property is sold. The land installment seller is paid first from the proceeds an amount necessary to satisfy the amount due on the land contract. The remaining proceeds are used to satisfy the mortgagee's indebtedness, and the installment buyer receives the balance of any remaining monies. In a few states, the mortgagee is obligated to pay the balance of the indebtedness owed to the seller before the foreclosure sale.

CASE EXAMPLE

Toble sold Randomacre to Hillside on land contract. Hillside mortgaged the property, and when he defaulted, he owed $40,000 on the land contract and $20,000 on the mortgage. The property was foreclosed and sold at public auction for $70,000. The proceeds were distributed as follows:

Tobler:	$40,000
Mortgagee:	20,000
Hillside:	10,000
Total	$70,000

Conveyance. The buyer's ultimate objective is to receive good title to the property. Upon performance of the contractual obligations, including payment of the last installment, the seller is obligated to give a good title to the property by conveying the deed to the buyer. This requirement is normally reflected in a clause that reads as follows:

> When the buyer has paid the full purchase price with interest due and in the manner required by the terms and conditions of this contract; and, if the buyer performs all other provisions required of the buyer by the terms and conditions of this contract, seller agrees to convey the above described property to the buyer by deed of general warranty, with release of dower, if any.

ADVANTAGES TO THE BUYER

Most purchasers are not financially able to raise the entire purchase price in one lump sum; consequently, they must obtain financing in order to purchase the realty. A buyer, however, may not be able to secure financing from a lending institution because of an inability to meet down payment requirements or because of an unsatisfactory credit rating; or the lender may refuse to extend credit because of the marginal value of the property.

The principal advantage that the installment contract offers to buyers is the ability to purchase the property. For little or no down payment, buyers are able to gain an interest in, and derive the benefit of, the property. The land installment contract increased in popularity as a financing tool in the early 1980s, when high interest rates decreased the borrowing power of many people. Its usage continued even in the face of declining interest rates.

ADVANTAGES TO THE SELLER

The land installment contract may also benefit the seller. Such benefits may include attraction of buyers, tax advantages and continued incidents of legal ownership.

Attract Buyers. The main advantage to sellers is that the land installment contract provides a means for increasing the demand for property by attracting buyers who could otherwise not purchase the property because of an inability to secure outside financing. The ability to set the schedule of repayment so that it is affordable to the buyer often places the seller in a position to increase the purchase price above the market level and/or charge a higher interest rate than the seller is paying on the mortgage. Normally, however, the property is priced in accordance with the market. The attractive terms often permit the sale of otherwise unattractive property.

Tax Break. Under an installment contract, the seller does not receive the entire purchase price in one lump sum. Payments ate extended over a period of years. Under an Internal Revenue Code section, a seller may elect to partially defer tax treatment for gains in an installment sale transaction. A taxpayer who elects the installment method of reporting need only report as income, in a given year, the proportion of the installment payments that the gross profit bears to the total contract price. Consequently, income is spread over a period of time. As a result, the seller may defer taxable income to a future time when overall income may be less. The seller consequently receives a welcome tax break.

CASE EXAMPLE

Barry Martin sells property to Sheila Cable for $100,000, payable $25,000 down with the remainder to be paid over 15 years at $5,000 a year. Martin had previously purchased the property for $75,000. His gross profit is $25,000 ($100,000 contract price – $75,000 original purchase price). Cable pays the $25,000 down payment. The proportion of the gross profit to the total contract price is 25 percent (25,000/100,000 = 25%). Martin, by electing the installment method, need report as income in the year of sale only $6,250 (25 percent of $25,000 down payment) and $1,250 in each succeeding year (25 percent of $5,000).

Incidents of Legal Ownership. The land installment contract secures the payment of the buyer's indebtedness and gives the seller certain incidents of legal ownership. As discussed earlier, the seller may assign the property subject to the contract or mortgage the property up to the indebtedness. This is attractive to a seller who may reap the benefits of incidents of ownership while involved in a sale of the property.

DISADVANTAGES TO THE BUYER

The land installment contract may present certain disadvantages to the buyer. These disadvantages may arise should the seller die, fail to transfer good title or neglect to record the contract.

Problems Created by the Death of the Seller. Although the land contract is enforceable against the seller's heirs upon death, as a practical matter enforcement may be very costly. The buyer may be forced to hire an attorney to accomplish the transfer. The beneficiaries may be difficult to locate, and the property may be tied up in probate for years. Should there be a large number of beneficiaries, the situation becomes more laden with concurrent ownership interests and difficulties. Since minor and incompetent beneficiaries may require the appointment of a guardian, resolution may be even further complicated and delayed. Similar problems are present when the seller assigns the installment contract to another who dies.

Unwillingness or Inability to Transfer Good Title. The seller might refuse to transfer the title to the buyer after fulfillment of the contract. The buyer, who is legally entitled to the deed, may be forced to institute suit seeking specific performance. Even worse, after the buyer pays the installments in conformity with the contract, the seller may not have good title. Normally, the seller has agreed to convey title to the buyer upon receiving the final payment. By prevailing authority, the seller is not required to maintain marketable title during the pendency of the contract, although a few courts have taken a contrary view. The buyer could obtain protection by insisting upon a contract provision requiring the seller to maintain marketable title or by obtaining title insurance.

Failure To Record. As stated earlier, the installment contract should be recorded to protect the buyer's interest. Sellers may try to discourage buyers from recording because in the event of default less difficulty attends to quieting title in their name if there has been no recording. In fact, some contracts may contain *in terrorem* clauses that prohibit recording at the expense of forfeiture. Although their validity is dubious, they undoubtedly discourage some buyers from recording. Some states by statute require the installment contract to be recorded and provide penalties for failure to do so, such as rescission of the contract.

   If the installment contract is recorded, the majority of states give the buyer's contract priority over most subsequent purchasers and lienors since they are on constructive notice of the buyer's interest. Further, the land installment buyer usually has priority over subsequent purchasers and lienors who have knowledge of the buyer's interest, even if the contract is unrecorded. In many jurisdictions the fact that the buyer is in possession gives subsequent purchasers constructive knowledge of the buyer's interest, even if the contract is not publicly recorded.

DISADVANTAGES TO THE SELLER

From the seller's viewpoint, the land installment contract is often a compromise sometimes negotiated as a result of an inability to sell the property for cash. Two reasons may exist for this inability. High market interest rates may make it impractical for purchasers to obtain conventional financing, or the purchaser's financial status may prevent him or her from obtaining a loan from a lending institution. Because the land contract often attracts buyers who are otherwise not able to purchase the property because of their financial status, risk of default is high. Default may result in the buyer's forfeiture of all rights in the property. The buyer's interest may revert to the seller, in which case the seller is burdened with the property once again and must reenter the real estate market, necessitating additional brokerage costs and perhaps attorney fees. In some jurisdictions, forfeiture is not an available remedy. Instead, judicial foreclosure of the property is necessary to cut off the buyer's interest. The cost of foreclosure makes it a burdensome remedy for the seller.

SELLER'S REMEDIES

A seller possesses several remedies against a buyer who fails to pay or who otherwise defaults under the terms of the installment contract, including specific performance of the contract, damages, rescission, forfeiture and foreclosure. These remedies were covered generally in Chapter 12. Forfeiture and foreclosure remedies, however, deserve special attention as seller's remedies under the land installment contract.

Forfeiture. Often included within the terms of a land contract is a forfeiture clause, which provides that in the event the buyer fails to abide by the terms of the contract, the seller has the right to terminate the contract, retake possession of the property and retain all prior payments. Traditionally, these forfeiture clauses have been upheld by the courts. When enforced, the defaulting buyer loses all equity in the property, and the seller often receives a substantial windfall. The forfeiture penalty may be very severe to a defaulting buyer.

CASE EXAMPLE

In 1971 Sellmer, the seller, entered into an installment sale contract with Donaldson, the buyer, for the purchase of a summer cottage on the Ohio River. The purchase price was $16,500 at the rate of 8 percent per annum for ten years. The contract called for a $2,000 down payment, and the monthly payments were $175. Donaldson, on several occasions, failed to make timely payments and failed to make three monthly installments in 1973. Donaldson failed to keep the property insured, contrary to a provision in the installment contract to do so. Additionally, Donaldson failed to keep the property in repair and left the property in an uninhabitable condition. Sellmer sued Donaldson, seeking a forfeiture and termination of the contract. The court held that because "Donaldson had wholly failed to perform his obligation to acquire adequate insurance and had allowed the property to deteriorate to such an extent that substantial repair was necessary before the house would even be habitable," forfeiture was a proper remedy. Consequently, the court ordered that more than $7,000 in payments made by Donaldson be forfeited to Sellmer and that the contract be terminated. *Donaldson v. Sellmer, 166 Ind. App. 60, 333 N.E. 2d 862 (1975).*

Most states have departed from automatic approval of the forfeiture remedy, and all states have mitigated its harshness by statute or judicial decision. Some states require a "grace period," within which the buyer may cure any breach. In those jurisdictions forfeiture is permitted only after compliance with procedural technicalities. The seller must notify the buyer of the intention to invoke forfeiture and of the grace period. If the buyer fails to correct the default within the specified period the statute permits, forfeiture is proper. The lengths of these grace periods vary from 30 days to a year. Some states graduate the grace period dependent upon the portion of the contract price the buyer has paid. In the event the seller affords the requisite statutory notice and there is no response by the buyer to cure the defect, some states permit forfeiture without judicial proceedings. Others require court action.

Another state statute eliminates forfeiture altogether by providing that the seller of a land installment contract shall be deemed to be a mortgagee and shall be subject to the same rules of foreclosure and to the same regulations, restraints and forms as are prescribed in relation to mortgages. Still, another statutory approach softening the hardship of forfeiture is the elimination of forfeiture as a remedy under certain conditions. This type of statute is the subject of the next case.

SMITH V. BLACKBURN
Ohio Court of Appeals
511 N.E. 132 (Ohio App. 1987)

BACKGROUND. Doris Blackburn entered into a land installment contract with the Smiths. After several late payments by Blackburn, the Smiths served a notice that the contract would be forfeited and thereafter instituted a suit seeking forfeiture. The trial court found in favor of Blackburn, holding that forfeiture was inappropriate.

DECISION. The court of appeals reversed the decision and remanded it to the trial court.

JUDGE GREY. The case raises an issue of statutory interpretation of [Revised Code] 5313.07. This section, simply put, says that when the vendee of a land contract has paid 20 percent of the purchase price, the vendor's remedy for default lies in foreclosure and not in forfeiture. The issue in this case is how that 20-percent figure is to be calculated.

. . .

The land contract was executed on a printed form which did not contain the words "purchase price," but Blackburn agreed to pay $20,000, with $2,000 down and $204.85 per month at 9 percent interest for 12 years. At the time of trial, it was stipulated that Blackburn had made the following payments: a down payment of $2,000; 23 monthly payments of $204.85 ($4,711.55 total) as per the contract to cover principal and interest; insurance premiums for two years of $320; and real estate taxes for 1984 and part of 1983 in the amount of $571.61.

The trial court, in determining whether the Smiths' action for forfeiture was properly brought . . . added together all the amounts paid by Blackburn, which totaled $7,603.16. The court ruled that since this amount was in excess of 20 percent of the purchase price, the Smiths had to bring an action in foreclosure and judicial sale. . . .

Blackburn asserts that she has paid $6,711.55—the cash down payment of $2,000, plus monthly payments totaling $4,711.55—which is in excess of 20 percent of $20,000, or $4,000. It must be stressed, however, that each monthly payment was to be applied under the terms of the contract, to *both* the principal amount *and* interest on the purchase price. The installment contract unambiguously describes the apportionment of each monthly payment to principal and interest. The new principal amount is calculated at the end of each month and interest on that amount is to be deducted from that month's payment. Whatever remains of the monthly payment is applied to reduce the principal amount.

...

The question is whether the statute contemplates interest payments being included in the "sum total" paid toward the purchase price. ...

Since the term "purchase price" is not defined in [the statute] its meaning may be expressly determined by the parties to the contract or by implication, *i.e.,* using the word's meaning. It is apparent from the agreement, the actions, and the briefs of both parties that the purchase price was $20,000. This figure is the basis for all other payments: the 10-percent down payment, the monthly payments on the remaining $18,000, the insurance on the property and the real estate taxes and assessments.

It was this figure which the parties agree to as the value of the premises in paragraph one, page two of the land installment contract.

Thus, with $20,000 being the "purchase price" pursuant to [the statute], the amounts paid toward it are to be determined in accordance with the terms of the contract. Under the agreement, only a portion of each payment is to be applied toward the principal amount of the "loan," the balance of the purchase price. Under Blackburn's formulation, "purchase price" would include all payments, interest as well as principal. We reject this formulation. The interest was agreed to, but as *interest* on the remaining balance of $18,000, not as a part of the purchase price. ...

The judgment of the [trial court] is reversed and the cause is remanded to that court with instructions to calculate 20 percent of the purchase price in accordance with this opinion. This court is aware that additional payments may have been made by the vendee during the pendency of this appeal and that these payments may have increased the total amount paid by the vendee to a sum that is in excess of 20 percent of the purchase price. In light of that possibility . . . we direct the [trial court] on remand to include in its calculations all payments made by the vendee during the pendency of this action.

JUDGMENT REVERSED AND THE CASE REMANDED.

Even when there is no statutory modification, courts are reluctant to uphold a forfeiture clause and often employ various rationales to relieve the defaulting buyer from a harsh result. If, for example, a seller consistently accepts late payments from the buyer and thereafter seeks forfeiture for delinquent payment, a court may hold that the seller has waived any rights under the contract for forfeiture by failing previously to object to delinquent payment. Other jurisdictions analogize a defaulting buyer in a land installment contract to a defaulting mortgagor and recognize an "equity of redemption period." In those jurisdictions courts determine the period of grace through tests of fairness and reason.

Case Example

In April 1967, the Allens (purchasers) entered into a land installment contract with the Ulanders (sellers) for the purchase of real estate. Under the terms of the contract, the Ulanders agreed to convey the real estate to the Allens after payment of $9,700 at the rate of $85 or more per month at 7 percent interest per annum. The contract further provided for forfeiture in the event the purchasers failed to make timely payments. Over a period of 7½ years the Allens paid more than $7,500 in principal and interest and built up an equity of $1,583. They also made improvements to the property, adding two bedrooms, a bathroom and paneling. The Allens failed to make five payments in 1974 and 1975, and the Ulanders instituted an action in forfeiture. The court, applying equitable notions, allowed the purchasers 30 days to deposit with the court a sum equal to five months' payments to avoid forfeiture. The court held that "where a purchaser under an installment land contract has acquired a substantial equitable interest in the property, the court has discretion to utilize a remedy similar to that permitted in foreclosure actions." *Ulander v. Allen, 37 Colo. App. 279, 544 P. 2d 1001 (1976).*

Still other equitable rationales may be invoked to support a refusal to recognize forfeiture. Some courts hold that, if the buyer would sustain a substantial net loss as a result of forfeiture, then forfeiture would be unconscionable; in that case the buyer is entitled to restitution. Under this view, if the seller's actual damages, based upon the fair market rental value of the property and other damages, are less than the buyer's payments, the buyer would be entitled to the difference.

Case Example

Mr. and Mrs. Hoyle, under an installment contract for the purchase of a motel, make total installment payments of $120,000 on a $345,000 purchase price. Additionally, they expend $30,000 on repairs and improvements to the premises. After four years, the Hoyles default on their installment payments and vacate the premises. The reasonable rental value of the motel is $30,000 per year. Under an equitable approach, since the $150,000 expenditure on payments and improvements is substantial, the buyer is entitled to restitution in the amount of $30,000, computed as follows: Buyer's total expenditures are $150,000, consisting of payments in the amount of $120,000 and improvements in the amount of $30,000. The reasonable rental value of the property is $30,000 × 4 years (the period of time in which the Hoyles occupied the premises), or $120,000. The difference between the total payments and the reasonable rental value is $30,000 payable to the Hoyles.

Finally, some courts have struck down the forfeiture clause simply on the basis that it constitutes an unconscionable penalty.

Foreclosure. As noted, some states by statute provide for foreclosure as the proper remedy for a seller against a defaulting installment buyer. Only a few states have recognized foreclosure by judicial decision as a seller's remedy in the event of the buyer's default. Indiana is one such state. In Indiana the courts reserve the remedy of forfeiture for cases of absconding or abandoning buyers or where only a minimum amount has been paid by the buyer while the seller is making expenditures for taxes, insurance and maintenance. In all other cases in that jurisdiction and in some other jurisdictions, the courts recognize judicial foreclosure as the proper remedy.

CASE EXAMPLE

Laura Virginia, seller, and Pam Osterholtz, purchaser, entered into a land contract for Whiteacre on the following terms: $10,000 down payment and $12,000 annually for five years, for a total of $70,000. Osterholtz paid $10,000 and made the first $12,000 installment but defaulted thereafter. Virginia instituted an action in forfeiture. The court held that foreclosure was the proper remedy. Under a foreclosure, if the property sold for $75,000 at a judicial sale, Virginia would receive $48,000 to satisfy the balance due on the contract and Osterholtz would receive the balance of $27,000. See *Sebastian v. Floyd, 585 S.W.2d 381 (Ky. 1979).*

BUYER'S REMEDIES

The buyer possesses several possible remedies against a seller who fails to convey title or otherwise defaults under the terms of the contract. The remedies of specific performance, rescission, damages and foreclosure will be examined.

Specific Performance. When the installment buyer completes the requirements under the installment contract, including payment of the last installment, he or she is entitled to the deed. If the seller does not convey the deed, a court may award specific performance, mandating the seller to execute a deed in the buyer's favor. Refusal to abide by the decree may result in contempt of court and punishment. The court may also execute a deed in the buyer's favor, or the very decree may act as the instrument that results in passage of title to the buyer.

Rescission. Another remedy for an installment buyer upon a seller's default is to elect rescission—that is, to have the contract terminated and the contract payments returned. In this instance, fairness often requires that a value for rental of the property be deducted from the amount due the buyer. The remedy of rescission is designed to return the parties to their original position. This remedy is especially desirable for the buyer when the subject real estate has depreciated in value below the contract price.

Damages. The installment buyer, in reliance upon the contract, may have spent money to improve the property. If the seller breaches under these circumstances and is unable to convey a marketable title, the buyer may prefer to sue for damages. A judgment for damages when properly certified and filed becomes a general lien on all real property the seller owns until the judgment is satisfied. As a lienor, the buyer may foreclose on any of the seller's real property to satisfy the judgment. Other means of satisfying the judgment include attachment and sale of the seller's personal property and garnishment of the seller's wages.

Foreclosure. The installment buyer has an equitable interest in the property. As such, the buyer possesses an equitable lien on the property securing his or her interest. Consequently, the buyer may foreclose on the property in the event of the seller's default and recover the purchase payments.

REVIEW AND DISCUSSION QUESTIONS

1. Describe the differences between a land installment contract and an ordinary real estate purchase contract.

2. Who is helped by the doctrine of "after acquired title"? In what ways?

3. (a) What is the primary advantage to a buyer who buys property on a land installment contract? (b) What are the advantages to a seller?

4. (a) What is the primary disadvantage to the buyer who sells property on a land installment contract? (b) What are the disadvantages to the seller?

5. What are some acts that might be considered a buyer's breach of a land installment contract?

6. Describe the seller's remedy of forfeiture and explain how the states have softened the impact of that remedy.

7. Describe the buyer's remedies in the event the seller defaults on a land installment contract.

CASE PROBLEMS

1. Donald Reed and LaVonne McAdow entered into a land installment contract for the sale of a parcel of land owned by Reed. The contract was never recorded. Subsequently, Reed assigned his entire interest in the land to Ohio Mortgage Company, which was unaware of the contract between Reed and McAdow. The assignment was not recorded. After the assignment of the land, Kagey Lumber Company obtained a judgment against Reed and is now in the process of placing a lien on the property. (a) Will Kagey's judgment become a lien on the property? Why or why not? (b) What are Kagey's rights in the property? Describe. (c) Is Ohio Mortgage Company subject to the provisions of the contract between Reed and McAdow? Discuss. *See Butcher v. Kagey Lumber Company, 164 Ohio St. 85, 128 N.E.2d 54 (1955).*

2. Moorman and Whitman signed a land installment contract for the sale of real estate owned by Moorman. The contract stated that the land consisted of three tracts totaling 460 acres. Whitman assigned his interest in the contract to Maxwell. The assignment, expressly authorized by the contract, contained a description of the land similar to that in the land installment contract. After three years, Maxwell paid Moorman the entire balance due under the land installment contract and received the deed to the property. Maxwell then attempted to sell the property to Fentress. Before the deal was consummated, Fentress notified Maxwell that the property contained only 355.9 acres rather than 460 acres, as stated in their contract. Maxwell and Fentress agreed to a reduction in the purchase price, and the contract was signed. Maxwell then attempted to persuade Moorman to return to him approximately

23 percent of the purchase price he paid. Moorman refused. (a) Can Maxwell successfully maintain an action against Moorman for return of the disputed portion of the purchase price? Explain. (b) Does Moorman have a cause of action against Whitman? Explain. *See Maxwell v. Moorman, 522 S.W.2d 441 (Ky. Ct. App. 1975).*

3. Newman entered into a land installment contract with Mountain Park Land Company to purchase a tract of timberland. After Newman paid approximately half of the money due to the company under the contract, the company, without the consent of Newman, cut down trees from the land and sold a substantial amount of the timber. As a result of the actions of Mountain Park, the land decreased in value. (a) Does Newman have a cause of action against Mountain Park? (b) If so, what is that cause of action and what are his possible remedies? *See Newman v. Mountain Park Land Co., 85 Ark. 208, 107 S.W. 391 (1908).* (c) What if Newman harvested the trees, inflicting the damage to the property during the pendency of the installment contract? Would Mountain Park have a cause of action against Newman? Explain. *See Reynolds v. Lawrence, 147 Ala. 216, 40 So. 576 (1906).*

4. Ben Schottenstein and Jack J. Devoe entered into a land installment contract. The terms of the contract stipulated that certain property would be conveyed in fee simple absolute by Schottenstein to Devoe in return for $21,500 payable in installments over a ten-year period. After signing the contract, Devoe learned that Schottenstein did not have legal title to the property at the time of the contract signing. Devoe therefore seeks to avoid the contract. (a) May he do so? Explain. (b) What is Schottenstein's counterargument? (c) What could Devoe have done if he knew of the state of Schottenstein's title prior to signing the contract? *See Schottenstein v. Devoe, 83 Ohio App. 193, 82 N.E.2d 552 (1948).*

5. Purchasers under a land installment contract made only 4 out of 12 monthly payments, failed to pay taxes and maintain insurance, and failed to pay sewer and water charges. In absence of a statute, what factors are relevant to determine the proper remedy available to the land installment seller? Explain. *See Grombone v. Krekel, 754 P.2d 777 (Colo. Ct. App. 1988).*

23

Fair Housing Laws

FAIR HOUSING

◆ **The term used to describe a national policy against most types of discrimination in housing.**

The second half of the 20th century has seen increasing involvement of government in housing in the United States. Types of housing regulations discussed elsewhere in the text include zoning and subdivision regulations, rent controls and mortgage regulations. During the same period, government has exhibited an interest in ensuring, through legislation, that no member of our society is refused an opportunity to obtain decent housing.

EQUAL PROTECTION

◆ **The constitutional mandate that all people be treated equally under the law.**

In the late 19th-century case of *Plessy v. Ferguson, 163 U.S. 537 (1896),* the U.S. Supreme Court affirmed the doctrine that "separate but equal" was the law of the land. This concept was used to separate the races in many sectors of American life, including public transportation, education and accommodations. In housing, some state and local governments passed laws confining blacks and whites to separate sections of cities for residential living. This practice was considered constitutional as long as both black and white sections were provided. Economic and social pressures also were factors separating the races in residential areas.

The separate-but-equal doctrine provided equality in theory, but it has been well documented that it had little relationship to equality in fact. Black and white schools were equal neither in physical plant nor in the quality of education children obtained in them. In housing as well, the quality and locations were not equal for blacks and whites.

In 1954, beginning with the school desegregation cases, the separate-but-equal doctrine was laid aside, and equal protection became the constitutional mandate. In these cases, the plaintiffs were black children who, pursuant to statutes in Kansas, South Carolina, Virginia and Delaware, attended schools segregated on the basis of race. In each of these states, with the exception of Delaware, federal district courts had denied relief to the plaintiffs, citing the separate-but-equal doctrine of *Plessy v. Ferguson.* In the Delaware case, the state supreme court adhered to the doctrine, but ordered plaintiffs admitted to the white schools because of their superiority to the black schools. Plaintiffs appealed to the U.S. Supreme Court, which rejected the language of *Plessy v. Ferguson.* In an important decision the court stated:

> We conclude that in the field of public education the doctrine of "separate but equal" has no place. Separate educational facilities are inherently unequal. Therefore, we hold that the plaintiffs and others similarly situated for whom the actions have been brought are, by reason of the segregation complained of, deprived of the equal protection of the laws guaranteed by the Fourteenth Amendment. *Brown v. Board of Education, 347 U.S. 483 (1954).*

After the decision in *Brown v. Board of Education,* the country began the slow process of racially integrating society. In the late 1950s and early 1960s, several states and cities enacted fair housing laws with varying degrees of coverage. These statutes were a prelude to the entry of the federal government into the fair housing arena. Since the federal government is now the focus for regulation of discrimination in housing, the remainder of this chapter will concentrate on several federal legislative enactments.

FEDERAL FAIR HOUSING LEGISLATION

It was more than ten years after *Brown v. Board of Education* before Congress became active in enacting the fair housing statute.

FAIR HOUSING ACT (1968) AS AMENDED

There are two major pieces of federal fair housing legislation. In 1968, Congress enacted the first comprehensive fair housing law in Title VIII of the Civil Rights Act of 1968, known also as the Fair Housing Act. The law prohibited discrimination and imposed liability on those who discriminated against persons seeking to buy or rent housing. One could not discriminate based on race, color, religion, or national origin. In 1974, Congress added sex or gender as a protected category. The Fair Housing Act of 1988 extended the categories of protection to include handicap and family status. It should be noted that states have fair housing laws too, and those laws may include additional protected classes.

Refusal to sell or rent residential property, or refusal to negotiate a sale or rental, or to otherwise make a dwelling unavailable for someone in a protected class is illegal conduct. In addition, a housing provider cannot discriminate in the setting of terms or conditions of the transaction.

C A S E   E X A M P L E

Filippo, a broker, refused to accept from a black person a purchase offer of $22,500, the price quoted to the buyer by Filippo's sales associate. Filippo instead told the black offeree that the selling price was $26,950. Later Filippo accepted a purchase order from a white buyer at $22,500 for the same property. As a result, Filippo's license was suspended for 45 days. Filippo appealed the suspension, but his appeal was rejected. *Filippo v. Real Estate Commission of District of Columbia, 223 A.2d 268 (D.C. 1966).*

It is illegal also to make or publish notices, statements, or advertisements that indicate a preference, limitation, or discrimination based on a statutorily protected class.

C A S E   E X A M P L E

Cartwright and Lindsay visited a real estate firm where they indicated to a sales associate an interest in purchasing property in a certain section of Detroit. The sales associate stated that the section was fine "if you like a busted community." When asked what was meant by busted community, the sales associate indicated that it was one into which blacks had moved. The sales associate also stated that housing values that community are down and will continue to go down and that, while the schools are OK, "You know what will happen eventually." The sales associate then suggested another community.

The act was amended in 1972 by a requirement that equal opportunity posters be displayed at brokerage houses, model home sites, mortgage lender offices and similar locations. The poster must contain the slogan "Equal Housing Opportunity" and must carry a brief equal housing opportunity statement. Failure to display such a poster will be treated as prima facie evidence of discrimination; that is, in the absence of evidence to the contrary it will be presumed that the broker discriminates in violation of the law.

Representation that a dwelling is not available for inspection, sale or rental, when in fact it is available, is also illegal. Other discriminatory acts explicitly made illegal under the law include *denying membership* or *limiting participation* in real estate brokerage firms or their multiple-listing pools, *blockbusting, redlining, discriminatory advertising,* and *steering.* The *Asbury v. Brougham* case presents an example of a situation where the facts are misrepresented by the agent of the lessor to a minority person seeking housing.

ASBURY V. BROUGHAM

U.S. Court of Appeals, Tenth Circuit
866 F.2d 1276 (1989)

BACKGROUND. Rosalyn Asbury tried to rent an apartment or a townhouse from Brougham Estates in Kansas City. The specific facts surrounding the refusal are discussed later in the case. Asbury charged that Brougham violated §1982 of the Federal Procedural Code and a section of the Fair Housing Act (1968) (FHA) by refusing to give her the opportunity to rent, to inspect, and to negotiate a rental of an apartment or townhouse because of her sex or race. Asbury was awarded $7,500 compensatory damages and $50,000 punitive damages by the jury at trial. Brougham contends that the evidence does not support the compensatory damages because Asbury failed to prove a discriminatory intent. Brougham challenged the punitive damages also because discriminatory motivation must be proven under §1982 to gain punitive damages. Brougham appealed to the Court of Appeals.

DECISION. The Tenth Circuit Court of Appeals affirmed the trial court.

DISTRICT JUDGE PARKER. §1982 and the FHA both prohibit discrimination on the basis of race. In order to prevail on a claim made under these statutes, plaintiff must prove a discriminatory intent. A violation occurs when race is a factor in a decision to deny a minority applicant the opportunity to rent or negotiate for a rental, but race need not be the only factor in the decision. In addition, the FHA specifically prohibits dissemination of false information about the availability of housing because of a person's race. Accordingly, failure to provide a minority applicant with the same information

about availability of a rental unit or the terms and conditions for rental as is provided to white "testers" results in false information being provided and is cognizable as an injury under the FHA.

The three-part burden of proof analysis established in *McDonnell Douglas Corp. v. Green* has been widely applied to FHA and §1982 claims. Under the *McDonnell Douglas* analysis, plaintiff first must come forward with proof of a prima facie case of discrimination. Second, if plaintiff proves a prima facie case, the burden shifts to defendants to produce evidence that the refusal to rent or negotiate for a rental was motivated by legitimate, non-racial considerations. Third, once defendants by evidence articulate non-discriminatory reasons, the burden shifts back to plaintiff to show that the proffered reasons were pretextual.

The proof necessary to establish a prima facie case under the FHA also establishes a prima facie case of racial discrimination under §1982. In order to establish her prima facie case, plaintiff had to prove that:

(1) she is a member of a racial minority;

(2) she applied for and was qualified to rent an apartment or townhouse in Brougham Estates;

(3) she was denied the opportunity to rent or to inspect or negotiate for the rental of a townhouse or apartment; and

(4) the housing opportunity remained available.

A review of the evidence in this case shows that plaintiff establishes her prima facie case. Defendants stipulated that Asbury is black.

Plaintiff testified that on February 23, 1984, she went to Brougham Estates with her daughter to obtain rental housing. At the rental office at Brougham Estates, Asbury encountered Wanda Chauvin, the manager, and explained to Chauvin that she was being transferred to Kansas City and needed to rent housing. Asbury told Chauvin that she needed to secure housing by the middle of March or the beginning of April. In response, Chauvin said there were no vacancies, but told Asbury she could call back at a later time to check on availability. Chauvin provided no information concerning availability of rental units that would assist Asbury in her efforts to rent an apartment or townhouse at Brougham Estates. Asbury asked for the opportunity to fill out an application, but Chauvin did not give her an application, again stating that there were no vacancies and that she kept no waiting list. Asbury also requested floor plans or the opportunity to view a model unit, and Chauvin refused. Instead, Chauvin suggested Asbury inquire at the Westminister Apartments, an apartment complex housing mostly black families. Although Chauvin did not ask Asbury about her qualifications, plaintiff was employed with the Federal Aviation Authority at a salary of $37,599. Based on her salary, defendants concede that Asbury would likely be qualified to rent an apartment or townhouse at Brougham Estates.

Defendants argue that Asbury was not rejected because Chauvin courteously invited her to call back. However, there is ample evidence in the record to support the jury's finding that defendant's failure or refusal to provide Asbury the opportunity to rent or inspect or negotiate for the rental of a townhouse or apartment constituted a rejection because of her race cognizable under §1982 and the FHA.

Defendants testified that families with a child are housed exclusively in the townhouses at Brougham Estates, and that there were no townhouses available on the date Asbury inquired. Asbury introduced evidence suggesting that both apartments and townhouses were available and, in addition, that exceptions previously had been created to allow children to reside in the apartments.

On February 24, 1984, the day after Asbury inquired about renting, Asbury's sister-in-law, Linda Robinson, who is white, called to inquire about the availability of two-bedroom apartments. The woman who answered the telephone identified herself as "Wanda" and invited Robinson to come to Brougham Estates to view the apartments. The following day, February 25, 1984, Robinson went to the rental office at Brougham Estates and met with Wanda Chauvin. Chauvin provided Robinson with four plans of one- and two-bedroom apartments at Brougham Estates. Robinson specifically asked Chauvin about rental to families with children, and Chauvin did not tell Robinson that children were restricted to the townhouse units. Robinson accompanied Chauvin to inspect a model unit and several available two-bedroom apartments. Upon inquiry by Robinson, Chauvin indicated that the apartments were available immediately and offered to hold an apartment for her until the next week.

Asbury also provided evidence indicating that townhouses were available for rent. On February 1, 1984, Daniel McMenay, a white male, notified Brougham Estates that he intended to vacate his townhouse. On April 4, 1984, Brougham Estates rented the townhouse vacated by McMenay to John Shuminski, a white male.

Since Asbury met her burden of proving a prima facie case of racial discrimination, the burden shifted to defendants to prove a legitimate, non-discriminatory reason for denial of housing.

Defendants claimed their legitimate, non-discriminatory reasons for rejecting Asbury arose out of the policies at Brougham Estates that families with one child could rent townhouses but not apartments, and that families with more than one child were not permitted to move into Brougham Estates. Defendants contended that in accordance with these rental policies, no appropriate housing was available for Asbury when she inquired. However, plaintiff introduced evidence indicating that exceptions to these rules had been made on several occasions; families with children had rented apartments, and families with more than one child had been permitted to move into Brougham Estates. The jury could therefore find that defendants' reasons for denying Asbury the opportunity to negotiate for rental were not legitimate and non-discriminatory.

Defendants also argue that evidence of a high percentage of minority occupancy in Brougham Estates conclusively rebuts the claim of intentional racial discrimination. Although such statistical data is relevant to rebutting a claim of discrimination, statistical data is not dispositive of a claim of intentional discrimination. Moreover, there was other evidence from which the jury could have determined that race was a motivating factor in defendants' decision to refuse to negotiate with Asbury for a rental unit.

Having reviewed the record in this case, we find that there was substantial evidence supporting and a reasonable basis for the jury's verdict awarding both compensatory and punitive damages, and we affirm the district court's decision to deny defendants' motion for a new trial.

AFFIRMED AND REMANDED.

◆ **Blockbusting.** Practice by which real estate agents attempt to exploit racial tensions, such as when African-Americans move into a previously all white neighborhood, through repeated solicitations for the sale of homes.

CASE EXAMPLE

Bowers and a number of other real estate firms in Northwest Detroit conducted solicitation campaigns in Northwest Detroit involving fliers, telephone calls and door-to-door canvassing. As part of their campaign, fliers were allegedly delivered to "Resident." One flier contained the legend "We think you may want a friend for a neighbor . . . know your neighbors." Another mailing also addressed to "Resident" purported to carry "neighborhood news." It announced that a real estate agency had just bought a house at a specific address in the recipient's neighborhood, that the named sellers had received cash and that the recipient might receive the same service. The recipients lived in changing neighborhoods. This conduct was judged to be illegal. *Zuch v. Hussey, 394 F. Supp. 1028 (D. Mich. 1975).*

◆ **Redlining.** Denial of a loan by a lending institution or the exacting of harsher terms for loans in certain parts of a city.

C A S E   E X A M P L E

The Laufmans, a white couple, purchased a home in a predominantly black neighborhood. When financing was denied by the Oakley Building and Loan Company, the Laufmans sued. They argued that the defendant had redlined areas in the community in which minority group families were concentrated.

The defendant moved for summary judgment. The court denied the motion. In denying the motion, the court stated that "although not altogether unambiguous, we read this [Sec. 3604 and 3605 of the Civil Rights Act of 1968] as an explicit prohibition of 'redlining.' " *Laufman v. Oakley Building and Loan Co., 408 F. Supp. 489 (1976).*

◆ **Steering. Channeling by a broker or salesperson of prospective home buyers toward, or away from, certain areas either to maintain homogeneity or to change the character of that area, usually for the purpose of enhancing sales opportunities.**

C A S E   E X A M P L E

The Village of Bellwood and six individuals brought suit against two real estate firms for steering black homebuyers to one area of the Village, and white homebuyers to another area. The realtors argued that the Village and the individuals, who were admittedly testers and not prospective homebuyers, were not economically injured and could not sue under the Fair Housing Act.

The U.S. Supreme Court held the conduct of the real estate firms was illegal steering under the Fair Housing Act and that the plaintiffs, contention that they were being denied the opportunity to live in an integrated community was adequate economic injury to bring the suit. *Gladstone Realtors v. Village of Bellwood, 441 U.S. 91 (1979).*

Exceptions. The Fair Housing Act of 1968 does not apply to the sale or rental of commercial or industrial properties. In addition, the act creates several exceptions to the prohibited conduct stated above.

A person may discriminate in the sale or rental of a dwelling, providing he or she can meet all these criteria:

▌ The person does not own more than three houses at any one time.

▌ The person is living in the house or was the last person to live there. If this residency requirement is not met, then the exception applies to only one sale every 24 months.

▌ In addition, the exempt person may not use a broker, an agent, or a sales associate to facilitate the sale.

Another exception occurs when the owner of a multiple-family dwelling with no more than four units resides in one of the units and rents out the other units.

FEDERAL HOUSING ACT ENFORCEMENT

AGGRIEVED PARTIES

The Fair Housing Act allows any aggrieved party to file a complaint against discriminatory practices. The term *aggrieved party* is broadly defined to include a victim, corporations, fair housing groups, testers, real estate professionals, local governments and the Secretary of HUD.

Prior to the Fair Housing Act Amendments of 1988, discrimination based on race, color, religion, sex, or national origin was prohibited. The new law adds the handicapped and familial status as classes protected from discrimination.

FAIR HOUSING ACT AND THE HANDICAPPED

Handicap-based discrimination was made illegal by the Fair Housing Act amendments of 1988. The protection applies broadly to those with a physical or mental disability that substantially limits one or more major life activities. Three categories of discrimination are recognized: direct discrimination, reasonable modification, and reasonable accommodation. Direct discrimination, by which a housing provider openly refuses a rental based on a physical or mental handicap, needs no further amplification.

Reasonable Modification. A landlord is required to permit a tenant, at the tenant's expense, to make a reasonable modification of the living space in order to have full use and enjoyment of the premises. A modification may be installing grab bars, ramps and alarms, or widening doorways. The modifications can go beyond the living unit itself, and include the laundry room or the garage.

The tenant must obtain the landlord's consent prior to making a modification. The landlord can withhold consent only where the modification is unreasonable due to the financial or administrative burden it imposes. If the modification would interfere with the landlord's or the next tenant's enjoyment of the premises, the handicapped tenant may be required to restore the premises to its original condition upon leaving.

There are special rules that apply to multifamily dwellings. A multifamily dwelling is defined as a building with four or more living units if the building has an elevator, or a ground floor dwelling with four or more units. Such a multifamily dwelling unit is required to have full handicap accessibility to common areas, and all entrances must be wheelchair accessible. Within individual units the law requires accessibility to all switches and environmental controls, reinforcement of bathroom walls to allow for future installation of grab bars, and sufficient widths in kitchens and bathrooms to afford wheelchair maneuverability. The statute provides that compliance with the American National Standards Institute standards for providing accessibility and usability for physically handicapped people is satisfactory.

Reasonable Accommodation. The Fair Housing Act mandates that a landlord or housing provider make reasonable accommodation of its rules, policies, practices, and services in order for a handicapped person to enjoy the unit. In contrast with a reasonable modification, the housing provider may be required to take affirmative measures to meet the reasonable accommodation specification. The handicapped person is entitled to an equal opportunity to use and enjoy the dwelling unit. The concept of reasonable accommodation is also used in applying section 504 of the Rehabilitation Act of 1973.

A housing provider may have to waive its "no pet policy" to accommodate a service or companion animal such as a "sight dog" for a blind person. Another example is that parking rules may have to be adjusted to accommodate a person with a mobility-related disability. In reasonable accommodation lawsuits, the courts have applied a type of balancing test. It will balance the needs of the handicapped person against the financial burden placed on the housing provider. The housing provider may be required to incur reasonable costs but will not have to assume an undue financial burden. In applying the balancing tests, the courts appear to favor the handicapped person, except under extreme circumstances.

Group Home Accommodations. The Fair Housing Act prohibits local governments from applying laws and regulations that discriminate against group homes of nonrelated persons. Land use regulations, including zoning provisions and special use permits, cannot effectively prohibit groups of disabled individuals from living in the residence of their choice. If the purpose or effect of the law is to exclude or restrict group homes, it violates the reasonable accommodation provision.

As with the reasonable accommodation provision applying to disabled individuals, the courts use a balancing test in group home cases. The courts seek to decide if the accommodation of its law to the group home imposes an undue hardship on the municipality. It will examine variables such as crime and safety concerns, negative impacts on real estate values, and the financial burden placed on the parties.

There is an exemption in the Fair Housing Act for restrictions regarding the maximum number of occupants permitted in a dwelling. The courts in interpreting the exemption have carefully confined it to regulations solely limiting the number of persons residing in a unit. The following case is an example of that narrow construction.

CITY OF EDMONDS V. OXFORD HOUSE, INC.

Supreme Court of the United States
115 S. Ct. 1776 (1995)

BACKGROUND. Oxford House operates a group home in the City of Edmonds, Washington, for 10 or 12 adults recovering from alcoholism and drug addiction. The City's zoning code provides that occupants of single-family dwelling units must compose a "family." It defines a family as either persons, regardless of number, related by genetics, adoption, or marriage, or a group of five or fewer unrelated persons. The city cited Oxford House for violation of this zoning code provision. Oxford House asserted reliance on the Fair Housing Act provisions protecting handicapped persons from discrimination. The definition of a handicapped person is broad enough to include the residents of Oxford House. The District Court found that the zoning regulation was within the Fair Housing Act exemption. The Court of Appeals reversed, finding for Oxford House, and holding that the exemption was inapplicable to this zoning restriction.

DECISION. The United States Supreme Court affirmed the Court of Appeals decision.

JUSTICE GINSBURG. The Fair Housing Act (FHA or Act) prohibits discrimination in housing against persons with handicaps. Section 3607(b)(1) of the Act entirely exempts from the FHA's compass "any reasonable local, State, or Federal restrictions regarding the maximum number of occupants permitted to occupy a dwelling." This case presents the question whether a provision in petitioner City of Edmonds' zoning code qualifies for §3607(b)(1)'s complete exemption from FHA scrutiny. The provision, governing areas zoned for single-family dwelling units, defines "family" as "persons [without regard to number] related by genetics, adoption, or marriage, or a group of five or fewer [unrelated] persons."

The defining provision at issue describes who may compose a family unit; it does not prescribe "the maximum number of occupants" a dwelling unit may house. We hold that §3607(b)(1) does not exempt prescriptions of the family-defining kind, i.e., provisions designed to foster the family character of a neighborhood. Instead, §3607(b)(1)'s absolute exemption removes from the FHA's scope only total occupancy limits, i.e., numerical ceilings that serve to prevent overcrowding in living quarters.

Discrimination covered by the FHA includes "a refusal to make reasonable accommodations in rules, policies, practices, or services, when such accommodations may be necessary to afford [handicapped] person[s] equal opportunity to use and enjoy a dwelling." Oxford House asked Edmonds to make a "reasonable accommodation" by allowing it to remain in the single-family dwelling it had leased. Group homes for recovering substance abusers, Oxford urged, need 8 to 12 residents to be financially and therapeutically viable. Edmonds declined to permit Oxford House to stay in a single-family residential zone, but passed an ordinance listing group homes as permitted uses in multifamily and general commercial zones.

The sole question before the Court is whether Edmonds' family composition rule qualifies as a "restrictio[n] regarding the maximum number of occupants permitted to occupy a dwelling" within the meaning of the FHA's absolute exemption. In answering this question, we are mindful of the Act's stated policy "to provide, within constitutional limitations, for fair housing throughout the United States." We also note precedent recognizing the FHA's "broad and inclusive" compass, and therefore according a "generous construction" to the Act's complaint-filing provision. Accordingly, we regard this case as an instance in which an exception to "a general statement of policy" is sensibly read "narrowly in order to preserve the primary operation of the [policy]."

Land use restrictions designate "districts in which only compatible uses are allowed and incompatible uses are excluded." These restrictions typically categorize uses as single-family residential, multiple-family residential, commercial, or industrial.

Land use restrictions aim to prevent problems caused by the "pig in the parlor instead of the barnyard." In particular, reserving land for single-family residences preserves the character of neighborhoods, securing "zones where family values, youth values, and the blessings of quiet seclusion and clean air make the area a sanctuary for people." To limit land use to single-family residences, a municipality must define the term "family"; thus family composition rules are an essential component of single-family residential use restrictions. Maximum occupancy restrictions, in contradistinction, cap the number of occupants per dwelling, typically in relation to available floor space or the number and type of rooms. These restrictions ordinarily apply uniformly to all residents of all dwelling units. Their purpose is to protect health and safety by preventing dwelling overcrowding.

Section 3607(b)(1)'s language—"restrictions regarding the maximum number of occupants permitted to occupy a dwelling"—surely encompasses maximum occupancy restrictions. But the formulation does not fit family composition rules typically tied to land use restrictions. In sum, rules that cap the total number of occupants in order to prevent overcrowding of a dwelling "plainly and unmistakably," fall within §3607(b)(1)'s absolute exemption from the FHA's governance; rules designed to preserve the family character of a neighborhood, fastening on the composition of households rather than on the total number of occupants living quarters can contain, do not.

Turning specifically to the City's Community Development Code, we note that the provisions Edmonds invoked against Oxford House, are classic examples of a use restriction and complementing family composition rule. These provisions do not cap the number of people who may live in a dwelling. In plain terms, they direct that dwellings be used only to house families. Captioned "USES," ECDC §16.20.010 provides that the sole "Permitted Primary Us[e]" in a single-family residential zone is "[s]ingle family dwelling units. " Edmonds itself recognizes that this provision simply "defines those uses permitted in a single

family residential zone." A separate provision caps the number of occupants a dwelling may house, based on floor area:

> Floor Area. Every dwelling unit shall have at least one room which shall have not less than 120 square feet of floor area. Other habitable rooms, except kitchens, shall have an area of not less than 70 square feet. Where more than two persons occupy a room used for sleeping purposes, the required floor area shall be increased at the rate of 50 square feet for each occupant in excess of two.

This space and occupancy standard is a prototypical maximum occupancy restriction. Edmonds nevertheless argues that its family composition rule, ECDC §21.30.010, falls within §3607(b)(1), the FHA exemption for maximum occupancy restrictions, because the rule caps at five the number of unrelated persons allowed to occupy a single-family dwelling. But Edmonds' family composition rule surely does not answer the question: "What is the maximum number of occupants permitted to occupy a house?" So long as they are related "by genetics, adoption, or marriage," any number of people can live in a house. Ten siblings, their parents and grandparents, for example, could dwell in a house in Edmonds' single-family residential zone without offending Edmonds' family composition rule.

Family living, not living space per occupant, is what ECDC §21.30.010 describes. Defining family primarily by biological and legal relationships, the provision also accommodates another group association: five or fewer unrelated people are allowed to live together as though they were family. This accommodation is the peg on which Edmonds rests its plea for §3607(b)(1) exemption. Had the City defined a family solely by biological and legal links, §3607(b)(1) would not have been the ground on which Edmonds staked its case. It is curious reasoning indeed that converts a family values preserver into a maximum occupancy restriction once a town adds to a related persons prescription "and also two unrelated persons."

Edmonds' zoning code provision describing who may compose a "family" is not a maximum occupancy restriction exempt from the FHA under §3607(b)(1).

AFFIRMED.

STATUTORY REMEDIES

It is in the area of remedies provided by the Fair Housing Act that the amendments of 1988 make their most significant changes. There are three distinct avenues open for redressing housing discrimination under the new law: administrative enforcement, Attorney General litigation and private litigation.

Administrative Enforcement. An aggrieved party may file a complaint of discrimination with HUD any time up to one year after its occurrence. The administrator will either transfer the complaint to a state or local agency, or begin an investigation. If the state or locality where the alleged discriminatory activity took place has a HUD-approved "substantially equivalent" fair housing program, the complaint is assigned to the nonfederal authorities.

If there is no substantially equivalent nonfederal program, HUD has 100 days to carry out an investigation of the complaint and to file a report of its findings. During the 100-day period, HUD must begin a process of conciliation attempting to obtain an agreement ending the dispute. Note that a state program must be substantially equivalent to the federal so that when a complaint is referred to the state a similar procedure is followed.

If no conciliation agreement is reached during the 100-day investigatory period, HUD must dismiss the complaint or file charges. If HUD files charges, the aggrieved party has 20 days to exercise an election to take this matter to federal court for a jury trial. If the aggrieved party does not choose to go to federal court, the case stays in the administrative arena and is assigned to an administrative law judge.

The administrative law judge has 120 days to commence a hearing on the charges filed. At the conclusion of the administrative hearing, the judge will make recommendations to HUD for resolution of the dispute. It is highly likely that HUD will accept the recommendations. The administrative law judge can award the complainant actual damages, an injunction or other equitable relief, and/or assess substantial civil penalties. The judge can also award the complainant attorney's fees. Once HUD approves the ruling, the parties have 30 days to appeal the case to the appropriate Federal Court of Appeals.

> **CASE EXAMPLE**
>
> Blackwell, a white, refused to sell his house to a black couple (Herrons). Instead, Blackwell leased the house to a white couple. The Herrons filed a complaint with HUD. The administrative law judge (ALJ) found for the Herrons, granting them $40,000 in actual damages and granting $20,000 to the white couple who leased the house for their embarrassment and economic loss; he also assessed a civil penalty of $10,000 against Blackwell.
>
> The Eleventh Circuit upheld the ALJ on all the relief granted. This is the first case decided by an ALJ under the 1988 Fair Housing Act Amendments enforcement procedures. Notice the flexibility the ALJ has in granting relief. *Secretary, HUD ex rel. Herron v. Blackwell, 908 F.2d 864 (1990).*

Attorney General Litigation. If, after HUD files a charge of discrimination, the aggrieved party exercises the election to have a jury trial, HUD will notify the Attorney General; the Attorney General has 30 days to file a civil action in federal court on behalf of the complainant.

In this type of litigation, the court may grant any relief that is available in private litigation (discussed in the next section), including actual and punitive damages, injunctions and other appropriate equitable remedies.

In addition to this type of civil action aimed at redressing a specific discriminatory action, the Attorney General may file suit where there is a pattern or practice of discrimination or there is a discriminatory denial of rights to a group of persons, raising issues of public importance.

Finally, the Attorney General has the authority to bring actions to enforce a conciliation agreement reached by the parties under the administrative process of the Act.

Private Litigation. An aggrieved party may bring a private enforcement action in federal district court within two years of the discriminatory action. The private lawsuit can be filed even though an administrative complaint is filed with HUD. If a conciliation agreement is entered on the HUD-filed complaint, or if a hearing commences before the administrative law judge, the private lawsuit must be terminated.

There are several advantages to the private litigation avenue for the complainant. The judge can appoint an attorney for the complainant when he or she is unable to retain one and can waive statutory costs and fees if complainant is financially unable to bear them. More important, the court can grant unlimited actual and punitive damages and can more liberally require the defendant to pay the aggrieved parties' attorney's fees.

REVIEW AND DISCUSSION QUESTIONS

1. Compare the theory and the reality of the policies of "separate but equal" with "equal protection."

2. Has discrimination in housing been completely banned by law?

3. Differentiate between blockbusting and steering.

4. Distinguish between reasonable modification and reasonable accommodation in protecting disabled persons from discrimination under the Fair Housing Act. Which one is likely to involve more disputes? Why?

5. From the perspective of an aggrieved party, how did the Fair Housing Act amendments of 1988 provide a greater incentive to redress discriminatory treatment?

CASE PROBLEMS

1. D. C. Williams and his wife, a black couple, wished to purchase lots in a subdivision being developed by the Matthews Company. The subdivision was not integrated. When they made an offer to purchase, a company official informed them that lots were sold only to builders. Although generally this was the case, some lots had been sold to individuals.

   Williams and his wife approached several white builders. Each of them refused to purchase and build for the Williams family, stating that they would get no more business in that area if they built for a black. Eventually Anderson, a black builder, agreed to purchase a lot and build the house that Williams and his wife wanted. The Matthews Company informed Anderson that it would not sell him the lot because he was not on the company's approved builder list. When Anderson attempted to find out what he had to do to become approved, he was informed that only the company president could do this and he was out of the country on a trip to the Orient for two months. The company had no policy for approval of builders but it did have an office memo indicating support for integration of the subdivision. The memo also indicated a belief that the issue was a sensitive one and should be handled at the level of company president.

   No public announcement had ever been made of the company's commitment to integration, and no black had ever acquired property in the subdivision. Has the Matthews Company violated any of the federal civil rights statutes? Discuss. *Williams v. Matthews Co., 499 F.2d 819 (8th Cir. 1974).*

2. Greenwood was a sales associate in an office visited by Bago, a prospective buyer. Bago expressed an interest in a property in a specific area of Detroit. Greenwood told Bago that she had some nice property listed outside the city. She stated, "The school system is poor in Detroit." Later she asked, "Do you read the newspapers? Even the police are afraid to live in the area, and they are supposed to protect us." Greenwood gave Bago several listings in Detroit and a suburb and suggested that he compare prices, indicating that prices were lower in Detroit because blacks lived there. Greenwood further indicated that she would sell him any property he was interested in, wherever it was located. What, if any, violation of fair housing legislation has Greenwood committed? Support your answer.

3. The City of Parma, a suburb of Cleveland, had a policy rejecting any proposal for low-income housing, even if it meant losing unrelated federal funding. In addition, local ordinances made construction of low-income housing economically infeasible. Was the Fair Housing Act violated? Note that §3604 (a) of that act makes it unlawful "to refuse to sell or rent . . . or otherwise make unavailable or deny, a dwelling to any person because of race, color, religion, sex, or national origin." Discuss. *United States v. City of Parma, 494 F. Supp. 1049 (D. Ohio 1980).*

4. Swanner owned several rental properties in Anchorage. On several occasions, he refused to rent to couples who intended to cohabit but were unmarried. Swanner contended that couples living together outside marriage were likely to engage in fornication, and that was repugnant to his religious beliefs. If you were Swanner, what would you argue in court? Does Swanner's conduct violate the Fair Housing Acts? *Swanner v. Anchorage Equal Rights Com'n, 874 P.2d 274 (1994).*

24

Land Use: The Constitution and the Plan

The basic tenets of U.S. property law can be traced back to feudal times in England. Between the king and the lowest serf was the great mass of landholders. The landholder was not an owner but had the right to use a parcel of land. In exchange for that right of use, certain duties were owed to the superior on the feudal scale. These duties might include providing military service or a portion of the crops grown on the land. Our system of private property has evolved from this scheme, in which each landholder owed certain obligations in exchange for the right of use, but the legal notion of private property in America took its own peculiar twist.

As in England, the landholder's *rights* gradually expanded into what we refer to as *ownership*. These rights eventually gave the owner almost absolute and unfettered control over his or her grant of land. William Blackstone, the great 18th-century authority on the common law, referred to a person's property right as "that sole and despotic dominion," thereby depicting the extensive freedom that accompanied land ownership. A person's ownership rights were never quite as absolute as Blackstone alleged, but the wide range of rights he connoted became indelibly etched in the minds of landowners in England and America.

The American difference applied not to the "rights" side of the equation but to the "duty" side. Almost from the inception of this country, a landowner owed no duty to anyone except to refrain from acts on the property that would significantly interfere with another landowner's use of his or her property. Once the purchase price was paid, the buyer of land owed no additional duty to the seller. Our concept of property has always emphasized the landowner's rights over any duties arising from that ownership.

Though most Americans still cling tenaciously to the idea of absolute ownership rights in land, those rights have eroded sharply in the 20th century. The subdivider of land usually places a significant number of restrictions on use in the deed to the new homeowner. Municipal codes place an array of restraints on an owner's property rights. For instance, zoning laws limit an owner's use of the land. Other statutes or local ordinances require an owner to hook up to a sewer, to desist from playing loud music late at night, to refrain from keeping farm animals and to get a permit in order to build an addition to the house, to name only a few. This chapter will describe some of the traditional private restrictions on an owner's use of real property. It will then discuss constraints created by the Federal Constitution. Finally, it will discuss the planning process that must precede most regulations.

PRIVATE RESTRICTIONS ON LAND USE

Many limitations on the use of land are the result of agreements between buyers and sellers. These limitations are often referred to as *private restrictions*. The term *private restrictions* is also used to refer to limitations on land use imposed by the common law.

RESTRICTIVE COVENANTS

◆ **Private agreements, usually placed in the deed by the seller when conveying land to the buyer, that restrict future use of that land.**

Parties to a real estate transaction are free to enter into any legal agreement that suits their particular situation. An agreement restricting the future use of the land is called a *restrictive covenant*.

A restrictive covenant is said to run with the land if it attaches to the land and is not dependent upon the continued ownership of the parties to the original deed. The buyer's successors in title would be bound by the covenant, and the seller's successors in title would continue to benefit from the covenant.

CASE EXAMPLE

Baum, as the original grantee of a subdivided parcel, covenanted in the deed to accept and pay for a seasonal water supply provided by the original grantor. Eagle Enterprises, the successor to the original grantor, sued Gross, the successor to the grantee Baum, to enforce the restrictive covenant relating to the supplying of water. Eagle Enterprises argues that the covenant attaches, or "runs with the land," thereby binding all subsequent owners to pay for supplying the water. Gross responds that the covenant bound only Baum and did not run with the land.

The court held that a restrictive covenant will run with the land if it meets three conditions: (1) the original parties must intend that it run with the land; (2) there must be privity of estate between the parties; and (3) the covenant must touch and concern the land. Although the court found that this particular covenant was personal and did not "touch and concern" the land, any covenant that meets the threefold test will be held to run with the land. *Eagle Enterprises, Inc. v. Gross, 39 N.Y.2d 505, 349 N.E.2d 816 (1976).*

Privity of estate is a phrase used to express the successive relationship of the parties to the land. For example, privity of estate exists between the grantor and grantee of an easement. The term *touch and concern the land* relates to the determination of whether the purported easement is peculiarly tied to the land itself or is rather a personal agreement between the parties and only incidentally concerns the land. The distinction between a personal covenant and one that touches and concerns the land is not always clear.

The restrictive covenant may carry a time limitation such as: "This covenant shall run with the land and be in effect for 20 years from the date of the conveyance." Usually, however, no termination period is stipulated, and the covenant lasts indefinitely.

Over the years, restrictive covenants have not been favored by the courts because they constituted an encroachment on the free transferability of land. Courts have never been enthusiastic about permitting land to be tied up with restrictions on use; when any doubt exists as to the meaning of the covenant, courts usually find against the party placing the restriction in the deed. Despite the clear intention of the parties in the *Eagle Enterprises* case described above, note the reluctance of the court to bind future parties where grounds existed for relieving the land from the restriction.

The use of restrictive covenants and the attitude of courts toward them may be shifting. Today a substantial amount of residential development takes place in the form of subdivisions. The developer usually places a broad range of restrictive covenants in the plat plan or the individual deeds of the homebuyers or both. The purpose of the restrictions is to protect other landowners in the subdivision from losing some of their property value because of the unorthodox activity of a neighbor in the subdivision. For example, a restrictive covenant might prohibit the landowners from raising pigs or other farm animals. To avoid conflicts caused by questionable land use during development or immediately after the subdivision is completed, developers are inclined to include restrictive covenants against everything not narrowly confined to normal single-family use. The developer thereby makes every subdivision owner the third-party beneficiary of the restrictive covenants in the deeds of the other homeowners in the tract. The covenants generally are part of the deed or are filed with the general plat plan for the development and then recorded, thereby giving notice to all parties having an interest in the land in the future. The covenant is now part of the chain of title and runs with the land indefinitely.

Traditionally, the person selling part of his or her land subject to restrictive covenants has the right to enforce the covenant in the courts. Similarly, any owner in the subdivision as the third-party beneficiary of the developer-homeowner contract has enforcement rights in the court. However, a modern practice is for the developer to create a group such as an architectural committee to administer the covenant procedure. The developer and some associates often constitute the committee. The committee is authorized to handle complaints and (sometimes) to permit deviations from the restrictions in the covenants. For example, the restrictive covenant may bar all buildings from the land except the house and attached garage, unless approved by the architectural committee. Upon request, the committee may permit the homeowner to build a small toolshed on the property.

One problem may arise from this practice when the developer conveys all the parcels in the tract and does not provide for transfer of membership on the committee to the local subdivision residents, creating a hiatus. Theoretically, any homeowner *can* enforce the covenant. If the courts follow their traditional inclination of disfavoring restrictive covenants, however, enforcement may be impossible. It is arguable that the covenantor intended the *committee* to be the mechanism for enforcement, but the committee is now defunct.

An additional problem is that, when restrictive covenants proliferate, people tend to ignore them. County or local zoning and building codes reduce the need for restrictive covenants by controlling major use changes or construction on residential land.

CASE EXAMPLE

Rachel assembles a four- by six-foot metal shed on her property to store her lawn mower and garden tools. Although the building is prohibited (without permission) by the restrictive covenant in Rachel's deed, it is common in her subdivision to own these sheds; in other words, "everyone ignores the covenant." The courts may not enforce the restrictive covenant on request by a neighbor because the homeowners have acquiesced in this noncompliance.

However, there are instances where Rachel will clearly be subject to the restrictive covenant and probably to a building code. When Rachel decides to build a second house on her lot, the covenant is violated and a building permit is required. The building inspector, in order to offer some measure of protection to other residents, oversees her plans. The building code, rather than the restrictive covenant, will probably become the enforcement mechanism.

Nevertheless, the restrictive covenants still provide a mechanism for an unhappy neighbor to complain, even concerning minor alterations like the small metal storage shed.

Restrictive covenants can be terminated in several ways. *All* the concerned parties may agree in writing to the termination. This approach may prove infeasible where the number of parties to the covenant is large. The covenants can also be terminated through condemnation of the land by a public agency having the power of eminent domain.

A common method of extinguishing these covenants is through nonuse or misuse. The character of the neighborhood may change, making continuation of the restrictions meaningless.

CASE EXAMPLE

DeMarco brought an action against adjacent property owners to have restrictive covenants limiting use to residential purposes declared void. Due to the construction of the Edsel Ford Freeway, replacing a two-lane country road, all surrounding land on the parties' street was in commercial use.

The court voided the restrictive covenant because the four-lane freeway had completely changed the character of the area. *DeMarco v. Pallazzo, 47 Mich. App. 444, 209 N.W. 2e 540 (1973).*

PUBLIC RESTRICTIONS IN LAND USE

In the 20th century, private restrictions were eclipsed in importance by public restrictions. Land use and development is controlled predominantly by legislation adopted at the state and local levels. Initially, control was by zoning codes; more recently, there has been a wide variety of other types of regulations.

Zoning and other regulatory legislation is examined in the next chapter. The remainder of this chapter is confined to three preconditions for a valid regulation. Any land use legislation must be a valid exercise of the police power, conform to federal and state constitutional limitations, and be preceded by a certain degree of planning.

THE POLICE POWER

The authority to regulate land use is almost exclusively provided by the police power. The police power is the inherent right of the state to regulate to protect the public health, safety or welfare of its citizens. The grant of authority under the police power is very broad, and it can be delegated to local governments.

To be a valid exercise of the police power, the legislative body must have a legitimate police power purpose, that is, a public health, safety or welfare reason for its enactment. It must prove also that there is a substantial connection, or nexus, between the legislatively stated purpose and the regulation enacted. For instance, if the law's stated purpose is highway safety, it must substantially promote highway safety.

Unlike the exercise of the power of eminent domain, the legislature regulating under the police power does not take the regulated property nor does it pay just compensation to the property owner. Though the U.S. Supreme Court in the Nollan Case discusses the situation as if it were a regulatory takings case (see next section), one can see from the test it applies that it involves the issue of a valid exercise of the police power.

NOLLAN V. CALIFORNIA COASTAL COMMISSION
U.S. Supreme Court
438 U.S. 825 (1987)

BACKGROUND. James and Marilyn Nollan leased a small beachfront bungalow in Ventura County, California. Subsequently, they entered into a contract to purchase the land from the owner, but the agreement was contingent on their ability to demolish the bungalow, now fallen into disrepair, and to replace it with a larger house. To achieve this end, they needed a permit from the California Coastal Commission (Commission). The Commission's function was to protect the coastal area from harmful development. The Commission granted the permit, but conditioned it on the Nollans' willingness to grant a public easement across the near-ocean portion of the lot. The Commission had conditioned all permit requests in the area in this fashion, apparently with the expectation of linking easements for public access along the shore and between two parks lying north and south of Nollan's land. The parks are about one-half mile apart.

The justification given by the Commission for the easement condition was that the new, larger house would further block the view of the ocean and worsen the public's ability to see that there was nearby public access to the beach. Also, it argued that the new house would further privatize the shorefront.

The Nollans sued, contending that the permit condition violated their property rights. The trial court found for the Nollans because there were inadequate facts to support the request for an easement. The Court of Appeal reversed the trial court.

DECISION. The United States Supreme Court reversed the California appellate court, ruling in favor of the Nollans.

JUSTICE SCALIA. Had California simply required the Nollans to make an easement across their beachfront available to the public on a permanent basis in order to increase public access to the beach, rather than conditioning their permit to rebuild their house on their agreeing to do so, we have no doubt there would have been a taking. To say that the appropriation of a landowner's premises does not constitute the taking of a property interest but rather, "a mere restriction on its use," is to use words in a manner that deprives them of all their ordinary meaning. Indeed, one of the principal uses of the eminent domain power is to assure that the government be able to require conveyance of just such interests, so long as it pays for them. We have repeatedly held that, as to property reserved by its owner for private use, "the right to exclude [others is] 'one of the most essential sticks in the bundle of rights that are commonly characterized as property.'"

Given, then, that requiring uncompensated conveyance of the easement outright would violate the Fourteenth Amendment, the question becomes whether requiring it to be conveyed as a condition for issuing a land use permit alters the outcome. We have long recognized that land use regulation does not effect a taking if it "substantially advance[s] legitimate state interests" and does not "den[y] an owner economically viable use of his land." Our cases have not elaborated on the standards for determining what constitutes a "legitimate state interest" or what type of connection between the regulation and the state interest satisfies the requirement that the former "substantially advance" the latter. They have made clear, however, that a broad range of governmental purposes and regulations satisfies these requirements. The Commission argues that among these permissible purposes are protecting the public's ability to see the beach, assisting the public in overcoming the "psychological barrier" to using the beach created by a developed shorefront, and preventing congestion on the public beaches. We assume, without deciding, that this is so.

If the Commission attached to the permit some condition that would have protected the public's ability to see the beach notwithstanding construction of the new house—for example, a height limitation, a width restriction, or a ban on fences—so long as the Commission could have exercised its police power (as we have assumed it could) to forbid construction of the house altogether, imposition of the condition would also be constitutional. Moreover, (and here we come closer to the facts of the present case), the condition would be constitutional even if it consisted of the requirement that the Nollans provide a viewing spot on their property for passersby with whose sighting of the ocean their new house would interfere. Although such a requirement, constituting a permanent grant of continuous access to the property, would have to be considered a taking if it were not attached to a development permit, the Commission's assumed power to forbid construction of the house in order to protect the public's view of the beach must surely include the power to condition construction upon some concession by the owner, even a concession of property rights, that serves the same end. If a prohibition designed to accomplish that purpose would be a legitimate exercise of the police power rather than a taking, it would be strange to conclude that providing the owner an alternative to that prohibition which accomplishes the same purpose is not.

The evident constitutional propriety disappears, however, if the condition substituted for the prohibition utterly fails to further the end advanced as the justification for the prohibition. The essential nexus is eliminated.

The Nollans' new house, the Commission found, will interfere with "visual access" to the beach. That in turn (along with other shorefront development) will interfere with the desire of people who drive past the Nollans' house to use the beach, thus creating a "psychological barrier" to "access." The Nollans' new house will also, by a process not altogether clear from the Commission's opinion but presumably potent enough to more than offset the effects of the psychological barrier, increase the use of the public beaches, thus creating the need for more "access." These burdens on "access" would be alleviated by a requirement that the Nollans provide "lateral access" to the beach.

Rewriting the argument to eliminate the play on words makes clear that there is nothing to it. It is quite impossible to understand how a requirement that people already on the public beaches be able to walk across the Nollans' property reduces any obstacles to viewing the beach created by the new house. It is also impossible to understand how it lowers any "psychological barrier" to using the public beaches, or how it helps to remedy an additional congestion on them caused by construction of the Nollans' new house. We therefore find that the Commission's imposition of the permit condition cannot be treated as an exercise of its land use power for any of these purposes. Our conclusion on this point is consistent with the approach taken by every other court that has considered the question, with the exception of the California state courts.

Justice Brennan argues that a person looking toward the beach from the road will see a street of residential structures, including the Nollans' new home, and conclude that there is no public beach nearby. If, however, that person sees people passing and repassing along the dry sand behind the Nollans' home, he will realize that there is a public beach somewhere in the vicinity. The Commission's action, however, was based on the opposite finding that the wall of houses completely blocked the view of the beach and that the person looking from the road would not be able to see it at all. Our cases describe the condition for abridgment of property rights through the police power as a "substantial advanc[ing]" of a legitimate State interest. We are inclined to be particularly careful about the adjective where the actual conveyance of property is made a condition to the lifting of a land use restriction, since in that context there is heightened risk that the purpose is avoidance of the compensation requirement, rather than the stated police power objective.

REVERSED.

islands, like the Isle of Palms. Historically, critical area demarcations had often shifted in response to shifting sands caused by storms. The Beachfront Management Act (Act) (1988), the law that brought the Lucas lots within the designated critical area, sought to set a baseline seaward from which the land was highly erodible and not appropriate for houses.

The Council denied Lucas' permit request, and Lucas sued claiming a regulatory taking. The trial court ruled that the permit denial deprived Lucas of all economic use of the lots and awarded him $1.2 million in "just compensation." The Supreme Court of South Carolina reversed, holding that the Act was designed to prevent a serious public harm. Given the validity of the Act's purpose, no compensation was due regardless of its effect on the land's economic value.

DECISION. The U.S. Supreme Court reversed, again ruling for Lucas.

JUSTICE SCALIA. Prior to Justice Holmes' exposition in *Pennsylvania Coal Co. v. Mahon (1922),* it was generally thought that the Takings Clause reached only a "direct appropriation" of property, or the functional equivalent of a "practical ouster of [the owner's] possession." Justice Holmes recognized in Mahon, however, that if the protection against physical appropriations of private property was to be meaningfully enforced, the government's power to redefine the range of interests included in the ownership of property was necessarily constrained by constitutional limits. If, instead, the uses of private property were subject to unbridled, uncompensated qualification under the police power, "the natural tendency of human nature [would be] to extend the qualification more and more until at last private property disappeared." These considerations gave birth in that case to the oft-cited maxim

that, "while property may be regulated to a certain extent, if regulation goes too far it will be recognized as a taking."

Nevertheless, our decision in Mahon offered little insight into when, and under what circumstances, a given regulation would be seen as going "too far" for purposes of the Fifth Amendment. In 70-odd years of succeeding "regulatory takings" jurisprudence, we have generally eschewed any set formula for determining how far is too far, preferring to "engage in . . . essentially ad hoc, factual inquiries." We have, however, described at least two discrete categories of regulatory action as compensable without case-specific inquiry into the public interest advanced in support of the restraint. The first encompasses regulations that compel the property owner to suffer a physical "invasion" of his property. In general (at least with regard to permanent invasions), no matter how minute the intrusion, and no matter how weighty the public purpose behind it, we have required compensation.

The second situation in which we have found categorical treatment appropriate is where regulation denies all economically beneficial or productive use of land. As we have said on numerous occasions, the Fifth Amendment is violated when land-use regulation "does not substantially advance legitimate state interests or denies an owner economically viable use of his land."

We have never set forth the justification for this rule. Perhaps it is simply, as Justice Brennan suggested, that total deprivation of beneficial use is, from the landowner's point of view, the equivalent of a physical appropriation. "For what is the land but the profits thereof?" Surely, at least, in the extraordinary circumstance when no productive or economically beneficial use of land is permitted, it is less realistic to indulge our usual assumption that the legislature is simply "adjusting the benefits and burdens of economic life," in a manner that secures an "average reciprocity of advantage" to everyone concerned.

On the other side of the balance, affirmatively supporting a compensation requirement, is the fact that regulations that leave the owner of land without economically beneficial or productive options for its use—typically, as here, by requiring land to be left substantially in its natural state—carry with them a heightened risk that private property is being pressed into some form of public service under the guise of mitigating serious public harm.

We think, in short, that there are good reasons for our frequently expressed belief that when the owner of real property has been called upon to sacrifice all economically beneficial uses in the name of the common good, that is, to leave his property economically idle, he has suffered a taking.

It is correct that many of our prior opinions have suggested that "harmful or noxious uses" of property may be proscribed by government regulation without the requirement of compensation. "Harmful or noxious use" analysis was, in other words, simply the progenitor of our more contemporary statements that "land-use regulation does not effect a taking if it 'substantially advances legitimate state interests'. . . ." The transition from our early focus on control of "noxious" uses to our contemporary understanding of the broad realm within which government may regulate without compensation was an easy one, since the distinction between "harm-preventing" and "benefit-conferring" regulation is often in the eye of the beholder.

When it is understood that "prevention of harmful use" was merely our early formulation of the police power justification necessary to sustain (without compensation) any regulatory diminution in value; and that the distinction between regulation that "prevents harmful use" and that which "confers benefits" is diffi-

cult, if not impossible, to discern on an objective, value-free basis; it becomes self-evident that noxious-use logic cannot serve as a touchstone to distinguish regulatory "takings"—which require compensation—from regulatory deprivations that do not require compensation.

Where the State seeks to sustain regulation that deprives land of all economically beneficial use, we think it may resist compensation only if the logically antecedent inquiry into the nature of the owner's estate shows that the proscribed use interests were not part of his title to begin with. It seems to us that the property owner necessarily expects the uses of his property to be restricted, from time to time, by various measures newly enacted by the State in legitimate exercise of its police powers.

Where regulations prohibit all economically beneficial use of land, any limitation so severe cannot be newly legislated or decreed (without compensation), but must inhere in the title itself, in the restrictions that background principles of the State's law of property and nuisance already place upon landownership.

On this analysis, the owner of a lake bed, for example, would not be entitled to compensation when he is denied the requisite permit to engage in a landfilling operation that would have the effect of flooding others' land. Nor would the corporate owner of a nuclear generating plant, when it is directed to remove all improvements from its land upon discovery that the plant sits astride an earthquake fault. Such regulatory action may well have the effect of eliminating the land's only economically productive use, but it does not proscribe a productive use that was previously permissible under relevant property and nuisance principles. The use of these properties for what are now expressly prohibited purposes was always unlawful.

The "total taking" inquiry we require today will ordinarily entail (as the application of state nuisance law ordinarily entails) analysis of, among other things, the degree of harm to public lands and resources, or adjacent private property, posed by the claimant's proposed activities, the social value of the claimant's activities and their suitability to the locality in question, and the relative ease with which the alleged harm can be avoided through measures taken by the claimant and the government (or adjacent private landowners) alike. The fact that a particular use has long been engaged in by similarly situated owners ordinarily imports a lack of any common-law prohibition (though changed circumstances or new knowledge may make what was previously permissible no longer so). So also does the fact that other landowners, similarly situated, are permitted to continue the use denied to the claimant.

It seems unlikely that common-law principles would have prevented the erection of any habitable or productive improvements on petitioner's land; they rarely support prohibition of the "essential use" of land. South Carolina must identify background principles of nuisance and property law that prohibit the uses he now intends in the circumstances in which the property is presently found. Only on this showing can the State fairly claim that, in proscribing all such beneficial uses, the Beachfront Management Act is taking nothing.

REVERSED.

JUST V. MARINETTE COUNTY

Supreme Court of Wisconsin
201 N.W.2d 761 (1972)

BACKGROUND. Marinette County adopted a shoreland zoning ordinance. Its purpose is to prevent deterioration of the state's navigable waters. The county passed the law in response to a state mandate to do so. The state mandate was triggered by its role as public trustee of the state's navigable waters. The County ordinance prohibited filling or draining of wetlands in a "conservancy district" without obtaining a permit. Ronald and Kathryn Just owned land that was a designated wetland in a conservancy district. The Justs began to fill their land without applying for a permit. They were ordered to stop. The Justs sued the County, contending that the shoreland zoning ordinance created a regulatory taking of their land. The trial court dismissed the action. The Justs appealed to the state Supreme Court.

DECISION. The Wisconsin Supreme Court affirmed the lower court's decision for Marinette County.

CHIEF JUSTICE HALLOWS. To state the issue in meaningful terms, it is a conflict between the public interest in stopping the despoliation of natural resources, which our citizens until recently have taken as inevitable and for granted, and an owner's asserted right to use property as he wishes. The protection of public rights may be accomplished by the exercise of the police power unless the damage to the property owner is too great and amounts to a confiscation. The securing or taking of a benefit not presently enjoyed by the public for its use is obtained by the government through its power of eminent domain. The distinction between the exercise of the police power and condemnation has been said to be a matter of degree of damage to the property owner. In the valid exercise of the police power reasonably restricting the use of property, the damage suffered by the owner is said to be incidental. However, where the restriction is so great the landowner ought not to bear such a burden for the public good, the restriction has been held to be a constructive taking even though the actual use or forbidden use has not been transferred to the government so as to be a taking in the traditional sense. Whether a taking has occurred depends upon whether "the restriction practically or substantially renders the land useless for all reasonable purposes."

Many years ago, Professor Freund stated in his work on The Police Power, "It may be said that the state takes property by eminent domain because it is useful to the public, and under the police power because it is harmful. . . . From this results the difference between the power of eminent domain and the police power, that the former recognizes a right to compensation, while the latter on principle does not." Thus the necessity for monetary compensation for loss suffered to an owner by police power restriction arises when restrictions are placed on property in order to create a public benefit rather than to prevent a public harm.

This case causes us to reexamine the concepts of public benefit in contrast to public harm and the scope of an owner's right to use of his property. In the instant case we have a restriction on the use of a citizen's property, not to secure a benefit for the public, but to prevent a harm from the change in the natural character of the citizen's property. We start with the premise that lakes and rivers in their natural state are unpolluted and the pollution which now exists is man made. The State of Wisconsin under the trust doctrine has a duty to eradicate the present pollution and to prevent further pollution in its navigable waters. This is not, in a legal sense, a gain or a securing of a benefit by the maintaining of the natural status quo of the environment. What makes this case different from most condemnation or police power zoning cases is the interrelationship of the wetlands, the swamps and the natural environment of shorelands to the purity of the water and to such natural resources as navigation, fishing, and scenic beauty. Swamps and wetlands were once considered wasteland, undesirable, and not picturesque. But as the people became more sophisticated, an appreciation was acquired that swamps and wetlands serve a vital role in nature, are part of the balance of nature and are essential to the purity of the water in our lakes and streams. Swamps and wetlands are a necessary part of the ecological creation and now, even to the uninitiated, possess their own beauty in nature.

Is the ownership of a parcel of land so absolute that man can change its nature to suit any of his purposes? An owner of land has no absolute and unlimited right to change the essential natural characters of his land so as to use it for a purpose for which it was unsuited in its natural state and which injures the rights of others. The exercise of the police power in zoning must be reasonable and we think it is not an unreasonable exercise of that power to prevent harm to public rights by limiting the use of private property to its natural uses.

This is not a case where an owner is prevented from using his land for natural and indigenous uses. The uses consistent with the nature of the land are allowed and other uses recognized and still others permitted by special permit. The shoreland zoning ordinance prevents to some extent the changing of the natural character of the land within 1,000 feet of a navigable river because of such land's interrelation to the contiguous water. The changing of wetlands and swamps to the damage of the general public by upsetting the natural environment and the natural relationship is not a reasonable use of that land which is protected by police power regulation. Nothing this court has said or held in prior cases indicated that destroying the natural character of a swamp or a wetland so as to make that location available for human habitation is a reasonable use of that land when the new use, although of a more economic value to the owner, causes a harm to the general public.

The Justs argue that their property has been severely depreciated in value. But this depreciation of value is not based on the use of the land in its natural state but on what the land would be worth if it could be filled and used for the location of a dwelling. While loss of value is to be considered in determining whether a restriction is a constructive taking, value based upon changing the character of the land at the expense of harm to public rights is not an essential factor or controlling.

The shoreland zoning ordinance preserves nature, the environment, and natural resources as they were created and to which the people have a present right. The ordinance does not create or improve the public condition but only preserves nature from the despoilage and harm resulting from the unrestricted activities of humans.

AFFIRMED.

It should be noted that the holding of the *Lucas* case is a narrow one. It holds that a regulatory taking occurs when all reasonable and beneficial economic use is denied the landowner; and then only when the proposed use was not already restricted by the state's nuisance and property law. It did make clear, however, that the harm/benefit type of analysis used by the court in the *Just* case was no longer appropriate in a *Lucas*-type situation. The conclusion reached by the *Just* case seems valid if the Justs retained some reasonable economic use. The differences in the two courts' general approach—economic vs. natural resource based—is a controversy probably not yet settled. Whichever theory is used, once a regulation is declared by a court to be a regulatory taking, the landowner is entitled to just compensation for the period the regulation was in effect.

By far the most important constitutional limitation in the land use area is the prohibition against regulatory takings. There are, however, other constitutional limitations that have played a lesser role in land use litigation, such as the equal protection clause. Most regulations attacked in court with an equal protection argument were adopted for economic reasons. In economic-based equal protection cases, the courts permit a regulation to differentiate between classes of persons (e.g., married and unmarried), but the classification must be reasonable and bear a rational relationship to a permissible state objective (e.g., public safety). In short, regulators may differentiate between classes but cannot discriminate against a group. It should be noted that this rational basis test does not apply in cases involving certain types of differentiations, such as those based on race or color. Differences based on race or color are subjected to a more rigorous test and are unlikely to survive judicial scrutiny.

Some state courts review land use regulations using a substantive due process standard. These courts examine the legislation under attack to see if in their view it is reasonable. So the courts actually second-guess the wisdom of the legislature in passing the law. The courts balance the benefit that the law can be expected to attain against the cost it will impose on society or individuals. Ideally, this is a repetition of the exact balancing process that the legislature carried out before adopting the law.

The federal courts and many state courts reject the notion of reviewing cases under a substantive due process standard. They contend that the wisdom of a law is within the purview of the legislative body and should not be overturned by a court unless it is arbitrary in nature. Whether these courts always refrain from reviewing the wisdom of land use laws despite what they say is a matter of some debate.

PLANNING

The cornerstone of any land use regulation is a plan. The law provides that regulations, especially zoning codes, must be based on a comprehensive plan. The regulator may organize, restrict or even prohibit development for public health, safety and welfare purposes, so long as the regulation is not arbitrary and is adopted pursuant to a plan.

There is no clear definition of what constitutes a comprehensive plan. Some state courts in zoning cases contend that the comprehensive plan need not be in writing, but may be inferred from the zoning map and the community's traditional land use patterns. In reality these courts pay only lip service to the planning requirement. It is a rare community that relies on a zoning map and past development patterns and develops in a truly planned fashion. Despite this fact, many states continue to minimize the planning requirement.

The Comprehensive Plan. Some states and municipalities take the planning requirement seriously and mandate the preparation and adoption of a bona fide comprehensive plan. A comprehensive, or master, plan has some standard characteristics. It deals with future physical development of the community, contains a textual statement of land-use policies and has a set of descriptive maps. The plan and maps are general in nature. A zoning code and map are usually adopted to make the plan operational and to add precision to the broad policies and maps contained in the plan.

LABONTA V. CITY OF WATERVILLE

Supreme Judicial Court of Maine
528 A. 2d 1262 (1987)

BACKGROUND. Shaw's Realty Company sought to locate a 170,000-square-foot shopping center on a parcel of land adjacent to Kennedy Memorial Drive in Waterville. A strip of land 800 feet deep along the drive was zoned for commercial use. The back portion of the parcel was zoned for residential use. Shaw petitioned the city council to rezone 8.1 acres of the land from residential to commercial. After holding public hearings on the proposed rezoning, the city council amended the zoning code by affirming Shaw's zone change request.

Robert LaBonta and a group of neighbors to the parcel filed suit to have the zone change overturned. They argued that the amendment was inconsistent with the city's comprehensive plan. In particular, it was inconsistent with the goal of protecting residential neighborhoods. The trial court found for the city.

DECISION. The Supreme Court of Maine affirmed the trial judge's opinion in favor of the city.

CHIEF JUSTICE MCKUSICK. The comprehensive plan, that section 4962(1)(A) requires every municipality to have as a prerequisite to zoning, is by definition "a compilation of policy statements, goals, [and] standards" with respect to issues relevant to land use regulation. The Waterville comprehensive plan sets forth a number of goals relevant to the rezoning requested by Shaw's, of which the protection of residential neighborhoods is but one. Particularly pertinent is the plan's emphasis on the need to expand economic opportunity in Waterville and to provide adequate space for commercial development. Even more specifically, the plan sets as a zoning goal for the City the commercial development along three arteries including Kennedy Memorial Drive, by stating the following:

"Commercial growth should continue to follow its present pattern of development with relation to three major traffic arteries of the City.

"Firstly, College Avenue has been, for years, the traditional node for newer commercial development. The present state of development and large volumes of traffic on that street preclude other types of use. Main Street, south of Route 95, and Kennedy Memorial Drive also have very large traffic volumes. While these streets do not have a long history of commercial development, their present state of rapidly progressing development has established them as major areas of commercial land use outside of the downtown area.

"By allowing for commercial development to occur in a coherent pattern in these areas of the City, other areas may be completely exempted from the pressures of this type of land use...."

From the transcript of the hearings conducted by the city council, it is clear that the council recognized and acted upon its responsibility to amend the zoning ordinance only in a way consistent with the comprehensive plan and the multiple goals stated therein. Faced with the multiple goals of protecting residential neighborhoods and promoting economic opportunity and commercial development along Kennedy Memorial Drive, the city council was not required to refrain from permitting any intrusion whatever upon an area previously zoned residential. Rather it had the job of accommodating these multiple goals in a way to advance the overall best interests of the City and its people as defined by the comprehensive plan read as a whole.

The test for the court's review of the city council's rezoning action is whether "from the evidence before it" the city council could have determined that the rezoning was in basic harmony with the [comprehensive] plan. In making that review of the record before the city council, the court will not substitute [its] judgment for that of the duly elected legislative body, the city council." The parties challenging the council's action have the burden of showing inconsistency between the rezoning and the comprehensive plan.

On the basis of the evidence before it, the city council is justified in concluding that the zoning change was in basic harmony with the comprehensive plan because the change struck a reasonable balance among the City's various zoning goals. On the one hand, the goal of promoting commercial development along Kennedy Memorial Drive (with the creation of additional job opportunities and the attraction of consumer dollars to Waterville) could not be fully achieved by the proposed shopping center within the 800-foot strip previously zoned commercial. The development of "one-stop shopping" means that a retail shopping area to be competitive must be large enough to offer customers a substantial variety of stores; and significant traffic flow advantages accrue to a deeper shopping center layout as compared to strip development. Also, recently imposed environmental regulations require the construction of a storm water retention basin, which in turn requires an additional area for a commercial establishment. On the other hand, the area that the city council rezoned commercial had been zoned residential for 58 years and still at the time of the rezoning no house had been built within it. The residents challenging the Waterville rezoning fail to persuade us that the city council's conclusion was not adequately supported by the evidence before it.

JUDGMENT AFFIRMED.

Generally, state legislation enables municipalities to enact zoning codes and other land use regulations, but makes comprehensive planning a precondition. In short, the planning and regulating are done locally under state authorization. There is a trend, however, for the states to become more involved in the land use planning and regulating process. During the 1970s, some state legislatures became dissatisfied with local planning and rescinded local power to do so. The rescission was usually for reasons of environmental protection and often applied to limited areas of the state. For example, New York placed land use control over the Adirondack Mountain region in the hands of a state-appointed regional agency, and California created the San Francisco Bay Conservation and Development Commission to plan and regulate future land use for the Bay Area.

This trend toward state control continues and is broadening. Some states have enacted comprehensive planning and land use systems applicable to the entire state, not confining them to environmental protection purposes.

Growth Management Systems. Several states have enacted comprehensive legislation setting up a system of growth management directed by the state. The leading state in this type of planning is Oregon. Oregon's system established a set of statewide planning goals and policies within which localities must operate. It established the state Land Conservation and Development Commission to oversee and guide the localities in this process. There are 19 goals with accompanying guidelines. The goals run the gamut from citizen involvement to land use planning to forest lands to energy conservation. Each locality must devise a land use plan and process consistent with these statewide goals.

The preparation of an EIS has become more manageable in recent years. Some communities have developed natural resource inventories that provide the scientific data to assist in preparing EISs. Many areas have private contractors available who specialize in preparing EISs.

Ultimate responsibility for preparing EISs lies with the government agency. The normal procedure is that the agency makes the threshold decision of whether to prepare an EIS. This decision may be facilitated by consulting the agency's EIS regulations, which will list projects necessitating EISs and those not requiring an EIS. For the types of actions not listed in its regulations, often called "unlisted actions," the agency prepares an environmental assessment. The environmental assessment (EA) is a mini-EIS whose purpose is to decide whether the proposed development action may have a significant effect on the quality of the environment. If the EA reveals that significant environmental impacts will not result, it terminates the process by issuing a "negative declaration." If the EA indicates that there may be significant environmental impacts, the agency must prepare an EIS. The preparation of the EIS is often preceded by a process called *scoping*. During scoping, the agency consults with all interested parties to determine what the significant impacts are likely to be (e.g., water pollution) and what the scope of those impacts is (e.g., within the Black River drainage area).

The EIS is initially prepared in draft form called a *DEIS*. The DEIS is circulated to relevant parties and is made available to the public. All parties have a specified period of time to respond to the DEIS. The agency then prepares a final EIS, known as an *FEIS*. The FEIS must address any shortcomings in the DEIS and respond to any reasonable comments made to the agency during the DEIS comment period. The FEIS is then considered by the agency decision maker along with other relevant information in determining whether to approve or to go ahead with the proposal.

REVIEW AND DISCUSSION QUESTIONS

1. Explain the rationale used for permitting one homeowner in a subdivision to sue a neighbor asserting a restrictive covenant in the neighbor's deed.
2. Why are courts unfavorably inclined toward restrictive covenants?
3. At this time which is the more important land use control factor—restrictive covenants or zoning? Why?
4. Distinguish between the power of eminent domain and a police power regulation.
5. Why do many courts refuse to review cases under a substantive due process standard?
6. When will a "regulatory taking" occur?
7. Discuss the purpose behind environmental impact assessment.

CASE PROBLEMS

1. Pursuant to a comprehensive plan, the City of Utica zoned an area "land conservation district." Within this district there were no automatically permitted uses. A special-use permit might be issued for several uses related to agriculture and recreation. Dur-Bar Realty

Company sued to have the zoning ordinance declared unconstitutional. Discuss. *Dur-Bar Realty Co. v. City of Utica, 57 A.D.2d 52, 394 N.Y.S.2d 913 (1977).*

2. Unlimited, Inc., applied for a building permit to construct a convenience store. Kitsap County granted the permit subject to two conditions: that Unlimited (1) provide an easement to owners of nearby commercially zoned property to facilitate the development of their land; and (2) dedicate, or give to the County, a strip of land for a county road extension. Unlimited sued the County contending that the conditions affected a taking of their property without due process of law. Discuss. *Unlimited v. Kitsap County, 30 Wash. App. 723, 750 P.2d 651 (1988).*

3. The City of Seattle adopted a greenbelt ordinance that required landowners to preserve from 50 to 70 percent of their land in its natural state without paying them compensation. The City asserted a valid police power purpose for the law. What test must be applied to these facts to determine whether a taking without due process of law has occurred? Discuss. *Allingham v. City of Seattle, 109 Wash.2d 947, 749 P.2d 160 (1988).*

4. A developer in New York City proposed to build a high-rise luxury condominium. New York State has a little-NEPA mandating the preparation of environmental impact statements (EISs) for some projects. The EIS examined the project's effects on the physical environment and found none that were significant. The EIS was challenged, however, because it did not discuss the impact that the project would have on the existing patterns of population concentration, distribution, growth or neighborhood character. The preparer of the EIS contended that these factors were not within the term *environment*. Discuss the pros and cons of the parties' positions in this case. *Chinese Staff and Workers Ass'n v. City of New York, 68 N.Y.2d 359, 502 N.E.2d 176, 509 N.Y.S. 449 (1986).*

25

Regulation of Land Development

Early in this century, state and local governments strayed to some degree from their laissez-faire attitude toward private land ownership. Prior to this time, Americans took seriously the 18th-century authority on the common law, William Blackstone, who pronounced private property rights as "that sole and despotic dominion." Though landowners never had quite the absolute rights alluded to by Blackstone, little land regulation existed. This system of nonregulation faded as the congestion, noise, pollution and other urban ills manifested themselves to city dwellers.

The chief tool selected to address these problems early in the century was zoning. The adoption of zoning codes proliferated after the U.S. Supreme Court in the 1926 case *Village of Euclid v. Ambler 275 U.S. 365* found constitutional a system that divided the community into use zones. Zoning has retained its primacy as a land use regulatory mechanism. Many modern zoning codes are not confined to separating land uses but address problems like protecting prime agricultural lands.

Zoning is no longer alone, whatever its form, in regulatory land use. Americans realized that zoning codes were not protecting the land from environmental degradation. Wetlands, prime agricultural lands, historical heritage and wildlife habitat were being lost at an alarming rate despite zoning. The result was legislation, in addition to zoning, addressing the special problems of environmental degradation.

This chapter discusses traditional zoning and its modern nuances. It describes some of the problems created by development for special types of land areas and discusses regulatory tools used to cope with these problems.

ZONING

◆ **The regulation by the public, usually a municipality, of structures and uses of land within designated zones.**

In its simplest form, traditional zoning divides the municipality into districts for residential, commercial and industrial uses. Within each of these districts, limitations are placed on the size and height of buildings, the siting of the buildings on the parcel, the density of development in the area, the minimum size of the parcel and perhaps the type of structure permitted on the site. The purchaser of a parcel of land must be aware not only of the restrictions revealed by a title search but also of the limitations placed on the land by the zoning code.

The power to zone is expressly given to each locality (municipality or county) by the state through *enabling legislation,* by which that state authorizes the locality to regulate in the area of land use control. That legislation requires the zoning code adopted by the locality to be consistent with a plan for development. The zoning districts are to be placed on a map pursuant to that plan, for the purpose of maintaining property values, matching designated use to the character of the land (low-density development in unsewered areas with relatively impermeable soil, for example) and promoting the environmental, cultural and economic welfare of the area in any other way.

Some courts have been lenient in approving zoning codes when the question pertains to the existence of a plan. They have not required a truly comprehensive plan in the modern sense. Often a zoning code and map drawn up by a qualified firm and adopted by the town has met with judicial approval, even though review of how to optimize local development or nondevelopment is lacking.

One reason for this judicial leniency has been that sparsely populated localities cannot reasonably afford to develop a comprehensive plan. Thus, the economic ability of the locality to generate a more comprehensive plan becomes relevant. The courts are not explicit on this point, but this economic constraint seems to underlie many decisions.

The three basic zoning classifications of residential, commercial and industrial have tended to proliferate. It is not uncommon now for localities to have 15 to 20 or more zones. The use permitted within a zone is often more narrowly confined, with separate zones for single-family houses on one acre, single-family houses on one-half acre, condominiums, garden-type apartments, double houses and so on. Separate zones are designated for shopping centers, office buildings, personal service shops (beauty parlors) and gas stations. For industry, the developer has to select the correct zone from among heavy manufacturing, light manufacturing, warehousing and the like. With this multitude of zones, the locality is able to exercise tighter control over the location of development. Careful examination of local zoning code definitions and requirements is essential because they tend to be highly variable.

One intrinsic problem with zoning that is magnified by the multiplication of zones is inflexibility. Theoretically, the municipality periodically studies the needs of the locality and develops a zoning code or makes amendments to the existing codes based on those needs. Those needs may change before the municipality undertakes to assess them, so that zones may be outdated and discourage more appropriate development.

In some areas of the country where condominiums came into vogue, there were no appropriate zones to accommodate them, and their development was therefore hindered. Other localities acted promptly to create special districts for condominiums, only to find them a passing fad and economically infeasible for the area. The result was that districts zoned for condominiums were then classified inappropriately.

states contend that zoning is an administrative decision and zone changes on individual parcels can be made by the appropriate agency, for example, the planning board.

Although a local government can initiate a zone change, generally the moving party is a landowner or developer. He or she tries to convince the legislative body that the proposed use makes more sense than the use designated in the zoning code. When granting a zone change, the legislature must be careful to establish the reasons for the change. The change must be presented as being justified by the current needs of the community. In this way, the zone change is assured of being consistent with the notion that the locality is continuing to plan for its land use.

F.S. PLUMMER CO., INC. v. TOWN OF CAPE ELIZABETH

Supreme Judicial Court of Maine
612 A.2d 856 (1992)

BACKGROUND. Prior to 1981, F.S. Plummer Co., Inc. (Plummer) purchased several undeveloped lots in an existing subdivision. The lots were zoned Residential A District. In 1981, the Town of Cape Elizabeth (Town) enacted comprehensive zoning amendments. As a result four of Plummer's lots were rezoned Resource Protection District (RPD) making it impossible to develop them for residential use. Plummer applied for a zone change, but the Town Council denied the application. Plummer sued the Town alleging a denial of due process, a lack of substantial evidence to support the denial of the application, and an abuse of discretion. The trial court agreed with Plummer and ordered the Town to reclassify the lots as residential.

DECISION. The Supreme Judicial Court of Maine reversed the trial court's decision.

JUSTICE RUDMAN. The ordinance itself is presumed to be constitutional. The burden is on Plummer to show by "clear and irrefutable evidence that it infringes on paramount law" and to establish "the complete absence of any

state of facts that would support … the ordinance. In order for the ordinance to be a valid exercise of the Town's police power it must 1) provide for the public welfare, 2) use means appropriate to the desired ends, and 3) not be exercised in an arbitrary or capricious manner.

Among the goals of the RPD is the protection of the environment and water quality. This goal provides for the public welfare and is a valid object of the exercise of the Town's police power. Restricting development in wetland areas is an appropriate means of achieving those objects.

Under the Town's zoning ordinance, the RPD consists of:

All other areas so designated on the official zoning map, and any apparent wetlands contiguous thereto … unless the applicant for a permit for use or development of any land within the foregoing descriptions shall demonstrate by way of an on-site survey that the land does not constitute either "wetlands" … or "Sebago Mucky Peat" type soil, or coastal dunes.

Plummer's property was designated as part of the RPD on the official zoning map. The ordinance provides a reasonable mechanism for landowners who feel their property was improperly included in the RPD to petition for its reclassification. Although Plummer was able to demonstrate that its property did not contain Sebago Mucky Peat, the Town found, and Plummer concedes the fact, that its property contains wetlands. Therefore, the Town Council's adoption of the ordinance cannot be said to be arbitrary or capricious and the Town's amendment of its zoning ordinance, the effect of which was the reclassification of Plummer's property, was a valid exercise of its police power.

To successfully challenge the Town Council's denial of its zone change request Plummer must show that the Town's decision was inconsistent with the comprehensive plan. The Town Council found that these lots contained wetlands, and that filling the lots could create run-off and flooding problems. The comprehensive plan states that "certain areas of the community should be excluded from development because of the natural conditions of the land. Where these conditions can be shown to have a substantial relationship to the public's health, safety and welfare (i.e., flood hazard or ability to support a subsurface disposal system) severe restrictions on development can and should be sustained." The comprehensive plan further contemplates that no development will occur in the RPD. We conclude that the Town Council's denial of Plummer's zone change request was in basic harmony with the comprehensive plan.

REVERSED.

VARIANCE

◆ **Permission obtained from the appropriate governmental authorities to deviate somewhat from the designations under the zoning code.**

In contrast to a zone change, a variance is not actually a change in the law. A variance is generally a modest deviation from the requirements of the zoning code. For instance, a landowner may gain a variance to allow him to set his proposed house back only 25 feet from the street rather than the 30 feet required under the zoning law. His parcel of land would continue to be zoned R-1 as it was before the variance.

Use variances can also be granted. Since they could permit a commercial use in a residential zone, however, they are more destructive to the local plan and are less likely to be granted.

Variances are granted by an administrative body in the locality. It may be called a *zoning board of appeals,* a *board of adjustment* or some similar title. In order to obtain a variance, the applicant must prove that the failure to grant it will cause him or her unnecessary hardship. In addition, the applicant must show that the new use will not reduce the value of surrounding properties and that the granting of it is within the public interest and not contrary to the spirit of the zoning code.

> ### CASE EXAMPLE
>
> The Town of Hampstead's zoning ordinance prohibits residential buildings higher than 1½ stories. The purpose of the regulation is to retain the view of and from the lake and to maintain the beauty and countrified atmosphere of the town. Alexander applied for a variance to put an additional full story on his one-story home. His variance application was denied by the town, and he sued to overturn the denial.
>
> The court held that the denial of the variance was based on protecting the lake view and was therefore not arbitrary. It went on to state that in order to obtain a variance, the applicant must prove the following: (1) no reduction in the value of surrounding properties would be suffered; (2) granting the permit would benefit the public interest; (3) denial of the variance would create unnecessary hardship for the applicant; (4) granting the permit would do substantial justice; and (5) the use must not be contrary to the spirit of the ordinance. *Alexander v. Town of Hampstead, 525 A.2d 276 (1987).*

The rule of law states that no one has a *right* to a variance, so courts will not overturn the administrator's decision to deny it unless the decision is arbitrary. This narrow scope of judicial review permits the zoning board wide latitude in approving and disapproving variances. Unless the zoning board strictly requires the applicant to meet the burden of proof mentioned above and unless it keeps foremost the goals intended to be accomplished in the zoning code, its wide latitude can lead to an undermining of the land use goals established for the locality.

GREY ROCKS LAND TRUST V. TOWN OF HEBRON

Supreme Court of New Hampshire
614 A.2d 1048 (1992)

BACKGROUND. William Robertie owned 35 acres of land on which five buildings were clustered near the town road. The land was along a channel, and Robertie operated a marina on it. The buildings were used for boat storage, boat repairs, and boat-related retail sales. The land was zoned Lake District and uses were limited to those that protected scenic, recreational, and environmental values or the natural and scenic resources of the town. The specifically stated permitted uses did not include a marina. In 1987, Robertie applied for an expansion of his commercial use of the property. The Town of Hebron denied the application because the marina was a nonconforming use and could not be expanded. The marina predated the zoning ordinance. In 1988, Robertie applied to the Zoning Board of Adjustment (ZBA) for a variance to build a boat storage building. The ZBA granted the variance.

Grey Rocks Land Trust (Grey Rocks) is an abutting landowner whose land is used for recreation and residential purposes. After losing their argument opposing the variance, Grey

Rocks sued to overturn the granting of the variance because Robertie had failed to prove that its denial would create an unnecessary hardship. The Superior Court upheld the ZBA.

DECISION. The New Hampshire Supreme Court reversed the decision concluding that the grounds for a variance had not been satisfied.

JUSTICE JOHNSON. "To obtain a variance under RSA 674:33 I(b), an applicant must satisfy each of five requirements: (1) that a denial of the variance would result in unnecessary hardship to the applicant; (2) that no diminution in value of surrounding properties would occur; (3) that the proposed use would not be contrary to the spirit of the ordinance; (4) that granting the variance would benefit the public interest; and (5) that granting the variance would do substantial justice."

This court has further defined the requirement that a denial of a variance [would] result in unnecessary hardship. The standard for establishing hardship is narrow. "For hardship to exist under our test, the deprivation resulting from application of the ordinance must be so great as to effectively prevent the owner from making any reasonable use of the land." Furthermore, the hardship must arise from "some unique condition of the parcel of land distinguishing it from others in the area. . . ." "The uniqueness of the land, not the plight of the owner, determines whether a hardship exists."

In order for the ZBA to have concluded that a hardship existed, it would have to have found that literal enforcement of the ordinance bars any reasonable use of the land. Thus, a showing that Robertie was making a reasonable use of the land at the time of the application for a variance would preclude a finding of hardship.

The uncontroverted fact that the Marina had been operating as a viable commercial entity for several years prior to the variance application is conclusive evidence that a hardship does not exist. The defendant Robertie was clearly making a reasonable use of his property prior to his application for a variance. A viable, nonconforming business fails to meet the strict standard for a finding of hardship established by cases such as *Governor's Island*.

In addition to failing to find that denying the variance would preclude any reasonable use of Robertie's property, the ZBA also failed to find that Robertie's land was unique. The ZBA stated in its submission of fact findings to the court that "[t]he Newfound Lake Marina is the only Marina located within the Town of Hebron." A nonconforming use, however, may not form the basis for a finding of uniqueness to satisfy the hardship test. The nonconforming use that is presently located on Robertie's land has nothing to do with the land itself. Therefore, because the record fails to reflect any other basis for finding that Robertie's land is unique, we hold that the ZBA erred as a matter of law in finding that Robertie satisfied the uniqueness prong of the hardship requirement.

The defendants next argue that, independent of the hardship requirement, the owner of a nonconforming use has a right to "[develop] [the] nonconforming use in a way that results in a mere intensification of the use that reflects a natural expansion and growth of trade."

"[I]n order to determine how much a nonconforming use may be expanded or changed, we must look to the facts existing when the nonconforming use was created. We must also consider the extent to which the challenged use reflects the nature and purpose of the prevailing nonconforming use, whether the challenged use is merely a different manner of using the original nonconforming use or whether it constitutes a different use, and whether the challenged use will have a substantially different impact upon the neighborhood."

We have never permitted an expansion of a nonconforming use that involved more than the internal expansion of a business within a pre-existing structure.

In the instant case, it is apparent from the aerial photographs, and the defendants concede in their brief, that the new building is located 450 feet closer to Grey Rocks than the five pre-existing buildings. Thus, the new building clearly has a greater aesthetic impact on the abutting property than the other five buildings. In this case, we hold that the new building will have "a substantially different impact upon the neighborhood."

Any expansion of a nonconforming use must be evaluated in the context of the zone in which it is located. The Lake District is intended to protect "scenic, recreational and environmental values" and to "encourage only such further development as will not harm the environment or destroy this district or any part thereof as a natural and scenic resource of the Town." We hold as a matter of law that the construction of a new building, such as the one proposed by the Marina, would substantially impair the natural scenic, recreational, and environmental values of the surrounding property, contrary to the purposes of the Lake District, and is therefore beyond the scope of the "natural expansion," to which the Marina is entitled.

REVERSED.

EXCEPTIONS IN ZONING
◆ **Permitted uses provided for in the ordinance that are inconsistent with the designated zone.**

Unlike variances or zone changes, exceptions are built right into the zoning ordinance. For instance, an R-1 (residential) zone may permit by exception the construction of a church, school or park within that district. The uses by exception are different from the uses allowed by the zoning code but are considered to be compatible with those uses. No special administrative permission is necessary. So long as the proposed use coincides with the exception detailed in the zoning code, the landowner will be allowed to construct the excepted use.

SPECIAL-USE PERMIT
◆ **A system whereby special exceptions to the zoning ordinance are granted by the land use administrator under a permit arrangement set forth in the zoning ordinance.**

It has become common in zoning codes to omit certain uses from any of the zoning classifications. These uses are allowed only by getting a permit, which entails obtaining the approval of local zoning officials. Hospitals, churches, schools, recreational facilities such as golf courses, and cemeteries are handled in this fashion. Some of these uses may not be offensive in any specific zone, but the permit process retains control for community officials over their location in those situations where they may be objectionable. The special-use permit provides for flexibility in locating these uses for the applicant and maintains public control at the same time.

The special-use permit can be attacked on the basis that it is spot zoning, that is, unplanned zoning. However, this approach can be distinguished in several ways. Generally special uses are enumerated as such in the zoning ordinance, giving rise to the notion that they may be appropriate uses in an array of zones, depending on surrounding conditions. Many of the uses are not intrinsically offensive; they are singled out for the special-use permit process so that they can be blended into the community in a planned way. This is the antithesis of spot zoning.

Even where the permitted use has greater potential for offending the area residents, such as a cemetery, jail or gas station, the purpose of segregating these uses in the zoning code is to ensure that they are placed on sites consistent with community needs.

VARIATIONS AND SPECIAL USES OF TRADITIONAL ZONING

The original purpose of traditional zoning was to keep different uses of land separate so that, for instance, an industrial use did not become a nuisance for nearby residential homeowners. Communities discovered that separating uses alone did not eliminate all their problems, nor did it provide them with ideal living conditions. Zoning, and variations of it, are being used to attack a wide variety of urban and suburban ills.

LARGE-LOT ZONING
♦ **A zoning classification that requires a minimum of one acre or more of land for each single-family house that is constructed.**

The selection of one acre as the minimum size for large-lot zoning and other zoning is somewhat arbitrary. Other writers may contend that it should be slightly larger or smaller. What size lot constitutes a questionable zoning classification may depend on the location of the property. For instance, city lots tend to be small, and rural lots tend to be much larger. In any event, at some point, depending on the environment, the minimum lot size may be so large that it raises a legal question as to whether or not the size can be justified under the police power.

Advantages. In many areas of the country, it is not uncommon to have zoning classifications requiring a minimum lot size of one, two or even five acres. Several legitimate public policy reasons can be given for mandatory lots of that size. Where municipal sewers and water are not available, the soil and geologic conditions may necessitate sparse development for nature to function adequately in supplying water and for cleansing wastewater. In some states where it is recognized as a salient reason for zoning, and in other states where it may be used merely as an additive reason, aesthetics may be offered as a reason for large-lot zoning. Sparse development on large, generously landscaped lots is attractive to almost everyone.

Large-lot zoning, despite the language contained in the purpose clause of a local code, may have a hidden motivation. Wealthy people prefer to live on large lots, which give better assurance of privacy in tranquil surroundings. The greater the financial means of the owner, the larger the residential lot is likely to be. It is quite natural for someone who can afford it to select a dream home in suburbia. Similarly, the desire to have amenities as well as to retain the market value of their properties causes others to desire comparable high-priced housing nearby.

A second purpose for this type of zoning is that sparse development on large lots tends to be less expensive in terms of the cost of public services. Though municipal sewer and water facilities, if available, may be more expensive, other community services, such as schools, fire and police, tend to be less expensive. A major share of municipal property taxes goes for schools, and taxpayers usually wish to keep these taxes down. Statistically, well-to-do people have relatively few children, and restricting developments to large lots enables residents to reduce school taxes.

Disadvantages. Hidden motivation may represent the negative side of large-lot zoning. The intent of such zoning, or at least a residual result, is discriminatory. Even when the intent of large-lot zoning is for the socially laudatory purpose of permitting people to enjoy the "fruits of their labor," one effect of such zoning is to exclude the poor and less financially advantaged.

Excluding the financially disadvantaged usually results in the exclusion of minority groups as well. A municipality that caters to the wealthy with large-lot zoning may be steering low- and middle-income housing and the resulting higher public service taxes into nearby communities. A community may feel that exclusive use of large-lot zoning will help prevent higher taxes, crime and congestion. These social ills do not go away, however; they are merely concentrated in communities that do not exclude through large-lot zoning.

Judicial Responses to Large-Lot Zoning. Though not yet widespread, there is a growing tendency among state courts to reject large-lot zoning as unconstitutional. The Pennsylvania and New Jersey courts have been leaders in this movement.

CASE EXAMPLE

The zoning ordinance in the Town of Concord required a minimum lot size of one acre along existing roads and three acres on the interior. Kit-Mar Builders were denied a request to rezone their property lots smaller than mandated by the code. Kit-Mar sued Concord, contending that the large-lot zoning was an unconstitutional taking of its property.

The Pennsylvania Supreme Court held that a zoning provision of this type is unconstitutional if either its purpose or its result is exclusionary. The only exception would be where the municipality can show some extraordinary justification for requiring large lots. An extraordinary justification would be where the natural conditions of the soil, for instance, cannot handle denser population and there is no other reasonable, nonexclusionary method of resolving the problem. *In re Kit-Mar Builders, Inc., 439 Pa. 466, 268 A.2d 765 (1970).*

Most Pennsylvania communities would be hard-pressed to satisfy the judicial burden of proving extraordinary justification.

The New Jersey courts have gone a step further. The New Jersey Supreme Court, in an opinion that has implications beyond large-lot zoning, has declared that developing communities must provide for their fair share of the low- and middle-income housing needs of their region. *South Burlington County N.A.A.C.P. v. Township of Mt. Laurel, 67 N.J. 151, 336 A.2d 713, appeal dismissed, 423 U.S. 808 (1975).* Taking a cue from the Pennsylvania courts, the opinion permits an exception when "peculiar circumstances" can be shown. *Peculiar circumstances* sounds very much like extraordinary justification. The legal basis of the court's ruling is that under state law citizens have a right to decent shelter, and rampant large-lot zoning could effect a denial of this right.

In short, large-lot zoning will be unacceptable where the community has not otherwise provided the housing, or potential for housing, for its share of the region's less financially advantaged people. The adoption of a regional approach to land use decision making has long been espoused by scholars and planners but had not previously received broad judicial approval.

If the New Jersey approach is broadly adopted, it will not sound the death knell for large-lot zoning. So long as a community is able to provide for its share of the regional housing needs elsewhere, it may continue to have large-lot zoning. In addition, there is nothing that prevents a developer from voluntarily building houses on large lots to satisfy a demand for such housing.

The U.S. Supreme Court, in *Agins v. City of Tiburon, 447 U.S. 254 (1980),* seemed less concerned than the above states about the potential disadvantages to large-lot zoning. It held that a regulation that limited an owner to as few as one house on a five-acre lot was legal. The court stated that where a regulation promoted a police power purpose and did not deny the owner of all reasonable economic use, no regulatory taking occurred. Also, New Jersey has since created an administrative mechanism for coping with the fair share housing program. Pennsylvania has been circumspect in recent years about striking down large-lot zoning.

PLANNED UNIT DEVELOPMENT (PUD)

◆ **An "overlay" zoning concept that enables a developer to obtain a higher density and more mixed use than the underlying zoning would allow, with more generous provision for green space.**

This definition of a PUD is necessarily vague. As it has evolved, the PUD has become many things. It is a term used to describe a development that clusters houses on undersized lots in order to provide more open space to the residents. The term is used to depict a development that permits various types of housing within the same tract, such as townhouses, apartments and single-family housing. In another community, it may be flexible enough to allow mixed uses, such as residential, commercial and even light industry (such as warehouses). Some zoning maps designate areas of the community as PUD zones, while other communities adopt a *floating-zone* concept in which the PUD becomes affixed to a particular land area

water lines and mandated drainage facilities, and the location of parks and open spaces. When the subdivider presents a plat plan to the planning board, the board determines whether the streets, sewers and so forth meet the conditions necessary for maintenance of the public health, safety and welfare.

Subdivision regulations generally take the form of standards, specifications and procedures set for street signs, streetlights, street trees, fire hydrants, storm drains, sanitary sewers, curbs, gutters and sidewalks. The regulations may require the developer to post a performance bond to ensure compliance with these rules. The final plat, or subdivision map, submitted by the developer will illustrate in detail all the improvements required under the subdivision rules.

CASE EXAMPLE

Sowin Associates applied to the Planning and Zoning Commission for subdivision approval of a plan for 11 lots on a 10-acre parcel. The parcel was zoned residential. The Commission denied subdivision approval because the development could cause off-site traffic congestion, decrease property values and was in disharmony generally with the area. The Associates' plan was apparently in conformity with the Town's subdivision regulations. Sowin Associates sued to reverse the Commission's denial.

The Court reversed the Commission's denial because Sowin Associates' plan conformed to the town's subdivision regulations. It stated that traffic congestion, decrease in property values and area disharmony are relevant considerations in a zoning matter determining the use of the land, but not in a subdivision matter. *Sowin Associates v. Planning and Zoning Commission, 23 Conn. App. 370, 580 A.2d 91 (1990).*

Subdivision Exactions and Impact Fees. Subdivision exaction is a requirement that a subdivider dedicate part of its land, or an in-lieu-fee payment, to the community to serve site-specific needs created by the subdivision.

An impact fee is a device requiring a subdivider to fund major, off-site infrastructure expansion that serves the community at large as well as the subdivision residents.

Approval of the developer's plat plan usually coincides with the community's agreement to accept title to all streets, streetlights and so forth when completed. Herein lies the *quid pro quo,* the equal exchange that enables the community to regulate a subdivision closely. The developer agrees to comply with the various subdivision regulations and expects in return that the community will accept a *dedication,* or transfer of title, of the infrastructure facilities, including roads, sewers, hydrants, and drainage structures. The transaction relieves the developer of continuing responsibility for maintaining these facilities.

A dedication, or *subdivision exaction,* which is becoming common now, is one for parks or open space. The planning board may insist that the developer dedicate a percentage of its land, or money in lieu of parkland, prior to granting approval of the final plat. This type of dedication has been approved as a reasonable extension of the transaction discussed above.

States take different approaches to how closely the need for the parkland must be tied to the demand created by the residents in the developer's subdivision. In states with a more flexible rule, the planning board can exact land based on future, as well as present, needs of the subdivision residents; that is, ten years from now 15 acres of open space per thousand people will be the standard rather than the present 10 acres per thousand. A recent U.S. Supreme Court case addressed the issue as a constitutional one.

DOLAN V. CITY OF TIGARD
Supreme Court of the United States
114 S.Ct. 2309 (1994)

BACKGROUND. The State of Oregon requires that its municipalities adopt comprehensive land use plans. The City of Tigard in its comprehensive plan includes a Central Business District Zone in which 15percent of a parcel must remain open space, and requires new development to facilitate the transportation plan by dedicating land for pedestrian/bicycle pathway. The plan further encourages measures to control flooding along Fanno Creek caused by an increase In impervious surface due to increased urbanization.

Florence Dolan owns a 1.67 acre parcel along Fanno Creek that is zoned as Central Business District. She operates a plumbing and electrical supply store on the premises, and applied for a permit to redevelop the site doubling the size of the store and paving. The City Planning Commission granted her a permit with the following conditions. Dolan must dedicate to the city the portion of her property along Fanno Creek that is within the 100-year floodplain; and dedicate an additional 15-foot strip of land adjacent to the floodplain for a pedestrian/bicycle pathway. The floodplain dedication can be used to satisfy the 15 percent open space requirement. The Commission's justification for the requested dedication was the increase of impervious surface in the floodplain of Fanno Creek caused by her expansion, and the assumed increase in use by Dolan's customers of the pathway as an alternative to using cars and increasing congestion.

The Land Use Board of Appeals, the Oregon Court of Appeals, and the Oregon Supreme Court each affirmed the validity of the Commission's permit conditions.

DECISION. The United States Supreme Court reversed the prior decision.

CHIEF JUSTICE REHNQUIST. The Takings Clause of the Fifth Amendment of the United States Constitution, made applicable to the States through the Fourteenth Amendment, provides: "[N]or shall private property be taken for public use, without just compensation." Without question, had the city simply required petitioner to dedicate a strip of land along Fanno Creek for public use, rather than conditioning the grant of her permit to redevelop her property on such a dedication, a taking would have occurred.

On the other side of the ledger, the authority of state and local governments to engage in land use planning has been sustained against constitutional challenge as long ago as our decision in *Euclid v. Ambler Realty Co. (1926)*. A land use regulation does not effect a taking if it "substantially advance[s] legitimate state interests" and does not "den[y] an owner economically viable use of his land." The conditions imposed were not simply a limitation on the use petitioner might make of her own parcel, but a requirement that she deed portions of the property to the city.

In evaluating petitioner's claim, we must first determine whether the "essential nexus" exists between the "legitimate state interest" and the permit condition exacted by the city. If we find that a nexus exists, we must then decide the required degree of connection between the exactions and the projected impact of the proposed development. We were not required to reach this question in *Nollan*, because we concluded that the connection did not meet even the loosest standard. Undoubtedly, the prevention of flooding along Fanno Creek and the reduction of traffic congestion in the Central Business District qualify as the type of legitimate public purposes we have upheld. It seems equally obvious that a nexus exists between preventing flooding along Fanno Creek and limiting development within the creek's 100-year floodplain. Petitioner proposes to double the size of her retail store and to pave her now-gravel parking lot, thereby expanding the impervious surface on the property and increasing the amount of stormwater run-off into Fanno Creek.

The same may be said for the city's attempt to reduce traffic congestion by providing for alternative means of transportation. In theory, a pedestrian/bicycle pathway provides a useful alternative means of transportation for workers and shoppers: "Pedestrians and bicyclists occupying dedicated spaces for walking and/or bicycling . . . remove potential vehicles from streets, resulting in an overall improvement in total transportation system flow."

The second part of our analysis requires us to determine whether the degree of the exactions demanded by the city's permit conditions bear the required relationship to the projected impact of petitioner's proposed development.

The city required that petitioner dedicate "to the city as Greenway all portions of the site that fall within the existing 100-year floodplain [of Fanno Creek] . . . and all property 15 feet above [the floodplain] boundary." In addition, the city demanded that the retail store be designed so as not to intrude into the greenway area. The city relies on the Commission's rather tentative findings that increased stormwater flow from petitioner's property "can only add to the public need to manage the [floodplain] for drainage purposes" to support its conclusion that the "requirement of dedication of the floodplain area on the site is related to the applicant's plan to intensify development on the site." Since state courts have been dealing with this question a good deal longer than we have, we turn to representative decisions made by them.

In some States, very generalized statements as to the necessary connection between the required dedication and the proposed development seem to suffice. We think this standard is too lax to adequately protect petitioner's right to just compensation if her property is taken for a public purpose.

Other state courts require a very exacting correspondence described as the "specifi[c] and uniquely attributable" test. Under this standard, if the local government cannot demonstrate that its exaction is directly proportional to the specifically created need, the exaction becomes "a veiled exercise of the power of eminent domain and a confiscation of private property behind the defense of police regulations." We do not think the Federal Constitution requires such exacting scrutiny, given the nature of the interests involved.

A number of state courts have taken an intermediate position, requiring the municipality to show a "reasonable relationship" between the required dedication and the impact of the proposed development. "The distinction, therefore, which must be made between an appropriate exercise of the police power and an improper exercise of eminent domain is whether the requirement has some reasonable relationship or nexus to the use to which the property is being made or is merely being used as an excuse for taking property simply because at that particular moment the landowner is asking the city for some license or permit."

We think the "reasonable relationship" test adopted by a majority of the state courts is closer to the federal constitutional norm than either of those previously discussed. But we do not adopt it as such, partly because the term "reasonable relationship" seems confusingly similar to the term "rational basis" which describes the minimal level of scrutiny under the Equal Protection Clause of the Fourteenth Amendment. We think a term such as "rough proportionality" best encapsulates what we hold to be the requirement of the Fifth Amendment. No precise mathematical calculation is required, but the city must make some sort of individualized determination that the required dedication is related both in nature and extent to the impact of the proposed development.

We turn now to analysis of whether the findings relied upon by the city here, first with respect to the floodplain easement, and second with respect to the pedestrian/bicycle path, satisfied these requirements. It is axiomatic that increasing the amount of impervious surface will increase the quantity and rate of storm-water flow from petitioner's property. Therefore, keeping the floodplain open and free from development would likely confine the pressures on Fanno Creek created by petitioner's development. The city not only wanted petitioner not to build in the floodplain, but it also wanted petitioner's property along Fanno Creek for its greenway system. The city has never said why a public greenway, as opposed to a private one, was required in the interest of flood control.

The difference to petitioner, of course, is the loss of her ability to exclude others. As we have noted, this right to exclude others is "one of the most essential sticks in the bundle of rights that are commonly characterized as property." It is difficult to see why recreational visitors trampling along petitioner's floodplain easement are sufficiently related to the city's legitimate interest in reducing flooding problems along Fanno Creek, and the city has not attempted to make any individualized determination to support this part of its request.

We conclude that the findings upon which the city relies do not show the required reasonable relationship between the floodplain easement and the petitioner's proposed new building.

With respect to the pedestrian/bicycle pathway, we have no doubt that the city was correct in finding that the larger retail sales facility proposed by petitioner will increase traffic on the streets of the Central Business District. The city estimates that the proposed development would generate roughly 435 additional trips per day. Dedications for streets, sidewalks, and other public ways are generally reasonable exactions to avoid excessive congestion from a proposed property use. But on the record before us, the city has not met its burden of demonstrating that the additional number of vehicle and bicycle trips generated by the petitioner's development reasonably relate to the city's requirement for a dedication of the pedestrian/bicycle pathway easement. The city simply found that the creation of the pathway "could offset some of the traffic demand ... and lessen the increase in traffic congestion." No precise mathematical calculation is required, but the city must make some effort to quantify its findings in support of the dedication for the pedestrian/bicycle pathway beyond the conclusory statement that it could offset some of the traffic demand generated.

Cities have long engaged in the commendable task of land use planning, made necessary by increasing urbanization particularly in metropolitan areas such as Portland. The city's goals of reducing flooding hazards and traffic congestion, and providing for public greenways, are laudable, but there are outer limits to how this may be done.

REVERSED.

As sources of funds for community improvement have disappeared over the past decade or so, communities are striving to create new tools to fund needed projects. The subdivision exaction tool addresses needs created by and within the subdivision. A new subdivision, along with other development in the area, generally creates the need for the construction or expansion of areawide but off-site improvements. Many communities authorize the collection of user impact fees from subdividers for such improvements as widening of nearby highways, expansion of water and sewage treatment facilities and construction of landfills. The user impact fee resembles payment in lieu of land fees used in subdivision exactions. Some differences between the two are: in-lieu fees finance on-site improvements, and user impact fees finance off-site projects; in-lieu fees are generally assessed based on the subdivision's acreage or number of lots, and user impact fees are based on the square footage of the proposed buildings or the number of bedrooms; and in-lieu fees are confined to residential subdivisions, while user impact fees are often applied to other types of development, too.

As with subdivision exactions, care must be taken to tie the size of the fee to the share of the cost of the improvement created by the subdivider. This caution is especially important in light of a recent U.S. Supreme Court case, *Nollan v. California Coastal Commission, 107 S.Ct. 3141 (1987)*. The Court decided that there must be a "substantial" connection between the government's stated purpose and the regulatory action. In this case, that means that there must be a substantial connection between the needs created by the subdivision and the specific subdivision's exaction or user impact fee. Insertion of the word *substantial* into the usual test for valid regulations provides the courts with the power to second-guess the regulators.

LAND ETHIC: ECOLOGICAL IMPERATIVES AND VALUE CHOICES

As this century comes to a close, there is a growing awareness that humans are part of a larger community. This community includes not only the other humans who inhabit the planet, but the flora (plants) and fauna (animals) that share our living space. Human life and that of the plants and other animals cannot exist without certain essential ingredients, including clean air and water, sunlight, livable habitat and the ozone layer, to mention a few. Humans, other animals, plants and these essential ingredients are all bound together in an intricate and inseparable web of relationships called *ecosystems*. Humans are important, but not the sole participants, in life on this planet.

The quality of life on the planet depends in large measure on the sensitivity and respect with which humans make decisions. No decisions are more important than those made about land. Land provides humans with their habitat, and it provides the habitat for the animals and plants that provide humans with the essential ingredients of existence, food and air.

During this century, humans have been less than sensitive and discreet in their decisions about land. In the long view, this insensitivity threatens life itself. In the future, protection of some types of lands from development—like wetlands, prime agricultural lands, floodplains, coastal areas and wildlife habitat—is an ecological imperative. Beyond these imperatives lie some important value choices about other types of land. The quality of human life seems to depend on retaining our history through preservation of landmarks and historical areas, protecting aesthetically pleasing areas and retaining diversity of land types.

The remainder of this chapter discusses some regulations aimed at protecting these ecological imperatives and environmental value choices. These regulations evidence an emerging land ethic that places future emphasis in land use decisions on environmental harmony. Protection of wetlands, the floodplain, the coastal zone and other critical areas, including prime farmland (discussed earlier), are ecological imperatives. Preservation of historical culture and scenic areas are community value choices.

WETLANDS

◆ **Lands that have groundwater levels at or near the surface for much of the year or that are covered by aquatic vegetation.**

Historically, wetlands, including treed swamps and grass-dominated marshlands, have been treated as wasteland. They were considered inaccessible areas whose major function was the breeding of insect pests. In recent years, however, we have begun to see wetlands in a different light. True, wetlands are breeding areas for mosquitoes, as is any depression that retains water, such as residential drain spouts. Nevertheless, wetlands are also an important natural resource.

Wetlands provide areas for storm waters to gather for their slow return to the ground-water and air. Therefore, they are important as flood control areas. High groundwater and storm waters do not disappear on the development of a site or on the laying of drainpipe. Drainpipe merely concentrates the water, shifting the wetness problem farther downstream in the watershed. Wetlands provide this retention function naturally.

In addition, wetlands provide highly productive wildlife habitats. Hunters, fishermen, bird-watchers, trappers and other recreationists find wetlands extremely important in supporting their leisure time habits. Wetlands provide an outdoor classroom for amateur and professional scientists and are aesthetically pleasant to many people. With public recognition of these resource values, and the setting aside of the traditional view of wetlands as areas to be filled and developed, legal methods for protecting these areas have evolved.

Many states passed legislation to control development in wetland areas. The technique generally adopted has been a permitting process. Prior to filling, dredging or otherwise substantially modifying a wetland area, the landowner must get a state, regional or local permit. Permits are not issued where development will cut deeply into the resource value of the wetland area, unless there is a strong counterbalancing reason for doing so. The state wetland protection systems vary, but they generally involve the preparation of wetlands inventories and maps and the issuance of guidelines or regulations for controlling the process of issuing permits. It should be realized that a permit process does not *automatically* curtail development on all wetlands, but it *may* result in a landowner's being unable to make full economic commodity use of his or her land.

The federal Clean Water Act of 1972, as amended, created a permit system administered by the U.S. Army Corps of Engineers for most dredging and filling activities in wetlands connected with navigable waters. The term *navigable waters* has been defined broadly under the statute to include any waters that have the capability of affecting interstate commerce. Prior to the issuance of any permit, the corps must prepare an environmental impact statement (EIS) that analyzes all environmental factors. One remedy the corps has utilized against landowners who fill without a permit is to compel the removal of the fill and the restoration of the wetland, an undertaking that can be extremely expensive. A controversy continues under federal law as to the technical definition of a wetland. The broader the definition of a wetland, the more land that will be subject to the permit system and to the possibility of restriction on development.

Some states and localities have used a zoning approach to control development in wetlands. These zones, which might be called *conservation and recreation districts,* allow only uses consistent with retaining the character of the wetland. Prior to 1970, the zoning approach, which lacked the flexibility of a permit system, was uniformly held to be an illegal taking without due process of law. The judicial rationale was that this type of zoning denied landowners all *reasonable* use of their land. Fishing, boating and hunting, which might have been allowed, were not "reasonable" uses.

More recently, most of the states' wetland measures, as well as the federal wetland permit procedures, have been upheld under judicial scrutiny. In addition, some life has been breathed into the zoning approach for controlling wetland development.

Traditional analysis states that the police power can be used to prevent public harm but not to grant a public benefit. In this case, as always with this type of analysis, whether the regulation involves a harm or benefit depends on who is doing the classifying. Today, most courts would find that protecting an ecologically important area like a wetland is preventing a public harm.

Another line of reasoning may bode well for the zoning approach to protecting wetlands. The one constant in "takings" analyses is the rule that the landowner cannot be deprived of all reasonable use. A serious question is raised as to whether or not filling for development is a reasonable use of a wetland. Also, what is reasonable in this area is a time-related notion, so yesterday's unreasonable use may become reasonable one day.

Wetlands are being controlled as special environments in most states where they are numerous. The techniques for control vary somewhat, but judicial approval for all the approaches seems to be growing.

FLOODPLAINS

◆ **Areas near waterways that are prone to flooding.**

Human beings have always tended to settle near streams, lakes and other bodies of water. The body of water provided a drinking supply, fishing and a convenient means of transportation. The first permanent settlements were made with a wary eye toward the ravages that a flood-swollen stream could cause. High, sheltered places near the water were favored over lower-lying areas that were more susceptible to flooding.

People slowly seemed to lose this sensitivity to the forces of nature. Settlements became more numerous in low-lying, flood-prone river valleys. Floods were either tolerated or, in more recent history, controlled by capital construction projects such as dams, levees and dikes that alleviated the problem. In recent years it has become clear that, although dams and dikes may postpone or prevent some floods, sooner or later the dike weakens or the dam is not massive enough to handle a severe storm, and a flood ensues.

The cost of removing people from the floodplains throughout the world is prohibitive. Many people would not be willing to leave even if economic constraints did not prevail. In recent years, governments have undertaken measures to protect those living on the floodplain and to discourage others from building new structures or from repairing flood-damaged structures within the floodplain.

Some communities have used zoning as a method of controlling growth on the floodplain. A "floodplain district" would prohibit building new structures or filling or damming within the floodplain. It would prohibit any residential use. The purposes of this zoning would be to protect people who might choose to live on the floodplain unaware of the hazards of doing so, to protect those near the floodplain who would be injured by obstructions in the flow of floodwater and to protect the public at large, who must bear the cost of disaster relief when persons on the floodplains lose their property because of flooding.

The legal question raised again is whether this type of regulation, which permits very limited economic use, denies all reasonable use of the land and thereby constitutes a taking. What is a reasonable use must be looked at in the context of the land involved. Floodplain lands, with their vulnerability to massive flood destruction, are not reasonably usable for residential or other permanent types of construction. Although this line of reasoning has not been adopted uniformly to protect the floodplain, it may represent the wave of the future.

Although this regulatory trend is aimed at keeping people out of the floodplain, the federal government is involved in protecting its residents. The national Flood Insurance Program makes flood insurance available to landowners in flood-prone communities, where such insurance was previously exorbitantly expensive or simply unavailable. In essence, unless an individual in a flood-prone area has flood insurance, he or she will not be able to get a mortgage from the bank. If a community does not participate in the flood insurance program, federal aid or loans for use within the federally described flood hazard area will not be made available. An additional regulatory hook in the system is that a community must agree to establish land use controls for the flood-prone area before it is able to participate in the insurance program. In short, the expectation is that insurance will replace disaster relief in some measure, and new construction on the floodplain will be discouraged. A contrary argument can be made though. By subsidizing insurance for those who live on the floodplain, the federal program encourages people to continue to live there.

BEVERLY BANK V. ILLINOIS DEPARTMENT OF TRANSPORTATION

Supreme Court of Illinois
144 Ill.2d 210, 579 N.E.2d 815 (1991)

BACKGROUND. Beverly Bank (Bank) owns two lots in the Village of Flossmoor, located in the Butterfield Creek floodway. The 100-year floodway is a model based on a statistical projection of the land that would be flooded by a worst storm likely to occur within any 100-year period. The lots are zoned for single-family use. In 1988, the Bank's application for an extension of a construction permit was denied because section 18(g) (state law) prohibits all new residential construction in the floodway. Bank sued and was successful in the lower court.

DECISION. The Illinois Supreme Court reversed the lower court, deciding for the defendant Department of Transportation.

JUSTICE CUNNINGHAM. Before the General Assembly enacted section 18g, the law required that any new construction in the 100-year floodway may only be permitted if it would not increase the flood level. Section 18g prohibits all new construction which is not an appropriate use. The legislation was enacted in the wake of severe flooding which occurred in the Chicago metropolitan area in September 1986 and August 1987.

The General Assembly specifically determined what would and would not be an appropriate use of the floodway:

"(3) 'Appropriate use of the floodway' means use for (i) flood control structures, dikes, dams and other public works or private improvements relating to the control of drainage, flooding or erosion; (ii) structures or facilities relating to the use of, or requiring access to, the water or shoreline, including pumping and treatment facilities, and facilities and improvements related to recreational boats, commercial shipping and other functionally dependent uses; and (iii) any other purposes which the Department determines, by rule, to be appropriate to the 100-year floodway, and the periodic inundation of which will not pose a danger to the general health and welfare of the user, or require the expenditure of public funds or the provision of public resources or disaster relief services. Appropriate use of the floodway does not include construction of a new building unless such building is a garage, storage shed or other structure accessory to an existing building and such building does not increase flood stages."

Plaintiff further argues that this court must not give "blind deference to the General Assembly's express prohibition of new, nonappropriate construction, but must balance the individual hardships imposed on plaintiff by application of section 18g against the benefit to be gained by the public. According to plaintiff, this court must engage in a case-by-case factual inquiry to determine whether section 18g is unconstitutional as applied to any given piece of property in the 100-year floodway on which the property owner wishes to construct a new residence.

If the court were to review, as plaintiff urges, the constitutionality of section 18g as it applies to a particular piece of property by engaging in an ad hoc factual determination, the court would, in effect, be holding the class-wide prohibition on new residential construction unconstitutional on its face for failing to provide for a variance or special use. The court may not judicially create exceptions to this prohibition by engaging in individual factual evaluations with regard to each parcel of land which lies within the floodway in each instance in which a property owner desires to build a house.

"It is well established that reasonable restraints on the use of property in the interest of the common good and bearing a real and substantial relation to the public health, safety, morals and general welfare constitute a valid exercise of the police power."

Defendant identifies several legitimate State interests, any of which, it argues, provide a reasonable basis for the prohibition of new residential construction in the 100-year floodway. In addition to the interest of reducing flood damage, defendant argues that the prohibition protects the health and welfare of those who would live in the new houses, reduces the expenditure of public funds, and limits the extent of emergency relief services required by the periodic inundation of flood waters.

Even if plaintiff were to successfully build the two proposed houses in the floodway at an elevation which would not flood, defendant points out, the homes would still be surrounded by moving water during the 100-year floods. Emergency vehicles would not have access to the homes, and the residents could find themselves stranded without food, clean water, or electricity. In such a situation, defendant points out, the residents would very likely need to relocate temporarily to emergency shelters provided by the State's disaster relief services. Defendant argues that each and all of the above rationales justify the challenged flood control legislation and sustain its validity.

We agree with defendant that the General Assembly has the authority to prohibit all new residential construction in the 100-year floodway. It is reasonable for the General Assembly to rely on the extensive research contained in the Governor's flood control task force report which documented the demographic and land use changes which have contributed to the increased flooding in the 100-year floodway. It is reasonable for the General Assembly to accept the recommendation of the task force that a central part in the response to the severe flooding which may occur in a 100-year flood event is the prohibition of all new residential construction in the floodway. It is also reasonable for the General Assembly to rely on the scientific study contained in the report which emphasized the importance of maintaining existing natural storage areas in the watershed to reduce flood damage.

Finally, plaintiff argues that defendant's refusal to grant the permit extension constitutes a taking of plaintiff's property without just compensation in violation of the Fifth Amendment to the United States Constitution.

As plaintiff acknowledges, the Fifth Amendment's prohibition of the taking of private property for public use without just compensation does not preclude the State from taking private property, but only requires the State pay compensation. The Fifth Amendment does not require that just compensation be paid in advance of, or even contemporaneously with, the taking. "If the government has provided an adequate process for obtaining compensation, and if resort to that process 'yield[s] just compensation,' then the property owner 'has no claim against the Government' for a taking."

We agree with defendant that the Court of Claims Act provides a constitutionally adequate mechanism by which plaintiff may obtain compensation should the facts reveal a taking of plaintiff's properties in the 100-year floodway. As defendant states, plaintiff has not been denied compensation; plaintiff has not sought compensation through the appropriate means.

REVERSED.

COASTAL ZONE
◆ **The area including coastal waters and the adjacent shorelands.**

The coastal zone environment is an extremely fragile area. It is an ecosystem of interconnected marshes, mudflats, beaches and dunes. Human activities that create pollution and siltation can destroy these fragile ecosystems and the quality of the coastal waters generally. To prevent this type of destruction, the federal and state governments have enacted regulatory schemes protecting the coastal zone.

The primary regulation in the area is the federal Coastal Zone Management Act of 1972 (CZMA). The purpose of the CZMA is to establish a fairly uniform system of state controls for coastal lands, including the Great Lakes. The program is administered by the National Oceanic and Atmospheric Administration. Participation in the program by the states is voluntary.

The CZMA requires the states to undertake coastal lands planning and to develop management programs for protection and development of these lands. The act provides for annual grants of up to 80 percent of the cost of the development and implementation of coastal zone management programs. The state programs must identify the boundaries of the coastal zone, define the permissible uses within the zone and establish the regulatory agencies and controls that will implement the plan. The program must identify procedures for designating specific areas for preservation or restoration due to their "conservation, recreational, ecological and esthetics values."

The CZMA was broadened in several ways by legislation enacted in 1980. The act expanded protection "to significant natural systems, including wetlands, floodplains, estuaries, beaches, dunes, barrier islands, coral reefs, and fish and wildlife habitat," within the coastal zone. The act expands the CZMA purposes "to minimize the loss of life and property" in flood-prone areas within the coastal zone.

This new law created Resources Management Improvement Grants, available to states for developing deteriorating urban waterfronts, for preserving and restoring important natural areas and for providing public access to beaches and other coastal areas.

In addition to federal regulatory activity in coastal areas, several states are active in coastal zone protection separate from the CZMA program. For instance, under state legislation, New Jersey and Delaware regulate certain industrial activities in the coastal area. In a separate development, the New Jersey Supreme Court in *Matthews and Van Ness v. Bay Head Improvement Assoc., 471 A.2d 355 (1984)* held that the public has a right of access to and use of the dry sand beach areas shoreward of the wet sand area generally recognized as public land.

CRITICAL AREAS
◆ **Areas legislatively identified as containing natural limitations, or ones that are important to maintaining the ecosystem.**

Beyond zoning codes, the normal approach toward regulation is a piecemeal one, that is, to adopt separate controls for wetlands, others for the flood-prone areas and still others for prime agricultural lands. A more systematic approach is to regulate all sensitive areas under a single, comprehensive set of rules. Some communities have adopted critical area controls to accomplish this end.

The first task that must be undertaken by a community prior to enacting critical area controls is to make policy determinations as to what types of lands or resources have special value to the community. The legislature then adopts a critical area controls system aimed at protecting these lands and resources. Normally, these include lands that have natural limitations for development (floodplains, steep slopes, lie on an earthquake fault), lands that are ecologically important (wetlands, habitat for endangered or threatened species of animals and plants) and lands that are prized by the community because of their economic value, scarcity or uniqueness (prime farmland, scenic vistas, historical sites). It should be noted that some of the areas identified as critical fit the category of ecological imperatives (wetlands), while others are products of community value choices (historical sites). The controls may contain a variety of types of regulations, including acquisition of some lands, zoning, and permits.

Once the types of lands to be protected are identified and the regulatory scheme is established, the specific geographic locations of the critical area sites must be identified. Usually, these sites are mapped. The critical area map can be overlayed onto the zoning map for use by the agency administering the critical area controls.

The advantages of critical area controls are that they are comprehensive and systematic. Prospective developers are put on notice as to those lands that are incompatible with development, thereby avoiding poor land investments and lost time.

The concept of critical area controls is not confined to local communities. Some states—including Florida, Maine, Maryland, Minnesota, Nevada, North Carolina, Oregon, Vermont and Wyoming—have enacted laws that make use of the concept. Other states—including New Jersey (Pinelands) and New York (Adirondack Mountains)—have singled out regions of the state for critical area controls. The Federal Land Policy and Management Act (1976) provides that the Bureau of Land Management identify critical environmental areas and promulgate regulations giving them special protection.

The use of critical area controls is growing, and they appear to provide a systematic addition to traditional land use regulations for protecting lands valued by the community.

HISTORIC PRESERVATION

◆ **The preservation of buildings, and perhaps archaeological sites, from destruction by new development.**

Though the historical preservation concept is applied more broadly, it is usually applicable to buildings in urban areas. In some regions of the country, communities have designated certain areas historic districts because of their economic and cultural significance. In effect, this is a type of zoning. Within historical districts, permits have to be obtained prior to making a significant change in the facade or structure of a building. Because the historical district usually enhances the economy of the affected area, and change is controlled only by a permit system rather than prohibited, the courts are unlikely to find a regulatory taking exists.

Historically significant buildings do not normally constitute an entire district but are scattered among other urban developments. Many cities have designated landmarks in the community and have established a regulatory scheme for preserving their historical significance. The landmark designation differs from a historical district in that in the former the burden falls unevenly on a limited number of landowners. Also, the benefits of the landmark designation may accrue to the area in general and not solely to the landmark owner. In a historical district, the burdens and benefits, at least theoretically, fall equally on all landowners within the district.

One approach to landmark protection, adopted by New York City, utilizes a concept known as *transferable development rights (TDRs)*. The TDR concept is somewhat variable and complex, so it will be oversimplified here. Each tract of land has a certain number or amount of development rights that attach to the land and are transferable. A landowner proposing to build a high-rise residential unit does not obtain enough development rights with the deed to develop to the maximum permitted by the zoning code. These rights, or TDRs, have to be purchased from other landowners—in this case, the ones who own the landmarks and are prohibited from fully utilizing the TDRs on their own property. In this fashion, the economic burden of owning a landmark (or a wetland, a scenic vista or an archaeological site) does not fall solely on the shoulders of the landmark owner. Landowners simply go into a ready market to purchase or sell TDRs.

Historical preservation is a relatively new concern in this country, and the law pertaining to it is evolving. Reasonably designated historical districts seem secure from judicial consternation. Landmarks legislation is legal and has found a potentially useful tool in the use of TDRs, but questions as to their legality and as to whether a convenient market arrangement will evolve for their purchase and sale create some uncertainty. Whatever the limitations, a growing number of communities are making the value choice to preserve the best of their historical heritage.

AESTHETICS

◆ **Originally, regulation to retain visual and scenic beauty.**

Traditionally, aesthetics is associated with a community's goal of maintaining its visual and scenic beauty. Regulation for aesthetic purposes may include a ban on billboards, set-back requirements for buildings in a zoning code, or fencing for junkyards. In recent years, two questions have occupied courts in reviewing aesthetic regulations. One is whether a regulation based solely on aesthetic purposes is a valid exercise of the police power, and the second question pertains to the precise meaning of the term *aesthetics,* since it appears to be broadening from its initial definition.

The validity of aesthetic regulations has evolved over the course of the 20th century. During the early part of this century, the courts indicated that a regulation based partially or exclusively on aesthetics was invalid. The main problem was that the courts perceived controls based on beauty and good taste to be too subjective for institutions that demanded objective standards. Toward the middle of the century, judicial attitudes shifted. Though aesthetics could not be the sole basis for a regulation, it was acceptable as a reason among other traditional reasons for regulating. If a community banned billboards because they threatened public safety and because they were ugly, an otherwise reasonable regulation was valid. Though the aesthetics-based part of the purpose was treated with suspicion and was referred to often as an unimportant makeweight, aesthetics clearly gained legitimacy as a regulatory purpose during this era.

Currently, another shift in judicial attitude toward aesthetics is occurring. It appears that a majority of state appellate courts have accepted aesthetics alone as a legitimate reason for exercising the community's police power, Communities can regulate billboards for the solitary purpose of improving the appearance of the area. The groundwork for the courts accepting aesthetics as a full-fledged regulatory purpose was laid by the U.S. Supreme Court in the case of *Berman v. Parker, 348 U.S. 26 (1954)*. The Court declared that the concept of public welfare in the police power was broad enough to encompass aesthetic regulations. In regard to public welfare, it states that the "values it represents are spiritual as well as physical, aesthetic as well as monetary. It is within the power of the legislature to determine that the community should be beautiful as well as clean, well-balanced as well as carefully patrolled."

The New York Courts were among the earliest to accept the principle that aesthetics can stand alone as a basis for regulation.

CASE EXAMPLE

McCormick owned 39 acres of land on Oseetah Lake in the Adirondack Mountains. McCormick applied to the Adirondack Park Agency (APA) for a permit to develop 32 lots on the tract. The APA granted the permit subject to a restriction against placing any boat houses on the shoreline of the lake. The sole basis for the restriction was that boat houses would interfere with the rustic or aesthetic quality of the area. McCormick protested the restriction in court.

The court upheld the APA decision, affirming a previous position that aesthetics alone could substantiate a zoning regulation. The court noted that a "regulation in the name of aesthetics must bear substantially on the economic, social and cultural patterns of the community or district." *Matter of McCormick v. Lawrence, 8 Misc.2d 64, 372 N.Y.S.2d 156 (1975)*.

This latter language regarding community economic, social and cultural patterns may simply be recognizing that an aesthetics regulation must be supported by a public health, safety or welfare reason, or it may be an attempt to provide some criteria for reviewing the reasonableness of this type of regulation. Regardless, aesthetics as the primary reason for a regulation is an expansion of the limitations existing under prior law.

Now that the judicial mist is beginning to clear around the question of whether aesthetics can stand alone, the mist is reappearing on another front. The definition of aesthetics as used by communities in their regulations, and by the courts in validating those regulations, seems to be expanding. The aesthetics language being used by legislatures and courts is not confined to visual beauty. The courts continue to wince at the potential for abuse of such a subjective concept.

One writer who has analyzed the cases has opined that aesthetics is a concept referring to our "shared human values" and has nothing to do with visual beauty. Historical buildings and wetlands are not preserved because they are visually beautiful, but because the community cherishes them, beautiful or not. Another writer analyzing the recent cases suggests that aesthetics is being used to express the desire of humans to live in harmony with their physical environment. Protection of coastal areas and wildlife habitat is a reflection of the attitude that humans must share the planet by necessity with their fellow creatures.

Whatever its precise definition, the concept of aesthetics provides communities with significant latitude for adopting controls to protect and preserve the natural environment.

REVIEW AND DISCUSSION QUESTIONS

1. The courts that have rejected large-lot zoning have retained an exception to their declaration of illegality. They have said that large-lot zoning is all right if there is some "extraordinary justification." What would constitute such a justification?

2. Why have courts been reluctant to approve regulations that are based solely on visual beauty?

3. If the floodplains are dangerous places to live, then we should have a policy against people living there. Discuss the implications of such a policy.

4. Contrast a zone change request with a variance request.

5. If a community wanted to permanently restrict the use of its prime farmland to agricultural use, can it legally do it? Support your answer.

CASE PROBLEMS

1. The Town of Preston passed a sign control ordinance. Section 8 of the ordinance stipulated that all existing signs within the town must conform to the sign ordinance within five years from the date of its enactment. Marvin Miller has a large, flashing, nonconforming sign that he does not wish to remove. What arguments should Marvin assert? Would he be successful?

2. S. Volpe & Company petitioned the board of appeals for a special permit to construct a golf course on its land. Golf courses were one of the specially permitted uses allowed under the Town of Wareham's zoning ordinance. The board denied the permit because the land included salt marshes and the golf course would destroy the ecology of the region and harm local fishing. What will be the result in court? *S. Volpe & Co. v. Board of Appeals of Wareham, 4 Mass. App. Ct. 57, 348 N.E.2d 807 (1976).*

3. Rogers owns a large single-family house in the suburbs. She plans to move to a more expensive house in a nearby suburb. To afford the new house, Rogers wants to convert her present home into a two-family apartment. The zoning classification for her house is R-2, that is, single-family house on a minimum lot size of 20,000 square feet. Advise Rogers on how to proceed. Is she likely to be successful under your suggested procedure?

4. Ima Nactivist, councillor for the Town of Riverview, introduced legislation at the town board meeting that, if enacted, would require the removal of all structures now existing on the floodplain in Riverview. The legislation included an array of dates on which types of structures would have to be removed, ranging from 1 to 15 years. Older and less valuable structures would be removed earlier, and newer and more valuable ones would be eliminated later. Cyrus Caselaw, town attorney, informed Ima that the proposed law was clearly unconstitutional. Ima retorted that Cyrus was misinformed. Discuss.

5. Bayswater proposed a cluster subdivision of 115 units on smaller-than-required lots and proposed to dedicate 60 acres to open space. The Planning Board has the authority to allow clustering so long as the unit density does not exceed the site's legal capacity if not clustered, and so long as open space is dedicated to the town. The 60 acres was largely steep slopes and wetlands. The Town Planning Board approved Bayswater's proposal as submitted, but required a $5,000 per unit subdivision exaction payment for parkland per another law. Bayswater refused to pay the in-lieu fee, contending that the 60 acres of open space in its proposal satisfies the parkland exaction portion of town law. Discuss. *Bayswater Realty and Capital Corp. v. Planning Board of the Town of Lewisboro, 544 N.Y.2d 613, 560 N.E.2d 1300 (1990).*

26

Environmental Law

Since the early 1970s, numerous federal laws have been enacted advocating protection of the physical environment. Several of these laws directly or indirectly affect real estate transactions. The impact of the Comprehensive Environmental Response, Compensation, and Liability Act (CERCLA) is the most dramatic; however, the Clean Water Act, the Clean Air Act, the Resource Conservation and Recovery Act, the National Environmental Policy Act (discussed in Chapter 24) and several others affect real estate decisions. Each of these federal laws may be paralleled or complemented by similar state laws.

COMPREHENSIVE ENVIRONMENTAL RESPONSE, COMPENSATION, AND LIABILITY ACT (CERCLA)

◆ A statute whose purpose is to provide a regulatory mechanism for cleaning up inactive waste sites that release hazardous substances into the environment.

The CERCLA, or Superfund Law, was enacted in 1980. It was significantly amended by the Superfund Amendments and Reauthorization Act, or SARA, in 1986. The purpose of CERCLA and SARA is to establish a regulatory mechanism for dealing with abandoned or inactive hazardous waste sites.

The public health and safety problem created by inactive hazardous waste sites was first brought to the public's attention by the discovery of significant health impacts of the Hooker Chemical site at Love Canal in New York. Since that time, literally thousands of inactive hazardous waste sites have been identified in every region of the country. Many of these sites leak hazardous materials into the water, air and soil in the surrounding area.

SUPERFUND

CERCLA mandated that a national inventory of hazardous waste sites be made. The inventory identified some 33,000 inactive hazardous waste sites. The Environmental Protection Agency (EPA) identified those sites in the inventory that merited remedial action and placed them on the National Priority List (NPL). A site is listed on the NPL if it receives a minimum score, currently 28.5, under a technical listing procedure called the Hazardous Ranking System (HRS). The major effect of being put on the NPL is that the site will be cleaned up and is eligible for the use of Superfund monies to facilitate the cleanup.

The Hazardous Substances Response Fund, or Superfund, was established to provide a source of funds for cleaning up hazardous waste sites. Under the law to date, Congress has made available over $12 billion to conduct cleanup activities. Approximately 87 percent of the Superfund monies comes from taxes on industry, principally the petroleum and chemical industries, which are the major sources of hazardous waste. The remainder of Superfund monies comes from Congressional appropriations from other federal tax revenues. Superfund can be used to pay for expenses incurred in planning for site cleanup and for the cleanup itself. Many states have their own version of Superfund that may provide additional cleanup funds.

IMPLEMENTING THE CLEANUP

Cleanup activities or response costs can be incurred by federal or state officials or private parties. If the party incurring the response costs wishes to be reimbursed by Superfund, by state funds or by the parties responsible for the hazardous waste, it must follow the National Contingency Plan (NCP).

The NCP originated in the Clean Water Act for cleaning up oil spills. Under CERCLA, it was adapted for use in cleaning up hazardous waste sites on land. The NCP provides a step-by-step procedure that must be followed in carrying out a removal action or a remedial action at the site. A removal action is immediate and interim measures are used to neutralize an imminent threat from the site. For example, a removal action may involve removing barrels that are leaking waste into a stream, or putting up a security fence to protect the public from the hazardous nature of the site. A remedial action is the permanent action taken to eliminate the threat created by the site to public health or safety, or to the environment.

A goal of CERCLA is to get the parties responsible for disposing of the hazardous waste to clean up the site. Unfortunately, the responsible parties may be unknown to the EPA or be unwilling to clean up the site. The EPA determines, however, who will conduct the cleanup action. The EPA may choose to clean up the site itself using Superfund monies, or EPA may negotiate an agreement with the state by which the state will carry out the cleanup activities. The EPA may insist that the responsible parties clean up the site. Where EPA cleans up the site using Superfund money, it subsequently seeks reimbursement (contribution) from the responsible parties. It currently recovers about 70 percent of its Superfund expenditures. Most of the remaining 30 percent covers the cost of orphan sites, those sites where the responsible parties cannot be identified.

LIABILITY

Any party who has incurred response costs from either a removal action or a remedial action may recover all or part of those costs from potentially responsible parties. In order to succeed, the plaintiff must prove five elements:

1. The place involved is a facility.
2. The facility caused a release or threat of a release of a hazardous substance.
3. The defendant is a potentially responsible party.
4. The damages sought were the necessary costs incurred responding to a release.
5. The plaintiffs followed the NCP.

First, the party must prove that the place involved in incurring the costs is a facility. The courts have broadly interpreted facility to be a typical hazardous waste disposal site but have also held such places as horse stables and spraying trucks to be facilities.

Second, there must be a release or the threat of a release of a hazardous substance from the facility. In addition to its own definition of what substances are hazardous, CERCLA uses the hazardous definitions contained in the Clean Water Act, the Resource Conservation and Recovery Act and other environmental laws. The release of the hazardous substance can be to any medium, including the soil, the groundwater or the wind.

Third, the defendant from whom response costs are sought must be a person covered by the law, or a potentially responsible party (PRP). PRPs are broadly defined to include past or present owners or operators of the facility, past or present generators of the waste disposed at the facility, and past or present transporters of waste to the facility, if the transporter selected that facility. It should be noted that a PRP does not have to participate in, or even know about, the disposal of the hazardous waste. Merely being an owner or operator at the time the hazardous waste was deposited on the site qualifies one as a PRP.

It is the broad definition of PRPs and the extent of their legal liability that has markedly changed real estate transactions in recent years. Owners may be lessors who knew nothing of the activities on the site, or in limited circumstances lenders to the owners of the facility who have foreclosed on a defaulted mortgage and taken title to the land to protect their investment, or parent corporations who participated in the management of its subsidiary corporation who was the facility owner.

When a PRP is held liable for response costs under CERCLA, the liability is strict, and joint and several. Strict liability means that the plaintiff need not show fault on the part of the defendant but only that they come within the definition of a PRP. Joint and several liability means that the plaintiff can sue any one or more of the PRPs without including all of them, and the PRPs sued are responsible for the total response costs. If the defendant PRPs know that other PRPs exist, it is up to them to bring them into the litigation. It is possible for a defendant PRP to prove that its waste is severable or divisible from all other waste at the facility. In the event that the defendant PRP can prove divisibility, it can only be held liable for the contribution of its waste to the response costs.

In order to hold a PRP liable for response costs, the plaintiff does not have to prove that the PRP's waste actually caused the release; only that a waste of the type deposited by the PRP was released. With the broad definition of PRP, the restrictive nature of strict, and joint and several liability, and the requirement that the plaintiff does not have to prove causation, CERCLA casts a wide, almost impenetrable, net.

The fourth element that the plaintiff must prove is that costs it seeks to recover were reasonably necessary to remedy the threat created by release from the facility. Finally, the plaintiff must follow the National Contingency Plan in expending the funds to clean up the site.

The following case explores the remedies available to the current owner of a hazardous waste site against those who owned the site when the waste was actually deposited.

CADILLAC FAIRVIEW/CALIFORNIA INC. V. DOW CHEMICAL CO.
Ninth Circuit Court of Appeals
840 F.2d 691 (1988)

BACKGROUND. In 1976, Cadillac Fairview purchased a site in Torrance, California. Later it learned that hazardous waste was deposited on the site and that it had migrated to the underlying soil and was a threat to cause substantial environmental and health problems. At the request of state officials, Cadillac Fairview hired engineers to do chemical testing at the site and to evaluate the hazards posed by the contamination. In addition, it erected a fence around the site and posted guards to keep trespassers off the site. It spent $70,000 on these removal activities.

The site had been purchased by the federal government in 1942 and a rubber-producing plant had been constructed on it. Dow Chemical operated the facility under a contract with the government; that contract authorized Dow to dump hazardous by-products of its production processes on the site. In 1955, Shell Oil purchased the site; it also deposited hazardous waste on the site until 1972. Cadillac Fairview purchased the site from a successor in title of Shell Oil.

Cadillac Fairview sued the federal government, Dow and Shell to recover its response costs and for an injunction ordering that all remedial action and costs of that action were the responsibility of the federal government, Dow and Shell. The federal district court dismissed Cadillac Fairview's suit for failure to state a cause of action.

DECISION. The Ninth Circuit Court of Appeals held that Cadillac Fairview was entitled to response costs for its removal action, but was not entitled to the injunction.

CIRCUIT JUDGE WALLACE. Section 107-(a)(2)(B) of CERCLA expressly creates a private claim against any person who owned or operated a facility at the time hazardous substances were disposed of at the facility for recovery of necessary costs of responding to the hazardous substances incurred consistent with the national contingency plan. Cadillac Fairview alleged that it incurred "necessary costs" of response within the meaning of section 107(a), and that Dow, Shell, and the federal defendants owned or operated the Site at the time that hazardous substances were deposited there. Despite these allegations, the district court dismissed Cadillac Fairview's suit against the private defendants for failure to state a claim under section 107(a).

The district judge based his decision to dismiss Cadillac Fairview's damages claims on its failure to await governmental action with respect to the Site before bringing suit. The court held that in order for a private response action to be "consistent with the national contingency plan," it must be "initiated and coordinated by a governmental entity, and not by a private individual acting alone." The court also stated that the costs incurred by Cadillac Fairview were not compensable response costs under section 107 because they did not constitute "cleanup costs" within the meaning of the national contingency plan.

Though the national contingency plan describes the role of lead agencies in examining information and determining appropriate responses to environmental hazards, we hold that such provisions do not constrain private parties seeking to recover response costs under section 107(a). We concluded that this reading of section 107(a) was supported both by "the lack of any procedure whereby a private party could seek to obtain prior governmental approval of a cleanup program" and by CERCLA's broad remedial purpose to promote private enforcement actions "independent of governmental actions financed by Superfund." In NL Industries, we reaffirmed our holding in *Wickland*, and rejected the argument that response costs cannot be deemed "necessary" in the absence of lead agency approval of the cleanup.

Shell argues that although no federal involvement is necessary, some ·significant state or local governmental action must precede a response action for which recovery is possible under section 107(a).

Shell, however, cites no authority for the proposition that significant state or local governmental action is a necessary prerequisite to a private action under section 107(a). Nor is there any mention of such a requirement in either section 107 or in the national contingency plan. We are thus reluctant to read a state or local governmental action requirement into the statute absent some strong indication that Congress intended that private parties await action by a state or local government before commencing a response action. Our examination of CERCLA's provisions leads us to conclude that significant state or local governmental action need not precede a response action for that action to be either "necessary" or "consistent with the national contingency plan."

Dow argues that without preliminary governmental action, a defendant can be forced to pay for cleanup actions that are inadequate or ill-conceived. This argument ignores the plain language of the statute. Section 107(a) does not allow recovery of any and all costs of response that a private party incurs. To recover costs under section 107(a), the party undertaking the response action must prove that the costs it incurred were "necessary" and that it incurred those costs in a manner "consistent with the national contingency plan." A response action is consistent with the plan for purposes of section 107 only if it satisfies criteria set forth in pertinent regulations.

We conclude, therefore, that the district court erred in ruling that some governmental entity must authorize and initiate a response action for that action to be necessary and consistent with the national contingency plan.

As an alternative ground for the dismissal of Cadillac Fairview's damages claims, the district court held that Cadillac Fairview failed to allege that it incurred "cleanup" costs within the meaning of section 107(a). We rejected the distinction between investigatory costs and on-site cleanup costs in *Wickland*. Section 107(a)(2)(B) allows recovery of "costs of response," which includes costs incurred "to monitor, assess, and evaluate the release or threat of release of hazardous substances," and costs of actions "necessary to prevent . . . damage to the public health . . . [including] security fencing or other measures to limit access." The testing and security expenditures alleged by Cadillac Fairview fall within the ambit of those defined by the section. The district court thus erred in holding that Cadillac Fairview failed to state a claim for recovery of those costs under section 107(a)(2)(B).

Cadillac Fairview also pleaded a claim for injunctive relief ordering Dow, Shell, CC&F, and the federal defendants to undertake appropriate response actions with respect to the Site in a manner consistent with the national contingency plan. The district court examined CERCLA's provisions and found that the only private remedy provided in CERCLA is the private cause of action for response costs described in section 107(a). Under section 107(a), the United States, a State, an Indian Tribe, or any other person may recover necessary costs of response incurred consistent with the national contingency plan. There is no mention of a right to injunctive relief in section 107(a). In contrast, under section 106(a), the President may require the Attorney General to seek injunctive relief "when the President determines that there may be an imminent and substantial endangerment to the public health or welfare or the environment." The district court concluded that the failure to provide for injunctive relief in section 107(a), coupled with the absence of any provision for a private right of action under section 106(a), mandated the conclusion that Congress did not intend to create a private cause of action for injunctive relief under CERCLA.

We conclude, therefore, that CERCLA 107(a) does not provide for a private right to injunctive relief against owners and operators as defined by section 107(a)(2). Section 106(a) and 107(a) indicate that when Congress wished to provide for injunctive relief under CERCLA, it knew how to do so and did so expressly. The district court's dismissal of Cadillac Fairview's claims for injunctive relief against Dow, Shell, CC&F, and the federal defendants is affirmed.

DEFENSES

The defenses for a PRP are few and narrow. The PRP may defend by proving that the release of a hazardous substance was caused by an act of God or of war. The law includes a "third-party" defense, which is equally narrow. If the PRP can prove that the release was caused solely by a third party having no contractual relationship to the PRP and that the PRP used due care with respect to the hazardous substance, including taking adequate precautions to prevent harm, it is not liable under CERCLA. Proving the lack of any contractual relationship, such as a lease, a deed or a shipping contract, is unlikely, unless the PRP is the victim of a midnight dumper.

SARA added a defense, called the *innocent landowner defense*, that is broader in nature. If the hazardous waste was placed on the site before the defendant PRP became the owner and the defendant did not know or have reason to know that the waste was on the site at the time of acquisition, or if the PRP is a government agency that obtained the land involuntarily (e.g., nonpayment of taxes), or is a person who acquired through inheritance or bequest, the defendant is not liable.

To meet the test "did not know or have reason to know," the defendant must undertake at the time of acquisition "all appropriate inquiry" into previous ownership and uses of the property consistent with good commercial and customary practice in an effort to minimize liability. All appropriate inquiry includes consideration of the specialized knowledge or experience of the defendant, the relationship of the actual purchase price to the market value of the property (if not contaminated), the obviousness of the presence of the hazardous waste and the ability to detect hazardous waste through appropriate inspection.

It appears that, at a minimum, the defendant at the time of acquisition must have visually inspected the property, checked government records concerning past ownership and uses of the property and made further inquiry if the purchase price was distinctly lower than the market prices of other property in the vicinity. In practice, it appears that a Phase I environmental site assessment (ESA) by a qualified professional is becoming the standard. The Phase I ESA is used to determine the environmental conditions on the property. It consists of a records review, site reconnaissance, interviews with current owners and occupants of the property and with local government officials, and a report.

If the PRP cannot meet the "all appropriate inquiry" test, but is a minor contributor to the waste at the facility, the EPA may enter a *de minimis* settlement with the otherwise innocent purchaser. The statute authorizes a de minimis settlement when the purchaser did not know of, conduct or permit the generation, transportation, storage, treatment or disposal of any hazardous substance at the site and did not otherwise contribute to the release of the hazardous substance. In the de minimis settlement, the PRP is required to pay a proportionately higher amount of the estimated response costs in exchange for avoiding the costs of litigation and the uncertainty of delay in settling the matter.

The following case includes a critical evaluation of CERCLA when it is applied to real estate owners and transactions. It points out some of the problems incurred when the government tried to affix liability for hazardous waste cleanup on the "potentially responsible parties" rather than letting it fall onto the taxpayers. As you read the case it might be enlightening to ask who should pay for cleaning up hazardous waste sites from the perspective of fairness, economic efficiency, and environmental protection.

UNITED STATES V. A&N CLEANERS AND LAUNDERERS, INC.
Federal District Court
854 F.Supp. 229 (1994)

BACKGROUND. Berkman, Petrillo and the Custos (Berkman defendants) each hold a one-third interest in a parcel of land as tenants in common. A&N Cleaners and Launderers, Inc. (A&N) operate a dry cleaning establishment in a building on the parcel. A floor drain traversed the entire length of the interior building and emptied into a dry well. The Village of Brewster well field was used to extract 300,000 to 400,000 gallons of water per day from the aquifer. In 1982, the well field was placed on the National Priorities List due to the presence of volatile halogenated organic compounds (VHOs) in the groundwater. The remedial investigation/feasibility study (RI/FS) revealed that the dry well was a significant source of the VHO contamination. The United States sued the Berkman defendants for costs incurred as owners of the site causing a release of hazardous substances.

The Berkman defendants argued that they were third parties who did not cause the release, and alternatively, that they were innocent landowners. These defenses are provided for in CERCLA.

DECISION. The Federal District Court found that the Berkman defendants could not rely on the two CERCLA defenses.

DISTRICT JUDGE SWEET. Under the "Third-Party Defense" set forth in CERCLA §107(b)(3), a defendant is not liable if it establishes that the release or threatened release was caused solely by:

(3) an act or omission of a third party other than an employee or agent of the defendant, or than one whose act or omission occurs in connection with a contractual relationship, existing directly or indirectly, with the defendant.

The second defense relevant to this case, the "Innocent Landowner Defense," is actually a special case of the Third-Party Defense. In 1986 Congress created an exception to the "no contractual relationship" requirement of the Third-Party Defense, thereby making it available to some owners who acquired the relevant property after the disposal or placement of hazardous substances occurred. CERCLA defines "contractual relationship" as including "land contracts, deeds or other instruments transferring title or possession," unless:

the real property on which the facility concerned is located was acquired by the defendant after the disposal or placement of the

hazardous substance on, in, or at the facility and. . . . [a]t the time the defendant acquired the facility the defendant did not know and had no reason to know that any hazardous substance which is the subject of the release or threatened release was disposed of on, in, or at the facility.

To qualify as an Innocent Landowner one must have undertaken "all appropriate inquiry into the previous ownership and uses of the property, consistent with good commercial or customary practice" at the time of transfer. "Good commercial or customary practice" is not defined in the statute, and the relevant legislative history is vague, indicating that "a reasonable inquiry must have been made in all circumstances, in light of best business and land transfer principles." In deciding whether a defendant has complied with this standard, courts consider any specialized knowledge or expertise the defendant has, whether the purchase price indicated awareness of the presence of a risk of contamination, commonly known or [from] reasonable information about the property, the obviousness of the presence of contamination at the property, and the ability to detect such contamination by appropriate inspection.

Landowners who meet the requirements will not be found to be in a "contractual relationship" with the party responsible for the release of hazardous substances at the property.

CERCLA's liability scheme was intended to ensure that those who were responsible for, and who profited from, activities leading to property contamination, rather than the public at large, should be responsible for the costs of the problems that they had caused.

In addition, Congress intended CERCLA's liability scheme to provide incentives for private parties to investigate potential sources of contamination and to initiate remediation efforts.

The imposition of strict liability solely on the basis of property ownership, however, does something other than cause handlers of dangerous substances to be responsible for the hazards they create. It transfers the costs of the national problem of remediating abandoned contaminated sites onto the shoulders of individuals involved in real estate transactions, many of whom had never violated any environmental regulation, thereby negating Congress' intention of making those responsible for causing contamination pay for its remediation.

CERCLA's narrow affirmative defenses do little to alleviate the unfairness of the statute's liability scheme, particularly in cases where liability is predicated solely on property ownership. By restricting the application of the Defenses to those that have complied with a series of ill-defined due care and investigatory requirements, CERCLA in practice imposes the costs of the public problem of ferreting out contaminated sites onto the private individuals involved in real estate transactions and ownership without even providing reasonable guidance on what these property owners must do to meet their obligations.

The only blameworthy activity that many property owners facing CERCLA liability have engaged in is the failure to comply with the host of amorphous and undefined due care requirements necessary for establishing CERCLA's affirmative defenses. Also, as demonstrated by the present case, the Government's access to the highly technical information necessary to identify contamination is often superior to that of the ordinary landowner. Rather than preventing blameworthy defendants

from escaping liability, shifting the burden of proof of causation to defendants merely helps ensure that the Government will recoup their Response Costs, "at the cost of imposing liability upon some individual defendants who caused no harm, but are unable to prove it by a preponderance of the evidence."

In addition to its unfairness, the liability structure of CERCLA is counterproductive. PRPs faced with disproportionate liability litigate tenaciously, prolonging or postponing remediation of contaminated sites and increasing dramatically the costs of remediation.

If Congress must shift the costs of ferreting out contamination from the general public to those involved in real estate transactions it should, at a minimum, define the scope of the required investigation.

Were the Berkman Defendants to have had a clear, intelligible mandate from Congress or the EPA regarding the investigation they should have conducted prior to purchasing the Property and the monitoring that they should have conducted since its purchase, it is doubtful that they would be before the Court at this time.

However, since the Berkman Defendants' liability is predicated on their unwitting ownership of contaminated property, rather than on any disposal of waste which might have occurred on the Property since they purchased it, they bear the burden of showing that a totally unrelated third party is the sole cause of the release of hazardous substances in question. The Berkman Defendants have failed in this burden. This conclusion precludes the application of either of the Defenses to the Berkman Defendants.

DAMAGES

Any person can recover response costs, including costs of assessing and planning the cleanup. The government can get an injunction to halt a release of a hazardous substance, or ensure an administrative order compelling a PRP to conduct the cleanup. If a PRP refuses to obey the administrative order to clean up, the government can recover punitive damages up to three times the actual cost of the cleanup. The federal government may also assess civil penalties of up to $25,000 per violation.

CERCLA places an affirmative obligation on federal and state governments to seek to recover natural resource damages caused by the release of a hazardous substance. The term *natural resources* is broadly defined to include injury to public "land, fish, wildlife, biota, air, water, groundwater, drinking water supplies" and other natural resources owned or held in trust by the federal and state governments. The President and the Governor of the relevant state must identify a trustee for natural resources. The trustees must agree on the natural resource damage and seek recovery against the PRPs. Superfund monies cannot be used to pay natural resource damages.

BROWNFIELD INITIATIVE

Many former industrial sites in urban communities have fallen into disuse and decay. These areas, referred to as *brownfields,* are often contaminated with hazardous waste. Due to the high cost of decontaminating brownfield sites, and the uncertainty caused by the CERCLA process, businesses are reluctant to locate new facilities on brownfield sites. These unproductive industrial areas add little to the tax base and economic life of the urban communities in which they are located.

Businesses tend to locate their new facilities on previously undeveloped sites in the suburbs or in rural areas. These previously undeveloped sites, or greenfields, already provide community services, as agricultural land, scenic areas, wetlands, floodplains, or open space. Arguably it makes more sense to redevelop the unproductive brownfield sites than to expand into greenfield areas.

Sensitive to these needs, the federal government is trying through administrative regulation to revitalize urban communities by encouraging the cleanup and redevelopment of brownfield sites. The Brownfields Initiative provides grants to communities as seed money to encourage redevelopment. The seed money is used for assessing contamination on abandoned sites, resolving liability concerns, and attracting redevelopers who will invest in the brownfields. The federal EPA is in the process of removing 27,000 low-priority, urban sites from the Superfund inventory, removing a stigma that may discourage redevelopers. Other incentives are currently under consideration. In short, unproductive urban real estate may be in for a period of revival, as the strictures of CERCLA are applied by the government in a less adversarial fashion, and with a sharper focus on reducing public health and environmental risk.

STATE CERCLA-TYPE STATUTES

Several states—including California, Connecticut, Illinois, Iowa, Missouri, and New Jersey—have enacted CERCLA-type laws that often focus on real estate transactions. Many other states have very recently adopted or are considering laws to make the real estate transaction a trigger that sets off an inquiry into the possible existence of hazardous waste on the site. For example, the California Torres Act requires that an owner of nonresidential property who knows or has reasonable cause to believe that a release of a hazardous waste from the site has occurred must give written notice to the buyers or lessees prior to concluding a real estate transaction with them. Failure to do so may result in civil penalties.

The model that most states appear to be following is New Jersey's Environmental Clean-up Responsibility Act (ECRA), which went into effect in 1983. The law applies to any industrial establishment, including manufacturing firms, warehousing businesses, utilities, repair operations and transportation and communication services. It applies when the industrial establishment engages in any conveyance of real estate; changes in ownership or operation; is acquired or taken over; has a lease expire; or goes into bankruptcy or ceases or transfers operations.

If the industrial establishment engages in one of the above activities, it must undertake an environmental audit to determine if its site is contaminated by hazardous waste. If contamination is found, the firm must develop a cleanup plan, which is subject to review and approval by a state agency. The transaction cannot be concluded until the state agency signs off on the audit or the cleanup plan. The firm must provide financial assurances equal to the anticipated cost of the cleanup to guarantee that cleanup actually occurs.

Failure to comply with the statute makes the real estate or other transaction voidable by either the state or the transferee. The industrial establishment may be liable for up to $25,000 per day in fines and is strictly liable for all cleanup and related costs.

Notice that the New Jersey law has as its trigger a real estate or some other business transaction. Under federal CERCLA, the trigger is the release of a hazardous substance from the site.

CLEAN WATER ACT

♦ **A statute whose purpose is to cleanse, maintain and enhance the quality of the nation's water resources.**

The Clean Water Act amendments, adopted in 1972 and amended several times since then, uses a system of effluent and water quality standards to limit pollution in the nation's surface waters. The chief focus of the law through 1987 was on regulating point sources of pollution. A point source is a discrete conduit (pipe) used to dispose of wastes.

STATUTORY STRUCTURE: INDUSTRIAL DISCHARGERS

Effluent standards are technology-based standards imposed on major industrial sources of water pollution. Major industrial sources were categorized by industry (e.g., chemical) or subcategory of industry (e.g., chemical-sulfuric acid). Each source within the designated category of industry was to adopt "best practicable technology" by 1977, and a stricter "best available technology" or "best conventional technology" by 1983. In some cases, these dates were extended by subsequent amendments to the 1972 law.

Water quality standards are ambient standards based upon a use of the body of water designated by the state. The state determines that a stream, or portion of it, should be used to supply drinking water to a municipality or as a trout stream or for some other designated use. In order to use the stream for the state-designated purpose, certain types of pollution (e.g., fecal coliform) cannot exceed established levels. The established level is the water quality standard needed to maintain the quality of the receiving water.

A point source of water pollution must conform to the stricter of the effluent standard or water quality standard. In reality, the source must adopt the effluent standard, but if necessary, due to the high quality demanded by state-designated use (drinking water) or stream conditions (many other sources of mercury in the stream) or other factor, the source must adopt the stricter water quality standard. The enforcement mechanism is that each major pollution source must get a permit that states a specific number limitation on each type of effluent.

At this time, most industrial sources have adopted the technology necessary to meet the effluent standard. Two significant areas of water pollution are inadequately addressed by the point source, technology-based standard approach. Due to a prior lack of understanding and to limitations on existing technology, toxics dumped into the water are only now beginning to be regulated. Nonpoint sources of pollution, those not emanating from a discrete conduit, are also by and large unregulated. Nonpoint sources of pollution come mainly from agricultural run-off, mining and timbering waste, and construction and road run-off.

In 1987, Congress, recognizing the continuing problems of toxic and nonpoint source pollution, amended the law to refocus attention on these pollution sources. The EPA must identify those waters that fail to meet water quality standards due to toxics and nonpoint sources of pollution. The states must then develop management programs to systematically eliminate the nonconformity of the identified waters to the water quality standards.

The effluent standards do not have a direct effect on land use, as they only designate the technology that must be used by a new industrial pollution source. However, the water quality standard, which concerns itself with the quality of the ambient water, may affect the location of water pollution sources. Industrial sources will have to be relatively clean in order to locate on a stream whose use is designated for drinking water or swimming. Others will be forced to locate on streams with lower water quality standards.

STATUTORY STRUCTURE: MUNICIPAL DISCHARGERS

In addition to industrial point sources of water pollution, Congress recognized, in 1972, that nontreatment or rudimentary treatment of municipal sewage was a major contributor to water pollution in surface waters. With the Clean Water Act, the country embarked on a major undertaking to provide secondary treatment for all municipal sewage. Secondary sewage treatment removes approximately 90 percent of all organic contaminants in the water.

Congress authorized the federal government to pay 75 percent of the cost of constructing publicly owned sewage treatment works (POTWs). The grants program has been changed to a revolving fund loan program. The revolving fund provides loans for up to 80 percent of the cost of construction of POTWs to complete the job of providing adequate treatment nationally. It should be emphasized that the current system is a loan arrangement, unlike the outright grants that were made by the federal government under the original law in 1972.

Real estate development can be curtailed if a community does not have a POTW capable of providing secondary treatment, or if the currently adequate POTW does not have the capacity to absorb the sewage from the new development.

CLEAN AIR ACT

◆ **A statute whose purpose is to cleanse, maintain and enhance the quality of the nation's air resource.**

The Clean Air Act, adopted in 1970 and amended in 1977 and 1990, mandates that the EPA regulate pollutants that are harmful to public health and welfare. The country is divided into air quality control regions for purposes of administering the act. The EPA assembled the full body of relevant information about pollutants it chose to regulate and issued the information as a *criteria document*. Based on these criteria, the EPA promulgated national ambient air quality standards (NAAQS) for what came to be called the *criteria pollutants*. There are six criteria pollutants: sulfur dioxide, nitrous oxide, carbon monoxide, ozone, particulates and lead.

There are two types of NAAQS. Primary standards are intended to protect public health, secondary standards are stricter than primary standards and exist to protect public welfare. Public welfare includes protecting soil, water, vegetation, wildlife, visibility and the like.

The states were to formulate state implementation plans (SIPs) for meeting the NAAQS. Primary standards were to be met by 1975 and secondary standards within a reasonable time (1977 was designated by the EPA). These dates were extended, and 25 years later, many regions continue to have trouble meeting one or more of the standards.

In the 1977 amendments to the Clean Air Act, Congress ordered the air quality control regions to be divided into those that attained and those that did not attain NAAQS. The regions are referred to as prevention of significant deterioration, or PSD, regions (attainment) and nonattainment regions. An industrial source of air pollution seeking to locate in an area needs to know whether it is a PSD region or a nonattainment region.

If the region is a clean air area, or PSD region, the law mandates that the air quality cannot be *significantly* deteriorated. The law divided PSD regions into three categories based on the anticipated economic growth in the area. In the Class I region, little to no additional criteria pollutant is allowed. In a Class II region, moderate increases are allowed, and in Class III regions, greater increases are permitted. The regional increments, or allowed deterioration, are specific number limitations and are permanent. In no case, however, may the pollution exceed NAAQS, regardless of the allowed regional increment.

Any major industrial developer seeking to locate in a PSD region must obtain a permit, agree to use best available control technology as defined by the EPA to limit its emissions, and prove that the NAAQS and the PSD regional increment will not be exceeded. The industrial applicant for a permit to pollute the air is required to do a full year of site monitoring prior to construction to determine existing levels of the pollutants in the area, to ensure that the PSD increment will not be exceeded.

If the industrial source tries to locate in a nonattainment region, it must obtain a permit. Although pollution sources are permitted to locate in a nonattainment region, it may be difficult to do so because the region must make regular progress toward achieving the NAAQS. Thus, the new source must find an offset for its pollution in the region and must adopt control technology that achieves the lowest rate of emission required of any source of its type in the country (called LAER). The source also runs the risk that it will be required to achieve greater control in the future because the NAAQS must ultimately be met.

In 1990, Congress passed major amendments to the Clean Air Act. The amendments address four continuing problems: urban smog, motor vehicle emissions, acid rain, and toxic air pollutants. At least two of these areas of regulation may affect the industrial real estate developer. The urban smog provisions apply to the remaining nonattainment regions. These regions must make annual progress toward achieving the NAAQS and must meet the standards within 3 to 20 years, depending on the severity of the current urban air pollution problems. A new industrial facility in a nonattainment region must show that its level of pollutants will be offset (and more) by reductions of other sources of pollution in the region in order to continue this region's progress toward meeting the NAAQS.

The acid rain provisions establish a permanent cap for sulfur dioxide emissions that is less than one-half of the current level of emissions. The mechanisms chosen to achieve the necessary reductions are controls on electric generating power plants. It does not appear at this time that the acid rain provisions will directly affect industrial facilities but may indirectly affect them by increasing the cost of energy or limiting its availability.

OTHER LEGISLATION

There are many other statutes—federal, state and local—that directly or indirectly affect real estate transactions. The National Environmental Policy Act (NEPA) requires the preparation of environmental impact statements; the National Flood Insurance Act mandates protection for floodplain areas; and the Coastal Zone Management Act protects coastal regions from unwise development; these are discussed in Chapter 23 and 24. The Resource Conservation and Recovery Act (RCRA) regulates active hazardous waste sites, active solid waste sites and underground storage tanks. The Endangered Species Act protects the habitat of endangered or threatened species of plants and wildlife. The Federal Insecticide, Fungicide and Rodenticide Act (FIFRA) regulates the application of these substances to the land and to the environment generally. The Safe Drinking Water Act establishes minimum standards to protect the quality of municipal drinking water supplies. These and other federal environmental laws are often complemented by similar or more restrictive state laws. A careful review of the array of environmental legislation is necessary to safely conclude real estate transactions today.

INDOOR POLLUTION

◆ **Pollution within buildings that may come from many sources and is now recognized as a serious health problem.**

Indoor pollution sources release gases or particles into the air. Several recent studies point to indoor air pollution as the number one environmental human health risk. Inadequate ventilation, high temperature or humidity can increase concentrations of these pollutants. The sources of indoor pollution are many. Among the most prominent are radon, asbestos, tobacco smoke, formaldehyde, lead, pesticides and household products.

The health risks created by indoor pollution are magnified because people spend approximately 90 percent of their time indoors, and those likely to spend the most time indoors—the young, the elderly and the chronically ill—are the most susceptible. The adverse effects range from headaches and fatigue to cancer and heart disease.

As the case for indoor pollution is substantiated and the information regarding its risks is more widely communicated, the likelihood of builders, architects, employers and landlords incurring legal liability increases. The legal theories likely to be used are negligence, breach of express or implied warranties, strict product liability, fraud or misrepresentation, and a host of others.

DRINKING WATER

The Safe Drinking Water Act was amended in 1986 to require the use of lead-free pipe, solder and flux in the installation of public water systems and in the plumbing of buildings connected to public water systems. In 1996 the law was amended to require that drinking water suppliers provide an annual report to all customers that identifies the level of contaminants in the water supplied, and a description of the health risks associated with those contaminants. A prospective home buyer will probably expect to see a copy of this report.

RADON

Radon is an odorless, colorless, radioactive gas that results from the natural decay of uranium below ground. It has been linked to lung cancer. In 1988, Congress amended the Toxic Substances Control Act with an act called the Indoor Radon Abatement Law. Although the law specifically states that it does not create a legal cause of action, it brings nationwide attention to the radon problem. The law sets the long-term goal of reducing indoor radon levels to that of the outside ambient air. The EPA is ordered to publish periodic updates on radon health risks and information on the methods available to measure and reduce those risks. The EPA has developed model construction standards and techniques for controlling radon levels. The statute provides money to assist states in developing programs to promote public awareness of radon risks and in developing feasible measures to mitigate the risk. Tests are now available for determining radon levels in buildings. A radon test is becoming a fairly common request by real estate purchasers.

ASBESTOS

Asbestos use in commercial building products began in the early 20th century and was common for many years. Asbestos can cause asbestosis (a scarring of lung tissue) and forms of lung and stomach cancer. Regulations recently promulgated by the Occupational Safety and Health Administration (OSHA) place significant responsibilities on building and facility owners, managers and lessors. Among the responsibilities for commercial builders are due diligence surveys and disclosures about presumed asbestos-containing materials. Otherwise regulation of asbestos removal and disposal are controlled by state law.

LEAD-BASED PAINTS

Historically, lead was added to paint to facilitate drying and endurance. It is a toxic metal that is linked, even in small amounts, to severe health and environmental risk. Lead-based paints were banned from use in residential units in 1978. New regulations that took full effect by the end of 1996 apply to all residences built before 1978. The regulations require that real estate agents and property owners disclose to purchasers and new tenants (including renewing tenants) all known lead-based paint and lead-based paint hazards in the residence. In addition, the agents and owners must provide a pamphlet, "Protect Your Family from Lead in Your Home," which contains low-cost tips for identifying and controlling lead-based paint hazards. Notification and disclosure language must appear in the contract or lease, and parties must verify in writing that the regulations requirements were met. Finally, home buyers will have ten days to conduct a lead-based paint inspection or risk assessment at their own expense before the contract becomes final. The right to inspect can be waived by the buyer.

REVIEW AND DISCUSSION QUESTIONS

1. Discuss how the Hazardous Substances Response Fund, or Superfund, is used to pay for cleaning up hazardous waste sites.
2. If a business is going to purchase a site that was previously used by an industrial firm, what precautionary steps would you suggest to avoid CERCLA liability?
3. If a party wants to recover money spent on response costs under CERCLA, what must it prove to win in court?
4. Can an innocent landowner be held liable for response costs under CERCLA? Discuss.
5. What are the chief problems left to be addressed in order to make the nation's water quality safe for public health and safety? Who is most likely to be affected by regulations addressing these problems?
6. How can air pollution controls affect real estate transactions?
7. What are the main sources of indoor pollution? Why is it critical that the problem of indoor pollution be remedied?

CASE PROBLEMS

1. Idarado Mining Co. operated a mine for the extraction of several metals, including zinc, lead, silver and gold. The operation of the 16-square-mile site created hazardous waste in the form of tailings, mine drainage and waste rock. The State of Colorado submitted several alternative plans to a court for cleaning up the site under CERCLA. The court approved one of the state's plans, stating that it was consistent with the National Contingency Plan and authorized the State to incur removal and remedial costs of nearly $2 million. The State completed the cleanup and sued Idarado for the response costs. Idarado contested some of the costs, including the costs of preparing the plans not approved by the court and the cost of restocking a stream with fish. Idarado's waste previously destroyed the stream's fishery. Is Idarado likely to be successful in challenging these response costs? Explain. *Colorado v. Idarado Mining Co., 735 F.Supp. 368 (1990).*

2. Complaints by neighbors near a site formerly owned by Bell Petroleum Services, Inc. (Bell), about discolored drinking water caused an investigation by the Environmental Protection Agency (EPA). The investigation revealed that the aquifer from which the drinking water was drawn was contaminated by chromium, a hazardous waste. The State of Texas and the EPA cooperatively cleaned up the site and then sued Bell for response costs. Bell denies responsibility because it no longer owns the site and because the governments did not prove that it was Bell's chromium waste that caused the contamination. Bell does not deny that it deposited chromium waste on the site. Discuss. *U.S. v. Bell Petroleum Services, Inc. 734 F.Supp. 771 (1989).*

3. Belvidere Steel Co. is seeking a site to expand its operations. It finds an apparently ideal site on the Little Lehigh River in northeastern Pennsylvania. The technical people have certified to the board of directors that the site is free of contamination from hazardous waste, has an excellent transportation system, and is otherwise ideally located for the manufacture of specialty steel. At this stage, you are called before the board to discuss the site as the technical expert on air and water pollution. What issues are you going to discuss with the board?

4. Ruth Arones, a real estate broker, has an "exclusive right to sell" contract to sell a house owned by Karl and Nan Lipper. The Lippers tell Arones that the house is airtight and therefore extremely energy efficient. Arones notices that the inside of the house has not been painted in some time and that the paint is chipping badly. Arones knows also that some houses in the vicinity have shown high levels of radon when tested. Arones has a young couple, who have two small children, interested in buying the house. You are a senior broker in Arones's firm and she relates these facts to you, seeking your advice on how to proceed. There are no applicable state statutes. How would you counsel Arones?

GLOSSARY

A

abstract of title A summary of all the recorded transactions, including deeds, mortgages, judgments and the like, that affect the title to a specific parcel of land.

acceleration clause A provision in a mortgage giving the mortgagee the right to declare the entire debt due and payable on default.

acceptance Assent to the terms of an offer.

accession Gradual increase in riparian or littoral property as a result of deposits of sediment made by a body of water.

accord An agreement to substitute a different kind of performance for that originally contracted for.

accretion The rights and principles the law uses to deal with changes in the size and shape of land due to natural causes.

acknowledgment In conveyancing, the act by which a person who has executed an instrument goes before an authorized officer, usually a notary public, and declares that the instrument is genuine and executed voluntarily.

action for rent or damages The landlord may permit, or be required to permit, the wrongdoing tenant to retain possession of the property and seek money damages for the landlord's injury.

actual notice Title information that is acquired personally by the interest holder.

adjudicated insane Has been declared insane by a court.

adjustable-rate mortgage (ARM) A type of flexible-rate mortgage.

administration of estates A general term used to describe the management and settlement of a decedent's estate by a person appointed by the courts.

administrative remedies Remedies provided by administrative agencies based on power granted in an enabling act.

administrator A person charged with administering the estate of an intestate decedent.

adverse possession Acquisition of title to real estate by means of wrongful occupancy for a period of time established by statute.

aesthetics Regulation to retain visual and scenic beauty.

affidavit of title A sworn statement verifying facts that satisfy certain objections to title.

after acquired title Title acquired by a grantor after the grantor attempts to convey good title.

agency A legal relationship in which one party, called the *principal,* authorizes another, called the *agent,* to act in the principal's behalf.

agency coupled with an interest An agency that cannot be revoked by the principal.

agricultural lands Lands that are actively being used for grazing and crop production.

alienation Transferring ownership, title or interest in real estate from one person to another.

allodial system A system in which land is owned without obligation to pay rents.

alluvion Land created by sediment left by a body of water.

amortization Repayment of a debt in periodic installments of interest and principal over a period of time.

annual percentage rate (APR) As defined in the "Truth-in-Lending" Act, the percentage that the total finance charge calculated on an annual basis bears to the amount of the loan or credit.

anticipatory breach A breach of contract that occurs as a result of repudiating a contract before the date due for performance.

appeal Process in which a higher court reviews alleged legal errors made by a lower court or an administrative agency.

architect A professional person to prepare the plans and specifications for the construction of a house.

assessments The regular monthly payments for upkeep of the common elements, as well as payments required for special expenses or improvements to those common elements.

assignee A party to whom a right is transferred.

assignment Transfer of property right from one person (the assignor) to another (the assignee).

assignor A party who transfers a right.

assumption A contract between a grantor/mortgagor and a grantee in which the grantee agrees to assume responsibility for the mortgage debt.

attachment (1) the process by which a secured party acquires a security interest in collateral; (2) the act of seizing a defendant's property by legal process to be held by a court to ensure satisfaction of a judgment that might be awarded.

attestation The act of witnessing the execution of an instrument and subscribing as a witness.

authority Term used in the law of agency denoting the agent's power to perform acts authorized by the principal. (*See also* express authority and implied authority.)

B

balloon payment The final payment under a contract, which is substantially larger than the previous installment payments.

bargain and sale deed A deed that conveys title but makes no warranties.

bilateral contract A contract involving a promise in exchange for a promise.

blockbusting Inducing (for profit) the sale or rental of any dwelling by indicating that a particular class of person (for example, non-white) has entered or will enter the neighborhood.

breach of contract The unexcused failure to perform an obligation under a contract.

broker An agent who facilitates a transaction between parties.

builder *See* contractor.

building code compliance Protects the public health, safety and welfare by regulating building and construction standards.

buyer's broker A broker who has contracted to locate real estate for a buyer.

bylaws The rules governing the internal operation of the condominium development.

C

call Term used to refer to the different monuments, courses and distances that make up a metes-and-bounds description.

capacity The legal ability to enter into a contract.

caveat emptor Let the buyer beware.

caveat venditor Let the seller beware.

certificate of title A statement of opinion by an attorney that describes the status of the title to a parcel.

certiorari, writ of A legal document in which a higher court orders a lower court to supply the record of a case that the higher court wishes to review.

chain of title The recorded history of events that affect the title to a specific parcel of land, usually beginning with the original patent or grant.

Clean Air Act A statute whose purpose is to cleanse, maintain and enhance the quality of the nation's air resource.

Clean Water Act A statute whose purpose is to cleanse, maintain, and enhance the quality of the nation's water resources.

closing The final state of the real estate purchase transaction, when the deed and the purchase money are exchanged.

coastal zone Area including coastal waters and the adjacent shorelands.

codification Collection and organization of judge-made law into a code or statute.

cognovit A confession of judgment that permits the landlord, upon default by the tenant, to obtain a judgment against the tenant without the need for formal legal proceedings.

commitment Used in mortgage financing to designate the lender's promise to loan a specified amount of money at an agreed-upon rate of interest.

common elements The parts of the development property that are necessary or convenient for the residents of the condominium and are owned in common by all the condominium residents.

common law (1) law based upon written opinions of appellate courts (*see* judge-made law); (2) the traditional nonstatutory law of England and the United States.

community property A form of co-ownership between husband and wife in which each has a one-half interest in property acquired through the labor of either during marriage.

Comprehensive Environmental Response, Compensation, and Liability Act (CERCLA) A statute providing for cleanup of inactive waste sites that release hazardous substances into the environment.

comprehensive plan A prerequisite for regulating land use. Its contents can range from a thorough master plan to a zoning code and map.

condemnation Legal action by which government acquires private property for a public use. Based on the right of eminent domain.

condominium The fee simple ownership of one unit in a multiple-unit structure, combined with an ownership of an undivided interest in the land and all other parts of the structure held in common with the owners of the other individual units in the structure.

condominium association The organization stipulated by statute to administer the operation of the common elements of the condominium.

consideration A promise, act or forbearance bargained for and given in exchange for a promise, act or forbearance.

construction mortgage A mortgage given to secure funds advanced to construct or improve a building.

constructive eviction An occurrence that results when the actions of the landlord so materially interfere with the tenant's enjoyment as to make the premises untenable.

constructive notice The knowledge of certain facts that might be discovered by a careful inspection of public records, provided that such information is within the history of title, or discovered by an inspection of the premises.

contingency clause A provision within a contract that makes performance under the contract conditional upon the occurrence of a stated event.

contract A promise or an agreement that the law will enforce.

contractor The person or firm that undertakes to construct a house at a given price.

contract for a deed *See* land installment contract.

contract zoning Zoning in which an applicant will be granted a requested zone change only after contracting with the community to comply with certain covenants.

cooperative A form of ownership in which the land and buildings are (usually) owned by a corporation; individual unit residents own stock in the corporation and have a proprietary lease in a specific unit or apartment.

co-ownership Ownership of real estate in which two or more people have undivided interests.

correlative right, doctrine of A legal doctrine that prohibits depletion of a common pool of oil or gas. Sometimes applied to water.

co-tenancy *See* co-ownership.

counteroffer A new offer made as a response to a person who has made an offer.

covenant of fitness of the premises An assurance that the premises are fit for habitation.

covenant of quiet enjoyment A warrant by the landlord that the tenant will have the premises free from interference by the landlord or anyone claiming better right to the premises than the landlord.

covenant to deliver possession The landlord promises to deliver the right of possession to the tenant at the time the lease is scheduled to start.

critical areas Areas legislatively identified as containing natural limitations, or ones that are important to maintaining the ecosystem.

curtesy A common law estate that provided a husband with a life interest in all his wife's real property at the time a child was born of the marriage.

D

damages Money recoverable by one suffering a loss or injury due to breach of the contract.

decisional law Law that evolves from published opinions of appellate courts. (*See* judge-made law.)

declaration A document required by state law, which must accompany and be recorded with the master deed for the condominium development.

dedication The grant of real property such as a public street to a governmental unit for public use.

deed A legal instrument that conveys title to real property upon delivery and acceptance by the grantee.

deed in lieu of foreclosure A deed in which a mortgagor conveys mortgaged real estate to the mortgagee, who promises in return not to foreclose on the mortgage debt, which is in default.

deed of trust A legal instrument in which a borrower transfers real property to a trustee as security for a debt. The lender is the beneficiary of the trust.

default Nonperformance of a duty or obligation as part of the mortgage transaction.

defeasible fee *See* fee simple defeasible.

deficiency judgment A money judgment awarded to the mortgagee when funds obtained as a result of a foreclosure sale are insufficient to pay the debt.

delivery Surrender of possession and control of a document to a third party.

Department of Veterans Affairs loan guarantees Guarantees provided by DVA to lenders that finance housing construction and purchases by veterans.

developer The person or firm that subdivides a parcel of land and prepares the site for construction.

disavow Avoid a contract.

discharge The release of contractual obligations.

diversity jurisdiction Power of federal courts to hear cases involving citizens of different states.

dominant estate The parcel of land that benefits from an easement appurtenant; also called *dominant tenement.*

dower Life estate of a widow in one third of any real estate to which her husband had legal title during marriage. (*See also* inchoate dower.)

dual agency A transaction in which an agent represents both principals.

due-on-sale clause A provision found in some mortgages requiring the mortgagor to pay off the mortgage debt if he or she sells the property.

duty to repair Tenant's obligation to leave premises in about the same condition as when received, reasonable wear and tear excluded.

E

earnest money A cash deposit evidencing a good-faith intention to complete a transaction.

easement A nonpossessory interest in real property; the right to use another's real property for a particular purpose.

easement appurtenant The right of an owner of a parcel of land to benefit from the use of another's land. (*See also* dominant estate and servient estate.)

easement by necessity An easement that permits the owner of a landlocked parcel to cross a parcel of land of which the landlocked parcel formerly was a part.

easement in gross An easement that exists as a personal right apart from a dominant estate.

ejectment A legal action to recover possession of real property.

elective share The share of a deceased spouse's property that the surviving spouse may claim if the decedent left no will or the surviving spouse did not receive the minimum specified by law.

eminent domain Right of the state to take private property for public use. Just compensation must be paid to the owner.

enabling legislation State statutory authorization granting a local government the right to regulate in a specific area.

environmental impact assessment A statement describing and analyzing the environmental impacts of a proposed action.

Equal Credit Opportunity Act Federal statute prohibiting discrimination in an applicant's credit transaction.

equal protection The constitutional mandate that all people be treated equally under the law.

equitable title The buyer's right to obtain ownership of real property upon payment of the purchase price.

equity of redemption The right of a mortgagor or another person with an interest in real estate to reclaim it after default but before foreclosure.

escheat Reversion to the state of title to property of a person dying without heirs or leaving a will.

escrow A process by which money and/or documents are held by a third party until the terms and conditions of an agreement are satisfied.

escrow agent The third party who is the depositary in an escrow transaction.

escrow agreement An agreement that directs the escrow agent regarding terms and conditions under which the deed or other instruments are to be delivered to the parties and the disposition of the deed or other instruments on default.

estate The extent and character of a person's ownership interest in real property. (*See also* future estate and life estate.)

estoppel certificate A statement by a mortgagor that he or she has no defense against paying the mortgage debt; also indicates the amount that remains unpaid.

eviction by the landlord The term usually associated with the legal procedure by which a landlord has the tenant removed from the premises because the tenant has breached the lease agreement.

evidence of title A document verifying ownership of property.

exceptions in zoning Permitted uses provided for in the ordinance that are inconsistent with the designated zone.

exclusive agency A listing in which the seller gives one broker authority to procure a buyer for property but also retains the right for himself or herself.

exclusive right to sell A listing in which the seller gives one broker authority to procure a buyer for property, but the broker is entitled to a commission if the seller procures the buyer.

exculpatory clause A lease clause by which the landlord attempts to excuse himself or herself from

liability for negligence in maintaining the leasehold premises.

executed A promise that has been performed.

executor Person appointed to administer the estate of a decedent who died testate.

executory An unperformed promise.

exemptions Transactions that would otherwise meet the definition of a security but that have been statutorily excused from the law's restrictions.

express authority Authority a principal confers upon an agent explicitly and distinctly. May be conferred orally or in writing.

express grant An easement created by an owner expressly granting in a deed a specific right to another to use the owner's property.

express reservation Property owner conveys title to another by deed specifically reserving an easement for himself or a third party within the deed.

F

fair housing The term used to express a national policy against most types of discrimination in housing.

federal question A legal dispute that involves the U.S. Constitution, a treaty, or a federal statute. Federal question cases are heard by federal courts.

fee simple (absolute) The most extensive estate in real property that an owner can possess.

fee simple defeasible A fee simple estate that terminates upon the occurrence of a specified condition; also called a *qualified fee*.

fee simple determinable A defeasible fee that terminates automatically if a stated act or event occurs.

fee simple subject to condition subsequent A fee that may be terminated by the grantor when a certain condition is fulfilled.

feudal system A system in which landowners pay rents to a superior.

FHA insurance Insurance provided lenders under Title II of the National Housing Act of 1943.

fiduciary duty A trustee's responsibility to act solely in the best interests of the owner or beneficiary of the trust.

finance charge Defined in the "Truth-in-Lending" Act as the monetary total of all charges a borrower must pay the lender for credit or a loan.

fixture An item that was personal property but has been permanently affixed to real property.

fixture filing A section of the UCC that allows a security interest to persist in goods (personal property) that later become fixtures.

flexible-rate mortgage A mortgage that contains a provision permitting the mortgagee to adjust the interest rate upward or downward in a manner specified in the mortgage.

floodplains Areas near waterways that are prone to flooding.

foreclosure A procedure in which property used as security for a debt is sold in the event of default to satisfy the debt.

foreclosure of mortgage Legal procedure by which a lender who has advanced funds with real property as security recovers in the event of default. (*See also* judicial foreclosure, power-of-sale foreclosure and strict foreclosure.)

forfeiture The loss of the right to a down payment on real estate as a result of a breach of contract.

fraud A deceptive act or statement deliberately made by one person in an attempt to gain an unfair advantage over another.

freehold estate An interest in real property created to last for an uncertain period of time.

future estate An interest in real property that will become possessory in the future.

G

general lien A lien that applies to all property that a person owns.

grantee Person who acquires title to real property by deed.

grantor Person who transfers title to real property by deed.

gross lease A lease in which a flat or fixed amount of rent is paid by the tenant.

ground lease A specialized type of net lease in which the lessor leases a piece of vacant land to the lessee, usually with the stipulation that the les*see* at his or her own expense will construct a building thereon.

growth management plans Comprehensive growth plans that dictate both when and where growth will occur.

H

historic preservation The preservation of buildings, and perhaps archaeological sites, from destruction by new development.

holdover tenant One who failed to vacate or surrender possession of the premises on the ending date of a term tenancy.

homestead laws Provide heads of families some exemptions from creditor's claims.

I

implied authority An agent's authority to do those acts necessary and proper to accomplish the express terms of the agency.

implied notice Legal notice that is imposed by the law when conditions exist that would lead a reasonable person to inquire further into the condition of the title.

implied warranty of habitability A warranty imposed by law on the landlord by which he or she warrants that a residential property is safe and sanitary and fit for living at the time the tenant enters and during the period of tenancy.

in pari delicto At equal fault.

in terrorem clause A clause in an installment contract that prohibits recording at the expense of forfeiture.

inchoate dower The expectant interest of a wife to dower.

indemnification The act of compensating another in the event of loss.

independent contractor A person who is retained to do a job, using his or her own judgment as to how the work will be done.

individual unit deed The deed for each individual condominium unit in the development.

indoor pollution Pollution within buildings that is recognized as a health problem.

innocent misrepresentation An unintentional misstatement of a material fact that induces justifiable reliance to the detriment of a party.

interpleader A legal procedure whereby a party deposits money into court so that the court can distribute it to the rightful owner.

inter vivos trust A trust that takes effect during the life of the creator.

intestate A person who dies without leaving a will.

intestate succession Distribution of property of a person who dies without leaving a will or whose will is invalid.

intrastate offering An exemption from registration under federal securities law where the offering is made solely to residents of the state by a resident offeror doing business in the same state.

involuntary alienation The transfer of title to land against the owner's wishes.

J

joint tenancy Co-ownership in which the entire estate passes to the survivor upon the death of the other joint tenant or tenants.

joint venture A business entity in which two or more persons agree to carry out a single undertaking for profit.

judge-made law Law based upon the written opinions of appellate courts, called *precedent.*

judgment creditor A plaintiff who has won a monetary judgment that has not yet been paid.

judgment lien A lien that attaches to real property of a defendant when a plaintiff wins a judgment in the jurisdiction in which the property is located.

judicial foreclosure A foreclosure ordered by a court.

judicial remedies Remedies provided by the courts.

jurisdiction The power of a court to hear a case.

just compensation The award to the owner when property is taken by the government through eminent domain.

L

land installment contract A contract in which the buyer pays the purchase price on an installment basis.

The seller/owner retains title until the purchase price is paid; also called *contract for a deed.*

landlord's lien Under common law, the lien known as the right of distress provided the landlord with a lien on the personal property of the tenant where there was a failure to pay rent.

large-lot zoning A zoning classification that requires a minimum of one acre or more of land for each single-family house that is constructed.

lease A contract, either written or oral, that transfers the right of possession of the premises to the les*see* or tenant.

leasehold estate An estate created when the owner of property, known as the *lessor* or *landlord,* conveys a possessory interest in the real property to another, known as the *lessee* or *tenant,* for a specific period of time in exchange for the tenant's payment of rent.

legal description A description of a parcel of land complete enough to locate and identify the premises.

legal notice A knowledge of another's interest in real property sufficient to make the adverse interest legally binding to the prospective purchaser or any other party acquiring interest in the property.

license A personal privilege to enter another's property for a specific purpose.

licensing laws State laws that require a person to obtain a license in order to act as a real estate broker or sales associate and regulate the conduct of those who act as brokers or sales associates.

lien A claim against another's property securing either payment of a debt or fulfillment of some other monetary charge or obligation. (*See also* general lien and specific lien.)

life estate An ownership interest in real property created to last for a person's life.

limited partnership A partnership formed according to the provisions of a state limited partnership act. The liability of a limited partner is limited to the amount he or she has invested.

limited warranty deed A deed in which the seller warrants against acts that he or she has done that might affect title; also called *special warranty deed.*

lis pendens, notice of A notice filed for the purpose of warning people that legal action has been taken that might affect title or possession of specified real property.

listing A contract between a seller and a broker authorizing the broker to find a buyer for real property upon specified terms in return for a fee if the broker is successful. (*See also* open listing.)

littoral lands Lands that border on an ocean, a sea or a lake.

long-term escrow A financing device that combines the land installment contract and the escrow.

M

marketable title Title that is free of liens or other encumbrances that interfere with the peaceful enjoyment of the property.

mechanic's lien The right of one who renders services or supplies materials in connection with improvements to real property to seek a judicial sale of the realty to satisfy unpaid claims.

memorandum A writing that contains essential terms in satisfaction of the Statute of Frauds.

metes and bounds A method of describing land using compass directions, monuments or landmarks, and linear measurements.

mistake Unintentional error.

mistakes in recording Errors made by the recorder.

mistakes in the instrument Errors made in the preparation of the instrument to be recorded.

mobile home A transportable structure built on a chassis and designed for year-round living.

mortgage A document that uses real property to secure payment of a debt.

mortgagee A lender who acquires an interest in a borrower's real property as security for repayment of a loan.

mortgage insurance Insurance provided by government agencies or private corporations protecting mortgage lenders against loss caused by a borrower's default.

mortgagor A borrower who gives a lender an interest in the borrower's real property to secure payment of a loan.

multiple-listing service An organization among brokers who have contracted to agree to share listings with each other.

N

negative amortization When periodic payments on an amortized loan do not cover all the interest that is due, the unpaid amount is added to the principal. This is referred to as *negative amortization.*

NEPA Statute requiring the preparation of a document detailing environmental data and analyzing that data regarding a proposed government action.

net lease As contrasted with the gross lease, a type of lease in which the tenant agrees to pay the taxes, insurance, repairs and other operating expenses of the premises.

nonconforming use A legal use that was established prior to zoning or prior to the present zoning classification and is permitted to continue despite its nonconformance with the zoning code.

note The borrower's written promise to repay a loan according to its terms.

notice statutes Statutes that provide that the subsequent buyer prevails over all interested parties who have not recorded their interest at the time the buyer accepts the conveyance and pays consideration for the land without notice of the preexisting conveyance.

novation An agreement in which a creditor agrees to discharge an existing debt and to substitute a new obligation and a new debtor in its place.

nuisance An unreasonable interference by one party with another's use or enjoyment of his or her land.

O

offer A proposal intended to create a contract upon acceptance by the person to whom it is made.

open-end mortgage A mortgage that permits the mortgagor to borrow additional funds, usually up to the original amount of the debt.

open listing A brokerage agreement that entitles the broker to a fee only if his or her activities bring about the sale. The property may be listed with several brokers.

option contract A contract that gives a person a designated period of time to buy or lease real property at a specified price.

optionee One who is the recipient of an option.

optionor One who agrees not to revoke an offer.

P

package mortgage A mortgage debt secured by both personal and real property.

parol evidence Oral or other evidence extraneous to a written contract.

parties' tort liability A civil duty to third parties to maintain premises in a reasonably safe condition.

partition A legal action in which a co-owner obtains a division of real property, terminating any interest of other co-owners in the divided portion. Each former co-owner's share is now owned individually.

partnership An association of two or more persons to organize a business venture and divide the profits.

party wall A single wall on the boundary of adjoining properties; it serves as a common support for buildings on each of two parcels.

per capita Distribution of an intestate's property in equal shares to persons who have the same relationship to the decedent without reference to the share an ancestor would have taken.

per stirpes Distribution of an intestate's property to persons who take only the share that an ancestor would have taken.

percentage lease A lease whose rental is based in part on the gross sales made by the tenant on the premises.

percolating water Water that passes through the ground, not flowing in a clearly defined underground stream or supplied by streams flowing on the surface.

perfection (1) Legal steps necessary to establish a valid mechanic's lien; (2) acts by which a secured party establishes priority in collateral over claims of third parties.

performance standards zoning Standards set to limit the adverse off-site impact of an owner's use. For example, standards can be established for odors, noise and signs.

periodic tenancy An estate from period to period, continuing from period to period until terminated by proper notice from one of the parties.

personal property Property that is not real property; generally characterized as having substance and being movable.

planned unit development (PUD) A concept involving a development larger than a traditional subdivision, generally permitting mixed uses within the development and attempting to provide a maximum amount of land for open space.

plat A map of a subdivision indicating boundaries of individual properties. Also includes details such as lot numbers, blocks, streets, public easements and monuments.

possession The right to occupy and control real estate to the exclusion of all others.

possibility of reverser A possibility that an estate based upon a condition may revert to the grantor if the grantee or those who take through the grantee breach the condition.

power of attorney A document authorizing a person, the attorney-in-fact, to act as agent on behalf of another as indicated in the instrument.

power-of-sale foreclosure Foreclosure based on terms in a mortgage giving a mortgagee or third party the power to sell the security if the borrower defaults.

power of termination The future interest that a grantor of an estate on condition subsequent has to terminate the estate if the condition occurs; also called *right of reentry*.

precedent A published opinion of an appellate court that serves as authority for determining a legal question in a later case that has similar facts.

prescription Acquisition of an easement through wrongful use of another's land for a period of time designated by statute.

prior appropriation Water rights doctrine giving primary rights to first users of water.

private offering An exemption from registration under federal securities law for offerings made to knowledgeable investors who have adequate information to evaluate fully the risks in the transaction.

probate The legal proceeding that establishes the validity of a will.

profit à prendre A nonpossessory interest in real property permitting the holder to remove part of the soil or produce of the land.

promissory estoppel A doctrine that prevents a party from denying that a promise is supported by consideration.

property Legal rights that a person possesses with respect to a thing; rights that have economic value.

prorate To divide or allocate proportionately.

prospectus A written document containing all the information necessary for an investor to make an independent and intelligent decision regarding a securities offering.

public use A use that benefits the community.

puffing Statements of opinion made by a seller to induce the purchaser to buy.

punitive damages Damages awarded as a punishment to the wrongdoer. Punitive damages are added to damages actually incurred.

purchase-money mortgage A mortgage given to a lender to secure part of the purchase price of real property, delivered contemporaneously with the transfer of title to the buyer.

Q–R

quitclaim deed An instrument that conveys whatever title the grantor has.

race-notice statutes Statutes that provide that a subsequent buyer will prevail only if he or she has no notice of the prior transaction at the time of conveyance.

ratify Approve a contract.

ready, willing and able Capable of present performance.

real estate escrow See escrow.

real estate investment trust (REIT) A tax shelter that exempts certain qualified real estate investment syndications from corporate taxes where 90 percent or more of the ordinary income is distributed annually to the beneficiaries or investors.

real estate purchase contract An agreement whereby a seller promises to sell an interest in realty by conveying a deed to the designated estate for which a buyer promises to pay a specified purchase price.

real estate sales associate A person employed by a real estate broker who lists and sells real estate.

real estate securities Any arrangement whereby a person invests money in a common enterprise involving real estate with the expectation of attaining profits from the efforts of a promoter or some other third party.

Real Estate Settlement Procedures Act (RESPA) A federal law that requires lending institutions to disclose certain information to purchasers of residential real estate and prohibits those institutions from engaging in certain fraudulent activities.

real property Land, buildings and other improvements permanently affixed to land.

real property rights Ownership or proprietary rights in land and anything permanently affixed to land.

recording statutes Laws that require the entry into books of public record the written instruments affecting the title to real property.

rectangular survey system System of land description that applies to most of the land in the United States.

redlining Denial of a loan by a lending institution or the exacting of harsher terms for loans in certain parts of a city.

reformation Change in lease agreement due to landlord's refusal to make repairs.

registration of securities The listing of an issuance that meets the definition of a security—and is not otherwise exempted—with the SEC and (perhaps) with state officials.

regulatory taking A regulation that deprives the owner of all reasonable use of the land constitutes a de facto taking of the property without due process of law under the Fifth and Fourteenth Amendments to the Constitution.

rejection An offeree's refusal or failure to accept an offer.

relation back A legal doctrine whereby the title acquired by a deed relates back to the moment of the first delivery to an escrow agent.

release of mortgage See satisfaction of mortgage.

reliction Land created when water recedes.

remainder A future interest in real estate created when a grantor conveys less than a fee simple and by the same instrument directs another estate to arise immediately upon the termination of the prior estate.

rent The compensation paid by the les*see* for the possession of the leased property.

rent paid in advance Rent payments due prior to the beginning of the lease period.

rent withholding The practice, allowed in a few states under limited circumstances, in which the tenant withholds rent as an inducement to force the landlord to perform repairs.

rescission A cancellation of a contract that results in the parties being restored to the position they were in before the contract was made.

respondeat superior, doctrine of The legal doctrine that an employer is liable for the wrongful acts of employees done within the scope of their employment.

restrictive covenant A provision in a deed limiting the uses that may be made of the property.

reversion A future interest in real estate created by operation of law when a grantor conveys a lesser estate than he or she possesses.

revocation An offeror's act of withdrawing an offer.

right of possession In all jurisdictions the right of possession implicitly resides in the tenant; that is, no one will have possessory rights inconsistent with those granted to the tenant.

right of reentry *See* power of termination.

right of survivorship A characteristic of some forms of co-ownership by which the surviving co-tenant acquires the entire estate.

riparian lands Lands that border on a stream or watercourse.

riparianism Water rights doctrine based on the idea that all owners of riparian lands are entitled to share equally in the use of water.

rollover mortgage A mortgage that must be refinanced every few years in order to adjust the interest rate up or down in response to prevailing market conditions.

rule of capture A legal principle of oil and gas law allowing a land owner the right to all oil and gas from wells on his or her land, including oil and gas migrating from the land of others.

run with the land Rights in real property that pass to successive owners are said to run with the land.

S

S corporation A corporation that has elected to be treated as a partnership for tax purposes.

satisfaction The performance of an agreement to substitute a different kind of performance for that originally contracted for.

satisfaction of mortgage A written statement by the mortgagee that the debt secured by the mortgage has been paid, also called a *release of mortgage.*

scienter In fraud action, knowingly making a false statement or asserting that something is true without actual knowledge.

section An area of land approximately one mile square, containing as nearly as possible 640 acres.

secured transaction A transaction in which the parties agree that personal property or fixtures will secure a loan or the purchase of an item on credit.

security deposit Money deposited by the tenant, usually at the inception of the lease, over and above the advance payment of rent for the security of the landlord.

segregation in housing The voluntary or enforced separation of one group from another in residential location based on religious association, ethnic background, race or a combination of these factors.

seisin Ownership of real property.

"separate but equal" facilities A concept that permitted the state to enforce separation of the races so long as each race was provided with "equal" services or facilities.

separate property In community property jurisdictions, property owned by either spouse prior to marriage and property acquired during marriage by gift, inheritance or will.

servient estate The parcel of land that is subject to an easement appurtenant; also called *servient tenement.*

settlement *See* closing.

settlement clerk The person who is designated to coordinate the exchange of documents at the closing.

special-use permit A system whereby special exceptions to the zoning ordinance are granted by the land use administrator under a permit arrangement.

specific lien A lien that applies only to a designated property.

specific performance A court decree mandating a party to perform according to the contract.

spot zoning A zone change permitted by the local legislature that is not in harmony with the comprehensive plan for that area.

Statute of Frauds A statute that necessitates that certain contracts, in order to be enforceable, be supported by a written memorandum and signed by the party against whom enforcement is sought.

Statutes of Descent and Distribution Provide for the distribution of an intestate's personal property; patterned after the English Statute of Distribution.

statutory law Law enacted by local and state legislative bodies and by Congress.

statutory right of redemption The right of a mortgagor to redeem the property after a foreclosure sale.

steering Channeling of prospective home buyers to or away from certain areas.

strict foreclosure A judicial procedure that terminates the mortgagor's equity of redemption and establishes the mortgagee's absolute title to mortgaged real property.

subdivision regulations Restrictions on the division of a parcel of land into two or more units. A subdivision will require prior approval by an administrator such as a planning board.

subject to As used in financing the purchase of real property, a sale in which an existing mortgage on the property is not paid off, the buyer paying only for the seller's equity.

sublease A transfer of part of the leasehold interest of the tenant, with the tenant retaining a reversionary interest.

subordination agreement As used in mortgage financing, an agreement in which a mortgagee surrenders a priority lien and accepts a junior position in relationship to other liens or claims.

substantial performance The amount of compliance under the terms of a contract that discharges a party from further obligation although failing to perform totally under the contract.

syndicate A group of investors who pool their resources to develop, manage or purchase real estate.

T

tax lien A lien imposed against real property for payment of taxes.

tenancy at sufferance Created when a person is wrongfully in possession of another's land without a valid lease.

tenancy at will A tenancy that exists until either party chooses to terminate it.

tenancy by the entirety Co-ownership of real property by husband and wife. The right of survivorship is a characteristic of a tenancy by the entirety.

tenancy in common A form of co-ownership in which each owner possesses an undivided right to the entire property. Shares of co-owners need not be equal, and no right of survivorship exists.

tenancy in partnership A form of co-ownership in which each partner owns partnership property along with all other partners.

tender An offer of money or property as required by the contract.

tenure An historic system of holding lands, a characteristic of which was the possessor's subordination to some superior to whom the possessor owed certain duties.

term tenancy An estate for a specified period of time that has a specific beginning date and a specific ending date. When the ending date arrives, the estate is terminated without notice by either party.

testamentary trust A trust that does not take effect until the death of the creator.

testate succession Transfer of property when a person dies leaving a will.

testator A person who dies leaving a will.

third-party beneficiary A person who is allowed to enforce a contract although not a party to it.

third-person guaranty of rent The landlord who has doubts about the capacity or reliability of the tenant in meeting the conditions of the lease may require a third person to guarantee performance.

title The totality of rights and obligations possessed by an owner; evidence of ownership.

title insurance The comprehensive indemnity contract that insures the titleholder against title defects and encumbrances that may exist at the time the policy is issued.

Torrens certificate A document issued under the Torrens system, a type of land title registration.

township An area of land approximately six miles square, containing as nearly as possible 23,040 acres and divided into 36 sections.

trade fixtures Items added to land or buildings by a tenant to be used in the tenant's trade or business.

traditional zoning Zoning based on classifying land into use districts, such as residential, commercial and industrial uses.

transferring development rights A system of land controls that permits the transfer of the right to develop from sites that are desired to be preserved to sites on which maximum development is desirable.

trespass A wrongful, physical invasion of the property of another.

trust A legal relationship in which a person transfers legal title to property to a trustee who manages it for the benefit of third parties, the beneficiaries of the trust. (*See also* inter vivos trust and testamentary trust.)

trustee The person responsible for managing a trust.

Truth-in-Lending Federal statute that requires lenders to disclose the cost of consumer credit.

U

unconscionable contract A contract that a court may render unenforceable because it is grossly unfair.

underground streams Subterranean waters that flow in clearly defined channels discoverable from the earth's surface.

undivided interest Interest of a co-owner that gives him or her the right to possession of the entire property along with other co-owners (*See* co-ownership.)

undue influence The exertion of dominion over another person that destroys that person's ability to exercise independent judgment.

Uniform Partnership Act A model act that establishes the legality of the partnership form of ownership.

uniform settlement statement A closing statement required for all federally related residential first mortgages.

unilateral contract A contract involving a promise in exchange for an act.

usury The practice of charging interest on a loan in excess of a rate allowed by law.

V

variable-rate mortgage A type of flexible-rate mortgage.

variance Permission obtained from the appropriate governmental authorities to deviate somewhat from the designations under the zoning code.

vendor's lien The right of a seller to a lien against land conveyed for any unpaid or unsecured portion of the purchase price.

voidable A contract that may be voided or validated at the option of a party.

W

waiver Intentional surrender of a known right or privilege.

warranty deed A deed that conveys title and warrants that title is good and free of liens and encumbrances. (*See also* limited warranty deed.)

waste Damage caused by the tenant, including failure to protect the premises from decay and ruin caused by the natural elements.

wetlands Lands that have groundwater levels at or near the surface for much of the year or that are covered by aquatic vegetation.

will A written instrument that permits distribution of an owner's property after death.

wraparound mortgage A second mortgage covering an existing mortgage that the lender agrees to service.

wrongful abandonment The tenant's vacating of the premises without justification and with the intention of no longer performing under the terms of the lease.

wrongful eviction An act that occurs when the landlord without justification deprives the tenant of the possession of the premises.

Z

zone change A zoning amendment made by the legislative body that created the zoning code.

zoning The regulation by the public, usually a municipality, of structures and uses of land within designated zones.

Alphabetical Index
of Cases

Adams v. Spillman, 366

Agins v. City of Tiburon, 505

Agrelius v. Mohesky, 340

Alameda County Water District v. Niles Sand and Gravel Co., Inc., 45–46

Alchemedes/Brookwood, Petition of, 402–3

Alexander v. Town of Hampstead, 500

Allen v. Allen Title Co., 296

Allingham v. City of Seattle, 493

Applebaum v. Zeigler, 289

Asbury v. Brougham, 460–63

Asher v. Herman, 298–99

Atlanta (City of) v. Atlanta Trailer City Trailer Park, 351

Austin v. United States, 181–83

Avila S. Condominium Ass'n v. Kappa Corp., 110

Bailey v. Eagle Mountain Telephone, Inc., 63–64

Balfour v. Balfour, 170

Bard v. Kent, 192

Bayswater Realty and Capital Corp. v. Planning Board of the Town of Lewisboro, 523

Beachwood Villas Condominium v. Poor, 93–95

Beals (J.M.) Enterprises, Inc. v. Industrial Hard Chrome, Ltd., 116–18

Bean v. Sears, Roebuck & Co., 262

Been Corp. v. Shader, 305

Beri, Inc. v. Salishan Properties, Inc., 244

Berk-Fink Realty Co. v. Ershowsky, 155

Berman v. Parker, 387, 521

Beverly Bank v. Illinois Department of Transportation, 516–17

Bishop v. Johnson, 359–61

Blackett v. Olanoff, 141–42

Blankenship v. Myers, 322–23

Boomer v. Atlantic Cement Co., 54

Bowman v. Holsopple, 33

Brasker v. Tanner, 366

Brown v. Board of Education, 459

Brown v. Burnside, 198

Bull v. Goldman, 442

Burgess v. Pine Island Corp., 349, 351

Burns v. Pugmire, 191

Bury v. Young, 342

Butcher v. Kagey Lumber Company, 456

Butkovich v. Summit County, 349–50

Cadillac Fairview/California Inc. v. Dow Chemical Co., 527–29

Cahion v. Ahmadi et al, 230–32

Canada v. City of Shawnee, 44

Cash v. Craver, 158–59

Cashman v. Kirby, 262

Caulfield v. Improved Risk Mutuals, Inc., 307

Chertok v. Kassabian, 277

China Doll Restaurant, Inc. v. Schweiger, 128

Chinese Staff and Workers Ass'n v. City of New York, 493

Clarence v. Larkin, 196–97

Claussen v. First American Title Guaranty Co., 297

Coffin v. Left Hand Ditch Co., 56

Collins v. Kares, 294

Colorado v. Idarado Mining Co., 540

Commonwealth v. Ulrich, 404

Corea v. Maggiore, 262

Cragin v. Powell, 362

Crisp Lumber Co. v. Bridges, 65

Cross v. Cross, 73

Cultum v. Heritage House Realtors, Inc., 199–201

Cummings v. Boyles, 375

Curtiss v. Feriss, 339

Daniels v. Deseret Federal Savings and Loan, 314

Davis v. DeVore, 363

Deetz v. Carter, 41
DeMarco v. Pallazzo, 476
Dennen v. Searle, 334
Derman Rug Co. Inc. v. Ruderman, 135
Devlin v. The Phoenix, Inc., 168
Dickerson Realtors, Inc. v. Frewert, 216
Dickinson v. Dodds, 172
Dolan v. City of Tigard, 509
Donaldson v. Sellmer, 451
Drew Associates of N.J. v. Travisano, 95
Duncan v. Rossuck, 270–71
Dur-Bar Realty Co. v. City of Utica, 493
Durell v. Freese, 167

Eagle Enterprises, Inc. v. Gross, 474–75
Easton v. Strassburger, 227
Edmonds (City of) v. Oxford House, Inc.,
    466–69
805 Third Avenue Co. v. M.W. Realty Assoc.,
    213
Eisenberg v. Comfed Mortgage Co., Inc.,
    286–87
Elmore v. Blume, 248
Euclid (Village of) v. Ambler, 494, 509
Ewing v. Adams, 122

Federal Land Bank of Omaha v. Swanson,
    24–26
Field v. Goat, 68
Filippo v. Real Estate Commission of District of
    Columbia, 460
Fincher v. Miles Homes, 447
Fountainbleau Hotel Corp. v. Forty-Five
    Twenty-Five Florida, 162–63
Franz v. Nelson, 337
Fuqua v. Fuqua, 302

Gagner v. Kittery Water District, 405
Ganser v. Zimmerman, 306
Garraway v. Yonce, 336
Garrett Tire Center, Inc. v. Herbaugh Supreme
    Court of Arkansas, 422–23
Gelber v. Cappeller, 307
Gibbens v. Hardin, 195
Gilbertie v. Zoning Board of Appeals, 496
Gilmer v. Anderson, 296
Gladstone Realtors v. Village of Bellwood, 464

Gokey v. Bessette, 152
Governor's Island, In re, 501
Graham v. Lyons, 398–99
Gregory v. Walker, 129
Grey v. Coastal States Holding Co., 111
Grey Rocks Land Trust v. Town of Hebron,
    500–502
Grindal, In re, 67–68
Groening v. Opsota, 255
Grombone v. Krekel, 457
Gruman v. Investors Diversified Services, Inc.,
    145–46

Haines v. Mensen, 347
Hall v. Wright, 252
Hamer v. Sidway, 180
Harper v. Rogers, 347
Hartman v. Wood, 303–4
Haslem v. Lockwood, 21–23
Hawaii Housing Authority v. Midkeff, 370
Henderson v. Estate of Henderson, 380–81
Hendricks v. Behee, 172
Herron v. Blackwell, 470
Hewgley v. Jose Vivo, 344–46
Hickox v. Bell, 446
Hidden Harbour Estates, Inc. v. Basso, 94
Hilgendorf v. Hague, 238
Hocking v. Dubois, 102–5
Hoffman v. Connall, 224–26
Housh v. Swanson, 151
Howey, In re, 103–5
HTM Restaurants, Inc. v. Goldman, Sachs
    and Company, 132
Huggans v. Weer, 364
Humber v. Morton, 5
Hunter Land Co. v. Laungenour, 42

Jacob & Youngs, Inc. v. Kent, 192
Johnson v. Marcel, 54–55
Jones v. Jones, 340–41
Joyce v. Ritchie Tower Properties, 102
Just v. Marinette County, 481, 484–86

Kasten Construction Co. Inc. v. Maple Ridge
    Construction Co. Inc., 289
Katz v. Walkinshaw, 45
Kelley v. The Ohio Oil Co., 49

Kerley v. Wolfe, 40
Kit-Mar Builders, Inc., In re, 504
Kittrel v. Scarborough, 387
Kline v. Burns, 134
Kramer v. Chabot, 261–63

LaBonta v. City of Waterville, 487–89
Laddon v. Rhett Realty, Inc., 213
LaFond v. Frame, 289
Laufman v. Oakley Building and Loan Co., 464
Lawing v. Jaynes, 404
Lawson v. Citizens So. Nat'l Bank of South
    Carolina, 255
Leben v. Nassau Savings & Loan Association,
    410–11
Lee v. Heftel Supreme Court of Hawaii, 14–16
Lee County Board of Review v. Property Tax
    Appeal Board, 31–33
Leon Realty, Inc. v. Hough, 249
Levandusky v. One Fifth Avenue Apartment
    Corp., 98–100
Loeb v. Conley, 391
Lone Star Development Corp. v. Miller, 274
Loretto v. Teleprompter Manhattan CATV
    Corp., 481
Lucas v. South Carolina Coastal Council, 480,
    481–84, 486
Lucy v. Zehmer, 175–76
Lundberg v. Northwestern National Bank, 437

McCormick v. Lawrence, In re, 521
McDaniel v. Lawyer's Title Guaranty Fund, 405
McDonnell Douglas Corp. v. Green, 461
McGinnis v. Frederick W. Berens Sales, Inc.,
    240
McIlroy v. Hamilton, 167
McKone v. Guertzgen, 443–44
McLain v. Real Estate Board of New Orleans,
    Inc., 8–10
McWilliams v. Barnes, 258
Management Clearing, Inc. v. Vance, 219
Marengo Cave Co. v. Ross, 368
Martin's Estate, In re, 377
Matthews and Van Ness v. Bay Head
    Improvement Assoc., 518
Maxwell v. Moorman, 456–57
Meinhard v. Salmon, 82
Merry v. County Board of Education, 306
Metropolitan Life Ins. Co. v. Reeves, 24

Mitchell v. Jerrolds, 63–64
Moore v. (Pa.) State Real Estate Commission,
    222
Morris v. Davis, 292
Morrison v. Jones, 354
Morrison v. Thoelke, 192
Mudusar v. V.G. Murray and Co., 135

Nelson v. Baker, 191
Nelson v. Davis, 307
Newman v. Mountain Park Land Co., 457
Nilsson v. Latimer, 56
Nollan v. California Coastal Commission, 387,
    477–79, 510, 512
Nolte v. Smith, 327
Normile v. Miller, 192
Northern Corporation v. Chugach Electric
    Association, 190–91
Northwest Bank v. Frederick, 415

Oellerich v. First Fed. Sav. Loan Assn., 438

Papa Gino's of America, Inc. v. Broadmanor
    Associates, Ltd., 125–27
Papalexion v. Tower West Condominium, 92
Pennsylvania Coal Co. v. Mahon, 482
Piedmont and Western Investment Corp.
    v. Carnes-Miller Gear Co., Inc., 347
Plessy v. Ferguson, 458–59
Plummer (F.S.) Co., Inc. v. Town of Cape
    Elizabeth, 498–99
Prah v. Maretti, 51–53
Prescott v. Smits, 114
Prima Paint Corp. v. Flood & Conklin
    Manufacturing Co., 15–16

Reed v. King, 256–57
Reichman v. Drake, 133
Reynolds v. Lawrence, 457
River Birch Associates v. City of Raleigh, 213
Rivers v. Beadle, 171
Rodesney v. Hall, 87
Rucker v. Corbin, 235
Salahutdin v. Valley of California, Inc., 227–29
Scantlin v. Superior Homes, 253
Schaefers v. Apel, 343–44
Schottenstein v. Devoe, 457
Sebastian v. Floyd, 455

Securities and Exchange Commission v. Ralston Purina Co., 106
Shelly v. Kramer, 19
Smith v. Blackburn, 452–53
Soergel v. Preston, 168
South Burlington County N.A.A.C.P. v. Township of Mt. Laurel, 505
Sowin Associates v. Planning and Zoning Commission, 508
Spencer v. Lyman Falls Power Co., 179
Stanley v. Schwalby, 393
State Roads v. Kamins, 373
Stephens County v. Mid-Kansas Oil and Gas Co., 48
Stuart v. Hamilton, 117
Sturgill v. Industrial Painting Corp., 306
Swanner v. Anchorage Equal Rights Com'n, 472

Takacs v. Takacs, 247
Tanners Realty Corporation v. Ruggerio, 192
Taylor v. Caldwell, 193
Teal v. Walker, 412
Tempe (City of) v. Baseball Facilities, Inc., 70
Tennant v. Lawton, 225
Terry v. Born, 184
Thomas Haverty Co. v. Jones, 185
Thrasher v. City of Atlanta, 37–38
Tillotson v. Stephens, 33
Towski v. Griffiths, 222
Trautwein v. Leavey, 173

Ulander v. Allen, 454
Union National Bank v. Derderian, 418
United States of America v. Bostian, 320–21

United States v. A&N Cleaners and Launderers, Inc., 530–32
United States v. Bell Petroleum Services, Inc., 540
United States v. Causby, 371–72
United States v. City of Parma, 471
United States v. Graham Mortgage Corp., 287
Unlimited v. Kitsap County, 493

Vega v. First Federal Savings and Loan Association, 289
Volpe (S.) & Co. v. Board of Appeals of Wareham, 522
Vulcan Metals Co. v. Simmons Mfg. Co., 254

Wagner v. Regency Inn Corp., 129
Walrath, In re, 79–80
Watson v. McCabe, 213
West Federal Savings & Loan Association v. Interstate Investment, Inc., 295
Western Tie & Timber Co. v. Campbell, 422–23
White v. Rehn, 213
Wickland, In re, 528–29
Williams v. Matthews, 471
Williams v. Van Hersh, 265
Williston Co-op Credit Union v. Fossum, 213
Wilson (Roland A.) & Assoc. V. Forty-O-Four Grand Corp., 246
Winkelman v. Allen, 236
Woodward, In re, 335

Young v. Garwacki, 148–50

Zaremba v. Konopka, 307
Zuch v. Hussey, 463

SUBJECT INDEX OF CASES

1 Introduction to Law and Legal Systems

Humber v. Morton, 5
Lee v. Heftel Supreme Court of Hawaii, 14–16
McLain v. Real Estate Board of New Orleans, Inc., 8–10
Prima Paint Corp. v. Flood & Conklin Manufacturing Co., 15–16

2 Real and Personal Property

Bowman v. Holsopple, 33
Federal Land Bank of Omaha v. Swanson, 24–26
Haslem v. Lockwood, 21–23
Lee County Board of Review v. Property Tax Appeal Board, 31–33
Metropolitan Life Ins. Co. v. Reeves, 24
Shelly v. Kramer, 19
Tillotson v. Stephens, 33

3 Land, Water and Air Rights

Alameda County Water District v. Niles Sand and Gravel Co., Inc., 45–46
Boomer v. Atlantic Cement Co., 54
Canada v. City of Shawnee, 44
Coffin v. Left Hand Ditch Co., 56
Deetz v. Carter, 41
Hunter Land Co. v. Laungenour, 42
Johnson v. Marcel, 54–55
Katz v. Walkinshaw, 45
Kelley v. The Ohio Oil Co., 49
Kerley v. Wolfe, 40
Nilsson v. Latimer, 56
Prah v. Maretti, 51–53
Stephens County v. Mid-Kansas Oil and Gas Co., 48
Thrasher v. City of Atlanta, 37–38

4 Estates in Land

Bailey v. Eagle Mountain Telephone, Inc., 63–64
Crisp Lumber Co. v. Bridges, 65
Field v. Goat, 68
Grindal, In re, 67–68
Mitchell v. Jerrolds, 63–64
Tempe (City of) v. Baseball Facilities, Inc., 70

5 Co-Ownership

Cross v. Cross, 73
Meinhard v. Salmon, 82
Rodesney v. Hall, 87
Walrath, In re, 79–80

6 Condominiums, Cooperatives, Time-Shares, and Real Estate Investments

Avila S. Condominium Ass'n v. Kappa Corp., 110
Beachwood Villas Condominium v. Poor, 93–95
Drew Associates of N.J. v. Travisano, 95
Grey v. Coastal States Holding Co., 111
Hidden Harbour Estates, Inc. v. Basso, 94
Hocking v. Dubois, 102–5
Howey, In re, 103–5
Joyce v. Ritchie Tower Properties, 102
Levandusky v. One Fifth Avenue Apartment Corp., 98–100
Papalexion v. Tower West Condominium, 92
Securities and Exchange Commission v. Ralston Purina Co., 106

7 The Leasehold

Beals (J.M.) Enterprises, Inc. v. Industrial Hard Chrome, Ltd., 116–18

China Doll Restaurant, Inc. v. Schweiger, 128
Ewing v. Adams, 122
Gregory v. Walker, 129
Papa Gino's of America, Inc. v. Broadmanor Associates, Ltd., 125–27
Prescott v. Smits, 114
Stuart v. Hamilton, 117
Wagner v. Regency Inn Corp., 129

8　The Landlord-Tenant Relationship

Blackett v. Olanoff, 141–42
Derman Rug Co. Inc. v. Ruderman, 135
Gokey v. Bessette, 152
Gruman v. Investors Diversified Services, Inc., 145–46
Housh v. Swanson, 151
HTM Restaurants, Inc. v. Goldman, Sachs and Company, 132
Kline v. Burns, 134
Mudusar v. V.G. Murray and Co., 135
Reichman v. Drake, 133
Young v. Garwacki, 148–50

9　Easements and Other Nonpossessory Rights

Berk-Fink Realty Co. v. Ershowsky, 155
Cash v. Craver, 158–59
Devlin v. The Phoenix, Inc., 168
Durell v. Freese, 167
Fountainbleau Hotel Corp. v. Forty-Five Twenty-Five Florida, 162–63
McIlroy v. Hamilton, 167
Soergel v. Preston, 168

10　Basic Contract Law

Austin v. United States, 181–83
Balfour v. Balfour, 170
Bard v. Kent, 192
Burns v. Pugmire, 191
Dickinson v. Dodds, 172
Hamer v. Sidway, 180
Hendricks v. Behee, 172
Jacob & Youngs, Inc. v. Kent, 192
Lucy v. Zehmer, 175–76
Morrison v. Thoelke, 192

Nelson v. Baker, 191
Normile v. Miller, 192
Northern Corporation v. Chugach Electric Association, 190–91
Rivers v. Beadle, 171
Spencer v. Lyman Falls Power Co., 179
Tanners Realty Corporation v. Ruggerio, 192
Taylor v. Caldwell, 193
Terry v. Born, 184
Thomas Haverty Co. v. Jones, 185
Trautwein v. Leavey, 173

11　Real Estate Purchase Contract

Brown v. Burnside, 198
Clarence v. Larkin, 196–97
Cultum v. Heritage House Realtors, Inc., 199–201
805 Third Avenue Co. v. M.W. Realty Assoc., 213
Gibbens v. Hardin, 195
Laddon v. Rhett Realty, Inc., 213
River Birch Associates v. City of Raleigh, 213
Watson v. McCabe, 213
White v. Rehn, 213
Williston Co-op Credit Union v. Fossum, 213

12　Agency and Brokerage

Beri, Inc. v. Salishan Properties, Inc., 244
Cahion v. Ahmadi et al, 230–32
Dickerson Realtors, Inc. v. Frewert, 216
Easton v. Strassburger, 227
Elmore v. Blume, 248
Hilgendorf v. Hague, 238
Hoffman v. Connall, 224–26
Leon Realty, Inc. v. Hough, 249
McGinnis v. Frederick W. Berens Sales, Inc., 240
Management Clearing, Inc. v. Vance, 219
Moore v. (Pa.) State Real Estate Commission, 222
Rucker v. Corbin, 235
Salahutdin v. Valley of California, Inc., 227–29

Tennant v. Lawton, 225
Towski v. Griffiths, 222
Wilson (Roland A.) & Assoc. v. Forty-O-Four Grand Corp., 246
Winkelman v. Allen, 236

13   Fraud and Deceit

Bean v. Sears, Roebuck & Co., 262
Cashman v. Kirby, 262
Corea v. Maggiore, 262
Groening v. Opsota, 255
Hall v. Wright, 252
Kramer v. Chabot, 261–63
Lawson v. Citizens So. Nat'l Bank of South Carolina, 255
McWilliams v. Barnes, 258
Reed v. King, 256–57
Scantlin v. Superior Homes, 253
Vulcan Metals Co. v. Simmons Mfg. Co., 254
Williams v. Van Hersh, 265

14   Closing the Real Estate Transaction

Applebaum v. Zeigler, 289
Chertok v. Kassabian, 277
Duncan v. Rossuck, 270–71
Eisenberg v. Comfed Mortgage Co., Inc., 286–87
Kasten Construction Co. Inc. v. Maple Ridge Construction Co. Inc., 289
LaFond v. Frame, 289
Lone Star Development Corp. v. Miller, 274
United States v. Graham Mortgage Corp., 287
Vega v. First Federal Savings and Loan Association, 289

15   Escrow Closing

Allen v. Allen Title Co., 296
Asher v. Herman, 298–99
Been Corp. v. Shader, 305
Caulfield v. Improved Risk Mutuals, Inc., 307
Claussen v. First American Title Guaranty Co., 297
Collins v. Kares, 294

Fuqua v. Fuqua, 302
Ganser v. Zimmerman, 306
Gelber v. Cappeller, 307
Gilmer v. Anderson, 296
Hartman v. Wood, 303–4
Merry v. County Board of Education, 306
Morris v. Davis, 292
Nelson v. Davis, 307
Sturgill v. Industrial Painting Corp., 306
West Federal Savings & Loan Association v. Interstate Investment, Inc., 295
Zaremba v. Konopka, 307

16   Liens Against Title

Blankenship v. Myers, 322–23
Daniels v. Deseret Federal Savings and Loan, 314
Nolte v. Smith, 327

17   Deeds

Agrelius v. Mohesky, 340
Bury v. Young, 342
Curtiss v. Feriss, 339
Dennen v. Searle, 334
Franz v. Nelson, 337
Garraway v. Yonce, 336
Haines v. Mensen, 347
Harper v. Rogers, 347
Hewgley v. Jose Vivo, 344–46
Jones v. Jones, 340–41
Piedmont and Western Investment Corp. v. Carnes-Miller Gear Co., Inc., 347
Schaefers v. Apel, 343–44
Takacs v. Takacs, 247
United States of America v. Bostian, 320–21
Woodward, In re, 335

18   Land Descriptions

Adams v. Spillman, 366
Atlanta (City of) v. Atlanta Trailer City Trailer Park, 351
Bishop v. Johnson, 359–61
Brasker v. Tanner, 366
Burgess v. Pine Island Corp., 349, 351
Butkovich v. Summit County, 349–50
Cragin v. Powell, 362

Davis v. DeVore, 363
Huggans v. Weer, 364
Morrison v. Jones, 354

19   Involuntary Transfers

Berman v. Parker, 387
Cummings v. Boyles, 375
Hawaii Housing Authority v. Midkeff,
    370
Henderson v. Estate of Henderson, 380–
    81
Kittrel v. Scarborough, 387
Marengo Cave Co. v. Ross, 368
Martin's Estate, In re, 377
Nollan v. California Coastal Comm'n,
    387
State Roads v. Kamins, 373
United States v. Causby, 371–72

20   Recording and Assurance of Title

Alchemedes/Brookwood, Petition of,
    402–3
Commonwealth v. Ulrich, 404
Gagner v. Kittery Water District, 405
Graham v. Lyons, 398–99
Lawing v. Jaynes, 404
Loeb v. Conley, 391
McDaniel v. Lawyer's Title Guaranty
    Fund, 405
Stanley v. Schwalby, 393

21   Mortgages

Garrett Tire Center, Inc. v. Herbaugh
    Supreme Court of Arkansas, 422–23
Leben v. Nassau Savings & Loan
    Association, 410–11
Lundberg v. Northwestern National Bank,
    437
Northwest Bank v. Frederick, 415
Oellerich v. First Fed. Sav. Loan Assn.,
    438
Teal v. Walker, 412
Union National Bank v. Derderian, 418
Western Tie & Timber Co. v. Campbell,
    422–23

22   Land Installment Contracts

Bull v. Goldman, 442
Butcher v. Kagey Lumber Company, 456
Donaldson v. Sellmer, 451
Fincher v. Miles Homes, 447
Grombone v. Krekel, 457
Hickox v. Bell, 446
McKone v. Guertzgen, 443–44
Maxwell v. Moorman, 456–57
Newman v. Mountain Park Land Co., 457
Reynolds v. Lawrence, 457
Schottenstein v. Devoe, 457
Sebastian v. Floyd, 455
Smith v. Blackburn, 452–53
Ulander v. Allen, 454

23   Fair Housing Laws

Asbury v. Brougham, 460–63
Brown v. Board of Education, 459
Edmonds (City of) v. Oxford House, Inc.,
    466–69
Filippo v. Real Estate Commission of
    District of Columbia, 460
Gladstone Realtors v. Village of
    Bellwood, 464
Herron v. Blackwell, 470
Laufman v. Oakley Building and Loan
    Co., 464
McDonnell Douglas Corp. v. Green, 461
Plessy v. Ferguson, 458–59
Swanner v. Anchorage Equal Rights
    Com'n, 472
United States v. City of Parma, 471
Williams v. Matthews, 471
Zuch v. Hussey, 463

24   Land Use: The Constitution and the
Plan

Allingham v. City of Seattle, 493
Chinese Staff and Workers Ass'n v. City
    of New York, 493
DeMarco v. Pallazzo, 476
Dur-Bar Realty Co. v. City of Utica, 493
Eagle Enterprises, Inc. v. Gross, 474–75
Just v. Marinette County, 481, 484–86
LaBonta v. City of Waterville, 487–89

Loretto v. Teleprompter Manhattan
CATV Corp., 481
Lucas v. South Carolina Coastal Council,
480, 481–84, 486
Nollan v. California Coastal Commission,
477–79
Pennsylvania Coal Co. v. Mahon, 482
Unlimited v. Kitsap County, 493

25 Regulation of Land Development

Agins v. City of Tiburon, 505
Alexander v. Town of Hampstead, 500
Bayswater Realty and Capital Corp. v.
Planning Board of the Town of
Lewisboro, 523
Berman v. Parker, 521
Beverly Bank v. Illinois Department of
Transportation, 516–17
Dolan v. City of Tigard, 509??
Euclid (Village of) v. Ambler, 494, 509
Gilbertie v. Zoning Board of Appeals, 496
Governor's Island, In re, 501
Grey Rocks Land Trust v. Town of
Hebron, 500–502

Kit-Mar Builders, Inc., In re, 504
McCormick v. Lawrence, In re, 521
Matthews and Van Ness v. Bay Head
Improvement Assoc., 518
Nollan v. California Coastal Commission,
510, 512
Plummer (F.S.) Co., Inc. v. Town of Cape
Elizabeth, 498–99
South Burlington County N.A.A.C.P. v.
Township of Mt. Laurel, 505
Sowin Associates v. Planning and Zoning
Commission, 508
Volpe (S.) & Co. v. Board of Appeals of
Wareham, 522

26 Environmental Law

Cadillac Fairview/California Inc. v. Dow
Chemical Co., 527–29
Colorado v. Idarado Mining Co., 540
United States v. A&N Cleaners and
Launderers, Inc., 530–32
United States v. Bell Petroleum Services,
Inc., 540
Wickland, In re, 528–29

INDEX

A

Abandonment
  and termination of deeds, 137–38
  and termination of easement, 165
  wrongful, 137–38
Abrahamson, Justice, 51–53
Absolute ownership, 48. *See also* Ownership
Abstract of title, 271, 276, 399–400. *See also*
  Title
Acceleration clause, 415
Acceptance, 170, 174–77, 338–40
Accession, 374–75
Accord, 189
Accretion, 374
Acknowledgment, 211, 337, 396
Act, 180
Action
  in ejectment, 20
  for rent, damages, 138
Actual eviction, 132
Actual fraud, 251–63
  damages for, 260–63
  intentional, 252–53
  material misrepresentation as, 259–60
  misstatement of material fact as, 253–54
  puffing as, 254–58
  punitive damages for, 262
  reliance and, 258–59
  remedies for, 260
Actual notice, 390
Adams, Justice, 340–42
Adams v. Spillman, 366
Adjoiners, 352, 353
Adjustable-rate mortgage (ARM), 420–21
Administrative adjudication, 6
Administrator, 384
Adverse possession, 367–69
Adverse use, 161
Advertising, 460
  credit, 430

implied authority and, 219–20
Aesthetics, 520–22
Affidavit of title, 277, 278
Affirmative covenants, 343–344
Affirmative easement, 153
After acquired title, 442
Agency, 214. *See also* Broker(s)
  coupled with an interest,
    238–39
  creation of, 215
  disclosure and, 232–33, 429
  dual, 229, 230–32
  exclusive, 217
  real estate transactions and, 214–15
  termination of, 237–39
Aggrieved parties, 465, 470
Agins v. City of Tiburon, 505
Agrelius v. Mohesky, 340
Agricultural lands zoning, 507
Air quality, 536–37
Air rights, 50–53
*Alameda County Water District v. Niles Sand
  and Gravel Co., Inc.,* 45–46
Alchemedes/Brookwood, Petition of, 402–3
Alexander v. Town of Hampstead, 500
Alienation. *See* Involuntary alienation;
  Voluntary alienation
Allen v. Allen Title Co., 296
Allingham v. City of Seattle, 493
Allodium, 57
Alluvion, 374
Almon, Justice, 230–32
Alternative dispute resolution,
  14–16
American Arbitration Association, 14
American National Standards Institute, 465
Ancient lights doctrine, 162
Andersen, Justice, 224–26
Annual percentage rate (APR), 430. *See also*
  Interest rates

Anticipatory breach, 184–85
Appeal, 7
Appellate court, 6, 7, 13
Applebaum v. Zeigler, 289
Appraisal, 417
Appurtenance, 312
APR. *See* Adjustable-rate mortgage
Arbitration, 14–16
Architect, 245–47
Architectural committee, 475
Asbestos, 539
Asbury v. Brougham, 460–63
Asher v. Herman, 298–99
Assessments, 92–95, 413
   for condominiums, 92–95
   for cooperatives, 96–100
Assignee, 183–84
Assignment, 144–46
   of contract, 183–84
   of land installment contract, 445–46
   of lease, 277
   of mortgage, 435–36
Assignor, 183
Assumption, 432–33, 434
Assurance of title, 399–403
Atlanta (City of) v. Atlanta Trailer City Trailer Park, 351
Attachment, 28, 321–22
Attestation, 211, 338, 383
Attorney
   boundary disputes and, 364–65
   certificate of title and, 271, 276–77
   closing, 268–69
   deed preparation by, 274
   escrow and, 294–300
   -in-fact, 338
   opinion of title, 276, 400
   recording by, 393–94
Attorney-General litigation, 470
Austin v. United States, 181–83
Authority, 218–20
   broker and, 199–201, 219–20
   express, 219
   implied, 219–20
Avila S. Condominium Association v. Kappa Corp., 110
Avulsion, 374

B

Bailey v. Eagle Mountain Telephone, Inc., 63
Balfour v. Balfour, 170
Balloon payment, 183, 441
Bard v. Kent, 192
Bargain and sale deed, 332
Baseline, 355
Bayswater Realty and Capital Corp. v. Planning Board of the Town of Lewisboro, 523
Beachwood Villas Condominium v. Poor, 93–95
Beals (J.M.) Enterprises, Inc. v. Industrial Hard Chrome, Ltd., 116–18
Bean v. Sears, Roebuck & Co., 262
Been Corp. v. Shader, 305
Bell, Justice, 37–38
Beneficial use, 42
Beri, Inc. v. Salishan Properties, Inc., 244
Berk-Fink Realty Co. v. Ershowsky, 155
Berman v. Parker, 387, 521
Beverly Bank v. Illinois Department of Transportation, 516–17
Bilateral contract, 179
Bill of Rights, 19
Bishop v. Johnson, 359–61
Blackett v. Olanoff, 141–42
Blackmun, Judge, 182–83
Blackstone, William, 18, 473
Blankenship v. Myers, 322–23
Blanket mortgage, 96, 97, 436
Blease, Judge, 256–57
Blockbusting, 460, 463
Blue-sky laws, 86, 101
Board of adjustment, 499
Boomer v. Atlantic Cement Co., 54
Boundaries, 362
Boundary disputes, 364–65
Bowman v. Holsopple, 33
Brasker v. Tanner, 366
Breach of contract, 184–88, 207
   anticipatory, 184–85
   substantial performance and, 185–86
Brennan, Justice, 479, 482
Broker(s)
   authority of, 199–201, 219–20
   closing, 268
   commission of, 8–10, 234–37
   decedent property and, 375–84

defined, 215
duties to buyer, 223–33
duties to seller, 221–23
as independent contractor, 316, 239–40,
   247–49
licensing laws for, 240–41
listing and, 216–18
new home construction sales and, 242–49
unauthorized practice of law by, 241–42
Brown v. Board of Education, 459
Brown v. Burnside, 198
Brownfield initiative, 533
Buchanan, Justice, 175–76
Builder, 247–49. *See also* Contractor
Building
   code compliance, 136
   construction of, 242–49
   permit, 248
   structure, 312
Burger, Chief Justice, 8–10
Burgess v. Pine Island Corp., 349, 351
Burns v. Pugmire, 191
Bury v. Young, 342
Business judgment rule, 99
Butcher v. Kagey Lumber Company, 456
Butkovich v. Summit County, 349–50
Buyer
   actions at cloasing, 277, 279
   of land contract
      advantages, 448
      disadvantages, 449–50
      remedies, 455–56
   preparation for closing, 269–73
Buyer's broker, 227–29
Bylaws, 90

C

*Cadillac Fairview/California Inc. v. Dow
   Chemical Co.,* 527–29
Cahion v. Ahmadi et al, 230–32
Call, 353
Canada v. City of Shawnee, 44
Capacity, to enter into contract, 170, 178–79,
   334–35
Cardine, Justice, 443
Cardoza, Benjamin, 81–82
Care, 222–23

Cash v. Craver, 158–59
Caulfield v. Improved Risk Mutuals, Inc., 307
Caveat emptor, 4–5, 134, 390
Caveat venditor, 5
CERCLA. *See* Comprehensive Environmental
   Response, Compensation, and Liability
   Act
Certificate of title, 271, 276–77
Chain of title, 90, 272, 389, 394–96, 475
Chertok v. Kassabian, 277
China Doll Restaurant, Inc. v. Schweiger, 128
*Chinese Staff and Workers Ass'n v. City of New
   York,* 493
Circuit court, 11
Circuits, 13
Civil Rights Act, 10
   Title VIII. *See* Fair Housing Act
Claimants, mechanic's lien, 310–11
Clarence v. Larkin, 196–97
Claussen v. First American Title Guaranty Co.,
   297
Clayton Act, 3
Clean Air Act, 536–37
Clean Water Act, 10, 39, 514, 526
   industrial dischargers, 534–35
   municipal dischargers, 535–36
Closing, 267–69
Closing
   action at, 276–77
   amount needed at, 273
   attorney's role in, 268–69
   broker's role in, 268
   contract, 211–12
   escrow, 267–68, 291–94
   evidence of title and, 274
   good faith estimates for, 281
   kickbacks and, 286
   possession and, 133, 207–8, 295–96
   post procedures for, 288
   preparation for, 269–76
   prorations and, 209–10
   Real Estate Settlement Procedures Act and,
      3, 279–87
   uniform settlement statment and, 281–85
Cloud on the title, 396
Coastal zone, 518
Coastal Zone Management Act, 518, 537

Code of Ethics, 224
Coffin v. Left Hand Ditch Co., 56
Cognovit, 131–32
Collins v. Kares, 294
Colorado v. Idarado Mining Co., 540
Commentaries on the Law of England, 18
Commerce Clause, 8
Commercial properties, 464
Commingling, 297
Commission
    broker's, 8–10, 234–37
    open listings and, 217–18
    procuring cause and, 235
Committee, 475
Common elements, 89, 90–91
Common law, 4
    limitations, 53–55
    percolating water, 43–44
Commonwealth v. Ulrich, 404
Communication, 171
Community-based strategic planning, 490
Community property, 77–78, 80
Community Reinvestment Act, 431
Competent grantor, 334
Comprehensive Environmental Response,
    Compensation, and Liability Act, 524
    brownfield initiative and, 533
    cleanup implementation of, 525
    damages under, 533
    defenses under, 529–32
    liability under, 526–29
    state statutes and, 534
    Superfund and, 525
Comprehensive plan, 487–90, 495
Compulsory partition, 74
Concealment, 256–57
Concurrent ownership, 71
Condemnation, 373–74
    and eminent domain, 3, 166, 369–74, 477,
        480–84
Condition, 300, 342
Conditional sales contract, 28. *See also* Security
    agreement
Condominium, 88–89, 495
    assessments for, 92–95
    association for, 91–92
    bylaws of, 90
    common elements of, 90–91
    compared to cooperative, 96–100

    declaration for, 89–90
    formation of, 89
    individual unit deed, 90
    security and, 101–5
Consent, 313
Conservation and recreation districts, 514
Consideration, 170, 179–81, 342–43
Constitutional limitations, 480–87
Constitutions, 2–3, 8
Construction, and sales, 242–49
Construction mortgage, 30, 89, 423–24
Constructive eviction, 132, 140–42
Constructive fraud, 251–63
Constructive notice, 288, 391–92, 395
Consumer Credit Protection Act of 1968, 429
Contiguity, 375
Contingency clause, 206–7
Continuous use, 161–62
Contract, 169–70
    assignment of, 183–84
    breach of, 184–88, 207
    for deed. *See* Land installment contract
    destruction of subject matter and, 173
    disavow, 178
    easement, 157–58
    elements of, 170–83
    enforceable, 295
    executory, 264
    interpretation of, 183
    privity of, 146
    land installment. *See* Land installment con-
        tract
    mortgage. *See* Mortgage
    real estate purchase. *See* Real estate pur-
        chase contract
    remedies for breach of, 186–88
    substantial performance and, 185–86
    valid, 118–19
Contractor, 247–49
    lien, 309–17
Convenience, 293
Conveyance, 165–66
    words of, 333–34
Cooperative, 95
    compared to condominium, 96–100
    financing, 96
Co-ownership, 71
    community property and, 77–78, 80
    estate tax problems of, 76

investment alternatives for, 80–86
joint tenancy, 72–74
partition, 74–75
real estate syndicate, 82–86
separate property, 78–80
tenancy by the entirety, 75–76
tenancy in common, 73–74
tenancy in partnership, 76–77
trust, 80–82
Corporate grantor, 335
Corporation, 215
Correlative rights doctrine, 44–46, 50
Corrigan, Judge, 79–80
Counteroffer, 173
County court, 11
Court
of common pleas, 11
of general jurisdiction, 11
of limited jurisdiction, 11
of special jurisdiction, 11, 13
Court opinion, 5–6. *See also* Precedent
Court structure, 7
federal, 7–8, 10, 13–14
state court, 7–8, 10, 11–13
trial and appellate courts, 7
Courts of Appeal, U.S., 13, 14
Covenant, 343–44
against encumbrances, 329
to deliver possession, 133
of fitness of premises, 133–34
of further assurances, 331
of quiet enjoyment, 132–33, 331
of right to convey, 329
of seisin, 329
termination of, 344
of warranty, 331
Cragin v. Powell, 362
Credit advertising, 430
Crisp Lumber Co. v. Bridges, 65
Critical areas, 518–19
Crockett, Justice, 350
Crops, 27
Cross v. Cross, 73
Cultum v. Heritage House Realtors, Inc., 199–
201
Cummings v. Boyles, 375
Cunningham, Justice, 516–17

Curtesy, 384. *See also* Dower
Curtis v. Feriss, 339
Cushman v. Kirby, 262
CZMA. *See* Coastal Zone Management Act

D

Daly, Judge, 126–27
Damages, 20, 187, 455–56
action for, 138
actual fraud, 260–63
assessment and, 93
under CERCLA, 533
lessee, 142–43
liquidated, 187–88
measure of, 150
punitive, 262
Daniels v. Deseret Federal Savings and Loan,
314–16
Date, of contract, 204
Davidson, Judge, 314–16
Davies, Judge, 403
Davis v. DeVore, 363
Dealer's talk. *See* Puffing
Death
land contract seller's, 450
of offeror, 173–74
power of attorney and, 204–5
proof of, 386
relation back and, 302
transfer of property and, 375–84
Deceit, 251. *See also* Actual fraud
Decisional law, 4
Declaration, 89–90
Dedication, 160–61, 508
Deed, 328
bargain and sale, 332
competent grantor, 334
consideration and, 170,
179–81, 342
covenants and, 132–34,
329–31, 342–44
delivery of, 295–96, 339–42
easement creation by, 156–58
escrow and, 58, 183, 341–42, 374, 378
elements of, 333–42
fiduciary, 332
form of, 208

general warranty, 208, 329–31
homestead exemption and,
    66–69, 93
individual unit, 90
in lieu of foreclosure, 419–20
land descriptions. *See* land descriptions
land installment contracts and, 441
legal descriptions in, 205,
    337, 348–64
mortgage, 408–9
preparation of, 274
quitclaim, 208, 275, 332–33, 391
real versus personal property and, 19029
of reconveyance, 437
recording of, 123, 392–97, 450
relation back, 302–4, 319
release of, 164, 436, 437
restrictions, 343
special warranty, 331
specific performance, 11, 170, 186, 455
tendering, 276
of trust, 409, 437
valid, 294
warranty, 303–4, 329–31
Deetz v. Carter, 41
Default, 411–12, 414–16, 450
    acceleration clause and, 415
    cognivit and, 131–32
    deed in lieu of foreclosure, 419–20
    equity of redemption and, 415, 453
    in land installment contract, 440–41
    statutory right of redemption and, 411, 416
    waiver and, 264
Defeasible fee, 60–61
Defective title, 333
Defenses, CERCLA, 529–32
Deficiency judgment, 417
Del Sole, Judge, 398–99
Delivery, 295–96, 338–41
DeMarco v. Pallazzo, 476
De minimis settlement, 530
Demolition, 312
Dennen v. Searle, 334
Department of Veterans Affairs, loan
    guarantees, 428
Depository Institution Deregulation and
    Monetary Control Act, 429
Derman Rug Co. Inc. v. Ruderman, 135
Descent and distribution, 376–78

Description, of premises, 119–20
Destruction, of subject matter, 173
Developer, 243–45
    government regulation and, 86
    growth management systems and, 490
    new home construction and, 242–49
    planned unit developments and, 505–6
    restrictive covenants and, 90, 343, 474–76
    subdivision and, 244, 507–12
    zone changes and, 497–99
Development regulation, 494
Devlin v. The Phoenix, Inc., 168
Dickerson Realtors, Inc. v. Frewert, 216
Dickinson v. Dodds,, 172
Dicta, 4
DIDMC. *See* Depository Deregulation and
    Monetary Control Act
Diminution in value test, 481
Disability, relation back and, 302
Disavow, contract, 178
Discharge, 188–91, 436–37
Disclosure, 232
    laws, 227
    meaningful, 429
    sample, 233
Discrimination. *See* Fair Housing Act
Distribution
    order of, 377–78
    per capita, 377
    per stirpes, 377
District court, 11
District Court, U.S., 13
Diversity jurisdiction, 10
Divorce, 76
    dower and, 66, 302–2, 332–33, 384
    tenancy by the entirety and, 75–76
Dolan v. City of Tigard, 509–12
Dominant estate (tenement), 154, 158
Donaldson v. Sellmer, 451
Douglas, Justice, 371–72
Dower, 66, 302–3, 332–33, 384
Drew Associates of N.J. v. Travisano, 95
Drinking water, 537, 538
Drugged person, 179
Dual agency, 229, 230–32
Due-on-sale clause, 432
Duncan v. Rossuck, 270–71
Dur-Bar Realty Co. v. City of Utica, 493
Duress, 177

Durrell v. Freese, 167
Duty to speak, 256
DVA. *See* Department of Veterans Affairs

E

EA. *See* Environmental assessment
Eagle Enterprises, Inc. v. Gross, 474–75
Earnest money, 210
Easement, 153–54
Easement
   appurtenant, 154
   deed and, 156–58
   in gross, 155–56
   by implication, 158–60
   implied from necessity, 159–60
   implied from prior use, 158–59
   party wall and, 155
   from plats and maps, 160,
     362–64
   by prescription, 161–63
   profit a prendre, 156
   termination of, 164–67
Easton v. Strassburger, 227
ECOA. *See* Equal Credit Opportunity Act
Ecological imperatives, 512–13
   for coastal zone, 518
   for critical areas, 518–19
   for floodplains, 514–17
   for wetlands, 513–14
Ecology, 490–91
Ecosystems, 512
Edmonds (City of) v. Oxford House, Inc., 466–
   69
Effluent standards, 534–35. *See also* Clean
   Water Act
Egan, Justice, 117–18
805 Third Avenue Co. v. M.W. Realty Assoc.,
   213
EIS. *See* Environmental impact statement
Eisenberg v. Comfed Mortgage Co., Inc., 286–
   87
Ejectment, action in, 20
Elective share, 65, 383–84
Elmore v. Blume, 248
Eminent domain, 3, 166, 369–74, 477, 480–84.
   See also Taking

Employer-employee relationship, 239–40, 245–
   46
Encumbrance, 272, 329
   chain of title and, 90, 272, 389, 394–96
   easement as, 156–58
   removal of, 274
Endangered Species Act, 537
Entitlement, 428
Environmental assessment, 491–92, 530
Environmental impact statement, 245, 514
Environmental law, 524
Environmental protection, 489
Environmental Protection Agency, 6, 525, 533,
   535, 538
Equal Credit Opportunity Act, 430–31
Equal protection, 458–59
Equal protection clause, 19
Equitable title, 441
Equity of redemption, 415
   default and, 411, 416
   period, 453
Erosion, 374
Escheat, 58, 378
Escrow, 183, 342
   closing, 267–68, 291–94
   deed and. *See* Deed
   earnest money and, 210
   long-term, 305
   mortgage and, 306
   relation back doctrine and, 302–4, 319
   requirements of, 294–300
   title passage and, 301–4
   transaction, 292–93
Escrow agent (holder), 288, 291, 296–99, 342
Escrow agreement, 299–300, 301
Estate
   administration of, 384–86
   privity of, 146
   tax problems in, 76
   for years, 113
Estates in land. *See also* Leasehold estate
   allodium, 57
   curtesy and, 384
   dower and, 60, 302–3, 332–33, 384
   feudalism, 57
   freehold, 59–69
   future estates, 61–64

homestead exemptions and, 66–69, 93
life estates, 59, 64–66
property interests and, 58–59
tenure and, 58
Estoppel, 164–65
promissory, 180–81
Euclid (Village of) v. Ambler, 494, 509–10
Eviction, 132, 207
constructive, 140–42
by landlord, 137
wrongful, 140
Evidence of title, 274. *See also* Certificate of
title; Title insurance
Ewing v. Adams, 122
Exceptions, zoning, 502
Excessive Fines Clause, Eighth Amendment,
182–83
Exclusive agency, 217
Exclusive possession, 112
Exclusive right to sell, 217
Exclusive-right-to-sell listing, 238
Exculpatory clause, 150–51
Execution, 317, 337–38
Execution lien, 317
Executor, 384
Executory contract, 264
Express authority, 219
Express grant, 157
Express reservation, 157–58
Express vendor's lien, 322

F

Fair housing, 458
Fair Housing Act
amended, 459–64
statutory remedies, 469–70
Fair market value, 373
Family rights, 383
Farmland, 507
Federal court, 7–8, 10. *See also* Court structure
jurisdiction of, 8
system, 13–14
Federal estate taxes, 325
Federal gift taxes, 325
Federal Home Loan Bank Board, 6, 420
Federal Housing Act enforcement, 465–70
Federal Housing Administration insurance,
427–28

Federal Insecticide, Fungicide and Rodenticide
Act, 537
Federal Land Bank of Omaha v. Swanson,
24–26
Federal Land Policy and Management Act, 519
Federal question jurisdiction, 10
Federal Reserve Board, 430–31
Federal Rules of Civil Procedure, 300
Federal tax lien, 325
Fee simple, 59, 60
absolute, 59, 60
determinable (with a special limitation), 61,
63–64
subject to condition subsequent, 61
FHA mortgage, 427–28
Fiduciary deed, 332
Fiduciary duty, 81–82, 228–29, 409
Field v. Goat, 68
FIFRA. *See* Federal Insecticide, Fungicide and
Rodenticide Act
*Filippo v. Real Estate Commission of District of
Columbia,* 460
Finance charge, 429–30
Financial Institutions Reform, Recovery and
Enforcement Act, 431
Financing
real and personal property distinction, 21
statement, 28, 29
Fincher v. Miles Homes, 447
FIRREA. *See* Financial Institutions Reform,
Recovery and Enforcement Act
First delivery, 295
First in time, first in right principle, 319, 414
Fixture, 23–26, 139–40
crops as, 27
filing, 29–30
secured transaction and, 27–29
Flaw, in title, 396
Flood Insurance Program, 515
Floodplains, 515–17
Forbearance, 180
Foreclosure, 188, 451
assessment and, 93
deed in lieu of, 419–20
judicial, 416–17
and land contract, 454–55, 456
power-of-sale, 417–18
strict, 418–19
tax liens, 325

Forfeiture clause, 451–54
Fountainbleau Hotel Corp. v. Forty-Five Twenty-Five Florida, 162–63
Franz v. Nelson, 337
Fraud, 119, 177, 194–95, 251–63
    damages for, 260–63
    intentional, 252–53
    material misrepresentation as, 259–60
    misstatement of material fact as, 253–54
    puffing as, 254–58
    punitive damages for, 262
    reliance and, 258–59
    remedies for, 260
Freehold estate, 59–69
    defeasible fee, 60–61
    fee simple, 59, 60
    future estate, 61–64
    life estate, 64–66
Freund, Professor, 485
Fructus industriales, 27
Fructus naturales, 27
Fuqua v. Fuqua, 302
Future estate, 59, 61–64

G

Gagner v. Kittery Water District, 405
Gallagher, Justice, 145–46
Gap, 395
Garraway v. Yonce, 336
Garrett Tire Center, Inc. v. Herbaugh Supreme Court of Arkansas, 422–23
Geiger, Justice, 31–33
Gelber v. Cappeller, 307
General common elements, 91
General lien, 187, 309. *See also* Liens
General power of attorney, 338
General warranty deed, 208, 329–31
Gibbens v. Hardin, 195
Gibson, Justice, 261–63
Gilbertie v. Zoning Board of Appeals, 496
Gilmer v. Anderson, 296
Ginsburg, Justice, 467–69
Gladstone Realtors v. Village of Bellwood, 464
Gokey v. Bessette, 152
Golden, Justice, 444
Good faith, 207, 221–22
    estimate, 281

purchase, 393
Goodman, Judge James A., 67–68
Goods, 27
Goodwin, Chief Judge, 103–5
Government
    fair housing laws and, 459–70
    syndicate regulation by, 86
Governor's Island, In re, 501
Grace period, 451
Graduated lease, 121, 127
Graham v. Lyons, 398–99
Grantee, 328
    chain of title and, 90, 272, 389, 394–96, 475
    closing and, 267–68, 291–92
    deed delivery and, 295–96, 338–41
    escrow and, 288, 291, 296–99, 341–42
    identifiable, 336
    privity of estate, 146
    quitclaim deed and, 208, 275, 332–33, 391
    recording and, 397–99
    relation back and, 302–4, 319
    title and, 301–4
Granting clause, 61, 333
Grantor, 328, 334
    chain of title and, 90, 272, 389, 394–96, 475
    closing and, 267–68, 291–92
    competency of, 173–74, 178, 334
    corporate, 335
    deed delivery and, 295–96, 338–41
    escrow and, 288, 291, 296–99, 341–42
    identifiable, 336
    legal description and, 205, 336–37, 348–51
    minors and, 178–79, 334
    privity of estate, 146
    quitclaim deed and, 208, 275, 332–33, 391
    recording and, 397–99
    relation back and, 302–4, 319
    title and, 301–4
Gregory v. Walker, 129
Grey, Judge, 452–53
Grey Rocks Land Trust v. Town of Hebron, 500–502
Grey v. Coastal States Holding Co., 111
Grindal, In re, 67–68
Groening v. Opsota, 255
Grombone v. Krekel, 457

Gross lease, 123–24
Ground lease, 124–25
Group home accommodations, 466
Growth management systems, 489–90
Gruman v. Investors Diversified Services, Inc.,
    145–46

H

Habitability, 147
Habitability warranty, implied, 134–35
Haines v. Mensen, 347
Hall v. Wright, 252
Hallows, Chief Justice, 484–86
Hamer v. Sidway, 180
Handicapped, 465–69
Harmful or noxious use, 483
Harper v. Rogers, 347
Hartman v. Wood, 303–4
Haslem v. Lockwood, 21–23
Hawaii Housing Authority v. Midkeff, 370
Hazard insurance, 209, 272–73
Hazardous Ranking System, 525
Hazardous Substances Response Fund. *See*
    Superfund
Hazardous waste, 526–29
Heirs, 378
Hendricks v. Behee, 172
Herron v. Blackwell, 470
Hewgley v. Jose Vivo, 344–46
Hickory v. Bell, 446
Hidden Harbour Estates, Inc. v. Basso, 94
High-water mark, 39
Hilgendorf v. Hague, 238
Hill, Judge, 159
Historical preservation, 519–20
Hocking v. Dubois, 102–5
Hoffman v. Connall, 224–26
Holding, 4
Holdover tenancy, 113, 115–18
Holmes, Justice, 482
Home construction, 242–49
Home Mortgage Disclosure Act, 431
Home warranty plan, 210
Homestead exemption laws, 66–69
Homestead laws, 93
Hopkins, Judge, 411
Housh v. Swanson, 151
Housing and Urban Development, Department
    of, 6

litigation, 470
    settlement costs booklet, 280
    substantially equivalent program of, 469
Howey, In re, 103–5
HTM Restaurants, Inc. v. Goldman, Sachs and
    Company, 132
HUD. *See* Housing and Urban Development,
    Department of
Huggans v. Weer, 364
Humber v. Morton, 5
Hunter Land Co. v. Laungenour, 42
Hurley, Judge, 93–95

I

Impact fees, 508–12
Implied agency rule, 176
Implied authority, 219–20
Implied notice, 391
Implied warranty of habitability, 134–35
Improvements, 36, 312, 317
In terrorem clauses, 450
Inchoate dower, 66
Inchoate lien, 313–14
Incidents of legal ownership, 449
Indemnification clause, 445
Independent contractor, 216, 239–40, 247–49
Index leases, 127
Individual unit deed, 90
Indoor pollution
    from asbestos, 539
    in drinking water, 538
    from lead-based paints, 539
    from radon, 538
Industrial discharges, 534–35
Industrial properties, 464
Injunction, 11
Innocent landowner defense, 529–32
Innocent misrepresentation, 177
Insanity
    contract and, 178
    of offeror, 173–74
    relation back doctrine and, 302
Inspection, 445
Inspection clause, 210
Insurance, 413
Insure, duty to, 139
Inter vivos trust, 81
Interlocutory judgment, 319
Internal Revenue Code, 10

condominium association and, 97
installment sales and, 449
Interpleading, 300
Intestate succession, 375–78, 379
descent and distribution, 375–84
escheat, 58
Intrastate offerings, 106
Involuntary alienation
accretion and, 374
adverse possession and, 367–69
eminent domain and, 369–74
Involuntary lien. *See* Judgment lien

J

Jacob & Youngs, Inc. v. Kent, 192
Johnson, Justice, 501–2
Johnson v. Marcel, 54–55
Joint interests, estate tax problems, 76
Joint tenancy, 72–73
Joint venture, 82, 84–85
Jones v. Jones, 340–42
Joyce v. Ritchie Tower Properties, 102
Judge-made law, 4, 6
Judgment creditor, 317
Judgment lien, 309, 317–22
Judicial foreclosure, 416–17
Junior lien, 419–20
Jurisdiction, 11, 13
Just compensation, 372–73
Just v. Marinette County, 481, 484–86
Justice court, 11

K

*Kasten Construction Co. Inc. v. Maple Ridge
Construction Co. Inc.,* 289
Katz v. Walkinshaw, 45
Kaye, Judge, 98–100
Kelley v. The Ohio Oil Co., 49
Kerley v. Wolfe, 40
Kickbacks, 286
Kit-Mar Builders, Inc., In re, 504
Kittrell v. Scarborough, 387
Kline, Justice, 228–29
Kline v. Burns, 134
Koch, Jr., Judge, 345–46
Kramer v. Chabot, 261–63

L

LaBonta v. City of Waterville, 487–89
Laches, 369
Laddon v. Rhett Realty, Inc., 213
LaFond v. Frame, 289
Land, 35–36. *See also* Estates in land; Real
property
accretion, 374
air rights, 50–53
mineral rights, 46–47
as natural resource, 36–38
oil and gas rights, 48–50
surface water on, 39–42
Land descriptions
boundary disputes and, 364–65
calls and, 353
legal, 205, 336–37, 348–51
metes and bounds, 352–54
rectangular survey system, 354–62
surveys, 273
Land installment contract, 183, 311, 323–24
after acquired title, 442
assignment of, 445–46
buyer
advantages, 448
disadvantages, 450
remedies, 455–56
indemnification, 445
mortgage, 446–48
price, 444
seller
advantages, 449
disadvantages, 450–51
remedies, 451–55
terms, 442–45
title problems, 441
waste, removal, inspection, 445
Landlord-tenant relationship, 130–32
Land ownership. *See* Estates in land
Land use. *See also* Zoning
aesthetics and, 520–22
Clean Air Act and, 536–37
Clean Water Act and, 10, 39, 514, 526,
534–36
growth management systems, 490
large-lot zoning, 503–5
planning, 487–92

private restrictions on, 474–76
public restrictions on, 476–92
restrictive covenants for, 90, 343, 474–76
subdivision regulations for, 507–12
Large-lot zoning, 503–5
Latent defects, 147
Laufman v. Oakley Building and Loan Co., 464
Law
  operation of, 189–91, 238
  precedent and, 2, 3–5
  sources of, 2–6
Lawful purpose, 181–83
Lawing v. Jayme, 404
*Lawson v. Citizens So. Nat'l Bank of South
    Carolina,* 255
Lead-based paints, 539
Lease. *See also* Landlord-tenant relationship;
    Leasehold estate
  assignment of, 277
  cognovit, 131–32
  elements of, 118–21
  graduated, 121, 127
  gross, 123–24
  ground, 124–25
  legal use of premises and, 121–22
  mortgage and, 414
  percentage, 125–27
  recording of, 123
  renewal of, 127–28
  right of possession and, 123
  survival clause for, 137–38
  types of, 123–27
Leased premises, sale of, 147–51
Leasehold estate, 112
  holdover tenant, 115–18
  periodic tenancy, 113–14
  tenancy at sufferance, 115
  tenancy at will, 114–15
  term tenancy, 112–13
Leben v. Nassau Savings & Loan Association,
    410–11
*Lee County Board of Review v. Property Tax
    Appeal Board,* 31–33
Lee v. Heftel Supreme Court of Hawaii, 14–16
Legal description, 205, 337, 348–64
Legal life estate, 65–66
Legal notice, 390–92
Legal purpose, 170
Leon Realty, Inc. v. Hough, 249

Lessee. *See also* Landlord-tenant relationship;
    Lease; Leasehold estate
  obligations of, 138–40
  remedies of, 140–43
Lessor, 119. *See also* Landlord-tenant
    relationship; Lease; Leasehold estate
  obligations of, 132–36
  remedies of, 137–38
  security for, 130–32
Letters of administration, 385
Letters testamentary, 385
*Levandusky v. One Fifth Avenue Apartment
    Corp.,* 98–100
Levy of execution, 317
Liability
  under CERCLA, 526–29
  leased premises and, 147–50
Liacos, Judge, 148–50
License, 166–67, 240–41
Lien, 308–9
  assessment as, 92–93
  claim or affidavit, 314–16
  cognivit and, 131–32
  express vendor's, 322
  general, 187, 309
  judgment, 309, 317–22
  junior, 419–20
  mechanic's, 309–17, 414, 424, 445
  mortgage as. *See* Mortgage
  partition and, 74–75
  relation back doctrine and, 302–4, 319
  upon sale, 93
  tax, 324–25, 413
  Torrens certificate and, 401–3
  types of, 309–26
  vendor's, 322–24
Lien theory, 408, 411, 432
Lien waiver, 313, 317
Life estate, 59, 64–66
  curtesy and, 384
  dower and, 66, 302–3, 332–33
Life tenant, 64
Limited common elements, 91
Limited liability, 83
Limited partnership, 83–84
Limited warranty deed, 331. *See also* Special
    warranty deed
Liquidated damages, 187–88
Liquidity, 427

Lis pendens, 320–21
Listing, 216–18
  exclusive, 217, 238
  multiple service, 218, 229
  open, 217–18
Littoral land, 39
Lively, Judge, 321
Livery of seisin, 58
Living trust, 81
Loan approval, 410
Loeb v. Conley, 391
Lone Star Development Corp. v. Miller, 274–75
Loretto v. Teleprompter Manhattan CATV Corp., 481
Low-water mark, 39
Loyalty, 221–22
Lucas v. South Carolina Coastal Council, 480, 481–84, 486
Lucy v. Zehmer, 175–76
Lundberg v. Northwestern National Bank, 437

M

McCormick v. Lawrence, In re, 521
McDaniel v. Lawyer's Title Guaranty Fund, 405
McDonnell Douglas Corp. v. Green, 461
McGinnis v. Frederick W. Berens Sales, Inc., 240
McIlroy v. Hamilton, 167
McKone v. Guertzgen, 443–44
McKusick, Chief Justice, 488–89
McLain v. Real Estate Board of New Orleans, Inc., 8–10
McWilliams v. Barnes, 258
Magistrate court, 11
Mail box rule, 176
Management Clearing, Inc. v. Vance, 219
Manifest intent, 174–76
Maps, 160
Marengo Cave Co. v. Ross, 368
Marketable title, 208, 271–72, 395
Martin's Estate, In re, 377
Master mortgage, 408–9
Master plan. *See* Comprehensive plan
Material fact, 223–24
  misrepresentation of, 259–60
  misstatement of, 253–54

Material supplier's lien, 309–17. *See also* Mechanic's lien
Matthews and Van Ness v. Bay Head Improvement Assoc., 518
Maxwell v. Moorman, 457
Mechanic's lien, 309–17, 414, 424, 445
Mediation, 14–16
Meeting of the minds, 174–76, 235
Meinhard v. Salmon, 82
Membership denial, 460
Memorandum, 195–98
Mental capacity, 335
Merger, 164, 436
Merry v. County Board of Education, 306
Metes and bounds, 352–54
Metropolitan Life Ins. Co. v. Reeves, 24
Miller, Justice, 304
Mineral deed, 47
Mineral lease, 47
Mineral reservation, 47
Mineral rights, 46–47
  acquisition of, 47
  options, 47
Minors
  contract and, 178–79
  deeds and, 334
Misrepresentation, 223, 251. *See also* Actual fraud
Mistake, 177
Mitchell v. Jerrolds, 63–64
Mobile Home Privilege Tax Act, 31–33
Mobile homes, 30–33
Moore v. State Real Estate Commission, 222
Morrison v. Jones, 354
Mortgage, 406–8
  abstract of title and, 271, 276, 399–400
  agency coupled with an interest and, 238–39
  annual percentage rate, 430. *See also* Interest rates
  application, 409–11
  assignment of, 144–46, 183–84, 435–36
  blanket, 96, 97, 436
  closing and, 277, 279
  commitment, 409–11
  credit advertising, 430
  deed and, 408–9
  discharge of, 188–91, 436–37

Equal Credit Opportunity Act and, 430–31
escrow, 306
expressed vendor's lien and, 322
finance charge for, 429–30
foreclosure of, 416–20
forms and content of, 408–9
homestead exemption and, 66–69, 93
insurance, 427
for land installment contract, 446–48
leases and, 414
loan regulations, 428–31
mechanic's lien and, 414
new home construction and, 242–49
note and, 407
partition and, 74–75
party rights, obligations under, 411–13
possession and, 207–8, 411–12
recording of, 393–94
release of, 409
sale of real estate and, 432–35
types of, 420–26
usury and, 428–29
Mortgagee, 407
Mortgagor, 407
Mudusar v. V.G. Murray and Co., 135
Multifamily dwellings, 465
Multiple listing service, 218, 229
Municipal court, 11
Municipal dischargers, 535–36
Municipal planning. *See* Planning

N

Nakayama, Justice, 15–16
National ambient air quality standards, 536–37
National Association of REALTORS®, 224, 227, 241
National Conference of Commissioners on Uniform State Law, 5
National Contingency Plan, 525, 528
National Environmental Policy Act, 491–92, 537
National Flood Insurance Act, 537
National Housing Act, 427
National Priority List, 525
Natural flow doctrine, 40–41
NCP. *See* National Contingency Plan
Negative easement, 153–54
Negligent misrepresentation, 264

Nelson v. Baker, 191
Nelson v. Davis, 307
Net lease, 124
New home construction, sales, 242–49
New York Rule, 317
Nilsson v. Latimer, 56
No-lien provision, 317
Nollan v. California Coastal Commission, 387, 477–79, 512
Nolte v. Smith, 327
Nonconforming use, 496–97, 501–2
Nonfreehold estate, 59–60
Nonownership theory, 48, 49
Nonpossessory rights, 153
Normile v. Miller, 192
Northern Corporation v. Chugach Electric Association, 191
Northwest Bank v. Frederick, 415
Notary public, 396
Notary seal, 276
Note, 407
Notice, 313
    actual, 390
    constructive, 288, 391–92, 395
    of judicial foreclosure, 416–17
    of lis pendens, 320–31
    of nonresponsibility, 311
    race, 392, 413
    statutes, 392–93
Novation, 188, 433, 434
NPL. *See* National Priority List
Nuisance, 51–53

O

Objective test, 174–75
Oellerich v. First Fed. Sav. Loan Assn., 438
Offer, 170–74, 409–10. *See also* Real estate purchase contract
Offeree, 171
Offeror, 171–72
    death of, 173
    insanity of, 173–74
Oil and gas ownership, 48–50
Open listing, 217–18
Open-end mortgage, 424–25
Operation of law, 238
Ownership, 18, 473
    forms of, 108
    interest and mechanic's lien, 311

oil and gas, 48–50
Ownership theory, 48

P

Package mortgage, 425
Papa Gino's of America, Inc. v. Broadmanor Associates, Ltd., 125–27
Papalexion v. Tower West Condominium, 92
Pari delicto, 181
Park, Judge, 22–23
Parker, Judge, 461–63
Parol evidence, 198–99, 205
Part performance, 198
Parties, 119
    against whom enforcement is sought, 198
    agency termination and, 237–38
    aggrieved, 465
    change of mind and, 294
    names of, 204–5
    operation of, 188–89
Partition, 74–75
Partnerships, 82, 83–84, 215, 335
Party wall, 155
Pearson, Justice, 200–201
Peculiar circumstances, 505
Pennsylvania Coal Co. v. Mahon, 482
Pennsylvania Rule, 316
Per capita distribution, 377
Percentage lease, 125–27
Percolating water, 43–46
Perfection, 28–29, 313–17
Performance bond, 245
Performance standards zoning, 506–7
Periodic tenancy, 113–14
Permissive waste, 139
Personal action, 20
Personal injury, 148–50
Personal property, 20–23, 27–29, 324–25
Personal representative, 384–85
Per stirpes distribution, 377
Phantom fees, 286
Piedmont and Western Investment Corp. v. Carnes-Miller Gear Co., 347
Pittman, John, 381
Planned unit development, 505–6
Planning, 487–92
Plat, 160, 362–64

Pledge, 28
Plessy v. Ferguson, 458–59
Plummer (F.S.) Co., Inc. v. Town of Cape Elizabeth, 498–99
Police power, 3, 477–79, 514
Possession, 207–8, 411–12
    of collateral, 28
    covenant to deliver to, 133
    right of, 123
    surrender of, 295–96
Possibility of reverter, 62
Potentially responsible party, 526, 529, 533
Power of attorney, 204–5, 338–39
Power of termination, 61, 62
Power-of-sale foreclosure, 417–18
Practice of law, unauthorized, 241–42
Prah v. Maretti, 51–53
Precedent, 2, 3–5
Premise
    description of, 119–20
    fitness of, 133–34
    inspection of, 273
    legal use of, 121–22
Prescott v. Smits, 114
Prescription, 161–63, 165
Price, 206
Price, Judge, 196–97
Prima Paint Corp. v. Flood & Conklin Manufacturing Co., 15–16
Principal meridian, 355
Principal-agent relationship, 246
Prior appropriation 40, 41–42, 43, 46
Priorities, 323–25, 413
Private nuisance doctrine, 51–53
Private offering, 106
Private restrictions, 474–76
Privity of contract, 146
Privity of estate, 146, 474–75
Probate court, 13, 384, 385–86
Procuring cause, 235
Profit a prendre, 156
Profits, 412
Promises, 254
Promissory estoppel, 180–81
Promissory note, 407
Property, 18–19
    description, 205

inspection, 210
real, 19–20
real and personal legal problems, 20–23
Property tax
duty to pay, 136
homestead exemption, 69
Proprietary lease, 95
Proration, 208–10
Prospectus, 107–8
Publicly owned sewage treatment works, 536
Public restrictions, 476–92
constitutional limitations of, 480–87
police power and, 477–79
Public use, 370–72
Puffing, 254–58
Punitive damages, 262
Pur autre vie, 64
Purchase money mortgage,
421–23
Purchase price, 453
Purtle, Judge, 422–23

Q

Quiet enjoyment, covenant of, 132–33
Quiet title action, 396, 401
Quitclaim deed, 208, 275, 332–34, 391
Quitrent, 58

R

Race to record, 392, 413
Radon, 538
Ranges, 357
Ratify, contract, 178
Rattigan, Judge, 45–46
Ready, willing and able buyer, 235–36
Real actions, 20
Real estate, 20, 36
Real Estate Investment Trust Act, 109
Real estate investment trusts, 82, 85, 109
Real estate purchase contract, 194–201. *See also* Contract
attestation and acknowledgment of, 211
closing of, 211–12
contingency clause in, 206–7
date of, 204
deed form for, 208
earnest money and, 210
evidence of title for, 208

home warranty plan for, 210
inspection clause in, 210
parties to, 204–5
possession and, 207–8
price and, 206
property description for, 205
proration of, 208–10
provisions of, 201–12
sample, 202–3
signing of, 211
unconscionable clauses in, 212
Real estate sales associate, 239–40
Real Estate Settlement Procedures Act, 3,
279–80
abusive practices and, 286–87
good-faith estimate and, 281
settlement costs booklet and, 280
uniform settlement statement and, 281–85
Real estate syndicates, 82–86
Real property, 20–23, 36
fixtures, 23–26
rights, 19–20
Reality of assent, 177
Reasonable accommodation,
465–66
Reasonable modification, 465
Reasonable relationship test, 511
Reasonable rent, 121
Reasonable time, 173
Reasonable use doctrine, 41, 44, 51–53
Recording
abstract of title, 271, 276,
399–400
acknowledgment, 211, 337, 396
chain of title, 90, 272, 389, 394–96, 475
of Deed. *See* Deed
of easement, 156–58
evidence of title. *See* Evidence of title
of land contracts, 450
of lease, 123
mistakes in, 396–99
process of, 393–94
statutes, 389–92
title insurance, 208, 271, 274
Torrens certificate, 401–3
types of, 392–93
Rectangular survey system,
354–62
Redemption

equity of, 415
    statutory right of, 416
Redlining, 460, 463–64
Reed v. King, 256–57
Reformation, 142–43
Registration statement, 107
Regulation Z, 429–30
Rehnquist, Chief Justice, 509–12
Reichman v. Drake, 133
REIT. *See* Real estate investment trust
Rejection, 172–73
Relation back doctrine, 302–4, 319
Release, 164, 436, 437
    of mortgage, 409
Reliance, 258–59
Reliction, 374
Remainder interest, 62
Rent, 121, 412
    action for, 138
    income from closing and, 209
    paid in advance, 130
    sales and, 464
    third person guaranty of, 131
    withholding, 143
Repair, duty to, 135–36, 138
Representation, 460
Rescission, 142–43, 177, 186, 253, 455
Resource Conservation and Recovery Act, 526,
    537
Restrictive covenants, 90, 343, 474–76
Revenue Act of 1939, 31–33
Reverse annuity mortgage, 426
Reverse mortgage, 426
Reversionary interest, 62, 118
Revised Uniform Limited Partnership Act, 83,
    84
Revocation, 172, 177
Reynolds v. Lawrence, 457
Right of election. *See* Elective share
Right of first refusal, 90
Right of possession, 112, 123
Right of reentry, 62
Right of survivorship, 72
Riparian land, 39
Riparian rights doctrine, 40–41, 46
River Birch Associates v. City of Raleigh, 213
Rivers v. Beadle, 171

Rodesney v. Hall, 87
Rollover mortgage, 426
Rucker v. Corbin, 235
Rudman, Justice, 498–99
Rule of capture, 49–50

S

Safe Drinking Water Act, 537, 538
Safe harbor, 107
Salahutdin v. Valley of California, Inc., 227–29
Sale
    and leaseback arrangement, 127
    of leased premises, 147–51
    price, 417
Sales associate, 239–40
    licensing, 241
Satisfaction of mortgage, 189, 409, 437
Scalia, Justice, 478–79, 482–84
Scantlin v. Superior Homes, 253
Schottenstein v. Devoe, 457
Scienter, 252–53
S corporation, 82, 83
Sebastian v. Floyd, 455
Second delivery, 302
Section, 357–62
Secured debts, 406–7
Secured transaction, 27–29
Securities, 86
    condominiums as, 101–2
    exemptions for, 105–7
    prospectus for, 107–8
    real estate as, 101
    registration of, 107
Securities Act of 1933, 86, 101, 103
Securities and Exchange Commission
    condominiums and, 101–2, 104–5
    exemptions, 105–7
*Securities and Exchange Commission v. Ralston
    Purina Co.,* 106
Securities Exchange Act of 1934, 86
Security agreement, 28, 29
Security deposit, 131, 208
    protection of, 412
Seisin, delivery of, 58
Seller
    land contract
        advantages of, 449

disadvantages of, 450–51
    remedies for, 451–55
    preparation for closing, 273–76
Separate property, 78–80
Servient estate (tenement), 154, 158
Settlement
    action at, 276–77
    amount needed at, 273
    attorney's role in, 268–69
    broker's role in, 268
    contract, 211–12
    escrow, 267–68, 291–94
    evidence of title and, 274
    good faith estimates for, 281
    kickbacks and, 286
    possession and, 133, 207–8, 295–96
    post procedures for, 288
    preparation for, 269–76
    prorations and, 209–10
    Real Estate Settlement Procedures Act and,
        3, 279–87
    uniform settlement statment and, 281–85
Settlement clerk, 269
Settlement costs booklet, 280
Settlement services, 287
Settlement statement, 281–85
Severance of joint tenancy, 73
Sewage treatment, 536
Shapiro, Justice, 298–99
Shelly v. Kramer, 19
Sherman Act, 3, 8–10
Signed will, 383
Site grading, 245
Skill, 222–23
Smith v. Blackburn, 452–53
Soergel v. Preston, 168
Solar energy, 162–63
Sound mind, 380–81. *See also* Capacity
South Burlington County N.A.A.C.P. v.
    Township of Mt. Laurel, 505
Sowin Associates v. Planning and Zoning
    Commission, 508
Spacing statutes, 50
Special partnership, 83
Special warranty deed, 331
Special-use permit, 502–3
Specific liens, 309
Specific performance, 11, 170, 186, 455
Spencer v. Lyman Falls Power Co., 179

Stanley v. Schwalby, 393
Stare decisis obligation, 3
State action, 92
State court, 7–8, 10
    intermediate appellate, 13
    supreme court, 13
    system, 11–13
    trial court, 11
Statement of lease term, 120–21
State Roads v. Kamins, 373
State statutes, 50
State supreme court, 13
State trial court, 11
Statute of Frauds, 119, 194–95, 198, 295. *See*
    also Actual fraud; Fraud
    names of parties, 204–5
    price and, 206
Statute of limitations, 204, 436
Statutes of descent and distribution, 376–78
Statute of Wills, 380
Statutory law
    codification of cases, 6
    court interpretation of, 5–6
    role of statutes in, 5
Statutory permit systems, 42–43
Statutory right of redemption, 411, 416
Steagall, Judge, 270–71
Steering, 460, 464
Stephens County v. Mid-Kansas Oil and Gas
    Co., 48
Stephenson, Justice, 55
Strict foreclosure, 418–19
Sturgill v. Industrial Painting Corp., 306
Subdivision, 244
    exactions, impact fees, 508–12
    regulations, 507–12
Subject to mortgage clause, 432, 433, 435
Sublease, 143–44
Substantial performance, 185–86
Subterranean water, 43–46
Superfund, 525
Superfund Amendments and Reauthorization
    Act, 524, 529–32
Superior court, 11
Supreme court
    state, 13
    U.S., 13–14
Surface water, 39–40
    rights theories, 40–42

Surrogate's court, 384
Survey, 273
Survival clauses, 137–38
Swanner v. Anchorage Equal Rights Commission, 472
Sweet, Judge, 531–32

T

Takacs v. Takacs, 347
Taking, 477, 480–87, 514
Tanners Realty Corporation v. Ruggerio, 192
Tax break, land contract, 449
Tax lien, 324–25, 413
Taylor v. Caldwell, 193
Teal v. Walker, 412
Tempe (City of) v. Baseball Facilities, Inc., 70
Tenancy at sufferance, 60, 115
Tenancy at will, 60, 114–15
Tenancy by the entirety, 75–76
Tenancy for years, 59
Tenancy from period to period, 59
Tenancy in common, 73–74, 82
Tenancy in partnership, 76–77
Tennant v. Lawton, 225
Tenure, 58–59
Term tenancy, 112–13
Termite inspection certificate, 275
Terry v. Born, 184
Testamentary trust, 81
Testate, 375
    succession, 378, 380–84
Testator, 375, 380
Third-party
    defense, 529–32
    guaranty of rent, 131
    related transactions, 143–51
Thomas Haverty Co. v. Jones, 185
Thrasher v. City of Atlanta, 37–38
Tillotson v. Stephens, 33
Time is of the essence, 211–12, 267
Time-shares, 100
Title
    assurance of, 399–403
    evidence of, 208
    land contracts and, 450
    passage, 301–4
    subject to prior rights, 390

transfer and death, 375–84
Title insurance, 208, 271, 274, 400–401, 441
Title theory, 408, 432
Torrens certificate, 401–3
Touch and concern the land, 474–75
Township, 355–57
Towski v. Griffiths, 222
Tract index, 394
Trade fixtures, 26
Transaction brokers, 232
Transactions
    secured, 27–29
    third-party related, 143–51
Transferable development rights, 520
Trespass, 54–55
Trial court, 7
Troutwein v. Leavey, 173
Trust, 80–82, 93
    in lieu of life estate, 65
Trustee, 81–82, 409
Truth-in-Lending Act, 3, 429

U

Ulander v. Allen, 454
Unconscionable contract, 212
Underground streams, 46
Undivided interest, 73
Undue influence, 177
Unencumbered title, 395–96
Uniform Commercial Code, 190, 212
    fixtures and, 27, 28, 29–30
    mobile homes and, 30
Uniform Limited Partnership Act, 83–84
Uniform Partnership Act, 77, 82, 335
Uniform Probate Code, elective share, 65
Uniform Residential Landlord and Tenant Act, 113, 131, 134
Uniform Settlement Statement, 281–85
Uniform Simultaneous Death Act, 386
Unilateral, 180
Uninterrupted use, 162
Union National Bank v. Derderian, 418
United States of America v. Bostian, 320–21
United States v. A&N Cleaners and Launderers, Inc., 530–32
United States v. Bell Petroleum Services, Inc., 540

United States v. Causby, 371–72
United States v. City of Parma, 471
United States v. Graham Mortgage Corp., 287
U.S. government survey system. *See*
     Rectangular survey system
Unity of interest, 73
Unity of possession, 73
Unity of time, 73
Unity of title, 73
Unlimited v. Kitsap County, 493
Urbigkit, Chief Justice, 443–44
Use variance, 499
Usury, 428–29
Utilities, 244–45, 275

V

Variable rate mortgage, 420, 421, 426
Variance, 499–502
*Vega v. First Federal Savings and Loan
     Association,* 289
Vendor's lien, 322–24
Vested interest, 62
Veterans Affairs loan guarantees, 428
Voidable contracts, 178–79
*Volpe (S.) & Co. v. Board of Appeals of
     Wareham,* 522
Voluntary alienation, 367. *See also* Deed
     conveyance
Voluntary partition, 74
Voluntary waste, 139
Vulcan Metals Co. v. Simmons Mfg. Co., 254

W

Wagner v. Regency Inn Corp., 129
Waiver, 264
Wallace, Judge, 527–29
Walrath, In re, 79–80
Warranty deed, 303–4, 329–31
Waste, 59, 64, 138–39, 207, 208
Water, 38–39
     quality standards, 535
     rights theories, 40–42

statutory permit systems,
     42–43
subterranean, 43–46
surface, 39–40
Watson v. McCabe, 213
*West Federal Savings & Loan Association v.
     Interstate Investment, Inc.,* 295
Wetlands, 491, 513–14
White, Justice, 24–26
White v. Rehm, 213
Wigginton, Judge, 360–61
Wilkins, Justice, 141–42
Will, 380–84
Williams, Judge, 63–64
Williams v. Matthews, 471
Williams v. Van Hersh, 265
Williston Co-op Credit Union v. Fossum, 213
*Wilson (Roland A.) & Assoc. v. Forty-O-Four
     Grand Corp.,* 246
Winkelman v. Allen, 236
Witnessed will, 383
Woodward, In re, 335
Wraparound mortgage, 183
Writ of certiorari, 14
Written will, 383
Wrongful abandonment, 137–38
Wrongful eviction, 140

Y–Z

Young, Judge, 286–87
Young v. Garwacki, 148–50
Zaremba v. Konopka, 307
Zone change, 497–99
Zoning, 244, 494–96
     of agricultural lands, 507
     board of appeals, 499
     exceptions in, 502
     large-lot, 503–5
     performance standards for, 506–7
     of planned unit development, 505–6
     subdivision regulations and, 507–12
Zuch v. Hussey, 463

Connecticut and American Impressionism

A COOPERATIVE EXHIBITION PROJECT CONCURRENTLY IN THREE LOCATIONS

The William Benton Museum of Art	Hurlbutt Gallery	Lyme Historical Society
The University of Connecticut, Storrs	Greenwich Library, Greenwich	Old Lyme
The Artists and The Landscape	**The Cos Cob Clapboard School**	**The Art Colony at Old Lyme**
March 17 - May 30, 1980	March 20 - May 31, 1980	March 21 - June 21, 1980

Lenders to the Exhibitions

Albright-Knox Art Gallery
Buffalo, New York

Addison Gallery of American Art,
Phillips Academy
Andover, Massachusetts

American Academy and Institute of
Arts and Letters

The Art Institute of Chicago

Associated American Artists
New York City

Babcock Galleries
New York City

Mr. and Mrs. John Bartol

Mrs. Anne Bonnet

Boston Public Library

The Brett Mitchell Collection, Inc.
Cleveland, Ohio

The Brooklyn Museum

Fenton L. B. Brown

Jeffrey R. Brown, Fine Arts
North Amherst, Massachusetts

The Bruce Museum
Greenwich, Connecticut

Mrs. Charles Burlingham

Mr. George Butler

N. Robert Cestone

Chapellier Galleries, Inc.
New York City

The Chrysler Museum
Norfolk, Virginia

The Cleveland Museum of Art

Thomas Colville Fine Paintings
New Haven, Connecticut

Stephen H. Condict III

James L. Coran

Corcoran Gallery of Art
Washington, D.C.

Mr. and Mrs. John H. Crawford III

The Currier Gallery of Art
Manchester, New Hampshire

Delaware Art Museum
Wilmington

Detroit Athletic Club
Detroit, Michigan

Diplomatic Reception Rooms,
Department of State
Washington, D.C.

Mr. and Mrs. Errett Dunlap

Nan Greacen Faure

The First Congregational Church
Old Lyme, Connecticut

Nancy Foote

Mr. and Mrs. William Marshall Fuller

John H. Garzoli

Gallery New World
Darien, Connecticut

Geist Collection
Chicago

Georgia Museum of Art,
The University of Georgia
Athens

Graham Gallery
New York City

Grand Central Art Galleries, Inc.
New York City

Grand Rapids Art Museum
Michigan

Robert P. Gunn

Mr. and Mrs. Alan W. Hall

Hammer Galleries
New York City

Hirshhorn Museum and Sculpture
Garden, Smithsonian Institution

Historical Society of the
Town of Greenwich
Connecticut

Helen S. Hyman

D. Clinton Hynes Fine Art
Chicago

Dr. and Mrs. A. Everette James, Jr.

Kennedy Galleries, Inc.
New York City

Lamb Collection
Chicago

Mr. and Mrs. James T. Larkin

Mr. and Mrs. Curtis A. Ley

Library of Congress

W. David Lindholm Collection

R. H. Love Galleries, Inc.
Chicago

Diane Tanenbaum Lux

Kenneth Lux Gallery
New York City

Lyman Allyn Museum
New London, Connecticut

Lyme Public Library
Lyme, Connecticut

Dr. Clark S. Marlor

Mead Art Museum,
Amherst College
Amherst, Massachusetts

Meredith Long & Company
Houston

The Metropolitan Museum of Art

Morris Collection
Chicago

Museum of Art,
Rhode Island School of Design
Providence

Museum of Fine Arts
Boston

Museum of Fine Arts
Springfield, Massachusetts

Walter A. Nelson-Rees

New Britain Museum
of American Art
New Britain, Connecticut

The New York Public Library

Old Lyme-Phoebe
Griffin Noyes Library
Old Lyme, Connecticut

The Parrish Art Museum
Southampton, New York

Elizabeth DuMond Perry

Phelan Collection
Chevy Chase, Maryland

The Phillips Collection
Washington, D.C.

Mr. and Mrs. Meyer P. Potamkin

Private Collections

San Diego Museum of Art

Mr. and Mrs. Milton Turner Schaeffer

Contents

S.K.T. Galleries
New York City

Smith College Museum of Art
Northampton, Massachusetts

Dr. Herbert J. Smokler

Ira Spanierman, Inc.
New York City

Stone Ledge Studio Art Galleries
Noank, Connecticut

Mrs. Ben Strouse

University Art Collections,
Arizona State University
Tempe

Clark Voorhees, Jr.

Robert C. Vose, Jr.

Wadsworth Atheneum
Hartford, Connecticut

The Washington County Museum of
Fine Arts
Hagerstown, Maryland

Webster Fine Art, Inc.
Chevy Chase, Maryland

Mrs. Robert P. Weimann, Jr.

Henry C. White II

Nelson Holbrook White

The Whitney Museum of American Art

Worcester Art Museum
Massachusetts

Preface 7

    Paul F. Rovetti, *Director*
    The William Benton Museum of Art

Chronology 8

Catalogue of the Exhibitions 10

The Artists and The Landscape 30

    Reflections on Impressionism, Its Genesis and
    American Phase 30

      Harold Spencer

    Catalogue 56

    Selections from the Exhibition 63

The Cos Cob Clapboard School 82

    The Cos Cob Clapboard School 82

      Susan G. Larkin

    Catalogue 100

    Selections from the Exhibition 105

The Art Colony at Old Lyme 114

    The Art Colony at Old Lyme 114

      Jeffrey W. Andersen

    Catalogue 138

    Selections from the Exhibition 142

Biographies of the Artists 150

Acknowledgments 180

Index of Artists 182

Photography Credits 183

Wilson Irvine painting in an Old Lyme Field

Preface

Connecticut, the beautiful,
God made of you a paradise

MILDRED HOBBS

In 1923 the author, antiquarian, and photographer, Wallace Nutting, commented in his book *Connecticut Beautiful* that many New Englanders believed Connecticut did little more than fill the space between Massachusetts and New York. He observed further, however, that Connecticut had peculiar beauties of her own that must be recognized. It is true those beauties did exist in 1923. The rolling hills of Connecticut were part of that beauty. Today, Connecticut's rolling hills are crisscrossed by interstate highways from south to north, from west to east, and at many places in between. Today her coastline has nuclear power plants raising their stacks against the prospect of Long Island Sound and many of her rivers are not filled with fish the way they used to be, but her beauty still exists. Yes, New Haven's elms are gone and many scenes of beauty that Wallace Nutting knew are gone, too. But there is a continuance of beauty that stretches on into today. There are still places little changed from the time they were painted by the artists shown in this exhibition.

Connecticut and American Impressionism is a celebration of the beauty of this state. We hope that it will recapture for a moment a view of the land which many have forgotten. As a native of Connecticut, I hope that this exhibition will rekindle an interest in what used to be and what ought to remain. The exhibition brings to light the work of many fine landscape painters whose work is not often seen. It is a cooperative venture which brings together for the first time works which indicate the place that Connecticut has in the history of American art, a place more important than many have realized.

Connecticut and American Impressionism as an exhibition is the culmination of the work of many people. As a cooperative effort three institutions have pooled their resources to bring to public view a broad range of art which is impressive in scope. The exhibition and this catalogue could have not been possible were it not for the goodwill and support of the trustees of the institutions involved and the financial aid of federal and state agencies. We are grateful to the trustees and staffs of the Hurlbutt Gallery of The Greenwich Library, of The Lyme Historical Society, and of the Benton Museum for all of their work. We are especially grateful to The National Endowment for the Humanities for its support, particularly of this catalogue, to the Connecticut Humanities Council for its aid in funding educational activities, and to the Connecticut Commission on the Arts for its contributions toward several aspects of this exhibition. We are grateful, too, to a number of private donors for their financial aid. An exhibition of this kind is extremely complex in its organization and would not in fact have been possible for any of our institutions to produce singly with our limited resources. The cooperative aspect of this exhibition has been its greatest strength and has allowed us to create something we believe will be of value in the future.

Acknowledgments for the aid of many people and institutions appear later in this catalogue but one person's work must be noted here. The work of Hildegard Cummings in the production of this exhibition and in many areas which supplement the exhibition has been far and beyond what was required. Her belief in this project and devotion to its completion deserve high praise. She has been a pivotal point around which everything swirled in great confusion. Her many hours devoted to this project have cost her hours of sleep and at times have been frustrating. It is accurate to say that this project could not have occurred were it not for Mrs. Cummings' work. To her and her alone go our thanks for the completion of this exhibition.

PAUL F. ROVETTI, *Director*
The William Benton Museum of Art
The University of Connecticut

Chronology

1882	J. Alden Weir first visits Windham		
1883	Weir in Branchville	Mark Twain, *Life on the Mississippi*	Brooklyn Bridge completed
1886	John Twachtman in Greenwich 1st French Impressionist exh. in U.S.		Haymarket Riot Geronimo surrenders
1888	Twachtman in Branchville	Edward Bellamy, *Looking Backward*	Blizzard of '88
1889	Twachtman settles in Greenwich	Andrew Carnegie, *The Gospel of Wealth*	
1890	Charles Davis in Mystic	Jacob Riis, *How the Other Half Lives*	Sherman Anti-Trust Act Battle of Wounded Knee
1892	Theodore Robinson in Cos Cob Twachtman-Weir Cos Cob classes Ernest Lawson in Cos Cob	"After the Ball is Over"	"The Four Hundred" U.S. Immigration Service opens on Ellis Island
1893	Twachtman-Weir Cos Cob classes Robinson and Lawson in Cos Cob	Stephen Crane, *Maggie, Girl of the Streets* Turner, *Significance of the American Frontier*	World's Columbian Expo, Chicago Financial panic and depression
1894	Hassam, Robinson, Lawson in Cos Cob		Edison introduces motion pictures
1896	Robinson dies Elmer MacRae in Cos Cob	Edward MacDowell, *Woodland Sketches*	Klondike Gold Rush
1897	Founding of The Ten	Sousa, "Stars and Stripes Forever"	
1898	First exhibition of The Ten Walter Griffin in Hartford Twachtman in Norwich	Westcott, *David Harum*	Spanish-American War U.S. annexes Hawaii
1899	Henry Ward Ranger in Old Lyme Twachtman at Holley House	Scott Joplin, "Maple Leaf Rag" Veblen, *Theory of the Leisure Class*	China Open-Door Policy
1900	Art colony begins at Old Lyme MacRae marries Constant Holley Charles Ebert to Greenwich	Dreiser, *Sister Carrie* Baum, *Wonderful Wizard of Oz*	
1901	Art colony grows at Old Lyme Twachtman at Holley House Griffin in Farmington	Frank Norris, *The Octopus* Booker T. Washington, *Up From Slavery*	Pan-American Expo, Buffalo McKinley assassinated
1902	Frank DuMond to Old Lyme Childe Hassam in Cos Cob 1st Old Lyme exhibition Twachtman dies	"In the Good Ol' Summertime" Owen Wister, *The Virginian*	
1903	Hassam in Old Lyme 20 artists in Old Lyme exhibition	Jack London, *Call of the Wild* Film: *Great Train Robbery*	Wright Brothers airplane flight Ranger develops coop apartments in New York City
1904	Hassam in Old Lyme Griffin in Old Lyme Ranger goes to Noank Emil Carlsen visits Weir in Windham Lyme Summer School of Art	Lincoln Steffens, *The Shame of the Cities* Ida Tarbel, *History of Standard Oil* "Meet Me in St. Louis, Louis" Henry James, *The Golden Bowl*	Universal Expo, St. Louis
1905	Hassam in Old Lyme, paints church Metcalf in Old Lyme Woodrow Wilsons in Old Lyme Carlsen in Falls Village	Edith Wharton, *House of Mirth*	Lewis and Clark Expo, Portland, Ore.
1906	Hassam, Metcalf, Simmons in Old Lyme Lyme Summer School to Woodstock, New York	Upton Sinclair, *The Jungle*	San Francisco earthquake and fire Pure Food and Drug Act

1907	Old Lyme church burns Lyme artists vote exhibition receipts toward church reconstruction	First Ziegfeld Follies *The Education of Henry Adams* Picasso, *Les Demoiselles d'Avignon*	Financial panic and depression
1908	Weir, *Building a Dam, Shetucket* Hassam, *Bridge at Old Lyme*	"Shine On Harvest Moon"	Penn Station under construction 1st group show of The Eight
1909	D. Putnam Brinley to Silvermine Hassam, *New Haven Green*	"By the Light of the Silvery Moon" Frank Lloyd Wright, Robie House	Admiral Dewey reaches North Pole Henry Ford mass produces cars
1910	Old Lyme colony still growing Old Lyme church reconstructed Ochtman summer school at Mianus Connecticut Academy of Fine Arts established		Boy Scouts of America founded Census shows 70% of Connecticut's population foreign-born or children of foreign-born
1912	Old Lyme exhibition week long now Greenwich Society of Artists formed	Zane Grey, *Riders of the Purple Sage*	*Titanic* sinks
1913	Mystic Art Association founded Nearly 40 artists in Old Lyme	Willa Cather, *O Pioneers*	Armory Show, New York City "New" Grand Central Station Federal Reserve System
1914	Lyme Art Association founded Hassam in Cos Cob Willa Cather in Cos Cob	W. C. Handy, "St. Louis Blues" Robert Frost, *North of Boston* Charles Ives, *Three Places in New England*	War begins in Europe Clayton Anti-Trust Act Opening of Panama Canal
1915	Hassam etches at Cos Cob Edward Rook, Gold Medal for *Laurel* at Panama-Pacific Expo Weir, *The Fishing Party,* c. 1915	Edgar Lee Masters, *Spoon River Anthology* Film: *Birth of a Nation*	*Lusitania* sunk by German submarine Revival of Ku Klux Klan Panama-Pacific International Expo, San Francisco (star attraction: Ford's assembly line for Model-T)
1917	Hassam in Cos Cob "Golden days" over for both Old Lyme and Cos Cob	T. S. Eliot, "Love Song of J. Alfred Prufrock"	U.S. enters World War I Russian Revolution
1918			Influenza kills half million in U.S.; 20 million worldwide WWI Armistice
1919	J. Alden Weir dies Ebert moves to Old Lyme	Sherwood Anderson, *Winesburg, Ohio*	Prohibition
1920	Guy C. Wiggins to Old Lyme Carlsen, *Connecticut Hillside,* c. 1920	Youmans, "Tea for Two" Sinclair Lewis, *Main Street*	Women's Suffrage Wall St. Bombing
1921	Lyme Art Gallery 1st self-financed art colony gallery	Eugene O'Neill, *Anna Christie* Booth Tarkington, *Alice Adams*	1st Sacco-Vanzetti Trial
1923	Grand Central Art Galleries established	Elmer Rice, *The Adding Machine*	Teapot Dome Scandal
1925	Metcalf dies	Dreiser, *An American Tragedy*	Scopes Trial
1927	Davis, *Countryside in Autumn,* c. 1927	Al Jolson, *The Jazz Singer*	Sacco and Vanzetti executed Lindburgh flight
1929		Hemingway, *Farewell to Arms* Faulkner, *Sound and the Fury*	Stock market collapses Museum of Modern Art founded
1933	Lawson in Hartford	O'Neill, *Ah, Wilderness!* Erskine Caldwell, *God's Little Acre*	Bank holiday Prohibition ended
1935	Hassam dies Griffin dies	Steinbeck, *Tortilla Flat* Odets, *Waiting for Lefty*	Will Rogers killed in plane crash Huey Long assassinated

Catalogue of the Exhibitions

Connecticut and American Impressionism is three art exhibitions concurrently in three locations, all celebrating the beauty of Connecticut, its vital role in the development of American Impressionist art at the turn of the century, and the importance of its early art colonies. This is the catalogue for all three exhibitions. The color reproductions grouped here are of works of art from all three exhibitions. Immediately following the essay related to each exhibition are the catalogue listings and additional plates for that exhibition. Catalogue numbers are consecutive throughout: *The Artists and The Landscape,* 1-95; *The Cos Cob Clapboard School,* 96-159; and *The Art Colony at Old Lyme,* 160-213. The Connecticut site of the work follows its date in the entry. Dimensions are given in inches and centimeters, height preceding width.

17   Charles H. Davis, *Countryside in Autumn,* c. 1927

4   Emil Carlsen, *Cherry Blossoms*

27   Will Howe Foote, *White's Point from Millstone Point,* c. 1920

29　Edmund Greacen, *Winter Landscape, Lieutenant River, Old Lyme*, 1917

33   Walter Griffin, *White Birch Trees, Old Lyme, Conn.*, c. 1907

35   Childe Hassam, *Bridge at Old Lyme,* 1908

44   Ernest Lawson, *The Duck Pond – Norfolk, Connecticut,* early 1930s

55   Theodore Robinson, *Sloop Cove,* c. 1894

66   John H. Twachtman, *November Haze,* c. 1897-98

62   John H. Twachtman, *From the Holley House,* c. 1890–1900

18

76   J. Alden Weir, *Building a Dam, Shetucket*, 1908

112   Childe Hassam, *The Holley Farm*, 1902

115   Childe Hassam, *The Mill Pond, Cos Cob, Connecticut,* 1902

167   William Chadwick, *On the Porch*, c. 1908

173   Will Howe Foote, *A Summer's Night,* c. 1906

178   Walter Griffin,
       Portrait of Mrs. Brown and Her Son, 1907

180   Childe Hassam, *Apple Trees in Bloom, Old Lyme,* 1904

195   Willard L. Metcalf, *Flying Shadows,* 1905

197   Willard L. Metcalf, *November*, 1905

202   Edward F. Rook, *Laurel,* c. 1905–10

Reflections on Impressionism, Its Genesis and American Phase

HAROLD SPENCER

In the spring of 1878 the young American painter Julian Alden Weir received a letter from Mary Cassatt,[1] the first major American Impressionist. She sent her regrets at being unable to send works to an exhibition to which she had been invited by Weir. She promised to do better the following year, and did, sending two works to the exhibition of the Society of American Artists in 1879. She also wrote:

I always have a hope that at some future time I shall see New York the artist's ground, I think you will create an American school.

It is doubtful that she was proposing a school of American Impressionists. She had only begun to paint in an Impressionist vein herself. Although histories of American art usually claim her, Mary Cassatt's career is essentially French. But within a decade other Americans, studying in France, would begin to absorb ideas from the French Impressionist movement and carry them back to the United States to establish the beginnings of an American phase of Impressionism on home ground. During the 1890s this new spirit gathered adherents and by the end of the decade was a conspicuous current in American painting.

In December of 1897 a group of painters resigned from the Society of American Artists, formed their own loose association, and mounted their first exhibition the following spring. They called themselves The Ten American Painters or simply The Ten. Although The Ten was not formed as an Impressionist group, its members were, coincidentally and in varying degrees, partisans of the movement. The membership of The Ten included Julian Alden Weir, John H. Twachtman, Childe Hassam, Willard Metcalf, Thomas Dewing, Edmund C. Tarbell, Frank W. Benson, Robert Reid, Joseph De Camp, and E. E. Simmons. When Twachtman died in 1902, his place was taken by William Merritt Chase. The Ten continued to exhibit together until 1918.

One of the reasons for forming this new association was dissatisfaction with the unwieldy nature of the annual exhibitions of the Society of American Artists. The Ten desired to hold smaller shows — some thirty or forty works — that would have coherence resulting from the mutually sympathetic tastes of the membership. One result of this affiliation was to make American Impressionism more conspicuous as a movement by being identified with a group.

Impressionism was christened in the spring of 1874 when several independent artists in France also chose to exhibit together. Prior to the exhibition, one of them, Edgar Degas, had viewed it as a "realist" Salon. But Claude Monet, in giving one of his paintings in the show the title *Impression: Sunrise,* unwittingly provided the tenacious but inadequate label for the group. An unfriendly critic, grasping at Monet's title, dubbed the artists "Impressionists" in a scathing review of the exhibition.[2] The term proved remarkably durable, even though the artists themselves later officially rejected it.[3] What these painters shared, apart from their identity as a group outside the circle of regular Salon artists, was their realist position as recorders of the immediate, transitory, commonplace world around them. Stylistically they were not a tightly cohesive enclave, but by 1874 some of them had drawn fairly close together in style and technique, while retaining distinct individual characteristics.

In view of the diversity of personal styles among the Impressionists, two major considerations are essential at the outset to an understanding of what is implied by the term "Impressionism." The first of these, already identified, is simply its original designation of a group of artists who exhibited together in Paris, with shifting participation even among its major figures, from 1874 until 1886. The second consideration is the concept of Impressionism as style and technique. This is really an abstraction based on certain features of Impressionist methods of transcribing visual appearances from nature into the work of art. While this concept is by no means identical with any single Impressionist's approach, it comes closest to that of Claude Monet, long viewed as the "typical" example.

In the light of French Impressionism, the American phase has normally been assessed as something different, and possibly too much emphasis in these assessments has been accorded its derivative features. Until very recently[4] the differences have usually redounded to the disadvantage of the Americans, because the criteria employed have been so exclusively drawn from the French prototype; but the nature of American Impressionism is such that it should also be examined in the context of entrenched American attitudes towards the art of painting already in the grain of American artists.

These reflections on Impressionism and its American phase aim at developing a general context for some works of art created by a group of American Impressionists who found the Connecticut scene a congenial environment. This special case — American Impressionists in Connecticut — is particularly inviting as a focus, for it brings together an interacting community of artists and a landscape they shared as a common subject.

To understand both the meanings and forms of American Impressionism, one must look back beyond the 1890s to the inheritances from earlier phases of American painting and look back to Europe as well for the sources of French Impressionism there. Some of these European sources nourished art in the United States even before American artists discovered Impressionism in France, and our understanding of the pattern of these interlacements as they pertain directly to American Impressionism is still far from complete. The scope of these comments is by necessity too limited to do much more than suggest the general nature and implications of this transatlantic web of relationships, but it is hoped that what follows will provide a minimal background for viewing American Impressionism in Connecticut with a fair perspective.

THE EUROPEAN SOURCES

Whenever western painting has represented the natural appearance of the material world, light has generally been a persistent factor in the process. It is obviously through illumination — natural or artificial — that objects in space become visible and space itself a visible dimension. During the centuries since the Renaissance, painting had been largely a matter of developing on a plane surface an equivalent image for the sensation of looking through space — as through a window — at objects disposed throughout a spatial dimension. By means of perspective in its variant forms, atmospheric and linear, the artist was enabled to establish an illusion of real space. Through the devices of tones, colors, and simulated textures, the artist recreated effects of light, atmosphere, and the substantial surfaces of things. The latter was generally achieved through matching to a convincing degree the local color of the object being depicted and through identifying its volumetric character by employing tonal gradients, from lighted to shadowed portions, that would at least approximate the material appearance of things in the "real" world. That this matching process has involved the invention of conventional devices like perspective systems and other signs — and an acceptance of these conventions by the viewer for the matching to make sense — should remind us how much pictorial "reality" is an abstraction of sorts and, therefore, provisional and subject to amendment.[5] The *techniques* of Impressionism constituted such an amendment to the currently accepted devices of picture making, and the initial protest against Impressionism, when it first came to the public's attention, was largely a reaction to an unfamiliar amendment.

The technical procedures of French Impressionist painting itself varied from artist to artist and went through a series of phases, each of which held lessons for American painters, although the American response, when it finally came, was conditioned by previous American practices and therefore somewhat fragmentary.

For the French Impressionists, subject matter was the intimate, visible world around them, but this alone would not differentiate Impressionism from earlier forms of realism. The distinction that sets apart Impressionism as a point of view is its particular approach to perceiving the substance of reality, its plein-air practice of painting out-of-doors (not always adhered to), and especially its technique of transcription.

During the early phases of Impressionism in the 1860s, the substance of its image of reality was rendered in terms of rather flat color shapes that were intended to match the tonal and chromatic variations of the retinal image, but somewhat simplified or summarized (fig. 1). The *solidity* of objects and the *qualities* of their surfaces were implied through these patches of matching, generalized color — a kind of pictorial "shorthand" notation that began to treat the problem of image-making almost as much in terms of the painted surface as in terms of a traditional illusionary depiction of solids and voids. The fact that the recognizability of things depicted in terms of these color shapes was not circumvented or appreciably distorted and that the images of these things retained their normal relationships and proportions, one to the other and to the spaces around them, kept Impres-

prominent place in the background of "impressionistic" painting generally.[12]

An early step in the direction of the out-of-doors confrontation with nature, so fundamental to Impressionist practices, took place in England during the latter part of the eighteenth century when the vogue of the Picturesque[13] pervaded the enjoyment of the out-of-doors, literary descriptions of nature, landscape design, and landscape drawing, painting, and printmaking. The very pervasiveness of the Picturesque points to its identity as an aesthetic attitude. The fact that its visual focus lay on the English countryside did not, however, make it a particularizing point of view. It was too generalized a formal principle for that. Its popularization owed much to the literary and amateur pictorial efforts of a country clergyman, the Reverend William Gilpin, whose numerous books on the subject[14] disseminated the Picturesque spirit to a widening audience. The essential visual ingredients in the Picturesque were roughness, irregularity, and sudden variations — the kinds of visual experiences that could be encountered in the unplanned countryside. Excursions of the gentry into the country in search of the Picturesque experience became a popular pleasure-hunt. However generalizing the Picturesque principles were, the eventual effect was to draw attention to the native landscape. The Picturesque thus cleared the way for the particularizations of such painters as John Constable,[15] who recorded not only the native appearance of his Suffolk countryside but the transitory changes wrought by the passing weather, for to him no two days were quite alike.

Constable's intensive studies of skies are evidence of his careful observation of natural phenomena, and the fact that there seems to be no transference of these studies directly to the skies of other works underscores the degree to which each painting carried with it its own peculiar "weather" and affirms the artist's ongoing preoccupation with the shifting particularities of time and place in his landscapes. This lent to his works that quality of immediacy which, paired with his technique of breaking down color areas into juxtaposed variations of hue, could still hold some lessons worthy of the notice of Claude Monet and Camille Pissarro in 1870-71, when they were in London.[16]

Three paintings by Constable were exhibited in the Paris Salon of 1824, where they drew praise from French artists, including Eugène Delacroix. What struck the French artists with peculiar force was not merely the strong sense of reality these works conveyed but the way in which that reality was rendered. Delacroix noted Constable's practice of mingling several variations of a color, juxtaposed to one another but not mixed,[17] an effect approximating, somewhat remotely, the broken color tints later utilized by the Impressionists.

Although the art of Joseph Mallord William Turner would appear, on the basis of his career-long involvement with light, the chromatic orchestrations of his later oil paintings, and his watercolors, to have been a likely precursor of Impressionism, his actual role remains problematic. Pissarro does admit that Turner had some influence,[18] but his remarks leave some question regarding the extent to which the Englishman was viewed as a kindred spirit. The fact that Turner was obviously an intense observer of atmospheric phenomena was apparently compromised for the Impressionists by the sublimity of his imaginative treatment of atmospheric effects. The romantic grandeur of many of his subjects and his effects were at odds with the Impressionists' interpretation of immediate and ordinary sensations from nature. Their orientation towards the natural phenomena was closer to Constable's. If Turner's chromatic treatment of light and the dissolving materiality of objects in his later work seem comparable to the more diaphanous phases of Monet's Impressionism, the Englishman's dramatics would leave even this relationship in doubt. It is worth noting, however, that when Pissarro became disenchanted with Neo-Impressionism and wrote to his son Lucien that he was going to the Louvre to look at works which might be useful to him in solving "the problem of dividing pure tone without harshness," he deplored the absence of Turners to study.[19]

Constable's work, on the other hand, had a profound but delayed effect on French landscape painting.[20] During the middle decades of the century, a group of painters working around the village of Barbizon by the forest of Fontainebleau began to celebrate the native French countryside as Constable had done in the valley of the meandering Stour. Like Constable, they had studied the great Dutch landscape tradition of the seventeenth century, but their debt to the more recent English example was equally evident in their work and in their devotion to locale.

In the atmospheric effects of the Barbizon painter Theodore Rousseau's works, Charles Baudelaire, reviewing the Paris Salon of 1846, found "memories of English painting,"[21] and similar observations have been made of other Barbizon artists. What these painters shared with Constable, in particular, was a balance between the materiality of things and the immateriality of the light that touched them — a dualism[22] that was eventually dissolved by the ascendancy of the Impressionist method of depicting light. It was this balance that may have appealed to American tastes when the Barbizon school attracted not only American painters during their European tours of study around mid-century but American collectors as well.[23]

When he reviewed the Paris Salon of 1859, Baudelaire again took note of Rousseau, but with criticism that seems to prefigure later objections to Impressionism. He deplored Rousseau's taking what he perceived to be a simple study after nature for a composition — "a little scrap of nature" — which Baudelaire deemed a "famous modern fault," implying thereby that others were at it too. Although he observed that few possessed this artist's sincere love for light, he found Rousseau's "luminous haze which sparkles as it is tossed about" upsetting to the "anatomy" of objects.[24] For Baudelaire, at least, the balance was not there.

With Charles-François Daubigny, the plein-air aspects of the Barbizon school have yet another parallel with the Impressionists: the artist, in his houseboat on the Oise, the Marne, and the Seine, painted the tranquil landscape along the rivers. Daubigny's paintings of river shorelines set a precedent for this subject to which Impressionists like Monet would frequently turn, for Monet, too, took to the river in a studio-boat. When Daubigny settled at Auvers-sur-Oise, he became the first of a succession of artists to discover its charms, among these the Impressionists Camille Pissarro, Berthe Morisot, and Armand Guillaumin. Paul Cézanne also painted there, as did the Dutch artist Vincent Van Gogh during his last troubled months. It was typical of both the French and American Impressionists that certain locales held a special appeal. Apart from their pursuit of nature's transient appearance, the sense of place remained strong, and place-names like La Grenouillère, Argenteuil, Pontoise, and Bougival in France, Cos Cob, Old Lyme, the Isles of Shoals, and Gloucester in New England readily evoke the images of Impressionist paintings.

By the time the leading Americans who came under the influence of Impressionism were studying in France, the French phase of Impressionism was already fully established and on view, joining the works of Courbet, Corot, Boudin, Jongkind, and the Barbizon painters as examples of recent developments in French art.

AMERICAN BACKGROUNDS

To view the American Impressionists as merely transplanting a movement and seeking its subject matter in locales that offered reasonable alternatives to the French painting grounds where they had first encountered and explored the new idiom would be, at best, only a half-truth. American Impressionism has its component of native tradition, which, if it sometimes parallels European developments and draws some sustenance from them along the way, is far from being a faint transatlantic echo. It drew upon earlier sources at home as well as sources abroad, and these home sources, as we devote more study to American Impressionism, may prove to have been more decisive in the shaping of our American version than adaptations from the contemporary French school.

John I. H. Baur asserted, in an essay[25] written over thirty years ago, that the "impressionistic" vision in American painting of the latter part of the nineteenth century grew out of an earlier tradition established by painters of "light and air" during the pre-Civil War era. He also noted "the obvious but rather superficial debt" that the American Impressionist movement owed to France but pointed out the "appreciable effect" on these same American Impressionists by the "limited impressionism" of the generation of Eastman Johnson and Winslow Homer, which in turn was stimulated by the example established through the pre-Civil War tradition of atmospheric emphasis in American landscape painting. Now, a full quarter of a century after the publication of a second article by Baur, his important essay on American luminism,[26] the attention being focused on the American Impressionists begs review and renewed appreciation of Baur's arguments. They still hold remarkably firm, and the observations he made decades ago are essential to any assessments now made of the American Impressionist movement, although one is compelled to reach farther back than the era of the luminists for some relevant considerations.

Native American landscape painting could be said to have begun with a sense of place. When our first real "school" of landscape painting developed around the central figure of Thomas Cole — the so-called Hudson River School, well under way in the early 1830s — it was the appearance of the native landscape that was celebrated along with its romantic content. Although compositional devices handed on from European classical and picturesque landscape traditions provided, more often than not, the underlying structure of these American works, details — to the extent that they transcended conventionalized idioms of representation — bespoke a familiarity with the native natural world. Details from nature overlying the conventional arrangements of composition were often derived from observations made of American scenery here and there and gathered together in the final work, a kind of landscape of assemblage, and not an altogether accurate replica of a specific American scene. Yet an authentic American appearance, by this method somewhat idealized, was evoked in many of these works.

Paintings based on scenes in the Catskills, on mountain lakes and the rocky gorges running back from the Hudson were of places that had about them still some aura of the untouched wilderness. This wilderness landscape was an image peculiar to the New World, a state of nature unlike that of Europe, which had so long felt the transforming presence of settled societies. The sentiments associated with the American wilderness were a medley of poetic, pietistic, and nationalistic feelings identified with the amplitude and variety of the American space stretching westward from the seaboard. It was a reciprocal relationship between the idea and the land, for the latter continually gave back its visual and material affirmations of these sentiments. Probably no other society in history had been so favored with this degree of accommodation from its environment. The natural wealth of the continent, in material resources as well as in its offerings of national adventure, individual opportunity, and national pride, seemed then, in the romantic climate of the nineteenth century, inexhaustible. But there were those who sensed its vulnerability. Thomas Cole, in his "Essay on American Scenery," [27] after cataloguing the visual and spiritually rewarding qualities of the land, played for a moment the prophet: "Where the wolf roams, the plough shall glisten; on the gray crag shall rise temple and tower — mighty deeds shall be done in the now pathless wilderness; and poets yet unborn shall sanctify the soil." [28] But then, at the end, he expressed his sorrow at the "ravages of the axe," [29] symbol of the aggressive frontier. Here, in its simplest form, was the troublesome predicament, for the national destiny, as it was perceived, could bring with it the transformation, if not the outright destruction, of something that had already been sanctified by philosophers and poets and extolled by the painters of landscape, something with which they felt the continent — and the new nation — had been providentially blessed.

For Cole, the wilderness to which the Old Testament prophets had retired to seek divine inspiration had its contemporary American counterpart — "a fitting place to speak of God." [30] While there was no thriving vein of religious painting along traditional lines in the United States, there was, in effect, a sacred landscape. In 1825 William Cullen Bryant would begin his poem, "A Forest Hymn," by saying: "The groves were God's first temples." He would conclude the poem with these lines:

. . . Be it ours to meditate,
In these calm shades, thy milder majesty,
And to the beautiful order of thy works
Learn to conform the order of our lives.

The philosophical content of the American romantic landscape was expressed in Ralph Waldo Emerson's *Nature,* [31] written in 1836, incorporating ideas that had been accumulating for years in his journals and lectures. As the initial statement of his New England transcendentalism, it has been called "a little manual of pantheism." [32] It was written after Emerson had returned from Europe, where he had met Carlyle, Coleridge, and Wordsworth. The substance of this little book bears traces of their ideas as well as varieties of Platonism and the mysticism of Swedenborg. But, these European sources aside, one discovers that the sensuous testing-ground of his philosophy of transcendentalism lay in his own luminous experience of the natural world. In communion with this nature, the poet found confirmation of a sacred unity wherein the microcosm of the human soul was but "part or particle of God."

Thus, the romantic landscape of the Hudson River School and its followers had acquired a train of content that went well beyond the mere representation — and, in some cases, aggrandisement — of American scenery in the northeastern United States. It was symbol — and sacred symbol, at that — and a genuine love for nature was deemed to nurture morality in the devout. All this was a heavy burden for landscape imagery to bear, and it would be illogical to assume that all such associations could be quickly or easily shed, especially when the literature that expressed many of these same sentiments was staple diet in American public education well into the twentieth century. The old ideas lingered on with varying degrees of adulteration and reached in the paintings of the American Impressionists the closing phase in a long continuity of romantic sentiments. The seasonal exodus from the New York studios to the New England countryside bore with it implications of renewal and sanctuary. The same landscape which could be invested with pantheistic associations and invite a pietistic communion, could also serve a less elevated function: it could be therapeutic. One could slip away to the retreats of nature in order to escape the round of materialistic pressures — in short, to take a vacation. Here the relationship of the seeker to the landscape setting resembles the leisurely pursuit of the Picturesque in eighteenth-century England.

Any reader of *The Crayon*, an American art journal published between January, 1855, and July, 1861, would have found in its pages, issue after issue, the recurring theme of nature's healing effects on the weary human spirit beset on every quarter by the drudgeries of life, the "clink of coin" and the "clatter of factories."[33] This *leitmotif* of nature as sanctuary pervades a great deal of American literature commonly read by Americans in the nineteenth century: works by Emerson, Thoreau, Bryant, Cooper, Hawthorne, Whittier.

W. J. Stillman, one of the publishers of *The Crayon*, related, some years after the event, the story of an outing he organized in the summer of 1858.[34] It was a distinguished party that included, in addition to Stillman and others, Ralph Waldo Emerson, Louis Agassiz, and James Russell Lowell. Stillman's account, and other sources,[35] make it clear that this experience, intimately in touch with nature, was a revitalizing communion and a memorable occasion for the participants.

The "philosophers' camp" of Stillman's outing had one distinct feature which set it quite apart from the solitary romantic's communion with nature. The key to Stillman's excursion was companionship and discourse — a social event. Here, at mid-century, is one indication of a process of socialization that was affecting the old romantic communion with nature. What, for Emerson in 1836, had been set largely in terms of private reflection amid a heightened awareness of nature, by 1858, on Stillman's outing, was experienced in concert.[36] This communal spirit would also be a distinctive feature of American Impressionism, as the artists gathered together for fellowship and work at Weir's farm in Branchville, at Cos Cob, and at Old Lyme.

Prevailing attitudes towards art and nature in America during the middle decades of the nineteenth century, a period coinciding with the birth and youth of the major American Impressionists, and therefore a formative background for their era of artistic maturity, can be extracted from *The Crayon*. Its pages testify to the prevalence of a moral view of nature and to the conviction that art and nature had edifying and purifying effects upon the human mind and spirit. But one of the most obvious features of *The Crayon* was its espousal of the ideas of the English critic John Ruskin,[37] and no serious study of American landscape of the nineteenth century can overlook his presence as a guiding sensibility. Widely read in America, Ruskin was an authoritative voice whose moralizing approach to art and advocacy of naturalism were shaping influences on American taste.

In 1855 Cole's successor as leader of the Hudson River School, Asher B. Durand, began publication in *The Crayon* of his nine "Letters on Landscape Painting,"[38] in which one can read that "the external appearance of this our dwelling place, apart from its wondrous structure and functions that minister to our well-being, is fraught with lessons of high and holy meaning"[39] and that the glories of nature are presented to us by "the Great Designer" as "types of the Divine attributes."[40] Yet by far the greater part of Durand's letters dwells on the obligation of the artist to observe and render with infinite dedication the particularities of nature itself. Here is a hint of the essential dichotomy of idealism and realism that has permeated so much of American art. It would be a fundamental quality in the luminist paintings of "light and air" that Baur viewed as having profound significance for later American landscape painting, including American Impressionism.

Although gently modulated light effects, creating atmospheric perspectives that fade off into luminous distance, and in some works a more theatrical light, intensifying the emotional impact of the sublime, were in the repertoire of the Hudson River School and in the spectacular landscapes of Church and Bierstadt, these luminist painters of "light and air" gave the phenomena of natural light and atmosphere a more essential, if less dramatic, role. Yet this role can be measured only as an equation of light and object, in which the effects of light create a unifying tone in paintings which, for all their apparent realism, impress one with their quiet and deliberate formality.

Fitz Hugh Lane and Martin Johnson Heade have often been regarded as exemplars of the luminist vein of American painting. Technically, according to Baur, luminists were "extreme realists, relying on infinitely subtle variations of tone and color to capture their magical effects" and spiritually they were "the lyrical poets of the American countryside and the most sensitive to its nuances of mood."[41] It is debatable whether the realistic component should be placed first in order of significance, since the form these artists realized is mainly a précis of nature so immaculate as to draw attention at once to its conceptual aspect. Luminist emphasis on the extreme clarity of objects generally accompanied a remarkable simplicity in the depiction of these forms, a simplicity that was not left lean but fleshed out with substantial detail. It had the clarity of an elaborately finished diagram, and it was this conceptual factor that lent the paintings of such luminists as Lane and Heade their unusual blend of reality and unreality — or of reality unnaturally heightened. It also imbued them with a quality that seemed to deny the active presence of the artist — as if the image had created itself — so meticulously and innocently were the surfaces of nature transcribed. The paintings of the major luminists suggest such a profound identification of the artist with the subject that we seem to be confronted in these works with "the poetry of things themselves,"[42] which links these artists to the universal vein of "naive" painting, wherein representation itself becomes a mystical act.

Luminist light was to some extent the by-product of the extreme clarity with which the objects in the painting were rendered and of the general tone that pervaded the pictures, the latter modifying the separateness of things by enveloping them in a unifying tonal scale. This unity and a predilection for reposeful scenes give the luminist works much of their poetry of quietism, augmented more often than not by the composition itself, by almost metrical cadences in the arrangements of forms and intervals.

The quietude of the luminist variety of realism marked a movement away from the theatricality to which romantic landscape had so frequently turned, although the heyday of luminist painting in the 1850s and 1860s was also shared by the spectacular landscapes of Church and Bierstadt. Luminist tendencies to court the unspectacular were closer to the spirit of the genre tradition of everyday subject matter that had been advanced in the paintings of William Sidney Mount and George Caleb Bingham. And the light-enhanced paintings of Winslow Homer from the mid-1860s through the 1870s and Eastman Johnson's work of the 1870s, particularly his extended series of cranberry pickers at work, suggests an intersection of the earlier genre tradition with the luminist concern for clarity and light.

While the dramatic emphasis both in subject matter and theatrical effects that pervaded so much of Hudson River School painting and the works of Church and Bierstadt had little in common with the gentle vision of the American Impressionist painters of landscape, these earlier landscapes have relevance for the later artists. The accumulation, over the years, of a romantic attachment to the varieties of American scenery and to this subject which seemed to have, above all others, a native validity, had provided some degree of national focus for generations of artists and their supportive clienteles. By establishing a tradition of American landscape painting, the earlier artists bequeathed to the American Impressionists a precedent upon which they were able to fashion their own variations in a changing environment. A pursuit of intimacy and a flight from grandeur mark the later work. In this, the American Impressionists shared choices not only with the luminists but with European tendencies after the romantic era of the earlier nineteenth century exhausted the heroic vision of the natural world. If American landscape painting of the late nineteenth century was drifting away from earlier pantheistic and moral associations, it would not abandon entirely the overtones of spiritual renewal that had become one of the stubborn connotations of contact with nature. The attractions of the changing seasons and the unruffled pastoral settings still abundant in the New England countryside, while offering intrinsic visual delights, would yet retain some attenuated strains of purified experience stolen from the increasing tempo of the metropolitan world, where artists maintained their studios close to the marketplace. If this new era of landscape painting was less ambitious of message-bearing content, it was not unmindful of the associative values that still clung to the image of the natural world. And if there was a hedonistic tone in the later work, something not unlike the simple enjoyment of a summer's stroll, it also carried with it therapeutic possibilities. Perhaps this constituted a large measure of its appeal. It did not address the troublesome issues of the day — as American literature was beginning to — but seemed to seek a refuge from them. In this respect, it was reaffirming older romantic sentiments about the *function* of landscape painting's relationship to its viewers.

PRELUDES TO AMERICAN IMPRESSIONISM

The generation of painters who became the core of American Impressionism did not have to contend with the violent opposition that the French Impressionists encountered when they made their debut in Paris in 1874. The Americans were not received with eagerness but neither were they too severely condemned. The reception was mixed but on the whole promising. There were several reasons for this.

In the first place, by the time the American Impressionists were becoming conspicuous on the home scene, there had already been some exposure to the new wave of French Impressionists through exhibitions in New York and Boston, and American collectors were beginning to acquire Impressionist paintings. Furthermore, the Barbizon school of painters, who formed a bridge to the Impressionists,[43] were not only in favor with Americans but were being avidly collected by the 1870s.

Secondly, there were American artists of established reputation whose affinity with the Impressionist vision, whether proponents of Impressionism or not, helped to establish a transition in taste that would make this newly imported idiom seem less aberrant to the American public than the French variety had appeared to its Parisian counterpart a few decades earlier.

And finally, the themes of American Impressionist landscape paintings were, by and large, the familiar commonplaces of the American countryside, village, and shore, or the urban pleasantries of park and boulevard. Their genre subjects celebrated the gentle pleasures of the good life: the home environment, intimate and untroubled, family and friends, the leisure moments on porch or picnic, the summer vacation. For these things there was already, in a climate of American optimism, well-being, and domestic pride, the predisposition for acceptance. These themes mirrored back to those attracted to the arts something of their own experience. Only the unfamiliar techniques of Impressionist painting — the spontaneity and sketchiness as opposed to the generally favored Salon finish and literalness — had to be overcome. But even here there had been some preparation.

In the middle of the nineteenth century, American artists studying abroad became acquainted with the Barbizon school of French painting. Barbizon painting, as Baudelaire had noted, often seemed rough and sketch-like. It went after general effects more than minutely naturalistic detail. Furthermore, Barbizon poetic sentiment, focused as it was on the appearance of the French pastoral countryside, the nearby forest of Fontainebleau, and the moods of nature this locale sustained, found a ready acceptance from Americans, whose own attitudes towards nature had been conditioned by a literary tradition that instilled values of a similar kind. There had been, too, a historic connection between poets and painters in America, as in the friendship between Bryant and Cole. And when painters like Cole and Durand wrote about the landscape, poetry — always close to the surface — frequently emerged. American poetry that had landscape for a major theme — that of Bryant, for example — abounds in imagery akin to the themes of Barbizon pastoral and forest landscape.[44] The same is true of Wordsworth's poetry of nature, treasured by American readers, where there is often that tinge of melancholy that invests so many Barbizon works with their faintly elegiac tone.[45] The Barbizon painter Jean Fran-

çois Millet would speak of "the sad fate of humanity — weariness"[46] that has the sound of the English poet in it: "the still, sad music of humanity."[47] In a letter of 1850, Millet wrote:

I would paint nothing that was not the result of an impression directly received from Nature, whether in landscape or in figures. The joyous side never shows itself to me; I know not if it exists, but I have never seen it. The gayest thing I know is the calm, the silence, which are so delicious, both in the forest and in the cultivated fields. You will confess that it always gives you a very dreamy sensation, and that the dream is a sad one, although very delicious.[48]

When the American painter William Morris Hunt was studying in France at mid-century, he became a close friend of Millet and moved from his studies in Paris to Barbizon and adopted the Barbizon manner for his own. On his return to the United States he did much, as an influential teacher and spokesman, to promote a taste for Barbizon painting in America. Hunt's social connections were such as to make his voice persuasive among those with the means to collect art, and the wealth of Barbizon painting that came into Boston collections can be credited largely to his efforts. George Inness, too, found the Barbizon spirit congenial. After his exposure to Barbizon painting — particularly that of Rousseau — during trips to France in the 1850s, his own work began to display Barbizon characteristics. Since both he and Hunt returned to the United States in the mid-1850s, the beginnings of Barbizon influence on American tastes could be dated from that time. By the 1870s it had become a fashionable style.

The Barbizon school's relationship to the genesis of Impressionism and the favor it found among American artists and collectors should be borne in mind as an important link, for its spirit continued to drift among the American Impressionists in the moodier tonal veins of their work. The founding father of the Old Lyme group that fostered so much American Impressionism, Henry Ward Ranger, was essentially a Barbizon painter,[49] although he would eventually exhibit some Impressionist tendencies; and Connecticut-born Dwight W. Tryon, a luminist in the early 1870s, was attracted to the Barbizon school during his period of European study (1877-1881). Impressionist handling and hints of Corot would later infuse his work with a delicate, airy poetry, the mood of which hold something of both luminist quietism and Barbizon melancholy. Alexander Wyant and Homer Dodge Martin were also influenced by the Barbizon manner, as well as by George Inness, and it would be difficult to separate the influences.

Barbizon characteristics have also been observed in the work of Albert Pinkham Ryder,[50] whose relationship to the artistic currents of his time, while attracting passing notice, has usually been accorded something like the status of a footnote to his solitary genius. The sentiment that resides in many of his themes is close to the elegiac note in so much of Barbizon painting. As Leo Stein noted in his eloquent memorial to Ryder,[51] there was a great deal of romantic pastoral matter in Ryder's work. Stein went on to say:

The crepuscular scenes that are so frequently painted, the autumnal afternoons, the carefully devised perspectives that lead into the pictures and beyond, all these are inducements, as are their equivalents in nature, to such a passage from the thing before the eye, and its intrinsic values, to a remoter field of emotional stimulation.

This is very near to being a digest of Barbizon subject and sentiment. In stating that Ryder's real subject was "a mood and not a fact copied from nature," Stein defined both Ryder's affinity with Barbizon feeling and his subjective distance from the school.

Finding in Ryder's painting "reminiscences of Corot and Turner," Stein also places him, however marginally, in the context of relationships we have already noted as part of the genesis of Impressionism. Ryder's direct relationship to some corners of American Impressionism also deserves attention, for his poetic vision probably had some as yet unmeasured effect on both Twachtman and Weir. His close friendship with Weir, in particular, is worthy of notice, and there are paintings by the latter that must be considered in the light of Ryder's example.[52]

A dandy grey eminence in the background of American painting during the last half of the century, James Abbott McNeill Whistler really belongs to the history of European art, since his career as an expatriate artist developed in the context of England, France, and Italy. Never an Impressionist in any orthodox sense, he was nonetheless sympathetic to that point-of-view and was always close to the leading edge of the art of his era. His effect on American painting in the latter part of the century has yet to be isolated and fully assessed, but in studies of American painters of the period he constantly emerges as an influential spirit. Because of his close involvement with European developments, it is difficult to extract his individual impact from the direct influences of these same developments on American painting. But whenever we encounter in American painting of the latter part of the century a delicate, harmonic arrangement of formal elements and a pronounced mood of reverie, in the musical sense of that term, one is tempted to look to Whistler as one of the generative sources. The soft, diffused tonalities of his *Nocturnes* and the suspended delicacies of his Venetian prints come to mind whenever we find similar characteristics in American Impressionist paintings and etchings.

By the 1890s Americans had been viewing for some time, in the works of Winslow Homer, one of the conspicuous concerns of French Impressionism: the representation of light as a freshly and economically recorded visual sensation. Homer's paintings of the last half of the 1860s (fig. 4) have often been cited as displaying features remarkably close to Monet's paintings of the same period.[53] Homer's trip to France (late 1866 to October, 1867) has raised questions about what he may have seen abroad that could have influenced the works painted on his return. The questions remain essentially unanswered, but speculations still hover.[54] The likelihood of his having seen the works of the younger French artists like Monet seems somewhat remote. About all that can be said is more of an observation than an argument: that if his work subsequent to the trip abroad does for a time exhibit a palette of higher key and his effects of light a more saturated brightness, these could just as well be an organic development of the tendency already inherent in his work. The artist's taciturn nature has left thus far no documentation to which the scholar can appeal. Nevertheless, Homer's gift for acute observation of visual sensation and his economy of means in rendering it palpable are at least parallel to the early phases of French Impressionism.

Furthermore, Homer's work was regularly on view in New York. Almost every year from 1863 to 1880, his paintings were in the National Academy exhibitions, although rarely well displayed. At the Water Color Society's shows between 1874 and 1881, he exhibited several watercolors almost every year.

Of the artists who have a peripheral relationship to American Impressionism, John La Farge occupies an important position. His paintings of the 1860s reveal a finely-tuned sensibility in handling nuances of natural light and during this period he experimented with outdoor painting. In paralleling the interests of the French Impressionists with respect to light, he shares with Homer — and at the same period — an independent American strain of proto-impressionism.

John Singer Sargent, the third member of the American triumvirate of expatriates that included

Fig. 4. Winslow Homer. *Long Branch, New Jersey*, 1869.
Oil on canvas, 16" x 21¾". Museum of Fine Arts, Boston,
Bequest of James Dennie.

Whistler and Cassatt, was also a conspicuous figure at the edge of American Impressionism. Although his career was truly cosmopolitan, his American absenteeism was not as total as Whistler's nor as sustained as Cassatt's. He was portraitist to the elite on both sides of the Atlantic. And in a limited way he was also an Impressionist.

Sargent visited Monet at Giverny in 1887, painted him at work, and admired the French master, whose paintings he may have known quite well long before their actual acquaintance.[55] During the 1880s, and especially after his meeting with Monet, Sargent's painting would often be close to the Impressionists in plein-airism and in high-keyed palette. His virtuoso execution, however, qualities the Impressionist aspect of his painting by drawing attention more to the brilliance of the performance than to evocations of transience and the transforming energy of light. The brushwork, instead of functioning like typical Impressionist microstructure, accommodates the inherent substance of things and thus tends to be interpretive of "object-ness" rather than of light as an enveloping presence.[56]

Nevertheless, Sargent's spontaneous style in his oils and in his lively watercolors places him close to Impressionism. His established reputation and the technical facility of his dashing brushwork that made him popular as a portraitist undoubtedly had some effect on the eventual appreciation of Impressionism in America.

Among American landscape painters whose work may have assisted materially in preparing a climate of acceptance for American Impressionism was George Inness. By the 1880s he was firmly established as an important American painter. But he was no friend of Impressionism. Sometime around 1884, in a letter to an editor,[57] he objected to being classed as an Impressionist and called Impressionism a "new fad" and an "evil extreme" in art. Acknowledging that all artists are subject to impressions and that some, like himself, seek to convey their impressions to others, Inness stated his own position in "the art of communicating impressions." The elements of this were "the solidity of objects and transparency of shadows in a breathable atmosphere through which we are conscious of spaces and distances." The Impressionist "pancake of color" was "humbug." Nonetheless, the poetically suggestive, soft-toned later work of Inness has often been compared to Impressionism.

While there is some justification for this comparison, it begs qualification,[58] not only in view of the artist's own statements but with respect to the tonal

Fig. 5.   George Inness. *Spring Blossoms,* 1889. Oil on
canvas, 30¼″ x 45¾″. The Metropolitan Museum of Art,
Gift of George A. Hearn in memory of Arthur Hoppock
Hearn, 1911.

vein of landscape painting to which his art, at this
phase of his career, truly belongs. It is the soft-edged
rendering and the absence of elaborate detail in his
late work that elicits the characterization of it as
"impressionistic."

Works painted during the last ten years of his life
(fig. 5) remind us of the misty tonalities of Whistler.
As Nicolai Cikovsky, Jr. has pointed out,[59] these late
works are not so much transcriptions of actual misty
atmospheric conditions (which one would expect of
the true Impressionist) but inventions of the artist, the
manifestations of his personal, subjective vision.[60] The
result is an ambience in which the "solidity of objects"
seems to be in the process of dissolving into some
enveloping essence, unifying object with surrounding
space. Light, the touchstone of Impressionism, is not
the determinant factor here, but in some respects there
is a parallel between this blending of object with a
general tonality and the dissolution of solidities into
the flickering, light-based microstructure of later Impressionist broken-color technique. The relationship
between these tonal works of Inness and Monet's
Impressionism from the 1880s on is, at the very least, a
cousinship of sorts and an indication of the gradual
erosion of the earlier sanctity of the object and sharply
defined descriptive passages in American painting — as

in luminism, for example. Only to this extent is Inness
"impressionistic."[61]

The subjective feeling in the later painting of George
Inness, while to some extent reflecting his personal
involvement with Swedenborgian spiritualism, is yet
another variation of the tradition of poetic sentiment in
American landscape painting that had been there almost from the beginning. The objective prose of
Winslow Homer, on the other hand, carried the
equally pervasive realistic vein of American landscape
painting into terse objective transcriptions of visual
sensation. Neither of these strains gave way entirely
before the imported features in American Impressionism but, instead, infused the latter with many of
those very qualities that distinguish it from its French
counterpart.

THE AMERICAN PHASE OF IMPRESSIONISM

As early as September of 1883 Americans had the
opportunity to see a number of French Impressionist
works in Boston as part of an International Exhibition
of Art and Industry held in the Mechanic's Building.[62]
This exhibition was shortly followed by one in New
York, the circumstances of which drew more attention.[63] In the fall of 1883 the French Government had

given the Statue of Liberty to this country, and since it was necessary to raise funds to provide an architectural base for the statue, a benefit exhibition was organized to be installed at the National Academy of Design. While the exhibition featured such artists as Géricault, Courbet, Corot, Millet, and the Barbizon painters who were then popular, it also included French Impressionists, who were made the real focus of the show.

The culminating event in the sequence of introductions to French Impressionism that the American public encountered in the late nineteenth century occurred in March of 1886, when the American Art Association opened an exhibition of French Impressionists at its Jackson Square location in New York.[64] Some three hundred paintings went on view, among them many of the undisputed masterpieces of French Impressionism,[65] which comprised about one-sixth of the exhibition. In May the exhibition continued at the National Academy of Design.

Although there was adverse criticism, there were also sympathetic voices, and sales amounted to about $18,000. This encouraged the organizers of the exhibition to plan another for the spring of 1887. This second exhibition, less radical in content than the first, was challenged by New York dealers, who opposed the shipping of foreign works duty-free,[66] as had been the case with the 1886 exhibition. The American Art Association, sponsor of both shows, had been founded as a non-profit organization in 1877, ostensibly for the purpose of encouraging American artists, but New York dealers, claiming that it was really an art business, not an educational enterprise, forced a compromise in the arrangements. The paintings came in duty-free, but no sales were allowed. The furor over the customs duty was good publicity, however, and attendance was good.

At the World's Columbian Exposition held in Chicago in 1893, the French Government sponsored an official showing of French art which contained not a single French Impressionist painting. "A Loan Collection of Foreign Masters," however, was gathered from private holdings in the United States: eighteen pictures, including works by Manet, Monet, Degas, Pissarro, Renoir, and Sisley. And the now growing number of American Impressionists, including the future members of The Ten, were well represented in the American section of the art palace.[67]

One visitor to the Exposition took note not only of Impressionism as a style but as an international phenomenon affecting the younger artists "of Russia, Norway, Sweden, Denmark, and America as well as the *plein air* school of Giverney [*sic*]."[68] This visitor was the American writer Hamlin Garland, and his observations, published the following year, have been called the movement's first all-out defense in English. This "blue-shadow idea" was, in Garland's view, a new wave signalling the ongoing vitality of art in an evolutionary process of changing styles.

The fundamental idea of the impressionists, as I understand it, is that a picture should be a unified impression. It should not be a mosaic, but a complete and of course momentary concept of the sense of sight . . . . It should be the stayed and reproduced effect of a single section of the world of color upon the eye . . . . They therefore strive to represent in color an instantaneous effect of light and shade as presented by nature, and they work in the open air necessarily. They are concerned with atmosphere always. They know that the landscape is never twice alike. Every degree of the progress of the sun makes a new picture . . . . Impressionists are, above all, colorists . . . . They do not paint leaves, they paint masses of color; they paint the *effect* of leaves upon the eye.[69]

The presence of an American phase of Impressionism, sensed at Chicago, seemed to be confirmed in the spring of 1898 when The Ten held their first group exhibition, appropriately, at the Durand-Ruel Galleries in New York. These artists had drawn together partly out of discontent with the restrictive atmosphere the Society of American Artists had acquired. They also desired to exhibit as a smaller, exclusive group displaying some mutuality of taste, but there was really considerable diversity among them — as there had been among the French Impressionists.[70] The same patterns of diversity appeared in other American Impressionists. To be sure, there was evidence enough of lessons gathered from the French but little indication of a studied orthodoxy in American versions of Impressionism. This may have had something to do with the manner in which Impressionism came to the artists— grafted on from outside the schools — and may explain why the question of an academic Impressionism does arise later when both the example and teaching of the American Impressionists became a part of the American student's formal training here.

Nevertheless, there were those who, early on, saw a school. One critic, Sadakichi Hartmann, in 1902, found the artists of the Boston circle around Edmund C. Tarbell — the "Tarbellites," as he called them — so similar that he facetiously professed to find some difficulty in distinguishing among them, "never sure which of them painted this or that picture."[71] Concerned primarily with figure painting, generally of elegant, wholesome women in light-filled interiors, on porches, or in gardens, the works in this vein by Tarbell and Frank W. Benson recall the gentle urbanity and optimism of the Victorian novels of American William Dean Howells. If there was any single quality most of the American Impressionists shared, it was that of optimism. That it was not otherwise suggests the degree to which their art was thoroughly committed to the pleasurable aspects of life and responsive to the native appeal of the rural landscape, for there was much about the age that could have turned an artist to more sober subjects.

The era of American Impressionism, from the 1890s into the early decades of the twentieth century, coincided with the period when the United States was emerging from self-containment into the status of an international power. The Spanish-American War was fought the same year as the first exhibition of The Ten. Urbanism and industrialization, which had accelerated sharply after the Civil War, were effecting substantial changes in the social and economic profiles of the country, and the great American fortunes were being made. Acquisitiveness was on conspicuous display, and if it was beginning to function in the arts, as fortunes begat patronage, it did not come all in a rush on the younger American painters.

But there were lingerings in the midst of change. During the last quarter of the nineteenth century, American poetry, song, and legend were still predominantly rural in tone and the vision of pastoral America was a treasure-trove of basic virtues. The cult of the self-made man[72] was a popular bit of savory and more often than not, if his success were urban, it was up from rural roots. It was a time that clung nostalgically to the old, simple, pastoral idealities even as the unmeasured vastness of the abstraction of power, which was to become the looming reality of the twentieth century, was already shaping itself within the idea of progress.

There had long been an optimistic American faith in progress. It was enshrined in the founding documents and in the American self-image as sanctuary of freedom and land of opportunity. When American Impressionism made its appearance, one gateway to individual freedom and opportunity had all but closed: the geographical frontier. But at the same time, a theoretical support for the idea of progress — the theory of social evolution — was being employed in the hurly-burly of a new frontier where "survival of the fittest" could be interpreted as an argument in favor of laissez-faire policies in business and industry.[73] Reaction came in the shape of various reform movements and a body of muckraking literature exposing

corruption in government as well as in business and industry. The American Federation of Labor was already on the scene, born in 1886 out of an earlier organization, and the continuing conflict between labor and management had begun. Sweatshop and slum were as much a part of the New York scene as Central Park and the new mansions of the wealthy.

In the fall of 1900 Sadakichi Hartmann challenged the American artist to discover the picturesqueness of the city of New York.[74] The tone of his remarks was thoroughly romantic, although the actual themes to which he called attention would have appeared to the general run of romantics as singularly unpromising subjects, more ugly than otherwise: the elevated railroad and its busy stations, the sea of roofs, the blocks of office buildings, and "the unfathomable and inexhaustible misery of the slums." He was actually addressing photographers, but his arguments read like an extended recipe for the kind of painting that would soon emerge from the studios of the so-called Ash Can School — The Eight who made their first appearance as a group in 1908 at the Macbeth Gallery in New York.[75] For some of them, the city was teeming with new, frequently impudent, subjects, and for the first time in American art the commonplaces of the urban scene became a major celebration. Half of the group had worked as newspaper artists[76] and the reporter's eye for the eccentricities of neighborhoods and the eccentrics in the crowd was evident in their work. Some, like Ernest Lawson (who studied with Twachtman) and William Glackens were Impressionists of sorts, and one, Maurice Prendergast, was clearly Post-Impressionist in outlook. There was considerable diversity in the group, with Arthur B. Davies, for example, serving as one of the organizers of the Armory Show that raised artistic issues at odds with the position generally assumed by The Eight.

While there is justification for viewing the vein of raw urban commonplaces in some of The Eight's paintings as diametric to the pastoral amenities of the American Impressionists who were ranging through rural Connecticut and the rest of New England, they both belong to an older, inclusive current of localism in American art. The sense of place was strong in each instance. But even as these two movements were conspicuous aspects in American painting of the early twentieth century, other American artists were confronting abroad the new modernist issues of European art, some hints of which could be seen in New York at exhibitions in the gallery of Alfred Stieglitz. At the New York Armory Show of 1913, the European section would make clear that dramatic changes had been affecting western art during the previous decade and a new wave of internationalism would soon be evident in American art, superseding both The Ash Can School and American Impressionism — not, however, to the complete exclusion of the native vein of localism, for its history would have a longer run beyond the limits of our focus here.[77]

The urban and industrial reshaping of the American scene may not appear to have had much effect on the American Impressionists as a whole, yet it would be wrong to assert that their art lay entirely outside the realities of the era, in some Never-Never Land of pastoral ideality. Many of them maintained studios in the city and the urban landscape was not entirely absent from their art, however much they may have gentled it. Indeed, it could be said that a substantial contribution to the spread of American Impressionism and its outreach to the American public lay in the nature of the city and in one technological development of American industry: the railroad.

During the era of American Impressionism there was excellent rail service from Manhattan into New England, and Connecticut, as the nearest neighbor, was attracting a good share of the vacation crowds from the metropolitan population. The city could be an uncomfortable place indoors as well as out during the summer months, and "escape" may well have been one impetus for much of the summer migration to the Connecticut shore and countryside. Its picturesque charms, which drew the artists in the first place, inevitably brought others to the region. Many were seasonal birds of passage, but others — like some of the artists — settled in until finally, years after the heyday of Impressionism, the automobile completed the work of a declining railroad system in suburbanizing the Connecticut shore and hinterland closest to the metropolitan area. The sight of the easels of artists and of art students from the summer schools in Connecticut may even have confirmed to many of the summer visitors that they had selected a properly picturesque spot for the summer recess.

There is some correlation between the growth of summer resorts in New England and the growth of plein-air painting so central to Impressionist methods, and the fact that so much of this art was produced in popular vacation areas in New England is worth noting. The history of the growth of many resort areas provides some evidence of a pattern in which the visits of artists and literary personalities preceded the onslaught of the larger vacation crowds.[78] Mount Desert Island in Maine, for example, was visited by several American painters before the Civil War, among others, Thomas Doughty in 1836, Thomas Cole in 1844, Fitz Hugh Lane in 1848 and on subsequent trips, and Frederic Church from the early 1850s to 1860, by which time it was becoming a well-known summer retreat.

In 1848 a summer hotel opened at Appledore, Isles of Shoals, New Hampshire, which soon became a favored summer sanctuary for such literary figures as James Russell Lowell, Nathaniel Hawthorne, and John Greenleaf Whittier. The poetry of Celia Thaxter, daughter of the hotel's proprietor, and her engaging personality made her a popular figure there. Childe Hassam, for whom this locale was a favorite painting ground, was one of her valued friends, and the artist painted her many times in the surroundings of Appledore. Her sonnet on Childe Hassam returned the tribute to the painter. William Morris Hunt, who had done so much to popularize a taste for Barbizon painting in America, spent his last days at the Thaxter home. Hunt, from 1856 to 1862, had also maintained a studio in another growing resort area — Newport, Rhode Island — which had become popular by the 1850s and which, by the end of the century, was displaying conspicuous opulence. Other Massachusetts areas like Cape Ann and Cape Cod attracted generations of artists as well as the vacation crowds.

Connecticut sites such as Greenwich, Cos Cob, Old Lyme, Mystic, Essex, and Noank in the late nineteenth and early twentieth centuries became centers of artistic activity and social interactions of a full range — from acceptance to rejection — among artists, writers, art students, vacationers, and old residents.

It has been said that the American Impressionists rarely associated with groups[79] This is hardly borne out by their history, and the organization of The Ten, which held together for so many years, is only one instance. The communal tone that prevailed in the art colonies at Cos Cob and Old Lyme was, in part, the social consequence of their founding by artists who were themselves a "clubby" breed. There was among them an easy camaraderie born of mutual friendships (particularly strong in the case of Weir, Twachtman, and Hassam) and a common experience abroad as students. There, as Americans, they had acquired a collective identity that extended to their professional lives on their return to the United States. This was maintained informally in the social life at Weir's farms in Branchville and Windham, at Holley House in Cos Cob, and at Florence Griswold's establishment in Old Lyme, but it went beyond such gatherings as these. For several of the artists, membership in The Players[80], where they mingled with theater and literary figures, and in the Salmagundi Club,[81] which brought together both artists and amateurs of the arts, was a feature of their social lives in New York. And they frequently exhibited their works in private clubs.

Even the fact that so many of them taught at the Art Students League, organized in 1875 by dissident students from the National Academy of Design, suggests some identification with communal purposes, given the "self-help" organizational structure of the school. Moreover, a sense of group identity was clearly affirmed by the secession of The Ten from the Society of American Artists, since, as we have indicated, they wished to mount more compact exhibitions of their works, rather than to be absorbed into the large, unwieldy annuals where the quality was invariably mixed and their identities as professionals compromised.

But one of the most unusual manifestations of community among these artists was the cooperative studio building on West 67th Street in New York, which was planned, financed, and owned by artists.[82] The idea for this particular structure originated around the turn of the century with Henry Ward Ranger, who was instrumental in the founding of the Old Lyme colony. He became president of this cooperative enterprise, and among the other stockholder-owners and occupants of its apartment-studios were Childe Hassam and Frank Vincent DuMond. The top floor was reserved for servants' quarters, while a frieze of Greek horsemen painted by V. V. Sewell, one of the owners, graced the main floor entrance hall, and the spacious studios were furnished with large comforting fireplaces. These were not bohemian "pads."

The original building had scarcely been completed, in 1903, when a second group of artists, including Robert Vonnoh, sponsored, with financial assistance from the first group, the construction of another studio building next to it, dubbed the "Atelier." The idea was so attractive that, by 1907, several similar apartment buildings had been constructed in New York.[83] While it may seem odd that some of the prominent American Impressionists should have contributed so substantially to the history of the American condominium, it was merely one of many manifestations of their action as a social and professional enclave, as knit together by certain common interests and tastes as they were solitary before the easel and individual as to style.

For many of these artists, the teacher's role became an important function. They had returned from studies abroad to settle in as professional artists at precisely the period when there had been a recent proliferation of art schools and departments of art at colleges and universities in the United States.[84] In 1868, when Mary Cassatt left America for her studies in Europe, there were barely a half dozen professional art schools in the country that could claim to be more than ephemeral institutions. Some twenty years later, when Theodore Robinson and Childe Hassam were exploring the Impressionist idiom in France, the number had trebled, even if one did not count the art departments established in a few of the universities. Thus, when the American Impressionists began to appear in numbers during the 1890s, the teaching of art in this country had increased dramatically and would continue to grow. These artists would constitute an important segment of the new artist-teacher population in the professional art schools and in the summer schools which sprang up at pictorially inviting locales conducive to the increasingly popular plein-air painting.[85]

In assessing the role these artists may have played in edging the artistic tastes of the American public towards an appreciation of Impressionism, it should be noted that in Connecticut many local art associations were organized during the period when American Impressionists were active in the state as artists and teachers.[86] These organizations generally aimed at promoting, locally or regionally, public interest in the arts through exhibitions, classes, and other activities. Some of these groups were chapters of the American Federation of Arts (organized in 1909 and incorporated in 1916) "to unite in closer fellowship all who are striving for the development of Art in America, either through production or the cultivation of appreciation . . . and to furnish a channel through which public opinion, instrumental in securing better legislation, may find expression."[87] The Connecticut Academy of Fine Arts, first organized in 1910 and incorporated in 1927, continues to hold its annual exhibitions, providing artists in the region an opportunity to exhibit their works to the Connecticut public in a professionally juried context. The record of its exhibitions indicates that some of the American Impressionists were actively involved, both as officers and as exhibitors.[88]

Evidence of the importance of Connecticut to the American Impressionists is, of course, best shown in the work produced in the state by some of its most important figures. John H. Twachtman, J. Alden Weir, Childe Hassam, Willard Metcalf, Theodore Robinson, and several others all painted many of their finest works in Connecticut, and, since landscape was a persistent theme, the sense of place was reflected in the work.

In response to urgings from Weir that he find some place of his own to "get acquainted with . . . grow up with," Theodore Robinson thought of Cos Cob.[89] Although he was active in Connecticut for only a brief period, it was at Cos Cob that he turned out some of his best American paintings. Robinson had made the acquaintance of Monet at Giverny, becoming one of a limited circle of Americans to have cultivated a friendship with the French master,[90] and by 1888 was painting in an Impressionist manner with Monet's encouragement. Until December of 1892, when he began his final residence in the United States, Robinson moved back and forth from Europe. The promise of reconciliation between the Impressionist touch he had acquired abroad and a native leaning towards descriptive realism was maturing in his work; but it was tragically cut off: fragile of health, his production limited, he died in the spring of 1896, less than two full years after the Cos Cob period.

Robinson's habit of working from photographs, which he used very much like traditional studies for a composition, marked off with a grid for scaling to the final work, seems to have been limited chiefly to his figural compositions, probably a matter of both convenience and economy. The practice was not uncommon in the nineteenth century, when photography began to be viewed as one of the artist's tools, even though there was frequent opposition to it as a compromising device. Speculation about an historical relationship betweeen photography and Impressionism raises interesting questions regarding light, perspective, focus, and transient effects. Robinson apparently utilized the photograph to hold in mind some sign of the permanent form of things freed from nature's transience.[91] This might be viewed, in the context of his art generally, as an indication of a haunting conflict between his acceptance of Impressionism as registering the transitory sensation and the traditional American respect for the materiality of things. The problem is complicated by the fact that the photograph does, indeed, register the fleeting moment, holds it back, as it were, outside of time. Be that as it may, Robinson's paintings of the yacht harbor and landings at Cos Cob seem to represent an interval of liberation from any conflicts in his art, for they are among his freshest, surest works.

Weir's advice to Robinson, that he find some place of his own to grow with, came out of the substance of his own life in Connecticut. He had acquired his farm in Branchville around the time of his marriage to Anna Dwight Baker of Windham in 1883. There and at Windham he painted regularly during the summer

Mr. and Mrs. J. Alden Weir in their Branchville home.

season and often at other times of the year. His landscapes are predominantly of these two locales, and his affection for them is registered in the mood of contentment they generally evoke. Their idyllic charm exemplifies the lingering romantic tone in so much of American Impressionism, which in Weir's case was particularly strong. While recognizing that the writer at the time was a young man in love, one finds Weir's remarks in a letter to his bride-to-be expressive of sentiments embodied in his later paintings of the Connecticut countryside. It was no passing fancy.

I recall those few hours we had in the charming little village of Windham, this is really the first Connecticut village that I have really ever known, & now I feel that a charm is connected with all villages, such as I have read of but never appreciated.[92]

There is here a hint of the degree to which rural Connecticut became for Weir — and others among his painter friends — a paradigm of rustic sanctuary. This — and their fond attachment to certain motifs which appear again and again in their paintings — links them to the temper of romanticism and to the imagery of American rustic poetry, just as the spirit of their gleanings from the countryside suggests affinities with the sentiments of the Picturesque. Their art held less of innovation than of continuities. In this respect, Weir's example is especially to the point.

J. Alden Weir was the first of the major American Impressionists — excepting expatriate Mary Cassatt — to study in Europe. In view of his subsequent role as one of the leaders in the circle of American Impressionists, his initial reaction to the French movement is illuminating. In 1874, when the French Impressionists made their debut, Weir was a student in Paris, but there seems to be no hint of his awareness of them until three years later, when he writes that he has been across the river to an exhibition of "Impressionalists." He had never seen "more horrible things." The artists did not observe drawing and form, he reported, but presented "an impression of what they call nature." He spent a quarter of an hour with works that included Renoir's *Le Moulin de la Galette* and "left with a headache."[93] These were the reactions of a young man totally immersed in studies of an academic nature under the oversight of Gérôme — the very antithesis of Impressionism. Weir was absorbing, in his visits to museums, lessons from the masters of the past and noting those artists of the present whom he was prepared to accept. The tone of his remarks has a youthful passion, but he would be nearly as disturbed towards the end of his career when he encountered the works of Matisse.[94] Weir did not leap quickly into new waters.

His report to his father from London in 1873, before going on to Paris, is also revealing.[95] He was both charmed and awed by the works of John Constable but found Turner's *Rain, Steam, and Speed* (1844, National Gallery, London) "very curious." He also expressed disappointment in Turner's *The Burial of Wilkie* (now *Peace – Burial at Sea,* 1842, Tate Gallery, London), which he had previously known through an engraving. Here Weir's innate conservatism shows through his sketchy comments. Both of these paintings by Turner are in his "impressionistic" manner. The former picture, with its unusual composition featuring a vague, dark train bearing down on a sharp diagonal out of a colorful mist, had from its first appearance been a controversial work, both "insane" and "magnificent" to the eyes of one reviewer.[96] Whereas the subject of *Peace – Burial at Sea* presumably had an acceptable romantic appeal to Weir, it would have appeared to him in an engraved version as less diaphanous than it actually was; and the deliberately sooty darkness of the sail-and-steam vessel would have seemed less startling in the half-tones of a print than when viewed in the ambience of Turner's opalescent sea and the veil of atmosphere around it. Weir was not yet at a point in his career when he could accept the more radical phase of Turner's work. His reaction to the Impressionists only a few years later is thus understandable, for it was traditional "drawing and form" that caught his appreciative eye during his student years.

His espousal of Impressionism — generally a somewhat guarded partisanship — required preparation.

This process undoubtedly began even during those early years in France through his warm friendship with Jules Bastien-Lepage,[97] whose careful draftsmanship was so respectful of the materiality of things. But Bastien-Lepage also advocated plein-air painting, and the combination represented a compromise between the old and the new. His palette, lightened by his adaptations of Impressionism, often emitted a cool, silvery tone similar to that in Corot's later landscapes, which could also be found later in some of Weir's paintings of landscape subjects around Branchville and Windham.

Weir's early respect for Mary Cassatt's painting, evidenced soon after his return from France by his invitation to her on the occasion of the 1878 annual exhibition of the Society of American Artists, implies that he was already favorably inclined towards painting that owed something to the example of Manet, as Cassatt's work did at the time. As a student, he had shown an interest in the works of such masters as Velasquez and Hals,[98] artists who were also important to Manet; and in 1881 Weir was instrumental in acquiring two important Manets for the collector Erwin Davis. Finally, Weir's own still-life painting *The Delft Plate* (1888, Museum of Fine Arts, Boston) is remarkably close to Manet in conception and handling. It had been a steady evolution, and around 1890 Weir's Impressionist period would begin.

In *Building a Dam, Shetucket* (cat. 76, illus. p. 19), Weir's restrained Impressionism had fully matured, and one understands why his good friend Albert Pinkham Ryder pronounced it one of the artist's best works.[99]

The subject would appear to be singularly unproductive of the idyllic mood Weir so successfully draws from the scene, as the scar of earth in the woods loses its ugliness in the mellow tones of summer light. One is reminded of Emerson's remark: "There is no object so foul that intense light will not make beautiful."[100] Space is compressed. Pattern emerges. It is finely orchestrated work, not the record of a transient moment. Here, as in Twachtman's visual poetry, is that subtle ambivalence through which reality and form drift alternately in and out of the consciousness of the viewer.

It has been said that Weir, Twachtman, Robinson, and Hassam brought to America "a pale, belated impressionism" and that their pictures, despite "a supposed devotion to particularity," had only "a vague, unlocalized prettiness."[101] Belated their Impressionism surely was, since by the time they emerged on the American scene, the French Impressionists — latterly "Independents" — had ceased to exhibit as a group. Given the stylistic variety among the French Impressionists themselves, it is risky, however, to be too doctrinaire in one's generalizations with respect to style, particularly when the inevitable comparisons so often hinge on qualitative judgments. As pointed out earlier, "Impressionism," as a stylistic term, is something of an abstraction. It serves best as a term of convenience of the most general nature, and this is as true of the French as it is of the American phase.

American Impressionism was not "unlocalized," for there is no mistaking its sense of place. To anyone on intimate terms with the New England countryside, the landscapes of the American Impressionists are still echoed in the land. As Charles Eldredge has noted, "these painters' eyes were opened to the simple pleasures and modest beauties of their own region."[102]

The Americans were Impressionists selectively. Plein-airism they adopted (although this was not exclusively an Impressionist practice); the technique of flickering brushwork they employed with widely varying degrees of commitment and in a variety of forms; as a group, they tended to emphasize the permanent form of things at least as much as they courted the transforming energy of light; they were not always "blue shadow" painters and often reverted to tonalism; optical mixtures they used now and then, but this seems never to have been a central issue; and they frequently pursued Impressionism's decorative potentialities to enhance the surfaces of their paintings, in some cases to the point of mannerism. But one feature seems fairly consistent: a tendency to retain something of the materiality of things. There are exceptions to this, but even in the bath of light and atmosphere, the resistant form of the object usually seeps through. This is demonstrated even in Hassam's work, which is often so close to being "typically" Impressionist in handling.

When Robinson was discovering Impressionism, Childe Hassam (already a mature artist before going to Paris in 1886 to study at the Académie Julian) was also beginning to explore an Impressionist palette and technique. His *Grand Prix Day* (1887, New Britain Museum of American Art; fig. 6), executed in a flashing technique, was shown in the Paris Salon of 1888 and again, in 1893, at the World's Columbian Exposition in Chicago. In this work, and in a smaller, sketchier version now in the Museum of Fine Arts, Boston, Hassam was on old home ground. Before going to Paris he had painted street scenes in varied

Fig. 6.   Childe Hassam. *Le Jour de Grand Prix,* 1887. Oil on canvas, 36″ x 48″. New Britain Museum of American Art.

49

Fig. 7. John H. Twachtman. *Arques-la-Bataille,* 1885.
Oil on canvas, 60″ x 78⅞″. The Metropolitan Museum
of Art, Purchase, 1968, Morris K. Jesup Fund.

moods of atmosphere and light.[103] Street scenes were always among his favorite subjects, a predilection he shares with some of the French Impressionists. But what is particularly notable about *Grand Prix Day* is the fact that although its surface is developed in the short touches of Impressionist brushwork, the various forms, even the fluttering passages of foliage, retain weight and density; and this is as true of the smaller work in Boston as of the Salon piece in New Britain. The pattern of light and dark is equally strong. The effect of light does not dissolve the weightiness of things, and even where individual forms are sketchily mingled together there is a massy denseness to the passages. There is much about it that recalls the objective vein in American painting (cf. fig. 4). Still, the accents of brilliant light, the general luminosity of the scene, and the lively brushwork indicate already an understanding of what some of the French Impressionists had been doing. Hassam developed considerable facility with the "stitchery" of broken color rendering and, in many of his American works, there is often a distinctive and deliberate touch in the brushwork, like a coded vocabulary more dash than dot. The technical aspects of Impressionism are less marked in others.

John H. Twachtman returned to the United States from Paris the same year Hassam arrived in the French capital, but his Impressionism, which began around 1890, would be an intensely subjective variety. He had developed in France a style that departed radically from his earlier Munich and Barbizon manners. His large canvas, *Arques-la-Bataille* (1885, The Metropolitan Museum of Art; fig. 7), stands as the masterwork of this period of his career. Sky, distant bank, river, and foreground are resolved into gently-toned horizontal bands, only slightly modulated here and there by quietly emergent details. This painting recalls the formal elegance of Whistler and the refinements of Far Eastern art (the latter especially evident in the deft calligraphic rendering of the grasses in the foreground) and prefigures the basic difference between Twachtman's mature American works and characteristics associated with French Impressionism. The lyricism of his later painting would be derived not from the immediate sensation but from a meditative concentration on his subjects that seems to suspend them somewhere between reality and dream, like fading after-images of a remembered fragment of nature. Of all the American Impressionists, Twachtman was the most poetic temperament, and his paintings in series

— of the pools and cascades on his Connecticut farm — often approach in form and feeling a level of abstraction nearly musical in tone.

Like Twachtman, Willard Metcalf was a painter of the seasons, but more literal in his approach. Although he became known as the "poet laureate" of the hilly New England landscape, there are few of those poetic transformations in his work that were so essential to Twachtman's vision. But his prose — if one may call it that — did not lack grace, or sensitivity to nature's quieter moods. Indeed, there were none among the American Impressionists who were more attuned to the nuances of spring light which had yet some edge of winter's chill left in it, to the lazy warmth of summer meadows, or to the almost submarine spectrum of moonlight.

The images created by these painters have a familiar look. They probably represent to most viewers who know the region their own remembered pleasures, even when the mood of the pictures derives from the more somber aspects of the year's cycle, for even melancholy can be a delicious sentiment, as Millet knew and as Twachtman's winter pools attest. Casual meanderings along Connecticut's shore and over its country roads can still reveal the native sources of these Impressionist images: the spring blossoms, laurel along the ledges, the light-filtered shade of trees at midsummer, the sparkle of some small brook, old farms weathered by the years, fields mottled by out-croppings of ledge and sectioned by the ubiquitous stone walls, village lanes that have somehow managed stubbornly to retain the charms of a gracious past, the flashing patterns of color and light in the bobbing yacht harbors, quiet stretches of wetlands along the shore, summer gardens and meadows flecked with wild flowers, autumn foliage, winter snows, forested hills, and over all the constantly shifting patterns of New England's skies.

While the painting techniques of these American Impressionists reveal, in widely varying degrees of adaptation, their gatherings from the European experience, their themes persistently call attention to continuities of much larger range than the decades of Impressionist activity itself. Their localisms are of the moment, of particular places and moments viewed with Impressionist immediacy, often on the spot "with the sight of simple seeing," to use Wallace Stevens' phrase.[104] But they also catalogue, as if by some conditioned seeking out of an American typology, the kinds of subjects that one could also find imbedded in American literature: vignettes drawn from the particularities of an experience of American places, yet

The waterfall on Twachtman's Greenwich farm.

rendered typical by their drift into a collective consciousness that has formed out of these fragments an American sense of place. That these images contain so many overtones of romantic sentiment is but the heritage from which no society can escape — its own history. The painting of American places was born in a romantic era and developed an iconography that could not be easily shed. A fair measure of it was fashioned in New England, and the fact that so much of American Impressionism came out of this region is a conjunction of some consequence.

Walt Whitman closed the Preface to the 1855 edition of his *Leaves of Grass* with these words: "The proof of the poet is that his country absorbs him as he has absorbed it." In its own time, American Impressionism was accorded its measure of affectionate proof even as it revealed its own affections in its sense of place. There may be some elusive reciprocal relationship in all this, as the landscape image of the land created expectation in return. Now, after a season of forgetfulness, we can only surmise to what degree the American Impressionists were instrumental in establishing a vision of New England that still lingers as an attractive image in the American mind.

1 Letter dated March 10, 187[8], from 13 Avenue Trudanie.Archives of American Art, microfilm reel 71, frame 1088.

2 Louis Leroy, *Charivari,* April 24, 1874.

3 Announced by Armand Silvestre, *"Le monde des arts,"* La Vie Moderne, April 24, 1879.

4 John I. H. Baur, *Leaders of American Impressionism* (Exh. cat., The Brooklyn Museum, 1937); F. Van Deren Coke, *Impressionism in America* (Exh. cat., University of New Mexico, 1975); reprinted *The American Impressionists* (Exh. cat., Hirschl and Adler Galleries, 1968); Donelson F. Hoopes, *The American Impressionists* (New York: Watson-Guptill Publications, 1972); Moussa M. Domit, *American Impressionist Painting* (Exh. cat., National Gallery of Art, 1973); Richard J. Boyle, *American Impressionism* (Boston: New York Graphic Society, 1974); Charles Eldredge, "Connecticut Impressionists: The Spirit of Place," *Art in America,* 62 (Sept.-Oct.,1974), 84-90; and William Gerdts, *American Impressionism* (exh. cat., Henry Art Gallery, University of Washington, 1980).

5 For a thorough treatment of this subject, see Ernst Gombrich, *Art and Illusion: A Study of the Psychology of Pictorial Representation,* 2nd ed., rev. (N.Y.: Bollingen Foundation, 1961).

6 For a discussion of Impressionist microstructure, see Fritz Novotny, "The Reaction Against Impressionism from the Artistic Point of View," *Problems of the 19th and 20th Centuries:* Vol. IV, *Studies in Western Art* (Princeton University Press, 1963), pp. 93-103.

7 Foremost among the color theories known to the Impressionists was that of Michel E. Chevreul, whose *De loi du contraste simultané des couleurs . . .* was published in Paris in 1839. (1st English ed., 1854.) Other influential publications were Charles Blanc, *Grammaire des arts du dessin* (1867), extending Chevreul's theories and dealing at length with optical mixtures; H. Von Helmholtz, *Handbuch der Physiologischen Optik* (1867); and Ogden N. Rood, *Modern Chromatics* (1879). Neo-Impressionism, which relied more heavily on scientific color theory, was developed during the 1880s by Georges Seurat, who employed Chevreul's circle of four basic colors and their intermediates: *blue,* blue-violet, violet, red-violet, *red,* red-orange, orange, yellow-orange, *yellow,* yellow-green, *green,* and blue-green. These colors were not mixed with one another but mixed individually with white to increase the range of values within each color. By mingling the separate dots of these colors, Seurat intended that the resultant microstructure would mix optically in the vision of the viewer. For a letter from Pissarro to Durand-Ruel on Neo-Impressionist objectives, see Lionello Venturi, *Les Archives de l'Impressionisme* (N.Y.: Editions Durand-Ruel, 1939), Vol. II, 24.

8 In an unpublished essay written for Durand-Ruel in January, 1873, Monet's friend, Armand Silvestre, placed early Impressionism in historical context, relating it to the art of Delacroix, Corot, Courbet, and Manet. Cited in Kermit Champa, *Studies in Early Impressionism* (New Haven: Yale University Press, 1973) p. 97.

9 ". . . *la représentation des choses* rélles et existantes," in *Courrier du Dimanche,* December 25, 1861.

10 Cf. Corot, *L'Hôtel Cabassus à Ville d'Avray* (1835-40, Louvre); Monet, *The Bridge at Bougival* (1869-70, The Currier Gallery of Art, Manchester, N.H.); and Pissarro, *Entrance to Village of Voisins* (1872, Louvre).

11 Frédérick Villot, as quoted in René Huyghe, *Delacroix* (N.Y.: Abrams, 1963), p. 129.

12 For comments on Anglo-French connections and on the presence of English artists and their works in France, see Prosper Dorbec, "Les Paysagistes Anglais en France," *Gazette des Beaux-Arts,* Series 4, 8 (1912), 257-81.

13 See Christopher Hussey, *The Picturesque; Studies in a Point-of-View* (London: G. P. Putnam's Sons, 1927). Jane Austen was attracted to William Gilpin's writings at an early age and occasionally alludes to the vogue of the Picturesque in her writings. See *Sense and Sensibility* (London: Oxford University Press, 1970), pp. 82-84, for a dialogue on the Picturesque; also *Northanger Abbey and Persuasion* (London: Oxford University Press, 1971), p. 100.

14 Books by William Gilpin include *An Essay upon Prints: Containing Remarks upon the Principles of Picturesque Beauty . . . ,* 2nd ed. (London: G. Scott, 1768); *Observations, Relative Chiefly to Picturesque Beauty . . . ,* 2 Vols. (London: R. Blamire, 1786); *Remarks on Forest Scenery* (London: R. Blamire, 1791); *Three Essays; on Picturesque Beauty; on Picturesque Travel; and on Sketching Landscape* (London: R. Blamire, 1792).

15 Although Constable's work does not adhere to the stereotypes of the Picturesque, there is evidence of Picturesque elements in his compositions and in his sketches, a natural relationship considering the origin and focus of the movement and Constable's early exposure to the Picturesque ideas of his acquaintance John T. Smith. During Constable's youth the cult of the Picturesque was at its height, and some of the artist's remarks on the landscape in his correspondence have overtones of Picturesque sentiment. Constable's library contained works by William Gilpin, Richard Payne Knight, Uvedale Price, and John T. Smith, the important English writers on the Picturesque. See Leslie Parris, Conal Shields, and Ian Fleming-Williams (eds.), *John Constable: Further Documents and Correspondence* (London: The Tate Gallery and Suffolk Records Society, 1975), pp. 25-52. On Smith's relationship to Constable, see Graham Reynolds, *Constable, The Natural Painter* (N.Y.: McGraw-Hill, 1965), p. 22; also, by same author, *Catalogue of the Constable Collection* (London: Her Majesty's Stationery Office, 1973), pp. 13, 19; R. B. Beckett, *John Constable and the Fishers: The Record of a Friendship* (London: Routledge and Kegan Paul, 1952), pp. 81-83, 124.

16 In a letter of 1903 to Wynford Dewhurst, who was preparing a book *(Impressionist Painting, Its Genesis and Development,* London, 1904), Pissarro remarked that Constable, Turner, and Old Crome had influenced the Impressionists in that these English painters shared their own aims

with regard to plein air, light, and fugitive effects. Shortly afterwards, writing to his son Lucien, Pissarro is less emphatic as to their influence. See Camille Pissarro, *Camille Pissarro: Letters to His Son Lucien,* ed. John Rewald with Lucien Pissarro, trans. Lionel Abel (N.Y.: Pantheon Books, 1943), pp. 355-56.

17 "Constable said that the superiority of the green he uses for his meadows derives from the fact that it is composed of a multitude of different greens. What causes the lack of intensity and of life in verdure as it is painted by the common run of landscapists is that they ordinarily do it with a uniform tint. What he said about the green of the meadows can be applied to all the other tones." *The Journal of Eugène Delacroix,* trans. Walter Pach (N.Y.: Crown, 1948), p. 730.

18 Letter to Lucien dated May 8, 1903. *Pissarro: Letters,* p. 356.

19 Letter to Lucien dated September 6, 1888. *Pissarro: Letters,* pp. 131-32.

20 In a letter to his father, dated Paris, June 3, 1874, J. Alden Weir wrote that "the French call Bonington and Constable the founders of the French school and their works are very much thought of." Weir was not referring to the Impressionists but to the Barbizon painters of landscape. For the relationships between the English and French landscape painters, see Prosper Dorbec, "Les paysagistes anglais en France," *Gazette des Beaux-Arts,* Series 4, 7 (1912), pp. 257-81. A brief account is in Jean Bouret, *The Barbizon School and 19th Century French Landscape Painting* (Greenwich, Conn.: New York Graphic Society, 1973), pp. 33-42.

21 Charles Baudelaire, *Art in Paris 1845-1862: Salons and Other Exhibitions Reviewed by Charles Baudelaire,* trans. Jonathan Mayne (London: Phaidon, 1965), p. 109.

22 Fritz Novotny, *Painting and Sculpture in Europe 1780-1880* (Baltimore: Penguin, 1960), pp. 104-05.

23 See Lois Fink, "American Artists in France, 1850-1870," *American Art Journal,* 5 (Nov. 1973), 32-49. Bouret, *The Barbizon School,* pp. 22-24, believes the U.S. and U.S.S.R. have more Barbizon works than other countries.

24 Baudelaire, p. 196.

25 John I. H. Baur, "Early Studies in Light and Air by American Landscape Painters," *Brooklyn Museum Bulletin,* 60 (Winter, 1948), 1-9.

26 John I. H. Baur, "American Luminism," *Perspectives USA,* 9 (Autumn, 1954), 90-98.

27 Thomas Cole, "Essay on American Scenery," *The American Monthly Magazine,* New Series, I (Jan., 1836), 1-12; reprinted in John McCoubrey (ed.), *American Art 1700-1960: Sources and Documents* (Englewood Cliffs, N.J.: Prentice-Hall, 1965), pp. 98-110; also in John Conron (ed.), *The American Landscape: A Critical Anthology of Prose and Poetry* (N.Y.: Oxford University Press, 1974), pp. 568-78.

28 Cole, (McCoubrey, p. 109), (Conron, pp. 577-78).

29 Cole, (Conron, p. 578). See also Barabara Novak, "The Double-Edged Axe," *Art in America,* 64 (Jan.-Feb. 1976), 45-50; and in the same issue, Donald B. Kuspit,

"19th-Century Landscape: Poetry and Property," 64-71.

30 Cole, (McCoubrey, pp. 99-100), (Conron, p. 569).

31 Ralph Waldo Emerson, *Nature* (Boston: James Munroe and Co., 1836).

32 Regis Michaud, *Emerson the Enraptured Yankee,* trans. George Boas (N.Y.: Harper and Bros., 1930), p. 133.

33 *The Crayon,* II, 4 (July 25, 1855), 47. And Emerson wrote: "Our hunting for the picturesque is inseparable from our protest against false society." *Emerson's Complete Works* (Boston: Riverside, 1833-1893), III, p. 171.

34 William J. Stillman, "The Philosophers' Camp," *Century Magazine,* 46 (1893), 598-606.

35 Charles Eliot Norton testified to Lowell's enthusiasm when he visited the latter shortly after his return. Charles Eliot Norton, *Letters,* I, pp. 182-83. As editor of *Atlantic Monthly,* Lowell encouraged numerous articles about nature. See Hans Huth, *Nature and the American* (Berkeley: Univ. of California Press, 1957), pp. 100-04, for an account of his interest. Emerson, in his poem "The Adirondacs," wrote: "The spiritual stars rise nightly shedding down/ A private beam into each several heart."

36 Emerson had acknowledged fairly late in 1837 that one could acquire new sharpness of perception if one had the advantage of the company of an artist. Emerson, *Journals,* IV, p. 321.

37 A handy anthology is *The Art Criticism of John Ruskin,* ed. Robert L. Herbert (Garden City, N.Y.: Doubleday Anchor, 1964).

38 *The Crayon,* I (1855): 1 (Jan. 3), 1-2; 3 (Jan. 17), 34-35; 5 (Jan. 31), 66-67; 7 (Feb. 14), 97-98; 10 (Mar. 7), 145-46; 14 (Apr. 4), 209-11; 18 (May 2), 273-75; 23 (June 6), 354-55; II, 2 (July 11), 16-17.

39 *Crayon,* p. 34.

40 *Crayon,* p. 34.

41 Baur, "American Luminism," p. 90.

42 Baur, "American Luminism," p. 97, quoting remarks by George Santayana on Lucretius.

43 Novotny, p. 101. See Madeleine Fidell-Beaufort and Janine Bailly-Herzberg, *Daubigny* (Paris: Editions Geoffroy-Dechaume, 1975) for works by this artist which bear comparision with the early phase of Impressionism. For specific references to this connection see Kermit Champa, *Studies in Early Impressionism* (New Haven: Yale University Press, 1973). pp. 59-60, 70-72, 75-77, 92-93.

44 Among others, Bryant's "Inscriptions for the Entrance to a Wood" (1817), "Autumn Woods" (1824), "A Summer Ramble" (1826), and "The Path" (1863).

45 For this tone in Wordsworth's landscape imagery and images comparable to those in Barbizon landscape, see *Prelude* (1799-1805), "Lines Composed a Few Miles Above Tintern Abbey" (1798), "When, to the Attractions of the Busy World" (1805-1815), and "Yarrow Visited" (1814-1815). In the Preface to *Lyrical Ballads* (1800) the poet eulogizes the rustic life close to nature. Bryant was indebted to Wordsworth's example, and once remarked that the English poet was "a sort of poetical master" to him. See *The Letters of William Cullen Bryant,* ed. William Cullen

Bryant II and Thomas G. Voss (N.Y.: Fordham University Press, 1975-1977), I, p. 235 (letter to Charles Folsom, dated March 20, 1827). For other references to the Wordsworth connection: I, pp. 114, 159; and II, pp. 342-45 (on Bryant's visit with Wordsworth in July, 1945).

46 Julia Cartwright, *Jean François Millet: His Life and Letters* (N.Y.: Macmillan, 1902), p. 106.

47 William Wordsworth, in "Lines Composed a Few Miles Above Tintern Abbey."

48 Cartwright, p. 106.

49 Compare Ranger's *Autumn Woodlands* (fig. 5) with Théodore Rousseau's *Sortie de Forêt à Fontainebleau, Soleil Couchant* (c. 1848, Louvre) and *Une Avenue, Forêt de l'Isle-Adam* (1849, Louvre); and Narcisse Diaz de la Peña's *Forest Scene* (1867, St. Louis Art Museum).

50 The critic Sadakichi Hartmann, recounting a visit to Ryder's studio, found that the artist's method seemed related to Diaz and Monticelli, of whom the former, Narcisse Diaz de la Peña, was one of the Barbizon group. See his *A History of American Art* (Boston: L. C. Page, 1902), I, p. 313. Nicolai Cikovsky, Jr., *George Inness* (N.Y.: Praeger, 1971), p. 61, states that Ryder, like Inness, was "nourished by Barbizon art." Ryder also admired Corot.

51 Leo Stein, "Albert Ryder," *The New Republic,* 14 (April 27, 1918), 385-86.

52 See, for example, J. Alden Weir, *Moonlight* (c. 1905, Chester Dale Collection, National Gallery of Art, Washington, D.C.). Boyle, p. 160, links Weir's *Pan and the Wolf* and *Fishing Party* to Ryder.

53 The most frequently cited work is Monet's *Women in a Garden* (1866-67, Louvre), with which one should compare such works by Homer as *The Morning Bell.* (c. 1866, Yale University Art Gallery), *Croquet Scene* (1866, The Art Institute of Chicago, *The Bridle Path, White Mountains* (1868, Sterling and Francine Clark Art Institute, Williamstown, Mass.), and *Long Branch, New Jersey,* 1869, Museum of Fine Arts Boston.).

54 On this problem see Barbara Novak, *American Painting of the Nineteenth Century* (N.Y.: Praeger, 1969) pp. 165-74, where arguments by Lloyd Goodrich and Albert Ten Eyck Gardner are also cited. Also John Wilmerding, *Winslow Homer* (Praeger, 1972), pp. 48-52.

55 Boyle, p. 210.

56 This is apparent in his dashing canvas of *Paul Helleu Sketching, and His Wife* (1889, The Brooklyn Museum). The flickering brushstrokes function primarily to indicate individual blades of grass, just as his handling of drapery, hats, and canoe supports the substantiality of these things with different brushwork. The slender rod supporting the artist's canvas is rendered with precision, emphasizing its whip-like resilience.

57 To "Editor Ledger" from Tarpon Springs, Florida, cited in George Inness, Jr., *The Life, Art and Letters of George Inness* (N.Y.: The Century Co., 1917), pp. 168-74.

58 Cikovsky, p. 62 ff.

59 Cikovsky, p. 62 ff.

60 His work was once described as "more of a painting than a picture." See "Some Living American Painters. Critical Conversations by Howe and Torrey," *Art Interchange,* 32 (April 1894), 102.

61 George Inness, Jr., p. 168, states: "That my father was an impressionist in the highest sense of the word cannot be doubted, but he abhorred the name and what it stood for in generally accepted terms."

62 Hans Huth, "Impressionism Comes to America," *Gazette des Beaux-Arts,* series 6, 29 (April 1946), 225-52, documents early U.S. exhibitons of French Impressionism.

63 Huth, "Impressionism . . . ," 231-35. William Merritt Chase and Carroll Beckwith were in charge of the arrangements for this exhibition, and the emphasis on the Impressionists was apparently Chase's idea.

64 Huth, "Impressionism . . .," 237-44. Arrangements were made with the French dealer Durand-Ruel in the summer of 1885.

65 Huth, "Impressionism . . .," 239, note 22. Among these works were Degas, *The Millinery Shop* (1886, The Art Institute of Chicago); Manet, *The Fifer,* (1866, Louvre) and *On the Balcony* (1869, Louvre); Renoir, *Dance at Bougival* (1883, Museum of Fine Arts, Boston) and *Luncheon of the Boating Party* (1881, Phillips Memorial Gallery, Washington, D.C.).

66 J. Alden Weir wrote a letter to the editor of *The Critic,* dated December 9, 1885, protesting the high duty on imported art works. AAA, reel 125/357.

67 Among the exhibitors were Weir, with 8 oils and 26 prints; Hassam, 6 oils and 4 watercolors; Vonnoh, 13 oils; Lilla Cabot Perry and Thomas Dewing, 7 works each; Chase, 6; Twachtman, 5; Reid, 4; Robinson, Metcalf, Tarbell, Benson, Simmons, and Ochtman, 3 each; and DeCamp, 1.

68 Hamlin Garland, *Crumbling Idols* (Chicago: Stone and Kimball, 1894), p. 121. "Impressionism," pp. 121-41.

69 Garland, 122-24.

70 Perhaps we attach too much significance to the word "Impressionist," given the casual nature of the christening of 1874 and the subsequent rejection of the term by the artists themselves. See notes 2 and 3.

71 Hartmann, pp. 240-41.

72 Merle Curti, *The Growth of American Thought,* 3rd ed. (N.Y.: Harper and Row, 1964), pp. 626-32.

73 Curti, pp. 552-63.

74 Sadakichi Hartmann, "A Plea for the Picturesqueness of New York," *Camera Notes and Proceedings,* 4 (October 1900), 91-97.

75 They included Robert Henri, John Sloan, George Luks, William Glackens, Everett Shinn, Ernest Lawson, Arthur B. Davies, and Maurice Prendergast.

76 Sloan, Luks, Glackens, and Shinn.

77 The "regionalism" of Grant Wood, Thomas Hart Benton, and John Steuart Curry, at its peak in the 1930s, is the most obvious example.

78 Huth, *Nature and the American,* pp. 105-28.

79 Hoopes, p. 8.

80 The Players was founded in 1888 by Lawrence

Barrett, Augustin Daly, and Edwin Booth (who donated his house at 16 Gramercy Place for the organization's quarters, reserving a suite for himself until his death in 1893). The membership was limited to artists, editors, authors, and playwrights, although other individuals of prominence were eligible.

81 The Salmagundi Club was founded in 1871 as a sketch class.

82 See 'Co-operative Studio Building for New York Artists,'' *The Commercial Advertiser* [New York], March 28, 1903, p. 5; and "Artists Who Pay No Rent," *Brooklyn Daily Eagle,* July 7, 1907. It was the cooperative idea alone that was new, since the studio building had long been a feature of both New York and Boston art scenes. The studios of the famous Tenth Street Building in New York, designed by Richard Morris Hunt in the late 1850s, had provided working quarters for such artists as Frederic Church, Albert Bierstadt, and Martin Johnson Heade; and during the American Impressionist era, William Merritt Chase had studios there. In 1902, Weir also occupied a studio in this building. Archives of American Art, reel 125/895.

83 *Brooklyn Daily Eagle,* July 7, 1907.

84 Pennsylvania Academy of Fine Arts (1805), National Academy of Design (1825), Maryland Institute (1826), Cooper Union (1859), School of the Art Institute of Chicago (1866), Yale School of Fine Arts (1866), Cincinnati Art Academy (1869), Massachusetts School of Art (1873), department of art at Syracuse University (1873), department of art at University of Illinois (1873), California School of Fine Arts (1874), Art Students League (1875), School of the Museum of Fine Arts, Boston (1876), department of art at University of Kansas (1877), Rhode Island School of Design (1877), Cleveland Institute (1882), Kansas City Art Institute (1885), Minneapolis Art Institute (1886), Corcoran School of Art (1887).

85 At the Art Students League (Twachtman, Weir, Chase, Metcalf, Hassam, DuMond, and Reid); at Cooper Union (Metcalf, Twachtman, Weir, Reid); at the Pennsylvania Academy of Fine Arts (Chase, Vonnoh, Robinson); at the Boston Museum School (Benson, Tarbell); and at numerous summer schools. They also reached out to other parts of the coutry: Lawson taught in Columbus, Georgia, in Kansas City, Missouri, and in Colorado Springs (as did Reid); Twachtman taught in Cincinnati; Carlsen in San Francisco. Tarbell was principal of the Corcoran School of Art from 1918 to 1925. Such an extensive record of teaching left a mark on the schools and the students, forming another generation of Impressionists, even as the mainstreams of American art had turned in other directions.

86 New Haven Paint and Clay Club (1900), Connecticut Arts Association, Danbury (1908), Connecticut Academy of Fine Arts (1910), The Greenwich Society of Artists and New Haven Brush and Palette Club (1912), Lyme Art Association and Municipal Art Commission of New Haven (1914), Silvermine Guild of Artists and Kent Art Association (1922), Mystic Art Association and Wilton Art Association (1924), Hartford Salmagundians (1928), Hartford Society of Women Painters, Art League of New Britain, and Darien Guild of the Seven Arts (1929).

87 *American Art Annual,* 31 (Washington, D.C.: The American Federation of Arts, 1935, for the year 1935), p. 23.

88 Henry C. White was one of the founding members and Guy Wiggins served as president from 1927 well into the 1930s. Several of the artists in the present exhibition exhibited regularly or occasionally.

89 Theodore Robinson, Diary, New York, April 11, 1895. Frick Art Reference Library, New York.

90 Besides John Signer Sargent, there was Lilla Cabot Perry and Theodore Butler, who married Monet's step-daughter.

91 "Painting directly from nature is difficult, as things do not remain the same, the camera helps to retain the picture in your mind." Quoted in John I. H. Baur, *Theodore Robinson* (Exh. cat., The Brooklyn Museum of Art, 1946), p. 36.

92 Letter to Anna Dwight Baker, posted May 16, 1882. Archives of American Art, microfilm 125, frame 42.

93 Letter of April 15, 1877.

94 Letter to C. E. S. Wood, dated January 30, 1915. AAA, 126/47-48. For his rejection of the Futurists, see letter to C. E. S. Wood, February 8, 1914. AAA, 126/8.

95 Letter dated September 26, 1873. AAA, 71/40-41.

96 *The* [London] *Times,* May 8, 1844.

97 Weir was instrumental in acquiring Bastien-Lepage's *Joan of Arc* (1879, The Metropolitan Museum of Art) for the collector Erwin Davis, who bequeathed it to the museum in 1889. Weir even considered having Bastien-Lepage serve as best man at his wedding to Anna Dwight Baker. In 1887, he helped raise money for a memorial to Bastien-Lepage, who died in 1884.

98 "Velasquez I admire" (letter, Paris, Dec. 14, 1873); Frans Hals "this great Dutch genius" (letter, Paris, around June, 1874); Velasquez's *infanta* "rich and wonderful in values" (letter, Paris, June 3, 1874); "I am now at Haarlem, the town that I revere! the birth-place of Frans Hals!" (letter, Haarlem, Jan. 2, 1875); a portrait by Velasquez was "all one could wish for in a portrait" (same letter); and in a letter to his father from Rotterdam, Jan. 8, 1875, Weir included a poem he had written in praise of Hals.

99 Letter to C. E. S. Wood, dated January 13, 1911. AAA, 126/861-62.

100 Emerson, *Nature,* p. 20.

101 John McCoubrey, *American Tradition in Painting* (N.Y.: George Braziller, 1963), p. 31.

102 Charles Eldredge "Connecticut Impressionists, The Spirit of Place," *Art in America,* 62 (Sept.-Oct. 1974), 89.

103 For example, *Rainy Day, Boston* (1885, The Toledo Museum of Art) and *Boston Common at Twilight* (1885-6, Museum of Fine Arts, Boston).

104 From "An Ordinary Evening in New Haven," in *Collected Poems of Wallace Stevens* (N. Y.: A. Knopf, 1964), p. 471.

Abrams, Lucien

1 *Landscape, Lieutenant River*
1915: Old Lyme
Oil on canvas, 26 x 32 (66 x 81.3)
Signed and dated LL: *Lucien Abrams 1915*
Lyman Allyn Museum

Bicknell, Frank A.

2 Mountain Laurel
c. 1910: Rogers Lake, Lyme
Oil on canvas, 24 x 30 (61 x 76.2)
Signed LR: *Frank A. Bicknell;* on stretcher in pencil:
*"Mountain Laurel" (Rogers Lake, Lyme, Conn.) by
Frank A. Bicknell*
Private Collection

Brinley, D. Putnam

3 *A Colonial Church*   ILLUS. P. 64
1910: Danbury
Oil on canvas, 31 x 25¼ (78.7 x 64.1)
Signed and dated LL: *D. Putnam Brinley '10*
Private Collection on Loan to the Bowdoin College
Museum of Art

"D. Putman Brinley . . . has been making an oil
painting of the First Congregational Church, working
from the lawn of the Porter residence opposite"
(*Danbury Evening News,* Sept. 29, 1910).

Carlsen, Emil

4 *Cherry Blossoms*   ILLUS. P. 12
n.d.: Probably Falls Village
Oil on canvas, 23⅛ x 23⅛ (58.7 x 58.7)
No signature
Hammer Galleries

5 *Connecticut Hillside*
1920s: Probably Falls Village
Etching, 3⅜ x 4⅜ (8.6 x 11.1)
No signature
The William Benton Museum of Art, Gift of Dr.
Gilbert Erlechman

This is from a portfolio of six etchings published in
1979, for the first time, from the original copper plates
executed by the artist.

6 *Connecticut Hillside*   ILLUS. P. 63
c. 1920: Probably Falls Village
Oil on canvas, 29¼ x 27⅜ (74.3 x 69.5)
Signed LR: *Emil Carlsen*
The Art Institute of Chicago, Walter H. Schulze
Memorial

7 *Connecticut Landscape*
1920s: Probably Falls Village
Etching, 3⅜ x 4⅜ (8.6 x 11.1)
No signature
The William Benton Museum of Art, Gift of Dr.
Gilbert Erlechman
See note for cat. 5.

8 *Landscape*
c. 1925–30: Probably Falls Village
Oil on canvas, 29¾ x 26 (75.6 x 66)
No signature
Hammer Galleries

Study for *The Garden of Gethsemene* (oil on canvas, 43"
x 37"), first exhibited in 1930 at the Carnegie Institute
and now in a private collection. The religious painting
depicts Christ, with a halo, in the lower left of the
landscape.

9 *Night, Old Windham*
1904: Windham Center
Oil on canvas, 50 x 40 (127 x 101.6)
Signed LR: *Emil Carlsen;* on reverse: *Emil Carlsen
Night, Old Windham 1904*
W. David Lindholm Collection, Courtesy of
R. H. Love Galleries, Inc., Chicago

The building at the right is almost certainly the
cottage on J. Alden Weir's property, where Carlsen
and his family stayed on their frequent visits to
Windham.

10 *Wood Interior*   ILLUS. P. 64
c. 1921: Falls Village
Oil on canvas, 32 x 25½ (81.3 x 64.8)
No signature
The Brett Mitchell Collection, Inc., Cleveland, Ohio

11 *Wyndham Church, Connecticut*   ILLUS. P. 65
1906–07 or 1911: Windham Center
Oil on canvas, 18 x 15⅛ (45.7 x 38.4)

Signed LL: *Emil Carlsen*
Smith College Museum of Art, Northampton, Massachusetts, Gift of Mrs. Daniel Fraad (Rita Rich '37), 1977
The subject is St. Paul's Episcopal Church, Plains Road, Windham Center, where J. Alden Weir and his family were members. Weir presented to the church oil studies for stained glass windows commemorating the death of his first wife, Anna Dwight Baker. There is no explanation for Carlsen's misspelling of **Windham** here, for the town name is correctly spelled **in his title for a 1904 painting (cat. 9).**

Chadwick, William

12 *Connecticut River, View from Ely's Ferry Road*
n.d.: Lyme
Oil on canvas, 30 x 40 (76.2 x 101.6)
Signed LR: *W. Chadwick*
Lyman Allyn Museum

13 *Old Lyme Church*   ILLUS. P. 65
c. 1917: Old Lyme
Oil on canvas, 30 x 30 (76.2 x 76.2)
Signed LR: *W. Chadwick*
Lamb Collection, Courtesy of R. H. Love Galleries, Inc., Chicago
The church in the background is the First Congregational Church of Old Lyme.

Clark, Walter

14 *Noank*
1900: Noank
Oil on canvas, 20 x 30 (50.8 x 76.2)
No signature
Collection of Dr. and Mrs. Everette James, Jr., Nashville, Courtesy of R. H. Love Galleries, Inc., Chicago

Davis, Charles H.

15 *Across the River in Mystic*   ILLUS. P. 66
c. 1918: Mystic
Oil on canvas, 20 x 36 (50.8 x 91.4)
Signed LL: *C. H. Davis;* on stretcher top: *C. H. D./915*
Collection of Mrs. Robert P. Weimann, Jr.

16 *A Bright Winter Morning*   ILLUS. P. 66
c. 1929: Mystic
Oil on canvas, 20 x 27 (50.8 x 68.6)
Signed LL: *C. H. Davis;* on reverse: *1164*
Thomas Colville Fine Paintings, New Haven

17 *Countryside in Autumn*   ILLUS. P. 11
c. 1927: Mystic
Oil on canvas, 40¹/₁₆ x 50⅛ (101.8 x 127.3)
Signed LL: *C. H. Davis;* label on stretcher top: *Chas. Davis, Countryside in Autumn, 1129*
The William Benton Museum of Art, Louise Crombie Beach Memorial Collection

A Davis painting with this title was exhibited at Doll and Richards Gallery, Boston, Feb. 23-Mar. 6, 1928. Cat. 17 was assigned to The University of Connecticut by the Ranger Fund Committee of the National Academy of Design in 1931 and reassigned permanently by the Smithsonian Art Commission in 1945.

18 *Morning Sunlight*   ILLUS. P. 67
c. 1895: Mystic
Oil on canvas, 20 x 30 (50.8 x 76.2)
Signed LL: *C. H. Davis;* on reverse: *397*
Museum of Fine Arts, Boston, Gift of the Estate of Mrs. George Hebron Chaplin, 1911

19 *Sketchbook*
1932-33: Mystic
Pencil and watercolor on paper, 8 x 10¼ closed (20.3 x 26)
Thomas Colville Fine Paintings, New Haven

Thomas Colville has pointed out that it was Davis's habit to record his work as numbered miniatures in sketchbooks like this one. He began the system in France and continued it until his death in August, 1933. This is his last sketchbook of this sort and includes the numbers 1228-1287. Numbers in the 390s and up certainly indicate American works.

20 *Wind Driven*
n.d.: Mystic
Oil on canvas, 50 x 40 (127 x 101.6)
Signed LL: *C. H. Davis*
John H. Garzoli

DuMond, Frank Vincent

21 *Autumn in Lyme*
1925: Lyme
Oil on canvas, 28 x 30 (71.1 x 76.2)
Signed LL: *Frank V. DuMond*
Collection of N. Robert Cestone, Rowayton

22 *Golden Afternoon in Old Lyme*
1903: Old Lyme
Oil on canvas, 28 x 36 (71.1 x 91.4)
Signed and dated LR: *Frank V. DuMond 1903*
Elizabeth DuMond Perry, Wilton

23 *Planting Season*   ILLUS. P. 67
1929: Grassy Hill, Lyme
Oil on panel, 24 x 30 (61 x 76.2)
Signed and dated LL: *Frank V. DuMond '29*
Collection of N. Robert Cestone, Rowayton
The scene depicted is on the artist's property.

Foote, Will Howe

24 *Connecticut Shore*   ILLUS. P. 68
c. 1920: Niantic Bay?
Oil on canvas board, 7 x 9 (17.8 x 22.9)
Signed LR: *Will Howe Foote*
Nan Greacen Faure

It is uncertain whether this painting and the remarkably similar view (cat. 56) by Foote's close friend Gregory Smith were painted at the same time. They could have been, because Old Lyme artists often did paint together in pairs or groups.

25 *The Golden Bough*
1921: Hamburg Cove, Lyme
Oil on canvas, 30 x 30 (76.2 x 76.2)
Signed LR: *Will Howe Foote*
Nancy Foote

26 *Summer*   ILLUS. P. 68
c. 1918: Old Lyme
Oil on canvas, 30 x 30 (76.2 x 76.2)
Signed LL: *Will Howe Foote*
S. K. T. Galleries

The scene is the Foote family garden in Old Lyme

27 *White's Point from Millstone Point*   ILLUS. P. 12
c. 1920: Millstone Point, Waterford
Oil on canvas, 18 x 16 (45.7 x 40.6)
Signed LR: *Will Howe Foote*
Phelan Collection

The artist's son, then a boy of ten or twelve, remembers having had to pose as "the female nude" for paintings like these and getting painful sunburns as reward. The Millstone nuclear power plant now sits where the artist did when he painted this scene.

Greacen, Edmund

28 *Noank Shipyard*   ILLUS. P. 69
1912: Noank
Oil on canvas, 20 x 24 (50.8 x 61)
Signed and dated LL: *Edmund Greacen/1912*
Grand Central Art Galleries

The Palmer Shipyard in Noank.

29 *Winter Landscape, Lieutenant River, Old Lyme*   ILLUS. P. 13
1917: Old Lyme
Oil on canvas, 22⅛ x 36⅛ (56.2 x 91.8)
Signed and dated LL: *Edmund Greacen/1917*
Nan Greacen Faure

30 *Winter Marshes, Old Lyme*   ILLUS. P. 70
c. 1910-14: Old Lyme
Oil on canvas, 24 x 29 (61 x 73.7)
No signature
Meredith Long & Co., Houston

Griffin, Walter

31 *Landscape–Old Lyme, Connecticut*
1908: Old Lyme
Hard point pastel, 6 x 12 (15.2 x 30.5)
Signed LL: *Walter Griffin*
Mr. and Mrs. Curtis A. Ley

32 *Summer*
1902: Hartford
Oil on panel, 6 x 8 (15.2 x 20.3)
Signed and dated on reverse: *Walter Griffin 1902/Hartford, Ct.*
Wadsworth Atheneum, Hartford, Gift of Mrs. Frank W. Cheney

33 *White Birch Trees, Old Lyme, Conn.*   ILLUS. P. 14
c. 1907: Old Lyme
Oil on canvas, 24 x 30 (61 x 76.2)
Signed LR: *Walter Griffin*
Mr. and Mrs. Milton Turner Schaeffer

Hassam, Childe

34 *Bridge at Old Lyme*
1922: Bow Bridge, Old Lyme
Etching and dry point, 8⅛ x 11⁵/₁₆ (20.6 x 43.8)
Initialled and dated in plate LL: *C. H. 1922;* monogrammed, margin LR
American Academy and Institute of Arts and Letters

35 *Bridge at Old Lyme*   ILLUS. P. 15
1908: Bow Bridge, Old Lyme
Oil on canvas, 24 x 27 (61 x 68.6)
Signed and dated LL: *Childe Hassam 1908*
The University of Georgia, Georgia Museum of Art, Eva Underhill Holbrook Collection of American Art, Gift of Alfred H. Holbrook, 1945

36 *Church at Old Lyme*
1924: Old Lyme
Etching, 7¼ x 6½ (18.4 x 16.5)
Monogrammed and dated in plate LL; monogrammed in pencil LR
Library of Congress
Same as cat. 182.

37 *Church at Old Lyme, Connecticut*   ILLUS. P. 70
1905: Old Lyme
Oil on canvas, 36 x 32 (91.4 x 81.3)
Signed and dated LR: *Childe Hassam 1905/Oct. 17*
Albright-Knox Art Gallery, Buffalo, New York, Albert H. Tracy Fund

38 *Landscape, Land of Nod*
1918: Branchville
Lithograph, 8⅞ x 14⅛ (22.5 x 36)
Signed and dated on stone: *Land of Nod/June 15, 1918/Childe Hassam;* monogrammed in pencil at edge LR (Griffith, 21. Edition of 55.)
Library of Congress

The subject is probably Nod Hill Road, where J. Alden Weir had his farm. Artists seem often to have referred to the area as the Land of Nod, an allusion to the mythical realm of pleasant dreams.

39 *Laurel in the Ledges*   ILLUS. P. 71
1906: Old Lyme
Oil on canvas, 20 x 30 (50.8 x 76.2)
Signed and dated LL: *Childe Hassam 1906*
Oliver B. James Collection of American Art, University Art Collections, Arizona State University, Tempe

40 *New Haven Green*   ILLUS. P. 71
1909: New Haven
Oil on canvas, 36 x 38½ (91.4 x 97.8)
Signed and dated LR: *Childe Hassam/N. H. 1909*
Detroit Athletic Club

Hassam's painting records the passing of "Quality
Row." The four buildings on the far side of the
Green, on Elm Street, between Church and Temple,
are (l. to r.): the New Haven Free Public Library
(under construction in 1909, dedicated in 1911), the
Thomas R. Trowbridge House (which stood until
1912), the Nathan Smith House, and the David C.
DeForest House (both torn down in 1910 to make way
for the County Courthouse). The three houses and
the Bristol House, which stood on the site of the
Library until 1907-08, were known as "Quality
Row." Hassam probably painted this from one of the
three Edward Malley Buildings. (Information from
Robert Egleston, Curator, New Haven Colony
Historical Society.)

41 *The Oak Tree*   ILLUS. P. 72
1905: Windham
Oil on canvas, 18 x 22 (45.7 x 55.9)
Signed and dated LL: *Childe Hassam 1905*
Private Collection

42 *Old Lace*
1915: Cos Cob
Etching, 7 x 7 (17.6 x 17.6)
Monogrammed and dated in plate LR;
monogrammed in pencil, margin LR.
Library of Congress

A view of the mill pond bridge in front of the Holley
House. Same as Cat. 117.

43 *Palmer's Dock, Cos Cob*
1915: Cos Cob
Etching and drypoint, 7⅞ x 5½ (20 x 14)
Initialled and dated in plate LC: *Cos Cob, C. H. 1915;*
monogrammed, margin LR
American Academy and Institute of
Arts and Letters

The dock is that of the Palmer & Duff Shipyard.

Lawson, Ernest
44 *The Duck Pond–Norfolk, Connecticut*   ILLUS. P. 15
Early 1930s: Norfolk
Oil on canvas laid on board, 16 x 40 (40.6 x 101.6)
Signed LL: *E. Lawson;* on reverse: *Duck Pond, Norfolk,
Conn. Ernest Lawson, 119 East 9th St., N.Y. City.*
Chapellier Galleries, Inc.

Lawson butted two canvases together to form a long
horizontal.

45 *Garden Landscape*   ILLUS. P. 72
n.d.: Greenwich?
Oil on canvas, 20 x 24 (50.8 x 61)
Signed LL: *E. Lawson*
The Brooklyn Museum

Lumis, Harriet R.
46 *October Haze, Connecticut*
c. 1918: Southeastern Connecticut?
Oil on canvas, 24 x 28 (61 x 71.1)
Signed LR: *Harriet R. Lumis*
Lamb Collection, Courtesy of R. H. Love Galleries,
Inc., Chicago

Metcalf, Willard L.
47 *May Pastoral*   ILLUS. P. 73
1907: Old Lyme
Oil on canvas, 37 x 39 (91.4 x 99)
Signed and dated LL: *W. L. Metcalf 1907*
Museum of Fine Arts, Boston, Charles Henry
Hayden Fund, 1908

48 *New England Afternoon*
c. 1925: Woodbury?
Oil on canvas, 38½ x 36 (97.8 x 91.4)
Signed LL: *W. L. Metcalf.*
Washington County Museum of Fine Arts,
Hagerstown, Maryland

"*New England Afternoon* scarcely needs a title, it is so
typical" (clipping from a 1926 Grand Rapids,
Michigan newspaper in artist's scrapbook, Archives of
American Art), and that makes the specific locale of
this painting hard to determine. Woodbury has been
suggested as the site, but certain elements are
disturbingly dissimilar.

49 *October*   ILLUS. P. 73
1908: Leete's Island
Oil on canvas, 26 x 29 (66 x 73.7)
Signed and dated LL: *W. L. Metcalf 1908*
Museum of Fine Arts, Springfield, Massachusetts,
Gift of the grandchildren of Frederick Harris.

Metcalf painted this picture of the Palatiah Leete house
(c. 1700) on Leete's Island in Guilford while boarding
at the nearby home of Mrs. Calvin Leete.

50 *The Trout Brook*   ILLUS. P. 72
1907: Probably Lyme
Oil on canvas, 26 x 28 (66 x 71.1)
Signed and dated LR: *W. L. Metcalf. 1907*
The Currier Gallery of Art, Manchester, New
Hampshire

Elizabeth G. de Veer has informed us that Metcalf
listed this painting as 1906 in his cash book,
presumably by mistake. Since he was often in Old
Lyme in both 1906 and 1907, the setting is probably
one in the neighborhood.

Ranger, Henry Ward
51 *Mason's Island from Noank*
c. 1900: Noank
Oil on wood panel, 12 x 16 (30.5 x 40.6)
Signed LL: *HWR*
Lyman Allyn Museum

52 *October, Mason's Island* ILLUS. P. 73
n.d.: Mason's Island
Oil on panel, 12 x 16 (30.5 x 40.6)
Estate stamp and number LL
Stone Ledge Studio Art Galleries, Noank

Robinson, Theodore

53 *Anchorage, Cos Cob, Ct.* ILLUS. P. 74
1894: Cos Cob
Oil on canvas, 20⅛ x 24⅛ (51.1 x 61.3)
Signed LR: *(Th. Robinson)*
Mr. and Mrs. William Marshall Fuller

54 *The E. M. J. Betty* ILLUS. P. 69
1894: Potter's Point, Cos Cob
Oil on canvas, 12¼ x 20 (31.1 x 50.8)
Signed and dated LR: *Th. Robinson/'94*
Geist Collection, Courtesy of R. H. Love Galleries,
Inc., Chicago

The subject is the last of the Cos Cob market boats,
The E. M. J. Beatty (the artist misspelled the name). It
made its last run just two years after this, in the year
that Robinson died.

55 *Sloop Cove* ILLUS. P. 16
c. 1894: Cos Cob
Oil on wood, 10¼ x 11¾ (26 x 29.8)
Signed LL: *Th. Robinson*
Private Collection

The cove was named for the oyster sloops that were
so often there. See the photograph on p. 87.

Smith, Edward Gregory

56 *Connecticut Shore* ILLUS. P. 68
c. 1920: Niantic Bay area?
Oil on canvas board, 10 x 13 (25.4 x 33)
Signed LR: *Edward G. Smith*
Nan Greacen Faure

See cat. 24.

Tryon, Dwight W.

57 *Glastonbury Meadows*
1881: Glastonbury
Oil on canvas, 15½ x 23½ (39.4 x 59.7)
Signed and dated LR: *D. W. Tryon/July, 1881*
Kenneth Lux Gallery

Twachtman, John H.

58 *Bridge in the Woods* ILLUS. P. 75
c. 1900: Round Hill, Greenwich
Oil on canvas, 26 x 14 (66 x 35.6)
No signature
Kennedy Galleries, Inc., New York City

Richard Boyle has said that Twachtman built this little
white bridge at the head of the pool on his farm in
about 1895. He painted it at least four times.

59 *The Dock, Bridgeport* ILLUS. P. 110
1889 or before: Bridgeport
Etching, 3⅞ x 6 (9.8 x 15.2)
Initialled in plate LL: *JHT*; initialled in pencil, margin
LR: *JHT per AT*
Prints Division, The New York Public Library, Astor,
Lenox, and Tilden Foundations

Same as cat. 143.

60 *Footbridge at Bridgeport* ILLUS. P. 76
1889 or before: Bridgeport
Pastel, 11¾ x 19½ (29.8 x 49.5)
Signed LR: *J. H. Twachtman*
Washington County Museum of Fine Arts,
Hagerstown, Maryland

There were several footbridges in Bridgeport during
the nineteenth century; Twachtman's closely
resembles the Stratford Avenue footbridge that
connected the older part of the city with East
Bridgeport. The etching (cat. 61) reverses the image.

61 *Footbridge, Bridgeport* ILLUS. P. 76
1889 or before: Bridgeport
Etching, 3¹⁵/₁₆ x 6 (10 x 15.2)
Initialled in plate LL: *J. H. T.*; initialled below plate
LR: *JHT & AT*
Addison Gallery of American Art, Phillips Academy,
Andover, Massachusetts, Gift of Mr. E. C. Shaw

Same as cat. 144. See note for cat. 60.

62 *From the Holley House* ILLUS. P. 18
c. 1890-1900: Cos Cob
Oil on canvas, 30 x 30 (76.2 x 76.2)
Signed LL: *J. H. Twachtman*
W. David Lindholm Collection

A view from the front terrace.

63 *The Harbor, Bridgeport*
1889 or before: Bridgeport
Etching, 4½ x 6⅝ (11.4 x 16.8)
Initialled in pencil, margin LR: *JHT per AT*
Prints Division, The New York Public Library, Astor,
Lenox, and Tilden Foundations

64 *Inner Harbor, Bridgeport*
1889 or before: Bridgeport
Etching, 6⅝ x 10⅛ (16.8 x 25.7)
No signature
Prints Division, The New York Public Library, Astor,
Lenox, and Tilden Foundations, Gift of J. Alden Weir,
1906

65 *The Little Bridge* ILLUS. P. 75
c. 1896: Round Hill, Greenwich
Oil on canvas, 25 x 25 (63.5 x 63.5)
Signed LR: *J. H. Twachtman*
The University of Georgia, Georgia Museum of Art,
Eva Underhill Holbrook Memorial Collection of
American Art, Gift of Alfred H. Holbrook, 1945

See note for cat. 58.

66 *November Haze*   ILLUS. P. 17
   c. 1897-98: Branchville
   Oil on canvas, 24¾ x 29¾ (62.9 x 75.6)
   Twachtman estate sale stamp in red LL
   R. H. Love Galleries, Inc., Chicago
   Formerly entitled *The Valley*.

67 *Spring*
   c. 1890-1900: Greenwich
   Oil on canvas, 18 x 15½ (45.7 x 39.4)
   Twachtman estate sale stamp in red LR
   Museum of Art, Rhode Island School of Design, Gift
   of Mrs. Gustav Radeke

68 *Twachtman's Home*
   c. 1890-1900: Round Hill, Greenwich
   Oil on canvas, 20 x 16 (50.8 x 40.6)
   Signed LL: *J. H. Twachtman*
   Robert C. Vose, Jr.

   Formerly entitled *Cottage Through the Trees*. The artist
   painted his house several times, sometimes even
   including the Stanford White portico he had added to
   the simple farmhouse.

69 *The Waterfall*
   c. 1890-1900: Round Hill, Greenwich
   Oil on canvas, 30 x 30⅛ (76.2 x 76.5)
   Signed LR: *J. H. Twachtman*
   Worcester Art Museum

70 *The Waterfall*   ILLUS. P. 70
   c. 1900: Round Hill, Greenwich
   Oil on canvas, 17 x 22 (43.2 x 55.9)
   Signed LR: *J. H. Twachtman*
   Addison Gallery of American Art, Phillips Academy,
   Andover, Massachusetts, The Candace C. Stimson
   Bequest

71 *Winter Silence*   ILLUS. P. 77
   c. 1890-1900: Round Hill, Greenwich
   Oil on canvas, 23 x 22½ (55.9 x 57.2)
   Signed LR: *J. H. Twachtman*
   Amherst College, Mead Art Museum

Vonnoh, Robert

72 *Pleasant Valley, Lyme, Connecticut*   ILLUS. P. 78
   1905 or after: Pleasant Valley, Lyme
   Oil on canvas, 24¼ x 30⅛ (61.6 x 76.5)
   Signed LR: *Vonnoh*
   Private Collection

   An inscription on the original stretcher (now
   unfortunately lost) is supposed to have read
   "September 30th, 1890," but that cannot be the date
   of this painting, since Vonnoh was then still in France.
   Indeed, the earliest time Vonnoh can be placed in Old
   Lyme is the summer of 1905.

Voorhees, Clark G.

73 *Essex Dock*
   1919: Essex?
   Oil on canvas, 18 x 25 (45.7 x 63.5)
   Signed LR: *Clark G. Voorhees*
   Clark Voorhees, Jr.

   The artist's son wonders if this painting might
   have been done at Newport, Rhode Island.

Walkley, David

74 *Quiambaug Cove Road*   ILLUS. P. 78
   1910: Stonington
   Oil on canvas, 20 x 24 (51 x 61)
   Signed LR: *David Walkley*
   Stone Ledge Studio Art Galleries, Noank

Weir, J. Alden

75 *The Ailanthus Tree*   ILLUS. P. 79
   c. 1906-08: Windham
   Oil on canvas, 29¾ x 25 (75.6 x 63.5)
   Signed LR: *J. Alden Weir*
   Private Collection

76 *Building a Dam, Shetucket*   ILLUS. P. 19
   1908: Shetucket River, Windham
   Oil on canvas, 31¼ x 40¼ (79.4 x 102.2)
   Signed LR: *J. Alden Weir*
   The Cleveland Museum of Art, Purchase from the
   J. H. Wade Fund

   The site must be the so-called Scotland Dam on
   Jerusalem Rd., not far from Weir's Windham home.
   Construction began in 1907 and ended in 1909. The
   Connecticut Light and Power Co. still operates the
   facility today. Despite its popular name, the dam is
   not in the town of Scotland but just over the line in
   Windham.

77 *The Farm*
   c. 1885-93: Branchville?
   Etching, image 2⅜ x 3¾ (5.9 x 9.4) (plate
   trimmed to plate marks)
   Initialled in plate LR
   Library of Congress

   After a pastel sketch by the artist.

78 *The Haystacks*
   c. 1885-89: Branchville or Windham
   Etching and drypoint, 5⅛ x 4½ (13.2 x 11.5)
   Initialled in plate LL; signed in pencil LL: *J. Alden Weir*
   Library of Congress

79 *Landscape*   ILLUS. P. 80
   1894: Windham area?
   Oil on canvas, 24 x 36 (61 x 91.4)
   Signed LR: *J. Alden Weir '94*
   New Britain Museum of American Art, Harriet
   Russell Stanley Fund

80 *Landscape*   ILLUS. P. 80
   1907: Willimantic?
   Watercolor, 18¾ x 14⅛ (47.6 x 35.9)
   Signed LC: *J. Alden Weir '07*
   Dr. Herbert J. Smokler

81 *Landscape and Farm*
   c. 1895: Probably Branchville
   Oil on canvas, 22 x 27 (55.9 x 68.6)
   Signed LR: *J. Alden Weir*
   Delaware Art Museum, Gift of the Friends of Art

82 *Norwich on the Thames*
   n.d.: Norwich
   Oil on canvas, 24 x 33½ (61 x 68.9)
   Signed LL: *J. Alden Weir*
   Mrs. Charles Burlingham

83 *Obweebetuck*
   c. 1908: From Weir's garden, Windham Center
   Oil on canvas, 24¼ x 33¾ (61.6 x 85.7)
   Signed LR: *J. Alden Weir*
   Corcoran Gallery of Art, Bequest of George M.
   Oyster, Jr.

   Weir painted this small mountain in Windham several
   times.

84 *Roscoe's Barn*
   c. 1885-89: Branchville?
   Etching, 3⅝ x 6¼ (9.3 x 16)
   Initialled in plate LL
   Library of Congress

85 *South Norwalk, #2*
   c. 1885-89: South Norwalk
   Etching, 5¼ x 3⅞ (13.4 x 9.9)
   Initialled in plate LR
   Library of Congress

   Weir may have created this image while he was
   waiting at the South Norwalk train station to transfer
   to the branch line that would take him to his farm
   near Ridgefield.

86 *The Train from Norwich*
   n.d.: Windham?
   Oil on canvas, 24¼ x 33¾ (61.6 x 85.7)
   No signature
   Mrs. Charles Burlingham

87 *The Webb Farm*
   c. 1885-89: Windham Center
   Etching and drypoint, 5¹⁵/₁₆ x 7⅞ (15.2 x 20)
   Signed in pencil LR: *J. Alden Weir*
   Library of Congress
   People named Webb owned a farm adjacent to Weir's
   farm in Windham Center. Same as cat. 157.

88 *Willimantic, Connecticut*   ILLUS. P. 80
   1903: Willimantic
   Oil on canvas, 20 x 24 (50.8 x 61)
   Signed LL: *J. Alden Weir*

Oliver B. James Collection of American Art,
University Art Collections, Arizona State University,
Tempe, Arizona

One of Weir's favorite subjects, this view is of the
mid-nineteenth-century American Thread Company
mills.

89 *The Wooden Bridge*
   c. 1885-89: Probably Branchville
   Etching, 4⅞ x 6⅞ (12.4 x 17.4)
   Signed in pencil LL: *J. Alden Weir*
   Library of Congress
   Same as cat. 158.

White, Henry C.
90 *The Connecticut River–Reflections*
   c. 1895-1900: Probably Hartford
   Pastel on gray paper, 10 x 13 (25.4 x 33)
   Signed by son LL: *Henry C. White per N. C. W.*
   Nelson Holbrook White

91 *Indian Summer*
   1892: Hartford
   Oil on panel, 12 x 16 (30.5 x 40.6)
   Signed LR: *H. C. White*
   Nelson Holbrook White

92 *New London Harbor*   ILLUS. P. 81
   c. 1924: New London
   Oil on board, 14 x 10 (35.6 x 25.4)
   Signed LR: *H. C. White*
   Lyman Allyn Museum

Wiggins, Guy C.
93 *North Pier–Noank, Connecticut*
   1925: Noank
   Oil on board, 8 x 10 (20.3 x 25.4)
   Signed LL: *Guy Wiggins*
   Gallery New World, Darien

94 *Mantle of Winter*
   1924: Hamburg Cove, Lyme
   Oil on canvas, 25⁵/₁₆ x 30 (64.2 x 76.2)
   Signed LL: *Guy Wiggins*
   The William Benton Museum of Art, Louise Crombie
   Beach Memorial Collection

   Reputedly a scene from the artist's studio window.

95 *Under Gray Skies*   ILLUS. P. 81
   n.d.: Hamburg Cove or Essex?
   Oil on canvas, 25½ x 30¼ (64.8 x 76.8)
   Signed LL: *Guy Wiggins*
   New Britain Museum of American Art, Estate of
   Frances Whittlesey

6   Emil Carlsen, *Connecticut Hillside,* c. 1920

15   Charles H. Davis, *Across the River in Mystic,* c. 1918

16   Charles H. Davis, *A Bright Winter Morning,* c. 1929

18　Charles H. Davis, *Morning Sunlight,* c. 1895

23　Frank Vincent DuMond, *Planting Season,* 1929

24 Will Howe Foote, *Connecticut Shore,* c. 1920   56 Edward Gregory Smith, *Connecticut Shore,* c. 1920

26 Will Howe Foote, *Summer,* c. 1918

28   Edmund Greacen, *Noank Shipyard,* 1912

54   Theodore Robinson, *The E. M. J. Betty,* 1894

30   Edmund Greacen, *Winter Marshes, Old Lyme,* c. 1910–14

37   Childe Hassam, *Church at Old Lyme, Connecticut,* 1905

39   Childe Hassam, *Laurel in the Ledges,* 1906

40   Childe Hassam, *New Haven Green,* 1909

41 Childe Hassam, *The Oak Tree*, 1905

45 Ernest Lawson, *Garden Landscape*

50 Willard L. Metcalf, *The Trout Brook*, 1907

72

47 Willard L. Metcalf, *May Pastoral*, 1907

49 Willard L. Metcalf, *October*, 1908

52 Henry Ward Ranger, *October, Mason's Island*

53   Theodore Robinson, *Anchorage, Cos Cob, Ct.*, 1894

65   John H. Twachtman, *The Little Bridge,* c. 1896

58   John H. Twachtman, *Bridge in the Woods,* c. 1900

60   John H. Twachtman, *Footbridge at Bridgeport,* c. 1889

61   John H. Twachtman, *Footbridge, Bridgeport,* c. 1889

A favored subject of Twachtman's, the busy Inner Harbor
of Bridgeport is shown here as it looked at the time he
was working there, c. 1888. The Stratford Avenue
footbridge in the center may have been one of
Twachtman's subjects.

70 John H. Twachtman, *The Waterfall,* c. 1900

71 John H. Twachtman, *Winter Silence,* c. 1890–1900

72　Robert Vonnoh, *Pleasant Valley, Lyme, Connecticut,* c. 1905

74　David Walkley, *Quiambaug Cove Road,* 1910

75   J. Alden Weir, *The Ailanthus Tree,* c. 1906–08

79 J. Alden Weir, *Landscape,* 1894

80 J. Alden Weir, *Landscape,* 1907

88 J. Alden Weir, *Willimantic, Connecticut,* 1903

92   Henry C. White, *New London Harbor,* c. 1924

95   Guy C. Wiggins, *Under Gray Skies*

The Cos Cob Clapboard School

SUSAN G. LARKIN

They were often noisy in the evening, those artists and writers who boarded at the Holley House. Cos Cob villagers out for an after-dinner stroll could hear the debates John Twachtman and Lincoln Steffens stirred up and the debaters' laughter once the argument was settled.[1] During the day, it was different. The sight of a painter and his easel at the end of the dock was as familiar to the villagers as the gulls wheeling over the harbor. They were not even astonished to find the artists painting their simple frame houses, a subject they chose so frequently that Childe Hassam called them "the Cos Cob Clapboard School of Art."[2] The villagers must occasionally have wondered though what brought these visitors to Cos Cob in the first place.

WHY A COLONY?

The art colony that gathered in Cos Cob beginning about 1890 had its origins an ocean away, in the European studios of the seventies and eighties. There, the art students who would become the first generation of American Impressionists — Twachtman, Hassam, Theodore Robinson and J. Alden Weir — enjoyed the camaraderie of the Paris and Munich academies. This good fellowship extended to vacations, when students went off together to paint outdoors in a picturesque spot. As a student at Munich's Royal Academy, Twachtman joined one such group in the summer of 1876, sharing a secularized monastery in southern Bavaria with the cattle of the local peasants.[3] He went to Italy as an instructor with another group, the followers of his own former teacher, Frank Duveneck.[4] Outside Paris, Twachtman worked in an informal colony which included two artists who were later to join him in Cos Cob — Robinson and Hassam—as well as a future Old Lyme artist, Willard Metcalf. Robert Louis Stevenson was also there, writing under a tree while his friends toiled at their canvases.[5] On their wedding trip, Twachtman and his bride, the former Martha Scudder of Cincinnati, joined the brothers J. Alden and John F. Weir for an etching and painting trip through Holland.[6]

After returning to the United States, the young artists continued their search for congenial companions at picturesque sites. Twachtman wrote to Weir in June, 1880, that he had finally settled at Nonquit Beach, Massachusetts, after searching the northern New England coast for an agreeable place to spend the summer. "I was on the point of going to Mt. Desert," he wrote, but "met an artist friend who wanted to know why I didn't go to Nonquit . . . . He told me that . . . other artists were down there."[7]

For its members, among them Twachtman, Weir and William Merritt Chase, New York's Tile Club provided the benefits of a colony from 1877 to 1887. Best remembered for its elaborate outings, which combined serious work with sometimes sophomoric pranks, the club was an important alliance among the avant-garde of its day.[8] J. Alden Weir touched on the benefits of such associations in a letter to his parents: "I begin to think that an artist can be bred a good workman anywhere if he has some healthy men to work with who are not influenced by the old pictures except in sentiment."[9]

This concept, that an artist might work best in an informal group, contradicted the stereotype of the lonely painter starving in his garret. If the work of a serious artist is essentially solitary, the more so if he has declared his independence of "the old pictures," then what did these men hope to gain by clustering together?

"Misery loves company" might be the simplest answer. While these high-spirited young men were anything but morose, they were generally misunderstood by the critics of their day and ignored by the wealthy collectors. Only from one another did they receive the encouragement that enabled them to keep working toward an original style. Moreover, banding together permitted small economies important to impecunious artists. A painter might be spared the expense of models' fees, for example, by painting his colleagues and their families. Most important, working together facilitated the cross-fertilization of ideas, spawning influences that were decisive in the careers of several Connecticut artists.

A colony required not only people, however, but also a place: a place where artists could find inexpensive living accommodations and, above all, a place worth painting. Cos Cob in the 1890s easily fulfilled the first requirement. At least three modest boarding houses served both summer visitors who could not afford the elaborate new hotels in nearby Greenwich and thrifty local residents who leased their homes to city people for the summer and moved into these neighborhood inns, whose rates were low enough to permit them to turn a profit on the season's rent.[10] The best known of these boarding houses was the rambling frame inn on Strickland Road owned by Edward Holley and his good-natured wife Josephine.[11]

The idea that their village was worth painting would probably never have occurred to the people of Cos Cob.[12] In the mid-nineteenth century, Greenwich was a prosperous farming community, producing fruit, vegetables, meat, milk, hay and grain for the New York market. The Upper Landing, at Mianus, was the main shipping point for city-bound produce, but oxcarts heaped with potatoes rumbled past the Holley House to Cos Cob's Lower Landing (fig. 1). The village bustled when the weekly market boats arrived,

as farmers came in from back country to unload their wagons, shop at one of the two general stores, and drop into Toby Burke's saloon.[13]

In addition to the market boats, oyster sloops and fishing schooners worked out of Cos Cob harbor, often dodging the canoes of children paddling over to Riverside to visit friends.[14] Until it burned in 1899, an eighteenth-century mill at the mouth of the tidal pond added the clank of its gears to the steady beat of the carpenter's hammer at the Palmer & Duff Shipyard (fig. 2). The smells of oakum and new-milled wheat and the clean salt breezes off Long Island Sound mingled with the fragrances of roses and hollyhocks in cottage gardens.

In short, Cos Cob was a village like many others along the New England coast in the last quarter of the nineteenth century. What brought artists here rather than to any of a dozen similar villages?

Quite literally, the railroad. The first train chuffed across the newly-completed Mianus River Bridge on December 27, 1848.[15] By 1870, when the first Cos Cob railroad station was built, it took about eighty minutes to get to midtown Manhattan.[16] A special train, added in 1882, made the run in just thirty-eight minutes—nine minutes faster than today's express.[17] About twenty trains a day linked Greenwich to the

Holley House. The Holley House in the snow (after 1899). The oldest part of the house was built in 1685. As a residence in constant use for nearly 300 years, the house combines architectural elements from a variety of periods. Now owned by the Historical Society of the Town of Greenwich, it is called the Bush-Holley House, after its first-known and last private owners.

Map of Cos Cob and Greenwich

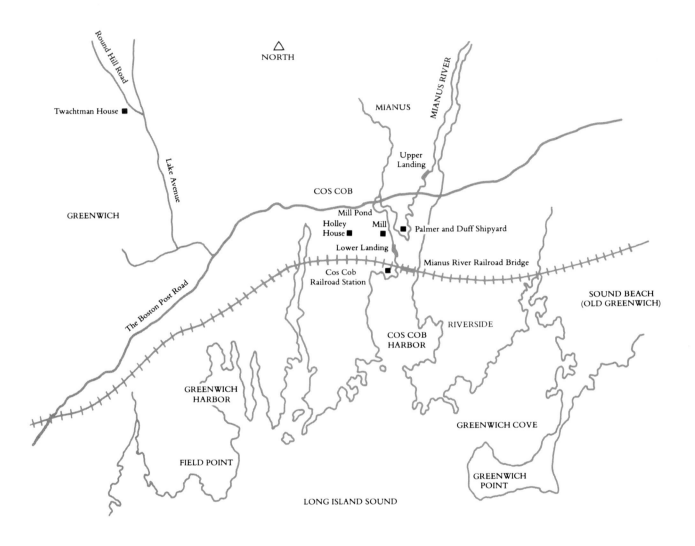

Fig. 1 **Cos Cob Lower Landing,** c. 1900. Cos Cob village as seen from the harbor: left to right, a waterfront warehouse used to store farm goods before shipment to New York; the lattice-framed building which housed Toby Burke's saloon on the ground floor and rooms for the Burke family and boarders above; and the post office. Only the post office building (now a private home) is still standing. The Holley House is out of the picture to the right.

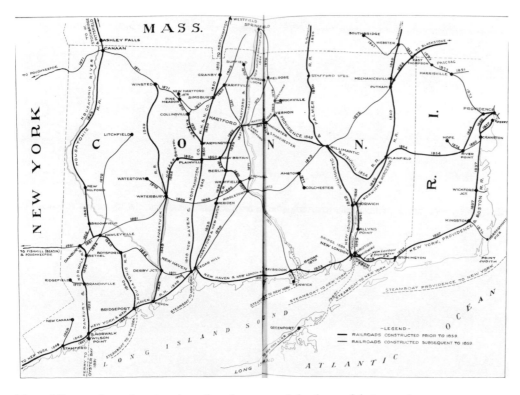

Map of Connecticut, showing the railroad routes and the dates of their opening

Cos Cob Mill. The mill as seen from the Holley House, with miller Edward P. Holley framed in the doorway. Limestone, like that piled to the right, was ground to make plaster.

Cos Cob Mill. Edward P. Holley inside the mill he managed in Cos Cob. Built in 1724, the tide-powered mill supplied meal to Revolutionary soldiers and early settlers in New York and Connecticut. It burned in 1899.

Fig. 2. **Palmer & Duff Shipyard.** Many of the boats that worked out of Cos Cob were built and repaired at Palmer & Duff's. One of the busiest spots in the village, the shipyard was a popular subject among the artists.

Oyster Sloop. The *Ann-Gertrude* is typical of the oyster sloops that worked out of Cos Cob and Greenwich harbors. In the early 1900s, more than thirty such sailboats worked off Greenwich shores.

Holley Ladies. Two generations of hostesses to two generations of artists: Josephine Holley (seated) and her daughter Constant, on the porch of the Holley House, c. 1899. Constant Holley married the artist Elmer MacRae in 1900.

Twachtman. John H. Twachtman in the Holley House, probably in the winter of 1901-02, wearing the heavy white turtleneck which was his habitual winter garb.

Shucking Oysters. The artists Charles Ebert, Walter Fitch, and Childe Hassam shuck oysters behind the Holley House (c. 1900-05), as a small friend looks on.

city, enabling artists to maintain studios there, stay in touch with their dealers, even teach, and still spend much of their time in the country.

TWACHTMAN SETTLES IN GREENWICH

The founder of the Cos Cob art colony, John Twachtman, may have considered the rail link from Greenwich to Branchville, where his close friend J. Alden Weir had spent summers since 1883,[18] as important as that to New York. The Twachtmans first lived in Greenwich in the summer of 1886. That September the family moved to Cos Cob.[19] Though there is no record of where they stayed, they could not have helped at least knowing of the Holleys' old house overlooking the mill pond.

Those were bad times financially for Twachtman, alleviated somewhat by a commission to work on a cyclorama in Chicago. After the project was completed, the family rented a place near Weir's Branchville home in 1888.[20] Weir had just bought an etching press,[21] and the two friends resumed the side-by-side printmaking they had enjoyed seven years earlier in Holland. They roamed the countryside around Branchville — Twachtman going as far afield as Bridgeport — recording their impressions on copper plates small enough to tuck into a pocket. Weir probably sketched *South Norwalk* (cat. 156) at the train station there while waiting to transfer from the main New York–New Haven line, which passed through Greenwich, to the branch line that would take him to his farm near Ridgefield. While Twachtman's etchings merely suggest the presence of man, Weir often used the medium for portraits of his friends. Twachtman created at least two etchings in Newport, where he conducted a summer class in 1889,[22] but when Weir was forced to drop printmaking in the early nineties because the close work strained his eyes,[23] Twachtman stopped as well.

Twachtman probably lived in Branchville only for the summer of 1888, moving back to Greenwich that fall. The strongest evidence for this dating is the painting *Icebound,* the first in a series depicting the waterfall on what was to become Twachtman's farm. *Icebound,* now in the collection of the Art Institute of Chicago, was first exhibited in June, 1889, suggesting that it was painted the previous winter.[24] Twachtman was not able to buy land until he had a secure source of income: the teaching career at the Art Students League which began in the fall of 1889 and continued until his death.[25]. However, he had probably lived as a tenant on the property known as Hangroot, which he bought in two installments — three acres with a house in

February, 1890, supplemented by an additional thirteen acres the following year.[26] His identification on the warrantee deed as "John Henry Twachtman of said town of Greenwich" further indicates that he had been a resident of the area before he became a landowner.

After years of renting, Twachtman undoubtedly knew what he wanted should he ever be able to buy. By all accounts he got it. The artist took his seven-year-old son Alden (named after Weir) to inspect the Round Hill Road property which is crossed by Horseneck Brook. As they walked over the land, Twachtman suddenly threw up his arms and shouted, "This is it!"[27] Twachtman eventually bought the farm and for the last twelve years of his life painted it again and again: the brook, with its rocky cascade and hemlock-fringed pool; the house, to which he added as his family grew; the gardens, where he and his wife puttered as happily as any modern suburbanites.[28]

For Twachtman, unlike Weir and many other turn-of-the-century artists, the country was home year-round. While Weir lived in Connecticut from about May to November, spending the remaining months in New York,[29] Twachtman enjoyed winter as well as summer on his farm. In a letter to Weir postmarked Greenwich, December 16, 1891, Twachtman wrote, "I can see how necessary it is to live always in the country — at all seasons of the year."[30] Twachtman spent as little time as possible in Manhattan — two days a week for his classes at the Art Students League,[31] plus occasional periods when he was preparing for an exhibition. His dislike of the city is reflected in a letter he wrote to Josephine Holley from the Players Club (he had been staying at the Holley House for several months while his family was travelling in Europe):

. . . in the morning I shall wake up and — no — not walk out onto the upper porch to see what the day is like — but look down into an air-shaft and when in the street see the ugly holes of the sub-way on Fourth Avenue. If the whole thing were only covered with snow and made beautiful.[32]

If Twachtman thought snow could improve Fourth Avenue, he was awed by its transformation of Round Hill Road. Eventually his students would share his love of snowy landscapes, and the Holley House would be nearly as crowded with young artists during the winter holidays as in the summer. Twachtman dashed off a note to Mrs. Holley on New Year's Day, 1899, telling her to expect thirty to thirty-five students.[33] At first, however, the Cos Cob art classes were held during the summer, probably beginning in 1890. J. Alden Weir shared the instruction, at least in 1892 and 1893.[34]

Most of the summer students were enrolled in Twachtman's and Weir's winter classes at the Art Students League. Weir taught painting at the League, but Twachtman handled Preparatory Antique, a required beginning course that involved drawing from plaster casts.[35] While Twachtman considered this tedious drill essential to an artist's training,[36] the class offered no opportunity for him to influence his students' style. If he exerted any such influence in the winter sessions, it was only in his criticism of the sketches he insisted they bring in from outside.[37] In Cos Cob, however, the emphasis was entirely different. The studio-weary young artists had come to paint outdoors, and Twachtman was in a position to direct any Impressionist tendencies they may have shown. The Greenwich artist "was the first teacher to bring the theories and methods of Impressionism before art students in this country."[38] He did so not at the Art Students League but in his classes at Cos Cob.

Ernest Lawson was among the first summer students. A classmate's appraisal of his Cos Cob work indicates the slant of the instruction there: "Ernest Lawson was the leading member of the class . . . for from the first he got hold of things, and painted canvases made of color and filled with light and air."[39] This approach explains both the Cos Cob school's appeal and its decline. While few can deny the charm of the delicate works produced under Twachtman's influence, young artists could successfully fill only so many canvases with "light and air." Twachtman's strength became his followers' weakness; his subtle understatement, their lack of anything to say.

Twachtman was a moody and demanding teacher, capable of cruelty to students who lacked talent. Teaching was never a joy to him but simply a means of

Fig. 3. **Japanese Tea Ceremony.** A tea ceremony on a Cos Cob porch decorated with paper fans, Japanese lanterns, hanging scrolls, Oriental rugs, and flowers. The Japanese man in the background was a student at the summer school. The kimono-clad young women, probably also art students, may have included the models for Childe Hassam's paintings *The Goldfish Window* and *Listening to the Orchard Oriole.*

Cos Cob, c. 1900. Cos Cob village as seen from across the millpond bridge (it doubled as a dam). Left to right: warehouses; Toby Burke's saloon; the post office; and the Holley House (partly hidden behind trees). The lattice of the Brush house is visible to the right of the barn.

supporting his family without having to paint saleable pictures. At Cos Cob, however, among his friends and better students, he was more relaxed than in New York.[40] The kindly J. Alden Weir also grudged the time teaching took from his painting,[41] but he was a popular instructor whose students' openness was praised by Mary Cassatt.[42] The two friends were magnets attracting their idealistic followers to Cos Cob.

Charles Ebert had been one of Twachtman's students in Italy even before he enrolled at the Art Students League.[43] Ebert's summers in Cos Cob resulted in a colony romance and his marriage in 1903 to another student, Mary Roberts. The Eberts settled in Greenwich, later becoming active in the Greenwich Society of Artists, before moving to Old Lyme in 1919.[44]

D. Putnam Brinley may have been the colony's only native son. The Riverside resident studied under Twachtman at the Art Students League — as did everyone who went through that school from 1890 to 1902 — but there is no firm evidence that he was a formal member of the Cos Cob classes. It is certain, however, that the lanky artist was a familiar sight to the Holley House group as he passed by on his way to visit a charming young writer whose family summered in the neighborhood.[45] Since the colony included both Brinley's teacher and his classmates, he must have painted with them at least occasionally.

If Brinley was unique in the colony as a native son, another student was valued for his foreignness. A Japanese man among Twachtman's summer students taught the Holleys' daughter the art of Oriental flower arrangement and conducted tea ceremonies for kimono-clad American young ladies[46] (fig. 3). The presence of the Japanese artist suggests a source of the kimonos Childe Hassam's models wore in such paintings as *Listening to the Orchard Oriole* (cat. 114, illus. p. 107). More important, the student was a direct source of information on the Japanese art Twachtman and Weir admired so enthusiastically.

From autumn, 1893, through spring, 1894, the Impressionist Theodore Robinson noted in his diary his long discussions of Japanese art with Twachtman and Weir, the hours they spent poring over Japanese prints together, even the dinner at Weir's New York house with Twachtman "and a Japanese gentleman who explained certain things about prints and books."[47] Each of the three American Impressionists purchased one or more Japanese prints,[48] but it was Twachtman whose poetic, evocative landscapes demonstrated the greatest Oriental influence.

Robinson was a frequent visitor to Greenwich from 1892 to 1894, sometimes staying with the Twachtmans, other times boarding in the neighborhood. Early in the summer of 1894, after the death of the Captain Merritt at whose home he had been boarding in Greenwich, he moved to Cos Cob, about four miles from Twachtman's house, taking a room at the Holleys'. "Holly [sic] house built in 1664 they say — some rather nice wood-work," he noted. "Walked around by the R.R. bridge to Mianus and back. Some fine things — little white boats near the Sound."[49]

So strongly did Robinson respond to the "fine things" he found in Cos Cob that he considered buying a house there, even making the rounds with a realtor. He decided instead to spend the next summer — the last of his life, as it turned out — in Vermont. That decision was probably unwise. The artist himself was dissatisfied with his Vermont work,[50] and a recent biographer has judged that "Perhaps Robinson's most successful American canvases are those which he painted at Cos Cob during the summer of 1894."[51]

THE EXCHANGE OF IDEAS

Robinson's sojourns in the Greenwich area influenced not only his work but also Twachtman's. Before he came to Connecticut, Robinson had painted near Monet's home in Giverny, a small town about as far from Paris as Greenwich is from New York. Though Robinson admired Monet's work, he remained more concerned with realism than the French master.[52] Robinson seems to have served, however, as a carrier of the French Impressionist influence to Twachtman, whose work reflected a modified Impressionism in the late 1880s, when Robinson returned briefly from France.[53]

Twachtman, in turn, may have guided Robinson away from excessive realism. After visiting his friend in October, 1893, Robinson admitted that some of Twachtman's paintings "make my things seem prosaic and heavy."[54] Twachtman was a master of artistic economy, suggesting rather than stating, retaining only those details that heightened the mood he hoped to convey. This characteristic is especially evident in *Waterfall* (cat. 151, illus. p.112), a painting as subtle as the Japanese art Twachtman so admired. By about 1893, Robinson, too, had ventured toward abstraction, most decisively in *Landscape* (cat. 136).

Twachtman may also have steered Robinson away from the sentimentality to which he was prone in paintings that included the human figure. In many of Robinson's French works, the figure (usually a pretty girl) is a major element, pushing the paintings to the borderline of nineteenth-century anecdotal art. Most of his Cos Cob canvases, on the other hand, are pure landscapes, as are nearly all of Twachtman's. In one that does contain a figure, *The E.M.J. Betty,* the human is a minor note subordinated to the total composition (cat. 54, illus. p. 69).

Robinson used photographs for most of his French figure paintings, a practice he followed in only one Greenwich work, a delightful study of Twachtman's daughters crossing the brook near their home (fig. 4). "Took photos of Margery and Elsie at brook, 5 p.m., crossing on the stepping stones," he noted on June 9, 1893. Six days later, perhaps after he had developed the film, Robinson recorded that he had "Commenced" a 'Stepping-Stones' with Elsie and Marjorie crossing a charming spot, overshadowed by hickory foliage."

Betraying their photographic origin, the poses in Robinson's figure studies are generally static: a peasant woman standing beside a well, two girls reading (rather uncomfortably) in the bow of a rowboat, a young woman in a picture hat lolling in tall meadow grass. *Stepping Stones,* on the other hand, portrays two barefoot children picking their way across a stream.

The squirmy age of the models justifies the preliminary snapshot; the finished work is as fresh and full of motion as its fair-haired young subjects.

Robinson's enjoyment of Cos Cob resulted not only from the satisfying work he did there but also from the companionship the colony offered. While staying at the Holley House, he took the train to Branchville to spend Sunday with the Weirs. Leonard Ochtman, the Dutch-born landscape painter who lived in the Mianus Valley, invited Robinson for dinner followed by a drive around Sound Beach. With two other artists, he sailed to Indian Harbor, stopping for a swim on the way home. Ernest Lawson, back in town briefly between trips to France, showed Robinson the paintings he had done abroad (Robinson was unimpressed). And ebullient Childe Hassam, with whom Robinson often dined in New York, might be up at Twachtman's place, helping to build the foundation for another addition.[55]

Hassam's first known Cos Cob works are *Smelt Fishers* and *The Red Mill,* dated 1896. His last work in the area was probably *Clarissa's Window,* an oil study of the Holley's granddaughter painted in 1923.[56] In the twenty-seven years between his first and last known

Fig. 4. Theodore Robinson, *Stepping Stones.* Oil on canvas, 21½" x 28½". Hirschl & Adler Galleries, New York City.

Cos Cob works, Hassam produced dozens of others in the village. Those pictures reflect crucial changes in the art colony and its world.

By the time Hassam painted *Smelt Fishers,* Robinson had died in poverty in New York City. Six years later, John Henry Twachtman, the dominant personality in the art colony, died in Gloucester, where he had been conducting a summer class.[57] Fortunately for the continuation of the colony, one of Twachtman's students, Elmer Livingston MacRae, had married the Holleys' daughter in 1900 and moved into the old house. Had Constant Holley married a Greenwich businessman, the art colony would probably have dwindled rapidly after Twachtman's death. Instead, for about twenty-five years, she and her husband continued to attract artists to Cos Cob.

And not only artists. The front porch of the Holley House resembled a humanities seminar, with painters, writers, actresses, editors and journalists discussing the most favorable conditions for the creation of art and the most graceful way to dive off the mill pond bridge. Lincoln Steffens, known for his exposés of urban corruption, liked the area so much he bought a home in Riverside. Naturalist Ernest Thompson Seton bought land in Cos Cob, where the local boys he organized as Woodcraft Indians camped out in real tepees and paddled birchbark canoes.[58] Don Seitz, business manager of the *New York World,* lived on Strickland Road just around the bend from the Holley House. Winfield S. Moody of the *Evening Sun* and *McClure's* art editor August Jaccacci also settled nearby. The potter Leon Gambetta Volkmar, Gilman Hall of *Ainslee's* and *Everybody's,* humor columnist Bert Leston Taylor, and writer Jean Webster were among the others who gathered at the Holley House.[59]

While most of the writers of the Cos Cob colony are little known today, the reputation of one has been enhanced by time. A now elderly lady who grew up in the neighborhood remembers "Willa Cather in her cape, passing the house, extending a courteous 'good morning.'"[60] J. Alden Weir's daughter also cited Cather as a regular visitor to the Holley House,[61] and a book inscribed to Constant Holley MacRae from Willa Cather in 1925 reflects the writer's affection for the family.[62] Cather mentions Cos Cob in her novel *The Song of the Lark,* albeit in an unflattering context. Landry, a minor character,

. . . was born, and spent the first fifteen years of his life, on a rocky Connecticut farm not far from Cos Cob. His father was an ignorant, violent man, a bungling father and a brutal husband The farmhouse, dilapidated and damp, stood in a hollow beside a marshy pond.[63]

Twachtman at Charades. Artists often played charades on the front porch of the Holley House. The singer is unidentified; his accompanist is John Henry Twachtman. (Original photograph is labeled November 7, 1890.)

Charades, c. 1902. Constant and Elmer MacRae play charades with guests on the Holley House porch. They seem to be voyagers on a steamship. Mrs. MacRae (the former Constant Holley) is the woman to the left; her husband is wearing the soft cap.

The marshy pond was undoubtedly the mill pond; the dilapidated house could have been almost any in Cos Cob, including the Holleys'.

Childe Hassam's *Couch on the Porch, Cos Cob* (now in a private collection) is said to depict Miss Cather. Painted at the Holley House in the summer of 1914, when Cather was writing *The Song of the Lark,* it shows a dark-haired woman lounging on a sofa reading a book. Because the model is facing away from the viewer, the most that can be said with certainty is that her hairstyle closely resembles the writer's.

GREENWICH BECOMES A SUBURB

While Hassam was portraying the new members of the colony, the village as he, Twachtman and Robinson had known it was changing rapidly. Theodore Robinson painted the last of the Cos Cob market boats, the *E.M.J. Beatty,* in 1894 (cat. 54, illus. p. 69). Just two years later, in the year Robinson died, it made its final run to New York.[64] The *Beatty's* retirement sealed Cos Cob's lingering decline as a shipping center for local farm produce. In the mid-1800s, the market boats carried as much as 28,000 bushels of potatoes, 210 tons of hay, and two tons of poultry a week from Greenwich to the city. The trains gradually displaced the boats as produce carriers until, by 1911, they were carrying more farm products in than out.[65] The trains had made Greenwich land more valuable as lawn than as pasture, and the town's population more than doubled between 1890 and 1920.[66] The railroad, which had helped make Cos Cob an art colony, was turning it into a suburb.

Many of the new residents were former summer people. Some were super-rich, like the collectors of French Impressionist art, the H. O. Havemeyers, but most were middle-class commuters. Steffens explained the colony's distinction between the area's older residents and its new ones:

The townspeople and fishermen were all right; they fitted into the land- and seascapes, but toward . . . the successful New Yorkers who were buying up Greenwich and modernizing that lovely old town, we were such snobs that after cutting us and then discovering that we were cutting them, they used to try to get in with us. And they couldn't.[67]

For their part, the townspeople and fishermen seem to have accepted the artists, despite their Yankee suspicion of outsiders.[68] Cos Cob youngsters felt as free to hang over a painter's shoulder as to play in the sailmaker's loft. One little girl, resting her head against Childe Hassam as he painted her house, declared that she knew he was an artist because he smelled like one.[69]

The chill between the colony and the commuters gradually diminished. The artists may have recognized the prosperous newcomers as potential collectors; the commuters, on the other hand, began to value the town's artistic reputation as an added status symbol. When Leonard Ochtman, Charles Ebert, Elmer MacRae, and others formed the Greenwich Society of Artists in 1912, an editorialist predicted smugly that "in time something like the atmosphere of Barbizon, Giverny, and of similar places abroad, should attach to the other charms which make Greenwich a naturally adorable place of residence."[70]

From the artists' point of view, the area was becoming less adorable with each new sign of modernization. At first, they adapted to the changes. When the railroad drawbridge over the Mianus River was being renovated, they were initially indignant that the construction destroyed the view and the quiet they had left the city to enjoy. Before long, however, Lincoln Steffens found "all the Cos Cob school with their easels set and painting the noisy, dirty bridge improvement."[71] Childe Hassam lavished as much sparkling light and color on his version of the construction site as on any garden scene (cat. 115, illus. p. 21). Perhaps the Cos Cob artists' ready acceptance of the bridge stemmed from their habit of seeking beauty in familiar subjects: a woodland brook rather than crashing surf; a modest saltbox rather than a grandiose mansion. As they became accustomed to the railroad bridge, they could find something to appreciate even in its graceless span.

The power plant was harder to accept. An ugly concrete pile built in 1906-07 to supply power to the New York–New Haven trains, its smokestacks showered soot for a mile around, graying Constant MacRae's cherished flowerbeds and making it more difficult than ever to keep the big house clean. But Childe Hassam didn't flinch even at this: his etching *Cos Cob* shows the ramshackle riverfront warehouses with the power-plant stacks belching smoke in the background (cat. 109, illus. p. 106). Hindsight tempts us to read the print as a symbol of the conflict between the picturesque old (the warehouses) and the ugly new (the smokestacks), but Hassam probably intended no such interpretation. He was a faithful recorder of what he saw; the smokestacks were there, so he included them.

THE ARMORY SHOW

Just as the colony's members and setting were changing, so was the art world. The instrument of change in this case was the 1913 Armory Show. Ironically, the Cos Cob colony, which had been the original means

Cos Cob Bridge and Power Plant. Theodore Robinson set his easel on the railroad bridge to paint *Low Tide, Riverside Yacht Club.* Later, Childe Hassam painted construction work on the bridge itself in *The Mill Pond, Cos Cob, Connecticut.* The power plant has been a source of pollution and community anger since it began operation in 1907.

for the spread of Impressionism in this country, energetically supported the event that hastened the style's decline.

The Armory Show grew out of the same impulse that had prompted Hassam, Twachtman and Weir to form The Ten in 1897: the desire to present the then-progressive artists to a wider public.[72] While The Ten aimed to lure buyers from the fashionable European painters to the largely ignored American Impressionists, the Armory Show's organizers were dedicated to exhibiting the avant-garde regardless of nationality. Twachtman, the first leader of the Cos Cob colony, had been one of The Ten's founders; now his successor as the colony's head, Elmer MacRae, took a leading role in the Armory Show's sponsoring organization, the Association of American Painters and Sculptors (AAPS).

The AAPS began in a series of conversations among Elmer MacRae, Henry Fitch Taylor, Jerome Myers, and Walt Kuhn in early December, 1911; its first official meeting was held on December 19 of that year.[73] The seventeen charter members included six who had worked in Cos Cob: MacRae, Taylor,[74] D. Putnam Brinley, Ernest Lawson, Allen Tucker, and J. Alden Weir. MacRae was elected treasurer; Weir, who was by then the dean of American Impressionists, was voted president *in absentia,* an office he promptly resigned.[75]

Exhibition was the new association's purpose, and its enthusiastic members were soon immersed in ar-

rangements for the International Exhibition of Modern Art, to be held in New York's 69th Regiment Armory from February 15 to March 15, 1913. Cos Cob artists were active on the committees: MacRae and Taylor served on the executive committee and, along with Tucker, on the catalogue committee; Lawson and MacRae worked on foreign exhibits; Brinley, Tucker and Taylor helped with domestic exhibits; MacRae was chairman of the sales committee, and Brinley was also a member of the publicity committee.[76] Mild-mannered Sandy MacRae devoted two years of hard work to the show and, along with AAPS president Arthur B. Davies, Walt Kuhn and Walter Pach, was one of the people most responsible for its success.

The Cos Cob colony was well represented not only in the Armory Show's organization but also in the exhibition itself. Besides the artists already named, Childe Hassam, Alden Twachtman, and the tonalist Hermann Dudley Murphy were included. Theodore Robinson and John Henry Twachtman were shown as forerunners of modern American art, along with James McNeill Whistler and Albert Pinkham Ryder, just as Monet, Degas and Pissarro were among those in the European historical section.[77] But while the contemporary European art revealed a radical break with Impressionism, many of the Americans were still working in the same mode as Twachtman and Robinson. That Twachtman was included in the historical rather than the contemporary section was merely an accident of his early death. Had his *Hemlock Pool* (cat. 145, illus. p. 23) been hung among the paintings of Lawson, Brinley and MacRae, it would not have looked "earlier," as would have been the case had a Monet, for example, been exhibited beside a Picasso.

Impressionism was not the only American school represented in the Armory Show, but since its heyday in the last ten years of the nineteenth century, no other style had forcefully succeeded it as the country's leading art form. The Ashcan School, which found its inspiration in city alleys rather than country lanes, marked a change in subject rather than style.[78] When American artists and collectors saw — many for the first time — works by Cézanne, Braque, Duchamp, Matisse and Kandinsky, the Ashcan School suddenly looked passé.[79] As for Impressionism, if anyone had insisted before the Armory Show that it was still the cutting edge of American art, that position was totally untenable by March 16, 1913.

The Armory Show stimulated the younger American artists to seek fresh modes of expression. To the older generation, however, much of the work seemed ludicrous. Childe Hassam dismissed the exhibition in a prose style perfectly suited to his opinion: "If any of it is good, it will stay on the Golden Bough of Art. So much of it is obviously insincere and on the fool-fringe of the Fine Arts that it will rot, and drop off the tree."[80]

HASSAM'S COS COB ETCHINGS

Though Hassam was uninfluenced by the Armory Show, he did not stop developing as an artist. At age fifty-six, at the midpoint of a successful career, he turned seriously to etching for the first time in the summer of 1915. Kerr Eby, who would go to the trenches to capture the horrors of two world wars in grimly realistic prints, had an etching press in his studio on the Cos Cob waterfront. The grandson of the art dealer Frederick Keppel (who later published etchings by Hassam, Twachtman and Weir), Eby offered Hassam technical advice and the use of his press. The younger artist's generosity extended even further — asked how he dried his proofs without flattening the ink, Hassam replied, "Well, as a matter of fact, I usually spread them out on Eby's bed."[81]

The twenty-five etchings Hassam produced in Cos Cob that summer include four sketches of Eby's studio and eighteen others of barns, houses and bridges. Long interested in early-American buildings, Hassam found the inspiration for his etchings not in Cos Cob's landscape but rather in its architecture. This choice of subject matter may also have been a reflection of

Hassam's personality. It is difficult to imagine the gregarious bon vivant alone on a secluded beach. If he depicted buildings, on the other hand, there were sure to be people nearby.

Hassam's Cos Cob etchings offer a composite portrait of the people and place he so loved: Constant MacRae carries a basket of flowers up the sun-dappled steps of the Holley House (cat. 119, illus. p. 108); Mrs. Hassam writes at a desk in her bedroom (cat. 122); the kimono-clad daughter of the local saloon keeper stands pensively at the dining-room mantel (cat. 121, illus. p. 108). The saloon is there, too (cat. 120, illus. p. 108), with an organ grinder playing outside — perhaps the same man Twachtman had hired years before for an impromptu dance on the Holleys' front porch.[82] Hassam's admiration for Cos Cob's built landscape is shown in his careful attention to architectural detail: the small glass panes surrounding a two-century old Dutch door; the lattice framing Toby Burke's saloon; the lacy railing of the mill pond bridge. Beyond this realism, however, he took an Impressionist's delight in the patterns of light and shade that played over the village and the people who gathered there.

ASSESSMENT

Hassam and a few other artists came to the Holley House to paint through the 1920s, but after the first World War, Cos Cob never regained its early vigor as an art colony. Though Leonard Ochtman, Will Howe Foote, and Frank DuMond held occasional classes in the village, the summer school's continuity had been broken with Twachtman's death.[83] Most of the colony's second generation had come to Cos Cob as students. Without a school, the colony lost this source of self-renewal.

Furthermore, the factors that had made Cos Cob an important gathering place for artists now worked against it. The train connection between Cos Cob and New York had made the area a convenient base for artists; by the twenties, the changes that followed the railroad had destroyed the very things the artists had come to paint. The Armory Show, to which Elmer MacRae had dedicated so much time, had revealed Impressionism to be an outmoded form. Cos Cob, identified with Impressionism, represented the past to the ambitious young artists who had glimpsed the future at the Armory Show.

Cos Cob was a popular painting site from the late 1880s through the 1920s, but for twenty-five years, from 1890 to 1915, it was not merely subject but also stimulus for some of the major art movements of the early twentieth century. The cross-influences between Twachtman and Robinson, as they painted and talked together in Greenwich and Cos Cob, had resulted in a uniquely American form of Impressionism which had been spread to a new generation of artists through Twachtman's Cos Cob classes. The Ten, formed by Cos Cob artists Twachtman, Hassam and Weir, had brought American Impressionism to the attention — if not to the walls — of collectors and curators. The mingling of artists, writers and journalists at the Holley House and their unselfconscious rapport with the villagers represented a community seldom achieved outside Utopian literature. The encouragement, technical advice and willing models the colony provided made Childe Hassam's first significant venture into etching so successful that his Cos Cob proofs remain among the best in American printmaking.[84] Finally, artists who had spent their formative years working in Cos Cob were prominent in the organization of the Armory Show, which radically altered the direction of American art. That the new direction should be opposite that of the colony's origins was an irony John Twachtman, its founder, would surely have appreciated.

Flag-Raising. This World War I flag-raising was in front of the Brush house. The war had a profound impact on the Cos Cob art colony. Kerr Eby enlisted in the Army in 1917 and made front-line prints that captured the ugliness of the war for people back home. D. Putnam Brinley was turned down for active duty because of height but served instead by camouflaging ships in Baltimore, then supervising, in France, the decoration of the French equivalent of USOs. Too old for active duty, Childe Hassam captured the patriotism of the time in his Flag Series. Prints of one of Hassam's flag paintings were sold for the benefit of a children's reading room in war-torn Brussels.

Brush House. The Brush house and store stood next to the Holley House. One of the oldest buildings in Cos Cob, the Brush house was a popular subject with the artists.

NOTES

1 Lincoln Steffens, *The Autobiography of Lincoln Steffens* (New York: Harcourt, Brace and Company, 1931), p. 437.

2 Adeline Adams, *Childe Hassam* (New York: American Academy of Arts and Letters, 1938), p. 93.

3 John Douglas Hale, "The Life and Creative Development of John H. Twachtman" (PhD dissertation, Ohio State University, 1957), p. 16. Available from University Microfilms.

4 Hale, p. 37.

5 Hale, pp. 53-54.

6 *John Henry Twachtman* (Exh. cat., The Cincinnati Art Museum, 1966), p. 32.

7 Quoted in Hale, p. 35.

8 Dorothy Weir Young, *The Life and Letters of J. Alden Weir* (New Haven: Yale University Press, 1960), p. 147.

9 Young, p. 144.

10 Mary Dodge Ficker, *Old Greenwich in the 1890's and 1900's* (Friends of the Greenwich Library Oral History Project, 1976), p. 3.

11 The oldest part of the house was built in 1685. It is now called the Bush-Holley House after its first known owner and the Holleys. The Historical Society of the Town of Greenwich bought the house from Mrs. Constant Holley MacRae in 1957 and has operated it since as a museum. It has been classified by the National Trust for Historic Preservation as one of the 300 most important historic buildings in the United States.

12 Cos Cob is a section of Greenwich. The town of Greenwich encompasses several sections, among them Cos Cob, Riverside, Mianus, and Old Greenwich (then Sound Beach), which are separate communities sharing a common town government. Confusingly for non-residents, "Greenwich" can refer both to the separate section called Greenwich and to the total area. The name Cos Cob is a corruption of Coe's cob, for the stone breakwater (cob) built by an early settler named John Coe to protect his property along the Mianus River.

13 Spencer P. Mead, *Ye Historie of Ye Town of Greenwich* (New York: The Knickerbocker Press, 1911; reprinted by Harbor Hill Books, Harrison, N. Y., 1979), pp. 332-33, 338.

14 For more information about oystering in Cos Cob, see Clarence Chard's *Oystering* (Friends of the Greenwich Library Oral History Project, 1976). The information about children crossing to Riverside in canoes is based on Katherine W. Brush's *The Strickland Road Area* (Oral History Project, 1974).

15 Mead, p. 336.

16 Carol Ashwell, "Pity the Poor Commuter in 1850," *The Link* (published by the Greenwich Junior Women's Club), November 1954, pp. 4-5.

17 *The Greenwich Graphic,* April 29, 1882, p. 3.

18 Young, p. 159 ff.

19 Hale, p. 62.

20 Hale, p. 63.

21 *John Henry Twachtman,* p. 32.

22 Hale, p. 69.

23 Margery A. Ryerson, "J. Alden Weir's Etchings," *Art in America,* 8 (August 1920), 244.

24 James L. Yarnall, "John H. Twachtman's *Icebound,*" *Bulletin of The Art Institute of Chicago,* 71 (Jan.-Feb. 1977), 2-5.

25 Hale, p. 69.

26 Warrantee Deeds, Greenwich Town Hall, Book 60, p. 165 and Book 61, p. 488.

27 Hale, p. 70.

28 Hale, pp. 73, 113.

29 Young, p. 165.

30 Young, p. 190.

31 Hale, p. 79.

32 Letter from John H. Twachtman to Josephine Holley, postmarked New York City, Jan. 17, 1902. Collection of the Historical Society of the Town of Greenwich.

33 Letter from John H. Twachtman to Josephine Holley, postmarked Greenwich, Jan. 1, 1899. Collection of the Historical Society of the Town of Greenwich.

34 Young, pp. 181, 185.

35 Allen Tucker, *John H. Twachtman* (New York: Whitney Museum of American Art, American Artists Series, 1931), p. 7. Beginning in 1894, Twachtman taught a similar class at Cooper Union (Hale, p. 141).

36 Charles DeKay, "John H. Twachtman," *Art World,* 9 (June 1918), 112.

37 Hale, p. 146.

38 Holger Cahill and Alfred H. Barr Jr., eds., *Art in America: A Complete Survey* (New York: Halcyon House, 1939), p. 87.

39 Tucker, p. 8.

40 Hale, p. 154.

41 Young, p. 141.

42 Young, p. xxii.

43 Hale, p. 268, note 3.

44 *Charles H. Ebert* (Exh. cat., Lyman Allyn Museum, 1979).

45 Elizabeth M. Loder, *D. Putnam Brinley: Impressionist and Mural Painter* (Published for The New Canaan Historical Society and The Silvermine Guild of Artists by University Microfilms International, 1979), pp. 1-2. Brinley married the young writer, Kathrine Sanger, in 1904.

46 This information is based on conversations with William E. Finch, Jr., curator of the Bush-Holley House, and Mrs. Yoneo Arai, who was a close friend of the MacRaes. It has not, unfortunately, been possible to identify the man by name.

47 Theodore Robinson, diary notation, New York City, April 8, 1894. Robinson's diary from 1892-1896 is available at the Frick Art Reference Library, New York.

48 Robinson, diary notations, New York City, Nov. 30, 1893 and Feb. 16, 1894; *John Henry Twachtman* (Exh. cat., Ira Spanierman Galleries, 1968), n.p.

49 Robinson, diary notation, Cos Cob, June 7, 1894.

50 Robinson, diary notation, New York City, Nov. 14, 1895.

51 *Theodore Robinson* (Exh. cat., Baltimore Museum of Art, 1973), p. xvii.

52 *Theodore Robinson* (Exh. cat., Brooklyn Museum, 1946; reprinted in *Three Nineteenth Century American Painters,* New York: Arno Press, 1969), p. 27.

53 Richard J. Boyle, "John H. Twachtman: An Appreciation," *American Art & Antiques,* Nov.-Dec. 1978, p. 74.

54 Robinson, diary notation, Greenwich, Oct. 31, 1893.

55 Robinson, diary notations, Cos Cob, May 30-Sept. 2, 1894.

56 The locations of *Smelt Fishers, The Red Mill* and *Clarissa's Window* are unknown. According to Hassam biographer Adeline Adams, *Clarissa's Window* was painted in 1923. A 1969 exhibition catalogue from Hammer Galleries dates the work 1913. It seems likely that 1923 is the correct date. Clarissa MacRae was born in 1904 or 1905. The model in the painting is certainly not eight years old, Clarissa's age in 1913, but about 18, her age in 1923. It is, of course, possible that the subject was not Clarissa but merely that the setting was her room.

57 Letter from John Twachtman to Josephine Holley, postmarked Gloucester, Mass., June 30, 1902. Collection of the Historical Society of the Town of Greenwich.

58 The Woodcraft Indians soon evolved into the first Boy Scouts of America. For more information, see Leonard S. Clark's *Seton's Indians* (Friends of the Greenwich Library Oral History Project, 1976).

59 Lincoln Steffens, "Cos Cob: An Art Colony," in *Autobiography,* pp. 436-42. For information on Volkmar, see *Greenwich Historic Collections,* vol. III, no. 1 (published by the Historical Society of the Town of Greenwich).

60 Katherine L. S. Lowell and Harry M. Lounsbury, *The Strickland Road Area* (Friends of the Greenwich Library Oral History Project, 1978), p. 81.

61 Young, p. 142.

62 The book, *The Best Stories of Sarah Orne Jewett,* selected and arranged with a preface by Willa Cather (Boston: Houghton Mifflin Co., 1925), is in the collection of the Historical Society of the Town of Greenwich.

63 Willa Cather, *The Song of the Lark* (Boston: Houghton Mifflin Co., 1943), p. 536.

64 *Before and After 1776: A Comprehensive Chronology of the Town of Greenwich 1640-1976* (The Historical Society of the Town of Greenwich, 1976), p. 68. Robinson titled his painting *The E.M.J. Betty;* the boat's actual name was the *E.M.J. Beatty.* Robinson's diary indicates that this casual approach to spelling was not uncharacteristic of him.

65 Mead, pp. 332-33.

66 Based on figures taken from "Study of Population Growth, Characteristics, Composition and Distribution" by Walter A. Wachter, Greenwich Town Planner, May 1944. Filed under Greenwich Census at the Greenwich Library.

67 Steffens, pp. 436-37.

68 Steffens, p. 439. See also Ficker, pp. 3-4.

69 Lowell and Lounsbury, p. 81.

70 Quoted in *The History of the Greenwich Art Society* (published by that organization in 1976), p. 8.

71 Steffens, p. 438.

72 Richard J. Boyle, *American Impressionism* (Boston: New York Graphic Society, 1974), pp. 147-48.

73 Milton W. Brown, *The Story of the Armory Show* (Published by The Joseph H. Hirshhorn Foundation, distributed by the New York Graphic Society, 1963), pp. 29-30.

74 Young, note, p. 142. This may be the same "Taylor" whom Robinson often mentions in his diary as a companion in Cos Cob.

75 Brown, pp. 30-32.

76 Brown, pp. 60, 63.

77 Brown, p. 93.

78 Brown, p. 105.

79 *The Armory Show Fiftieth Anniversary Exhibition* (Exh. cat., Munson-Williams-Proctor Institute, 1963), p. 35.

80 Adams, p. 69.

81 Quoted by Dorothy Keppel in "Kerr Eby," *Print Collector's Quarterly: An Anthology of Essays on Eminent Printmakers of the World,* vol. 4 (Millwood, N.Y.: kto press, 1977), p. 20013. According to Keppel, Eby worked with Hassam in Cos Cob in 1919, after Eby returned from World War I. Hassam, however, began experimenting with etching in 1915, indicating that Eby lived in Cos Cob before he enlisted in June, 1917. It is possible, of course, that he also worked in Cos Cob after the war.

82 Hale, p. 122.

83 Twachtman had not conducted summer classes at Cos Cob in unbroken succession. He taught at Norwich, Connecticut, in 1898 and in Gloucester, Massachusetts, during the summers of 1900, 1901, and 1902. However, there had been a sense of continuity to the sessions.

84 *Childe Hassam as Printmaker* (Exh. cat., Metropolitan Museum of Art, 1977), unpaged.

Brinley, D. Putnam

96 *Daisy Field*
1909: Silvermine
Oil on board, 8¾ x 7¾ (22.2 x 19.7)
Signed and dated LL: *D. Putnam Brinley '09*
Private Collection

97 *The Emerald Pool*
1912: Silvermine
Oil on canvas, 43 x 48 (109.2 x 121.9)
Signed and dated LR: *D. Putnam Brinley 1912*
Private Collection

Exhibited at the Armory Show, 1913.

98 *A May Morning*
c. 1912: Silvermine
Oil on canvas, 32 x 30 (81.3 x 76.2)
Signed LL: *D. Putnam Brinley*
Historical Society of the Town of Greenwich, Gift of
Mrs. Albert A. Loder, Jr.

Also titled *Silvermine River.*

99 *Midsummer Moonlight*
1910: Riverside Yacht Club, Riverside
Oil on canvas, 31 x 25 sight (78.7 x 63.5)
Signed and dated LL: *D. Putnam Brinley '10*
Private Collection

Clark, Walter

100 *Greenwich*   ILLUS. P. 105
1893: Greenwich
Oil on canvas, 32 x 28 (81.3 x 71.1)
Signed LL: *Walter Clark*
Collection of Dr. and Mrs. A. Everette James, Jr.,
Nashville, Courtesy of R. H. Love Galleries, Inc.,
Chicago

101 *The Sound at Greenwich*
1893: Greenwich
Oil on canvas, 26 x 32 (66 x 81.3)
Signed LL: *Walter Clark;* inscribed on reverse:
Greenwich, Looking Toward Belle Haven 1893
Collection of Walter A. Nelson-Rees and James L.
Coran, Courtesy of R. H. Love Galleries, Inc.,
Chicago

Ebert, Charles

102 *Along Shore, Greenwich*
c. 1912: Greenwich
Oil on canvas, 30 x 42 (76.2 x 106.7)
No signature
Private Collection

103 *Betty on the Dock*
c. 1914: Probably Cos Cob
Watercolor, 10 x 13¾ (25.4 x 34.9)
No signature
Lyman Allyn Museum

Betty is the artist's daughter.

104 *Mary Roberts Ebert with Betty*   ILLUS. P. 106
c. 1906: Greenwich
Oil on canvas, 30 x 27 (76.2 x 68.6)
No signature
Robert P. Gunn

105 *Sunlight, Moonlight, Water, Connecticut*
c. 1917; Probably Greenwich
Oil on canvas, 30 x 36 (76.2 x 91.4)
Signed LR: *Ebert*
Private Collection

Eby, Kerr

106 *The Boat House*
1917: Probably Cos Cob
Etching, 5¾ x 8 (14.6 x 20.2)
Signed and dated in plate LR: *Eby 17;* signed in pencil,
margin LC: *Per Eby imp.*
Library of Congress

Foote, Will Howe

107 *Cos Cob Shipyard*
1903: Cos Cob
Oil on canvas, 25½ x 30¼ (64.8 x 76.8)
Signed LR: *Will Howe Foote 1903*
Stephen H. Condict III

Originally entitled *A Gray Day, Cos Cob.*

Hassam, Childe

108 *The Colonial Table*
1915: Cos Cob
Etching, 6¹⁵/₁₆ x 10 (17.6 x 25.4)

Monogrammed and dated in plate UL: *CH Cos Cob 1915;* monogrammed in pencil, margin LR: *CH imp.*
The Metropolitan Museum of Art, Gift of Mrs. Childe Hassam, 1940

A room in the Holley House.

109 *Cos Cob*   ILLUS. P. 106
1915: Cos Cob
Etching, 6⅞ x 5 (17.44 x 12.7)
Monogrammed and dated in plate LR: *Cos Cob CH 1915;* monogrammed in pencil, margin LR: *CH imp.*
Historical Society of the Town of Greenwich

A view of Kerr Eby's studio in a Cos Cob waterfront warehouse. The smokestacks of the railroad power plant are visible in the upper right background. Hassam did not reverse his drawing on the etching plate, so this print is a mirror image of the actual scene.

110 *Cos Cob Dock*
1915: Cos Cob
Etching, 8⅜ x 6¼ (21.3 x 15.9)
Monogrammed in plate, LC: *CH Cos Cob;* monogrammed in pencil, margin LR: *CH imp.*
Mr. and Mrs. Errett Dunlap

A view of Kerr Eby's waterfront Cos Cob studio.

111 *The Dutch Door*
1915: Cos Cob
Etching, 8⅜ x 9⅞ (21.3 x 25.1)
Monogrammed in pencil, margin LR: *CH imp.*
Historical Society of the Town of Greenwich

Helen Burke, daughter of the saloon owner Toby Burke, standing in the front door of the Holley House.

112 *The Holley Farm*   ILLUS. P. 20
1902: Cos Cob
Pastel, 18 x 22 (45.7 x 55.9)
Signed and dated LL: *Childe Hassam 1902*
Diplomatic Reception Rooms, Department of State, Washington, D.C.

Hassam gave this pastel, one of at least six he did in Cos Cob during the summer and fall of 1902, to J. Alden Weir.

113 *Late Afternoon, Cos Cob*
1902: Cos Cob
Pastel on tan paper, 17 x 21 sight (43.2 x 53.3)
Signed and dated LL: *Childe Hassam 1902*
Historical Society of the Town of Greenwich

A fall view of the Cos Cob mill pond from the grounds of the Holley House.

114 *Listening to the Orchard Oriole*   ILLUS. P. 107
1902: Cos Cob
Oil on canvas, 32 x 26 (81.3 x 66)
Signed and dated LR: *Childe Hassam 1902*
Mr. and Mrs. Alan W. Hall, Rockport, Indiana

115 *The Mill Pond, Cos Cob, Connecticut*   ILLUS. P. 21
1902: Cos Cob
Oil on canvas, 26¼ x 18¼ (66.7 x 46.4)
Signed and dated LL: *Childe Hassam 1902*
Mr. George Butler

116 *The Old House*
1915: Cos Cob
Etching, 6 x 7¾ (15.2 x 19.7)
Monogrammed and dated in plate LR: *Cos Cob CH Oct. 2, 1915;* signed in pencil, margin LL: *Childe Hassam;* monogrammed, margin LR: *CH imp.*
Historical Society of the Town of Greenwich

The Holley House (now called the Bush-Holley House). Hassam did not reverse his drawing on the etching plate.

117 *Old Lace*
1915: Cos Cob
Etching, 6¾ x 6¾ (17.1 x 17.1)
Monogrammed and dated in plate LR: *Cos Cob CH Nov. 5, 1915;* monogrammed in pencil, margin LR: *CH imp.*
Associated American Artists, New York City

A view of the mill pond bridge in front of the Holley House. Same as cat. 42.

118 *The Red Store*
1916: Cos Cob
Watercolor, 14½ x 22 (36.8 x 55.9)
Signed and dated UR: *Childe Hassam, 1916*
Collection of Babcock Galleries, New York City

A view of the Brush house, a mid-eighteenth-century building next to the Holley House, with its adjacent store. For John Twachtman's treatment of the same house and store, see cat. 142 and 148.

119 *The Steps*   ILLUS. P. 108
1915: Cos Cob
Etching, 10⅞ x 7⅝ (27.6 x 19.4)
Monogrammed and dated in plate: *Sept. 19, 1915 Cos Cob CH*
Print Department, Boston Public Library

Mrs. Elmer MacRae carrying a basket of flowers up the steps of the Holley House.

120 *Toby's, Cos Cob*   ILLUS. P. 108
1915: Cos Cob
Etching, 7 x 8⅞ (17.8 x 22.5)
Monogrammed and dated in plate LL: *CH Cos Cob 1915;* monogrammed in pencil, margin LR: *CH imp.*
The Metropolitan Museum of Art, Gift of Mrs. Childe Hassam, 1940

A former Cos Cob resident (Mrs. Katherine L. S. Lowell) called Toby's "a very respectable saloon . . . . They never had the police down there or anything of that kind . . . . People went in for their drink and their beer and didn't fall over the dock."

121 *The White Kimono*   ILLUS. P. 108
1915: Cos Cob
Etching, 7⅜ x 10⅞ (18.7 x 27.6)
Monogrammed and dated in plate CR: *CH 1915;*
monogrammed in pencil, margin LR: *CH imp.*
Associated American Artists, New York City

Helen Burke, daughter of Toby, the saloon owner,
lived with her family above the saloon but is shown
here standing at the dining room mantel in the Holley
House. A year before, Hassam had done a painting of
a similar scene, *In the Old House,* but the model there
wore a white dress of the period. The print is a mirror
image of the actual setting.

122 *The Writing Desk*
1915: Cos Cob
Etching, 10 x 7 (25.4 x 17.8)
Monogrammed and dated in plate, UR: *Cos Cob CH
1915;* monogrammed in pencil, margin LR: *CH imp.*
Historical Society of the Town of Greenwich

A portrait of Mrs. Hassam at the Holley House.

Lawson, Ernest

123 *Yacht Club–Night, Greenwich*   ILLUS. P. 22
c. 1894: Greenwich
Oil on canvas, 20 x 24 (50.8 x 61)
Signed LL: *Ernest Lawson;* on stretcher: *Yacht
Club–Night, Greenwich*
Webster Fine Art, Inc.

MacRae, Elmer L.

124 *Boats at a Landing*
1906: Cos Cob
Oil on canvas, 20 x 20 (50.8 x 50.8)
Signed LR: *E. L. MacRae/1906*
The Whitney Museum of American Art, New York,
Gift of Mr. and Mrs. Raymond J. Horowitz

125 *Fairy Stories*   ILLUS. P. 109
1912: Probably Cos Cob
Oil on canvas, 28⅜ x 36⅛ (71.8 x 91.6)
Signed and dated LR: *E. L. MacRae 1912*
The Parrish Art Museum, Littlejohn Collection

Also entitled *Fairy Tales,* this painting was exhibited in
the Armory Show, 1913. It probably depicts
the artist's wife, his twin daughters, and another,
younger child.

126 *Holley House–Blizzard*
1912: Cos Cob
Oil on canvas, 26 x 31½ sight (66 x 80)
Signed and dated LR: *E. L. MacRae 1912*
Mr. and Mrs. John Bartol

127 *The Upper Porch at the Holley House*
1908: Cos Cob
Oil on canvas, 24 x 28 sight (60 x 71.1)
Signed and dated LL: *E. L. MacRae 1908*
Private Collection

128 *Sketchbook*
1906: Cos Cob
Pencil and crayon on paper, sheet size 8⅛ x 6¾
(20.6 x 17)
Signed and dated inside front cover: *E. L. MacRae
Dec. 1906*
Historical Society of the Town of Greenwich

A bound sketchbook of 59 sheets with 10 drawings.

129 *Sketchbook*
c. 1906: Cos Cob
Pencil and crayon on paper, sheet size 10 x 7½
(25.4 x 19)
No signature
Historical Society of the Town of Greenwich

A bound sketchbook of 60 sheets with 21 drawings, all
of the artist's twin daughters, Clarissa and Constant,
born October 31, 1904.

130 *Village Green*
1910: Cos Cob
Oil on canvas, 25½ x 31½ (64.8 x 80)
Signed and dated LR: *E. L. MacRae 1910*
Historical Society of the Town of Greenwich

A view of the green in front of the Holley House.

Ochtman, Leonard

131 *Connecticut Salt Marshes*
1899: Probably Cos Cob or Riverside
Oil on canvas, 16⅛ x 22 (40.9 x 55.9)
Signed LL: *Leonard Ochtman 1899*
The Metropolitan Museum of Art, Gift of Mr. and
Mrs. Maurice Glickman, 1979

132 *December Sunset*   ILLUS. P. 109
1918: Cos Cob
Oil on canvas, 36 x 52 (91.4 x 132.1)
Signed and dated LL: *Leonard Ochtman 1918*
D. Clinton Hynes Fine Art, Chicago

Also entitled *December Sun.*

133 *Haystacks*
c. 1900: Cos Cob?
Oil on canvas, 24¼ x 36 (61.6 x 91.4)
Signed LL: *Leonard Ochtman*
Private Collection, Chicago, Courtesy of R. H. Love
Galleries, Inc., Chicago

134 *October Morning*
1919: Probably Cos Cob
Oil on canvas, 24 x 30 (61 x 76.2)
No signature
The Bruce Museum, Greenwich

135 *Summer Play on the Beach*
n.d.: Greenwich
Oil on board, 12 x 16 (30.5 x 40.6)
Signed LL: *Leonard Ochtman*
Grand Central Art Galleries

Robinson, Theodore

136 *Landscape*
c. 1893-95: Greenwich area?
Oil on canvas, 18 x 22 (45.7 x 55.9)
No signature
Mrs. Ben Strouse

137 *Sketchbook*   ILLUS. P. 110
June, 1894: Cos Cob
Pencil on paper, sheet size 4 x 6½ (10.2 x 15.2)
Signed and dated inside front cover: *Theo. Robinson/ Cos Cob, June '94*
Ira Spanierman, Inc.

A bound sketchbook of 33 sheets with 27 drawings. In this book, small enough to tuck into a pocket, Robinson made quick drawings of the Cos Cob shoreline. His concern with the varying effects of daylight on the Sound is shown in some careful notations he made of the hour when he made a sketch.

Twachtman, John H.

138 *Branchville, Connecticut*
1889 or before: Branchville
Etching, 3⅞ x 4⅝ (9.8 x 11.7)
Initialled in pencil: *J. H. T. per A. T.*
Associated American Artists, New York City

The artist's son, Alden Twachtman, signed all prints in the posthumous 1921 edition published by Keppel & Co., New York City.

139 *The Cabbage Patch*   ILLUS. P. 22
c. 1897-98: Round Hill, Greenwich
Oil on canvas, 25 x 25 (63.5 x 63.5)
No signature
Helen S. Hyman

Twachtman found his subject in his own garden.

140 *Cascade*
c. 1890-1900: Greenwich
Pastel, 10¼ x 8¼ (26 x 21)
No signature
The Whitney Museum of American Art, New York, Gift of Mr. and Mrs. Raymond J. Horowitz.

141 *Cos Cob*
c. 1898: Cos Cob
Oil on canvas, 12 x 16 (30.5 x 40.6)
Signed LR: *J. H. Twachtman*
Morris Collection, Courtesy of R. H. Love Galleries, Inc., Chicago

142 *Country House in Winter, Cos Cob*   ILLUS. P. 110
n.d.: Cos Cob
Oil on canvas, 25 x 25 (63.5 x 63.5)
Signed LL: *J. H. Twachtman*
Addison Gallery of American Art, Phillips Academy, Andover, Massachusetts, Gift of Anonymous Donor

Same subject as cat. 118 and 148.

143 *The Dock, Bridgeport*   ILLUS. P. 110
1889 or before: Bridgeport
Etching, 3⅞ x 5⅞ (9.8 x 14.9)
Initialled in plate LL: *J. H. T.*
Mr. and Mrs. James T. Larkin

Part of the 1921 Keppel edition, even though Alden Twachtman did not sign this print. He did initial another copy of the same print, cat. 59.

144 *Footbridge, Bridgeport*   ILLUS. P. 76
1889 or before: Bridgeport
Etching, 3⅞ x 5⅞ (9.8 x 14.9)
Initialled in plate LL: *J. H. T.* initialled in pencil, margin LR: *J.H.T. per A.T.*
Mr. and Mrs. James T. Larkin

Same as cat. 61. See note for cat. 60.

145 *Hemlock Pool*   ILLUS. P. 23
1902: Round Hill, Greenwich
Oil on canvas, 30 x 25 (76.2 x 63.5)
Signed LR: *J. H. Twachtman*
Addison Gallery of American Art, Phillips Academy, Andover, Massachusetts, Gift of Anonymous Donor

Exhibited in the Armory Show, 1913.

146 *Landscape*
n.d.: Probably Greenwich
Pastel on tan paper, 11¼ x 17½ sight (2.6 x 44.4)
Signed LR: *J. H. Twachtman*
Ira Spanierman, Inc.

147 *Landscape with Trees*
n.d.: Probably Greenwich
Pastel on tan paper, 9¼ x 11⅞ sight (23.5 x 30.2)
No signature
Ira Spanierman, Inc.

148 *October*   ILLUS. P. 111
c. 1901: Cos Cob
Oil on canvas, 30 x 30 (76.2 x 76.2)
No signature
The Chrysler Museum, Norfolk, Virginia

The Brush house and store.

149 *Old Mill, Branchville*   ILLUS. P. 111
1889 or before: Branchville
Etching, 4¼ x 3 (10.8 x 7.6)
Initialled in plate LL: *J.H.T.;* initialled in pencil, margin LR: *JHT per AT.*
Mr. and Mrs. James T. Larkin

150 *Tiger Lilies*
c. 1895: Probably Greenwich
Oil on canvas, 30 x 22 (76.2 x 55.9)
Signed LC: *J. H. Twachtman*
Mr. and Mrs. Meyer P. Potamkin

Theodore Robinson may have been referring to this clump of lilies in his diary notation for July 4, 1893, a day he spent with the Twachtmans in Greenwich: "Red lilies in the road, near the house, brilliant in sunlight."

151 *The Waterfall*   ILLUS. P. 112
1890s: Round Hill, Greenwich
Oil on canvas, 22 x 30 (55.9 x 76.2)
Twachtman estate sale stamp LR
Hirshhorn Museum and Sculpture Garden,
Smithsonian Institution

Weir, J. Alden

152 *The Back Lots*
1918: Branchville
Oil on canvas, 24½ x 33¾ (62.2 x 85.7)
Signed LL: *J. Alden Weir*
Mrs. Charles Burlingham

153 *The Fishing Party*   ILLUS. P. 113
c. 1915: Weir's Pond, Branchville
Oil on canvas, 28 x 23 (71.1 x 58.4)
Signed LR: *J. Alden Weir*
The Phillips Collection, Washington, D.C.

With a $2500 first prize from the Boston Art Club in
1896 for a painting a newspaper described as
"Impressionism minus its violence," Weir built a
fishing pond at Branchville. It became known as "The
Boston Art Club Pond," and he further improved it
with a small dock, boathouse, and the little bridge in
this painting. A devoted angler, Weir kept tackle on
hand for his guests. There were countless fishing
parties at Branchville, but usually the participants
were men. The pond, still intact, is currently the
property of a land developer, so its future is uncertain.

154 *Landscape*
n.d.: Branchville
Oil on canvas, 37 x 59 (99 x 15)
Signed LR: *J. Alden Weir/Branchville*
Geist Collection, Courtesy of R. H. Love Galleries,
Inc., Chicago

155 *Portrait of Theodore Robinson*   ILLUS. P. 112
n.d.
Drypoint, 6⅞ x 5 (17.6 x 12.9)
Signed in pencil, margin LR: *J. Alden Weir*
Library of Congress

156 *South Norwalk, #1*
c. 1885-89: South Norwalk
Etching, 5¼ x 3⅞ (13.4 x 9.9)
Initialled in plate LR
Library of Congress

See the note for cat. 85.

157 *The Webb Farm*
c. 1885-89: Windham Center
Etching and drypoint, trimmed to 5¹⁵⁄₁₆ x 7⅞
(15.2 x 20)
Signed in pencil LR: *J. Alden Weir*
Prints Division, The New York Public Library, Astor,
Lenox and Tilden Foundations, Gift of the Artist,
1906.

Same as cat. 87.

158 *The Wooden Bridge*
c. 1885-89: Probably Branchville
Etching, trimmed to 4⅞ x 6⅞ (12.4 x 17.4)
Signed in pencil LL: *J. Alden Weir*
Prints Division, The New York Public Library, Astor,
Lenox and Tilden Foundations, Gift of the Artist,
1906.

Same as cat. 89.

Winslow, Henry

159 *Cos Cob*
1906: Cos Cob
Etching, 5 x 8⅞ (12.7 x 22.6)
Signed and dated in plate LL: *Winslow 06 Coscob;*
signed in pencil LR: *Henry Winslow*
Print Department, Boston Public Library

100   Walter Clark, *Greenwich,* 1893

104   Charles Ebert, *Mary Roberts Ebert with Betty,* c. 1906

109   Childe Hassam, *Cos Cob,* 1915

114   Childe Hassam, *Listening to the Orchard Oriole,* 1902

119   Childe Hassam, *The Steps,* 1915

120   Childe Hassam, *Toby's, Cos Cob,* 1915

121   Childe Hassam, *The White Kimono,* 1915

125   Elmer L. MacRae, *Fairy Stories,* 1912

132   Leonard Ochtman, *December Sunset,* 1918

137   Theodore Robinson, *Sketch of Mianus River Bridge,* 1894

143   John H. Twachtman, *The Dock, Bridgeport,* c. 1889

142   John H. Twachtman, *Country House in Winter, Cos Cob*

149　John H. Twachtman, *Old Mill, Branchville,*
c. 1889

148　John H. Twachtman, *October,* c. 1901

151   John H. Twachtman, *The Waterfall*, 1890s

155   J. Alden Weir, *Portrait of Theodore Robinson*

112

153   J. Alden Weir, *The Fishing Party*, c. 1915

In a scene strikingly reminiscent of *The Fishing Party*,
Weir's daughters are seen here on the way to the pond on
his Branchville farm.

The Art Colony at Old Lyme

JEFFREY W. ANDERSEN

THE AMERICAN BARBIZON

"I want you to see a little of this beautiful country, where pictures are made — your station is Lyme,"[1] wrote the American painter Henry Ward Ranger from Old Lyme, Connecticut in late August, 1899 to his New York agent William Macbeth. Little did Macbeth know that Ranger was excitedly making plans to establish in Old Lyme[2] an art colony that would come to be known as the "American Barbizon." After many years in Europe, spent absorbing the styles of nineteenth-century Dutch art and of the French Barbizon, Ranger began his search for a place in New England that combined the contemplative qualities of the Forest of Fontainebleau with the hazy atmosphere of the Dutch lowlands. To Ranger's eye, Old Lyme was perfect.

That summer Ranger saw Old Lyme as a small village inconspicuously spread over a "strikingly diversified"[3] terrain bounded by where the Connecticut River meets the Long Island Sound (map, p. 115). He

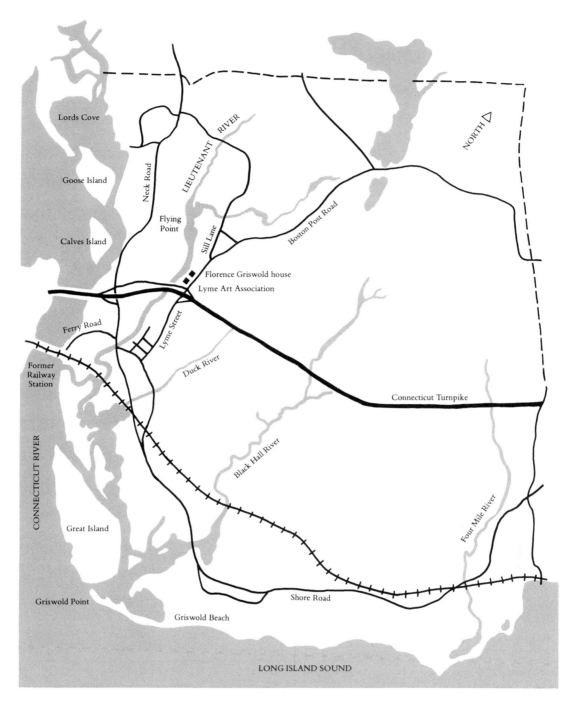

Fig. 1. **Lyme Street,** c. 1905. When the Lyme art colony began, "there was hardly a house on this street that didn't need shingling," recalled one of the artists. Only four new houses had been built on the street in the previous thirty years. Old Lyme was in sad shape — the victim of a declining shipbuilding industry that had once brought great prosperity to the town.

Old Lyme is located at the confluence of the Connecticut River and the Long Island Sound in Southeastern Connecticut.

delighted in the network of ambulating rivers that had earlier brought prosperity to the town as a shipbuilding center but had gradually reverted to a more natural state as the industry declined. The Lieutenant, Duck, and Black Hall Rivers all lazily flowed into the wide Connecticut near the Sound. Ranger was struck by broad expanses of salt meadows and lowland estuaries. There the summer light brilliantly shimmered and hung like an eyelid over the water. To the north, open meadows wound up to the picturesque hills dotted with tall cedars, mature oaks, and exposed granite precipices. Tucked away among the woods and upland pastures were ancient homesteads bordered by stone fences made from the rocky soil. "The variety in the landscape would drive an artist to distraction. It is a singular mixture of the wild and the tame, of the austere and the cheerful,"[4] prophetically wrote a visitor to Lyme in 1876.

Old Lyme represented to Ranger the consummate place for his generation of American landscapists, at least for those with similar Barbizon leanings, to come together in a picturesque rural setting to sketch and paint (fig. 1). Henry Ward Ranger's choice of Old Lyme as his "new Fontainebleau in Connecticut"[5] marked the beginning of events that would have far reaching effects on the character of this New England village and on the scores of landscape artists who flocked there in the early decades of the twentieth century. Ranger's leadership of the colony was soon overshadowed, however, by the arrival of the influential American Impressionist Childe Hassam in 1903. Hassam, along with Impressionists Willard Metcalf and Walter Griffin, led the conversion of the colony's viewpoint from Barbizon to Impressionism. Under their direction the art colony at Old Lyme became identified as a center of American Impressionism, providing a stylistic vocabulary that the colony would assiduously cling to long after Impressionism had ceased to be a vital force in American art. Because of this idiomatic shift, Ranger's contribution to the colony is often overlooked — to the detriment of both an historical and stylistic understanding of the art colony at Old Lyme.

When Ranger arrived in Old Lyme that summer of 1899, he took his room and board in Miss Florence Griswold's home, a Late Georgian mansion on the town's main street, whose dilapidated state failed to disguise its graceful proportions and handsomely colonnaded grand portico (fig. 3). Both the house and Miss Griswold were to become central figures in the development of the art colony.

Fig. 2. **Florence Griswold in about 1915.** "She wasn't beautiful. She wasn't strong. She wasn't self-reliant. But though they said she was sixty, she didn't look fifty. Her greying wavy black hair swept loosely back in a low coil, her well-marked eyebrows, her slender nose, her delicately modeled chin, her sensitive mouth, and her smiling black eyes, these were the features we all remembered" (Arthur Heming, *Miss Florence and the Artists of Old Lyme).*

Fig. 3. **Florence Griswold House.** Designed by Samuel Belcher and built in 1817, this grand porticoed Late Georgian mansion was purchased by Captain Robert Griswold in 1841. His daughter, Florence, was born in the house on Christmas Day, 1850. With the family fortune diminishing, Florence, her two sisters, and her mother opened up a girls' finishing school in 1878. Following Henry Ward Ranger's arrival in 1899, the house was transformed into the home of one of the best known art colonies in the country.

Miss Griswold (fig. 2), born on Christmas Day, 1850, was descended from one of New England's first families, whose lineage reads like a "Who's Who" of Connecticut politics, law, and commerce. Her father, Captain Robert Griswold, purchased the house for his new bride, Helen Powers Griswold, in 1841 and Miss Griswold had grown up there. Florence Griswold and her two sisters, Louise and Adele, enjoyed a cultivated and affluent upbringing in Old Lyme. Their father was a prosperous packet boat captain whose ships plied the Atlantic waterways to London, where he reputedly had a second family to support. This bigamous arrangement, while perhaps convenient to a man spending half his life at sea, may partially explain why he had nothing but the house to leave his wife and daughters upon his death in 1882. Perhaps a more plausible reason was the forced obsolescence of the packet boat trade by the ocean steamer in the late 1860s and 1870s. Circumstances were so lean for the Griswold family that in the fall of

1878 Mrs. Griswold and her three daughters opened up the Griswold Home School, a finishing school devoted to instruction in music, theater, literature, languages and the home arts.[6] They ran the school for fourteen years, although it was never especially successful. Later the house was open to summer visitors and run informally as a boarding house. The 1890s were hard on Florence: Louise died in 1896, Adele moved away, and her mother died in 1899. Thus when Ranger arrived that summer, Florence was feeling the personal loss of her mother and the strain of impoverished circumstances that made it practically impossible to take care of the Griswold estate and its ten or eleven acres.

How Ranger heard about the Griswold house is not known, though we do know that his friend and fellow artist Clark Voorhees had stayed in the house with his mother and sister during the summer of 1896[7] and most likely recommended the place to him. In any event, upon his arrival at Old Lyme, Ranger quickly

Fig. 4. **Henry Ward Ranger.** Ranger on the back porch of the Griswold House, 1903-04.

saw the potential of bringing to fruition his dream of gathering together a coterie of similarly minded plein-airists to form an art colony that he envisioned as the "American Barbizon." Everything was right — the local countryside, its close proximity to and from New York by train, the availability of the house and outbuildings which could function as studios, and the personality of Miss Griswold, who enthusiastically shared Ranger's dream. Ranger returned to New York that fall and like a real estate salesman sensing an approaching closure, excitedly extolled the virtues of Old Lyme to his artist friends, recruiting them to return to the place "where pictures are made" in the spring of 1900. Joining him during that spring and summer were Lewis Cohen, Alphonse Jongers, Henry Rankin Poore, Louis Paul Dessar and William Howe.[8]

Critics in the first decade of this century referred to these painters as "tonalists" because of their use of limited color scales and delicate modulations of light to create effects of mood.[9] One art critic even went so far

as to label Henry Ward Ranger the leader of "The Tonal School of America."[10] Actually, as Wanda Corn has pointed out, Ranger and his group were really a second generation of tonalists, successors to the tonalist traditions of George Inness, Dwight Tryon, and Alexander Wyant, who tempered this influence with their Barbizon methods of plein-air sketching and rough textural effects.[11]

Ranger (fig. 4), an imposing figure with his husky frame and fully bearded face, punctuated only by an ever-present cigar, thrived on his position as master of this new colony — freely dispensing critiques of his company's work and expounding on the art of everything from painting to playing horseshoes, the latter of which occupied a good deal of his time behind the Griswold house (fig. 6). Ranger was always his own best advocate. Writing to Macbeth of a Montreal dealer's opinion of his work, "He said in substance that my work would stand with the *best* and that no one now was doing better, hardly anyone so well . . . he finds my work thoroughly original *as I know it is* in spite of Damn Fool Criticism which can't get beyond the surface of things."[12] Ranger had built up a considerable following among collectors for his forest interiors that were carefully and consistently arranged to lead the viewer's eye from the painting's darkened edges to a hazy light-filled distant central plane — often a pool, stream or break in the woods (fig. 5). Unfortunately, many of these paintings appear more to be compositional variants of Diaz de la Peña's Barbizon forest interiors than personal translations of the Connecticut woods.

The circle of artists coming to Old Lyme grew rapidly. In 1901, Allen B. Talcott, Will Howe Foote (William Howe's young nephew), Cullen Yates, and Clark Voorhees (fig. 7) joined the group. Word was undoubtedly spread further by the showing of Old Lyme pictures at the National Academy of Design annual exhibition in January, 1902. Allen Talcott wrote to Florence Griswold telling her of the show. "Are you coming to New York? I hope you will. I think you would be proud of your colony of Artists as they are represented at the Academy . . . . Fourteen pictures I believe by a very small group of men."[13] That winter other artists eagerly sought to prepare for a spring or summer visit to Old Lyme by writing Miss Griswold, or "Miss Florence" as they affectionately addressed her, requesting accommodations and studio space or by seeking introductions from one of the colonists. "I have the pleasure of announcing that Mr. and Mrs. DuMond[14] have decided that they wish to spend the summer in Lyme with you . . . . They will come about

Fig. 6. **Pitching Horseshoes.** Pitch quoits (horseshoes) was a favorite pastime among the artists. Henry Poore (left) and Henry Ward Ranger are depicted here. The colony also had its own baseball team, as well as track and field days that were highlighted by paper medals awarded to entries in the fat man's race. Ranger was frequently in the running.

Fig. 5. Henry Ward Ranger, *Autumn Woodlands,* 1902. Oil on canvas, 28″ x 36″. Lyme Historical Society, Gift of Israel E. Liverant.

Fig. 7. **Cohen and Voorhees.** Lewis Cohen and Clark Voorhees on the front walk of the Griswold House, equipped with knapsack and painting supplies for a day of plein-air work.

Fig. 8. **Hassam on Front Porch.** Childe Hassam seated on the front porch of the Griswold House with Mrs. Beardsley (left) and Helen Freeman. Miss Freeman later married the painter Will Howe Foote.

Fig. 9. **Phoebe Griffin Noyes Library.** Built in 1898 on Old Lyme's main street, the Library played host to the art colony's annual summer exhibitions from 1902 to 1920.

the first of June and will probably stay until the first of October. . . . The DuMonds will be a great acquisition to our colony and I assure you that they improve on acquaintance," wrote Talcott to Miss Griswold.[15] Besides the DuMonds, the 1902 season brought, along with the others mentioned, Jules Turcas, Bruce Crane, George Bruestle, Frank Bicknell, and Arthur Heming and Harry Hoffman, who became lifelong best friends.

While many of these early colonists first became acquainted with each other through the National Academy of Design or the Art Students League, certainly more than a few met in the Paris academies and ateliers. For instance, Clark Voorhees met Will Howe Foote in 1898 or 1899 and, at that time, Voorhees spoke of Old Lyme and showed Foote a sketch of the Old Lyme church that he had brought with him.[16] Artistic training in the conservative Académie Julian or École des Beaux-Arts was an educational requisite for American artists in the last quarter of the nineteenth century. Here they absorbed the Barbizon traditions under the strict tutelage of the academy masters Boulanger and Lefebvre, among others.[17] Many of the first painters coming to Old Lyme, having recently returned to America, perceived the colony as an opportunity to extend their neo-Barbizon and tonalist palettes. Working predominantly in richly muted brown tones, for which they were nicknamed the "Brown Gravy School," the depiction of huge twisted oaks, rocky upland pastures, and farm animals dominated the moody, textured canvases of the artists who made up the short-lived "American Barbizon" art colony.

IMPRESSIONISM AT OLD LYME

Childe Hassam was already one of the leading American painters when he arrived in Old Lyme in 1903 (fig. 8). Although he had had his first one-man exhibition only three years before, he had participated in more than eighty group shows[18] and wielded considerable influence as "the strongest exponent of the school of Monet in America."[19] Actually, Hassam never met Monet. His own conversion to Impressionism came from viewing the works of Monet, Sisley, and other French Impressionists in the Parisian galleries while he was a student in Paris from 1886 to 1889. Returning stateside in 1889, Hassam applied to his own painting the French Impressionist techniques of employing high-keyed and broken colors to render the transient effects of light and atmosphere. Hassam was far from a facile imitator, however, and it was through his choice of subject matter, his carefully controlled perspective, and his robust handling of paint that a distinctly American sensitivity emerged. Self-described as the "Marco Polo" of American art,[20] Hassam had a tireless passion for painting exuberant interpretations of the American landscape, cityscape, and seashore. Nowhere is this more apparent than in his paintings of New England. Here he was on his own turf. Born and raised in Dorchester, Massachusetts, Hassam was fascinated by the shimmering summer light that typifies the New England seaside. Using color schemes that vibrated with intensity, Hassam brilliantly recorded the sun-drenched summer days and moonlit nights on the Isles of Shoals, Gloucester, Provincetown, and Newport. He reveled in the outdoor summer resort life of these places where he could satisfy his passion for ocean swimming. One can sense his relish for the outdoor life from the following description of his day on Appledore Island in the Isles of Shoals off Portsmouth, New Hampshire:

I eat the north side of a haddock for breakfast, a bucket of fish chowder for dinner and a few boiled live lobsters for supper. About noontime there can be seen *(from a distance)* a good-sized purple lobster cooking in the seaweed in a certain part of the island.[21]

Hassam came to Old Lyme on one of his peripatetic searches for seaside places to record with his brush and was clearly impressed by the similarity of the countryside to that around Weir's farm in Branchville.[22] Immediately he took a great liking to Miss Florence, who in turn treated Hassam as one of her favorites for years to follow. Because of his stature, Hassam was given the best studio on the property, affording a handsome view of the Lieutenant River. His painting *Apple Trees in Bloom, Old Lyme* (1904) shows a view of the studio with the Lieutenant River in the background (cat. 180, illus. p. 26).

Hassam left for the Isles of Shoals late in the summer of 1903, leaving behind a painting of the Lieutenant River bridge that was to be included in the second annual art exhibition in the Phoebe Griffin Noyes Library, a recently built Colonial Revival building on Old Lyme's main street (fig. 9). The first exhibition had been organized at Allen Talcott's urging, who felt that the colonists should show the people of the village what they were up to.[23] Open on August 27 and 28, 1902, the show displayed recent Lyme paintings by twelve artists and marked the debut of the first art colonial summer exhibition in America (figs. 10 and 11). Additional features were prized "antiques and curios" consisting of china, silver, jewelry, laces, miniatures, and old manuscripts lent by local residents.[24] By all accounts, the

Fig. 10. **First Exhibition Poster.**
The 1902 poster for the first summer art colony exhibition in America.

Fig. 11. **Second Annual Library Exhibition,**
1903. Starting in 1902 and continuing until 1921, the local library was temporarily transformed each summer into an art gallery. This photograph shows the main reading room. Velvet drapes created additional hanging space, and shadow boxes were used to set off each picture.

Fig. 12. **Exhibition Poster,**
1903. Though not advertised, Childe Hassam was included in this exhibition. The eight women exhibitors were students in The Lyme Summer School of Art.

Fig. 13. **Afternoon Tea,** c. 1904. During the art colony exhibitions, afternoon teas were held on the lawn of the library.

122

exhibition was a huge success. Tourists came in droves by carriage or train. A stage carried visitors to and from the train station free of charge, stopping along the way at the Old Lyme Inn, which did a booming business serving meals. A fifty cent admission charge was levied to view the exhibition, with proceeds going to the Library. Members of the sponsoring Ladies' Library Association served elegant teas on the lawn (fig. 13). Apparently some members thought the admission price was a bit steep, for the following year, in 1903, the charge was cut in half. The antiques were dropped as the roster of painters jumped to twenty — eight of them female artists, mostly pupils in the Lyme Summer School of Art (fig. 12).[25]

As preparations were underway for the 1903 exhibition, Ranger and his group were back at the Griswold house joking that Hassam's bright colored landscape would stick out like a sore thumb against their predominantly brown-toned canvases. They were right. It did stick out, but not unfavorably. As one reviewer describes:

A striking feature of this exhibition is the wonderful harmony that prevails throughout the major part of the collection. One noticeable exception, however, during the recent exhibition, was the picture The Old Bridge by the impressionist Childe Hassam, a delightful bit of open-air realism and strangely prominent in lieu of its environment.[26]

Although Hassam's arrival at Old Lyme initiated the colony's conversion to Impressionism, there were actually several factors already contributing to the change. Since the 1890s Impressionism was being taught at the Art Students League by such influential American painters as J. Alden Weir, John Twachtman and William Merritt Chase. Robert Vonnoh, a later member of the Lyme group, was teaching Impressionist practices at the Pennsylvania Academy of Fine Arts. The author Hamlin Garland extolled the virtues of European and American Impressionism in the World's Columbian Exposition at Chicago in 1893. The Ten American Painters, later described as a "kind of Academy of American Impressionism,"[27] was formed in 1897-98 for the purpose of holding its own group exhibitions apart from the conservative National Academy and the declining Society of American Artists. Group exhibitions of The Ten at Durand-Ruel and Montross Galleries in New York City attracted widespread public and critical attention.

All of these pioneering events contributed to a developing Impressionist trademark at Old Lyme, but Hassam was the catalyst around whom the style coalesced. His many friends began to gravitate to Old Lyme — painters like Willard Metcalf and Walter Griffin, both contemporaries of Hassam in their early forties and Impressionists who sharpened the colony's new focus. Fellow members of The Ten, Edward Simmons and J. Alden Weir, came at Hassam's request. Simmons stayed the summer of 1906 and Weir came briefly one summer en route to his farm in Windham, Connecticut.[28] Word of Old Lyme was being passed among a new breed of American art-school–trained painters who looked up to Hassam and Metcalf as accomplished masters. Successive waves of these young American Impressionists, all in their twenties and early thirties, began to arrive in Lyme hoping to schedule their visits at a time when Hassam, Metcalf, or Griffin would be there. William Chadwick, Edward Rook, Gifford Beal, Guy Wiggins, and Robert Nisbet first came to Old Lyme between 1903 and 1906. The 1910 and 1911 seasons brought the arrival of Everett Warner, George Burr, Gregory Smith, Edmund Greacen and Chauncey Ryder. Soon following were Lawton Parker, Katherine Langhorne Adams, Wilson Irvine, Martin Borgord, and Lucien Abrams, among others. "Under Hassam," observed Donelson Hoopes, "the shoreline of Connecticut became a kind of Giverny of America."[29] Attracted by the colony's camaraderie and its plein-air attitude, many of these painters elected to take permanent residence in Old Lyme. Later they formed the rank and file of the Lyme Art Association, when it was organized in 1914. These actions, in a sense, institutionalized the art colony and perpetuated the identification of Old Lyme as a center of American Impressionism.

Unlike Hassam, both Metcalf and Griffin were relatively unrecognized when they arrived in Old Lyme, at least in terms of commercial success. Certainly the fact that each of them was able to gain critical acclaim and commercial progress while at Old Lyme did a great deal to lure others to the colony. Griffin's years in Old Lyme were full of fruitful experimentation. Adopting a pointillist technique similar to that of Hassam, Griffin created hard point pastels that were highly praised for their freely expressive characteristics. He even chose to translate this technique in his full-length commissioned Portrait of Mrs. Brown and Her Son, 1907 (cat. 178, illus. p. 25), where short strokes of color suggest an outdoor backdrop for the otherwise formal portrait. Griffin's pointillist strokes became much tighter in rendering the subjects' white summer outfits. He then refined this technique in order to produce a consciously realistic treatment of the face and hands of the two figures. Thus, in one painting, Griffin ran the gamut from French pointillism to academic realism. *Portrait of Mrs. Brown and Her Son* illustrates the primacy that the American Impressionists attached to maintaining a degree of structural form in contrast with their French counterparts, who dissolved form for a "unified appearance of the total scene."[30]

Metcalf came to Old Lyme following a year spent in Maine working in relative isolation — he referred to this experience as his "Renaissance," the start of his "new" approach to landscape painting. By 1905, rumors were widespread in art circles that Metcalf was about to "break through." Recognition came the next year in November, 1906, at his near sell-out exhibition of Lyme canvases at the St. Botolph Club in Boston. Critics waxed eloquent about Metcalf's "immense improvement."[31] The next summer an article on the Lyme colony noted that

One explanation of the remarkable jump Lyme has taken is that Willard Metcalf sold in three days $8,000 worth of Lyme landscapes in the St. Botolph Club last winter. This made Lyme sound like Standard Oil, and with no less enthusiasm than the gold hunters of '49, the picture makers have chosen Lyme as a place to swarm.[32]

Following right on the heels of the St. Botolph Club exhibition, Metcalf received the gold medal and first prize at the Corcoran Gallery in Washington for *May Night,* a romantic moonlight portrayal of Miss Florence Griswold's house (fig. 14). Not only did the award provide national recognition for Metcalf, but, as Metcalf's biographer, Elizabeth G. de Veer, has stated, it "convinced innumerable other artists that they, too, could succeed by painting and learning in so happy an environment" as Old Lyme.[33]

A dramatic illustration of Hassam's and Metcalf's pervasive influence on the colony is seen in the stylistic changeover in the works of all but the most committed of Ranger's group. Suddenly in some, and more gradually in others, a perceptible chromatic shift from a muted tonalist palette to a brighter though oftentimes restrained Impressionism can be observed. Frank Vincent DuMond's palette changed from tonalist landscapes full of allegorical details to brightly hued impressionistic renderings of the Lyme countryside around his Grassy Hill home overlooking the Long Island Sound (cat. 169, illus. p. 143). Will Howe Foote, initially establishing himself by painting academic portraits and tonalist landscapes, later fully adopted Impressionism at Old Lyme and, like many of the Lyme painters, stayed with it for the rest of his career. Foote's high-keyed figure composition *Hydrangeas*

(cat. 172) is closely aligned to the works of the American Impressionists Richard Miller and Frederick Frieseke (the latter an expatriate painter who settled next door to Monet at Giverny) in its genteel sentiment and its use of flat patterned designs of color. Arthur Dawson, Bruce Crane, Allen Talcott, Gifford Beal, Clark Voorhees, William Robinson, George Bruestle, and Frank Bicknell are a few of the Lyme painters who defected from Ranger's Barbizon camp to embrace, in varying degrees, the values of American Impressionism.[34]

Fig. 14.   Willard L. Metcalf. *May Night,* 1906. Oil on canvas, 39½″ x 36⅜″. Corcoran Gallery of Art, Washington, D.C. *May Night* depicts the moonlit facade of the Griswold House with Miss Florence approaching on the stone walk. Metcalf offered the picture to Miss Florence in order to pay his summer's board bill. "I won't take it," she said. "It's the best thing you've ever done." When *May Night* was shown the following winter at the Corcoran Gallery, it won the first Corcoran Gold Medal and a cash prize of $1000. Purchased by the same gallery later that year for $3000, the painting represented a turning point in Metcalf's career.

Ranger's effect on the colony was not altogether lost by this general stylistic shift. His Barbizon-influenced mode of painting had important consequences for the development of an Old Lyme style. Writing about the colony, Robin Richman proposed that an Old Lyme style eventually evolved out of a synthesis of the French Barbizon and Impressionist idioms, tempered by the American landscape tradition with its structural concerns and emphasis on realism.[35]

In general, then, the Lyme artists started with the Barbizon plein-air direct impression-of-nature approach, overlaid this with the techniques of Impressionism, but, because of American traditions, retained certain principles of structure, and, in doing so, were unwilling to sacrifice realism to achieve the French Impressionist dissolution of form. One needs to look at this generic characterization of "the style of Old Lyme" in relation to the values of American Impressionism. They share common ground right down the line. Indeed, the art colony at Old Lyme developed not a rare hybridized style unique to its own boundaries but, rather, one that was a component part of the overall fabric of Impressionism in America. The importance of this movement to Old Lyme was that it provided a cohesive focus — a focus that was at first exhilarating but would eventually evolve into an artistic stalemate for the colony.

LIFE AT THE "HOLY HOUSE"

Just as Ganne's Inn at Barbizon and the Hotel Baudy at Giverny had played host to European plein-air colonies, the Griswold mansion hosted the art colony at Old Lyme. Designated the "Holy House" by Childe Hassam as a takeoff on the Holley House in Cos Cob,[36] the Griswold house became the communal heart of the colony. Nearly all rooms in the old mansion were converted into guest bedrooms, including the third floor attic, where bachelor artists stayed in a maze of small rooms lit only by dormer windows or fanlights. Circuitous paths, overgrown with wild tangles of roses, vines, and weeds, led to the orchard, flower gardens, and to the barns that were cleverly transformed into working studios (map, p. 126). Beyond the studios, paths wound down to the Lieutenant River, where three old rowboats, christened across their stern "The Small Pox," "The Scarlet Fever," and the "Prickly Heat," lined the shore.[37]

Descriptions of the house never failed to mention its down-at-the-heels appearance (fig. 3). "The patched roof, the crumbling cornice, the decayed pillars, the dilapidated shutters, the rotten steps, and the broken windows spoke loudly of the ravages of time."[38] The artist and writer Arthur Heming, upon first entering the house in 1902, recalled with lavish detail the appearance of the spacious central hallway:

I saw two old sofas that had gouged holes in the wall plaster with their restless backs, while their wobbly legs seemed to be vainly reaching out after their runaway casters, as several cats and dogs slept soundly and breathed heavily among the chaos of faded and tattered cushions and ripped and gaping upholstery. A tall, gloomy looking hatrack . . . threatened at any moment to cast an avalanche of old clothing across the hall.[39]

What the Griswold mansion lacked in housekeeping, it made up in its lively esprit de corps, coupled with the gracious personality of Miss Florence. Picnics, games of horseshoes and baseball, and canoeing on the Lieutenant River were especially popular among the colony members (figs. 15, 17-20). Evenings were full of impromptu musical and theatrical entertainment they produced. The artists devised a parlor amusement that they called The Wiggle Game — pieces of paper, each drawn with several unconnected lines or "wiggles," were passed out with the object being to use the "wiggles" to create humorous caricatures. (fig. 21).

Some of the practical jokes the artists played on each other are legendary. Before Ranger left in a huff for Noank in 1904, claiming that Old Lyme had become "too civilized" for his taste,[40] Hassam and others got in some good-natured teasing. Hassam vociferously referred to Ranger and Henry Poore as members of the "baked-apple school of art."[41] One prank involved catching a box turtle and painting his shell with colored spots. Carefully concealed until he was dry and had a fine coat of varnish, the turtle was turned loose near the front porch. Finding the turtle, Ranger immediately "recognized" the scientific name of the breed, and the men suggested it be sent to Yale for study. No, announced Ranger, it should be left here to propagate, being such a rare breed.[42] Henry Poore was very proud of his dogmatically conservative tract *Pictorial Composition* (1903), and he couldn't look at someone's work without commenting how it should have an "exit" here and an "entrance" over there to make it right. One day Poore began his usual criticism, this time on one of William Robinson's canvases. Robinson interrupted with a tart response: "Poore, there is something I am going to tell you, whenever the fellows want a real good laugh, they just go and read your book."[43]

Unsuspecting newcomers to this fraternity were especially fresh fodder for the pranksters. No one was spared, not even the distinguished Dr. Woodrow

The Grounds of the Florence Griswold House

Fig. 15. **Costumed Artists.** Impromptu dress-up parties, with costumes borrowed from trunks full of old clothes Miss Florence had in her attic, often ended in mock parades down the main street of town.

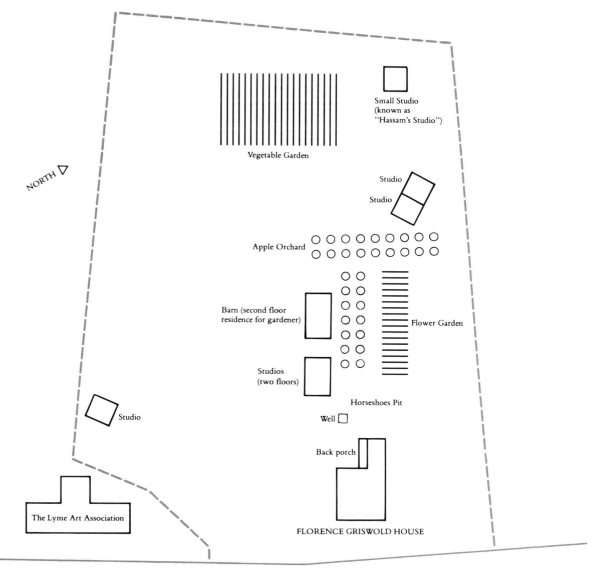

NORTH ▽

Small Studio
(known as
"Hassam's Studio")

Vegetable Garden

Studio

Studio

Apple Orchard

Barn (second floor
residence for gardener)

Flower Garden

Studios
(two floors)

Horseshoes Pit

Well

Studio

Back porch

The Lyme Art Association

FLORENCE GRISWOLD HOUSE

Lyme Street

Fig. 18. **Boating Picnic.** A boating picnic at Hamburg Cove in Lyme about 1903. Pictured from left to right: Childe Hassam, Ekhart Wilcox, Will Howe Foote, Harry Hoffman (in white hat), Clark Voorhees, Arthur Heming, Gifford Beal, Florence Griswold, art students Adele Williams and Mrs. Manners, Allen Talcott, Carleton Wiggins, and Henry Poore.

Fig. 16. **Griswold House.** This is Florence Griswold's home as it appeared at the turn of the century. A barn at the left was later converted to an artist's studio. Her property extended behind the house to the banks of the Lieutenant River.

Fig. 19. **Canoeing.** Canoeing on the Lieutenant River was a popular pastime, especially on romantic moonlit nights. Harry Hoffman proposed to Miss Beatrice Pope from a canoe on one such evening. This photograph includes Childe Hassam (paddling, right) and Florence Griswold (second from left).

Fig. 17. **Old Lyme Group Portrait.** Early members of the colony posing for an informal group portrait. Standing (left to right): Childe Hassam, Frank Vincent DuMond, William Howe, Henry Ward Ranger, and Henry Poore. Seated: Clark Voorhees, Will Howe Foote, Harry Hoffman, and Arthur Heming.

Fig. 20. **Trip to the Beach.** The artists and their wives starting on a trip to the bathing beach in Old Lyme, c. 1905–06, where the "mosquitoes were terrible," according to the inscription on the reverse of this photograph.

127

Fig. 21. **The Wiggle Game.** The Lyme painters challenged each other to matches of the Wiggle Game. The rules were simple. Someone would start the play by drawing several unconnected lines on a piece of paper. This would be passed to a player who, by connecting the "Wiggles," had to create a humorous caricature.

Wilson, then president of Princeton University, whose family spent the summers of 1905, 1909, and 1910 at Miss Florence's so that Mrs. Wilson could study landscape painting under Frank DuMond. Dr. Wilson's customary breakfast was a bowl of shredded wheat. Heming relates how he "selected a nice little bunch of excelsior from a newly arrived packing case, put it in a bowl, poured cream over it, and served it to the future President of the United States."[44] Woodrow Wilson and his family became longtime friends of Miss Florence and occasionally returned to Old Lyme to pay her a visit. Later, when Wilson was President of the United States, he brought his second wife for a brief visit to Old Lyme. They docked on the Lieutenant River and walked up to Miss Florence's house. On the way back, Mrs. Wilson was overheard to comment that she did not see how anyone could stand to stay in such a "dreadfully filthy" place.[45]

Housekeeping deficiencies aside, Florence Griswold personified the ideal hostess. Meals were always ample and frequently lavish spreads, with the menu being a roast one night, a turkey the next, and a ham the third.[46] Presiding at the head of the table, Miss Florence was a talented conversationalist who could draw upon her well-rounded knowledge of literature, music, botany, and the fine arts to enliven the dinner

Fig. 22. **Miss Florence and Artists.** A group of Lyme artists with Florence Griswold in the dining room of her home, c. 1920-25. From left to right: Bruce Crane, Florence Griswold, Henry R. Poore, William Robinson, Ernest Albert, Lydia Longacre. By the 1920s, the Old Lyme group was composed mostly of older men (all depicted here were in their sixties) and the vitality of the earlier days had passed.

talk (fig. 22). Her cheerfully optimistic personality invariably aroused the loyalty of her guests. Letters to her from many of the artists glow with nearly reverential praise. "One very great cause I have for Thanksgiving," wrote Allen Talcott, "is that some good spirit brought me to your door and that I was privileged to be with you and to share your delightful hospitality which has all the charm of being a guest with the freedom of being at home."[47] She went out of her way to help "her boys" as she called them—offering encouragement and endeavoring to sell their paintings from her front hallway "gallery" (fig. 23).

She readily extended credit to artists who repeatedly endured long periods between sales of their work. This, along with the fact that her rates were far too low, contributed to her habitual indebtedness. Turning a profit, however, was not nearly so important in her mind as creating for her colony of artists a pleasant environment where "every day is so in line with work."[48] To this end she devoted herself and very successfully so. Like the MacDowell Colony in Peterborough, New Hampshire, which flourished under the attentive patronage of Marian MacDowell, it was Florence Griswold, always willing to extend herself on an artist's behalf, who played a central role in fostering the creative development of the art colony at Old Lyme. Indeed, she was in every way as she described herself: the "keeper of the artist colony."[49]

THE LYME SUMMER SCHOOL OF ART

In the years before and after the turn of the century, summer art schools proliferated up and down the east coast. An odd mixture of youthful art students, Sunday-painters, and vacationists seeking a country holiday flocked to Cape Ann's Rockport and Gloucester, Cape Cod's Provincetown, scenic points along the Maine coast, Cos Cob, Old Lyme, and to the more inland landscape schools of New Hope, Pennsylvania, and Woodstock, New York. The summer school was a boon to many of these places for, as Karal Ann Marling has written, "summer schools were dependable sources of income, not only for towns on the skids, which rented student rooms and meals, but also for artists, whose paychecks normally came irregularly from windfall sales and the odd prize."[50]

A look at The Lyme Summer School of Art,[51] sponsored by the Art Students League in New York, bears this out. Under the direction of Frank Vincent DuMond, assisted by Will Howe Foote, the school had forty or fifty students from all over the country by 1904.[52] Quarters were available in private homes, except for the few who could afford to stay in the Old

Fig. 23. **Front Hallway "Gallery,"** c. 1910. Miss Florence used her front hallway as a "gallery" where she sold paintings by the Lyme artists and sometimes old furniture. The end of the hall opened up to a back porch, where meals were served during the summer.

Lyme Inn, a first-class summer hotel. A house next to the Inn served meals for students. The League rented the town's band room for indoor classes. Suddenly local barns were in great demand as studios. Farmers gladly complied with this demand, no doubt laughing to themselves at the sight of an art student standing in front of an easel and canvas, sharing a barn with the livestock. One Yankee farmer, obviously sensing a good thing, reportedly tried to charge rent to any hopeful artist wishing to paint "private views" of his land.

Emulating the established Lyme colonists, students scattered over the countryside in search of yet-unseen sketching grounds. A favorite job of the young boys in town was "caddying" for female pupils by carrying their packs of painting accoutrements to a chosen spot, agreeing to return at an appointed time. Fifteen cents was the usual pay for such a favor. Twice a week

Fig. 24. **Sketching Class Postcard.**
This scene of an outdoor sketching class on the eastern bank of the Connecticut River in Old Lyme was reproduced as a postcard. Included is a model with a parasol posing for the students at the river's edge. Students swarmed Old Lyme during the summer months seeking instruction from such painter-teachers as Frank Vincent DuMond, Will Howe Foote, Henry Poore, and Robert Nisbet.

classes gathered at a selected outdoor site for criticism or for talks on how to depict the natural effects of sunset and moonlight (fig. 24). A contemporaneous account of the Saturday afternoon criticisms tells how "the week's output is lined up on the walls of the old band room where their creators come prepared for the worst."[53] From his experience of directing summer art schools in the 1890s, Frank DuMond understood the value of publicity to the success of his outdoor summer school at Lyme. By writing and by granting interviews, he promoted the artists' colony and the "painterliness" of Old Lyme. Speaking of the Lyme colony, he said:

I know of no colony in Europe, where art colonies are as thick as blackberries, that can compare with it, and I have scoured the country over there pretty thoroughly with my classes. The woody parts of Lyme resemble Barbizon somewhat, but the woody parts are only one feature. If artists continue to go there for two thousand years they will find something new to paint, and each one who comes finds something which has been overlooked by everybody else.[54]

Though the success of DuMond's summer school boosted the depressed local economy, it also threatened to disrupt the harmony of the colony. Many of the colonists jealously felt that their ranks were being invaded by lowly students and amateurs, or "blots," as they were called. The quietude of the Old Lyme countryside was a primary attraction for the artists painting there. In their minds, students, with their easels and umbrellas visible from every horizon, jeopardized the possibilities of engaging in a serious rapport with the countryside. Walter Griffin's wife, Lillian Baynes Griffin, summed up the colony's position: "The question is, will Lyme be able to hold its

own, and continue as a place where the best American painters congregate to produce their work, or will it be swamped by the dilettantes and art students?"[55] Given this attitude, it is no wonder that The Lyme Summer School of Art was relatively short-lived — existing for only four seasons. Through John Carlson's recommendation, the Art Students League moved its summer school to a more receptive Woodstock, New York, where it flourished under Birge Harrison's direction.

The Lyme art colonists sought to seclude themselves in a setting where they could work relatively uninterrupted and enjoy the rustic pleasures of nature. While many of these artists were dependent upon teaching as a source of consistent income, more than a few viewed the activity as a somewhat bothersome annoyance that got in the way of their own painting. And the last thing they wanted was to be constantly reminded of this dependence by sharing their quarters with students. Willard Metcalf, prior to his own success that eliminated any need for pupils, clearly illustrates this point in a letter to Florence Griswold:

I heard yesterday from Mr. Browning who is going to Lyme — with his wife — and who is to receive my assistance this summer. [He] is very anxious to have you accommodate them. It is a somewhat delicate matter for me to speak of: for Mr. B. is a charming man but I should prefer not to have to see him at every meal, as he is *studying* art.[56]

Occupancy in the Griswold mansion was the best measure of one's acceptance by the colony of painters. During the colony's most active years from 1900 to 1915, the artists had an informal understanding with Miss Florence that group approval was a prerequisite

Fig. 25. **Bow Bridge.** At one time or another, just about every one of the Old Lyme group painted a picture of this country bridge that spanned the Lieutenant River. The abutments of the old bridge are still visible to the north of the Connecticut Turnpike where it crosses the river.

of staying in the house. With very few exceptions, students were prohibited. Students treated this situation with a mixture of humor and hopefulness: "On passing the 'Holy House' we students bow in mock humility, each of us secretly hoping that some day we would be of enough importance . . . to be a resident there."[57]

The colony's clannish posture was extended to just about everyone except the local natives. Summer tourists were labeled as hoi polloi to be regarded with a sort of haughty indifference. Curious reporters were avoided even more, for according to Hassam, "What they really want to know is about one's home life, whether you wear spats or puttees, whether you are married or divorced and how many times if so. What breakfast food you take too!"[58] Even DuMond himself acknowledged the situation by noting that "the greatest care is taken by us all to keep undesirable people away."[59] One should keep in mind that the art colony, almost by definition, was clubbish in its role as a protected retreat. Other colonies exhibited this characteristic. At Cos Cob, for example, the artists and writers of that colony turned up their noses at the successful New Yorkers who were buying up Greenwich and turning it into a modern community.[60]

A colony, whether artistic, literary, or theatrical in nature, functions as a temporary retreat from the day-to-day complexities of the outside world to a fraternal place offering a communally supportive environment that only a group of sympathetic colleagues can provide. Tantamount to its success is the need to have a self-conscious identity as a defined group. Banding together, usually with a shared point of view, art colonists sought to create an environment ideally suited to all their particular needs as artists. Whether staying for a few days or a few months, the painters who came to Old Lyme regarded it as a special place where circumstances provided fruitful artistic opportunity. Their shared point of view was built upon an appreciation of the "sense of place" of the local countryside, upon the privacy it offered, and upon the infinite seasonal nuances it revealed. Indeed it is the identification of place that embodies Old Lyme as an Impressionist art center.

OLD LYME'S SENSE OF PLACE

In the minds of the art public, Childe Hassam's *Church at Old Lyme* series and Willard Metcalf's *May Night* came to personify Old Lyme as an art colony and as the quintessential New England village. Purchased by such important American museums as the Corcoran Gallery of Art in Washington, the Smith College Museum of Art in Northhampton, Massachusetts, and the Albright Art Gallery in Buffalo, these paintings considerably advanced Hassam's and Metcalf's careers. But, perhaps more important, they came to be viewed as archetypes, as standards to be used by artists and the public alike in recognizing the colony's work. This, in turn, induced other artists to try their hand at painting the same subject. Besides the Old Lyme Church and the Griswold house, the Lieutenant River with its picturesque Bow Bridge (fig. 25), the laurel at Flying Point, and Bradbury's Mill Pond were particularly popular painting subjects. The manner and approach differs, but the scene remains the same.

It is too convenient to dismiss the repetitiveness as pandering to commercial interests that demanded yet another view of Old Lyme's version of Motif #1. Rather, it is more likely that the Lyme artists' motivation stemmed from a mixture of artistic respect for

Hassam and Metcalf, from the geographic proximity of these sites to their residences and studios (map, 132), and from a shared aesthetic sense. The result is not a collective lack of imagination on the part of the art colony but rather a cohesive artistic identity achieved through the shared experience of painting subjects that somehow embodied a particular sense of place, each in its own way unique.

For Childe Hassam, the Congregational Church at Old Lyme, designed by the New England architect Samuel Belcher, with its white clapboard facade and attenuated spire rising high above the village, evoked childhood memories of the church in his hometown of Dorchester, Massachusetts.

Some of the white churches were actual . . . masterpieces of architecture . . . . As a very young boy [I] looked at this New England Church and without knowing it appreciated partly its great beauty as it stood there against one of our radiant North American clear blue skies and as it still stands there now.[61]

Hassam and others who painted the Old Lyme church venerated it as something that was substantial in beauty, classical in form and, above all, permanent.

Hassam's reaction to the loss of the church by fire at midnight July 2, 1907, was genuine bereavement.

Who is the devil who did it? I was very much disgusted with humanity when I heard of it. And I don't need to say that I always had a real and pagan delight in the many and beautiful aspects of that old church. They cannot rebuild it — never! And the fine and immemorial elms — Oh! It is a pity.[62]

While other members of the colony shared Hassam's despair, they chose not to heed his advice that it could never be rebuilt. That summer the artists voted that the receipts from their annual exhibition, amounting to several thousand dollars, should go toward reconstructing the old church.

Metcalf's *May Night* was the prototype for the plentiful number of moonlight views of the Griswold

Old Lyme's main street lies just east and parallel to the Lieutenant River, which was a shipbuilding center in the 19th century. In 1970, the Old Lyme Historic District was formed to preserve the historic center of the village. Favorite painting sites of the art colony, together with the location of some of the artists' houses, are noted on the map.

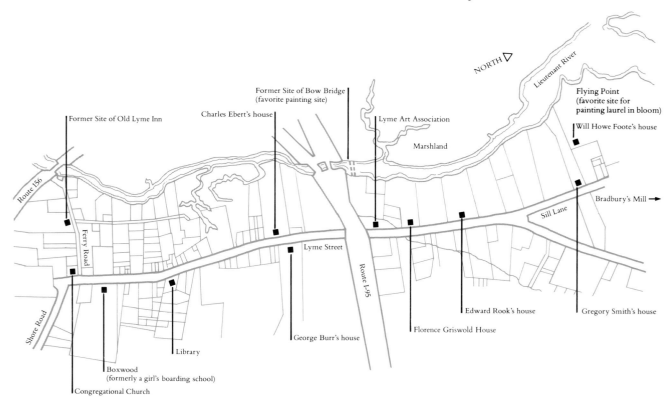

house, and one can see the direct influence it had on Will Howe Foote's *A Summer's Night* (cat. 173, illus. p. 25) and Clark Voorhees' *Moonlight Mystery* (cat. 208, illus. p. 149). Each painting establishes a sense of high drama by contrasting shadowed foliage with the almost phosphorescent glow of the moonlit facade. By elevating the house to a temple-of-the-gods status, they have gone beyond the Impressionist's objective interest in the visual sensation of light into a poetic realm aligned to the romantic and tonalist traditions of American painting. Certainly the Lyme Impressionists' predilection for moonlight scenes suggests that it was a stylistic trademark of the colony. While the romantic and atmospheric qualities of moonlight had an undeniable appeal to the American Impressionist, it is easy to overestimate this. A more prosaic reason for painting such scenes is offered in one of Hassam's letters to Weir: "We are all doing moonlights. The weather has been so bad that we have been forced to it."[63]

Hassam's remark illustrates the effect weather and seasonal changes had on landscape painting in Old Lyme. From spring's first buds to the laurel season in June to the autumn colors of October, it was the cycle of nature that dictated the painter's visit to Lyme. Though a few stayed on at Miss Florence's at least part of the long winter, most returned to their New York studios, which, for many, were in the cooperatively owned Studio Association building, a twelve-story structure overlooking Central Park at West 67th Street. The building was a nexus of activity for prominent American artists. Metcalf, Ranger, Talcott, Dessar, Beal, Vonnoh, and many other Lyme painters had their studios there at one time or another during the early years of the century.[64] "Lyme teas" were hosted in these studios during the winter. A few Lyme artists, at least those prosperous enough to do so, went south for the winter where the brilliant light, turquoise water, and whitewashed buildings of the Caribbean were especially suited to their Impressionist palette. The extension of Lyme art colony associations far beyond the confines of the "Holy House" is a testament to the group's strongly held communal identity.

But it is back at the Griswold house that one finds the most tangible representation of the colony's group identity — the painted panels decorating the doors and walls of the old house (fig. 26). The panels bear a striking resemblance to the ones begun just a few years earlier at the Salmagundi Club in New York, a club that many of the Lyme artists belonged to.[65] In the Griswold mansion, Ranger provided the initial stimulus by painting a moonlit Bow Bridge on a front hallway panel. He then challenged Henry Poore to

Fig. 26. **Griswold House Dining Room.** The dining room of the Florence Griswold House, now the museum headquarters of the Lyme Historical Society, once served as the central gathering place for Old Lyme artists. Panels painted by the colonists line the room, and the peculiar mix of furnishings approximate those pictured in photographs from the early years of this century.

continue the scene on the adjacent panel. Poore promptly executed a dog barking at the moon, tying the panels into a unified composition. William Howe then painted a portrait of a large bull across two panels on a door in the front parlor. Before long all of the doors were spoken for. Across the mantel of the dining room, Henry Poore began painting *The Fox Chase* — a humorous caricature study of the colony in a helter-skelter chase over the hills of Old Lyme (fig. 27). Metcalf suggested studding the dining room walls with a double row of panels. One by one the panels were completed by "those fortunate enough to be asked by the . . . charter members of the Holy House clan."[66] An incorrectly held assumption is that the artists painted the panels in lieu of room and board payments. In fact, artists were proud to contribute a painting to the ensemble — it represented a mark of artistic approval by their colleagues. For years William Howe periodically sent requests to Florence Griswold to make more picture postcards of his "cattle" door panel so he could send copies to his friends.[67]

LINGERING TRADITIONS

Old Lyme, by the end of the first decade and into the second decade of the twentieth century, was one of the most highly acclaimed art colonies in America. Art periodicals, magazines, and newspapers all over the country reviewed the colony's annual exhibitions that had grown from a two-day event in 1902 to five days in 1905 and then to a week by 1912. Each year more

Fig. 27. **The Fox Chase.** Painted by Henry R. Poore across the narrow eight-foot long mantle in the dining room of the Griswold House, *The Fox Chase* is a visual chronicle of the humor, fellowship, and group identity of the Lyme art colony. On the far right the "Holy House" is visible in the background, below which the inscription "School of Lyme" (denoting the colony's stylistic identity, not the Lyme Summer School of Art) is placed squarely between two bottles—a full one labeled "Mastic" and a nearly empty one labeled "Rye." Poore depicted each group member in a characteristic pose or attire for easy recognition. Edward Rook, teased for his consistently large canvases, is obscured by one of his paintings. William Howe is seated at his easel painting a model—not a lithe young female figure but a sorry looking old cow purchased from a local farmer. With his shirt draped over his easel, Hassam stands bare from the waist up, looking at the approaching crowd. Seeing the half-nude Hassam, Matilda Browne throws her hands up in shock. The outline of the Old Lyme Congregational Church rises from a clump of trees. Painted between 1901 and 1905, the mural had an organic quality, as new colony members were added or, in one case, deleted, because the artist left without paying his bill.

Fig. 28. **Lyme Art Gallery.** Designed by Charles A. Platt and erected in 1921, the Lyme Art Gallery was America's first art gallery to be self-financed by a summer art colony. Miss Florence, who is seated in the doorway, served as a gallery agent for many years.

and more collectors, dealers, art enthusiasts, and curious onlookers came from New York, Boston, New England summer spots, and elsewhere to attend the "Exhibition of Pictures Painted Principally in Old Lyme and the surrounding Country."[68] Train schedules between Lyme and New Haven, Hartford, and New London were printed on the exhibition announcements. Season admission tickets were sold. Proceeds from the exhibitions often totaled several thousand dollars and, at times, rivaled the take from the National Academy's shows in New York.

Accompanying this success was Old Lyme's gradual transition from a transient art center to a place of permanent residence for artists.[69] Land values mounted, local agriculture declined, business facilities multiplied and the summer tourist trade prospered. As this growing community of artists got involved in civic affairs,[70] the townspeoples' initial suspicions about the colony were put to rest. The situation was quite different at first, as Florence Griswold reflected:

A few relatives and friends didn't quite approve of the artists at first. There was an undercurrent of opposition at first. Those who felt offended by their arrival in the town had the impression, I believe, that these men were like the wild young men they had heard or read about . . . . However, it wasn't long before these same people became charmed with the personalities of these well-educated, widely traveled and talented group of men who were far from wild and whose every endeavor was to do serious work. The Lyme group, fortunately, has never had any of the triflers. They supported and patronized the splendid library, also the other institutions of the town, they loved and painted the beautiful church and soon became homeowners, taxpayers and leading citizens who with vigor backed up every worthwhile cause. So you see, at first the artists adopted Lyme, then Lyme adopted the artists, and now, today, Lyme and art are synonymous.[71]

The colony dreamed of having its own building especially designed as a gallery.[72] In 1914, the Lyme Art Association was formed with the goal of raising funds to build a gallery.[73] World War I stalled its efforts but by 1920 the association's plans began to take shape. Fittingly, the artists decided to erect the gallery on land

adjacent to the Griswold house, land that Miss Florence had given to the association in 1918.[74] Designed by the New York architect Charles A. Platt,[75] the attractively skylighted Lyme Art Gallery officially opened on August 6, 1921, and became America's first self-financed art gallery built by a summer art colony (fig. 28).

Given the bright prospects of a handsome new gallery, it is ironic that by this time the art colony's once-influential role had slackened considerably. A victim of its own resistance to change, the colony was eclipsed by the more progressive art currents of the Ash Can School's urban realism and by a new generation of modernists who were influenced by the successive waves of European abstract art that flooded America in the teens and twenties. Institutionalized through the Lyme Art Association, the colony turned inward and clung to its nineteenth-century principles of visual expression, its members confident that their mode of depicting nature's moods would eventually triumph over the social reformist values of The Eight and the "excesses" of the modernists.

While the emergence of an Old Lyme style initially provided a valid cohesive focus for the colony, by the 1920s it had become somewhat of a formula marked by a stiff academic Impressionism. The big draws of the colony, Metcalf and Hassam, had stopped exhibiting — Metcalf in 1909 and Hassam in 1912 (though both were incorrectly advertised as exhibitors through 1913). Those who stayed continued to work largely in the Impressionist idiom, but few attempted to extend their vision or break new ground, preferring instead quietly to maintain the established directions of the Old Lyme landscape tradition by painting "interpretations of [Old Lyme's] contours and moods."[76]

By the 1930s the art association was having financial difficulties and the art colony existed only as a historical phenomenon. The ebullient atmosphere of the "Holy House" had long since passed, though hundreds of people visited the house each year. The elderly Miss Florence guided visitors through the gallery of pictures that lined the doors and walls of her art colonial shrine. Thus the precedent for the house to

serve as a museum had already been established when the Florence Griswold Association was founded in 1936, a year before Miss Florence's death, with the immediate objective of providing for her care, and the long-range goal of operating the house as a museum, a function for which it is used today by the Lyme Historical Society.

The reasons behind the proliferation of art colonies in America between 1890 and 1910 are varied and only a few can be suggested here. In part, the summer colony was an outgrowth of the Barbizon and Impressionist tenets of plein-air painting and the direct impression of nature, popularized by the American painters' exposure to these trends in Europe and in the art schools at home. Fueled by their aversion to conditions in overcrowded and industrial cities, artists who shared the period's "cult of the outdoors" took off for rustic country settings to bathe at the fountain of rejuvenation — that of nature itself. Wedded to this summer exodus from the city was the artist's impulse to create a congenial environment suited to his every need, what Karal Ann Marling called the "art colonial dream." And, too, an important factor was the Impressionists' new awareness of the American landscape, built not upon the grandiose theatricality of the Hudson River School but on expressing a painter's intimate personal reaction to the native characteristics of the land.

Old Lyme was a chosen place in this new awareness of the American landscape that nurtured art colonies across a land that ranged from the exotic primitive scenery of Taos and Santa Fe, to the mountainous Woodstock, to the rugged coast of Gloucester, to the sand dunes and free spirit of Provincetown. At their best, the painters at Old Lyme sensitively recorded their reactions to the landscape — communicating the subtleties, effectively rendering light in all its forms from luminous summer days to moonlit winter nights, and finding harmony with both the contemplative and expressive characteristics of the Connecticut countryside. If we accept Joshua Taylor's judgment that "all art to be universal must be intensely local," then there is value in examining this body of work as a strand of the rich fabric of American art.

1 Macbeth Gallery, New York, Archives of American Art (microfilm reel NMc10, frame 788).

2 Old Lyme is a part of the region historically known as Lyme that once incorporated the present towns of East Lyme, Hadlyme, South Lyme, Old Lyme, and Lyme.

3 John Warner Barber, *Connecticut Historical Collections* (New Haven: Durrie and Peck and J. W. Barber, 1838), p. 333.

4 *Lyme — A Chapter of American Genealogy* (Old Lyme: Old Lyme Bicentennial Commission, 1976), p. 50. Reprinted from *Harper's New Monthly Magazine,* 52 (1876), 309-21.

5 Grace L. Slocum, "An American Barbizon: Old Lyme and its Artist Colony," *New England Magazine,* 34 (July 1906), 563.

6 Memorial pamphlet, *Louise Augusta Griswold: Born October 8, 1841, Died April 12, 1896* (Old Lyme: privately printed, 1896), p. 3. (Lyme Historical Society [hereafter referred to as LHS] Archives.)

7 *The* [Lyme, Connecticut] *Sound Breeze,* October 13, 1896.

8 Robin Richman's excellent introduction for *The Art Colony at Old Lyme, 1900-1935* (Exh. cat., Lyman Allyn Museum, 1966) refers to Cohen, Jongers, and Poore returning with Ranger in 1900. A letter from William H. Howe to Florence Griswold, June 18, 1901 (Florence Griswold Papers, LHS Archives) mentions that Howe and Dessar and their wives were also guests in 1901.

9 For a discussion of tonalism and its relation to the art colony at Old Lyme, consult Mary Muir, "Tonal Painting, Tonalism, and Tonal Impressionism" (Master's Thesis, University of Utah, 1978), pp. 167-172.

10 Clara Ruge, "The Tonal School of America," *International Studio,* 27 (1906), lvii-lxviii.

11 *The Color of Mood; American Tonalism 1880-1910* (Exh. cat., M. H. De Young Memorial Museum and the California Palace of the Legion of Honor, 1972), pp. 22-23.

12 Macbeth Gallery, *AAA,* frame 806.

13 Letter from Allen B. Talcott to Florence Griswold, January 11, 1902 (Florence Griswold Papers, LHS Archives).

14 Frank Vincent DuMond had just resumed teaching at the Art Students League in New York. His wife, Helen Xavier, was also an artist.

15 Talcott letter to Florence Griswold, January 20, 1902 (Florence Griswold Papers, LHS Archives).

16 Notes from conversation with Will Howe Foote, September, 1954 (Lyme Art Association Papers, LHS Archives).

17 For an excellent discussion of the Barbizon movement in America, see Peter Bermingham, *American Art in the Barbizon Mood* (Exh. cat., National Collection of Fine Arts, 1975). For general background on French Barbizon art, see Robert L. Herbert, *Barbizon Revisited* (Exh. cat., Museum of Fine Arts, Boston, 1962).

18 *Childe Hassam 1859-1935* (Exh. cat., University of Arizona Museum of Art, 1972), p. 20.

19 L. Mechlin, "Contemporary American Landscape Painting," *International Studio,* 39 (November, 1909), 6.

20 Letter from Childe Hassam to Florence Griswold, March 20, 1906 (Florence Griswold Papers, LHS Archives).

21 Hassam letter to Florence Griswold, May 2, 1907 (Florence Griswold Papers, LHS Archives).

22 Childe Hassam Papers, Archives of American Art (microfilm reel NAA 1).

23 Notes on the Florence Griswold House by Harry Hoffman, August 5, 1954 (Lyme Art Association Papers, LHS Archives), p. 7.

24 1902 Lyme, Connecticut Exhibition Poster, (LHS Archives).

25 1903 Lyme, Connecticut Exhibition Poster, (LHS Archives). An interesting note is that, in subsequent years, art students were not invited to exhibit their work.

26 *The Sound Breeze,* April 2, 1904.

27 E. P. Richardson, *Painting in America* (New York: Crowell, 1956), p. 306.

28 Conversation with Mrs. Charles Burlingham, September 21, 1979.

29 Donelson Hoopes, *The American Impressionists* (New York: Watson-Guptill Publications, 1972), p. 16.

30 *American Impressionist Painting* (Exh. cat., National Gallery of Art, 1973), p. 16.

31 Willard Metcalf Papers, Archives of American Art (microfilm roll N70/13, frame 507).

32 Metcalf Papers, AAA, frame 510.

33 *Willard Leroy Metcalf: A Retrospective* (Exh. cat., The Museum of Fine Arts, Springfield, Massachusetts, 1976), p. xviii. Elizabeth G. de Veer is preparing a definitive biography and catalogue raisonné on Metcalf that will be an important contribution to our understanding of this underrated American artist.

34 For further discussion of this stylistic changeover at Old Lyme and for examples of some of the Lyme artists not included in this exhibition, refer to *The Art Colony at Old Lyme, 1900-1935* (Exh. cat., Lyman Allyn Museum, 1966).

35 *Art Colony at Old Lyme,* p. 16.

36 Statement by Nelson C. White, personal conversation, Old Lyme, Connecticut, September 19, 1979.

37 Arthur Heming, *Miss Florence and the Artists of Old Lyme* (Essex: Pequot Press, 1971), p. 7. When Heming read of Florence Griswold's death in 1937, he wrote this account of her and the early years of the colony. The unpublished manuscript was discovered in a box of old papers and subsequently published by the Lyme Historical Society.

38 Heming, p. 2.

39 Heming, p. 2.

40 Statement by Mrs. Truman Handy, former student of Ranger, personal interview by Dale Tuller, Old Lyme, Connecticut, May 31, 1978 (LHS Archives).

41 Marion Grant, *The Florence Griswold House,* unpublished monograph, p. 15 (LHS Archives).

42 Notes on the Florence Griswold House by Gregory

Smith (Lyme Art Association Papers, LHS Archives), p. 10.

43 Notes by Gregory Smith, p. 9.

44 Heming, p. 25.

45 Notes by Gregory Smith, p. 8.

46 Statement by Dr. Matthew Griswold, cousin and personal physician of Florence Griswold, personal interview, Old Lyme, Connecticut, September 26, 1979.

47 Letter from Allen Talcott to Florence Griswold, Thanksgiving Day, 1901 (Florence Griswold Papers, LHS Archives).

48 Letter from Willard Metcalf to Florence Griswold, August 20, 1907 (Florence Griswold Papers, LHS Archives).

49 Calendar Entry by Florence Griswold, October 11, 1911 (LHS Archives).

50 Karal Ann Marling, *Woodstock An American Art Colony 1902-1977* (Exh. cat., Vassar College Art Gallery, 1977) p. 3 of introduction.

51 The Brooklyn artist, Joseph Boston, opened an earlier summer school of art in Old Lyme in June, 1894, under the auspices of the Brooklyn Institute of Arts and Sciences. Classes were held in the new high school building and students sought accommodations in the nearby Pierpont House or in private homes. The school lasted only one summer and then moved in 1895 to Belle Island — a small island at the mouth of Norwalk Harbor, Connecticut (Lyme Art Association Papers, LHS Archives.)

52 Slocum, p. 576.

53 *The Sound Breeze,* April 2, 1904.

54 *The New York City Sun,* November 24, 1907.

55 Metcalf Papers, AAA microfilm reel N70/13, frame 510.

56 Letter from Metcalf to Florence Griswold, May 3, 1905 (Florence Griswold Papers, LHS Archives).

57 *The [Portland] Oregon Sunday Journal,* March, 1913.

58 Letter from Hassam to Florence Griswold, March 20, 1906 (Florence Griswold Papers, LHS Archives).

59 *The New York Sun,* November 24, 1907.

60 Charles Eldredge, "Connecticut Impressionists: The Spirit of Place," *Art in America,* 62 (Sept.-Oct., 1974), p. 86.

61 Hassam Papers, *AAA,* microfilm reel NAA 1.

62 Heming, p. 67.

63 Letter from Childe Hassam to J. Alden Weir, July 7, 1906, Archives of American Art (microfilm reel NAA1).

64 "New York Studios of New England Artists," *New England Magazine,* 44 (April 1911), 201.

65 William Henry Shelton, *The Salmagundi Club* (Boston: Houghton Mifflin, 1918), pp. 86-87.

66 *The Sound Breeze,* April 2, 1904.

67 Letter from William H. Howe to Florence Griswold, January 28, 1921 (Florence Griswold Papers, LHS Archives).

68 1910 Ninth Annual Lyme Exhibition Announcement (LHS Archives).

69 A few of the artists who purchased or built houses in the Lyme/Old Lyme area between 1900 and 1920 were Gregory Smith, Harry Hoffman, Will Howe Foote, William Chadwick, Allen Talcott, Louis Paul Dessar, Clark Voorhees, Frank DuMond, Lewis Cohen, Frederic Ramsdell, Jules Turcas, George Burr, Charles Ebert, Lucien Abrams, Frank Bicknell, Wilson Irvine, George Bruestle, Arthur Dawson, Robert and Bessie Potter Vonnoh, Carleton Wiggins, Oscar Fehrer, and Edward Rook.

70 Resident artists served on town committees, became involved with community churches, and had an increasing voice in town affairs. For instance, Gregory Smith and Allen Talcott were at different times elected Justice of the Peace, and Smith was a central figure in town politics for years. Clark Voorhees acted as president of the local library, an organization that many of the artists' wives were associated with. The artists Thomas W. Ball, Bicknell, Foote, Smith, and Voorhees, as well as Florence Griswold, were founding members of the Old Lyme Fire Department, organized in 1923.

71 *The Deep River New Era,* July 16, 1937.

72 From the beginning, the Lyme painters had found the library less than ideal for showing their work, "owing to lack of proper lighting, restricted wall space, and the trouble caused by the necessary disarrangement of the library fixtures before each exhibition." (Lyme Art Association brochure, 1914.)

73 The Lyme artists appointed a committee in 1913 to study the prospects of building a gallery. It was reported that $15,000 was needed to construct a modest gallery. A benefit exhibition of Lyme pictures held in New York proved to be unsuccessful. Following its incorporation, the Lyme Art Association sent a carefully worded fund-raising appeal to the "Friends of the Colony." The association recognized that it could only be successful if its interests were closely identified with the needs of the townspeople. The appeal stressed that though the promotion of art was the association's primary objective, "of nearly equal importance to its members is the desire that Lyme itself may benefit by the erection of a structure . . . in which lectures, conferences, and also social meetings, dances, private theatricals and other forms of entertainment may be held." (Lyme Art Association brochure, 1914.)

74 Deed, Florence Griswold to Lyme Art Association, January 13, 1918 (photocopy in 1933-34 scrapbook, Lyme Art Association).

75 Platt was initially trained as a painter and etcher, at the National Academy of Design, Art Students League, and then in Paris under Boulanger and Lefebvre. He was associated with a number of the Lyme artists through the National Academy of Design and other art organizations in New York. For further information on Platt, see: Royal Cortissoz, *Monograph of the Work of Charles A. Platt* (New York: The Architectural Book Publishing Co., 1913).

76 *Twenty-Fourth Annual Exhibition of Paintings* (Exh. cat., Lyme Art Association, 1925), p. 1.

Abrams, Lucien

160 *The Orchard*
1916: Behind the Florence Griswold House, Old Lyme
Oil on canvas, 26¼ x 32¼ (66.7 x 81.9)
Signed and dated LL: *Lucien Abrams/16*
Lyme Historical Society

Bicknell, Frank A.

161 *Lieutenant River, Old Lyme*
n.d.: Old Lyme
Oil on panel, 22¼ x 61 (56.5 x 154.9)
Signed LR: *Frank A. Bicknell ANA*
Private Collection

Framed in three sections by the artist.

Borgord, Martin

162 *To Miss. Florence*
July, 1916: Florence Griswold House interior, Old Lyme
Oil on panel, 15¾ x 11¾ (40 x 29.8)
Inscribed, signed and dated LR: *To Miss. Florence/Martin Borgord/July 1916*
Private Collection

Burr, George

163 *Old Lyme Garden*   ILLUS. P. 142
n.d.: Behind the artist's house, Old Lyme
Oil on panel 12 x 9 (30.5 x 22.9)
Signed LR: *G Burr;* on reverse: *G Burr/Old Lyme Garden*
Lyme Historical Society

164 *President Wilson's Daughters*
c. 1910: Hamburg Cove, Lyme
Oil on panel, 8½ x 10⅝ (21.6 x 27)
Signed LR: *G. B. Burr*
Lyme Historical Society, Gift of Mr. and Mrs. Abraham Adler

On reverse: an oil portrait of the artist's son, George Watson Burr.

Chadwick, William

165 *Front Parlor, Florence Griswold House, Old Lyme*
n.d.: Florence Griswold House, Old Lyme
Oil on canvas, 24 x 30 (61 x 76.2)
No signature

Lyme Historical Society, Gift of Mrs. Elizabeth Chadwick O'Connell

The woman seated on the sofa is believed to be the artist's wife, Pauline Bancroft Chadwick, in which case the painting would date after 1910, the year of their marriage.

166 *Griswold Beach, Old Lyme*   ILLUS. P. 142
n.d.: Griswold Beach, Old Lyme
Oil on board, 14⅛ x 18 (35.9 x 45.7)
Signed LR: *W. Chadwick*
Lyme Historical Society, Gift of the Artist

167 *On the Porch*   ILLUS. P. 24
c. 1908: Back Porch of the Florence Griswold House, Old Lyme
Oil on canvas, 24 x 30 (61 x 76.2)
Signed LR: *W. Chadwick*
Lyme Historical Society, Gift of Mrs. Elizabeth Chadwick O'Connell

DuMond, Frank Vincent

168 *Path to the Sound*
1906: Grassy Hill, Old Lyme
Oil on board, 12 x 16 (30.5 x 40.6)
Signed and dated LR: *Frank V. DuMond '06*
Robert P. Gunn

169 *Top of the Hill, Old Lyme*   ILLUS. P. 143
c. 1906: Grassy Hill, Old Lyme
Oil on board, 12 x 16 (30.5 x 40.6)
No signature; on reverse, in artist's hand (?): *22/Gate to the Hilltop*
Lyme Historical Society

Ebert, Charles

170 *Old Lyme Church*
c. 1923: Old Lyme
Oil on canvas 30 x 36 (76.2 x 91.4)
Signed LR: *Ebert*
The First Congregational Church of Old Lyme

171 *Portrait of Betty*
c. 1917: Monhegan, Maine
Oil on canvas, 36 x 30 (91.4 x 76.2)
No signature
Lyme Historical Society, Gift of Mr. and Mrs. Robert H. Bartels

Foote, Will Howe

172 *Hydrangeas*
c. 1914: Old Lyme
Oil on canvas, 30 x 30 (76.2 x 76.2)
Signed LL: *Will Howe Foote*
S.K.T. Galleries

173 *A Summer's Night*　ILLUS. P. 25
c. 1906: Florence Griswold House, Old Lyme
Oil on canvas, 34 x 30 (86.4 x 76.2)
Signed LR: *Will Howe Foote*
Lyme Historical Society, Gift of the Artist
Also titled *The Griswold House by Moonlight*.

Greacen, Edmund

174 *The Artist's Wife*
c. 1910-13: Old Lyme
Oil on board, 13¾ x 14 (34.9 x 35.6)
Signed by daughter LR: *Edmund Greacen by N.G.*
Nan Greacen Faure

175 *Bow Bridge*
c. 1910-14: Old Lyme
Oil on canvas, 20 x 24 (50.8 x 61)
No signature
Mrs. Anne Bonnet

176 *The Old Garden*
c. 1912: Behind the Florence Griswold House, Old Lyme
Oil on canvas, 30¼ x 30¼ (76.9 x 76.9)
Signed LR: *Edmund Greacen*
Lyme Historical Society, Gift of
Mrs. Edmund Greacen, Jr.

Griffin, Walter

177 *Early Autumn Landscape*
1905: Old Lyme
Hardpoint pastel on cardboard, 6 x 8 (15.2 x 20.3)
Signed LL: *W. Griffin; on reverse: Walter Griffin/1905*
Lyme Historical Society

178 *Portrait of Mrs. Brown and Her Son*　ILLUS. P. 25
1907: Old Lyme
Oil on canvas, 72 x 37¾ (182.9 x 95.9)
Signed and dated LL: *Walter Griffin–1907; on reverse UL: Portrait of Virginia Bätjer Brown./wife of Luther Connah Brown./and their son Anson Swan Brown./1907; on reverse UR: Painted by Walter Griffin/Old Lyme. Conn.*
Lyme Historical Society, Gift of
Mrs. John B. Johnson

This portrait was commissioned by Luther Connah Brown and is one of Griffin's few portraits from his Old Lyme period.

179 *Untitled*
1905: Old Lyme
Hardpoint pastel on brown paper, 10⅜ x 14½ (26.4 x 36.9)
Inscribed, signed and dated LL: *To Miss Florence Griswold/Walter Griffin '05*
Lyme Historical Society

Hassam, Childe

180 *Apple Trees in Bloom, Old Lyme*　ILLUS. P. 26
1904: Old Lyme
Oil on panel, 24 x 30 (61 x 76.2)
Signed and dated LL: *Childe Hassam 1904;* monogrammed and dated on reverse
Private Collection

The building at the right is Hassam's studio on the Florence Griswold property overlooking the Lieutenant River. See cat. 188.

181 *The Bridge Over the Lieutenant River*
1905: Old Lyme
Oil on canvas, 19⅞ x 23⅞ (50.5 x 60.6)
Signed and dated LL: *Childe Hassam 1905*
Private Collection

182 *Church at Old Lyme*
1924: Old Lyme
Etching on heavy Japan paper, 7¼ x 6½ (18.4 x 16.5)
Monogrammed and dated in plate LL; monogrammed in pencil LR
Lyme Historical Society, Given in memory of Daniel Woodhead, Jr. and Henry B. Day.
Same as cat. 36.

183 *Church at Old Lyme*
1906: Old Lyme
Pastel on green paper, 12 x 8⅞ (30.5 x 22.5)
Signed and dated LL: *Childe Hassam, 1906*
Albright-Knox Art Gallery, Buffalo, New York, Gift of Mrs. Theodore G. Kenefick, 1962

184 *Church at Old Lyme*　ILLUS. P. 143
1906: Old Lyme
Oil on canvas, 30⅛ x 25¼ (76.5 x 63.8)
Signed and dated LR: *Childe Hassam 1906*
The Parrish Art Museum, Littlejohn Collection

185 *Moonlight on the Sound*
1906: Long Island Sound, possibly from Cos Cob
Oil on canvas, 20 x 30⅛ (51 x 76.5)
Signed and dated LL: *Childe Hassam 1906*
Private Collection

186 *The Old Lyme Church in Moonlight*
1905: Old Lyme
Oil on canvas, 23½ x 19½ (59.7 x 49.6)
Signed LL: *Childe Hassam; on reverse: CH 1905*
Private Collection

187 *Stone Bridge, Old Lyme, Connecticut*   ILLUS. P. 143
1905: Adjacent to Florence Griswold House,
Old Lyme
Oil on canvas, 18 x 22 (45.7 x 55.9)
Signed and dated LL: *Childe Hassam 1905*
San Diego Museum of Art, Gift of the Parker
Foundation

The subject of this painting is the small bridge and
brook that winds between the Florence Griswold
House and the Lyme Art Gallery. A different view of
the brook is found in Metcalf's *November* (cat. 197).

Hoffman, Harry

188 *Childe Hassam's Studio*   ILLUS. P. 144
1909: Behind the Florence Griswold House, Old Lyme
Oil on canvas, 24 x 18 (61 x 45.7)
Signed LL: *H. Hoffman* on stretcher, reverse: *Hassam's
Studio – Old Lyme 1909*
Lyme Historical Society, Gift of the Artist

This is the same subject as cat. 180.

Irvine, Wilson H.

189 *The Pool*   ILLUS. P. 145
c. 1913: Lyme
Oil on canvas, 26¾ x 23⅜ (67.9 x 59.4)
Signed LL: *Irvine*
Graham Gallery

Irvine painted this across the road from his house in
Lyme.

190 *School Days*
n.d.: Lyme
Oil on canvas, 34 x 36½ (86.4 x 92.7)
Signed LR: *Irvine*
Lyme Public Library

Jongers, Alphonse

191 *The Harpist, Portrait of Miss Florence Griswold*
1903: Florence Griswold House, Old Lyme
Oil on canvas, 35½ x 27¼ (90.2 x 69.5)
Signed UR: *Alphonse Jongers.*
Lyme Historical Society, Gift of the Lyme Art
Association

Also titled *The Lady of Lyme.*

Langhorne, Katherine

192 *Landscape*
c. 1912: Old Lyme
Oil on canvas, 25 x 30½ (63.5 x 77.5)
Signed LR: *K. Langhorne*
Old Lyme-Phoebe Griffin Noyes Library

Metcalf, Willard L.

193 *Child In Sunlight*   ILLUS. P. 145
August, 1915: Pleasure Beach, Waterford
Oil on canvas, 25 x 21 (63.5 x 53.3)
Signed LL: *W.L.M.;* on reverse: *Rosalind Metcalf.
3 years 9 mos. Aug. 1915*
Lyme Historical Society, Gift of Mrs. Henriette
Metcalf

194 *Church Across the Fields*   ILLUS. P. 146
1908: Probably Old Lyme
Oil on panel, 14½ x 16½ (36.9 x 41.9)
Signed and dated LL: *W. L. Metcalf 1908*
Mr. and Mrs. John H. Crawford III

If the church here is that in Old Lyme, it could have
existed only in the artist's memory, since the actual
structure had not yet been rebuilt after its destruction
by fire in 1907.

195 *Flying Shadows*   ILLUS. P. 27
1905: Near Lyme
Oil on canvas, 26 x 29 (66 x 73.7)
Signed and dated LL: *W. L. Metcalf. '05*
Jeffrey R. Brown, Fine Arts

Metcalf titled a second painting *Flying Shadows* as well
(illus., Patricia Jobe Pierce, *The Ten,* p. 90).

196 *Lyme Hillside*
1906: Lyme
Pastel on gray paper, 5⅛ x 6⅞ (13 x 17.4)
Signed and dated LR: *W. L. Metcalf '06*
Lyme Historical Society

197 *November*
1905: Old Lyme   ILLUS. P. 28
Oil on canvas, 26 x 21½ (66 x 54.6)
Signed and dated LL: *W. L. Metcalf 1905*
Diane Tanenbaum Lux

See note for cat. 187.

198 *Springtide in Connecticut*
1909: Leete's Island
Oil on canvas, 40 x 43 (101.6 x 109.2)
Signed LL: *W. L. Metcalf*
Grand Rapids Art Museum, Gift of Willard F. Keeney

Original title: *Spring Fields.* Elizabeth G. de Veer, who
provided the information about the original title, says
Metcalf painted a smaller version of the same subject,
c. 1910, titled *Springtide (time) in Connecticut.*

Ranger, Henry Ward

199 *Meetinghouse Hill*
1902: Meetinghouse Hill, Old Lyme
Oil on panel, 5¼ x 8¾ (13.3 x 22.2)
Signed LL: *H.W.R.*
Old Lyme-Phoebe Griffin Noyes Library

200 *Somber Harmony*
c. 1902-03: Old Lyme
Oil on panel, 11¹⁵⁄₁₆ x 16¹⁄₁₆ (30.3 x 40.8)
Monogrammed and signed LL: *HWR*
The William Benton Museum of Art, Louise Crombie
Beach Memorial Collection

Robinson, William S.

201 *Laurel*   ILLUS. P. 146
c. 1908: Near Old Lyme
Oil on canvas, 20 x 24 (50.8 x 61)

Signed LL: *Wm. S. Robinson;* on reverse (within circle): *F/22/1921*
Lyme Historical Society, Gift of Miss Hyla Snyder

Rook, Edward F.

202 *Laurel*   ILLUS. P. 29
c. 1905-10: Old Lyme (Possibly the Lieutenant River)
Oil on canvas, 40¼ x 50¼ (102.2 x 127.6)
Signed LR: *Edward Rook*
Hammer Galleries

203 *Mill Dam*
n.d.: Bradbury's Mill Dam, Old Lyme
Oil on canvas, 26½ x 36½ (67.3 x 92.7)
Inscribed and signed LR: *To Miss Florence Griswold/Edward F. Rook*
Fenton L. B. Brown

Rook painted at least two other versions of this scene (*Flume In Snow* and *Swirling Waters,* cat. 204). Consequently, the site came to be known among fellow Lyme artists as "Rook's Mill."

204 *Swirling Waters*   ILLUS. P. 147
c. 1917: Bradbury's Mill Pond, Old Lyme
Oil on canvas, 30¼ x 38⅝ (76.8 x 98.1)
Signed LL: *Edward F. Rook*
Lyme Historical Society, Gift of Mrs. Chauncey B. Garver

Ryder, Chauncey F.

205 *Winter Landscape*
n.d.: Connecticut?
Oil on canvas, 20¼ x 30¼ (51.4 x 76.8)
Signed LR: *Chauncey F. Ryder*
New Britain Museum of American Art, Estate of Miss Frances Whittlesey

Smith, Edward Gregory

206 *The Bow Bridge*   ILLUS. P. 148
c. 1912-15: Old Lyme
Oil on canvas, 36 x 40 (91.4 x 101.6)
Signed LL: *Gregory Smith*
Private Collection

Voorhees, Clark G.

207 *Lyme Hills*   ILLUS. P. 148
n.d.: Lyme
Oil on board, 6⅛ x 8¾ (15.5 x 22.2)
Signed LR: *C. G. Voorhees*
Fenton L. B. Brown

208 *Moonlight Mystery*   ILLUS. P. 149
n.d.: Old Lyme
Oil on board, 18 x 23¾ (45.7 x 60.2)
Signed LR: *Clark G. Voorhees*
Clark Voorhees, Jr.

209 *My Garden*   ILLUS. P. 149
c. 1914: Old Lyme
Oil on canvas, 28¾ x 36 (73 x 91.4)
Signed LR: *Clark G. Voorhees*
Clark Voorhees, Jr.

At least two other colonists, Will Howe Foote and Matilda Browne, painted Voorhees' garden. Voorhees later painted an almost identical view, entitled *Honeysuckle and Roses.*

White, Henry C.

210 *Autumn Sketch*
1892: Waterford
Oil on panel, 12 x 16 (30.5 x 40.6)
No signature
Henry C. White II

211 *Lieutenant River – Lyme*
c. 1904-05: Lyme
Pastel, 9 x 11 (22. 9 x 27.9)
No signature
Nelson Holbrook White

Wiggins, Guy C.

212 *Church on the Hill*
n.d.: Grassy Hill, Lyme
Oil on canvas, 32 x 27 (81.3 x 68.9)
Signed LL: *Guy C. Wiggins*
Lyman Allyn Museum

213 *Street Fair*
c. 1910: Old Lyme
Oil on board, 8 x 10 (20.3 x 25.4)
Signed on reverse: *Guy Wiggins*
Collection of Dr. Clark S. Marlor

163   George Burr, *Old Lyme Garden*

166   William Chadwick, *Griswold Beach, Old Lyme*

142

184   Childe Hassam, *Church at Old Lyme,* 1906

169   Frank Vincent DuMond,
      Top of the Hill, Old Lyme, c. 1906

187   Childe Hassam,
      Stone Bridge, Old Lyme, Connecticut, 1905

188   Harry Hoffman, *Childe Hassam's Studio*, 1909

193   Willard L. Metcalf, *Child in Sunlight,* August, 1915

189   Wilson H. Irvine, *The Pool,* c. 1913

145

194   Willard L. Metcalf, *Church Across the Fields*, 1908

201   William S. Robinson, *Laurel,* c. 1908

204   Edward F. Rook, *Swirling Waters,* c. 1917

206   Edward Gregory Smith, *The Bow Bridge,* c. 1912–15

207   Clark G. Voorhees, *Lyme Hills*

208   Clark G. Voorhees, *Moonlight Mystery*

209   Clark G. Voorhees, *My Garden,* c. 1914

Biographies of the Artists

Childe Hassam once remarked to Florence Griswold that what people really want to know about artists "is about one's home life, whether you wear spats or puttees, whether you are married or divorced and how many times if so. What breakfast food you take too!" Short biographies of artists, by contrast, are usually terse lists of an artist's training, awards and exhibitions. The notes that follow are often a mix of trivia with the material of a formal resume, and the pattern can change from entry to entry. It cannot be helped. In some instances, a good deal is known about an artist, and then the intent is to present new or corrected information or insight into the artist's attitudes. Suggestions for further reading are highly selective. In many instances, however, information is so scant that virtually every tidbit is offered, and no further reading can sensibly be suggested for the general reader.

Although we consulted as many secondary sources as possible, we concentrated on primary sources — oral history, letters, diaries, and other materials in archives such as those of the National Academy of Design and the Archives of American Art. The Lyme Historical Society Archives have been especially useful. A search for information about any Old Lyme artist must begin there. Because there is so much still to be learned, we encourage persons with questions or with new or different information about the art and artists presented here to get in touch with any of our three institutions.

Throughout these notes, when a state name does not follow that of a city or town, it should be understood that Connecticut is meant.

Abrams, Lucien

Born June 10, 1870,
  Lawrence, Kansas.
Died April 14, 1941,
  New Haven.
In Old Lyme, 1915-41.

When Lucien Abrams graduated from Princeton in 1896, the university offered him a post as instructor of Latin — a subject he excelled in. Intent on becoming an artist, Abrams declined the offer and spent the next two winters studying at the Art Students League in New York. Like so many of the Old Lyme group, Abrams later enrolled at the Académie Julian in Paris, where he received instruction from Benjamin Constant and Jean-Paul Laurens. Yet years later, Abrams would note that "My art was developed, not in the schools, but by independent study before nature, not trying to copy, but to interpret, to find order in chaos, and put it in plastic form."

Since his family had considerable means, Abrams was able to live and travel in Europe from the time of his enrollment in the Académie Julian in 1894 until 1915. He was strongly influenced by Whistler during a short period at the latter's art school in Paris. It is true, nevertheless, that most of his study was done independently during his extensive travels through Europe. He painted in Belgium, Provence, Brittany, Southern France, Italy, and Spain. In 1905-06 he spent six months in Algeria. In museums he studied the Old Masters and developed a keen sense of art connoisseurship. Particularly interested in the French Impressionists, Abrams over the years amassed an important collection of paintings by Auguste Renoir, now in the Marion Koogler McNay Art Institute in San Antonio, Texas.

From 1902 until 1914, Lucien Abrams exhibited annually in Paris at the Salon d'Automne and the Salon des Indépendants. His participation in French art circles no doubt contributed to the influences of Impressionism, Post-Impressionism, and Fauvism that are evident in his work. Abrams said that his aim was "to interpret the beauty of reality; to place it in expressive form before others."

The Old Lyme landscapes of his mature years reflect this aim most clearly. Using a lean palette — he once said that he had tried to limit himself to five colors — marked by rich shades of blue, green, red, and white, Abrams worked with swatches of paint, alternating in thickness, that produce harmonies of bold color. Unfortunately this approach does not translate well in his figure studies, where his deficiencies as a draftsman become apparent.

Abrams was a relative latecomer to Old Lyme, arriving in 1915, when he was forty-five years old. He and his wife, Charlotte Gina Onillon, a native of Paris and a graduate of the Sorbonne, had just recently been married. They purchased a summer residence in Old Lyme that commanded a fine view of Long Island Sound. Abrams was an active member of the Lyme Art Association and exhibited there every year from 1915 until the 1930s.

Abrams had one-man exhibitions in this period at Pabst Galleries in San Antonio, Texas, where he had a winter home, and at Durand-Ruel Galleries, New York. His work was recently featured in the 1978 exhibition *Three American Impressionists: From Paris to Old Lyme* at A. M. Adler Fine Art, Inc., New York. Abrams was a member of the American Federation of Artists, the Lyme Art Association, and the Princeton Club of New York City. He died in New Haven, April 14, 1941.

Further reading:
Three American Impressionists: From Paris to Old Lyme; Lucien Abrams, George Burr, Charles Ebert. Exh. cat., A. M. Adler Fine Art, Inc., New York City, 1978.

Adams, Katherine Langhorne

Born 1885, Plainfield, N.J.
Still living?
In Old Lyme, 1912-13.

Katherine Langhorne exhibited only twice in Old Lyme, in 1912 and 1913, and little is known about her association with the colony, except that she coped readily with a male artist who mistakenly entered her bedroom in the Griswold House one night, having been misdirected by forgetful Miss Florence. She studied at the Art Students League under John Henry Twachtman and Frank Vincent DuMond and was also enrolled in summer courses, possibly in either Cos Cob or Old Lyme. She exhibited at the National Academy of Design as early as 1912, and in 1915 two of her works were included in the Panama-Pacific International Exposition in San Francisco. Although it is not known whether she studied in Paris, she travelled throughout Europe as well as in Japan, and much later, in the 1930s, she lived for a while in Buenos Aires.

Around 1916 Katherine Langhorne married Benjamin Pettengill Adams, moved to New York, and thereafter exhibited under her married name. Three exhibitions of her paintings were held during the 1920s at the Milch, Babcock, and Montross Galleries in New York. Her eleven paintings at Milch included both New York City and New England country subject matter. Reviewing her 1928 exhibit at Babcock Galleries, which featured views of the Palisades, a critic for *Art News* commented on the relative abstraction of her landscapes:

Mrs. Adams' interpretations of nature show the influence of her teacher, Twachtman, as well as an excellent sense of Oriental elimination. For those in quest of photographic accuracy these seasonal studies of the Palisades will offer little that is recognizable or satisfying. For those to whom landscape painting at its best is but a state of mind, Mrs. Adams' work loses nothing by its departure from the minutiae of the earlier exponents of Hudson River scenery.

Katherine Langhorne Adams was also represented in exhibitions at the Pennsylvania Academy of Fine Arts, the Art Institute of Chicago, and the National Association of Women Painters and Sculptors, where she won the Marcia Tucker Prize in 1935 and an honorable mention the following year.

With her husband, she had moved in the 1920s to Sneden's Landing, Palisades, New York, where she designed the stone house they had built there. Her plan won first prize in a contest sponsored by *House Beautiful* magazine for "the best small house East of the Mississippi." Later, she lived in Fairfield, Connecticut, and Alexandria, Virginia.

Further reading:
"Exhibitions in New York," *American Art News,* 20 (Jan. 14, 1922), 1.
"Katherine Langhorne Adams, Alfredo Cini, Babcock Galleries," *Art News,* 26 (May 12, 1928),11.

Bicknell, Frank Alfred

Born Feb. 17, 1866, Augusta,
  Maine.

Died Apr. 9, 1943, Essex.

In Old Lyme, c. 1902-c. 1940.

Frank Bicknell remains mysterious. He is frequently described as tall, handsome, and outgoing, but no photograph of him has been located. He lived in Old Lyme for nearly forty years, yet little can be said about his life there, nor, indeed, about his life before that.

Bicknell was born in Augusta, Maine, in 1866, and later moved to Malden, Massachusetts, where he studied art with Albion H. Bicknell, presumably a relative. In 1887 he exhibited at the National Academy of Design. The following year he moved from Malden to New York City, and by 1893 he was in Paris studying at the Académie Julian under Bouguereau and Robert Fleury. His entry in New York's National Academy exhibition that year depicted an old washhouse along the River Eure-Chartres, suggesting a Barbizon approach not unlike that of his first teacher and namesake.

In 1894 his address was the Salmagundi Club in New York, possibly indicating his recent return to this country, and his entry in the National Academy annual that year was *An Old Apple-Orchard, France* (which he priced at $500, an amount roughly four times that he had put on his earlier paintings).

Curiously, Bicknell's address for the next few years was "The Tower," Madison Square Garden, one of the newest, most celebrated buildings in the city. The Spanish tower that architect Stanford White designed to crown what was essentially an amusement center that included a theater, restaurant, concert hall and roof garden (where White would be killed in 1906, victim of a jealous husband) was the second tallest structure in the city, lit up at night, and topped by a controversial nude Diana sculpted by Augustus Saint-Gaudens. Stanford White had a sumptuous apartment in "The Tower." Rents there must have been steep. Was Bicknell a wealthy man?

He had money enough to travel to Japan during this period, for paintings he exhibited at the National Academy in the late 1890s are of Japanese subjects, and some artists' dictionaries of the early 1900s note his trip to Japan.

Bicknell came to Old Lyme early, about 1902, and after that seemed to limit his travels to the eastern United States, often Maine or Cape Cod. A bachelor, Bicknell often referred to the other colonists as "the family." Arthur Heming, whose reminiscences of Old Lyme were published posthumously in 1971, described a typical evening

in the Griswold House living room after a hard day's work. The group around the fireplace: Metcalf, Woodrow Wilson, Hassam, "Uncle" Howe, DuMond, Robinson, and Rook. "Mrs. Wilson, Mrs. DuMond, Miss Pope and Bicknell were having a rubber of bridge, and Miss Florence was playing the piano while Hoffman was accompanying her upon his flute." Mrs. Wilson bought some of Bicknell's paintings.

Bicknell and Miss Florence became good friends. His trips to Old Lyme meant a good deal to him. In a 1907 letter from North Hackensack, New Jersey, where he then had a winter home, he wrote:

My dear Miss Florence:
Can you — and will you stow me away somewhere in the big house about the last week in Septembre? Or the first week of Octobre at the latest? Please do not say *no* — Put me in the Barn if you will — but come to Lyme I must sometime this Autumn.

Inexplicably, in about 1919, Bicknell began to teach. He became Associate Professor at the College of Fine Arts, Carnegie Institute of Technology, for six years, and apparently he taught no more after that.

Bicknell was a member of many organizations, among them the Lotos Club, the Salmagundi Club, the MacDowell Club, the National Arts Club, the Academy of National Art, the American Art Association of Paris, the Pittsburgh Art Association, and the Chicago Water Color Society. He was elected to associate membership in the National Academy of Design in 1913.

After 1916, Bicknell's home in Old Lyme was one that had belonged to fellow artist Lewis Cohen, a Barbizon painter who bequeathed the place to him. Until failing health forced Bicknell to give it up, he was a prominent member of the Old Lyme group, who specialized in painting the local landscape at different times of day and in different seasons of the year. He died in 1943 in a nursing home in Essex. If there had been relatives, certainly his history would be better remembered. Neither his personality nor his accomplishments as an artist are yet well enough known.

Borgord, Martin

Born Feb. 8, 1869, Guasdal,
  Norway.

Died Mar. 25, 1935, Riverside,
  Cal.

In Old Lyme, summers, 1916,
  1918.

Martin Borgord, although virtually unknown today, was early in this century recognized as a prominent painter and sculptor. Born in Norway, Borgord studied in Paris under Jean-Paul Laurens and later under William Merritt Chase. By 1899 the influential art dealer William Macbeth, who was devoted to the cause of promoting American art, was representing Borgord in New York. While maintaining a part-time studio in Holland in the years following, Borgord assumed directorships both of the Art School of the Carnegie Institute and the Allegheny (Pennsylvania) School of Painting. (One cannot be more specific about this artist, especially concerning dates.)

Borgord was honored in Paris with a medal from the Salon in 1905 and, years later in 1924, with a one-man exhibition of his paintings and sculptures at the Galerie de Marsan. He exhibited at New York's National Academy of Design in 1913 and again in 1919. His membership affiliations also reflect the international stamp of the man, for he belonged not only to New York's exclusive Salmagundi Club but to the St. Lucas Society in Amsterdam, the Allied Art Association, and the American Art Association of Paris.

A painter of landscapes, portraits, still lifes, and marines, Borgord was represented by two Dutch scenes in the Lyme group exhibition of 1916. He exhibited again in 1918. Why he came to Old Lyme or what his relationship was with the other members of the art colony has yet to be determined. Nevertheless, Borgord spent several weeks in Old Lyme during the height of the laurel season in the summer of 1916, working in a studio behind Florence Griswold's house. A writer for the *Hartford Courant* interviewed him then and described one of the canvases he saw as "a brilliant colorful impression of a lady standing amidst the laurel bed." The artist explained his most recent painting interests to the reporter: "I formerly worked for effects of dark and light; now I paint entirely for unusual effects and harmonies of color." (Had the Impressionism of Old Lyme influenced him or had he come to Old Lyme for support of his new ideas?) The reviewer admired Borgord's work for what he termed its "consummate draughtsmanship, and great reserve, that rare ability to show absolute truth of relations within a restricted scale of values."

Further reading:
Macbeth Papers. Archives of American Art microfilm copy.

Brinley, Daniel Putnam

Born Mar. 8, 1879,
  Newport, R.I.
Died July 31, 1963, Norwalk.
In Riverside, c. 1880-1900;
  in Silvermine, 1909-63.

"A very tall, distinguished-looking man with sparkling blue eyes and beautiful long-fingered hands, he was kind, generous, and full of fun." That is the way D. Putnam Brinley's niece, Elizabeth Loder, describes him. Known to his friends as "Put," he was proud that he was the great-great-grandson of history's "Old Put," General Israel Putnam, the Revolutionary War hero from Connecticut.

Brinley is unique among the artists of Cos Cob in that he was a resident of the area. He grew up in Riverside, just across the Mianus River from Cos Cob. His wife, Kathrine Gordon Sanger (an author of travel books and a "dramatic recitalist" whose professional name was Gordon Brinley), had spent summers with her family near the Holley House, where artists gathered.

Brinley studied at the Art Students League 1900-02 under John Twachtman, Bryson Burroughs, Kenyon Cox, H.

Siddons Mowbray, and others. His interest was in landscape painting, and he probably attended the Art Students League summer school in Cos Cob in 1902. He travelled to Europe in 1904 to complete his training, but except for one life class at the Accademia di Belle Arti in Florence, he explored the galleries, museums, and churches independently. In Paris between 1905-08, he became involved with the New Society of American Artists, along with Edward Steichen, John Marin, Max Weber, and others. Although his own art was never avant-garde, Brinley helped to establish several progressive art associations in Paris and worked especially hard to find alternatives to the conservative and exclusive academic exhibition system. When he and his wife returned to New York in July, 1908, Brinley spent the rest of that summer painting in Woodstock, New York, where Birge Harrison was conducting the Art Students League summer school.

In 1909 Brinley and his wife "were sighing for summer in a green world" and remembered that Charles Caffin, the art critic, had told them in Paris about the beauties of Silvermine. They rented a house "little and white, facing the sheds of a disused mill — Blanchards." Thereafter they generally spent spring, summer, and fall in Silvermine, winters in New York. The sculptor Solon Borglum was a neighbor, and Brinley joined the group called "The Knockers," which met every Sunday morning in Borglum's barn studio for frank discussions of the artists' work. The group evolved into the Silvermine Guild of Artists, which Brinley served as president in 1923. In 1913 the Brinleys built, on the Silvermine River, a Tudor-style house that they named Datchet House, after the name of the English village where a Brinley ancestor lived in 1640. The house was featured in *House Beautiful, International Studio,* and *Arts and Decoration.*

During his first summer in Silvermine, even as he became friends with Borglum, a conservative artist, Brinley became a member of Alfred Stieglitz's progessive Little Galleries of the Photo-Secession at 291 Fifth Avenue; he was included in a group exhibiton at 291 in March, 1910. That same month, the Madison Art Gallery, under the direction of former Cos Cob artist Henry Fitch Taylor, hung Brinley's first one-man exhibition.

Brinley was a charter member of the Association of American Painters and Sculptors and active in the preparations for the Armory Show. Though he was sympathetic to modernist trends, his own art remained Impressionist until after the Armory Show. His *The Emerald Pool* (cat. 97) is reminiscent of Twachtman's *Hemlock Pool* (cat. 145, illus. p. 23). His *A Colonial Church* (cat. 3, illus. p. 64) is so like any of Hassam's *Church at Old Lyme* paintings that even the Brinley family thought for a long time that the subject was the Congregational Church at Old Lyme. The modernist European art in the Armory show had a decided effect on Brinley's work. He intensified color, flattened forms, and tightened his compositions, although he continued the emphasis on decorative pattern which was a major element in his later murals. Brinley was also a founding member of the Grand Central Art Galleries, a member of the MacDowell Club, the National Arts Club, and the National Academy of Design.

Critics generally praised Brinley's work, finding it both poetic and "thoroughly and gratefully American" because of "the beauty he finds everywhere he looks in our

American landscape," such as in "our homely white Colonial houses . . . our mountain laurel and our huddled clumps of slim birches." Brinley did like it here and said so: "Much travel in Europe and in America has shown me no area more satisfying for permanent residence, or more loveable, than the countryside reached by the tree-shaded roads linking Norwalk and New Canaan, Connecticut."

Further reading:
Daniel Putnam Brinley: The Impressionist Years. Exh. cat., Bowdoin College Museum of Art, 1978.
Loder, Elizabeth M. *D. Putnam Brinley: Impressionist and Mural Painter.* Published for the New Canaan Historical Society and the Silvermine Guild of Artists by University Microfilms International, 1979.

Burr, George Brainerd

Born Aug. 7, 1876,
Middletown.
Died 1939, Old Lyme.
In Old Lyme, 1910-39.

George Burr had a gallery of sketches that he collected and carefully hung on the walls of his Old Lyme house. Most of them were given to him by artist friends, often in exchange for one of his own sketches. Requesting a drawing from his friend Edmund Greacen, Burr wrote, "I like a sketch to look like what it is — a sketch, so don't finish except for name." George Burr's paintings reveal a similar strong interest in expressing a rough, unfinished quality. Most adept with smaller canvases, Burr created lively textured landscape and figure paintings by employing a translucent background over which strong dabs of paint were loosely applied, frequently exposing the canvas.

Burr had been introduced to and influenced by the modern movements of German Expressionism and French Fauvism when he lived in Germany and France during the first decade of the twentieth century. Consequently his choice of color was at times more daring than that of most of the Old Lyme group. He readily experimented with intense blues, purples, and reds that convey an expressionistic mood in much of his work.

The son of a prominent Middletown, Connecticut, banker, George Burr had left for Europe as a young man to study architecture in the Royal Architect's office in Berlin. He met and became engaged to Lucretia Phinney, who was studying German on a college scholarship. After their marriage in America, they returned to Berlin. Burr had decided against being an architect and began art studies first at the Berlin and then the Munich Academy of Fine Arts, continued them at the Colarossi Academy in Paris, and, later, at the Art Students League in New York. While in Europe, he and his wife lived for many summers in Holland, chiefly at Volendam. They often spent winters on the island of Capri in southern Italy.

After living in Europe for fourteen years, George Burr decided in 1910 to bring his family back to his native New England, and he believed Old Lyme would be a good place to settle and establish his art career in America. He and his wife purchased "Cricket Lawn," an 1844 cottage-style house on the main street. For many of the local artists, the Burr home became a center of activity. George Burr had a fine sense of humor, he was a tennis enthusiast, and both he and his wife were active in town affairs.

Burr was invited to contribute to the annual local art exhibition his first summer in Old Lyme. He became an active member of the art colony and of the Lyme Art Association when it was formed in 1914. He won the Association's Goodman Prize in 1933. In addition to painting, Burr developed considerable talent as an etcher and had some critical success with his colored etchings and monotypes.

Burr's professional memberships also included the Allied Artists Association and the Salmagundi Club. Twenty-one examples of his work were displayed in 1978 at A. M. Adler Fine Art, Inc., New York, in the exhibition *Three American Impressionists: From Paris to Old Lyme.*

Further reading:
Three American Impressionists: From Paris to Old Lyme; Lucien Abrams, George Burr, Charles Ebert. Exh. cat., A. M. Adler Fine Art, Inc., New York City, 1978.

Carlsen, Emil

Born Oct. 19, 1853,
Copenhagen, Denmark.
Died Jan. 2, 1932,
New York City.
In Windham periodically, early 1900s; summers in Falls Village, 1905-32.

Emil Carlsen (who did not use his first name, Sören) studied architecture at Denmark's Royal Academy for four years before emigrating to the United States in 1872 at the age of nineteen, but he enjoyed painting and there were painters in his family. Carlsen decided on an art career after an unsatisfying stint as an architect's assistant in Chicago. He worked briefly under Danish painter Lauritz Holst in Chicago and, by 1874, was the first teacher of drawing and painting at the school that became part of the Chicago Art Institute. In 1875 he went to Paris for six months, where he saw the work of Chardin, which would influence his own still lifes, and where, by his own account, he painted "assiduously" from nature. When he returned to this country, he set up a studio in New York to begin his career in art.

For many years that career did not thrive. Carlsen soon moved to Boston, but his luck did not improve. He auctioned his paintings to try to pay bills, worked in Boston as a designer and engraver, and then, in Paris, painted commissioned still lifes for Blakeslee and other

American dealers. While in Paris from 1884-86, he enrolled at the Académie Julian, where he associated not only with Americans like Willard Metcalf but with many French artists. His palette brightened considerably.

Largely self-taught himself, Carlsen spent many of the next thirty-five years teaching others. He became director of the San Francisco Art Association's school in 1887, where, except for a brief stay in New York, he taught for four years. Believing that sales and exhibition opportunities were limited in the Bay Area, in 1891 he moved east permanently. He began to teach both at the National Academy of Design and at the Pennsylvania Academy of Fine Arts. In 1896 he married Luella May Ruby in New York City, and in 1901 their son Dines, who would become an artist himself, was born.

Almost fifty by then, Carlsen had a reputation as a fine still-life painter, but after 1900 landscapes became increasingly important in his work. Honors came in quick succession: Member, Society of American Artists, 1902; Associate, National Academy of Design, 1904; Academician, N.A.D., 1906; Member, National Institute of Arts and Letters, 1906. His many prizes ranged from a gold medal for a still life at the Louisiana Purchase Exposition in St. Louis, 1904, to the medal of honor for a seascape at the Panama-Pacific International Exposition in San Francisco, 1915. He exhibited at Folsom Gallery and at Macbeth Gallery in New York, at Vose Galleries in Boston, and, after 1926, at Grand Central Art Galleries in New York, where he was an artist member of that cooperative. Group exhibitions were often with major figures of American Impressionism, including his close friends Metcalf, J. Alden Weir, who fondly called him "Old Carlsen," and Childe Hassam, who liked to refer to Carlsen as the "Dane of American artists."

It was after his marriage that Carlsen began to spend time away from cities, and it was to Connecticut he came with his wife and son. He probably visited Weir at Branchville, but after Weir inherited his father-in-law's large house in Windham, Carlsen and his family went there frequently and even spent two or three summers in the early 1900s in a cottage on the grounds. Weir's youngest daughter remembers well that the artists enjoyed painting together in the neighborhood during the day and socializing with the families in the evening. Carlsen wrote Weir at least one special letter of thanks "for the many years we had your house at Windham." He probably painted the cottage in *Night, Old Windham* (cat. 9).

Carlsen not only liked the idea of summers in the country, but he also seemed interested in the idea of artists working together in idyllic surroundings. The reason he bought a home in Falls Village, his son told people in that northwestern Connecticut town, was that one day in or before 1905 Carlsen had set out to see Old Lyme, where friends told him an art colony had developed. The railroad ticket agent had misunderstood Carlsen's request and sold him a ticket to Lime Rock. When he realized the mistake, Carlsen decided to explore Lime Rock and neighboring Falls Village anyway, and he liked what he saw so much he bought a house in Falls Village in 1905. No art colony was there, but in later years art associations would develop both at Lime Rock and at nearby Kent. Carlsen frequently exhibited in their annual exhibitions.

Carlsen and his family spent winters in New York City and occasionally travelled abroad or to Vermont or Maine, but he considered Falls Village his home and found most of his landscape subjects in the nearby woods, brooks, and hills until his death in 1932.

Further reading:
The Art of Emil Carlsen, 1853-1932. Exh. cat., Wortsman Rowe Galleries, San Francisco, 1975. Includes reprints of essays by Eliot Clark, Duncan Phillips, F. Newlin Price and others.

Chadwick, William
Born 1879, Dewsbury,
  Yorkshire, England.
Died Aug. 3, 1962, Old Lyme.
In Old Lyme, summers,
  1902-10; permanently,
  1915-62.

In 1902, William Chadwick, at twenty-three, was introduced to Old Lyme through colleagues at the Art Students League in New York. At the time Chadwick's painting interests focused on portraiture and figure subjects. During that first of many summers spent in Old Lyme, Chadwick began experimenting with landscape painting, no doubt influenced by the many well-respected landscapists already attracted to the growing art colony.

For the next several years Chadwick shared studio residences in New York with Will Howe Foote and Harry Hoffman and spent summers with them at the Griswold House in Old Lyme. The painters and their families were close friends all their lives, and all of them eventually made Old Lyme their permanent home. As Richard H. Love has noted, however, "at this time they established a working orbit between New York City and Connecticut, not vastly different from the precedent set by Twachtman, Robinson and Weir."

Chadwick studied with Joseph DeCamp at the Art Students League, and the artist's early painting shows the mark of his instructor's Boston School style. While in Old Lyme, Chadwick gradually absorbed the influences of the colony's older painters, particularly Willard Metcalf and Walter Griffin. Incorporating elements from both the Boston and Old Lyme Schools, Chadwick developed his own conservative impressionistic style, marked by delicate and subtle tones.

Chadwick married Pauline Bancroft of Wilmington, Delaware, in June of 1910, and, two years later, the couple left for a lengthy trip to Europe. Most of their time abroad was spent in Italy, where they were visited by Metcalf and Griffin.

In 1915 Chadwick and his wife purchased a house on Johnny Cake Hill in Old Lyme. For the next forty years the artist resolutely carried on the Impressionist tradition, painting the seasonal changes in the countryside around Old Lyme. Additionally, Chadwick made frequent sketching trips to Monhegan Island, Maine, Vermont, and Bermuda, often with one or more of his artist friends, such as Foote, Hoffman, or Charles Ebert.

The Telfair Academy in Savannah, Georgia, hosted Chadwick's first one-man show in February, 1927. One month later basically the same show was presented at the Wilmington (Delaware) Society of Fine Arts. Both exhibitions were highly praised by local critics.

Although William Chadwick never had great commercial success, he was well respected by his artist-colleagues in the Lyme Art Association. Following the painter's death in 1962, the association held a memorial show of Chadwick's paintings in 1963. Referring to the exhibition, the artist Nelson C. White wrote:

William Chadwick's work is distinguished for a sensitive and subtle Impressionism . . . . he evokes the mood of the shifting seasons, effects of sunshine and cloud shadows, the laurel of late spring and the snow of winter.

Chadwick recently gained national exposure in a major retrospective, *William Chadwick, 1879-1962: An American Impressionist,* that opened at the Lyme Historical Society in August, 1978, and circulated to several museums in the eastern United States. The exhibition was organized by R. H. Love Galleries of Chicago. Chadwick's work is represented in the Lyme Historical Society, the Lyman Allyn Museum, and the National Collection of Fine Arts.

Further reading:
An Exhibition of Paintings by William Chadwick. Exh. cat., Wilmington [Delaware] Society of Fine Arts, 1927.
Love, Richard H. *William Chadwick, 1879-1962: An American Impressionist.* Exh. cat., R. H. Love Galleries, Chicago, 1978.

Clark, Walter

Born 1848, Brooklyn, N.Y.
Died 1917, New York City?
In Cos Cob, periodically from
    1890, summer of 1893; in
    Noank sometime.

Walter Clark spent three years studying engineering at the Massachusetts Institute of Technology before he travelled to Europe to study art and architecture in 1869. He journeyed on to India, China, and Japan, then settled briefly in Wyoming for a stint as a sheep rancher before returning to New York to continue his artistic training in earnest. He studied at the National Academy of Design under Lemuel Wilmarth and Jonathan Hartley, the son-in-law of the tonalist George Inness. Inness's influence became more direct in the early 1880s, when Clark had a studio in New York adjacent to that of the older artist.

By the 1890s, Clark was beginning to turn from tonalism toward Impressionism, probably as a result of working beside his friends John Twachtman, Edward Potthast, and Joseph R. DeCamp. During the summers, Walter Clark and his son Eliot (born 1883) painted in such artists' colonies as Cos Cob, Chadd's Ford, Gloucester, and Ogunquit, Maine. (Drawing on his personal familiarity with many of his father's friends, Eliot Clark would later write perceptive criticisms of the work of Twachtman, Hassam, Robinson, Weir, and others.)

Walter Clark was highly respected during his lifetime. He was a member of the National Academy, the Society of American Artists, and the Salmagundi Club. He received a silver medal at the Pan-American Exposition in Buffalo in 1901, the Inness Gold Medal of the National Academy of Design in 1902, and a silver medal at the St. Louis Exposition in 1904.

Further reading:
Love, Richard H. Monograph on Walter Clark and Eliot Clark to be published in 1980.

Davis, Charles Harold

Born Jan. 7, 1856,
    Amesbury, Mass.
Died Aug. 5, 1933, Mystic.
In Mystic, 1890-1933.

In 1890 Charles H. Davis moved to Mystic to live year-round. The story is that Davis, intending to settle somewhere in his native New England, studied maps and statistics to find the place that best answered his requirements of topography and climate. It was Mystic.

Davis was then thirty-four years old and just back from France. His American training had been limited to two or three years under Otto Grundmann at the Boston Museum of Fine Arts in the late 1870s. His schoolteacher father had had to struggle to find the tuition for the Museum School, but Davis did so well there that in 1880 a businessman from his hometown offered him a thousand dollars to study in Paris. Davis enrolled at the Académie Julian under Boulanger and Lefebvre. Soon, however, he ended his formal training and moved to the Barbizon region outside Paris, where he began painting the simple, glowing landscapes that characterize Barbizon art. One was accepted for the Salon the following spring, and Davis found enough buyers for others he began to send home that he was able to stay abroad for a decade, a success few young American artists could boast of. He was married in 1884 to a Frenchwoman, Angèle Lagarde.

How Davis responded to French Impressionism is still unknown, but the Barbizon style lingered in his work after he moved to Mystic. Around 1895 a change is perceptible to purer color, more light, and what Davis himself called an "eloquent arrangement" more faithful to mood than to naturalistic detail.

Once in Mystic, Davis was content to stay. (There were a few trips, however, including one in 1928 to Wales.) An art critic reported that, "With a walking stick and a bit of grass between his teeth, he may be seen almost any day, summer or winter, wandering over hill and dale, storing his memory full of choice spots . . . where the spirit of beauty dwells." He painted about nine hundred landscapes in the Mystic area during his career, usually recording them as numbered miniature sketches (cat. 19).

In a period when artists joined social clubs, kept winter and summer studios, and travelled widely, Davis belonged only to the Lotos Club and never had a city studio. While Davis stayed home, however, his scenes of Mystic travelled to Macbeth Gallery in New York, Doll & Richards in Boston and museums and major exhibitions in places as far flung as San Francisco, Chicago, Atlanta, St. Louis, and Paris, where they regularly won prizes. Davis's prize list is exceptionally long and impressive, beginning with the 1887 Paris Salon and continuing almost annually until his death in 1933. He was a member of the National Academy of Design and of the Society of American Artists. He also became a member of the Grand Central Art Galleries in New York, a pioneer cooperative organized by artists and businessmen in 1923.

On home ground, Davis could be outgoing. Early on he held art classes in Mystic that attracted so many students that *Connecticut Magazine* commented in August, 1899, that "The pallet and easel have become familiar sights along the river, and the village streets, and among the hills." In 1900, two years after his wife died, Davis married one of his students, Frances Thomas, who exhibited regularly in Mystic art exhibitions and was, for a time, a paid reviewer of those at Old Lyme.

Davis was good friends with Henry Ward Ranger of Noank and with artists at Old Lyme. He persuaded other artists to settle in Mystic and is credited with starting several on their careers. In 1913, with his doctor friend, George Leonard, Davis founded the Mystic Art Association, which was initially financed by a tearoom run by townswomen on exhibition afternoons. "Uncle Charlie" was apparently never too busy to listen to and encourage younger artists in Mystic. Always interested in spreading the good word about art, he willed his library of more than eight hundred art reference books to the nearest major public library, in Westerly, Rhode Island, where the books are still in circulation. Davis died in Mystic in 1933.

Further reading:
"Charles H. Davis — Landscapist," *International Studio,* 75 (June 1922), 176-83.
Gillet, Louis Bliss. "Charles H. Davis." *American Magazine of Art,* 27 (March 1934), 105-12. Also in *Memorial Exhibition: Paintings by Charles H. Davis* (Exh. cat., Macbeth Gallery, New York City, 1934).

DuMond, Frank Vincent
Born Aug. 20, 1865,
  Rochester, N.Y.
Died Feb. 6, 1951,
  New York City.
In Lyme, 1902-41.

"Now while it's nice and quiet here," Frank DuMond wrote to his parents from Lyme in August, 1909, "I'm finishing a little picture which I think of sending to our annual Lyme show. It's purely of the imagination and is

that cherished land where all is peace and beauty. We all seem to yearn for it and that I suppose is a very good reason for painting it." Since the places DuMond painted were those he really knew, the landscape of Lyme figures large in his work, imbued with imagination, certainly, but also with the spirit of place. His palette lightened at Old Lyme, too.

DuMond lived in a part of Lyme called Grassy Hill and commuted to New York's Art Students League, where he was a favorite teacher. One of his host of students (that included artists as diverse as John Marin, Kenneth Hayes Miller, and Georgia O'Keeffe) said that "His dedication to teaching was such that he showed more stamina . . . at 86 than most of us in our 20s. As well as doing his own painting and holding his regular classes, he had an extra late-afternoon session in the League basement once a week. Present and past students would bring in work painted outside of class, and . . . he would go over them one at a time for the benefit of all." He taught for more than fifty years at the Art Students League, maintaining a schedule that often required him to take the night ferry from New London in order to be in New York in time for his classes. The DuMonds also had an apartment in the cooperative building on W. 67th St. DuMond was an original stock-holder there and helped finance the Hotel des Artistes as well.

DuMond was born in Rochester, New York, in 1865. He went to New York in 1884 to study at the Art Students League and became an illustrator, first for the *New York Daily Graphic,* then for *Century* and for *Harper's Weekly.* In 1888 he went to Paris to study at the Académie Julian under Boulanger, Constant, and Lefebvre. In 1892 *Harper's* editor, who was president of the Art Students League, persuaded DuMond to teach there. He was twenty-seven years old. Besides teaching, he continued his illustration career for a time, eventually doing the art work for Mark Twain's *Joan of Arc.*

In the 1890s DuMond also taught summer classes in France, first for the Art Students League and then privately. Students in those classes literally worked from dawn to dusk, since they were expected to be outdoors each day to paint both sunrise and sunset and attend drawing and other lessons between. Such schedules were not unusual for students of landscape painting in the period.

DuMond for a time did many murals, for places such as The Lotos Club, Central Park Studios, and the Hotel des Artistes in New York City. His fifteen-foot mural for the Court of the Universe at the Panama-Pacific Exposition in San Francisco in 1915 was "Conquest of the Pacific Coast." He had already received a number of awards: a gold medal at the 1890 Paris Salon (for a religious painting called "Holy Family"), gold medals at the Boston Exposition of 1892 and the Atlanta Exposition of 1895, two silver medals at the Pan-American Exposition in Buffalo in 1901, and another at the St. Louis Exposition of 1904. He was director of the department of fine arts for the Lewis and Clark Exposition in Portland, Oregon, in 1905, and a member of the awards jury at the Panama-Pacific Exposition. He was a member of the National Academy of Design and the Society of American Artists, as well as of several other professional groups, and he belonged, as well, to the Lotos, Players, Salmagundi, and Century Clubs.

DuMond and his family first went to Old Lyme in 1902. With Will Howe Foote as his assistant, DuMond directed the Lyme Summer School of Art, which became known as the foremost in the country. By 1904 the school had forty or fifty students. By 1906 it was feared that the great number of students would spoil the "place where the best American painters congregate," and the Art Students League was persuaded to move the school to Woodstock, New York. DuMond and others continued to give private lessons in Lyme. He was so highly thought of as a teacher that Mrs. Woodrow Wilson reputedly had come to Lyme just to study with him. DuMond apparently taught summer clases in Lyme until at least 1915. He bought his Grassy Hill home several years earlier.

Between world wars, he taught summer sessions in Cape Breton, Nova Scotia. In about 1939 he was apparently at Kent and Essex for summer classes, and later he had a popular summer school in Pownal, Vermont. He combined his favorite sport of fly-fishing with painting and was known for a series on salmon fishing in the 1940s. He moved to New York in 1941, at least for the winters. In 1952, a year after DuMond's death, the Art Students League sponsored a memorial exhibition of his work.

Further reading:
Abrams, Herbert E. "Teachings of Frank Vincent DuMond: Penetrating Light." *American Artist,* 38 (March 1974), 36-45.
Frank Vincent DuMond. Exh. cat., Art Students League, 1949.
Frank Vincent DuMond Papers. Archives of American Art microfilm copy.
A Memorial Exhibition of Paintings by F. V. DuMond, N.A. Exh. cat., Art Students League, 1952.

Ebert, Charles H.

Born July 21, 1873,
  Milwaukee, Wisc.
Died Oct. 2, 1959, Preston.
In Greenwich, c. 1900-19; in
Old Lyme, 1919-59.

Charles Ebert moved from New York to Greenwich around 1900 and thereafter made Connecticut his home. While in Greenwich, Ebert studied under John Twachtman and stayed seasonally at the Holley House, where he was introduced to Julian Alden Weir and Childe Hassam. Under their influence, especially that of Twachtman, Ebert painted the local countryside, experimenting with bold brushwork and unusual atmospheric effects.

In 1903, Ebert married another of Twachtman's pupils, Mary Roberts, and in 1919 the couple moved to Old Lyme. By this time the art colony had long since made its conversion to Impressionism, and its importance as a center of American art was already diminishing. While in Old Lyme, both of the Eberts exhibited regularly at the Lyme Art Association.

Beginning in 1909, the Eberts spent most of their summers on Monhegan Island, off the coast of Maine, meeting there at times other Old Lyme Impressionists, including Walter Griffin and Frank Bicknell. The rocky seacoast, engulfed in mist and dotted with fishermen's huts, especially suited Charles Ebert's interest in capturing brilliant color, picturesque scenery, and fleeting atmospheric conditions.

Ebert's early art training began in 1892-93 at the Art Academy of Cincinnati. He then spent a year in New York at the Art Students League and moved in 1894 to Paris, where he studied at the Académie Julian under Benjamin Constant and Jean-Paul Laurens. Upon his return to the United States in 1896, Ebert opened a studio in New York City and tried to earn a living as a free-lance illustrator. He eventually landed a full-time position as political cartoonist for *Life* magazine. Mary Roberts Ebert, whose own finances were secure, persuaded her husband to abandon illustration in order to devote his full attention to painting.

Ebert first exhibited at the National Academy of Design in 1907. Following this recognition, his paintings were included in exhibitions at such major museums as the Art Institute of Chicago, the Pennsylvania Academy of Fine Arts, and the Carnegie Institute. Additionally, Ebert was awarded a bronze medal at the Buenos Aires Exposition of 1910 and a silver medal at the San Francisco Panama-Pacific Exposition in 1915. He was a member of the Lyme Art Association, Salmagundi Club, and Allied Art Association, and he was a founder of the Greenwich Art Society. A retrospective exhibition of his work was organized by the Lyman Allyn Museum, New London, in 1979.

Further reading:
Charles H. Ebert 1873-1959. Exh. cat., Lyman Allyn Museum, 1979.
Raynor, Vivien, "Rediscovering an Impressionist." *New York Times,* November 4, 1979, Sec. 2, p. 20.
Three American Impressionists: From Paris to Old Lyme; Lucien Abrams, George Burr, Charles Ebert. Exh. cat., A. M. Adler Fine Art, Inc., New York City, 1978.

Eby, Kerr

Born Oct. 19, 1889,
  Tokyo, Japan.
Died Nov. 18, 1946, Norwalk.
In Cos Cob, c. 1913-1917;
  settled in Westport after
  World War I.

Born in Japan of Canadian Methodist missionaries, Kerr Eby did not come to the United States until 1907, when he was eighteen years old. The maternal grandson of print dealer Frederick Keppel, Eby (who never used his first name, Harold) studied at Pratt Institute and the Art Students League. In the summer of 1915, and probably for two years before and after that time, he had a studio in a waterfront warehouse just across the road from the Holley House.

In Cos Cob the young printmaker not only produced such etchings as *Backyards* but — perhaps more important

— offered Childe Hassam the technical advice that helped make the older artist's first serious venture into etching so successful. The twenty-five prints Hassam produced in Cos Cob in 1915 include a portrait of Eby in his studio, a self-portrait of Hassam there, and two views of the building's exterior.

Eby was also a source of first-hand information about Japan. The Cos Cob colony had admired Japanese art ever since the years of Twachtman's and Weir's summer classes. A Japanese artist had been a member of the colony at the turn of the century, and Hassam's Cos Cob models had dressed in kimonos as early as 1902. Eby's dinner-table accounts of Japanese life undoubtedly renewed the Holley House group's interest in Oriental art. Two of Hassam's 1915 etchings depict a young Cos Cob woman dressed in a white kimono.

Eby enlisted in the Army in 1917, serving as a sergeant in the Corps of Engineers. He returned to the front lines in the Second World War as an artist-war correspondent with the Marines in the Pacific. Ironically, the pacifist artist was to become as well known for his grimly realistic depictions of war as for his peaceful Connecticut landscapes.

Between the wars Eby lived in Westport, where he captured on the etching plate views of that area when it was still largely farmland. Like many of the Cos Cob artists, Eby seemed to prefer winter landscapes, but unlike the painters, who were challenged by white, he was concerned with line: the intricate mesh of bare branches against the sky, the zigzag of a rail fence across a snowy field. His Connecticut landscapes often include houses, as do Hassam's, but whereas Hassam enjoyed architecture for itself, Eby often used buildings to evoke a mood just short of sentimentality. He was a popular artist during his lifetime. His prints commanded as high a price the year after his death as they do today.

Further reading:
The Stamp of Whistler Exh. cat., Allen Memorial Art Museum, Oberlin College, 1977.
Keppel, Dorothy. "Kerr Eby." *Print Collector's Quarterly,* Vol. 4. Millwood, N.Y.: to press, 1977, pp. 2005-17.

Foote, Will Howe

Born June 29, 1874,
  Grand Rapids, Mich.
Died Jan. 27, 1965, Sarasota, Fla.
In Old Lyme, 1901-65; in
  Cos Cob, 1903.

Will Howe Foote was one of the earliest artists at Old Lyme and one who adopted the town as home. He first went there the summer of 1901 with his uncle, William H. Howe, a painter of cattle, who had been told about the beauties of the countryside by Henry Ward Ranger. Foote had himself heard of Old Lyme when he had met Clark Voorhees in France. He and his uncle were both from Grand Rapids,

Michigan, where Foote's father was an executive in the furniture industry that made the city famous. Encouraged to be an artist by his father, he began his professional training at the Art Institute of Chicago in 1894. He became friends there with a fellow Michigan student, Frederick Frieseke, who would study with him again at the Art Students League in New York, where Foote worked in 1895-96 under H. Siddons Mowbray and Kenyon Cox.

In 1897 he and Frieseke went to the Académie Julian in Paris, where Foote studied under Jean-Paul Laurens and Benjamin Constant. He was at Julian's until 1900, except for an Italian trip, summers at Laren, Holland, or Etaples, France, and a short period at Whistler's school in Paris. He exhibited twice at the Old Salon, and when he returned to the United States in 1900, he had a one-man exhibition in his hometown.

Will Howe Foote's paintings were well received on his return from abroad. He exhibited frequently at the National Academy of Design and became an associate member in 1910. His awards included a bronze medal at the St. Louis Exposition in 1904 and a silver medal at the Panama-Pacific Exposition in San Francisco in 1915.

Once he visited Old Lyme, Foote returned every summer. In 1902 he was hired as assistant to Frank DuMond at the Lyme Summer School of Art, which was sponsored by the Art Students League of New York. Sometime in 1903 he also taught a session in Cos Cob. After 1906, when the League moved its Lyme classes to Woodstock, New York, Foote continued in Old Lyme as a private instructor.

In 1907 he was married to Helen Kirtland Freeman, whom he had met a year or two earlier when she had come to the Lyme art colony as a student of Henry Rankin Poore. Fellow artist William Chadwick was best man at the wedding. The Footes began building a house on Sill Lane in Old Lyme and upon its completion in 1909 spent every spring, summer and fall there, where Foote devoted full time to painting. The Gregory Smiths, old friends from Grand Rapids, arrived in Old Lyme in 1910 and became neighbors.

Foote's early works in Connecticut, such as *A Summer's Night* (cat. 173, illus. p. 25) reflect the artist's interest in soft, atmospheric scenes dominated by a single, overriding tone. The arrival of Childe Hassam and Walter Griffin influenced Foote as it did many other Old Lyme artists, and his palette consequently lightened, becoming at times as high key as in *Summer* (cat. 26, illus. p. 68). Throughout his experimentation with light and color, however, Foote's interest in form, mass, and simple geometric arrangements continued.

Considering that he lived there so long, Foote painted the Old Lyme countryside relatively little. He was not fond of working with green, a color omnipresent in Connecticut in summer. Furthermore, he disliked New England winters so much that he avoided nearly all of them, favoring the Caribbean, Mexico, or the American Southwest.

Though his work had been included in a Macbeth Gallery exhibition in 1914, Foote, who had money of his own, never had nor wanted a dealer. When sales of his pictures fell off badly during the 1920s, Foote declined invitations to exhibit in museums and galleries, feeling it not worth the trouble and expense of crating and shipping. After 1933 he exhibited only at the annual exhibitions of the Lyme Art Association. He continued to experiment with subject matter and technique, but he destroyed all but what he judged to be his best work.

Foote was the last survivor of the original Old Lyme group. He had been active in the town's civic affairs as well as in its art colony. He was a charter member of the local volunteer fire department. He died in 1965 at ninety years of age and is buried next to his wife in the Duck River Cemetery in Old Lyme. After his death, memorial exhibitions of his work were held both in Grand Rapids and in Old Lyme. In 1978 S.K.T. Galleries of New York organized a Foote retrospective that travelled to the Lyme Historical Society the following year.

Further reading:
Foote, Will Howe. Personal interview. Old Lyme, September, 1954. Transcript, Lyme Historical Society Archives.
Smith, Ann Youngdahl. "Will Howe Foote, American Impressionist." *American Art Review,* (forthcoming in 1980).
Will Howe Foote 1874-1965. Exh. cat., S.K.T. Galleries, New York City, 1978.

Greacen, Edmund W.

Born Sept. 18, 1876,
New York City.
Died Oct. 4, 1949,
White Plains, N.Y.
In Old Lyme, 1910-17.

Edmund Greacen grew up in a New York City brownstone, staffed by Irish servants, that stood where part of Rockefeller Center is now. His father was an Irish immigrant of Scottish Presbyterian descent who married a rich American and, through his own shrewd judgment in the wholesale shoe trade, increased her fortune. Following a private school education, Greacen studied at New York University, where he received a bachelor of arts degree, but where his main interests seem to have been the high hurdles, banjo playing, his fraternity, and similar extracurricular activities. Eager to participate in the Spanish-American War after graduation, he was sent on an around-the-world tour by his father, who hoped travel would allay his son's enthusiasm for soldiering. Greacen had already filled three sketchbooks, and his interest in art evidently did grow on the trip. In 1899, at the age of twenty-three, he enrolled at the Art Students League, and, soon after, at the art school run by William Merritt Chase, where he studied with Chase, Robert Henri, Louis Mora, Frank DuMond, and Everett Shinn.

In late 1904 Greacen married Ethol Booth of New Haven and the following spring sailed with her, Chase, and about three dozen of Chase's other students to Spain, on one of the art study tours that Chase became famous for. The Greacens stayed on in Europe, mainly in France, until 1909. Greacen became strongly attracted to Impressionism, and, in 1907, he moved his family to Giverny to be near Monet, who greatly influenced him even though the American saw little of the aging French master himself. He was close,

however, to Monet's stepdaughter Suzanne and her American husband, artist Theodore Butler, as well as to other American painters in the village.

On his return to this country in 1909, Greacen participated in group exhibitions in New York and elsewhere. He was in the Artists' Independent Exhibition of 1910, his Impressionist work there markedly different from the realism and social commentary of artists like John Sloan, George Luks, George Bellows, and Stuart Davis that made up the rest of the exhibition. Greacen had a one-man exhibition at the Folsom Galleries on Fifth Ave. in 1911 and, in 1914, another at the Toledo Museum of Art in Ohio, where he received warm praise. He began doing some of the "portraits" of formal gardens of the wealthy that he became noted for.

Between 1910 and 1917, Old Lyme and the Griswold House became the Greacen family's haven from city living, a kind of American Giverny. They enjoyed the conviviality and the scenery, and they went to Old Lyme as often as they could for days or weeks at a time, in all seasons. Greacen painted some of his loveliest landscapes in Lyme and neighboring places.

World War I disrupted Greacen's career. A school of art he established in 1917 lasted only about a year. He served six months in France with the French YMCA (the U. S. Army had turned down his application for active service because he was over forty). After the war, however, several honors came to him, among them election to associate membership in the National Academy of Design in 1920 (full membership, 1935) and, in 1921, the $1,000 Shaw Purchase Prize of the Salmagundi Club.

In 1922, the same year he had a one-man exhibition at Macbeth Gallery, Greacen suggested and organized a pioneer artists' cooperative, a non-profit gallery where established artists could keep their work on continuous exhibition. Artists would contribute works of art as yearly dues, and businessmen would provide capital. The gallery, established the following year and located on the top floor of Grand Central Station, came to be known (and still is, though now in the Biltmore Hotel) as Grand Central Art Galleries. It had as many as twenty exhibition rooms at times and was influential in furthering interest in American art. Travelling exhibitions from Grand Central later went to at least twenty cities, among them Hartford and New Britain in this state. In 1924 Greacen began a related art school, also called Grand Central — the largest of its kind in New York City — which opened with 200 students, grew to more than 900, and lasted twenty years, until Greacen's health failed. Among the many artists who taught there, besides Greacen himself, were Ivan Olinsky, Louis Mora, Arshile Gorky, and Greacen's daughter, Nan Greacen Faure. Greacen believed in teaching technical competence but wanted to avoid forcing students to be either "modern" or "conservative."

His responsibilities at Grand Central increasingly kept him in New York City, and he became more an indoor painter, often doing portraits as well as poetic cityscapes. Old Lyme was only a memory. From 1937 on, Greacen's health was impaired by a series of strokes. For a few years the Greacens moved to Florida's Gulf Coast, but they returned to the New York area shortly before the artist died in 1949.

Teddy Greacen laughed when one of his last students asked whether he looked through a piece of gauze when he painted. The artist knew that his kind of painting looked strange to art students of the post-World-War society, but he also knew that he still believed what he had once written: ". . . some of us like the fleeting beauty of the moment."

A retrospective exhibition of Greacen's work was organized by the Cummer Gallery of Art in Jacksonville, Florida, in 1972.

Further reading:
Edmund W. Greacen, N.A.: American Impressionist, 1876-1949. Exh. cat., Cummer Gallery of Art, Jacksonville, Fla., 1972.

Griffin, Walter

Born Jan. 14, 1861,
    Portland, Me.
Died May 18, 1935,
    Portland, Me.
In Hartford and Farmington,
    c. 1898-c. 1906; in Old Lyme
    periodically, 1904-08.

Biographers usually designate Walter Griffin's Old Lyme period as the first important phase of his career. Yet Griffin was an established artist when he came to this state and was in Connecticut at least five years before going to Old Lyme. In 1903 his work was in an exhibition at the Wadsworth Atheneum, Hartford, featuring "four of Connecticut's best-known artists" (the others: Allen Talcott, Charles Noel Flagg, and William Gedney Bunce).

Griffin's father was a carver of ship figureheads in Maine and a member of a Sunday painting group, "The Brush-uns," which Griffin joined as a youngster. In 1877, when he was sixteen, he began five years of study at the school of the Boston Museum of Fine Arts. In 1882 he enrolled at the National Academy of Design in New York, where he worked under and became close friends with Montague Flagg, a nephew of Washington Allston. Other friends were William Merritt Chase, Willard Metcalf, Emil Carlsen, Childe Hassam, Robert Brandegee, and Charles Foster.

Griffin went to France in 1887 and studied with Raphael Collin, and, at the École des Beaux-Arts, with Jean-Paul Laurens. He exhibited at the 1889 Salon. By then he had already discovered the villages of Barbizon and Fleury and become friends with François Millet. A year or so later he settled in Fleury and established art classes. Mostly he stayed in France until 1897.

By 1898 Griffin was in Hartford. He had a studio in the gas company building at 700 Main St. and taught at the school of the Art Society of Hartford (now Hartford Art School of the University of Hartford). Though classes were often held in the Morgan Memorial building of the Wadsworth Atheneum, they were never administered by the museum, and Griffin was never director or curator of the Wadsworth Atheneum, as some have reported. While records of the Art Society are incomplete, Griffin is listed as late as the 1905-06 year as the school's only instructor, with a gifted former student as his assistant — Louis Orr, the future etcher.

Griffin must soon have felt at home in Hartford. His friends Robert Brandegee and Charles Foster were living in nearby Farmington, and Montague Flagg's half-brother, Charles Noel Flagg, had organized and was directing the Connecticut League of Art Students. Faculty and students regularly went out to Farmington to sketch, paint, and talk art with Brandegee and Foster. In 1899 Griffin was married in Hartford to Lillian Baynes, who had served as secretary-treasurer of the summer art school he had opened in Quebec in 1897 or 1898 and continued at least through 1899.

Griffin loved Farmington. In November, 1900, he published a rhapsodic tribute to that village about ten miles west of Hartford: "I have never been able to help comparing the two villages with which I am most familiar, — Barbizon, France, and Farmington . . . Farmington might be called the Barbizon of America." Only Farmington was better, he asserted, "typical of what is best in our villages."

These words and others by Griffin appeared in a monthly called *Farmington Magazine,* an idea of Robert Brandegee's that lasted a couple of years in 1900-02. Griffin's wife was listed as associate editor in the first number, November, 1900, and Griffin not only contributed essays on art for the first six months, but his cover design was used throughout the run. He advertised portfolios of sketches he had done of "interesting features of Farmington," priced at $5.00, available at the local drug store or on order from his Hartford studio. He also talked about Farmington as a favorite "colony" for artists from "Hartford, Boston, New York, and other cities . . . Almost every day their white umbrellas have been seen near the river, through the town, and among the hills." He proposed annual summer exhibitions of Farmington art, which never materialized.

Griffin visited Farmington often. He took part in painting scenes on door and wall panels in a local home, as he was to do again in Old Lyme later. He is listed among the Hartford guests at an exclusive reception in 1901 for President Theodore Roosevelt at the Farmington home of Roosevelt's sister, Mrs. William S. Cowles. He is remembered by some of the village's older citizens.

In 1903 several of Griffin's friends were in Old Lyme. Allen Talcott began going in 1901, and Childe Hassam and Henry White arrived in 1903. Perhaps Griffin visited, for William Chadwick remembered that Griffin came down early on. The summer of 1904 Griffin was certainly there and exhibited in the annual exhibition. He then exhibited regularly until 1910 and again from 1915-17. Old Lyme and its artists influenced Griffin and he them. His oils brightened, and he did fine drawing in hard point pastels. He decided to give up teaching in order to devote himself to art.

By 1908, however, Griffin's marriage was awry. He and his wife had stayed in New York in the cooperative studio apartments on W. 67th St., where Ranger, Hassam, and other friends lived. But in late February, 1908, Griffin wrote to Florence Griswold that the Players Club would be his address for a while. In early June, 1909, he sent her $30 against his bill, advised her to rent his Old Lyme studio and room, and gave Portland, Maine, as his address "until further notice." So 1908 seems to mark the end of Griffin's Old Lyme period, though he exhibited again and as late as 1918 was writing Miss Florence that he would surely visit her even though he could not summer with her.

Thereafter Griffin lived abroad more than at home: 1909-10, Norway (his Old Lyme friend William Singer was there); 1913, Venice (William Gedney Bunce was there); 1911-18, Boigneville, France (Griffin was mistakenly arrested as a war spy, acquitted, and in the United States for part of this period); 1918-22, Stroudwater, Maine; and 1923-33, France (periodically). The village of Contes, sixteen miles inland from Nice, became his favorite painting site after 1926. Griffin's last two years were spent in Maine, in failing health, but he painted until nearly the end. Exhibitions had been frequent and well received. Awards and honors had come steadily. He had been an Academician of the National Academy since 1922. Griffin was honored by the Academy soon after he died in 1935, with a joint memorial exhibition for him and for his old friend, Childe Hassam.

Further reading:
Lovejoy, Rupert. "The Life and Work of Walter Griffin, 1861-1935." *American Art Review,* 2 (Sept.-Oct. 1975), 92-107.
Merrick, L. "Walter Griffin, Artiste." *International Studio,* 62 (August 1917), xlv-xlviii.
Walter Griffin, 1861-1935: Maine Impressionist. Exh. cat., William A. Farnsworth Library and Art Museum, Rockland, Me., 1978.

Hassam, Childe

Born Oct. 17, 1859,
Dorchester, Mass.

Died Aug. 27, 1935,
Easthampton, N.Y.

In Cos Cob periodically,
1894-1923; in Old Lyme,
summers, 1903-c.1907.

Childe Hassam (he did not use his first name, Frederick) was the son of a prosperous Boston merchant and collector of American antiques. Soon after high school he went to work for a wood-engraver, producing business letterheads and newspaper mastheads. Later he worked as an illustrator, creating popular work for periodicals such as *Harper's* and *Scribner's.* He studied art at the Lowell Institute and took an evening life-class at the Boston Arts Club before studying painting privately with I. M. Gaugengigl. In 1883 Hassam painted in England, Scotland, Holland, Italy, and Spain. Soon after, he married Kathleen Maud Doane and, in 1886, returned to Europe. While earning a living in Paris as a painter and illustrator, he enrolled at the Académie Julian, where he studied under Boulanger and Lefebvre.

During this second trip to Europe he became friends with John Twachtman, Theodore Robinson, Willard Metcalf, and other artists with whom he would later paint in Cos Cob and Old Lyme. Hassam painted what was prob-

ably his first Impressionist picture, *Le Jour du Grand Prix,* which was awarded a gold medal at the 1888 Paris Salon (fig. 6). Certainly influenced by Claude Monet and the French, Hassam's work remained distinctively American, marked by his personal exploitation of Impressionist ideas, as he himself asserted:

I have to de-bunk the idea that I learned to paint in France. I learned to paint in Boston before I ever went to France. I have to de-bunk the idea that I use dots of color, so called, or what is known as impressionism (everybody who paints and sees is probably an impressionist) but none of those men who are supposed to have painted with dots and dashes ever really did do just that. There are only two or three who ever tried it and they gave it right up. It never amounted to anything.

Hassam continued to paint in France until 1889. After winning a bronze medal in the Paris Exposition that year, he returned to the United States and settled in New York. New York remained his primary residence for most of his life, for unlike many of his colleagues Hassam loved the city. "To me New York is the most wonderful city in the world," he declared. "No street, no section of Paris or any other city I have seen is equal to New York."

Nonetheless, the enthusiastic athlete and gregarious bon vivant spent much of his time travelling to places where he might find picturesque subjects and enjoy country living, congenial companionship, and outdoor exercise. One of Hassam's favorite sites for these pursuits is described in a letter to his close friend, J. Alden Weir, with whom he often visited in Branchville and in Windham. He writes from Old Lyme, in questionable French, of the special ambience he feels there: *"Venez donc passer quelque temps ici! Temps superbe! La très bonne chère et une société comme il n'y en a pas une seconde!"* He liked his studio there, too — "just the place for high thinking and low living." Though his association with Old Lyme was relatively brief, it had far-reaching effects on the development of that art colony.

Another favored spot for painting and relaxation was Cos Cob, which he visited on and off for more than twenty years. Cos Cob was especially significant in Hassam's development as a printmaker, for he turned seriously to etching for the first time there in the summer of 1915. In both places, architecture — classic New England churches as well as ramshackle waterfront warehouses — occupied as much of his time as landscape. He also painted figure studies in both the Holley House and Florence Griswold's "Holy House."

Known to his friends as Muley, a nickname from Tile Club days that apparently referred to his strong opinions, Hassam enjoyed popularity in his time and is remembered both as an artist and as a unique personality. Artist Arthur Heming describes "a spruce-looking man of medium height and powerful build" who was affectionately called "the old devil" by a servant at the Griswold House. At Miss Florence's he liked to rummage through the trunks in the attic for an old flowered dressing gown or stove-pipe hat to wear down the street to the post office in order to startle the townspeople. Whether at Old Lyme, Cos Cob, Appledore, New Hampshire, or Easthampton, New York, he could be counted on to keep things lively.

Hassam's popularity as an artist is shown by the numerous awards and honors he received for his work, as well as by the widespread acceptance he won from contemporary critics. Together with J. Alden Weir and John Twachtman, Hassam founded The Ten in 1897. He was a member of the American Water Color Society, the Society of American Artists, the National Academy of Design, and the Association of American Painters and Sculptors.

Finally, he was an artist interested in American art education. He willed his own collection of work to the American Academy of Arts and Letters, a group of nearly 450 paintings, pastels, and decorative panels. At his direction, the collection was sold, at prices set by Macbeth and Milch galleries, for the purchase of works by contemporary American and Canadian artists to be given to museums of the United States. Like the Ranger Fund, Hassam's generous bequest has benefited numbers of public museum collections in this country and has fostered interest in American art.

Further reading:

Adams, Adeline. *Childe Hassam.* N.Y.: American Academy of Arts and Letters, 1938.

Childe Hassam, 1859-1935. Exh. cat., University of Arizona Museum of Art, 1972.

Cortissoz, Royal. *Catalogue of the Etchings and Dry-Points of Childe Hassam, N.A.* N.Y.: Charles Scribner's Sons, 1925.

Hoopes, Donelson. *Childe Hassam.* N.Y.: Watson-Guptill Publications, 1979.

Hoffman, Harry Leslie

Born Mar. 16, 1871,
  Cressona, Pa.
Died Mar. 6, 1964, Old Lyme.
In New Haven, 1895-97; in
  Old Lyme, summers. 1902-09;
  permanently, 1910-64.

Harry Hoffman, back in Old Lyme after a short period of study at the Académie Julian in Paris in 1903, invited Willard Metcalf to critique his recent work. "The trouble with you, Hoffman," Metcalf advised, "is you're going around with a ball and chain tied to your feet. Go out and paint what you see and forget your theories."

Only a few months before, Hoffman had concluded his first one-man show — a small exhibition at the American Art Association in Paris. Besides studying in Paris, he had worked at Yale under John Ferguson Weir (father of J. Alden) and at the Art Students League with Frank Vincent DuMond. Given Hoffman's solid art education, Metcalf's remark must have jolted the young artist. Under Metcalf's guidance, Hoffman soon became a proponent of Impressionism, painting such brightly rendered canvases as *Childe Hassam's Studio* (cat. 189, illus. p. 144).

Harry Hoffman first came to Old Lyme in 1902 with his good friend Arthur Heming. Both were students of DuMond and that first year stayed in a private home and took their meals at Florence Griswold's house. They evidenced promise as artists and were quickly drawn into the new colony's membership. Hoffman returned each sum-

mer, though once at least, when he was very short of money, he nearly made a switch to a career that could have parted him from Old Lyme forever. The former Yale athlete wrote to Heming, who was already at the Griswold House: "Have just been offered good pay to pitch for a professional baseball team. Shall I accept?" Heming was appalled and says he saved Hoffman for the art world by arranging for him to model for the sculptor Tait McKenzie, who had an order to do an athletic figure during his Old Lyme summer, and to take down, in shorthand, DuMond's Saturday afternoon lectures to his summer class. Luckily, Hoffman was a man of several talents.

Another of them came in handy when he was courting his wife. Despite protestations to his friends at the Griswold House that he intended to work hard at art in the summers and "steer clear of girls," he was immediately attracted to a Miss Beatrice Pope from East Orange, New Jersey, who arrived for a stay at Miss Florence's one summer. Arthur Heming, whose remembrances of Old Lyme are sometimes heightened, says the girl was the daughter of a woman who had spent a quiet summer with Miss Florence back in the days when she ran a girls' boarding school. She wanted her daughter to recuperate from too many dinners and dances at a country place that had no men, and Miss Florence and the artists thought it would be a good joke not to tell her about the new art colony that was in the house, eagerly awaiting the arrival of her young daughter. Since the young lady's sister Florence was one of three women who came to Old Lyme around 1905 to study art with Henry Rankin Poore, Heming's version of the Hoffman-Pope romance may be fanciful.

Still, his memory of the two young people canoeing in the moonlight on the Lieutenant River is probably not far-fetched. He says Hoffman, who thought of becoming a professional flutist for a time, serenaded his lady on the flute with "Lo, Hear the Gentle Lark!" In little more than a week, the two were engaged, and to Hoffman's surprise, he had fallen in love with a girl who was wealthy. His money troubles were over.

When he married Beatrice Pope in 1910, her family set up the newlyweds in a spacious house on a hilltop off Sill Lane in Old Lyme. They made this their permanent home after a lengthy honeymoon in Spain (where Hoffman was mistakenly arrested as a spy while sketching in a forbidden spot in Palos). Following the tradition established in the Griswold House, Hoffman decorated his own house with panel paintings over the doors and on the wainscoting.

By the 1920s Hoffman had achieved a reputation for highly unusual paintings of underwater life. Having fashioned a bucket with a glass bottom that he floated on the water's surface, he made rapid notes in watercolor of what he observed. These sketches became the basis of several hundred paintings of the undersea. Hoffman accompanied the eminent naturalist William Beebe on research trips to the Galapagos Islands, Bermuda, and British Guiana in order to pursue his speciality. He was entranced by the colors he saw under the ocean's surface:

. . . Not one color, nor was it one tint or shade. It was all colors, but in the same value. And the only way to paint it was impressionistically, using broken colors of light pink, green, violet, and blue. These colors thin out in the distance so that they merge into the disappearing iridescence.

The artist received a prestigious gold medal at the Panama-Pacific Exposition in 1915, the 1924 Eaton Purchase Prize of the Lyme Art Association, and the Landscape Prize of the New Haven Paint and Clay Club in 1925. He was elected an associate of the National Academy of Design in 1930. His friends were equally proud of Hoffman's role in assisting Florence Griswold when she was old and about to lose her house. He was instrumental in promoting, and served as treasurer for, the fund "Miss Florence's artists" established in order to buy the Griswold House, assure her of a home in it for life, and preserve it as a museum after her death.

Although many of the American Impressionists lived long lives, Hoffman had one of the longest. He lived to be ninety-two and had been in Old lyme more than sixty years when he died in 1964.

Further reading:
Hoffman, Harry L. Personal Interview. Old Lyme, August 5, 1954. Transcript, Lyme Historical Society Archives.
"The Painter Who Found a New World Underseas." *New Haven Register,* May 19, 1963.

Irvine, Wilson Henry

Born Feb. 28, 1869, Byron, Ill.
Died Aug. 21, 1936, Lyme.
In Lyme, summers, 1914-17;
    permanently, 1918-36.

Looking through a glass prism one day in his studio in Lyme, Wilson Irvine became fascinated by the rainbow-like effects. He began to view his subjects through the crystal to create what he called "prismatic paintings." His first exhibition of these jewel-like canvases with heavy impasto (paintings that compare closely with Walter Griffin's work between 1915 and 1930) was a one-man show at the Grand Central Art Galleries in 1930. Critics labelled these paintings "curiosities" and predicted that nothing would come of the experiment. Irvine nevertheless persisted in using the technique and won a fair measure of acceptance for his "prismatic paintings" in the later years of his career.

Wilson Irvine had a keenly imaginative mind. He invented and patented a tree swing made of canvas straps that was manufactured by a Chicago firm. In the 1920s he experimented with what he called "aqua-prints," in which he controlled the process of making marbleized paper in order to introduce naturalistic subject matter. Always looking for new modes of visual expression, Irvine warned that "any painter who in this day and age clings tenaciously to the one thing which he can do best, in a technical sense, and is satisfied, is not only standing still, he is actually retrograding."

Like so many of the American Impressionists, Irvine was largely self-taught. The only formal training he had was in evening classes at the Art Institute of Chicago. It has yet to

be determined how long Irvine studied or how he established his career in Chicago, but he must have developed a good reputation. He was a member of nearly every Chicago art organization of his day, including the Cliff Dwellers and the Chicago Arts Club, and he served as President for both the Palette and Chisel Club and the Chicago Society of Artists.

Irvine and his family first came to Lyme in the summer of 1914, when the artist was forty-five years old. The reasons for this move have not been discovered. But within a few years he bought a permanent home in the Hamburg section of Lyme, where he and his family became good friends with such neighboring artists as Robert and Bessie Potter Vonnoh and Guy Wiggins. (By the second decade of this century, many of the artists associated with the Old Lyme colony had moved to the more rural Hamburg, attracted by its picturesque cove of water and its open countryside, and disappointed by Old Lyme's increasing "progress." As early as 1909 Woodrow Wilson was complaining about the noise of motor cars roaring down the main street, something that had not been a problem on his first visit in 1905.)

Irvine specialized in painting landscapes, particularly of the Connecticut countryside in spring. Critics frequently noted his ability to paint subtle atmospheric mists and to render tree forms truthfully. Both of these characteristics are in evidence in *The Pool* (cat. 189, illus. p. 145). He loved to paint outdoors, especially "when there's a kind of hazy beauty in the air."

Not much is known about Irvine's exhibition history. He received a silver medal at the Panama-Pacific Exposition of 1915, and in 1926 he was elected an associate of the National Academy of Design. He exhibited regularly with the Lyme Art Association. He is represented in the collections of such museums as the Art Institute of Chicago, the Phoenix Art Museum, the William Benton Museum of Art, and the Lyme Historical Society. Irvine died in Lyme in 1936.

Further reading:
Aqua-Prints by Wilson Irvine. Exh. cat., Albert Roullier Galleries, New York City, n.d.
Wilson Irvine Papers. Archives of American Art microfilm copy.

Jongers, Alphonse

Born Nov. 17, 1872,
    Mézières, France.
Died Oct. 2, 1945,
    Montreal, Canada.
In Old Lyme, 1900-04.

The portraitist, Alphonse Jongers, was one of the Lyme art colony's charter members, coming to Old Lyme at Henry Ward Ranger's suggestion in the spring of 1900.

Born in France, Jongers trained under Delaunay and Gustave Moreau at the École des Beaux Arts, and then studied for two years in Spain. Jongers moved to French Canada in 1895, where at the age of twenty-three he opened a studio in Montreal. It was probably there that Ranger and Jongers met and became friends, as Ranger travelled to Montreal frequently in the late 1890s. In 1900, just before making his first of several trips to Old Lyme with Ranger, Jongers moved to New York City. His first known exhibition in New York was a March, 1902, group show of seven painters (including fellow Lyme artists Louis Paul Dessar, George Bogert, and Ranger) at Durand-Ruel Galleries.

Between 1900 and 1904, Jongers spent each summer in Old Lyme. In 1903 he persuaded Florence Griswold to pose for her portrait, playing the harp her father had brought from England (cat. 191). He was unable to finish before returning to the city and asked Miss Florence to send the harp to his New York studio in order to complete the canvas. The portrait was sold to George A. Hearn and hung with the Hearn Collection at the Metropolitan Museum of Art. In 1918 the painting was sold to a New Haven dealer, who in turn sold it to the Lyme Art Association. As a tribute to Florence Griswold, the Association gave her the painting.

Jongers played an important role in the early "Barbizon" years of the Lyme art colony. He also painted portraits of Henry Ward Ranger, now in the National Portrait Gallery and the National Academy of Design, as well as a portrait of Louis Paul Dessar in the National Academy. Additionally, Jongers is represented in the Metropolitan Museum of Art, National Collection of Fine Arts, and the Montreal Museum of Fine Arts. He was a member of the Society of American Artists and was elected an Associate of the National Academy of Design in 1906. He received a silver medal at the the St. Louis Exposition in 1904 and the third class medal at the Paris Salon of 1909.

Jongers returned to Montreal in 1924, where he was successful enough to be called "one of Canada's leading portrait painters." Two years after his death in 1945, a memorial exhibition of his work was held at the Montreal Art Association.

Further reading:
"Alphonse Jongers Memorial Exhibition." *Montreal Art Association Bulletin,* No. 43 (Dec. 1947), pp. 2-3.
"Among the Artists." *American Art News,* 3 (Nov. 26, 1904), 2.

Langhorne, Katherine
see Adams, Katherine Langhorne

Lawson, Ernest
Born Mar. 22, 1873, Halifax, Nova Scotia.
Died Dec. 18, 1939, Miami Beach, Fla.
In Cos Cob c. 1892-93, 1894; in Hartford, 1933; in Norfolk, 1934.

Ernest Lawson studied under John Twachtman and J. Alden Weir in the Cos Cob summer school, probably in 1892 and 1893, and his time in Cos Cob shaped his entire career. His first studies had been at the Kansas City Art Institute. In 1890, he had enrolled at the Art Students League in New York, where his teachers were Twachtman, Weir, Willard Metcalf, and H. Siddons Mowbray. Undoubtedly it was as a result of his association with Twachtman and Weir at the League that Lawson went to Cos Cob, where, for the first time, he painted landscapes out-of-doors. He never forgot Weir's reaction to his first — "the worst I have ever seen" — nor that Weir had gone on to say, "You are trying to get the whole world on one canvas. Simplify everything and stick to your first impression." Though Lawson admired Weir, it appears that Twachtman had the greater influence on him. Critic Hilton Kramer believes "The crucial influence on Lawson was Twachtman's . . . and he never strayed very far from this basic influence in a long lifetime of painting." Like Twachtman, Lawson became known for his winter landscapes. Unlike his teacher, however, Lawson often employed bright colors robustly applied. His palette was so brilliant that one contemporary critic referred to him as "Lawson of the Crushed Jewels."

Lawson was already imbued with the Impressionist philosophy when he left for France in 1893. He studied briefly at the Académie Julian before going off on his own to continue the open-air painting he had enjoyed in Cos Cob. In Paris, he shared a studio with the novelist Somerset Maugham, who used him as the model for the artist Frederick Lawson in *Of Human Bondage.*

Lawson returned to the United States in 1894, believing it was time to come home:

As far as influence goes, we can get too much. . . . I want to keep my individuality and at the same time get as much of the best French influence as will be consistent with it. As with medicine, French influence kills if taken in too large a dose — witness most of our best artists who have become to all intents and purposes Frenchmen in work and thought. Now I will go back again to Connecticut and see what I can do.

Lawson returned to Greenwich. He was there for a few months, then sailed for Europe again. He had just married one of his art teachers from Kansas, and she wanted very much to go. Four years later, he settled in Washington Heights, New York, where he painted the views of the Hudson River in winter which became his best-known work. In 1908, he exhibited at Macbeth Gallery with The Eight, a group named in parody of The Ten and comprised of Lawson, six urban realists under the leadership of Robert Henri, and the highly individual post-Impressionist Maurice Prendergast. Lawson was the only pure landscape painter in the group and closely linked with the late Impressionists against whose sentimentality and prettiness The Eight were in mild rebellion. He had met the others of The Eight through William Glackens.

A charter member of the Association of American Painters and Sculptors, Lawson helped with the preparations for the 1913 Armory Show, in which he exhibited. He was elected a full member of the National Academy of Design in 1917.

Troubled by personal and financial problems, Lawson moved about frequently, especially in his later years. He had continued to visit Connecticut periodically and may have spent summers here between 1906-09. Occasionally in the 1920s he exhibited in Connecticut Academy of Fine Arts exhibitions. And in 1933 he taught in Hartford for an organization (as yet unidentified) that he said was made up entirely of women artists, writers, and sculptors. He was not happy: "I have spent a good deal of time in Hartford, but it did add to my sorrow that there were any number of applicants for the teaching job willing to take $100 a month. I had to take that or nothing." Furthermore, he had to go to a reception in his honor. "Hundreds of women, mostly middle-aged. As I was the only man you can imagine how I adored it. We all made little speeches and drank tea." Still, the Connecticut landscape was pleasing. "Leaves are beginning to bud, how I wish you were here, as next month is the best in the North."

A year or so later he was painting in Norfolk as a houseguest of Dr. Edward Quintard, a prominent physician who liked to paint and write poetry. He visited the family often on weekends and gave Quintard some painting lessons. An exhibition of Lawson's Norfolk landscapes (along with several of his Nova Scotia scenes) was held in the town in 1934. A tea celebrated the opening and a special catalogue (listing 21 paintings) was published. Two years later, in 1936, Lawson moved to Coral Gables, Florida, where he had spent time each year since 1931.

Lawson wrote a Credo which he subtitled "The Power to See Beautifully and Idealistically." "Color is my specialty," he said in part. "It affects me like music affects some persons — emotionally . . . . We don't actually copy nature in art. Nature merely suggests something to us, to which we add our own ideas. Impressions from nature are merely jumping off points for artistic creations."

Further reading:
Berry-Hill, Henry and Sidney. *Ernest Lawson, American Impressionist.* Leigh-on-Sea, England: F. Lewis, Publishers, Ltd., 1968.
DuBois, Guy Pène. *Ernest Lawson.* American Artists Series. N.Y.: Whitney Museum of American Art, 1932.
Ernest Lawson: Retrospective. Exh. cat., ACA Galleries, New York City, 1976.
Karpiscak, Adeline Lee. *Ernest Lawson, 1873-1939; A Retrospective Exhibition.* Exh. cat., University of Arizona Museum of Art, 1979.

Lumis, Harriet Randall

Born May 29, 1870, Salem.
Died April 6, 1953,
    Springfield, Mass.
In Connecticut steadily,
    1870-92; periodically,
    1892-1953.

Although Harriet Randall Lumis lived most of her adult life in Springfield, Massachusetts, she considered Connecticut a second home. She was born and grew up in the state, her birthplace the country village of Salem, near Norwich. The interest she showed in sketching from nature when she first attended school at Bacon Academy in Colchester was encouraged by her father. But when she was a boarding student at the Connecticut Literary Institution at Suffield in the early 1880s, she reluctantly chose not to enroll in art courses: "To be sure I was filled with a great desire to paint the atrocious flower pieces . . . but my family thought music the most fitting medium." Her family by then had moved to a farm a little north of Colchester, in Hebron. In 1892 Harriet Randall was married to Fred Williams Lumis, a native of Norwich, who had just settled in Springfield, Massachusetts, where he would become an architect and the city's building commissioner. It was there that her art career began.

In 1883 the Lumises enrolled in an evening drawing class sponsored by the Springfield school system. The training was academic but the experience developed Harriet Lumis's early interest in art into a total commitment. She had several instructors in Springfield — among them Mary Hubbard, James Hall, Roswell Gleason Shurleff, and Willis S. Adams — all academic draftsmen or tonalist painters. In 1910, at forty years old, and again in 1911, she went to Mianus in Cos Cob to study with Leonard Ochtman in the New York Summer School. Ochtman, something of a tonalist himself, nonetheless shared with Cos Cob artists such as Twachtman and Hassam a desire to depict specific locales in a subtle, intimate way. Lumis began to share those attitudes. She developed an interest in American Impressionism.

Once she committed herself to Impressionism — just at the time that it was essentially over as a force in American art — she remained fiercely loyal to its ideas and style for the rest of her long life. In 1949 she would help found an Academic Artists' Association in Springfield to support realistic art against what she called modernist "propaganda."

In 1913 Lumis began to participate in the exhibitions of the fairly young Connecticut Academy of Fine Arts and she soon became an active member. She was stimulated by the professional contacts with artists such as Charles Noel Flagg, Henry C. White, and Guy Wiggins. Presumably her strong interest in the Connecticut Academy led her to help form a similiar group in Springfield in 1919, the Springfield Art League.

Lumis won more recognition in the 1920s. She was elected to the National Association of Women Painters and Sculptors in 1921. In 1925 she won her first major prize — in a Connecticut Academy annual. She was fifty-five years old. Her training had been limited and had come late, and her exhibition activity had been essentially local. Springfield commercial galleries had, however, shown her work with that of artists such as Charles H. Davis, Bruce Crane, and Birge Harrison. Her reputation had grown slowly but steadily. Her style, never static, had become personal.

Lumis continued her training (at the Breckinridge Summer School of Art, Gloucester, Massachusetts) and she increased her participation in exhibitions, including those at the National Academy of Design, the Pennsylvania Academy of Fine Arts, and the Women's National Exposition in St. Louis (1926). The Chicago department store Carson, Pirie Scott began to sell her art. She had several one-woman exhibitions at the Jasper Rand Art Museum in Westfield, Massachusetts.

After her husband died in 1938, Lumis taught landscape painting until her own death in 1953, because she needed the income. Despite developments in American art in the 1940s, she taught only American Impressionism, because she still believed so completely in its ideals. Throughout her career, she painted near her home or on the Massachusetts shore, but she often visited family and friends in Connecticut, and when she was in the state she painted local scenes. Richard H. Love, who organized a major retrospective of her work in 1977, says that a significant part of Lumis's work was done in the state that had been her girlhood home.

Further reading:
Harriet Randall Lumis, 1870-1953; An American Impressionist. (Exh. cat., R. H. Love Galleries, Chicago, 1977).

MacRae, Elmer Livingston

Born July 16, 1875, New York City.

Died Apr. 2, 1953, Greenwich.

In Cos Cob permanently, 1896-1953.

Little is known about Elmer MacRae's early life. He studied for a time at the Art Students League with John Twachtman, Carroll Beckwith, Robert Blum, and H. Siddons Mowbray. Sometime in the early 1890s he came to Cos Cob for two summers of outdoor landscape classes with Twachtman. In 1896 he settled in the village, and four years later he married Constant Holley, the daughter of the owners of the boardinghouse that was the informal headquarters of the Cos Cob colony. MacRae never again lived anywhere but the Holley House.

Like Twachtman, whom he succeeded as leader of the art colony, MacRae found the inspiration for his landscapes on home ground. He also executed many portraits, especially of his wife and twin daughters. Just as his landscapes capture familiar scenes of daily life (a man chopping firewood while hens scratch under an apple tree), so the portraits show the artist's fair-haired little girls engaged in the everyday activities of a country childhood.

Contemporary critics found greater merit in MacRae's pastels than in his oils. Reviewing an exhibit at the Madison Art Gallery in March, 1910, a writer in the *New York Post* remarked that MacRae showed most individuality when working with colored chalks. "He has used them," the critic wrote, "to give suggestions of color and form; instead of chalking the scenes to death, his light touch gives them life." Perhaps influenced by Whistler and the French Impressionists, Twachtman and Hassam had also worked in pastel in Cos Cob. MacRae's interest in the medium went further: he was one of the founders and the first secretary-treasurer of the American Pastel Society.

In addition to his participation in the Pastellists (as they were called), MacRae was active in other arts organiza-

tions. He was a charter member of the Greenwich Society of Artists and served on its first council. More important, he was a founder of the organization which sponsored the Armory Show, the Association of American Painters and Sculptors (AAPS).

As the association's treasurer and an active member of several exhibition committees, MacRae was largely responsible for the day-to-day preparations for the Armory Show. Other members of the AAPS, especially Arthur B. Davies, Walt Kuhn, and Walter Pach, had selected the contemporary European art which would completely change the American art world when it was shown in New York, Boston, and Chicago in 1913. Without MacRae's dedicated attention to the Armory Show's organization, however, the ground-breaking exhibition would probably not have been the success that it was.

Ten of MacRae's works, including *Fairy Stories* (cat. 125, illus. p. 109), were exhibited in the Armory Show. MacRae also exhibited at the Holley House in October of 1908, 1909, and 1910; with D. Putnam Brinley at a New Canaan restaurant in 1909; and in group shows at the Madison Art Gallery in New York in March and November, 1910. A posthumous retrospective of his work was held at the Milch Gallery from March 23 to April 18, 1959.

Further reading:
Elmer Livingston MacRae: Forgotton Artist of the Armory Show. Exh. cat., Milch Galleries, New York City, 1959.

Metcalf, Willard Leroy

Born July 1, 1858, Lowell, Mass.

Died Mar. 9, 1925, New York City.

In Old Lyme, 1905-07; Leete's Island periodically, 1908-09; **Waterford, summers, 1910-c. 1915; northwestern Ct. periodically 1910-25.**

Beginning in 1904, Willard Metcalf kept a scrapbook of newspaper clippings and magazine notices of his exhibitions and prizes. On the inside cover he had written, "A partial history of the Renaissance," an allusion to the new direction his art had taken in 1904, when he was forty-six years old. He seems to have determined in about 1903 to confront nature as it was in New England. "He would leave the city as if for a campaign," the art critic Royal Cortissoz reported, "and bring back his sheaves with something of the air of a fighter who had conquered another step in his march." In 1904 he painted mostly near Boothbay, Maine, living at times in a tent beside the Damariscotta River, and when he exhibited twenty-one paintings (not all of them new) in his first New York one-man exhibition at Fishel, Adler, and Schwartz Gallery in 1905, critics like Cortissoz said that "it was plain he had greatly widened his range . . . a sympathy more alert and more penetrating." A year after Metcalf's renaissance began, he went to Old Lyme.

Further reading:
Bell, R. H. *Art-Talks With Ranger*. N.Y.: G. P. Putnam and Sons, 1914.
Bromhead, Harold W. "Henry W. Ranger." *International Studio,* 19 (July 1906), xxxiii-xliv.
Daingerfield, Elliott. "Henry W. Ranger, Painter." *Century Magazine,* 97 (Nov. 1918), 82-89.
Henry Ward Ranger Centennial Exhibition, 1858-1958. Exh. cat., National Collection of Fine Arts, 1958.

Robinson, Theodore

Born July 3, 1852, Irasburg, Vt.
Died Apr. 2, 1896, New York City.
In Greenwich, summer, 1893, and periodically, fall and winter, 1893-95; in Cos Cob, summer, 1894.

Theodore Robinson, an American painter intimately familiar with the Giverny of Claude Monet, eventually came home to look for the American version. He concluded that it was to be found in Vermont, the state where he had been born, but many people believe his best American work was done in the Greenwich area between 1893-95.

Notes in his diary reveal that things did not always go well for him there. The American landscape was "ragged" compared with that of Giverny, and the light was different. The domestic architecture of "little square, box-shaped white houses" was not picturesque in the European way. Besides, Robinson was very ill with the asthma that would kill him prematurely in 1896. He had to fight, within himself, a sentimental strain. He was keenly aware of the difficulties of combining the techniques of French Impressionism with the attitudes inherent in the American landscape tradition. He had been using photographs as an aid to figure painting since the 1880s but was now having ambivalent feelings about using the camera at all. In Cos Cob or neighboring Greenwich, however, despite all difficulties, he found an ambience that made his times there among the most satisfactory of his life.

Theodore Robinson's family moved from Vermont to Wisconsin when he was three years old. In about 1870 he studied briefly at the Art Institute of Chicago until his chronic asthma forced him to stop. In 1874 he enrolled at the school of the National Academy of Design in New York. Soon after, he was a member of the splinter group that broke with the Academy to form the Art Students League, whose name he suggested.

Robinson spent much of his adult life in Europe. In 1876 he left New York for Paris, where he studied under Carolus-Duran and Gérôme and exhibited in the Salons of 1877 and 1879. In Venice, where he lived for about a year, he became friends with Whistler. He returned to the United States in 1879 and spent the next five years teaching and working on decorative commissions, often with Will Low

and John LaFarge, until he could save enough money to return to France. He began exhibiting in the National Academy of Design in 1881.

Robinson lived in France again from 1884 to 1892, except for a couple of brief visits to New York. Beginning in 1887, he worked in Giverny, the small town where Monet designed the gardens and lily pond he was to paint again and again. Influenced by Monet, with whom he became good friends in 1888, Robinson adopted a lightened palette and an Impressionist concern with light. He retained his typically American interest in realism, however, never letting color govern form to the extent that Monet did.

As important as the French Impressionist influence on Robinson's own work was the impact his Impressionist work had on that of other American artists. His Giverny paintings, shown at the Society of American Artists annual exhibition in 1888, were among the first Impressionist works by an American exhibited in New York. He was the first American Impressionist to receive a major honor — The Webb Prize for landscape, in 1890, awarded by the Society of American Artists. More important, on his return to the United States, Robinson was able to influence American artists directly.

When he came back in 1892, he spent time with his friends John Twachtman and J. Alden Weir in Connecticut. He was with them the summers of 1893 and 1894 and as early as 1892, when he painted a winter scene of Twachtman's house at Round Hill. The three friends discussed Monet's theories. They looked closely at one another's work. Twachtman and Weir, both respected teachers, passed on to students attitudes they learned from Robinson. Robinson himself did some teaching: summer classes in 1893 and 1894 for the Brooklyn Arts School; and then, from late 1894, at the Pennsylvania Academy of Fine Arts, where Robert Vonnoh, another pioneer American Impressionist, must have known exactly what he was doing when he persuaded Robinson to take over classes he had already introduced to Impressionism.

Being back in his native country worked on Robinson, too. He was profoundly affected by the Connecticut landscape, especially that around Cos Cob. According to Sona Johnston, curator of the Baltimore Museum's 1973 Robinson retrospective, "The Connecticut shore was for him an ideal setting in an artistic sense . . . . He had never spent an extended period of time at the shore, and it is obvious that he was inspired by the qualities of the intense light reflecting off the water and its effect on the surrounding landscape." Twachtman, Weir, and other friends urged Robinson to settle in Cos Cob, but he decided instead to spend the summer of 1895 near relatives in Vermont. He died in New York the following spring; his physician had to wire his friends to collect enough money for his funeral.

Further reading:
Baur, John I. H. *Theodore Robinson, 1852-1896*. Exh. cat., Brooklyn Museum, 1946. Reprinted by Arno Press, New York, in *Three Nineteenth Century American Painters,* 1969.
Clark, Eliot. *Theodore Robinson: His Life and Art*. Chicago: R. H. Love Galleries, 1979.
Johnston, Sona. *Theodore Robinson, 1852-1896*. Exh. cat., Baltimore Museum of Art, 1973.
Theodore Robinson, Diaries, 1892-1896. Available at Frick Art Reference Library, New York City.

Robinson, William S.

Born Sept. 15, 1861, East
Gloucester, Mass.
Died Jan. 11, 1945, Biloxi,
Miss.
In Old Lyme, summers,
c. 1905-20; permanently,
c. 1921-37.

In his lifetime, William Robinson was the recipient of numerous awards and exhibition prizes. After his death in 1945, however, his name all but faded from the American art scene. Though at times he painted seascapes and maritime subjects in Gloucester, Massachusetts, and Monhegan, Maine, he was especially fond of, and skilled at, painting the Old Lyme hillsides and pasturelands, and the laurel that grew along the banks of the Lieutenant River — subjects especially suited to his Impressionist palette and brushwork.

In his early career, Robinson developed his talents as a marine artist while he held a number of teaching positions. He taught at several Boston area schools during the early 1880s and from 1885-89 was an instructor at the Maryland Institute in Baltimore. He then travelled abroad and studied at the Académie Julian under Benjamin Constant and Jules Lefebvre. Robinson first exhibited at the National Academy of Design in 1891, shortly after his return to the United States. In the 1890s he taught at the Drexel Institute, Pennsylvania Academy of the Fine Arts, and Columbia University's Teachers College. He continued to exhibit his Barbizon-influenced landscapes and seascapes. Robinson told William Macbeth in 1893: "I do marines, that is surf and boat subjects, also Dutch fisherfolk."

Beginning around 1905, Robinson made yearly journeys from New York to Old Lyme. He always stayed at the Florence Griswold House, working in a studio across the brook from the Lyme Art Association. Robinson was a charter member of this organization and later became its president. Additionally, he was president of the American Watercolor Society from 1914 through 1921 and a member of the National Arts Club, Salmagundi Club, and Lotos Club. He was elected an associate of the National Academy of Design in 1907 and a full academician in 1911.

His canvases received many awards, including honorable mentions at the Paris Exposition of 1900 and the Pan-American Exposition in Buffalo in 1901; a bronze medal at the St. Louis Exposition in 1904; and silver medals at the 1910 International Exposition in Buenos Aires and the 1915 Panama-Pacific Exposition in San Francisco. Robinson was also the recipient of a number of prizes from the National Academy of Design, Salmagundi Club, and Lyme Art Association. In 1925 one of his paintings of mountain laurel was awarded the Lyme Art Association's Museum Purchase Prize and was given to the Cleveland Museum of Art.

In about 1921 Robinson seems to have moved to Old Lyme year-round, staying, as usual, in the Griswold House, until Miss Florence died in 1937. He lived in Biloxi, Mississippi, during the final years of his life.

Rook, Edward F.

Born Sept. 21, 1870,
New York City.
Died Oct. 25, 1960,
Old Lyme.
In Old Lyme, 1903-60.

The artists at Old Lyme generally had two kinds of thoughts about Edward Rook — that he was one of the finest painters in their group and that he had one of the most interesting personalities. As artist Nelson C. White phrases it, "Mr. Rook was noted for his originality of approach to almost every subject, not only in his art but in his daily life." His training in art was conventional for American painters of the time. He had studied in the 1880s with Benjamin Constant and Jean-Paul Laurens, probably at the Académie Julian. Except for one or two visits home, Rook remained in France until the end of 1900. He did exhibit a painting in the 1898 exhibition of the Pennsylvania Academy of Fine Arts, which was awarded the Temple Gold Medal.

In 1901, on Valentine's Day, Rook was married to Edith Sone. The following summer they traveled to the Canadian Rockies, then down the Pacific coast to California. Rook won a bronze medal that same year at the Pan-American Exposition in Buffalo. Near the end of 1902, the Rooks went to Mexico, where they lived for eleven months. Rook came from a family of means and apparently could afford to do pretty much as he liked.

Edward Rook and his wife were in Old Lyme in late October of 1903. Why they chose to go there is not clear, but they obviously liked it, because in April, 1905, they moved to Old Lyme, "made it our residence." And it was there they stayed, their travels over, Mrs. Rook even behaving like a recluse at times. Rook continued to exhibit at major expositions: he won two silver medals at the Universal Exposition, St. Louis, in 1904; a silver medal at the International Fine Arts Exposition, Buenos Aires, in 1910; and a gold medal at the Panama-Pacific International Exhibition, San Francisco, in 1915. He was also an active member of the Lyme Art Association. He did not have a New York gallery dealer, and since he deliberately set his prices high, he sold relatively little. He is represented, however, in the permanent collections of several American museums and of the Lotos Club, to which he belonged. He painted landscapes, still lifes, and marines.

Rook was made a full member of the National Academy of Design in 1924, the same year he and his wife moved into a new home they had built in Old Lyme. The house was the talk of the town because Rook, who had grown passionately fond of automobiles, had designed the garage as the focus of the structure. The house, arranged tightly against either side of and over the garage, acted as a kind of picture frame for it. Rook owned three cars, among them a Hupmobile and a Locomobile. At night he raised their hoods and spotlighted the engines so he could admire the machinery, which he thought very beautiful. He never

171

learned to drive and had to hire driver-mechanics, most of whom dismayed him because of their casual attitude toward the machines.

Rook was essentially a gentle, courtly man, which seems to have made his vagaries all the more endearing to his friends. He loved mountain laurel, as did many of the Impressionist artists, and shared their frustration that the flowers often faded faster than they could be painted. Sometimes Rook tied pink cotton balls onto laurel bushes for a "second blooming," so he could finish a painting.

Rook stories are plentiful. One that is often told has to do with a sheet of plate glass lying on the ground near Rook's back door. Artist Gregory Smith asked what it was all about. "Why, that is for the rats, sir," said Rook. Smith pressed for an explanation. "That is to cover the garbage pail, don't you see. The garbage pail is sunk in the ground and the plate glass is to cover it. And the rats can come. That is to torment them. They can see the garbage but they can't get it."

It tormented some of Rook's friends that though he worked hard at his art, he never worked much at exhibiting it or promoting his reputation. Some of his paintings have only recently begun to appear in galleries again. Someday the work of this painter, so admired by his peers for its proficiency and vision, will have to be reassessed.

Ryder, Chauncey Foster

Born Feb. 29, 1868,
Danbury.

Died May 18, 1949,
Wilton, N.H.

In Old Lyme, summers,
1910-11.

Chauncey Ryder was born in Danbury in 1868, but his family soon moved to New Haven, where he spent most of his early years. Later he moved to Chicago, where he was married to Mary Dole Keith in 1891. Shortly after their marriage, he enrolled in evening classes at the Art Institute. Then, probably in the mid-90s, he spent two years at Smith's Art Academy in Chicago, first as a student and then as an instructor. (One cannot be more specific about details of Ryder's early training and experience.)

In 1901, when Ryder was thirty-three years old, he and his wife sold their house and all its contents in order to finance a move to Paris. It must have been a now-or-never act of desperation. Certainly it indicates how important study in Paris was to Americans who hoped to become artists. Ryder was probably at least ten years older than most students at the Académie Julian when he enrolled. He worked there for two years under Jean-Paul Laurens and Raphael Collin. In 1903 the first work he submitted to the Paris Salon was accepted, and he continued to exhibit there regularly until 1907. To augment his income, he gave art lessons.

Ryder's work was recognized in 1907 by William Macbeth of Macbeth Galleries in New York, and from that point on he met with more success. Macbeth not only ran one of the only two galleries devoted to American art, but he worked hard to promote the artists he represented and to win respect for American art. He even produced, to that end, a serial publication called *Art Notes,* which remarked on many exhibitions other than his own and often chided American art collectors for "buying European." After he began his association with Macbeth, Ryder maintained studios in both New York and Paris for the next several years.

Little is known about Ryder's association with Old Lyme except that it was brief. He exhibited with the Lyme artists' group in both 1910 and 1911, stayed in Miss Florence Griswold's house, and painted one of the panels in her dining room. He must have been looked up to by the artists in Old Lyme, because participation in the annual exhibitions was by invitation, and permission to stay in the Griswold House was far from automatic. Most important, to be asked to paint one of the panels was considered a rare privilege.

The summer of 1910 must have been a busy one for Ryder, for besides visiting Old Lyme, he spent time in Ipswich, Massachusetts, and Monhegan, Maine, as well as Wilton, New Hampshire, where he bought a summer studio. From then on Ryder spent most of April through November there, painting the New Hampshire landscape. In 1911, however, he seems to have visited Old Lyme again briefly.

Ryder sold at least one of his paintings in Old Lyme — to Mrs. Woodrow Wilson. By this time he had developed a sketch-like style of landscape painting that was unique. A contemporary art critic said, "Ryder paints with a freedom and a facility which is not deterred by quibbling details. He is always lyrical and poetic in his approach, and often achieves a certain luminous quality . . . transforming a whole scene into something of other-worldly loveliness."

His oils with loosely-defined forms, usually small in size, sold well. Some larger, more diverse, compositions were acquired by major museums, including the Art Institute of Chicago, the Metropolitan Museum of Art, and the Pennsylvania Academy of Fine Arts.

Ryder received numerous awards and prizes, including a silver medal at the Panama-Pacific Exposition in 1915; the Salmagundi Club Show Prize in 1926; the National Academy of Design Obrig Prize in 1933; and a gold medal at the Paris International Exposition in 1937. He was named an associate of the National Academy of Design in 1915 and a full academician in 1920. He was also a member of the Salmagundi Club, the National Arts Club, the Lotos Club, and Allied Artists of America. Although best known for his oil paintings, Ryder was a proficient draftsman, printmaker, and watercolorist.

Further reading:
Chauncey F. Ryder, N.A. 1868-1949. Exh. cat., Pierce Galleries, Hingham, Mass., 1977.
Pisano, Ronald G. "Chauncey Foster Ryder: Peace and Plenty." *American Art and Antiques,* 1 (Sept.-Oct. 1978), 76-83.

Smith, Edward Gregory

Born May 2, 1880,
  Grand Rapids, Mich.
Died Nov. 7, 1961,
  Boiling Springs, Pa.
In Old Lyme, 1910-61.

Gregory Smith (he always called himself that, though he signed some paintings with his full name) moved to Old Lyme from his hometown of Grand Rapids, Michigan, in 1910, at the encouragement of his friend Will Howe Foote. Smith, who was thirty at the time, had studied a couple of years at the Chicago Art Institute and was anxious to meet the many well-known artists staying in Old Lyme.

Gregory Smith admired a number of the artists associated with the colony, particularly Childe Hassam and Willard Metcalf. He respected Metcalf's ability to record the essence of the New England countryside — from panoramic views to intimate woodland scenes. Metcalf's interest in painting both moonlight scenes and winter landscapes influenced Smith to make these his specialty. Hassam's imprint on Smith is illustrated in Smith's painting of the *Bow Bridge* (cat. 206, illus. p. 148). Both painters utilized strong apostrophe-like brushwork and high-key colors to record a sense of veiled luminosity.

When Smith and his wife Annie first came to Old Lyme, they rented the Brick Store, a local landmark that was near the present site of the Lyme Art Association. They frequently had meals at Miss Florence Griswold's house and Gregory Smith sometimes boarded there with other colony members for several months at a time when Mrs. Smith took the children to Florida. Admired for his sharp wit, Smith was often in on the antics and practical jokes the artists played on one another.

In 1916 the Smiths built a house and studio on Sill Lane in Old Lyme, where they lived for the rest of their lives. A beautiful arbor connected the studio to the house. Tragically, a fire in 1925 totally destroyed the studio and most of the work the artist had accumulated to that time.

Although Smith was not so commercially successful as some of the Old Lyme group, the artists held him in high regard as a painter. Several of the most prestigious exhibition prizes of the Lyme Art Association were awarded him, including the W. S. Eaton Purchase Prize in 1922, the Woodhull Adams Memorial Prize in 1927, and the Goodman Prize in 1931 and 1936. In 1977 a small retrospective of Smith's work was shown at the Lyme Historical Society.

Smith served as president of the Lyme Art Association for more than twenty years, from 1934-58. Later he managed the association's gallery and enjoyed a bit of local fame with his "Janitor" series of newspaper articles about the activities of the association. Smith also had an absorbing interest in politics and was involved for years in Republican activities in Old Lyme. He was a charter member of the Old Lyme Volunteer Fire Department, organized in 1923.

Further reading:
Notes on the Florence Griswold House by Gregory Smith. Lyme Art Association Papers. Lyme Historical Society Archives.
Paintings by Gregory Smith. Exh. cat., Lyme Historical Society, 1978.

Tryon, Dwight W.

Born Aug. 13, 1849, Hartford.
Died July 1, 1925, South
  Dartmouth, Mass.
In Hartford and East
  Hartford, 1849-73;
  periodically, 1873-c. 1920.

The landscapes that Dwight W. Tryon painted cannot be labelled Impressionist but are subtle and lyrical and reveal a deep love of nature, especially in its delicate, elusive phases. They relate closely to those of the American Impressionists, who followed him in time. "The personality of this painter of poetic landscapes might have disconcerted you," said artist Henry C. White of his teacher and friend in the biography *The Art and Life of Dwight William Tryon,* because "he was short, rather thick-set and muscular . . . . His hands, wide, with short, thick fingers, blunt at the ends, callused and gnarled as those of any sailor or farmer, gave no evidence whatever of his mastery of minute and delicate craftsmanship."

Tryon had had to develop that remarkable mastery mostly on his own. He wanted to be an artist but worked as a bookkeeper and clerk in a Hartford bookstore. He once confided his ambition to Mark Twain, a customer of the store, who found the idea lamentable. Tryon persisted and by 1873 was able to open a studio in Hartford, marry, and work full-time at art. He exhibited and sold pictures both in Hartford and New York and began to teach private students such as Henry C. White. In 1876 he went to Paris, where he studied with Jacquesson de la Chevreuse, a favorite pupil of Ingres, and at the École des Beaux-Arts. He also worked briefly with Daubigny, Harpignies, and Guillemet.

In 1881 he returned to New York and set up a studio in the Rembrandt Building on W. 57th St., where Thomas Dewing was a neighbor. Two years later he made South Dartmouth, Massachusetts, his summer home, and two years after that he joined the faculty of Smith College in Northampton, where he was for many years head of the Art Department, until his retirement in 1923. He began to spend many summers exploring Buzzards Bay on his own cruising sloop.

Tryon was elected a full member of the National Academy of Design in 1891. His prize list is long and impressive, and he is represented in the collections of major museums. His New York dealer was Montross, and his work was collected by Charles L. Freer, who intended to devote a room to it in the Freer Gallery in Washington,

D.C., because he believed Tryon's art, along with that of Whistler, Dewing, and Abbott Thayer, was most in sympathy with the Oriental work that made up most of his famous collection. (The plan was not carried out after Freer's death.) When Tryon died, he presented an entire art museum to Smith College. Tryon Gallery was completed a year after the artist's death but was demolished a few years ago to make way for the modern building that now houses the Smith College Museum of Art.

It is clear that from the mid-1870s on, Tryon never again had a home of his own in Connecticut. That he learned to love nature as he was growing up in this state is obvious. That he continued to visit is a conjecture based on the fact that he had family in Hartford (his family's clothing business, Stackpole, Moore, Tryon, is still operating). That he did visit and even painted in Connecticut after 1873 is demonstrated by *Glastonbury Meadows,* 1881 (cat. 57).

Further reading:
Dwight W. Tryon: A Retrospective Exhibition. Exh. cat., The William Benton Museum of Art, The University of Connecticut, 1971.
White, Henry C. *The Life and Art of Dwight William Tryon.* Boston: Houghton Mifflin Co., 1930.

Twachtman, John Henry

Born Aug. 4, 1853,
 Cincinnati, Ohio.
Died Aug. 8, 1902,
 Gloucester, Mass.
In Greenwich area,
 c. 1886-1902; Norwich,
 summer, 1898.

John Henry Twachtman was introduced to art by his German-immigrant father, who painted landscapes and still-lifes on window shades. The younger Twachtman began working in the window-shade factory at age fourteen, meanwhile taking night courses in drawing at the Ohio Mechanics Institute. He enrolled at the McMicken School of Design in 1871, where one of his instructors was the Munich-trained artist Frank Duveneck, who eventually took him as a private student. Following the pattern of American artists of his period, Twachtman went to Europe to complete his studies, working at Munich's Royal Academy from 1875-77. The following year he painted in Venice with Duveneck and William Merritt Chase. The paintings of this early, or Munich, period are characterized by dark colors thickly applied. Twachtman showed one typically brownish-black example to a friend years later, chuckling, "That is sunny Venice, done under the influence of the Munich school."

The artist made a conscious effort to rid himself of the somber Munich palette and to improve his drawing by enrolling in the Académie Julian in Paris in 1883. Together with his wife, who was a painter and etcher, he lived in Paris from 1883-85, spending the holidays painting in the French countryside with such new friends as Childe Hassam, Theodore Robinson, and Willard Metcalf. The paintings from this transitional, or French, period (which lasted until the late 1880s) were the artist's most popular during his lifetime. The paint is applied in thin washes; the color range is limited to cool, silvery greens and grays; the composition is simplified, tending toward abstraction, and the predominant influences seem to be Oriental art and the American expatriate James McNeill Whistler. Despite its relative popularity, however, Twachtman rejected the style as "too easy."

It was not until he settled in Greenwich in the late 1880s that Twachtman developed his mature, individual style. The paintings of Twachtman's Greenwich period are characterized by a brighter palette, apparently influenced by Theodore Robinson's experience of French Impressionism. As important as any purely artistic influence, however, was Twachtman's discovery of a landscape which perfectly suited his personal vision. The intimate scale of the Greenwich countryside and its varied but not extreme seasonal changes married perfectly with the artist's sensitivity to nuances of color and mood. Unlike French Impressionists, who travelled from one scenic village to another in search of the picturesque, Twachtman found ample inspiration on his own seventeen-acre farm on Round Hill Road. Again and again he painted his simple farmhouse, with the new portico Stanford White designed for it; the brook just beyond, which cascaded over the rocks and formed a hidden moss-rimmed pool; the white lattice bridge he built at the head of the pool; and even the cabbage patch he and his wife had in their garden. Although he painted the same scene in all seasons, he especially enjoyed winter landscapes, both for the challenge of exploring the variations of white and for the natural abstraction of form under a blanket of snow. (He never sold this farm, as some have reported. It was his joy — and the main subject of his art until he died.)

Twachtman attracted other artists to the Greenwich area when he established summer painting classes in Cos Cob in about 1890. J. Alden Weir, whom Twachtman had met in Paris in 1876, often shared the instruction, and the two close friends visited back and forth between Greenwich and Weir's place in Branchville. Before settling in Greenwich, Twachtman had spent the summer of 1888 in Branchville near Weir, where they had experimented with etching on a press Weir had acquired. Twachtman became especially fond of the harbor area of Bridgeport and executed prints of scenes there, either before or shortly after he moved to Greenwich. Ten years or so later he could easily have visited Weir at Windham, for in 1898 Twachtman served as the instructor at Norwich of the first summer school of the Art Students League ever held outside New York City..

Twachtman's final, or Gloucester, period is named for the Massachusetts town where he conducted summer classes in 1900, 1901, and 1902. The pictures of the last two years of his life, whether painted in Greenwich, Cos Cob, or Gloucester, mark a return to the use of black — nearly abandoned since his youthful Munich period — the new use of brighter colors with greater value contrasts, and more forceful brushwork.

Twachtman was a painter's painter, always admired by fellow artists and knowledgeable amateurs. He never achieved financial success or approval by the established critics during his lifetime. He was never elected to the National Academy, although Weir proposed his name repeatedly. He was a member of the Society of American Artists, the New York Etching Club, the Tile Club, the Players Club, and a founder of The Ten. He died in Gloucester, Massachusetts, in 1902, at the age of forty-nine.

Further reading:
Boyle, Richard J. *John Henry Twachtman.* N.Y.: Watson-Guptill Publications, 1979.
Hale, John Douglas. "The Life and Creative Development of John H. Twachtman." PHD dissertation, Ohio State University, 1957. Available from University Microfilms.
John Henry Twachtman Exh. cat., Cincinnati Art Museum, 1966.
Ryerson, Margery. "John H. Twachtman's Etchings." *Art in America,* 8 (Feb. 1920), 92-96.

Vonnoh, Robert

Born Sept. 17, 1858, Hartford.
Died Dec. 28, 1933,
    Nice, France.
In Old Lyme summers,
    c. 1905-c.1925.

Robert Vonnoh, one of the first Americans to adopt Impressionism, was born in Hartford in 1858 to German parents. The family soon moved to Boston, where Vonnoh studied at the Massachusetts Normal Art School. In 1881 he enrolled at the Académie Julian in Paris, where he worked under Boulanger and Lefebvre, but when his money ran out in 1883, he returned to Boston and taught at several local art schools. He began to establish himself as a portrait painter.

By 1887 he was able to go to Paris for four more years. He participated in various European exhibitions, won honorable mention in the Salon of 1889, and bronze medals for two consecutive years in Paris expositions. He encountered French Impressionism during this second Paris stay, but he must have been aware of it already because Hamlin Garland (who met Vonnoh in Boston in about 1885 through the landscape painter John Enneking) wrote of these younger artists' violent criticism of "the 'Old Hat' schools of Munich" and their keen interest in the "new technique in the use of color" that was "the latest word from Paris." Enneking's friend, Lilla Cabot Perry, staged an informal impressionist exhibition in her home with a group of paintings by John Breck, which "widened the influence of the new school," according to Garland.

By 1891 Vonnoh was back in America, exhibiting landscapes at a Boston gallery in November; they were "a record of impressions gathered out of doors during summer holydays in France in '89 and '90 and in this country the present year" (Vonnoh wrote in the preface to the checklist) "painted earnestly and sincerely with a desire to secure interesting effects of light and color as presented in certain phases of Nature."

That same year Vonnoh became principal instructor in portrait and figure painting at the Pennsylvania Academy of Fine Arts, where he remained until at least the end of 1894, when he persuaded Theodore Robinson to take his place two days a week. In Philadelphia his pupils included Robert Henri, E. W. Schofield, W. E. Redfield, John Sloan, William Glackens, and Maxfield Parrish.

Vonnoh was married to Bessie O. Potter in 1899. She was a noted sculptor with whom he would often exhibit in future. They would become the first husband-wife members of the National Academy. There is evidence that the Vonnohs were in Old Lyme in 1906, but the couple probably first went there the summer of 1905. Statements that credit Vonnoh with being one of the founders of the colony in 1900 cannot be substantiated. Bessie Potter Vonnoh herself wrote that the colony was "famous" and "old" when she and her husband first visited there and that they met the Woodrow Wilson family at the Florence Griswold House — that could not have happened before 1905.

Although the Vonnohs did not participate in the annual Old Lyme art exhibitions until 1917, they returned to town regularly for at least twenty years and had a summer home in the area. They also had a place in Grez-sur-Loing, a French village beloved by the earlier generation of Barbizon painters, but Bessie Vonnoh wrote that she and her husband did not get to their French house from World War I until 1923. Instead, they went to Lyme to be among many of their friends.

Once the Vonnohs began to exhibit in Lyme Art Association exhibitions, they did so regularly for about a dozen years, and Robert Vonnoh occasionally exhibited with the Connecticut Academy of Fine Arts as well. In 1920 he won its top prize. His retrospective exhibitions of 1923 and 1926 traveled from New York to Kansas to California. These were one-man exhibitions, the first since his marriage not to include Bessie Potter Vonnoh's sculptures. That gives some credence to rumors that the Vonnoh marriage failed at some point, although there was never a divorce. Sometime after 1925 Robert Vonnoh seems to have moved permanently to Grez — alone and with failing eyesight. He died in Nice in 1933. His career had included both portraiture and landscapes that were sometimes so heavy with impasto they were described as reliefs in oil.

Further reading:
Vonnoh, Bessie Potter. "Tears and Laughter Caught in Bronze." *The Delineator,* October, 1925, pp. 8 ff.
"The Vonnohs." *International Studio,* 54 (Dec. 1914), 48-52.
"Vonnoh's Half-Century." *International Studio,* 77 (June, 1923), 231-33.

Voorhees, Clark Greenwood

Born May 29, 1871,
    New York City.
Died July 17, 1933, Old Lyme.
In Old Lyme,
    summers, 1896, 1901-03;
    permanently, 1904-33.

Clark Voorhees was the first artist to discover Old Lyme — in the spring of 1896, while exploring the Connecticut shoreline by bicycle. He liked what he saw so much he arranged to stay at the Griswold House, which Miss Florence had recently opened to boarders, and spent all that summer and part of the fall painting in the neighborhood.

Unlike most of the group that would come to Old Lyme, Clark Voorhees had not at first wanted a career in art. He had studied at the Sheffield Scientific School of Yale University, then gone on for a master's degree at Columbia University, where he had done some teaching in chemistry as well. Not until 1894, the year before he received his advanced degree, did Voorhees study art (with Irving Wiles of New York City). By 1896, however, he had turned from the possibility of a career in science and enrolled at the Académie Julian in Paris, under Benjamin Constant and Jean-Paul Laurens. He had determined to be an artist.

Voorhees was in Old Lyme again for at least part of each summer between 1901-03, staying at the Griswold House. He had met Will Howe Foote earlier in Europe and perhaps knew some of the other artists from New York who were working in Old Lyme. At any rate, Voorhees knew the area from his earlier stay.

He was married to Maud Christine Folson in August, 1904, and the couple moved to Lyme. They restored a 1740 gambrel-roof cottage situated at the edge of the Connecticut River, and the house and garden eventually became subjects for several of the artist's paintings, such as *My Garden* (cat. 209, illus. p. 149).

Although Voorhees stayed in Connecticut year-round at first, he maintained club memberships in New York City and had an active exhibition schedule outside Old Lyme. Beginning in 1901 he exhibited regularly at the National Academy of Design, and he was also represented in exhibitions at the Carnegie Institute and the Art Institute of Chicago. He was awarded a bronze medal at the St. Louis World's Fair in 1904, the Hallgarten Prize at the National Academy in 1905, and the Eaton Purchase Prize of the Lyme Art Association in 1929. His memberships included the Salmagundi Club, the Century Club, the Stockbridge (Massachusetts) Art Association, and the artists' cooperative, Grand Central Art Galleries, of which he was a founder in 1923.

Beginning in 1919, Voorhees and his family spent winters in Somerset, Bermuda, where Voorhees established another studio and apparently gained an excellent reputation. In the art section of the British Commonwealth Exposition in 1925, Bermuda chose to be represented solely by the work of Clark Voorhees. Both in Bermuda and in Old Lyme, Voorhees did painting that ranged from moonlit tonalist landscapes to high impressionistic studies. Though he was best known for his oils, he began to etch as well in his later years and produced many prints.

Despite his travels to New York City, Newport, Rhode Island, Bermuda, and other places, Voorhees was devoted to the art colony and to Old Lyme and played an active role in both. He exhibited with the Lyme group from the outset and served as the Art Association's secretary for several years. He was a charter member of the local volunteer fire department. In 1919 he was elected a trustee of the local library, which represented an acceptance by the town of the artists in their midst. Minutes for the meeting in which

Voorhees won his board membership state that "After discussion on the question of having the artists now resident in Lyme represented on the corporation, as tending to bind them more closely to the interests of the Library, it was decided to elect one of them." The experiment must have worked well, because by 1927 Voorhees was president of the library board.

Walkley, David Birdsey
Born Mar. 2, 1849,
Rock Creek, Ohio.
Died Mar. 23, 1934,
Rock Creek, Ohio.
In Cos Cob and Falls Village,
1890s; in New London,
c. 1900-02; in Mystic,
c. 1902-c. 1915.

David Walkley was born in 1849 in Rock Creek, Ohio, near Ashtabula. Like many others in northeastern Ohio, he was descended from early Connecticut settlers, one of whom had bought property in Haddam in 1668 that became known as Walkley Hill.

In 1867 Walkley began four years of study at the Pennsylvania Academy of Fine Arts, after which he had a studio in Philadelphia for a year. He moved to Cleveland and maintained a studio there for six more years. In 1878 he was able to go to Paris for further study, first at Mosler's Academy, then at the Académie Julian under Gustave Boulanger and Jules Lefebvre. On his return to the United States, Walkley taught for six years at the Pittsburgh School of Design. In 1884 he was married to May Remington, one of his students, and, following a trip to Paris, they settled in New York City, where Walkley's studio was on the present site of Saks Fifth Avenue store. Walkley renewed his studies, working at the Art Students League under William Merritt Chase. Then he taught at the League for a number of years.

He exhibited regularly in New York, Philadelphia, and Pittsburgh galleries, at the National Academy of Design, Pennsylvania Academy of Fine Arts, Art Club of Philadelphia, the World's Columbian Exhibition of 1892, and museums such as the Art Institute of Chicago and the Corcoran Gallery of Fine Art. He was a member of the Salmagundi Club and the Society of American Artists.

Walkley decided to get his family out of New York City sometime in the late 1880s or early 1890s. A daughter remembers that the family spent brief periods in Cos Cob, Port Chester, N.Y., and Falls Village before settling in New London for a couple of years around the turn of the century. Walkley wanted a place picturesque for painting and beneficial for the family. He worried about his wife and three daughters because he was frequently away, teaching or working abroad in places like Holland and Wales. When New London eventually proved unsatisfactory because rents were high, Walkley hired a boat and sailed the Sound looking for a better place. He liked West Mystic and found a place to rent there of the first person he asked. The family stayed for many years in a fine old house that overlooked the water (rent was twelve dollars a month). Walkley's studio was on the upper floor. Thus Walkley became one of the earliest artists to settle in the Mystic area year-round.

Walkley occasionally painted in Stonington, Noank, and Mason's Island as well as Mystic. He found Henry Ward Ranger and J. Eliot Enneking to be very friendly. Walkley's daughter says Charles Davis, always a guiding spirit for Mystic artists, was nevertheless a man who kept mostly to himself.

By 1926, Walkley, at seventy-seven years old, was back in the Ohio town where he had been born. In 1928 he spent the winter painting in Phoenix, Arizona. He died in Rock Creek, Ohio, in 1934, after an art career that had endured more than sixty years.

Weir, J. Alden

Born Aug. 30, 1852,
West Point, N.Y.

Died Dec. 8, 1919,
New York City.

In Windham and Branchville,
1882-1918; in Cos Cob,
1892-93.

Julian Alden Weir was part of a distinguished family of artists, a founding member of The Ten American Painters, a president of the National Academy of Design, and a president and trustee of the Metropolitan Museum of Art. He travelled widely in Europe but concluded that "Europe palls on me. For some there is no place like home." He spent winters in New York City, but home was also Connecticut, where he spent many months of his life and where he found the inspiration for much of his art. "Here shall we rest and call *content* our home" was the epigram painted over the front door of one of his country houses. He was unusual in that he maintained two homes in this state — one at Branchville in the southwest, the other at Windham Center in the east.

Weir was a son of Robert W. Weir, noted artist and instructor of art at the military academy at West Point, and his brother was the artist John Ferguson Weir, who taught at the School of Fine Arts at Yale University from 1869-1913. He studied with his father and then, in the late 1860s and early 1870s, at the National Academy of Design in New York. In 1873 he went to Paris and worked under Gérôme at the École des Beaux-Arts and became friends with Jules Bastien-Lepage. He describes days in Paris that regularly included eight hours of drawing from a model, three hours of painting in the studio, and sometimes a lecture on perspective. Little wonder that he was appalled, when he first saw Impressionist work in 1877, at its lack of concern for drawing and form.

Weir returned to America in 1877 but made several more trips abroad, including one in 1881, where he painted in Holland with his brother John, Bastien-Lepage, and John Twachtman. In 1882 he fell in love with Anna Dwight Baker, whose family had homes both in New York City and in Windham Center, Connecticut, and his visits to her country home mark the beginning of his association with this state. Their marriage took place in 1883, the list of wedding ushers ranging from artists like William Merritt Chase to architect Stanford White to Elliott Roosevelt, younger brother of Theodore. Weir made a home for his bride in Branchville, near Ridgefield, where he had acquired some hundred and fifty acres from the art collector, Erwin Davis, in exchange for an Old Master painting. Through the years Weir enlarged and improved the house and built a fishing pond. Though Weir had stayed at the Holley House in Cos Cob before his marriage and taught in Cos Cob later, he was never closely associated with any art colony. (He visited Old Lyme only for a day or two.) But he entertained so many artist friends that he experienced much of the fellowship and stimulation that art colonies provided their members.

Anna Weir died in February, 1892, leaving Weir with three little daughters to raise. In 1893, he married Anna's sister, Ella Baker (Twachtman was best man), and thus continued his association with Windham. Weir inherited the property there, and then he had two Connecticut homes and two country studios. Several of the artists who visited him in Branchville, such as Childe Hassam, Albert Pinkham Ryder, and John Singer Sargent, also visited Windham. Emil Carlsen and his family were frequent guests there.

In 1892 and 1893 Weir taught summer classes with Twachtman at Cos Cob, and for four years, beginning with the summer of 1897, he held summer art classes at Branchville. From his return to America until 1898, he taught at the Cooper Union and at the Art Students League, for a total of about twenty years.

In 1897, with Hassam and Twachtman, Weir seceded from the Society of American Artists and founded The Ten American Painters. His own career was distinguished, and he was an artist who succeeded both in portraiture and in the Impressionist landscapes he had begun to do by the 1890s. Several prominent artists considered him their best friend and looked to him for advice (some, like Ryder, also for needed sustenance). Twachtman once wrote from Paris that he was taking Weir's advice and working hard at life drawing; Carlsen, often gently admonished by Weir for drawing too much, occasionally was able to achieve a looseness (as in *Cherry Blossoms,* cat. 4, illus. p. 12) that surpassed what Weir himself could do.

Weir's youngest daughter remembers that the family used to divide each summer fairly evenly between Branchville and Windham. The artist sometimes travelled between the two places by train, sometimes by horse. Weir's letters reveal he also visited one place or the other at additional times of year. Both places were working farms, with the help of hired hands, and Windham, at least, had dairy cattle and an apple orchard. Weir, who developed heart disease, spent the last summer and fall of his life at Windham. In October, when he was too weak to walk, he was carried outside by farmhands to a hammock back of the house, where he lay for hours near his fragrant grapevines, looking past oaks and elms toward Obweebetuck, the mountain he had painted several times. Dorothy Weir Young, the daughter who published his letters, wrote that she often heard him say as he lay there, "What a beautiful world it is." He died in New York City in December, 1919, and is buried in the Windham Center cemetery.

The Metropolitan Museum of Art held a major memorial exhibition in 1924.

Further reading:
Baur, John I.H. *Leaders of American Impressionism: Mary Cassatt, Childe Hassam, John H. Twachtman, J. Alden Weir.* Exh. cat., The Brooklyn Museum, 1937.
Clark, Eliot. "The Work of J. Alden Weir." *Art in America,* 8 (Aug. 1920), 232-42.
Phillips, Duncan. *Julian Alden Weir: An Appreciation of His Life and Works.* Phillips Publications Number One. N.Y.: E. P. Dutton & Co., 1922. Includes essays by Emil Carlsen, Royal Cortissoz, Childe Hassam, and J. B. Millet.
    Young, Dorothy Weir. *The Life and Letters of J. Alden Weir.* New Haven: Yale University Press, 1960.

White, Henry C.

Born Sept. 15, 1861, Hartford.

Died Sept. 28, 1952, Waterford.

In Hartford until 1914; summers in Waterford, 1891-1914; spring and fall in Old Lyme, 1903-07; to Waterford year-round 1914.

Henry C. White was the son of Judge John Hurlburt White and Jennie M. Cooke. For two years after his graduation from Hartford High School in 1882, he was clerk of the Hartford Probate Court his father presided over. His art training had begun at fourteen with private lessons in 1875 from Dwight Tryon, who became a life-long friend. White is the author of the major biography, *The Life and Art of Dwight William Tryon,* published in 1930.

From 1884-86 White studied in New York, privately with Tryon and at the Art Students League with Kenyon Cox and George de Forest Brush. In 1889 he became a teacher of drawing at Hartford High School and built his first studio. That same year he was married to Grace Holbrook. He began to spend summers in Waterford in 1891, except for 1896 and 1897, when he traveled in England, France, Holland, Belgium, Germany, and Italy. On his return in 1897 he gave up high school teaching, taught briefly at the school of the Art Society of Hartford, and held a private drawing class in his studio.

Although White traveled frequently, sketching as he went, he was essentially a painter and etcher of the Connecticut landscape and shore. From 1903-07 he spent spring and fall in Old Lyme. He experienced his favorite seasons three times over each year. Spring in Hartford was followed a week or two later by spring at Old Lyme, then finally at Waterford. Late autumn was the other time of year he would be always outdoors sketching in pencil or pastel. Summer was his least favorite season for art because summer greens were "Too much spinach!" His oil paintings were usually done in the studio, a composite of remembered impressions.

In 1903 White and his family stayed at the Florence Griswold House in Old Lyme. Later they rented what was called the Brick Store, farther down Main Street. White's Knox, the first automobile in Old Lyme, was sheltered in a barn opposite a tree called "Barbizon Oak," because artists like Ranger, Dessar, "Uncle" Howe, and White painted it so often. Though the Whites' extended stays in Old Lyme lasted only through 1907, they remained close friends with the artists. Charles Davis of Mystic was also a friend. White designed for Davis' sailboat an ingenious folding mast that enabled the Mystic artist to float his boat under the low bridge in his town with no trouble. At least once, too, White traveled to Greenwich to visit and paint with John Twachtman.

When White realized, early in his career, that he could exhibit at important shows and galleries without fear of rejection, he stopped seeking such status and limited himself to occasional one-man exhibitions. Yet his influence on art in Connecticut was strong. He was a founder and officer of the Connecticut Academy of Fine Arts, which, from its beginnings in 1910, developed into an important showcase for artists in Connecticut and neighboring states. He painted until he was nearly eighty.

Though he asserted that Impressionism had touched him little, he shared with the American Impressionists their attitudes towards nature and some of their techniques. His son, Nelson C. White, a landscape artist in Waterford, has said that "fleeting, evanescent effects" were what moved his father, but that "his castles in the air, if you will, had foundations under them, as Thoreau so wisely recommended."

Further reading:
Henry C. White, 1861-1952: Memorial Exhibition. Exh. cat., Lyman Allyn Museum, New London, 1954.

Wiggins, Guy C.

Born Feb. 23, 1883, Brooklyn, N.Y.

Died Apr. 25, 1962, St. Augustine, Fla.

In Lyme, 1905-37; in Essex, 1937-62.

Guy Wiggins had a long and successful career as an Impressionist artist and teacher in New York and in Connecticut, but he once told his son (also an artist named Guy) that "painting is a wonderful hobby, but a damned difficult way to make a living." (Perhaps he was thinking of the way he had sent his son through Loomis Chaffee School in Windsor — with a series of paintings.) Ironically, although his work includes many fine Connecticut landscapes, he is best remembered for some snow scenes of New York City. Like many other American Impressionists, Wiggins had one foot in the city and the other in the country.

Wiggins was born in Brooklyn, New York, went to England with his family as a boy, received an English grammar school education, and traveled widely abroad. He was the son of a prominent artist, Carleton Wiggins, a painter in the Barbizon style who studied with George Inness and admired Anton Mauve and Dwight Tryon. The father and his family had been early and regular visitors to the Old Lyme colony, and the elder artist had settled in

Lyme permanently by 1915, where he was active in the Lyme Art Association and in the social life of the colony. Carleton Wiggins' palette had brightened under the influence of Old Lyme Impressionism, but in general his work remained tonal and his subjects were truly pastoral, his paintings often of sheep in a meadow. The son, by contrast, became strongly attracted to Impressionism and stayed with it long after it was considered outmoded. Eventually in 1920, he and his family also settled in Lyme. Some twenty years later he relocated in Essex.

For a time Wiggins had some serious training as a draftsman, for he studied architecture at Polytechnic Institute in Brooklyn, perhaps to avoid competing with his father as an artist. His own art talent had manifested itself early and stunningly. He had been only eight years old when New York critics publicly praised some watercolors done in France and Holland. Soon his interest in art exceeded that in architecture, and he studied at the National Academy of Design, first under William Merritt Chase and later under Robert Henri.

Wiggins quickly won recognition. By the time he was twenty he had a work in the permanent collection of the Metropolitan Museum of Art. He was elected to full membership in the National Academy of Design in 1919. Awards came steadily, such as the prestigious Norman Wait Harris Bronze Medal from the Art Institute of Chicago in 1917. His prize list is long.

Wiggins was especially busy in the years before World War I, working on commissions from New York patrons for scenes painted "on location" in England (he met his wife on one of these trips), but he found time to be at Old Lyme and exhibit there, and he became involved as well with the Connecticut Academy of Fine Arts, established in 1910. He showed *Building the Ship, Noank* in the premier exhibition, and for the second annual exhibition, in which he entered another Noank scene, he was on both the jury and the hanging committee. Subsequently, besides jurying, he won prizes in Academy exhibitions and served as president (beginning in 1927 into the 1930s). He also belonged to the New Haven Paint and Clay Club.

By 1920 Wiggins had decided to make his home on an old farm in Hamburg Cove, a picturesque area in Lyme township. He still spent time in New York, and most of his New York snow scenes probably date from the early 1920s. In an interview published in the *Detroit News* in 1924 (specific date unknown), he talked about these pictures:

One cold, blustering, snowy winter day I was in my New York studio trying to paint a summer landscape. Things wouldn't go right and I sat idly looking out of a window at nothing. Suddenly I saw what was before me — an elevated railroad track, with a train dashing madly through the whirling blizzard-like snow that made hazy and indistinct the row of buildings on the far side of the street . . . . Well, when I gave an exhibition a short time afterward . . . the winter canvases were sold before anything else. In a week, so to say, I was established as a painter of city winter scenes, and I found it profitable. Then suddenly I felt a revulsion against them and I stopped. Everyone said I was a fool and was shutting the door upon opportunity, maybe fame. Just the same I couldn't go on with winter stuff and that was all there was to it.

Although he spoke of the New York pictures as though they were history, he sometimes again felt the urge "to brush up a little snow" in order to pile up a little cash. Indeed, he may have changed his attitude completely, for

he also once told someone that New York during a snowfall was his favorite subject. But since Connecticut landscapes and New York snow scenes are about equal in number in his work, and comprise most of it, the pastoral quality in parts of our state clearly appealed to Wiggins. Some say the Connecticut landscapes are his best work.

In 1930 Wiggins, though he still listed a winter New York address in the *American Art Annual*, was advertising there the "Guy Wiggins Art School: New Haven (winter); Lyme (summer)." Hartford artist James Goodwin McManus often taught the summer classes with him at Hamburg Cove.

In 1937, at the age of fifty-four, Wiggins resettled in Essex and moved his art school there year-around. He invited for his students' benefit such guests as George Luks, Bruce Crane, Eugene Higgins and John Noble. He formed the Essex Painters Society. In Essex he is reputed to have lived with his second wife in a "beach wagon." He died while on vacation in St. Augustine, Florida, in 1962 and is buried in Old Lyme. People who knew him still talk about him as "the ebullient Wiggins." His artistic reputation surpasses both that of his father and of his son.

Further reading:
Guy C. Wiggins, American Impressionist. Exh. cat., Campanile Galleries, Inc., Chicago, 1970.
Paintings by Three Generations of Wiggins, 1870's-1970's. Exh. cat., Loomis Chaffee School and New Britain Museum of Art, 1979.
Walt, Adrienne L. "Guy Wiggins: American Impressionist." *American Art Review*, 4 (Dec. 1977), 100-13.

Winslow, Henry

Born July 13, 1874,
    Boston, Mass.
Died after 1953?
In Cos Cob, 1906; in South
    Norwalk, 1908.

The little-known artist, poet, and critic Henry Winslow studied with Whistler in Paris and exhibited in the Paris Salons and London's Royal Academy. As a student of Whistler — the flamboyant pre-Impressionist who ranks among history's greatest printmakers — Winslow developed a deep interest in etching. His book *The Etching of Landscapes,* published by the Chicago Society of Etchers in 1914, includes a perceptive criticism of Whistler.

Winslow lived in New York City sometime after the turn of the century. He visited Connecticut at least twice. His etching *Cos Cob,* dated 1906, depicts the shipyard and shoreline from a vantage point within a dockside shed. An etching of South Norwalk's waterfront is dated 1908.

Until Winslow, no one in the Cos Cob colony had produced prints there. Twachtman and Weir had created some etchings before 1890, but neither worked in that medium in Cos Cob. Later, Kerr Eby had an etching press in the village, which he shared with Hassam in 1915. The extent of Winslow's work in the Cos Cob area and his relationship with the Cos Cob group of artists have yet to be determined.

Further reading:
The Stamp of Whistler. Exh. cat., Allen Memorial Art Museum, Oberlin College, 1977, pp. 264-65.

Acknowledgments

Old Lyme artist with portable studio, c. 1910. Several of the artists had such studios designed to keep them warm on winter sketching trips.

Acknowledgments of help to a project as complex as *Connecticut and American Impressionism* can be only cursory — though debts are great and gratitude is deep. There is no adequate way to thank the host of people who have supported this cooperative exhibition project in one way or another. The long list of names that follows is very selective. We have not forgotten that we had even more help, and we appreciate it. Special thanks, of course, go to the lenders to these exhibitions, for they made the project possible. Although we regret that some institutions and individuals were unable or unwilling to lend art or provide information that would have contributed to the special scope of these exhibitions, we are delighted by the splendid cooperation we encountered generally. Help came to us generously and wholeheartedly — from our many lenders, both of works of art and of historical photographs, from staff of the funding agencies, from curators, gallery staff, researchers, librarians, and artists' relatives who answered countless questions, and from people who provided special editorial, secretarial, printing, design, and photographic services.

While the entire staffs of the three organizing institutions contributed to this project, the project coordinator and the curators of the three exhibitions wish to thank a few people particularly. We would have been lost without the secretarial skills of Leslie Arriola, Lyme Historical Society, and of Theresa Roy, The William Benton Museum of Art. Libby Cryer, Dodie Headington, Pat Mudge, Pam Koob, and Margaret Mosely volunteered their help with the Hurlbutt Gallery exhibition in several essential ways. At the Lyme Historical Society, Bonnie MacAdam collaborated on every aspect of exhibition organization and catalogue preparation. At The William Benton Museum of Art, William Devlin was responsible for assembling the historical photographs for the catalogue and all exhibitions, George E. Mazeika deftly handled the myriad of registraral details for all three exhibitions, and Paul F. Rovetti not only provided solid support throughout but, time and again, provided solutions to what the rest of us thought were unsolvable problems.

The Benton Museum also thanks the students in Art 283, a special topics course on American Impressionism in Connecticut taught by Harold Spencer in the fall of 1978, for basic research in preparation for the Benton exhibition: Denise Cornwall, Patricia Cyr-Devoe, Patricia Hall, Janie Horowitz, Harwood Johnson, Donna Madonna, Peggie Prior, and Prudence Sloane. Special thanks to Patricia Cyr-Devoe, Janie Horowitz, and Harwood Johnson for continuing help in the spring of 1979.

For extra courtesies, patience, and contributions, we all thank the following:

James H. Allyn
Sperry and Doris Andrews
Patricia Appleton, Malcolm Grear
Designers
Jean Baldwin, Guilford Free Library
Ann Barnsley Bartels
Judith Barter, Mead Art Museum,
Amherst College
Lucinda Berkpile, New Haven Colony
Historical Society
Berry-Hill Galleries
E. Irving Blomstrann
William Bocchino, Hoffman Printing
M. A. Bossler, Detroit Athletic Club
Patricia Burr Bott
Fenton L. B. Brown
Jeffrey R. Brown
Margaret Brown
Virginia Burgess
John D. Burke
Cora Weir Burlingham
Lawrence Campbell, Art Students
League
N. Robert Cestone, New World Gallery
Peter Chase, Old Lyme-Phoebe Griffin
Noyes Library
Carol Clark, Amon Carter Museum
Jack Clark, The Bruce Museum
Abby Ann Cole
Thomas Colville
Lucy Crosbie
Elizabeth Daily, Graham Gallery
Danbury Scott-Fanton Museum and
Historical Society
Monica B. Davies
Elizabeth G. de Veer
Frances Donald, Greenwich Library
Diane Drisch, Wadsworth Atheneum
Esther Duffy, Greenwich Library
Sue Dunlap, Greenwich Art Society
Robert Egleston, New Haven Colony
Historical Society
Paul Elliker
Nina Evans
Nan Greacen Faure
Rene Faure
Charles Ferguson, New Britain
Museum of American Art
William E. Finch, Jr., Historical Society
of the Town of Greenwich
Freeman Foote
Nancy Forster, Sotheby Parke-Bernet
Jon Freshour, Library of Congress
Robert Gilmore
Joan Gould, Metropolitan Museum
of Art

Robert Graham, Graham Gallery
Ruth N. Greacen
Greenwich Arts Council
Greenwich Art Society
Joyce Knight Gruberman, R. H. Love
Galleries, Inc.
Mary Guck, Grand Central Art
Galleries
Robert P. Gunn
Ted Hendrickson
Historical Society of the Town
of Greenwich
Ay-Whang Hsia, Wildenstein & Co.
Ira Spanierman Gallery
Jan Irvine
Colta Ives, Metropolitan Museum of
Art
Mr. & Mrs. Edwin C. M. Jasinski
Anne Johnson
Dale Johnson, Metropoliton
Museum of Art
Leslie Joncus
Sandra Joncus, Waterford Public
Library
Emily Jostrand
David Kolch, Lyman Allyn Museum
Antoinette M. Kraushaar, Kraushaar
Galleries
Iris Krenzis, Hammer Galleries
Barbara Krulik, National Academy
of Design
Charles Lay
Barbara Limeburner
W. David Lindholm
Irene Chapellier Little, Chapellier
Galleries
Elizabeth M. Loder
Richard H. Love
Patti L. Maloof, Smithsonian
Institution, Juley Archives
Virginia Mann, Silvermine Guild of
Artists
Clark S. Marlor
Edgar de N. Mayhew, Lyman Allyn
Museum
Cathy McLearn
Henriette Metcalf
Jo Miller
Mrs. William Morrison, Wilton
Historical Society
Mary Muir
Mohini Mundkur, University of
Connecticut Library
Robert M. Murdock
William Newkirk, Malcolm Grear
Designers

Marion Nicholson, Greenwich Library
Joseph Occhipinti, Salmagundi Club
Elizabeth Chadwick O'Connell
Barbara Ornstein
David Palmquist, Bridgeport Public
Library
William Petersen, Mystic Seaport
Museum, Inc.
Arthur Phelan
Patricia Pierce, Pierce Galleries
Robert R. Preato, Grand Central Art
Galleries
Alexander R. Raydon, Raydon Gallery
Elizabeth Ridgeway, Windham
Historical Society
Elizabeth Roth, New York Public
Library
Ida Rubin
Robert B. Russell, Jr.
Schweitzer Gallery
Mitchell Shaneen
Ann Youngdahl Smith, Mattatuck
Museum
Gregory and Ann Smith
Ray W. Smith
Harve Stein, Stone Ledge Art Studio &
Gallery
Marion Stock, Falls Village-Canaan
Historical Society
Diana Strazdes, Museum of Fine Arts,
Boston
John W. Streetman, III, Evansville
Museum of Arts and Science
Melinda Kahn Tally, Davis & Long Co.
George B. Tatum
Lois Tinkham
University of Connecticut Library,
Interlibrary Loan Staff
University of Connecticut Photo Lab
Clark Voorhees, Jr.
Abbot Williams Vose
Robert C. Vose
Robert C. Vose, Jr.
Alice Waldecker, Norfolk
Historical Society
Nelson C. White
Grace W. Williamson
Sandy Wilson
Nicole Wise
Mahonri Young
Walter Zervas, New York Public
Library

Index of Artists

Abrams, Lucien pp. 123, 137, 151; cat. nos. **1, 160**

Adams, Katherine Langhorne pp. 123, 151-52; cat. no. **192**

Bicknell, Frank Alfred pp. 121, 124, 137, 152, 158; cat. nos. **2, 161**

Borgord, Martin pp. 123, 152-53; cat. no. **162**

Brinley, Daniel Putnam pp. 91, 95-96, 153-54, 167; cat. nos. **3, 96-99;** illus. p. 64

Burr, George Brainerd pp. 123, 137, 154; cat. nos. **163-64;** illus. p. 142

Carlsen, Emil pp. 55, 154-55, 161, 177; cat. nos. **4-11;** illus. pp. 12, 63-65

Chadwick, William pp. 123, 137, 155-56, 159, 161; cat. nos. **12-13, 165-67;** illus. pp. 24, 65, 142

Clark, Walter p. 156; cat. nos. **14, 100-01;** illus. p. 105

Davis, Charles Harold pp. 156-57, 166, 169, 177-78; cat. nos. **15-20;** illus. pp. 11, 66-67

DuMond, Frank Vincent pp. 46, 55, 96, 118, 121, 124, 128-31, 136-37, 152, 157-59; cat. nos. **21-23, 168-69;** illus. pp. 67, 143

Ebert, Charles pp. 91, 94, 98, 137, 156, 158; cat. nos. **102-05, 170-71;** illus. p. 106

Eby, Kerr pp. 96, 99, 158, 179; cat. no. **106**

Foote, Will Howe pp. 96, 118, 121, 124, 129, 133, 136-37, 155-56, 158-60, 173, 176; cat. nos. **24-27, 107, 172-73;** illus. pp. 12, 25, 68

Greacen, Edmund W. pp. 123, 154, 160-61; cat. nos. **28-30, 174-76;** illus. pp. 13, 69-70

Griffin, Walter pp. 116, 123, 130, 158-59, 161-62; cat. nos. **31-33, 177-79;** illus. pp. 14, 25

Hassam, Childe pp. 30, 45-46, 48-50, 54-55, 82, 88, 91-99, 116, 120-21, 123, 125, 127, 131-33, 135-37, 152, 156-59, 161-63, 168-69, 173-74, 177, 179; cat. nos. **34-43, 108-22, 180-87;** illus. pp. 15, 20-21, 26, 49, 70-72, 106-08, 143

Hoffman, Harry Leslie pp. 121, 136-37, 152, 155-56, 163-64; cat. no. **188;** illus. p. 144

Irvine, Wilson Henry pp. 6, 123, 137, 164; cat. nos. **189-90;** illus. p. 145

Jongers, Alphonse pp. 118, 164-65; cat. no. **191**

Lawson, Ernest pp. 44, 54-55, 89, 92, 95-96, 165-66; cat. nos. **44-45, 123;** illus. pp. 15, 22, 72

Lumis, Harriet Randall pp. 166-67; cat. no. **46**

MacRae, Elmer Livingston pp. 93-96, 167; cat. nos. **124-30;** illus. p. 109

Metcalf, Willard Leroy pp. 30, 46, 51, 54-55, 82, 116, 123-24, 130-33, 135-37, 152, 161-63, 165, 167-68, 173-74; cat. nos. **47-50, 193-98;** illus. pp. 27-28, 72-73, 124, 145-46

Ochtman, Leonard pp. 54, 92, 94, 96, 166, 168-69; cat. nos. **131-35;** illus. p. 109

Ranger, Henry Ward pp. 39, 46, 54, 114, 116-119, 123-25, 133, 136, 157, 159, 161, 164, 169-70, 177-78; cat. nos. **51-52, 199-200;** illus. pp. 73, 119

Robinson, Theodore pp. 46-49, 54-55, 82, 91-92, 94-99, 156, 162, 168, 170, 174-75; cat. nos. **53-55, 136-37;** illus. pp. 16, 69, 74, 92, 110

Robinson, William S. pp. 124-25, 152, 171; cat. no. **201;** illus. p. 146

Rook, Edward F. pp. 123, 137, 152, 171-72; cat. nos. **202-04;** illus. cover, pp. 29, 147

Ryder, Chauncey Foster pp. 123, 172; cat. no. **205**

Smith, Edward Gregory pp 123, 136-37, 159, 171, 173; cat. nos. **56, 206;** illus. pp. 68, 148

Tryon, Dwight W. pp. 39, 118, 173-74, 178; cat. no. **57**

Twachtman, John Henry pp. 30, 40, 45-46, 48, 50-51, 54-55, 82, 88-93, 95-99, 123, 153, 156, 158-59, 162-63, 165, 167-68, 170, 174-75, 177, 179; cat. nos. **58-71, 138-51;** illus. pp. 17-18, 22-23, 50, 70, 75-77, 110-12

Vonnoh, Robert pp. 46, 54-55, 123, 133, 137, 164, 170, 175; cat. no. **72;** illus. p. 78

Voorhees, Clark Greenwood pp. 117-18, 120-21, 124, 133, 137, 159, 175-76; cat. nos. **73,** 207-09; illus. pp. 148-49

Walkley, David Birdsey pp. 169, 177-78; cat. no. **74;** illus. p. 78

Weir, Julian Alden pp. 30, 37, 40, 45-48, 53-55, 82, 89-93, 95-98, 121, 123, 133, 137, 155-56; 158-59, 162-63, 165, 168, 170, 174, 177-79; cat. nos. **75-89, 152-58;** illus. pp. 19, 79-80, 112-13

White, Henry C. pp. 55, 161, 166, 173, 178; cat. nos. **90-92, 210-11;** illus. p. 81

Wiggins, Guy C. pp. 55, 123, 164, 166, 178-79; cat. nos. **93-95, 212-13;** illus. p. 81

Winslow, Henry p. 179; cat. no. **159**

Photographic Credits

Photographers:

E. Irving Blomstrann: p. 49; 15, **17,** 24, color 29, 49, 56, 76, 79, 80, 95

Bramac Studio: 23

Chisholm and Kenyon, Inc.:   30

Donahue Studios, Inc.;   114

Greenberg, Wrazen and May: 37

Helga Photo Studios, Inc.:   p. 92

Ted Hendrickson: pp. 119, 128, 134-5; 41, 75, 163, 166, **167,** 169, **173, 178,** 188, 193, 201, 204, 206, 208, 209

Frank Kelly: 50

R. H. Love Galleries, Bruce C. Bachman Photography: 13, **66,** 100

Louis S. Martel: 104

Quiriconi-Tropea Photographers: 132

R. K. Arnold Newspictures: 40

T. Rose: 26

I. Serisawa Photography: 39, 88

David Stansbury: 11

Studio Nine, Inc.:   28, 54, **115**

Joseph Szasfai: 16

Taylor and Dull, Inc.:   58

The following photographs are through the courtesy of:

Addision Gallery of American Art, Phillips Academy, Andover, Mass.: 61, 70, 142, **145**

Amherst College, Mead Art Museum: 71

Amon Carter Museum: 53

Art Institute of Chicago: 6

Brett Mitchell Collection: 10

Brooklyn Museum: 45

Fenton L. B. Brown: 207

Jeffrey Brown: **195**

Chapellier Galleries: **44**

The Chrysler Museum at Norfolk, Va.;   148

Cleveland Museum of Art: **76**

Corcoran Gallery of Art: p. 124; 83

Mr. and Mrs. John H. Crawford III: 194

Davis and Long Co.:   **55**

Diplomatic Reception Rooms, Dept. of State, Washington, D.C.:   **112**

University of Georgia, Georgia Museum of Art: **35,** 65

Graham Gallery: 189

Hammer Galleries: **4, 202**

Hirshhorn Museum and Sculpture Garden, Smithsonian Institution: 151

Hirschl-Adler Gallery: **197**

Historical Society of Town of Greenwich: 109

Ira Spanierman Gallery: 137

Library of Congress: 155

W. David Lindholm Collection: **62**

Elizabeth Loder: 3

Lyman Allyn Museum: 92

Mary Baskett Gallery: 143

Metropolitan Museum of Art: pp. 32 (fig. 1), 42, 50; 119, 120, 121, 149

Museum of Fine Arts, Boston: pp. 32 (fig. 3), 41; 18, 47

National Gallery of Art: p. 32 (fig. 2)

Parrish Art Museum: 125, 184

Phelan Collection: **27**

Phillips Collection: 153

San Diego Museum of Art: 187

Schweitzer Gallery: 72

Sotheby Parke Bernet, Inc.:   139

Stone Ledge Studio Art Galleries: 52, 74

Vose Galleries of Boston: **33**

Washington County Museum of Fine Arts: 60

Webster Fine Art, Inc.:   **123**

Wildenstein Gallery: **180**

Supplementary Photographs:

Sperry and Doris Andrews: pp. 47, 113

Art Students League: p. 157

Ann Barnsley Bartels: p. 158

Patricia Burr Bott: p. 154 (George Burr)

Historical Collections, Bridgeport Public Library: p. 76

Nan Greacen Faure: p. 160

Freeman Foote: p. 159

Greenwich Art Society: p. 168

Historical Society of the Town of Greenwich: pp. 51, 83, 85, 86, 87, 88, 90, 93, 95, 97, 174

Ira Spanierman Gallery: 170

Jan Irvine: pp. 6, 164

Mr. and Mrs. Edwin C. M. Jasinski: p. 166

Ann Johnson: p. 171

Peter A. Juley and Son Collection, Smithsonian Institution: pp. 154 (Emil Carlsen), 156, 162, 163, 165, 167, 172, 173 (Gregory Smith), 175 (Clark Voorhees), 178 (Guy Wiggins)

Elizabeth Loder: p. 153

Lyme Historical Society: title page, pp. 114 116, 117, 118, 119, 120, 122, 124, 126, 127, 128, 129, 130, 131, 133, 134, 151, 169, 180

National Academy of Design: p. 175 (Robert Vonnoh)

Betty Chadwick O'Connell: p. 155

Phoebe Griffin Noyes Library: p. 122 (Interior of library)

Mr. and Mrs. Gregory Smith: p. 177

Vose Galleries of Boston: p. 161

Nelson H. White: p. 173, 177

Mrs. Grace W. Williamson: p. 176 (David Walkley)